Lecture Notes in Computer Science 7575

Commenced Publication in 1973
Founding and Former Series Editors:
Gerhard Goos, Juris Hartmanis, and Jan van Leeuwen

Andrew Fitzgibbon Svetlana Lazebnik
Pietro Perona Yoichi Sato
Cordelia Schmid (Eds.)

Computer Vision – ECCV 2012

12th European Conference on Computer Vision
Florence, Italy, October 7-13, 2012
Proceedings, Part IV

Springer

Volume Editors

Andrew Fitzgibbon
Microsoft Research Ltd., Cambridge, CB3 0FB, UK
E-mail: awf@microsoft.com

Svetlana Lazebnik
University of North Carolina, Dept. of Computer Science
Chapel Hill, NC 27599, USA
E-mail: lazebnik@cs.unc.edu

Pietro Perona
California Institute of Technology
Pasadena, CA 91125, USA
E-mail: perona@caltech.edu

Yoichi Sato
The University of Tokyo, Institute of Industrial Science
Tokyo 153-8505, Japan
E-mail: ysato@iis.u-tokyo.ac.jp

Cordelia Schmid
INRIA, 38330 Montbonnot, France
E-mail: cordelia.schmid@inria.fr

ISSN 0302-9743 e-ISSN 1611-3349
ISBN 978-3-642-33764-2 e-ISBN 978-3-642-33765-9
DOI 10.1007/978-3-642-33765-9
Springer Heidelberg Dordrecht London New York

Library of Congress Control Number: 2012947663

CR Subject Classification (1998): I.4.6, I.4.8, I.4.1-5, I.4.9, I.5.2-4, I.2.10, I.3.5, F.2.2

LNCS Sublibrary: SL 6 – Image Processing, Computer Vision, Pattern Recognition, and Graphics

Typesetting: Camera-ready by author, data conversion by Scientific Publishing Services, Chennai, India

Printed on acid-free paper

Springer is part of Springer Science+Business Media (www.springer.com)

Foreword

The European Conference on Computer Vision is one of the top conferences for researchers in this field and is held biennially in alternation with the International Conference on Computer Vision. It was first held in 1990 in Antibes (France) with subsequent conferences in Santa Margherita Ligure (Italy) in 1992, Stockholm (Sweden) in 1994, Cambridge (UK) in 1996, Freiburg (Germany) in 1998, Dublin (Ireland) in 2000, Copenhagen (Denmark) in 2002, Prague (Czech Republic) in 2004, Graz (Austria) in 2006, Marseille (France) in 2008, and Heraklion (Greece) in 2010. To our great delight, the 12th conference was held in Florence, Italy.

ECCV has an established tradition of very high scientific quality and an overall duration of one week. ECCV 2012 began with a keynote lecture from the honorary chair, Tomaso Poggio. The main conference followed over four days with 40 orals, 368 posters, 22 demos, and 12 industrial exhibits. There were also 9 tutorials and 21 workshops held before and after the main event. For this event we introduced some novelties. These included innovations in the review policy, the publication of a conference booklet with all paper abstracts and the full video recording of oral presentations.

This conference is the result of a great deal of hard work by many people, who have been working enthusiastically since our first meetings in 2008. We are particularly grateful to the Program Chairs, who handled the review of about 1500 submissions and co-ordinated the efforts of over 50 area chairs and about 1000 reviewers (see details of the process in their preface to the proceedings). We are also indebted to all the other chairs who, with the support of our research teams (names listed below), diligently helped us manage all aspects of the main conference, tutorials, workshops, exhibits, demos, proceedings, and web presence. Finally we thank our generous sponsors and Consulta Umbria for handling the registration of delegates and all financial aspects associated with the conference.

We hope you enjoyed ECCV 2012. Benvenuti a Firenze!

October 2012

Roberto Cipolla
Carlo Colombo
Alberto Del Bimbo

Preface

Welcome to the proceedings of the 2012 European Conference on Computer Vision in Florence, Italy! We received 1437 complete submissions, the largest number of submissions in the history of ECCV. Forty papers were selected for oral presentation and 368 papers for poster presentation, resulting in acceptance rates of 2.8% for oral, 25.6% for poster, and 28.4% in total.

The following is a brief description of the review process. After the submission deadline, each paper was assigned to one of 54 area chairs (28 from Europe, 21 from the USA and Canada, and 4 from Asia) with the help of the Toronto Paper Matching System (TMS). TMS, developed by Laurent Charlin and Richard Zemel, is beginning to be used by an increasing number of conferences, including NIPS, ICML, and CVPR. To ensure the best possible assignment of papers to area chairs, the program chairs manually selected several area chair candidates for each paper based on the suggestions generated by TMS. After automatic load balancing and conflict resolution, each AC was finally assigned approximately 30 papers closely matching their expertise.

Area chairs then made reviewer suggestions (an average of seven per paper), which were load-balanced and conflict-resolved, giving 3 reviewers for each paper and a maximum of 11 papers per reviewer. The ACs were assisted in this process by TMS, which was also used for automatically selecting potential reviewers, matching each submitted paper based on the reviewers' representative publications. These suggestions came from a pool of potential reviewers composed from names of people who have reviewed for recent vision conferences, self-nominations (any member of the community could fill out a form on the ECCV website asking to be a reviewer), and nominations by ACs. From an initial pool of 863 reviewers, 638 ended up reviewing at least one paper. This was the first time that TMS had been used this extensively in the review process for a vision conference (CVPR 2012 used a restricted version of the system for assigning papers to area chairs), and in the end, we were very pleased with its performance. An important improvement over previous conferences was that initial reviewer suggestions were generated entirely in parallel by the ACs, without the "race" for good reviewers that the previous methods have implicitly encouraged. Area chairs were then given the opportunity to correct infelicities in the load balancing before the final list was generated. We extend our heartfelt thanks to the area chairs, who participated vigorously in this process, to maximize the quality of the review assignments.

For the decision process, we introduced one major innovation. We replaced the physical area chair meeting and the conventional AC buddy system with virtual meetings of AC triplets (this system was first tried out for BMVC 2011 and found to work very well). After the conclusion of the review, rebuttal, and discussion periods, the AC triplets met on the phone or on Skype (and, in just one case, in person), jointly discussed all their papers, and made acceptance/rejection decisions. Thus, the reviews and consolidation reports for each paper were carefully examined by three ACs, ensuring a fair and thorough assessment. A program chair assisted in each AC triplet meeting to maintain the consistency in the decision process and to provide any necessary support. Furthermore, each triplet recommended a small number of top-ranked papers (typically one to three) for oral presentation, and the program chairs took these candidates and made the final oral vs. poster decisions.

Double-blind reviewing policies were strictly maintained throughout the entire process – neither the area chairs nor the reviewers knew the identity of the authors, and the authors did not know the identity of the reviewers and ACs. Based on feedback from authors, reviewers, and area chairs, we believe we successfully maintained the integrity of the paper selection process, and we are very excited about the quality of the resulting program.

We wish to thank everyone involved for their time and dedication to making the ECCV 2012 program possible. The success of ECCV 2012 entirely relied on the time and effort invested by the authors into producing high-quality research, on the care taken by the reviewers in writing thorough and professional reviews, and on the commitment by the area chairs to reconciling the reviews and writing detailed and precise consolidation reports. We also wish to thank the general chairs, Roberto Cipolla, Carlo Colombo, and Alberto Del Bimbo, and the other organizing committee members for their top-notch handling of the event.

Finally, we would like to commemorate Mark Everingham, whose untimely death has shocked and saddened the entire vision community. Mark was an area chair for ECCV and also an organizer for one of the workshops; his hard work and dedication were absolutely essential in enabling us to put together a high-quality conference program. We salute his record of exemplary service and intellectual contributions to the discipline of computer vision. Mark, you will be missed!

October 2012

Andrew Fitzgibbon
Svetlana Lazebnik
Pietro Perona
Yoichi Sato
Cordelia Schmid

Organization

General Chairs

Roberto Cipolla	University of Cambridge, UK
Carlo Colombo	University of Florence, Italy
Alberto Del Bimbo	University of Florence, Italy

Program Coordinator

Pietro Perona	California Institute of Technology, USA

Program Chairs

Andrew Fitzgibbon	Microsoft Research, Cambridge, UK
Svetlana Lazebnik	University of Illinois at Urbana-Champaign, USA
Yoichi Sato	The University of Tokyo, Japan
Cordelia Schmid	INRIA, Grenoble, France

Honorary Chair

Tomaso Poggio	Massachusetts Institute of Technology, USA

Tutorial Chairs

Emanuele Trucco	University of Dundee, UK
Alessandro Verri	University of Genoa, Italy

Workshop Chairs

Andrea Fusiello	University of Udine, Italy
Vittorio Murino	Istituto Italiano di Tecnologia, Genoa, Italy

Demonstration Chair

Rita Cucchiara	University of Modena and Reggio Emilia, Italy

Industrial Liaison Chair

Björn Stenger	Toshiba Research Europe, Cambridge, UK

Web Chair

Marco Bertini	University of Florence, Italy

Publicity Chairs

Terrance E. Boult	University of Colorado at Colorado Springs, USA
Tat Jen Cham	Nanyang Technological University, Singapore
Marcello Pelillo	University Ca' Foscari of Venice, Italy

Publication Chair

Massimo Tistarelli	University of Sassari, Italy

Video Processing Chairs

Sebastiano Battiato	University of Catania, Italy
Giovanni M. Farinella	University of Catania, Italy

Travel Grants Chair

Luigi Di Stefano	University of Bologna, Italy

Travel Visa Chair

Stefano Berretti	University of Florence, Italy

Local Committee Chair

Andrew Bagdanov	MICC, Florence, Italy

Local Committee

Lamberto Ballan
Laura Benassi
Marco Fanfani
Andrea Ferracani
Claudio Guida
Lea Landucci
Giuseppe Lisanti
Iacopo Masi
Fabio Pazzaglia
Federico Pernici
Lorenzo Seidenari
Giuseppe Serra

Area Chairs

Simon Baker	Microsoft Research, USA
Horst Bischof	Graz University of Technology, Austria
Michael Black	Max Planck Institute, Germany
Richard Bowden	University of Surrey, UK
Michael S. Brown	National University of Singapore, Singapore
Joachim Buhmann	ETH Zurich, Switzerland
Alyosha Efros	Carnegie Mellon University, USA
Mark Everingham	University of Leeds, UK
Pedro Felzenszwalb	Brown University, USA

Rob Fergus	New York University, USA
Vittorio Ferrari	ETH Zurich, Switzerland
David Fleet	University of Toronto, Canada
David Forsyth	University of Illinois at Urbana-Champaign, USA
Kristen Grauman	University of Texas at Austin, USA
Martial Hebert	Carnegie Mellon University, USA
Aaron Hertzmann	University of Toronto, Canada
Derek Hoiem	University of Illinois at Urbana-Champaign, USA
Katsushi Ikeuchi	The University of Tokyo, Japan
Michal Irani	The Weizmann Institute of Science, Israel
David Jacobs	University of Maryland, USA
Sing Bing Kang	Microsoft Research, USA
David Kriegman	University of California, San Diego, USA
Kyros Kutulakos	University of Toronto, Canada
Christof Lampert	Institute of Science and Technology, Austria
Ivan Laptev	INRIA, France
Victor Lempitsky	Yandex, Russia
Steve Lin	Microsoft Research, China
Jitendra Malik	University of California, Berkeley, USA
Jiří Matas	Czech Technical University, Czech Republic
Yasuyuki Matsushita	Microsoft Research, China
Tomas Pajdla	Czech Technical University, Czech Republic
Patrick Pérez	Thomson-Technicolor, France
Marc Pollefeys	ETH Zurich, Switzerland
Jean Ponce	Ecole Normale Supérieure, France
Long Quan	Hong Kong Univ. of Science and Technology, China
Deva Ramanan	University of California, Irvine, USA
Stefan Roth	TU Darmstadt, Germany
Carsten Rother	Microsoft Research, UK
Yoav Schechner	Technion, Israel
Bernt Schiele	Max Planck Institute, Germany
Christoph Schnörr	University of Heidelberg, Germany
Stan Sclaroff	University of Boston, USA
Josef Sivic	Ecole Normale Supérieure, France
Peter Sturm	INRIA, France
Carlo Tomasi	Duke University, USA
Antonio Torralba	Massachusetts Institute of Technology, USA
Tinne Tuytelaars	University of Leuven, Belgium
Jakob Verbeek	INRIA, France
Yair Weiss	The Hebrew University of Jerusalem, Israel
Christopher Williams	University of Edinburgh, UK
Ramin Zabih	Cornell University, USA
Lihi Zelnik	Technion, Israel
Andrew Zisserman	University of Oxford, UK
Larry Zitnick	Microsoft Research, USA

Reviewers

Vitaly Ablavsky
Lourdes Agapito
Sameer Agarwal
Amit Agrawal
Karteek Alahari
Karim Ali
Saad Ali
S. Ali Eslami
Daniel Aliaga
Neil Alldrin
Marina Alterman
Jose M. Alvarez
Brian Amberg
Cosmin Ancuti
Juan Andrade
Mykhaylo Andriluka
Anton Andriyenko
Elli Angelopoulou
Roland Angst
Relja Arandjelovic
Helder Araujo
Pablo Arbelaez
Antonis Argyros
Kalle Åström
Vassilis Athitsos
Josep Aulinas
Shai Avidan
Tamar Avraham
Yannis Avrithis
Yusuf Aytar
Luca Ballan
Lamberto Ballan
Atsuhiko Banno
Yinzge Bao
Adrian Barbu
Nick Barnes
João Pedro Barreto
Adrien Bartoli
Arslan Basharat
Dhruv Batra
Sebastiano Battiato
Jean-Charles Bazin
Fethallah Benmansour
Alexander Berg
Tamara Berg
Hakan Bilen
Matthew Blaschko
Michael Bleyer
Liefeng Bo
Daniele Borghesani
Terrance Boult
Lubomir Bourdev
Y-Lan Boureau
Kevin Bowyer
Edmond Boyer
Steven Branson
Mathieu Brédif
William Brendel
Michael Bronstein
Gabriel Brostow
Matthew Brown
Thomas Brox
Marcus Brubaker
Darius Burschka
Tiberio Caetano
Barbara Caputo
Stefan Carlsson
Gustavo Carneiro
Joao Carreira
Yaron Caspi
Carlos Castillo
Jan Cech
Turgay Celik
Ayan Chakrabarti
Tat Jen Cham
Antoni Chan
Manmohan Chandraker
Ming-Ching Chang
Lin Chen
Xilin Chen
Daozheng Chen
Wen-Huang Cheng
Yuan Cheng
Tat-Jun Chin
Han-Pang Chiu
Minsu Cho
Tae Choe
Ondrej Chum
Albert C.S. Chung
John Collomosse
Tim Cootes
Florent Couzine-Devy
David Crandall
Keenan Crane
Antonio Criminisi
Shengyang Dai
Dima Damen
Larry Davis
Andrew Davison
Fernando De la Torre
Joost de Weijer
Teofilo deCampos
Vincent Delaitre
Amael Delaunoy
Andrew Delong
David Demirdjian
Jia Deng
Joachim Denzler
Konstantinos Derpanis
Chaitanya Desai
Thomas Deselaers
Frederic Devernay
Thang Dinh
Santosh Kumar Divvala
Piotr Dollar
Justin Domke
Gianfranco Doretto
Matthijs Douze
Tom Drummond
Lixin Duan
Olivier Duchenne
Zoran Duric
Pinar Duygulu
Charles Dyer
Sandra Ebert
Michael Elad
James Elder
Ehsan Elhamifar
Ian Endres

Olof Enqvist
Sergio Escalera
Jialue Fan
Bin Fan
Gabriele Fanelli
Yi Fang
Ali Farhadi
Ryan Farrell
Raanan Fattal
Paolo Favaro
Rogerio Feris
Sanja Fidler
Robert Fisher
Pierre Fite-Georgel
Boris Flach
François Fleuret
Wolfgang Förstner
Andrea Fossati
Charless Fowlkes
Jan-Michael Frahm
Jean-Sebastien Franco
Friedrich Fraundorfer
William Freeman
Oren Freifeld
Mario Fritz
Yasutaka Furukawa
Andrea Fusiello
Adrien Gaidon
Juergen Gall
Andrew Gallagher
Simone Gasparini
Peter Gehler
Yakup Genc
Leifman George
Guido Gerig
Christopher Geyer
Abhijeet Ghosh
Andrew Gilbert
Ross Girshick
Martin Godec
Roland Goecke
Michael Goesele
Siome Goldenstein
Bastian Goldluecke
Shaogang Gong
German Gonzalez
Raghuraman Gopalan
Albert Gordo
Lena Gorelick
Paulo Gotardo
Stephen Gould
Helmut Grabner
Etienne Grossmann
Matthias Grundmann
Jinwei Gu
Steve Gu
Li Guan
Peng Guan
Matthieu Guillaumin
Jean-Yves Guillemaut
Ruiqi Guo
Guodong Guo
Abhinav Gupta
Mohit Gupta
Tony Han
Bohyung Han
Mei Han
Edwin Hancock
Jari Hannuksela
Kenji Hara
Tatsuya Harada
Daniel Harari
Zaid Harchaoui
Stefan Harmeling
Søren Hauberg
Michal Havlena
James Hays
Xuming He
Kaiming He
Varsha Hedau
Nicolas Heess
Yong Heo
Adrian Hilton
Stefan Hinterstoisser
Minh Hoai
Jesse Hoey
Anthony Hoogs
Joachim Hornegger
Alexander Hornung
Edward Hsiao
Wenze Hu
Changbo Hu
Gang Hua
Xinyu Huang
Rui Huang
Wonjun Hwang
Ichiro Ide
Juan Iglesias
Ivo Ihrke
Nazli Ikizler-Cinbis
Slobodan Ilic
Ignazio Infantino
Michael Isard
Hervé Jégou
C.V. Jawahar
Rodolphe Jenatton
Hueihan Jhuang
Qiang Ji
Jiaya Jia
Hongjun Jia
Yong-Dian Jian
Hao Jiang
Zhuolin Jiang
Shuqiang Jiang
Sam Johnson
Anne Jorstad
Neel Joshi
Armand Joulin
Frederic Jurie
Ioannis Kakadiaris
Zdenek Kalal
Joni-K. Kamarainen
Kenichi Kanatani
Atul Kanaujia
Ashish Kapoor
Jörg Kappes
Leonid Karlinsky
Kevin Karsch
koray kavukcuoglu
Rei Kawakami
Hiroshi Kawasaki
Verena Kaynig
Qifa Ke
Ira Kemelmacher-Shlizerman

Aditya Khosla
Tae-Kyun Kim
Jaechul Kim
Seon Joo Kim
Kris Kitani
Jyri Kivinen
Hedvig Kjellstrom
Jan Knopp
Kevin Koeser
Pushmeet Kohli
Nikos Komodakis
Kurt Konolige
Filip Korc
Andreas Koschan
Adriana Kovashka
Josip Krapac
Dilip Krishnan
Zuzana Kukelova
Neeraj Kumar
M. Pawan Kumar
Junghyun Kwon
Dongjin Kwon
Junseok Kwon
Florent Lafarge
Shang-Hong Lai
Jean-Francois Lalonde
Michael Langer
Douglas Lanman
Diane Larlus
Longin Jan Latecki
Erik Learned-Miller
Seungkyu Lee
Kyong Joon Lee
Honglak Lee
Yong Jae Lee
Bastian Leibe
Ido Leichter
Frank Lenzen
Matt Leotta
Vincent Lepetit
Anat Levin
Maxime Lhuillier
Rui Li
Stan Li
Hongsheng Li
Ruonan Li
Hongdong Li
Feng Li
Yunpeng Li
Fuxin Li
Li-Jia Li
Zicheng Liao
Shengcai Liao
Jongwoo Lim
Joseph Lim
Yen-Yu Lin
Dahua Lin
Daniel Lin
Haibin Ling
James Little
Ce Liu
Xiaobai Liu
Ming-Yu Liu
Xiaoming Liu
Tyng-Luh Liu
Yunlong Liu
Wei Liu
Jingen Liu
Marcus Liwicki
Liliana Lo Presti
Roberto Lopez-Sastre
Jiwen Lu
Zheng Lu
Le Lu
Simon Lucey
Julien Mairal
Michael Maire
Subhransu Maji
Yasushi Makihara
Dimitrios Makris
Tomasz Malisiewicz
Jiri Matas
Iain Matthews
Stefano Mattoccia
Thomas Mauthner
Steven Maybank
Walterio Mayol-Cuevas
Scott McCloskey
Stephen McKenna
Gerard Medioni
Jason Meltzer
Talya Meltzer
Heydi Mendez-Vazquez
Thomas Mensink
Fabrice Michel
Branislav Micusik
Krystian Mikolajczyk
Niloy Mitra
Anurag Mittal
Philippos Mordohai
Francesc Moreno-Noguer
Greg Mori
Bryan Morse
Yadong Mu
Yasuhiro Mukaigawa
Lopamudra Mukherjee
Andreas Müller
Jane Mulligan
Daniel Munoz
A. Murillo
Carlo Mutto
Hajime Nagahara
Vinay Namboodiri
Srinivasa Narasimhan
Fabian Nater
Shawn Newsam
Kai Ni
Feiping Nie
Juan Carlos Niebles
Claudia Nieuwenhuis
Ko Nishino
Sebastian Nowozin
Jean-Marc Odobez
Peter O'Donovan
Sangmin Oh
Takeshi Oishi
Takahiro Okabe
Takayuki Okatani
Aude Oliva
Carl Olsson
Bjorn Ommer
Eng-Jon Ong
Anton Osokin
Matthew O'Toole
Mustafa Özuysal

Maja Pantic
Caroline Pantofaru
George Papandreou
Toufiq Parag
Vasu Parameswaran
Devi Parikh
Sylvain Paris
Minwoo Park
Dennis Park
Ioannis Patras
Ioannis Pavlidis
Nadia Payet
Kim Pedersen
Ofir Pele
Shmuel Peleg
Yigang Peng
Amitha Perera
Florent Perronnin
Adrian Peter
Maria Petrou
Patrick Peursum
Tomas Pfister
James Philbin
Justus Piater
Hamed Pirsiavash
Robert Pless
Thomas Pock
Gerard Pons-Moll
Ronald Poppe
Fatih Porikli
Mukta Prasad
Andrea Prati
Jerry Prince
Nicolas Pugeault
Novi Quadrianto
Vincent Rabaud
Rahul Raguram
Srikumar Ramalingam
Narayanan Ramanathan
Marc'Aurelio Ranzato
Konstantinos Rapantzikos
Nikhil Rasiwasia
Mohammad Rastegari
James Rehg
Erik Reinhard
Xiaofeng Ren
Christoph Rhemann
Antonio Robles-Kelly
Emanuele Rodolà
Mikel Rodriguez
Antonio Rodriguez-Sanchez
Marcus Rohrbach
Javier Romero
Charles Rosenberg
Bodo Rosenhahn
Samuel Rota Bulò
Peter Roth
Amit Roy-Chowdhury
Dmitry Rudoy
Olga Russakovsky
Bryan Russell
Chris Russell
Radu Rusu
Michael Ryoo
Mohammad Sadeghi
Kate Saenko
Amir Saffari
Albert Salah
Mathieu Salzmann
Dimitris Samaras
Aswin Sankaranarayanan
Benjamin Sapp
Radim Sara
Scott Satkin
Imari Sato
Eric Saund
Daniel Scharstein
Walter Scheirer
Kevin Schelten
Raimondo Schettini
Konrad Schindler
Joseph Schlecht
Frank Schmidt
Uwe Schmidt
Florian Schroff
Rodolphe Sepulchre
Uri Shalit
Shiguang Shan
Ling Shao
Abhishek Sharma
Eli Shechtman
Yaser Sheikh
Alexander Shekhovtsov
Ilan Shimshoni
Takaaki Shiratori
Jamie Shotton
Nitesh Shroff
Zhangzhang Si
Leonid Sigal
Nathan Silberman
Karen Simonyan
Vivek Singh
Vikas Singh
Maneesh Singh
Sudipta Sinha
Greg Slabaugh
Arnold Smeulders
Cristian Sminchisescu
William A. P. Smith
Kevin Smith
Noah Snavely
Cees Snoek
Michal Sofka
Qi Song
Xuan Song
Anuj Srivastava
Michael Stark
Bjorn Stenger
Yu Su
Yusuke Sugano
Ju Sun
Min Sun
Deqing Sun
Jian Sun
David Suter
Yohay Swirski
Rick Szeliski
Yuichi Taguchi
Yu-Wing Tai
Jun Takamatsu
Hugues Talbot
Robby Tan

Xiaoou Tang
Marshall Tappen
Jonathan Taylor
Christian Theobalt
Tai-Peng Tian
Joseph Tighe
Radu Timofte
Sinisa Todorovic
Federico Tombari
Akihiko Torii
Duan Tran
Tali Treibitz
Bill Triggs
Nhon Trinh
Ivor Tsang
Yanghai Tsin
Aggeliki Tsoli
Zhuowen Tu
Pavan Turaga
Ambrish Tyagi
Martin Urschler
Raquel Urtasun
Jan van Gemert
Daniel Vaquero
Andrea Vedaldi
Ashok Veeraraghavan
Olga Veksler
Alexander Vezhnevets
Sara Vicente
Sudheendra Vijayanarasimhan
Pascal Vincent
Carl Vondrick
Chaohui Wang
Yang Wang
Jue Wang
Hanzi Wang
Song Wang
Gang Wang
Hongcheng Wang
Jingdong Wang
Lu Wang
Yueming Wang
Ruiping Wang
Kai Wang
Alexander Weiss
Andreas Wendel
Manuel Werlberger
Tomas Werner
Gordon Wetzstein
Yonatan Wexler
Oliver Whyte
Richard Wildes
Oliver Williams
Thomas Windheuser
David Wipf
Kwan-Yee K. Wong
John Wright
Shandong Wu
Yi Wu
Changchang Wu
Jianxin Wu
Ying Wu
Jonas Wulff
Jing Xiao
Jianxiong Xiao
Wei Xu
Li Xu
Yong Xu
Yi Xu
Yasushi Yagi
Takayoshi Yamashita
Ming Yang
Ming-Hsuan Yang
Qingxiong Yang
Jinfeng Yang
Weilong Yang
Ruigang Yang
Jianchao Yang
Yi Yang
Bangpeng Yao
Angela Yao
Mohammad Yaqub
Lijun Yin
Kuk-Jin Yoon
Tianli Yu
Qian Yu
Lu Yuan
Xiaotong Yuan
Christopher Zach
Stefanos Zafeiriou
Andrei Zaharescu
Matthew Zeiler
Yun Zeng
Guofeng Zhang
Li Zhang
Lei Zhang
Xinhua Zhang
Shaoting Zhang
Jianguo Zhang
Ying Zheng
S. Kevin Zhou
Changyin Zhou
Shaojie Zhuo
Todd Zickler
Darko Zikic
Henning Zimmer
Daniel Zoran
Silvia Zuffi

Sponsoring Companies and Institutions

Gold Sponsors

Google

NATIONAL ROBOTICS ENGINEERING CENTER (NREC)

Silver Sponsors

Adobe

Microsoft Research

MITSUBISHI ELECTRIC

MOBILEYE

NVIDIA

POINT GREY

technicolor

TOSHIBA Leading Innovation

TOYOTA

Bronze Sponsors

DATALOGIC INDUSTRIAL AUTOMATION

IBM Research

ST life.augmented

Institutional Sponsors

Università degli Studi di Firenze

UNIVERSITY OF CAMBRIDGE

ENTE CASSA DI RISPARMIO DI FIRENZE

Table of Contents

Poster Session 4

Oral Session 4: Actions and Activities

Poster Session 5

Tracking Feature Points in Uncalibrated Images with Radial Distortion

Miguel Lourenço and João Pedro Barreto

Institute for Systems and Robotics,
Dept. of Electrical and Computer Engineering,
University of Coimbra, Portugal
{miguel,jpbar}@isr.uc.pt

Abstract. The appearance of moving features in the field-of-view (FoV) of the camera may substantially change due to different camera poses. Typical solutions for tracking image points involve the assumption of an image motion model and the estimation of the motion parameters using image alignment techniques. While for conventional cameras this suffices, the radial distortion that arises in cameras with wide FoV lenses makes the standard motion models inaccurate. In this paper, we propose a set of motion models that implicitly encompass the distortion effect arising in this type of imaging devices. The proposed motion models are included in a standard image alignment framework for performing feature tracking in cameras presenting significant distortion. Consolidation experiments in repeatability and structure-from-motion scenarios show that the proposed RD-KLT trackers significantly improve the tracking performance in images presenting radial distortion, with minimal computational overhead when compared with a state-of-the-art KLT tracker.

1 Introduction

Tracking image keypoints across frames is useful in computer and robotic vision applications such as optical flow [1, 2], object tracking [3], and 3D reconstruction [4]. The interest in feature tracking dates back to [1, 2], where the authors propose the well known KLT tracker for computing optical flow between spatially and temporally close frames. The original KLT method assumes a translation model and iteratively estimates the displacement vector using image alignment techniques. Several improvements [5–8] have been proposed to the original method, specially aiming at reducing its computational complexity [5, 6] and improving tracking in wide-baseline situations [7, 8].

Wide field-of-view (FoV) cameras became increasingly popular due to their benefits in vision systems. Panoramic cameras proved to be highly advantageous in egomotion estimation [9, 10], and in surveillance systems due the thorough visual coverage of the environments [11]. However, the projection in cameras with wide angle lens presents strong radial distortion (RD) caused by the bending of the light rays when crossing the optics. The distortion increases with the distance to the center of distortion, and it is typically described by nonlinear terms that are function of the image radius.

A. Fitzgibbon et al. (Eds.): ECCV 2012, Part IV, LNCS 7575, pp. 1–14, 2012.

Image alignment techniques applied in a feature tracking context rely on the assumption of a motion model that determines the degree of deformation tolerated by the tracker. Several motion models have been used in the literature, ranging from a low complexity translation model [1, 2] to an affine motion model [5, 6, 8]. As discussed in [12] the performance of local feature tracking can be improved through the designed of specialized motion models. Unfortunately, the standard motion models do not compensate the RD effect arising in cameras equipped with unconventional optics.

Despite of these facts, the KLT tracker has been applied in the past to images with significant RD [13, 14]. While some simply ignore the effect of RD during registration [14], others correct the distortion in a pre-processing step before applying the KLT [13]. Although the later approach is quite straightforward, the distortion rectification requires the interpolation of the image signal, which is computationally expensive and unreliable since the synthetically corrected images contain artificially interpolated pixel intensities [15].

In this paper we focus on the problem of feature tracking in images presenting significant radial distortion. Our contributions are the following:

(i) We propose an extension of the affine motion model for describing the patches deformation that fuses feature motion with image distortion. It is proved that the proposed RD compensated motion model verifies the requirements to be used inside the efficient inverse compositional KLT framework [5, 6] whenever the calibration is known in advance. Unfortunately, the particular structure of this warp does not allow to calibrate the distortion during tracking, as we will discuss later;

(ii) To cope with this problem, we also propose an approximation to the ideal theoretical model that enables to robustly calibrate distortion during tracking. To the best of our knowledge this is the first work showing that is possible to estimate RD using solely low-level feature motion;

(iii) Extensive repeatability [16] and structure-from-motion experiments [15] show that the tracking performance can be significantly improved through a proper RD compensation, with a computational overhead of 15% when compared with a standard KLT algorithm.

The structure of this paper is as follows: Section 2 reviews the adopted camera model and the literature related with the KLT. Section 3 derives the RD compensated motion models and explains how to include them in the inverse compositional KLT. In section 4, the proposed RD-KLT trackers are evaluated in a representative set of repeatability [16] and structure-from-motion (SfM) experiments [15]. Finally, section 5 presents the conclusions of our work.

Notation: Matrices are represented by symbols in sans serif font, e.g. M, and image signals are denoted by symbols in typewriter font , e.g. $\mathtt{I}$. Vectors and vector functions are typically represented by bold symbols, and scalars are indicated by plain letters, e.g $\mathbf{x} = (x, y)^\mathsf{T}$ and $\mathbf{f}(\mathbf{x}) = (f_x(\mathbf{x}), f_y(\mathbf{x}))^\mathsf{T}$. $\mathbf{0}$ is specifically used to represent a null vector.

2 Background

In this section, we review the adopted camera model and the KLT framework using direct and inverse image alignment. We also summarize standard image motion models, and discuss the importance of the local template updates and pyramidal image representation for achieving reliable tracking.

2.1 The Division Model for Radial Distortion

We assume that the image distortion can be described using the 1st order division model with the amount of distortion being quantified by a single parameter ξ (typically $\xi < 0$). Let $\mathbf{x} = (x, y)^\mathsf{T}$ and $\mathbf{u} = (u, v)^\mathsf{T}$ be corresponding points in distorted and undistorted images expressed with respect to a reference frame with origin in the center of the image [17]. $\mathbf{f}$ is a vector function that maps points from the distorted image $\mathtt{I}$ to its undistorted counterpart $\mathtt{I}^u$:

$$\mathbf{u} = \mathbf{f}(\mathbf{x}) = (1 + \xi \mathbf{x}^\mathsf{T}\mathbf{x})^{-1}\mathbf{x}. \tag{1}$$

The function is bijective and the inverse mapping from $\mathtt{I}$ to $\mathtt{I}^u$ is given by[18]:

$$\mathbf{x} = \mathbf{f}^{-1}(\mathbf{u}) = 2(1 + \sqrt{1 - 4\xi\mathbf{u}^\mathsf{T}\mathbf{u}})^{-1}\mathbf{u}. \tag{2}$$

Given that the radius of $\mathbf{x}$ is $r = \sqrt{\mathbf{x}^\mathsf{T}\mathbf{x}}$, the corresponding undistorted radius is

$$r^u = (1 + \xi r^2)^{-1} r. \tag{3}$$

Henceforth, and in order to make the compression undergone by a particular image more intuitive, the amount of distortion will be quantified by

$$\%\,\mathrm{RD} = \frac{r_M^u - r_M}{r_M^u} \times 100 = -\xi r_M \times 100 \tag{4}$$

with r_M being the distance from the center to an image corner (maximum distorted radius) [15].

2.2 Kanade-Lucas-Tomasi Algorithm

Feature tracking between temporally adjacent images is typically formulated as a non-linear optimization problem whose cost function is the sum of the squared error between a template $\mathtt{T}$ and incoming images $\mathtt{I}$. The goal is to compute

$$\epsilon = \sum_{\mathbf{x} \in \mathcal{N}} \Big[\mathtt{I}(\mathbf{w}(\mathbf{x}; \mathbf{p})) - \mathtt{T}(\mathbf{x})\Big]^2, \tag{5}$$

where $\mathbf{p}$ denotes the components of the image warping function $\mathbf{w}$, and $\mathcal{N}$ denotes the integration region of a feature. Lucas and Kanade proposed to optimize

Eq. 5 by assuming that a current $\mathbf{p}$ motion vector is known and iteratively solve for $\delta\mathbf{p}$ increments on the warp parameters, with Eq. 5 begin approximated by

$$\epsilon = \sum_{\mathbf{x}\in\mathcal{N}} \left[\mathtt{I}(\mathbf{w}(\mathbf{x};\mathbf{p}+\delta\mathbf{p}))-\mathtt{T}(\mathbf{x})\right]^2 \approx \sum_{\mathbf{x}\in\mathcal{N}} \left[\mathtt{I}(\mathbf{w}(\mathbf{x};\mathbf{p}))+\nabla\mathtt{I}\frac{\partial\mathbf{w}}{\partial\mathbf{p}}\delta\mathbf{p}-\mathtt{T}(\mathbf{x})\right]^2. \quad (6)$$

Differentiating ϵ with respect to $\delta\mathbf{p}$, and after some algebraic manipulations, a closed-form solution for $\delta\mathbf{p}$ can be obtained:

$$\delta\mathbf{p} = \mathcal{H}^{-1} \sum_{\mathbf{x}\in\mathcal{N}} \left[\nabla\mathtt{I}\frac{\partial\mathbf{w}(\mathbf{x};\mathbf{p})}{\partial\mathbf{p}}\right]^{\mathsf{T}} \Big(\mathtt{T}(\mathbf{x}) - \mathtt{I}(\mathbf{w}(\mathbf{x};\mathbf{p}))\Big), \quad (7)$$

with $\mathcal{H} = \sum_{\mathbf{x}\in\mathcal{N}} \left[\nabla\mathtt{I}\frac{\partial\mathbf{w}(\mathbf{x};\mathbf{p})}{\partial\mathbf{p}}\right]^{\mathsf{T}} \left[\nabla\mathtt{I}\frac{\partial\mathbf{w}(\mathbf{x};\mathbf{p})}{\partial\mathbf{p}}\right]$ being a 1st order approximation of the Hessian matrix, and the parameter vector being additively updated $\mathbf{p}^{i+1} \leftarrow \mathbf{p}^{i} + \delta\mathbf{p}$ at each iteration i. This method is also known as *forward additive* KLT [5, 6] and it requires to re-compute $\mathcal{H}$ at each iteration due its dependence with incoming image $\mathtt{I}$.

For efficiently solving Eq. 6, Baker and Matthews [5, 6] proposed an *inverse compositional alignment* method that starts by switching the roles of $\mathtt{T}$ and $\mathtt{I}$

$$\epsilon = \sum_{\mathbf{x}\in\mathcal{N}} \left[\mathtt{I}(\mathbf{w}(\mathbf{x};\mathbf{p})) - \mathtt{T}(\mathbf{w}(\mathbf{x};\delta\mathbf{p}))\right]^2 \approx \sum_{\mathbf{x}\in\mathcal{N}} \left[\mathtt{I}(\mathbf{w}(\mathbf{x};\mathbf{p})) - \mathtt{T}(\mathbf{w}(\mathbf{x};\mathbf{0})) - \nabla\mathtt{T}\frac{\partial\mathbf{w}}{\partial\mathbf{p}}\delta\mathbf{p}\right]^2. \quad (8)$$

The increments $\delta\mathbf{p}$ are then computed as:

$$\delta\mathbf{p} = \mathcal{H}^{-1} \sum_{\mathbf{x}\in\mathcal{N}} \left[\nabla\mathtt{T}\frac{\partial\mathbf{w}(\mathbf{x};\mathbf{0})}{\partial\mathbf{p}}\right]^{\mathsf{T}} \Big(\mathtt{I}(\mathbf{w}(\mathbf{x};\mathbf{p})) - \mathtt{T}(\mathbf{x})\Big), \quad (9)$$

with $\mathcal{H} = \sum_{\mathbf{x}\in\mathcal{N}} \left[\nabla\mathtt{T}\frac{\partial\mathbf{w}(\mathbf{x};\mathbf{0})}{\partial\mathbf{p}}\right]^{\mathsf{T}} \left[\nabla\mathtt{T}\frac{\partial\mathbf{w}(\mathbf{x};\mathbf{0})}{\partial\mathbf{p}}\right]$, and $\mathbf{w}(\mathbf{x};\mathbf{0})$ being the identity warp. $\mathcal{H}$ is computed using the template gradients and, therefore, it is constant during the registration procedure, leading to a significant computational improvement when compared with the forward additive KLT. Finally, the warp parameters are updated as follows:

$$\mathbf{w}(\mathbf{x};\mathbf{p}^{i+1}) \leftarrow \mathbf{w}(\mathbf{x};\mathbf{p}^{i}) \circ \mathbf{w}^{-1}(\mathbf{x};\delta\mathbf{p}). \quad (10)$$

Although the update rule of the inverse compositional alignment is computationally more costly than a simple additive rule, Baker and Matthews [5, 6] show that the overall computational complexity of the inverse formulation is significantly lower than that of the forward additive KLT.

The motion model $\mathbf{w}$ used for feature tracking determines the degree of image deformation tolerated during the registration process. The original contribution of Lucas and Kanade [1, 2] assumes that the neighborhood $\mathcal{N}$ around a feature point $\mathbf{x}$ moves uniformly and, therefore, the authors model the image motion using a simple translation model. However, the deformation that it tolerates is not sufficient when the tracked image region is large, or the video sequence undergoes considerable changes in scale, rotation and viewpoint. In these situations, the affine motion model [5, 6, 8] is typically adopted

$$\mathbf{w}(\mathbf{x};\mathbf{p}) = (\mathsf{I} + \mathsf{A})\mathbf{x} + \mathbf{t}, \tag{11}$$

where the parameter vector is $\mathbf{p} = (a_1, .., a_4, t_x, t_y)^{\mathsf{T}}$, $\mathtt{I}$ is a 2×2 identity matrix, and $\mathsf{A} = \begin{pmatrix} a_1 & a_2 \\ a_3 & a_4 \end{pmatrix}$. In this paper, we propose an extension to the affine motion model that accounts for the RD effect arising in cameras equipped with wide FoV lenses.

For long-term feature tracking, the template update is a critical step to keep plausible tracks. An inherent problem to the template update step is the localization drift introduced whenever the template is updated [19]. High-order motion models tend to be more flexible in terms of the deformation tolerated during the registration process, with the templates being updated less frequently [19, 5, 6]. We carefully choose the frequency of the template update using the squared error of Eq. 5, as detailed in [8].

Despite of the warp complexity, the registration process may fail to converge when the initialization of the warp parameters $\mathbf{p}^0$ is not close enough to the current motion parameters, i.e. $\mathbf{p}^0$ is not in the convergence region $\mathcal{C}$ where the 1st order approximation of Eq. 8 is valid [5, 6]. To attenuate this effect we adopt a pyramidal tracking framework [7], where several image resolutions are built by downsampling the image by factors of 2. A L-levels pyramidal tracking algorithm proceeds from the coarse to the finest pyramid level, with the coarsest feature position being given by $\mathbf{x}^L = 2^{-L}\mathbf{x}$. The registration proceed at each pyramid level, with the result begin propagated to next level as $\mathbf{x}^{L-1} = 2\,\mathbf{x}^L$ (for further details see [7]). Since the integration region $\mathcal{N}$ is kept constant across scales, the pyramidal framework greatly improves the probability of $\mathbf{p}^0$ belonging to $\mathcal{C}$, which by consequence increases the tracking success.

3 RD-KLT: Feature Tracking in Radial Distorted Images

In this section, we derive an extension to the affine motion model for cameras equipped with wide FoV lenses. It is proved that the derived RD model met the necessary requirements to be used in the inverse compositional KLT framework whenever the distortion calibration is known. As it will be discussed, this warping function does not allow to estimate the ξ during tracking due to its particular structure. Therefore, we also propose an approximation to the ideal theoretical model that enables to accurately estimate the distortion coefficient, at a negligible lost of tracking performance.

3.1 Mapping Composition for Deriving an RD Compensated Motion Model

Let's consider the standard situation where two undistorted images $\mathtt{I}^u$ and $\mathtt{I}^{u'}$ that are related by a generic motion function $\mathbf{w}$ such that $\mathtt{I}^u(\mathbf{u}) = \mathtt{I}^{u'}(\mathbf{w}(\mathbf{u};\mathbf{p}))$. We now consider that $\mathtt{I}^u$ and $\mathtt{I}^{u'}$ are the warping result of the original distorted images $\mathtt{I}$ and $\mathtt{I}'$. Using the distortion function of Eq. 1, we know that corresponding undistorted and distorted coordinates are related by $\mathbf{u} = \mathbf{f}(\mathbf{x})$, so we can re-write the mapping relation as $\mathtt{I}^u(\mathbf{u}) = \mathtt{I}^{u'}(\mathbf{w}(\mathbf{f}(\mathbf{x});\mathbf{p}))$. Since $\mathtt{I}^u(\mathbf{u}) = \mathtt{I}(\mathbf{x})$, with $\mathbf{x} = \mathbf{f}^{-1}(\mathbf{u})$, we can finally write directly the mapping relation between two distorted image signals as $\mathtt{I}(\mathbf{x}) = \mathtt{I}'(\mathbf{f}^{-1}(\mathbf{w}(\mathbf{f}(\mathbf{x});\mathbf{p})))$. Therefore, the RD compensated motion model that related the two distorted image signals can be expressed using the following function composition:

$$\mathbf{x}' = \mathbf{v}_\xi(\mathbf{x};\mathbf{p}) = \Big(\mathbf{f}^{-1} \circ \mathbf{w} \circ \mathbf{f}\Big)(\mathbf{x};\mathbf{p}). \tag{12}$$

3.2 cRD-KLT - Calibrated RD-KLT

In case the ξ coefficient is known in advance, the parameter vector $\mathbf{p}$ of $\mathbf{v}_\xi$ comprises the same parameters of the original motion of Eq. 11. The efficient inverse compositional KLT algorithm requires that the proposed set of warps form a *group* with respect to composition [5, 6]. The RD compensated motion model verifies the necessary *group* requirements:

(i) Identity - $\mathbf{v}_\xi(\mathbf{x};\mathbf{0}) = \mathbf{x}$
(ii) Invertibility - $\mathbf{v}_\xi(\mathbf{x};\mathbf{p})^{-1} = (\mathbf{f}^{-1} \circ \mathbf{v} \circ \mathbf{f})^{-1} = \mathbf{f}^{-1} \circ \mathbf{v}^{-1} \circ \mathbf{f}$
(iii) Composition - $\mathbf{v}_\xi(\mathbf{x};\mathbf{p}) \circ \mathbf{v}_\xi(\mathbf{x};\delta\mathbf{p}) = \mathbf{f}^{-1} \circ \mathbf{w}(\mathbf{x};\mathbf{p}) \circ \mathbf{w}(\mathbf{x};\delta\mathbf{p}) \circ \mathbf{f}$

It can be observed that the function composition to obtain the RD compensated model can be applied to any family of warps $\mathbf{w}$ that form group. By replacing our motion model $\mathbf{v}_\xi$ in the inverse composition KLT, it is straightforward to obtain the closed-form solution for $\delta\mathbf{p}$, which is given by:

$$\delta\mathbf{p} = \mathcal{H}_d^{-1} \sum_{\mathbf{x}\in\mathcal{N}} \left[\nabla\mathtt{T}\frac{\partial \mathbf{v}_\xi(\mathbf{x};\mathbf{0})}{\partial \mathbf{p}}\right]^{\mathsf{T}} \Big(\mathtt{I}(\mathbf{v}_\xi(\mathbf{x};\mathbf{p})) - \mathtt{T}(\mathbf{x})\Big) \tag{13}$$

with $\mathcal{H}_d = \sum_{\mathbf{x}\in\mathcal{N}} \left[\nabla\mathtt{T}\frac{\partial \mathbf{v}_\xi(\mathbf{x};\mathbf{0})}{\partial \delta\mathbf{p}}\right]^{\mathsf{T}} \left[\nabla\mathtt{T}\frac{\partial \mathbf{v}_\xi(\mathbf{x};\mathbf{0})}{\partial \mathbf{p}}\right]$, and the Jacobian $\frac{\partial \mathbf{v}_\xi(\mathbf{x};\mathbf{0})}{\partial \mathbf{p}}$ being evaluated at $\mathbf{p} = \mathbf{0}$. Finally, the motion parameters are updated at each iteration as follows:

$$\mathbf{v}_\xi(\mathbf{x};\mathbf{p}^{i+1}) \leftarrow \mathbf{v}_\xi(\mathbf{x};\mathbf{p}^i) \circ \mathbf{v}_\xi^{-1}(\mathbf{x};\delta\mathbf{p}) = \mathbf{f}^{-1} \circ \mathbf{w}(\mathbf{x};\mathbf{p}^i) \circ \mathbf{w}^{-1}(\mathbf{x};\delta\mathbf{p}) \circ \mathbf{f}. \tag{14}$$

3.3 Difficulties in Extending cRD-KLT to Handle Non-calibrated Images

The cRD-KLT considers a warping function $\mathbf{v}_\xi$ that compensates the radial distortion, applies the motion model, and then restores the non-linear image deformation (see Fig. 1(a)). As it will be shown in the evaluation section, this approach is highly effective for performing image alignment of local patches in cameras with lens distortion, improving substantially the tracking accuracy and repeatability if compared with standard KLT. However, it has the drawback of requiring prior knowledge of the distortion parameter ξ, which implies a partial camera calibration. A strategy to overcome this limitation is to use the differential image alignment to estimate both the motion and the image distortion. This passes by extending the vector $\mathbf{p}$ of model parameters in order to consider ξ as a free variable in addition to the motion variables. In this case the warping function becomes $\mathbf{v}(\mathbf{x};\, \mathbf{q})$ with the difference with respect to $\mathbf{v}_\xi(\mathbf{x}, \mathbf{p})$ being only the vector $\mathbf{q} = (\mathbf{p}, \xi)$ of free parameters to be estimated.

Unfortunately, the model $\mathbf{v}(\mathbf{x};\, \mathbf{q})$ cannot be used for image registration using inverse compositional alignment. The problem is that any vector of parameters $\mathbf{q}$ of the form $\mathbf{q} = (\mathbf{0},\, \xi)$ is a null element that turns the warping function into the identity mapping

$$\mathbf{v}(\mathbf{x};\, (\mathbf{0},\, \xi)) = \mathbf{x},\, \forall_\xi.$$

This means that the Jacobian of $\mathbf{v}(\mathbf{x};\, \mathbf{q})$ evaluated for any $\mathbf{q}$ such that $\mathbf{p} = \mathbf{0}$ is singular and, consequently, $\mathcal{H}_d$ is non-invertible precluding the use of inverse compositional alignment. An alternative would be to use the forward additive framework, since the only requirement needed is the differentiability of the warp with respect to the motion parameters [5, 6]. Unfortunately, the computational complexity of this approach is significantly higher than that of the efficient inverse formulation. Instead of using the forward additive registration, the next section proposes to approximate the warp $\mathbf{v}(\mathbf{x};\, \mathbf{q})$ by assuming that the distortion is locally linear in a small neighborhood around the feature point.

3.4 uRD-KLT - Uncalibrated RD-KLT

This section shows that it is possible to avoid the singular Jacobian issue by replacing the $\mathbf{v}(\mathbf{x}; \mathbf{q})$ by a suitable approximation of the desired composed warping. As it will be experimentally shown, this approximation has minimum impact in terms of error in image registration, enabling to use inverse compositional alignment to estimate both motion and distortion in an accurate and robust manner.

Let's assume that in a small neighborhood $\mathcal{N}$ around a feature $\mathbf{c}$ the distortion effect can be approximated by

$$\mathbf{f}(\mathbf{x}) \approx \mathbf{g}_\mathbf{c}(\mathbf{x}) = (1 + \xi \mathbf{c}^\mathsf{T} \mathbf{c})^{-1} \mathbf{x}. \quad (15)$$

Remark that by replacing the radius of each point $\mathbf{x}$ by the radius of the central point $\mathbf{c}$ of the window $\mathcal{N}$ the non-linear function $\mathbf{f}$ becomes a projective transformation $\mathbf{g}_\mathbf{c}(\mathbf{x})$ as shown in Fig. 1(b). This is a perfectly plausible approximation whenever the distance between the feature point $\mathbf{c}$ and the center of the image is substantially larger than the size of the neighborhood $\mathcal{N}$. In the situations where this is not verified, the effect of distortion is negligible, and the

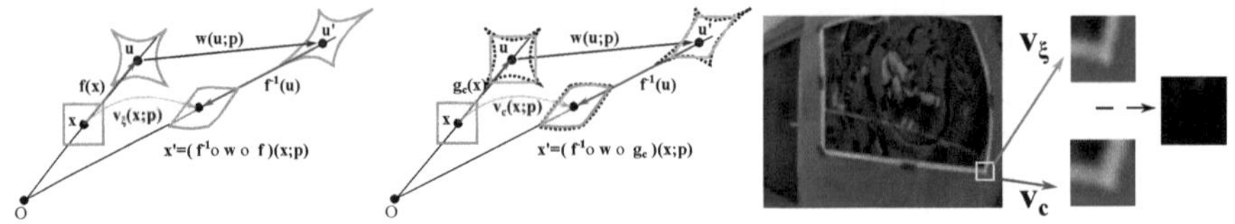

(a) $\mathbf{v}_\xi$ (b) $\mathbf{v_c}$ (c) $\mathbf{v}_\xi - \mathbf{v_c}$

Fig. 1. Schematic difference between the (a) accurate and the (b) approximate RD compensated motion model. The black dashed lines in (b) represent the patches using the accurate RD model. (c) shows the difference between the accurate and the approximate models for a corner patch of an image with high distortion.

approximation does not introduce significant error. Replacing $\mathbf{f}$ by $\mathbf{g_c}$ in Eq. 12 yields the following approximation to the ideal theoretical model (see Fig.1(b)):

$$\mathbf{v_c}(\mathbf{x};\mathbf{q}) = \Big(\mathbf{f}^{-1} \circ \mathbf{w} \circ \mathbf{g_c}\Big)(\mathbf{x};\mathbf{q}). \tag{16}$$

In this case, the warp has single null element, and the Jacobian is not singular when evaluated in $\mathbf{q} = \mathbf{0}$, leading to an invertible $\mathcal{H}_d$. Remark that replacing $\mathbf{f}^{-1}$ by $\mathbf{g}_c^{-1}$ would again lead to a motion model with singular Jacobian and non-invertible $\mathcal{H}_d$.

Estimation of the Warp Parameters: The next step concerns the estimation of the increments $\delta\mathbf{q}$ of parameter vector $\mathbf{q}$. Due to the global nature of the RD, the distortion coefficient ξ must be simultaneously estimated for the N features being tracked, while keeping each the vector $\mathbf{p}$ specific for each feature. Recall that we want to compute the increment $\delta\mathbf{q}$ using the inverse compositional algorithm, through the following closed-form solution:

$$\delta\mathbf{q} = \mathcal{H}_d^{-1} \sum_{N} \left[\nabla \mathtt{T} \frac{\partial \mathbf{v_c}(\mathbf{x};\mathbf{0})}{\partial \mathbf{p}}\right]^{\mathsf{T}} \Big(\mathtt{I}(\mathbf{v_c}(\mathbf{x};\mathbf{q})) - \mathtt{T}(\mathbf{x})\Big). \tag{17}$$

For each image feature, this equation can be re-written as

$$\mathsf{B}_{n\times n}\delta\mathbf{q}_{n\times 1} = \mathbf{e}_{n\times 1}, \tag{18}$$

where $\mathsf{B}_{n\times n} = \mathcal{H}_d = \big(\mathsf{H}_{n\times n-1}\ \mathbf{h}_{n\times 1}\big)$, and n is the number of parameters of $\mathbf{q}$. By performing a proper block-by-block stacking, the observation of all the N tracked features lead to the following system:

$$\underbrace{\begin{pmatrix} \mathsf{H}^1_{(n\times n-1)} & 0 & \cdots & 0 & \mathbf{h}^1_{(n\times 1)} \\ 0 & \mathsf{H}^2_{(n\times n-1)} & & & \mathbf{h}^2_{(n\times 1)} \\ \vdots & & \ddots & & \vdots \\ 0 & \cdots & 0 & \mathsf{H}^N_{(n\times n-1)} & \mathbf{h}^N_{(n\times 1)} \end{pmatrix}}_{\mathsf{B}_{nN\times(n-1)N+1}} \underbrace{\begin{pmatrix} \delta\mathbf{p}^1 \\ \delta\mathbf{p}^2 \\ \vdots \\ \delta\mathbf{p}^N \\ \delta\xi \end{pmatrix}}_{\delta\mathbf{q}^t_{(n-1)N+1\times 1}} = \underbrace{\begin{pmatrix} \mathbf{e}^1 \\ \mathbf{e}^2 \\ \vdots \\ \mathbf{e}^N \end{pmatrix}}_{\mathbf{e}^t_{nN\times 1}} \tag{19}$$

These systems of linear equations are typically solved through the computation of the pseudo-inverse $\delta\mathbf{q}^t = \mathsf{B}^\dagger\mathbf{e}^t = (\mathsf{B}^\mathsf{T}\mathsf{B})^{-1}\mathsf{B}^\mathsf{T}\mathbf{e}^t$. However, the explicit computation of the pseudo-inverse is computational expensive and subject to residual errors [20]. We solve the system of linear equations using the gaussian elimination method [20]. Since we have an over-constrained problem, we compute $\mathsf{B}^\mathsf{T}\mathsf{B}\delta\mathbf{q}^t = \mathsf{B}^\mathsf{T}\mathbf{e}^t$. Through Cholesky decomposition, we factorize $\mathsf{B}^\mathsf{T}\mathsf{B} = \mathsf{L}^\mathsf{T}\mathsf{L}$, with L being an upper triangular matrix. The updates $\delta\mathbf{q}^t$ are computed after solving an upper and lower triangular system, which are fast to compute [20].

Update of the Warp Parameters: The final step of the algorithm concerns the update the current parameters estimative. In theory [5, 6], the incremental warp $\mathbf{v_c}(\mathbf{x}; \delta\mathbf{q})$ must be composed with the current warp estimative. We relax this composition requirement and use an approximate relation to update the warp parameters. We start from the relation given in [5, 6]

$$\mathbf{v_c}(\mathbf{x}; \mathbf{q}^{i+1}) \leftarrow \mathbf{v_c}(\mathbf{x}; \mathbf{q}^{i}) \circ \mathbf{v_c}^{-1}(\mathbf{x}; \delta\mathbf{q}) \equiv \mathbf{v_c}(\mathbf{v_c}(\mathbf{x}; -\delta\mathbf{q}); \mathbf{q}^{i}). \tag{20}$$

Using this equation, we can formulate the parameters update as an additive step through the computation of a Jacobian matrix $\mathsf{J}_\mathbf{q}$ that maps the inverse compositional increment $\delta\mathbf{q}$ to its additive first-order equivalent $\mathsf{J}_\mathbf{q}\delta\mathbf{q}$ [5, 6], with the warp parameters being additively updated as $\mathbf{q}^{i+1} \leftarrow \mathbf{q}^{i} + \mathsf{J}_\mathbf{q}\delta\mathbf{q}$.

4 Experimental Validation

A tracking algorithm must be able to perform long-term feature tracking with high pixel accuracy [16]. Typically, the tracking performance is benchmarked through the evaluation of the tracking repeatability and the sub-pixel accuracy achieved during the image registration process [16]. This section compares the standard KLT algorithm against the proposed cRD-KLT and uRD-KLT trackers in sequences with different amounts of RD. All the trackers are directly used in the images with distortion, without ant type of rectification or pre-processing. We perform experiences in sequences of planar scenes, where it is possible to obtain ground truth to assess repeatability [16], and scenes with depth variation, where we evaluate the accuracy of Structure-from-Motion [15] . In addition, we describe an experience in self-calibration using the uRD-KLT tracker that can be helpful in practical surveillance scenarios. The three methods under evaluation were implemented using the affine motion model and a squared integration window $\mathcal{N}$ of 11×11 inside a pyramidal image registration with 4 resolution levels. Since our main goal is to perform feature (position) tracking rather than the template itself, we monitor the health of the template through the evaluation of the squared error of Eq. 5, with a new template being captured at the last feature position whenever required.

4.1 Repeatability Analysis in Planar Scenes

This experiment evaluates the reliability of the feature tracking algorithms using images of planar scenes. This means that every 2 images are related by an homography that is used to verify the correctness and localization accuracy of the tracked features. For the computation of the ground truth homographies, we apply a robust estimation algorithm [21] that uses hundreds of correspondences obtained with sRD-SIFT, which provide precisely located features in radial distorted images [15]. The trackers are tested using four levels of distortion (0%, 10%, 25% and 45 %), with each level comprising 3 types of motion: slow translation, fast translation and generic camera motion.

We start by extracting 150 features using the Shi-Tomasi detection criteria [2], and track them along the 600 frames of each sequence. The reliability of the tracks are measured using the following metrics:

(i) *Repeatability* measures the ratio of correct points in the frame f using the ground truth homography H_1^f that provides the mapping from view 1 to f. The repeatability is measured as:

$$\mathcal{R} = \frac{\#(||\mathbf{x}_f - \mathsf{H}_1^f \mathbf{x}_1|| < \mathcal{D})}{\#(\mathsf{H}_1^f \mathbf{x}_1)}, \tag{21}$$

where $||\cdot||$ denotes the euclidean distance and $\mathcal{D} = 2$ pixels.

(ii) The *Sub-pixel accuracy* is measured for the points N that are reliably tracked. At frame f, we evaluate the RMS of the euclidean distance between consecutive feature positions as:

$$\mathcal{S}_{err} = \sqrt{\frac{\sum(||\mathbf{x}_f - \mathsf{H}_1^f \mathbf{x}_1||)^2}{N}}; \tag{22}$$

(iii) The *Photometric error* $\mathcal{A}_{err}$ is measured as the RMS of the squared error of Eq. 5 of the N tracked features.

We also include the computational time (FPS - frame per second) of the different methods for tracking the 150 features and the RD estimation for each level of distortion obtained using the uRD-KLT. The image sequences presenting distortion are calibrated using the Single Image Calibration (SIC) proposed in [22], which provides the ground truth for the distortion estimation.

Table 1 shows the repeatability results obtained in the planar image sequences. The conventional KLT tracker performs well in low distortion sequences, or when the motion between frames is smooth. In such cases, the distortion changes smoothly between two points locations, and the template update process enables to keep plausible tracks. However, when more complex motions, such as fast translation or affine camera motions are considered, the distortion changes more abruptly between two feature locations, precluding an effective performance of the registration process with direct consequences in the tracking results. As we increase the distortion and the complexity of the motion, the KLT starts loosing performance, which proves the importance of compensating distortion during tracking.

The compensation of distortion during registration, either by knowing RD calibration, or by performing it on-the-fly, brings improvements in all the evaluation parameters. The deformation tolerated by the RD compensated motion

Table 1. Performance evaluation in the planar scenes. The results are organized by type of motion (vertically) and corresponding amount of distortion (horizontally). The results presented are the RMS of the evaluation metric computed over the 600 frames. The distortion estimation and computational time are averaged over the 3 sequences with the same RD. The computational times were measured in a Intel Core i7-2600 CPU @3.4GHz.

				Slow Trans			Fast Trans			Affine Motion		
		%RD	FPS	$\mathcal{R}$	$\mathcal{S}_{err}$	$\mathcal{A}_{err}$	$\mathcal{R}$	$\mathcal{S}_{err}$	$\mathcal{A}_{err}$	$\mathcal{R}$	$\mathcal{S}_{err}$	$\mathcal{A}_{err}$
0%	**KLT**	—	6.11	0.98	0.21	0.014	0.95	0.27	0.021	0.90	0.35	0.032
	uRD-KLT	0.6±1.4	5.32	0.98	0.23	0.018	0.95	0.31	0.028	0.90	0.39	0.035
10%	**KLT**	—	6.09	0.98	0.38	0.038	0.92	0.58	0.055	0.90	0.59	0.045
	cRD-KLT	9.8	6.03	0.98	0.30	0.021	0.98	0.47	0.028	0.98	0.43	0.027
	uRD-KLT	9.4±0.48	5.28	0.98	0.32	0.021	0.98	0.47	0.028	0.98	0.43	0.027
25%	**KLT**	—	6.07	0.98	0.42	0.049	0.88	0.56	0.047	0.69	0.85	0.051
	cRD-KLT	24.7	6.02	0.99	0.33	0.026	0.98	0.43	0.026	0.90	0.55	0.027
	uRD-KLT	24.5±1.3	5.24	0.99	0.33	0.026	0.98	0.45	0.027	0.90	0.58	0.034
45%	**KLT**	—	5.95	0.87	0.81	0.051	0.76	1.15	0.065	0.64	1.27	0.076
	cRD-KLT	44.3	5.95	0.95	0.56	0.029	0.91	0.70	0.038	0.84	0.65	0.047
	uRD-KLT	44.2 ± 2.9	5.19	0.95	0.58	0.031	0.89	0.75	0.041	0.84	0.66	0.049

models allow to compensate the pernicious effects of distortion, which in practice is translated in accurate estimations of the feature motion parameters. This is visible in the lower appearance error and spatial accuracy achieved by the RD-KLT trackers. Since the registration is more accurate, the appearance error is lower, and the template update is less frequent, minimizing the inherent error in localization introduced by this process. It can also be observed that uRD-KLT performs slightly worse than the cRD-KLT algorithm in the sequences with high distortion and more complex motion. The differences in sub-pixel precision and photometric error are due to the use of the approximated RD motion model, which becomes slightly more imprecise as we increase distortion. Nevertheless, the difference is almost marginal without practical influence in the repeatability.

The 3 methods were implemented in Matlab/MEX files. The C-MEX files include operations that are transversal to the 3 methods, namely the interpolation routines, image gradient computation and image pyramid building. The computational time of the cRD-KLT ($\approx$ 1.11 milliseconds (ms)/feature) is slightly higher than the conventional KLT ($\approx$ 1.10 ms/feature). The small differences are explained by the different motion models used, which in our case is a non-linear mapping function that requires a little more computation. The uRD-KLT ($\approx$ 1.27 ms/feature) presents a computational overhead of $\approx$ 15%, which is a consequence of performing the RD estimation globally using Eq. 19. Nevertheless, it has the obvious advantage of not requiring distortion calibration for performing efficient feature tracking.

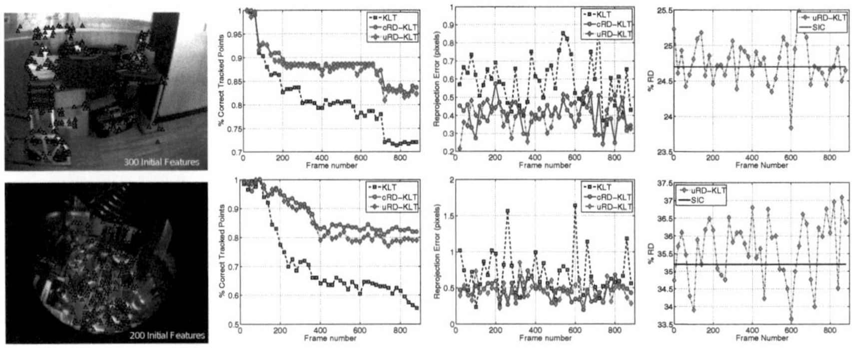

(a) Example image (b) Ratio of Inliers (c) Reproj. Error (d) RD estimation

Fig. 2. SfM experiments with a 25% distortion sequence and with a endoscopic sequence with 35% of RD. It can be observed that the RD-KLT tracker permit to long-term feature tracking (b) at a high precision accucary (c). (d) compares the distortion estimation form uRD-KLT with the explicit calibration results [22].

4.2 Structure-from-Motion (SfM)

Tracking features have been successfully applied to camera motion estimation and 3D scene reconstruction [21], with accurate point correspondence across frames being of key importance [21]. In this paper, the motion estimation is carried by a sequential SfM pipeline that uses as input the tracked points obtained by the 3 competing tracking methods. The objective is to recover the motion of two sparse sequences of 45 frames (sampled uniformly from sequences of 900 frames). The first sequence is obtained using a mini-lens that presents RD $\approx 25\%$, and the second sequence is captured using a boroscope with RD $\approx 35\%$, commonly used in medical endoscopy and industrial inspection.

The SfM pipeline iteratively adds new consecutive frames with a 5-point RANSAC initialization (using 2 views) [23], a scale factor adjustment (using 3 views) [21], and a final refinement with a sliding window bundle adjustment. Figure 2 shows that the motion estimation results. It can be observed that the RD-KLT trackers provide a lower re-projection error meaning that the extra parameter in the RD motion models permits a better convergence of the registration process in images presenting significant amounts of distortion. Finally, it can be seen in Fig. 2(d) that the distortion is robustly estimated, with the results being close to the ones obtained with the explicit calibration from [22].

4.3 RD Calibration for Surveillance Applications

Surveillance systems largely benefit with the usage of wide-angle lens that, due their wide FoV, enable a complete visual coverage of the environments [11]. In this final experiment, we show that using the uRD-KLT can be advantageous for estimating the distortion of a steady camera using the moving objects of

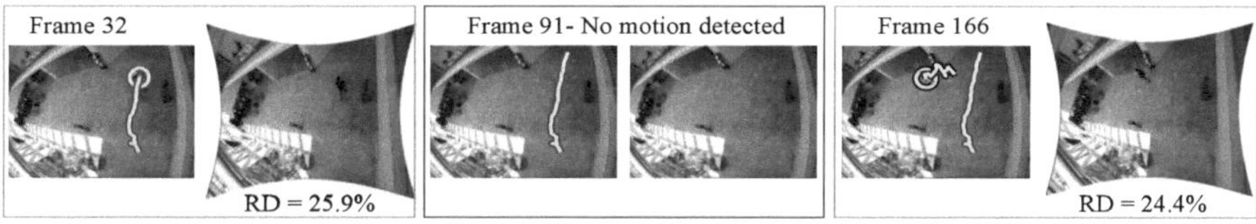

Fig. 3. Tracking experiment in a surveillance scenario from CAVIAR project. Distortion estimation is performed when significant motion is detected in the environment. Image inside the same bounding box concern the same instant of time. In each bounding box, the tracking results are shown on the left image, and the distortion estimation on the right image.

the scene. We test the algorithm using a sequence of the CAVIAR project[1], for which the RD calibration is unknown. We detect corner points at each frame sequence and initialize the uRD-KLT. If the points do not move in the next two frames, we re-initialize the tracker. The tracking results can be observed in Fig. 3. In each pair of bounded images, the original image (left image) shows the tracking results and the correspondent rectified image is shown on the right. In the middle block of images, the RD distortion estimated is negligible since no motion is detected and, therefore, the registration framework does not have any clues about how the local patches are deformed under the action of distortion.

5 Conclusions

This article presented for the first time an extension to the conventional KLT algorithm for point feature tracking in images with radial distortion. This was achieved by modifying the warping functions in order to account for both the motion and the non-linear image deformation arising in cameras with wide-angle lenses. Comparative experiments show that our RD-KLT tracker performs almost as well as the standard KLT tracker in sequences of correct perspective images, and achieves substantially better results in sequences with any amount of non-linear distortion. This is accomplished with minimum computational overhead. Such improvements in tracking are of strong importance for applications and domains that employ cameras equipped with mini-lens, fish-eye lenses, or boroscopes (e.g. robotics, medical applications, etc). In addition, we show for the first time that it is possible to accurately calibrate the image distortion while tracking low-level point features.

Acknowledgments. The authors acknowledge the Portuguese Science Foundation (FCT) that generously funded this work through grants PTDC/EIA-CCO/109120/2008 and SFRH/BD/63118/2009.

[1] Available at `http://homepages.inf.ed.ac.uk/rbf/CAVIARDATA1/`

References

1. Lucas, B.D., Kanade, T.: An Iterative Image Registration Technique with an Application to Stereo Vision. In: DARPA Image Understanding Workshop, pp. 121–130 (1981)
2. Shi, J., Tomasi, C.: Good features to track. In: IEEE-CVPR, pp. 593–600 (1994)
3. Yilmaz, A., Javed, O., Shah, M.: Object Tracking: A survey. ACM Comput. Surv. 38 (2006)
4. Pollefeys, M., Van Gool, L., Vergauwen, M., Verbiest, F., Cornelis, K., Tops, J., Koch, R.: Visual Modeling with a Hand-Held Camera. IJCV 59, 207–232 (2004)
5. Baker, S., Matthews, I.: Equivalence and Efficiency of Image Alignment Algorithms. In: IEEE-CVPR, vol. 1, pp. 1090–1097 (2001)
6. Baker, S., Matthews, I.: Lucas-Kanade 20 Years On: A Unifying Framework. IJCV 56, 221–255 (2004)
7. Bouguet, J.Y.: Pyramidal Implementation of the Lucas Kanade Feature Tracker Description of the algorithm (2000)
8. Hwangbo, M., Kim, J.S., Kanade, T.: Gyro-aided feature tracking for a moving camera: fusion, auto-calibration and GPU implementation. IJRR 30, 1755–1774 (2011)
9. Gluckman, J., Nayar, S.: Egomotion and Omnidirectional Cameras. In: IEEE-ICCV (1998)
10. Baker, P., Fermuller, C., Aloimonos, Y., Pless, R.: A Spherical Eye from Multiple Cameras (Makes Better Models of the World). In: IEEE-CVPR (2001)
11. Caron, G., Eynard, D.: Multiple camera types simultaneous stereo calibration. In: IEEE-ICRA, pp. 2933–2938 (2011)
12. García Cifuentes, C., Sturzel, M., Jurie, F., Brostow, G.J.: Motion models that only work sometimes. In: BMVC (2012)
13. Koeser, K., Bartczak, B., Koch, R.: Robust GPU-assisted camera tracking using free-form surface models. Journal of Real-Time Image Processing 2, 133–147 (2007)
14. Behrens, A., Bommes, M., Stehle, T., Gross, S., Leonhardt, S., Aach, T.: Real-time image composition of bladder mosaics in fluorescence endoscopy. Computer Science - Research and Development 26, 51–64 (2011)
15. Lourenco, M., Barreto, J.P., Vasconcelos, F.: sRD-SIFT: Keypoint Detection and Matching in Images With Radial Distortion. In: IEEE-TRO (2012)
16. Gauglitz, S., Höllerer, T., Turk, M.: Evaluation of Interest Point Detectors and Feature Descriptors for Visual Tracking. IJCV 94, 335–360 (2011)
17. Willson, R.G., Shafer, S.A.: What is the center of the image? J. Opt. Soc. Am. A 11, 2946–2955 (1994)
18. Barreto, J.P.: A Unifying Geometric Representation for Central Projection Systems. CVIU 103, 208–217 (2006)
19. Matthews, L., Ishikawa, T., Baker, S.: The Template Update Problem. IEEE-TPAMI 26, 810–815 (2004)
20. Davis, T.A.: Direct Methods for Sparse Linear Systems. Fundamentals of Algorithms, vol. 2. Society for Industrial and Applied Mathematics (2006)
21. Ma, Y., Soatto, S., Kosecka, J., Sastry, S.: An Invitation to 3D Vision: From Images to Geometric Models. Springer (2003)
22. Barreto, J.P., Roquette, J., Sturm, P., Fonseca, F.: Automatic Camera Calibration Applied to Medical Endoscopy. In: BMVC (2009)
23. Nistér, D.: An Efficient Solution to the Five-Point Relative Pose Problem. IEEE-TPAMI 26 (2004)

Divergence-Free Motion Estimation

Isabelle Herlin[1,2], Dominique Béréziat[3], Nicolas Mercier[1,2], and Sergiy Zhuk[4]

[1] INRIA , B.P. 105, 78153 Le Chesnay, France
[2] CEREA, Joint Laboratory ENPC - EDF R&D, Université Paris-Est, 77455 Marne la Vallée Cedex 2, France
[3] Université Pierre et Marie Curie, 75005 Paris, France
[4] IBM Research, Dublin Tech. Campus, Damastown, Dublin 15, Ireland

Abstract. This paper describes an innovative approach to estimate motion from image observations of divergence-free flows. Unlike most state-of-the-art methods, which only minimize the divergence of the motion field, our approach utilizes the vorticity-velocity formalism in order to construct a motion field in the subspace of divergence free functions. A 4DVAR-like image assimilation method is used to generate an estimate of the vorticity field given image observations. Given that vorticity estimate, the motion is obtained solving the Poisson equation. Results are illustrated on synthetic image observations and compared to those obtained with state-of-the-art methods, in order to quantify the improvements brought by the presented approach. The method is then applied to ocean satellite data to demonstrate its performance on the real images.

1 Introduction

A fluid is called incompressible if its velocity field has zero divergence. A fluid is said incompressible if its motion is characterised by a null divergence. For instance, atmosphere and ocean are such incompressible fluids that are daily observed by a large number of satellites providing 2D observations of these systems. The 2D incompressible hypothesis still remains a good approximation for ocean satellite sequences if no or small vertical motion occurs (no upwelling and downwelling). This is the geostrophic assumption. Introducing the divergence-free heuristics for motion estimation methods is then a promising issue for such data sequences.

If the divergence-free assumption is assumed to be valid on an image sequence, it should be implemented through the whole computational process. However, in most of image processing methods, the velocity field $\mathbf{w}$ is estimated by solving a brightness transport equation with additional regularisation terms. In order to satisfy the divergence-free hypothesis, these terms constrain the divergence to be as small as possible, but its value is not zero. In the data assimilation framework, motion is estimated as a compromise between heuristics on the dynamics of $\mathbf{w}$ and the image observations [1]. If the motion field is divergence-free, it is then only characterised by its vorticity ξ, according to the Helmholtz orthogonal decomposition [2]. In this paper, we then propose to replace the heuristics on the

A. Fitzgibbon et al. (Eds.): ECCV 2012, Part IV, LNCS 7575, pp. 15–27, 2012.

dynamics of $\mathbf{w}$ by their equivalent on the vorticity ξ. As temporal integration of vorticity requires an additional knowledge of the velocity field, an algebraic method is described, based the projection of vorticity on a reduced basis, that converts vorticity to velocity. The divergence-free motion estimation problem is then formalised as a cost function to be minimised. Its gradient is computed from an adjoint variable [3]. The output is the vorticity field computed over the whole assimilation window, corresponding to the input image sequence. The motion field is obtained from that vorticity field solving the Poisson equation.

During the last two decades, many authors investigated the issue of fluid flow motion estimation, see for instance [4] for a survey. On one hand, transport brightness equations, based on fluid flow laws, have been proposed as alternatives to the famous brightness constancy assumption [5]. For instance, a 2D brightness transport equation may be derived from the 3D continuity equation in radiography fluid flow imagery [6,7]. The 2D continuity equation has also been proposed due to its robustness to rotational motion [8,9]. For Sea Surface Temperature (SST) oceanographic images, a 2D brightness transport equation is derived from a 3D model of ocean surface temperature [10]. On another hand, regularisation techniques, dedicated to fluid motion estimation, have been intensively studied. On 2D image sequences, a notable result is due to Suter [11], which proposed to restrain the divergence and the curl of $\mathbf{w}$ or their variations to be as small as possible. Each term having its own weight value, the user decides to constrain the divergence or/and the vorticity to be either low value or spatially regular. Suter's solution is computed with a variational technique and a B-spline decomposition. Additionally, Isambert *et al.* [12] proposed a B-spline multi-scale approach and a partition of unity to define control points, used to derive the solution. A multi-resolution div-curl regularisation combining Markov Random Field and Gauss-Seidel relaxation is described in [13]. The div-curl regularisation has also been used for 3D images of fluid flow [14,15], on which the incompressible assumption is verified. In [14], 3D velocity is computed from 3D Cine CT images using a L_2 regularisation under divergence-free constraint. In [15], motion is computed with a 3D div-curl regularisation function and stochastic models. To constrain motion having exact null divergence, alternatives to div-curl regularisation are proposed in the literature. Ruhnau *et al.*, in [16], solves the optical flow equation under the constraints of Stokes equation and null divergence. Amimi, in [6], characterises the divergence-free motion as deriving from a stream function that verifies the optical flow equation.

More recently, variational data assimilation methods were applied to estimate motion using a dynamic equation on the velocity field. Ruhnau *et al.*, in [17], define a filtering method, based on an evolution equation of vorticity. The vorticity being initialised with a null value at $T = 0$, the method minimises, at each observation date, an energy function under the constraint of null divergence. This function includes three terms: optical flow equation, spatial regularity of vorticity, and coherency with the evolution equation of vorticity. The authors explain that estimations are reliable after around ten observations, which makes the method not usable for shorter sequences. In [18], velocities and temperature are computed from Shallow-Water and transport equations and temperature values are compared to SST image acquisitions. The velocity field is regularised with a second order div-curl norm. In [19], vorticity and divergence are both components of the state vector. The vorticity dynamics is described by a 2D approximation of the Navier-Stokes equations, that requires the simultaneous knowledge of velocity and vorticity. The divergence is supposed to be function of a Gaussian random variable and the authors use the heat equation to describe its dynamics. The computation of motion from vorticity and divergence is then performed in the Fourier domain using the Biot-Savart law. The comparison of the state vector with the image observations is achieved by the optical flow equation. In Papadakis *et al.* [20], a pure divergence-free model is defined for periodic motion field: motion is characterised by its vorticity value, which is the only component of the state vector, and the 2D Navier-Stokes equations provide the dynamic model. An error term on the dynamics is considered as a control of the optimisation problem. Images are assimilated using the optical flow equation as observation equation. The underlying assumption is that motion is constant between two consecutive acquisitions, which is however not coherent with the dynamic model.

This paper describes a divergence-free motion estimation approach, based on the Euler equations, and relying on an algebraic method to derive the motion vector from its vorticity value. The state vector $\mathbf{X}$ includes the vorticity value ξ and a pseudo-image I_s: $\mathbf{X} = \left(\xi \; I_s\right)^T$. I_s is supposed to have the same temporal evolution as the studied image sequence. In the paper, the heuristics of transport of grey level values by the motion field is applied. During the assimilation process, values of I_s are compared to image observations in order to constrain the motion estimation process. The paper will discuss the impact of including the pseudo-image I_s in the state vector on the quality of results. The assumption of Lagrangian constancy for $\mathbf{w}$ is used, from which an evolution equation of vorticity ξ is derived.

Section 2 describes the divergence-free image model used for motion estimation on an image sequence. As the evolution equations involve the velocity $\mathbf{w}$, the algebraic method that computes $\mathbf{w}$ from its vorticity ξ is described. Section 3 explains how the solution is obtained by minimising a cost function with a strong 4D-Var (for a perfect model with no error on the dynamics) data assimilation method. Section 4 details the numerical aspects required for an effective implementation by interested Readers. Section 5 quantifies results on synthetic data and discusses the estimation obtained on oceanographic satellite data. Comparisons with state-of-the-art methods are provided, that justify the interest of our approach.

2 Problem Statement

This section describes the divergence-free model, that represents motion on an image sequence.

Let us denote $\Omega \times [0, t_N]$ the bounded space-time domain on which images, vorticity and motion fields are defined.

2.1 Divergence-Free Model

Vorticity characterises a rotational motion while divergence characterises sinks and sources in a flow. 2D motion $\mathbf{w} = \left(u\ v\right)^T$ is described by its vorticity, $\xi = \frac{\partial v}{\partial x} - \frac{\partial u}{\partial y}$, under the hypothesis of null divergence [2]. ξ is chosen as the first component of the state vector $\mathbf{X}$ of the model. Deriving the evolution law for ξ requires heuristics on the velocity $\mathbf{w}$. The Lagrangian constancy hypothesis, $\frac{d\mathbf{w}}{dt} = 0$, is considered in the paper. It can be expanded as: $\frac{\partial \mathbf{w}}{\partial t} + (\mathbf{w}.\nabla)\mathbf{w} = 0$:

$$\frac{\partial u}{\partial t} + u\frac{\partial u}{\partial x} + v\frac{\partial u}{\partial y} = 0 \tag{1}$$

$$\frac{\partial v}{\partial t} + u\frac{\partial v}{\partial x} + v\frac{\partial v}{\partial y} = 0 \tag{2}$$

Let us compute the y-derivative of Eq. (1), subtract it from the x-derivative of Eq. (2), and replace the quantity $\frac{\partial v}{\partial x} - \frac{\partial u}{\partial y}$ by ξ, we obtain:

$$\frac{\partial \xi}{\partial t} + u\frac{\partial \xi}{\partial x} + v\frac{\partial \xi}{\partial y} + \xi\left(\frac{\partial u}{\partial x} + \frac{\partial v}{\partial y}\right) = 0 \tag{3}$$

that is rewritten in a conservative form as:

$$\frac{\partial \xi}{\partial t} + \nabla.(\xi\mathbf{w}) = 0 \tag{4}$$

The pseudo-image I_s is transported by motion with the same heuristics as the image sequence: this is the well known optical flow constraint equation [5], expressed as:

$$\frac{\partial I_s}{\partial t} + \nabla I_s.\mathbf{w} = 0 \tag{5}$$

and rewritten as:

$$\frac{\partial I_s}{\partial t} + \nabla.(I_s\mathbf{w}) = 0 \tag{6}$$

under the divergence-free hypothesis.

The model is then defined by the state vector $\mathbf{X} = \left(\xi\ I_s\right)^T$ and its evolution system:

$$\frac{\partial \xi}{\partial t} + \nabla.(\xi\mathbf{w}) = 0 \tag{7}$$

$$\frac{\partial I_s}{\partial t} + \nabla.(I_s\mathbf{w}) = 0 \tag{8}$$

2.2 Algebraic Computation of w

When the state vector is integrated in time with Eqs. (7,8), from an initial condition defined at date 0, the knowledge of ξ, I_s and $\mathbf{w}$ is required at each time step. The velocity field $\mathbf{w}$ should then be computed from the scalar field ξ at each time step. A stream function φ is first defined as the solution of the Poisson equation:

$$-\Delta\varphi = \xi \tag{9}$$

Then, $\mathbf{w}$ is derived from φ by:

$$\mathbf{w} = \left(\frac{\partial\varphi}{\partial y} \; -\frac{\partial\varphi}{\partial x}\right)^T \tag{10}$$

In the literature (see for instance in [20]) Eq. (9) is usually solved in the Fourier domain with pseudo-spectral methods assuming periodic boundary conditions. However, this periodicity property is inadequate in our context, as there is no reason having a motion field with periodicity of the image domain's size. An algebraic solution of the Poisson equation is proposed in the following, in order to allow vorticity having Dirichlet boundary conditions with null value [21].
An eigenfunction, ϕ, of the linear operator $-\Delta$ has to verify $-\Delta\phi = \lambda\phi$, where λ is the corresponding eigenvalue. Explicit solutions of this eigenvalue problem are the family of bi-periodic functions $\phi_{n,m}(x,y) = \sin(\pi n x)\sin(\pi m y)$ with the associated eigenvalues $\lambda_{n,m} = \pi^2 n^2 + \pi^2 m^2$. These functions form an orthogonal basis of a subspace of $L_2(\Omega)$, space of square-integrable functions defined on Ω. They have null values on the domain boundary. Let $(a_{n,m})$ be the coefficients of ξ in the basis $(\phi_{n,m})$: $\xi(x,y) = \sum\limits_{n,m} a_{n,m}\phi_{n,m}(x,y)$. It comes:

$$\varphi(x,y) = \sum_{n,m} \frac{a_{n,m}}{\lambda_{n,m}} \phi_{n,m}(x,y) \tag{11}$$

and eq. (9) is verified:

$$-\Delta\varphi(x,y) = -\sum_{n,m} \frac{a_{n,m}}{\lambda_{n,m}} \Delta\phi_{n,m}(x,y) = \sum_{n,m} \frac{a_{n,m}}{\lambda_{n,m}} \lambda_{n,m}\phi_{n,m}(x,y) = \xi \tag{12}$$

At each date, having knowledge of ξ and $(\phi_{n,m})$, the values of $(a_{n,m})$ are first computed. Then φ is derived by Eq. (11), using the $(\lambda_{n,m})$ values.

3 4D-Var Data Assimilation

In order to determine $\mathbf{X}$, the 4D-Var framework considers a system of three equations to be solved.
The first equation describes the evolution in time of the state vector $\mathbf{X}$. This is given by Eqs. (7,8). For sake of simplicity, the system is summarised by introducing the evolution model M for the state vector $\mathbf{X}$:

$$\frac{\partial \mathbf{X}}{\partial t} + M(\mathbf{X}) = 0 \tag{13}$$

Let us consider having some knowledge on the state vector value at initial date 0, which is described by a background value $\mathbf{X}_b(x,y)$. As this initial condition is uncertain, the second equation of the system involves an error term ϵ_B:

$$\mathbf{X}(x,y,0) = \mathbf{X}_b(x,y) + \epsilon_B(x,y) \tag{14}$$

The error $\epsilon_B(x,y)$ is supposed to be Gaussian with zero-mean and covariance function $B(x,y)$. If estimating motion from an image sequence, the only knowledge that is available is the background of the component I_s, that is chosen as the first image of the sequence: $I(x,y,t_1)$. The background equation, Eq. (14), reduces to:

$$I_s(x,y,0) = I(x,y,t_1) + \epsilon_{B_I}(x,y) \tag{15}$$

with B_I the part of B related to I_s.

The last equation, named observation equation, links the state vector to the studied image sequence $I(x,y,t)$: the pseudo-image I_s has to be almost identical to the image observation $I(x,y,t)$. It is expressed as:

$$I_s(x,y,t) = I(x,y,t) + \epsilon_R(x,y,t) \tag{16}$$

Image acquisitions are noisy and their underlying dynamics could be different from the one described by Eq. (8). The observation error, ϵ_R, is used to model these uncertainties. It is supposed Gaussian and characterised by its variance $R(x,y,t)$.

In order to discuss how Eqs. (13,15,16) are solved by the data assimilation method, the state vector and its evolution equation are first approximated in time with an Euler scheme. The space variables x and y are further omitted for sake of simplicity. Let dt be the time step, the state vector at discrete index k, $0 \leq k \leq N_t$, is denoted $\mathbf{X}(k) = \mathbf{X}(k \times dt)$. The discrete evolution equation is:

$$\mathbf{X}(k+1) = \mathbf{X}(k) - dtM(\mathbf{X}(k)) = Z_k(\mathbf{X}(k)) \tag{17}$$

with $Z_k(\mathbf{X}(k)) = \begin{pmatrix} \xi(k) - dt\nabla.(\xi(k)\mathbf{w}(\xi(k))) \\ \mathbf{q}(k) - dt\nabla.(\mathbf{q}(k)\mathbf{w}(\xi(k))) \end{pmatrix}$.

N_{obs} image observations $I(t_i)$ are available from the image sequence, at indexes $t_1 < \cdots < t_i < \cdots < t_{N_{\mathrm{obs}}}$. Looking for $\mathbf{X} = (\mathbf{X}(0), \cdots, \mathbf{X}(N_t))$ solving Eqs.(17,15,16) is expressed as a constrained optimisation problem: the cost function

$$\begin{aligned} J(\mathbf{X}) =& \frac{1}{2}\int_\Omega B_I^{-1}(I_s(0) - I(t_1))^2 dxdy \\ &+ \frac{1}{2}\sum_{i=1}^{N_{\mathrm{obs}}} \int_\Omega R^{-1}(t_i)(I_s(t_i) - I(t_i))^2 dxdy \end{aligned} \tag{18}$$

has to be minimised over Eq. (17). The first term of J comes from Eq. (15) and the second one from Eq. (16), which is valid at observation indexes t_i.

From Eq. (17), we derive:

$$\mathbf{X}(k) = Z_{k-1} \cdots Z_0[\mathbf{X}(0)] \tag{19}$$

expressing that the state vector at index k only depends on $\mathbf{X}(0)$. The constrained optimisation problem (18) is then rewritten as an unconstrained one: minimisation of the cost function:

$$\begin{aligned} J(\mathbf{X}(0)) =& \frac{1}{2}\int_{\Omega} B_I^{-1} \left(H\mathbf{X}(0) - I(t_1)\right)^2 dxdy \\ &+ \frac{1}{2}\sum_{i=1}^{N_{\text{obs}}} \int_{\Omega} R^{-1}(t_i) \left(HZ_{t_i-1} \cdots Z_0[\mathbf{X}(0)] - I(t_i)\right)^2 dxdy \end{aligned} \tag{20}$$

where H stands for the projection of the state vector X on its component I_s. Using calculus of variation, the gradient of J is obtained from its directional derivative:

$$\begin{aligned} \langle \nabla J_{\mathbf{X}(0)}, \eta \rangle = & \int_{\Omega} (H\eta)^T B_I^{-1} (H\mathbf{X}(0) - I(t_1)) dxdy \\ & + \sum_{i=1}^{N_{\text{obs}}} \int_{\Omega} \left(H \frac{\partial Z_{t_1-1}}{\partial \mathbf{X}} \cdots \frac{\partial Z_0}{\partial \mathbf{X}} \eta \right)^T \times \\ & R^{-1}(t_i) \left(HZ_{t_i-1} \cdots Z_0[\mathbf{X}(0)] - I(t_i)\right) dxdy \end{aligned} \tag{21}$$

Introducing the adjoint operator, defined by $\langle Af, g \rangle = \langle f, A^* g \rangle$, we factorise η in the previous equation and obtain:

$$\begin{aligned} \nabla J_{\mathbf{X}(0)} = H^T B_I^{-1} (H\mathbf{X}(0) - I(t_1)) \\ + \sum_{i=1}^{N_{\text{obs}}} \left(\frac{\partial Z_0}{\partial \mathbf{X}} \right)^* \cdots \left(\frac{\partial Z_{t_i-1}}{\partial \mathbf{X}} \right)^* H^T R^{-1}(t_i) (HZ_{t_i-1} \cdots Z_0[\mathbf{X}(0)] - I(t_i)) \end{aligned} \tag{22}$$

Let us introduce the auxiliary variable λ defined by:

$$\lambda(k) = \left(\frac{\partial Z_k}{\partial \mathbf{X}} \right)^* \lambda(k+1) + H^T R^{-1}(k) \left(H\mathbf{X}(k) - I(k)\right), \tag{23}$$

$\lambda(N_t) = 0$, and $H^T R^{-1}(k)(H\mathbf{X}(k) - I(k))$ being only taken into account at observation indexes t_i. It can be easily proved that the gradient reduces to:

$$\nabla J_{\mathbf{X}(0)} = H^T B_I^{-1} (H\mathbf{X}(0) - I(t_1)) + \lambda(0) \tag{24}$$

The cost function J is minimised using an iterative steepest descent method. At each iteration, the forward time integration of $\mathbf{X}$ provides the value of J, then a backward integration of λ computes $\lambda(0)$ and provides ∇J. An efficient solver [22] is used to perform the steepest descent given J and ∇J. Full details are given in [3] about the derivation of ∇J.

4 Numerical Implementation

The numerical scheme applied for the forward time integration of $\mathbf{X}$ is described in the following. As the evolution equations of vorticity and pseudo-image, Eqs. (7) and (8), are similar, the description is only given for the first one. A source splitting is first applied. Given a time interval $[t_1, t_2]$, we integrate successively the two equations:

$$\frac{\partial \xi^*}{\partial t} + \frac{\partial (u\xi^*)}{\partial x} = 0 \quad t \in [t_1, t_2] \tag{25}$$

$$\frac{\partial \xi^{**}}{\partial t} + \frac{\partial (v\xi^{**})}{\partial y} = 0 \quad t \in [t_1, t_2] \tag{26}$$

with $\xi^*(x, y, t_1) = \xi(x, y, t_1)$ and $\xi^{**}(x, y, t_1) = \xi(x, y, t_1)$. $\xi(x, y, t_2)$ is then approximated as $\xi(x, y, t_2) = \xi^{**}(x, y, t_2) + (\xi^*(x, y, t_2) - \xi(x, y, t_1))$.

Let f be a function defined on the space-time domain $\Omega \times [0, t_N]$. Let dx and dy be the spatial discretisation steps, supposed equal without any loss of generality: $dx = dy$. The discrete representation of f is $f^k_{i,j} = f(i \times dx, j \times dx, k \times dt)$ with $1 \leq i \leq N_x$, $1 \leq j \leq N_y$ and $0 \leq k \leq N_t$. With these notations, Eqs. (25,26) are approximated as in [23]:

$$\xi^*_{i,j} = \xi^k_{i,j} - \frac{dt}{dx}((F^u)^k_{i+1,j} - (F^u)^k_{i,j}) \tag{27}$$

$$\xi^{**}_{i,j} = \xi^k_{i,j} - \frac{dt}{dx}((F^v)^k_{i,j+1} - (F^v)^k_{i,j}) \tag{28}$$

with $F^u = u\xi$ and $F^v = v\xi$. A non-central scheme of order 3 (see [24]) is used to approximate fluxes (F^u) and (F^v) from the discrete representations of ξ and $\mathbf{w}$. $(F^u)^k_{i+1,j}$ is equal to:

$$\begin{array}{ll} u^k_{i+1,j}[\xi^k_{i,j} + d_0(\nu^k_{i+1,j})(\xi^k_{i+1,j} - \xi^k_{i,j}) + \\ \quad d_1(\nu^k_{i+1,j})(\xi^k_{i,j} - \xi^k_{i-1,j})] & \text{if} \quad u^k_{i+1,j} \geq 0 \end{array} \tag{29}$$

$$\begin{array}{ll} u^k_{i+1,j}[\xi^k_{i+1,j} + d_0(\nu^k_{i+1,j})(\xi^k_{i,j} - \xi^k_{i+1,j}) + \\ \quad d_1(\nu^k_{i+1,j})(\xi^k_{i+1,j} - \xi^k_{i+2,j})] & \text{if} \quad u^k_{i+1,j} < 0 \end{array} \tag{30}$$

with $d_0(\nu) = \frac{1}{6}(2-\nu)(1-\nu)$, $d_1(\nu) = \frac{1}{6}(1-\nu)^2$ and $\nu^k_{i+1,j} = \frac{dt}{dx}|u^k_{i+1,j}|$. The same formulation is applied for $(F^u)^k_{i,j}$, $(F^v)^k_{i,j+1}$ and $(F^v)^k_{i,j}$.

Eqs. (27,28), and those obtained from the approximation of Eq. (8), provide the discrete operator Z_k. The adjoint operator $\left(\frac{\partial Z_k}{\partial \mathbf{X}}\right)^*$ is automatically generated from the discrete operator Z_k by an efficient automatic differentiation software (see [25]).

5 Results

5.1 Synthetic Experiment

The divergence-free model is run from the initial conditions displayed in Figure 1. This provides a sequence of five synthetic observations (the first one is the initial

Fig. 1. Pseudo-image, vorticity and motion field at $t = 0$. Positive vorticity values are coloured in red and negative one in blue.

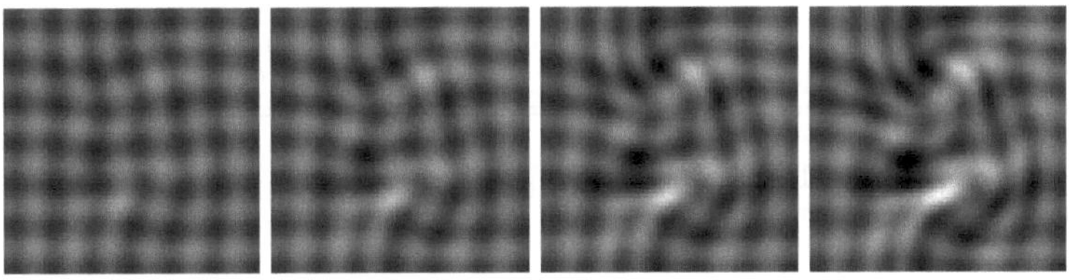

Fig. 2. Four observations of the twin experiment

condition and the four others are displayed on Figure 2) and the ground-truth of vorticity, motion and pseudo-image over the whole temporal window.

An assimilation experiment, named twin experiment, is performed with these five observations in order to retrieve the vorticity and motion fields. For that experiment, the background of vorticity is set to zero and the one of pseudo-image is the first observation. The result of the assimilation process is the state vector $\mathbf{X}(k) = \left(\xi(k)\ I_s(k)\right)^T$ and its associated motion vector $\mathbf{w}(k)$ over the same temporal interval than the image sequence. Statistics on the misfit between motion results and ground truth demonstrate the validity of the method: the average of the angular error and relative norm error are respectively 0.18° and 0.65%.

In order to compare our approach with state-of-the-art methods, a gaussian noise is added to the original observations, whose standard deviation is around one third of the image range. This provides the new observations displayed on Figure 3. In Table 1, the error between the motion result, obtained by data assimilation with these noisy images, and the ground truth is given for our approach and six state-of-the-art methods. In all cases, the optimal parameter values have been used. The first five one are image processing methods that rely on a L_2 regularisation of motion [5,26] or on a second-order regularisation of the divergence [12,13,11]. We also compare with [20] that applies data assimilation for a divergence-free model, whose state vector reduces to vorticity, with the optical flow equation as observation equation. Results demonstrate the improvement obtained with our formalism.

As the method presented in Papadakis *et al.* [20] is the most similar to our approach, it is important to explain why we obtain better results. As said before, we assume that N_{obs} image observations $I(t_i)$ are available at temporal indexes

Fig. 3. Noisy observations of the twin experiment

Table 1. Error analysis: misfit between motion results and ground truth

Method	Angular error (in deg.) Mean	Std. Dev.	Relative norm error Mean (in %)	Endpoint error Mean
Horn *et al* [5]	30.38	29.29	73	0.81
Sun *et al* [26]	11.31	12.54	60	0.6
Papadakis *et al* [20]	17.01	28.36	56	0.55
Corpetti *et al* [13]	7.19	10.78	26	0.26
Isambert *et al* [12]	6.71	14.35	42	0.37
Suter [11]	6.88	14.28	45	0.45
Our approach	3.32	10.5	5	0.04

$t_1 < \cdots < t_i < \cdots < t_{N_{\text{obs}}}$. At each observation date, our observation equation is $I_s(t_i) = I(t_i) + \epsilon_R(t_i)$ while [20] uses:

$$\frac{\partial I}{\partial t}(t_i) + \nabla I(t_i).\mathbf{w}(t_i) = \epsilon_R(t_i) \tag{31}$$

The temporal gradient in Eq. (31) being computed from the image sequence, it involves at least two frames, for instance t_i and t_{i+1}. Then, Eq. (31) implicitly assumes that motion is constant from t_i to t_{i+1}, which is not coherent with the evolution equation (Navier-Stokes equations) of vorticity and motion used in the dynamic model. Inconsistency of equations in the data assimilation system has a negative impact on results.

5.2 Application to Oceanographic SST Satellite Images

The approach has also been applied on satellite data. Observations are images acquired by NOAA/AVHRR sensors over Black Sea[1], and measure the Sea Surface Temperature (SST) with a spatial resolution of about 1 km at nadir. In the upper layer of the Black Sea, horizontal motion is around $30\,{}^{\text{cm}}/_{\text{s}}$ for mesoscale eddies, while vertical motion is around $10^{-4}\,{}^{\text{cm}}/_{\text{s}}$ and can be neglected. The 2D divergence-free assumption, or geostrophic equilibrium, is then roughly verified and the method is applicable. For the assimilation experiment, the background

[1] Data have been provided by E. Plotnikov and G. Korotaev from the Marine Hydrophysical Institute of Sevastopol, Ukraine.

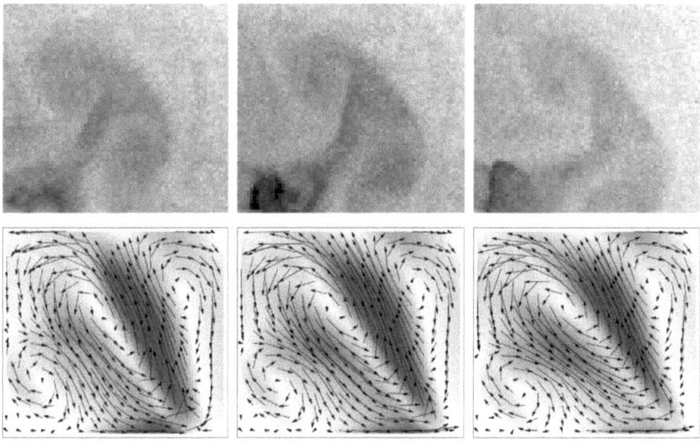

Fig. 4. Exp. 1. Observations and motion result at $t = 1, 3, 5$.

Table 2. Correlation between pseudo-images and observations

Date	1	2	3	4	5
Experiment 1	0.96	0.94	0.93	0.94	0.94
Experiment 2	0.99	0.93	0.94	0.97	–

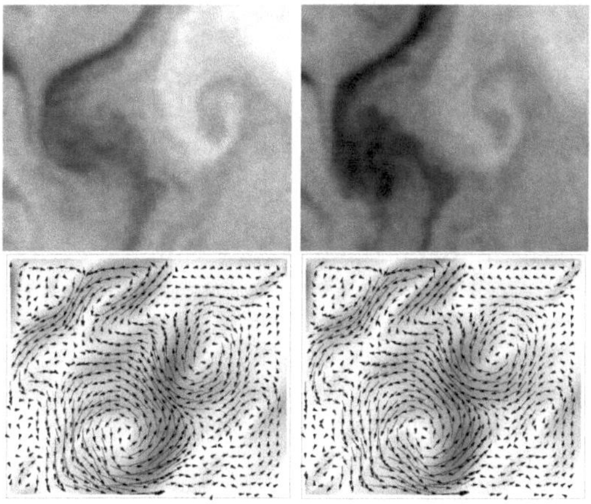

Fig. 5. Exp. 2. Observation and motion results at $t = 1, 3$.

of vorticity is set to zero and the one of pseudo-image is the first acquisition of the sequence.

Two experiments are described: the first one with five observations (part is displayed on Figure 4) and the second one with four observations (see Figure 5). The result of motion estimation is displayed on the same figures. Visualization is made with the coloured representation tool of the Middlebury database[2], superposed with the vector representation. As explained in Section 3, the method computes the initial condition for velocity and pseudo-image that achieves the best compromise between dynamics and observations. Therefore, at acquisition dates, pseudo-images are not exactly equal to the satellite acquisitions. Their correlation measures if the structures (edges) are correctly assessed, and motion accurately estimated. Results are given in Table 2: correlation values are close to 1, proving that the motion retrieved by our method is coherent with the dynamics underlying the evolution displayed by the observations.

6 Conclusion

The paper describes an image assimilation approach to estimate divergence-free motion on satellite acquisitions. An image model is designed: its state vector includes the vorticity and a pseudo-image, whose importance has been discussed in the results section. Motion is computed from vorticity by an algebraic method. The divergence value is then exactly null during the whole process. This allows to avoid Tikhonov regularity constraints on the divergence and the difficulty to correctly assess the constraint weights. The image assimilation technique performs a compromise between the image model and the acquired image observations in order to derive motion from an image sequence.

The method has been quantified on synthetic experiments, applied on satellite acquisitions and positively compared to well-known state-of-the-art methods.

Three main perspectives are envisaged. First, the cost of the algebraic computation of $\mathbf{w}$ from the vorticity will be decreased by limiting the set of projection fields to be taken into account for retrieving $\mathbf{w}$ from ξ. Second, model reduction, with a Galerkin projection on a subspace including only these projection fields, will be applied. This reduction will allow to perform data assimilation at lower cost, on long temporal assimilation windows. Last, other optimisation techniques, such as the minimax method are considered in order to also derive the estimation of uncertainty on the motion result.

References

1. Béréziat, D., Herlin, I.: Solving ill-posed image processing problems using data assimilation. Numerical Algorithms 56, 219–252 (2011)
2. Deriaz, E., Perrier, V.: Divergence-free and curl-free wavelets in two dimensions and three dimensions: application to turbulent flows. Journal of Turbulence 7, 1–37 (2006)
3. Le Dimet, F.X., Talagrand, O.: Variational algorithms for analysis and assimilation of meteorological observations: Theoretical aspects. Tellus 38A, 97–110 (1986)
4. Heitz, D., Mémin, E., Schnörr, C.: Variational fluid flow measurements from image sequences: synopsis and perspectives. Experiments in Fluids 48, 369–393 (2010)
5. Horn, B., Schunk, B.: Determining optical flow. Art. Int. 17, 185–203 (1981)

[2] `http://vision.middlebury.edu/flow/`

6. Amini, A.: A Scalar Function Formulation for Optical Flow. In: Eklundh, J.-O. (ed.) ECCV 1994. LNCS, vol. 801, pp. 125–131. Springer, Heidelberg (1994)
7. Wildes, R., Amabile, M.: Physically based fluid flow recovery from image sequences. In: CVPR, pp. 969–975 (1997)
8. Del Bimbo, A., Nesi, P., Sanz, J.: Optical flow computation using extended constraints. Trans. on Image Processing 5, 720–739 (1996)
9. Schunck, B.: The motion constraint equation for optical flow. In: ICPR (1984)
10. Vigan, X., Provost, C., Bleck, R., Courtier, P.: Sea surface velocities from Sea Surface Temperature image sequences. Journal of Geophysical Research 105, 19499–19514 (2000)
11. Suter, D.: Motion estimation and vector splines. In: CVPR, pp. 939–942 (1994)
12. Isambert, T., Herlin, I., Berroir, J.P.: Fast and stable vector spline method for fluid flow estimation. In: ICIP, pp. 505–508 (2007)
13. Corpetti, T., Mémin, E., Pérez, P.: Dense estimation of fluid flows. Pat. Anal. and Mach. Int. 24, 365–380 (2002)
14. Song, S., Leahy, R.: Computation of 3-D Velocity Fields from 3-D Cine CT Images of a Human Heart. Trans. on Medical Imaging 10, 295–306 (1991)
15. Gupta, S.N., Prince, J.L.: On div-curl regularization for motion estimation in 3-D volumetric imaging. In: ICIP, vol. 1, pp. 929–932 (1996)
16. Ruhnau, P., Schnörr, C.: Optical stokes flow estimation: An imaging-based control approach. Experiments in Fluids 42, 61–78 (2007)
17. Ruhnau, P., Stahl, A., Schnörr, C.: Variational estimation of experimental fluid flows with physics-based spatio-temporal regularization. Measurement Science and Technology 18, 755–763 (2007)
18. Huot, E., Herlin, I., Mercier, N., Plotnikov, E.: Estimating apparent motion on satellite acquisitions with a physical dynamic model. In: ICPR, pp. 41–44 (2010)
19. Papadakis, N., Mémin, E.: Variational assimilation of fluid motion from image sequence. SIAM Journal on Imaging Sciences 1, 343–363 (2008)
20. Papadakis, N., Corpetti, T., Mémin, E.: Dynamically consistent optical flow estimation. In: ICCV, pp. 1–7 (2007)
21. McOwen, R.: Partial Differential Equations: Methods and Applications, ch. 4. Prentice Hall (2003)
22. Zhu, C., Byrd, R., Lu, P., Nocedal, J.: L-BFGS-B: a limited memory FORTRAN code for solving bound constrained optimization problems. Technical Report NAM-11, EECS Department, Northwestern University (1994)
23. LeVeque, R.: Numerical Methods for Conservative Laws, 2nd edn. Lectures in Mathematics. ETH Zürich. Birkhaüser Verlag (1992)
24. Hundsdorfer, W., Spee, E.: An efficient horizontal advection scheme for the modeling of global transport of constituents. Monthly Weather Review 123, 3,554–3,564 (1995)
25. Hascoët, L., Pascual, V.: Tapenade 2.1 user's guide. Technical Report 0300, INRIA (2004)
26. Sun, D., Roth, S., Black, M.: Secrets of optical flow estimation and their principles. In: ECCV, pp. 2432–2439 (2010)

Visual Tracking via Adaptive Tracker Selection with Multiple Features

Ju Hong Yoon[1], Du Yong Kim[2], and Kuk-Jin Yoon[1]

[1] Computer Vision Lab., Gwangju Institute of Science and Technology, Korea
[2] Applied Computing Lab., Gwangju Institute of Science and Technology, Korea
{jhyoon,kjyoon}@gist.ac.kr, duyongkim@gmail.com

Abstract. In this paper, a robust visual tracking method is proposed to track an object in dynamic conditions that include motion blur, illumination changes, pose variations, and occlusions. To cope with these challenges, multiple trackers with different feature descriptors are utilized, and each of which shows different level of robustness to certain changes in an object's appearance. To fuse these independent trackers, we propose two configurations, tracker selection and interaction. The tracker interaction is achieved based on a transition probability matrix (TPM) in a probabilistic manner. The tracker selection extracts one tracking result from among multiple tracker outputs by choosing the tracker that has the highest tracker probability. According to various changes in an object's appearance, the TPM and tracker probability are updated in a recursive Bayesian form by evaluating each tracker's reliability, which is measured by a robust tracker likelihood function (TLF). When the tracking in each frame is completed, the estimated object's state is obtained and fed into the reference update via the proposed learning strategy, which retains the robustness and adaptability of the TLF and multiple trackers. The experimental results demonstrate that our proposed method is robust in various benchmark scenarios.

Keywords: Visual tracking, multiple features, transition probability matrix, robust likelihood function, tracker interaction, appearance learning.

1 Introduction

Visual tracking is an important research topic in the field of computer vision because of its wide application in surveillance, robotics, human-computer interface, vehicle tracking, medical imaging, and so on. Due to the characteristics of the various vision applications, visual tracking is required to deal with practical challenges originating from dynamic circumstances such as object and/or background illumination changes, object pose variation, occlusions, and motion blur [22] as shown in Fig. 1. Therefore, many researchers have discussed how to improve the performance of visual trackers by using multiple features in an efficient manner [4–15]. Despite decades of research, how to use multiple features to achieve a robust visual tracking is still an open problem.

In this paper, we propose a new visual tracking framework that fuses multiple trackers and features intelligently. We assume that each feature shows strong discriminating power under the conditions to which it is best suited. For instance, the histogram of

A. Fitzgibbon et al. (Eds.): ECCV 2012, Part IV, LNCS 7575, pp. 28–41, 2012.

(a) Pose and illumination changes (♯120,297) (b) Occlusion and motion blur (♯771,873)

Fig. 1. Example of our tracking results in *tiger1* and *liquor* seqs

oriented gradients (HOG) is robust to pose variation when the object's shape is consistent [21]; the Haar-like feature is robust to occlusion since it is part-based [20]; and the intensity is a good enough feature descriptor when there is small amount of pose variation and noise, because it contains redundant visual information [3].

In our method, each tracker is implemented with a different feature based on a particle filter. Our objective is then to integrate these multiple trackers and features to achieve robust visual tracking in dynamic environment changes. To achieve the efficient fusion, we propose two configurations, 1) Tracker Selection and 2) Tracker Interaction, in a Bayesian framework. The tracker selection chooses one of the tracking results from the multiple trackers according to tracker probability. The tracker that has the highest tracker probability is selected. The tracker interaction provides communication between the trackers based on a transition probability matrix (TPM) [2] with a conventional resampling technique [25]. The purpose of the tracker interaction is to prevent unreliable trackers from drifting. Since each tracker is implemented based on the particle filter, the interaction between the trackers is represented by three actions: keeping its own samples, taking samples from other trackers, and giving samples to other trackers. Here, the role of the TPM is to determine the aforementioned actions of each tracker.

The changes in an object's appearance affect the reliability of trackers. Hence, we need to reflect the variations in the reliability of trackers in the tracker fusion by updating the TPM and tracker probability. The update is executed in a recursive Bayesian form based on a tracker likelihood function (TLF) that measures the current fidelity of a tracking output from each tracker. We consider two terms, flexibility and stability when designing the TLF. This concept is successfully used in [4]. To embody this concept, we propose using two types of appearance models. The first focuses on flexibility and is computed based on recent object appearances that reflect an instantaneous object appearance. The second appearance model is obtained by using a reconstructed appearance based on an appearance dictionary, i.e., a set of representative appearance templates [16]. Due to the reconstructed appearance, we can measure robustly each tracker's reliability, although occlusion or outliers exist in the object's appearance. Hence, the latter appearance model is more stable and conservative than the former. These reference properties are maintained via the proposed learning strategy.

The contributions of this paper are summarized as follows. First, we propose a new tracking framework to integrate multiple trackers and features that consist of tracker selection and interaction. Second, a robust TLF is proposed to measure tracker reliability robustly even though occlusions or outliers occur in the object's appearance. Third, a simple but effective learning strategy is proposed to maintain the references used in each tracker and the TLF.

The remainder of the paper is organized as follows. We explain the differences between our method and related studies in Section 2. The overall framework and its components are specifically explained in Section 3. Experimental results are shown in Section 4 with the performance evaluation of the proposed tracking method and comparison with the state-of-the-art trackers.

2 Related Work

During the last decade, many elaborate tracking frameworks have been proposed to achieve robust visual tracking by using multiple features [4–15]. Among these, some of studies that are closely most related to our approach are briefly explained in this section. The methods that integrate trackers or features have been proposed using Condensation [1] or other Bayesian filters; they can be categorized into three kinds: a single tracker with multiple observations [6–8, 14], and multiple trackers in parallel [9, 10, 15] or in cascade[11, 12].

In [6–8, 14], the multiple feature observations are fused into a product form within a single tracker framework, and the reliability of each feature is not measured. However, measuring the reliability of each feature is important since some features are very weak to specific changes in an object's appearance, such as motion blur, illumination change, etc. In our method, the current fidelity of each tracker with a different feature is reflected in a fusion process to achieve robustness. Du et al. [11] proposed using Linked Hidden Markov Models which enable the conjunction of particle filters with a belief propagation. Thus, trackers can interact with other trackers, and each tracker is connected with certain trackers in a fixed order to achieve robust performance. The approach in [12] sequentially estimates the rectangular template, color space, color distribution, and the contour of the object. Finally, all of the samples are unified to compute the final estimated state at each frame. The tracker order is critical to the performance of both methods: if the order is changed, then the performance will be degraded. However, in our method, each tracker operates in parallel and independently. Hence, other features or trackers can be added easily if the trackers are formulated within Condensation or Bayesian filters; moreover, they are fully connected and interact with each other via the TPM, and therefore, the order is not an issue. In [9, 10], the authors proposed combining two trackers based on tracker interaction, and fusing the tracking outputs. In contrast, our method provides a more general multiple tracker integration because it can fuse more than three trackers without modification. Kwon et al. [15] proposed using different trackers whose observations are hue, saturation, intensity, and edge, respectively. All trackers operate in parallel and interact with each other. However, it may seem ad-hoc because the interaction is conducted if the uniformly generated value is smaller than the selected threshold. In contrast, we try to avoid the heuristic interaction. In our method, the interaction is conducted based on the TPM which represents how trackers interact with other trackers; the TPM is recursively updated to cope with the current fidelity of each tracker, which may change at each frame.

3 Proposed Visual Tracking Framework

The purpose of visual tracking is to estimate an object motion state x_k in image sequences. To formulate this problem, we adopt Bayesian filtering in which the posterior probability $p(x_k|Z_k)$ is recursively updated as follows:

$$p(x_k|Z_{1:k}) \propto p(Z_k|x_k) \int p(x_k|x_{k-1})p(x_{k-1}|Z_{1:k-1})dx_{k-1}, \tag{1}$$

where the state x_k is represented as $x_k = [p_{X,k}, p_{Y,k}, \theta_k, s_k, \alpha_k, \phi_k]^{\mathrm{T}}$ where each parameter denotes (X, Y) position, rotation angle, scale, aspect ratio, and skew direction, respectively. Z_k denotes an observation. $p(x_k|x_{k-1})$ represents the object motion model that transits the previous state x_{k-1} to the new state x_k. $p(Z_k|x_k)$ is the observation likelihood that measure similarity between the state and the observation.

In our method, we utilize multiple observation models based on multiple features. Each observation(feature) model is assigned to one single tracker. If we use M features, M trackers are used totally. To efficiently unify M trackers into one framework, we consider two configurations, i.e., 1) Tracker Selection and 2) Tracker Interaction based on the interacting multiple model (IMM) filter [17] and (1) is reformulated as

$$\begin{aligned} p(x_k|Z_{1:k}) &\triangleq \sum_{i=1}^{M} T_k^{(i)} \underbrace{p(x_k|Z_{1:k}, m_k = i)}_{\text{i-th tracker posterior probability}} \propto \sum_{i=1}^{M} T_k^{(i)} \underbrace{p(Z_k|x_k, m_k = i)}_{\text{observation likelihood model}} \\ &\times \int \underbrace{p(x_k|x_{k-1}, m_k = i)}_{\text{motion model}} \underbrace{\sum_{j=1}^{M} \omega_{k-1|k-1}^{(j,i)} p(x_{k-1}|Z_{1:k-1}, m_{k-1} = j)\, dx_{k-1}}_{\text{interacted prior}}, \end{aligned} \tag{2}$$

where $m_k \in \{1, ..., M\}$ is a tracker index and each tracker is formulated with the interacted prior, the motion model, and the observation likelihood. These trackers are integrated on interaction coefficients $\omega_{k-1|k-1}^{(j,i)} \triangleq P\{m_k = i|m_{k-1} = j, Z_{1:k-1}\}$ expressed in a form of matrix called a transition probability matrix (TPM) $\Omega_{k-1} = [\omega_{k-1}^{(j,i)}], i, j = 1, ..., M$. All tracker posterior probabilities are unified with tracker probabilities $T_k^{(i)} \triangleq P\{m_k = i|Z_{1:k}\}$ ($P\{\}$ denotes the discrete probability). Then, from (2), we can obtain the tracking result $\hat{x}_k$ as

$$\begin{aligned} \hat{x}_k &= \hat{x}_k^{(\hat{m}_k)}, \;\; \hat{m}_k = arg\max_i T_k^{(i)}, \\ \hat{x}_k^{(i)} &= arg\max_{x_k} p(x_k|Z_{1:k}, m_k = i), \;\; i = 1, ..., M, \end{aligned} \tag{3}$$

where M tracking outputs $\hat{x}_k^{(i)}$ are obtained by the maximum a posteriori estimate from the posterior probability of each tracker $p(x_k|Z_{1:k}, m_k = i)$.

To estimate the current object state x_k based on (2), we also need to estimate the TPM Ω_k and the selected tracker index m_k as shown in Fig. 2. For the practical implementation, we approximate multiple trackers based on the particle filter and estimate the object state $\hat{x}_k^{(i)}$ in 3.1. Since the object appearance and background continuously changes, the tracker probability and interaction coefficients are adaptively updated by

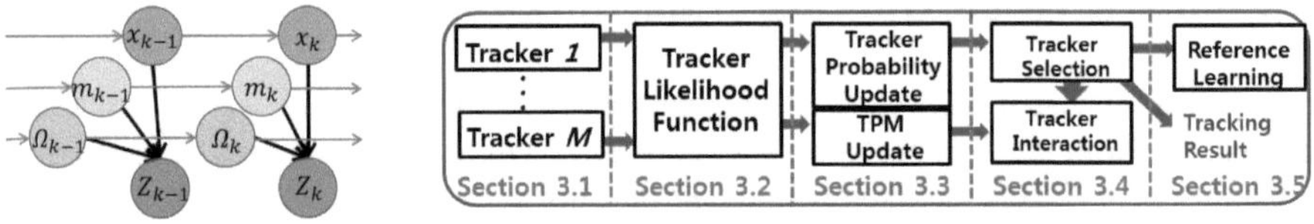

(a) Graphical model (b) Tracking procedure

Fig. 2. Left: (a) Graphical model of our method: Hidden(state x_k, tracker index m_k, TPM Ω_k); Observation (image frame, Z_k). Right: (b) Overall procedure of the proposed tracking algorithm

evaluating each tracker reliability measured by the robust TLF in 3.2 and 3.3. After that, we integrate multiple trackers based on both updated tracker probabilities and the TPM. We obtain one tracking result according to the tracker probabilities as in (3). The tracker interaction is conducted based on the updated TPM and the selected tracking result via the proposed tracker interaction in 3.4. The tracking result is fed into the reference update to reflect changes of the object appearance via the proposed learning strategy in 3.5. The overall procedure of the proposed method is shown in Fig. 2.

3.1 Single Tracker

Each tracker is formulated based on the interacted prior, motion model, and observation likelihood model as expressed in (2).

Interacted Prior: The interacted prior in (2) is computed based on the TPM via the proposed interaction method in 3.4.

Motion Model: To achieve a robust state motion transition $p(x_k|x_{k-1}, m_k = i)$, we simply adopt two motion models (zero- and first-order motion model) in terms of (X,Y) translation. The zero-order motion is identical to the random walk motion. The first-order motion utilizes the prior information of (X,Y) translation that is simply obtained by computing the difference between estimated X and Y positions at $k-1$ and $k-2$. More efficient usage of multiple motion models for visual tracking is referred to [23].

Observation Likelihood Model: A different feature is used to represent the object appearance in each tracker. The object appearance is extracted from the image as

$$Z_k^{(i)} = Vec(F^{(i)}(I(x_k))) + v_k^{(i)}, \;\; i = 1, ..., M \tag{4}$$

where $Vec()$ is vectorization; $I(x_k)$ denotes an image template based on x_k; $F^{(i)}()$ is the i-th feature extraction; $v_k^{(i)}$ is unknown noise. To deal with this high dimensionality of appearance, we use the incremental PCA subspace learning method [3]. In the incremental PCA based observation likelihood model, we compute the mean and principal eigenvectors and incrementally update them to cope with the object appearance changes as proposed in 3.5. Based on the template mean $\bar{O}^{(i)}$ and L principal eigenvectors $g_l^{(i)}, l = 1, ..., L$, the observation likelihood based on i-th tracker is given as

$$\begin{aligned} p(Z_k|x_k, m_k = i) &= exp(-\rho_T \| Z_k^{(i)} - \textstyle\sum_l c_l g_l^{(i)} \|^2), \\ c_l &= (g_l^{(i)})^{\mathrm{T}}(Z_k^{(i)} - \bar{O}^{(i)}), \;\; l = 1, ..., L, \end{aligned} \tag{5}$$

where ρ_T is the control parameter and c_l is the coefficient from the projection of the template mean to each principal eigenvector.

Particle Approximation: The i-th tracker posterior probability $p(x_k|Z_{1:k}, m_k = i)$ is approximated as a set of N samples as $\{x_{q,k}^{(i)}, w_{q,k}^{(i)}\}_{q=1}^{N}$ where $x_{q,k}^{(i)}$ and $w_{q,k}^{(i)}$ are the state sample and sample weight, respectively. Then, each tracker estimates the object state $\hat{x}_k^{(i)}$ in (3). As a result, we obtain M candidate states (i.e., $\hat{x}_k^{(i)}, i = 1, ..., M$) from M trackers.

In the next subsection, the tracker reliabilities are measured based on the M candidate states by using the robust TLF.

3.2 Robust Tracker Likelihood Function (TLF) on Flexibility and Stability

We can compute the normalized j-th feature appearance $z_k^{(i,j)}$ with respect to i-th tracker output as

$$z_k^{(i,j)} = \frac{Vec(F^{(j)}(I(\hat{x}_k^{(i)})))}{\|Vec(F^{(j)}(I(\hat{x}_k^{(i)})))\|}, \quad i, j = 1, ..., M \tag{6}$$

where $z_k^{(i,j)} \in \Re^{d^{(j)}}$ and $d^{(j)}$ is the dimension of j-th feature. In this section, we measure these appearances based on the i-th tracker output to analyze the tracker reliability and adaptively reflect the measured reliability in the tracker probability and TPM update in 3.3. This measure is called the tracker likelihood function (TLF) in (8) in which we consider two appearance models to manage the abrupt appearance changes of the object as well as the occlusion or outliers.

First, we assume that the recent object appearance is similar to the current object appearance. We call this reference template an "instantaneous reference" made of the recent object appearance and denote it as $f_{I,k}^{(j)}$ where j is the feature index. In this paper, we obtain this reference by simply averaging the object appearances in recent frames.

Secondly, to achieve stability in occlusions or other temporal outliers, we consider the reconstructed appearance that is a linear combination of the appearances called a "reconstructing reference" $f_{R,k}^{(j)}$ with coefficients $\alpha_k^{(i,j)}$ where i is the tracker index. To compute these coefficients, we adopt L1 minimization because it is robust to a wide range of image corruption, especially to occlusions [16, 19].

$$\min \|D_k^{(j)} c_k^{(i,j)} - z_k^{(i,j)}\|_2^2 + \lambda \|c_k^{(i,j)}\|_1 \tag{7}$$

where $D_k^{(j)} = [f_{R,k}^{(j)}, I^{(j)}]$ consists of a j-th feature dictionary and non-object (trivial) appearance template sets, i.e, $I^{(j)} \in \Re^{d^{(j)} \times d^{(j)}}$ [16]. The corresponding coefficients are represented as $c_k^{(i,\zeta)} = [\alpha_k^{(i,j)^{\mathrm{T}}}, \beta_k^{(i,j)^{\mathrm{T}}}]^{\mathrm{T}}$ where $\beta_k^{(i,j)} \in \Re^{d^{(j)}}$ are non-object coefficients. Here, $f_{R,k}^{(j)} = [f_{1,k}^{(j)}, ..., f_{r,k}^{(j)}] \in \Re^{d^{(j)} \times r}$ denotes the dictionary of j-th feature containing a set of r normalized representative appearance templates and $\alpha_k^{(i,j)} = [\alpha_{1,k}^{(i,j)}, ..., \alpha_{r,k}^{(i,j)}]^{\mathrm{T}} \in \Re^r$ denotes the object appearance coefficients. Then, we can obtain the j-th feature reconstructed appearance for the i-th tracker tracking result as $f_{R,k}^{(j)} \alpha_k^{(i,j)}$.

Based on the two appearance models, we calculate the TLF as follows:

$$\begin{aligned} p(Z_k|m_k = i, \Omega_{k-1}, Z_{1:k-1}) &\triangleq p_{TLF}(Z_k|\hat{x}_k^{(i)}) \approx p_I(Z_k|\hat{x}_k^{(i)}) p_R(Z_k|\hat{x}_k^{(i)}) \\ &= \prod_{j=1}^{M} p(Z_k|\hat{x}_k^{(i)}, f_{I,k}^{(j)}) p(Z_k|\hat{x}_k^{(i)}, f_{R,k}^{(j)}) \propto exp(-\rho(E_{I,k}^{(i)} + E_{R,k}^{(i)})), \end{aligned} \tag{8}$$

where ρ is the control parameter and

$$E_{I,k}^{(i)} = \sum_{j=1}^{M} (f_{I,k}^{(j)} - z_k^{(i,j)})^{\mathrm{T}} (f_{I,k}^{(j)} - z_k^{(i,j)}) \tag{9}$$

$$E_{R,k}^{(i)} = \sum_{j=1}^{M} (f_{R,k}^{(j)} \alpha_k^{(i,j)} - z_k^{(i,j)})^{\mathrm{T}} (f_{R,k}^{(j)} \alpha_k^{(i,j)} - z_k^{(i,j)}) \tag{10}$$

3.3 The Update of Tracker Probability and TPM

According to the tracker reliability affected by the dynamic environments in visual scene, the tracker probabilities and their interaction should changes. Thus, we update tracker probability and the TPM based on current tracker reliabilities (represented by the TLF $p_{TLF}(Z_k|\hat{x}_k^{(i)})$ in (8)) as follows.

Tracker Probability Update: The tracker probability update is defined by considering tracker reliabilities and the interactions between trackers as

$$T_k^{(i)} = C^{-1} p_{TLF}(Z_k|\hat{x}_k^{(i)}) \sum_{j=1}^{M} \omega_{k-1}^{(j,i)} T_{k-1}^{(j)}, \tag{11}$$

where C is the normalization term. Hence, the sum of all tracker probabilities is 1.

TPM Update: According to [2], the TPM is assumed to be an unknown random matrix with some prior distribution. Hence, in a Bayesian framework, the TPM posterior probability $p(\Omega|Z_{1:k})$ can be represented as a recursive form

$$p(\Omega|Z_{1:k}) = \frac{p(Z_k|\Omega, Z_{1:k-1})}{p(Z_k|Z_{1:k-1})} p(\Omega|Z_{1:k-1}) \tag{12}$$

For the practical implementation, the TPM posterior is approximated based on a first-order, second-order, or numerical integration (NI) approach. Among them, the NI is more robust and accurate than other approaches [2]. In the NI, the TPM posterior is expressed as the set of N_Φ fixed grid samples, Φ_q, i.e., $\{\Phi_q, \kappa_{q,k}\}_{q=1}^{N_\Phi}$ where $\kappa_{q,k}$ is the sample weight and updated as (The derivation of (13) is given in detail in the supplement material)

$$\begin{aligned} \kappa_{q,k} &= \frac{T_{k-1}^{\mathrm{T}} \Phi_q \Lambda_k}{T_{k-1}^{\mathrm{T}} \Omega_{k-1} \Lambda_k} \kappa_{q,k-1}, \\ \Omega_k &= \left(\sum_{g=1}^{N_\Phi} \kappa_{g,k}\right)^{-1} \sum_{q=1}^{N_\Phi} \kappa_{q,k} \Phi_q, \end{aligned} \tag{13}$$

where Ω_k is the estimated current TPM, $\Lambda_k = [p_{TLF}(Z_k|\hat{x}_k^{(1)}), ..., p_{TLF}(Z_k|\hat{x}_k^{(M)})]^{\mathrm{T}}$ is the set of the TLFs, and $T_{k-1} = [T_{k-1}^{(1)}, ..., T_{k-1}^{(M)}]^{\mathrm{T}}$ is the set of the tracker probabilities. Each value of the TPM samples $\phi_q^{(j,i)} \in \Phi_q$ is chosen within $[0, 1]$ while satisfying $\sum_{j=1}^{M} \phi_q^{(j,i)} = 1$. In the experiments, the 216 TPM samples are used and fixed for all benchmark sequences, and they are given in the supplementary material due to the limitation of the paper length.

Algorithm 1. Tracker Interaction

given $\{x_{q,k}^{(i)}, w_{q,k}^{(i)}\}_{q=1}^{N}$, $i = 1, ..., M$ ▷ Sample representation of i-the tracker
given $\omega_k^{(j,i)} \in \Omega_k$, $j, i = 1, ..., M$ ▷ Updated TPM
for $i = 1 : M$ **do**
  for $q = 1 : N$ **do**
    $w_{q,k}^{*(i)} = w_{q,k}^{(i)} Kernel(Hx_{q,k}^{(i)} - H\hat{x}_k, R)$
  end for
  $w_{q,k}^{*(i)} := w_{q,k}^{*(i)} / \sum_{g=1}^{N} w_{g,k}^{*(i)}$, $q = 1, ..., N$
end for
for $i = 1 : M$ **do**
  $\tilde{x}_k^{(i)} = \phi$
  for $j = 1 : M$ **do**
    $X = Resampling(\{x_{q,k}^{(j)}, w_{q,k}^{*(j)}\}_{q=1}^{N},\ N \times \omega_k^{(j,i)})$
    $\tilde{x}_k^{(i)} := \tilde{x}_k^{(i)} \cup X$
  end for
end for
Output $\{x_{q,k}^{(i)}, \frac{1}{N}\}_{q=1}^{N} := \{\tilde{x}_{q,k}^{(i)}, \frac{1}{N}\}_{q=1}^{N}, i = 1, ..., M$ ▷ Interacted prior of i-th tracker
$H = \begin{bmatrix} 1\,0\,0\,0\,0\,0 \\ 0\,1\,0\,0\,0\,0 \end{bmatrix}$, Range: $R = \sqrt{(2 \times q_{\mathrm{x}})^2 + (2 \times q_{\mathrm{y}})^2}$

3.4 Multiple Tracker Integration via Tracker Selection and Interaction

The multiple trackers are integrated via the tracker selection and interaction based on the updated tracker probability and TPM in Section 3.3.

Tracker Selection. The tracker selection picks one tracker whose tracker probability is the highest among updated tracker probabilities in (3). The output of the selected tracker $\hat{x}_k$ is the estimated object motion state at the current frame.

Tracker Interaction. The trackers interact with each other based on the TPM via the proposed tracker interaction in Algorithm 1. First, before the interaction based on the TPM, we remove the samples far from the selected tracking result $\hat{x}_k$ in terms of the position by using the uniform kernel with respect to the range R defined in Algorithm 1 where q_{x} and q_{y} are standard deviations that are set according to the object translation motion along x- and y- coordinates. In this paper, R is at most 12. H is the position conversion matrix that extracts position parameters by $[p_{X,k}, p_{Y,k}]^{\mathrm{T}} = H\hat{x}_k$. Then, each tracker interacts based on the TPM and the conventional resampling technique [25]. Here, N is the number of samples used in each tracker. The TPM provides the information that how many samples are transferred or kept. For instance, $N \times \omega_k^{(i,i)}$ represents that $N \times \omega_k^{(i,i)}$ samples are kept in the i-th tracker sample set after interaction. $N \times \omega_k^{(j,i)}$ represents that $N \times \omega_k^{(j,i)}$ samples from the j-th tracker are transferred to the i-th tracker. If the i-tracker is robust for some frames, then $\omega_k^{(i,i)}$ becomes greater than $\omega_k^{(j,i)}, j \neq i$ after the TPM update. Hence, most of the i-th tracker samples are kept and the i-th tracker obtain a few samples from other trackers. Finally, We select samples according to the interaction coefficients $\omega_{k-1}^{(j,i)}$ of the TPM via resampling technique that is conventionally used in the particle filtering so that reliable samples with high weights in each tracker will survive.

3.5 Reference Learning

In this paper, we also propose a simple but effective reference learning strategy. The three kinds of reference (i.e., tracker reference, instantaneous reference, and reconstructing reference) are incrementally updated based on the estimated M features that is obtained by $\hat{f}_k^{(j)} = z_k^{(\hat{m},j)}, j = 1, ..., M$ in (6) where $\hat{m}$ is the index of the selected tracker in (3).

Tracker References: We update each tracker reference by using the incremental PCA [3]. Here, the reference of the selected tracker is not updated whereas the references of all other trackers are updated. This concept provides two benefits — sufficient learning and the alleviation of accumulation error in the reference. As mentioned in [4], the accumulation error is inevitable when the reference is updated. However, if the reference represents the object appearance properly, the reference does not need to be updated. In our tracking scheme, we assume that the reference of the selected tracker represents the current appearance of the object well; thus, we only update the references of other (not selected) trackers.

Instantaneous References: Each instantaneous reference is obtained by taking mean value of the recently estimated appearance. Hence, it is simply computed by $f_{I,k+1}^{(j)} = MEAN(\hat{f}_{k-\delta}^{(j)}, ..., \hat{f}_k^{(j)})$ where δ is a constant value[1].

Reconstructing References: Inspired from [18], the reconstructing references $f_{R,k}^{(j)}$ are updated by measuring noises of the estimated features. In [18], they decide whether the reference is updated or not by exploring the non-zero elements in the non-object reference coefficients, if there is occlusion, the reference vector contains many non-zero elements. In this paper, the noises are measured based on the non-object reference coefficient vector $\beta_k^{(\hat{m},j)} \in \Re^{d^{(j)}}$ in (7) where $\hat{m}$ is the index of the selected tracker. We count non-zero elements in $\beta_k^{(\hat{m},j)}$, and then compute a noise ratio $R_{noise}^{(j)}$ by $R_{noise}^{(j)} = B^{(j)}/d^{(j)}$ where $B^{(j)}$ is the number of non-zero elements. When the noise ratio $R_{noise}^{(m)}$ is smaller than the certain threshold[1] γ, one representative appearance template (i.e., $f_{i,k}^{(j)} \in f_{R,k}^{(j)}$) that has the lowest coefficient is replaced by $\hat{f}_k^{(j)}$.

4 Experimental Results

Using the benchmark sequences[2,3,4], we evaluate our tracking method, which is simply called "Adaptive Tracker Selection (ATS)". We employ three trackers with different features to implement the ATS: Tracker 1, 2, and 3 are associated with HOG, intensity, and Haar-like feature, respectively. As mentioned in the introduction, we select these

[1] We used the parameter $\delta = 10$ and the threshold $\gamma = 0.3$ in the experiments.

[2] http://vision.ucsd.edu/~bbabenko/project_miltrack.shtml

[3] http://homepages.inf.ed.ac.uk/rbf/CAVIARDATA1/

[4] http://www.gpu4vision.org

features because they are enough to deal with occlusion, motion blur, pose variation, and illumination changes. Each tracker is implemented based on a particle filter using 300 samples. To approximate the TPM, we use 216 TPM samples, which are given in the supplementary material. The initial tracker probability $T_0^{(m)}$ is set to 1/3. The reconstructing reference of each feature contains 25 appearance templates. The parameter ρ in (8) is set to 2.

In 4.1, we discuss the computational time of our method. In 4.2, we analyze the ATS, focusing on the TPM, and show how the TPM manages multiple trackers of different features. Then, in 4.3, we present our comparative studies of a single tracker with multiple observations (S-MO) and a single tracker with a HOG, Intensity, and Haar-like observation, respectively (S-HOG, S-I, and S-Haar). It should be noted that they are implemented based on the IVT [3] framework with two motion models used in the ATS. Moreover, we compare our ATS to state-of-the-art trackers, i.e., MIL[27], TLD[28], L1Track[16], VTD[15], and PROST[4]. For the quantitative comparison, two performance indices are selected: mean distance errors and the percentage of correctly tracked frames according to a PASCAL score[4, 24]. The PASCAL score is obtained by evaluating to what extent the tracking template overlaps the ground truth template as a ratio [4]. Then, if the PASCAL score is greater than 0.5 in a certain frame, that frame is counted as a correctly tracked frame.

4.1 Computational Time

We implement our method using MATLAB 2010a. The most computation time is spent on feature extraction, especially for HOG and Haar features, and non-optimized code is used. The computation time of the S-MO method that uses the same features (HOG, Haar, Intensity) is comparable with that of the proposed ATS. When we use 900 samples, the S-MO takes about 2.76 sec/frame. The ATS takes about 3.26 sec/frame. Hence, it seems that our tracker integration scheme does not require a large amount of computational time.

4.2 Analysis on TPM

We explore how the TPM manages multiple trackers of different features for a certain change in object appearance. In Fig. 3, the changes in the values of diagonal coefficients ($\omega_k^{(i,i)}$) of the TPM are shown according to changes in object appearance over time. If $\omega_k^{(i,i)}$ decrease, then $\omega_k^{(j,i)}, n \neq m$ increases because $\sum_{j=1}^{M} \omega_k^{(j,i)} = 1$; hence, the i-th tracker becomes more dependent on other trackers. If the i-th tracker is not robust, then the $\omega_k^{(i,i)}$ value decreases. The maximum and minimum values of a diagonal coefficient are 0.7 and 0.2, respectively. Note that $\omega_k^{(1,1)}$, $\omega_k^{(2,2)}$, and $\omega_k^{(3,3)}$ denotes HOG tracker, Intensity tracker, and Haar tracker, respectively. In CAVIAR seq., there are few changes in appearance in many frames; hence, the Intensity tracker tracks the object most accurately. However, between $\sharp$ 190 and $\sharp$ 220, an occlusion occurs; thus, $\omega_k^{(1,1)}$ and $\omega_k^{(2,2)}$ decrease whereas $\omega_k^{(3,3)}$ increases. In woman seq. [26], an occlusion occurs repeatedly. When the occlusion first occurs, the $\omega_k^{(1,1)}$ and $\omega_k^{(2,2)}$ decrease and $\omega_k^{(3,3)}$ increases because the Haar feature is more robust than other features in occlusion. If there is only

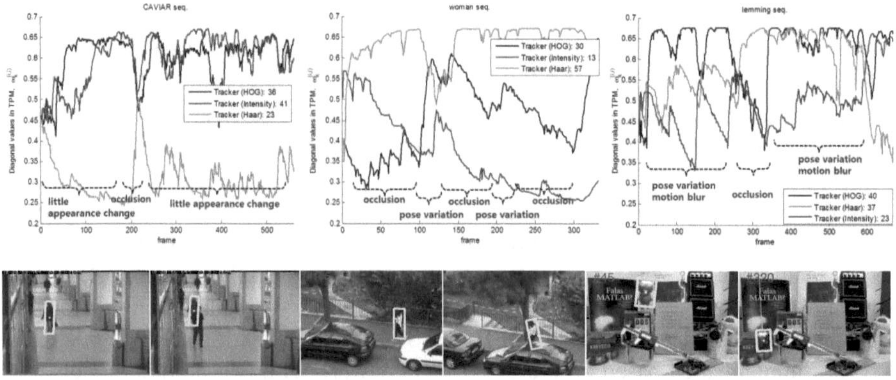

(a) CAVIAR seq. (♯140,♯210) (b) woman seq. (♯105,♯155) (c) lemming seq. (♯45,♯320)

Fig. 3. 1) Changes of diagonal coefficients in the TPM: $\omega_k^{(1,1)}$(HOG:Blue), $\omega_k^{(2,2)}$(Intensity:Red), $\omega_k^{(3,3)}$(Haar:Green), 2) Numbers inside the box denote percentage of tracker selections

a small pose variation with no occlusion, the $\omega_k^{(1,1)}$ and $\omega_k^{(2,2)}$ start to increase. In lemming seq., there are frequent motion blurs and occlusions for short durations. In motion blurs, the HOG tracker is more robust than other features because the outer shape of the lemming is consistent. When the occlusion occurs around ♯300, $\omega_k^{(3,3)}$ increases.

4.3 Quantitative and Qualitative Evaluations

According to the overall results, the trackers that use on a single feature (i.e., MILTrack, TLD, L1Track) yield limited performances in various appearance changes as shown in Table 1 and Fig. 4. The trackers that use multiple featuers (i.e., VTD, PROST, S-MO, ATS) generate better results.

Occlusion: The target in the *CAVIAR* and *woman* seqs. undergoes heavy occlusions. As shown in Table 1, the S-Haar tracks the object perfectly because the Haar-like feature is robust when only occlusion exists. However, the S-HOG and S-I fail to track it since both these features are weak to occlusions. In Fig. 4, the VTD also fails to track in

Table 1. "A"("B"): "A"- the mean distance error in pixel; "B"- the percentage of correctly tracked frames based on Pascal score [24]. Red is the best result and blue is the second-best result.

Sequence	MIL	TLD	L1Track	VTD	PROST	S-I	S-HOG	S-Haar	S-MO	ATS
tiger1	15 (62)	12 (45)	44 (17)	44(21)	-	51 (37)	19 (66)	9 (80)	31 (39)	5 (94)
david	16 (62)	8 (96)	26 (58)	26 (68)	-	6 (90)	4 (91)	69 (36)	4 (100)	3 (100)
girl	27 (68)	26 (46)	13 (99)	15(98)	-	49 (50)	17 (87)	27 (74)	28 (76)	11 (100)
coke11	18 (32)	10 (48)	54 (5)	76(5)	-	63 (14)	9 (68)	12 (46)	10 (68)	7 (85)
CAVIAR	-	40 (19)	4 (100)	29 (41)	-	12 (65)	19 (41)	3 (100)	3 (100)	2 (100)
woman	-	-	252 (13)	108 (15)	-	92 (16)	124 (15)	4 (100)	4 (100)	2 (100)
board	115 (51)	142 (11)	255 (3)	83 (34)	39 (75)	146 (19)	16 (93)	35 (71)	84 (32)	16 (92)
box	196 (3)	17 (90)	150 (15)	66 (36)	13 (91)	104 (37)	10 (95)	69 (26)	86 (28)	9 (91)
lemming	15 (83)	146 (4)	212 (13)	83 (52)	25 (71)	20 (40)	68 (75)	174 (18)	111 (48)	11 (86)
liquor	165 (20)	20 (77)	181 (19)	103 (28)	21 (85)	521(22)	101 (29)	712 (22)	63 (23)	4 (98)

occlusions because it allows all the recent appearances including the occluded parts. In contrast, the ATS considers stability; hence, it can deal with the occlusion problem by measuring tracker reliability.

Pose Variation: In *girl* seq., the object repeatedly undergoes pose variation, but its outer shape is consistent. Thus, the S-HOG faithfully tracks the object as shown in Table1. The ATS successfully uses the HOG feature and shows a much better performance than the S-MO because the ATS measures the tracker reliability and updates the TPM. Based on the TPM, the more robust tracker can support other trackers.

Illumination Change: In *david* seq., the object appearance has illumination changes with little pose variation. The S-HOG robustly tracks the object because the outer shape of the object is consistent even when the illumination changes. The S-I also adapts well to the illumination changes because it is implemented based on the IVT [3]. Hence, the S-MO and ATS also perfectly track the object because these two features are robust.

Complex Changes: In practice, most image sequences contain various changes in appearance. Hence, the appropriate use of multiple features is very important. The *tiger1*

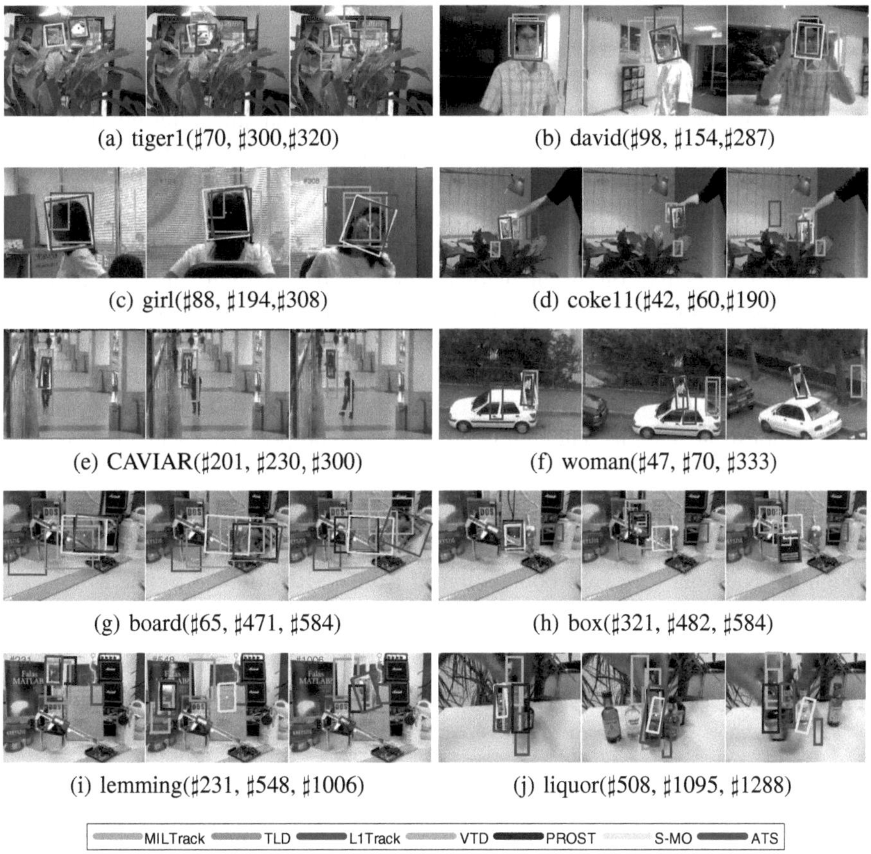

Fig. 4. Tracking results of different algorithms: ATS (the proposed method)

and *coke11* seqs. contain occlusions, illumination changes, and pose variations. The ATS measures the tracker reliability and updates the TPM as to which trackers can interact. Using this mechanism, the ATS shows better results than the S-MO, especially in these complicated situations. In the *board*, *box*, and *lemming* seqs., the object's appearance undergoes drastic motion blur and pose variation, but their shape is consistent. Hence, the S-HOG shows the best results in the *board* and *box* seqs. In terms of the PASCAL score, S-HOG faithfully tracks the object in the *lemming* seq. Overall, the ATS demonstrates the best performance because it utilizes not only the HOG feature but also other features in the appropriate situations. The *liquor* seq. contains the most severe motion blur and occlusions; hence, most of trackers fail to track the object. In contrast, PROST reliably tracks the object because it is designed to include flexibility, moderate adaption, and stability in the object appearance model to deal with various changes in appearance. Thus, the PROST tracker resembles the ATS, which also considers the flexibility and stability but in a different manner. In particular, in ATS the reliability and flexibility information are used more efficiently because it employs multiple features with multiple tracker based on the interactions. This leads to better results.

5 Conclusions

In this paper, we propose a robust visual tracking method that integrates multiple trackers based on multiple features via tracker interaction and selection. The tracker interaction is conducted based on the TPM and prevents individual tracker divergence. The TPM update and tracker selection are computed by investigating each tracker's reliability based on the TLF. To cover various kinds of changes in object appearance, the TLF is formulated based on instantaneous references for flexibility and reconstructing references for stability. Thus, the proposed tracking method can select the best among multiple trackers even if the object's appearance changes drastically. In addition, the proposed learning strategy enhances the performance of individual trackers and sustains the flexibility and stability of the two reference models in the TLF. The experimental results demonstrate that, in challenging sequences, the proposed tracking method tracks the object more robustly than other trackers.

Acknowledgments. This research was supported by Basic Science Research Program through the National Research Foundation of Korea(NRF) funded by the Ministry of Education, Science and Technology(2009-0065038).

References

1. Isard, M., Blake, A.: Condensation - conditional density propagation for visual tracking. IJCV 29(1), 5–28 (1998)
2. Jilkov, V.P., Li, X.R.: Online Bayesian estimation of transition probabilities for markovian jump systems. IEEE Transactions on Signal Processing 52(6), 307–315 (2004)
3. Ross, D., Lim, J., Lin, R.-S., Yang, M.-H.: Incremental learning for robust visual tracking. IJCV 77, 125–141 (2008)

4. Santner, J., Leistner, C., Saffari, A., Pock, T., Bischof, H.: Prost: Parallel robust online simple tracking. In: CVPR, pp. 723–730 (2010)
5. Spengler, M., Schiele, B.: Towards robust multi-cue integration for visual tracking. Machine Vision and Applications 14(1), 50–58 (2003)
6. Giebel, J., Gavrila, D.M., Schnörr, C.: A Bayesian Framework for Multi-cue 3D Object Tracking. In: Pajdla, T., Matas, J. (eds.) ECCV 2004. LNCS, vol. 3024, pp. 241–252. Springer, Heidelberg (2004)
7. Brasnett, P., Mihaylova, L., Canagarajah, N., Mihaylova, L., Canagarajah, N., Bull, D.: Particle filtering with multiple cues For object tracking. In: Proc. of SPIE's Annual Symp. EI ST, pp. 430–441 (2005)
8. Wang, H., Suter, D.: Efficient visual tracking by probabilistic fusion of multiple cues. In: International Conference on Pattern Recognition, pp. 892–895 (2006)
9. Leichter, I., Lindenbaum, M., Rivlin, E.: A general framework for combining visual trackers - the "black boxes" approach. IJCV 67(3), 343–363 (2006)
10. Badrinarayanan, V., Perez, P., Clerc, F.L., Oisel, L.: Probabilistic color and adaptive multi-feature tracking with dynamically switched priority between cues. In: ICCV, pp. 1–8 (2007)
11. Du, W., Piater, J.: A Probabilistic Approach to Integrating Multiple Cues in Visual Tracking. In: Forsyth, D., Torr, P., Zisserman, A. (eds.) ECCV 2008, Part II. LNCS, vol. 5303, pp. 225–238. Springer, Heidelberg (2008)
12. Moreno-Noguer, F., Sanfeliu, A., Samaras, D.: Dependent multiple cue integration for robust tracking. PAMI 30(4), 670–685 (2008)
13. Stenger, B., Woodley, T., Cipolla, R.: Learning to track with multiple observers. In: CVPR, pp. 2647–2654 (2009)
14. Zelniker, E.E., Hospedales, T.M., Gong, S., Xiang, T.: A unified Bayesian framework for adaptive visual tracking. In: BMVC, pp. 18.1–18.11 (2009)
15. Kwon, J., Lee, K.M.: Visual tracking decomposition. In: CVPR, pp. 1269–1276 (2010)
16. Mei, X., Ling, H.: Robust visual tracking using l1 minimization. In: ICCV, pp. 1436–1443 (2009)
17. Bar-Shalom, Y., Li, X.R., Kirubarajan, T.: Estimation with applications to tracking and navigation. Wiley, New York (2001)
18. Mei, X., Ling, H., Wu, Y., Blasch, E., Bai, L.: Minimum error bounded efficient l1 tracker with occlusion detection. In: CVPR, pp. 1257–1264 (2011)
19. Kim, S.-J., Koh, K., Lustig, M., Boyd, S., Gorinevsky, D.: An interior-point method for large-scale l1 regularized least squares. IEEE Journal on Selected Topics in Signal Processing 1(4), 606–617 (2007)
20. Yang, M.-H.: Face detection. In: Encyclopedia of Biometrics, pp. 303–308 (2009)
21. Dalal, N., Triggs, B.: Histograms of oriented gradients for human detection. In: CVPR, pp. 886–893 (2005)
22. Yilmaz, A., Javed, O., Shah, M.: Object tracking: a survey. ACM Computing Surveys 38(4) (2006)
23. Cifuentes, C.G., Sturzel, M., Jurie, F., Brostow, G.J.: Motion models that only work sometimes. In: BMVC (2012)
24. Everingham, M., Van Gool, L.J., Williams, C.K.I., Winn, J.M., Zisserman, A.: The pascal visual object classes (voc) challenge. IJCV 88(2), 303–338 (2010)
25. Doucet, A., Godsill, S., Andrieu, C.: On sequential Monte Carlo sampling methods for Bayesian filtering. Statistics and Computing 10(3), 197–208 (2000)
26. Adam, A., Rivlin, E., Shimshoni, I.: Robust fragments-based tracking using the integral histogram. In: CVPR, pp. 798–805 (2006)
27. Babenko, B., Yang, M.-H., Belongie, S.: Visual tracking with online multiple instance learning. In: CVPR, pp. 983–990 (2009)
28. Kalal, Z., Matas, J., Mikolajczyk, K.: P-n learning: bootstrapping binary classifiers by structural constraints. In: CVPR, pp. 49–56 (2010)

Image Enhancement Using Calibrated Lens Simulations

Yichang Shih[1,2], Brian Guenter[1], and Neel Joshi[1]

[1] Microsoft Research
[2] MIT CSAIL

Abstract. All lenses have optical aberrations which reduce image sharpness. These aberrations can be reduced by deconvolving an image using the lens point spread function (PSF). However, fully measuring a PSF is laborious and prohibitive. Alternatively, one can simulate the PSF if the lens model is known. However, due to manufacturing tolerances lenses differ subtly from their models, so often a simulated PSF is a poor match to measured data. We present an algorithm that uses a PSF measurement at a single depth to calibrate the nominal lens model to the measured PSF. The calibrated model can then be used to compute the PSF for any desired setting of lens parameters for any scene depth, without additional measurements or calibration. The calibrated model gives deconvolution results comparable to measurement but is much more compact and require hundreds of times fewer calibration images.

1 Introduction

Lens aberrations limit the quality of images formed by lenses. These aberrations are inherent in the physics of optical image formation and vary as a function of lens settings. Image deconvolution can be used to reduce many aberrations if the lens point spread function (PSF) is known. Recovering both the PSF and deblurred image from a single image input (blind-deconvolution) is ill-posed and as a result can be unreliable.

An alternative is to measure the PSF of a lens. Indirect method such as that of Joshi et al. [11] over-smooth the PSF unacceptably as a result of regularization needed in their method. Direct methods include using a laser, beam spreader, and precision collimator system to create a single illumination point for measuring the PSF one point at a time. These methods require precise hardware and are very slow. The more commonly used, faster method is to capture an image of a grid of back illuminated pinholes, such as shown in Fig. 5. Each photograph captures many samples of the PSF across the entire field of view. The complete PSF can be measured by systematically varying the lens parameters to cover all possible permutations.

Unfortunately, making a pinhole target small enough so that they image less than a pixel is very difficult, especially for close focusing distance.[1]. Not being able to measure near the lens[2], where the PSF varies most rapidly, is a significant limitation to direct measurement of PSFs.

[1] e.g. for a 2 micron pixel sensor to measure closer than 10 times the focal length of a lens, ones needs pinholes less than 20 microns in diameter. This is difficult both due to due to manufacturing limits and that diffraction through the pinhole becomes a factor.

[2] Typically on the order of a few feet for common focal length and sensor sizes.

A. Fitzgibbon et al. (Eds.): ECCV 2012, Part IV, LNCS 7575, pp. 42–56, 2012.

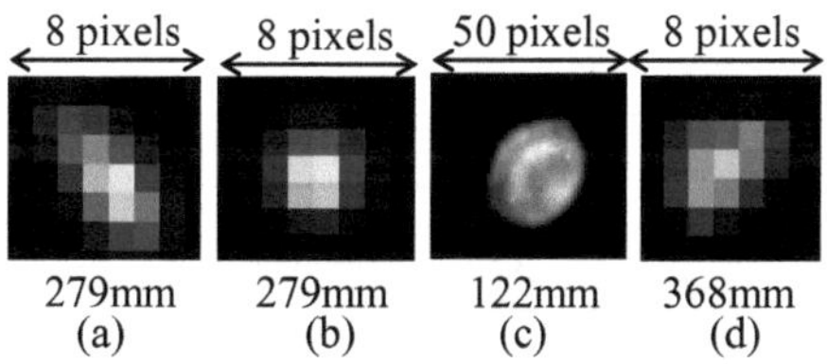

Fig. 1. Measured PSFs show that real lenses violate many common assumptions about the invariance of the PSF. The PSF is measured at (a) corner of a focused plane at 279mm, (b) center of the same focused plane, (c) corner of a de-focused plane (focusing at 279mm but imaged at 122mm), and (d) corner of a focused plane at 368mm.

An equally serious problem is the sheer number of photographs necessary to adequately sample the PSF. Simulations with the commercial Zemax lens design software has shown that lens PSF varies substantially as a function of lens parameters, including aperture, focal length, focusing distance, and illuminant spectrum. The latter two parameters have generally been ignored in previous work in this area but they affect the PSF as strongly as the first two. As a result, literally hundreds of images are needed to properly measure the multidimensional parameter space of a lens.[3]

In addition, because the focusing distance and illuminant spectrum dimensions are difficult to sample along their full range, extrapolation beyond the captured data values will almost certainly be necessary. While interpolation is potentially possible, extrapolation is unlikely to work well, given the complex changes in the shape and amplitude of the PSF as a function of these two parameters.

An alternative is to simulate the lens PSF for any desired setting of lens parameters by using optics simulation on an accurate CAD model of the lens. The CAD model is called the lens prescription. The primary difficulty with using the lens prescription directly is that manufacturing tolerances [17] cause any particular physical lens to differ from the nominal CAD lens design, which causes dramatic PSF variations between nominally identical lenses, as shown in Fig. 4. As a consequence simply using the nominal lens prescription to generate PSF's for deconvolution doesn't give very good results.

Our approach is to use the lens prescription as a starting point for calibration process that adjusts the lens prescription to fit a single measurement of the PSF. The lens prescription fitting is done only once per lens. Once we have the lens prescription we can compute the PSF at any point on the image plane, for any combination of lens parameters: aperture, focal length, focusing distance, and illuminant. The technique overview is illustrated in Fig. 2.

This method has many advantages over direct PSF measurement because it requires far fewer calibration pictures (one versus hundreds), the fitted lens prescription is more compact than a full set of measured PSF images (a few hundred bytes versus hundreds of KBytes), and the PSF can be computed for arbitrary lens parameters, while mea-

[3] An accurate PSF measurement would require at least an additional 5 samples in the focusing distance dimension (aperture, focal length, focusing distance). At least another 3 samples would be necessary along the spectral dimension. A very conservative estimate of the total number of pictures required to accurately measure a lens PSF is $3 * 5^3 = 375$. In practice far more would be necessary for fast lenses that focus at close distances.

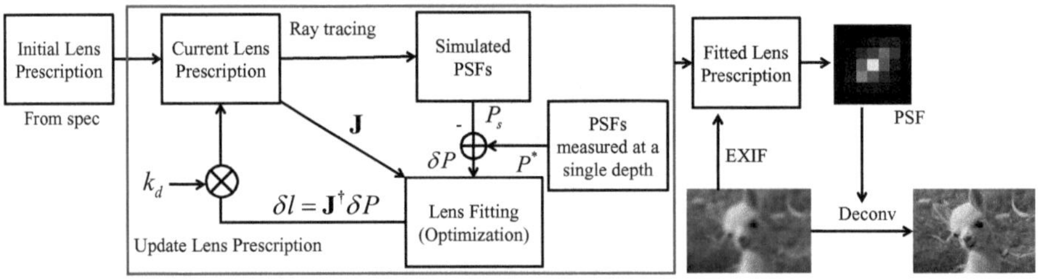

Fig. 2. Algorithm and system overview. Our lens prescription calibration process is illustrated in the blue outline. The process takes measured PSFs at a single depth as input. The process only need to be done once. We compute PSFs using calibrated lens prescription and EXIF info from the new input photo (focusing distance, aperture size, and white balance as approximate illuminant spectrum) for image enhancement.

sured PSF's only cover the range of lens parameters that were sampled and cannot be effectively extrapolated beyond this range.

For consumer level cameras lens manufacturers can use our method to calibrate each lens before it leaves the factory. For computer vision research applications lens prescriptions are frequently available for machine vision style lenses[4] so researchers can use the method to calibrate their systems.

The key contribution of this paper is the use of optics simulation combined with the fitting algorithm, which makes it possible to use a single calibration photograph to generate synthetic PSF's for any combination of lens settings.

2 Related Work

Much of the recent work in image deblurring has been in measuring and removing blur due to camera motion [7,21] or scene motion [15,16], while less attention has been paid towards correcting for blur due to lens aberrations, which is the situation we consider in this work.

Aberrations can be removed by deconvolving with the lens PSF [20]. Because of the high dimensionality of the PSF function and the difficulty of PSF measurement, corrections are usually performed by fitting the PSFs to a parametric model [13,4,2].

The closest related works are those of single image calibration and measurement methods [11,3,12]. These works show how to estimate optical blur functions or chromatic abberation either blindly or through a calibration process.

Simple spatially invariant parametric models are not accurate measures of image blur [11,13]. Perhaps the most closely related works are those that have used or created lens models for image correction [6,10,9,5,14,13]. Several commercial products, such as PTLens, DXO, and Adobe Photoshop, perform image corrections using non-physical low order parametric models tuned to various lens profiles. Due to their non-physical nature, these methods can only produce limited improvements [13].

[4] Edmund Optics makes lens prescriptions available for research purposes. All our lenses were purchased there.

Kee et al. [13] address this issue by presenting a spatially-varying parametric model fitted from estimated PSFs. Instead of estimating PSF from edge response in their work, we directly measure PSFs to avoid over-blurred PSFs [11]. We fits a lens CAD model so that we can predict PSFs at arbitrary aperture, focal length, focusing distance, illuminant spectrum. The latter two are ignored in Kee et al.'s work. Our method only requires a single photograph, which makes the calibration process far less laborious.

3 PSF Simulation

Several previous works have made simplifying assumptions about the lens point spread function [4,2,19]. These simplifications include: 1) a simple canonical PSF shape, such as a 2D Gaussian, or pillbox, 2) a constant PSF across the image plane, 3) that the PSF is invariant as a function of distance to the focused object plane, and 4) that the defocused PSF is a scaled version of the focused PSF.

Real lenses violate all these assumptions. In Fig. 1, we show the measured PSF of a lens at two image positions, two focus/defocus distances, and two focal plane depths. Even on the optical axis, there are significant differences between the PSF; off-axis the differences are dramatic. Perhaps most surprisingly, the PSF is strongly dependent on the distance the lens is focused.

In the general case, the PSF of a fixed focal length lens is a 6 dimensional function of the light wavelength, (λ), image plane coordinates, (x, y), lens aperture, a, lens to object distance, d_{obj}, and back focal distance, d_{bf}. One can measure PSFs for a particular lens by taking measurements of the lens response over these 6 dimensions, using specialized equipment [22], but such methods are only accurate in limited working volumes and require a vast amount of data to be collected.

Modern lenses are designed using lens CAD models and are precisely specified by a set of parametric values called the *lens prescription*. Our method takes a single photograph to calibrate the lens prescription. The fitted lens model is used to generate PSFs at any desired lens parameter values. Given this specification, obtaining accurate PSFs becomes a software process instead of a complicated measurement process.

3.1 Lens Prescriptions

The lens prescription describes the optical properties of the lens: the size, curvature, index of refraction, and type of coating of each element. To account for chromatic aberration, a dispersion function models the variation of the index of refraction, n, with light wavelength, λ. The most commonly used functions are polynomials in either the Schott

$$n^2 = a_0 + a_1\lambda^2 + a_2\lambda^{-22} + a_3\lambda^{-4} + a_4\lambda^{-6} + a_5\lambda^{-8} \tag{1}$$

or the Sellmeier 1 form

$$n^2 - 1 = \frac{K_1\lambda^2}{\lambda^2 - L_1} + \frac{K_2\lambda^2}{\lambda^2 - L_2} + \frac{K_3\lambda^2}{\lambda^2 - L_3}. \tag{2}$$

We model the effect of the following parameters: 1) geometric properties of each optical surface: diameter, radius of curvature, offset along optical axis, and offset perpendicular to optical axis, 2) coefficients of the dispersion function of each material, 3) index of

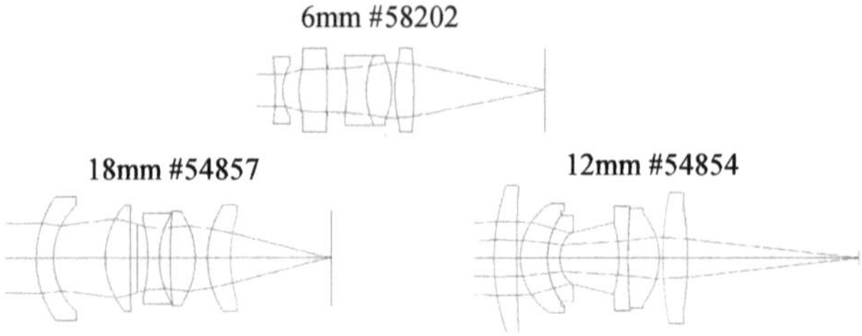

Fig. 3. The 3 lenses we tested. All three lenses are stock Edmund Optics lenses – the part numbers are shown.

refraction and thickness of each antireflection coating material, and 4) lens back focal distance.

Our simulator currently models lens elements with spherical surfaces[5] and a single layer antireflection coating. We simulated three lenses from the Edmund Optics catalog[6]: a high resolution 6mm microvideo lens, a medium resolution 12mm microvideo lens, and a high resolution 18mm double Gauss lens. The optical layouts of all three shown in Fig. 3.

3.2 PSFs Computation with a Lens Prescription

Existing commercial software products, such as ZEMAX, can be used to simulate lenses, but as these products are costly and not instrumented to be used easily for an optimization or calibration procedure. Thus we have implement at standard lens simulator algorithm that uses the same principles as Zemax [8].

Given the focal length, aperture, focusing distance, and white balance that is stored in the EXIF header of the image file, we can simulate the image plane PSF of each of the virtual object points. We note that we do not need the full scene depth only the focal depth, since we only seek to remove aberrations and focal plane artifacts as opposed to defocus debluring – there are no limitations on the scene depth range. These PSF's are fed into the deconvolution algorithm to correct lens aberrations. In the interest of space, and as the contribution of our work is the calibration process and not the simulation, we describe the simulation details in our supplementary materials.

Because the PSF is dependent on wavelength we simulate the PSF at 18 wavelengths for each color channel and sum these incoherently to give the final PSF for each color channel. Our measurements are done with sequential RGB illumination from a three color LED lamp, so that artifacts due to demosaicing would not be confounded with the results of the image corrections; however, our methods can be easily be used with Bayer demosaicked images.

We assume most sensor has a microlens array as an anti-aliasing filter to create a 100% fill-factor. We thus model our sensor response linear to light intensity. We do

[5] Aspherical surfaces are used in very high quality (and cost) glass lenses and in low cost plastic injection molded lenses. The majority of lenses between these extremes use only spherical surfaces.

[6] Chosen because they are typical machine vision lenses, and because Edmund Optics provides lens prescriptions for research purposes.

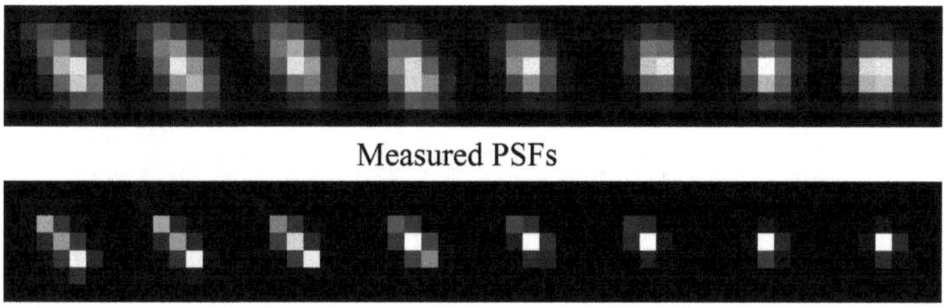

Fig. 4. Mismatch between a measured PSF and one simulated using the nominal, manufacturer provided lens prescription. Left to right in the two figures corresponds to the PSF being sampled from corner to center.

not directly consider other effects. More in-depth study is a good suggestion for future work.

3.3 Mismatch with Measured PSFs

We measured actual lens PSFs and compared them with the simulated PSFs, as shown in Fig. 4. The measurement setup and method are described in Sec. 5. Note that the simulated PSFs are very different from measured PSFs. The mismatch is caused by variations within manufacturing tolerances and fabrication errors during lens production. Variation between nominally identical lenses can be quite large and also different from the lens specification [17].

4 Lens Prescription Calibration

We notate our simulation by using the function $S(l, x)$, which takes a lens prescription l and light source positions x as input, and outputs the corresponding point spread functions P. Let l^* and l_s denote the actual and nominal lens specification, respectively. The object of the lens fitting step is to find $\delta l^* \equiv l^* - l_s$.

Our optimization method minimizes the L2 norm between the measured and the simulated PSFs by adjusting the lens prescription. Denoting the measured PSFs as P^*, the objective function is

$$\delta l^* = \arg\min_{\delta l} \|S(l_s + \delta l, x) - P^*\|_2. \tag{3}$$

Given that δl is very small and S is smooth around l_s, the first order approximation on $S(l_s + \delta l, x)$ is

$$S(l_s + \delta l, x) \approx S(l_s) + \frac{\partial S}{\partial l}\delta l, \tag{4}$$

where $S(l_s)$ is the PSF simulated using the nominal lens prescription, and $\frac{\partial S}{\partial l}$ is the Jacobian at l_s, which is denoted by $\mathbf{J}$. In practice, since there is no simple analytical form of $S(l_s)$, we perturb lens prescription and compute the PSF difference over the lens prescription variation to form the Jacobian matrix. Denoting $\delta P = P^* - S(l_s)$ as the difference between simulated and measured PSFs and combining Eq. 3 and Eq. 4 gives

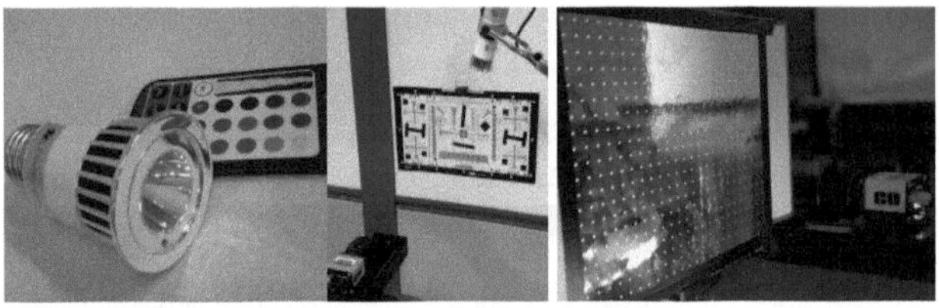

Fig. 5. Experimental Setup. Left: 3-color LED to illuminate resolution charts. Middle: Image collection setup. Right: A precisely constructed pinhole grid pattern. Note: when collecting data, the only light present is due to the LED illuminant.

$$\delta l^* = \arg\min_{\delta l} \|\mathbf{J}\delta l - \delta P\|_2 = \mathbf{J}^\dagger \delta P. \tag{5}$$

The calibration process first calculates the Jacobian, and then applies the Jacobian pseudo-inverse to the difference between measured and simulated PSFs. In practice, S is not linear to l, so we multiply δl by a damping factor $k_d < 1$ [18], and iterate several times until convergence, which typically takes 3 to 5 iterations. The optimization scheme is shown in Fig. 2.

We fit the following parameters in the lens prescription: 1) Radius of curvature, XY offset (perpendicular to the optical axis), and Z offset (parallel to optical axis) of each optical element, 2) Coefficients of the dispersion function formula, and 3) Camera back focal length.

Because we assume spherical lenses, surface tilting can be modeled by a combination of X, Y, and Z offsets. The dispersion function affects chromatic abberation as different wavelengths have different refraction indices. Chromatic abberation is most affected by the first derivative of the dispersion function $\frac{dn}{d\lambda}$, so as a simplification we only optimize this first derivative for each glass.

5 Lens Measurements

The PSF measurement setup is shown in Fig. 5. This consists of an Edmund Optics 5MP monochrome camera. To obtain color images we use a three-color LED illuminant, also shown in Fig. 5.

We found our camera to be relatively noisy due to its small (2.2 μm) pixel size. To correct fixed pattern noise, we captured a textureless white card at two exposure levels and fit a per-pixel offset and gain. Each pixel is corrected to have the same offset and gain. We averaged several images in sequence to reduce the remaining temporally varying noise components.

We tested three different multi-element lenses, shown in Fig. 3, that cover a range of properties that are typically seen in consumer camera lenses. All are off-the-shelf parts purchased from Edmund Optics. We used these lenses because Edmund Optics will provide prescriptions for their lenses, while manufacturers such as Canon will not.

For each image, we measure the object distance and estimate the back focal distance. With these parameters we simulate the point-spread function.

To calibrate and measure our simulated point spread functions we use several precisely constructed calibration targets. To measure effective image resolution, we use a standard I3A/ISO Resolution Test Chart from BHPhoto. To measure impulse responses, we laser-cut $0.1mm$ diameter pinholes into an aluminized Mylar sheet, which was then mounted on a flat acrylic backing coated with a diffusing material. We backlit this target with our LED light source illustrated in Fig. 5.

5.1 Calibration

We calibrated the 3 lenses shown in Fig. 3. The number of variables in 3 lenses are 33, 36, 43 for lenses (a), (b), (c) in Fig. 3, respectively. Non-linear optimization of this number of variables is challenging. The damping factor, k_d, is set to 0.7, and we iterated 5 times.

The calibration process takes 84, 53, and 67 measured PSF samples as input for lens (a), (b), (c), respectively. The numbers depend on the field of view of the lenses. These PSFs are measured at a single focusing distance and captured with a single image. The un-calibrated PSFs has more significant differences at corners, so we sample more densely at the corners than at the center. While we use a single photograph and focal plane for calibration, the extension to multiple planes is straightforward. The object distances are 279mm, 711mm, 863mm for lenses (a), (b), (c), respectively, to make sure the light sources can cover the whole field of view.

The manufacturing tolerance of each parameter is on the order of 1% [17], so we set the offsets to be 0.5% for radius, $10^{-5}m$ for XYZ offsets, 1% of dispersion at the red frequency[7] for the dispersion function offset, and $10^{-5}m$ for back focal length. The numerical derivatives are approximated with a two sided finite difference.

Both PSF computation and Jacobian calculation can be performed in parallel. Running the calibration on a 4-core machine takes about 6 hours for each lens. Because the simulation and calibration are easily parallelized larger clusters will dramatically reduce this time.

6 Results

In this section, we discuss several experiments used to show that our calibration process is accurate and stable. In lieu of comparing to less accurate parametric models, we have choosen to compare directly to groundtruth measurements, as we felt this was the most rigorous way to show the accuracy of our simulated kernels after calibration. We performed three cross validation experiments to show there is no over-fitting, that we are calibrating accurately, and that the calibration is stable across changes in the lens focus and illuminant spectrum. As appropriate, figures show the corresponding blur kernel sampled from the PSF as an inset image. Please see our supplemental materials for additional results.

Fig. 6 shows the results of image enhancement by deconvolving with simulated PSFs. As was done in the work of Joshi et al. [11], we use Lucy-Richardson deconvolution as this method is less forgiving of errors in blur kernels and thus best conveys the accuracy of the kernel. The results show that compared with the PSF simulated from

[7] In physics, dispersion is defined as $\frac{dn(\lambda)}{d\lambda}$.

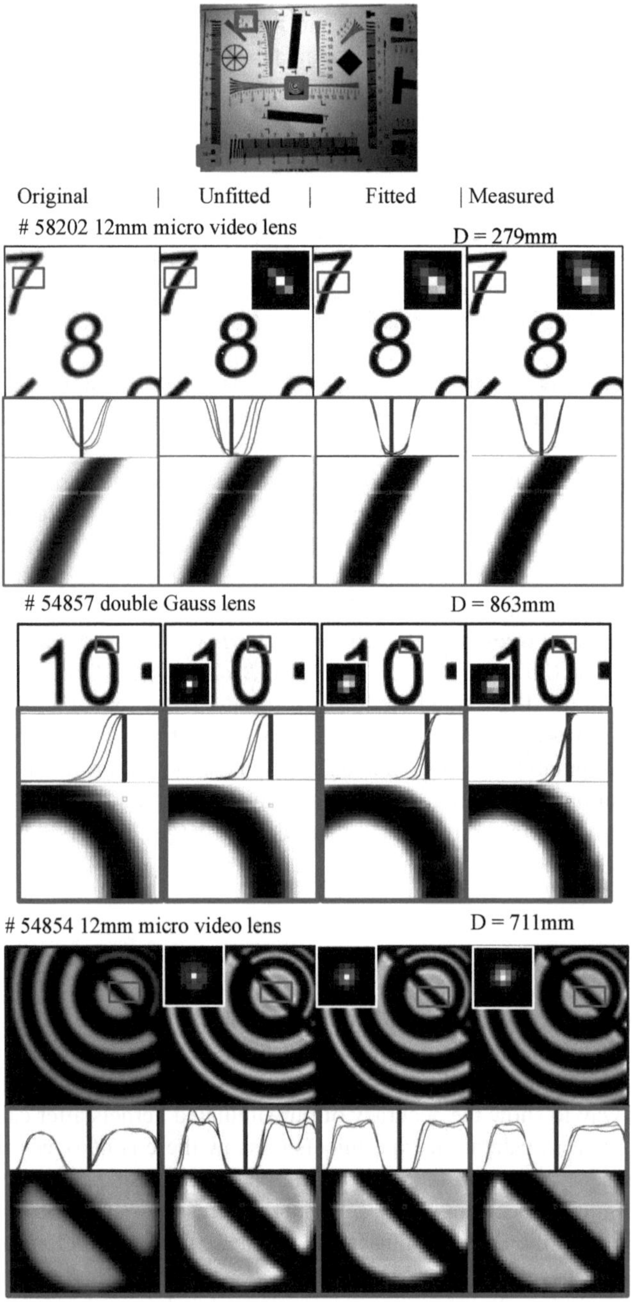

Fig. 6. Cross validation across the image plane. Original images taken at D (first col.), images deconvolved with PSFs simulated using nominal (un-calibrated) and calibrated lens prescription (second and third col.), and with measured PSFs (fourth col.). The 1-D horizontal slice of insets shows the calibrated version sharpens the image and reduces the chromatic aberration in all lenses.

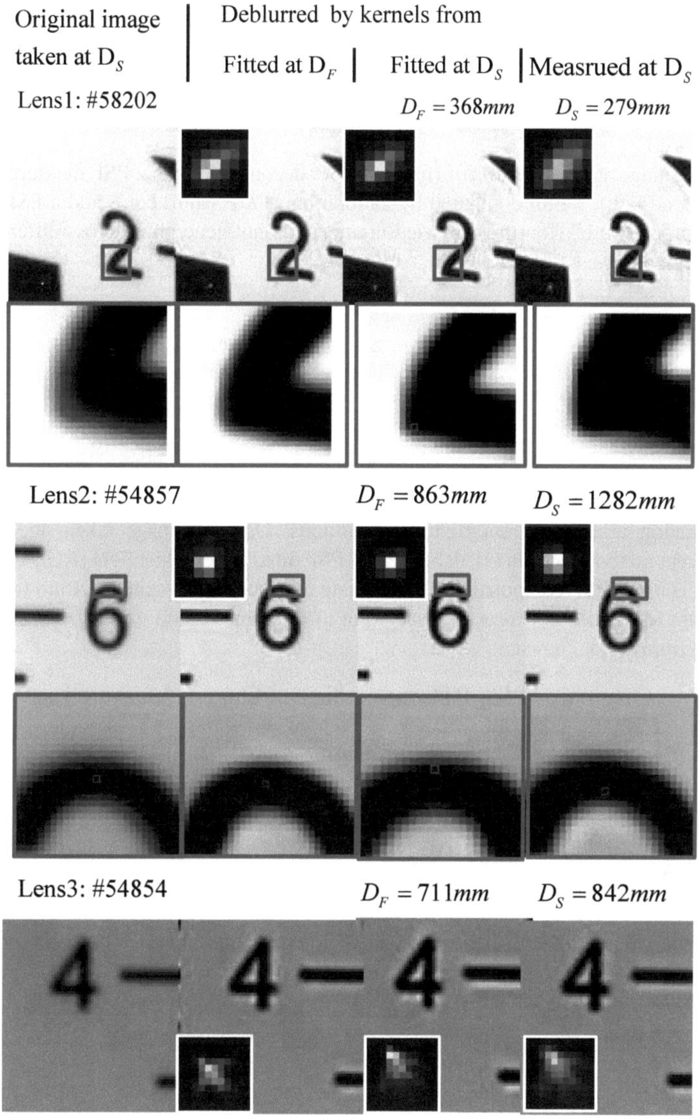

Fig. 7. We calibrated at two different depths D_F and D_S, respectively, then took an image at depth D_S, and deconvolved it using PSFs synthesize at D_S. Original images (first col.), images deconvolved using the PSFs from each calibration (second and third col.), and images deconvolved by PSF measured at D_S, i.e., the "groundtruth" (fourth col.). The image enhancement is equally good regardless of which depth is used for fitting.

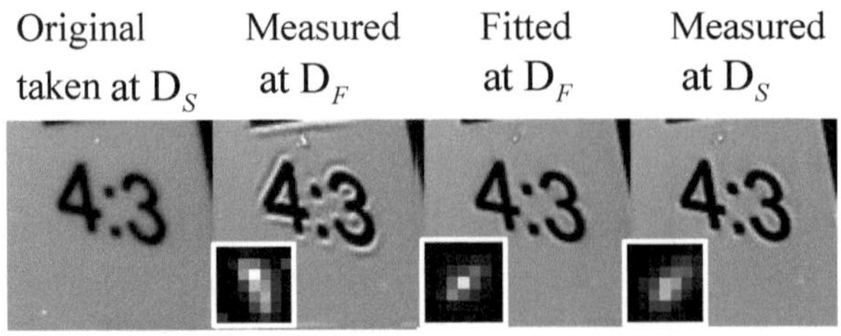

Fig. 8. For an image at $D_S = 368mm$ (first col.), we deconvolve with a PSF measured at $D_F = 279mm$ (second col.), a PSF computed by calibration at D_F (third col.), and a PSF measured at D_S, i.e. "groundtruth" (fourth col.). Measurements do not generalize across different depths, while our method does.

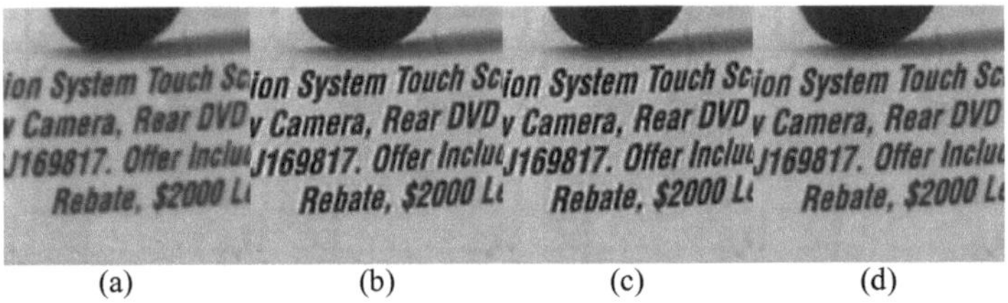

Fig. 9. Validation under different lighting conditions. Original image taken under incandecent/fluorescent mixed spectrum (a), deblurred by PSF fitted under white light (RGB LED)(b), deblurred results using PSF computed by approximate tungsten/fluorescent spectrum (c) and white light spectrum (d), instead of measured spectrum in (b). Our method gives good results even if the eaxt spectrum is not known.

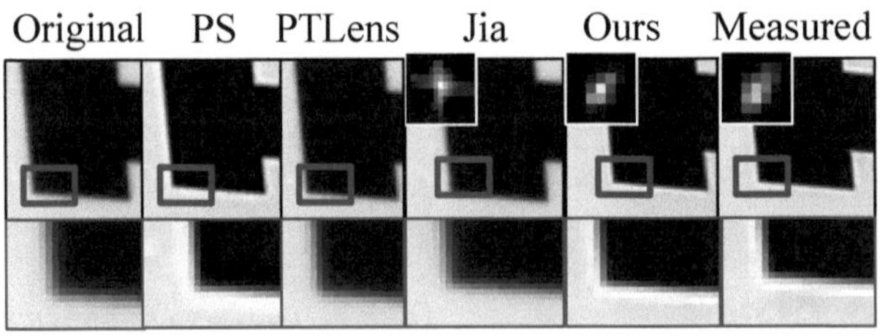

Fig. 10. Comparison with Photoshop smart sharpening (lens blur mode), PTLens chromatic aberration removal, Jia et al.'s robust motion deblurring.

Fig. 11. Geometric distortion can be easily corrected for using our method

Fig. 12. Image enhancement results of a newspaper and a National Geographic magazine cover. We take a image (first col.), and fit lens prescriptions at two different depths, respectively, and use them to enhance the image (second and third col.). The insets show reduced abberations and chromatic aberrations.

the lens specification, the PSF from the calibrated lens prescription is closer to the results using the measured PSF. Compared with original images, while the PSF from the un-calibrated lens introduced artifacts when used for deconvolution, our method simultaneously sharpen the image and reduces chromatic aberration with few artifacts just as when using the measured PSF.

In Fig. 7, we show the results after calibrating a lens to get two prescriptions P_a and P_b respectively for two corresponding measured depths D_F and D_S. We then took an image at depth D_S, and deconvolved it with the PSF synthesized at D_S using the prescriptions from both calibration runs, i.e. fitting at the the same depth D_S and a different depth D_F. In all cases and all lenses, regardless of what depth is used for fitting, the deconvolution results significantly reduce chromatic aberrations and sharpen the image. In these experiments, we use a range of depth differences between D_F and D_S – 33% for the #58202, 50% for the #54857, and 8% for the #54854. To the best of our knowledge, no existing parametric model can predict the PSF at different depths, while our method can.

In Fig. 8, we show the result of taking an image at D_S and deconvolving it with the PSF measured at D_F. The result includes noticeable artifacts. The purpose of this experiment is to illustrate that the assumption that PSF shape is invariant to focused plane distance is over simplified. One cannot simply measure the PSF at one depth and use it to enhance images from other depths. This shows the importance of our work: one can calibrate the lens prescription at one depth and later simply compute PSFs at different depths to enhance images.

In Fig 12, we show results using more natural images. We also include results for these images of the same cross validation process discussed above. In all cases, our method reduces or removes chromatic aberration and sharpens the images. We compare our method with existing methods in Fig. 10. In Fig.11, we show that our method can easily correct for geometric distortion using the correspondences from ray tracing.

In Fig. 9, we show how our our method can be used to correct images taken under a different illuminant spectrum than was used for calibration. The lens prescription calibrated using measurement under white light spectrum works well on images taken under incandecent fluorescent mixed spectrum. In Fig. 9 we show our method does not even require accurate spectrum information, but we can instead simulate a PSF using standard illuminant spectrum [1] given the white-balance mode of a camera (florescent, tungsten, etc.). The approximate fluorescent mixed spectrum [1] and white light spectrum (Figs. 9 (c)(d).) generate comparable results to using actual measure spectrum information (Fig. 9 (b).)

7 Conclusions

Our method improves image quality by deblurring images using point-spread functions computed with wave optics and a calibrated lens model. These point-spread functions model all optical aberrations. Previous work has addressed these optical artifacts as separate problems, while our approach unifies all of these corrections into one process.

Our method requires roughly two orders of magnitude fewer calibration images than strictly measurement based methods. Our fitted lens model generalizes to conditions far outside of those captured during calibration. After calibration the PSF can easily be simulated at any desired focus distance, lens aperture, or image plane position. We have demonstrated that the match between our fitted model and a measured PSF is very good, even when the lens calibration and PSF simulation are done at different depths.

Unlike previous methods, ours generalizes to illumination spectra different from that used to capture the calibration image. Ideally the precise illumination spectrum would be known but one can still improve images significantly if the lighting spectrum is unknown.

References

1. `http://www.cis.rit.edu/research/mcsl2/online/cie/fluorescents.html`
2. Banham, M.R., Katsaggelos, A.K.: Digital image restoration. IEEE Signal Processing Magazine 14(2), 24–41 (1997)
3. Brauers, J., Seiler, C., Aach, T.: Direct psf estimation using a random noise target. In: Digital Photography, p. 75370 (2010)
4. Cannon, M.: Blind deconvolution of spatially invariant image blurs with phase. IEEE Transactions on Acoustics, Speech, and Signal Processing [see also IEEE Transactions on Signal Processing] 24(1), 58–63 (1976)
5. Cathey, W.T., Dowski, E.R.: New paradigm for imaging systems. Appl. Opt. 41(29), 6080–6092 (2002)
6. Conchello, J.-A., Lichtman, J.W.: Optical sectioning microscopy. Nature Methods 2(12), 920–931 (2005)
7. Fergus, R., Singh, B., Hertzmann, A., Roweis, S.T., Freeman, W.T.: Removing camera shake from a single photograph. ACM Trans. Graph. 25, 787–794 (2006)
8. Goodman, J.W.: Introduction to Fourier Optics (2005)
9. Hanrahan, P., Ng, R.: Digital correction of lens aberrations in light field photography. In: International Optical Design, p. WB2. Optical Society of America (2006)
10. Hausler, G.: A method to increase the depth of focus by two step image processing. Optics Communications 6, 38–42 (1972)
11. Joshi, N., Szeliski, R., Kriegman, D.J.: Psf estimation using sharp edge prediction. In: IEEE Conference on Computer Vision and Pattern Recognition, CVPR 2008, pp. 1–8 (2008)
12. Kang, S.: Automatic removal of chromatic aberration from a single image. In: IEEE Conference on Computer Vision and Pattern Recognition, CVPR 2007, pp. 1–8. IEEE (2007)
13. Kee, E., Paris, S., Chen, S., Wang, J.: Modeling and removing spatially-varying optical blur. In: 2011 IEEE International Conference on Computational Photography (ICCP), pp. 1–8. IEEE (2011)
14. Krist, J.E.: Deconvolution of hubble space telescope images using simulated point spread functions. Astronomical Data Analysis Software and Systems (1992)
15. Levin, A.: Blind motion deblurring using image statistics. In: NIPS, pp. 841–848 (2006)
16. Levin, A., Sand, P., Cho, T.S., Durand, F., Freeman, W.T.: Motion-invariant photography. ACM Trans. Graph. 27, 71:1–71:9 (2008)
17. McGuire Jr., J., et al.: Designing easily manufactured lenses using a global method. In: International Optical Design Conference. Optical Society of America (2006)
18. Meiron, J.: Damped least-squares method for automatic lens design. JOSA 55(9), 1105–1107 (1965)
19. Nayar, S.K., Watanabe, M., Noguchi, M.: Real-time focus range sensor. IEEE Trans. Pattern Anal. Mach. Intell. 18, 1186–1198 (1996)

20. Scalettar, B., Swedlow, J., Sedat, J., Agard, D.: Dispersion, aberration and deconvolution in multi-wavelength fluorescence images. Journal of Microscopy 182(1), 50–60 (1996)
21. Xu, L., Jia, J.: Two-Phase Kernel Estimation for Robust Motion Deblurring. In: Daniilidis, K., Maragos, P., Paragios, N. (eds.) ECCV 2010, Part I. LNCS, vol. 6311, pp. 157–170. Springer, Heidelberg (2010)
22. Zhou, C., Lin, S., Nayar, S.: Coded aperture pairs for depth from defocus. In: ICCV, Kyoto, Japan (October 2009)

Color Constancy, Intrinsic Images, and Shape Estimation

Jonathan T. Barron and Jitendra Malik

UC Berkeley
{barron,malik}@eecs.berkeley.edu

Abstract. We present **SIRFS** (shape, illumination, and reflectance from shading), the first unified model for recovering shape, chromatic illumination, and reflectance from a single image. Our model is an extension of our previous work [1], which addressed the achromatic version of this problem. Dealing with color requires a modified problem formulation, novel priors on reflectance and illumination, and a new optimization scheme for dealing with the resulting inference problem. Our approach outperforms all previously published algorithms for intrinsic image decomposition and shape-from-shading on the MIT intrinsic images dataset [1, 2] and on our own "naturally" illuminated version of that dataset.

1 Introduction

In 1866, Helmholtz noted that "In visual observation we constantly aim to reach a judgment on the object colors and to eliminate differences of illumination" ([3], volume 2, p.287). This problem of color constancy — decomposing an image into illuminant color and surface color — has seen a great deal of work in the modern era, starting with Land and McCann's Retinex algorithm [4, 5]. Retinex ignores shape and attempts to recover illumination and reflectance in isolation, assumptions shared by nearly all subsequent work in color constancy [6–11]. In this paper we present the first algorithm for recovering shape in conjunction with surface color and color illumination given only a single image of an object, which we call "shape, illumination, and reflectance from shading" (SIRFS).

There are many early works regarding color constancy, such as gamut mapping techniques [6], finite dimensional models of reflectance and illumination [7], and physically based techniques for exploiting specularities [8]. More recent work uses contemporary probabilistic tools, such as modeling the correlation between colors in a scene [9], or performing inference over priors on reflectance and illumination [10]. All of this work shares the assumptions of Retinex that shape (and to a lesser extent, shading) can be ignored or abstracted away.

Color constancy can be viewed as a subset of the intrinsic images problem: decomposing a single image into its constituent "images": shape, reflectance, illumination, etc [13]. Over time, the computer vision community has reduced this task to just the decomposition of an image into shading and reflectance. Though

A. Fitzgibbon et al. (Eds.): ECCV 2012, Part IV, LNCS 7575, pp. 57–70, 2012.

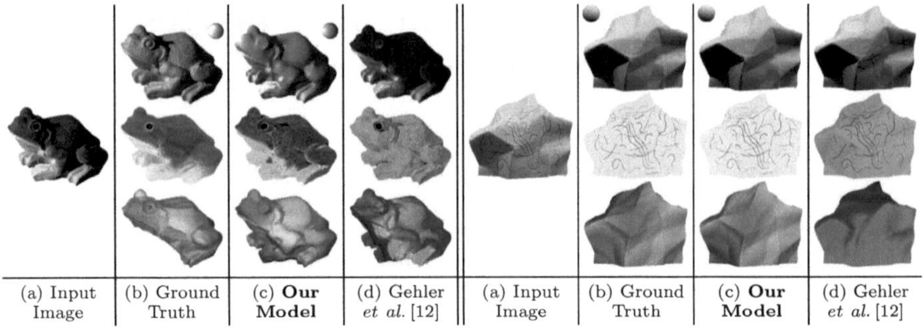

Fig. 1. Two objects from our datasets. Given just the masked input image (a), our model produces (c): a depth-map, reflectance image, shading image, and illumination model that together exactly explain the input image (illumination is rendered on a sphere, and shape is shown as a pseudocolor visualization where red is near and blue is far). Our output looks very similar to (b), the ground-truth explanation of the image — in some cases, nearly indistinguishable. The top-performing intrinsic image algorithm (d) performs much worse on our datasets, and only estimates shading and reflectance (we assume ground-truth illumination is known for (d), and run a shape-from-shading algorithm on shading to produce a shape estimate). Many more similar results can be seen in the supplementary material.

this simplified "intrinsic images" problem has seen a great deal of progress in recent years [2, 12, 14, 15] all of these techniques have critical difficulties with non-white illumination — that is, they do not address color constancy. Additionally, none of these techniques recover shape or illumination, and instead consider shading in isolation.

Another special case of intrinsic images is shape-from-shading (SFS) [16], in which reflectance and illumination are assumed to be known and shape is recovered. This problem has been studied extensively [17, 18], and very recent work has shown that accurate shape can be recovered under natural, chromatic illumination [19], but the assumptions of known illumination and uniform reflectance severely limit SFS's usefulness in practice.

Perceptual studies show that humans use spatial cues when estimating lightness and color [20, 21]. This suggests that the human visual system does not independently solve the problems of color constancy and shape estimation, in contrast to the current state of computer vision.

Clearly, these three problems of color constancy, intrinsic images, and shape from shading would benefit greatly from a unified approach, as each subproblem's strength is another's weakness. We present the first such unified approach, by building heavily on the "shape, albedo, and illumination from shading" (SAIFS) model of our previous work [1], which addresses this problem for grayscale images and white illumination. We extend this technique to color by: trivially modifying the rendering machinery to use color illumination, introducing novel priors for reflectance and illumination, and introducing a novel multiscale inference scheme for solving the resulting problem. We evaluate on the MIT intrinsic images dataset [1, 2], and on our own variant of the MIT dataset in which we have re-rendered the objects under natural, chromatic illuminations produced from real-world environment maps. This additional dataset allows us to evaluate on images produced under natural illumination, rather than the "laboratory"-style controlled illumination of the MIT dataset.

We will show that our unified model outperforms all current techniques for the task of recovering shape, reflectance, and, optionally, illumination. By exploiting color in natural reflectance images, we do better than the grayscale technique of [1] at disambiguating between shading and reflectance. By explicitly modeling shape and illumination we are able to outperform "intrinsic image" algorithms, which only consider shading and reflectance and perform poorly as a result. By modeling chromatic illumination we are able to exploit chromatic shading information, and thereby produce improved shape estimates, as demonstrated in [19]. For these reasons, when faced with images produced under natural, non-white illumination the performance of our algorithm actually *improves*, while intrinsic algorithms perform much worse. See Figure 1 for examples of the output of our algorithm and of the best-performing intrinsic image algorithm.

In Section 2, we present a modification of the problem formulation of [1]. In Sections 3, 4, and 5 we motivate and introduce three novel priors on reflectance images: one based on local smoothness, one based on global sparsity or entropy, and one based on the absolute color of each pixel. In Section 6 we introduce a prior on illumination, and in Section 7 we present a novel multiscale optimization technique that is critical to inference. In Section 8 we show results for the MIT dataset and our own version of the MIT dataset with natural illumination, and in Section 9 we conclude.

2 Problem Formulation

Our problem formulation is an extension of the "SAIFS" problem formulation of [1], which is itself an extension of the "SAFS" formulation of [22]. We optimize over a depth map, reflectance image, and model of illumination such that cost functions on those three quantities are minimized, and such that the input image is exactly recreated by the output shape, albedo, and illumination.

More formally, let R be a log-reflectance map, Z be a depth-map, and L be a model of illumination, and $S(Z, L)$ be a "rendering engine" which produces a log-shading image given depth-map Z and illumination L. Assuming Lambertian reflectance, the log-intensity image I is equal to $R + S(Z, L)$. I is observed, and $S(\cdot)$ is defined, but Z, R, and L are unknown. We search for the most likely (or equivalently, least costly) explanation for image I, which corresponds to solving the following optimization problem:

$$\begin{aligned} \underset{Z,R,L}{\text{minimize}} \quad & g(R) + f(Z) + h(L) \\ \text{subject to} \quad & I = R + S(Z, L) \end{aligned} \tag{1}$$

where $g(R)$ is the cost of reflectance R (roughly, the negative log-likelihood of R), $f(Z)$ is the cost of shape Z, and $h(L)$ is the cost of illumination L. To optimize Equation 1, we eliminate the constraint by rewriting $R = I - S(Z, L)$, and minimize the resulting unconstrained optimization problem using multiscale L-BFGS (see Section 7) to produce depth map $\hat{Z}$ and illumination $\hat{L}$, with which we calculate reflectance image $\hat{R} = I - S(\hat{Z}, \hat{L})$. When illumination is known, L is fixed. This problem formulation differs from that of [1] in that we have a single model of illumination which we optimize over and place priors on, rather than a distribution over "memorized" illuminations. This is crucial, as the huge variety of natural chromatic illuminations makes the previous formulation intractable.

To extend the grayscale model of [1] to color, we must redefine the prior on reflectance $g(R)$ to take advantage of the additional information present in color reflectance images, and to address the additional complications that arise when illumination is allowed to be non-white. Because illumination is a free parameter in our problem formulation, we must define a prior on illumination $h(L)$. We use the same $S(Z, L)$ and a modified version of $f(Z)$ as [1] (see the supplementary material).

Our prior on reflectance will be a linear combination of three terms:

$$g(R) = \lambda_s g_s(R) + \lambda_e g_e(R) + \lambda_a g_a(R) \tag{2}$$

where the λ weights are learned using cross-validation on the training set. $g_s(R)$ and $g_e(R)$ are our priors on local smoothness and global entropy of reflectance, and can be thought of as multivariate generalizations of the grayscale model of [1]. $g_a(R)$ is a new "absolute" prior on each pixel in R that prefers some colors over others, thereby addressing color constancy.

3 Local Reflectance Smoothness

The reflectance images of natural objects tend to be piecewise smooth — or equivalently, variation in reflectance images tends to be small and sparse. This insight is fundamental to most intrinsic image algorithms [2, 4, 5, 14, 23], and is used in our previous works [1, 22]. In terms of color, variation in reflectance tends to manifest itself in both the luminance and chrominance of an image (white transitioning to blue, for example) while shading, assuming the illumination is white, affects only the luminance of an image (light blue transitioning to dark blue, for example). Past work has exploited this insight by building specialized models that condition on the chrominance variation of the input image [2, 5, 12, 14, 15]. Effectively, these algorithms use image chrominance as a substitute for reflectance chrominance, which means that they fail when faced with non-white illumination, as we will demonstrate. We instead simply place a multivariate prior over differences in reflectance, which avoids this non-white illumination problem while capturing the color-dependent nature of reflectance variation.

Our prior on reflectance smoothness is a multivariate Gaussian scale mixture (GSM) placed on the differences between each reflectance pixel and its neighbors. We will maximize the likelihood of R under this model, which corresponds to minimizing the following cost function:

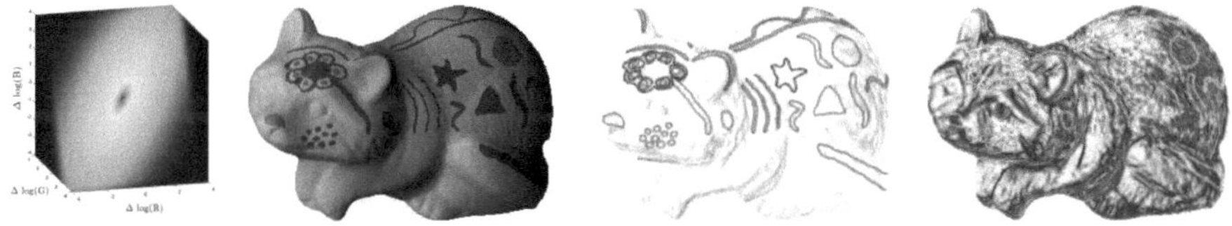

(a) Our GSM smoothness prior | (b) R - a proposed reflectance image | (c) $g_s(R)$ - cost under our model | (d) $\nabla g_s(R)$ - influence under our model

Fig. 2. Our smoothness prior is a multivariate Gaussian scale mixture on the differences between nearby reflectance pixels (Figure 2(a)). This distribution prefers nearby reflectance pixels to be similar, but its heavy tails allow for rare non-smooth discontinuities. We see this by analyzing some image R as seen by our model. Strong, colorful edges, such as those caused by reflectance variation, are very costly (have a low likelihood) while small edges, such as those caused by shading, are more likely. But in terms of *influence* — the gradient of cost with respect to each reflectance pixel — we see an inversion: because sharp edges lie in the tails of the GSM, they have little influence, while shading variation has great influence. This means that during inference our model attempts to explain shading in the image by varying shape, while ignoring sharp edges in reflectance. Additionally, because this model captures the correlation between color channels, chromatic variation has less influence than achromatic variation (because it lies further out in the tails), making it more likely to be ignored during inference.

$$g_s(R) = \sum_i \sum_{j \in N(i)} \log \left(\sum_{k=1}^{K} \boldsymbol{\alpha}_k \, \mathcal{N}\left(R_i - R_j \, ; \mathbf{0}, \boldsymbol{\sigma}_k \, \Sigma\right) \right) \tag{3}$$

Where $N(i)$ is the 5×5 neighborhood around pixel i, $R_i - R_j$ is a 3-vector of the log-RGB differences from pixel i to pixel j, $K = 40$ (the GSM has 40 discrete Gaussians), $\boldsymbol{\alpha}$ are mixing coefficients, $\boldsymbol{\sigma}$ are the scalings of the Gaussians in the mixture, and Σ is the covariance matrix of the entire GSM (shared among all Gaussians of the mixture). The mean is 0, as the most likely reflectance image should be flat. The GSM is learned on the reflectance images in our training set. The differences between this model and that of [1] are: 1) we have a multivariate rather than univariate GSM, to address color, 2) we're placing priors on the differences between all pairs of reflectance pixels within a window, rather than placing a prior on the magnitude of the gradient of reflectance at each pixel, as this produces better results, and 3) we have one single-scale prior, as multiscale priors no longer improve results when using our improved optimization technique. A visualization and explanation of the effect of this smoothness prior can be found in Figure 2.

4 Global Reflectance Entropy

The reflectance image of a single object tends to be "clumped" in RGB space, or equivalently it can be approximated by a set of "sparse" exemplars. This motivates the second term of our model of reflectance: a measure of global entropy which we minimize. We will build upon our previous model [1], but different forms of this idea have been used in intrinsic images techniques [23, 12], photometric stereo [24], shadow removal [25], and color representation [26]. As in [1], we build upon the entropy measure of Principe and Xu [27], which is a model of quadratic entropy (or Rényi entropy) for a set of points assuming a Parzen window. This can be thought of as a "soft" and differentiable generalization of Shannon entropy, computed on a set of points rather than a histogram.

A naive extension of the one-dimensional entropy model of [1] to three dimensions is not sufficient: The RGB channels of natural reflectance images are highly correlated, causing a naive isotropic entropy measure to work poorly. To address this, we pre-compute a whitening transformation from training reflectance images and compute an isotropic entropy measure in this whitened space during inference, effectively giving us an anisotropic entropy measure. Formally, our cost function is non-normalized Rényi entropy in the space of whitened reflectance:

$$g_e(R) = -\log\left(\sum_i \sum_j \exp\left(-\frac{\|\mathrm{W}R_i - \mathrm{W}R_j\|_2^2}{4\sigma_e^2}\right)\right) \tag{4}$$

Where W is the whitening transformation learned from training reflectance images, as follows: Let X be a $3 \times n$ matrix of the pixels in the reflectance images in our training set. We compute the covariance matrix $\Sigma = \mathrm{XX}^{\mathrm{T}}$ (ignoring centering), take its eigenvalue decomposition $\Sigma = \Phi\Lambda\Phi^{\mathrm{T}}$, and from that construct the whitening transformation $\mathrm{W} = \Phi\Lambda^{1/2}\Phi^{\mathrm{T}}$. σ_e is the bandwidth of the Parzen window, which determines the scale of the clusters produced by minimizing this entropy measure, and is tuned through cross-validation. See Figure 3 for a motivation of this model.

These Rényi measures of entropy are quadratically expensive to compute naively, so others have used the Fast Gauss Transform [25] and histogram-based techniques [1] to approximate it in linear time. The histogram-based technique appears to be more efficient than the FGT-based methods, and provides a way to compute the analytical gradient of entropy, which is crucial for optimization. We therefore use a 3D generalization of the algorithm of [1] to compute

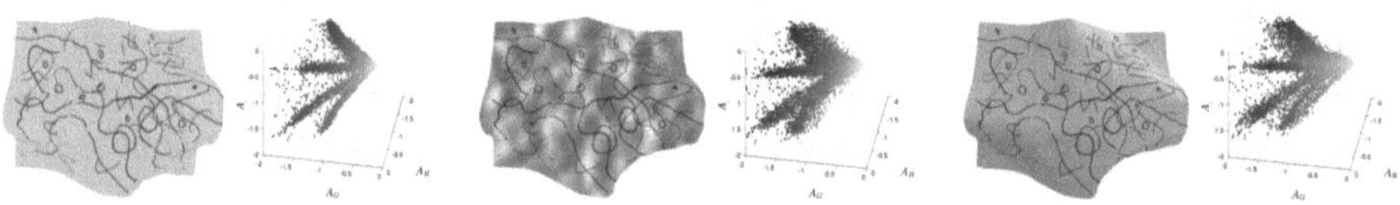

(a) Correct Everything $g_e(R) = 0.913$ (b) Wrong Shape $g_e(R) = 1.325$ (c) Wrong Light $g_e(R) = 2.366$

Fig. 3. Reflectance images and their corresponding log-RGB scatterplots. Mistakes in estimating shape or illumination produce shading-like or illumination-like artifacts in the inferred reflectance, causing the the RGB distribution of the inferred reflectance to be "smeared", and causing entropy (and therefore cost) to increase.

our entropy measure. The resulting technique looks very similar to the bilateral grid [28] used in high-dimensional Gaussian filtering, and can be seen in the supplementary material.

5 Absolute Color

The previously described priors were imposed on *relative* properties of reflectance: the differences between adjacent or non-adjacent pixels. Though this was sufficient for past work, now that we are attempting to recover surface color and non-white illumination we must impose an additional prior on *absolute* reflectance: the raw log-RGB value of each pixel in the reflectance image. Without such a prior (and the prior on illumination presented in Section 6) our model would be equally pleased to explain a white pixel in the image as white reflectance under white illumination as it would blue reflectance under yellow illumination, for example.

This sort of prior is fundamental to color-constancy, as most basic color constancy algorithms can be viewed as minimizing a similar sort of cost: the gray-world assumption penalizes reflectance for being non-gray, the white-world assumption penalizes reflectance for being non-white, and gamut-based models penalize reflectance for lying outside of a gamut of previously-seen reflectances. We experimented with variations or combinations of these types of models, but found that a simple density model on whitened log-RGB values worked best.

Our model is a 3D thin-plate spline (TSP) fitted to the distribution of whitened log-RGB reflectance pixels in our training set. Formally, to train our model we minimize the following:

$$\underset{\mathrm{F}}{\text{minimize}} \quad \left(\sum_{i,j,k} \mathrm{F}_{i,j,k} \cdot \mathrm{N}_{i,j,k} \right) + \log \left(\sum_{i,j,k} \exp\left(-\mathrm{F}_{i,j,k}\right) \right) + \lambda \sqrt{J(\mathrm{F}) + \epsilon^2}$$

$$J(\mathrm{F}) = \mathrm{F}_{xx}^2 + \mathrm{F}_{yy}^2 + \mathrm{F}_{zz}^2 + 2\mathrm{F}_{xy}^2 + 2\mathrm{F}_{yz}^2 + 2\mathrm{F}_{xz}^2 \tag{5}$$

Where F is a 3D TSP describing cost (or non-normalized negative log-likelihood), N is a 3D histogram of the whitened log-RGB reflectance in our training data, and $J(\cdot)$ is the TSP bending energy cost (made more robust by taking its square root, with ϵ^2 added to make it differentiable everywhere). Minimizing the sum of the first two terms is equivalent to maximizing the likelihood of the training data, and minimizing the third term causes the TSP to be piece-wise smooth. The smoothness multiplier λ is tuned through cross-validation.

During inference, we maximize the likelihood of the reflectance image R by minimizing its cost under our learned model:

$$g_a(R) = \sum_i \mathrm{F}(\mathrm{W}R_i) \tag{6}$$

where $\mathrm{F}(\mathrm{W}R_i)$ is the value of F at the coordinates specified by the 3-vector $\mathrm{W}R_i$, the whitened reflectance at pixel i (W is the same as in Section 4). To make this function differentiable, we compute $\mathrm{F}(\cdot)$ using trilinear interpolation. A visualization of our model and of the colors it prefers can be seen in Figure 4.

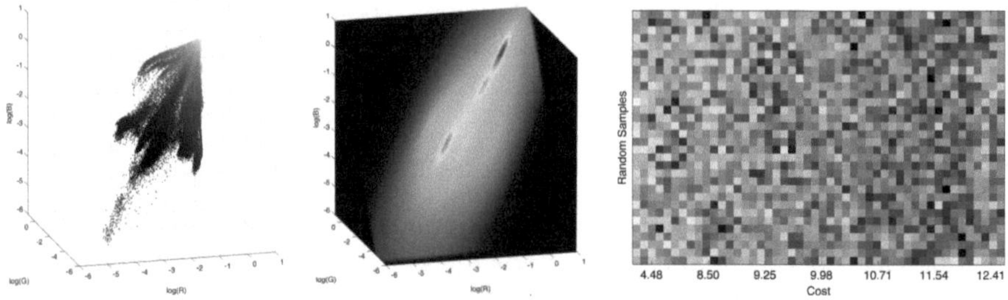

(a) Training reflectances (b) Our PDF of reflectance (c) Reflectances sorted by cost

Fig. 4. A visualization of our "absolute" prior on reflectance. On the left we have the log-RGB reflectance pixels in our training set, and a visualization of the 3D thin-plate spline PDF that we fit to that data. Our model prefers reflectances that are close to white or gray, and that lie within gamut of previously seen colors. Though our prior is learned in whitened log-RGB space, here it is shown in unwhitened coordinates, hence its anisotropy. On the right we have randomly generated reflectances, sorted by their cost (negative log-likelihood) under our model. Our model prefers less saturated, more subdued colors, and abhors brightly lit neon-like colors. The low-cost reflectances look like a tasteful selection of paint colors, while high-cost reflectances don't even look like paint at all, but instead appear almost glowing and luminescent.

6 Priors over Illumination

In our previous work, inference with unknown illumination involved maximizing an expected complete log-likelihood with respect to a memorized set of ~100 illuminations taken from the training set. That framework was an effective way of both optimizing with respect to illumination (as the posterior distribution over illuminations was re-evaluated at each step in optimization, effectively "moving" the light around) and of regularizing illumination in a non-parametric way (as only previously seen illuminations were considered). However, that framework requires an extremely expensive marginalization over a set of illuminations, which causes inference to be extremely slow — hours per image. That framework also scales linearly with the complexity of the illumination, so modeling the variety of natural, colorful illuminations makes inference impossibly slow. For these reasons, in this paper we adopt a simplified model (Equation 1) in which we explicitly optimize over a single model of illumination in conjunction with shape. This allows us to model and recover a very wide variety of natural illuminations (see Figure 5), while making inference effectively as fast as if illumination were known — around 5 minutes per image. Unfortunately, this model also requires us to explicitly define $h(L)$, our prior on illumination.

We use a spherical-harmonic (SH) model of illumination, so L is a 27 dimensional vector (9 dimensions per RGB channel). In contrast to traditional SH illumination, we parametrize log-shading rather than shading. This choice makes optimization easier as we don't have to deal with "clamping" illumination at 0,

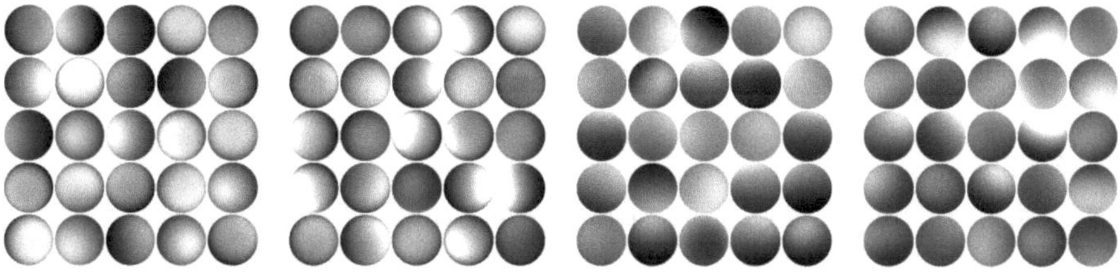

(a) "Lab" Data (b) "Lab" Samples (c) "Natural" Data (d) "Natural" Samples

Fig. 5. We use two datasets: the "laboratory"-style illuminations of the MIT intrinsic images dataset [2, 1] which are harsh, mostly-white, and well-approximated by point sources, and a new dataset of "natural" illuminations, which are softer and much more colorful. We model illumination using just a multivariate Gaussian on spherical harmonic illumination. Shown here are some example illuminations from our datasets and samples from our models, all rendered on Lambertian spheres. The samples looks superficially similar to the data, suggesting that our model is reasonable.

and it allows for easier regularization as the space of log-shading SH illuminations is surprisingly well-modeled by a simple multivariate Gaussian. Training our model is extremely simple: we fit a multivariate Gaussian to the SH illuminations in our training set. During inference, the cost we impose is the negative log-likelihood under that model:

$$h(L) = \lambda_L (L - \boldsymbol{\mu}_L)^{\mathrm{T}} \Sigma_L^{-1} (L - \boldsymbol{\mu}_L) \tag{7}$$

where $\boldsymbol{\mu}_L$ and Σ_L are the parameters of the Gaussian we learned, and λ_L is the multiplier on this prior (learned through cross-validation). Separate Gaussians and multipliers are learned from the illuminations in our two different datasets (see Section 8). See Figure 5 for a visualization of our training data and of samples from our learned models.

The Gaussians we learn for illumination mostly describe a low-rank subspace of SH coefficients. For this reason, it is important that we optimize in the space of whitened illumination. Whitened illumination is used as the internal representation of illumination during optimization, but is transformed to un-whitened space when calculating the loss function.

7 Multiscale Optimization

Here we present a novel multi-scale optimization method that is simpler, faster, and finds better local optima than the previous coarse-to-fine techniques we have presented [1, 22]. Our technique seems similar to multigrid methods [29], though it is extremely general and simple to implement. We will describe our technique in terms of optimizing $f(X)$, where f is some loss function and X is some n-dimensional signal.

Let us define $\mathcal{L}(X, h)$, which constructs a Laplacian pyramid from a signal, $\mathcal{L}^{-1}(Y, h)$, which reconstructs a signal from a Laplacian pyramid, and $\mathcal{G}(X, h)$, which constructs a Gaussian pyramid from a signal. Let h be the filter used in constructing and reconstructing these pyramids. Instead of minimizing $f(X)$ directly, we reparameterize X as $Y = \mathcal{L}(X, h)$, and minimize $f'(Y)$:

$$[\ell, \nabla_Y \ell] = f'(Y): \tag{8}$$
$$X \leftarrow \mathcal{L}^{-1}(Y, h) \text{ // reconstruct the signal from the pyramid}$$
$$[\ell, \nabla_X \ell] \leftarrow f(X) \text{ // compute the loss and gradient with respect to the signal}$$
$$\nabla_Y \ell \leftarrow \mathcal{G}(\nabla_X \ell, h) \text{ // backpropagate the gradient onto the pyramid}$$

We then solve for $\hat{X} = \mathcal{L}^{-1}(\arg\min_Y f'(Y), h)$ using L-BFGS. Other gradient-based techniques could be used, but L-BFGS worked best in our experience.

The choice of h, the filter used for our Laplacian and Gaussian pyramids, is crucial. We found that 5-tap binomial filters work well, and that the choice of the magnitude of the filter dramatically affects multiscale optimization. If $\|h\|_1$ is small, then the coefficients of the upper levels of the Laplacian pyramid are so small that they are effectively ignored, and optimization fails. If $\|h\|_1$ is large, then the coarse scales of the pyramid are optimized and the fine scales are ignored. The filter that we found worked best is: $h = \frac{1}{4\sqrt{2}}[1, 4, 6, 4, 1]$, which has twice the magnitude of the filter that would normally be used for Laplacian pyramids. This increased magnitude biases optimization towards adjusting coarse scales before fine scales, without preventing optimization from eventually optimizing fine scales.

Note that this technique is substantially different from standard coarse-to-fine optimization, in that *all* scales are optimized simultaneously. As a result, we find much lower minima than standard coarse-to-fine techniques, which tend to keep coarse scales fixed when optimizing over fine scales. Our improved optimization also lets us use simple single-scale priors instead of multiscale priors, as was necessary in our previous work [1].

This optimization technique is used to solve Equations 1 and 5. When optimizing Equation 1 we initialize Z to 0 and L to $\boldsymbol{\mu}_L$, and optimize with respect to a vector that is a concatenation of $\mathcal{L}(Z, h)$ and a whitened version of L. For both problems, naive single-scale optimization fails badly.

8 Results

We evaluate our algorithm using the MIT intrinsic images dataset [1, 2]. The MIT dataset has very "laboratory"-like illumination — lights are white, and are placed at only a few locations relative to the object. Natural illuminations display much more color and variety (see Figures 5 and 6).

We therefore present an additional pseudo-synthetic dataset, in which we have rendered the objects in the MIT dataset using natural, colorful illuminations taken from the real world. We took all of the environment maps from the sIBL Archive[1], expanded that set of environment maps by shifting and mirroring

[1] `http://www.hdrlabs.com/sibl/archive.html`

them, and varying their contrast and saturation (saturation was only decreased, never increased), and produced spherical harmonic illuminations from the resulting environment maps. After removing similar illuminations, the illuminations were split into training and test sets. Each object in the MIT dataset was randomly assigned an illumination (such that training illuminations were assigned to training objects, etc), and each object was re-rendered under its new illumination, using that object's ground-truth shape and reflectance.

Our experiments can be seen in Table 1, in Figure 1, and in the supplementary material. We present four sets of experiments, with either the "laboratory" illumination of the basic MIT dataset or our "natural" illumination dataset, and with the illumination either known or unknown. We use the same training and test split as in [1], with our hyperparameters tuned to the training set, and with the same parameters used in all experiments and all figures.

For the known-lighting case our baselines are a "flat" baseline of $Z = 0$, four intrinsic image algorithms (these produce shading and reflectance images, and we then run the SFS algorithm of [1] using the recovered shading and known illumination to recover shape), the achromatic technique of our previous work [1], and the shape-from-contour algorithm of [1]. For unknown illumination, the only existing baseline is our previous work [1]. We present two simplifications of our model in which we apply the smoothness and entropy albedo priors of [1] to the RGB or YUV channels of color reflectance (while still using our absolute color and illumination priors), to demonstrate the importance of our multivariate models. We also present an ablation study in which priors on reflectance

Table 1. A comparison of our model against others, on the "laboratory" MIT intrinsic images dataset [1, 2] and our own "natural" illumination variant, with the illumination either known or unknown. Shown are the geometric means of five error metrics (excluding L-MSE when illumination is known) across the test set, and an "average" error (the geometric mean of the other mean errors). N-MSE, L-MSE, s-MSE, and r-MSE measure shape, illumination, shading, and reflectance errors, respectively, and rs-MSE is the error metric of [2], (where it is called "LMSE") which measures shading and reflectance errors. These metrics are explained in detail in the supplementary material.

Laboratory Illumination Dataset

Algorithm	N-MSE	s-MSE	r-MSE	rs-MSE	L-MSE	Avg.
Known Illumination						
Flat Baseline	0.6141	0.0572	0.0452	0.0354	-	0.0866
Retinex [2, 5] + SFS [1]	0.8412	0.0204	0.0186	0.0163	-	0.0477
Tappen *et al.* 2005 [14] + SFS [1]	0.7052	0.0361	0.0379	0.0347	-	0.0760
Shen *et al.* 2011 [15] + SFS [1]	0.9232	0.0528	0.0458	0.0398	-	0.0971
Gehler *et al.* 2011 [12] + SFS [1]	0.6342	0.0106	0.0101	0.0131	-	0.0307
Barron & Malik 2012A [1]	0.2032	0.0142	0.0160	0.0181	-	0.0302
Shape from Contour [1]	0.2464	0.0296	0.0412	0.0309	-	0.0552
Our Model (Complete)	0.2151	0.0066	0.0115	0.0133	-	0.0215
Unknown Illumination						
Barron & Malik 2012A [1]	0.1975	0.0194	0.0224	0.0190	0.0247	0.0332
Our Model (RGB)	0.2818	0.0090	0.0118	0.0149	0.0098	0.0213
Our Model (YUV)	0.2906	0.0110	0.0171	0.0182	0.0126	0.0263
Our Model (No Light Priors)	0.5215	0.0301	0.0273	0.0285	0.2059	0.0758
Our Model (No Absolute Prior)	0.3261	0.0124	0.0195	0.0189	0.0166	0.0301
Our Model (No Smoothness Prior)	0.2727	0.0105	0.0179	0.0223	0.0125	0.0270
Our Model (No Entropy Model)	0.2865	0.0109	0.0161	0.0152	0.0141	0.0255
Our Model (White Light)	0.2221	0.0082	0.0112	0.0136	0.0085	0.0188
Our Model (Complete)	0.2793	0.0075	0.0118	0.0144	0.0100	0.0205

Natural Illumination Dataset

Algorithm	N-MSE	s-MSE	r-MSE	rs-MSE	L-MSE	Avg.
Known Illumination						
Flat Baseline	0.6141	0.0246	0.0243	0.0125	-	0.0463
Retinex [2, 5] + SFS [1]	0.4258	0.0174	0.0174	0.0083	-	0.0322
Tappen *et al.* 2005 [14] + SFS [1]	0.6707	0.0255	0.0280	0.0268	-	0.0599
Gehler *et al.* 2011 [12] + SFS [1]	0.5549	0.0162	0.0150	0.0105	-	0.0346
Gehler *et al.* 2011 [12] + [11] + SFS [1]	0.6282	0.0163	0.0164	0.0106	-	0.0365
Barron & Malik 2012A [1]	0.2044	0.0092	0.0094	0.0081	-	0.0195
Shape from Contour [1]	0.2502	0.0126	0.0163	0.0106	-	0.0271
Our Model (Complete)	0.0867	0.0022	0.0017	0.0026	-	0.0054
Unknown Illumination						
Barron & Malik 2012A [1]	0.2172	0.0193	0.0188	0.0094	0.0206	0.0273
Our Model (RGB)	0.2373	0.0086	0.0072	0.0065	0.0104	0.0159
Our Model (YUV)	0.3064	0.0095	0.0088	0.0072	0.0110	0.0183
Our Model (No Light Priors)	0.3722	0.0141	0.0149	0.0118	0.1491	0.0424
Our Model (No Absolute Prior)	0.1914	0.0124	0.0106	0.0036	0.0136	0.0165
Our Model (No Smoothness Prior)	0.2700	0.0084	0.0071	0.0065	0.0090	0.0157
Our Model (No Entropy Prior)	0.2911	0.0080	0.0067	0.0054	0.0109	0.0155
Our Model (White Light)	0.6268	0.0211	0.0207	0.0089	0.0647	0.0437
Our Model (Complete)	0.2348	0.0060	0.0049	0.0042	0.0084	0.0119

or illumination are removed, and in which illumination is forced to be white (achromatic) during inference.

For our "natural" illumination dataset, we use the same baselines (except for [15], as their code was not available). We also evaluate against the intrinsic image algorithm of Gehler *et al.* [12] after having run a contemporary white-balancing algorithm [11] on the input image, which shows that a "color constancy" algorithm does not fully address natural illumination for this task.

For the "laboratory" case, our algorithm is the best-performing algorithm whether or not illumination is known. Surprisingly, performance is slightly better when illumination is unknown, possibly because optimization is able to find more accurate shapes and reflectances when illumination is allowed to vary. The shading and reflectances produced by Gehler *et al.* [12] seem equivalent to ours with regards to rs-MSE, s-MSE, and r-MSE (the metrics that consider shading and reflectance). However, when SFS is performed on their shading, the resulting shapes are much worse than ours in terms of N-MSE (the metric that consider shape). This appears to happen because, though this algorithm produces very accurate-looking shading images, that shading is often inconsistent with the known illumination or inconsistent with itself, causing SFS to produce a contorted shape. We see that treating color intelligently works better than a naive RGB or YUV model, and much better using only grayscale images (Barron and Malik 2012A [1]). The ablation study shows that all priors contribute positively: removing any reflectance prior hurts performance by 30-50%, and removing the illumination prior completely cripples the algorithm. Constraining the illumination to be white helps performance on this dataset, but would presumably make our model generalize worse on real-world images.

For the "natural" illumination case, we outperform all other algorithms by a very large margin — our error is less than 40% of the best-performing intrinsic image algorithm (20% if illumination is known). This shows the necessity of explicitly modeling chromatic illumination. While our complete model outperforms all other models, the "white light" case often underperforms many other models, even the achromatic model of [1]. This shows that attempting to use color information in the presence of non-white illumination without taking into consideration the color of illumination can actually *hurt* performance. For example, in the "laboratory" MIT dataset, our model performs equivalently to Gehler *et al.* in some error metrics, but in the "natural" illumination case, Gehler *et al.* and the other intrinsic image algorithms all perform significantly worse than our model. Because these intrinsic image algorithms rely heavily on color cues and assume illumination to be white, they suffer greatly when faced with colorful "natural" illuminations. In contrast, our model actually performs as well or better in the "natural" illumination case, as it can exploit color illumination to better disambiguate between shading and illumination (Figure 2), and produce higher-quality shape reconstructions (Figure 6). See the supplementary material for many examples of the output of our model and others, for all four experiments.

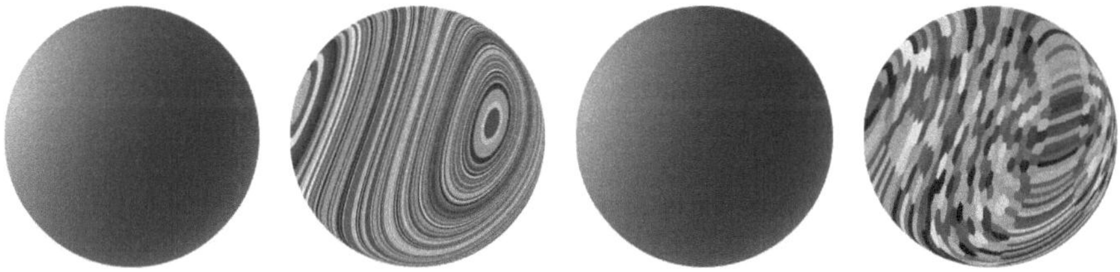

(a) Achromatic illumination (b) Achromatic isophotes (c) Chromatic illumination (d) Chromatic isophotes

Fig. 6. Chromatic illumination dramatically helps shape estimation. Achromatic isophotes (K-means clusters of log-RGB values) are very elongated, while chromatic isophotes are usually more tightly localized. Therefore, under achromatic lighting a very wide range of surface orientations appear similar, but under chromatic lighting only similar orientations appear similar.

9 Conclusion

We have extended our previous work [1] to present the first unified model for recovering shape, reflectance, and chromatic illumination from a single image, unifying the previously disjoint problems of color constancy, intrinsic images, and shape-from-shading. We have done this by introducing novel priors on local smoothness, global entropy, and absolute color, a novel prior on illumination, and an efficient multiscale optimization framework for jointly optimizing over shape and illumination.

By solving this one unified problem, our model outperforms all previously published algorithms for intrinsic images and shape-from-shading, on both the MIT dataset and our own "naturally" illuminated variant of that dataset. When faced with images produced under natural, chromatic illumination, the performance of our algorithm improves dramatically because it can exploit color information to better disambiguate between shading and reflectance variation, and to improve shape estimation. In contrast, other intrinsic image algorithms (which incorrectly assume illumination to be achromatic) perform very poorly in the presence of natural illumination. This suggests that the "intrinsic image" problem formulation may be fundamentally limited, and that we should refocus our attention towards developing models that jointly reason about shape and illumination in addition to shading and reflectance.

Acknowledgements. J.B. was supported by NSF GRFP and ONR MURI N00014-10-10933.

References

1. Barron, J.T., Malik, J.: Shape, albedo, and illumination from a single image of an unknown object. In: CVPR (2012)
2. Grosse, R., Johnson, M.K., Adelson, E.H., Freeman, W.T.: Ground-truth dataset and baseline evaluations for intrinsic image algorithms. In: ICCV (2009)

3. van Helmholtz, H.: Treatise on physiological optics, 2 vols., translated. Optical Society of America, Washington, DC (1924)
4. Land, E.H., McCann, J.J.: Lightness and retinex theory. JOSA (1971)
5. Horn, B.K.P.: Determining lightness from an image. Computer Graphics and Image Processing (1974)
6. Forsyth, D.A.: A novel algorithm for color constancy. IJCV (1990)
7. Maloney, L.T., Wandell, B.A.: Color constancy: a method for recovering surface spectral reflectance. JOSA A (1986)
8. Klinker, G., Shafer, S., Kanade, T.: A physical approach to color image understanding. IJCV (1990)
9. Finlayson, G., Hordley, S., Hubel, P.: Color by correlation: a simple, unifying framework for color constancy. TPAMI (2001)
10. Brainard, D.H., Freeman, W.T.: Bayesian color constancy. JOSA A (1997)
11. Gijsenij, A., Gevers, T., van de Weijer, J.: Generalized gamut mapping using image derivative structures for color constancy. IJCV (2010)
12. Gehler, P., Rother, C., Kiefel, M., Zhang, L., Schoelkopf, B.: Recovering intrinsic images with a global sparsity prior on reflectance. In: NIPS (2011)
13. Barrow, H., Tenenbaum, J.: Recovering intrinsic scene characteristics from images. In: Computer Vision Systems (1978)
14. Tappen, M.F., Freeman, W.T., Adelson, E.H.: Recovering intrinsic images from a single image. TPAMI (2005)
15. Shen, J., Yang, X., Jia, Y., Li, X.: Intrinsic images using optimization. In: CVPR (2011)
16. Horn, B.K.P.: Shape from shading: A method for obtaining the shape of a smooth opaque object from one view. Technical report, MIT (1970)
17. Brooks, M.J., Horn, B.K.P.: Shape from shading. MIT Press (1989)
18. Zhang, R., Tsai, P., Cryer, J., Shah, M.: Shape-from-shading: a survey. TPAMI (1999)
19. Johnson, M.K., Adelson, E.H.: Shape estimation in natural illumination. In: CVPR (2011)
20. Gilchrist, A.: Seeing in Black and White. Oxford University Press (2006)
21. Boyaci, H., Doerschner, K., Snyder, J.L., Maloney, L.T.: Surface color perception in three-dimensional scenes. Visual Neuroscience (2006)
22. Barron, J.T., Malik, J.: High-frequency shape and albedo from shading using natural image statistics. In: CVPR (2011)
23. Shen, L., Yeo, C.: Intrinsic images decomposition using a local and global sparse representation of reflectance. In: CVPR (2011)
24. Alldrin, N., Mallick, S., Kriegman, D.: Resolving the generalized bas-relief ambiguity by entropy minimization. In: CVPR (2007)
25. Finlayson, G.D., Drew, M.S., Lu, C.: Entropy minimization for shadow removal. IJCV (2009)
26. Omer, I., Werman, M.: Color lines: Image specific color representation. In: CVPR (2004)
27. Principe, J.C., Xu, D.: Learning from examples with quadratic mutual information. In: Workshop on Neural Networks for Signal Processing (1998)
28. Chen, J., Paris, S., Durand, F.: Real-time edge-aware image processing with the bilateral grid. In: SIGGRAPH (2007)
29. Terzopoulos, D.: Image analysis using multigrid relaxation methods. TPAMI 8, 129–139 (1986)

A Fast Illumination and Deformation Insensitive Image Comparison Algorithm Using Wavelet-Based Geodesics

Anne Jorstad[1], David Jacobs[1], and Alain Trouvé[2]

[1] University of Maryland, College Park, MD, USA
[2] Ecole Normale Supérieure de Cachan, France

Abstract. We present a fast image comparison algorithm for handling variations in illumination and moderate amounts of deformation using an efficient geodesic framework. As the geodesic is the shortest path between two images on a manifold, it is a natural choice to use the length of the geodesic to determine the image similarity. Distances on the manifold are defined by a metric that is insensitive to changes in scene lighting. This metric is described in the wavelet domain where it is able to handle moderate amounts of deformation, and can be calculated extremely fast (less than 3ms per image comparison). We demonstrate the similarity between our method and the illumination insensitivity achieved by the Gradient Direction. Strong results are presented on the AR Face Database.

1 Introduction

The presence of lighting changes and deformations complicates the task of general image comparison. We present a fast algorithm that can handle illumination variation and moderate amounts of deformation in an efficient wavelet-based geodesic framework. Expressing the image matching cost in the wavelet domain allows us to derive an algorithm where the complete cost calculation requires only $O(n)$ table lookups, for n the number of pixels in one image.

Considering images as points on a high dimensional image manifold, defining a metric to give local structure to the manifold allows paths to be calculated between images along the manifold; see Fig. 1. Computer Vision literature frequently uses geodesics in a Manifold Learning framework, where many given images are assumed to lie on a manifold and paths are defined by edges through sets of known images. In this work, we are given only two images, and we consider the geometry of the manifold, as induced by the chosen metric, to calculate the length of the path between them. It is natural to use the length of the geodesic, or locally shortest path, to define the similarity between two images, and geodesics provide significant information about the ways in which images differ. Points along a geodesic curve are images that have morphed part way from the first image to the second, and changes such as lighting and deformations can be introduced gradually through time. Being able to construct and manipulate geodesics has many applications, including accurate image interpolation [17], the ability to extract nonlinear statistics from a set of images on a manifold [18], and image registration [1]. In this work we aim to measure geodesic lengths on an image manifold, and provide a framework that can then be extended for further applications.

A. Fitzgibbon et al. (Eds.): ECCV 2012, Part IV, LNCS 7575, pp. 71–84, 2012.

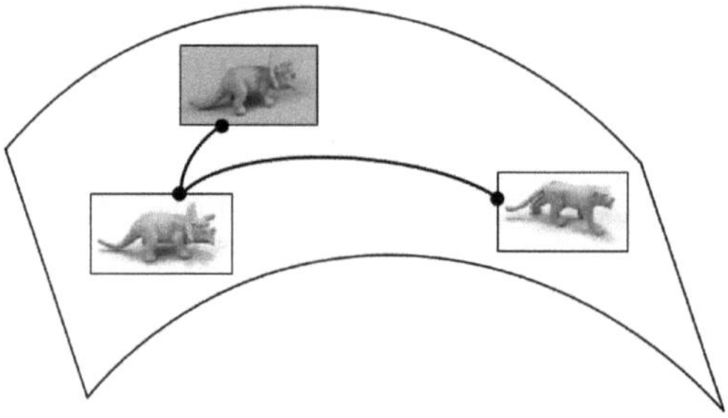

Fig. 1. A high-dimensional manifold, where each point on the manifold is an $M \times N$-dimensional image, and geodesics connecting more similar images are shorter (images from [8])

Due to their high dimensionality, calculating geodesic distances can be a very expensive task directly, but we show that by working in the wavelet domain with a well-chosen metric, we can solve this problem very efficiently. To define an appropriate manifold of images, we will use a metric that is insensitive to changes in lighting and moderate amounts of deformation. The metric depends on image gradients, as gradients are less sensitive to changes in lighting than are direct pixel intensities. We will achieve results similar to those from the illumination-insensitive Gradient Direction, but here we also have a meaningful geodesic in addition to a simple difference value. We will show that our lighting cost is insensitive to moderate amounts of deformation when accumulated over several scales.

A geodesic-based image comparison framework has been considered in the past in works including [1]. Wavelets have been used to obtain insensitivity to group actions in works such as [2], and an efficient approximation of the somewhat deformation-insensitive Earth Mover's Distance has been calculated in the wavelet domain in [15]. The insensitivity of the gradient to lighting change has been shown numerous times such as in [10], where normalized gradients are used as features so that the SIFT descriptors are invariant to affine changes in illumination. We modify the gradient-based lighting-insensitive metric presented in [7]. Handling illumination changes and deformations together in an Optical Flow framework has been studied in works such as [13], but our proposed algorithm can be computed several orders of magnitude faster than these previous methods, while still providing accurate matching costs.

The primary contributions of this work are threefold: 1) a method using geodesics to calculate an illumination-insensitive image comparison cost similar to the Gradient Direction, but useful for applications where manipulating geodesics is required; 2) the insight that local dependencies can be removed by using an appropriate wavelet domain to express an image matching cost function based on gradient terms, allowing the cost computation to be separated into independent problems at every point location in wavelet space; and 3) a very fast calculation of this image comparison cost.

2 Geodesics for Object Identification

Identifying objects in pairs of images is made challenging by changes in pose, lighting, deformations, and occlusions. If these changes could be introduced gradually over the course of several images, they would be much easier to handle. If we consider the manifold of images of a single class of object, where every point on the manifold is some instance of that object, then paths through the manifold connecting two images would consist of a continuum of images morphing from the first image to the second, like a video playing over time. The similarity of two instances of an object could then be defined by the length of the geodesic connecting them on the manifold, where shorter paths imply more similar objects; see Fig. 1.

Given a manifold of $M \times N$-dimensional images, we define a metric on this manifold so that it has a quantifiable structure, making it a Riemannian manifold [4]. The metric defines how costly it is to take an infinitesimal step in any given direction from any given point, and can be thought of as an $M \times N$-dimensional topographical map, where walking up a hill in one direction costs more than walking downwards in a different direction. On the Euclidean plane, the metric is $d(p_1, p_2) = \|p_2 - p_1\|_2$, but a metric can be defined in many ways as long as it is a locally linear metric. The metric chosen to define the manifold can be constructed to heavily penalize certain types of image variations, while allowing other variations to have low costs. For example, we would like an image metric that allows scene lighting to change at little cost, while object instance changes should come with a very high cost.

The length L of a path $I(t)$ from $t = 0$ to $t = 1$ on a manifold is defined, for any given metric $\|\cdot\|$, to be

$$L(I(0), I(1)) = \int_0^1 \left\| \frac{dI}{dt} \right\| dt. \tag{1}$$

In order to calculate the geodesic path connecting $I(0)$ and $I(1)$, we must find the minimum cost path $I(t)$ along the manifold. This becomes an optimization problem, where we want to solve $I_{\text{geod}}(t) = \arg\min_{I(t)} L(I(0), I(1))$. Geometrically, a geodesic is a curve whose tangent vectors $\frac{dI}{dt}$ have constant length [4]. It can be shown that the length of the geodesic $I_{\text{geod}}(t)$ is also equal to

$$L_{\text{geod}}(I(0), I(1)) = \min_{I(t)} \sqrt{2E(I(t))}, \tag{2}$$

a function of the energy E of the curve [19], where energy is defined as

$$E(I(t)) = \frac{1}{2} \int_0^1 \left\| \frac{dI}{dt} \right\|^2 dt, \tag{3}$$

which is familiar from classical mechanics where kinetic energy is $\frac{1}{2}mv^2$. The relation (2) can be understood intuitively because the tangent vectors all have constant length c, and so if $\int_0^1 \|c\| dt$ is minimal, then $\frac{1}{2} \int_0^1 \|c\|^2 dt$ must also be minimal, as squaring is a monotonic function. Therefore,

$$I_{\text{geod}}(t) = \arg\min_{I(t)} \int_0^1 \left\| \frac{dI}{dt} \right\| dt = \arg\min_{I(t)} \frac{1}{2} \int_0^1 \left\| \frac{dI}{dt} \right\|^2 dt. \tag{4}$$

We will choose an appropriate energy function and use the relation from (2) to help us calculate geodesic distances on the image manifold.

The metric defining the manifold on which the geodesics live can be adjusted for various applications, making this an elegant framework to handle an often messy problem, allowing images to update gradually and continuously through time. In the next sections we will discuss the metric and optimization schemes chosen to efficiently solve this problem.

3 A Lighting-Insensitive Metric

A pixel-based metric proposed in [7] was designed to be insensitive to changes in scene illumination, which the authors combined with a regularization term to handle deformations in an Optical Flow-like framework, calling the combined method the Deformation and Lighting Insensitive (DLI) metric. The lighting-insensitive (LI) term relating two images I_1 and I_2 was presented as

$$E_{\text{LI}}(I_1, I_2) = \frac{1}{2} \sum_{x,y} \frac{\|\nabla \delta I(x,y)\|^2}{\|\nabla I(x,y)\|^2 + \epsilon^2}, \tag{5}$$

where $\nabla \delta I$ and ∇I are defined in terms of I_1 and a second image $\hat{I_2}$ that is I_2 warped to match I_1 as closely as possible under certain constraints, so $\delta I = \hat{I_2} - I_1$ and $\nabla I = \nabla I_1$. The small constant ϵ is of the order of the noise in the image, and ensures that the denominator is never zero.

Using image gradients instead of intensities directly is known to be less sensitive to changes in lighting, for example from [10]. The Gradient Direction is a cost function commonly used when insensitivity to illumination change is desired. The direction of the image gradient $\theta = \tan^{-1}\left(\frac{I_y}{I_x}\right)$ is calculated at each pixel, then used in a sum-of-squared-differences image comparison, defining a cost between a given pair of images. This measure is invariant to adding a constant value to the image, or multiplying the image by a scalar, desirable properties for being insensitive to changes in scene illumination. However, it can be argued that a small change in illumination should be penalized less harshly than a large change in illumination.

The metric E_{LI} has similar properties to the Gradient Direction, but is able to respond to different gradient relations appropriately, scaling the gradient of the image change δI by the norm of the image gradient. Changing from a small to a medium gradient norm will be penalized more severely than changing from a medium to a large gradient norm. Comparing two smooth image regions should have a low cost, while comparing a smooth region to a jagged region should have a high cost. The image gradient is small at pixels that correspond to smooth regions of an object, and although a change in scene lighting will result in different pixel intensities, the relative intensities of the pixels will remain similar, and the gradient will remain small, so both the numerator and the denominator will be small, resulting in a low matching cost, and the desired property holds. In an image region where there is a geometric boundary, such as at the edge of a building, a change in scene lighting could affect the distinct surfaces in very different ways, but as the gradient is likely to be large across this boundary, matching a larger $\nabla \delta I$ is permissible at a lower cost as it will be weighted by the image gradient in the denominator. In an image region where there is an albedo change but little geometric

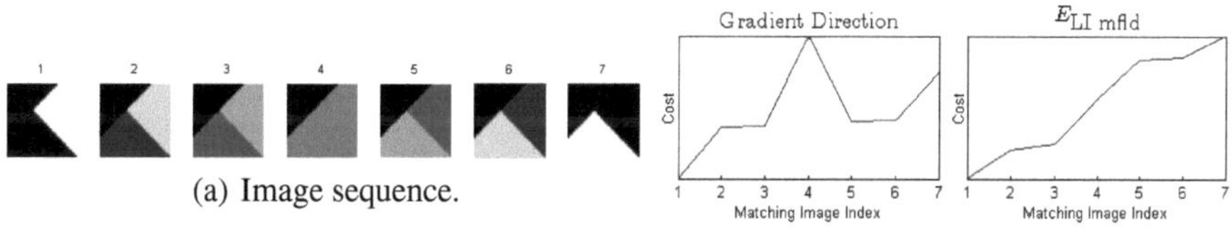

(a) Image sequence.

(b) Image matching costs.

Fig. 2. (a) Image sequence, where each image is compared to image 1, the leftmost image. (b) Gradient Direction and $E_{\mathrm{LI\,mfld}}$ costs for each image pair in the image sequence.

change, for example a colored stripe on a white wall, the gradient across this boundary may be large, but as the scene lighting changes, $\nabla\delta I$ will scale with ∇I, so as long as the pixels being compared correspond to the same points in the scene, the matching cost will remain low.

To understand the difference in behavior between the Gradient Direction and our new cost $E_{\mathrm{LI\,mfld}}$, we provide a simple toy example Fig. 2, which could represent a series of images captured as a lighting source moves from one side of a building to another across a corner. Costs are calculated from the leftmost image in Fig. 2(a) to all images in the sequence, and these costs are presented in Fig. 2(b). As the change in intensity gets larger, the cost of $E_{\mathrm{LI\,mfld}}$ steadily increases, and when the order of the intensity magnitudes reverses (from image 3 to image 5), this causes a jump in the costs. With Gradient Direction (mod π), the cases where two image regions have the same intensity (images 4 and 7) cause the comparison cost value to blow up, while otherwise the direction of the gradients and hence the costs are not discriminative.

We will use this metric to define a manifold that is insensitive to changes in illumination. Along any curve $I(t)$ (a continuum of images) on the manifold, for small step $\delta t > 0$, $\delta I(t) = I(t+\delta t) - I(t)$. The relation between two images from (5) defines a Riemannian structure on images using the infinitesimal norm

$$\|\delta I\|_{\mathrm{LI}}^2 = \frac{1}{2}\sum_{x,y}\frac{\|\nabla\delta I(x,y)\|^2}{\|\nabla I(x,y)\|^2+\epsilon^2}. \tag{6}$$

Using this term in the energy function from (3), the energy of a curve $I(t)$ on this manifold is

$$E_{\mathrm{LI\,mfld}}(I(t)) = \lim_{\delta t\to 0^+}\frac{1}{2}\int_0^{1-\delta t}\frac{\|\delta I\|_{\mathrm{LI}}^2}{(\delta t)^2}dt. \tag{7}$$

We search for geodesics on this manifold in order to determine the distance $L_{\mathrm{geod}}(I(0), I(1))$ between any given pair of input images $I(0)$ and $I(1)$. To calculate the geodesic from (4) we must therefore solve

$$I_{\mathrm{geod}}(t) = \arg\min_{I(t)}\lim_{\delta t\to 0^+}\frac{1}{2}\int_0^{1-\delta t}\sum_{x,y}\frac{\|\nabla\delta I(x,y,t)\|^2}{\|\nabla I(x,y,t)\|^2+\epsilon^2}\frac{1}{(\delta t)^2}dt. \tag{8}$$

3.1 Behavior of the Metric

In this section we will discuss the behavior of the geodesics defined by this lighting-insensitive metric at a single point location (x, y). When the image gradient is near zero, the metric is dominated by the $\frac{1}{\epsilon^2}$ term, and the cost scales nearly linearly with the change in the gradient.

In regions where the image gradients are large, the behavior is more exponential. This can be seen analytically without loss of generality if we consider the case where the gradient is zero in the y dimension in both images, so that there is no change in gradient direction and $\nabla I = I_x$. For clarity let $\epsilon^2 = 0$, and take $I' = \lim_{\delta t \to 0^+} \frac{\delta I}{\delta t}$. This reduces (8) to

$$\arg\min_{I(t)} \frac{1}{2} \int_0^1 \left(\frac{I'_x}{I_x} \right)^2 dt, \tag{9}$$

which can be solved using the Euler-Lagrange equation [3], a technique that converts a functional to be minimized into a differential equation describing the minimizing function. Specifically, given a functional J of the form $J(f) = \min_{f(t)} \int_0^1 F(t, f(t), f'(t))dt$, the function $f(t)$ that minimizes $J(f)$ is described by the equation $\frac{\partial F}{\partial f} - \frac{d}{dt}\frac{\partial F}{\partial f'} = 0$. Applying the Euler-Lagrange equation to (9), the resulting differential equation can be simplified to

$$(I'_x)^2 - I_x I''_x = 0. \tag{10}$$

It can be shown that $I_x(t) = ce^{rt}$ satisfies this equation for $c, r \in \mathbb{R}$, and any set of boundary conditions $I(0)$ and $I(1)$ will determine the specific values of these variables. We therefore see that when the value of ϵ is small with respect to the magnitudes of $\nabla \delta I$ and ∇I, the gradient of I behaves like an exponential, meaning that I changes exponentially with time. So the cost function we seek to minimize is near linear when the image gradients are near zero, and near exponential when the image gradients are larger, which penalizes scene lighting variation as desired.

3.2 Disadvantages of Direct Optimization

The most straightforward way to minimize (8) is to use a gradient descent optimization scheme. However, for input images of size $M \times N$, the geodesic path $I(t)$ has dimension $M \times N \times T$, for T the number of time steps used to discretize the geodesic. Calculations with $\nabla E_{\text{LI mfld}}$ are cumbersome and easily get trapped in local minima. We avoid these computations by moving the problem into the wavelet domain, where we will show that it can be expressed as $M \times N$ distinct 1D problems that are straightforward to solve.

4 Optimization in the Wavelet Domain

We show that moving the norm $E_{\text{LI mfld}}$ into the wavelet domain results in a function that can be minimized over each independent variable separately, thereby vastly simplifying the minimization calculations and resulting in a very fast computation. We will also find that this representation provides insensitivity to moderate amounts of deformation.

4.1 Background on Wavelets

For our purposes, wavelets are a set of orthonormal functions that allow local analysis of a function according to scale; for details see [11]. At every scale the wavelet transform

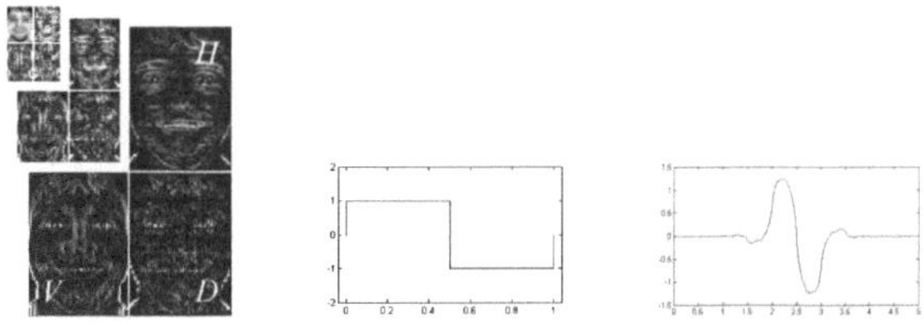

(a) (b) (c)

Fig. 3. (a) 2D Haar wavelet decomposition to three scales, (b) 1D Haar wavelet, (c) 1D biorthogonal spline wavelet

has three outputs, defined in the horizontal H, vertical V and diagonal D directions, and a downsampled version of the input that is then processed at the next scale; see Fig. 3(a). Wavelet functions used to filter an image can be constructed in a wide variety of forms, but for our purposes we consider only functions that have the same general form as a derivative filter. The 1D Haar wavelet at one scale (see Fig. 3(b)) is exactly a simple finite difference filter, and so filtering with a Haar wavelet is equivalent to downsampling by two and filtering with a finite difference filter in each dimension, i.e. extracting the gradient at every other pixel. The critical observation here is that each term of this wavelet transform is independent. Wavelet basis functions can be chosen to be orthogonal, and in this case changing the value of the wavelet coefficient at one location at one scale affects no other coefficients at any scale, for its support of two adjacent points at the next coarsest scale is downsampled by two, so these points influence no other coefficient. This allows us to define gradients in terms of independent wavelet coefficients. If we filter with a smoother wavelet of a similar gradient-like shape, such as the biorthogonal spline wavelet (see Fig. 3(c)), this can be considered to be filtering with a smoothed gradient filter, with desirable continuity properties. In this work we will use the family of biorthogonal spline wavelets (with orders nr = 1, nd = 3).

4.2 The Lighting Metric in the Wavelet Domain

We rewrite the function $E_{\text{LI mfld}}$ (7) in terms of wavelet coefficients. If these coefficients are defined so that $H(m,n)$ is the horizontal component and $V(m,n)$ is the vertical component of a 2D gradient-like wavelet calculated via a discrete wavelet transform, then $H \approx I_x$ and $V \approx I_y$, where each has been downsampled by a factor of two. Using the L^2 norm, E_{LI} can be rewritten approximately as

$$E_{\text{wav}}(I) = \frac{1}{2}\sum_{m,n} \frac{\delta H^2 + \delta V^2}{H^2 + V^2 + \epsilon^2}, \tag{11}$$

where H and V depend on point locations (m,n), but we leave this out of the notation for clarity, as (m,n) are fixed inside the sum. The converted cost function does not make use of the diagonal component of the 2D wavelet decomposition, as all terms are expressible using only H and V.

In the wavelet domain, each wavelet basis location is now independent of its neighbors, as the local descriptions of the gradients are handled during the wavelet filtering, a result of the orthogonality of the wavelets as described in the previous section. A primary

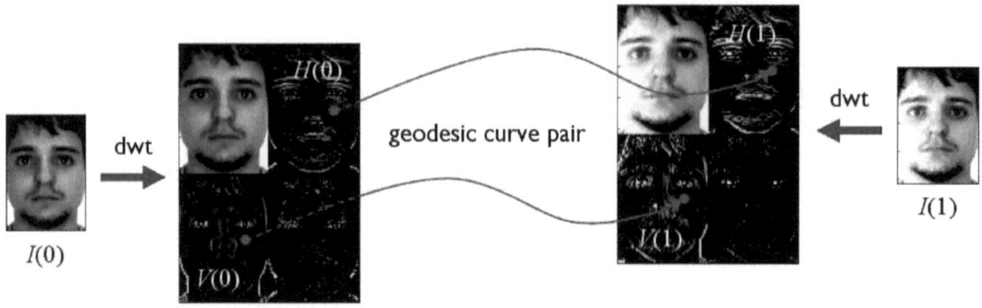

Fig. 4. Algorithm schematic: The discrete wavelet transform (dwt) is applied to the input images to generate the horizontal and vertical components H and V of the wavelet decomposition at one scale. At each point pair location in $H(0), V(0)$, the geodesic curve is calculated to the corresponding point location in $H(1), V(1)$. These curves are then integrated, and the resulting values from each point pair are summed for the total image matching cost.

contribution of this work is the insight that using the wavelet domain to express an image matching cost function based on gradients allows the similarity computation to be separated into independent problems at every point location in wavelet space. We recall that the terms comprising the cost function in the wavelet domain are sampled from the original terms at every other pixel. Again taking $H' = \lim_{\delta t \to 0^+} \frac{\delta H}{\delta t}$ and $V' = \lim_{\delta t \to 0^+} \frac{\delta V}{\delta t}$ so that the $\frac{1}{(\delta t)^2}$ term cancels, the minimization problem (8) can be rewritten as

$$I_{\text{geod}}(t) = \frac{1}{2} \sum_{m,n} \operatorname*{arg\,min}_{H(t),V(t)} \int_0^1 \frac{H'^2 + V'^2}{H^2 + V^2 + \epsilon^2} dt. \tag{12}$$

where H and V are curves through time, and each individual point on the curves is in $\mathbb{R}^{M \times N}$. The $M \times N \times T$ dimensional problem of (8) has now been separated into $M \times N$ independent continuous 1D problems to be summed, one for each location (m, n) in the wavelet domain. The geodesic path at each point location is defined by two 1D curves, $H(t)$ and $V(t)$, which are coupled, meaning that their geodesic paths are co-dependent and are optimized together; see Fig. 4. We can calculate the geodesic path for each point location separately, and then the full geodesic path of the image as a whole is simply the combination of all these distinct paths. The starting and ending values $H(0)$, $H(1)$, $V(0)$, $V(1)$ are the coefficients from the wavelet decompositions of the given images $I(0)$ and $I(1)$, and so this reduces to a series of boundary value problems.

The minimization problem in (12) is a functional of a form that can be easily converted to a set of differential equations using the Euler-Lagrange equation [3], as described in Sec. 3, which can then be solved numerically. We chose to first convert the relation into polar coordinates, as this proved to be more stable to solve numerically. Defining $r = \sqrt{H^2 + V^2}$ and $\theta = \tan^{-1} \frac{V}{H}$, the inner functional to be minimized becomes

$$\operatorname*{arg\,min}_{r(t),\theta(t)} \int_0^1 \frac{r'^2 + r^2\theta'^2}{r^2 + \epsilon^2} dt. \tag{13}$$

Following the vector form of the Euler-Lagrange equation, the differential equations that describe the curves $r(t)$ and $\theta(t)$ that together minimize the term inside the sum for a single point location (m, n) are

$$r'' = r\theta'^2 + (rr'^2 - r^3\theta'^2)(r^2 + \epsilon^2)^{-1},$$
$$\theta'' = 2r^{-1}r'\theta'(r^2(r^2 + \epsilon^2) - 1). \tag{14}$$

This pair of second order equations can be solved as a system of four first order equations using any numerical integration scheme, and we chose to use the Boundary Value Problem solver from MATLAB. The output is a pair of numerical 1D curves $r(t)$ and $\theta(t)$, starting at $r(0), \theta(0)$ and ending at $r(1), \theta(1)$, that can be converted back to 1D curves $H(t), V(t)$, and that minimizes the cost from (12). This process is repeated for each wavelet domain point (m, n) separately. We now have $M \times N$ pairs of geodesic curves. A visual schematic of the algorithm can be seen in Fig. 4.

Once all the optimal curves have been found, it remains to integrate along each of them to calculate the cost contribution from each location, and sum these point costs for the overall value of the energy of the image matching. These integrations can be computed numerically, discretizing the curve into T segments and summing the value of the cost function at each of these segments. Once the total energy is calculated, we recall the relation from (2) and return the square root of twice the energy value as the true geodesic length.

4.3 Limiting Behavior

When ϵ is reduced to 0, equation (13) decouples into two separate problems:

$$\arg\min_{r(t)} \int_0^1 \frac{r'^2}{r^2} dt \quad \text{and} \quad \arg\min_{\theta(t)} \int_0^1 \theta'^2 dt. \tag{15}$$

These equations are optimized by exponential curves in $r(t)$ and linear curves in $\theta(t)$, and when the boundary values are included, the optimal curves are

$$r(t) = r_0 e^{\ln \frac{r_1}{r_0} t} = r_0 \left(\frac{r_1}{r_0}\right)^t \quad \text{and} \quad \theta(t) = (\theta_1 - \theta_0)t + \theta_0. \tag{16}$$

These functions can be integrated analytically, resulting in a total energy of

$$E = \left(\ln \frac{r_1}{r_0}\right)^2 + (\theta_1 - \theta_0)^2, \tag{17}$$

a value determined entirely by the boundary points, invariant to the path connecting them. This is observed to be exactly the cost of the Gradient Direction plus a constant term depending on the ratio of the lengths of the H and V terms in the two images. So we expect the cost reported here to be very similar to the Gradient Direction, but more highly penalizing cases where the difference in gradient norms between the two images is large, while the Gradient Direction is invariant to uniform scalar changes in intensity magnitude. It is reasonable and often desirable to have cases where a uniform intensity change is small be penalized less than cases where the magnitude is large. When the magnitude of r is the same at corresponding pixels in both images, the cost is exactly that of the Gradient Direction. In this limiting case when $\epsilon = 0$ the geodesic path is not meaningful, but for all positive ϵ a geodesic path does exist. When the gradient norms are small, we prefer the linear penalty incurred by the ϵ term, as discussed in Sec. 3.1, so that small amounts of noise in smooth regions do not bias the measure.

In practice when ϵ is positive, these properties are consistent, but the geodesic cost is influenced by its entire path on the manifold. The cost to rotate by an angle θ when $r_1 = r_2$ is essentially constant, regardless of the magnitude of r_1. The cost to go from (r_1, θ_1) to (r_2, θ_2) is close to the cost of rotating a constant r by $\theta_2 - \theta_1$ plus the cost of scaling from r_1 to r_2 without any rotation.

4.4 Deformation Insensitivity

The algorithm presented above provides a way to compare images that is insensitive to changes in scene illumination. We now claim that this algorithm can also handle moderate amounts of deformation. Expanding our function to include several scales s of wavelet coefficients, where larger scales correspond to coarser levels of the decomposition, the function to be minimized is now

$$I_{\text{geod}}(t) = \frac{1}{2} \sum_{m,n} \sum_{s} \underset{H(t),V(t)}{\arg\min} \lambda_s \int_0^1 \frac{H'^2 + V'^2}{H^2 + V^2 + \epsilon^2} dt. \tag{18}$$

We choose the weighting coefficient to be $\lambda_s = 2^s$, which we justify from its similarity to the Wavelet Earth Mover's Distance weighting as discussed below, and because it was observed empirically to provide the most accurate results. Using several scales increases accuracy because we can now consider both global image properties from the coarse scales, and edge details from the finer scales. In our experiments we use the first three scales of the wavelet transform. The resulting algorithm now involves a separate geodesic curve construction and integration for each scale and location.

Further, we argue that simply using wavelets adds moderate deformation insensitivity. Deformations within the support of each wavelet basis function are handled together during the wavelet transform, so deformations localized to these region have little overall impact on the wavelet coefficients. A similar observation was made previously when the Earth Mover's Distance was explored in the wavelet domain. The Earth Mover's Distance (EMD) algorithm [14] provides a way to compare two distributions by measuring the distance and quantity of "mass" that must be moved in order to convert one distribution into the other, where "mass" is thought of as whatever is populating the bins of a histogram. This similarity measure captures certain types of deformation, where no particular geometric structure is preserved or favored, but local changes in mass cost significantly less than global structure modifications.

The Wavelet EMD [15] approximates the Earth Mover's Distance in the wavelet domain, converting an algorithm of complexity $O(n^3 \log n)$ into an $O(n)$ algorithm without any significant performance difference, where n is the number of points in an image, and its cost depends on wavelet coefficients at all scales. At each individual scale, it limits the distance individual mass units can move to the span of the wavelet at that scale. The weighting on the magnitude of each scales' wavelet coefficients in the distance calculation is $2^{2s} = 4^s$, similar to the weighting we incorporated into our multiscaled cost function (18), where our base is 2 instead of 4. When the image gradients are small, our proposed cost function is essentially linear, as discussed in Sec. 3.1, meaning that it behaves similarly to the Wavelet EMD, and we understand how our new metric is able to handle moderate amounts of deformation, as this is the purpose of the Earth Mover's Distance. When the image gradients are larger, the new metric becomes more exponential, which allows the image comparison to be penalized less heavily when large lighting changes are present.

5 The Faster Algorithm

We will now discuss how to optimize our calculations to create a very computationally efficient algorithm. For any given pair of starting input values $H(0), V(0)$ and ending input values $H(1), V(1)$, the geodesic curve connecting them is always the same, so the cost of this input is always the same. This means that the geodesic curves can be calculated and integrated offline, and at run time the only computation that has to be performed is to look up the value of the integral for the given $(H(0), V(0), H(1), V(1))$. To further reduce the amount of space and time required, at every point we convert the input $(H(0), V(0), H(1), V(1))$ into polar coordinates, $(r_1, r_2, \theta_1, \theta_2)$, and then rotate so that $\theta_2 = 0$, as these rotated values preserve the relation between the points and will result in the same output cost. This allows us to generate a lookup table of integral values that depends on only three values $(r_1, r_2, \Delta\theta)$ instead of four.

We discretize the space of r values into 40 bins of exponentially increasing size in the range $[0, 1.5]$, as this is the range of wavelet coefficient values observed in practice for images with pixel values in $[0, 1]$, with coarser scales generally consisting of smaller values. We used $\epsilon = 0.01$ in our experiments. The space of $\Delta\theta$ values we discretize into 80 bins of uniform size in the range $[0, 2\pi)$. The resulting costs are symmetric about $\Delta\theta = \pi$, so we really only have to store the first half of these values, and the lookup table to be stored is of dimension $40 \times 40 \times 40$. The online calculation at each location (m, n) in wavelet space consists of converting $(H(0), V(0), H(1), V(1))$ into polar coordinates $(r_1, r_2, \Delta\theta)$, looking up the corresponding integral value in the table, and adding this value to the overall cost being calculated.

This calculation is limited principally by the speed at which a given machine can perform a lookup in a $40 \times 40 \times 40$ array, which is in general a very fast operation. The cost of this calculation is on the order of milliseconds, fast enough to use in practice when many image comparisons must be computed very quickly. On a 3.16 GHz machine running MATLAB in serial, this takes on average 1.3×10^{-3} seconds for a pair of images with 5000 pixels each. We emphasize that the lookup table is application-independent; once it has been generated, which takes 1.5 hours, the same table can be used for any pair of images from any domain.

6 Experiments

One class of object that is regularly presented with large amounts of lighting variation and moderate amounts of deformation is the human face. Although nothing in our algorithm is specific to faces, the limited amount of deformation present with expression change, along with potentially high variations due to lighting change, make them a relevant application of our work. We use a common face dataset studied for this problem,

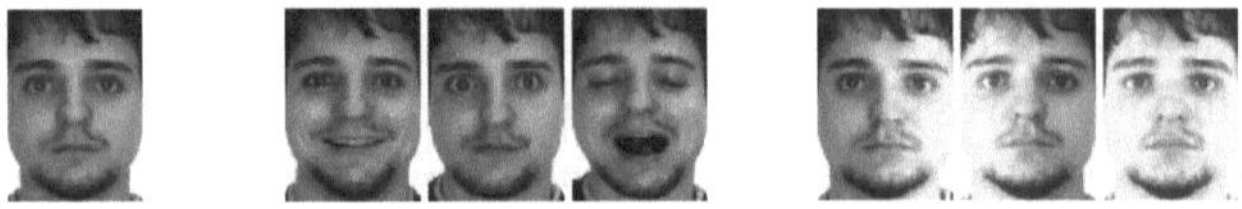

(a) neutral (b) expressions (c) lightings

Fig. 5. The variations of one person from the AR Face Database [12]

the subset of the AR Face Database [12] that contains variation in expression and lighting. We reduce the size of the standard cropped AR images by a factor of two in each dimension, as face recognition algorithms routinely perform the best on images of this scale, and so the images we compare are 83×59 pixels in dimension, and are smoothed slightly before processing. We use a neutral face from each of the 100 people in the dataset as gallery images, and the three variations in expression and the three variations in lighting for each person comprise the test set; see Fig. 5. The identity of each test image is determined by the gallery image returning the lowest cost pairing.

The algorithm presented here is a fast method for comparing images in the presence of lighting change and moderate deformations, and so we compare to other lighting and deformation insensitive algorithms that do not require training data. It was shown in [5] that the Gradient Direction method, described in Sec. 3, consistently performs better than the other standard pixel-based lighting-insensitive methods (Self-Quotient, luminance map estimation, Eigenphases, Whitening), so we compare to Gradient Direction. We also compare to the results of the Deformation and Lighting Insensitive metric (E_{DLI}) [7], and we expect our calculations to be much faster. Other works that present a cost function to handle both lighting change and deformations include that of [20], which calculates image point correspondences using edge maps and Gabor jet information, and [16] which uses mutual information to combine binary edge features with grayscale information. We also compare to simple image differencing and to normalized cross-correlation [9], where the template is a full image, as these methods are frequently used to compare images when many comparisons must be completed very fast. As our method is based on an L^2 metric, we use the L^2 norm on each of these measures for valid comparison. Results on the AR Face Database are presented in Table 1 for both algorithm speed and accuracy.

We see that our method achieves more accurate results than the Gradient Direction method on the lighting variation images, and significantly more accurate results on the expression variation images, as expected. This confirms the insensitivity of the method to lighting change, with the added benefit that we are able to construct geodesic information which allows for meaningful extensions such as mapping and interpolating large image variations. The accuracy of the method is also above that of the E_{DLI} work where the lighting metric was first presented, which also handled deformations explicitly, and our calculations here are 10^3 times faster than that work, making our method useful in template matching applications where the original method was prohibitively slow.

The previous best results on this dataset, as far as the authors are aware, were produced by Pixel-Level Decisions in [6], where simple thresholding was applied to pixel differences of a chosen image property. Standard deviation calculated within a window around each pixel was the property that provided the best results. The differences between these standard deviations at every pixel location in each image were computed,

Table 1. Identification results on the AR Face Database. The *Time* column reports the MATLAB calculation time of a single image pair comparison in seconds, except in two cases where time was not reported and we were unable to reproduce the authors' results.

Method	*Time (sec)*	*Expression*	*Lighting*	*Overall*
Image Differencing	3.1×10^{-5}	83.0%	9.0%	46.0%
Normalized Cross-Correlation [9]	7.2×10^{-3}	84.0%	59.3%	71.7%
Significant Jet Point [20]	–	80.8%	91.7%	86.3%
Binary Edge Feature and MI [16]	–	78.5%	97.0%	87.8%
Gradient Direction [5]	3.8×10^{-4}	85.0%	95.3%	90.2%
E_{DLI} [7]	1.0×10^{0}	89.6%	98.9%	94.3%
Proposed Method	1.3×10^{-3}	93.7%	96.7%	95.2%
Pixel Level Decisions [6]	5.6×10^{-4}	98.0%	94.0%	96.0%
Proposed Method thresholded	1.3×10^{-3}	97.3%	97.0%	97.2%

and the total number of pixel differences less than a pre-determined threshold were counted for the final similarity value. We present these results here to demonstrate that the surprisingly strong results achieved from this extremely simple algorithm can be applied to other pixel-based methods, and we use a similar thresholding step on our results as well. [6] also suggests compensating for local error by repeating the procedure with the images shifted a few pixels in every direction, but we do not compare these results as they are not relevant to the ideas in this paper. However, this repeated shifting could be applied to improve the results of any of the these methods. As the threshold value for our point costs in wavelet space, we use the cost value that counts the lowest 20% of the point costs across all images, as this was the value used by [6]. The exact threshold value is not sensitive, and we observed that all values thresholding 9% to 47% of the costs resulted in overall accuracies within 1% of each other, and the ideal threshhold on this dataset, if hand-picked, results in an overall accuracy of 98.0%. We see in Table 1 that this simple thresholding extension removes 58.6% of the errors in our method.

The proposed algorithm performs well with variations in lighting, and also handles moderate amounts of deformation. Many methods perform very poorly on the scream category of this database, but the multiscaled method presented here achieved 83.0% accuracy in this case, and 93.0% with thresholding, higher than either Gradient Direction (57.0%) or the E_{DLI} metric (79.6%), which was designed to handle deformations.

Not only does the proposed algorithm produce accurate identification results, but the computation time required is extremely small. We emphasize that no training data or learning stage is required for the method proposed in this paper.

7 Conclusion

We have presented a fast algorithm for handling illumination changes and moderate deformations applicable to any class of images. Geodesic distances were calculated between pairs of images, as defined on an image manifold given structure by an illumination-insensitive metric that was based on the change in image gradients. The metric was calculated in the wavelet domain, where each point location contributed independently to the overall image comparison cost, allowing geodesic costs to be computed extremely efficiently using a pre-calculated lookup table. Using wavelets at multiple scales allowed for insensitivity to moderate deformations in a manner similar to the Wavelet Earth Mover's Distance. Strong results were presented on the AR Face Database, where our algorithm is seen to be both extremely fast and accurate. Using geodesics to calculate image comparisons instead of simple pixel differences allows our method to be incorporated into a wide array of applications where having information along a morphing path is relevant. Because this algorithm is so fast, it could also be applied successfully in situations where Normalized Cross-Correlation is often used, where many image comparisons must be computed in a very short amount of time.

Acknowledgments. This work was supported by US Office of Naval Research MURI Grant N00014-08-10638, and by National Science Foundation Grant No. 0915977.

References

1. Beg, M., Miller, M., Trouvé, A., Younes, L.: Computing Large Deformation Metric Mappings via Geodesic Flows of Diffeomorphisms. IJCV 61, 139–157 (2005)
2. Bruna, J., Mallat, S.: Classification with Scattering Operators. In: CVPR (2011)
3. Courant, R., Hilbert, D.: Methods of Mathematical Physics, vol. I. ch. IV. Interscience Publishers, Inc. (1955)
4. do Carmo, M.: Riemannian Geometry. Birkhäuser (1992)
5. Gopalan, R., Jacobs, D.: Comparing and Combining Lighting Insensitive Approaches for Face Recognition. CVIU 114, 135–145 (2010)
6. James, A.P.: Pixel-Level Decisions Based Robust Face Image Recognition. In: Oravec, M. (ed.) Face Recognition, ch. 5, pp. 65–86. INTECH (2010)
7. Jorstad, A., Jacobs, D., Trouvé, A.: A Deformation and Lighting Insensitive Metric for Face Recognition Based on Dense Correspondences. In: CVPR (2011)
8. LeCun, Y., Huang, F., Bottou, L.: Learning Methods for Generic Object Recognition with Invariance to Pose and Lighting. In: CVPR (2004)
9. Lewis, J.: Fast Normalized Cross-Correlation. Vision Interface (1995)
10. Lowe, D.: Distinctive Image Features from Scale-Invariant Keypoints. IJCV 60 (2004)
11. Mallat, S.: A Wavelet Tour of Signal Processing. Elsevier (2009)
12. Martinez, A., Kak, A.C.: PCA versus LDA. PAMI 23, 228–233 (2001)
13. Negahdaripour, S.: Revised Definition of Optical Flow: Integration of Radiometric and Geometric Cues for Dynamic Scene Analysis. PAMI 20, 961–979 (1998)
14. Rubner, Y., Tomasi, C., Guibas: The Earth Mover's Distance as a Metric for Image Retrieval. IJCV (2000)
15. Shirdhonkar, S., Jacobs, D.: Approximate Earth Mover's Distance in Linear Time. In: CVPR (2008)
16. Song, J., Chen, B., Wang, W., Ren, X.: Face Recognition by Fusing Binary Edge Feature and Second-Order Mutual Information. In: IEEE Conf. on Cybernetics and Intelligent Systems, pp. 1046–1050 (2008)
17. Tung, T., Matsuyama, T.: Dynamic Surface Matching by Geodesic Mapping for 3D Animation Transfer. In: CVPR (2010)
18. Turaga, P., Veeraraghavan, A., Chellappa, R.: Statistical Analysis on Stiefel and Grassmann Manifolds with Applications in Computer Vision. In: CVPR (2008)
19. Younes, L.: Shapes and Diffeomorphisms. Springer (2010)
20. Zhao, S., Gao, Y.: Significant Jet Point For Facial Image Representation and Recognition. In: International Conference on Image Processing, pp. 1664–1667 (2008)

Large-Scale Gaussian Process Classification with Flexible Adaptive Histogram Kernels

Erik Rodner, Alexander Freytag, Paul Bodesheim, and Joachim Denzler

Computer Vision Group, Friedrich Schiller University Jena, Germany
{firstname.lastname}@uni-jena.de
http://www.inf-cv.uni-jena.de

Abstract. We present how to perform exact large-scale multi-class Gaussian process classification with parameterized histogram intersection kernels. In contrast to previous approaches, we use a full Bayesian model without any sparse approximation techniques, which allows for learning in sub-quadratic and classification in constant time. To handle the additional model flexibility induced by parameterized kernels, our approach is able to optimize the parameters with large-scale training data. A key ingredient of this optimization is a new efficient upper bound of the negative Gaussian process log-likelihood. Experiments with image categorization tasks exhibit high performance gains with flexible kernels as well as learning within a few minutes and classification in microseconds for databases, where exact Gaussian process inference was not possible before.

Keywords: Large-scale Gaussian Processes, Histogram Intersection Kernels, Hyperparameter Optimization, Bayesian Modeling.

1 Introduction

Non-linear learning with histogram kernels is currently one of the main techniques for solving complex visual recognition tasks [1–3]. This is mainly because histogram kernels, such as the histogram intersection kernel (HIK), exploit the property that histograms are normalized and lie in a very specific subspace [4], which allows providing a more suitable measure of similarity compared to standard kernels. For learning, SVM classifiers are the most prominent technique. However, it has been shown that full Bayesian techniques, *e.g.*, Gaussian process (GP) methods, do offer two important advantages: (1) they allow hyperparameter optimization by maximizing the marginal likelihood of the model, and (2) the uncertainty of the estimate can be predicted. Their main disadvantage is the cubic runtime of the learning step, which prevents them from being used in large-scale scenarios. Nevertheless, due to the large number of available image data, current tasks and research is shifting more and more towards large-scale learning scenarios, where the final goal is to efficiently handle several thousands to millions of training examples [5].

We present how to perform multi-class GP classification and hyperparameter optimization with large-scale datasets without any sparse approximation. The

A. Fitzgibbon et al. (Eds.): ECCV 2012, Part IV, LNCS 7575, pp. 85–98, 2012.

memory and runtime requirements of our methods are sub-quadratic allowing for scalability. The approach is based on fast multiplications of the histogram intersection kernel matrix with an arbitrary vector. This allows for solving the GP inference equations by utilizing iterative solvers. Furthermore, we demonstrate that hyperparameter optimization with the complete GP model can also be performed in an efficient manner by exploiting an upper bound of the determinant of the kernel matrix. The upper bound depends on terms, which can be efficiently calculated. The main contributions of this paper are as follows:

1. We show how to perform training and classification in a Bayesian manner with Gaussian processes and histogram intersection kernels in sub-quadratic and constant time, respectively.
2. Hyperparameter optimization for large-scale datasets with efficient GP marginal likelihood optimization is presented, which allows for linear kernel combination and feature relevance determination.
3. We demonstrate the advantages of parameterized histogram intersection kernels.

Additionally, Gaussian process classification with label regression [6] is extended towards handling imbalanced learning data. The remainder of our paper is organized as follows. In Sect. 2, we give a short overview of related work on efficient GP classification and exploiting the efficiency of the histogram intersection kernel. Gaussian processes for classification and the key concepts of the efficiency of the histogram intersection kernel are reviewed in Sect. 3 and 4. In Sect. 5, we demonstrate how GP classifiers can be trained, optimized, and evaluated in a fast manner by making use of the HIK properties. Experimental results for medium as well as large-scale classification tasks are shown in Sect. 6 highlighting the suitability of our efficient computations for various scenarios. A summary of our findings and a discussion of future research directions conclude the paper.

2 Related Work

Fast Learning and Classification with HIK. To overcome the drawback of time-consuming classification with kernel methods, Vedaldi and Zisserman [7] presented how to approximate the values of the histogram intersection kernel with explicit feature transformations. In contrast, Maji *et al.* [8] exploited the properties of HIK directly for calculating SVM decision scores in $\mathcal{O}(D\log(m))$ time compared to $\mathcal{O}(Dm)$ for standard SVM inference with m being the number of support vectors and D being the number of feature dimensions. Going one step further, Wu [9] presented fast SVM training by using the HIK properties to reformulate the SVM dual problem. The current paper, which was inspired by both works, shows that the special properties of the HIK can also be exploited for GP classification and even for hyperparameter optimization.

Generalized HIK and Hyperparameter Optimization. Barla *et al.* [10] applied the HIK for image classification and proved it to be a Mercer kernel for images having the same size. Since that time, a lot of improvements on this kernel have been proposed, *e.g.*, HIK with polynomial transformations [1] or the weighted multi-level extension known as pyramid match kernel (PMK) [2]. We show how to further generalize the HIK with arbitrary feature transformations and weights for each dimension. Therefore, our work is similar to [4], where a cross-validation procedure is proposed to estimate multiple weights of histogram kernels. In contrast, our hyperparameter optimization is based on a Bayesian model and can be utilized for large-scale scenarios, which is especially necessary when trying to estimate a large number of hyperparameters.

Fast GP Classification and Regression. GP classifiers require a computation time and memory cubically and quadratically in the number of training examples. Therefore, their direct application to large-scale problems is limited. A growing number of publications deal with tackling this problem by introducing sparse approximations assuming conditional independence between sets of certain variables. These variables could be specified examples of the training set or can be learned during training [11]. Although these techniques lead to impressive results, the necessary independence assumptions neglect information provided in training and test data. The only work we are aware of tackling full large-scale GP inference is the greedy block technique of Bo and Sminchisescu [12], which does not require storing the full kernel matrix in memory. However, kernel values have to be calculated explicitly, which is not necessary in our case. In experiments, we show that their method can be improved by orders of magnitude in computation time by exploiting HIK properties.

3 GP Regression and Hyperparameter Optimization

Let $\mathcal{X}$ be the space of all possible input data, *e.g.*, D-dimensional feature vectors. Given n training examples $\boldsymbol{x}^{(i)} \in \mathbf{X} \subset \mathcal{X}$ as well as corresponding binary labels $y_i \in \{-1, 1\}$, we would like to predict the label y_* of an unseen example $\boldsymbol{x}^* \in \mathcal{X}$. We now assume that f is a sample of a GP prior, *i.e.*, $f \sim \mathcal{GP}(0, K)$ with covariance function K, and that labels y_i are conditionally independent given $f(\boldsymbol{x}^{(i)})$. Furthermore, a simple additive Gaussian noise model with variance σ^2 is used:

$$p(y_i \mid f_i) = \mathcal{N}(y_i \mid f_i, \sigma^2) \ . \tag{1}$$

We follow [6] and solve a given binary classification problem as a regression problem, which regards y_i as real-valued function values instead of discrete labels. This is advantageous, because in this case the GP model assumptions lead to analytical solutions of the involved marginalizations and allow for directly predicting the expectation μ_* of the posterior of the label y_* given a new example $\boldsymbol{x}^*$ [13]:

$$\mu_* = \boldsymbol{k}_*^T (\mathbf{K} + \sigma^2 \cdot \mathbf{I})^{-1} \boldsymbol{y} = \boldsymbol{k}_*^T \boldsymbol{\alpha} \ . \tag{2}$$

The vector $\boldsymbol{k}_*$ contains the kernel values $(\boldsymbol{k}_*)_i = K(\boldsymbol{x}^{(i)}, \boldsymbol{x}^*)$ corresponding to a test example $\boldsymbol{x}^*$, $\mathbf{K}$ is the kernel matrix of the training data, and $\boldsymbol{y}$ is the vector containing all training labels.

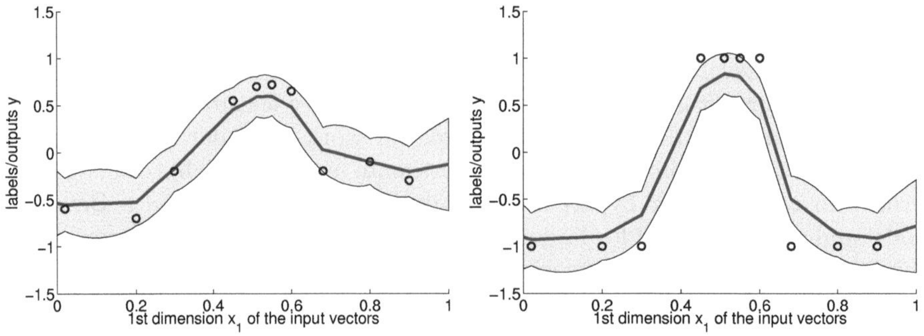

Fig. 1. Piecewise linearity of the regression function when using Gaussian process regression applied to the histogram intersection kernel: 2-dimensional input vectors $\boldsymbol{x}$ are used but due to the normalization $\|\boldsymbol{x}\|_1 = 1$, we only display the predictive mean (*red graph*) and confidence areas (*shaded area*) derived from the predictive variance with respect to the first dimension of the input vectors. Training points are shown as *blue dots* and the noise variance is set to 0.1.

Hyperparameter Optimization. In this paper, we use kernel functions that depend on hyperparameters $\boldsymbol{\eta}$, which have an important impact on the resulting classification model. In contrast to SVM techniques, the GP framework allows for finding their optimal values by likelihood maximization instead of expensive cross-validation. For GP regression, the negative log-likelihood is given by [13]

$$-\log p(\boldsymbol{y} \mid \mathbf{X}, \boldsymbol{\eta}) = \frac{1}{2}\boldsymbol{y}^T \left(\tilde{\mathbf{K}}_\eta\right)^{-1} \boldsymbol{y} + \frac{1}{2}\log\det\left(\tilde{\mathbf{K}}_\eta\right) + \frac{n}{2}\log 2\pi \tag{3}$$

with $\tilde{\mathbf{K}}_\eta$ being the parameterized kernel matrix having the noise variance σ^2 added to the main diagonal.

Multi-class Classification. Multi-class classification can be done by utilizing the one-vs-all technique [6], which also offers to perform model selection by joint optimization of hyperparameters with all involved binary problems [6]. The objective function is simply the sum of all binary negative log-likelihoods.

Imbalanced Datasets. If the number of positive and negative samples during training differs, the resulting decision function becomes biased towards the class more prominent in the training data. Especially for large-scale datasets with some hundred positive examples but several thousand negatives, this bias becomes crucial for the overall accuracy. To overcome this behavior, we propose using different noise levels for positive and negative examples, *i.e.*, the diagonal matrix $\mathbf{N}$ is added to the kernel matrix with $N_{ii} = 2\sigma^2 \cdot \left(\frac{|\{j \mid y_i = y_j\}|}{n}\right)$. By rewriting GP regression into a regularized least-squares problem [13, p. 144], this balancing strategy leads to an equal sum of positive and negative weights. Due to the lack of space, we refer to the supplementary material[1] for detailed derivations.

[1] Supplementary material: `http://www.inf-cv.uni-jena.de/gp_hik.html`

4 Efficient Kernel Calculations with Histogram Kernels

Kernel methods are one of the fundamental tools used to handle the complexity of visual recognition. It has been shown that the histogram intersection kernel

$$K^{\text{hik}}(\boldsymbol{x}, \boldsymbol{x}') = \sum_{d=1}^{D} \min(x_d, x'_d) \ , \tag{4}$$

which is often used to compare histogram feature vectors $\boldsymbol{x}, \boldsymbol{x}' \in \mathbb{R}^D$, allows for efficient classification and learning with support vector machines (SVM) [8, 9]. In our approach, we use the HIK directly in the previously presented GP framework as a covariance function. Figure 1 shows two examples of GP regression and classification with this model. The interesting observation is that the regression function estimated by the predictive mean given in Eq. (2) is piecewise linear. We exploit this property for speeding up GP regression and hyperparameter optimization in Sect. 5.

In the following, we briefly review the techniques of [8, 9] for speeding up the computation of kernel terms and extend them towards using parameterized generalizations of the HIK.

Fast Kernel Calculation. As we have seen in Eq. (2), similar to SVM and many other kernel methods, the predictive mean is a weighted sum of kernel values. The HIK allows for decomposing it in two parts [8]:

$$\boldsymbol{k}_*^T \boldsymbol{\alpha} = \sum_{i=1}^{n} \alpha_i \sum_{d=1}^{D} \min(x_d^{(i)}, x_d^*) = \sum_{d=1}^{D} \Big(\sum_{\{i: x_d^{(i)} < x_d^*\}} \alpha_i x_d^{(i)} + x_d^* \sum_{\{j: x_d^{(j)} \geq x_d^*\}} \alpha_j \Big) \ . \tag{5}$$

We can now significantly reduce the computational costs using the following trick. Let us assume that permutations π_d are given which rearrange the training examples such that they are sorted in an ascending order in each dimension d. Then, we can rewrite Eq. (5) as

$$\boldsymbol{k}_*^T \boldsymbol{\alpha} = \sum_{d=1}^{D} \Big(\underbrace{\sum_{i=1}^{r} \alpha_{\pi_d^{-1}(i)} x_k^{(\pi_d^{-1}(i))}}_{\doteq A(d,r)} + x_d^* \underbrace{\sum_{i=r+1}^{n} \alpha_{\pi_d^{-1}(i)}}_{\doteq B(d,r)} \Big) \ , \tag{6}$$

with r being the number of examples that are smaller than x_d^* in dimension d. Thus, Eq. (6) proves the piecewise linearity of the predictive mean of Gaussian process regression with HIK. If we precompute the two terms of the linear function during learning, evaluating the scores for test examples can be done with a few evaluations of A and B for each dimension. Given the vector $\boldsymbol{\alpha}$, the resulting computation time for building A and B is dominated by sorting in $\mathcal{O}(D\, n \log n)$ operations. In terms of memory usage, we only have to store $\mathcal{O}(D\, n)$ elements in contrast to the kernel matrix of size $\mathcal{O}(n^2)$. For calculating the score of a new example, we need $\mathcal{O}(D \log n)$ operations to find the correct position r in each dimension and compute the linear function in Eq. (6) by evaluating A and B. Similar considerations hold for multiplications of an arbitrary vector $\boldsymbol{v} \in \mathbb{R}^n$ with the kernel matrix $\mathbf{K}$, which can be done in $\mathcal{O}(D \cdot n)$. Furthermore, we can exploit sparsity of feature vectors with a careful implementation.

Quantization of the Feature Space. If we assume that feature values in dimension d are bounded by $x^*_d \in [l_d, u_d]$, the evaluation can be further speeded up by quantizing the feature space [8]. Using a quantization for each dimension with q bins, only q different outputs are possible for Eq. (6). With already computed matrices A and B, we can proceed with building a final lookup table T of dimension $D \times q$. Due to the already given permutations π_d, we can perform this within $\mathcal{O}\left(D \max\left(q, n\right)\right)$ operations. As a result, the time spent for evaluating the score of a new test example decreases to $\mathcal{O}(D)$. Consequently, for a given number of dimensions the score of a new test example can be computed in constant time independent of n.

Very General Histogram Intersection Kernels. Boughorbel *et al.* [1] show that the HIK equipped with any positive valued function g:

$$K^{\text{ghik}}(\boldsymbol{x}, \boldsymbol{x}') = \sum_{d=1}^{D} \min\left(g\left(x_d\right), g\left(x'_d\right)\right) \quad , \tag{7}$$

still remains a positive-definite kernel. If g is an automorphism, the relative order of the training elements stays valid after evaluating g. Therefore, the proposed techniques can also be applied to these generalized variants of the HIK and we can even use the same quantization by storing the original feature values. Two common examples of such functions are the powered absolute value $g_{|.|,\eta}(x) = |x|^\eta$ and the exponential $g_{e,\eta}(x) = \frac{\exp(\eta|x|)-1}{\exp(\eta)-1}$. In the remaining sections, we refer to them as generalized HIK (G-HIK) and exponential HIK (EXP-HIK). The kernel function given in Eq. (7) can be generalized even further by considering functions $g^{(d)}$ for each dimension. For example, $g^{(d)}(x_d) = \eta_d \cdot x_d$ with $\eta_d \geq 0$ allows for individually weighting input dimensions:

$$K^{\text{weights}}(\boldsymbol{x}, \boldsymbol{x}') = \sum_{d=1}^{D} \eta_d \cdot \min\left(x_d, x'_d\right) \quad . \tag{8}$$

In subsequent sections, we present how to optimize the parameters $\boldsymbol{\eta}$ even for large-scale training data. Together with the kernel function in Eq. (8), this allows for linear kernel combination [6] and automatic relevance determination [13].

5 Efficient GP Multi-class Classification

In this section, we demonstrate that GP regression and hyperparameter optimization can be performed efficiently when using histogram intersection kernels. An overview is shown in Fig. 2, whereas Table 1 summarizes the asymptotic computation times necessary for each step.

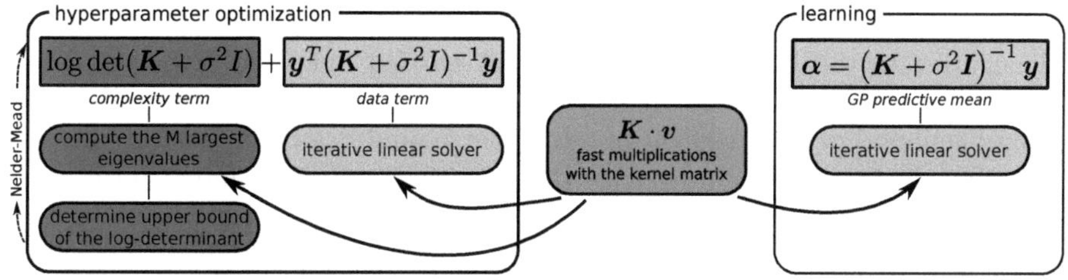

Fig. 2. Main outline of GP classification and hyperparameter optimization using fast multiplications with the kernel matrix

Table 1. Overview of asymptotic runtimes for training, testing, and optimization of hyperparameters for baseline GP compared to our approach. D denotes the number of dimensions, n the number of training examples, M the number of classes, and T_1 and T_2 the number of iterations used for the linear solver and the optimizer, respectively

	Asymptotic runtime	
Evaluation step	GP baseline	GP + HIK + Quantization
Training (Sect. 5.1)	$\mathcal{O}(\mathbf{n}^3 + \mathbf{n}^2 D)$	$\mathcal{O}(\mathbf{n}D(T_1 M + \log \mathbf{n}))$
Hyperparameter opt. (Sect. 5.2)	$\mathcal{O}((\mathbf{n}^3 + \mathbf{n}^2 D)T_2)$	$\mathcal{O}(\mathbf{n}MDT_1T_2)$
Testing (Sect. 5.1)	$\mathcal{O}(\mathbf{n}MD)$	$\mathcal{O}(MD)$

5.1 Learning and Classification

Inference with a GP model requires two steps: (1) solving the linear equation system $\tilde{\mathbf{K}}_\eta \cdot \boldsymbol{\alpha} = \boldsymbol{y}$ and (2) calculating the scalar product $\boldsymbol{k}_*^T \boldsymbol{\alpha}$. For large-scale datasets, storing the full kernel matrix is impossible and applying a Cholesky decomposition with a runtime of $\mathcal{O}(n^3)$ far from being practical. As we have seen in Sect. 4, multiplications with the kernel matrix can be done in linear time with histogram intersection kernels. Therefore, we use an iterative linear solver to tackle step 1. Wu [9] used a coordinate descent method to solve the quadratic program related to SVM learning. In contrast, our experiments show that a linear conjugate gradients (CG) method converges faster. The total asymptotic runtime for learning is $\mathcal{O}(nD(T_1 M + \log n))$ including sorting. The total number of iterations T_1 of the CG method depends on the condition number of the kernel matrix and we also see that the runtime performance of our method is linear in the number of classes M. We stop the CG method when the maximum norm of the residual drops below 10^{-2}.

After estimation of the coefficients $\boldsymbol{\alpha}$, we use the quantization algorithm of [8] reviewed in Sect. 4 allowing for computing $\boldsymbol{k}_*^T \boldsymbol{\alpha}$ in constant time (step 2). In our experiments, we choose an equidistant quantization with $q = 100$.

5.2 Large-Scale Hyperparameter Optimization

To optimize kernel hyperparameters with a large-scale dataset, we have to minimize the negative GP log-likelihood as given in Eq. (3). Due to the computational demand of evaluating Eq. (3) for large-scale datasets, we bound the negative log-likelihood with an efficiently computable function from above. Finding suitable hyperparameters is then done by minimizing this upper bound instead of the real negative log-likelihood. Optimization is carried out with a method that does not require any gradient information, because calculating the gradient of the log-likelihood or the gradient of our upper bound is a costly operation. Evaluating the log-likelihood requires the calculation of two different terms, the logarithm of the kernel matrix determinant and the data term involving the labels $\boldsymbol{y}$. The latter one is easy to compute, because it simply involves solving the same linear system as required for learning. However, the determinant of the kernel matrix is difficult to handle and we require some upper bound on it.

Efficient Upper Bound of the Log-Determinant. Computing the determinant of a matrix is a costly algebraic operation, even with fast matrix multiplications [14]. Due to this reason, we use the upper bound provided by Bai and Golub [15], which turns out to be efficiently computable for histogram intersection kernel matrices. If the eigenvalues λ_i of $\mathbf{D}$ can be bounded by $0 < \lambda_i \leq \beta$, an upper bound of the log-determinant is given by:

$$\log\det(\mathbf{D}) \leq \begin{bmatrix}\log\beta \ \log\bar{t}\end{bmatrix} \begin{bmatrix}\beta & \bar{t} \\ \beta^2 & \bar{t}^2\end{bmatrix}^{-1} \begin{bmatrix}\mu_1 \\ \mu_2\end{bmatrix} \doteq \mathrm{ub}(\beta, \mu_1, \mu_2) \tag{9}$$

where $\mu_1 = \mathrm{tr}\,(\mathbf{D})$, $\mu_2 = \|\mathbf{D}\|_F^2$, and $\bar{t} = \frac{\beta\mu_1 - \mu_2}{\beta n - \mu_1}$ [15]. It is interesting to note that this bound is tight for regularized rank-1 matrices $\mathbf{D} = \boldsymbol{u}\boldsymbol{u}^T + \tau\mathbf{I}$ [15]. For very complex classification tasks, we often observe a similar structure of the kernel matrix, which suggests that the bound is suitable in those scenarios.

To calculate the bound for the regularized kernel matrix $\tilde{\mathbf{K}}_{\boldsymbol{\eta}}$, we need the largest eigenvalue λ_1, the trace, and the squared Frobenius norm. We first compute the largest eigenvalue λ_1 with the Arnoldi iteration, which only requires matrix vector products. In our experiments, the algorithm needed approximately 10 steps to converge for various settings. Furthermore, it is easy to verify that the trace of the histogram intersection kernel matrix is the sum of all features values. The squared Frobenius norm is not directly available, but we can approximate it by $\tilde{\mu}_2 = \sum_{i=1}^{M} \lambda_i^2 \approx \sum_{i=1}^{n} \lambda_i^2 = \mu_2$ with M being the number of classes of the classification task and λ_i being the eigenvalues of the kernel matrix in decreasing order, *i.e.*, $\lambda_1 \geq \ldots \geq \lambda_n$. The motivation for this approximation is as follows: if we have M classes with very compact clusters and large distances between each other, the kernel matrix should obey a simple block structure of rank M leading to M non-zero eigenvalues. Due to the fact that our approximation of μ_2 is also a lower bound of $\|\mathbf{D}\|_F^2$, the necessary computations in Eq. (9) are still well-defined and it can be proved that we still have a proper upper bound of the log-determinant (see supplementary material for a detailed proof):

Theorem 1 (Upper bound with $\tilde{\mu}_2$). *For a given positive definite matrix $\mathbf{D} \in \mathbb{R}^{n \times n}$ with trace μ_1 and squared Frobenius norm μ_2 the following holds:*

$$\log\det(\mathbf{D}) \leq \mathrm{ub}(\beta, \mu_1, \mu_2) \leq \mathrm{ub}(\beta, \mu_1, \tilde{\mu}_2) \quad \text{if} \quad \tilde{\mu}_2 \leq \mu_2 \ . \tag{10}$$

To summarize, we need to perform the following steps to efficiently bound the negative GP log-likelihood in each iteration of the hyperparameter optimization method:

1. Compute the data term by utilizing the CG method.
2. Compute the trace μ_1 as the sum of all feature values.
3. Calculate the first M eigenvalues with the Arnoldi iteration.
4. Approximate the Frobenius norm with the sum of squared eigenvalues.
5. Compute the bound given in Eq. (9) with the approximated Frobenius norm.

In our experiments, the resulting upper bound of the negative GP log-likelihood was successfully used for hyperparameter optimization, which we show in the next section.

6 Experiments

We conducted experiments with several image categorization datasets. The results can be summarized as follows:

1. Using our approach, training, classification, and optimization of hyperparameters is significantly faster and has only linear memory requirement compared to baseline GP, allowing for learning on large-scale datasets.
2. Conjugate gradients with fast HIK matrix multiplications outperforms the methods of [9] and [12] in terms of convergence speed.
3. The log-determinant approximation given in Eq. (9) allows for hyperparameter optimization leading to significant performance gains.
4. Generalized histogram intersection kernels improve the classification performance significantly compared to standard HIK.
5. Determining feature relevance can be done efficiently with GP likelihood optimization and a weighted HIK.

6.1 Experimental Setup

The histogram intersection kernel is well suited for comparing histograms [4]. Therefore, all of our image categorization experiments use bag of visual words (BoV) features computed using the toolkit provided with the ILSVRC'10 database [5]. Although all types of histogram features can be utilized, we choose this basic representation without any incorporation of spatial information to focus the experiments on the machine learning part. We use the visual codebook provided with 1,000 elements. Note that the dimension of the feature vectors is an important factor for the computation time of GP large-scale inference, and the speed-up of our techniques is higher for low-dimensional features (see Table 1). As an optimization method we use the Nelder-Mead technique [16].

For multi-class classification, we use the average recognition rate (ARR) as a performance measure. Binary classification tasks are evaluated using the area under the ROC curve (AUC). To provide a fair comparison, computation times for all methods were measured on a single-core Intel 2.6GHz machine with a careful C++ implementation allowing for flexible data sizes.

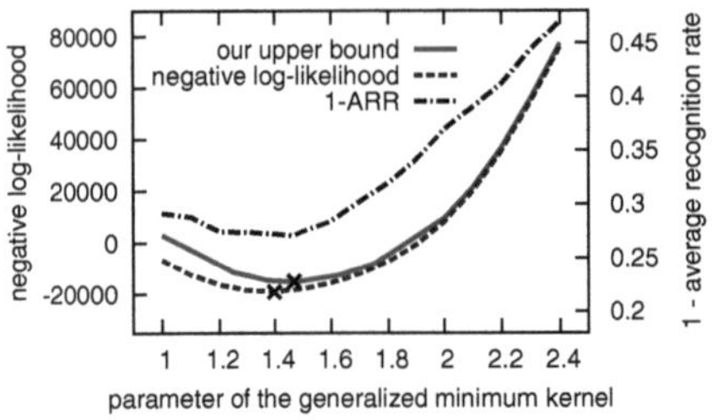

Approach	ARR
GP with HIK	70.8%
GP with optimized G-HIK	72.9%
GP with optimized EXP-HIK	**74.0%**
BoV baseline [18]	64.1%
GIST features [18]	73.0%
SPMK [18]	73.4%

Fig. 3. Experiments with the normalized 15Scenes database: (*left*) comparison between upper bounded negative GP log-likelihood and real negative log-likelihood, (*right*) results of GP with adaptive kernels

6.2 Experiments with the Normalized 15Scenes Database

We use the 15Scenes database [17] for preliminary results on a medium-scale database. We follow the suggestion of [18] and scale all images to a size of 256×256 pixels to get results, which are not biased on different characteristic image sizes for specific categories. Training is done with 100 examples for each category resulting in 1,500 examples in total.

Verifying the Bound of the Negative Log-Likelihood. A first experiment evaluates the upper bound of the negative GP log-likelihood presented in Sect. 5.2. The left plot in Fig. 3 shows the correct negative log-likelihood, our upper bound with respect to the hyperparameter η of a generalized HIK, and the average recognition rate when using the hyperparameter value for classification of the test set. It can be seen that our bound is sufficient for hyperparameter optimization in this setup, because the minima and the corresponding average recognition rates displayed only differ slightly. For higher values of η, our bound converges to the exact value because the influence of the log-determinant term compared to the data term of the log-likelihood decreases. Consequently, possible approximation errors become less important and the data term can be computed without any approximation even for large-scale datasets.

Different Generalized HIK. The table on the right hand side of Fig. 3 gives an overview of the recognition performance we achieved on this dataset with standard HIK, G-HIK, and EXP-HIK. The hyperparameters of G-HIK and EXP-HIK have been optimized with our GP likelihood optimization technique. The latter approach resulted in the best performance and is even comparable to the result of the spatial pyramid matching kernel (SPMK) given by [18]. This highlights the power of generalized HIK and our hyperparameter optimization, because we do not incorporate any position information in our features as done in the SPMK framework.

Using the standard biased 15Scenes database with the splits and features provided by [9], we achieve an average performance of 80.0% and 79.9% with and without optimization, respectively. In contrast, the SVM solver of [9], which

Table 2. Evaluation on 200 binary classification tasks derived from the ImageNet database. Computation times are given as median values of measurements for each task (learning) and each test example (classification).

	10,090 examples ($\ell = 10$)			**50,050 examples** ($\ell = 50$)		
Method	AUC	learning time	classif. time	AUC	learning time	classif. time
GP with HIK (Cholesky)	0.836	> 3.5h	1.1s	-	-	-
GP with HIK	0.836	64s	$44\mu s$	0.856	321s	$44\mu s$
GP with optimized G-HIK	0.865	435s	$44\mu s$	0.883	2815s	$44\mu s$
GP with optimized EXP-HIK	**0.889**	579s	$44\mu s$	**0.893**	2578s	$44\mu s$

also exploits HIK properties, achieved a recognition rate of 81.3%. Nonetheless, it should be noted that our approach focuses on Bayesian inference and Bayesian hyperparameter optimization, which offers a probabilistic formulation with a wide range of further applications and extensions, *e.g.*, active and transfer learning [6, 19] as well as incorporating other noise models [13].

6.3 Large-Scale Experiments with the ImageNet Database

We also test our approach on the part of the ImageNet dataset that was used for the ILSVRC'10 competition. This dataset contains in total 150,000 images from 1,000 different categories. We apply our method to binary classification tasks of this dataset, because learning with all categories turns out to be still impractical even with our fast kernel calculations. Binary tasks are derived in a one-vs-all manner, *i.e.*, we use all images of a single class as positive examples and ℓ examples from each of the other 999 categories as negative examples. In this manner, we derive 200 tasks from the first 200 categories and use the average AUC value achieved on the ILSVRC'10 validation dataset with 50,000 examples as the resulting performance value.

The results are shown in Table 2 for $\ell = 10$ and $\ell = 50$ with 10,090 and 50,050 examples in total. First it should be noted that standard GP regression for $\ell = 50$ is not directly applicable because of limiting memory capacity ($\ell = 50$ results in a $9GB$ kernel matrix). In contrast, it can be seen that we are able to learn GP classifiers within a few minutes. Furthermore, our GP likelihood optimization method is able to handle large datasets and provides significant performance gains with hyperparameter optimization (paired t-test, $p < 10^{-7}$).

6.4 Evaluation of Linear Solvers with Fast HIK Multiplications

In the following, we compare the performance of conjugate gradients with fast HIK matrix multiplications as presented in Sect. 4 and two other coordinate descent approaches [9, 12]: (1) the coordinate descent method of [9] applied to GP and (2) the greedy block coordinate descent (GBCD) approach of [12]. The first one was originally presented for fast SVM learning with HIK and directly operates on the lookup table T (Sect. 4). GBCD calculates parts of the kernel matrix on the fly to solve sub-problems. For our experiments, the size of the

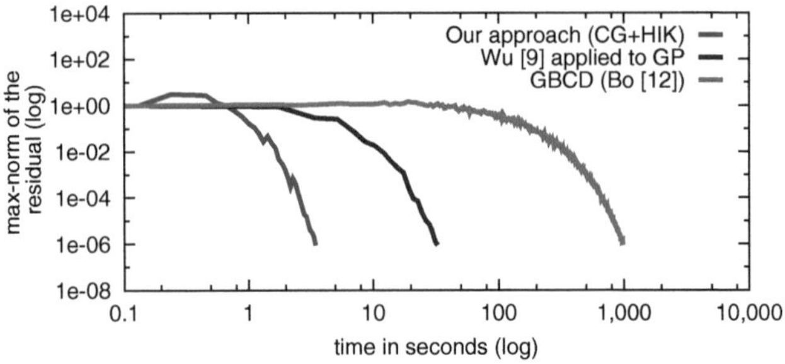

Fig. 4. Evaluation of the runtime and convergence of linear solvers: (1) our conjugate gradients method, (2) the coordinate descent method of [9], and (3) greedy block coordinate descent [12]. Note that our approach and [9] exploit fast HIK matrix multiplications, while [12] can be applied for every kernel function

sub-problems is set to 10 and the number of components κ for greedy selection is 20. We also tested other values, but did not achieve a significant speed-up. We use a binary classification task from the ILSVRC'10 database with $\ell = 1$ (see previous paragraph) and solved the linear system $\tilde{\mathbf{K}}_{\boldsymbol{\eta}} \cdot \boldsymbol{\alpha} = \boldsymbol{y}$ with all three methods. Figure 4 shows the residual of the linear system with respect to the computation time needed. Termination is done when the maximum norm of the residual drops below 10^{-6}.

As can be seen in Fig. 4 there are orders of magnitude between all three methods. Conjugate gradients reaches a solution in 3.7 seconds, which is superior to the coordinate descent method of [9] applied to GP, which converges after 32*s*. GBCD is slow (convergence after 16 minutes) due to the long time needed for explicit calculation of kernel values for 1,000-dimensional features. In the experiments of [12], only low-dimensional features ($D \leq 37$) were utilized. However, GBCD can be applied for large-scale GP regression with arbitrary kernel functions. It should also be noted that solving the linear system of GP regression needs more time than solving the optimization problem related to SVM. This is due to the additional sparsity constraints of SVM. However, the GP framework offers a proper Bayesian model with the previously mentioned advantages.

6.5 Feature Relevance Estimation

We have already seen that Gaussian Processes allow for hyperparameter optimization in a Bayesian manner. In this experiment, we show the suitability of GP equipped with optimized weighted HIK for efficient feature relevance determination leading to superior results to those of SVM-based estimations.

Since there is no exact gradient information during the optimization available, the Nelder-Mead method converges poorly for huge numbers of parameters to be optimized. Consequently, computing feature relevance for features with thousands of dimensions, as in our previous experiments, is almost impossible right now. Nevertheless, as a proof of concept we follow the same synthetic experimental setup as in [4]: for different numbers of training examples, we randomly

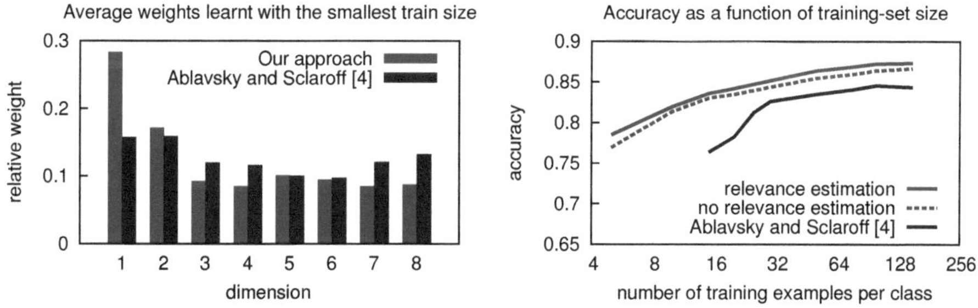

Fig. 5. Relevance determination with very generalized histogram intersection kernels and GP hyperparameter optimization. The first two features contain most of the discriminative information: (*left*) feature weights estimated with 5 examples per class, (*right*) performance compared to non-weighted histogram intersection kernels. Results are averaged over 500 runs.

sample eight-dimensional feature vectors with relevant information only available in the first two dimensions. The performance is estimated with 500 tests. For the specific random distributions, we refer the reader to [4] and references therein. The results of our experiments can be seen in Fig. 5.

The information included in each dimension is well reflected by the estimated relative weights η_i, which can be seen in the plot on the left hand side. Furthermore, the plot on the right hand side shows the recognition accuracy for standard and weighted HIK with respect to the training size. The improvement is highly significant with $p < 10^{-7}$ using the paired t-test. In comparison with [4], our approach additionally leads to more consistent weights and higher accuracies.

7 Conclusions and Future Work

This paper presented how Gaussian Processes equipped with the histogram intersection kernel can be speeded up significantly. The involved strategies allow for training and classification in sub-quadratic and constant time with few memory requirements. This significantly overcomes the main drawbacks of GP for large-scale scenarios (cubic and quadratic runtime for training and classification, quadratic demand of memory). We further developed an efficient method for optimizing hyperparameters in a Bayesian manner by exploiting the benefits of HIK and GP as well as by providing an efficient bound of the GP marginal log-likelihood. We demonstrated the suitability of our approach on several datasets. It turned out that we are able to find suitable parameters for different parameterized histogram intersection kernels even for large-scale datasets resulting in a significant improvement of the recognition performance. Furthermore, we successfully applied our framework to feature relevance determination showing superior results compared to state-of-the-art [4]. Our approach allows for large-scale classification with GP, which was proved in our ImageNet experiments.

Future work will focus on calculating approximate gradient information of the likelihood to allow optimization with respect to a large number of parameters. Furthermore, multi-class classification could be speeded up by using label trees [20] or similar techniques. Finally, we want to extend our approach to fast computation of the predictive variance for estimating classification uncertainties. This would allow for active learning applications.

Acknowledgments. We thank Esther and Matthias Wacker for their optimization toolbox as well as the reviewers for very useful suggestions.

References

1. Boughorbel, S., Tarel, J.P., Boujemaa, N.: Generalized histogram intersection kernel for image recognition. In: ICIP, pp. III-161–III-164 (2005)
2. Grauman, K., Darrell, T.: The pyramid match kernel: Efficient learning with sets of features. J. Mach. Learn. Res. 8, 725–760 (2007)
3. Wang, G., Hoiem, D., Forsyth, D.: Learning image similarity from flickr groups using fast kernel machines. TPAMI 99 (2012)
4. Ablavsky, V., Sclaroff, S.: Learning parameterized histogram kernels on the simplex manifold for image and action classification. In: ICCV, pp. 1473–1480 (2011)
5. Berg, A., Deng, J., Fei-Fei, L.: Large scale visual recognition challenge (2010), `http://www.imagenet.org/challenges/LSVRC/2010/`
6. Kapoor, A., Grauman, K., Urtasun, R., Darrell, T.: Gaussian processes for object categorization. IJCV 88, 169–188 (2010)
7. Vedaldi, A., Zisserman, A.: Efficient additive kernels via explicit feature maps. In: CVPR, pp. 3539–3546 (2010)
8. Maji, S., Berg, A., Malik, J.: Classification using intersection kernel support vector machines is efficient. In: CVPR, pp. 1–8 (2008)
9. Wu, J.: A Fast Dual Method for HIK SVM Learning. In: Daniilidis, K., Maragos, P., Paragios, N. (eds.) ECCV 2010, Part II. LNCS, vol. 6312, pp. 552–565. Springer, Heidelberg (2010)
10. Barla, A., Odone, F., Verri, A.: Histogram intersection kernel for image classification. In: ICIP, pp. 513–516 (2003)
11. Quiñonero Candela, J., Rasmussen, C.E.: A unifying view of sparse approximate gaussian process regression. J. Mach. Learn. Res. 6, 1939–1959 (2005)
12. Bo, L., Sminchisescu, C.: Greedy block coordinate descent for large scale gaussian process regression. In: Uncertainty in Artificial Intelligence (2008)
13. Rasmussen, C.E., Williams, C.K.I.: Gaussian Processes for Machine Learning. Adaptive Computation and Machine Learning. The MIT Press (2006)
14. Yuster, R.: Matrix sparsification for rank and determinant computations via nested dissection. In: IEEE Symp. on Foundations of Computer Science, pp. 137–145 (2008)
15. Bai, Z., Golub, G.: Bounds for the trace of the inverse and the determinant of symmetric positive definite matrices. Annals of Num. Mathematics 4, 29–38 (1997)
16. Nelder, J., Mead, R.: A simplex method for function minimization. Computer Journal 7, 308–313 (1965)
17. Lazebnik, S., Schmid, C., Ponce, J.: Beyond bags of features: Spatial pyramid matching for recognizing natural scene categories. In: CVPR, pp. 2169–2178 (2006)
18. Quattoni, A., Torralba, A.: Recognizing indoor scenes. In: CVPR, pp. 413–420 (2009)
19. Rodner, E., Denzler, J.: One-Shot Learning of Object Categories Using Dependent Gaussian Processes. In: Goesele, M., Roth, S., Kuijper, A., Schiele, B., Schindler, K. (eds.) DAGM 2010. LNCS, vol. 6376, pp. 232–241. Springer, Heidelberg (2010)
20. Bengio, S., Weston, J., Grangier, D.: Label embedding trees for large multi-class tasks. In: NIPS, pp. 163–171 (2010)

Background Subtraction with Dirichlet Processes

Tom S.F. Haines and Tao Xiang

Electronic Engineering and Computer Science, Queen Mary, Uni. of London
{thaines,txiang}@eecs.qmul.ac.uk

Abstract. Background subtraction is an important first step for video analysis, where it is used to discover the objects of interest for further processing. Such an algorithm often consists of a background model and a regularisation scheme. The background model determines a per-pixel measure of if a pixel belongs to the background or the foreground, whilst the regularisation brings in information from adjacent pixels. A new method is presented that uses a Dirichlet process Gaussian mixture model to estimate a per-pixel background distribution, which is followed by probabilistic regularisation. Key advantages include inferring the per-pixel mode count, such that it accurately models dynamic backgrounds, and that it updates its model continuously in a principled way.

1 Introduction

Background subtraction can be defined as separating a video stream into the regions unique to a particular moment in time (the foreground), and the regions that are always present (the background). It is primarily used as an interest detector for higher level problems, such as automated surveillance, intelligent environments and motion analysis. The etymology of *background subtraction* derives from the oldest method, where a single static image of just the background is subtracted from the current frame, to generate a difference image. If the absolute difference exceeds a threshold the pixel in question is declared to belong to the foreground. Such an approach fails because the background is rarely static. Background variability has many underlying causes [1,2]:

Dynamic background, where objects such as trees blow in the wind, escalators move and traffic lights change colour.
Noise, as caused by the image capturing process. It can vary over the image due to photon noise and varying brightness.
Camouflage, where a foreground object looks very much like the background, e.g. a sniper in a ghillie suit.
Moved object, where the background changes, e.g. a car could be parked in the scene, and after sufficient time considered part of the background, only to later become foreground again when driven off.
Bootstrapping. As it is often not possible to get a frame with no foreground an algorithm should be capable of being initialised with foreground objects in the scene. It has to learn the correct background model over time.

A. Fitzgibbon et al. (Eds.): ECCV 2012, Part IV, LNCS 7575, pp. 99–113, 2012.

Illumination changes, both gradual, e.g. from the sun moving during the day, and rapid, such as from a light switch being toggled.
Shadows are cast by the foreground objects, but later processing is typically not interested in them.

The background subtraction field is gargantuan, and has many review papers [3,4,5,2]. Stauffer & Grimson [6] is one of the best known approaches - it uses a Gaussian mixture model (GMM) for a per-pixel density estimate (DE) followed by connected components for regularisation. This model improves on using a background plate because it can handle a *dynamic background* and *noise*, by using multimodal probability distributions. As it is continuously updated it can *bootstrap*. Its mixture model includes both foreground and background components - it classifies values based on their mixture component, which is assigned to the foreground or the background based on the assumption that the majority of the larger components belong to the background, with the remainder foreground. This assumption fails if objects hang around for very long, as they quickly dominate the distribution. The model is updated linearly using a fixed learning rate parameter - it is not very good with the *moved object* problem. Connected components converts the intermediate foreground mask into regions via pixel adjacency, and culls all regions below a certain size, to remove spurious detections. This approach to noise handling combined with its somewhat primitive density estimation method undermines *camouflage* handling, as it often thinks it is noise, and also prevents it from tracking small objects. No capacity exists for it to handle *illumination changes* or *shadows*. The above can be divided into 4 parts - the model, updating the model, how pixels are classified, and regularisation; alternate approaches for each will now be considered in turn.

The Model: Alternative DE methods exist, including different GMM implementations [7] and kernel density estimate (KDE) methods, either using Gaussian kernels [8,9] or step kernels [10,7]. Histograms have also been used [11], and alternatives to DE include models that predict the next value [1], use neural networks [12], or hidden Markov models [13]. An improved background model should result in better performance regarding *dynamic background*, *noise* and *camouflage*. This is due to better handling of underfitting and/or overfitting, which improves generalisation to the data stream. Whilst better than Stauffer & Grimson [6] the above methods still suffer from over/under-fitting. KDE and histogram methods are particularly vulnerable, as they implicitly assume a constant density by using fixed size kernels/bins. GMM methods should do better, but the heuristics required for online learning, particularly regarding the creation of new components, can result in local minima in the optimisation, which is just as problematic.

Our Approach: We present an approach that uses a Dirichlet process Gaussian mixture model (DP-GMM) [14] for per-pixel density estimation. This is a non-parametric Bayesian method [15] that automatically estimates the number of mixture components required to model the pixels background colour distribution. Consequentially it correctly handles multi-modal *dynamic backgrounds* with regular colour/luminance changes, such as trees waving in the wind. As a fully Bayesian model over-fitting is avoided, improving robustness to *noise* and classifying pixels precisly, which helps to distinguish noise from *camouflage*. He et al. [16] recently also used DP-GMMs for background subtraction, in a block-based method. They failed to leverage the potential advantages however (Discussed below), and used computationally unmanageable methods - despite their efforts poor results were obtained.

Model Update: Most methods use a constant learning rate to update the model, but some use adaptive heuristics [7,17], whilst others are history based [1,16], and build a model from the last n frames directly. Adapting the learning rate affects the *moved object* issue - if it is too fast then stationary objects become part of the background too quickly, if it is too slow it takes too long to recover from changes to the background. Adaptation aims to adjust the rate depending on what is happening. Continuously learning the model is required to handle the *bootstrapping* issue.

Our Approach: Using a DP-GMM allows us to introduce a novel model update concept that lets old information degrade in a principled way. One side effect of this and the use of Gibbs sampling is that no history has to be kept [1,16], avoiding the need to store and process hundreds of frames. It works by capping the confidence of the model, i.e. limiting how certain it can be about the shape of the background distribution. This allows a stationary object to remain part of the foreground for a very long time, as it takes a lot of information for the new component to obtain the confidence of pre-existing components, but when an object moves on and the background changes to a component it has seen before, even if a while ago, it can use that component immediately. Updating the components for gradual background changes continues to happen quickly, making sure the model is never left behind. Confidence capping works because non-parameteric Bayesian models, such as DP-GMMs, have a rigorous concept of a new mixture component forming - parametric models [6,7] have to use heuristics to simulate this, whilst KDE based approaches are not compatible [8,9,10,7] as they lack a measure of confidence.

Pixel Classification: The use of a single density estimate that includes both foreground (fg) and background (bg), as done by Stauffer & Grimson [6] is somewhat unusual - most methods stick to separate models and apply Bayes rule [11], with the foreground model set to be the uniform distribution as it is unknown. **Our approach:** We follow this convention, which results in a probability of being bg or fg, rather than a hard classification, which is passed through to the regularisation step. Instead of using Bayes rule some works use a threshold [8]. Attempts at learning a foreground model also exist [9], and some models generate a binary classification directly [12].

Regularisation: Some approaches have no regularisation step [18], others have information sharing between adjacent pixels [12] but no explicit regularisation. Techniques such as eroding then dilating are common [2], and more advanced techniques have, for instance, tried to match pixels against neighbouring pixels, to compensate for background motion [8]. When dealing with a probabilistic fg/bg assignment probabilistic methods should be used, such as the use of Markov random fields (MRF) by Migdal & Grimson [19] and Sheikh & Shah [9].

Our Approach: We use the same method - the pixels all have a random variable which can take on one of two labels, fg or bg. The data term is provided by the model whilst pairwise potentials indicate that adjacent pixels should share the same label. Differences exist - previous works use Gibbs sampling [19] and graph cuts [9], whilst we choose belief propagation [20], as run time can be capped; also we use an edge preserving cost between pixels, rather than a constant cost, which proves to be beneficial with high levels of noise. Cohen [21] has also used a Markov random field, but to generate a background image by selecting pixels from a sequence of frames, rather than for regularisation.

2 Methodology

2.1 Per-Pixel Background Model

Each pixel has a density estimate constructed for it, to model $P(x|\text{bg})$ where x is the value of the pixel. The Dirichlet process Gaussian mixture model (DP-GMM) [14] is used. It can be viewed as the Dirichlet distribution extended to an infinite number of components, which allows it to learn the true number of mixtures from the data. For each pixel a stream of values arrives, one with each frame - the model has to be continuously updated with incremental learning.

Figure 1a represents the DP-GMM graphically using the *stick breaking* construction; it can be split into 3 columns - on the left the priors, in the middle the entities representing the Dirichlet process (DP) and on the right the data for which a density estimate is being constructed. This last column contains the feature vectors (pixel colours) to which the model is being fitted, x_n, which come from all previous frames, $n \in \mathcal{N}$. It is a generative model - each sample comes from a specific mixture component, indexed by $Z_n \in \mathcal{K}$, which consists of its probability of being selected, V_k and the Gaussian distribution from which the value was drawn, η_k. The conjugate prior, consisting of μ, a Gaussian over its mean, and Λ, a Wishart distribution over its inverse covariance matrix, is applied to all η_k. So far this is just a mixture model; the interesting part is that $\mathcal{K}$, the set of mixture components, is infinite. Conceptually the stick breaking construction is very simple - we have a stick of length 1, representing the entire probability mass, which we keep breaking into two parts. Each time it is broken one of the parts becomes the probability mass for a mixture component - a value of V_k, whilst the other is kept for the next break. This continues forever. α is the concentration parameter, which controls how the stick is broken - a low value puts most of the probability mass in a few mixture components, whilst a high value spreads it out over many. Orthogonal to the stick length each stick is associated with a draw, η_k, from the DP's base measure, which is the already mentioned conjugate prior over the Gaussian.

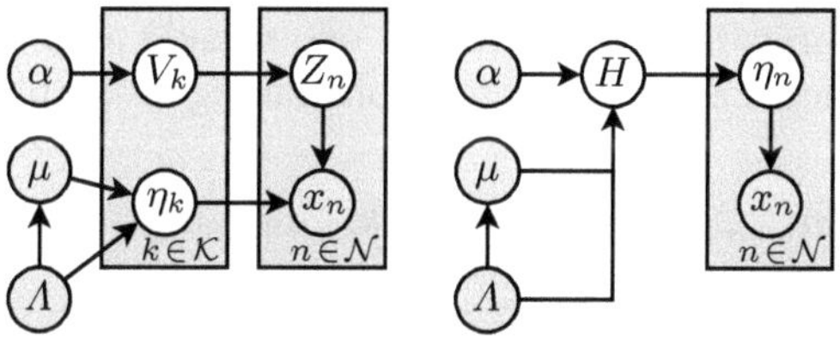

(a) Stick breaking (b) Chinese restaurant

Fig. 1. Two versions of the DP-GMM graphical model

Whilst the stick breaking construction offers a clean explanation of the model the Chinese restaurant process (CRP) is used for the implementation[1]. This is the model with the middle column of Figure 1a integrated out, to give Figure 1b. It is named by analogy. Specifically, each sample is represented by a customer, which turns up and sits at a table in a Chinese restaurant. Tables represent the mixture components, and a customer chooses either to sit at a table where customers are already sitting, with probability proportional to the number of customers at that table, or to sit at a new table, with probability proportional to α. At each table (component) only one dish is consumed, which is chosen from the menu (base measure) by the first customer to sit at that table. Integrating out the draw from the DP leads to better convergence, but more importantly replaces the infinite set of sticks with a computationally tractable finite set of tables.

Each pixel has its own density estimate, updated with each new frame. Updating proceeds by first calculating the probability of the current pixel value, x, given the current background model, then updating the model with x, weighted by the calculated probability - these steps will now be detailed.

Mixture Components: The per-pixel model is a set of weighted mixture components, such that the weights sum to 1, of Gaussian distributions. It is integrated out however, using the Chinese restaurant process for the mixture weights and the conjugate prior for the Gaussians. Whilst the literature [23] already details this second part it is included for completeness. $x \in [0,1]^3$ represents the pixels colour, and independence is assumed between the components for reasons of speed. This simplifies the Wishart prior to a gamma prior for each channel i, such that

$$\sigma_i^{-2} \sim \Gamma\left(\frac{n_{i,0}}{2}, \frac{\sigma_{i,0}^2}{2}\right), \quad \mu_i|\sigma_i^2 \sim \mathcal{N}\left(\mu_{i,0}, \frac{\sigma_i^2}{k_{i,0}}\right), \quad x_i \sim \mathcal{N}(\mu_i, \sigma_i^2), \tag{1}$$

where $\mathcal{N}(\mu, \sigma^2)$ represents the normal distribution and $\Gamma(\alpha, \beta)$ the gamma distribution. The parameters $n_{i,0}$ and $\sigma_{i,0}$, $i \in \{0,1,2\}$, are the Λ prior from the graphical model, whilst $\mu_{i,0}$ and $k_{i,0}$ are the μ prior.

[1] Variational methods [22] offer one approach to using the stick breaking construction directly. This is impractical however as historic pixel values would need to be kept.

Evidence, x, is provided incrementally, one sample at a time, which will be weighted, w. The model is then updated from having m samples to $m+1$ samples using

$$n_{i,m+1} = n_{i,m} + w, \qquad k_{i,m+1} = k_{i,m} + w,$$

$$\mu_{i,m+1} = \frac{k_{i,m}\mu_{i,m} + wx_i}{k_{i,m} + w}, \qquad \sigma^2_{i,m+1} = \sigma^2_{i,m} + \frac{k_{i,m}w}{k_{i,m} + w}(x_i - \mu_{i,m})^2. \tag{2}$$

Note that $n_{i,m}$ and $k_{i,m}$ have the same update, so one value can be stored to cover both, for all i. Given the above parameters, updated with the available evidence, a Gaussian may be drawn, to sample the probability of a colour being drawn from this mixture component. Instead of drawing it the Gaussian is integrated out, to give

$$x_i \sim \mathcal{T}\left(n_{i,m}, \mu_{i,m}, \frac{k_{i,m}+1}{k_{i,m}n_{i,m}}\sigma^2_{i,m}\right), \tag{3}$$

where $\mathcal{T}(v, \mu, \sigma^2)$ denotes the three parameter student-t.

Background Probability: To calculate the probability of a pixel, $x \in [0,1]^3$, belonging to the background (bg) model the Chinese restaurant process is used. The probability of x given component (table) $t \in T$ is

$$P(x|t, \text{bg}) = \frac{s_t}{\sum_{i \in T} s_i} P(x|n_t, k_t, \mu_t, \sigma^2_t), \tag{4}$$

$$P(x|n_t, k_t, \mu_t, \sigma^2_t) = \prod_{i \in \{0,1,2\}} \mathcal{T}\left(x_i | n_{t,i}, \mu_{t,i}, \frac{k_{t,i}+1}{k_{t,i}n_{t,i}}\sigma^2_{t,i}\right), \tag{5}$$

where s_t is the number of samples assigned to component t, and n_t, μ_t, k_t and σ_t are the parameters of the prior updated with the samples currently assigned to the component. By assuming the existence of a dummy component, $t = \text{new} \in T$, that represents creating a new component (sitting at a new table) with $s_{\text{new}} = \alpha$ this is the Chinese restaurant process. The student-t parameters for this dummy component are the prior without update. Finally, the mixture components can be summed out

$$P(x|\text{bg}) = \sum_{t \in T} P(x|t, \text{bg}). \tag{6}$$

The goal is to calculate $P(\text{bg}|x)$, not $P(x|\text{bg})$, hence Bayes rule is applied,

$$P(\text{bg}|x) = \frac{P(x|\text{bg})P(z\text{bg})}{P(x|\text{bg}) + P(x|\text{fg})}, \tag{7}$$

noting that pixels can only belong to the background or the foreground (fg), hence the denominator. $P(x|\text{bg})$ is given above, leaving $P(\text{bg})$ and $P(x|\text{fg})$. $P(\text{bg})$ is an implicit threshold on what is considered background and what is considered foreground, and is hence considered to be a parameter[2]. $P(x|\text{fg})$ is unknown and hard to estimate, so the uniform distribution is used, which is a value of 1, as the volume of the colour space is 1 (See subsection 2.3).

[2] Though it is simply set to 0.5 for the majority of the experiments.

Model Update: To update the model at each pixel the current value is assigned to a mixture component, which is then updated - s_t is increased and the posterior for the Gaussian updated with the new evidence. Assignment is done probabilistically, using the term for each component from Equation 4, including the option of a new mixture component. This is equivalent to Gibbs sampling the density estimate, except we only sample each value once on arrival. Updates are weighted by their probability of belonging to the background (Equation 7). Sampling each value just once is not an issue, as the continuous stream of data means the model soon converges.

A learning rate, as found in methods such as Stauffer & Grimson [6], is not used; instead, unique to a DP-GMM, the confidence of the model is capped. This can be interpreted as an adaptive update [7,17], but it is both principled and very effective. In effect we are building a density estimate with the ability to selectively forget, allowing newer data to take over when the background changes. It works by capping how high s_t can go, noting that s_t is tied to n_t and k_t, so they also need to be adjusted. When this cap is exceeded a multiplier is applied to all s_t, scaling the highest s_t down to the cap. Note that σ_t^2 is dependent on k_t, as it includes k_t as a multiplier - to avoid an update σ_t^2/k_t is stored instead. The effectiveness is such that it can learn the initial model with less than a second of data yet objects can remain still for many minutes before being merged into the background, without this impeding the ability of the model to update as the background changes. Finally, given an infinite number of frames the number of mixture components goes to infinity, so the number is capped. When a new component is created the existing component with the lowest s_t is replaced.

2.2 Probabilistic Regularisation

The per-pixel background model ignores information from a pixels neighbourhood, leaving it susceptible to noise and camouflage. To resolve this a Markov random field is constructed, with a node for each pixel, connected using a 4-way neighbourhood. It is a binary labelling problem, where each pixel either belongs to the foreground or the background. The task is to select the most probable solution, where the probability can be broken up into two terms. Firstly, each pixel has a probability of belonging to the background or foreground, directly obtained from the model as $P(\text{bg}|x)$ and $1 - P(\text{bg}|x)$, respectively. Secondly, there is a similarity term, which indicates that adjacent pixels are likely to have the same assignment,

$$P(l_a = l_b) = \frac{h}{h + m * d(a,b)}, \tag{8}$$

where l_x is the label of pixel x, h is the half life, i.e. the distance at which the probability becomes 0.5 and $d(a,b)$ is the Euclidean distance between the two pixels. m is typically 1, but is decreased if a pixel is sufficiently far from its neighbours that none provides a $P(l(a) = l(b))$ value above a threshold. This encourages a pixel to have a similar label to its neighbours, which filters out noise. Various methods can be considered for solving this model. Graph cuts [24] would give the MAP solution, however we use belief propagation instead [20], as it runs in constant time given an iteration cap, which is important for a real time implementation; it is also more amenable to a GPU implementation.

2.3 Further Details

The core details have now been given, but other pertinent details remain.

The Prior: The background model includes a prior on the Gaussian associated with each mixture component. Instead of treating this as a parameter to be set it is calculated from the data. Specifically, the mean and standard deviation (SD) of the prior are matched with the mean and SD of the pixels in the current frame,

$$n_{i,0} = k_{i,0} = 1, \qquad \mu_{i,0} = \frac{1}{|F|}\sum_{x \in F} x_i, \qquad \sigma^2_{i,0} = \frac{1}{|F|}\sum_{x \in F}(x_i - \mu_{i,0})^2, \tag{9}$$

where F is the set of pixels in the current frame. To change the prior between frames the posterior parameters must not be stored directly. Instead offsets from the prior are stored, which are then adjusted after each update such that the model is equivalent. The purpose then is to update the distribution that mixture components return to as they lose influence, to keep that in line with the current lighting level.

Lighting Change: The above helps by updating the prior, but it does nothing to update the evidence. To update the evidence a multiplicative model is used, whereby the lighting change between frames is estimated as a multiplier, then the entire model is updated by multiplying the means, $\mu_{i,m}$, of the components accordingly. Light level change is estimated as in Loy et al. [25]. This takes every pixel in the frame and divides its value by the same pixel in the previous frame, as an estimate of the lighting change. The mode of these estimates is then found using mean shift [26], which is robust to the many outliers.

Colour Model: A simple method for filtering out shadows is to separate the luminance and chromaticity, and then ignore the luminance, as demonstrated by Elgammal et al. [8]. This tends to ignore too much information; instead the novel step is taken of reducing the importance of luminance. In doing so luminance is moved to a separate channel; due to the DE assuming independence between components this is advantageous, as luminance variation tends to be higher than chromatic variation. To do this a parametrised colour model is designed. First the r, g, b colour space is rotated so luminance is on its own axis

$$\begin{pmatrix} l \\ m \\ n \end{pmatrix} = \begin{pmatrix} \sqrt{3} & \sqrt{3} & \sqrt{3} \\ 0 & \sqrt{2} & -\sqrt{2} \\ -2\sqrt{6} & \sqrt{6} & \sqrt{6} \end{pmatrix} \begin{pmatrix} r \\ g \\ b \end{pmatrix}, \tag{10}$$

then chromaticity is extracted

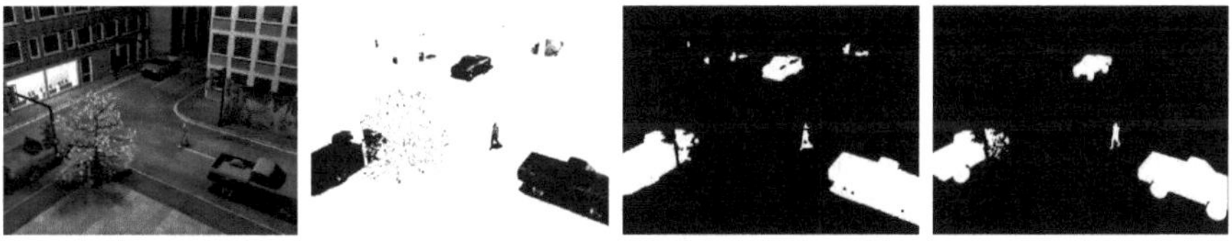

(a) Input video frame. (b) $P(\text{bg}|\text{model})$ - output of the DP-GMM for each pixel. (c) Foreground mask generated by the presented approach. (d) Ground truth foreground mask.

Fig. 2. Frame 545 from the bootstrap sequence

Table 1. Brief summaries of all the algorithms compared against

Barnich [10]	KDE with a spherical kernel. Uses a stochastic history.
Collins [27]	Hybrid frame differencing / background model.
Culibrk [28]	Neural network variant of Gaussian KDE.
Kim [18]	'Codebook' based; almost KDE with a cuboid kernel.
Li 1 [11]	Histogram based, includes co-occurrence statistics. Lots of heuristics.
Li 2 [29]	Refinement of the above.
Maddalena [12]	Uses a self organising map, passes information between pixels.
Stauffer [6]	Classic GMM approach. Assigns mixture components to bg/fg.
Toyama [1]	History based, with region growing. Has explicit light switch detection.
Wren [30]	Incremental spatio-colourmetric clustering (tracking) with change detection.
Zivkovic [7]	Refinement of Stauffer [6]. Has an adaptive learning rate.

$$l' = 0.7176\, l, \qquad \begin{pmatrix} m' \\ n' \end{pmatrix} = \frac{0.7176}{\max(l, f)} \begin{pmatrix} m \\ n \end{pmatrix}, \tag{11}$$

where 0.7176 is the constant required to maintain a unit colour space volume[3]. To obtain chromaticity the division should be by l rather than $\max(l, f)$, but this results in a divide by zero. Assuming the existence of noise when measuring r, g, b the division by l means the variance of m' and n' is proportional to $\frac{1}{l^2}$. To limit variance as well as extract chromaticity, we have two competing goals - the use of $\max(l, f)$ introduces f, a threshold on luminance below which capping variance takes priority. Given this colour space it is then parametrised by r, which scales the luminance to reduce its importance against chromaticity

$$[l, m, n]_r = [r^{\frac{2}{3}} l', r^{-\frac{1}{3}} m', r^{-\frac{1}{3}} n']. \tag{12}$$

The volume of the colour space has again been held at 1. Robustness to shadows is obtained by setting r to a low value, as this reduces the importance of brightness changes.

3 Experiments

Three sets of results are demonstrated - the synthetic test of Brutzer et al. [2] and two real world tests - *wallflower* from Toyama et al. [1] and *star* from Li et al. [29].

---

[3] The post processor assumes a uniform distribution over colour, and hence needs to know the volume. Note that this constant does not account for f, but then it makes very little difference to the volume.

Table 2. Synthetic experimental results - f-measures for each of the 9 challenges. The results for other algorithms were obtained from the website associated with Brutzer et al. [2], though algorithms that never got a top score in the original chart have been omitted. The numbers in brackets indicate which is the best, second best etc. The mean column gives the average for all tests - the presented approach is 27% higher than its nearest competitor.

method	basic	dynamic background	bootstrap	darkening	light switch	noisy night	camouflage	no camouflage	h.264, 40kbps	*mean*
Stauffer [6]	.800 (3)	.704 (5)	.642 (5)	.404 (7)	.217 (6)	.194 (6)	.802 (4)	.826 (4)	.761 (6)	.594 (7)
Li 1 [11]	.766 (5)	.641 (6)	.678 (4)	.704 (3)	.316 (3)	.047 (7)	.768 (6)	.803 (6)	.773 (4)	.611 (5)
Zivkovic [7]	.768 (4)	.704 (5)	.632 (6)	.620 (6)	.300 (4)	.321 (3)	.820 (3)	.829 (3)	.748 (7)	.638 (3)
Maddalena [12]	.766 (5)	.715 (3)	.495 (7)	.663 (5)	.213 (7)	.263 (5)	.793 (5)	.811 (5)	.772 (5)	.610 (6)
Barnich [10]	.761 (6)	.711 (4)	.685 (3)	.678 (4)	.268 (5)	.271 (4)	.741 (7)	.799 (7)	.774 (3)	.632 (4)
DP, no post	.836 (2)	.827 (2)	.717 (2)	.736 (2)	.499 (2)	.346 (2)	.848 (2)	.851 (2)	.781 (2)	.715 (2)
DP	**.853** (1)	**.853** (1)	**.796** (1)	**.861** (1)	**.603** (1)	**.788** (1)	**.864** (1)	**.867** (1)	**.827** (1)	**.812** (1)
DP, con com	.855	.872	.722	.818	.500	.393	.847	.851	.838	.744
DP, rgb	.850	.859	.783	.807	.445	.334	.852	.857	.848	.737

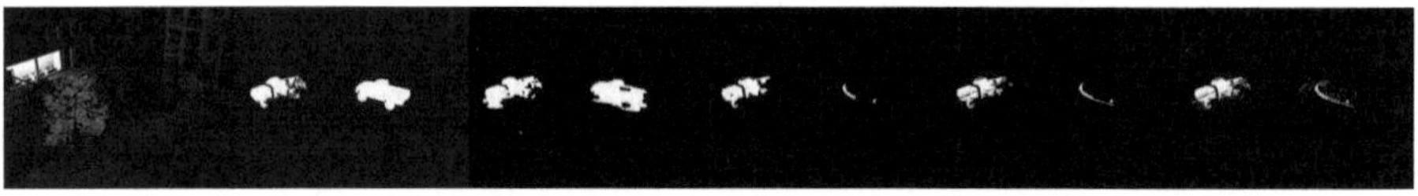

(a) Input (b) Ground truth (c) DP (d) DP, rgb (e) DP, con com (f) DP, no post

Fig. 3. Frame 990 from the noisy night sequence

Brutzer et al. [2] introduced a synthetic evaluation procedure for background subtraction algorithms, consisting of a 3D rendering of a junction, traversed by both cars and people - see Figure 2. Despite being synthetic it simulates, fairly accurately, 9 real world problems, and has the advantage of ground truth for all frames. The f-measure is reported for the various approaches in Table 2, and is defined as the harmonic mean of the recall and precision. Table 1 summarises all the algorithms compared against during all the experiments. For this test we used one set of parameters for all problems, rather than tuning per problem[4]. As can be seen, the presented approach takes the top position for all scenarios, being on average 27% better than its nearest competitor, and in doing so demonstrates that it is not sensitive to the parameters chosen. The algorithm without regularisation is also included in the chart[5] - in all cases a lack of regularisation does not undermine its significant lead over the competition, demonstrating that the DP-GMM is doing most of the work, but that regularisation always improves the score, on average by 13%. It can be noted that the largest performance gaps between regularisation being off and being on appears for the nosiest inputs, e.g. noisy night, light switch, darkening and h264. These are the kinds of problems encountered in surveillance applications. As a further point of comparison *DP, con com* is included, where the post-processing has been swapped for the connected components method of Stauffer & Grimson [6]. Interestingly for the simpler problems it does very well, sometimes better than the presented method,

[4] The original paper tuned one parameter per problem - we are at a disadvantage.

[5] The other algorithms on the chart have had their post-processing removed, so it can be argued that this is the fairer comparison to make, though Brutzer et al. [2] define post-processing such that our regularisation method is allowed.

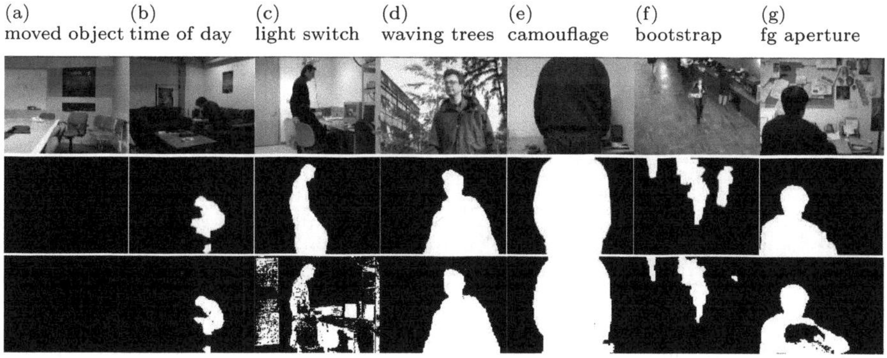

Fig. 4. Results for the *wallflower* dataset - on the top row is the image, on the second row the ground truth and on the third row the output of the presented algorithm. Toyama et al. [1] provide the outputs for other algorithms.

Table 3. Results for the *wallflower* dataset [1], given as the number of pixels that have been assigned the wrong class. Again, weaker algorithms have been culled from the original, though the positions continue to account for the missing methods. On average the presented approach makes 33% less mistakes than its nearest competitor.

method	moved object	time of day	light switch	waving trees	camouflage	bootstrap	foreground aperture	*mean*
Frame difference	**0** (1)	1358 (12)	2565 (3)	6789 (16)	10070 (12)	2175 (4)	4354 (9)	3902 (8)
Mean + threshold	**0** (1)	2593 (15)	16232 (11)	3285 (13)	1832 (3)	3236 (9)	2818 (5)	4285 (9)
Mixture of Gaussians	**0** (1)	1028 (10)	15802 (8)	1664 (8)	3496 (6)	2091 (3)	2972 (6)	3865 (7)
Block correlation	1200 (11)	1165 (11)	3802 (4)	3771 (15)	6670 (11)	2673 (8)	2402 (4)	3098 (5)
Eigen-background	1065 (10)	895 (7)	1324 (2)	3084 (12)	1898 (4)	6433 (11)	2978 (7)	2525 (3)
Toyama [1]	**0** (1)	986 (8)	**1322** (1)	2876 (11)	2935 (5)	2390 (6)	**969** (1)	1640 (2)
Maddalena [12]		453 (2)		293 (3)				
Wren [30]		654 (6)		298 (4)				
Collins [27]		653 (5)		430 (6)				
Kim [18]		492 (3)		353 (5)				
DP	**0** (1)	596 (4)	15071 (6)	265 (2)	1735 (2)	1497 (2)	1673 (3)	2977 (4)
DP, tuned	**0** (1)	**330** (1)	3945 (5)	**184** (1)	**384** (1)	**1236** (1)	1569 (2)	**1093** (1)

but when it comes to the trickier scenarios the presented is clearly better. To justify the use of the parametrised colour model *DP, rgb* shows the full model run using *rgb* instead of ours. The consequences are similar to those for connected components. Figure 3 shows all the variants for a frame from noisy night. It can be observed that the main advantage of the presented post processor is its ability to go from a weak detection that falls below the implicit threshold to a complete object, using both the colour and model uncertainty of the moving object.

The frame shown in Figure 2 has been chosen to demonstrate two weaknesses with the algorithm. Specifically, its robustness to shadows is not very effective - whilst this can be improved by reducing the importance of luminance in the colour space this has the effect of reducing its overall ability to distinguish between colours, and damages performance elsewhere. The second issue can be seen in the small blobs at the top of the image - they are actually the reflections of objects in the scene. Using a DP-GMM allows it to learn a very precise model,

(a) cam (b) ft (c) ws (d) mr (e) lb (f) sc (g) ap (h) br (i) ss

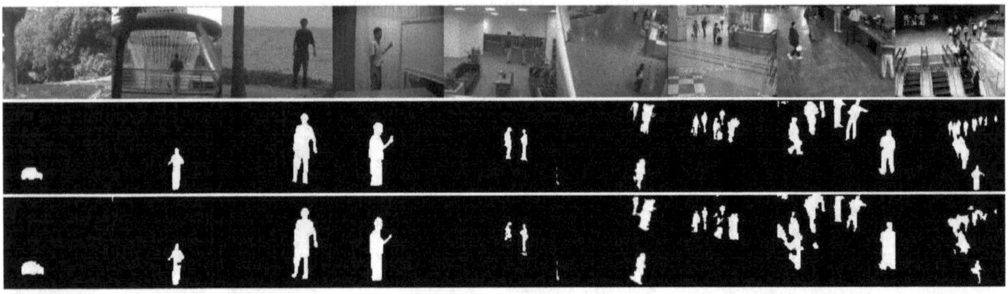

Fig. 5. Results for the *star* dataset - with the same frames as Culibrk et al. [28] and Maddalena & Petrosino [12], for a qualitative comparison. Layout is identical to Figure 4. The videos are named using abbreviations of their locations.

Table 4. Results for the *star* dataset [29,12]; refer to Figure 5 for exemplar frames, noting that *lb* has abrupt lighting changes. The average improvement of *DP, tuned* over its nearest competitor is 4%.

method	cam	ft	ws	mr	lb	sc	ap	br	ss	*mean*
Li 2 [29]	.1596 (5)	.0999 (6)	.0667 (6)	.1841 (6)	.1554 (6)	.5209 (6)	.1135 (6)	.3079 (6)	.1294 (6)	.1930 (6)
Stauffer [6]	.0757 (6)	.6854 (3)	.7948 (4)	.7580 (4)	.6519 (2)	.5363 (5)	.3335 (5)	.3838 (5)	.1388 (5)	.4842 (5)
Culibrk [28]	.5256 (4)	.4636 (5)	.7540 (5)	.7368 (5)	.6276 (4)	.5696 (4)	.3923 (4)	.4779 (4)	.4928 (4)	.5600 (4)
Maddalena [12]	.6960 (3)	.6554 (4)	.8247 (3)	.8178 (3)	.6489 (3)	.6677 (2)	**.5943** (1)	.6019 (3)	**.5770** (1)	.6760 (2)
DP	.7567 (2)	.7049 (2)	.9090 (2)	.8203 (2)	.5794 (5)	.6522 (3)	.5484 (3)	.6024 (2)	.5055 (3)	.6754 (3)
DP, tuned	**.7624** (1)	**.7265** (1)	**.9134** (1)	**.8371** (1)	**.6665** (1)	**.6721** (1)	.5663 (2)	**.6273** (1)	.5269 (2)	**.6998** (1)

so much so that it can detect the slight deviation caused by a reflection, when it would be preferable to ignore it. Further processing could avoid this.

Despite its low resolution (160×120) the *wallflower* [1] data set is one of the few real world options for background subtraction testing. It tests one frame only for each problem, by counting the number of mistakes made[6]; testing on a single frame is hardly ideal. There are seven tests, given in Figure 4 for a qualitative evaluation. Quantitative results are given in Table 3. Previously published results have been tuned for each problem, so we do the same in the *DP, tuned* row, but results using a single set of parameters are again shown, in the *DP* row, to demonstrate its high degree of robustness to parameter selection. For 5 of the 7 tests the method takes 1st, albeit shared for the moved object problem.

On foreground aperture it takes 2nd, beaten by the Toyama [1] algorithm. This shot consists of a sleeping person waking up, at which point they are expected to transition from background to foreground. They are wearing black and do not entirely move from their resting spot, so the algorithm continues to think they are background in that area. The regularisation helps to shrink this spot, but the area remains. It fails with the light switch test, which is interesting as no issue occurs with the synthetic equivalent. For the presented approach lighting correction consists of estimating a single multiplicative constant - this works outdoors where it is a reasonable model of the sun, but indoors where light bounces around and has

[6] For the purpose of comparison the error metrics used by previous papers [1] have been used.

a highly non-linear effect on the scene it fails. It is therefore not surprising that the synthetic approach, which simulates a sun, works, whilst the indoor approach, which includes light coming through a door and the glow from a computer monitor, fails. Examining the output in Figure 4 it can be noted that it has not failed entirely - the test frame is only the 13th frame after the light has been switched on, and the algorithm is still updating its model after the change.

Finally, the *star* evaluation [29] is presented, which is very similar to the *wallflower* set - a video sequence is shared. The sequences are generally much harder though, due to text overlays, systemic noise and some camera shake, and fewer algorithms have been run on this set. It has a better testing procedure, as it provides multiple test frames per problem, with performance measured using the average similarity score for all test frames, where similarity $= \text{tp}/(\text{tp} + \text{fn} + \text{fp})$. The presented approach[7] takes 1st 7 times out of 9, beaten twice by Maddalena et al. [12]. Its two weak results can probably be attributed to camera shake, as the presented has no robustness to shaking, whilst Maddalena et al. [12] does, due to model sharing between adjacent pixels. The light switch test in this data set does not trip it up this time - the library where it occurs has a high ceiling and diffuse lighting, making multiplicative lighting much more reasonable. Complex dynamic backgrounds clearly demonstrate the strength of a DP-GMM, as evidenced by its 3 largest improvements (*cam*, *ft* and *ws*).

Using a DP-GMM is computationally demanding - the implementation obtains 25 frames per second with 160×120, and is $O(n)$ where $n = wh$ is the number of pixels[8]. This is not a major concern, as real time performance on high resolution input could be obtained using a massively parallel GPU implementation. Indeed, an incomplete effort at this has already increased the speed by a factor of 5, making 320×240 real time.

4 Conclusions

This work represents the cutting edge background subtraction method[9]. It takes the basic concept of the seminal work of Stauffer & Grimson [6] and applies up to date methods in a mathematically rigorous way. The key advantage is in using DP-GMMs, which handle new mixture components forming as more information becomes available, and build highly discriminative models. Using a confidence cap handles the dynamics of a scene much better than a heuristic approach to model updates. Despite its thorough theoretical basis implementation remains relatively simple[10]. Certain improvements can be considered. Combining information between pixels only as a regularisation step does not fully exploit the information available, and so a rigorous method of spatial information

---

[7] As for *wallflower* we tune per-problem, as the competition has done the same; results for a single set of parameters are again presented.

[8] Run on a single core of an Intel i7 2.67Ghz.

[9] Code is available from `http://www.thaines.com`

[10] 186 lines of C for the DP model and 239 lines for the post-processing.

transmission would be desirable. This would be particularly helpful when handling mild camera shake. Sudden complex lighting changes are not handled, which means it fails to handle some indoor lighting changes.

References

1. Toyama, K., Krumm, J., Brumitt, B., Meyers, B.: Wallflower: Principles and practise of background maintenance. In: ICCV, pp. 255–261 (1999)
2. Brutzer, S., Hferlin, B., Heidemann, G.: Evaluation of background subtraction techniques for video surveillance. In: CVPR (2011)
3. Cheung, S.C.S., Kamath, C.: Robust techniques for background subtraction in urban traffic video. In: VCIP, vol. 5308, pp. 881–892 (2004)
4. Karaman, M., Goldmann, L., Yu, D., Sikora, T.: Comparison of static background segmentation methods. In: VCIP, vol. 5960, pp. 2140–2151 (2005)
5. Herrero, S., Bescós, J.: Background Subtraction Techniques: Systematic Evaluation and Comparative Analysis. In: Blanc-Talon, J., Philips, W., Popescu, D., Scheunders, P. (eds.) ACIVS 2009. LNCS, vol. 5807, pp. 33–42. Springer, Heidelberg (2009)
6. Stauffer, C., Grimson, W.E.L.: Adaptive background mixture models for real-time tracking. In: CVPR, vol. 2, pp. 637–663 (1999)
7. Zivkovica, Z., Heijden, F.: Efficient adaptive density estimation per image pixel for the task of background subtraction. Pattern Recognition Letters, 773–780 (2006)
8. Elgammal, A., Harwood, D., Davis, L.: Non-parametric model for background subtraction. In: Frame-rate Workshop, pp. 751–767 (2000)
9. Sheikh, Y., Shah, M.: Bayesian modeling of dynamic scenes for object detection. PAMI 27(11), 1778–1792 (2005)
10. Barnich, O., Droogenbroeck, M.V.: Vibe: A powerful random technique to estimate the background in video sequences. In: Acoustics, Speech and Signal Processing, pp. 945–948 (2009)
11. Li, L., Huang, W., Gu, I.Y.H., Tian, Q.: Foreground object detection from videos containing complex background. In: Proc. Multimedia, pp. 2–10 (2003)
12. Maddalena, L., Petrosino, A.: A self-organizing approach to background subtraction for visual surveillance applications. IEEE Tran. IP 17(7), 1168–1177 (2008)
13. Kato, J., Watanabe, T., Joga, S., Rittscher, J., Blake, A.: An hmm-based segmentation method for traffic monitoring movies. PAMI 24(9), 1291–1296 (2002)
14. Escobar, M.D., West, M.: Bayesian density estimation and inference using mixtures. J. American Statistical Association 90(430), 577–588 (1995)
15. Teh, Y.W., Jordan, M.I.: Hierarchical Bayesian Nonparametric Models with Applications. In: Bayesian Nonparametrics. Cambridge University Press (2010)
16. He, Y., Wang, D., Zhu, M.: Background subtraction based on nonparametric bayesian estimation. In: Int. Conf. Digital Image Processing (2011)
17. Lee, D.S.: Effective gaussian mixture learning for video background subtraction. PAMI 27(5), 827–832 (2005)
18. Kim, K., Chalidabhongse, T.H., Harwood, D., Davis, L.: Background modeling and subtraction by codebook construction. In: ICIP, vol. 5, pp. 3061–3064 (2004)
19. Migdal, J., Grimson, W.E.L.: Background subtraction using markov thresholds. In: Workshop on Motion and Video Computing, pp. 58–65 (2005)
20. Felzenszwalb, P.F., Huttenlocher, D.P.: Efficient belief propagation for early vision. In: CVPR, vol. 70(1), pp. 41–54 (2004)

21. Cohen, S.: Background estimation as a labeling problem. In: ICCV, pp. 1034–1041 (2005)
22. Blei, D.M., Jordan, M.I.: Variational inference for dirichlet process mixtures. Bayesian Analysis, 121–144 (2005)
23. Gelman, A., Carlin, J.B., Stern, H.S., Rubin, D.B.: Bayesian Data Analysis. Chapman & Hall (2004)
24. Boykov, Y., Veksler, O., Zabih, R.: Fast approximate energy minimization via graph cuts. PAMI 23, 1222–1239 (2001)
25. Loy, C.C., Xiang, T., Gong, S.: Time-delayed correlation analysis for multi-camera activity understanding. IJCV 90(1), 106–129 (2010)
26. Comaniciu, D., Meer, P.: Mean shift: A robust approach toward feature space analysis. PAMI 24(5), 603–619 (2002)
27. Collins, R.T., Lipton, A.J., Kanade, T., Fujiyoshi, H., Duggins, D., Tsin, Y., Tolliver, D., Enomoto, N., Hasegawa, O., Burt, P., Wixson, L.: A system for video surveillance and monitoring. Technical report, CMU (2000)
28. Culibrk, D., Marques, O., Socek, D., Kalva, H., Furht, B.: Neural network approach to background modeling for video object segmentation. Neural Networks 18(6), 1614–1627 (2007)
29. Li, L., Huang, W., Gu, I.Y.H., Tian, Q.: Statistical modeling of complex backgrounds for foreground object detection. IEEE Tran. IP 13(11), 1459–1472 (2004)
30. Wren, C.R., Azarbayejani, A., Darrell, T., Pentland, A.P.: Pfinder: Real-time tracking of the human body. PAMI 19(7), 780–785 (1997)

Mobile Product Image Search by Automatic Query Object Extraction

Xiaohui Shen[1], Zhe Lin[2], Jonathan Brandt[2], and Ying Wu[1]

[1] Northwestern University, Evanston, IL 60208, USA
{xsh835,yingwu}@eecs.northwestern.edu
[2] Advanced Technology Labs, Adobe, San Jose, CA 95110, USA
{zlin,jbrandt}@adobe.com

Abstract. Mobile product image search aims at identifying a product, or retrieving similar products from a database based on a photo captured from a mobile phone camera. Application of traditional image retrieval methods (e.g. bag-of-words) to mobile visual search has been shown to be effective in identifying duplicate/near-duplicate photos, near-planar and textured objects such as landmarks, books/cd covers. However, retrieving more general product categories is still a challenging research problem due to variations in viewpoint, illumination, scale, the existence of blur and background clutter in the query image, etc. In this paper, we propose a new approach that can simultaneously extract the product instance from the query, identify the instance, and retrieve visually similar product images. Based on the observation that good query segmentation helps improve retrieval accuracy and good search results provide good priors for segmentation, we formulate our approach in an iterative scheme to improve both query segmentation and retrieval accuracy. To this end, a weighted object mask voting algorithm is proposed based on a spatially-constrained model, which allows robust localization and segmentation of the query object, and achieves significantly better retrieval accuracy than previous methods. We show the effectiveness of our approach by applying it to a large, real-world product image dataset and a new object category dataset.

1 Introduction

Mobile product image search has recently become an interesting research topic due to the unprecedented development of smart phones and applications along with the increasing popularity of online shopping. In an ideal scenario, a user can simply take a picture of a product using a mobile phone to promptly identify the product and/or retrieve visually similar products from the database.

Traditional image retrieval methods typically adopt the bag-of-words model initially introduced in [1]. In this model, local features such as SIFT [2] are extracted from the query image and assigned to their closest visual words in a visual vocabulary. The query image is accordingly represented by a global histogram of visual words, and matched with database images by *tf-idf* weighting using inverted files[3,4].

A. Fitzgibbon et al. (Eds.): ECCV 2012, Part IV, LNCS 7575, pp. 114–127, 2012.

(a) Examples of database images, with aligned products and clean background.

(b) Examples of query images taken by mobile phones, with different backgrounds, viewpoint and illumination.

Fig. 1. Examples of database images and query images in mobile product image search

The bag-of-words model works well for retrieving duplicate/near-duplicate images and near-planar/highly-textured objects. However, its performance is generally poor when directly applied to mobile product image search. The mobile product image search problem has the following distinct characteristics compared to general image search:

1. The products in the database images are mostly well aligned and captured in studio environments with controlled lighting. The background is often clean, and the texture details are clear. See Fig. 1(a) for an example.
2. Mobile query images are usually taken under very different lighting conditions with cluttered background. There may exist large viewpoint variations between the query and database images. Moreover, motion blur and out-of-focus blur are very common in images captured by mobile phones. Fig. 1(b) shows some examples of mobile query images.
3. Product instances are often non-planar (e.g. shoes) and/or less textured (e.g. clothes), hence the standard RANSAC-based verification can easily fail.
4. Some product instances (e.g. shoes) are visually very similar to each other, and only a small portion of visual features can discriminate them, so we need a fine-grained discrimination strategy for correct identification.

As a result, when we use the bag-of-words model to perform mobile product image search, the results may be largely affected by the features extracted from the background of the query images. Even when we specify the location of the product in the query image, the features around the occluding boundaries of the product may still be largely different from those extracted from clean background. One can segment the query object by manual labeling. However, simple labeling (e.g., specifying the object by a bounding rectangle, as in [5]) does not necessarily guarantee accurate segmentation results, while extensive and careful labeling largely increases the burden for the users.

To this end, in this paper, a new approach is proposed to simultaneously retrieve visually similar product images, and localize/identify the product instance in the query image. In our approach, each retrieved database image predicts a location and an outline shape (or mask) for the query object. The center location and the support region of the query object can then be inferred by a weighted object mask voting and aggregation scheme while removing the outliers. Based on that, the query object is automatically segmented and filled with clean background, which is used to refine the search results in the next round. Since better search results yield better query object extraction, and vice versa, the above two procedures are performed in an iterative and interleaved way, hence forming a closed-loop adaptation between query object extraction and object retrieval.

We collected two datasets for experimental validation: a large, real-world product image database for identical object retrieval, and a new object category dataset sampled from Caltech256 [6] for object category retrieval[1]. Experimental results on these two datasets show that our automatic query extraction yields even better results than manual segmentation with a bounding rectangle as initialization in retrieval accuracy, while our iterative approach significantly outperforms previous methods.

2 Related Work

Previous image retrieval research mostly focuses on duplicate image, or near-planar and textured object retrieval with applications to web image search and personal photo management. The standard bag-of-words model [1] is heavily explored for these tasks, and many of its variations are introduced to further improve the performance. They either encode spatial information[4,7,8,9,10], use better feature quantization[11,12,13,14], or better vocabularies [15] to refine the search results. Query expansion [16,17] is a common post-processing technique to increase the recall while improving the retrieval precision.

While general image search has been well-studied, research efforts devoted to mobile product image search are still limited. Some search engines for product images have recently been developed [18,19,20]. However, in these works, the query images are very similar to the database images (i.e., captured in the same settings). Google Goggles[2] and Amazon Flow[3] are well-known commercial mobile product image search engines, but are working robustly only for a few near-planar, textured object categories such as logos/trademarks, books/CD covers, landmarks, artworks, text, etc. In [21], a new database for mobile visual search is proposed, in which the objects are still limited to planar categories such as books and CD covers. Retrieving more general object categories (either severely non-planar, non-rigid, or less-textured objects) from mobile phones is still an open research question, and a search engine specifically designed for mobile product image search for more challenging object categories is highly demanded.

---

[1] We will make both of our datasets publicly available

[2] `www.google.com/mobile/goggles/`

[3] `http://flow.a9.com`

On the other hand, object segmentation [22] is integrated with other vision problems such as object detection, categorization and recognition. Reference images are used in [23,24] to perform co-segmentation. In [25,26], poselet and image contours are aggregated to segment the object. [27,28] propose simultaneous object detection and segmentation, while [29,30] introduce algorithms for concurrent object recognition and segmentation. However, they all assume the example images are of known category labels, and/or are not addressed in the context of image retrieval where the database consists of thousands to millions of unlabeled images. In the context of image retrieval, some approaches have been proposed to localize the object in the database images, either by sub-image search [31,7] or by generalized Hough voting [10]. However, to the best of our knowledge, there is no previous work to simultaneously localize, identify and automatically segment the object from the query image during large-scale search. In [17], the failure cases in query expansion are automatically recovered by removing background confusers from the top retrieval results, but the method assumes the confuser textures coexist in many database images, which is not valid in our case; also, no clear object boundary can be easily obtained using their method, which is critical for mobile product image search.

3 Formulation

In this section, we present our simultaneous query object extraction and retrieval algorithm. The query object location and its support map is estimated by aggregating votes from the top-retrieved database images. The estimated object support map is then used to generate a trimap for GrabCut [22], by which the query object is segmented.

3.1 Query Object Localization from Database Images

In [10], a spatially-constrained similarity measure is proposed to simultaneously retrieve and localize the objects in the database images, in which the object in the query image is manually specified by a bounding rectangle. In this paper, we propose that when the object location, scale and/or pose in the query image is unknown, the similarity measure can be further extended to localize the query object with the help of the top-retrieved database images. Robust query object localization serves as a good prior for segmentation, and good object segmentation allows more accurate retrieval by using the spatially constrained model and reducing the influence of background clutter.

Our retrieval framework falls under the category of approaches using local feature, visual vocabulary and inverted file. We denote the query image by Q and a database image by D, respectively. Let $\{f_1, f_2, \cdots, f_m\}$ be the local features extracted from Q, and $\{g_1, g_2, \cdots, g_n\}$ be the local features extracted from D. In order to encode relative feature locations in the image similarity, we use the spatially-constrained similarity measure defined in [10]:

$$S(Q,D|\mathbf{T}) = \sum_{k=1}^{N} \sum_{\substack{(f_i,g_j) \\ f_i \in Q, g_j \in D \\ w(f_i)=w(g_j)=k \\ ||\mathbf{T}(L(f_i))-L(g_j)||<\varepsilon}} \frac{\mathrm{idf}^2(k)}{\mathrm{tf}_Q(k)\cdot \mathrm{tf}_D(k)} \tag{1}$$

where k denotes the k-th visual word in the vocabulary. $w(f_i) = w(g_j) = k$ means that f_i and g_j are both assigned to visual word k. $\mathrm{idf}(k)$ is the inverse document frequency of k, $\mathrm{tf}_Q(k)$ and $\mathrm{tf}_D(k)$ are the term frequencies (i.e., number of occurrence) of k in Q and D respectively. $L(f) = (x_f, y_f)$ is the 2D image location of f. The spatial constraint $||\mathbf{T}(L(f_i)) - L(g_j)|| < \varepsilon$ means that the locations of two matched features should be sufficiently close under a certain transformation[4]. Therefore, all the matched feature pairs that violate that transformation would be filtered out.

The approximate optimal transformation $\mathbf{T}^*$ (maximizing the score in Eqn. 1) between Q and D is obtained by generalized Hough voting[10], while the database images are simultaneously ranked by the maximum scores in Eqn. 1.

Similar to [10], we use the generalized Hough voting algorithm to localize the object in the query. The spatial constraint $||\mathbf{T}(L(f_i)) - L(g_j)|| < \varepsilon$ is equivalent to $||(L(f_i)) - \mathbf{T}^{-1}(L(g_j))|| < \varepsilon$. To localize the object in the query image, we need to first find the optimal $\mathbf{T}^{*-1}$. We decompose $\mathbf{T}^{-1}$ to rotation angle, scale factor and translation. For simplicity of illustration, we ignore the rotation angle in the following description. The scale factor is uniformly quantized to 4 bins in the range of 1/2 and 2, and a voting map indicating the probability of the object support pixels is generated for each of the quantized scale factors.

Our object extraction process is illustrated in Fig. 2. Suppose that $w(f_i) = w(g_i)$ in Fig. 2(a) and (b). We assume that the product objects in the database images are mostly around the image center. Therefore, the image center is also considered as the object center c in D. Since $w(f_i) = w(g_i)$, given a certain scale factor s, if (f_i, g_i) obeys the transformation $\mathbf{T}^{-1}$, the object center in Q would be $L(f_i) + s \cdot \overrightarrow{L(g_i)c}$, where $\overrightarrow{L(g_i)c}$ denotes the vector from $L(g_i)$ to c in D. Therefore, we cast a vote for each matched feature pair on the corresponding center location in Q, with voting score $\frac{\mathrm{idf}^2(k)}{\mathrm{tf}_Q(k)\cdot \mathrm{tf}_D(k)}$. If all the (f_i, g_i) pairs obey the same transformation, the voted object center would be very consistent, see $(f_i, g_i)(i = 1, 2, 3)$ for examples. On the contrary, if a feature pair is not spatially consistent with others, it will vote for a different location ((f_4, g_4) and (f_5, g_5)). After voting from all matched feature pairs, we choose the location with the maximum score as the best estimated object center in Q. It is straightforward to verify that the maximum score at the estimated location is exactly the similarity measure defined in Eqn. 1 given the pre-quantized scale factor s. To choose the

[4] We only consider scale change and translation for simplicity of illustration, but rotation can be easily handled by max pooling on retrieval scores of multiple rotated versions of the query as in [10].

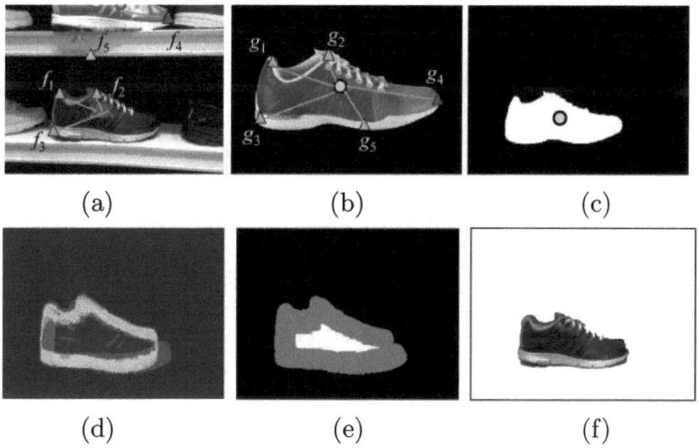

Fig. 2. Illustration of query object localization and extraction. (a) query image Q, (b) database image D, (c) voted mask of D on the object support map of Q, (d) query object support map by aggregating the voted masks of the top retrieved database images, (e) generated trimap based on the support map, (f) segmentation result using GrabCut with the trimap in (e).

best scale factor, we only need to select the scale corresponding to the voting map which generates the largest maximum score.

Based on the above process, each D has a prediction of the object location in the query image, which can be characterized by a vector $[x_c, y_c, s]^T$, where, (x_c, y_c) is the location of the object center in the query, and s is the relative scale factor between the query object compared with the object in D.

3.2 Query Object Extraction and Retrieval

In product image search, the database images mostly have clean background. The background color can be easily identified by finding the peak of the color histogram built upon the entire image, and the mask of the object can be accordingly obtained by comparing with the background color. Once we have the mask of the object in D as well as the estimated object location $[x_c, y_c, s]^T$, a transformed object mask can be voted at the estimated query location (x_c, y_c) with scale factor s, see Fig. 2(c) for example.

However, not all the top retrieved images can correctly localize the query object, especially when irrelevant objects are retrieved. Therefore, the outliers need to be excluded. Although sophisticated outlier removal methods such as spatial verification using RANSAC can be adopted here, the computational cost of these methods is typically high, and RANSAC does not handle non-planar, non-rigid, and less textured objects very well. Therefore, we only use their location predictions $[x_c, y_c, s]^T$ to effectively remove the outliers.

Consider that top N retrieved images are used to localize the query object, we get N location predictions $[x_c^i, y_c^i, s^i]^T (i = 1 \cdots N)$. Let $[\bar{x}_c, \bar{y}_c, \bar{s}]^T$ be the median values of all the predictions. For each $[x_c^i, y_c^i, s^i]^T$, if the squared distance

(a) (b) (c) (d) (e) (f) (g)

Fig. 3. Our query object localization method is robust to retrieved irrelevant objects. (a) Query images, (b)-(f) top 5 retrieved images, (g) voted object support maps.

$$D = (x_c^i - \bar{x}_c)^2 + (y_c^i - \bar{y}_c)^2 + \lambda(s^i - \bar{s})^2 > \tau \tag{2}$$

the corresponding database images will be removed from localization. In Eqn. 2 τ is a predefined threshold, and λ is a weight parameter.

We iterate this outlier removal and vote aggregation process multiple times to refine the object location, in which the median values $[\bar{x}_c, \bar{y}_c, \bar{s}]^T$ are updated after removing some outliers in each iteration. Once the outliers are removed, each inlier database image accumulates a mask at the estimated location with a weight. The weight can be determined as square root of the inverse of the rank, to assign more confidence on votes from higher ranked images. This process generates a soft map indicating the query object support region (Fig. 2(d)).

This algorithm is very simple, but can very effectively localize the object in the query image. See Fig. 3 for an example, even when irrelevant objects are retrieved, the location map can still accurately localize the object.

Once the object support map is generated, we use it to generate a trimap for GrabCut [22]. We first normalize the support map to a gray-scale image and perform dilation on the map. The pixels below a threshold (< 50) are set as background. Erosion is also performed, and the pixels above a high threshold (> 200) are set as foreground. All the other regions are labeled as uncertain. See Fig.2(e) for an example, the black regions represent the background, and the white and gray regions indicate the foreground and uncertain areas, respectively. In more challenging retrieval tasks (e.g., retrieving objects of the same semantic category but with large appearance changes, see Fig. 3), since shape information is not obvious in the estimated support map, to avoid false foreground labeling, only background and uncertain regions are labeled. Such a trimap is used as an input for GrabCut, and the final segmentation result is obtained as shown in Fig.2(f). Experimental results show that the overall segmentation results using our trimap are better than GrabCut with manual initialization.

We then extract the query object, fill the query image with a clean background and re-extract features from the new query image, in order to obtain better feature consistency across object boundaries, which are then used to perform search using Eqn. 1 in the next round. By reducing the background influence, the retrieval performance is dramatically improved. Therefore we can further use the refined search results to update the query object localization and segmentation.

(a) Examples of database images.

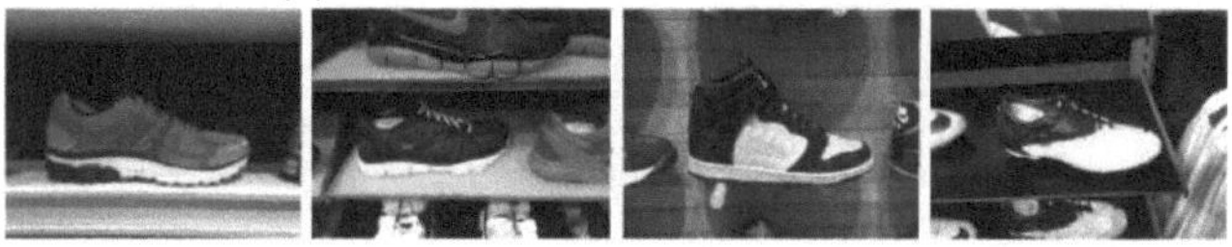

(a) Examples of query images.

Fig. 4. Example images in the sports product image dataset

By performing query object extraction and object search in an iterative way, the results of localization, segmentation and retrieval are simultaneously boosted. We stop the iteration when the difference between the segmentation masks of two consecutive iterations is smaller than a certain threshold. We found that in many cases, the differences of the segmented masks at the first two iteration steps are already small enough to stop the search. And most of the segmented results remain stable beyond the third iteration.

4 Experiments

We evaluated our method on two product image datasets, and compared it with the baseline bag-of-words retrieval method, the state-of-the-art spatial model as well as the query extraction method by GrabCut with manual initialization in terms of both segmentation and retrieval accuracy.

4.1 Datasets

We collected two datasets for product image search. The first one is a real-world sports product image (SPI) dataset, with 10 categories (hats, shirts, trousers, shoes, socks, gloves, balls, bags, neckerchief and bands) and 43953 catalog images. The objects in the database images are all well aligned, with clean background. See Fig. 4 for some examples. We also collected 67 query images captured with a mobile phone in local stores under various backgrounds, illumination and viewpoints. The objects in the query images are all shoes, and each has one exact same instance in the database, while there are totally 5925 catalog images in the shoe category. The task hence is to retrieve the same product from the database

(a) Examples of database images.

(a) Examples of query images.

Fig. 5. Example images in the object category search dataset

images. Cumulative Match Characteristic Curve (CMC) is used for performance evaluation, since it is equivalent to a 1:1 identification problem.

The second dataset is an object category search (OCS) dataset. Given a single query object, objects with the same semantic category need to be retrieved from the database. We collected 868 product images from Caltech 256 [6], in which the objects are positioned at the image center, with clean background. We also collected 60 query images for 6 categories from internet (each category has 10 queries). The query images contain background clutter, and the objects have large appearance differences, which makes it a very challenging task for object retrieval. See Fig. 5 for some examples. The number of relevant database images for the 6 categories ranges from 18 to 53. Average precision at rank k , i.e., the percentage of relevant images in the top-k retrieved images, is used to evaluate the performance on this dataset.

4.2 Results on the Sports Product Image Dataset

We use combined sparse and dense SIFT descriptors [2] as features[5] and hierarchical k-means clustering [3] to build the vocabulary. SIFT descriptors are computed with the "gravity" constraint [32]. The vocabulary on this dataset has 10580 visual words, which is used throughout all the experimental evaluations. Top 10 retrieved database images are used for query object localization.

We compared our method with the baseline bag-of-words method, and the spatially-constrained model with original query images [10]. We also manually segment the query object using GrabCut with a bounding rectangle as initialization, and then use the extracted object to perform search. Fig. 6(a) shows

[5] Sparse SIFT features are computed from DoG interest regions, and dense SIFT features are computed from a densely sampled regions in multiple scales across the image frame. Dense features are very useful for handling non-textured products.

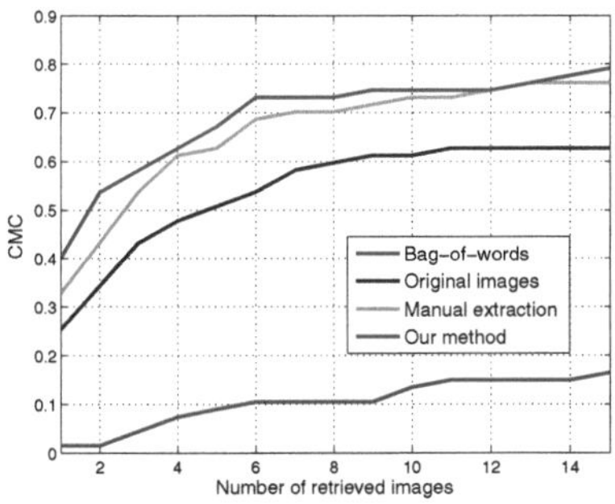

(a)

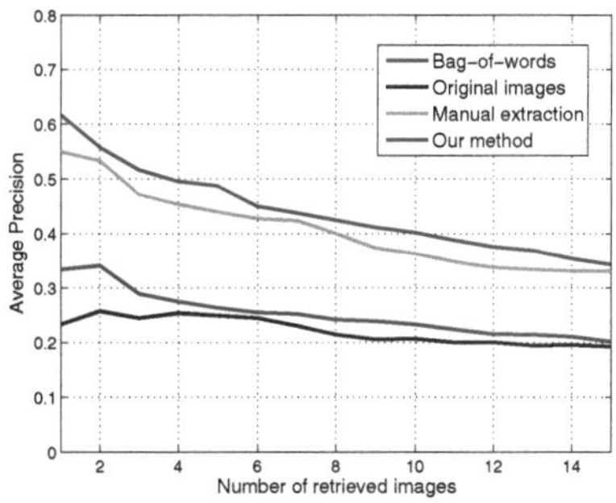

(b)

Fig. 6. Performance evaluation on the two mobile product image dataset. "Original Images" refers to the method in [10] using the original query image as a whole. (a)CMC curve on the sports product image dataset. Our method obtained significantly better performance than other methods. (b)Average precision at rank k on the object category search dataset. Our method consistently yields better precision.

the CMC for all the methods, in which the x-axis indicates the number of retrieved images k, and the y-axis indicates the probabilities that the correct catalog object appears in the top k retrieved images. It shows that the standard bag-of-words model cannot retrieve the correct object well for mobile product images. The spatially-constrained model removes some falsely matched features by more precise spatial matching, therefore largely improves the performance. However, it is still severely affected by the features extracted from the background and the object/background boundaries. Our method, by automatically extracting the query object, further improves the performance, and even outperforms the retrieve approach with manually initialized query object segmentation. In our method, 40% of the query images rank the correct catalog object at top 1, while the percentages for manual extraction and using original images are 32.8% and 25.3% respectively. When we consider the top 6 retrieved images, 73% of the query images have their correct catalog object ranked in top 6 with our method. The CMC curve only shows the results for top 15, as images with low ranks are far less important in most applications. There are still 20% of queries that cannot retrieve their relevant images in the top 15. This is because the viewpoint, lighting condition and image resolution are too different between the query and the database images. Further study can be conducted for these cases, e.g. investigating viewpoint or illumination robust features for product images.

Fig. 7 shows some examples of our query object extraction. We can see our object support maps accurately indicate the object regions, even when there are irrelevant objects in the top retrieved list (see the second row for an example). As a result, we can accurately extract the query object, and in many cases achieve more accurate performance than manually initialized segmentation.

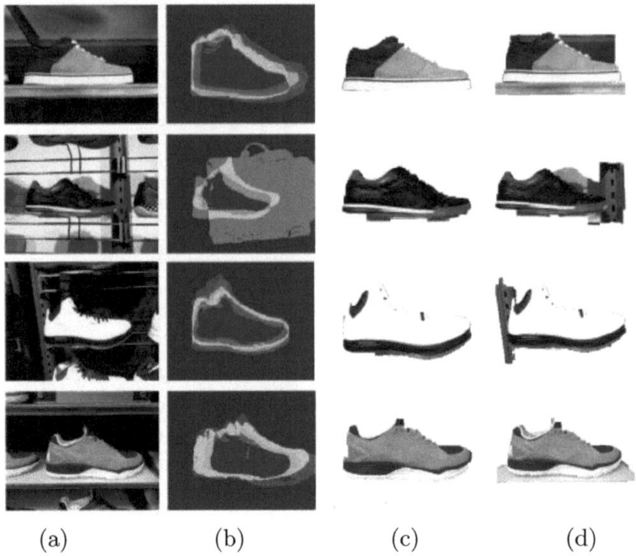

Fig. 7. Examples of query object extraction on the sports product image dataset. (a) original query images, (b) object support maps, indicating the object regions, (c) automatic object cut using the support maps in (b), (d) GrabCut with manual initialization. Since the trimaps provided by our method are more accurate, the segmentation results are even better than manual extraction.

4.3 Results on the Object Category Search Dataset

The implementation on this dataset is the same as the first dataset. Fig. 6(b) shows the average precision at rank k, i.e., the average percentage of relevant objects appearing in the top-k retrieved images, for all the four methods.

In this dataset, the appearance variation is very large within one category. As a result, the spatially-constrained model, which is mainly targeted for instance retrieval instead of object category retrieval, is not sufficient. We can see that the performance of this spatial model is slightly worse than the bag-of-words model. The average precision at rank k for these two methods remains 20% to 30%, which indicates that the retrieval task for this dataset is quite difficult.

By using our simultaneous segmentation and retrieval method, the average precision is dramatically improved, as shown in Fig. 6(b). Similar to the sports product image search dataset, our method still produces better retrieval performance than manual query object extraction, which demonstrates the effectiveness of our method on this challenging task.

Some examples of query object extraction are provided in Fig. 8. We can see that, when the object appearance does not change significantly within the semantic category, our object support map can accurately estimate the query object regions (the top two rows). Meanwhile, when the object appearance variation is large and the initial search results are noisy, our filtering process using Eqn. 2 can remove some irrelevant objects that incorrectly localize the query

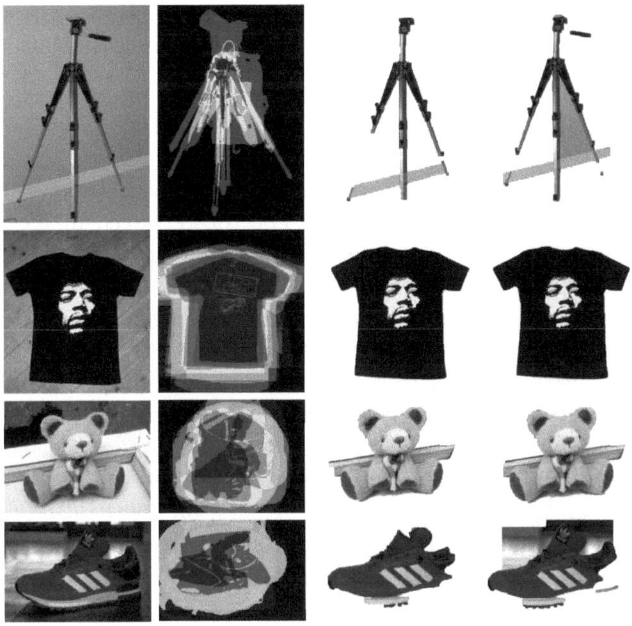

(a) (b) (c) (d)

Fig. 8. Examples of query object extraction on the object category search dataset. (a) original images, (b) object support maps, indicating the object regions, (c) automatic cut using the support maps in (b), (d) GrabCut with manual initialization. Even when the appearance variation is very large where many irrelevant objects are retrieved, our method can still successfully localize and extract the query object.

object, and the query object location can still be accurately estimated (the bottom two rows). As a result, we can still get comparable segmentation results as the manually initialized extraction method.

4.4 Complexity

Compared with the bag-of-words model, the additional storage in the indexing file is the location for each feature, which can be encoded by a 1-byte integer as in [10]. Therefore the additional storage for a database with 45k images is less than 2 MB. The additional memory cost in the retrieval process is the voting maps for each database image when optimizing $\mathbf{T}^{-1}$, which has the size of 16×16 with floating values. When we use 4 scale bins, i.e., generating 4 voting maps for each database image, the additional memory cost for the 45k-image dataset is much less than the size of the inverted file. Since we need to perform one or two iterations of search, the retrieval time would be multiple times of the initial search time, but the absolute retrieval time is still very short. The most time-consuming step of our method is the GrabCut segmentation. Excluding Grabcut, with 3.4G CPU, the search procedure for one iteration step takes 0.380s on average on the sports product image database with 45k images, and the whole process for each query can be performed within 3 seconds without code optimization.

5 Conclusions

We proposed a simple yet effective method to automatically extract the query object for mobile product image search. The top-retrieved images are used to localize the object in the query image with a spatially-constrained model. By extracting the query object, the influence of background clutter on visual features and retrieval accuracy is removed, and the retrieval performance is significantly improved. Experiments show that our method achieves more than 200% improvement over the baseline bag-of-words model, and even outperforms the method with manually initialized query object extraction.

Besides background clutter and small intra-class difference, there are still other issues in mobile product image search, such as the existence of image blur, and large viewpoint variation, image resolution and lighting condition. To improve the performance and make the product image search system practical, more research will be conducted to address these issues in our future work.

Acknowledgements. This work is partially supported by Adobe Systems Incorporated, and in part by National Science Foundation grant IIS- 0347877, IIS-0916607, US Army Research Laboratory and the US Army Research Office under grant ARO W911NF- 08-1-0504, and DARPA Award FA 8650-11-1-7149.

References

1. Sivic, J., Zisserman, A.: Video google: A text retrieval approach to object matching in videos. In: ICCV (2003)
2. Lowe, D.G.: Distinctive image features from scale-invariant keypoints. IJCV 60, 91–110 (2004)
3. Nistér, D., Stewénius, H.: Scalable recognition with a vocabulary tree. In: CVPR (2006)
4. Philbin, J., Chum, O., Isard, M., Sivic, J., Zisserman, A.: Object retrieval with large vocabularies and fast spatial matching. In: CVPR (2007)
5. He, J., Lin, T.H., Feng, J., Chang, S.F.: Mobile product search with bag of hash bits. In: ACM MM (2011)
6. Griffin, G., Holub, A., Perona, P.: Caltech-256 object category dataset. Technical Report 7694, California Institute of Technology (2007)
7. Lin, Z., Brandt, J.: A Local Bag-of-Features Model for Large-Scale Object Retrieval. In: Daniilidis, K., Maragos, P., Paragios, N. (eds.) ECCV 2010, Part VI. LNCS, vol. 6316, pp. 294–308. Springer, Heidelberg (2010)
8. Zhang, Y., Jia, Z., Chen, T.: Image retrieval with geometry-preserving visual phrases. In: CVPR (2011)
9. Cao, Y., Wang, C., Li, Z., Zhang, L., Zhang, L.: Spatial-bag-of-features. In: CVPR (2010)
10. Shen, X., Lin, Z., Brandt, J., Avidan, S., Wu, Y.: Object retrieval and localization with spatially-constrained similarity measure and k-nn reranking. In: CVPR (2012)

11. Philbin, J., Chum, O., Isard, M., Sivic, J., Zisserman, A.: Lost in quantization: Improving particular object retrieval in large scale image databases. In: CVPR (2008)
12. Wang, X., Yang, M., Cour, T., Zhu, S., Yu, K., Han, T.X.: Contextual weighting for vocabulary tree based image retrieval. In: ICCV (2011)
13. Jégou, H., Harzallah, H., Schmid, C.: A contextual dissimilarity measure for accurate and efficient image search. In: CVPR (2007)
14. Philbin, J., Isard, M., Sivic, J., Zisserman, A.: Descriptor Learning for Efficient Retrieval. In: Daniilidis, K., Maragos, P., Paragios, N. (eds.) ECCV 2010, Part III. LNCS, vol. 6313, pp. 677–691. Springer, Heidelberg (2010)
15. Mikulík, A., Perdoch, M., Chum, O., Matas, J.: Learning a Fine Vocabulary. In: Daniilidis, K., Maragos, P., Paragios, N. (eds.) ECCV 2010, Part III. LNCS, vol. 6313, pp. 1–14. Springer, Heidelberg (2010)
16. Chum, O., Philbin, J., Sivic, J., Isard, M., Zisserman, A.: Total recall: Automatic query expansion with a generative feature model for object retrieval. In: ICCV (2007)
17. Chum, O., Mikulík, A., Perd'och, M., Matas, J.: Total recall II: Query expansion revisited. In: CVPR (2011)
18. Jing, Y., Baluja, S.: Pagerank for product image search. In: WWW (2008)
19. Lin, X., Gokturk, B., Sumengen, B., Vu, D.: Visual search engine for product images. In: Multimedia Content Access: Algorithms and Systems II (2008)
20. Girod, B., Chandrasekhar, V., Chen, D., Cheung, N.M., Grzeszczuk, R., Reznik, Y., Takacs, G., Tsai, S., Vedantham, R.: Mobile visual search. IEEE Signal Processing Magazine 28 (2011)
21. Chandrasekhar, V., Chen, D., Tsai, S., Cheung, N.M., Chen, H., Takacs, G., Reznik, Y., Vedantham, R., Grzeszczuk, R., Bach, J., Girod, B.: The stanford mobile visual search dataset. In: ACM Multimedia Systems Conference (2011)
22. Rother, C., Kolmogorov, V., Blake, A.: Grabcut: Interactive foreground extraction using iterated graph cuts. In: SIGGRAPH (2004)
23. Batra, D., Kowdle, A., Parikh, D., Luo, J., Chen, T.: icoseg: Interactive cosegmentation with intelligent scribble guidance. In: CVPR (2010)
24. Rother, C., Kolmogorov, V., Minka, T., Blake, A.: Cosegmentation of image pairs by histogram matching-incorporating a global constraint into MRFs. In: CVPR (2006)
25. Bourdev, L.D., Malik, J.: Poselets: Body part detectors trained using 3D human pose annotations. In: ICCV (2009)
26. Brox, T., Bourdev, L.D., Maji, S., Malik, J.: Object segmentation by alignment of poselet activations to image contours. In: CVPR (2011)
27. Wu, B., Nevatia, R.: Simultaneous object detection and segmentation by boosting local shape feature based classifier. In: CVPR (2007)
28. Opelt, A., Pinz, A., Zisserman, A.: A Boundary-Fragment-Model for Object Detection. In: Leonardis, A., Bischof, H., Pinz, A. (eds.) ECCV 2006. LNCS, vol. 3952, pp. 575–588. Springer, Heidelberg (2006)
29. Leibe, B., Leonardis, A., Schiele, B.: Combined object categorization and segmentation with an implicit shape model. In: ECCV Workshop on Statistical Learning in Computer Vision (2004)
30. Yeh, T., Lee, J.J., Darrell, T.: Fast concurrent object localization and recognition. In: CVPR (2009)
31. Lampert, C.H.: Detecting objecs in large image collections and videos by efficient subimage retrieval. In: ICCV (2009)
32. Perd'och, M., Chum, O., Matas, J.: Efficient representation of local geometry for large scale object retrieval. In: CVPR (2009)

Analyzing the Subspace Structure of Related Images: Concurrent Segmentation of Image Sets*

Lopamudra Mukherjee[1], Vikas Singh[2], Jia Xu[2], and Maxwell D. Collins[2]

[1] University of Wisconsin-Whitewater
[2] University of Wisconsin-Madison
mukherjl@uww.edu, vsingh@biostat.wisc.edu,
{jiaxu,mcollins}@cs.wisc.edu

Abstract. We develop new algorithms to analyze and exploit the joint subspace structure of a set of related images to facilitate the process of concurrent segmentation of a large set of images. Most existing approaches for this problem are either limited to extracting a single similar object across the given image set or do not scale well to a large number of images containing multiple objects varying at different scales. One of the goals of this paper is to show that various desirable properties of such an algorithm (ability to handle *multiple* images with *multiple* objects showing *arbitary* scale variations) can be cast elegantly using simple constructs from linear algebra: this significantly extends the operating range of such methods. While intuitive, this formulation leads to a hard optimization problem where one must perform the image segmentation task together with appropriate constraints which enforce desired algebraic regularity (e.g., common subspace structure). We propose efficient iterative algorithms (with small computational requirements) whose key steps reduce to objective functions solvable by *max-flow* and/or nearly *closed form identities*. We study the qualitative, theoretical, and empirical properties of the method, and present results on benchmark datasets.

1 Introduction

Image segmentation is among the most widely studied problems in the computer vision community. The classical setting, which is how this problem is generally formalized in the literature, is *unsupervised*: one assumes that the underlying model requires no user involvement. While a completely automated solution still remains the de-facto objective, given the difficulty (and ill-posedness) of the task, in recent years we have seen a small but noticeable shift towards interactive image segmentation methods [1]. The goal here is to segment *a given image* with only nominal user interaction. Clearly, obtaining the best segmentation for *one* image is important – but we must note that the proliferation of massive image sharing platforms have created a significant shift in how image data typically

* This work is supported via NIH R21AG034315, NSF RI 1116584, NSF CGV 1219016, UW-ICTR and W-ADRC. M.D.C. was supported by the UW CIBM Program.

A. Fitzgibbon et al. (Eds.): ECCV 2012, Part IV, LNCS 7575, pp. 128–142, 2012.

Fig. 1. A set of images with two actors showing quasi-independent scale variations

presents itself. Images today are rarely generated as independent samples, but rather manifest as 'collections'. Since shared content is pervasive in such sets, modern algorithms must clearly go beyond the analysis of one image at a time. This strategy already works well in image categorization and object recognition problems [2], where leveraging large training corpora of images for the learning task is common. On the image segmentation front, the multiple image focused developments are relatively more recent and fall under the umbrella term of Cosegmentation [3]. The premise of Cosegmentation is that when many images containing the same foreground object are available, such shared content may be able to much reduce the need for user guidance [4].

Cosegmentation refers to segmenting a "similar" object from a set of images jointly, with an additional global constraint which forces the foreground appearance models to be similar. Both the unsupervised and the supervised versions of the problem have been actively studied in the last few years [4,5,6,7,8,9,10,11]. On the unsupervised side [3,8], cosegmentation approaches generally operate under the assumption that the background regions in the images are *disparate*: this is essential to rule out the case where the entire image is segmented as the foreground (the appearance models match trivially and the global constraint is less meaningful). Supervised (or weakly supervised) cosegmentation methods [4,10,11,12], on the other hand, address this issue via some interactive user scribble. In conjunction with the choice of appropriate pixel-wise features and/or wrapper inference methods, these models account quite well for changes in illumination, shape and scale variations, and reliably segment an object of interest from multiple images jointly. However, note that this body of work primarily addresses the setting where the set of images contains *a single object of interest.* Heuristic modifications aside, the core mathematical justification behind most existing models [11,7,4,13] does *not* carry through to multiple objects unless we make the impractical assumption that the scale of all objects varies identically across the image set. We show an illustrative example and discuss these details shortly.

Consider the set of images in Fig. 1 which we wish to segment jointly. These images consist of two actors (a dog and a deer), where each exhibits substantial scale changes depending on how close it is to the camera. In some images, one of the actors is temporarily occluded or not in the field of view (i.e., scale is zero). This example is not atypical – a surprisingly large number of image sets (including many instances in the popular iCoseg dataset [4]) consist of more than a single object of interest which co-occur across the image set. Viewing this as a multi-class Cosegmentation entails running the model for each class, one by one, which is often cumbersome if user interaction is needed. This is also an impediment in adapting Cosegmentation in analyzing video data. The algorithms described in this paper are motivated by some of these issues.

The main **contribution** of this paper is to make Cosegmentation approaches applicable to a significantly more general setting. Rather than ask that the foregrounds 'share' a parametric (or non-parametric) model [4], impose rank deficiency of the matrix of object appearances [13], or compare images pairwise [3,7] **(a)** we propose new formulations to identify the subspace(s) spanned by a small set of basis appearance models that can best reconstruct the entire set of composite foregrounds (pertaining to multiple objects) in the images. For such a strategy to work, three key components, namely, i) sparse basis subset selection, ii) subspace reconstruction, and iii) image segmentation must happen in tandem. This leads to an interesting (albeit difficult) optimization model. **(b)** We show how effective solutions can be derived for both the supervised and unsupervised versions based on subspace clustering, sparse representation methods and the theory of *maximizing* submodular functions. This provides an elegant framework which permits general non-parametric appearance model *compositions*, that is, the foreground may include tens of objects, at arbitrary scales.

2 Related Work

Initial methods for cosegmentation performed figure-ground labeling of a given pair of images, and enforced a matching (mutual consistency) requirement on the appearance models of the foreground. Various objectives and solution strategies have since been proposed (see [8] for a technical summary), and shown to work well when the number of images is limited to two. This special case is restrictive, and more recent works have extended the ideas to multiple image segmentation. The first step was taken by [4] which suggested constructing a shared mixture model to encode the appearance of a similar foreground object in all images. As noted by [8], this algorithm also shares the background model across the given set of images – a potential problem when the images do not have a substantial shared baseline. Vicente [8] proposed a solution to this problem for the two image setting. Contemporary to these results, [9] identified a nice relationship of Cosegmentation with maximum margin clustering, but the method is computationally quite expensive (especially for a large number of images). Chu [5] showed a small set of results using a method which looks for common patterns in a pre-processing step. Recently, [13] and [11] presented multi-image formulations of the problem. While [13] performs a sequence of iterations involving a segmentation step followed by a rank decomposition of the appearance model matrix, [11] scores similarities between a large set of proposal segmentations. But neither framework is directly generalizable to the *multi-object instances* in the iCoseg dataset or the type of examples shown in Fig. 1. Finally, a few recent papers have incorporated co-saliency [14], used cosegmentation for image classification [15], and extended the algorithms for the cosegmentation of shapes (see [16] for an example of this line of work). Table 1 summarizes the state of the art for the problem to place the contribution of this paper in context.

Table 1. State of the art for Cosegmentation; note that [5] is not included above because that method runs an offline common pattern discovery, and then adjusts a unary term in the segmentation. [9] is potentially applicable to multi-class segmentation, but is computationally expensive, cf. [9], section 3.2. and so only one object case was tackled. Hochbaum [10] does not seem straightforward to adapt for multiple objects. We very recently learnt of works [17,18] which detects multiple objects. These works are not discussed and evaluated here.

Article	≥ 2 objects	Images	Objective function	Solution Method
Rother [3]	No	2	Graph-cuts plus ℓ_1 norm	Trust-region method
Mu [6]	No	2	Quadratic energy plus generative model	Markov Chain Monte Carlo
Mukherjee [7]	No	2	Graph-cuts plus ℓ_2 norm	Linear Program
Vicente [8]	No	2	Graph-cuts plus generative model	EM like procedure
Hochbaum [10]	No[seebelow]	2	Joint segmentation with similarity reward	Pseudoflow
Batra [4]	No	Multiple	Graph-cuts plus GMM	Iterative Graph-cuts
Vicente [11]	No	Multiple	Similarity of proposal segmentation pairs	Graph-cuts, A* inference, Random forests
Joulin [9]	No[seebelow]	Multiple	Discriminative clustering	Convex relaxation of SDP
Mukherjee [13]	No	Multiple	Graph-cuts with a rank one constraint	Iterative network flow and SVD
Chang [14]	No	Multiple	Graph cuts with saliency prior	Graph cuts
This work	Yes	Multiple	—	—

3 Subspaces of Multiple Object Foreground

Most existing cosegmentation literature performs joint segmentation of all images and simultaneously regularizes the objective based on coherence among the segmented foreground appearance models of the respective images. Assume that $E_{\text{seg}}(\cdot)$ denotes an appropriate segmentation energy (summed over all images), and $C(\cdot)$ is the cosegmentation regularizer which expresses a measure of coherence among the foreground appearance models of the images provided. For example, [3] and [4] use a MRF energy for $E_{\text{seg}}(\cdot)$ and a mixture model based penalty for $C(\cdot)$, but various other options have also been proposed. Since the common building block of our algorithms is the subspace structure of similar foreground regions across images, it seems natural to approach this problem by identifying special forms of $C(\cdot)$ that offer this behavior.

Our first task is to decide on an appropriate representation (i.e., description) for the objects or foregrounds within the images. For both the object-level appearance model as well as the descriptor of the entire foreground, we make use of a visual dictionary over textons (very similar to the object recognition literature [19]). Filter bank responses, when clustered, provides a "texton histogram" where cluster centers with their corresponding covariances define a *visual word* (or a histogram bin). Distinct objects correspond to distinct distributions over k texton bins [12]. Based on this construct, assume that the histograms of each unique object which may appear in the images are provided as $\{m_1, \cdots, m_d\}$ for d objects, where for an object l, $m_l \in \mathbb{R}^k$. With this definition, it follows directly that the foreground in each to be segmented image (say, $f^{[i]}$ in image i) must be a vector in $\mathbb{R}^k$, and can be expressed as $f^{[i]} = \alpha_1 m_1 + \ldots + \alpha_d m_d$

(note that we are operating on the same set of dictionary of visual words or texton bins). Clearly, $\alpha_l = 0$ implies that the l-th object is missing in the i-th image and $\alpha_l > 0$ gives a scaled version of the object-wise texton histogram. This discussion does not yield an implementable algorithm yet (because neither the object-wise texton histogram nor the foreground regions are known).

The Subspace Structure of Foregrounds. Denote the set of foreground appearance vectors for s images as $\{F(:,1), \cdots, F(:,s)\} = \{f^{[1]}, \cdots, f^{[s]}\}$. Let us consider a simple example (two objects, three images) to see the subspace structure by focusing on the three respective foregrounds, $f^{[1]}$, $f^{[2]}$, and $f^{[3]}$, assuming that the object models in these foregrounds are indexed by m_1 and m_2. We have $f^{[1]} = \theta_1 m_1 + \theta_2 m_2$, $f^{[2]} = \theta_3 m_1 + \theta_4 m_2$, and $f^{[3]} = \theta_5 m_1 + \theta_6 m_2$ for some set of constants $\{\theta_1, \cdots, \theta_6\}$. Observe that the three foregrounds share the same basis in m_1 and m_2, and so we may write $f^{[3]}$ as a linear combination of $f^{[1]}$ and $f^{[2]}$. Also, $f^{[1]}$ is expressable by combining $f^{[2]}$ and $f^{[3]}$, and similarly $f^{[2]}$ in terms of $f^{[1]}$ and $f^{[3]}$ (a change of basis argument). Denote the coefficients of these linear combinations by a matrix, C whose (j,i)-th entry denotes the contribution of foreground $f^{[j]}$ in expressing $f^{[i]}$. So, the requirement that *every* foreground appearance model should be expressable as a linear combination of a set of basis texton histograms can be achieved by asking that each $f^{[i]}$ (individual columns of F) must be reconstructable as *a linear combination of all other* $f^{[j]}$ where $j \neq i$ ($f^{[i]}$ does not contribute in its own reconstruction). This can be written as $F = FC$ with the condition that the diagonal entries of C must be identically zero, i.e., $\text{diag}(C) = 0$ (where $F \in \mathbb{R}^{k \times s}$ and $C \in \mathbb{R}^{s \times s}$). If the columns of F lie in the *same subspace*, this constraint is satisfied. However, the linear form also permits the identification of *multiple* subspaces into which the columns of F can be 'clustered'. The latter interpretation is strongly related to recent developments in subspace clustering [20,21]. Finally, to permit small variations in the appearance models and make the model robust, we have $F = \hat{F} + \zeta$ where F is composed of a main component $\hat{F}$ plus a noise matrix ζ.

As a final ingredient, we also need to algebraically express the foreground vectors $F(:,i)$ as a function of the segmentation. For each image, we have the texton histogram of the entire image where rows (and columns) correspond to histogram bins (and image pixels) respectively. We denote this as a binary matrix $Z^{[i]}$, where $Z^{[i]}(b,p) = 1$ implies pixel p is assigned to visual word b (like the similarity indicator used in [10]). Let the unknown segmentation indicator variable for image i be $\mathbf{x}^{[i]}$. Then, each entry of $Z^{[i]}\mathbf{x}^{[i]}$ is the dot product of a row a in $Z^{[i]}$ with $\mathbf{x}^{[i]}$, and provides the number of pixels from bin a assigned to foreground. So, $Z^{[i]}\mathbf{x}^{[i]} = F(:,i) = f^{[i]}$. With these components, multi-object multi-image scale free cosegmentation takes the simple form as in (1):

$$
\begin{aligned}
&\min_{\mathbf{x},C,\zeta} \quad \sum_i E_{\text{seg}}(\mathbf{x}^{[i]}) + \|\zeta\|^2 \qquad\qquad (1)\\
&\text{subject to} \quad \text{diag}(C) = 0, \quad \text{rank}(C) \leq \kappa \text{ (a small constant)}.\\
&\qquad\qquad F = \hat{F} + \zeta, \quad \hat{F} = \hat{F}C, \quad Z^{[i]}\mathbf{x}^{[i]} = F(:,i),
\end{aligned}
$$

where the rank constraint offers a regularization on C, with similar motivation as in the subspace clustering literature [20]. The non-convex rank constraint is replaced by its convex relaxation: the nuclear norm. We will ensure fidelity between F and $\hat{F} + \zeta$ as well as between $\hat{F}$ and $\hat{F}C$ as soft constraints by penalizing their respective differences in the objective. The constraint $\hat{F} = \hat{F}C$ is a seemingly difficult quadratic form of two matrix *variables*. But even when included in the objective, it has a suprisingly simple solution because of the structure of C, as described shortly.

For concreteness of the presentation below, we now decide on the form of $E_{\text{seg}}(\mathbf{x}^{[i]})$ in (1). In this paper, we use the Markov Random Field segmentation, popular for a variety of computer vision applications, see [22]. Other linear forms are possible as long as the the optimal *real*-valued solution can be found in polynomial time in Step 2 below. The main descent steps of the optimization are:

1) Choose a matrix $\hat{F}$ based on some initialization (e.g., the matrix of all ones).

2) With $\hat{F}$ given, optimize $\min_{\mathbf{x}} \ \sum_i E_{\text{seg}}(\mathbf{x}^{[i]}) + \|F - \hat{F}\|^2$ s.t $\mathbf{x} \in [0, 1]$, to recover $\mathbf{x}$. We do not solve for C since $\hat{F}$ is given. Using $\mathbf{x}$, calculate each column of F as $Z^{[i]}\mathbf{x}^{[i]}$.

3) Then, optimize (2) to recover $\hat{F}$ and C,

$$\min_{\hat{F},C} \ \gamma_1\|F - \hat{F}\|^2 + \gamma_2\|\hat{F} - \hat{F}C\|^2 + \|C\|_* \ \text{ s.t.} \qquad \text{diag}(C) = 0 \qquad (2)$$

keeping F fixed. $\|C\|_*$ is nuclear norm. The user specified constants γ_1, γ_2 penalize the soft constraints.

4) Repeat Steps 2–3 until convergence (or negligible change in solution).

Properties. It turns out that the core of the procedure (Step 2 and Step 3) can be performed very efficiently. Let us first analyze Step 2. When E_{seg} is MRF, Step 2 with $\mathbf{x} \in [0, 1]$ is a Quadratic Pseudoboolean function (for which fast implementations are already available). Interestingly, Step 3 also turns out to be very easily solvable as shown by [21] (cf. Lemma 2). In fact, in Step 3, the solution of $\hat{F}$ and C such that it satisfies the constraints above can be obtained from a singular value decomposition of F. Since both steps are optimally solvable, we obtain the following simple result:

Lemma 1. *The objective value of the relaxed version of (1) is non-increasing with each iteration.*

Beyond Lemma 1, convergence to a stationary point requires making use of the *persistence* property from [23,24] to show that the set of solutions is finite. Then, the stationary point statement follows by arguments similar to results for convergence of k-means, as shown in [13].

4 Supervised Cosegmentation with Dictionaries of Appearance Models

The preceding model, while interesting, needs discriminative backgrounds across the given image set. This criteria is not satisfied in many datasets depicting multiple objects, where some images may be temporally related and therefore share a common background. This issue does not have an easy solution in the unsupervised setup, but can be addressed effectively by endowing the model with some form of weak supervision to make the problem well posed.

Consider a situation where the user interacts with the model on a few images in the set (the level of supervision is comparable to a GrabCut type scribble interaction [4]), which is then used to derive an approximate texton-based appearance model of the objects of interest. We call this setup cosegmentation with a *precise* dictionary. Note that 'precise' refers not to the quality of the appearance model, rather the fact that the dictionary consists *only* of appearance models of objects likely to appear in the set. We also study a more general version of the problem: it assumes the availability of a larger *overcomplete* dictionary made up of a diverse (and redundant) collection of appearance models. We give a brief overview of the precise dictionary version next, and then discuss its extensions.

Given a small collection of approximate appearances of objects as vectors (distributions over texture visual words), $\mathbf{M} = \{m_1, \cdots, m_d\}$, we want to segment the foreground from unseen images (where objects may appear at arbitrary scales). This problem can be written out as follows (γ is a constant):

$$\min_{\mathbf{x}^{[i]},\lambda} \quad E_{\text{seg}}(\mathbf{x}^{[i]}) + \gamma \|F(:,i) - \sum_{m_j \in \mathbf{M}} \lambda_j m_j\|^2 \quad \text{s.t.} \qquad F(:,i) = Z^{[i]}\mathbf{x}^{[i]}, \quad \mathbf{x}^{[i]} \in [0,1]. \tag{3}$$

The objective penalizes the difference of the unknown foreground $F(:,i)$ (for a fixed i) from a linear combination of the given basis vectors (object appearances). Since $\mathbf{M}$ is known, this problem can be solved very efficiently for the MRF objective as well as other segmentation functions considered in [25]. For instance, if we use MRFs for segmentation, we can obtain provably partially optimal solutions. To do this, we first substitute the basis set $\mathbf{M}$ with an orthogonal basis $\mathbf{M}'$ (using Gram-Schmidt). Then, the penalty term $\gamma\|F - \sum_{m_j \in \mathbf{M}} \lambda_j m_j\|^2$ is interpretable as the *distance* of the vector $F(:,i)$ to the subspace spanned by the vectors in $\mathbf{M}$ or the orthogonal set $\mathbf{M}'$. The advantage of using $\mathbf{M}'$ is that such a distance can be computed in closed form by projecting $F(:,i)$ on to this subspace expressing it as a linear combination of its projection to the orthogonal basis vectors. That is, $\text{proj}_{\mathbf{M}'}(F(:,i)) = \sum_{m_j \in \mathbf{M}'} \lambda_j m_j$ where $\lambda_j = \frac{F(:,i) \cdot m_j}{m_j \cdot m_j}$. For any image i in a given set, the objective function, therefore, takes the form,

$$\min_{\mathbf{x}^{[i]}} \quad E_{\text{seg}}(\mathbf{x}^{[i]}) + \gamma_1 \|F(:,i) - \text{proj}_{\mathbf{M}'}(F(:,i))\|^2, \tag{4}$$

which can be written as a Pseudoboolean function [23] in $\mathbf{x}$, and permits network flow-based solutions. Next, we build upon the ideas above, where the final optimization core will solve a problem similar in form to (4) as a module.

4.1 Cosegmentation with Overcomplete Dictionary

Knowledge of precisely which basis vectors will be used in representing the unknown foreground regions, while useful as a first step, restricts applicability of Cosegmentation in several circumstances. For example, consider a temporal image sequence consisting of two main actors (objects), as shown in Fig. 1. In some of the frames, one of the actors may be outside the field of view; therefore, it is not a good idea to use *all* available basis vectors to segment *every* image in the given set. Rather, we would like the algorithm to identify the *smallest* subset of bases that can be linearly combined to define the foreground of the images (restricting the model complexity). Further, such dictionaries are not difficult to construct using datasets such as MSRC Object Categories, Pascal VOC, and iCoseg using just weak supervision. Once a large universe of approximate object appearance models is available, the goal is to cosegment a given set of images, where the foreground is composed of *a small subset* of appearance models A from our dictionary, D. This problem shares similarities to the *dictionary selection* problem in [26,27,28], but with salient differences. In [26], the goal is to identify a sparsifying sub-dictionary by selecting dictionary columns from multiple candidate bases, and then representing the signal as a sparse reconstruction of the chosen bases.

$$\min_{\mathbf{x}^{[i]},\lambda} \quad \sum_i E_{\text{seg}}(\mathbf{x}^{[i]}) + \gamma_1 \sum_i \|F(:,i) - \sum_{m_j \in A, A\subseteq D, |A|\leq\beta} \lambda_j m_j\|^2 \tag{5}$$

$$\text{s.t.} \quad \forall i \;\; F(:,i) = Z^{[i]}\mathbf{x}^{[i]}, \quad \mathbf{x}^{[i]} \in [0,1]. \tag{6}$$

But here, the to-be-reconstructed vector F is *not* fixed, rather needs to be solved in conjuction with other terms. Further, finding the sparse representation standalone is insufficient; instead, it needs to interact with $E_{\text{seg}}(\mathbf{x}^{[i]})$[1].

Combinatorial Properties. If we use MRF for $E_{\text{seg}}(\cdot)$, in the current setup it is a submodular function [29]. So, we focus on the second part of the objective and define the following function: $L(F(:,i),A) = \|F(:,i) - \sum_{m_j\in A}\lambda_j m_j\|^2$. Note that, given F, the subset of D which best approximates it, can be written as $\hat{A} = \arg\min_{A\in D,|A|\leq\beta}\sum_i L(F(:,i),A)$. Let ϕ be the null set. We define an additional function $G(F(:,i),D) = L(F(:,i),\phi) - \min_{A\in D,|A|\leq\beta} L(F(:,i),A)$ which reduces variance between the linear combination of the chosen bases and the signal to be approximated. This function, when maximized also provides an equivalent sparse representation of the signal. It turns out that such a function is *approximately* sub-modular (see [26]) and its 'deviation' from submodularity is a function of the maximum *incoherency* $\mu = \max_{\forall u,v,u\neq v} \langle m_u, m_v\rangle$. With these tools in hand, we can directly make the following observation.

[1] The choice of extracting $A \subset D$ instead of regularizing the ℓ_1-norm of λ was driven by empirical feedback. Using a Lasso penalty (relaxation of ℓ_0 norm) involves solving a linear program which may become a bottleneck in vision applications. Second, while penalizing large values in λ (a consequence of ℓ_1) has the undesirable effect of making the model less immune to scale changes, giving unsatisfactory performance.

Observation 1. *The model in (5) can be expressed in the form:* $\min E - G$, *where* E *(same as* E_{seg}*) is submodular,* G *is approximately submodular (*$-G$ *is approximately super-modular), and so* $E - G$ *is a sum of submodular and (approximately) supermodular terms.*

Next, we show how the sub-supermodular function approximation method proposed by [30] can be extended to our problem. To do this, we substitute the supermodular term with its (approximately) modular approximation. This function is defined, wrt to a fixed subset A, as $\Psi(F(:,i),A) = L(F(:,i),\phi) - L(F(:,i),A)$, and can be shown to be approximately modular (see [26]). In our model, the important advantage is that the term $E - \Psi$ can replace the objective $E - G$, which is now approximately submodular (a sum of submodular and approximately modular terms). In addition, it is similar in form to (3), since when the set A is fixed, the problem reduces to a precise dictionary setup. Therefore, efficient methods from §4 are directly applicable. Based on these properties, we adopt the following iterative procedure:

1) Solve the function E and get an initial estimate for $F_{[t]}$ (t refers to the iteration number).
2) Solve $A_{[t]} = \arg\max_{A \subseteq D} G(F_{[t]}, D)$. This can be done using the procedure described in [26]. Note that since $G(F_{[t]}, D) = \psi(F_{[t]}, A_{[t]})$, we have $E - G(F_{[t]}, D) = E - \psi(F_{[t]}, A_{[t]})$.
3) Solve the optimization problem $\min_{\mathbf{x}} E - \psi(:, A_{[t]})$ keeping $A_{[t]}$ fixed, using a procedure similar to §4. Denote the optimal solution by $\mathbf{x}_{[t+1]}$ and the matrix of new foreground vectors as $F_{[t+1]}$.
4) Repeat Steps 2–3 until convergence (or negligible change in solution).

We can now prove the following result:

Proposition 1. *The objective function value is monotonically non-increasing with the iterations.*

Proof (sketch). Note that after Step 3, we get

$$F_{[t]} - G(F_{[t]}, D) = E_{[t]} - \psi(F_{[t]}, A_{[t]}) \geq E_{[t+1]} - \psi(F_{[t+1]}, A_{[t]}).$$

This is because as we are solving the optimization problem in Step 3 to optimality. Further,

$$E_{[t+1]} - \psi(F_{[t+1]}, A_{[t]}) \geq E_{[t+1]} - G(F_{[t+1]}, D).$$

This is true because in Step 2, $A_{[t+1]} = \arg\max_{A \subseteq D} G(F_{[t+1]}, D)$; therefore, $G(F_{[t+1]}, D) \geq \psi(F_{[t+1]}, A_{[t]})$; otherwise replacing $A_{[t+1]}$ by $A_{[t]}$ improves the solution of $G(F_{[t+1]}, D)$ trivially and the solution converges. Therefore, we directly have $E_{[t]} - G(F_{[t]}, D) \geq E_{[t+1]} - \psi(F_{[t+1]}, A_{[t]}) \geq E_{[t+1]} - G(F_{[t+1]}, D)$, and so the iterations either decrease the objective value at each step or the iterations converge.

Generating Class Specific Labels: The reader will notice that while our algorithms identifies multiple objects at arbitary scale variations in a set of images, the output is in the form of a *joint* foreground indicator vector, rather than class specific indicator vectors. But class specific indicators can be obtained from such an output, if desired. The main task is to divide the joint foreground indicator vector $F(:,i)$ of image i, into the constituent class specific indicator vectors. To do this, we project the foreground indicator vector $F(:,i)$ on to the basis vectors, to obtain foreground appearance model for each object individually (say $F_d(:,i)$ for object class d). We can then decompose the indicator vector $\mathbf{x}^{[i]}$, into an indicator vector for each object class $\mathbf{x}_d^{[i]}$, satisfying the property that they agree with the object-wise models above, i.e., $Z^{[i]}\mathbf{x}_d^{[i]} \simeq F_d(:,i)$. This is essentially a least squares problem of the form $Ax \simeq b$. It turns out the the LHS coefficient matrix (A) of this form has a totally unimodular property, therefore if we round the RHS (b) to integral values, such a least squares problem will have an exact solution.

5 Evaluations

Our experiments were designed to assess the model's performance on several benchmark datasets, using existing methods as a baseline. Broadly, the setup consists of: evaluation of (a) the unsupervised algorithms in §3, and (b) the supervised algorithms with exact and overcomplete dictionaries in §4 – §4.1. We demonstrate some examples for the unsupervised model, but mainly focus our attention to the more broadly applicable methods from Section 4.1, which were evaluated on the entire iCoseg dataset [4] and a subset of MSRC object categories. In addition, we also include comparison of our supervised method with fully supervised SVM. We used texture-based appearance models as described in Section 3 using agglomerative information bottleneck from [19]. The unary terms for the MRF objective were created using the GMMs from the Grabcut implementation in OpenCV using the training data (when available) or by specifying a box centered on the image covering 60% area (in the unsupervised setting). All segmentations were done at the pixel level (no superpixels were used).

Subspace Cosegmentation of Multiple Objects. We performed a preliminary evaluation of this model using a small number of examples collected from the internet.

Since the algorithm assumes that only the foreground regions are similar (and the background is disparate), we extracted images from several video sequences which were temporally separated. Representative examples (from Toy Story) are shown in Fig. 2 where there is significant pose/shape variation in the objects; further two of the images consist of only one character. The model performs favorably relative to [9] (also an unsupervised approach).

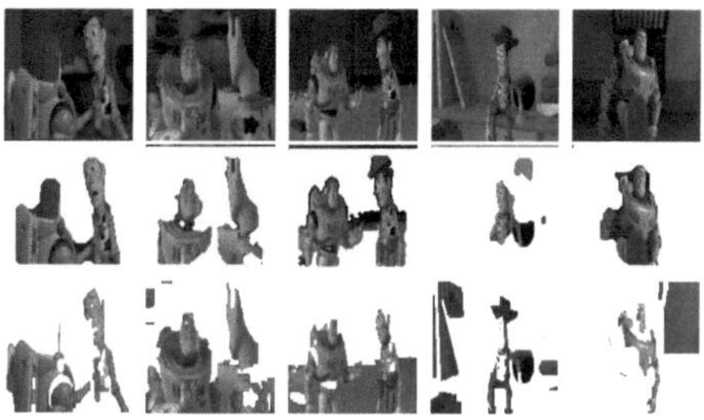

Fig. 2. Results of the algorithm in Section 3 (Row 2) relative to segmentation obtained from [9] (Row 3).

Fig. 3. Some results of the model in §4.1 on multi-object Liverpool (cols 1-4) and Soccer sets (cols 5-8)

Cosegmentation with Appearance Dictionaries. These experiments are a rigorous assessment of the model because the dataset includes deformable objects, and significant variations in pose, viewpoint, as well as scale. Interestingly, not all images contain all objects which allow properly evaluating all properties of our algorithm in §4.1.

ICoseg. The iCoseg dataset contains 38 image categories with up to 40 images in each class. For each class, we created a small training set consisting of up to 2 training examples (from the ground truth) to generate the dictionary (this can also be derived from scribble guidance [1]). We illustrate comparisons of our approach with three other methods from [11], [8], and [9]. Among these the cosegmentation method of [11] uses training data but by a very different procedure. Since the performance of any cosegmentation method varies among different classes, similar to other papers [4] we report the results for each class. Also, consistent with common practice [11,4,13], we report accuracy as the percentage of pixels in the image (both foreground and background) which were correctly classified. (note that results in [11] included a subset of all images in each class). Since the model decomposes into independent runs in §4.1, it is not limited by how many images can be segmented at once. In Table 2, we summarize our accuracy summaries after segmenting all $\sim$ 640 images from all classes in iCoseg. Overall, compared to the accuracy numbers reported for each class in [11] (and also [8], [9]), our model performs well and yields better accuracy in all but two classes. Some visual results are presented in Figure 3 to illustrate its qualitative performance on images with multiple objects (including scenes where an object is missing). Note that for the Liverpool and the Women Soccer images shown, the ground truth provided in iCoseg only asks for detecting one object. To detect all objects, we created a dictionary with only one training example for each team (by running a Grabcut with a few scribbles, and retaining results from the first iteration). Even though the training examples were not perfect, the results in Fig. 3 indicate the algorithm can identify multiple objects with

Table 2. Segmentation accuracy summaries for image classes from iCoseg dataset

class	Ours	[11]	[8]	[9]	class	Ours	[11]	[8]	[9]
Balloon	**95.17**%	90.10%	89.30%	85.20%	Kite Panda	**93.37**%	90.20%	70.70%	73.20%
Baseball	**95.66**%	90.90%	69.90%	73.0%	Panda	**92.83**%	92.70%	80.00%	84.00%
Brown bear	88.52%	**95.30**%	87.3%	74.0%	Skating	**96.64**%	77.50%	69.9%	82.1%
Elephants	**87.65**%	43.10%	62.3%	70.1%	Statue	**96.64**%	93.80%	89.3%	90.6%
Ferrari	**89.95**%	89.90%	77.7%	85.0%	Stonehenge1	**92.67**%	63.30%	61.1%	56.6%
Gymnastics	**92.18**%	91.70%	83.4%	90.9%	Stonehenge2	84.87%	**88.80**%	66.9%	86.0%
Kite	**94.63**%	90.3%	87.0%	87.0%	Taj Mahal	**94.07**%	91.1%	79.6%	73.7%

relative ease, and is mostly immune to situations where one or more objects are not visible in a scene.

Approach	Sheep	Car	Cow	Flowers	Plane	Dog	Bird
Ours	89.0%	**80.1%**	87.8%	86.5%	**87.1%**	**93.5%**	94.8%
[11]	**93.0%**	79.6%	**94.2%**	–	83.0%	93.1%	**95.3%**

Fig. 4. Segmentation accuracy on MSRC

MSRC Object Categories. The MSRC dataset contains several categories of objects, but in each object class, the constituent images are much more diverse compared to ICoseg. For example, the Flowers class includes flowers of different colors and shapes: in such cases, for cosegmentation to yield very high accuracy, far richer visual features may be needed. To make our models applicable, we created a dictionary having one representative image of each unique type which provided $4-5$ training examples per class – all other images in the class were then presented to the model for segmentation. The accuracy is summarized for the subset of classes tested are shown in Fig. 4 using the recent work of [11] (which also used training) as a baseline. Overall, this suggests that the performance of our algorithm is similar to [11]. Finally, we observe that both methods are limited only by the underlying visual features that enable (a) comparing proposal segmentations in [11] and (b) comparing appearance descriptors in ours. Examples from MSRC and iCoseg is shown in Fig. 5.

Results on Comparison with Fully Supervised SVM. Since the algorithms described in Sections 4 and 5 are essentially supervised, we compare our method with a fully supervised algorithm such as SVM. SVMs were run on images from the ICoseg dataset, since the background and foregrounds are both fixed for such images. For each image group, we select five images as the training set (note that for experiments using our method, we used no more than two training image). For each training image, we compute a texton feature descriptor (17 features) for each pixel and train a classifier based on that (we use the built-in svmtrain function in Matlab with SMO as the solver). After that, we use the learned classifier and test it on the remaining image set. Figure 6 shows some representative images. In general, the results of SVM are about $10-15\%$ worse than our method and also worse than any other baseline used in the main paper. This is somewhat expected as our algorithm imposes an appearance model

Fig. 5. Results of the algorithm in §4.1 on the ICoseg (cols 1-5) and MSRC (cols 6-8)

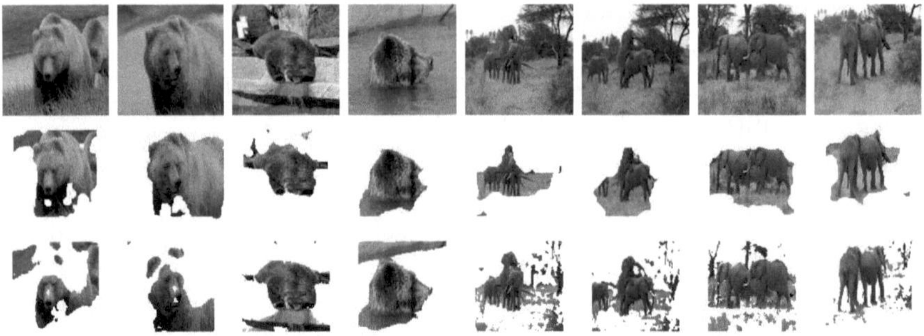

Fig. 6. Results of the comparison of our algorithm with fully supervised SVM on three datasets from Icoseg: Rows 1 shows the original images, Rows 2 shows the results of our approach and Rows 3 shows the results using SVM

constraint on the entire set of pixels labeled as foreground by asking that they span a subspace given by a subset of known appearances. But similar patches routinely co-occur in the foreground and background, which throws off the results of SVM substantially in the absence of any terms that make the solution behave like a valid segmentation (e.g., homogeneity).

Other Comments. Our results above show that the model yields results that are superior or competitive with the state of the art on two benchmark datasets. The run-time increases near linearly with each image; the main cost is minimizing a QPB function which takes $5 - 20s$ per image per iteration (convergence in 5 iterations). No superpixels were used, the segmentation was performed at the pixel level. Other than these experiments, we evaluated how often the "correct" basis vectors $A \subset D$ are chosen by the algorithm during segmentation. To do this, we manually found correspondences between each image in the test and training class for MSRC data. The number of histogram bin centers in [19] was fixed to 500. Feedback for MSRC experiments suggested that for the 125 images in Fig. 4, the model identified the correct basis subset over 90% of the time.

6 Discussion

We propose new algorithms for simultaneous segmentation of multiple objects from image collections, by analyzing and exploiting their shared subspace structure. Our models, for both unsupervised and supervised setting, extend the current state of the art for such approaches, which until now, has been limited to identifying a single common object. We believe this makes idea of cosegmentation applicable to a much wider class of problems, therefore significantly extends the operating range of such methods. Experiments on benchmark datasets show that algorithm performs well on a variety of image sets.

References

1. Rother, C., Kolmogorov, V., Blake, A.: "GrabCut": interactive foreground extraction using iterated graph cuts. ACM Trans. on Graphics 23, 309–314 (2004)
2. Gehler, P.V., Nowozin, S.: On feature combination for multiclass object classification. In: ICCV (2009)
3. Rother, C., Minka, T., Blake, A., Kolmogorov, V.: Cosegmentation of image pairs by histogram matching: Incorporating a global constraint into MRFs. In: CVPR (2006)
4. Batra, D., Kowdle, A., Parikh, D., Luo, J., Chen, T.: iCoseg: Interactive co-segmentation with intelligent scribble guidance. In: CVPR (2010)
5. Chu, W.-S., Chen, C.-P., Chen, C.-S.: MOMI-Cosegmentation: Simultaneous Segmentation of Multiple Objects among Multiple Images. In: Kimmel, R., Klette, R., Sugimoto, A. (eds.) ACCV 2010, Part I. LNCS, vol. 6492, pp. 355–368. Springer, Heidelberg (2011)
6. Mu, Y., Zhou, B.: Co-segmentation of Image Pairs with Quadratic Global Constraint in MRFs. In: Yagi, Y., Kang, S.B., Kweon, I.S., Zha, H. (eds.) ACCV 2007, Part II. LNCS, vol. 4844, pp. 837–846. Springer, Heidelberg (2007)
7. Mukherjee, L., Singh, V., Dyer, C.R.: Half-integrality based algorithms for cosegmentation of images. In: CVPR (2009)
8. Vicente, S., Kolmogorov, V., Rother, C.: Cosegmentation Revisited: Models and Optimization. In: Daniilidis, K., Maragos, P., Paragios, N. (eds.) ECCV 2010, Part II. LNCS, vol. 6312, pp. 465–479. Springer, Heidelberg (2010)
9. Joulin, A., Bach, F., Ponce, J.: Discriminative clustering for image co-segmentation. In: CVPR (2010)
10. Hochbaum, D.S., Singh, V.: An efficient algorithm for co-segmentation. In: ICCV (2009)
11. Vicente, S., Kolmogorov, V., Rother, C.: Object cosegmentation. In: CVPR (2011)
12. Collins, M.D., Xu, J., Grady, L., Singh, V.: Random walks based multi-image segmentation: Quasiconvexity results and gpu-based solutions. In: CVPR (2012)
13. Mukherjee, L., Singh, V., Peng, J.: Scale invariant cosegmentation for image groups. In: CVPR (2011)
14. Chang, K., Liu, T., Lai, S.: From cosaliency to cosegmentation: An efficient and fully unsupervised energy minimization model. In: CVPR (2011)
15. Chai, Y., Lempitsky, V., Zisserman, A.: Bicos: A bi-level co-segmentation method for image classification. In: ICCV (2011)
16. Glasner, D., Vitaladevuni, S., Basri, R.: Contour based joint clustering of multiple segmentations. In: CVPR (2011)
17. Kim, G., Xing, E.P., Fei-Fei, L., Kanade, T.: Distributed cosegmentation vis submodular optimization on anisotropic diffusion. In: ICCV (2011)
18. Joulin, A., Bach, F., Ponce, J.: Multi-class cosegmentation. In: CVPR (2012)
19. Winn, J., Criminisi, A., Minka, T.: Object categorization by learned universal visual dictionary. In: ICCV (2005)
20. Liu, G., Lin, Z., Yu, Y.: Robust subspace segmentation by low-rank representation. In: ICML (2010)
21. Favaro, P., Vidal, R., Ravichandran, A.: A closed form solution to robust subspace estimation and clustering. In: CVPR (2011)
22. Boykov, Y., Veksler, O., Zabih, R.: Fast approximate energy minimization via graph cuts. PAMI 23 (2001)

23. Boros, E., Hammer, P.: Pseudo-Boolean optimization. Disc. Appl. Math. 123, 155–225 (2002)
24. Rother, C., Kolmogorov, V., Lempitsky, V., Szummer, M.: Optimizing binary MRFs via extended roof duality. In: CVPR (2007)
25. Hochbaum, D.: Polynomial time algorithms for ratio regions and a variant of normalized cut. PAMI 32 (2010)
26. Cevher, V., Krause, A.: Greedy dictionary selection for sparse representation. IEEE J. of Selected Topics in Signal Processing 5, 979–983 (2011)
27. Jenatton, R., Mairal, J., Obozinski, G., Bach, F.: Proximal methods for sparse hierarchical dictionary learning. In: ICML (2010)
28. Krause, A., Cevher, V.: Submodular dictionary selection for sparse representation. In: ICML (2010)
29. Kolmogorov, V., Zabih, R.: What energy functions can be minimized via graph cuts? PAMI 26 (2004)
30. Narasimhan, M., Bilmes, J.: A submodular-supermodular procedure with applications to discriminative structure learning. In: UAI (2005)

Artistic Image Classification: An Analysis on the PRINTART Database

Gustavo Carneiro[1], Nuno Pinho da Silva[2], Alessio Del Bue[3], and João Paulo Costeira[2,*]

[1] Australian Centre for Visual Technologies, The University of Adelaide, Australia
[2] Instituto de Sistemas e Robótica, Instituto Superior Técnico, Portugal
[3] PAVIS, Istituto Italiano di Tecnologia (IIT), Italy

Abstract. Artistic image understanding is an interdisciplinary research field of increasing importance for the computer vision and the art history communities. For computer vision scientists, this problem offers challenges where new techniques can be developed; and for the art history community new automatic art analysis tools can be developed. On the positive side, artistic images are generally constrained by compositional rules and artistic themes. However, the low-level texture and color features exploited for photographic image analysis are not as effective because of inconsistent color and texture patterns describing the visual classes in artistic images. In this work, we present a new database of monochromatic artistic images containing 988 images with a global semantic annotation, a local compositional annotation, and a pose annotation of human subjects and animal types. In total, 75 visual classes are annotated, from which 27 are related to the theme of the art image, and 48 are visual classes that can be localized in the image with bounding boxes. Out of these 48 classes, 40 have pose annotation, with 37 denoting human subjects and 3 representing animal types. We also provide a complete evaluation of several algorithms recently proposed for image annotation and retrieval. We then present an algorithm achieving remarkable performance over the most successful algorithm hitherto proposed for this problem. Our main goal with this paper is to make this database, the evaluation process, and the benchmark results available for the computer vision community.

1 Introduction

Artistic image understanding is a field of research that stimulates the development of interdisciplinary work. In this paper, we consider artistic image to be an artistic expression represented on a flat surface (e.g., canvas or sheet of paper) in the form of a painting, printing, or drawing. Even though we have observed a increasing interest in this area, there is still a lack of common evaluation

* This work was supported by the FCT (ISR/IST plurianual funding) through the PIDDAC Program funds and FCT Project PRINTART (PTDC/EEA-CRO/098822/2008).

A. Fitzgibbon et al. (Eds.): ECCV 2012, Part IV, LNCS 7575, pp. 143–157, 2012.

Fig. 1. Examples of a scene depicting the same artistic theme "The Annunciation". Figure (a) shows a real photo of the scene, while in figure (b) a painting is displayed, and (c) shows an art print.

Fig. 2. Examples of the global, local and pose annotations made by the art historians. More training samples are provided in the supplementary material.

databases and procedures, similar to the ones found in photographic image retrieval and annotation, such as: Pascal VOC, Imagenet, TinyImages, Lotus Hill, SUN database to cite a few. Different from photographic images, art images can be better constrained based on compositional rules and themes. However, the texture and color patterns of visual classes (e.g., sky, sea, sand) are not consistently expressed in the artistic images, which makes the exploitation of low-level image features more challenging. In fact, current art image processing has shown that texture and color patterns in artistic images are more effectively used to classify painting styles [1] or artists [2] than to identify visual classes. For instance, Fig. 1 shows examples of a photo, a painting, and a print of a scene depicting the artistic theme "The Annunciation". Notice how the low-level features in the photographic image are more likely to successfully represent visual classes in the photo than in the artistic images.

We define artistic image understanding as a process that receives an artistic image and outputs a set of global, local and pose annotations. The global annotations consist of a set of artistic keywords describing the contents of the image. Local annotations comprise a set of bounding boxes that localize certain visual classes, and pose annotations consist of a set of body parts that indicate the

Fig. 3. Influence of Japanese art prints (a) on impressionist paintings (b), and of monochromatic art prints (c) on tile panel paintings (d)

pose of humans and animals in the image (see Fig. 2). Another process involved in the artistic image understanding is the retrieval of images given a query containing an artistic keyword. Systems developed for such end are of paramount importance to art historians for the task of analyzing artistic production, or can be part of an augmented reality method that provides information of an object of art given a digital picture of it.

A visual art form that is particularly important for the analysis of art images is printmaking. Printmaking is the process of creating prints from the impression that the print creator has of a painting (i.e., the print produced is similar to the original painting, but not identical). Cheap paper production and advancements in graphical arts resulted in an intensive use of printmaking methods over the last five centuries, which generated prints that have reached a significantly large number of artists. The main consequence of this wide availability of prints is their influence over several generations of artists, who have used them as a source of inspiration for their own production. For instance, Fig. 3 displays the influence of Japanese art prints on impressionist artists of the XIX century [3], and the influence of monochromatic art prints on artistic tile painters in Portugal. Therefore, a system that can automatically annotate and retrieve art prints has the potential to become a key tool for the understanding of the visual arts produced in the last five centuries.

In this paper, we present a new annotated database composed of artistic images that will be available for the computer vision community in order to start a comprehensive and principled investigation on artistic image understanding. Given the expert knowledge required for annotating this kind of images, it is not possible to use crowdsourcing tools (e.g., Amazon mechanical turk). Hence, art historians annotated 988 monochromatic artistic images, representing prints of religious themes made between the XV and XVII centuries in Europe. In this multi-label multi-class problem, 75 visual classes are annotated, from which 27 are related to the theme of the art image, and 48 are visual classes that can be

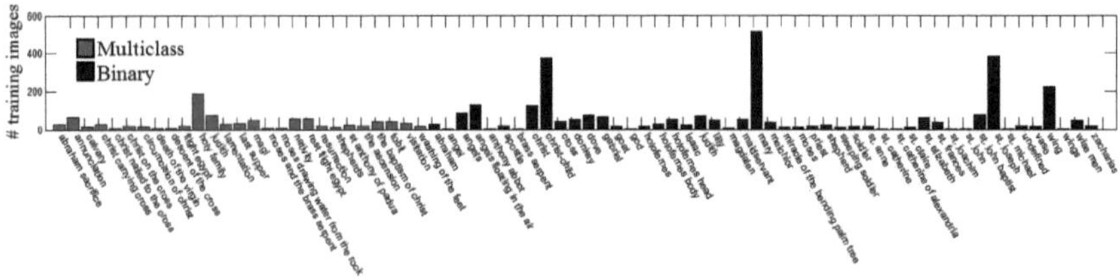

Fig. 4. Number of training images per class

localized in the image with bounding boxes. Out of these 48 classes, 40 visual classes have pose annotation, where 37 denote human subjects and 3 represent animal types. Figure 2 shows an example of the global, local and pose annotations produced by an art historian. We suggest error measures for the problems of global image annotation, image retrieval, local visual object detection, and pose estimation. Moreover, we test several methodologies and report their error measures that will be used as benchmarks for the problem. Specifically, we consider the following methodologies: random, bag of features [4], label propagation [5], inverted label propagation [6], matrix completion [7], and structural learning [8]. In particular, we introduce an improved inverted label propagation method that produces the best results, both in the automatic (global, local and pose) annotation and retrieval problems. This database will be freely available on the web [9], together with a table containing up-to-date results, a list of suggested error measures (with the respective code), and links to the evaluated techniques.

Literature Review. The current focus of art image analysis is on the forgery detection problem [10,2] and on the classification of painting styles [1]. The methodologies being developed can be regarded as adaptations of systems that work for photographic images, where the main changes are centered on the type of feature used and on spatial dependencies of local image descriptors. A particularly similar database to the one presented in this paper is the ancient Chinese painting data-set used for the multi-class classification of painting styles [11], which consists of monochromatic art images. Another important reference for our paper is the work by Yelizaveta et al. [12], which handles the multi-class classification of brush strokes, but they do not consider the multi-label problem being handled in our paper. Recently, Carneiro [6] shows a methodology for art image retrieval and *global* annotation, but he did not propose a database of artistic images, nor did he investigate local and pose annotation problems.

2 Database Collection and Evaluation Protocols

The artistic image database comprises 988 images with global, local and pose annotations (Fig. 2). All images have been collected from the Artstor digital image library [13], and annotated by art historians. The first stage consists of a global annotation containing one multi-class problem (theme with 27 classes) and 48 binary problems (Fig. 4 shows the class names and the respective number of training images). All these 48 binary problems comprise visual classes that can be localized in the image with bounding boxes forming the local annotation, as depicted in the central frame of Fig. 2. Finally, out of these 48 visual classes, 37 are annotated with the pose of the human subject and 3 are annotated with animal pose. The pose annotation is composed of torso and head (both represented by a bounding box), as shown in the right frame of Fig. 2.

Notation. The training set is represented by $\mathcal{D} = \{(\mathbf{x}, \mathbf{y}, \mathcal{L}, \mathcal{P})_i\}_{i=1}^{|\mathcal{D}|}$, where $\mathbf{x}_i$ is a feature vector representing an image I_i, $\mathbf{y}_i$ is the global annotation of that image representing the M multi-class and binary problems, so $\mathbf{y}_i = [\mathbf{y}_i(1), ..., \mathbf{y}_i(M)] \in \{0,1\}^Y$, where each problem is denoted by $\mathbf{y}_i(k) \in \{0,1\}^{|\mathbf{y}_i(k)|}$ with $|\mathbf{y}_i(k)|$ denoting the dimensionality of $\mathbf{y}_i(k)$ (i.e., $|\mathbf{y}_i(k)| = 1$ for binary problems and $|\mathbf{y}_i(k)| > 1$ with $\|\mathbf{y}_l\|_1 = 1$ for multi-class problems). This means that binary problems involve an annotation that indicates the presence or absence of a visual class, while multi-class annotation regards problems that one and only one of the possible classes is present. The set $\mathcal{L}_i$ represents the local annotation of image I_i denoted by a set of bounding boxes, each related to one of the binary classes of $\mathbf{y}_i$. Specifically, we have $\mathcal{L}_i = \{\mathbf{l}_{i,j}\}_{j=1}^{|\mathcal{L}_i|}$ with $\mathbf{l}_{i,j} = [y, \mathbf{b}]$, where $y \in \{1, ..., Y\}$ represents the visual class of the bounding box, $\mathbf{b} = [\mathbf{z}, w, h]$ with $\mathbf{z} \in \Re^2$ being the top-left corner and w and h, the width and height of the box, respectively. Finally, the set $\mathcal{P}_i = \{\mathbf{p}_{i,j}\}_{j=1}^{|\mathcal{P}_i|}$ denotes the pose annotation of image I_i, where $\mathbf{p}_{i,j} = [y, \mathbf{b}^{head}, \mathbf{b}^{torso}]$, where $\mathbf{b}^{head}$ denotes the bounding box of the head, and $\mathbf{b}^{torso}$ is the bounding box of the torso annotation. An annotated test set is represented by $\mathcal{T} = \{(\widetilde{\mathbf{x}}, \widetilde{\mathbf{y}}, \widetilde{\mathcal{L}}, \widetilde{\mathcal{P}})_i\}_{i=1}^{|\mathcal{T}|}$, but the annotations in the test set are used only for the purpose of methodology evaluation.

The label cardinality of the database, computed as $LC = \frac{1}{|\mathcal{D}|+|\mathcal{T}|} \sum_{i=1}^{|\mathcal{D}|+|\mathcal{T}|} \|\mathbf{y}_i\|_1$, is 4.22, while the label density $LD = \frac{1}{(|\mathcal{D}|+|\mathcal{T}|)Y} \sum_{i=1}^{|\mathcal{D}|+|\mathcal{T}|} \|\mathbf{y}_i\|_1$, is 0.05, where $Y = 75$ and $|\mathcal{D}| + |\mathcal{T}| = 988$.

2.1 Annotation and Retrieval Problems

For computing the error measures, 10 different training and test sets are available, with training sets comprising $|\mathcal{D}| = 889$ images (90% of the annotated images) and test sets with $|\mathcal{T}| = 99$ images (10% of the annotated images). The results are reported based on the performance computed over the test set $\mathcal{T}$ after training the methodology with the training set $\mathcal{D}$. Below, we define the error measures for the global annotation, retrieval, local and pose annotation.

Global Annotation. The global annotation process of a test image $\widetilde{\mathbf{x}}$ is achieved by finding $\mathbf{y}^*$ that solves the following optimization problem:

$$\begin{aligned} &\text{maximize } p(\mathbf{y}|\widetilde{\mathbf{x}}) \\ &\text{subject to } \mathbf{y} = [\mathbf{y}(1), ..., \mathbf{y}(M)] \in \{0,1\}^Y, \\ &\qquad \|\mathbf{y}(k)\|_1 = 1 \text{ for } \{k \in \{1, ..., M\} | |\mathbf{y}(k)| > 1\}, \end{aligned} \tag{1}$$

where $p(\mathbf{y}|\widetilde{\mathbf{x}})$ is a probability function that computes the confidence of annotating the test image $\widetilde{\mathbf{x}}$ with vector $\mathbf{y}$. We assess the *label-based global annotation* of each visual class y using the following precision, recall and F1 measures:

$$pga(y) = \frac{\sum_{i=1}^{|\mathcal{T}|}(\pi_y \odot \mathbf{y}_i^*)^\top \widetilde{\mathbf{y}}_i}{\sum_{i=1}^{|\mathcal{T}|}\pi_y^\top \mathbf{y}_i^*},\ rga(y) = \frac{\sum_{i=1}^{|\mathcal{T}|}(\pi_y \odot \mathbf{y}_i^*)^\top \widetilde{\mathbf{y}}_i}{\sum_{i=1}^{|\mathcal{T}|}\pi_y^\top \widetilde{\mathbf{y}}_i},\ fga(y) = \frac{2pga(y)rga(y)}{pga(y)+rga(y)}, \tag{2}$$

where $\pi_y \in \{0,1\}^Y$ is one at the yth position and zero elsewhere, and $\odot$ denotes the element-wise multiplication operator. The values of $pga(y)$, $rga(y)$ and $fga(y)$ are averaged over the visual classes. Notice in (2) that we only assess the result class by class independently. We also need to measure the performance considering all the annotated classes jointly. The following *example-based global annotation* measures (precision, recall and F1) are used in order to assess the performance in multi-label problems [14]:

$$pge = \frac{1}{|\mathcal{T}|}\sum_{i=1}^{|\mathcal{T}|}\frac{(\mathbf{y}_i^*)^\top \widetilde{\mathbf{y}}_i}{\|\mathbf{y}_i^*\|_1},\ rge = \frac{1}{|\mathcal{T}|}\sum_{i=1}^{|\mathcal{T}|}\frac{(\mathbf{y}_i^*)^\top \widetilde{\mathbf{y}}_i}{\|\widetilde{\mathbf{y}}_i\|_1},\ fge = \frac{1}{|\mathcal{T}|}\sum_{i=1}^{|\mathcal{T}|}\frac{2(\mathbf{y}_i^*)^\top \widetilde{\mathbf{y}}_i}{\|\mathbf{y}_i^*\|_1+\|\widetilde{\mathbf{y}}_i\|_1}. \tag{3}$$

Image Retrieval. The retrieval problem is defined as the most relevant test image returned from $\mathcal{T}$ given a query represented by a vector $\mathbf{q}$, as in:

$$\widetilde{\mathbf{x}}^* = \arg\max_{\widetilde{\mathbf{x}} \in \mathcal{T}} p(\widetilde{\mathbf{x}}|\mathbf{q}), \tag{4}$$

where $p(\widetilde{\mathbf{x}}|\mathbf{q})$ computes the probability of returning the image $\widetilde{\mathbf{x}} \in \mathcal{T}$ given the query vector $\mathbf{q} \in \{0,1\}^Y$. Although $\mathbf{q}$ can represent any combinations of classes, in this paper, we restrict $\mathbf{q}$ to have only one class (i.e., $\|\mathbf{q}\|_1 = 1$). The *label-based retrieval* is evaluated from the following precision and recall measures computed using the first $Q \leq |\mathcal{T}|$ images retrieved (sorted by $p(\widetilde{\mathbf{x}}|\mathbf{q})$ in (4) in descending order):

$$pr(\mathbf{q}, Q) = \frac{\sum_{i=1}^{Q}\delta(\widetilde{\mathbf{y}}^\top \mathbf{q} - \mathbf{1}^\top \mathbf{q})}{Q},\ \text{and}\ rr(\mathbf{q}, Q) = \frac{\sum_{i=1}^{Q}\delta(\widetilde{\mathbf{y}}^\top \mathbf{q} - \mathbf{1}^\top \mathbf{q})}{\sum_{i=1}^{|\mathcal{T}|}\delta(\widetilde{\mathbf{y}}^\top \mathbf{q} - \mathbf{1}^\top \mathbf{q})}, \tag{5}$$

where $\delta(.)$ is the Kronecker delta function. These precision and recall measures are used to compute the mean average precision (MAP), which is defined as the average precision over all queries, at the ranks that the recall changes.

Local Annotation. The local annotation aims at finding the bounding boxes of the visual classes present in the image. The following optimization problem finds the local annotation $\mathcal{L}^*$ given the test image and its global annotation:

$$\text{maximize}\ p(\mathcal{L}|\mathbf{y}, \widetilde{\mathbf{x}}), \tag{6}$$

where each k that $|\mathbf{y}(k)| = 1$ and $\mathbf{y}(k) = 1$ has a respective bounding box $\mathbf{l}_j^* \in \mathcal{L}^*$. The *label-based local annotation* of each visual class y is assessed with the following precision, recall and F1 measures [15]:

$$pla(y) = \frac{\sum_{i=1}^{|\mathcal{T}|}a(\mathbf{l}_i^*(y) \bigcap \widetilde{\mathbf{l}}_i(y))}{\sum_{i=1}^{|\mathcal{T}|}a(\widetilde{\mathbf{l}}_i(y))},\ rla(y) = \frac{\sum_{i=1}^{|\mathcal{T}|}a(\mathbf{l}_i^*(y) \bigcap \widetilde{\mathbf{l}}_i(y))}{\sum_{i=1}^{|\mathcal{T}|}a(\widetilde{\mathbf{l}}_i(y))},\ fla(y) = \frac{2pla(y)rla(y)}{pla(y)+rla(y)}, \tag{7}$$

where the function $a(\mathbf{l})$ returns the area (in pixels) of the bounding box defined by $\mathbf{l}$ (see above in Sec. 2), and operator $\bigcap$ returns the intersection between the bounding boxes from estimation $\mathbf{l}_i^*(y)$ and from ground truth $\widetilde{\mathbf{l}}_i(y)$ in the test image (note that both boxes are related to class y). The values of $pla(y)$, $rla(y)$ and $fla(y)$ are then averaged over the visual classes. Notice that in (7) we only assess the result class by class independently. We also need to measure the performance considering all the annotated classes jointly. The following *example-based local annotation* measures (precision, recall and F1) are used in order to assess the performance in multi-label problems:

$$ple = \frac{1}{|\mathcal{T}|}\sum_{i=1}^{|\mathcal{T}|}\sum_{y=1}^{Y}\frac{a(\mathbf{l}_i^*(y)\bigcap\widetilde{\mathbf{l}}_i(y))}{a(\mathbf{l}_i^*(y))},\ rle = \frac{1}{|\mathcal{T}|}\sum_{i=1}^{|\mathcal{T}|}\sum_{y=1}^{Y}\frac{a(\mathbf{l}_i^*(y)\bigcap\widetilde{\mathbf{l}}_i(y))}{a(\widetilde{\mathbf{l}}_i(y))},$$
$$fle = \frac{1}{|\mathcal{T}|}\sum_{i=1}^{|\mathcal{T}|}\sum_{y=1}^{Y}\frac{2(a(\mathbf{l}_i^*(y)\bigcap\widetilde{\mathbf{l}}_i(y)))}{a(\mathbf{l}_i^*(y))+a(\widetilde{\mathbf{l}}_i(y))}. \quad (8)$$

Pose Annotation. Finally, for the pose annotation, we assume the knowledge of global and local annotations in order to arrive at the pose annotation $\mathcal{P}^*$, as follows:

$$\text{maximize } p(\mathcal{P}|\mathcal{L},\mathbf{y},\widetilde{\mathbf{x}}), \quad (9)$$

where each k that $|\mathbf{y}(k)| = 1$ and $\mathbf{y}(k) = 1$ has a respective bounding box $\mathbf{l}_j \in \mathcal{L}$, and the head and torso bounding boxes are within the local annotation bounding box. The *label-based pose annotation* of the *head* visual class is assessed with the following precision, recall and F1 measures [15]:

$$ppa(y,head) = \frac{\sum_{i=1}^{|\mathcal{T}|} a(\mathbf{p}_i^*(y,head)\bigcap\widetilde{\mathbf{p}}_i(y,head))}{\sum_{i=1}^{|\mathcal{T}|} a(\mathbf{p}_i^*(y,head))},$$
$$rpa(y,head) = \frac{\sum_{i=1}^{|\mathcal{T}|} a(\mathbf{l}_i^*(y,head)\bigcap\widetilde{\mathbf{l}}_i(y,head))}{\sum_{i=1}^{|\mathcal{T}|} a(\widetilde{\mathbf{p}}_i(y,head))}, \quad (10)$$
$$fpa(y,head) = \frac{2ppa(y,head)rpa(y)}{ppa(y,head)+rpa(y,head)},$$

and similarly for *torso*, where the function $a(\mathbf{p}(y,head))$ returns the area (in pixels) of the bounding box defined by $\mathbf{p}$ (see above in Sec. 2), and operator $\bigcap$ returns the intersection between the bounding boxes from estimation $\mathbf{p}_i^*(y,head)$ and from ground truth $\widetilde{\mathbf{p}}_i(y,head)$ in test image i (note that both boxes are related to class y). The values of $ppa(y)$, $rpa(y)$ and $fpa(y)$ are then averaged over the visual classes. Notice in (10) that we only assess the result class by class independently. We also need to measure the performance considering all the annotated classes jointly. The following *example-based pose annotation* measures (precision, recall and F1) are used in order to assess the performance in multi-label problems:

$$ppe = \frac{1}{|\mathcal{T}|}\sum_{i=1}^{|\mathcal{T}|}\sum_{y=1}^{Y}\sum_{m\in\{head,torso\}}\frac{a(\mathbf{p}_i^*(y,m)\bigcap\widetilde{\mathbf{p}}_i(y,m))}{a(\mathbf{p}_i^*(y,m))},$$
$$rpe = \frac{1}{|\mathcal{T}|}\sum_{i=1}^{|\mathcal{T}|}\sum_{y=1}^{Y}\sum_{m\in\{head,torso\}}\frac{a(\mathbf{p}_i^*(y,m)\bigcap\widetilde{\mathbf{p}}_i(y,m))}{a(\widetilde{\mathbf{p}}_i(y,m))}, \quad (11)$$
$$fpe = \frac{1}{|\mathcal{T}|}\sum_{i=1}^{|\mathcal{T}|}\sum_{y=1}^{Y}\sum_{m\in\{head,torso\}}\frac{2(a(\mathbf{l}_i^*(y,m)\bigcap\widetilde{\mathbf{l}}_i(y)))}{a(\mathbf{p}_i^*(y,m))+a(\widetilde{\mathbf{p}}_i(y,m))}.$$

3 Image Annotation and Retrieval Procedures

In this section, we describe the image representation and the different methodologies used to solve for the annotation and retrieval problems.

3.1 Image Representation

The images are represented with the spatial pyramid [16] (with three levels), which is an extension of the bag of visual words [4], where each visual word is formed with a collection of local descriptors. The local descriptors are extracted with the scale invariant feature transform (SIFT) [17] using a uniform grid over the image and scale space in order to have 10000 descriptors per image. The vocabulary is built by gathering the descriptors from all images and running a hierarchical clustering algorithm with three levels, where each node in the hierarchy has 10 descendants [18]. This results in a directed tree with $1+10+100+1000 = 1111$ vertexes, and the image feature is formed by using each descriptor of the image to traverse the tree and record the path (note that each descriptor generates a path with 4 vertexes). The histogram of visited vertexes is weighted by the node entropy (i.e., vertexes that are visited more often receive smaller weights). The spatial pyramid representation is achieved by tiling the image in three levels, as follows: the first level comprises the whole image, the second level divides the image into 2×2 regions, and the third level breaks the image into 3×1 regions. This tiling has shown the best results in the latest Pascal VOC image classification competitions [19]. This means that there are 8 histograms describing an image, represented by $\mathbf{x} \in \Re^X$, where $X = 8 \times 1111$.

3.2 Methodologies

We explored different annotation methodologies that have recently shown state-of-the-art results in several photographic image annotation processes. Specifically, we evaluate the performance of inductive and transductive methodologies, and use a random annotation approach for comparison. For the inductive learning, we study the performance of bag of feature and structural learning approaches. The transductive methodology is tested with different types of label propagation methods.

Random. The random global annotation takes into consideration the priors of the visual classes as follows:

$$\text{Multiclass: } \{k : |\mathbf{y}(k)| > 1\} \qquad\qquad \text{Binary: } \{k : |\mathbf{y}(k)| = 1\}$$
$$\mathbf{y}^*(k) = \begin{cases} \pi_1, & r < p(\mathbf{y}(k) = \pi_1) \\ \vdots & \\ \pi_{|\mathbf{y}(k)|}, & \sum_{j=1}^{|\mathbf{y}(k)|-1} p(\mathbf{y}(k) = \pi_j) \leq r < 1 \end{cases}, \quad \mathbf{y}^*(k) = \begin{cases} 1, & r < p(\mathbf{y}(k) = 1) \\ 0, & \text{otherwise} \end{cases}, \tag{12}$$

where $r \sim \mathcal{U}(0,1)$ (with $\mathcal{U}(0,1)$ denoting the uniform distribution between 0 and 1), $p(\mathbf{y}(k) = \pi_j) = \frac{1}{|\mathcal{D}|} \sum_{i=1}^{|\mathcal{D}|} \mathbf{y}(k)_i^\top \pi_j$ (with $\pi_j = 1$ for binary problems and

$\pi_j \in \{0,1\}^{|\mathbf{y}(k)|}$ with zeros everywhere except at the jth position). The retrieval is done by first computing the global annotations for the test images in the set $\mathcal{T}$, and then the images are ranked based on the Hamming distance between query and test image annotations, as in:

$$\Delta(\mathbf{q}, \mathbf{y}) = \|\mathbf{q} - \mathbf{y}^*\|_1. \tag{13}$$

The local and pose annotations are achieved for each visual class by first selecting the training image with the smallest value for

$$i^* = \arg \min_{j \in \{1,...,|\mathcal{D}|\}} \Delta(\mathbf{y}^*, \mathbf{y}_j), \tag{14}$$

and assign $\mathcal{L}^* = \mathcal{L}_{i^*}$ and $\mathcal{P}^* = \mathcal{P}_{i^*}$. The acronym for this approach is **RND**.

Bag of Features. The bag of features model is based on Y support vector machine (SVM) classifiers using the one-versus-all training method. Specifically, we train the Y classifiers (each classifier for each label) $p(\mathbf{y}(k) = \pi_j | \widetilde{\mathbf{x}}, \theta_{SVM}(k,j))$, for $k \in \{1, ..., M\}$, $j \in \{1, ..., |\mathbf{y}(k)|\}$, $\pi_j \in \{0,1\}^{|\mathbf{y}(k)|}$ (with the jth element equal to one and rest are zero), and the annotation and retrieval use the same methods in (1) and (4), respectively, replacing $p(\mathbf{y}|\widetilde{\mathbf{x}})$ by $p(\mathbf{y}(k) = \pi_j | \widetilde{\mathbf{x}}, \theta_{SVM}(j))$. The penalty factor of the SVM for the slack variables is determined via cross-validation, where the training set $\mathcal{D}$ is divided into a training and validation sets of 90% and 10% of $\mathcal{D}$, respectively. This model roughly represents the state-of-the-art approach for image annotation and retrieval problems [20]. The extension to the retrieval problem is based on (13), and the local and pose annotations follow the method in (14). The acronym for this approach is **BoF**.

Label Propagation. The label propagation encodes the similarity between pairs of images using the graph Laplacian, and estimate the annotations of test image using transductive inference. This method has been intensively investigated, and we only present the main developments, which are the following. Find the annotation matrix $\mathbf{F}^*$ using the following optimization problem [5]:

$$\begin{array}{ll} \text{minimize} & 0.5 \operatorname{tr}(\mathbf{F}^\top (\mathbf{D} - \mathbf{W}) \mathbf{F}) \\ \text{subject to} & \mathbf{f}_i = \mathbf{y}_i, \text{ for } i = 1, ..., |\mathcal{D}| \end{array}, \tag{15}$$

where $\mathbf{W}, \mathbf{F}, \mathbf{D} \in \Re^{(|\mathcal{D}|+|\mathcal{T}|)\times(|\mathcal{D}|+|\mathcal{T}|)}$ with $\mathbf{W}_{ij} = \exp\{-0.5\,\|\mathbf{x}_i - \mathbf{x}_j\|_2^2/\sigma^2\}$ such that the index for the training set is from 1 to $|\mathcal{D}|$ and for the test set from $|\mathcal{D}|+1$ to $|\mathcal{D}|+|\mathcal{T}|$, $\mathbf{D}$ is a diagonal matrix with its (i,i)-element equal to the sum of the ith row of $\mathbf{W}$, and tr(.) computes the trace of a matrix. This problem has the closed form solution $\mathbf{F}^* = \beta(\mathbf{I} - \alpha(\mathbf{D} - \mathbf{W}))^{-1}\mathbf{Y}$, where $\mathbf{I}$ denotes the identity matrix,and α and β are regularization parameters such that $\alpha + \beta = 1$. In the experiments,this approach is named **LP**. The problem in (15) has been extended in order to include label correlation [21,22], as follows

$$\text{minimize } 0.5\operatorname{tr}(\mathbf{F}^\top(\mathbf{D}-\mathbf{W})\mathbf{F}) + (1-\mu)\operatorname{tr}((\mathbf{F}-\mathbf{Y})\Lambda(\mathbf{F}-\mathbf{Y})) + \mu\operatorname{tr}(\mathbf{F}\mathbf{C}\mathbf{F}^\top), \tag{16}$$

where Λ is a matrix containing ones in the diagonal from indices 1 to $|\mathcal{D}|$, and zero otherwise, and $\mathbf{C} \in [-1,1]^{Y \times Y}$ containing the correlation between classes.The problem in (16) has closed form solution $\mathbf{F}^* = (\mathbf{D} - \mathbf{W})^{-1}\mathbf{Y}(\mathbf{I} - \mu\mathbf{C})$, where μ is a regularization parameter. We represent this approach by **LP-CC** in the experiments. After finding $\mathbf{F}^*$, we need to define the values for $\mathbf{y}_i^*$ for each test image. We tried some alternatives present in the literature, but obtained the best performance with class mass normalization [23], which adjusts the class distributions to match the priors. The extension to the retrieval problem is based on (13), and the local and pose annotations follow the approach described in (14).

Inverted Label Propagation. By inverting the problem described in (15), it is possible to produce the global, local, and pose annotations simultaneously. Specifically, instead of inferring the labels of the test images (using matrix $\mathbf{F}$ in Eq. 15), the inverted label propagation returns a vector representing the probability of landing in one of the training images after starting the random walk process from a test image. Furthermore, the similarity between annotations (which in LP requires a reformulation of the problem) is incorporated in the adjacency matrix. Then, the annotation can be finalized using the training images annotations weighted by the probability of random walk process. Recently, Carneiro [6] has formulated the global annotation problem with the combinatorial harmonic (CH) approach [24], which computes the probability that a random walk starting at the test image $\widetilde{\mathbf{x}}$ first reaches each of the database samples $(\mathbf{x}, \mathbf{y}, \mathcal{L}, \mathcal{P})_i \in \mathcal{D}$. Assuming that the test image is represented by $\widetilde{\mathbf{x}}$, the adjacency matrix in this inverted problem is defined by taking into consideration both the image and label similarities, as in:

$$\mathbf{U}(j,i) = I_y(\mathbf{y}_i, \mathbf{y}_j) \times I_x(\mathbf{x}_i, \mathbf{x}_j) \times I_x(\mathbf{x}_j, \widetilde{\mathbf{x}}), \tag{17}$$

where $I_y(\mathbf{y}_i, \mathbf{y}_j) = \sum_{k=1}^{M} \lambda_k \times \mathbf{y}(k)_i^\top \mathbf{y}(k)_j$ (λ_k is the weight associated with the label k), and $I_x(\mathbf{x}_i, \mathbf{x}_j) = \sum_{d=1}^{X} \min(\mathbf{x}_i(d), \mathbf{x}_j(d))$ (i.e., this is the histogram intersection kernel over the spatial pyramid representation described in Sec. 3.1). Note that the matrix $\mathbf{U}$ in (17) is row normalized. The computation of the CH solution extends the adjacency matrix in (17), as in: $\widetilde{\mathbf{U}} = \begin{bmatrix} \mathbf{U} & \widetilde{\mathbf{u}} \\ \widetilde{\mathbf{u}}^T & 0 \end{bmatrix}$, where $\widetilde{\mathbf{u}}$ is the un-normalized initial distribution vector defined as $\mathbf{u} = [I_x(\mathbf{x}_1, \widetilde{\mathbf{x}}), ..., I_x(\mathbf{x}_{|\mathcal{D}|}, \widetilde{\mathbf{x}})]^\top$. Our goal is to find the distribution $\mathbf{g}^* \in \Re^{|\mathcal{D}|}$ ($\|\mathbf{g}^*\|_1 = 1$), representing the probability of first reaching each of the training images in a random walk procedure, where the labeling matrix $\mathbf{G} = \mathbf{I}$ (i.e., an $|\mathcal{D}| \times |\mathcal{D}|$ identity matrix) denotes a problem with $|\mathcal{D}|$ classes, with each training image representing a separate class. The estimation of $\mathbf{g}^*$ is based on the minimization of the following energy function:

$$E([\mathbf{G}, \mathbf{g}]) = \frac{1}{2} \left\| [\mathbf{G}, \mathbf{g}] \widetilde{\mathbf{L}} \begin{bmatrix} \mathbf{G}^T \\ \mathbf{g}^T \end{bmatrix} \right\|_2^2, \tag{18}$$

where $\widetilde{\mathbf{L}}$ is the Laplacian matrix computed from the the adjacency matrix $\widetilde{\mathbf{U}}$. This Laplacian matrix can be divided into blocks of the same sizes as in $\widetilde{\mathbf{U}}$, that is $\widetilde{\mathbf{L}} = \begin{bmatrix} \mathbf{L}_1 & \mathbf{B} \\ \mathbf{B}^T & \mathbf{L}_2 \end{bmatrix}$. Solving the following optimization problem produces $\mathbf{g}^*$ [24]:

$$\begin{aligned} &\text{minimize} \;\; E([\mathbf{G}, \mathbf{g}]) \\ &\text{subject to } \mathbf{G} = \mathbf{I}, \end{aligned} \tag{19}$$

which has the closed form solution [24]: $\mathbf{g}^* = (-\mathbf{L}_2^{-1}\mathbf{B}^T\mathbf{I})^\top$. Note that $\mathbf{g}^* \in [0,1]^{|\mathcal{D}|}$ and $\|\mathbf{g}^*\|_1 = 1$. In order to annotate the test image, one can use class mass normalization [6], but we propose an alternative way, which is to simply take the annotation of the training sample $\mathbf{y}_{i^*}, \mathcal{L}_{i^*}, \mathcal{P}_{i^*}$ with $i^* = \arg\max \mathbf{g}^*$. This allows to produce global, local and pose annotations, and the extension to the retrieval problem is based on (13). In the experiments, this approach is named **ILP-O**. Note that the original ILP [6] (with class mass normalization) is denoted by **ILP**.

Matrix Completion. The matrix completion formulation consists of forming a joint matrix with annotation and features $\mathbf{Z} = \begin{bmatrix} \mathbf{Z}_\mathbf{y} & \mathbf{Z}_{\mathbf{y}^*} \\ \mathbf{Z}_\mathbf{x} & \mathbf{Z}_{\widetilde{\mathbf{x}}} \end{bmatrix}$, where the goal is to find the values for $\mathbf{Z}_{\mathbf{y}^*} = [\mathbf{y}_1^* ... \mathbf{y}_{|\mathcal{T}|}^*]$ giving [7]:

$$\begin{aligned} &\text{minimize} \;\; \text{rank}(\mathbf{Z}) \\ &\text{subject to } \mathbf{Z}_\mathbf{y} = [\mathbf{y}_1 ... \mathbf{y}_{|\mathcal{D}|}], \; \mathbf{Z}_\mathbf{x} = [\mathbf{x}_1 ... \mathbf{x}_{|\mathcal{D}|}], \; \mathbf{Z}_{\widetilde{\mathbf{x}}} = [\widetilde{\mathbf{x}}_1 ... \widetilde{\mathbf{x}}_{|\mathcal{T}|}]. \end{aligned} \tag{20}$$

In (20), the non-convex minimization objective function rank is replaced by the convex nuclear norm $\|\mathbf{Z}\|_* = \sum_{k=1}^{min\{|\mathcal{D}|, Y+X\}} \sigma_k(\mathbf{Z})$, where the $\sigma_k(\mathbf{Z})$ are the singular values of $\mathbf{Z}$. Moreover, the equality constraints for $\mathbf{Z}_\mathbf{x}$ and $\mathbf{Z}_{\widetilde{\mathbf{x}}}$ are replaced by squared losses, and the one for $\mathbf{Z}_\mathbf{y}$ is relaxed to a logistic loss. After finding $\mathbf{Z}_{\mathbf{y}^*}$, we need to define the values for $\mathbf{y}_i^*$ for each test image, and we obtained the best results with class mass normalization [23]. This approach is extended for the retrieval problem using (13), and the local and pose annotations follow the approach described above in (14). This approach is represented by the acronym **MC** in the experiments.

Structural Learning. The structural learning formulation follows the structured SVM implementation [8], which is based on the margin maximization quadratic problem, defined by:

$$\begin{aligned} &\min_{\mathbf{w}, \xi} \;\; \|\mathbf{w}\|^2 + C \sum_{i=1}^{|\mathcal{D}|} \xi_i \\ &s.t. \;\; \mathbf{w}^\top \Psi(\mathbf{y}_i, \mathbf{x}_i) - \mathbf{w}^\top \Psi(\mathbf{y}, \mathbf{x}_i) + \xi_i \geq \Delta(\mathbf{y}_i, \mathbf{y}), \;\; i = 1 ... |\mathcal{D}|, \;\; \forall \mathbf{y} \in \{0,1\}^Y, \\ &\qquad \xi_i \geq 0, \;\; i = 1 ... |\mathcal{D}| \end{aligned} \tag{21}$$

where $\Delta(\mathbf{y}_i, \mathbf{y}) = \|\mathbf{y}_i - \mathbf{y}\|_1$ (13), $\Psi(\mathbf{y}, \mathbf{x}) = \mathbf{x} \otimes \mathbf{y} \in \Re^{X \times Y}$ (i.e., this is a tensor product combining the vectors $\mathbf{x}$ and $\mathbf{y}$ by replication the values of $\mathbf{x}$ in every dimension $y \in \{1, ..., Y\}$ where $\mathbf{y}^\top \pi_y = 1$), C is penalty for non-separable points, and ξ_d denotes the slack variables to deal with non-separable problems. The retrieval problem is based on (13), and the local and pose annotations follow (14). We represent this approach with the acronym **SL** in the experiments.

4 Experiments

In the experiments, we first compare the results of the global annotation and retrieval using all methods listed in Sec. 3.2 with the 10-fold cross validation experimental setup described in Sec. 2. For the **BoF**, we used the code implemented by Vedaldi and Fulkerson [25]. We implemented the code for **LP** following the algorithm by Zhou et al. [5]. For **LP-CC** we used the method by Wand et al. [21]. For **ILP** we follow the methodology by Carneiro [6], which was extended in this paper to produce the **ILP-O**. The **MC** was implemented based on the code MC-1 by Goldberg et al. [7], and for the **SL**, we used the code SVM^{struct} available from the page *svmligh.joachims.org/svm_ struct.html.* All regularization parameters in the algorithms above are learned via cross validation.

5 Discussion and Conclusions

According to the experiments, our extension of the inverted label propagation produces the best results. However, we note that the small training sets do not allow the inductive methodologies to build robust models for the majority of visual classes, and we believe that this is the main reason why **BoF** and **SL** do not produce the best results. We believe, that the superior performance of the inverted linear propagation is explained by the similar images from the same theme, containing the similar composition, visual classes and setting. Such similarities in art images arise from the artists' influence network. Therefore, given that the random walk process is highly likely to select the most similar images, the global annotation is often correct for the query image. The results for the local and pose annotation present an interesting challenge for the community. For

Table 1. Retrieval and global annotation performances in terms of the average ± standard deviation of measures (2)-(5) computed in a 10-fold cross validation experiment (the best performance for each measure is highlighted).

	Retrieval	Label-based global annotation			Example-based global annotation		
Models	Label MAP	Average Precision	Average Recall	Average F1	Average Precision	Average Recall	Average F1
RND	0.08 ± .06	0.06 ± .01	0.07 ± .01	0.06 ± .01	0.26 ± .02	0.21 ± .01	0.22 ± .01
BoF	0.12 ± .05	0.14 ± .11	0.10 ± .06	0.11 ± .08	0.35 ± .03	0.26 ± .08	0.30 ± .05
LP	0.11 ± .01	0.12 ± .02	0.12 ± .02	0.12 ± .02	0.32 ± .03	0.28 ± .02	0.26 ± .02
LP-CC	0.11 ± .01	0.13 ± .02	0.14 ± .02	0.13 ± .02	0.27 ± .03	0.26 ± .03	0.25 ± .03
ILP	0.14 ± .02	0.19 ± .03	**0.35 ± .03**	0.25 ± .04	0.24 ± .02	**0.48 ± .05**	0.30 ± .02
ILP-O	**0.18 ± .04**	**0.26 ± .05**	0.26 ± .05	**0.26 ± .05**	**0.39 ± .03**	0.39 ± .04	**0.38 ± .03**
MC	0.17 ± .01	0.24 ± .03	0.11 ± .02	0.15 ± .02	0.37 ± .02	0.28 ± .02	0.32 ± .02
SL	0.14 ± .01	0.18 ± .04	0.14 ± .03	0.16 ± .03	0.34 ± .04	0.31 ± .04	0.32 ± .04

Table 2. Local Annotation performance in terms of the average ± standard deviation of measures (7)-(8) computed in a 10-fold cross validation experiment (the best performance for each measure is highlighted).

	Label-based local annotation			Example-based local annotation		
Models	Average Precision	Average Recall	Average F1	Average Precision	Average Recall	Average F1
RND	$0.04 \pm .01$	$0.04 \pm .01$	$0.04 \pm .01$	$0.13 \pm .03$	$0.18 \pm .04$	$0.15 \pm .02$
BoF	$\mathbf{0.25 \pm .08}$	$0.05 \pm .03$	$0.07 \pm .03$	$\mathbf{0.28 \pm .05}$	$0.17 \pm .06$	$0.20 \pm .04$
LP	$0.12 \pm .05$	$0.06 \pm .02$	$0.08 \pm .02$	$0.21 \pm .02$	$0.19 \pm .04$	$0.20 \pm .02$
LP-CC	$0.08 \pm .02$	$0.06 \pm .01$	$0.07 \pm .01$	$0.12 \pm .02$	$0.17 \pm .04$	$0.14 \pm .02$
ILP	$0.06 \pm .03$	$0.10 \pm .03$	$0.07 \pm .03$	$0.13 \pm .02$	$0.19 \pm .03$	$0.16 \pm .02$
ILP-O	$0.15 \pm .05$	$\mathbf{0.16 \pm .05}$	$\mathbf{0.15 \pm .05}$	$0.21 \pm .03$	$\mathbf{0.24 \pm .03}$	$\mathbf{0.23 \pm .03}$
MC	$0.07 \pm .01$	$0.03 \pm .01$	$0.04 \pm .01$	$0.12 \pm .03$	$0.14 \pm .06$	$0.13 \pm .03$
SL	$0.09 \pm .00$	$0.06 \pm .01$	$0.07 \pm .01$	$0.18 \pm .03$	$0.20 \pm .04$	$0.19 \pm .01$

Table 3. Pose Annotation performance in terms of the average ± standard deviation of measures (10)-(11) computed in a 10-fold cross validation experiment (the best performance for each measure is highlighted).

	Label-based Pose annotation			Example-based Pose annotation		
Models	Average Precision	Average Recall	Average F1	Average Precision	Average Recall	Average F1
RND	$0.00 \pm .01$	$0.00 \pm .01$	$0.00 \pm .01$	$0.00 \pm .02$	$0.00 \pm .01$	$0.00 \pm .01$
BoF	$0.01 \pm .01$	$0.01 \pm .01$	$0.01 \pm .01$	$0.01 \pm .01$	$0.01 \pm .01$	$0.01 \pm .01$
LP	$0.00 \pm .00$	$0.00 \pm .00$	$0.00 \pm .00$	$0.00 \pm .00$	$0.00 \pm .00$	$0.00 \pm .00$
LP-CC	$0.00 \pm .00$	$0.00 \pm .00$	$0.00 \pm .00$	$0.00 \pm .00$	$0.00 \pm .00$	$0.00 \pm .00$
ILP	$0.01 \pm .01$	$0.01 \pm .01$	$0.01 \pm .01$	$0.01 \pm .01$	$0.01 \pm .01$	$0.01 \pm .01$
ILP-O	$\mathbf{0.05 \pm .04}$	$\mathbf{0.08 \pm .06}$	$\mathbf{0.06 \pm .05}$	$\mathbf{0.06 \pm .02}$	$\mathbf{0.07 \pm .02}$	$\mathbf{0.06 \pm .02}$
MC	$0.00 \pm .00$	$0.00 \pm .00$	$0.00 \pm .00$	$0.00 \pm .00$	$0.00 \pm .00$	$0.00 \pm .00$
SL	$0.00 \pm .00$	$0.00 \pm .00$	$0.00 \pm .00$	$0.00 \pm .00$	$0.00 \pm .00$	$0.00 \pm .00$

instance, exploring context cues may improve these results. Another point that can be explored is the use of people and face detectors in art images (we applied several state-of-the-art people and face detectors, but only obtained uninspiring results). In order to stimulate even more the research in this sub-field, we plan to add the delineation of arms and legs for the pose annotation. One final point, which is not evaluated in this work, concerns the image representation. Recently, wavelets produced excellent results on the forgery detection problem [2], but a more systematic comparison to other features is still necessary.

In conclusion, we believe that this database has the potential to spur a new sub-field of art image analysis within the computer vision community. The error measures and results provided can be used by the community to assess the progress made in this area. We believe that proper art image understanding has the potential to influence a more complete general image understanding.

The Table 1 shows the results (2)-(5) described for the global annotations process. The local annotation results explained in (7)-(8) are shown in Tab. 2, and the experimental results for the pose annotation are displayed in Tab. 3 using the measures (10)-(11). Figures 5 and 6 shows examples of retrieval and annotation results produced by the proposed **ILP-O**.

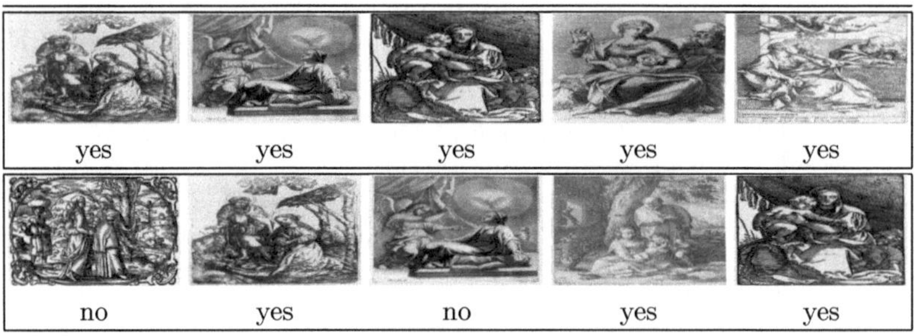

Fig. 5. Retrieval results of the **ILP-O**. Each row shows the top five matches to the following queries (from top to bottom): *'Holy Family'*, and *'Christ child'*. Below each image, it is indicated whether the image is annotated with the class.

Fig. 6. Annotation result of **ILP-O**. Note that the global annotation shown produced a perfect match with respect to the art historian's annotation.

Acknowledgments. The authors thank D. Lázaro and R. Carvalho for their help with the art history issues. We acknowledge the matrix completion code by R. Cabral. Finally, we thank D. Lowe for valuable suggestions on the development of this work.

References

1. Graham, D., Friedenberg, J., Rockmore, D., Field, D.: Mapping the similarity space of paintings: image statistics and visual perception. Visual Cognition 18, 559–573 (2010)
2. Li, J., Yao, L., Hendriks, E., Wang, J.: Rhythmic brushstrokes distinguish van gogh from his contemporaries: Findings via automated brushstroke extraction. IEEE TPAMI (accepted for publication in 2012)
3. Baumann, F., et al.: Degas Portraits. Merrell Holberton, London (1994)
4. Csurka, G., Dance, C., Fan, L., Willamowski, J., Bray, C.: Visual categorization with bags of keypoints. In: Workshop on Statistical Learning in Computer Vision, ECCV, pp. 1–22 (2004)
5. Zhou, D., Bousquet, O., Lal, T., Weston, J., Scholkopf, B.: Learning with local and global consistency. In: NIPS, pp. 321–328 (2004)
6. Carneiro, G.: Graph-based methods for the automatic annotation and retrieval of art prints. In: Proceedings of the ACM ICMR (2011)
7. Goldberg, A.B., Zhu, X., Recht, B., Xu, J., Nowak, R.D.: Transduction with matrix completion: Three birds with one stone. In: NIPS, pp. 757–765 (2010)

8. Tsochantaridis, I., Joachims, T., Hofmann, T., Altun, Y.: Large margin methods for structured and interdependent output variables. JMLR 6, 1453–1484 (2005)
9. http://printart.isr.ist.utl.pt
10. Johnson, C., Hendriks, E., Berezhnoy, I., Brevdo, E., Hughes, S., Daubechies, I., Li, J., Postma, E., Wang, J.: Image processing for artistic identification: Computerized analysis of Vincent Van Goghs brushstrokes. IEEE Sig. Proc. Ma., 37–48 (2008)
11. Li, J., Wang, J.: Studying digital imagery of ancient paintings by mixtures of stochastic models. IEEE Trans. Image Processing 13, 340–353 (2004)
12. Yelizaveta, M., Tat-Seng, C., Jain, R.: Semi-supervised annotation of brushwork in paintings domain using serial combinations of multiple experts. In: ACM Multimedia, pp. 529–538 (2006)
13. http://www.artstor.org
14. Nowak, S., Lukashevich, H., Dunker, P., Rüger, S.: Performance measures for multilabel evaluation: a case study in the area of image classification. In: Multimedia Information Retrieval, pp. 35–44 (2010)
15. Everingham, M., Van Gool, L.J., Williams, C., Winn, J., Zisserman, A.: The pascal visual object classes (voc) challenge. IJCV 88, 303–338 (2010)
16. Lazebnik, S., Schmid, C., Ponce, J.: Beyond bags of features, spatial pyramid matching for recognizing natural scene categories. In: CVPR (2006)
17. Lowe, D.: Distinctive image features from scale-invariant keypoints. IJCV 60, 91–110 (2004)
18. Nistér, D., Stewénius, H.: Scalable recognition with a vocabulary tree. In: CVPR, pp. 2161–2168 (2006)
19. http://pascallin.ecs.soton.ac.uk/challenges/VOC/
20. de Sande, K.V., Gevers, T., Smeulders, A.: The university of amsterdams concept detection system at imageclef 2009. In: CLEF Working Notes 2009 (2009)
21. Wang, H., Huang, H., Ding, C.: Image annotation using multi-label correlated green's function. In: ICCV, pp. 2029–2034 (2009)
22. Zha, Z., Mei, T., Wang, J., Wang, Z., Hua, X.: Graph-based semi-supervised learning with multi-label. In: ICME, pp. 1321–1324 (2008)
23. Zhu, X., Ghahramani, Z., Lafferty, J.: Semi-supervised learning using gaussian fields and harmonic functions. In: ICML, pp. 912–919 (2003)
24. Grady, L.: Random walks for image segmentation. IEEE Trans. Pattern Anal. Mach. Intell. 28, 1768–1783 (2006)
25. Vedaldi, A., Fulkerson, B.: VLFeat: An open and portable library of computer vision algorithms (2008)

Detecting Actions, Poses, and Objects with Relational Phraselets

Chaitanya Desai and Deva Ramanan

University of California at Irvine, Irvine CA, USA
{desaic,dramanan}@ics.uci.edu

Abstract. We present a novel approach to modeling human pose, together with interacting objects, based on compositional models of local visual interactions and their relations. Skeleton models, while flexible enough to capture large articulations, fail to accurately model self-occlusions and interactions. Poselets and Visual Phrases address this limitation, but do so at the expense of requiring a large set of templates. We combine all three approaches with a compositional model that is flexible enough to model detailed articulations but still captures occlusions and object interactions. Unlike much previous work on action classification, we do not assume test images are labeled with a person, and instead present results for "action detection" in an unlabeled image. Notably, for each detection, our model reports back a detailed description including an action label, articulated human pose, object poses, and occlusion flags. We demonstrate that modeling occlusion is crucial for recognizing human-object interactions. We present results on the PASCAL Action Classification challenge that shows our unified model advances the state-of-the-art for detection, action classification, and articulated pose estimation.

Action recognition is often cast as a k-way classification task; a person is either riding a bike, running, or talking on the phone, etc. For example, the PASCAL Action classification challenge requires one to label a human bounding-box (provided at test-time) with an action class. Such a formulation is limiting for two reasons. First, it assumes manual annotation of test data. In "real-world" unconstrained images, **detection** is crucial: how many people are riding a bike in this image, and where are they? Second, one may be interested in richer descriptions beyond a k-way class label. For instance, is this person riding a bike or about to mount it? Is he gripping the handlebar with one or both hands? Part of what makes this problem hard is that (1) humans can articulate and interact with objects in a variety of ways and (2) the resulting occlusions from those articulations and interactions are hard to model.

In this work, we present a novel approach to modeling human pose, together with interacting objects. Our model detects possibly multiple person-object instances in a single image and generates detailed spatial reports for each such instance. See Fig. 1 for an example of the output our model generates on a test image, *without* the benefit of any test annotation. Our approach unifies several recent lines of thought with classic models of human pose.

A. Fitzgibbon et al. (Eds.): ECCV 2012, Part IV, LNCS 7575, pp. 158–172, 2012.

Fig. 1. Our model detects multiple people-objects, action class labels, human and object pose, and occlusion flag. The above result was obtained without any manual annotation of human bounding boxes at test-time. White edges connect human body parts. Light-blue edges connect object parts to each other and to the human. We define a *single* compositional model for each action class (in this case, `RidingHorse`) that is able to capture large changes in articulation, viewpoint and occlusions. We denote occluded parts by an open circle. For example, our model correctly predicts that a different leg of each rider is occluded behind his horse.

Articulated Skeletons have dominated contemporary approaches for human pose estimation, popularized through 2D pictorial structure models that allow for efficient inference given tree-structured spatial relations [1]. We specifically follow the flexible mixtures of parts (FMP) framework of [2], which augments a standard pictorial structure with local part mixtures. While such methods are flexible enough to capture large variations in appearance due to pose, they still fail to accurately capture self-occlusions of limbs and occlusions due to interacting objects.

Visual Phrases implicitly model occlusions and interactions through the use of a "composite" template that spans both a person and an interacting object [3]. Traditional approaches use separate templates for a person and object; in such cases, it may be difficult to model geometric and appearance constraints that arise from their interaction. Consider a person riding a horse; the person's legs tend to be occluded, while visible body parts tend to take on a riding pose. A single, global composite captures such constraints, but one may need a large number of composites to capture all possible person-horse interactions (a standing vs. galloping horse, an upright vs. crouched rider, etc.).

Poselets encode visual composites of parts rather than visual composites of objects [4]. A torso-arm composite implicitly captures interactions and occlusions that are difficult to model with separate templates for the arm and torso. By composing together different poselets, one can generate a large number of global composites. While such models are successful at detection, it is not clear if they can be used for detailed spatial reasoning, such as pose estimation. One reason is that a large number of poselets may be needed to capture all body poses. Another is that such methods lack a relational model that forces an anatomically-consistent arrangement of poselets to fire in a given detection.

Our Approach combines the strengths of all three approaches. We break up global person+object composites into local patches or "phraselets," which can in turn be composed together to yield an exponentially-large set of composites. Notably, we enforce anatomically-consistent *relations* between phraselets to generate valid composites. We do so by defining phraselets as part mixtures in a FMP model, where local part mixture labels are obtained by "Poselet-like" clustering of global configurations of pose and nearby objects. To capture occlusions, we define separate phraselet mixtures for visible and occluded parts.

For example, we may learn different phraselets corresponding to hands gripping a handlebar, hands occluding torsos, and hands pointing away from the body. Our model includes relational constraints between phraselets; the presence of a handlebar phraselet induces a particular human body pose, as well as the presence of leg phraselets corresponding to legs occluded by bike-frames. Classic part models assume local appearance is independent of geometry; a hand looks the same regardless of the geometry of the remaining body. This makes occlusions and interactions difficult to model. Phraselets differ in that they encode dependencies between geometry and appearance through relational constraints.

Our Model Reports action class labels, articulated pose, object part locations, and part-occlusion flags. Notably, our models do *not* require a bounding-box annotation around a person at test-time. We show that our single model outperforms state-of-the-art methods for diverse tasks including visual composite detection (c.f. Visual Phrases), articulated pose estimation (c.f. FMP), and action classification (c.f. Poselets).

1 Related Work

Part models have a rich history in the context of pose-estimation. We refer the reader to a recent book chapter for a contemporary review [5]. Pictorial structures [1] are the dominant approach. Similar to [6], we learn part models in a discriminative framework. However, we follow a supervised learning framework for learning parts and relations, as in [2, 7]. Recent works have explored integrating relational part models with coarse-scale parts (rather than traditional limb models) [8]. This can also be integrated into a hierarchical, coarse-to-fine representation [9, 10]. Our model differs in that we consider only "fine" local representations, but focus on representing multi-modal appearances with mixture models. We show that one can represent an large set of coarse template by mixing and matching smaller patches. Our model jointly addresses detection, action classification, and pose estimation, similar to part-models that jointly reason about actions and pose [8], and detection and pose [9, 11].

Poselets were introduced and developed through [4, 12, 13]. We generate phraselets by clustering configurations of pose and nearby objects, unlike Poselets which clusters only pose. We consider action recognition as in [13], but also report human pose and object locations in a unified framework. Our phraselets differ in that they provide explicit reports of local occlusions. Perhaps most importantly, our model reports back an explicit articulated pose, while Poselets

Fig. 2. We show bike handles from PASCAL 2011 `RidingBike` action clustered using global configurations of pose and objects. Bike handles belonging to the same cluster are all assigned the same mixture label t^i as described in Sec. 2. Our clusters naturally encode changes in viewpoint, as well as different semantic object types; for example, the bottom-center and bottom-right clusters encode similar viewpoints, but different bicycle types (road bikes versus motorbikes). This is because each type induces different human poses, captured by our clustering algorithm.

does not. Poselets are detected independently of each other, making it difficult to extract a globally-consistent pose. Our relational model makes use of dynamic programming to force phraselets to fire in a globally-consistent manner.

Many approaches jointly recognize human pose and interacting objects. [14–16] describe contextual models for doing so, but assume that local part appearances are independent of the interaction. Such approaches typically assume a single instance of a person-object in the image. Our work differs in that we reason about multiple person-objects and detailed part occlusions of both the object and person. The latter allows us to better reason about occlusions arising from interactions. Visual phrases [3] takes a "brute-force" approach to modeling occlusions and pose interactions by defining a global template encompassing both the person and object. This approach may require a separate template for each combination of constituent objects and articulated pose. We instead use local mixtures and co-occurrence relations to reason about such interactions.

2 Phraselet Clustering

We describe our approach for learning phraselets, or mixtures of local patches, specific to a given activity such as bike riding. We assume we are given images from an activity with keypoint labels spanning both the human body and any interacting objects. Typical keypoint labels may include *head, lt shoulder, rt elbow, lt ankle, etc* for the central figure and *front wheel, rear wheel, bike handle* for the bike. More details on the parts we collect keypoint locations for are given

(a) Visible elbow phraselets (b) Occluded elbow phraselets

Fig. 3. We show left-elbow phraselets learned from the `Running` action class in PASCAL VOC 2011. Our occluded clusters capture changes in the appearance of elbows resulting arising from viewpoint and occlusion.

in Sec. 5. We assume these keypoint labels are with a visibility flag denoting if a particular keypoint is occluded or not.

Let $i \in \{1, 2, \ldots K\}$ be the one of the K parts of the person and/or the object specific to an activity. Let us write $p_n^i = (x, y)$ and $o_n^i \in \{0, 1\}$ for the pixel position and visibility flag of the ith part in training image n, respectively. We write $t_n^i \in \{1, 2, \ldots M\}$ for a mixture or phraselet label. For the remainder of this section, we describe a method for obtaining mixture labels. Our intuition is that global changes in the geometric configuration of the human body and nearby object will produce local changes in appearance of a part i, and hence should be captured by t_i. For example, the local appearance of the hand will be affected by the orientation and type of bicycle (e.g., different bicycles can have different types of handlebars). We construct a feature vector associated with each part in each image, and cluster these vectors to derive mixture labels. To make the clustering scale invariant, we estimate a scale for each part in each image $s_n^i = \text{scale}_i * \text{headlength}_n$, where scale_i is the canonical scale of a part measured in human head-lengths, and head-length_n is the length of the head in image n. For example, we use $\text{scale}_i = 1$ for body parts and $\text{scale}_i = 2$ for bicycle wheels. We now write the feature vector for part i in image n as:

$$x_n^i = \left[\text{Dist Visible}\right]^T \tag{1}$$

$$\text{where} \quad \text{Dist} = \{w_{ij} d_{ij} : j = 1..K\}, \quad \text{Visible} = \{w_{ij} o_n^j : j = 1..K\} \tag{2}$$

$$\text{and} \quad w_{ij} = e^{-T_i ||d_{ij}||^2}, \quad d_{ij} = \frac{(p_n^j - p_n^i)}{s_n^i}$$

Dist is a 2K-vector of (weighted) pixel displacements of each of the K parts from part i, normalized for scale. *Visible* is a K-vector of (weighted) binary occlusion flags. All terms are Gaussian-weighted by w_{ij} such that parts closer to part i have a larger influence in the global descriptor x_n^i. We found it useful to vary the variance of the gaussian (given by T_i) across each part, but use a fixed set across all activities For a given part i, we run K-means on all such features extracted from a training set of images.

Occlusion: Many parts are not visible in certain images. Such part instances may pollute a cluster if both visible and occluded parts are clustered together. Because we believe that occlusions will generate large changes in appearance, we simply separate x_n^i vectors into two sets, where part i is occluded or not, and separately run K means for each set. We generate $K = 6$ visible clusters and $K = 4$ occluded clusters for each part. This ensures that clusters/mixtures 1-6 are visible, while mixtures 7-10 are occluded. We show examples of visible clusters in Fig. 2. In Fig. 3, we compare visible and occluded clusters for the *left elbow* across images of people `Running`. We pad the image so that our model can find parts truncated by the image border; we treat truncation and occlusion identically, so that truncated patches along the border are added to the pool of occluded patches to be clustered.

Relationship to Past Work: Our clustering algorithm is closely aligned to the Poselet clustering algorithm of [12], but with several key differences. Firstly, we consider the global configuration of the person *and* interacting object, rather than just the person. Secondly, we explicitly construct clusters corresponding to occluded parts. This allows us to generate such occlusion labels for detected parts at test time simply by reading off the estimated mixture label. Thirdly, and perhaps most importantly, our clusters consist of small patches that are forced to fire in globally-consistent arrangements, following a relational model described in the next section. This allows us to extract globally-consistent estimates of articulated poses. Our relational model also allows us to compose together a small number of phraselets with small spatial support into a large number of composites with large spatial support - we use roughly 100 template patches per activity, while Poselets requires roughly 1000 templates. One concern may be that phraselets are less discriminative than Poselets due to their small spatial support. However, a collection of phraselets can *learn* to behave like a single, larger Poselet by enforcing rigid relational constraints, as we show next.

3 Relational Model

We now build an activity-specific model for scoring a collection of part mixtures, or phraselets. We would like to enforce consistent relations between phraselets, including spatial constraints on the geometric arrangement of parts, as well as appearance constraints on which mixtures can co-occur. Crucially, these constraints depend on each other; mixture appearance affects the spatial geometry and vice versa (e.g., a handlebar should be explained by an occluded phraselet only if the hand and handlebar lie spatially near each other). To encode such constraints, we follow the framework of [2], which describes a deformable part model that reasons about relations between local mixtures of parts. In this section, we review [2] and show how it can be used to build a relational model for phraselets.

Let I be an image, $p^i = (x, y)$ is the pixel location for part i and t^i is the mixture component of part i, derived from the previously described clustering algorithm. Suppose E is the edge structure defining relational constraints between the K parts. The score associated with a configuration of phraselets is written as

$$S(I, p, t) = b(t) + \sum_{i=1}^{K} \alpha_{t^i}^i \cdot \phi(I, p^i) + \sum_{i,j \in E} \beta_{t^i, t^j}^{ij} \cdot \psi(p^i - p^j) \quad (3)$$

(a) Running (b) RidingBike (c) Walking (d) Phoning

(e) RidingHorse (f) UsingComp. (g) TakingPhoto (h) Jumping

Fig. 4. Visualizations of our learned models and tree-structured relations. Our activity-specific tree connects part templates spanning both, the human and the object. Red edges connect parts of the human to each other. Green edges connect parts of an object to each other and to the human. Note that we are showing one (out of an exponential number of) combinations of local templates for each activity. For example, the selected phraselet mixtures in **(e)** correspond to a left-facing horse, but the same model generates other views by swapping out different mixtures at different spatial locations (as shown in Fig. 1).

Appearance Relations: We write $b(t) = \sum_{ij \in E} w^{ij}_{t^i t^j}$ for a "prior" over mixture combinations, which factors into a sum of pairwise compatibility terms. This term might encode, for example, that curved handlebars tend to co-occur with road bicycles, while flat handlers tend to co-occur with motorbikes. Given that $\phi(I, p^i)$ is a feature vector (e.g., HOG [17]) extracted from pixel location p^i, the first sum from (3) computes the score of placing template $\alpha^i_{t^i}$, tuned for mixture t^i for part i, at location p^i.

Spatial Relations: We write $\psi(p^i - p^j) = \begin{bmatrix} dx \; dy \; dx^2 \; dy^2 \end{bmatrix}^T$ for a quadratic deformation vector computed from the relative offset of locations p^i and p^j. We can interpret $\beta^{ij}_{t^i,t^j}$ as a quadratic spring model that switches between a collection of springs tailored for a particular pair of mixtures (t^i, t^j). Because the spring depends on the mixture components, spatial constraints are dependent on local appearance. For example, this dependency encodes the constraint that people may be posed differently for different types of bikes. Mixture-specific springs also encode self-occlusion constraints arising from viewpoint changes. For instance, our model can capture the fact that the right hip of a person is more likely to be occluded when it lies near a visible left hip, because such an spatial arrangement and mixture assignment is consistent with a right-facing person.

4 Inference and Learning

Inference corresponds to maximizing (3) with respect to p and t. When the relational graph is a tree, one can do this efficiently with dynamic programming, as described in [1, 2]. We omit the equations for a lack of space, but emphasize that our inference procedure returns back both part locations and part mixture labels. While the inferred mixture labels in [2] are ignored, we use them to infer occlusion flags for each part.

Structure Learning: Given a collection of K parts per activity, we would like to learn an activity-specific tree-based edge structure E connecting these K parts. The Chow-Liu algorithm is a well-known approach for learning tree models by maximizing mutual information [1, 18] of a given set of variables. In our case, we find the maximum-weight spanning tree in a fully connected graph whose edges are labeled with the mutual information between $z^i = (p^i, t^i)$ and $z^j = (p^j, t^j)$. Hence *both* spatial consistency and appearance consistency are used when learning the relational structure.

Once we learn an activity-specific tree, we learn the templates and relations for that tree using a structured prediction objective function. Let $z_n = \{(p_n^1, t_n^1)...(p_n^k, t_n^k)\}$ be a particular assignment of locations and types for all k parts in image n. Note that the scoring function in (3) is linear in the parameters $\theta = (\{w\}, \{\alpha\}, \{\beta\})$, and therefore can be expressed as $S(I_n, z_n) = \theta \cdot \Phi(I_n, z_n)$. We learn a model of the form:

$$\begin{aligned} &\underset{\theta,\xi_i \geq 0}{\operatorname{argmin}} && \frac{1}{2}\theta^T \cdot \theta + C \sum_n \xi_n && (4) \\ \text{s.t.} \quad &\forall n \in \text{positive images} && \theta \cdot \Phi(I_n, z_n) \geq 1 - \xi_n \\ &\forall n \in \text{negative images}, \forall z && \theta \cdot \Phi(I_n, z) \leq -1 + \xi_n \end{aligned}$$

The above constraint states that positive examples should score better than 1 (the margin), while negative examples, for all configurations of part positions and mixtures, should score less than -1. We collect negative examples from images consisting of people performing activities other than the one of interest. This form of learning problem is known as a structural SVM, and there exist many well-tuned solvers such as the cutting plane solver of SVMStruct in [19] and the stochastic gradient descent solver in [6]. We use the dual coordinate-descent QP solver of [2]. We show example models and their learned tree structure in Fig. 4 for 8 actions chosen from the PASCAL 2011 Action Classification competition.

5 Experiments

We consider 8 out of the 10 actions outlined in the PASCAL 2011 action classification competition. The actions considered correspond to the 8 models shown in Fig. 4. We train activity specific models as described in Sec. 4 for each of the 8 actions using PASCAL 2011-train data. In addition to the standard human joints, we model bike parts (*handle, front wheel, rear wheel*), horse parts (*nose, top-head, butt*) and computer screen (*whole object*) for their respective action classes. We model the full human body for most actions, but model only the upper body for actions with heavy occlusions and truncation (`Phoning`, `UsingComputer`, and `TakingPhoto`). We evaluate multiple aspects of our model, including detection, action classification, pose estimation, and occlusion prediction. To evaluate the

Fig. 5. We show detection results obtained without *any* manual annotation of test images. We follow the notational conventions of Fig. 1, including open circles to denote occluded parts. Each row shows the N best detections for a single action model (denoted by the row's label). Our compositional models are able to capture large changes in viewpoint and articulation that are present even within a single action class.

Fig. 6. We show 2 of the top false positives for a few actions. We plot ground-truth (red boxes) and predictions (blue boxes) belonging to only the action class denoted in each row. Many mistakes are due to imprecise bounding-box localization (`RidingHorse`) or confusion of action classes with similar poses (`Walking`). The latter is denoted by the lack of a red box. Some mistakes are due to inconsistencies and ambiguities in the ground-truth annotation. Consider the right image in the `RidingBike`/`TakingPhoto` rows; both images are annotated with a single action even though the person appears to be engaged in two actions (`TakingPhoto` and `RidingBike`/`RidingHorse`). This causes our predictions to be marked as false positives.

latter two, we introduce novel evaluation schemes for evaluating poses under occlusion. Because the web-based PASCAL evaluation server is no longer evaluating entries on the 2011-test, we evaluate results on 2011-val. To do so, we have manually annotated both the train and val set with part locations and occlusion flags.

5.1 Action Detection

For this task, our goal is to detect person-object composites in a test image. We use our models to produce composite candidates by running them as scanning-window detectors (without any manual annotation at test time), and applying NMS to generate a sparse set of non-overlapping detections. We visualize high scoring correct detections in Fig. 5 and false positives in Fig. 6. Ground truth person-object composites are obtained by considering a tight box around parts spanning the person and the object. To compare against groundtruth, we regress a rectangle using the part locations of the person and the object for each person-object detection.

We quantitatively evaluate our models using PASCAL's standard criteria of average precision (AP). We compare our models against a visual phrase (VP) baseline [3], trained for each action class. For those action classes without objects, this is equivalent to a standard DPM [6]. In both cases, we use defaults of 4 global mixtures and 6 parts per mixture. From Fig. 7, we see that our model outperforms these state-of-the-art baselines by a significant margin for most classes. The improvement is more modest for some classes (`Running`,`RidingBike`),

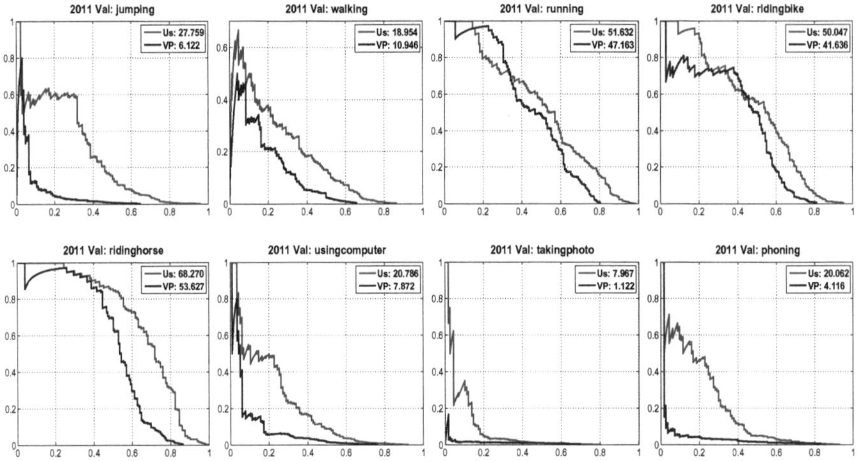

Fig. 7. Detection results on 2011 PASCAL-val set. Our model significantly outperforms a state-of-the-art visual phrase (VP) baseline [3].

perhaps because they exhibit less pose variation and so are well modeled by the global mixtures of the DPM.

5.2 Action Classification

We compare our model against 2 other baselines apart from (VP/DPM): (1) FMP, the flexible articulated model of [2] applied to the joint person-object composite. (2) FMP+occ, which is obtained as follows: The FMP model estimates local mixtures by clustering the relative position of a part i wrt its parent j. FMP+occ also does this, but partitions the set of training data into visible/occluded instances of part i, and separately clusters each. This allows the FMP model to report visibility states using estimated part mixtures, analogous to our own model. To allow comparison to past work, we evaluate results following the protocol of PASCAL, assuming human bounding-boxes are given at test-time. We score each bounding box with the highest-scoring overlapping pose of each action model. For the (VP) baseline, we also give it access to a bounding box around the person-object composite. We present results on the 2011-val in Table 1. Our model outperforms state-of-the-art baselines, including DPM/VP on 7/8 actions. We also report numbers on 2010 test data using PASCAL's evaluation server, shown in Table 2 and compare to reported performance of [13]. Our numbers are comparable, even though [13] is trained using a large external dataset and includes additional post-processing steps (such as contextual re-scoring). Other state-of-the-art methods for action classification exist, but some may make intimate use of the annotated human bounding box on the test-image (say, to define a coordinate system to extract spatial features). We advocate action detection as a more realistic evaluation.

5.3 Person-Object Pose Estimation

Qualitative results of our pose-estimation are shown in Fig 5. In general, our model rather accurately estimates parts of both the person and the object. Notably, our model also returns occlusion labels for each part (given by its estimated mixture label). We quantitatively evaluate both aspects of pose estimation below.

Occlusion-Aware Pose Evaluation: Standard benchmarks for pose estimation require an algorithm to report back the location of all parts, including those that may be occluded. See for example, the now-standard criteria of probability of a correct pose (PCP) [20]. We argue that a proper benchmark should only score visible parts. This is particularly relevant for human-object interactions because occlusions are rather common. We introduce a novel scheme for evaluating models and ground-truth poses that return a variable number of parts. Let n_g be the number of visible parts in the ground truth pose, and n_h be the number of visible parts in the hypothesized pose. Let k be the number of correctly matching parts across the two that are in correspondence and sufficiently overlap. We evaluate this pose using the fraction of correct parts $\frac{k}{.5(n_g+n_h)}$. One can show this is equivalent to the F_1 score, or harmonic mean of precision (the fraction of predicted parts that correctly match) and recall (the fraction of ground-truth parts that are correctly matched).

Results under our F_1 score are shown in Table 3. This evaluation penalizes algorithms for predicting an occluded part as visible; hence, it somewhat combines pose estimation with aspect estimation. Under this setting, our model outperforms all variants. The base FMP algorithm, like most algorithms for articulated pose estimation, reports a fixed set of parts. One may argue that it is artificially penalized under our F_1 score. However, FMP+occ *is* capable of predicting a vis-

Table 1. Class-specific AP results. In general our model strongly outperforms our baselines except for *UsingComp.* We suspect that this category exhibits less pose variation, and so is well-modelled by a global template.

Action classification on PASCAL 2011-val set

	Run.	R. Bike	R. horse	Phoning	TakingPhoto	UsingComp.	Walk.	Jump.
Us	69	81.7	90.3	32.9	24.3	45	40.3	49.6
FMP + occ	64.3	69.4	87.6	27.6	17.3	32.5	30.0	42.6
FMP	62.5	66.9	84.7	21.3	11.7	30.5	29.02	44.2
DPM/VP	63.2	66.4	79.7	21.2	12.1	43.5	32.1	28.8

Table 2. AP across various models on the PASCAL 2010 set. Our model is comparable to Poselets, even though the later is trained with a large external dataset and uses various post-processing steps for contextual res-coring.

Action classification on PASCAL 2010-test set

	Run.	R. Bike	R. horse	Phoning	TakingPhoto	UsingComp.	Walk.
Us	82.8	82.2	87.0	47.8	33.7	54.5	66.9
Poselets	85.6	83.7	89.4	49.6	31.0	59.1	67.9

Table 3. Pose estimation across various models on 8 actions from PASCAL 2011, scored using F_1 score. The numbers reported are average F_1 scored over all test instances belonging to the action of interest. Algorithms are penalized for predicting the location of an occluded part in a test image. Our model outperforms state-of-the-art FMP model[2] by a significant margin, even when its augmented to encode occlusions.

Occlusion-aware F1 score

	Run.	R. Bike	R. horse	Phoning	TakingPhoto	UsingComp.	Walk.	Jump.
Us:	**66.8**	**49.2**	**65.3**	**41.4**	**30.8**	**41.2**	**44.8**	**40.3**
FMP+occ:	64.7	45	61.9	31.5	22.1	40.2	32.9	38.1
FMP	59.2	42.4	51.2	24.4	21.2	28.4	24.3	29.1

Table 4. Pose estimation across various models on 8 actions from PASCAL 2011, scored using PCP. Algorithms are required to predict the location of all parts (including occluded ones) in a test image. See text for details.

PCP score

	Run.	R. Bike	R. horse	Phoning	TakingPhoto	UsingComp.	Walk.	Jump.
Us:	**68.7**	**50.7**	**64.7**	**39.9**	**28.9**	**43.1**	**45.4**	**40.7**
FMP+occ:	67.7	45.1	59.8	29.7	20.7	39.7	33.1	38.9
FMP	63.4	45.6	56.6	27.4	23.8	35.8	32.6	37.2

ibility label per part, by construction, just as our model. We see that this model performs significantly better than FMP, but is still considerably lower than our final model.

We also score PCP in Table 4, which requires an algorithm to report locations of all parts, regardless of their visibility. Our algorithm still outperforms the 2 baselines. *This suggests our model accurately predicts the locations of even occluded parts.* Interestingly, we still see a substantial improvement in performance from FMP to FMP+occ for most actions. In retrospect, this may seem obvious. Parts undergoing occlusions look different than when they are visible, and so one should train separate visual mixtures for such cases. One might suspect that these visual mixtures should have zero-weight, to ensure that no image evidence is scored during an occlusion. We take the view that the learning algorithm should determine this using training data. It may be that occluded parts still generate a characteristic gradient pattern (e.g., T-junctions), which can be captured by a template. Note that FMP+occ approach, in some sense, is a partial "phraselet" clustering since global knowledge of occluders is used to influence local appearance modeling.

Benchmark Pose Estimation: One could argue our phraselet model is directly applicable to pose estimation, without regard to interacting objects or actions. To evaluate this, we trained and evaluated our model on the PARSE benchmark [21]. We achieve a PCP score of 77.4%, outperforming the previous state-of-the-art FMP model at 74.9% (reported in [2]).

6 Conclusion

We have presented a novel approach to modeling human pose, together with interacting objects, based on compositional models of local visual interactions and their relations. Our modeling framework captures the complex geometry, appearance, and occlusions that arise in person-object interactions. We effectively use such models to detect person-object composites, estimate action class labels, articulated pose, object pose, and occlusion labels within a single, unified framework. We demonstrate compelling performance on diverse tasks including detection, classification, and pose estimation, as evidenced by comparing to state-of-the-art models especially tuned for those tasks.

Acknowledgements. We thank Yi Yang for fruitful discussions, and Deepa Desai for graciously annotating images. Funding for this research was provided by NSF Grant 0954083, ONR-MURI Grant N00014-10-1-0933, and the Intel Science and Technology Center - Visual Computing.

References

1. Felzenszwalb, P., Huttenlocher, D.: Pictorial structures for object recognition. IJCV (2005)
2. Yang, Y., Ramanan, D.: Articulated pose estimation with flexible mixtures-of-parts. In: CVPR (2011)
3. Sadeghi, M., Farhadi, A.: Recognition using visual phrases. In: CVPR (2011)
4. Bourdev, L., Malik, J.: Poselets: Body part detectors trained using 3D human pose annotations. In: ICCV (2009)
5. Ramanan, D.: Part-based models for finding people and estimating their pose. In: Visual Analysis of Humans (2011)
6. Felzenszwalb, P.F., Girshick, R.B., McAllester, D., Ramanan, D.: Object detection with discriminatively trained part based models. IEEE PAMI (2009)
7. Kumar, M., Zisserman, A., Torr, P.: Efficient discriminative learning of parts-based models. In: CVPR (2010)
8. Yang, W., Wang, Y., Mori, G.: Recognizing human actions from still images with latent poses. In: CVPR (2010)
9. Sun, M., Savarese, S.: Articulated part-based model for joint object detection and pose estimation. In: ICCV (2011)
10. Wang, Y., Tran, D., Liao, Z., Forsyth, D.: Discriminative hierarchical part-based models for human parsing and action recognition. In: JMLR (2012)
11. Tran, D., Forsyth, D.: Configuration estimates improve pedestrian finding. In: NIPS (2007)
12. Bourdev, L., Maji, S., Brox, T., Malik, J.: Detecting People Using Mutually Consistent Poselet Activations. In: Daniilidis, K., Maragos, P., Paragios, N. (eds.) ECCV 2010, Part VI. LNCS, vol. 6316, pp. 168–181. Springer, Heidelberg (2010)
13. Maji, S., Bourdev, L., Malik, J.: Action Recognition from a Distributed Representation of Pose and Appearance. In: CVPR (2011)
14. Bangpeng, Y., Fei-Fei, L.: Modeling mutual context of object and human pose in human-object interaction activities. In: CVPR (2010)

15. Gupta, A., Kembhavi, A., Davis, L.S.: Observing human-object interactions: Using spatial and functional compatibility for recognition. IEEE PAMI (2009)
16. Prest, A., Schmid, C., Ferrari, V.: Weakly supervised learning of interactions between humans and objects. IEEE PAMI (2011) (in press)
17. Dalal, N., Triggs, B.: Histograms of oriented gradients for human detection. In: CVPR (2005)
18. Chow, C., Liu, C.: Approximating discrete probability distributions with dependence trees. IEEE Transactions on Information Theory (1968)
19. Joachims, T., Finley, T., Yu, C.: Cutting plane training of structural SVMs. Machine Learning (2009)
20. Ferrari, V., Marin-Jimenez, M., Zisserman, A.: Progressive search space reduction for human pose estimation. In: CVPR (2008)
21. Ramanan, D.: Learning to parse images of articulated bodies. In: NIPS (2007)

Action Recognition with Exemplar Based 2.5D Graph Matching

Bangpeng Yao and Li Fei-Fei

Department of Computer Science, Stanford University
{bangpeng,feifeili}@cs.stanford.edu

Abstract. This paper deals with recognizing human actions in still images. We make two key contributions. (1) We propose a novel, 2.5D representation of action images that considers both view-independent pose information and rich appearance information. A 2.5D graph of an action image consists of a set of nodes that are key-points of the human body, as well as a set of edges that are spatial relationships between the nodes. Each key-point is represented by view-independent 3D positions and local 2D appearance features. The similarity between two action images can then be measured by matching their corresponding 2.5D graphs. (2) We use an exemplar based action classification approach, where a set of representative images are selected for each action class. The selected images cover large within-action variations and carry discriminative information compared with the other classes. This exemplar based representation of action classes further makes our approach robust to pose variations and occlusions. We test our method on two publicly available datasets and show that it achieves very promising performance.

1 Introduction

Humans can effortlessly recognize many human actions from still images, such as "playing violin" and "riding a bike". In recent years, much effort has been made in computer vision [1–8] with the goal of making this process automatic. Automatic recognition of human actions in still images has many potential applications, such as image search and personal album management.

Considering the close relationship between actions and human poses, in this paper, we aim to develop a robust action recognition approach by modeling human poses. The idea of using human poses for action recognition has been studied in some previous work which either detect local pose features [4, 6] or model the spatial configuration between human body parts and objects [2, 3, 7, 8]. However, while such approaches sound promising, the winning method [9] in the recent PASCAL challenge [10] simply treats action recognition as an image classification problem, without explicitly modeling human poses.

The challenges in modeling human poses for action recognition are illustrated in Fig.2. On the one hand, because of the variations of camera angles, the same human pose can correspond to very different body parts configurations on the 2D image plane, which poses challenges in reliable measurement of action similarities. On the other hand, human poses in the same action can change drastically,

A. Fitzgibbon et al. (Eds.): ECCV 2012, Part IV, LNCS 7575, pp. 173–186, 2012.

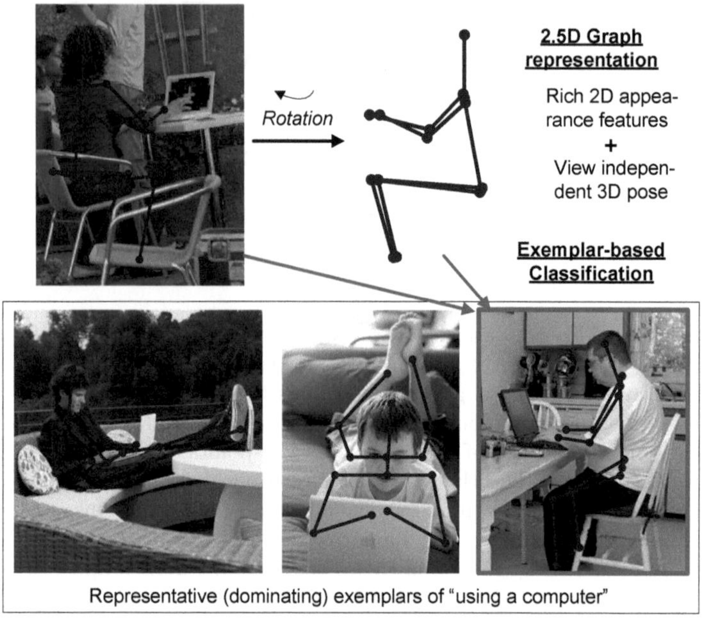

Fig. 1. An overview of our action recognition algorithm. We represent an action image as a 2.5D graph consisting of view-independent 3D pose and 2D appearance features. In recognition, the 2.5D graph is matched with a set of exemplar graphs for each action class, allowing more robust handling of within-action variations.

while very similar human poses might correspond to many different human actions, and therefore it is difficult to build a single pose model to distinguish one action from all the others.

In this paper, we propose a novel action recognition approach (Fig.1) to address the above two challenges. Specifically, we make two key contributions:

- **2.5D graph for action image representation.** We propose a 2.5D graph representation for action images. The nodes of the graph are key-points of the human body represented by view-independent 3D positions and rich 2D appearance features. The edges are relative distances between the key-points. Estimating the similarity between two action images then becomes matching their corresponding graphs.
- **Exemplar-based action classification.** Considering that a single pose model is not enough to distinguish one action from all the others, we propose an exemplar based approach for action classification. For each action class, we select a minimum set of "dominating images" that are able to cover all within-class pose variations and capture all between-class distinctions.

The rest of this paper is organized as follows. Related work is discussed in Sec.2. The 2.5D graph representation of action images and exemplar-based action recognition algorithm are elaborated in Sec.3 and Sec.4, respectively. Experiments are represented in Sec.5. We conclude our paper in Sec.6.

(a) (b)

Fig. 2. **(a)** The same action might contain very large pose variations. **(b)** Due to different camera angles, even the same human pose looks differently in 2D images.

2 Related Work

Human poses have been used for action recognition in existing literatures. Both global silhouette [2] and local pose units [4, 6] have been adopted for distinguishing different human actions. In [3, 7], action recognition is treated as a human-object interaction problem, where spatial relationships between different body parts and objects are modeled. The interactions are also represented as a set of bases of action attribute-object-pose in [5]. While most of such approaches rely on annotations of human poses, a weakly-supervised method was proposed to model human-object interactions in [8]. All those methods, however, model human poses in 2D only, and therefore are difficult to deal with the within-class pose variations caused by camera angle changes, as shown in Fig.2(b).

There has been some work for view-independent action recognition, mostly dealing with videos. [11] renders Mocap data from multiple viewpoints, which is time and storage consuming. [12] projects 2D features to a 3D visual hull. Manifold based warping methods are adopted in [13]. View-invariant feature descriptors have also been proposed [14, 15]. Most of such methods rely on temporal information, and therefore are not suitable to our problem.

In this work, we aim at view-independent action recognition from single images. We extract key-points of the human body [16] and then convert the 2D key-points to 3D positions without any supervision [17, 18]. The 3D positions of key-points allow us to rotate human skeletons from different views to the same view-point (Fig.1), hence making view-independent matching possible. Inspired by [19], where it shows that the combined pose and appearance features help improve action recognition performance, our 2.5D action graph is constructed by combining the view-independent 3D human skeletons and 2D appearance features [20, 21]. 2.5D graph representations have been used in computer vision systems before [22–24]. While most of these papers focus on modeling scene layers or rigid objects such as human faces, our method is designed for recognizing articulated objects such as human bodies.

While the majority of work in computer vision are model based, exemplar based methods have also been applied in object recognition [25–27] and video classification [28]. Different from most previous work where all training samples are treated as candidate exemplars, our method aims at selecting a compact

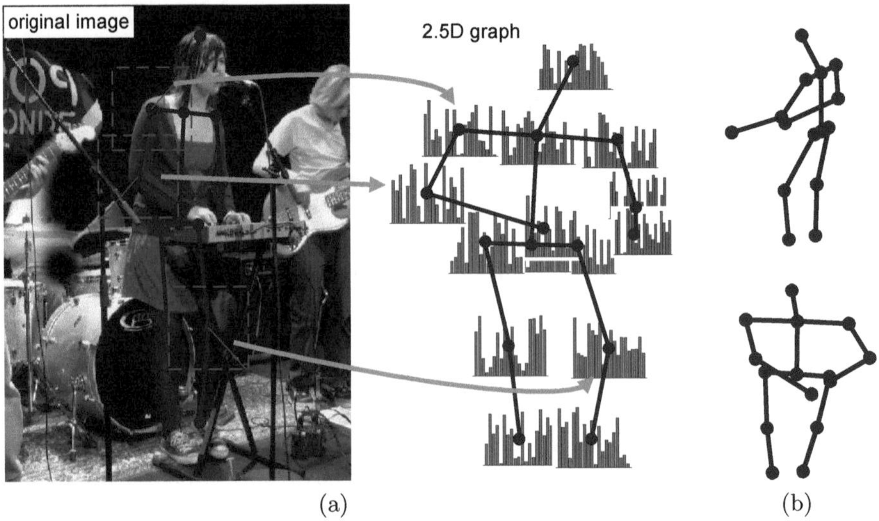

Fig. 3. (a) Illustration of an image and its corresponding 2.5D action graph. The histograms represent appearance features extracted from the corresponding image regions. **(b)** The human body skeleton from the other views.

set of images for each action class that are able to cover the within-class pose variation and capture all between-class distinctions. We show that the problem is essentially a minimum dominating set problem [29], and can be solved by using an improved reverse heuristic algorithm [30].

3 A 2.5D Graph of Human Poses and Appearances

3.1 The 2.5D Graph Representation

The term, *2.5D graph*, is borrowed from stereoscopic vision [31]. It refers to the outcome of reconstructing 3D information from 2D but the appearance cues are still 2D. A graphical illustration of our 2.5D representation of action images are shown in Fig.3. It combines view-independent 3D configuration of human skeletons and 2D appearance features.

A 2.5D graph $\mathcal{G}^{\mathcal{I}}$ representing an action image $\mathcal{I}$ consists of V nodes connected by E edges. The nodes correspond to a set of key points of the human body, as shown in Fig.3. A node v is represented by the 3D position of this node $\mathbf{l}_v^{\mathcal{I}}$ and 2D appearance features $\mathbf{f}_v^{\mathcal{I}}$ extracted in a local image region surrounding this point. An edge e is a three-dimensional vector $\Delta\mathbf{l}_e^{\mathcal{I}} = \mathbf{l}_v^{\mathcal{I}} - \mathbf{l}_{v'}^{\mathcal{I}}$, where node v and node v' are connected by e. Note that our model allows the human body to rotate in 3D (as shown in Fig.3(b)), which will result in different 3D positions of key-points and hence edge vectors. Also, because some key points might be outside of the boundary of the image, we introduce an auxiliary variable $h_v^{\mathcal{I}}$ for each v, and a $h_e^{\mathcal{I}}$ for each e. $h_v^{\mathcal{I}} = 1$ if key-point v is within the boundary of image $\mathcal{I}$, otherwise $h_v^{\mathcal{I}} = 0$. Similarly, $h_e^{\mathcal{I}} = 1$ if and only if both two points connected by e are within the image boundary.

Implementation Details. We consider 15 key-points of human bodies: top head, left-middle-right shoulders and hips, left-right elbows, wrists, knees, and ankles. Given an image, the 3D position of these points are obtained by first using pictorial structure [16] to estimate their positions in 2D, and then using the method in [17] with additional constraints [32] to recover the depth information. The key-point locations are then normalized such that the center of the torso is at $(0, 0, 0)$, and the height of the torso (distance between middle shoulder and middle hip) is 100 pixels. Although human pose estimation itself is challenging and the 3D points we obtain are not perfect, our approach can still achieve very good action recognition performance, even comparing with the setting that uses ground-truth key-point locations. We will show this in Sec.5.

The detailed process of using pictorial structure to estimate 2D key-points locations is as follows. Following the standard settings in [10], we assume that there is a bounding box surrounding each person whose action is to be recognized. As in [33], the image is normalized by extending the bounding box to contain $1.5\times$ the original size of the bounding box, and cropping and resizing it such that the large image dimension is 300 pixels. To deal with the situation that the legs are outside of the image boundary, we train a full human detector and an upper body detector excluding the key-points below hips. Given a normalized image, if the calibrated response score obtained from the full body detector is larger than 0.8 times of the score obtained from the upper body detector, we regard that the full human body is visible, otherwise upper body only. Because of the provided bounding boxes of the humans, the detection results are very reliable in almost all the images. Based on whether full body or only upper body is visible, we use the appropriate pictorial structure [16] model to estimate the location of the key points, considering or ignoring the key-points below hips. In our experiments (Sec.5), we re-train a pictorial structure model on each dataset, where the body part detectors are obtained using the deformable part models [34].

The appearance feature $\mathbf{f}_v^{\mathcal{I}}$ is a two-level spatial pyramid [21] of SIFT [20] features with locality-constrained linear coding [35] in a 60×60 image region centered at point v of image $\mathcal{I}$. We consider two image sizes, one is the normalized image of which the larger dimension is 300 pixels, the other is the image where the length of the torso is 100 pixels. We use a 512 codebook size for SIFT features, and therefore the dimensionality for $\mathbf{f}_v^{\mathcal{I}}$ is 2560. If the point i is outside of the image boundary, then all values of $\mathbf{f}_v^{\mathcal{I}}$ are set to 0.

3.2 Measuring Similarity of 2.5D Graphs

To use the 2.5D graph constructed in Sec.3.1 for action recognition (details in Sec.4), we need to match a graph $\mathcal{G}^{\mathcal{I}}$ to a "template graph" $\mathcal{G}^{\mathcal{M}}$ and compute their similarity. As described in Sec.3.1, the graph $\mathcal{G}^{\mathcal{I}}$ is denoted by $\{\mathbf{f}_v^{\mathcal{I}}, h_v^{\mathcal{I}}, v = 1, \cdots, V; \Delta\mathbf{l}_e^{\mathcal{I}}, h_e^{\mathcal{I}}, e = 1, \cdots, E\}$. The template graph $\mathcal{G}^{\mathcal{M}}$ is denoted as $\{\mathbf{f}_v^{\mathcal{M}}, h_v^{\mathcal{M}},$

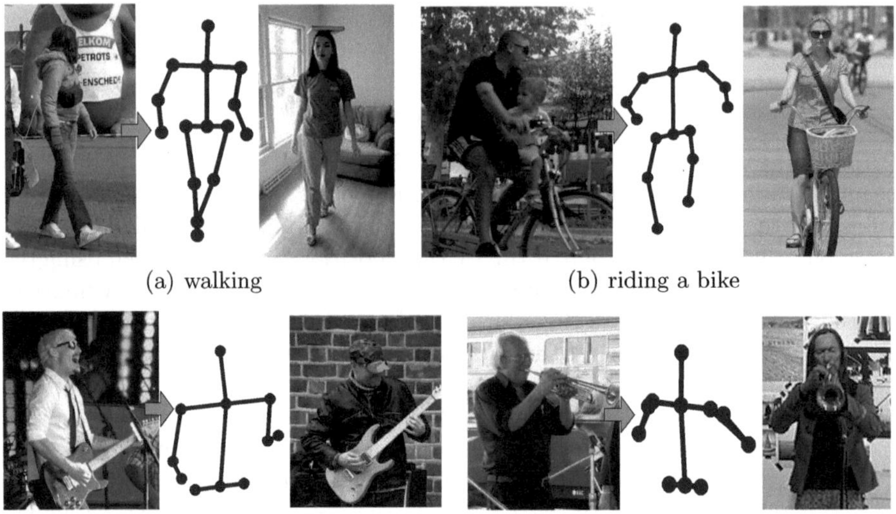

(a) walking (b) riding a bike (c) playing guitar (d) playing trumpet

Fig. 4. The 3D representation of human body key-points allows us to rotate one image to the same view-point of the other image, and thus achieve view-independent similarity matching. In each subfigure, from left to right: human in profile view, its pose in frontal view, and the other human with the same action in the frontal view.

$\mathbf{w}_v^{\mathcal{M}}, v = 1, \cdots, V; \Delta \mathbf{l}_e^{\mathcal{M}}, h_e^{\mathcal{M}}, \mathbf{w}_e^{\mathcal{M}}, e = 1, \cdots, E\}$, where $\mathbf{w}_v^{\mathcal{M}}$ and $\mathbf{w}_e^{\mathcal{M}}$ are the feature weights for the corresponding node and edge. How to obtain the weights will be described in Sec.4.

When matching the similarity between $\mathcal{G}^{\mathcal{I}}$ and $\mathcal{G}^{\mathcal{M}}$, we deal with the 2D appearance features (nodes) and 3D pose features (edges) separately. The similarity between the appearance features if node v is simply the weighted histogram intersection between $\mathbf{f}_v^{\mathcal{I}}$ and $\mathbf{f}_v^{\mathcal{M}}$, denoted as $\mathbf{w}_v^{\mathcal{M}} \cdot I\left(\mathbf{f}_v^{\mathcal{I}}, \mathbf{f}_v^{\mathcal{M}}\right)$. For the pose features, as shown in Fig.4, the 3D representation allows us to rotate the 3D key-point locations $\{\mathbf{l}_v^{\mathcal{I}}\}_{v=1}^{V}$ to the same view-point of $\{\mathbf{l}_v^{\mathcal{M}}\}_{v=1}^{V}$, and then match the view-independent similarity score.

Let $\mathbf{L}^{\mathcal{I}}$ and $\mathbf{L}^{\mathcal{M}}$ be $V \times 3$ matrices of the 3D positions of the key-points in $\mathcal{I}$ and $\mathcal{M}$. We want to find a 3×3 rotation matrix $\mathbf{R}^*$ that rotates $\mathbf{L}^{\mathcal{I}}$ to the same view of $\mathbf{L}^{\mathcal{M}}$, i.e.

$$\mathbf{R}^* = \arg\min_{R} \|\mathbf{L}^{\mathcal{M}} - \mathbf{R}\mathbf{L}^{\mathcal{I}}\|^2 \tag{1}$$

We use a least-square method [36] to find $\mathbf{R}^*$. Let $\mathbf{U}\mathbf{D}\mathbf{V}^T$ a singular decomposition of ${\mathbf{L}^{\mathcal{M}}}^T\mathbf{L}^{\mathcal{I}}$, and define $\mathbf{S} = \mathbf{I}$ if $\det({\mathbf{L}^{\mathcal{M}}}^T\mathbf{L}^{\mathcal{I}}) \geq 0$, otherwise $\mathbf{S} = \mathrm{diag}(1, \cdots, 1, -1)$. Then we have $\mathbf{R}^* = \mathbf{U}\mathbf{S}\mathbf{V}^T$. Fig.4 gives some example results of rotating an image to similar view-points of the other images.

Combining the similarity values obtained from appearance and pose features, the similarity between $\mathcal{G}^{\mathcal{I}}$ and $\mathcal{G}^{\mathcal{M}}$ is

$$\mathcal{S}\left(\mathcal{G}^{\mathcal{I}}, \mathcal{G}^{\mathcal{M}}\right) = \exp\left\{\sum_{v} h_v^{\mathcal{I}} h_v^{\mathcal{M}} \cdot \mathbf{w}_v^{\mathcal{M}} \cdot I\left(\mathbf{f}_v^{\mathcal{I}}, \mathbf{f}_v^{\mathcal{M}}\right) + \sum_{e} h_e^{\mathcal{I}} h_e^{\mathcal{M}} \cdot \mathbf{w}_e^{\mathcal{M}} \cdot \left(\mathbf{R}^* \Delta \mathbf{l}_e^{\mathcal{I}} - \Delta \mathbf{l}_e^{\mathcal{M}}\right)\right\} \quad (2)$$

$\mathcal{S}(\cdot,\cdot)$ is not symmetric, i.e. in most situations $\mathcal{S}\left(\mathcal{G}^{\mathcal{I}}, \mathcal{G}^{\mathcal{M}}\right) \neq \mathcal{S}\left(\mathcal{G}^{\mathcal{M}}, \mathcal{G}^{\mathcal{I}}\right)$.

4 Exemplar-Based Action Recognition

4.1 Dominating Sets of Action Classes

We adopt an exemplar-based approach for action recognition. Exemplar-based approaches allow using multiple exemplars to represent an action class, enabling more flexibility in overcoming the challenge of large within-action pose variations (Fig.2(b)). Rather than matching a testing image with all the training images as in most previous exemplar-based systems, for each action class, we select a small set of representative training images that are able to cover all pose variations of this action while maximizing the distinction between this action and all the others. Selecting such images is equivalent to the *minimum dominating set problem* [29, 30] in graph theory, and therefore we call those images *dominating images*, denoted as $Dom(k)$ for class k.

To formally define the dominating images of human actions, we first define the *coverage set* of an image $\mathcal{I}$, $Cov(\mathcal{I})$. The images in $Cov(\mathcal{I})$ belong to the same class as $\mathcal{I}$, and each image has a larger similarity value with $\mathcal{I}$ than all the images of different classes. Mathematically speaking, assume we have a set of training images $\{\mathcal{I}_1, \cdots, \mathcal{I}_N\}$, where each $\mathcal{I}_i$ is associated with an action class label $y_i \in \{1, \cdots, K\}$. The coverage set of $\mathcal{I}$ is defined as

$$Cov\left(\mathcal{I}\right) = \left\{\mathcal{I}_i \mid \mathcal{S}\left(\mathcal{G}^{\mathcal{I}_i}, \mathcal{G}^{\mathcal{I}}\right) > T + \eta,\ T = \max_{\forall j, y_j \neq y} \mathcal{S}\left(\mathcal{G}^{\mathcal{I}_j}, \mathcal{G}^{\mathcal{I}}\right)\right\}, \quad (3)$$

where T is the maximum similarity between $\mathcal{I}$ and images of the other classes. $\eta > 0$ controls the margin of the similarity difference. As shown in Fig.5, $Cov\left(\mathcal{I}\right)$ defines a set of images where the 3D pose configurations and visual appearances are similar to $\mathcal{I}$. For an action class k, the dominating image set $Dom(k)$ are a minimum set of images such that the joint of their coverage sets contain all the images of class k, i.e.

$$\forall\, \mathcal{I}_i \text{ where } y_i = k,\ \exists\, \mathcal{I}_j \in Dom(k) \text{ such that } \mathcal{S}\left(\mathcal{G}^{\mathcal{I}_i}, \mathcal{G}^{\mathcal{I}_j}\right) > T_j + \eta \quad (4)$$

If there exist another $\widetilde{Dom}(k)$ satisfies the above condition, $|Dom(k)| \leq |\widetilde{Dom}(k)|$, where $|Dom(k)|$ is the number of images in $Dom(k)$.

Fig. 5. Illustration of the dominating images of "using a computer". The images surrounded by red, blue, and green rectangles are dominating images. Dotted ellipses representing the corresponding coverage sets. The images surrounded by gray are images of the other actions, which are used to define the boundary of the coverage sets.

4.2 Obtaining Minimum Dominating Sets for Each Action

Our method of obtaining the minimum dominating sets consists of two steps. Firstly, we learn image-specific feature weights $\mathbf{W}^{\mathcal{I}} = \{\mathbf{w}_v^{\mathcal{I}}, v = 1, \cdots, V; \mathbf{w}_e^{\mathcal{I}}, e = 1, \cdots, E\}$ for each image $\mathcal{I}$ to maximize $|Cov(\mathcal{I})|$. Then we use an improved reverse heuristic method [30] to find the images that belong to $Dom(k)$ for each class k. We elaborate on the two steps separately.

For each image $\mathcal{I}$, $\mathbf{W}^{\mathcal{I}}$ maximizes the distinction between $\mathcal{I}$ and images of the other action classes. Finding a globally optimal $\mathbf{W}^{\mathcal{I}}$, however, is not a convex problem, because which images belong to $Cov(\mathcal{I})$ is uncertain. We therefore resort to a suboptimal solution which aims at separating within-class similarities from between-class similarities. We compute the histogram intersections of appearance features and distances of the key-point 3D positions between $\mathcal{I}$ and each image $\mathcal{I}_i$. This results to a feature vector

$$\left[h_v^{\mathcal{I}_i} h_v^{\mathcal{I}} \cdot I\left(\mathbf{f}_v^{\mathcal{I}_i}, \mathbf{f}_v^{\mathcal{I}}\right), v = 1, \cdots, N; h_e^{\mathcal{I}_i} h_e^{\mathcal{I}} \cdot \mathbf{R}^* \Delta \mathbf{l}_e^{\mathcal{I}_i} - \Delta \mathbf{l}_e^{\mathcal{I}}, e = 1, \cdots, E\right]. \quad (5)$$

If $\mathcal{I}_i$ and $\mathcal{I}$ belong to the same class, this vector is regarded as a positive sample, otherwise negative. We then train a binary SVM classifier to discriminate positive samples from negative samples. The obtained SVM feature weights are $\mathbf{W}^{\mathcal{I}}$.

Based on $\mathbf{W}^{\mathcal{I}}$ learned for each image that belong to class k, i.e. $y = k$, we can compute their coverage sets (Eq.3) and then find $Dom(k)$. But finding the minimum dominating set is also a NP-hard problem. We use the improved reverse heuristic (IRH) method [30], which selects the samples in $Dom(k)$ iteratively for each k. The heuristic rule is, on the one hand, the images have large coverage sets are more likely to be selected; on the other hand, the images that are covered

- For each class $k \in \{1, \cdots, K\}$, denote all the images of this class as $Im(k)$.
- Initialize $Dom(k) = \emptyset$.
  1. Compute $Cov(\mathcal{I})$ and $Reach(\mathcal{I})$ for each $\mathcal{I} \in Im(k)$;
  2. Find $\mathcal{I}^* \in Im(k)$ that maximizes $Cov(\mathcal{I}) - \lambda \cdot Reach(\mathcal{I})$;
  3. Add $\mathcal{I}^*$ to $Dom(k)$, and remove all $\mathcal{I} \in Cover(\mathcal{I}^*)$ from $Im(k)$;
  4. If $Im(k) \neq \emptyset$, return to step 1.

Fig. 6. The improved reverse heuristic method for selecting dominating images for each action class

by many other ones are less likely to be selected. In order to incorporate the latter heuristic rule, we define the reachability of an image $\mathcal{I}$,

$$Reach\left(\mathcal{I}\right) = \left\{\mathcal{I}_i \mid \mathcal{S}\left(\mathcal{G}^{\mathcal{I}}, \mathcal{G}^{\mathcal{I}_i}\right) > T_i + \eta,\ y_i = y\right\} \tag{6}$$

Based on the coverage set and reachability set of each image, the IRH method are shown in Fig.6.

4.3 Action Recognition Using the Dominating Sets

To recognize the human action in a test image $\mathcal{I}'$, we construct a 2.5D graph for this image and match it with the dominating images in all the action classes. The action class that correspond to the largest normalized similarity is the recognition result, i.e.

$$k' = \arg\max_{k} \mathcal{S}(\mathcal{I}', k), \text{ where } \mathcal{S}(\mathcal{I}', k) = \arg\max_{\mathcal{I}_i \in Dom(k)} \frac{\mathcal{S}(\mathcal{I}', \mathcal{I}_i)}{T_i} \tag{7}$$

5 Experiments

We carry out experiments on two publicly available datasets: the people playing musical instrument (PPMI) dataset [37] and the PASCAL VOC 2011 action classification dataset [10]. In all the experiments described below, all training processes are conducted on only training images, including human pose estimation, etc. Please refer to Sec.3 and Sec.4 for implementation details of our approach. On both datasets, we use mean Average Precision (mAP) for performance evaluation.

5.1 Results on the PPMI Dataset

The PPMI dataset [37] is a collection of images of people interacting with twelve different musical instruments: bassoon, cello, clarinet, erhu, flute, French horn, guitar, harp, recorder, saxophone, trumpet, and violin. It is a 24-class classification problem. For each instrument, there are images of people playing the instrument, as well as images of people holding the instrument but not playing. We use the normalized images on this dataset. For each class, there are 100 images for training and 100 images for testing.

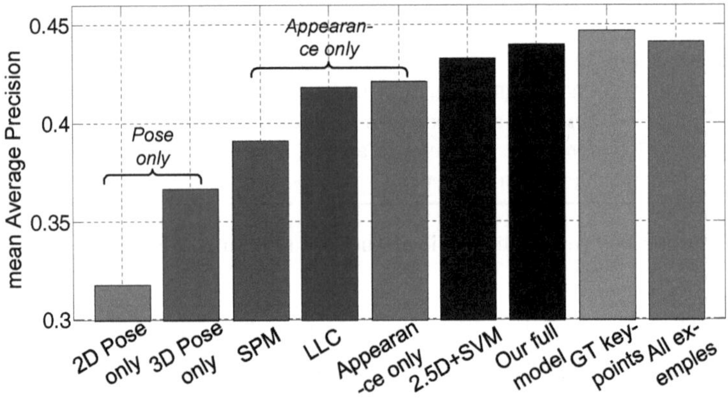

Fig. 7. Comparison of different methods on the PPMI dataset. The performances are evaluated by mean Average Precision. Magenta colors indicate existing methods. Green, blue, and cyan colors indicate our method or control experiments.

We compare our approach with a number of control settings and some state-of-the-art classification systems described below.

- *Bag-of-Words (BOW) baseline:* Extract SIFT features [20] and use bag-of-words for classification. The codebook size for SIFT features is 1024.
- *Locality-constrained linear (LLC) coding + spatial pyramid:* Image features are multi-scale, multi-resolution color-SIFT [38] features with locality-constrained linear coding [35]. The features are max-pooled on a three-level image pyramid [21] with linear SVM for classification. This is the best result reported in the website of the dataset.
- *Control - 3D pose only:* 2D image appearances are not used for image representation. Everything else is the same as our method. This is equivalent to setting $I\left(\mathbf{f}_v^{\mathcal{I}}, \mathbf{f}_v^{\mathcal{M}}\right)$ to $\mathbf{0}$ in Eq.2.
- *Control - 2D pose only:* Using only the original 2D locations for recognition, without rotating 3D key-point positions when matching two images.
- *Control - 2D appearance only:* The location of 3D key-points are not used for image representation. Everything else is the same as our method. This is equivalent to setting $\left(\mathbf{R}^* \Delta\mathbf{l}_e^{\mathcal{I}} - \Delta\mathbf{l}_e^{\mathcal{M}}\right)$ to 0 in Eq.2.
- *Control - 2.5D graph + SVM:* Using the 2.5D graph for image representation, and train a multiclass classifier based on 2D appearances and 3D poses.
- *Control - using ground-truth key-points:* Instead of using pictorial structure to estimate the 2D key-point locations. We use ground-truth positions of key-points.
- *Control - using all training images as exemplars:* Instead of selecting dominating images for each action, we match a testing image to all training images for classification.

The mAP of different methods are shown in Fig.7. Our method outperforms the existing methods by achieving a 43.9% mAP, even comparing with LLC, which

Fig. 8. Examples of dominating images selected from the PPMI training set

is the current best result on this dataset. Because the images of people playing some musical instruments are very similar (e.g. playing saxophone and playing bassoon, as shown in Fig.8.), using human pose only cannot achieve very good performance on this dataset. But 3D poses achieve much better results than 2D poses. Using the local appearance features extracted based on the key-point positions, our appearance feature performs comparable with LLC. The full 2.5D graph representation, which combines the 3D position information and 2D appearance information, outperforms both methods that use any one of them. This shows that our method effectively captures the complementary information between poses and appearances. Our full model also performs better than training a multiclass SVM classifier on the 2.5D graph features, demonstrating the effectiveness of the exemplar-based classification.

In Fig.7, our method is only 0.7% worse than the approach that uses ground-truth key-point locations to construct the 2.5D graphs. This shows that although our 2.5D graphs are constructed based on imperfect key-point locations (using the criteria in [39], our key-point detection accuracy is 65.7%), it can still achieve satisfactory recognition performance. Finally, our method performs comparable with the approach that uses all training images as exemplars. But our classification is much faster because we only need to match each testing image with 3.6 images (the average number of selected dominating images) per class, as compared with matching 100 images in the "all-exemplars" setting.

Fig.8 shows the dominating images selected from some action classes. On the classes of people playing the instrument, human poses are very similar in each class. Therefore the dominating images mainly capture with-class appearance variations. On the classes of people holding the instruments but not playing, the variations in both human pose and image appearance are captured.

5.2 Results on the PASCAL Dataset

The PASCAL 2011 action dataset contains around 8,000 images of ten actions: "jumping", "phoning", "playing instrument", "reading", "riding bike", "riding horse", "running", "taking photo", "using computer", and "walking". The dataset also contains images that do not belong to any of the ten actions. All images are downloaded from flickr, and represent very large variations in both human pose and appearance.

We compare our approach with a number of methods that achieve good performance on the challenge [10]. The results are shown in Table 1. We observe that our method performs the best on three out of the ten classes, especially on the classes of "jumping" and "playing instrument" which contain large human pose variations, and obtains the highest mean average precision over all the classes. On the classes of "riding a horse" and "riding a bike", our method does not perform as good as ATTR_PART, which explicitly detects objects such as horses and bikes in the images and relies on independent dataset to train the object detectors. Table 1 also shows that using pose features only, our method achieves better performance thatn POSELETS, demonstrating the effectiveness of our view-independent 3D pose representation.

Table 1. Results on the PASCAL 2011 action dataset. The numbers are percentage of mean average precision. The best results are marked by bold fonts.

Action	HOBJ_ DSAL	CON- TEXT	RF_ SVM	POSE_ LETS	ATTR_ PART	Our Method		
						Pose	App.	Full
jumping	71.6	65.9	66.0	59.5	66.7	64.6	68.9	**72.4**
phoning	**50.7**	41.5	41.0	31.3	41.1	41.2	44.5	48.3
playing instrument	77.5	57.4	60.0	45.6	60.8	68.3	72.9	**77.7**
reading	37.8	34.7	41.5	27.8	42.2	36.0	39.2	**43.2**
riding bike	86.5	88.8	90.0	84.4	**90.5**	81.4	86.6	89.0
riding horse	89.5	90.2	92.1	88.3	**92.2**	80.4	87.1	90.0
running	83.8	**87.9**	86.6	77.6	86.2	79.4	83.0	86.8
taking photo	25.1	25.7	28.8	**31.0**	28.8	21.6	25.1	27.9
using computer	58.9	54.5	62.0	47.4	**63.5**	51.5	56.9	60.5
walking	59.2	59.5	**65.9**	57.6	64.2	52.8	59.7	62.1
mean	64.1	60.6	63.4	55.1	63.6	57.7	62.4	**65.8**

6 Conclusion

In this paper, we propose a 2.5D graph for action image representation. The 2.5D graph integrates 3D view-independent pose features and 2D appearance features. An exemplar-based approach is used for action recognition, where a small set of images that are able to cover the large with-action pose variations are used as the exemplars for each class. One direction of future research is to study how the alignment of 3D positions can provide better usage of 2D appearance features.

Acknowledgement. This research is partially supported by an ONR MURI grant, the DARPA CSSG program, an NSF CAREER grant (IIS-0845230), a research sponsorship from Intel to L.F-F., and the SAP Stanford Graduate Fellowship and Microsoft Research PhD Fellowship to B.Y.

References

1. Ikizler, N., Cinbis, R.G., Pehlivan, S., Duygulu, P.: Recognizing actions from still images. In: ICPR (2008)
2. Gupta, A., Kembhavi, A., Davis, L.S.: Observing human-object interactions: Using spatial and functional compatibility for recognition. IEEE T. Pattern Anal. Mach. Intell. 31, 1775–1789 (2009)
3. Yao, B., Fei-Fei, L.: Modeling mutual context of object and human pose in human-object interaction activities. In: CVPR (2010)
4. Yang, W., Wang, Y., Mori, G.: Recognizing human actions from still images with latent poses. In: CVPR (2010)
5. Yao, B., Jiang, X., Khosla, A., Lin, A.L., Guibas, L.J., Fei-Fei, L.: Human action recognition by learning bases of action attributes and parts. In: ICCV (2011)
6. Maji, S., Bourdev, L., Malik, J.: Action recognition from a distributed representation of pose and appearance. In: CVPR (2011)
7. Delaitre, V., Sivic, J., Laptev, I.: Learning person-object interactions for action recognition in still images. In: NIPS (2011)
8. Prest, A., Schmid, C., Ferrari, V.: Weakly supervised learning of interactions between humans and objects. IEEE T. Pattern Anal. Mach. Intell. 34, 601–614 (2012)
9. Yao, B., Khosla, A., Fei-Fei, L.: Combining randomization and discrimination for fine-grained image categorization. In: CVPR (2011)
10. Everingham, M., Van Gool, L.J., Williams, C.K.I., Winn, J., Zisserman, A.: The PASCAL Visual Object Classes Challenge 2011 (VOC2011) Results (2011)
11. Natarajan, P., Nevatia, R.: View and scale invariant action recognition using multiview shape-flow methods. In: CVPR (2008)
12. Yan, P., Khan, S.M., Shah, M.: Learning 4D action feature models for arbitaray view action recognition. In: CVPR (2008)
13. Gong, D., Medioni, G.: Dynamic manifold warping for view invariant action recognition. In: ICCV (2011)
14. Weinland, D., Özuysal, M., Fua, P.: Making Action Recognition Robust to Occlusions and Viewpoint Changes. In: Daniilidis, K., Maragos, P., Paragios, N. (eds.) ECCV 2010, Part III. LNCS, vol. 6313, pp. 635–648. Springer, Heidelberg (2010)
15. Junejo, I.N., Dexter, E., Laptev, I., Perez, P.: View-independent action recognition from temporal self-similarities. IEEE T. Pattern Anal. Mach. Intell. 33, 172–185 (2011)
16. Sapp, B., Toshev, A., Taskar, B.: Cascaded Models for Articulated Pose Estimation. In: Daniilidis, K., Maragos, P., Paragios, N. (eds.) ECCV 2010, Part II. LNCS, vol. 6312, pp. 406–420. Springer, Heidelberg (2010)
17. Taylor, C.J.: Reconstruction of articulated objects from point correspondences in a single uncalibrated image, vol. 80, pp. 349–363 (2000)
18. Bourdev, L., Malik, J.: Poselets: Body part detectors trained using 3D human pose annotations. In: ICCV (2009)
19. Yao, A., Gall, J., Fanelli, G., van Gool, L.: Does human action recognition benefit from pose estimation? In: BMVC (2011)

20. Lowe, D.G.: Distinctive image features from scale-invariant keypoints. Int. J. Comput. Vision 60, 91–110 (2004)
21. Lazebnik, S., Schmid, C., Ponce, J.: Beyond bags of features: Spatial pyramid matching for recognizing natural scene categories. In: CVPR (2006)
22. Szeliski, R., Anandan, P., Baker, S.: From 2D images to 2.5D sprites: A layered approach to modeling 3D scenes. In: MMCS (1999)
23. Duan, Y., Qin, H.: 2.5D active contour for surface reconstruction. In: VMV (2003)
24. Zafeiriou, S., Petrou, M.: 2.5D elastic graph matching. Comput. Vis. Image Und. 115, 1062–1072 (2011)
25. Sung, K.K., Poggio, T.: Example-based learning for view-based human face detection. IEEE T. Pattern Anal. Mach. Intell. 20, 39–51 (1998)
26. Frome, A., Singer, Y., Sha, F., Malik, J.: Learning globally-consistent local distance functions for shape-based image retrieval and classification. In: ICCV (2007)
27. Malisiewicz, T., Gupta, A., Efros, A.A.: Ensemble of exemplar-SVMs for object detection and beyond. In: ICCV (2011)
28. Willems, G., Becker, J.H., Tuytelaars, T., van Gool, L.: Exemplar-based action recognition in video. In: BMVC (2009)
29. Hedetniemi, S.T., Laskar, R.C.: Bibliography on domination in graphs and some basic definitions of domination parameters. Discrete Math. 86, 257–277 (1990)
30. Yao, B., Ai, H., Lao, S.: Building a Compact Relevant Sample Coverage for Relevance Feedback in Content-Based Image Retrieval. In: Forsyth, D., Torr, P., Zisserman, A. (eds.) ECCV 2008, Part I. LNCS, vol. 5302, pp. 697–710. Springer, Heidelberg (2008)
31. Read, J.C.A., Phillipson, G.P., Serrano-Pedraza, I., Milner, A.D., Parker, A.J.: Stereoscopic vision in the absence of the lateral occipital cortex. PLoS One 5 (2010)
32. Lee, H.J., Chen, Z.: Determination of human body posture from a single view. Comp. Vision, Graphics, and Image Proc. 30, 148–168 (1985)
33. Delaitre, V., Laptev, I., Sivic, J.: Recognizing human actions in still images: a study of bag-of-features and part-based representations. In: BMVC (2010)
34. Felzenszwalb, P.F., Girshick, R.B., McAllester, D., Ramanan, D.: Object detection with discriminatively trained part-based models. IEEE T. Pattern Anal. Mach. Intell. 32, 1627–1645 (2010)
35. Wang, J., Yang, J., Yu, K., Lv, F., Huang, T., Gong, Y.: Learning locality-constrained linear coding for image classification. In: CVPR (2010)
36. Umeyama, S.: Least-squares estimation of transformation parameters between two point patterns. IEEE T. Pattern Anal. Mach. Intell. 13, 376–380 (1991)
37. Yao, B., Fei-Fei, L.: Grouplet: A structured image representation for recognizing human and object interactions. In: CVPR (2010)
38. Burghouts, G.J., Geusebroek, J.M.: Performance evaluation of local colour invariants. Comput. Vis. Image Und. 113, 48–62 (2009)
39. Ferrari, V., Marin-Jimenez, M., Zisserman, A.: Progressive search space reduction for human pose estimation. In: CVPR (2008)

Cost-Sensitive Top-Down/Bottom-Up Inference for Multiscale Activity Recognition

Mohamed R. Amer[1], Dan Xie[2], Mingtian Zhao[2],
Sinisa Todorovic[1], and Song-Chun Zhu[2]

[1] Oregon State University, Corvallis, Oregon
{amerm,sinisa}@onid.orst.edu
[2] University of California, Los Angeles, California
{xiedan,mtzhao,sczhu}@ucla.edu

Abstract. This paper addresses a new problem, that of multiscale activity recognition. Our goal is to detect and localize a wide range of activities, including individual actions and group activities, which may simultaneously co-occur in high-resolution video. The video resolution allows for digital zoom-in (or zoom-out) for examining fine details (or coarser scales), as needed for recognition. The key challenge is how to avoid running a multitude of detectors at all spatiotemporal scales, and yet arrive at a holistically consistent video interpretation. To this end, we use a three-layered AND-OR graph to jointly model group activities, individual actions, and participating objects. The AND-OR graph allows a principled formulation of efficient, cost-sensitive inference via an explore-exploit strategy. Our inference optimally schedules the following computational processes: 1) direct application of activity detectors – called α process; 2) bottom-up inference based on detecting activity parts – called β process; and 3) top-down inference based on detecting activity context – called γ process. The scheduling iteratively maximizes the log-posteriors of the resulting parse graphs. For evaluation, we have compiled and benchmarked a new dataset of high-resolution videos of group and individual activities co-occurring in a courtyard of the UCLA campus.

1 Introduction

This paper addresses a new problem. Our goal is to detect and localize all instances of a queried human activity present in high-resolution video. The novelty of this problem is two-fold: (i) the queries can be about a wide range of activities, including actions of individuals, their interactions with objects and other people, or collective activities of a group of people; and (ii) all these various types of activities may simultaneously co-occur in a relatively large scene captured by high-resolution video. The video resolution allows for digital zoom-in (or zoom-out) for examining fine details (or coarser scales), as needed for recognition. We call this problem multiscale activity recognition.

With the recent rapid increase in the spatial resolution of digital cameras, and growing capabilities of capturing long video footage, the problem of multiscale activity recognition becomes increasingly important for many applications, including video surveillance and monitoring. While recent work typically focuses on short videos of

A. Fitzgibbon et al. (Eds.): ECCV 2012, Part IV, LNCS 7575, pp. 187–200, 2012.

a particular activity type, there is an increasing demand for developing principled approaches to interpreting long videos of spatially large, complex scenes with many people engaged in various, co-occurring, individual and group activities. The key challenge of this new problem is complexity of inference. It is infeasible to apply sliding windows for detecting all activity instances at all spatiotemporal scales of the video volume.

To address the above challenge, we account for the compositional nature of human activities, and model them explicitly with the AND-OR graph [1–3]. The AND-OR graph is suitable for our purposes, because it is capable of compactly representing many activities, each recursively defined in terms of spatial layouts of human-human or human-object interactions. Modeling the temporal structure of activities is left for the future work. The recursion ends with primitive body parts and objects. Also, its hierarchical structure allows for a principled formulation of cost-sensitive inference. Our formulation rests on two computational mechanisms. First, following the work of [4], we express inference in terms of the α, β, and γ processes. The three processes are specific to each node in the AND-OR graph, where

1. α(node): detecting the activity directly from video features extracted from the video part associated with the node;
2. β(node): bottom-up binding of parts of the activity represented by the node;
3. γ(node): prediction of the activity represented by the node from the context provided by a parent node.

Second, we specify an explore-exploit (E^2) strategy for cost-sensitive inference. The E^2 strategy optimally schedules the sequential computation of α, β, and γ, such that the log-posteriors of the resulting parse graphs are maximized. In this way, the E^2 strategy digitally zooms-in or zooms-out at every iteration, conditioned on previous moves, and thus resolves ambiguities in all hypothesized parse graphs.

To initiate research on this important problem, we have collected and annotated a new dataset of high-resolution videos of various, co-occurring activities taking place in a courtyard of the UCLA campus [5]. Fig. 1 shows an example, cropped out frame from our UCLA Courtyard dataset. As can be seen, the cropped-out part shows a vast space wherein students are standing in a line to buy food, walking together in a campus tour led by a guide, or sitting and reading on the staircase. In other parts of the same video (not shown), people may be riding bicycles or scooters, buying soda from a vending machine, or jogging together. The video has a high resolution to allow activity recognition at different spatial and temporal scales. For example, it may be necessary to exploit the high resolution for digital zoom-in, and thus disambiguate particular objects defining the queried activity (e.g., buying a soda or a snack from the vending machine).

Prior Work – Multiscale activity recognition has received scant attention in the literature. Recent work typically studies prominently featured, single-actor, punctual or repetitive actions [6]. Activities with richer spatiotemporal structure have been addressed using graphical models, including Deformable Action Templates [7], Sum Product Networks [8], and AND-OR graphs [2, 3]. However, this work considers only one specific scale of human activities. Our work is related to recent methods for recognizing group and individual activities using context [9–11], and identifying objects in videos based on activity recognition [12]. There are two major differences. First, that work

Fig. 1. An example from our UCLA Courtyard dataset, showing multiple co-occurring group activities, primitive actions, and objects. Overlaid over the original frame, the purple marks the group walking together, the magenta marks the group standing in a line for food, the beige marks the group going to class, and the light blue marks the UCLA Courtyard tour. Within the dashed boxes, we show that each of these group activities consists of individual actions of group participants, where some of them interact with objects, e.g., carry backpacks.

considers only two semantic levels – namely, either context and activities, or activities and objects. We jointly consider three semantic levels: objects, individual actions, and group activities. Second, prior work typically focuses on simple videos showing a single activity (or object) in the entire video. Our high-resolution videos, instead, show a spatially large scene with multiple co-occurring activities of many people interacting with many objects over a relatively long time interval. We advance recent work on localizing single-actor, punctual, and repetitive activities [13] by parsing significantly more challenging videos with co-occurring activities at different scales.

Our work builds upon an empirical study of the α, β, and γ process for face detection in still images, presented in [4]. That work considered only one object class (i.e., faces), whereas we seek to recognize a multitude of activity and object classes. Our extensions include: (i) a new formulation of the expected gains of α, β, and γ, and specifying the E^2 strategy for cost-sensitive inference of the AND-OR graph.

In the sequel, Sec. 2 defines the AND-OR graph. Sec. 3 presents our inference. Sec. 4 specifies low-level detectors used in inference, and the computation of α, β, and γ. Sec. 5 formulates the E^2 strategy. Sec. 6 specifies our learning. Sec. 7 presents our experimental evaluation.

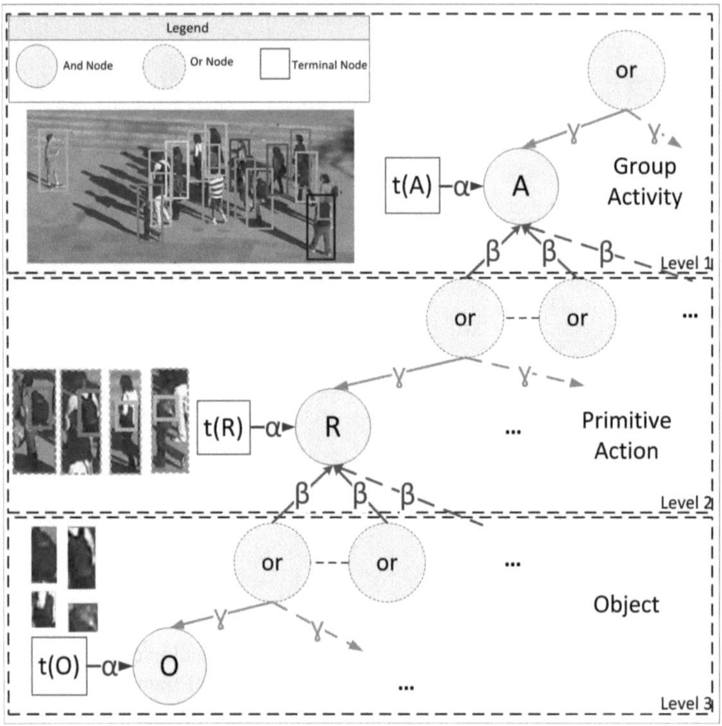

Fig. 2. The AND-OR graph of group activities $\mathcal{A}$, primitive actions $\mathcal{R}$, and objects $\mathcal{O}$. t is the terminal node representing a detector of the corresponding activity or object. Detector responses $t(\cdot)$ constitute the α process. The top-down γ process is aimed at predicting and localizing the corresponding primitive action (or object), based on context provided by the detected group activity (or primitive action). The bottom-up β process is aimed at inferring the corresponding primitive action (or group activity), based on detections of participating objects (or primitive actions).

2 AND-OR Graph

This section presents the AND-OR graph following the notation and formalism presented in [4]. The AND-OR graph, illustrated in Fig. 2, organizes domain knowledge in a hierarchical manner at three levels. Group activities, $a \in \mathcal{A}$, (e.g., Standing-in-a-line) are defined as a spatial relationship of a set of primitive actions (e.g., a group of people Standing, in a certain Pose, Orientation, and at certain Displacement). They are represented by nodes at the highest level of the graph. Primitive actions, $r \in \mathcal{R}$, (e.g., Riding-a-bike) are defined as punctual or repetitive motions of a single person, who may interact with an object (e.g., Bike or Phone). They are represented as children nodes of the group-activity nodes. Objects, $o \in \mathcal{O}$, include body parts and tools or instruments that people interact with while conducting a primitive action. Object nodes are placed at the lowest level of the AND-OR graph, and represent children of the primitive-action nodes. Modeling efficiency is achieved by sharing children nodes among multiple parents, where AND nodes encode particular configurations of parts, and OR nodes account for alternative configurations.

More formally, the AND-OR graph is $\mathcal{G} = (\mathcal{V}_{NT}, \mathcal{V}_T, \mathcal{E}, \mathcal{P})$, where $\mathcal{V}_{NT}$ is a union set of non-terminal AND and OR nodes. An AND node is denoted as $\wedge$, and an OR node is denoted as $\vee$. Let $l = 1, ..., L$ denote a level in $\mathcal{G}$, where $l-1$ is the level closer to the root than level l. Then, a parent of $\wedge^l$ is denoted as $\wedge^{l-}$. Similarly, ith child of $\wedge^l$ is denoted as $\wedge_i^{l+}$. We also use $X_{\wedge^l}$ to denote a descriptor vector of the video part associated with node $\wedge^l$, including the information about location, scale and orientation relative to the video part associated with the parent node $\wedge^{l-1}$. $\mathcal{V}_T = \{t_{\wedge_i} : \forall \wedge_i \in \mathcal{V}_{NT}\}$ is a set of terminal nodes connected to the corresponding non-terminal nodes, where each $t_{\wedge_i}$ represents a detector applied to the video part associated with $\wedge_i$. $\mathcal{E}$ is a set of edges of $\mathcal{G}$. A parse graph, pg, is a valid instance of the grammar $\mathcal{G}$. $\mathcal{P}$ is the probability over the space of all parse graphs. The edge set of a parse graph is a union of switching edges $\mathcal{E}_{\text{switch}}(\text{pg})$, decomposition edges $\mathcal{E}_{\text{dec}}(\text{pg})$, and relation edges $\mathcal{E}_{\text{rel}}(\text{pg})$, $\mathcal{E}(\text{pg}) = \mathcal{E}_{\text{switch}}(\text{pg}) \cup \mathcal{E}_{\text{dec}}(\text{pg}) \cup \mathcal{E}_{\text{rel}}(\text{pg})$, as explained below.

The prior probability of a parse graph is defined as $p(\text{pg}) = \frac{1}{Z}\exp(-E(\text{pg}))$, where the partition function is $Z = \sum_{\text{pg}} \exp(-E(\text{pg}))$, and the total energy is

$$E(\text{pg}) = -\sum_l \Big[\sum_{(\vee^l,\wedge^l)\in\mathcal{E}_{\text{switch}}(\text{pg})} \log p(\wedge^l|\vee^l) + \sum_{(\wedge^l,\wedge^{l-})\in\mathcal{E}_{\text{dec}}(\text{pg})} \log p(X_{\wedge^l}|X_{\wedge^{l-}}) \\ + \sum_{(\wedge_i^{l+},\wedge_j^{l+})\in\mathcal{E}_{\text{rel}}(\text{pg})} \log p(X_{\wedge_i^{l+}}, X_{\wedge_j^{l+}})\Big]. \tag{1}$$

In (1), the first term denotes the probability that OR node $\vee^l$ selects AND node $\wedge^l$, the second term defines parent-child statistical dependencies, and the third term defines pairwise dependencies between pairs of children of $\wedge^l$.

Given an input video frame, I, with domain defined on lattice Λ, the likelihood of a parse graph is defined as $p(I|\text{pg}) = \prod_{t\in\mathcal{V}_T(\text{pg})} p(I_{\Lambda_t}|t)$, where $\Lambda_t \in \Lambda$ is video domain occupied by the terminal node t.

3 Inference

Given a video, we conduct inference frame by frame. Temporal characteristics of activities are implicitly accounted for via descriptor vectors, which collect visual cues from space-time windows centered around spatial domains, $\Lambda_t \in \Lambda$, occupied by every terminal node t. Similar to the derivation in [4], the video frame, I_Λ, contains an unknown number, K, of instances of the queried activities at different spatial scales. Each inferred instance is represented by a parse graph in the world representation, $W = (K, \{\text{pg}_k : k = 1, 2, \ldots, K\})$. Under the Bayesian framework, we infer W by maximizing its posterior probability, $W^* = \arg\max_{W\in\Omega} p(W)p(I_\Lambda|W)$, where Ω is the space of solutions.

The prior of W is defined as $p(W) = p(K)\prod_{k=1}^K p(\text{pg}_k)$, where $p(K) \propto \exp(-\lambda_0 K)$ is the prior of the number of parse graphs, and $p(\text{pg}_k)$ is defined by (1). To compute the likelihood $p(I_\Lambda|W)$, we define foreground lattice $\Lambda_{\text{fg}} = \cup_k \Lambda_{\text{pg}_k}$, and background lattice $\Lambda_{\text{bg}} = \Lambda \setminus \Lambda_{\text{fg}}$, and use a generic background pdf, $q(I)$, as

$$p(I_\Lambda|W) = p(I_{\Lambda_{\text{fg}}}|W)q(I_{\Lambda_{\text{bg}}})\frac{q(I_{\Lambda_{\text{fg}}})}{q(I_{\Lambda_{\text{fg}}})} = q(I_\Lambda)\prod_{k=1}^K \frac{p(I_{\Lambda_{\text{pg}_k}}|\text{pg}_k)}{q(I_{\Lambda_{\text{pg}_k}})} \tag{2}$$

where $p(I_{\Lambda_{\mathrm{pg}_k}}|\mathrm{pg}_k)$ means that domain Λ_{pg_k} is explained away by the parse graph pg_k, and $q(I_{\Lambda_{\mathrm{pg}_k}})$ explains domain Λ_{pg_k} as background.

In inference, we sequentially infer the parse graphs, one at a time, and augment W. The inference of a parse graph is formulated as

$$\mathrm{pg}^* = \arg \max_{\mathrm{pg}\in\Omega(\mathrm{pg})} \left[\log p(\mathrm{pg}) + \log \frac{p(I_{\Lambda_{\mathrm{pg}}}|\mathrm{pg})}{q(I_{\Lambda_{\mathrm{pg}}})} \right], \tag{3}$$

where $p(\mathrm{pg})$ is defined by (1). The likelihood ratio in (3) can be factorized over terminal nodes, $t \in \mathcal{V}_T(\mathrm{pg})$, representing detector responses over the corresponding video parts. Specifically, we can write $\log \frac{p(I_{\Lambda_{\mathrm{pg}}}|\mathrm{pg})}{q(I_{\Lambda_{\mathrm{pg}}})} = \sum_{t\in\mathcal{V}_T(\mathrm{pg})} \log \frac{p(p(I_{\Lambda_t}|t)}{q(I_{\Lambda_t})} = \sum_{t\in\mathcal{V}_T(\mathrm{pg})} \psi(t)$, where $\psi(t)$ denotes the confidence of detector t applied at video part I_{Λ_t}. From (1) and (3), we have:

$$\mathrm{pg}^* = \arg \max_{\mathrm{pg}\in\Omega(\mathrm{pg})} \sum_l \Big\{ \underbrace{\log p(\wedge^l|\vee^l)}_{\text{AND-OR graph structure}} + \underbrace{\psi(t_{\wedge^l})}_{\alpha^l} + \underbrace{\Big[\underbrace{\psi(t_{\wedge^{l-}})}_{\alpha^{l-}} + \underbrace{\log p(X_{\wedge^l}|X_{\wedge^{l-}})}_{\gamma^{l-}} \Big]}_{\text{zoom-out}}$$
$$\underbrace{+ p(N^l) \sum_{i=1}^{N^l} \Big[\underbrace{\log p(X_{\wedge_i^{l+}}|X_{\wedge^l})}_{\gamma_i^{l+}} + \underbrace{\psi(t_{\wedge_i^{l+}})}_{\alpha_i^{l+}} + \sum_{i\neq j} \underbrace{\log p(X_{\wedge_i^{l+}}, X_{\wedge_j^{l+}})}_{\beta_{ij}^{l+}} \Big]}_{\text{zoom-in}} \Big\} \tag{4}$$

Equation (4) specifies the α^l, β^l, and γ^l processes at level l of the AND-OR graph. Confidences of the activity detectors constitute α^l process. The top-down γ^l process is aimed at predicting and localizing the corresponding primitive action (or object), based on the context of the group activity (or primitive action). For example, to zoom-out for examining the context of a primitive action, it is necessary to detect the action's contextual group activity, α^{l-}, and to estimate the likelihood of the corresponding parent-child configuration γ^{l-}. The bottom-up β^l process is aimed at inferring the corresponding group activity (or primitive action), based on its children primitive actions (or objects), and their configuration. For example, to zoom-in for examining individual actions within a group activity, it is first necessary to detect the primitive actions α_i^{l+}, $i = 1, ..., N^l$, then, estimate the likelihood of the corresponding parent-child configuration γ_i^{l+}, and finally estimate the likelihood of their configuration β_{ij}^{l+}, $i, j = 1, ..., N^l$.

4 Computing α, β, γ

For each level l of the AND-OR graph, we define a set of α^l detectors aimed at detecting corresponding activities. As the α's are independent across the three levels of our AND-OR graph, we specify three different types of detectors. All detectors have access to the Deformable-Parts-Model (DPM) person detector [14], and a multiclass SVM classifier aimed at detecting a person's facing direction. The person detector is initially applied to each frame using the scanning procedure recommended in [14]. A person's facing direction is classified by an 8-class classifier, learned by LibSVM on HOGs (the 5-fold cross-validation precision of orientation is 69%).

For detecting objects, we train the DPM on bounding boxes of object instances annotated in training videos, and apply this detector in a vicinity of every people detection. For each object detection, we use the above SVM to identity the object's orientation.

For detecting primitive actions, we apply the motion-appearance based detector of [15] in a vicinity of every people detection. From a given window enclosing a person detection, we first extract motion-based STIP features [16], and describe them with HOG descriptors. Then, we extract KLT tracks of Harris corners, and quantize the motion vectors along the track to obtain a descriptor called the Sequence Code Map. The descriptors of STIPs and KLT tracks are probabilistically fused into a relative location probability table (RLPT), which captures the spatial and temporal relationships between the features. Such a hybrid descriptor is then classified by a multiclass SVM to detect the primitive actions of interest.

For detecting group activities, we compute the STV (Space-Time Volume) descriptors of [17] in a vicinity of every people detection, called an anchor. STV counts people, and their poses, locations, and velocities, in different space-time bins surrounding the anchor. Each STV is oriented along the anchor's facing direction. STVs calculated per frame are concatenated to capture the temporal evolution of the activities. Since the sequence of STVs captures a spatial variation over time, the relative motion and displacement of each person in a group is also encoded. Tracking STVs across consecutive frames is performed in 2.5D scene coordinates. This makes detecting group activities robust to perspective and view-point changes. The tracks of STVs are then classified by a multiclass SVM to detect the group activities of interest.

The β process binds pairs of children nodes $(\wedge_i^{l+}, \wedge_j^{l+})$ of parent $\wedge^l$. This is evaluated using the Gaussian distribution $p(X_{\wedge_i^{l+}}, X_{\wedge_j^{l+}}) = N(X_{\wedge_i^{l+}} - X_{\wedge_j^{l+}}; \mu_{\beta^l}, \Sigma_{\beta^l})$.

The γ process predicts ith child $\wedge_i^{l+}$ conditioned on the context of parent $\wedge^l$. This is evaluated using the Gaussian distribution $p(X_{\wedge_i^{l+}}|X_{\wedge^l}) = N(X_{\wedge_i^{l+}} - X_{\wedge^l}; \mu_{\gamma^l}, \Sigma_{\gamma^l})$.

5 The E^2 Strategy for Cost-sensitive Inference

The E^2 strategy optimally schedules a sequential computation of α, β, and γ processes, such that the posterior distributions of K parse graphs in W are iteratively maximized. We make the assumption that every process carries the same computational cost.

More formally, given a query, q, the E^2 strategy sequentially selects an optimal move at a given state, which results in another state. The set of states, $\mathbb{S}_q$, that can be visited are defined by all AND nodes which form the transitive closure of node $\wedge_q$ representing q in the AND-OR graph. Thus, a state $s \in \mathbb{S}_q$ represents an AND node in the transitive closure of $\wedge_q$. A move, $m \in \mathbb{M}_s$, at state s, is defined by the edges in the AND-OR graph that directly link $\wedge_s$ to its parents and children nodes in $\mathbb{S}_q$. For example, a move to ith child node of $\wedge_s$ means running the detector defined by the terminal node $t_{\wedge_i}$, i.e., zooming-in and computing the α process of the child. Similarly, a move to lth parent node of $\wedge_s$ means zooming-out and running the detector $t_{\wedge_l}$.

We make the assumption that we have access to a *simulator*, which deterministically identifies next state s' (i.e., next AND node) after taking move m at state s. This simulator computes the log-posterior of K parse graphs in W, given by (4), from all α, β, and γ processes available until a given iteration. Since the simulator will always account for available detector responses in (4), the E^2 strategy should not repeat the moves which have already been taken. Since the moves are Markovian, we keep a record of detectors that have already been used $\mathbb{M}_{\text{used}}$.

A relatively small number of moves $|\mathbb{M}_s|$ at each state $s \in \mathbb{S}_q$ allows for a robust estimation of expected utilities of taking the moves, denoted as $\mathbb{Q}_q = [\mathbb{Q}(s, m; q)]$. $\mathbb{Q}_q$ is then used for guiding the scheduling of optimal moves in inference. One of the strengths of Q-learning is that it is able to compute $\mathbb{Q}_q$ without requiring a model of the environment. We specify a reward $\mathbb{R}_t(s, m; q)$ for taking move $m \in \mathbb{M}_s$ in state $s \in \mathbb{S}_q$, which results in the next state $s' \in \mathbb{S}_q$, and evaluate this reward for a given set of training parse graphs, $\{\text{pg}_t : t = 1, ..., T\}$. The reward is defined using the sigmoid function: $\mathbb{R}_t(s, m; q) = \left(1 + \exp^{-\left(\log p(\text{pg}_t|\mathbb{M}_{\text{used}}) - \log p(\text{pg}_t|\mathbb{M}'_{\text{used}})\right)}\right)^{-1}$, where $\log p(\text{pg}_t|\mathbb{M}_{\text{used}})$ denotes the log-posterior distribution of tth training parse graph, given all detector responses in $\mathbb{M}_{\text{used}}$. Then, the Q-learning is run T times over all parse graphs $\{\text{pg}_t\}$, and $\mathbb{Q}_q$ is updated as, for $t = 1, ..., T$:

$$\mathbb{Q}(s, m; q) \leftarrow \mathbb{Q}(s, m; q) + \eta_s \left(\mathbb{R}_t(s, m; q) + \rho \max_{m'} \mathbb{Q}(s', m'; q) - \mathbb{Q}(s, m; q)\right), \quad (5)$$

where η_s is the learning rate, and ρ is the discounting factor. We estimate η_s as the inverse of the number of times state s has been visited, and set $\rho = 1$.

The E^2 strategy is summarized in Alg. 1. The initial state $s^{(0)} \in \mathbb{S}_q$ is assumed to be the query node in the AND-OR graph. The first move $m^{(0)} \in \mathbb{M}_s$ is defined as running the detector of the query. For selecting optimal moves in the following iterations, $\tau = 1, 2, ..., \mathcal{B}$, the E^2 strategy flips a biased coin, and, if the outcome is "heads", takes the best expected move $m^{(\tau+1)} = \arg\max_m \mathbb{Q}(s^{(\tau)}, m; q)$, otherwise takes any allowed move in state $s^{(\tau)}$. In both cases, the move is selected from the allowed set of previously unselected moves $\mathbb{M}_{s^{(\tau)}} \setminus \mathbb{M}_{\text{used}}$. We specify the probability of "heads" to be $\epsilon = 0.75$, and thus enable a mechanism for avoiding local optima. For the selected move $m^{(\tau+1)}$, our simulator evaluates the log-posterior of the parse graphs, $\{\text{pg}_k^{*(\tau+1)} : k = 1, ..., K\}$, over all available α, β, and γ processes, given by (4). If these K log-posteriors are above a certain threshold, δ, estimated in training, the algorithm can terminate before the allowed number of iterations $\mathcal{B}$. We do not study here the right values of δ and $\mathcal{B}$.

In our empirical evaluations, we have observed that the E^2 strategy produces a reasonable scheduling of α, β and γ. Fig. 3a, shows our evaluation of the E^2 strategy for the query Walking, under different time budgets, on the UCLA Courtyard dataset. Fig. 3b shows our sensitivity to ϵ values averaged over 10 different types of queries about group activities, primitive actions, and objects, for the allowed budget of 100 iteration steps, on the UCLA Courtyard dataset.

Algorithm 1. E^2 Strategy

Input: Query q; budget $\mathcal{B}$; Bernoulli "success" probability ϵ;
expected utilities $\mathbb{Q}_q = [\mathbb{Q}(s, m; q)]$; threshold δ
Output: All instances of q, inferred by the parse graphs, $\{\text{pg}_k^{*(\mathcal{B})} : k = 1, ..., K\}$

Initialize: $\tau = 0$; state $s^{(0)}$; move $m^{(0)}$; $\mathbb{M}_{\text{used}} = \emptyset$;
Compute $\{\text{pg}_k^{*(0)} : k = 1, ..., K\}$ given by (4) ;
while $(\tau < \mathcal{B})$ **or** $(\forall k,\ \log p(\text{pg}_k^{*(\tau)} | \mathbb{M}_{\text{used}}) \leq \delta)$ **do**
  Toss a biased coin with $p(\text{"heads"}) = \epsilon$;
  if *("heads")* **then**
    Select the best expected move $m^{(\tau+1)} = \arg\max_{m \in \mathbb{M}_{s^{(\tau)}} \setminus \mathbb{M}_{\text{used}}} \mathbb{Q}(s^{(\tau)}, m; q)$;
  else
    Select randomly a move $m^{(\tau+1)} \in \mathbb{M}_{s^{(\tau)}} \setminus \mathbb{M}_{\text{used}}$;
  end
  $\mathbb{M}_{\text{used}} = \mathbb{M}_{\text{used}} \cup \{m^{(\tau+1)}\}$;
  Evaluate $\{\text{pg}_k^{*(\tau+1)} : k = 1, ..., K\}$ for $\mathbb{M}_{\text{used}}$, given by (4);
  $\tau = \tau + 1$;
end

6 Learning the Model Parameters

This section explains how to learn parameters of the pdf's appearing in (4).

We learn the distribution of the AND-OR graph structure, $p(\wedge^l | \vee^l)$, as the frequency of occurrence of pairs $(\wedge^l, \vee^l)$ in training parse graphs. The prior over the number of children nodes $p(N^l)$ is assumed exponential. Its ML parameter is learned on the numbers of corresponding children nodes of $\wedge^l$ in training parse graphs.

Learning α: For learning α^l, at a particular level l of the AND-OR graph, we use annotated sets of positive and negative training examples, $\{T_{\alpha^l}^+, T_{\alpha^l}^-\}$. $T_{\alpha^l}^+$ consists of labeled bounding boxes around corresponding group activities ($l = 1$), or primitive actions ($l = 2$), or objects ($l = 3$). Parameters of a classifier used for α^l detector (e.g., DPM of [14]) is learned on $\{T_{\alpha^l}^+, T_{\alpha^l}^-\}$ in a standard way for that classifier (e.g., using the cutting-plane algorithm for learning the structural latent SVM).

Learning γ: For learning γ^l of a primitive action (or object), we use training set T_{γ^l}. T_{γ^l} consists of pairs of descriptor vectors, $\{(X_{\wedge^l}, X_{\wedge_i^{l-}})\}$, extracted from bounding boxes annotated around instances of the primitive action (or object), and its contextual group activity (or primitive action) occurring in training videos. The descriptors capture the relative location, orientation, and scale of the corresponding pairs of training instances. T_{γ^l} is used for the ML learning of the mean and covariance, $(\mu_{\gamma^l}, \Sigma_{\gamma^l})$, of the Gaussian distribution $p(X_{\wedge^l} | X_{\wedge^{l-}})$.

Learning β: For learning β^l, we use two training sets: T'_{β^l}, and $T''_{\beta^{l+}}$. For a group activity (or primitive action), T'_{β^l} consists of pairs of descriptor vectors, $\{(X_{\wedge^l}, X_{\wedge_i^{l+}}) : i = 1, ..., N^l\}$, extracted from bounding boxes annotated around instances of the group activity (or primitive action), and its constituent primitive actions (or objects) occurring

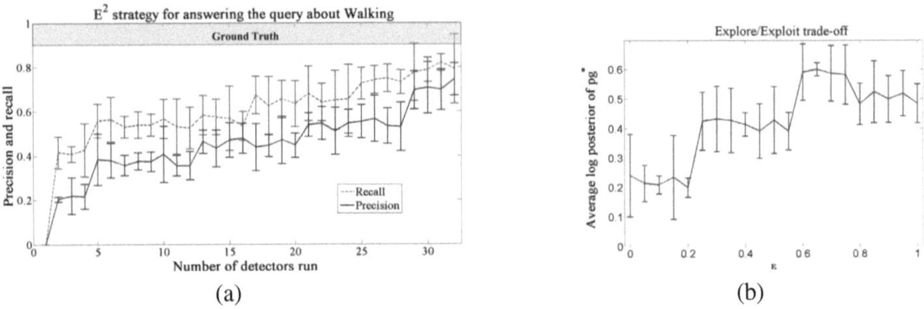

Fig. 3. Evaluation on the UCLA Courtyard dataset: (a) Precision and recall under different time budgets for the query Walking, averaged over all parse graphs. Our precision and recall increase as the number of detectors used reaches the maximum number 33. (b) Average log-posterior of ground-truth parse graphs of 10 different queries about group activities, primitive actions, and objects, for the budget of 100 iterations. The best results are achieved for $\epsilon \in [0.6 - 0.8]$.

in training videos. For a particular group activity (or primitive action), $T''_{\beta^{l+}}$ consists of all pairs of descriptor vectors, $\{(X_{\wedge_i^{l+}}, X_{\wedge_j^{l+}}) : i, j = 1, ..., N^l\}$, extracted from bounding boxes annotated around pairs of children of primitive actions (or objects) comprising the group activity (or primitive action). The descriptors capture the relative location, orientation, and scale of the corresponding pairs of training instances. T'_{β^l}, and $T''_{\beta^{l+}}$ are used for the ML learning of the means and covariances, $(\mu'_{\beta^l}, \Sigma'_{\beta^l})$ and $(\mu''_{\beta^l}, \Sigma''_{\beta^l})$, of the Gaussian distributions $p(X_{\wedge_i^{l+}} | X_{\wedge^l})$ and $p(X_{\wedge_i^{l+}}, X_{\wedge_j^{l+}})$.

7 Results

Existing benchmark datasets are not suitable for our evaluation. Major issues include: (1) unnatural, acted activities in constrained scenes; (2) limited spatial and temporal coverage; (3) limited resolution; (4) poor diversity of activity classes (particularly for multi-object events); (5) lack of concurrent events; and (6) lack of detailed annotations. For example, the VIRAT Ground dataset shows only single-actor activities (e.g., entering a building, parking a vehicle). The resolution of these videos (1280 × 720 or 1920 × 1080) is not sufficient to allow for digital zoom-in. Other surveillance datasets such as, VIRAT Aerial and CLIF, are not appropriate for our problem, since they are recorded from a high altitude where people are not visible. Other datasets (e.g, KTH, Weizmann, Youtube, Trecvid, PETS04, Olympic, CAVIAR, IXMAS, Hollywood, UCF, UT-Interaction or UIUC) are also not adequate, since they are primarily aimed at evaluating video classification. To address the needs of our evaluation, we have collected and annotated a new dataset, as explained below.

UCLA Courtyard Dataset [5]: The videos show two distinct scenes from a bird-eye viewpoint of a courtyard at the UCLA campus. The videos are suitable for our evaluation, since they show human activities at different semantic levels, and have a sufficiently high resolution to allow inference of fine details. The dataset consists of a 106-minute, 30 fps, 2560 × 1920-resolution video footage. We provide annotations in terms of bounding boxes around group activities, primitive actions, and objects in each frame. A bounding box is annotated with the orientation and pose, where we use 4 orientation classes for groups, 8 orientations for people, and 7 poses for people. Each frame is also annotated with the ground plane, so as to allow finding a depth of each individual or group. The following group activities are annotated: 1. Walking-together, 2. Standing-in-line, 3. Discussing-in-group, 4. Sitting-together, 5. Waiting-in-group, and 6. Guided-tour. The following primitive actions are annotated: 1. Riding-skateboard, 2. Riding-bike, 3. Riding-scooter, 4. Driving-car, 5. Walking, 6. Talking, 7. Waiting, 8. Reading, 9. Eating, and 10. Sitting. Finally, the following objects are annotated: 1. Food, 2. Book, 3. Car, 4. Scooter, 5. Bike, 6. Food Bus, 7. Vending Machine, 8. Food Menu, 9. Bench, 10. Stairs, 11. Table, 12. Chair, 13. Bottle, 14. Phone, 15. Handbag, 16. Skateboard, and 17. Backpack. For each group activity or primitive action, the dataset contains 20 instances, and for each object the dataset contains 50 instances. We split the dataset 50-50% for training and testing.

We also use the Collective Activity Dataset [17] that consists of 75 short videos of crossing, waiting, queuing, walking, talking, running, and dancing. This dataset tests our performance on a collective behavior of individuals under realistic conditions, including background clutter, and transient occlusions. For training and testing, we use the standard split of $2/3$ and $1/3$ of the videos from each class. The dataset provides labels of every 10th frame, in terms of bounding boxes around people performing the activity, their pose, and activity class.

The Collective Activity Dataset mostly shows a single group activity per video. We increase its complexity by synthesizing a composite dataset. The composite videos represent a concatenation of multiple original videos randomly placed on a 2×2 grid, as shown in Fig. 4. The composite videos show four co-occurring group activities. We formed 20 such composite sequences of multiple co-occurring group activities, and used 50% for training and 50% for testing.

We evaluate our performance for varying time budgets: $\mathcal{B} = \{1, 15, \infty\}$. $\mathcal{B} = 1$ means that we are allowed to run only the detector directly appropriate for the query (e.g., the detector of Riding-bike). This is our baseline. $\mathcal{B} = \infty$ means that we run the E^2 strategy as long as all detectors and their integration via the α, β, and γ processes are not executed. Finally, $1 < \mathcal{B} < \infty$ means that the E^2 strategy is run for $\mathcal{B}$ iterations.

We evaluate: i) Classification accuracy and ii) Recall and precision of activity detection. For detection evaluation, we compute a ratio, ρ, of the intersection and union of detected and ground-truth time intervals of activity occurrences. True positive (TP) is declared if the activity is correctly recognized, and $\rho > 0.5$, otherwise we declare false positive (FP). Note that this also evaluates localization of the start and end frames of activity occurrences.

Table 1 shows our precision, false positive rates, and running times, under varying time budgets, on the UCLA Courtyard dataset. As the budget increases, we observe better performance. The E^2 strategy gives slightly worse results in a significantly less amount of time, than the full inference with unlimited budget. Thus, the E^2 strategy improves the accuracy-complexity trade-off.

Table 2 compares our classification accuracy and running times with those of the state of the art [9, 11, 17] on the Collective Activity Dataset. For this comparison, we

Table 1. Average precision, and false positive rates on the UCLA Courtyard Dataset for primitive actions and group activities. The larger the time budget, the better precision.

	Query about group activities						
E^2 **strategy**	Standing-in-line	Guided-tour	Discussing	Sitting	Walking	Waiting	**Time**
$\mathcal{B} = 1$, Precision	62.2%	63.7%	68.1%	65.3%	69.4%	61.2%	5s
$\mathcal{B} = 1$, FP	7.2%	2.3%	9.8%	12.6%	8.1%	10.4%	5s
$\mathcal{B} = 15$, Precision	65.4%	66.1%	69.0%	68.7%	70.3%	66.5%	75s
$\mathcal{B} = 15$ FP	10.1%	4.7%	11.1%	11.1%	8.7%	10.9%	75s
$\mathcal{B} =$, Precision	68.0%	70.2%	75.1%	71.4%	78.6%	72.6%	230s
$\mathcal{B} = \infty$, FP	13.6%	10.3%	17.1%	13.7%	10.1%	12.2%	230s

	Query about primitive actions										
E^2 **strategy**	Walk	Wait	Talk	Drive Car	Ride S-board	Ride Scooter	Ride Bike	Read	Eat	Sit	**Time**
$\mathcal{B} = 1$, Precision	63.3%	61.2%	58.4%	65.8%	63.5%	60.1%	56.8%	55.3%	60.9%	54.3%	10s
$\mathcal{B} = 1$, FP	12.1%	16.2%	11.4%	3.4%	10.2%	11.6%	6.2%	8.2%	2.2%	5.3%	10s
$\mathcal{B} = 15$, Precision	67.6%	63.4%	62.3%	67.2%	67.1%	65.9%	59.3%	61.2%	66.3%	59.2%	150s
$\mathcal{B} = 15$, FP	14.2%	17.1%	15.1%	7.1%	13.8%	13.2%	9.3%	10.3%	4.3%	7.1%	150s
$\mathcal{B} = \infty$, Precision	69.1%	67.7%	69.6%	70.2%	71.3%	68.4%	61.4%	67.3%	71.3%	64.2%	330s
$\mathcal{B} = \infty$, FP	18.7%	20.2%	17.9%	9.7%	17.1%	16.3%	12.3%	12.1%	7.7%	9.0%	330s

Table 2. Average classification accuracy, and running times on the Collective Activity Dataset [17]. We use $\mathcal{B} = \infty$.

Class	**Our**	[11]	[18]	[9]	[17]
Walk	74.7%	38.8%	72.2%	68%	57.9%
Cross	77.2%	76.4%	69.9%	65%	55.4%
Queue	95.4%	78.7%	96.8%	96%	63.3%
Wait	78.3%	76.7%	74.1%	68%	64.6%
Talk	98.4%	85.7%	99.8%	99%	83.6%
Run	89.4%	N/A	87.6%	N/A	N/A
Dance	72.3%	N/A	70.2%	N/A	N/A
Avg	83.6%	70.9%	81.5%	79.1%	65.9%
Time	165s	N/A	55s	N/A	N/A

Table 3. Average precision, and false positive rates on the Composite Collective Activity dataset. We use $\mathcal{B} = \infty$.

Class	**Our**	**Our** FP-Rate	[18]	[18] FP-Rate
Walk	65.3%	8.2%	58.1%	12.2%
Cross	69.6%	8.7%	61.5%	15.5%
Queue	76.2%	5.2%	65.5%	8.7%
Wait	68.3%	7.7%	59.2%	8.2%
Talk	82.1%	6.2%	67.5%	7.1%
Run	80.4%	8.8%	72.1%	10.2%
Dance	63.1%	10.2%	55.3%	12.9%
Avg	72.1%	6.7%	62.7%	10.6%

Fig. 4. Our results on detecting group activities of the Composite Collective Activity dataset, for $\mathcal{B} = \infty$. The figure shows a single frame (not 4 frames) from the Composite dataset. A total of 7 co-occurring activity instances are detected. The detections are color coded. Top left: we detect the co-occurring Walking and Waiting. Top right: we detect the co-occurring Queuing, Talking, and Waiting. Bottom row: we detect Crossing (left), and Talking (right).

allow infinite budget in inference, and do not account for objects, since this information is not available to the competing approaches. As can be seen, we our performance is superior in reasonable running times. Figures 4 and 5 illustrate our qualitative results.

Fig. 5. Our results on an example video from the UCLA Courtyard dataset, under unlimited time budget. Detections are color coded, where the codes are given below each frame. Top left: results of the α's of group activities using the input poses and person detections. Top right: results of the α's of 10 objects. Bottom left: results of the α's of primitive actions. Bottom right: results for group activities and primitive actions of all parse graphs. (Best viewed zoomed-in, in color.)

8 Conclusion

We have formulated and addressed a new problem, that of multiscale activity recognition, where the main challenge is to make inference cost-sensitive and scalable. Our approach models group activities, individual actions, and participating objects with the AND-OR graph, and exploits its hierarchical structure to formulate a new inference algorithm. The inference is iterative, where the direct application of activity detectors, bottom-up and top-down computational processes are optimally scheduled using an explore-exploit (E^2) strategy. For evaluation, we have compiled a new dataset of 106-minute, 30 fps, 2560×1920-resolution video footage. The dataset alleviates the shortcomings of existing benchmarks, since its videos show unstaged human activities of different semantic scales co-occurring in a vast scene, and have a sufficiently high resolution to allow for digital zoom-in (or zoom-out) for examining fine details (or coarser scales), as needed for recognition. The E^2 strategy improves the accuracy-complexity trade-off of full inference of the AND-OR graph. We have also reported competitive results on the benchmark Collective activities dataset.

Acknowledgement. This research has been sponsored in part by grants DARPA MSEE FA 8650-11-1-7149 and ONR MURI N00014-10-1-0933.

References

1. Zhu, S.C., Mumford, D.: A stochastic grammar of images. Found. Trends. Comput. Graph. Vis. 2, 259–362 (2006)
2. Gupta, A., Srinivasan, P., Shi, J., Davis, L.: Understanding videos, constructing plots learning a visually grounded storyline model from annotated videos. In: CVPR (2009)
3. Si, Z., Pei, M., Yao, B., Zhu, S.C.: Unsupervised learning of event AND-OR grammar and semantics from video. In: ICCV (2011)
4. Wu, T., Zhu, S.C.: A numerical study of the bottom-up and top-down inference processes in and-or graphs. IJCV 93, 226–252 (2011)
5. UCLA Courtyard Dataset (2012), `http://vcla.stat.ucla.edu/Projects/Multiscale_Activity_Recognition/`
6. Wu, X., Xu, D., Duan, L., Luo, J.: Action recognition using context and appearance distribution features. In: CVPR (2011)
7. Yao, B., Zhu, S.C.: Learning deformable action templates from cluttered videos. In: ICCV (2009)
8. Amer, M., Todorovic, S.: Sum-product networks for modeling activities with stochastic structure. In: CVPR (2012)
9. Lan, T., Wang, Y., Yang, W., Mori, G.: Beyond actions: Discriminative models for contextual group activities. In: NIPS (2010)
10. Ryoo, M.S., Aggarwal, J.K.: Stochastic representation and recognition of high-level group activities. IJCV 93, 183–200 (2011)
11. Choi, W., Shahid, K., Savarese, S.: Learning context for collective activity recognition. In: CVPR (2011)
12. Sivic, J., Zisserman, A.: Efficient visual search for objects in videos. Proceedings of the IEEE 96, 548–566 (2008)
13. Yao, A., Gall, J., Van Gool, L.J.: A hough transform-based voting framework for action recognition. In: CVPR (2010)
14. Felzenszwalb, P.F., Girshick, R.B., McAllester, D., Ramanan, D.: Object detection with discriminatively trained part-based models. IEEE Transactions on Pattern Analysis and Machine Intelligence 32, 1627–1645 (2010)
15. Matikainen, P., Hebert, M., Sukthankar, R.: Representing Pairwise Spatial and Temporal Relations for Action Recognition. In: Daniilidis, K., Maragos, P., Paragios, N. (eds.) ECCV 2010, Part I. LNCS, vol. 6311, pp. 508–521. Springer, Heidelberg (2010)
16. Laptev, I., Marszalek, M., Schmid, C., Rozenfeld, B.: Learning realistic human actions from movies. In: CVPR (2008)
17. Choi, W., Shahid, K., Savarese, S.: What are they doing?: Collective activity classification using spatio-temporal relationship among people. In: ICCV (2009)
18. Amer, M., Todorovic, S.: A Chains model for localizing group activities in videos. In: ICCV (2011)

Activity Forecasting

Kris M. Kitani, Brian D. Ziebart, James Andrew Bagnell, and Martial Hebert

Carnegie Mellon University, Pittsburgh, PA 15213 USA
{kkitani,bziebart}@cs.cmu.edu, {dbagnell,hebert}@ri.cmu.edu

Abstract. We address the task of inferring the future actions of people from noisy visual input. We denote this task *activity forecasting.* To achieve accurate activity forecasting, our approach models the effect of the physical environment on the choice of human actions. This is accomplished by the use of state-of-the-art semantic scene understanding combined with ideas from optimal control theory. Our unified model also integrates several other key elements of activity analysis, namely, destination forecasting, sequence smoothing and transfer learning. As proof-of-concept, we focus on the domain of trajectory-based activity analysis from visual input. Experimental results demonstrate that our model accurately predicts distributions over future actions of individuals. We show how the same techniques can improve the results of tracking algorithms by leveraging information about likely goals and trajectories.

Keywords: activity forecasting, inverse optimal control.

1 Introduction

We propose to expand the current scope of vision-based activity analysis by exploring models of human activity that reason about the *future.* Although reasoning about future actions often requires a large amount of contextual prior knowledge, let us consider the information that can be gleaned from *physical scene features* and prior knowledge of *goals.* For example, in observing pedestrians navigating through an urban environment, we can predict with high confidence that a person will *prefer* to walk on sidewalks more than streets, and will

Fig. 1. Given a single pedestrian detection, our proposed approach forecasts plausible paths and destinations from noisy vision-input

A. Fitzgibbon et al. (Eds.): ECCV 2012, Part IV, LNCS 7575, pp. 201–214, 2012.

most certainly avoid walking into obstacles like cars and walls. Understanding the concept of human *preference* with respect to physical scene features enables us to perform higher levels of reasoning about future human actions. Likewise, our knowledge of a *goal* also gives us information about what a person might do. For example, if an individual desires to approach his car parked across the street, we know that he will prefer to walk straight to the car as long as the street is walkable and safe. To integrate these two aspects of prior knowledge into modeling human activity, we leverage recent progress in two key areas of research: (1) semantic scene labeling and (2) inverse optimal control.

Semantic scene labeling. Recent semantic scene labeling approaches now provide a robust and reliable way of recognizing physical scene features such as pavement, grass, tree, building and car [1], [2]. We will show how the robust detection of such features plays a critical role in advancing the representational power of human activity models.

Inverse optimal control. Work in optimal control theory has shown that human behavior can be modeled successfully as a sequential decision-making process [3]. The problem of recovering a set of agent preferences (the reward or cost function) consistent with demonstrated activities, can be solved via Inverse Optimal Control (IOC) – also called Inverse Reinforcement Learning (IRL) [4] or inverse planning [5]. What is especially intriguing about the IOC framework is that it incorporates concepts, such as *immediate rewards* (what do I gain by taking this action?), *expected future rewards* (what will be the consequence of my actions in the future?) and *goals* (what do I intend to accomplish?), which have close analogies to the formation of human activity. We will show how the IOC framework expands the horizon of vision-based human activity analysis by integrating the impact of the environment and goals on future actions.

In this work, we extend the work of Ziebart *et al.* [6] by incorporating vision-based physical scene features and noisy tracker observations, to forecast activities and destinations. This work is different from traditional IOC problems because we do not assume that the state of the actor is fully observable (e.g., video games [7] and locations in road networks [6]). Our work is also different from Partially Observable Markov Decision Process (POMDP) models because we assume that the *observer* has noisy observations of an actor, where the actor is fully aware of his own state. In a POMDP, the actor is uncertain about his own state and the observer is not modeled. To the best of our knowledge, this is the first work to incorporate the uncertainty of vision-based observations within a robust IOC framework in the context of *activity forecasting.* To this end, we propose a Hidden variable Markov Decision Process (hMDP) model which incorporates uncertainty (e.g., probabilistic physical scene features) and noisy observations (e.g., imperfect tracker) into the activity model. We summarize our contributions as follows: (1) we introduce the concept of inverse optimal control to the field of vision-based activity analysis, (2) we propose the hMDP model and a hidden variable inverse optimal control (HIOC) inference procedure to deal with uncertainty in observations and (3) we demonstrate the performance of forecasting, smoothing,

Homotopy classes **Our approach**

Fig. 2. Qualitative comparison to homotopy classes. Trajectories generated by distinct homotopy classes and trajectories generated by physical attributes of the scene. Physical attributes are able to encode agent preferences like using the sidewalk.

destination forecasting and knowledge transfer operations in a single framework on real image data.

As a proof-of-concept, we focus on trajectory-based human activity analysis [8]. We take a departure from traditional motion-based approaches [9], [10] and explore the interplay between features of the environment and pedestrian trajectories. Previous work [11], [12], has shown that modeling the impact of the social environment, like actions of nearby pedestrians, can improve priors over pedestrian trajectories. Our work is complementary in that, our learned model explains the effect of the *static environment*, instead of the dynamic environment like moving people, on future actions. Other work uses trajectories to infer the functional features of the environment such as road, sidewalk and entrance [13]. Our work addresses the inverse task of inferring trajectories from physical scene features. Work exploring the impact of destinations, such as entrances and exits, of the environment on trajectories has shown that knowledge of goals yields better recognition of human activity [14], [15]. Gong *et al.* [16] used potential goals and motion planning from homotopy classes to provide a prior for tracking under occlusion. Our work expands the expressiveness of homotopy classes in two significant ways, by generating a distribution over all trajectories including homotopy classes, and incorporating observations about *physical scene features* to make better inference about paths. Figure 2 depicts the qualitative difference between shortest distance paths of 'hard' homotopy classes and 'soft' probability distributions generated by our proposed approach. Notice how the distribution over potential trajectories captures subtle agent preferences such as walking on the sidewalk versus the parking lot, and keeping a safe distance from cars.

There is also an area of emerging research termed *early recognition*, where the task is to classify an incoming temporal sequence as early as possible while maintaining a level of detection accuracy [17], [18], [19]. Our task of *activity forecasting* differs in that we are recovering a *distribution over a sequence of future actions* as opposed to classifying a partial observation sequence as a discrete activity category. In fact, our approach can forecast possible trajectories before any pedestrian observations are available.

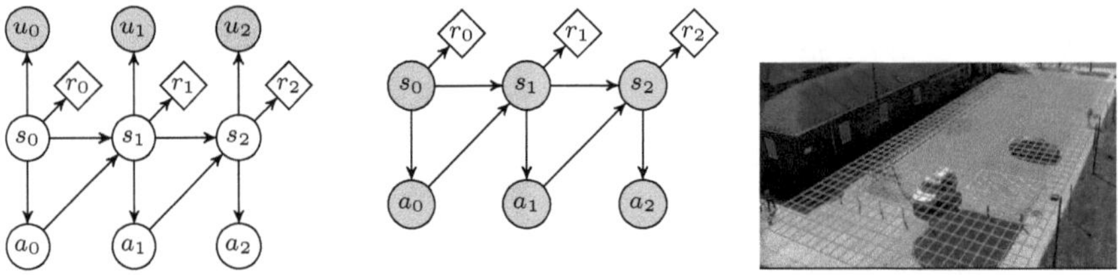

(a) Proposed hMDP (b) MDP (c) state representation

Fig. 3. Underlying graphical model and state representation for IOC. (a) Proposed hMDP: agent knows own state s, action a and reward (or cost) r but only noisy measurements of the state u are observed, (b) MDP: agent state and actions are fully observed and (c) ground plane is discretized into cells which represent states.

2 Preliminaries

Markov Decision Processes and Optimal Control. The Markov decision process (MDP) [20] is used to express the dynamics of a decision-making process (Figure 3b). The MDP is defined by an initial state distribution $p(s_0)$, a transition model $p(s'|s,a)$ (shorthand $p^{s'}_{s,a}$) and a cost function $r(s)$. Given these parameters, we can solve the *optimal control* problem by learning the optimal policy $\pi(a|s)$, which encodes the distribution of action a to take when in state s. To be concrete, Figure 3c depicts the state and action space defined in this work. The state s represents a physical location in world coordinates $s = [x, y]$ and the action a is the velocity $a = [v_x, v_y]$ of the actor. The policy $\pi(a|s)$ maps states to actions, describing which direction to move (action) when an actor is located at some position (state). The policy can be deterministic or stochastic.

Inverse Optimal Control. In the inverse optimal control problem, the cost function is not given and must be discovered from demonstrated examples. Various approaches using structured maximum margin prediction [21], feature matching [4] and maximum entropy IRL [3] have been proposed for recovering the cost function. We build on the maximum entropy IOC approach in [6] and extend the model to deal with noisy observations. We make an important assumption about the form of the cost function $r(s)$, which enables us to translate from observed physical scene features to a single cost value. The cost function:

$$r(s;\boldsymbol{\theta}) = \boldsymbol{\theta}^\top \boldsymbol{f}(s), \tag{1}$$

is assumed to be a weighted combination of feature responses $\boldsymbol{f}(s) = [f_1(s) \cdots f_K(s)]^\top$, where each $f_k(s)$ is the response of a physical scene feature, such as the soft output of a grass classifier, and $\boldsymbol{\theta}$ is a vector of weights. By learning the parameters of the cost function, we are learning how much a physical scene feature affects a person's actions. For example, a feature such as car and building, will have large weights because they are high cost and should be avoided. This explicit modeling of the effect of physical scene features on actions via the cost function sets this approach apart from traditional motion-based models of pedestrian dynamics.

3 Hidden Variable Inverse Optimal Control (HIOC)

In a vision-based system, we do not have access to the true state, such as the location of the actor, or the true action, such as the velocity of the actor. Instead, we only have access to the output of a noisy tracking algorithm. Therefore, we deal with observation uncertainty via a hidden state variable (Figure 3a). Using this hidden model, HIOC determines the *reliability* of observed states, in our case tracker detections, by adjusting its associated cost weight. For example, if the tracker output has low precision, the corresponding weight parameter will be decreased during training to minimize the reliance on the tracker output.

In the maximum entropy framework, the distribution over a state sequence $\boldsymbol{s}$ is defined as:

$$p(\boldsymbol{s};\boldsymbol{\theta}) = \frac{\prod_t e^{r(s_t)}}{Z(\boldsymbol{\theta})} = \frac{e^{\sum_t \boldsymbol{\theta}^\top \boldsymbol{f}(s_t)}}{Z(\boldsymbol{\theta})}, \tag{2}$$

where $\boldsymbol{\theta}$ are the parameters of the cost function, $\boldsymbol{f}(s_t)$ is the vector of feature responses at state s_t and $Z(\theta)$ is the normalization function. In other words, the probability of generating a trajectory $\boldsymbol{s}$ is defined to be proportional to the exponentiated sum of features encountered over the trajectory.

In our hMDP model (Figure 3a), we add state observations $\boldsymbol{u}$ to represent the uncertainty of being in a state. This implies a joint distribution over states and observations as:

$$p(\boldsymbol{s},\boldsymbol{u};\boldsymbol{\theta}) = \frac{\prod_t p(u_t|s_t) e^{\boldsymbol{\theta}^\top \boldsymbol{f}(s_t)}}{Z(\boldsymbol{\theta})} = \frac{e^{\sum_t \left\{\boldsymbol{\theta}^\top \boldsymbol{f}(s_t) + \theta_o \log p(u_t|s_t)\right\}}}{Z(\boldsymbol{\theta})}, \tag{3}$$

where the observation model $p(u_t|s_t)$ is a Gaussian distribution. Notice that by pushing the observation model into the exponent as $\log p(u_t|s_t)$ it can also be interpreted as an auxiliary 'observation feature' with an implicit weight of one, $\theta_o = 1$. However, we increase the expressiveness of the model by allowing the weight parameter θ_o of observations to be adjusted at training.

3.1 Training and Inference

In the training step, we recover the optimal cost function parameters $\boldsymbol{\theta}$ and consequentially an optimal policy $\pi(a|s)$, by maximizing the entropy of the conditional distribution or equivalently the likelihood maximization of the observations under the maximum entropy distribution,

$$p(\boldsymbol{s}|\boldsymbol{u};\boldsymbol{\theta}) = \frac{e^{\left\{\sum_t \boldsymbol{\theta}^\top \boldsymbol{f}'(s_t)\right\}}}{Z(\boldsymbol{\theta})}, \tag{4}$$

where the feature vector $\boldsymbol{f}'(s_t)$ now includes the tracker observation features.

To maximize the entropy of (4), we use exponentiated gradient descent to iteratively minimize the gradient of the log-likelihood $\mathcal{L} \triangleq \log p(\boldsymbol{s}|\boldsymbol{u};\boldsymbol{\theta})$. The

Algorithm 1. Backwards pass	**Algorithm 2.** Forward pass

$V(s) \leftarrow -\infty$
for $n = N, \ldots, 2, 1$ **do**
$V^{(n)}(s_{goal}) \leftarrow 0$
$Q^{(n)}(s,a) = r(s;\boldsymbol{\theta}) + E_{P^{s'}_{s,a}}[V^{(n)}(s')]$
$V^{(n-1)}(s) = \text{soft max}_a\, Q^{(n)}(s,a)$
end for
$\pi_\theta(a\|s) = e^{Q(s,a)-V(s)}$
	$D(s_{initial}) \leftarrow 1$
	for $n = 1, 2, \ldots, N$ **do**
	$D^{(n)}(s_{goal}) \leftarrow 0$
	$D^{(n+1)}(s) = \sum_{s',a} P^{s}_{s',a}\pi_\theta(a\|s')D^{(n)}(s')$
	end for
	$D(s) = \sum_n D^{(n)}(s)$
	$\hat{\mathbf{f}}_\theta = \sum_s \boldsymbol{f}(s)D(s)$

gradient can be shown to be the difference between the *empirical* mean feature count $\bar{\mathbf{f}} = \frac{1}{M}\sum_m^M \boldsymbol{f}(\boldsymbol{s}_m)$, the average features accumulated over M demonstrated trajectories, and the *expected* mean feature count $\hat{\mathbf{f}}_\theta$, the average features accumulated by trajectories generated by the parameters, $\nabla\mathcal{L}_\theta = \bar{\mathbf{f}} - \hat{\mathbf{f}}_\theta$. We update $\boldsymbol{\theta}$ according to the exponentiated gradient, $\boldsymbol{\theta} \leftarrow \boldsymbol{\theta}e^{\lambda\nabla\mathcal{L}_\theta}$, where λ is the step size and the gradient is computed using a two-step algorithm described next. At test time, the learned weights are held constant and the same two-step algorithm is used to compute the forecasted distribution over future actions, the smoothing distribution or the destination posterior.

Backward pass. In the first step (Algorithm 1), we use the current weight parameters $\boldsymbol{\theta}$ and compute the expected cost of a path ending in s_g and starting in $s_i \neq s_g$. Essentially, we are computing the expected cost to the goal from every possible starting location. The algorithm revolves around the repeated computation of the *state log partition function* $V(s)$ and the *state-action log partition function* $Q(s,a)$ defined in Algorithm 1. Intuitively, $V(s)$ is a soft estimate of the expected cost of reaching the goal from state s and $Q(s,a)$ is the soft expected cost of reaching the goal after taking action a from the current state s. Upon convergence, the maximum entropy policy is $\pi_\theta(a|s) = e^{Q(s,a)-V(s)}$.

Forward pass. In the second step (Algorithm 2), we propagate an initial distribution $p(s_0)$ according to the learned policy $\pi_\theta(a|s)$. Let $D^{(n)}(s)$ be defined as the *expected state visitation count* which is a quantity that expresses the probability of being in a certain state s at time step n. Initially, when n is small, $D^{(n)}(s)$ is a distribution that sums to one. However, as the probability mass is absorbed by the goal state, the sum of the state visitation counts quickly converges to zero. By computing the total number of times each state was visited $D(s) = \sum_n D^{(n)}(s)$, we are computing the unnormalized marginal state visitation distribution. We can compute the *expected* mean feature count as a weighted sum of feature counts $\hat{\mathbf{f}}_\theta = \sum_s \boldsymbol{f}(s)D(s)$.

3.2 Destination Forecasting from Noisy Observations

In novel scenes, the destination of an actor is unknown and must be inferred. For each activity, a prior on potential destinations $p(s_g)$, may be generated (e.g., points along the perimeter of a car for the activity 'approach car') and, in principle, a brute force application of Bayes' rule enables computing the posterior

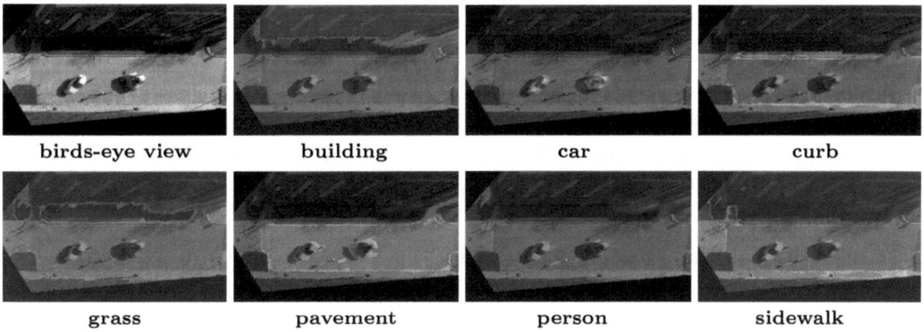

Fig. 4. Classifier feature response maps. Top left is the original image

over both destinations and intermediate states. A naive application, however, is quite expensive as we may wish to consider a large number of possible goals – potentially every state.

Fortunately, the structure of the proposed maximum entropy model enables efficient inference. Following Ziebart *et al.* [6], we approximate the posterior over goals using a ratio of partition functions, one with and one without observations:

$$p(s_g|s_0, u_{1:t}) \propto p(u_{1:t}|s_0, s_g) \cdot p(s_g) \quad (5)$$

$$\propto e^{V_{u_{1:t}}(s_g) - V(s_g)} \cdot p(s_g), \quad (6)$$

where $V_{u_{1:t}}(s_g)$ is the state log partition of s_g given the initial state is s_0 and the observations $u_{1:t}$ and $V(s_g)$ is the state log partition of s_g without any observations. The ratio of log partition functions measure the 'progress' made toward a goal by adding observations. In deterministic MDPs, where the action decisions may be randomized but the state transitions follow deterministically from a state-action pair, we can invert the role of goal and start locations for an agent. Doing so enables computing the partition functions required in time *independent* of the number of goals. Using this inversion property, the state partition values for each goal can be computed efficiently by inverting the destination and start states and running Algorithm 1.

4 Experiments

We evaluate the four tasks of activity analysis, namely, (1) forecasting, (2) smoothing, (3) destination prediction and (4) knowledge transfer, using our proposed unified framework. For our evaluation we use videos from the VIRAT ground dataset [22]. Our dataset consists 92 videos from two scenes, shown in Figure 1. Scene A consists of 56 videos and scene B consists of 36 videos. Each scene dataset consists of three activities categories: *approach car*, *depart car* and *walk through*. In all experiments, 80% of the data was used for training and the remaining 20% used for testing using 3-fold cross validation.

The physical attributes were extracted using the scene segmentation labeling algorithm proposed by Munoz *et al.* [1]. In total 9 semantics labels were used, including grass, pavement, sidewalk, curb, person, building, fence, gravel, and car. For each semantic label, four features were generated, including the raw probability and three types of 'distance-to-object' features. The distance feature is computed by thresholding the probability maps and computing the exponentiated distance function (with different variance). A visualization of the probability maps used as features is shown in Figure 4. For the smoothing task, the pedestrian tracker output is blurred with three different Gaussian filters which contribute three additional features. By adding a constant feature to model travel time, the total number of features used is 40.

Our state space is the 3D floor plane and as such, 2D image features, observations and potential goals are projected to the floor plane (camera parameters are assumed to be known) for all computations. For the activities *depart car* and *walk through* potential goals are set densely around the outer perimeter of the floor plane projection. For the activity *approach car*, connected components analysis is used to extract polygonal shape contours of detected cars, whose vertices are used to define a set of potential goals.

4.1 Metrics and Baselines

In each of the experiments, we have one demonstrated path, a sequence of states s_t and actions a_t, generated by a pedestrian for a specific configuration of a scene. We compare the demonstrated path with the probabilistic distribution over paths generated by our algorithm using two different metrics: first is probabilistic and evaluates the likelihood of the demonstrated path under the predicted distribution, the second performs a more deterministic evaluation by estimating the physical distances between a demonstrated path and paths sampled from our distribution. We use the negative log-loss (NLL) of a trajectories, as in [6] as our probabilistic comparison metric. The negative log-loss:

$$\mathrm{NLL}(\boldsymbol{s}) = E_{\pi(a|s)}\left[-\log \prod_t \pi(a_t|s_t) \right], \tag{7}$$

is the expectation of the log-likelihood of a trajectory $\boldsymbol{s}$ under a policy $\pi(a|s)$. In our example, this metric measures the probability of drawing the demonstrated trajectory from the learned distribution over all possible trajectories. We also compute the modified Hausdorff distance (MHD) as a physical measure of the distance between two trajectories. The MHD allows for local time warping by finding the best local point correspondence over a small temporal window (± 15 steps in our experiments). When the temporal window is zero, the MHD is exactly the Euclidean distance. We compute the mean MHD, by taking the average MHD between the demonstrated trajectory and 5000 trajectories randomly sampled from our distribution. The units of the MHD are in pixels in the 3D floor plane, not the 2D image plane. We always divide our metrics by the trajectory length so that we can compare metrics across different models and trajectories of different lengths.

We compare against a maximum entropy Markov model (MEMM) that estimates the policy based on environmental attribute features and tracker observation features. The policy is computed by:

$$\pi(a|s) \propto \exp\{\boldsymbol{w}_a^\top \boldsymbol{F}(s)\}. \quad (8)$$

where the weight vector $\boldsymbol{w}_a$ is estimated using linear regression and $\boldsymbol{F}(s)$ is a vector of features for all neighboring states of s. This model only takes into the account the features of the potential next states when choosing an action and has no concept of the future beyond a one-step prediction model.

We also compare against a location-based Markov motion model, which learns a policy from observed statistics of states and actions in the training set:

$$\pi(a|s) \propto c(a, s) + \alpha, \quad (9)$$

where $c(a, s)$ is the number of times the action a was observed in state s and α is a pseudo-count used to smooth the distribution via Laplace smoothing.

4.2 Forecasting Evaluation

Evaluating the true accuracy of a *forecasting distribution* over all future trajectories is difficult because we do not have access to such 'ground truth' from the future. As a proxy, we measure how well a learned policy is able to describe a single annotated test trajectory. We begin experiments in a constrained setting, were we fix the start and goal states to evaluate forecasting performance in isolation. Unconstrained experiments are performed in section 4.4. We compare our proposed model against the MEMM and the Markov motion model. Figure 5a and Table 1a show how our proposed model outperforms the baseline models. Note that tracker observations are not used in this experiment since we are only evaluating the performance of *forecasting* and not *smoothing*.

Qualitative results of activity forecasting are depicted in Figure 6. Our proposed model is able to leverage the physical scene features and generate a distribution that preserves actor preferences learned during training. Since many pedestrians used the sidewalk in the training examples, our model has learned that sidewalk areas have greater rewards or lower cost than paved parking lot areas. Notice that although it would be faster and shorter to walk diagonally across the parking lot, in terms of actor preferences it is more optimal to use the sidewalk. Without the use of informative physical scene features, we would need to learn motion dynamics with a Markov motion model from a large amount of demonstrated trajectories. Unfortunately, the Markov motion model degenerates to a random walk when there are not enough training trajectories for this particular configuration of the scene.

4.3 Smoothing Evaluation

In our smoothing evaluation, we measure how the computed smoothing distribution accounts for noisy observations and generates an improved distribution over

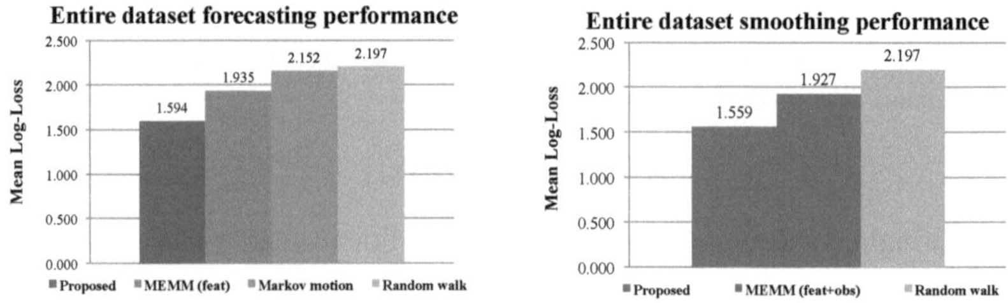

Fig. 5. Mean NLL of forecasting and smoothing performance

Fig. 6. Comparing forecasting distributions. The travel time only MDP ignores physical attributes of the scene. The Markov motion model degenerates to a random walk when train data is limited.

trajectories. We run our experiments with a state-of-the-art super-pixel tracker (SPT) [23] and an in-house template-based tracker to show how the smoothing distribution improves the quality of estimated pedestrian trajectories. Again, we fix the start and goal states to isolate the performance of smoothing. Our in-house tracker is conservative and only keeps strong detections of pedestrians, which results in many missing detections. Many gaps in detection causes the MHD between the observed trajectory and true trajectory to be large without smoothing. In contrast, the trajectories of the SPT have no missing observations due to temporal filtering but have a tendency to drift away from the pedestrian. As such, the SPT has much better performance compared to our in-house tracker before smoothing. Figure 7 shows a significant improvement for both trackers after smoothing. Despite that fact that our in-house tracker is not as robust as

Table 1. Average NLL per activity category and dataset (A and B) for (a) forecasting and (b) smoothing performance

(a) Forecasting	Proposed	MEMM	MarkovMot
approach (A)	**1.657**	1.962	2.157
depart (A)	**1.618**	1.940	2.103
walk (A)	**1.544**	2.027	2.174
approach (B)	**1.519**	1.780	2.180
depart (B)	**1.519**	1.903	2.115
walk (B)	**1.707**	1.997	2.182

(b) Smoothing	Proposed	MEMM
approach (A)	**1.602**	1.942
depart (A)	**1.594**	1.923
walk (A)	**1.483**	2.022
approach (B)	**1.465**	1.792
depart (B)	**1.513**	1.882
walk (B)	**1.695**	2.001

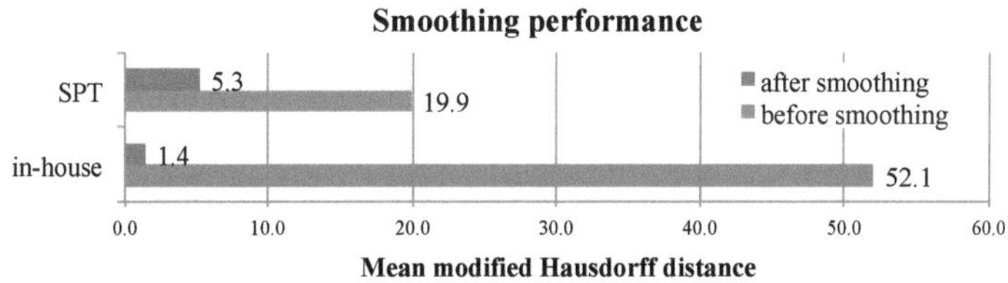

Fig. 7. Improvement in tracking accuracy with the smoothing distribution

Fig. 8. Destination forecasting and path smoothing. Our proposed approach infers a pedestrians likely destinations as more noisy observations become available. Concurrently, the *smoothing distribution* (likely paths up to the current time step t) and the *forecasting distribution* (likely paths from t until the future) are modified as observations are updated.

SPT, the MHD after smoothing is actually better than the SPT post-smoothing. This is due to the fact that our tracker only generates confident, albeit sparse, detections. The distributions generated by our approach also outperforms the MEMM, as shown in Table 1b.

4.4 Destination Forecasting Evaluation

In the most general case, the final destination of a pedestrian is not know in advance so we must reason about probable destinations as tracker observations become available. In this experiment we hold the start state and allow the destination state to be inferred by Equation (6). Figure 8 shows a visualization of destination forecasting, and consequentially, the successive updates of the forecasting and smoothing distributions. As noisy pedestrian tracker observations are acquired, the posterior distribution over destinations, the forecasting and smoothing distributions are updated. Quantitative results shown in Figure 9 show that the MHD quickly approaches a minimum for most activity categories, after about 30% of the noisy tracker trajectory has been observed. This indicates that we can forecast a person's likely path to a final destination after observing only a third of the trajectory.

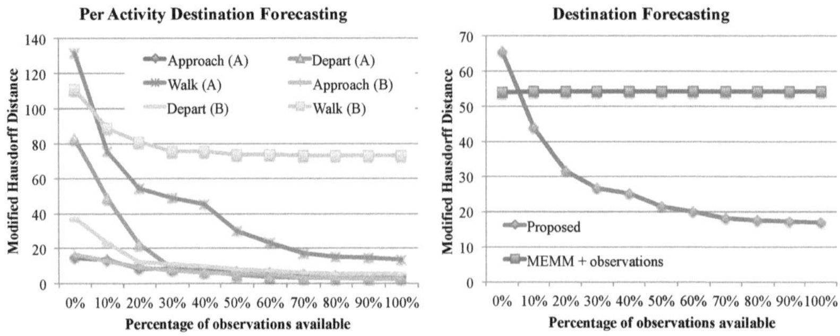

Fig. 9. Destination forecasting performance. Modified Hausdorff distance is the average distance between the ground truth trajectory and sampled trajectories from the inferred distribution. (a) per activity category performance over datasets, (b) average performance over the entire dataset.

Table 2. MHD for knowledge transfer performance. (a) forecasting and (b) smoothing. Proposed approach can be applied to novel scenes with comparable performance.

(a) Forecasting	TEST	
TRAIN	Scene A	Scene B
Scene A	**9.8520**	**7.4925**
Scene B	10.4358	8.9774
$\|\Delta\|$	0.584	1.485

(b) Smoothing	TEST	
TRAIN	Scene A	Scene B
Scene A	**3.2582**	**6.4705**
Scene B	4.9194	7.2837
$\|\Delta\|$	1.661	0.813

Fig. 10. Knowledge transfer examples of forecasting in novel scenes

4.5 Knowledge Transfer

Since our proposed method encapsulates activities in terms of physical scene features and not physical location, we are also able to generalize to novel scenes. This is a major advantage of our approach over other methods that use scene-specific motion dynamics. In this experiment we use two locations: scene A and scene B, and show that learned parameters can be transferred in both directions with similar performance. Table 2 shows that the transferred parameters perform on par with scene specific parameters. With respect to forecasting performance, the average MHD between a point of the ground truth and a point of a trajectory sampled from the forecasting distribution, is degraded by 0.584 pixels. It is interesting to note that in the case of training on scene A and transferring to scene B, the transferred model actually performs slightly better. We believe that this is caused by the fact that we have more training trajectories from scene A. In Figure 10 we also show several qualitative results of trajectory forecasting and destination forecasting on novel scenes. Even without observing a single trajectory from the scene, our approach is able to generate plausible forecasting distributions for activities such as walking through the scene or departing from a car.

5 Conclusion

We have demonstrated that tools from inverse optimal control can be used for computer vision tasks in activity understanding and forecasting. Specifically, we have modeled the interaction between moving agents and semantic perception of the environment. We have also made proper modifications to accommodate the uncertainty inherent to tracking and detection algorithms. Further, the resulting formulation, based on a hidden variable MDP, provides a unified framework to support a range of operations in activity analysis: smoothing, path and destination forecasting, and transfer, which we validated both qualitatively and quantitatively. Our initial work focused on paths in order to generate an initial validation of the approach for computer vision. Moving forward, however, our proposed framework is general enough to handle non-motion representations such as sequences of discrete action-states. Similarly, we limited our evaluation to physical attributes of the environments, but an exciting possibility would be to extend the approach to activity features, similar to those used in crowd analysis, or other semantic attributes of the environment.

Acknowledgement. This research was supported in part by NSF QoLT ERC EEEC-0540865, U.S Army Research Laboratory under the Collaborative Technology Alliance Program, Cooperative Agreement W911NF-10-2-0016 and Cooperative Agreement W911NF-10-2-0061. We especially thank Daniel Munoz for sharing and preparing the semantic scene labeling code.

References

1. Munoz, D., Bagnell, J.A., Hebert, M.: Stacked Hierarchical Labeling. In: Daniilidis, K., Maragos, P., Paragios, N. (eds.) ECCV 2010, Part VI. LNCS, vol. 6316, pp. 57–70. Springer, Heidelberg (2010)
2. Munoz, D., Bagnell, J.A., Hebert, M.: Co-inference for Multi-modal Scene Analysis. In: Fitzgibbon, A., Lazebnik, S., Perona, P., Sato, Y., Schmid, C. (eds.) ECCV 2012, Part VI. LNCS, vol. 7577, pp. 668–681. Springer, Heidelberg (2012)
3. Ziebart, B., Ratliff, N., Gallagher, G., Mertz, C., Peterson, K., Bagnell, J., Hebert, M., Dey, A., Srinivasa, S.: Planning-based prediction for pedestrians. In: IROS (2009)

4. Abbeel, P., Ng, A.: Apprenticeship learning via inverse reinforcement learning. In: ICML (2004)
5. Baker, C., Saxe, R., Tenenbaum, J.: Action understanding as inverse planning. Cognition 113(3), 329–349 (2009)
6. Ziebart, B., Maas, A., Bagnell, J., Dey, A.: Maximum entropy inverse reinforcement learning. In: AAAI (2008)
7. Levine, S., Popovic, Z., Koltun, V.: Nonlinear inverse reinforcement learning with Gaussian processes. In: NIPS (2011)
8. Morris, B., Trivedi, M.: A survey of vision-based trajectory learning and analysis for surveillance. Transactions on Circuits and Systems for Video Technology 18(8), 1114–1127 (2008)
9. Ali, S., Shah, M.: Floor Fields for Tracking in High Density Crowd Scenes. In: Forsyth, D., Torr, P., Zisserman, A. (eds.) ECCV 2008, Part II. LNCS, vol. 5303, pp. 1–14. Springer, Heidelberg (2008)
10. Zen, G., Ricci, E.: Earth mover's prototypes: A convex learning approach for discovering activity patterns in dynamic scenes. In: CVPR (2011)
11. Mehran, R., Oyama, A., Shah, M.: Abnormal crowd behavior detection using social force model. In: CVPR (2009)
12. Pellegrini, S., Ess, A., Schindler, K., Van Gool, L.J.: You'll never walk alone: Modeling social behavior for multi-target tracking. In: ICCV (2009)
13. Turek, M.W., Hoogs, A., Collins, R.: Unsupervised Learning of Functional Categories in Video Scenes. In: Daniilidis, K., Maragos, P., Paragios, N. (eds.) ECCV 2010, Part II. LNCS, vol. 6312, pp. 664–677. Springer, Heidelberg (2010)
14. Huang, C., Wu, B., Nevatia, R.: Robust Object Tracking by Hierarchical Association of Detection Responses. In: Forsyth, D., Torr, P., Zisserman, A. (eds.) ECCV 2008, Part II. LNCS, vol. 5303, pp. 788–801. Springer, Heidelberg (2008)
15. Kaucic, R., Amitha Perera, A., Brooksby, G., Kaufhold, J., Hoogs, A.: A unified framework for tracking through occlusions and across sensor gaps. In: CVPR (2005)
16. Gong, H., Sim, J., Likhachev, M., Shi, J.: Multi-hypothesis motion planning for visual object tracking. In: ICCV (2011)
17. Xing, Z., Pei, J., Dong, G., Yu, P.: Mining sequence classifiers for early prediction. In: SIAM International Conference on Data Mining (2008)
18. Ryoo, M.: Human activity prediction: Early recognition of ongoing activities from streaming videos. In: ICCV (2011)
19. Hoai, M., De la Torre, F.: Max-margin early event detectors. In: CVPR (2012)
20. Bellman, R.: A Markovian decision process. Journal of Mathematics and Mechanics 6(5), 679–684 (1957)
21. Ratliff, N., Bagnell, J., Zinkevich, M.: Maximum margin planning. In: ICML (2006)
22. Oh, S., Hoogs, A., Perera, A., Cuntoor, N., Chen, C., Lee, J., Mukherjee, S., Aggarwal, J., Lee, H., Davis, L., et al.: A large-scale benchmark dataset for event recognition in surveillance video. In: CVPR (2011)
23. Wang, S., Lu, H., Yang, F., Yang, M.H.: Superpixel tracking. In: ICCV (2011)

A Unified Framework for Multi-target Tracking and Collective Activity Recognition

Wongun Choi and Silvio Savarese

Electrical and Computer Engineering, University of Michigan, Ann Arbor, USA
{wgchoi,silvio}@umich.edu

Abstract. We present a coherent, discriminative framework for simultaneously tracking multiple people and estimating their collective activities. Instead of treating the two problems separately, our model is grounded in the intuition that a strong correlation exists between a person's motion, their activity, and the motion and activities of other nearby people. Instead of directly linking the solutions to these two problems, we introduce a hierarchy of activity types that creates a natural progression that leads from a specific person's motion to the activity of the group as a whole. Our model is capable of jointly tracking multiple people, recognizing individual activities (*atomic activities*), the interactions between pairs of people (*interaction activities*), and finally the behavior of groups of people (*collective activities*). We also propose an algorithm for solving this otherwise intractable joint inference problem by combining belief propagation with a version of the branch and bound algorithm equipped with integer programming. Experimental results on challenging video datasets demonstrate our theoretical claims and indicate that our model achieves the best collective activity classification results to date.

Keywords: Collective Activity Recognition, Tracking, Tracklet Association.

1 Introduction

There are many degrees of granularity with which we can understand the behavior of people in video. We can detect and track the trajectory of a person, we can observe a person's pose and discover what *atomic activity* (*e.g.*, *walking*) they are performing, we can determine an *interaction activity* (*e.g.*, *approaching*) between two people, and we can identify the *collective activity* (*e.g.*, *gathering*) of a group of people. These different levels of activity are clearly not independent: if everybody in a scene is walking, and all possible pairs of people are approaching each other, it is very likely that they are engaged in a gathering activity. Likewise, a person who is gathering with other people is probably walking toward a central point of convergence, and this knowledge places useful constraints on our estimation of their spatio-temporal trajectory.

Regardless of the level of detail required for a particular application, a powerful activity recognition system will exploit the dependencies between different levels of activity. Such a system should reliably and accurately: (i) identify stable and coherent trajectories of individuals; (ii) estimate attributes, such as poses, and infer atomic activities; (iii) discover the interactions between individuals;

A. Fitzgibbon et al. (Eds.): ECCV 2012, Part IV, LNCS 7575, pp. 215–230, 2012.

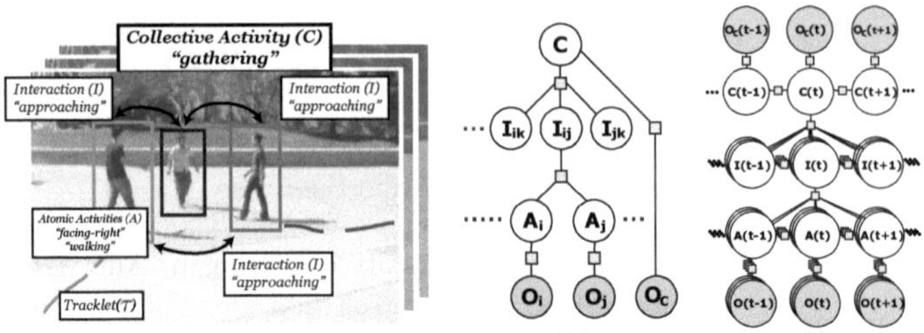

(a) (b) (c)

Fig. 1. In this work we aim at jointly and robustly tracking multiple targets and recognizing the activities that such targets are performing. **(a)**: The collective activity *“gathering”* is characterized as a collection of interactions (such as *“approaching”*) between individuals. Each interaction is described by pairs of atomic activities (e.g. *“facing-right”* and *“facing-left”*). Each atomic activity is associated with a spatial-temporal trajectory (tracklet τ). We advocate that high level activity understanding helps obtain more stable target trajectories. Likewise, robust trajectories enable more accurate activity understanding. **(b)**: The hierarchical relationship between atomic activities (A), interactions (I), and collective activity (C) in one time stamp is shown as a factor graph. Squares and circles represent the potential functions and variables, respectively. Observations are the tracklets associated with each individual along with their appearance properties O_i as well as crowd context descriptor O_c [1, 2] (Sec.3.1). **(c)**: A collective activity at each time stamp is represented as a collection of interactions within a temporal window. Interaction is correlated with a pair of atomic activities within specified temporal window (Sec.3.2). Non-shaded nodes are associated with variables that need to be estimated and shaded nodes are associated with observations.

(iv) recognize any collective activities present in the scene. Even if the goal is only to track individuals, this tracking can benefit from the scene's context. Even if the goal is only to characterize the behavior of a group of people, attention to pairwise interactions can help.

Much of the existing literature on activity recognition and tracking [3–11] avoids the complexity of this context-rich approach by seeking to solve the problems in isolation. We instead argue that tracking, track association, and the recognition of atomic activities, interactions, and group activities must be performed completely and coherently. In this paper we introduce a model that is both principled and solvable and that is the first to successfully bridge the gap between tracking and group activity recognition (Fig.1).

2 Related Work

Target tracking is one of the oldest problems in computer vision, but it is far from solved. Its difficulty is evidenced by the amount of active research that continues to the present. In difficult scenes, tracks are not complete, but are fragmented into tracklets. It is the task of the tracker to associate tracklets in order to assemble complete tracks. Tracks are often fragmented due to occlusions. Recent algorithms address this through the use of detection responses [12, 13], and pairwise interaction models [3–8]. The interaction models, however, are limited to a few hand-designed interactions, such as attraction and repulsion. Methods such as [14] leverage the consistency of the flow of crowds with models from physics, but do not attempt to associate tracklets or understand the actions of individuals. [15, 16] formulate the problem of multi-target tracking into a min-cost flow network based on linear/dynamic programming. Although both model interactions between people, they still rely on heuristics to guide the association process via higher level semantics.

A number of methods have recently been proposed for action recognition by extracting sparse features [17], correlated features [18], discovering hidden topic models [19], or feature mining [20]. These works consider only a single person, and do not benefit from the contextual information available from recognizing interactions and activities. [21] models the pairwise interactions between people, but the model is limited to local motion features. Several works address the recognition of planned group activities in football videos by modelling the trajectories of people with Bayesian networks [9], temporal manifold structures [10], and non-stationary kernel hidden Markov models [22]. All these approaches, however, assume that the trajectories are available (known). In collective activity recognition, [23] recognizes group activities by considering local causality information from each track, each pair of tracks, and groups of tracks. [1] classifies collective activities by extracting descriptors from people and the surrounding area, and [2] extends it by learning the structure of the descriptor from data. [24] models a group activity as a stochastic collection of individual activities. None of these works exploit the contextual information provided by collective activities to help identify targets or classify atomic activities. [11] uses a hierarchical model to jointly classify the collective activities of all people in a scene, but they are restricted to modelling contextual information in a single frame, without seeking to solve the track identification problem. Finally, [25] recognizes the overall behavior of large crowds using a social force model, but does not seek to specify the behaviour of each individual.

Our Contributions. are four-fold: we propose (i) a model that merges for the first time the problems of collective activity recognition and multiple target tracking into a single coherent framework; (ii) a novel path selection algorithm that leverages target interactions for guiding the process of associating targets; (iii) a new hierarchical graphical model that encodes the correlation between activities at different levels of granularity; (iv) quantitative evaluation on a number of challenging datasets, showing superiority to the state-of-the-art.

3 Modelling Collective Activity

Our model accomplishes collective activity classification by simultaneously estimating the activity of a group of people (*collective activity* C), the pairwise relationships between individuals (*interactions activities* I), and the specific activities of each individual (*atomic activities* A) given a set of observations O (see Fig.1). A collective activity describes the overall behavior of a group of more

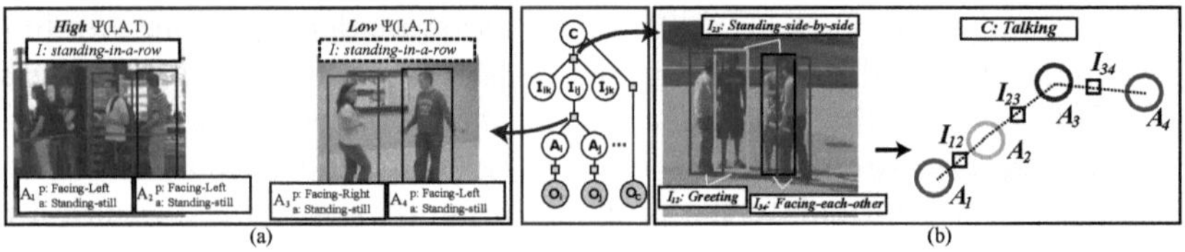

Fig. 2. (a): Each interaction is represented by a number of atomic activities that are characterized by an action and pose label. For example, with interaction I = *standing-in-a-row*, it is likely to observe two people with both p = *facing-left* and a = *standing-still*, whereas it is less likely that one person has p = *facing-left* and the other p = *facing-right*. **(b)**: Collective activity C is represented as a collection of interactions I. For example, with C = *talking* collective activity, it is likely to observe the interaction I_{34} = *facing-each-other*, and I_{23} = *standing-side-by-side*. The consistency of $C, I_{12}, I_{23}, I_{34}$ generates a high value for $\Psi(C, I)$.

than two people, such as *gathering*, *talking*, and *queuing*. Interaction activities model pairwise relationships between two people which can include *approaching*, *facing-each-other* and *walking-in-opposite-directions*. The atomic activity collects semantic attributes of a tracklet, such as poses (*facing-front*, *facing-left*) or actions (*walking*, *standing*). Feature observations $O = (O_1, O_2, ...O_N)$ operate at a low level, using tracklet-based features to inform the estimation of atomic activities. Collective activity estimation is helped by observations O_C, which use features such as spatio-temporal local descriptors [1, 2] to encode the flow of people around individuals. At this time, we assume that we are given a set of tracklets $\tau_1, ..., \tau_N$ that denote all targets' spatial location in 2D or 3D. These tracklets can be estimated using methods such as [6]. Tracklet associations are denoted by $T = (T_1, T_2, ..., T_M)$ and indicate the association of tracklets. We address the estimation of T in Sec.4.

The information extracted from tracklet-based observations O enables the recognition of atomic activities A, which assist the recognition of interaction activities I, which are used in the estimation of collective activities C. Concurrently, observations O_c provide evidence for recognizing C, which are used as contextual clues for identifying I, which provide context for estimating A. The bi-directional propagation of information makes it possible to classify C, A, and I robustly, which in turn provides strong constraints for improving tracklet association T. Given a video input, the hierarchical structure of our model is constructed dynamically. An atomic activity A_i is assigned to each tracklet τ_i (and observation O_i), an interaction variable I_{ij} is assigned to every pair of atomic activities that exist at the same time, and all interaction variables within a temporal window are associated with a collective activity C.

3.1 The Model

The graphical model of our framework is shown in Fig.1. Let $O = (O_1, O_2, ...O_N)$ be the N observations (visual features within each tracklet) extracted from video V, where observation O_i captures appearance features $s_i(t)$, such as histograms of oriented gradients (HoG [26]), and spatio-temporal features $u_i(t)$, such as a bag of video words (BoV [17]). t corresponds to a specific time stamp within the set of frames $\mathcal{T}_V = (t_1, t_2, ..., t_Z)$ of video V, where Z is the total number of frames in V. Each observation O_i can be seen as a realization of the underlying atomic activity A_i of an individual. Let $A = (A_1, A_2, ..., A_N)$. A_i includes pose labels $p_i(t) \in \mathcal{P}$, and action class labels $a_i(t) \in \mathcal{A}$ at time $t \in \mathcal{T}_V$. $\mathcal{P}$ and $\mathcal{A}$ denote the set of all possible pose (e.g, *facing-front*) and action (e.g, *walking*) labels, respectively. $I = (I_{12}, I_{13}, ..., I_{N-1N})$ denotes the interactions between all possible (coexisting) pairs of A_i and A_j, where each $I_{ij} = (I_{ij}(t_1), ...I_{ij}(t_Z))$ and $I_{ij}(t) \in \mathcal{I}$ is the set of interaction labels such as *approaching*, *facing-each-other* and *standing-in-a-row*. Similarly, $C = (C(t_1), ..., C(t_Z))$ and $C(t_i) \in \mathcal{C}$ indicates the collective activity labels of the video V, where $\mathcal{C}$ is the set of collective activity labels, such as *gathering*, *queueing*, and *talking*. In this work, we assume there exists only one collective activity at a certain time frame. Extensions to modelling multiple collective activities will be addressed in the future. T describes the target (tracklet) associations in the scene as explained in Sec.3.

We formulate the classification problem in an energy maximization framework [27], with overall energy function $\Psi(C, I, A, O, T)$. The energy function is modelled as the linear product of model weights w and the feature vector ψ :

$$\Psi(C, I, A, O, T) = w^T \psi(C, I, A, O, T) \tag{1}$$

$\psi(C, I, A, O, T)$ is a vector composed of $\psi_1(\cdot), \psi_2(\cdot), ..., \psi_m(\cdot)$ where each feature element encodes local relationships between variables and w, which is learned discriminatively, is the set of model parameters. High energy potentials are associated with configurations of A and I that tend to co-occur in training videos with the same collective activity C. For instance, the *talking* collective activity tends to be characterized by interaction activities such as *greeting*, *facing-each-other* and *standing-side-by-side*, as shown in Fig.2.

3.2 Model Characteristics

The central idea of our model is that the atomic activities of individuals are highly correlated with the overall collective activity, through the interactions between people. This hierarchy is illustrated in Fig.1. Assuming the conditional independence implied in our undirected graphical model, the overall energy function can be decomposed as a summation of seven local potentials: $\Psi(C, I)$, $\Psi(C, O)$, $\Psi(I, A, T)$, $\Psi(A, O)$, $\Psi(C)$, $\Psi(I)$, and $\Psi(A)$. The overall energy function can easily be represented as in Eq.1 by rearranging the potentials and concatenating the feature elements to construct the feature vector ψ. Each local potential corresponds to a node (in the case of unitary terms), an edge (in the case of pairwise terms), or a high order potential seen on the graph in Fig.1.(c): 1) $\Psi(C, I)$ encodes the correlation between collective activities and interactions (Fig.2.(b)). 2) $\Psi(I, A, T)$ models the correlation between interactions and atomic activities (Fig.2.(a)). 3) $\Psi(C)$, $\Psi(I)$ and $\Psi(A)$ encode the temporal smoothness prior in each of the variables. 4) $\Psi(C, O)$ and $\Psi(A, O)$ model the compatibility of the observations with the collective activity and atomic activities, respectively.

Collective - Interaction $\Psi(C, I)$: The function is formulated as a linear multi-class model [28]:

$$\Psi(C, I) = \sum_{t \in \mathcal{T}_V} \sum_{a \in \mathcal{C}} w_{ci}^{a} \cdot h(I, t; \triangle t_C) \mathbb{I}(a, C(t)) \tag{2}$$

where w_i is the vector of model weights for each class of collective activity, $h(I, t; \triangle t_C)$ is an $\mathcal{I}$ dimensional histogram function of interaction labels around time t (within a temporal window $\pm \triangle t_C$), and $\mathbb{I}(\cdot, \cdot)$ is an indicator function, that returns 1 if the two inputs are the same and 0 otherwise.

Collective Activity Transition $\Psi(C)$: This potential models the temporal smoothness of collective activities across adjacent frames. That is,

$$\Psi(C) = \sum_{t \in \mathcal{T}_V} \sum_{a \in \mathcal{C}} \sum_{b \in \mathcal{C}} w_{c}^{ab} \; \mathbb{I}(a, C(t)) \; \mathbb{I}(b, C(t+1)) \tag{3}$$

Interaction Transition $\Psi(I) = \sum_{i,j} \Psi(I_{ij})$: This potential models the temporal smoothness of interactions across adjacent frames. That is,

$$\Psi(I_{ij}) = \sum_{t \in \mathcal{T}_V} \sum_{a \in \mathcal{I}} \sum_{b \in \mathcal{I}} w_{i}^{ab} \; \mathbb{I}(a, I_{ij}(t)) \; \mathbb{I}(b, I_{ij}(t+1)) \tag{4}$$

Interaction - Atomic $\Psi(I, A, T) = \sum_{i,j} \Psi(A_i, A_j, I_{ij}, T)$: This encodes the correlation between the interaction I_{ij} and the relative motion between two atomic motions A_i and A_j given all target associations T (more precisely the trajectories of T_k and T_l to which τ_i and τ_j belong, respectively). The relative motion is encoded by the feature vector ψ and the potential $\Psi(A_i, A_j, I_{ij}, T)$ is modelled as:

$$\Psi(A_i, A_j, I_{ij}, T) = \sum_{t \in \mathcal{T}_V} \sum_{a \in \mathcal{I}} w_{ai}^{a} \cdot \psi(A_i, A_j, T, t; \triangle t_I) \; \mathbb{I}(a, I_{ij}) \tag{5}$$

where $\psi(A_i, A_j, T, t; \triangle t_I)$ is a vector representing the relative motion between two targets within a temporal window $(t - \triangle t_I, \; t + \triangle t_I)$ and w_{ai}^{a} is the model parameter for each class of interaction. The feature vector is designed to encode the relationships between the locations, poses, and actions of two people. See [29] for details. Note that since this potential incorporates information about the location of each target, it is closely related to the problem of target association. The same potential is used in both the activity classification and the multi-target tracking components of our framework.

Atomic Prior $\Psi(A)$: Assuming independence between pose and action, the function is modelled as a linear sum of pose transition $\Psi_p(A)$ and action transition $\Psi_a(A)$. This potential function is composed of two functions that encode the smoothness of pose and action. Each of them is parameterized as the co-occurrence frequency of the pair of variables similar to $\Psi(I_{ij})$.

Observations $\Psi(A, O) = \sum_i \Psi(A_i, O_i)$ and $\Psi(C, O)$: these model the compatibility of atomic (A) and collective (C) activity with observations (O). Details of the features are explained in Sec.7.

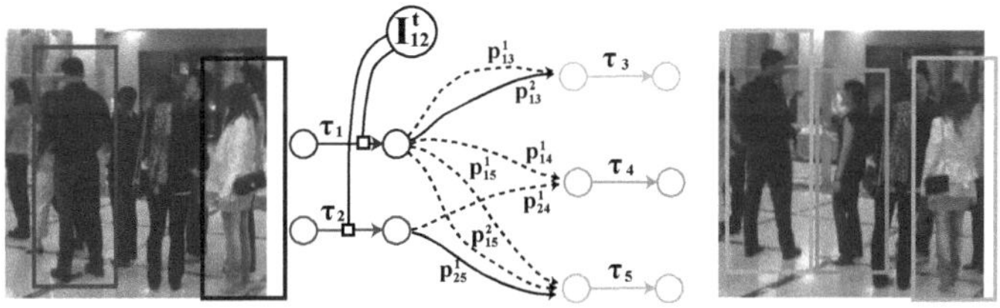

Fig. 3. The tracklet association problem is formulated as a min-cost flow network [15, 16]. The network graph is composed of two components: tracklets τ and path proposals p. In addition to these two, we incorporate interaction potential to add robustness in tracklet association. In this example, the interaction "standing-in-a-row" helps reinforce the association between tracklets τ_1 and τ_3 and penalizes the association between τ_1 and τ_4.

4 Multiple Target Tracking

Our multi-target tracking formulation follows the philosophy of [30], where tracks are obtained by associating corresponding tracklets. Unlike other methods, we leverage the contextual information provided by interaction activities to make target association more robust. Here, we assume that a set of initial tracklets, atomic activities, and interaction activities are given. We will discuss the joint estimation of these labels in Sec.5.

As shown in Fig.3, tracklet association can be formulated as a min-cost network problem [15], where the edge between a pair of nodes represents a tracklet, and the black directed edges represent possible links to match two tracklets. We refer the reader to [15, 16] for the details of network-flow formulations.

Given a set of tracklets $\tau_1, \tau_2, ..., \tau_N$ where $\tau_i = \{x_{\tau_i}(t_0^i), ..., x_{\tau_i}(t_e^i)\}$ and $x(t)$ is a position at t, the tracklet association problem can be stated as that of finding an unknown number M of associations $T_1, T_2, ..., T_M$, where each T_i contains one or more indices of tracklets. For example, one association may consist of tracklets 1 and 3: $T_1 = \{1, 3\}$. To accomplish this, we find a set of possible paths between two non-overlapping tracklets τ_i and τ_j. These correspond to match hypotheses $p_{ij}^k = \{x_{p_{ij}^k}(t_e^i + 1), ..., x_{p_{ij}^k}(t_0^j - 1)\}$ where the timestamps are in the temporal gap between τ_i and τ_j. The association T_i can be redefined by augmenting the associated pair of tracklets τ_i and τ_j with the match hypothesis p_{ij}. For example, $T_1 = \{1, 3, 1\text{-}2\text{-}3\}$ indicates that tracklet 1 and 3 form one track and the second match hypothesis (the solid edge between τ_1 and τ_3 in Fig. 3) connects them. Given human detections, we can generate match hypotheses using the K-shortest path algorithm [31] (see [29] for details).

Each match hypothesis has an associated cost value c_{ij}^k that represents the validity of the match. This cost is derived from detection responses, motion cues, and color similarity. By limiting the number of hypotheses to a relatively small value of K, we prune out a majority of the exponentially many hypotheses that could be generated by raw detections. If we define the cost of entering and exiting a tracklet as c_{en} and c_{ex} respectively, the tracklet association problem can be written as :

$$\hat{f} = \operatorname*{argmin}_{f} c^T f = \operatorname*{argmin}_{f} \sum_{i} c_{en} f_{en,i} + \sum_{i} c_{ex} f_{i,ex} + \sum_{i,j} \sum_{k} c_{ij}^k f_{ij}^k$$

$$s.t.\ f_{en,i}, f_{i,ex}, f_{ij}^k \in \{0,1\},\ f_{en,i} + \sum_{j} \sum_{k} f_{ji}^k = f_{i,ex} + \sum_{j} \sum_{k} f_{ij}^k = 1$$

where f represent the flow variables, the first set of constraints is a set of binary constraints and the second one captures the inflow-outflow constraints (we assume all the tracklets are true). Later in this paper, we will refer to $\mathbb{S}$ as the feasible set for f that satisfies the above constraints. Once the flow variable f is specified, it is trivial to obtain the tracklet association T through a mapping function $T(f)$. The above problem can be efficiently solved by binary integer programming, since it involves only a few variables, with complexity $O(KN)$ where N (the number of tracklets) is typically a few hundred, and there are $2N$ equality constraints. Note that the number of nodes in [15, 16] is usually in the order of tens or hundreds of thousands.

One of the novelties of our framework lies in the contextual information that comes from the interaction activity nodes. For the moment, assume that the interactions I_{12}^t between A_1 and A_2 are known. Then, selecting a match hypothesis f_{ij}^k should be related with the likelihood of observing the interaction I_{12}^t. For instance, the *red* and *blue* targets in Fig.3 are engaged in the *standing-in-a-row* interaction activity. If we select the match hypothesis that links *red* with *pink* and *blue* with *sky-blue* (shown with solid edges), then the interaction will be compatible with the links, since the distance between *red* and *blue* is similar to that between *pink*/*sky-blue*. However, if we select the match hypothesis that links *red* with *green*, this will be less compatible with the *standing-in-a-row* interaction activity, because the *green*/*pink* distance is less than the *red*/*blue* distance, and people do not tend to move toward each other when they are in a queue. The potential $\Psi(I, A, T)$ (Sec.3.2) is used to enforce this consistency between interactions and tracklet associations.

5 Unifying Activity Classification and Tracklet Association

The previous two sections present collective activity classification and multi-target tracking as independent problems. In this section, we show how they can be modelled in a unified framework. Let $\hat{y}$ denote the desired solution of our unified problem. The optimization can be written as:

$$\hat{y} = \operatorname*{argmax}_{f,C,I,A} \underbrace{\Psi(C, I, A, O, T(f))}_{Sec.3} - \underbrace{c^T f}_{Sec.4},\ s.t.\ f \in \mathbb{S} \quad (6)$$

where f is the binary flow variables, $\mathbb{S}$ is the feasible set of f, and C, I, A are activity variables. As noted in the previous section, the interaction potential $\Psi(A, I, T)$ involves the variables related to both activity classification (A, I) and tracklet association (T). Thus, changing the configuration of interaction and atomic variables affects not only the energy of the classification problem, but also the energy of the association problem. In other words, our model is capable of propagating the information obtained from collective activity classification to target association and from target association to collective activity classification through $\Psi(A, I, T)$.

5.1 Inference

Since the interaction labels I and the atomic activity labels A guide the flow of information between target association and activity classification, we leverage the structure of our model to efficiently solve this complicated joint inference problem. The optimization problem Eq.6 is divided into two sub problems and solved iteratively:

$$\{\hat{C}, \hat{I}, \hat{A}\} = \underset{C,I,A}{\operatorname{argmax}} \Psi(C, I, A, O, T(\hat{f})) \ AND \ \hat{f} = \underset{f}{\operatorname{argmin}} c^T f - \Psi(\hat{I}, \hat{A}, T(f)), \ s.t. \ f \in \mathbb{S} \quad (7)$$

Given $\hat{f}$ (and thus $\hat{T}$) the hierarchical classification problem is solved by applying iterative Belief Propagation. Fixing the activity labels A and I, we solve the target association problem by applying the Branch-and-Bound algorithm with a tight linear lower bound (see below for more details).

Iterative Belief Propagation. Due to the high order potentials in our model (such as the Collective-Interaction potential), the exact inference of the all variables is intractable. Thus, we propose an approximate inference algorithm that takes advantage of the structure of our model. Since each type of variable forms a simple chain in the temporal direction (see Fig.1), it is possible to obtain the optimal solution given all the other variables by using belief propagation [32]. The iterative belief propagation algorithm is grounded in this intuition, and is shown in detail in Alg.1.

Target Association Algorithm. We solve the association problem by using the Branch-and-Bound method. Unlike the original min-cost flow network problem, the interaction terms introduce a quadratic relationship between flow variables. Note that we need to choose at most two flow variables to specify one interaction feature. For instance, if there exist two different tails of tracklets at the same time stamp, we need to specify two of the flows out of seven flows to compute the interaction potential as shown in Fig.3. This leads to a non-convex binary quadratic programming problem which is hard to solve exactly (the Hessian H is not a positive semi-definite matrix).

Algorithm 1. Iterative Belief Propagation

Require: Given association $\hat{T}$ and observation O.
  Initialize C^0, I^0, A^0
  while Convergence, k++ **do**
    $C^k \Leftarrow \operatorname{argmax}_C \Psi(C, I^{k-1}, A^{k-1}, O, \hat{T})$
    for all $\forall i \in A$ **do**
      $A_i^k \Leftarrow \operatorname{argmax}_A \Psi(C^k, I^{k-1}, A, A_{\setminus i}^{k-1}, O, \hat{T})$
    end for
    for all $\forall i \in I$ **do**
      $I_i^k \Leftarrow \operatorname{argmax}_I \Psi(C^k, I, I_{\setminus i}^{k-1}, A^k, O, \hat{T})$
    end for
  end while

$$\underset{f}{\operatorname{argmin}} \frac{1}{2} f^T H f + c^T f, \; s.t. \; f \in \mathbb{S} \tag{8}$$

To tackle this issue, we use a Branch-and-Bound (BB) algorithm with a novel tight lower bound function given by $h^T f \leq \frac{1}{2} f^T H f, \; \forall f \in \mathbb{S}$. See [29] for details about variable selection, lower and upper bounds, and definitions of the BB algorithm.

6 Model Learning

Given the training videos, the model is learned in a two-stage process: i) learning the observation potentials $\Psi(A, O)$ and $\Psi(C, O)$. This is done by learning each observation potential $\Psi(\cdot)$ independently using multiclass SVM [28]. ii) learning the model weights w for the full model in a max-margin framework as follows. Given a set of N training videos (x^n, y^n), $n = 1, ..., N$, where x^n is the observations from each video and y^n is a set of labels, we train the global weight w in a max-margin framework. Specifically, we employ the cutting plane training algorithm described in [33] to solve this optimization problem. We incorporate the inference algorithm described in Sec.5.1 to obtain the most violated constraint in each iteration [33]. To improve computational efficiency, we train the model weights related to activity potentials first, and train the model weights related to tracklet association using the learnt activity models.

7 Experimental Validation

Implementation Details. Our algorithm assumes that the inputs O are available. These inputs are composed of collective activity features, tracklets, appearance feature, and spatio-temporal features as discussed in Sec.3.1. Given a video, we obtain tracklets using a proper tracking method (see text below for details). Once tracklets O are obtained, we compute two visual features (the histogram of oriented gradients (HoG) decriptors [26] and the bag of video words (BoV) histogram [17]) in order to classify poses and actions, respectively. The HoG is extracted from an image region within the bounding box of the tracklets and the BoV is constructed by computing the histogram of video-words within the spatio-temporal volume of each tracklet. To obtain the video-words, we apply PCA (with 200 dimensions) and the k-means algorithm (100 codewords) on the cuboids obtained by [17]. Finally, the collective activity features are computed using the STL descriptor [1] on tracklets and pose classification estimates. We adopt the parameters suggested by [1] for STL construction (8 meters for maximum radius and 60 frames for the temporal support). Since we are interested in labelling one collective activity per one time slice (i.e. a set of adjacent time frames), we take the average of all collected STL in the same time slice to generate an observation for C. In addition, we append the mean of the HoG descriptors obtained from all people in the scene to encode the shape of people in a certain activity. Instead of directly using raw features from HoG, BoV, and STL, we train multiclass SVM classifiers [33] for each of the observations to keep the size

Table 1. Comparison of collective and interaction activity classification for different versions of our model using the dataset [1] (left column) and the newly proposed dataset (right column). The models we compare here are: i) *Graph without* O_C. We remove observations (STL [1]) for the collective activity. ii) *Graph with no edges between* C *and* I. We cut the connections between variables C and I and produce separate chain structures for each set of variables. iii) *Graph with no temporal edges.* We cut all the temporal edges between variables in the graphical structure and leave only hierarchical relationships. iv) *Graph with no temporal chain between* C *variables.* v) Our full model shown in Fig.1.(d) and vi) baseline method. The baseline method is obtained by taking the max response from the collective activity observation (O_C).

	Dataset [1]				New Dataset			
Method	Ovral (C)	Mean (C)	Ovral (I)	Mean (I)	Ovral (C)	Mean (C)	Ovral (I)	Mean (I)
without O_C	38.7	37.1	40.5	37.3	59.2	57.4	49.4	41.1
no edges between C and I	67.7	68.2	42.8	37.7	67.8	54.6	42.4	32.8
no temporal chain	66.9	66.3	42.6	33.7	71.1	68.9	41.9	46.1
no temporal chain between C	74.1	75.0	54.2	48.6	77.0	76.1	**55.9**	**48.6**
full model ($\triangle t_C = 20$, $\triangle t_I = 25$)	**79.0**	**79.6**	**56.2**	**50.8**	**83.0**	**79.2**	53.3	43.7
baseline	72.5	73.3	-	-	77.4	74.3	-	-

Table 2. Comparison of classification results using different lengths of temporal support $\triangle t_C$ and $\triangle t_I$ for collective and interaction activities, respectively. Notice that in general larger support provides more stable results.

	Dataset [1]				New Dataset			
Method	Ovral (C)	Mean (C)	Ovral (I)	Mean (I)	Ovral (C)	Mean (C)	Ovral (I)	Mean (I)
$\triangle t_C = 30$, $\triangle t_I = 25$	79.1	79.9	56.1	50.8	80.8	77.0	**54.3**	**46.3**
$\triangle t_C = 20$, $\triangle t_I = 25$	79.0	79.6	**56.2**	**50.8**	**83.0**	**79.2**	53.3	43.7
$\triangle t_C = 10$, $\triangle t_I = 25$	77.4	78.2	56.1	50.7	81.5	77.6	52.9	41.8
$\triangle t_C = 30$, $\triangle t_I = 15$	76.1	76.7	52.8	40.7	80.7	71.8	48.6	34.8
$\triangle t_C = 30$, $\triangle t_I = 5$	**79.4**	**80.2**	45.5	36.6	77.0	67.3	37.7	25.7

of parameters within a reasonable bound. In the end, each of the observation features is represented as a $|\mathcal{P}|$, $|\mathcal{A}|$, and $|\mathcal{C}|$ dimensional features, where each dimension of the features is the classification score given by the SVM classifier. In the experiments, we use the SVM response for C as a baseline method (Tab.1 and Fig.4).

Given tracklets and associated pose/action features O, a temporal sequence of atomic activity variables A_i is assigned to each tracklet τ_i. For each pair of coexisting A_i and A_j, I_{ij} describes the interaction between the two. Since I is defined over a certain temporal support ($\triangle t_I$), we sub-sample every 10th frames to assign an interaction variable. Finally, one C variable is assigned in every 20 frames with a temporal support $\triangle t_C$. We present experimental results using different choices of $\triangle t_I$ and $\triangle t_C$, (Tab.2). Given tracklets and observations (O and O_C), the classification and target association take about a minute per video in our experiments.

Datasets and Experimental Setup. We present experimental results on the public dataset [1] and a newly proposed dataset. The first dataset is composed of 44 video clips with annotations for 5 collective activities (*crossing*, *waiting*, *queuing*, *walking*, and *talking*) and 8 poses (*right*, *right-front*, ..., *right-back*). In addition to these labels, we annotate the target correspondence, action labels and interaction labels for all sequences. We define the 8 types of interactions

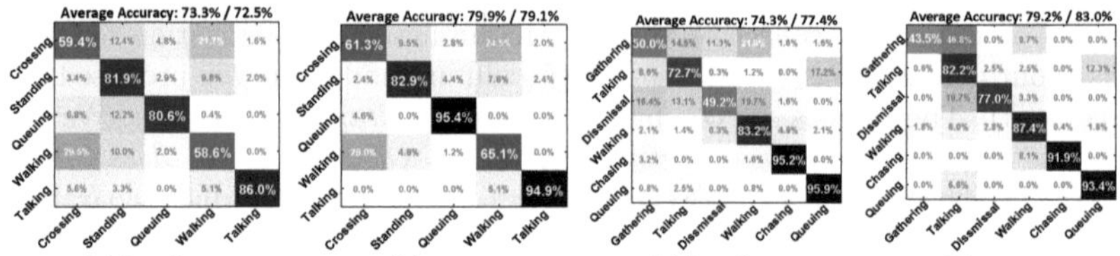

(a) baseline (b) ours (c) baseline (d) ours

Fig. 4. (a) and (b) shows the confusion table for collective activity using baseline method (SVM response for C) and proposed method on dataset [1], respectively. (c) and (d) compare the two methods on newly proposed dataset. In both cases, our full model improves the accuracy significantly over the baseline method. The numbers on top of each table show *mean-per-class* and *overall* accuracies.

as *approaching* (AP), *leaving* (LV), *passing-by* (PB), *facing-each-other* (FE), *walking-side-by-side* (WS), *standing-in-a-row* (SR), *standing-side-by-side* (SS) and *no-interaction* (NA). The categories of atomic actions are defined as: *standing* and *walking*. Due to a lack of standard experimental protocol on this dataset, we adopt two experimental scenarios. First, we divide the whole set into 4 subsets without overlap of videos and perform 4-fold training and testing. Second, we divide the set into separate training and testing sets as suggested by [11]. Since the first setup provides more data to be analysed, we run the main analysis with the setup and use the second for comparison against [11]. In the experiments, we use the tracklets provided on the website of the authors of [6, 1].

The second dataset is composed of 32 video clips with 6 collective activities: *gathering*, *talking*, *dismissal*, *walking together*, *chasing*, *queueing*. For this dataset, we define 9 interaction labels: *approaching* (AP), *walking-in-opposite-direction* (WO), *facing-each-other* (FE), *standing-in-a-row* (SR), *walking-side-by-side* (WS), *walking-one-after-the-other* (WR), *running-side-by-side* (RS), *running-one-after-the-other* (RR), and *no-interaction* (NA). The atomic actions are labelled as *walking*, *standing still*, and *running*. We define 8 poses similarly to the first dataset. We divide the whole set into 3 subsets and run 3-fold training and testing. For this dataset, we obtain the tracklets using [16] and create back projected 3D trajectories using the simplified camera model [34].

Results and Analysis. We analyze the behavior of the proposed model by disabling the connectivity between various variables of the graphical structure (see Tab.1 and Fig.4 for details). We study the classification accuracy of collective activities C and interaction activities I. As seen in the Tab.1, the best classification results are obtained by our full model. Since the dataset is unbalanced, we present both overall accuracy and mean-per-class accuracy, denoted as Ovral and Mean in Tab.1 and Tab.2.

Next, we analyse the model by varying the parameter values that define the temporal supports of collective and interaction activities ($\triangle t_C$ and $\triangle t_I$). We run different experiments by fixing one of the temporal supports to a reference value and change the other. As any of the temporal supports becomes larger, the collective and interaction activity variables are connected with a larger number

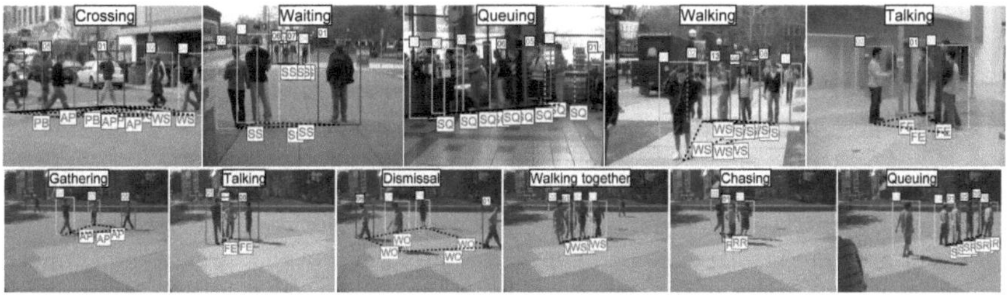

Fig. 5. Anecdotal results on different types of collective activities. In each image, we show the collective activity estimated by our method. Interactions between people are denoted by the dotted line that connects each pair of people. To make the visualization more clear, we only show interactions that are not labelled as NA (*no interaction*). Anecdotal results on the dataset [1] and the newly proposed dataset are shown on the top and bottom rows, respectively. Our method automatically discovers the interactions occurring within each collective activity; Eg. *walking-side-by-side* (denoted as WS) occurs with *crossing* or *walking*, whereas *standing-side-by-side* (SS) occurs with *waiting*. See text for the definition of other acronyms.

of interactions and atomic activity variables, respectively, which provides richer coupling between variables across labels of the hierarchy and, in turn, enables more robust classification results (Tab.2). Notice that, however, by increasing connectivity, the graphical structure becomes more complex and thus inference becomes less manageable.

Since previous works adopt different ways of calculating the accuracy of the collective activity classification, a direct comparison of the results may not be appropriate. [1] and [2] adopt leave-one-video-out training/testing and evaluate per-person collective activity classification. [11] train their model on three fourths of the dataset, test on the remaining fourth and evaluate per-scene collective activity classification. To compare against [1, 2], we assign the per-scene collective activity labels that we obtain with four-fold experiments to each individual. We obtain an accuracy of 74.4% which is superior than 65.9% and 70.9% reported in [1] and [2], respectively. In addition, we run the experiments on the same training/testing split of the dataset suggested by [11] and achieve competitive accuracy (80.4% overall and 75.7% mean-per-class compared to 79.1% overall and 77.5% mean-per-class, respectively, reported in [11]). Anecdotal results are shown in Fig.5.

Tab.3 summarizes the tracklet association accuracy of our method. In this experiment, we test three different algorithms for tracklet matching : pure match, linear model, and full quadratic model. *Match* represents the max-flow method without interaction potential (only appearance, motion and detection scores are used). *Linear* model represents our model where the quadratic relationship is ignored and only the linear part of the interaction potentials is considered

(a) (b)

Fig. 6. The discovered interaction *standing-side-by-side* (denoted as SS) helps to keep the identity of tracked individuals after an occlusion. Notice the complexity of the association problem in this example. Due to the proximity of the targets and similarity in color, the *Match* method **(b)** fails to keep the identity of targets. However, our method **(a)** finds the correct match despite the challenges. The input tracklets are shown as a solid box and associated paths are shown in dotted box.

Table 3. Quantitative tracking results and comparison with baseline methods (see text for definitions). Each cell of the table shows the number of match errors and Match Error Correction Rate (MECR) $\frac{\#\ error\ in\ tracklet\ -\ \#\ error\ in\ result}{\#\ error\ in\ tracklet}$ of each method, respectively. Since we focus on correctly associating each tracklet with another, we evaluate the method by counting the number of errors made during association (rather than detection-based accuracy measurements such as recall, FPPI, etc) and MECR. An association error is defined for each possible match of a tracklet (thus at most two per tracklets, previous and next match). This measure can effectively capture the amount of fragmentization and identity switches in association. In the case of a false alarm tracklet, any association with this track is considered to be an error.

	Match (baseline)	*Linear* (partial model)	*Quadratic* (full model)	*Linear GT*	*Quad. GT*	*Tracklet*
Dataset [1]	1109/28.73%	974/37.40%	894/42.54%	870/44.09%	736/52.70%	1556/0%
New Dataset	110/81.79%	107/82.28%	104/82.78%	97/83.94%	95/84.27%	604/0%

(e.g. those interactions that are involved in selecting only one path). The *Quadratic* model represents our full Branch-and-Bound method for target association. The estimated activity labels are assigned to each variable for the two methods. We also show the accuracy of association when ground truth (GT) activity labels are provided, in the fourth and fifth columns of the table. The last column shows the number of association errors in the initial input tracklets. In these experiments, we adopt the same four fold training/testing and three fold training/testing for the dataset [1] and newly proposed dataset, respectively. Note that, in the dataset [1], there exist 1821 tracklets with 1556 match errors in total. In the new dataset, which includes much less crowded sequences than [1], there exist 474 tracklets with 604 errors in total. As the Tab.3 shows, we achieve significant improvement over baseline method (*Match*) using the dataset [1] as it is more challenging and involves a large number of people (more information from interactions). On the other hand, we observe a smaller improvement in matching targets in the second dataset, since it involves few people (typically $2 \sim 3$) and is less challenging (note that the baseline (*Match*) already achieves 81% correct match). Experimental results obtained with ground truth activity labels (*Linear GT* and *Quad. GT*) suggest that better activity recognition would yield more accurate tracklet association. Anecdotal results are shown in Fig.6.

8 Conclusion

In this paper, we present a new framework to coherently identify target associations and classify collective activities. We demonstrate that collective activities provide critical contextual cues for making target association more robust and stable; in turn, the estimated trajectories as well as atomic activity labels allow the construction of more accurate interaction and collective activity models.

Acknowledgement. We acknowledge the support of the ONR grant N00014111 0389 and Toyota. We appreciate Yu Xiang for his valuable discussions.

References

1. Choi, W., Shahid, K., Savarese, S.: What are they doing?: Collective activity classification using spatio-temporal relationship among people. In: VSWS (2009)
2. Choi, W., Shahid, K., Savarese, S.: Learning context for collective activity recognition. In: CVPR (2011)
3. Scovanner, P., Tappen, M.: Learning pedestrian dynamics from the real world. In: ICCV (2009)
4. Pellegrini, S., Ess, A., Schindler, K., van Gool, L.: You'll never walk alone: Modeling social behavior for multi-target tracking. In: ICCV (2009)
5. Leal-Taixe, L., Pons-Moll, G., Rosenhahn, B.: Everybody needs somebody: Modeling social and grouping behavior on a linear programming multiple people tracker. In: Workshop on Modeling, Simulation and Visual Analysis of Large Crowds, ICCV (2011)
6. Choi, W., Savarese, S.: Multiple Target Tracking in World Coordinate with Single, Minimally Calibrated Camera. In: Daniilidis, K., Maragos, P., Paragios, N. (eds.) ECCV 2010, Part IV. LNCS, vol. 6314, pp. 553–567. Springer, Heidelberg (2010)
7. Khan, Z., Balch, T., Dellaert, F.: MCMC-based particle filtering for tracking a variable number of interacting targets. PAMI (2005)
8. Yamaguchi, K., Berg, A.C., Berg, T., Ortiz, L.: Who are you with and where are you going? In: CVPR (2011)
9. Intille, S., Bobick, A.: Recognizing planned, multiperson action. CVIU (2001)
10. Li, R., Chellappa, R., Zhou, S.K.: Learning multi-modal densities on discriminative temporal interaction manifold for group activity recognition. In: CVPR (2009)
11. Lan, T., Wang, Y., Yang, W., Mori, G.: Beyond actions: Discriminative models for contextual group activities. In: NIPS (2010)
12. Wu, B., Nevatia, R.: Detection and tracking of multiple, partially occluded humans by bayesian combination of edgelet based part detectors. IJCV (2007)
13. Ess, A., Leibe, B., Schindler, K., van Gool, L.: A mobile vision system for robust multi-person tracking. In: CVPR (2008)
14. Rodriguez, M., Ali, S., Kanade, T.: Tracking in unstructured crowded scenes. In: ICCV (2009)
15. Zhang, L., Li, Y., Nevatia, R.: Global data association for multi-object tracking using network flows. In: CVPR (2008)
16. Pirsiavash, H., Ramanan, D., Fowlkes, C.: Globally-optimal greedy algorithms for tracking a variable number of objects. In: CVPR (2011)
17. Dollar, P., Rabaud, V., Cottrell, G., Belongie, S.: Behavior recognition via sparse spatio-temporal features. In: VS-PETS (2005)

18. Savarese, S., DelPozo, A., Niebles, J., Fei-Fei, L.: Spatial-temporal correlatons for unsupervised action classification. In: WMVC (2008)
19. Niebles, J.C., Wang, H., Fei-Fei, L.: Unsupervised learning of human action categories using spatial-temporal words. IJCV (2008)
20. Liu, J., Luo, J., Shah, M.: Recongizing realistic actions from videos "in the wild". In: CVPR (2009)
21. Ryoo, M.S., Aggarwal, J.K.: Spatio-temporal relationship match: Video structure comparison for recognition of complex human activities. In: ICCV (2009)
22. Swears, E., Hoogs, A.: Learning and recognizing complex multi-agent activities with applications to american football plays. In: WACV (2011)
23. Ni, B., Yan, S., Kassim, A.: Recognizing human group activities with localized causalities. In: CVPR (2009)
24. Ryoo, M.S., Aggarwal, J.K.: Stochastic representation and recognition of high-level group activities. IJCV (2010)
25. Ramin Mehran, A.O., Shah, M.: Abnormal crowd behavior detection using social force model. In: CVPR (2009)
26. Dalal, N., Triggs, B.: Histograms of oriented gradients for human detection. In: CVPR (2005)
27. LeCun, Y., Chopra, S., Hadsell, R., Ranzato, M., Huang, F.: A tutorial on energy-based learning. MIT Press (2006)
28. Weston, J., Watkins, C.: Multi-class support vector machines (1998)
29. Choi, W., Savarese, S.: Supplementary material. In: ECCV (2012)
30. Singh, V.K., Wu, B., Nevatia, R.: Pedestrian tracking by associating tracklets using detection residuals. In: IMVC (2008)
31. Yen, J.Y.: Finding the k shortest loopless paths in a network (Management Science)
32. Felzenszwalb, P., Huttenlocher, D.: Efficient belief propagation for early vision. IJCV (2006)
33. Joachims, T., Finley, T., Yu, C.N.: Cutting-plane training of structural svms. Machine Learning (2009)
34. Hoiem, D., Efros, A.A., Herbert, M.: Putting objects in perspective. IJCV (2008)

Camera Pose Estimation Using First-Order Curve Differential Geometry

Ricardo Fabbri[1], Benjamin B. Kimia[1], and Peter J. Giblin[2]

[1] Brown University
Division of Engineering
Providence RI 02912, USA
{rfabbri,kimia}@lems.brown.edu
[2] University of Liverpool
Liverpool, UK
pjgiblin@liverpool.ac.uk

Abstract. This paper considers and solves the problem of estimating camera pose given a pair of point-tangent correspondences between the 3D scene and the projected image. The problem arises when considering curve geometry as the basis of forming correspondences, computation of structure and calibration, which in its simplest form is a point augmented with the curve tangent. We show that while the standard resectioning problem is solved with a minimum of three points given the intrinsic parameters, when points are augmented with tangent information only two points are required, leading to substantial computational savings, *e.g.*, when used as a minimal engine within RANSAC. In addition, computational algorithms are developed to find a practical and efficient solution shown to effectively recover camera pose using both synthetic and realistic datasets. The resolution of this problem is intended as a basic building block of future curve-based structure from motion systems, allowing new views to be incrementally registered to a core set of views for which relative pose has already been computed.

Keywords: Pose Estimation, Camera Resectioning, Differential Geometry.

1 Introduction

A key problem in the reconstruction of structure from multiple views is the determination of relative pose among cameras as well as the intrinsic parameters for each camera. The classical method is to rely on a set of corresponding points across views to determine each camera's intrinsic parameter matrix $\mathcal{K}_{im}$ as well as the relative pose between pairs of cameras [11]. The set of corresponding points can be determined using a calibration jig, but, more generally, using isolated keypoints such as Harris corners [10] or SIFT/HOG [17] features which remain somewhat stable over view and other variations. As long as there is a sufficient number of keypoints between two views, a random selection of a few feature correspondences using RANSAC [7,11] can be verified by measuring the number of inlier features. This class of isolated feature point-based methods are currently in popular and successful use through packages such as the Bundler and used in applications such as Phototourism [1].

A. Fitzgibbon et al. (Eds.): ECCV 2012, Part IV, LNCS 7575, pp. 231–244, 2012.

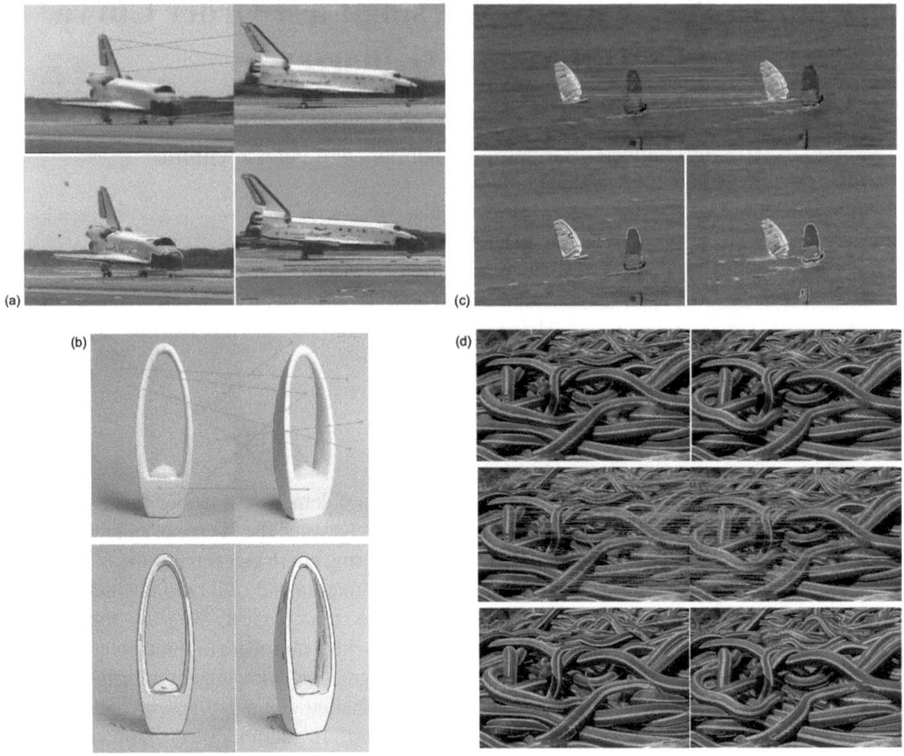

Fig. 1. (a) Views with wide baseline separation may not have enough interest points in common, but they often do share common curve structure. (b) There may not always be sufficient interest points matching across views of homogeneous objects, such as for the sculpture, but there is sufficient curve structure. (c) Each moving object requires its own set of features, which may not be sufficient without a richly textured surface. (d) Non-rigid structures face the same issue.

Two major drawbacks limit the applicability of interest points. First, it is well-known that in practice the correlation of interest points works for views with a *limited baseline*, according to some estimates no greater than 30° [18], Figure 1(a). In contrast, certain image curve fragments, *e.g.*, those corresponding to sharp ridges, reflectance curves, *etc*, persist stably over a much larger range of views. Second, the success of interest point-based methods is based on the presence of an abundance of features so that a sufficient number of them survive the various variations between views. While this is true in many scenes, as evidenced by the popularity of this approach, in a non-trivial number of scenes this is not the case, such as *(i)* Homogeneous regions, *e.g.*, from man-made objects, corridors, *etc.*, Figure 1(b); *(ii)* Multiple moving objects require their own set of features which may not be sufficiently abundant without sufficient texture, Figure 1(c); *(iii)* Non-rigid objects require a rich set of features per roughly non-deforming patch, Figure 1(d). In all these cases, however, there is often sufficient **image curve structure**, motivating augmenting the use of interest points by developing a parallel technology for the use of image curve structure.

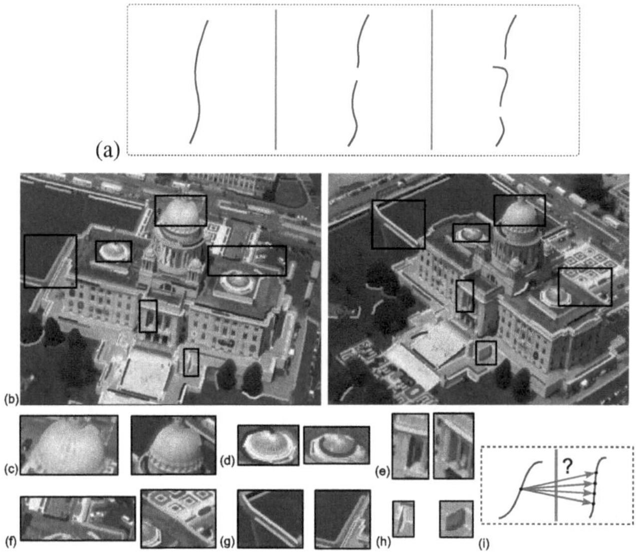

Fig. 2. Real challenges in using curve fragments in multiview geometry: (a) instabilities with slight changes in viewpoint, shown for two views in (b) and zoomed in (c-h), such as a curve in one view broken into two in another, a curve linked onto background, a curve detected in one view but absent in another, a curve fragmented into several pieces at junctions in one view but fully linked in another, different parts of a curve occluded in different views, and a curve undergoing deformation from one view to the other. (i) Point correspondence ambiguity along the curve.

The use of image curves in determining camera pose has generally been based on epipolar tangencies, but these techniques assume that curves are closed or can be described as conics or other algebraic curves [14, 15, 19, 21]. The use of image curve fragments as the basic structure for auto-calibration under general conditions is faced with two significant challenges. First, current edge linking procedures do not generally produce curve segments which persist stably across images. Rather, an image curve fragment in one view may be present in broken form and/or or grouped with other curve fragments. Thus, while the underlying curve geometry correlates well across views, the individual curve fragments do not, Figure 2(a-h). Second, even when the image curve fragments correspond exactly, there is an intra-curve correspondence ambiguity, Figure 2(i). This ambiguity prevents the use of corresponding curve points to solve for the unknown pose and intrinsic parameters. Both these challenges motivate the use of *small curve fragments*.

The paradigm explored in this paper is that small curve fragments, or equivalently points augmented with differential-geometric attributes[1], can be used as the basic image structure to correlate across views. The intent is to use curve geometry as a complementary approach to the use of interest points in cases where these fail or are not available. The value of curve geometry is in correlating structure across *three* frames or more

[1] Previous work in exploring local geometric groupings [22] has shown that tangent and curvature as well as the sign of curvature derivative can be reliably estimated.

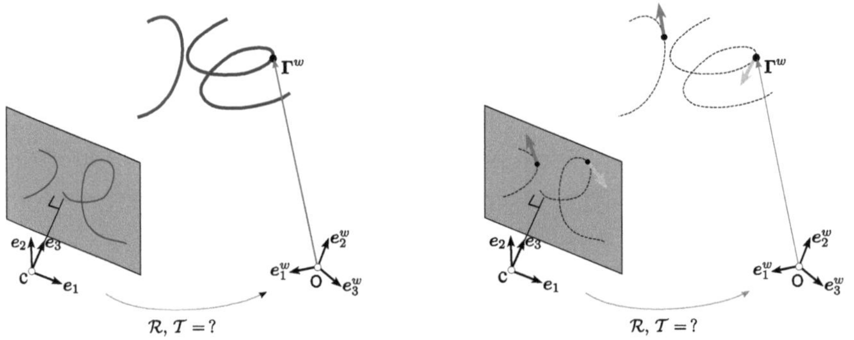

Fig. 3. The problem of determining camera pose $\mathcal{R}$, $\mathcal{T}$ given space curves in a world coordinate system and their projections in an image coordinate system (left), and an approach to that consisting of (right) determining camera pose $\mathcal{R}$, $\mathcal{T}$ given 3D point-tangents (*i.e.*, local curve models) in a world coordinate system and their projections in an image coordinate system.

since the correspondence geometry in two views is unconstrained. The differential geometry at two corresponding points in two views reconstruct the differential geometry of the space curve they arise from [4] and this constrains the differential geometry of corresponding curves in a third view.

The fundamental questions underlying the use of points augmented with differential-geometric attributes are: how many such points are needed, what order of differential geometry is required, *etc*. This paper explores the use of first-order differential geometry, namely points with tangent attributes, for determining the pose of a single camera with respect to the coordinates of observed 3D point-tangents. It poses and solves the following:

Problem: For a camera with known intrinsic parameters, how many corresponding pairs of point-tangents in space specified in world coordinates, and point-tangents in 2D specified in image coordinates, are required to establish the pose of the camera with respect to the world coordinates, Figure 3.

The solution to the above problem is useful under several scenarios. First, when many views of the scene are available and there is a reconstruction available from two views, *e.g.*, as in [5]. In this case a pair of point-tangents in the reconstruction can be matched under a RANSAC strategy to a pair of point-tangents in the image to determine pose. The advantage as compared to using three points from unorganized point reconstruction and resectioning is that *(i)* there are fewer edges than surface points and *(ii)* the method uses two rather than three points in RANSAC, requiring about half the number of runs for the same level of robustness, *e.g.*, 32 runs instead of 70 to achieve 99.99% probability of not hitting an outlier in at least one run, assuming 50% outliers (in practical systems it is often necessary to do as many runs as possible, to maximize robustness). Second, the 3D model of the object may be available from CAD or other sources, *e.g.*, civilian or military vehicles. In this case a strategy similar to the first scenario can be used. Third, in stereo video sequences obtained from precisely calibrated binocular cameras, the reconstruction from one frame of the video can be used to determine the camera pose in subsequent frames.

2 Related Work

Previous work has generally relied on matching *epipolar tangencies* on *closed curves*. Two corresponding points γ^1 in image 1 and γ^2 in image 2 are related by $\gamma^{2\top} E \gamma^1 = 0$, where E is the *essential matrix* [16]. This can be extended to the differential geometry of two curves, $\gamma^1(s)$ in the first view and a curve $\gamma^2(s)$ in a second view, *i.e.*,

$$\gamma^{1\top}(s) E \gamma^2(s) = 0. \tag{2.1}$$

The tangents $\boldsymbol{t}^1(s)$ and $\boldsymbol{t}^2(s)$ are related by differentiation

$$g^1(s)\boldsymbol{t}^{1^\top}(s) E \gamma^2(s) + \gamma^{1\top}(s) E g^2(s) \boldsymbol{t}^2(s) = 0, \tag{2.2}$$

where $g^1(s)$ and $g^2(s)$ are the respective speeds of parametrization of the curves $\gamma^1(s)$ and $\gamma^2(s)$. It is clear that when one of the tangents $\boldsymbol{t}^1(s)$ is along the epipolar plane, *i.e.*, $\boldsymbol{t}^{1^\top}(s) E \gamma^2(s) = 0$ at a point s, then $\gamma^{1\top}(s) E \boldsymbol{t}^2(s) = 0$. Thus, epipolar tangency in image 1 implies tangency in image 2 at the corresponding point, Figure 4.

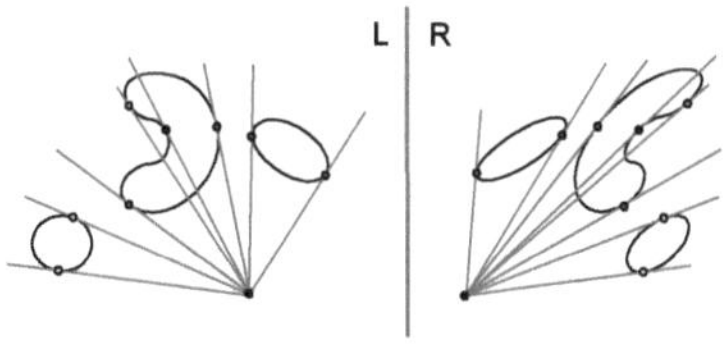

Fig. 4. Correspondence of epipolar tangencies in curve-based camera calibration. An epipolar line on the left must correspond to the epipolar line on the right having tangency on the corresponding curve, marked with the same color. This works for both static curves and occluding contours.

The epipolar tangency constraint was first proposed in [19] who use linked edges and a coarse initial estimate E to find a sparse set of epipolar tangencies, including those at corners, in each view. They are matched from one view to another manually. This is then used to refine the estimate E, see Figure 5, by minimizing $\gamma^{1\top}(s) E \gamma^2(s)$ over all matches in an iterative two-step scheme: the corresponding points are kept fixed and E is optimized in the first step and then E is kept fixed and the points are updated in a

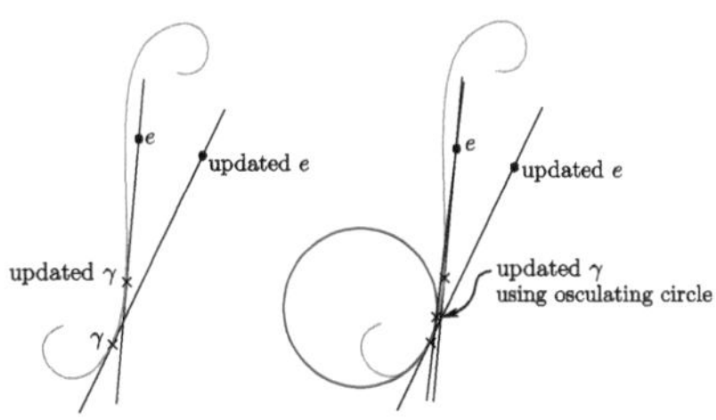

Fig. 5. The differential update of epipolar tangencies through curvature information

second step using a closed form solution based on an approximation of the curve as the osculating circle. This assumes that closed curves are available.

Kahl and Heyden [14] consider the special case when four corresponding conics are available in two views with unknown intrinsic parameters. In this approach, each pair of corresponding conics provides a pair of tangencies and therefore two constraints. Four pairs of conics are needed. If the intrinsic parameters are available, then the absolute conic is known giving two constraints on the epipolar geometry, so that only 3 conic correspondences are required. This approach is only applied to synthetic data which shows the scheme to be extremely sensitive even when a large number of conics (50) is used. Kaminski and Shashua [15] extended this work to general algebraic curves viewed in multiple uncalibrated views. Specifically, they extend Kruppa's equations to describe the epipolar constraint of two projections of a general algebraic curve. The drawback of this approach is that algebraic curves are restrictive.

Sinha *et. al.* [21] consider a special configuration where multiple static cameras view a moving object. Since the epipolar geometry between any pair of cameras is fixed, each hypothesized pair of epipoles representing a point in 4D is then probed for a pair of epipolar tangencies across video frames. Specifically, two pairs of tangencies in one frame in time and a single pair of tangencies in another frame provide a constraint in that they must all intersect in the same point. This allows for an estimation of epipolar geometry for each pair of cameras, which are put together for refinement using bundle adjustment, providing intrinsic parameters and relative pose. This approach, however, is restrictive in assuming well-segmentable silhouettes.

We should briefly mention the classic results that three 2D-3D point correspondences are required to determine camera pose [7], in a procedure known as *camera resectioning* in the photogrammetry literature (and by Hartley and Zisserman [11]), also known as *camera calibration* when this is used with the purpose of obtaining the intrinsic parameter matrix $\mathcal{K}_{im}$, where the camera pose relative to the calibration jig is not of interest. This is also related to the perspective n-point problem (PnP) originally introduced in [7] which can be stated as the recovery of the camera pose from n corresponding 3D-2D point pairs [12] or alternatively of depths [9].

Notation: Consider a sequence of n 3D points $(\boldsymbol{\Gamma}_1^w, \boldsymbol{\Gamma}_2^w, \ldots, \boldsymbol{\Gamma}_n^w)$, described in the world coordinate system and their corresponding projected image points $(\gamma_1, \gamma_2, \ldots, \gamma_n)$ described as points in the 3D camera coordinate system. Let the rotation $\mathcal{R}$ and translation $\mathcal{T}$ relate the camera and world coordinate systems through

$$\boldsymbol{\Gamma} = \mathcal{R}\boldsymbol{\Gamma}^w + \mathcal{T}, \tag{2.3}$$

where $\boldsymbol{\Gamma}$ and $\boldsymbol{\Gamma}^w$ are the coordinates of a point in the camera and world coordinate systems, respectively. Let $(\rho_1, \rho_2, \ldots, \rho_n)$ be the depth defined by

$$\boldsymbol{\Gamma}_i = \rho_i \gamma_i, \qquad i = 1, \ldots, n. \tag{2.4}$$

In general we assume that each point γ_i is a sample from an image curve $\gamma_i(s_i)$ which is the projection of a space curve $\boldsymbol{\Gamma}_i(S_i)$, where s_i and S_i are arclengths along the image and space curves, resp.

The direct solution to P3P, also known as the *triangle pose problem*, given in 1841 [8], equates the sides of the triangle formed by the three points with those of the vectors in the camera domain, *i.e.*,

$$\begin{cases} \|\rho_1\gamma_1 - \rho_2\gamma_2\|^2 = \|\boldsymbol{\Gamma}_1^w - \boldsymbol{\Gamma}_2^w\|^2 \\ \|\rho_2\gamma_2 - \rho_3\gamma_3\|^2 = \|\boldsymbol{\Gamma}_2^w - \boldsymbol{\Gamma}_3^w\|^2 \\ \|\rho_3\gamma_3 - \rho_1\gamma_1\|^2 = \|\boldsymbol{\Gamma}_3^w - \boldsymbol{\Gamma}_1^w\|^2 \end{cases} \tag{2.5}$$

This gives a system of three quadratics (conics) in unknowns ρ_1, ρ_2, and ρ_3. Following traditional methods going back to the German mathematician Grunert in 1841 [8] and later Finsterwalder in 1937 [6], by factoring out one depth, say ρ_1, this can be reduced to a system of two quadratics in two unknowns – depth ratios $\frac{\rho_2}{\rho_1}$ and $\frac{\rho_3}{\rho_1}$. Grunert further reduced this to a single quartic equation and Finsterwalder proposed an analytic solution.

Table 1. The number of 3D–2D point correspondences needed to solve for camera pose and intrinsic parameters

Case	Unknowns	Min. # of Point Corresp.	Min. # of Pt-Tgt Corresp.
Calibrated ($\mathcal{K}_{im}$ known)	Camera pose $\mathcal{R}$, $\mathcal{T}$	3	2 (this paper)
Focal length unknown	Pose $\mathcal{R}$, $\mathcal{T}$ and f	4	3 (conjecture)
Uncalibrated ($\mathcal{K}_{im}$ unknown)	Camera model $\mathcal{K}_{im}$, $\mathcal{R}$, $\mathcal{T}$	6	4 (conjecture)

In general, the camera resectioning problem can be solved using **three** 3D $\leftrightarrow$ 2D point correspondences when the intrinsic parameters are known, and **six** points when the intrinsic parameters are not known. It can be solved using **four** point correspondences when only the focal length is unknown, but all the other intrinsic parameters are known [3], Table 1. We now show that when intrinsic parameters are known, **only a pair of point-tangent correspondences are required to estimate camera pose.** We conjecture that future work will show that 3 and 4 points, respectively, are required for the other two cases, Table 1. This would represent a significant reduction for a RANSAC-based computation.

3 Determining Camera Pose from a Pair of 3D–2D Point-Tangent Correspondences

Theorem 1. *Given a pair of 3D point-tangents* $\{(\boldsymbol{\Gamma}_1^w, \boldsymbol{T}_1^w), (\boldsymbol{\Gamma}_2^w, \boldsymbol{T}_2^w)\}$ *described in a world coordinate system and their corresponding perspective projections, the 2D point-tangents* $(\gamma_1, \boldsymbol{t}_1)$, $(\gamma_2, \boldsymbol{t}_2)$, *the pose of the camera* $\mathcal{R}$, $\mathcal{T}$ *relative to the world coordinate system defined by* $\boldsymbol{\Gamma} = \mathcal{R}\boldsymbol{\Gamma}^w + \mathcal{T}$ *can be solved up to a finite number of solutions*[2], *by solving the system*

$$\begin{cases} \gamma_1^\top \gamma_1 \rho_1^2 - 2\gamma_1^\top \gamma_2 \rho_1 \rho_2 + \gamma_2^\top \gamma_2 \rho_2^2 = \|\boldsymbol{\Gamma}_1^w - \boldsymbol{\Gamma}_2^w\|^2, \\ Q(\rho_1, \rho_2) = 0, \end{cases} \tag{3.1}$$

[2] assuming that the intrinsic parameters $\mathcal{K}_{im}$ are known

where $\mathcal{R}\boldsymbol{\Gamma}_1^w + \mathcal{T} = \boldsymbol{\Gamma}_1 = \rho_1\gamma_1$ *and* $\mathcal{R}\boldsymbol{\Gamma}_2^w + \mathcal{T} = \boldsymbol{\Gamma}_2 = \rho_2\gamma_2$, *and* $Q(\rho_1, \rho_2)$ *is an eight degree polynomial. This then solves for* $\mathcal{R}$ *and* $\mathcal{T}$ *as*

$$\begin{cases} \mathcal{R} = \left[(\boldsymbol{\Gamma}_1^w - \boldsymbol{\Gamma}_2^w)\ \boldsymbol{T}_1^w\ \boldsymbol{T}_2^w\right]^{-1} \cdot \\ \quad \left[\rho_1\gamma_1 - \rho_2\gamma_2\ \rho_1\frac{g_1}{G_1}\boldsymbol{t}_1 + \frac{\rho_1'}{G_1}\gamma_1\ \rho_2\frac{g_2}{G_2}\boldsymbol{t}_2 + \frac{\rho_2'}{G_2}\gamma_2\right] \\ \mathcal{T} = \rho_1\gamma_1 - \mathcal{R}\boldsymbol{\Gamma}_1^w, \end{cases}$$

where expressions for four auxiliary variables $\frac{g_1}{G_1}$ *and* $\frac{g_2}{G_2}$, *the ratio of speeds in the image and along the tangents, and* ρ_1 *and* ρ_2 *are available.*

Proof. We take the 2D-3D point-tangents as samples along 2D-3D curves, respectively, where the speed of parametrization along the image curves are g_1 and g_2 and along the space curves G_1 and G_2. The proof proceeds by *(i)* writing the projection equations for each point and its derivatives in the simplest form involving $\mathcal{R}$, $\mathcal{T}$, depths ρ_1 and ρ_2, depth derivatives ρ_1' and ρ_2', and speed of parametrizations G_1 and G_2, respectively; *(ii)* eliminating the translation $\mathcal{T}$ by subtracting point equations; *(iii)* eliminating $\mathcal{R}$ using dot products among equations. This gives six equations in six unknowns: $(\rho_1, \rho_2, \rho_1\frac{g_1}{G_1}, \rho_2\frac{g_2}{G_2}, \frac{\rho_1'}{G_1}, \frac{\rho_2'}{G_2})$; *(iv)* eliminating the unknowns ρ_1' and ρ_2' gives four quadratic equations in four unknowns: $(\rho_1, \rho_2, \rho_1\frac{g_1}{G_1}, \rho_2\frac{g_2}{G_2})$. Three of these quadratics can be written in the form:

$$\begin{cases} Ax_1^2 + Bx_1 + C = 0 & (3.2) \\ Ex_2^2 + Fx_2 + G = 0 & (3.3) \\ H + Jx_1 + Kx_2 + Lx_1x_2 = 0, & (3.4) \end{cases}$$

where $x_1 = \rho_1\frac{g_1}{G_1}$ and $x_2 = \rho_2\frac{g_2}{G_2}$ and where A through L are only functions of the two unknowns ρ_1 and ρ_2. Now, Eq. 3.4 represents a rectangular hyperbola, Fig. 6, while Eqs. 3.2 and 3.3 vertical and horizontal lines in the (x_1, x_2) space. Fig. 6 illustrates that only one solution is possible which is then analytically written in terms of variables A–L (not shown here). This allows expressing $\rho_1\frac{g_1}{G_1}$ and $\rho_2\frac{g_2}{G_2}$ in terms of ρ_1 and ρ_2 – a degree 16 polynomial – but this is in fact divisible by $\rho_1^4\rho_2^4$, leaving a polynomial Q of degree 8. Furthermore, we find that $Q(-\rho_1, -\rho_2) = Q(\rho_1, \rho_2)$, using the symmetry of the original equations. This, together with the unused equation (the remaining one of four) gives the system 3.1. The detailed proof is given in the supplementary material.

Proposition 1. *The algebraic solutions to the system* (3.1) *of Theorem 1 are also required to satisfy the following inequalities arising from imaging and other requirements enforced by*

$$\rho_1 > 0,\ \rho_2 > 0 \tag{3.5}$$

$$\frac{g_1}{G_1} > 0,\ \frac{g_2}{G_2} > 0 \tag{3.6}$$

$$\frac{\det[\rho_1\gamma_1 - \rho_2\gamma_2\ \ \rho_1\frac{g_1}{G_1}\boldsymbol{t}_1 + \frac{\rho_1'}{G_1}\gamma_1\ \ \rho_2\frac{g_2}{G_2}\boldsymbol{t}_2 + \frac{\rho_2'}{G_2}\gamma_2]}{\det\left[\boldsymbol{\Gamma}_1^w - \boldsymbol{\Gamma}_2^w\ \boldsymbol{T}_1^w\ \boldsymbol{T}_2^w\right]} > 0. \tag{3.7}$$

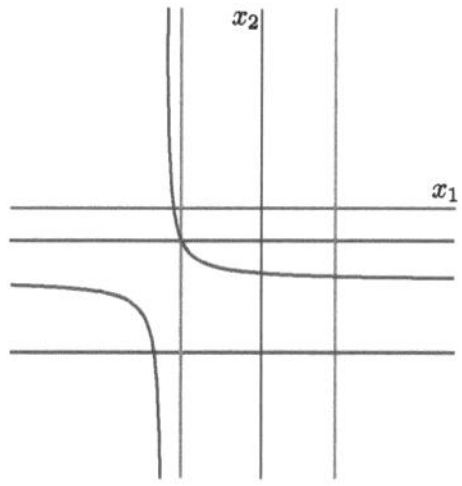

Fig. 6. Diagram of the mutual intersection of Equations 3.2–3.4 in the x_1–x_2 plane

Proof. There are multiple solutions for ρ_1 and ρ_2 in Eq. 3.1. Observe that if $\rho_1, \rho_2, \mathcal{R}, \mathcal{T}$ are a solution, then so are $-\rho_1$, $-\rho_2$, $-\mathcal{R}$, and $-\mathcal{T}$. Only one of these two solutions are valid, as the camera geometry enforces positive depth, $\rho_1 > 0$ and $\rho_2 > 0$; solutions are sought only in the top right quadrant of the ρ_1–ρ_2 space. In fact, the imaging geometry further restricts the points to lie in front of the camera.

Second, observe that the matrix $\mathcal{R}$ can only be a rotation matrix if it has determinant $+1$ and is a reflection if it has determinant -1. Using (3.2), $\det(\mathcal{R})$ can be written as

$$\det \mathcal{R} = \frac{\det \left[\rho_1 \boldsymbol{\gamma}_1 - \rho_2 \boldsymbol{\gamma}_2 \;\; \rho_1 \frac{g_1}{G_1} \boldsymbol{t}_1 + \frac{\rho_1'}{G_1} \boldsymbol{\gamma}_1 \;\; \rho_2 \frac{g_2}{G_2} \boldsymbol{t}_2 + \frac{\rho_2'}{G_2} \boldsymbol{\gamma}_2 \right]}{\det \left[\boldsymbol{\Gamma}_1^w - \boldsymbol{\Gamma}_2^w \;\; \boldsymbol{T}_1^w \;\; \boldsymbol{T}_2^w \right]}.$$

Finally, the space curve tangent $\boldsymbol{T}$ and the image curve tangent $\boldsymbol{t}$ must point in the same direction: $\boldsymbol{T} \cdot \boldsymbol{t} > 0$, or, as in the supplementary material, $\frac{g_1}{G_1} > 0$ and $\frac{g_2}{G_2} > 0$.

4 A Practical Approach to Computing a Solution

Equations 3.1 can be viewed as the intersection of two curves in the $\rho_1 - \rho_2$ space. Since one of the curves to be intersected is shown to be an ellipse, it is possible to parametrize it by a bracketed parameter and then look for intersections with the second curve which is of degree 8. This gives a higher-order polynomial in a *single* unknown which can be solved more readily than simultaneously solving the two equations of degree 2 and 8.

Proposition 2. *Solutions ρ_1 and ρ_2 to the quadratic equation in* (3.1) *can be parametrized as*

$$\begin{cases} \rho_1(t) = \dfrac{2\alpha t \cos\theta + \beta(1-t^2)\sin\theta}{1+t^2} \\ \rho_2(t) = \dfrac{-2\alpha t \sin\theta + \beta(1-t^2)\cos\theta}{1+t^2}, \end{cases} \qquad -1 \le t \le 1$$

where

$$\tan(2\theta) = \frac{2(1+\boldsymbol{\gamma}_1^\top \boldsymbol{\gamma}_2)}{\boldsymbol{\gamma}_1^\top \boldsymbol{\gamma}_1 - \boldsymbol{\gamma}_2^\top \boldsymbol{\gamma}_2}, \qquad 0 \le 2\theta \le \pi,$$

and

$$\alpha = \frac{\sqrt{2}\|\boldsymbol{r}_1^w - \boldsymbol{r}_2^w\|}{\sqrt{(\gamma_1^\top\gamma_1 + \gamma_2^\top\gamma_2) + (\gamma_1^\top\gamma_1 - \gamma_2^\top\gamma_2)\cos(2\theta) + 2\gamma_1^\top\gamma_2\sin(2\theta)}}, \qquad \alpha > 0,$$

$$\beta = \frac{\sqrt{2}\|\boldsymbol{r}_1^w - \boldsymbol{r}_2^w\|}{\sqrt{(\gamma_1^\top\gamma_1 + \gamma_2^\top\gamma_2) - (\gamma_1^\top\gamma_1 - \gamma_2^\top\gamma_2)\cos(2\theta) - 2\gamma_1^\top\gamma_2\sin(2\theta)}}, \qquad \beta > 0.$$

Proof. An ellipse centered at the origin with semi-axes of lengths $\alpha > 0$ and $\beta > 0$ and parallel to the coordinates x and y can be parametrized as

$$x = \frac{2t}{1+t^2}\alpha, \quad y = \frac{(1-t^2)}{1+t^2}\beta, \qquad t \in (-\infty, \infty), \tag{4.1}$$

with ellipse vertices identified at $t = -1$, 0, 1 and ∞, as shown in Figure 7. For a general ellipse centered at the origin, the coordinates must be multiplied with the rotation matrix for angle θ, obtaining

$$\begin{cases} \rho_1 = \dfrac{2\alpha t\cos\theta + \beta(1-t^2)\sin\theta}{1+t^2} \\ \rho_2 = \dfrac{-2\alpha t\sin\theta + \beta(1-t^2)\cos\theta}{1+t^2}. \end{cases} \qquad -1 \le t \le 1$$

Figure 7 illustrates this parametrization. Notice that the range of values of t we need to consider certainly lies in $[-1, 1]$ and in fact in a smaller interval where $\rho_1 > 0$ and $\rho_2 > 0$. Note that t and $-\frac{1}{t}$ correspond to opposite points on the ellipse.

The parameters α, β, and θ for the ellipse in (3.1) can then be found by substitution of ρ_1 and ρ_2, details of which are found in the supplementary material.

Both equations in (3.1) are symmetric with respect to the origin in the (ρ_1, ρ_2)-plane and the curves will intersect in at most $2 \times 8 = 16$ real points, at most 8 of which will be in the positive quadrant, as we in fact require $\rho_1 > 0$ and $\rho_2 > 0$.

The parametrization of the ellipse given in Proposition 2 allows us to reduce the two Equations 3.1 to a single polynomial equation in t. Substituting for ρ_1, ρ_2 in terms of t

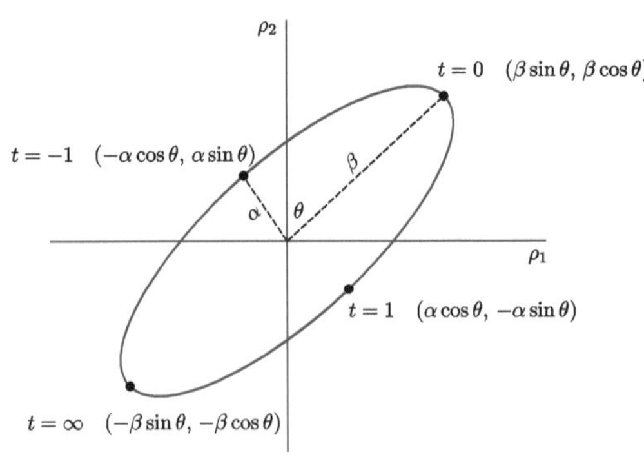

Fig. 7. Diagram illustrating a parametrization of the ellipse by a parameter t

into $Q = 0$ gives an equation in t for which, in fact, all the denominators are $(1+t^2)^{12}$, so that these can be cleared leaving a polynomial in $\tilde{Q}(t)$ of degree 16. The symmetry with respect to the origin in the (ρ_1, ρ_2)-plane becomes, in terms of t, a symmetry with respect to the substitution $t \to -1/t$, which gives diametrically opposite points of the ellipse. This implies that $\tilde{Q}$ has the special form

$$\tilde{Q}(t) = q_0 + q_1 t + q_2 t^2 + \cdots + q_{16} t^{16}, \tag{4.2}$$

where $q_i = -q_{16-i}$ for i odd. At most 8 solutions will lie in the range $-1 < t \leq 1$, and indeed we are only interested in solutions which make $\rho_1 > 0$ and $\rho_2 > 0$.

5 Experiments

We use two sets of experiments to probe camera pose recovery using 2D-3D point-tangent correspondences. First, we use a set of synthetically generated 3D curves consisting of a variety of curves (helices, parabolas, ellipses, straight lines, and saddle curves), as shown in Figure 8. Second, we use realistic data.

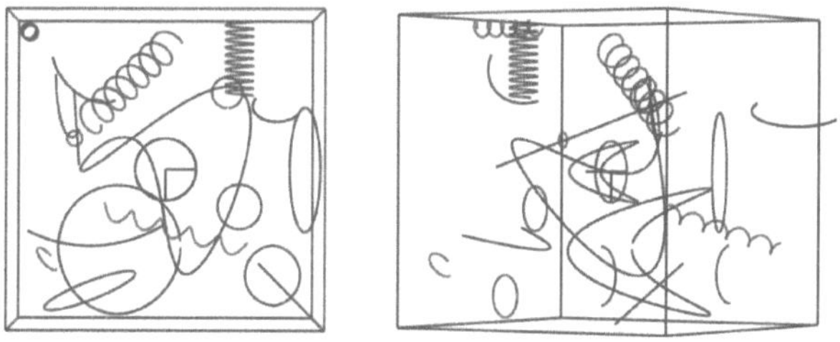

Fig. 8. Sample views of the synthetic dataset. Real datasets have also been used in our experiments, reported in further detail in the **supplemental material.**

The synthetic 3D curves of Figure 8 are densely sampled and projected to a single 500×400 view, and their location and tangent orientation are perturbed to simulate measurement noise in the range of $0 - 2$ pixels in location and $0 - 10°$ in orientation. Our expectation in practice using the publically available edge detector [22] is that the edges can be found with subpixel accuracy and edge orientations are accurate to less than $5°$.

In order to simulate the intended application, pairs of 2D-3D point-tangent correspondences are selected in a RANSAC procedure from among 1000 veridical ones, to which 50% random spurious correspondences were added. The practical method discussed in Section 4 is used to determine the pose of the camera $(\mathcal{R}, \mathcal{T})$ inside the RANSAC loop. Each step takes $90ms$ in Matlab on a standard 2GHz dual-core laptop. What is most significant, however, is that only 17 runs are sufficient to get 99% probability of hitting an outlier-free correspondence pair, or 32 runs for 99.99% probability. In practice more runs can easily be used depending on computational requirements. To assess the output of the algorithm, we could have measured the error of the estimated pose compared to the ground truth pose. However, what is more meaningful is the impact of the measured pose on the *measured* reprojection error, as commonly used in the field to validate the output of RANSAC-based estimation. Since this is a controlled experiment, we measure final reprojection error not just to the inlier set, but to the entire pool of 1000 true correspondences. In practice, a bundle-adjustment would be run to refine the pose estimate using all inliers, but we chose to report the raw errors without nonlinear least-squares refinement. The distribution of reprojection error is plotted for various levels of measurement noise, Figure 9. These plots show that the relative camera pose can be effectively determined for a viable range of measurement errors, specially since these results are typically optimized in practice through bundle adjustment. Additional information can be found in the supplemental material.

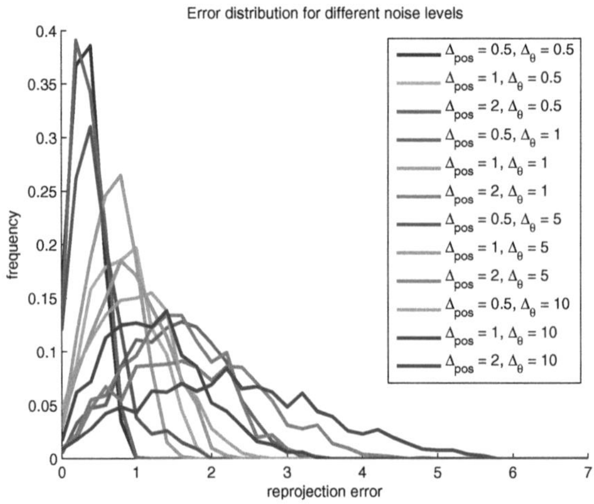

Fig. 9. Distributions of reprojection error for synthetic data without bundle adjustment, for increasing levels of positional and tangential perturbation in the measurements. **Additional results are reported in the supplemental material.**

Second, we use data from a real sequence, the "Capitol sequence", which is a set of 256 frames covering a 90° helicopter fly-by from the Rhode Island State Capitol, Figure 2, using a High-Definition camera (1280 × 720). Intrinsic parameters were initialized using the Matlab Calibration toolbox from J. Bouguet (future extension of this work would allow for an estimation of intrinsic parameters as well). The camera parameters were obtained by running Bundler [1] essentially out-of-the-box, with calibration accuracy of $1.3px$. In this setup, a pair of fully calibrated views are used to reconstruct a 3D cloud of 30 edges from manual correspondences. Pairs of matches from 3D edges to observed edges in novel views are used with RANSAC to compute the camera pose with respect to the frame of the 3D points, and measure reprojection error. One can then either use multiple pairs or use bundle adjustment to improve the reprojection error resulting from our initial computation of relative pose. Figure 10 shows the reprojection error distribution of our method for a single point-tangent pair after RANSAC, before and after running bundle-adjustment, versus the dataset camera from bundler (which is

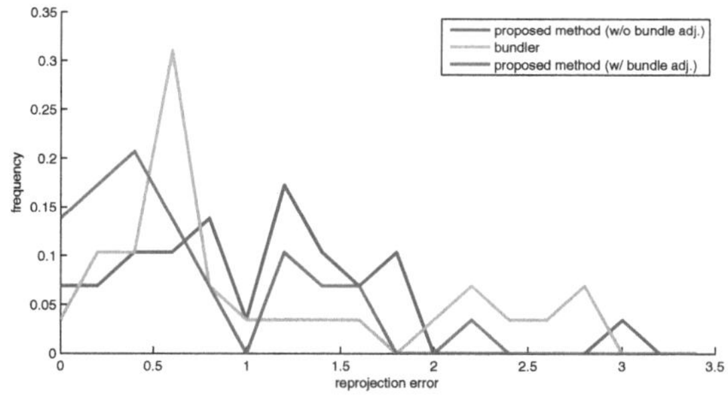

Fig. 10. The reprojection error distribution for real data (Capitol sequence) using only two point-tangents, before and after bundle adjustment. **Additional results are reported in the supplemental material.**

bundle-adjusted), for the Capitol sequence. The proposed approach achieved an average error of $1.1px$ and $0.76px$ before and after a metric bundle adjustment, respectively, as compared to $1.3px$ from Bundler. Additional information and results can be found in the supplemental material.

6 Future Directions

The paper can be extended to consider the case when intrinsic parameters are unknown. Table 1 conjectures that four pairs of corresponding 3D-2D point-tangents are sufficient to solve this problem. Also, we have been working on the problem of determining trinocular relative pose from corresponding point-tangents across 3 views. We conjecture that three triplets of correspondences among the views are sufficient to establish relative pose. This would allow for a complete curve-based structure from motion system starting from a set of images without any initial calibration.

Acknowledgments. The support of NSF grant 1116140, CNPq/Brazil proc. 200875/2004-3, FAPERJ/Brazil E26/112.082/2011, E26/190.180/2010, and the UERJ visiting professor grant are gratefully acknowledged.

References

1. Agarwal, S., Snavely, N., Simon, I., Seitz, S.M., Szeliski, R.: Building Rome in a day. In: ICCV 2009 (2009)
2. Ayache, N., Lustman, L.: Fast and reliable passive trinocular stereovision. In: ICCV 1987 (1987)
3. Bujnak, M., Kukelova, Z., Pajdla, T.: A general solution to the p4p problem for camera with unknown focal length. In: CVPR 2008 (2008)
4. Fabbri, R., Kimia, B.B.: High-Order Differential Geometry of Curves for Multiview Reconstruction and Matching. In: Rangarajan, A., Vemuri, B.C., Yuille, A.L. (eds.) EMMCVPR 2005. LNCS, vol. 3757, pp. 645–660. Springer, Heidelberg (2005)
5. Fabbri, R., Kimia, B.B.: 3D curve sketch: Flexible curve-based stereo reconstruction and calibration. In: CVPR 2010 (2010)

6. Finsterwalder, S., Scheufele, W.: Das ruckwartseinschneiden im raum. Sebastian Finsterwalder zum 75, 86–100 (1937)
7. Fischler, M.A., Bolles, R.C.: Random sample consensus: a paradigm for model fitting with applications to image analysis and automated cartography. Commun. ACM 24(6), 381–395 (1981)
8. Grunert, J.A.: Das pothenotische problem in erweiterter gestalt nebst Über seine anwendungen in der geodäsie. Archiv der für Mathematik and Physik 1, 238–248 (1841)
9. Haralick, R.M., Lee, C.-N., Ottenberg, K., Nölle, M.: Review and analysis of solutions of the three point perspective pose estimation problem. IJCV 13(3), 331–356 (1994)
10. Harris, C., Stephens, M.: A combined edge and corner detector. In: Alvey Vision Conference (1988)
11. Hartley, R., Zisserman, A.: Multiple View Geometry in Computer Vision. Cambridge University Press (2000)
12. Horaud, R., Conio, B., Leboulleux, O., Lacolle, B.: An analytic solution for the p4p problem. CVGIP 47(1), 33–44 (1989)
13. Hu, Z.Y., Wu, F.C.: A note on the number of solutions of the noncoplanar p4p problem. PAMI 24(4), 550–555 (2002)
14. Kahl, F., Heyden, A.: Using conic correspondence in two images to estimate the epipolar geometry. In: ICCV 1998 (1998)
15. Kaminski, J.Y., Shashua, A.: Multiple view geometry of general algebraic curves. IJCV 56(3), 195–219 (2004)
16. Longuet-Higgins, H.C.: A computer algorithm for reconstructing a scene from two projections. Nature 293, 133–135 (1981)
17. Lowe, D.G.: Distinctive image features from scale-invariant keypoints. IJCV 60(2), 91–110 (2004)
18. Moreels, P., Perona, P.: Evaluation of features detectors and descriptors based on 3D objects. IJCV 73(3), 263–284 (2007)
19. Porrill, J., Pollard, S.: Curve matching and stereo calibration. IVC 9(1), 45–50 (1991)
20. Robert, L., Faugeras, O.D.: Curve-based stereo: figural continuity and curvature. In: CVPR 1991 (1991)
21. Sinha, S.N., Pollefeys, M., McMillan, L.: Camera network calibration from dynamic silhouettes. In: CVPR 2004 (2004)
22. Tamrakar, A., Kimia, B.B.: No grouping left behind: From edges to curve fragments. In: ICCV 2007 (2007)

Beyond Feature Points: Structured Prediction for Monocular Non-rigid 3D Reconstruction

Mathieu Salzmann[1] and Raquel Urtasun[2]

[1] NICTA
[2] TTI Chicago

Abstract. Existing approaches to non-rigid 3D reconstruction either are specifically designed for feature point correspondences, or require a good shape initialization to exploit more complex image likelihoods. In this paper, we formulate reconstruction as inference in a graphical model, where the variables encode the rotations and translations of the facets of a surface mesh. This lets us exploit complex likelihoods even in the absence of a good initialization. In contrast to existing approaches that set the weights of the likelihood terms manually, our formulation allows us to learn them from as few as a single training example. To improve efficiency, we combine our structured prediction formalism with a gradient-based scheme. Our experiments show that our approach yields tremendous improvement over state-of-the-art gradient-based methods.

1 Introduction

Monocular non-rigid surface reconstruction has received increasing attention in recent years. Existing approaches to tackling this problem can be classified into (i) non-rigid structure-from-motion techniques [4,27,8] that exploit the availability of multiple images of different deformations to reconstruct both 3D points and camera motion, and (ii) template-based methods [23,18,5] that rely on a reference image with known 3D shape to perform reconstruction from a single additional image of the deformed surface. In most cases, the aforementioned methods are specifically designed to handle feature point correspondences, and as a consequence, cannot make use of richer image information, such as full surface texture, or surface boundaries. More importantly, these methods become unsuitable when too few feature points can be reliably detected and matched.

Several attempts have been proposed to leverage more complex image likelihoods [20,21]. However, the resulting methods rely on gradient-based optimization schemes that can easily get trapped in the many local maxima of these complex, non-smooth likelihoods. As a consequence, these methods have only been used either for frame-to-frame tracking, where the previous frame provides a good initialization [20], or when large amounts of training data are available to learn a discriminative predictor that produces a good initialization [21].

In contrast, in this paper we propose to employ a global optimization framework to exploit complex image likelihoods for monocular non-rigid reconstruction. As our optimization is more global than gradient-based methods, it is also more robust to local maxima, thus yielding accurate reconstructions even in the

A. Fitzgibbon et al. (Eds.): ECCV 2012, Part IV, LNCS 7575, pp. 245–259, 2012.

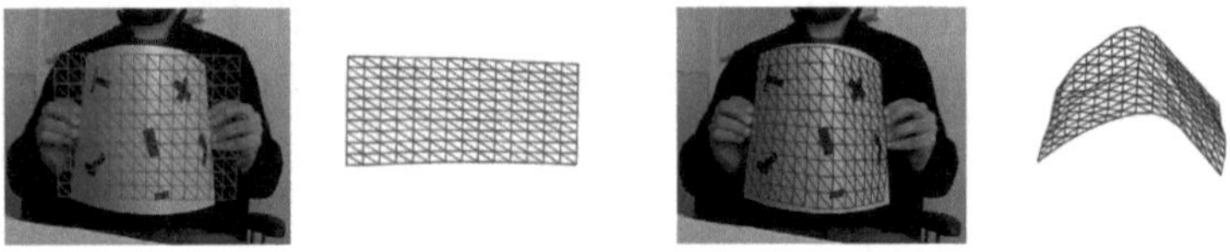

Fig. 1. Reconstructing a piece of cardboard from a single input image. (Left) Reconstruction obtained with a gradient-based method. (Right) Our reconstruction.

absence of a good initialization, as illustrated in Fig. 1. More specifically, we represent a surface as a triangulated mesh and formulate the 3D reconstruction problem as inference in a conditional Markov random field (CRF), where the variables to recover are the rotations and translations of the individual mesh facets. To handle such continuous variables, we adopt particle convex belief propagation [16] as our inference algorithm: We iteratively draw random samples around the current solution for each variable, compute the MAP estimate of the discrete CRF defined by these samples using convex belief propagation [12], and update the current solution with this MAP estimate. This strategy lets us effectively explore the 3D shape space even when no good initialization is provided. Furthermore, given very few training pairs of images and 3D shapes, we employ a structured prediction learning algorithm [11] to find the weights of the individual terms in the likelihood, thus avoiding having to set them manually as is traditionally done in 3D reconstruction algorithms (e.g., [20,18,21,5]).

To reduce the computational burden of performing global optimization on large graphs (i.e., fine meshes), we introduce a coarse-to-fine scheme that combines the advantages of global optimization and gradient-based approaches. Our strategy consists in first performing structured prediction with a coarse mesh, and then using the coarse solution as initialization to a gradient-based method. Since our coarse structured prediction yields a good initial shape estimate, this strategy has proven very effective in practice. We demonstrate the benefits of our approach in a variety of scenarios ranging from well-textured surfaces to very poorly-textured ones. Comparison against gradient-based techniques clearly shows that our approach is much better adapted to 3D reconstruction from a single image than state-of-the-art methods.

2 Related Work

Monocular non-rigid 3D shape recovery is a very challenging problem with many ambiguities due to noisy measurements, as well as to the wide range of deformations that objects may undergo. Throughout the years, approaches to tackling this problem have evolved, starting from the early methods that attempted to model the physical behavior of deformable surfaces [13,17,14,15], to the more recent ones that tried to learn this behavior from data [6,3].

In recent years, two main trends have emerged for non-rigid 3D shape recovery: Non-rigid structure-from-motion (NRSfM) and template-based reconstruction. NRSfM techniques [4,27,25,1,8] work under the assumption that multiple images of the surface undergoing different deformations are available. These methods try to recover the 3D locations of feature points, as well as the camera motion. As in our approach, [24] also reconstructs individual triangles, but in the NRSfM setting. [19] utilizes discrete optimization for NRSfM. However, their discrete problem is not directly for reconstruction purposes, but only to assign feature points to local patches. As opposed to NRSfM, template-based approaches [23,18,5] work with a single input image, but assume that the camera is calibrated and that a reference image with known surface shape is available. A successful shape prior in these methods is to encourage the surface to deform isometrically. Our work falls into the template-based category and exploits a similar isometry prior. However, whereas all the above-mentioned methods rely on feature points, our approach lets us exploit much richer image information.

Techniques that employ different sources of information, such as shading [26] or contours [10], have been developed. However, contour-based approaches are only applicable to a specific class of surfaces, and shape-from-shading methods make strong assumptions on the lighting conditions. More directly related to our approach are the methods of [20,21], where general image losses were also employed. However, due to the non-convexity of such losses and the use of a gradient-based method, [20] was only applied in a frame-to-frame tracking scenario. Furthermore, both techniques heavily rely on the availability of relatively large amounts of training data to learn either a deformation model [20], or a discriminative predictor to initialize a gradient-based method [21]. While we also exploit training data to learn the weights of the different terms in our likelihood, we require much fewer training examples. Furthermore, we utilize a global optimization method, which lets us reconstruct surfaces from individual images.

3 Structured Prediction for Non-rigid Surfaces

In this section, we introduce our surface parametrization and then present our structured prediction approach to non-rigid 3D reconstruction. Finally, we describe the gradient-based method used to refine the structured prediction results.

3.1 Surface Parametrization

We represent non-rigid surfaces as triangulated meshes, and, following a popular and effective trend [23,18,5], encourage the surface to deform isometrically by preserving the distances between neighboring mesh vertices. Furthermore, as our method falls into the template-based category, we assume that we are given a reference image in which the 3D shape of the surface is known.

Since the mesh already forms a graph, it might seem natural to use the 3D vertex positions as variables. However, some image likelihoods, such as template matching, are defined over a facet. Therefore, employing a parametrization in terms of 3D vertices will require 3-way potentials, i.e., terms that involve three variables. As the complexity of message passing inference in graphical models is

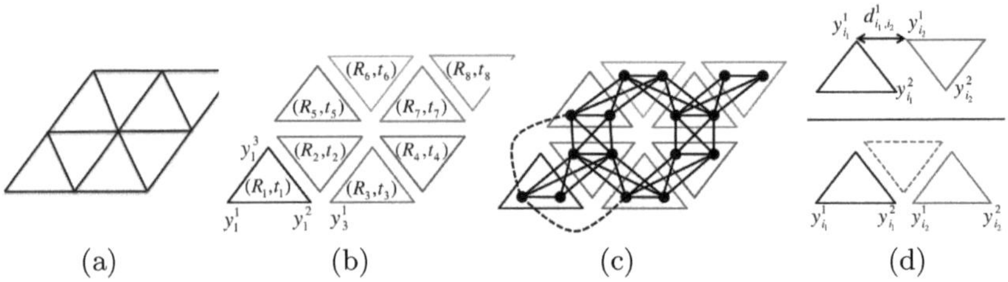

Fig. 2. Structured prediction with a mesh. (a) Triangulated mesh. (b) Parametrization in terms of facet rotations and translations. (c) Graphical model. Note that, to avoid clutter, only two longer range (dashed) edges are shown. (d) Illustration of the facet coherence potential (top) and the smoothness potential (bottom).

a function of the order of the potentials, as well as of the cardinality of the label set for each random variable, employing 3-way potentials is computationally prohibitive, thus making this parametrization unappealing. Instead, as illustrated in Fig. 2(a,b), we parametrize the surface in terms of the rotations and translations of the mesh facets, which, as shown below, only requires pairwise potentials.

More specifically, the 3D location of the kth vertex of facet i is given by

$$\mathbf{y}_i^k = \mathbf{R}_i(\tilde{\mathbf{y}}_i^k - \tilde{\mathbf{c}}_i) + \mathbf{t}_i \triangleq \mathbf{R}_i\bar{\mathbf{y}}_i^k + \mathbf{t}_i \ , \tag{1}$$

where $\mathbf{R}_i$ and $\mathbf{t}_i$ are the rotation matrix and translation of the facet, respectively, $\tilde{\mathbf{y}}_i^k$ is the location of the k^{th}vertex of facet i in the reference mesh, and $\tilde{\mathbf{c}}_i$ is the centroid of facet i in the reference mesh. We represent the rotation $\mathbf{R}_i$ in terms of a 3D vector of Euler angles $\boldsymbol{\theta}_i$. Note that other parameterizations, such as quaternions are also possible. The location of a 3D mesh vertex can then be obtained by averaging the above locations over all the facets that contain this vertex. Of course, this requires preventing the rotations and translations of these facets from disagreeing over the location of the shared vertex. As will be shown in the next section, this can be expressed as a pairwise potential.

3.2 Non-rigid 3D Reconstruction as Inference in a Graphical Model

Given our parametrization in terms of facet rotations and translations, we now describe our approach to non-rigid 3D reconstruction. We formulate monocular shape recovery as an inference problem in a CRF, where the random variables are continuous. The joint distribution over the random variables can be factorized into a product of non-negative potentials

$$p(\mathbf{z}) = p(\mathbf{R}, \mathbf{t}) = Z^{-1}\prod_i \psi_i(\mathbf{z}_i)\prod_\alpha \psi_\alpha(\mathbf{z}_\alpha) \ , \tag{2}$$

where $\mathbf{z} = (\mathbf{R}, \mathbf{t})$ is the set of all random variables, with $\mathbf{R}$ and $\mathbf{t}$ containing the rotations and translations for all facets, and Z is the partition function. The potentials $\psi_i(\mathbf{z}_i)$ and $\psi_\alpha(\mathbf{z}_\alpha)$ encode functions over single variables and groups of variables, respectively. Inference is performed by computing the MAP estimate

$$\mathbf{z}^* = \text{argmax}_\mathbf{z} \prod_i \psi_i(\mathbf{z}_i)\prod_\alpha \psi_\alpha(\mathbf{z}_\alpha) \ . \tag{3}$$

To solve our inference problem over continuous variables, we rely on particle convex belief propagation (PCBP) [16]. PCBP is an iterative algorithm that works as follows: Particles are sampled around the current solution for each random variable. These samples act as labels in a discrete CRF which is solved to convergence using convex belief propagation [12]. The current solution is then updated with the MAP estimate returned by convex BP. This process is repeated for a fixed number of iterations. In practice, we use the distributed message passing algorithm of [22] to solve the discrete CRF at each iteration.

Algorithm 1 depicts PCBP for our formulation of non-rigid 3D reconstruction. In the algorithm, we denote by $\hat{\mathbf{R}}_i$ and $\hat{\mathbf{t}}_i$ the discretized variables, which are grouped in the set $\hat{\mathbf{z}}$. At each iteration, to increase the accuracy of the reconstruction, we decrease the values of the standard deviations σ_r and σ_t of the Gaussian distributions from which the discretized random variables are drawn.

Algorithm 1. PCBP for non-rigid 3D reconstruction

Set N, η_r and η_t
Initialize $\mathbf{R}_i$ and $\mathbf{t}_i$ from the template mesh $\forall i$, as well as σ_r and σ_t
for $s = 1$ to #iters **do**
  Draw N random samples of Euler angles $\boldsymbol{\theta}_i^j \propto \mathcal{N}(0, \sigma_r)$, $\forall i$
  Compute the candidate discretized rotations $\hat{\mathbf{R}}_i^j = \mathbf{R}_i^j(\boldsymbol{\theta}_i^j)\mathbf{R}_i$, $\forall i, j$
  Draw N random samples of candidate discretized translations $\hat{\mathbf{t}}_i^j \propto \mathcal{N}(\mathbf{t}_i, \sigma_t)$, $\forall i$
  Solve the discrete CRF: $(\hat{\mathbf{R}}^*, \hat{\mathbf{t}}^*) = \text{argmax}_{\hat{\mathbf{z}}} \prod_i \psi_i(\hat{\mathbf{z}}_i) \prod_\alpha \psi_\alpha(\hat{\mathbf{z}}_\alpha)$
  Update $\mathbf{R}_i \leftarrow \hat{\mathbf{R}}_i^*$ and $\mathbf{t}_i \leftarrow \hat{\mathbf{t}}_i^*$, $\forall i$
  Update $\sigma_r \leftarrow \eta_r \sigma_r$ and $\sigma_t \leftarrow \eta_t \sigma_t$
end for

An artifact of using discretized variables with non-smooth potentials is that a solution around a local maximum might have a higher value than one around the global maximum. The iterative scheme will then re-sample around this relatively bad solution and, with decreasing σ_r and σ_t, potentially be driven away from the global maximum. To circumvent this issue, we introduce a scheme that keeps track of multiple solutions at each iteration of PCBP. Given all the discrete candidates for all the variables, we find an approximate MAP solution using convex BP. We then remove the labels corresponding to this solution and find an approximate solution to the MAP problem defined by the remaining labels. This can be done in an iterative manner, thus yielding M solutions around which we can then sample N/M values for the next iteration of PCBP. Note that even if we could solve the NP-hard discrete inference problem exactly, these solutions would not necessarily truly be the M best ones, since combinations of their labels are not considered as potential solutions (e.g., the second solution cannot contain labels used in the first solution). However, this allows for more variety in the candidate solutions, and the labels can potentially be combined at the next PCBP iteration. Note that other algorithms, such as [9,2], could also be used to generate candidate solutions. In the last iteration of PCBP, we only compute a single MAP estimate, which we take as our final reconstruction.

In the remainder of this section, we describe the different potentials that we used in our experiments. In particular, we define three types of image potentials to handle feature point correspondences, template matching and surface boundary likelihoods. These likelihoods are the ones typically used in gradient-based methods [20,21]. Additionally we employ two types of shape potentials encoding coherence of the facets and surface smoothness. Taken together, these potentials yield a graph such as the one depicted by Fig. 2(c). For clarity, we describe the potentials in the log domain, i.e., $w^T \phi = log(\psi)$. We define a weight for each type of potential, and as described later, learn the weights using [11].

Feature Point Correspondences: Although our main focus is to go beyond feature point correspondences, we show that our formulation also remains pairwise in this case. We make use of the template mesh to establish correspondences between a 3D point expressed in barycentric coordinates with respect to the facet it lies on and a 2D point in the input image. In the camera referential, the fact that a 3D point j on facet i reprojects at image location (u^j, v^j) can be written as

$$\mathbf{A} \sum_{k=1}^{3} b_j^k \mathbf{y}_i^k = \mathbf{A} \sum_{k=1}^{3} b_j^k \left(\mathbf{R}_i \bar{\mathbf{y}}_i^k + \mathbf{t}_i \right) = d^j \left(u^j \; v^j \; 1 \right)^T , \tag{4}$$

where b_j^k is the barycentric coordinate of point j with respect to the k^{th}vertex $\mathbf{y}_i^k$ of facet i to which the point belongs, $\mathbf{A}$ is the matrix of known internal camera parameters, and d^j is an unknown scalar encoding depth.

We define pairwise potentials $\phi^r_{\alpha_i}(\mathbf{R}_i, \mathbf{t}_i)$ by summing the negative reprojection errors of each detected feature point belonging to one particular facet. To this end, let us define the projection of point j on facet i as

$$\hat{u}^j(\mathbf{R}_i, \mathbf{t}_i) = \frac{\mathbf{A}_1 \sum_{k=1}^{3} b_j^k \left(\mathbf{R}_i \bar{\mathbf{y}}_i^k + \mathbf{t}_i \right)}{\mathbf{A}_3 \sum_{k=1}^{3} b_j^k \left(\mathbf{R}_i \bar{\mathbf{y}}_i^k + \mathbf{t}_i \right)} , \quad \hat{v}^j(\mathbf{R}_i, \mathbf{t}_i) = \frac{\mathbf{A}_2 \sum_{k=1}^{3} b_j^k \left(\mathbf{R}_i \bar{\mathbf{y}}_i^k + \mathbf{t}_i \right)}{\mathbf{A}_3 \sum_{k=1}^{3} b_j^k \left(\mathbf{R}_i \bar{\mathbf{y}}_i^k + \mathbf{t}_i \right)} , \tag{5}$$

where $\mathbf{A}_k$ is the kth row of $\mathbf{A}$. The potential for facet i can then be written as

$$\phi^r_{\alpha_i}(\mathbf{R}_i, \mathbf{t}_i) = - \sum_{j \in \mathcal{F}(i)} \left\| \left(\hat{u}^j(\mathbf{R}_i, \mathbf{t}_i) - u^j \; , \; \hat{v}^j(\mathbf{R}_i, \mathbf{t}_i) - v^j \right) \right\|_2^2 , \tag{6}$$

where $\mathcal{F}(i)$ is the set of feature points belonging to facet i. This potential is pairwise, as it is a function of the rotation and translation of a single facet.

Template Matching: For template matching, each facet in the reference mesh is treated as a template. We compute the normalized cross-correlation between the texture under the facet in the reference image and the texture under the deformed facet in the input image. This can be done by sampling the barycentric coordinates of the facet and retrieving the intensity values at the 2D image locations corresponding to the projected sampled 3D facet points. In our formalism, the intensity values for facet i can be stored in a vector $\mathbf{q}_i$, such that each element j is given by $\mathbf{q}_i^j = I\left(\hat{u}^j(\mathbf{R}_i, \mathbf{t}_i), \hat{v}^j(\mathbf{R}_i, \mathbf{t}_i)\right)$, where $I(u, v)$ is the intensity value at image location (u, v), and $(\hat{u}^j, \hat{v}^j)$ are the projections of the points at the sampled barycentric coordinates.

Let $\hat{\mathbf{q}}_i$ and $\tilde{\mathbf{q}}_i$ be the mean subtracted vectors of intensity values in the input image and in the reference image, respectively. A template matching potential for facet i can then be written as

$$\phi^t_{\alpha_i}(\mathbf{R}_i, \mathbf{t}_i) = (\hat{\mathbf{q}}_i^T \tilde{\mathbf{q}}_i) \left(\sum_j \left(\hat{\mathbf{q}}_i^j\right)^2 \sum_j \left(\tilde{\mathbf{q}}_i^j\right)^2 \right)^{-1/2} . \tag{7}$$

As for correspondences, this potential only depends on the rotation and translation of a single facet, and is therefore pairwise. Note that this potential truly depends on the locations of 3 vertices. Therefore, had we used vertex locations to parametrize our problem instead of facet rotations and translations, we would not be able to decompose this term in a sum of unary and pairwise potentials.

Surface Boundary: To account for object boundaries, we make use of the distance transform D of the edge image obtained from the input image with Canny's algorithm. D encodes the distance of each pixel to the closest edge, which has the advantage of being smoother than the edge image itself. We sample the barycentric coordinates of the boundary mesh edges, and project the resulting 3D points in D. Given the barycentric coordinates b_j^k of points sampled on an edge belonging to facet i, we can then write the edge potential

$$\phi^e_{\alpha_i}(\mathbf{R}_i, \mathbf{t}_i) = -D\big(\hat{u}^j(\mathbf{R}_i, \mathbf{t}_i), \hat{v}^j(\mathbf{R}_i, \mathbf{T}_i)\big) , \tag{8}$$

where $(\hat{u}^j, \hat{v}^j)$ are the projected sampled barycentric coordinates, which now only depend on the 2 vertices that define the mesh edge (i.e k ranges up to 2 in Eq. 5). Once again, this potential depends on a single facet, and is thus pairwise.

Facets Coherence: As mentioned in Section 3.1, optimizing the rotations and translations of the mesh facets independently may lead to disagreements over the location of the vertices shared by neighboring facets. As a consequence, 3D vertices belonging to multiple facets, computed by averaging the locations predicted by the facets, will be distant from the individual predictions. To prevent this, we include a potential that encourages facets sharing an edge to agree on the predictions of the two vertices defining the edge. Since this involves two facets, it may seem that the resulting potential will be of order 4 (i.e., 2 rotations and 2 translations). However, as shown below, our formulation has the advantage of decomposing the potential into a sum of unary and pairwise terms.

Let i_1 and i_2 be the indices of two facets sharing a mesh edge, as illustrated in Fig. 2(d). Let us denote by $\mathbf{y}^1_{i_1}$ and $\mathbf{y}^1_{i_2}$ the first pair of corresponding vertices in the two facets. The squared distance between these corresponding points can be written as

$$(d^1_{i_1,i_2})^2 = \left\|\mathbf{y}^1_{i_1} - \mathbf{y}^1_{i_2}\right\|_2^2 = \left\|\mathbf{R}_{i_1}\bar{\mathbf{y}}^1_{i_1} + \mathbf{t}_{i_1} - \mathbf{R}_{i_2}\bar{\mathbf{y}}^1_{i_2} - \mathbf{t}_{i_2}\right\|_2^2 . \tag{9}$$

By expanding the previous squared distance, we obtain

$$\begin{aligned}(d^1_{i_1,i_2})^2 = {} & \bar{\mathbf{y}}^{1^T}_{i_1}\mathbf{R}^T_{i_1}\mathbf{R}_{i_1}\bar{\mathbf{y}}^1_{i_1} + \mathbf{t}^T_{i_1}\mathbf{t}_{i_1} + \bar{\mathbf{y}}^{1^T}_{i_2}\mathbf{R}^T_{i_2}\mathbf{R}_{i_2}\bar{\mathbf{y}}^1_{i_2} + \mathbf{t}^T_{i_2}\mathbf{t}_{i_2} + 2\bar{\mathbf{y}}^{1^T}_{i_1}\mathbf{R}^T_{i_1}\mathbf{t}^1_{i_1} \\ & + 2\bar{\mathbf{y}}^{1^T}_{i_1}\mathbf{R}^T_{i_1}\mathbf{R}_{i_2}\bar{\mathbf{y}}^1_{i_2} + 2\bar{\mathbf{y}}^{1^T}_{i_1}\mathbf{R}^T_{i_1}\mathbf{t}_{i_2} + 2\mathbf{t}^T_{i_1}\mathbf{R}_{i_2}\bar{\mathbf{y}}^1_{i_2} + 2\mathbf{t}^T_{i_1}\mathbf{t}_{i_2} + 2\bar{\mathbf{y}}^{1^T}_{i_2}\mathbf{R}^T_{i_2}\mathbf{t}_{i_2} .\end{aligned} \tag{10}$$

Note that the first and third terms are constant due to the properties of rotation matrices. More importantly, note that all the terms are only functions of at most two variables. Therefore, the resulting potential obtained by summing the squared distances of both pairs of corresponding vertices, written as

$$\phi^c_{\alpha_{i_1,i_2}}(\mathbf{R}_{i_1}, \mathbf{t}_{i_1}, \mathbf{R}_{i_2}, \mathbf{t}_{i_2}) = -(d^1_{i_1,i_2})^2 - (d^2_{i_1,i_2})^2 \,, \tag{11}$$

is a sum of unary and pairwise terms.

Surface Smoothness: In addition to enforcing coherence of the facets, one might also want to encode some knowledge about the possible surface deformations. A classical example of this was introduced in the Active Contour Model [13], where the contour is encouraged to remain smooth by penalizing a quadratic function that approximates the sum of the square of the curvature along the contour. Following a similar idea, and assuming that the mesh forms a regular grid, we enforce smoothness by encouraging two aligned edges (i.e., horizontal or vertical edges in the grid) to remain straight.

Let i_1 and i_2 be the indices of two facets, each of which contains one of two aligned edges, as illustrated in Fig. 2(d). Furthermore, without loss of generality, let us assume that $\mathbf{y}^2_{i_1}$ and $\mathbf{y}^1_{i_2}$ correspond to the vertex shared by both facets. An energy encoding the squared curvature of these two edges can be written as

$$\begin{aligned} c^2_{i_1,i_2} &= \left\| -\mathbf{R}_{i_1}\bar{\mathbf{y}}^1_{i_1} - \mathbf{t}_{i_1} + \mathbf{R}_{i_1}\bar{\mathbf{y}}^2_{i_1} + \mathbf{t}_{i_1} + \mathbf{R}_{i_2}\bar{\mathbf{y}}^1_{i_2} + \mathbf{t}_{i_2} - \mathbf{R}_{i_2}\bar{\mathbf{y}}^2_{i_2} - \mathbf{t}_{i_2} \right\|^2_2 \\ &= \left\| -\mathbf{R}_{i_1}\bar{\mathbf{y}}^1_{i_1} + \mathbf{R}_{i_1}\bar{\mathbf{y}}^2_{i_1} + \mathbf{R}_{i_2}\bar{\mathbf{y}}^1_{i_2} - \mathbf{R}_{i_2}\bar{\mathbf{y}}^2_{i_2} \right\|^2_2 \,, \end{aligned} \tag{12}$$

where we computed the location of the vertex shared by the two edges as the average over both facet predictions. Note that the translation variables have cancelled each other out. As a consequence, it is obvious that this decomposes into a sum of terms that involve at most two variables. Therefore, we can write the smoothness potential

$$\phi^s_{\alpha_{i_1,i_2}}(\mathbf{R}_{i_1}, \mathbf{R}_{i_2}) = -c^2_{i_1,i_2} \,, \tag{13}$$

which is purely pairwise, since the unary terms involving the rotations become constant (i.e., as before, $\bar{\mathbf{y}}^{1^T}_{i_1} \mathbf{R}^T_{i_1} \mathbf{R}_{i_1} \bar{\mathbf{y}}^1_{i_1} = cst$).

Other shape regularizers have been used for 3D reconstruction and could possibly be incorporated into our formalism. However, as shown in our experiments, these general potentials are sufficient to perform accurate 3D reconstruction.

3.3 Learning the Potential Weights

Given a few training examples where both image and ground-truth 3D shape are available, structured prediction methods can also be used to learn the weights of the different potentials of interest. This is in contrast with most existing approaches to non-rigid 3D reconstruction where the weights are typically set manually. We rely on the family of structured prediction problems introduced in [11] to learn our weights. In particular, we make use of their CRF formulation with ℓ_2 regularization (i.e., following the notation of [11], $\epsilon = 1$ and $p = 2$). Since this formulation is designed for discrete variables, we draw N sample rotations and translations for each facet, and keep them fixed for the entire procedure.

In addition to the potentials defined above, learning the weights requires a loss function encoding the error of a configuration with respect to the ground-truth reconstruction. Here, we use a squared point-to-point distance. More specifically, for each facet i, the loss can be written as

$$\Delta(\mathbf{R}_i, \mathbf{t}_i) = \sum_{k=1}^{3} \left\| \mathbf{R}_i \bar{\mathbf{y}}_i^k + \mathbf{t}_i - \breve{\mathbf{y}}_i^k \right\|_2^2 , \tag{14}$$

where $\breve{\mathbf{y}}_i^k$ is the ground-truth location of the vertex corresponding to the kth vertex of facet i. It can easily be checked that this loss also consists of a sum of unary and pairwise terms. See [11] for more details on the learning method.

As shown in our experimental evaluation, only very few training examples are required to learn the potential weights. This is in contrast with reconstruction techniques that exploit learned deformation models, such as [20], which typically require many more training examples. This makes our approach more practical to deploy in general scenarios.

3.4 Shape Refinement with Gradient-Based Optimization

Performing PCBP on large graphs (i.e., fine meshes) can quickly become computationally prohibitive. To overcome this issue, we follow a simple coarse-to-fine strategy: We first compute an initial solution on a coarse mesh using the structured prediction approach described above, and then refine this solution using a gradient-based method. Since structured prediction provides us with a good initial shape estimate, a gradient-based method becomes very well suited. More specifically, we follow the gradient-based approach of [23] for inextensible surfaces, which directly optimizes the 3D locations of the mesh vertices. This approach was extended in [21] to handle more general image likelihoods than the reprojection error of feature points for which it was originally designed.

Let $\mathbf{y}$ be the $3N_v$-dimensional vector of mesh vertices, initialized with our subdivided coarse structured prediction. We refine the 3D surface shape by solving the optimization problem

$$\begin{aligned} \min_{\mathbf{y}} \; & - \sum_i w_i \phi'_i(\mathbf{y}) - \sum_\alpha w_\alpha \phi'_\alpha(\mathbf{y}) \\ \text{s. t. } & \|\mathbf{y}^j - \mathbf{y}^k\|_2^2 = l_{j,k}^2 \;\; \forall (j,k) \in \mathcal{E} , \end{aligned} \tag{15}$$

where $l_{j,k}$ is the known reference distance between vertices $\mathbf{y}^j$ and $\mathbf{y}^k$, and $\mathcal{E}$ is the set of mesh edges. ϕ'_i and ϕ'_α are the same potentials as for structured prediction, but expressed in terms of the mesh vertices.

Following [23,21], we obtain the solution to this optimization problem by iteratively linearizing the constraints and performing a few (i.e., 100 in practice) gradient descent steps in the null space of the linearized constraints. This scheme is carried out until convergence, or until a maximum number of iterations has been reached. More details on the overall procedure can be found in [23,21].

4 Experimental Evaluation

We demonstrate the effectiveness of our method in various scenarios including feature point correspondences, as well as more complex image likelihoods with well- and poorly-textured surfaces. For all our experiments, we ran 20 iterations of PCBP, and initialized $\sigma_r = \pi/8$ and $\sigma_t = 10$, with $\eta_r = \eta_t = 0.75$. We used $N = 100$ states, except for the real images where $N = 200$. For the first iteration, we used the reference shape as initialization, thus yielding identity rotation matrices and translations corresponding to the centroids of the facets. At each iteration, we kept either $M = 1$ or $M = 3$ solutions around which to re-sample. Corresponding results are denoted by Ours 1 Best and Ours 3 Best.

We compare our results against two baselines. The first one, later denoted by Shen09, corresponds to [23] initialized with the reference shape, with the extension of [21] to allow for more general image likelihoods than feature point reprojection error. The second baseline, later denoted by Salz10, follows the method of [21] and uses a Gaussian process (GP) predictor to initialize the shape before gradient-based optimization. To learn the GP predictor, we used the same training shapes as to learn the potential weights, and employ either noisy 2D point locations, or PHOG descriptors as input. To confirm that a simple coarse-to-fine optimization scheme is not enough to solve the problem, we also compare our results with a coarse-to-fine version of [23], denoted by Shen09 CTF. For all the baselines, we used the same image likelihoods as for our method, together with the weights learned with our CRF formulation.

In the remainder of this section, we present our results on synthetic data, motion capture data, and real images. 3D reconstruction errors are computed as the mean vertex-to-vertex distance between the ground-truth meshes and the reconstructions, averaged over 100 test images and for 5 train/test partitions.

Synthetic Data: As a first example, we consider the case of a 100×100mm mesh made of two facets, whose common edge act as a hinge, as depicted by Fig. 3(a). Deformations of this mesh were generated by randomly setting the angle between the two facets, as well as the global motion of the mesh. In this scenario, neither smoothness potential nor coarse-to-fine scheme were used.

To evaluate the performance of our approach on the popular problem of 3D reconstruction from feature point correspondences, we projected the deformed meshes in a 512×512 image using a known camera, added zero mean Gaussian noise with standard deviations $\{0, 2, 6, 10\}$ pixels to the 2D projections of the vertices, and used these noisy 2D locations as image measurements. We learned our potential weights and the GP predictor of Salz10 with $\{1, 5, 10\}$ training examples. Fig. 3(b,c) depict the 3D reconstruction errors as a function of the 2D measurement noise and of the number of training examples. Our approach outperforms the baselines, especially when keeping multiple solutions throughout

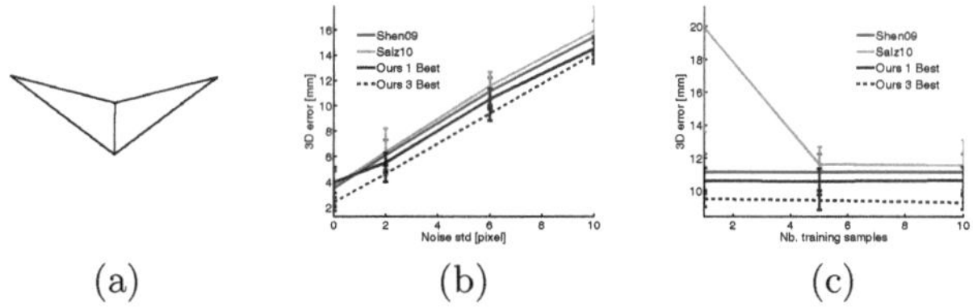

Fig. 3. Reconstructing a 2×2 **mesh from correspondences.** (a) Sample deformed mesh. 3D error as a function of (b) the 2D input noise, and (c) the number of training examples. Note that with few training examples, Salz10 performs poorly. In contrast, our approach performs well independently of the number of training examples.

the PCBP iterations. Note that with few training examples, Salz10 performs quite poorly. In contrast, our approach is very robust to the number of training examples; Even a single one is enough for us to learn the potential weights.

While feature point correspondences are an interesting source of information, our goal here is to address the problem of using more complex image likelihoods. To this end, we applied two different textures to the deformed meshes to create synthetic images such as those depicted in Fig. 4(a,d). We then added uniform random noise to the image intensities with maximum values of $\{0, 100, 200\}$. For all approaches, we used template matching and boundary likelihoods to reconstruct the surfaces. Fig. 4(b,c,e,f) depict the 3D errors as a function of the noise variance and of the number of training examples. In the well-textured case, our method yields a huge improvement over the baselines, thus fully showing the benefits of global optimization over local one. While improvement for the poorly-textured images is slightly smaller, it remains quite large. The lack of texture yields more ambiguities, which explains why keeping multiple solutions throughout PCBP yields significantly better results.

Motion Capture Data: The second set of experiments was performed using data obtained with a motion capture system [7]. The data consists of 3D reconstructions of reflective markers placed in a 9×9 regular grid of 160×160mm on a piece of cardboard deformed in front of 6 infrared cameras. Therefore, as opposed to the previous experiments, the deformations come from a real surface. Since no images are provided with the 3D data, we synthesized well- and poorly-textured images as before. In this experiment, we made use of our coarse-to-fine scheme, and performed our initial structured prediction with a 3×3 mesh. We used 5 training examples to learn the potential weights. We performed reconstruction with and without the smoothness prior to evaluate the performance of our algorithm when relying only on image information, in addition to the facet coherence term which is equivalent to the distance constraints of the baselines. Furthermore, since for the same deformation, a fine mesh is actually smoother than a coarse one, we also computed results by increasing the smoothness weight manually for refinement. Note that this was also performed for the baselines. Fig. 5(a,b) depict the 3D errors with no smoothness for the well-textured surface with a coarse mesh and after refinement, respectively. Our approach yields much more accurate reconstructions than the baselines. In Fig. 5(c-e), we show

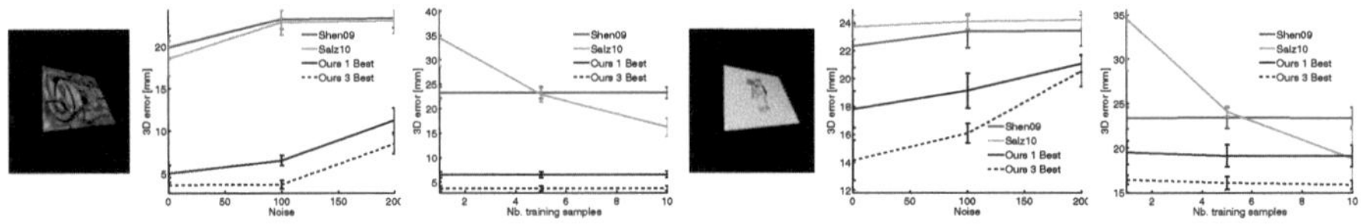

(a) (b) (c) (d) (e) (f)

Fig. 4. Reconstructing a 2 × 2 mesh from well- and poorly-textured images. (a) Sample well-textured input image. 3D error as a function of (b) the 2D input noise, and (c) the number of training examples. (d-f) Similar figures for the poorly-textured case. Note that our results are much more accurate than the baselines.

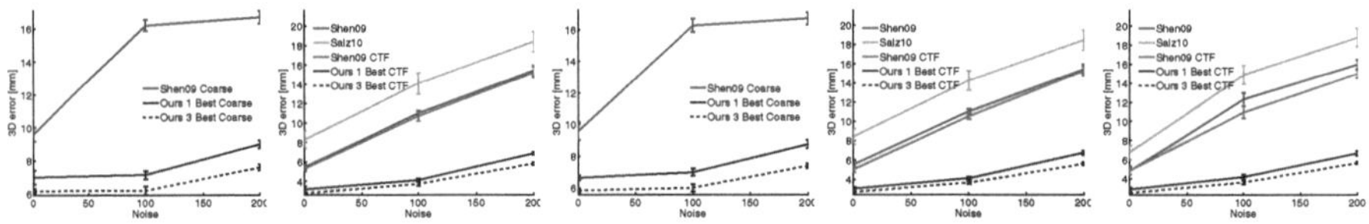

(a) (b) (c) (d) (e)

Fig. 5. Reconstructing a piece of cardboard from well-textured images. 3D error when (a) using a coarse (3 × 3) mesh and no smoothness, and (b) refining the results of (a) with a gradient-based method. (c-d) Similar results as (a-b) but with smoothness. (e) 3D errors when manually increasing the influence of the smoothness term for refinement. Shen09 and Salz10 were directly obtained using a fine mesh. Note that our coarse results give a much better initialization for the refinement step.

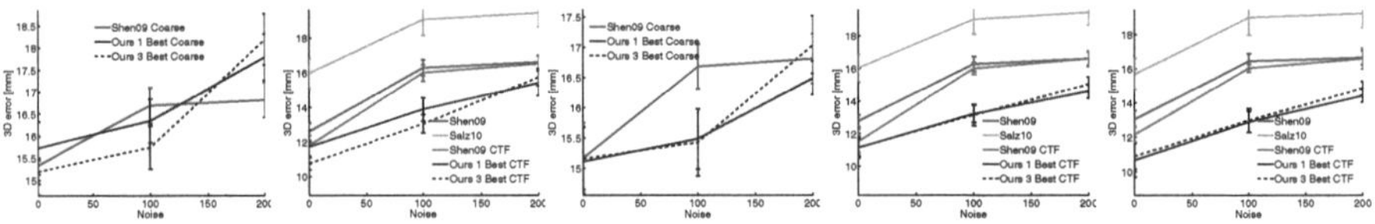

(a) (b) (c) (d) (e)

Fig. 6. Reconstructing a piece of cardboard from poorly-textured images. Similar plots as in Fig. 5. Note that here, the smoothness term has more influence on our results. Interestingly, increasing smoothness does not help the baselines significantly.

the 3D errors when using the smoothness term. Note that with this nice texture, smoothing has very little effect on the results. Fig. 6 depicts similar results for a poorly-textured surface; Without smoothness, our coarse results are roughly on par with Shen09. Interestingly, however, we outperform the baselines after refinement. This shows that our coarse results still provide a better initialization than the coarse version of Shen09. Note that with this poorly-textured surface, smoothness improves reconstruction, which seems natural since image information is much weaker. This, however, is not noticeably the case for the baselines.

Real Images: Finally, to show that our approach can also be applied to real images, we used two sequences of different deforming materials [7]. While these are video sequences, all the images were treated independently and initialized

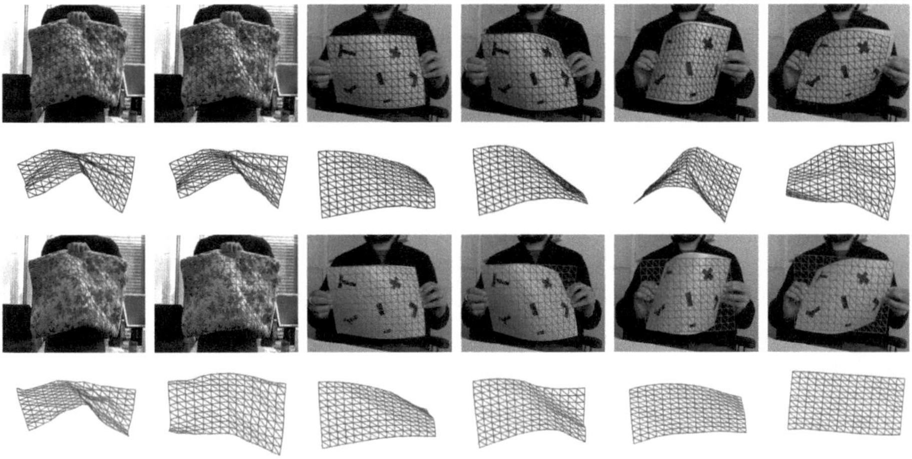

Fig. 7. Reconstructing surfaces from real images. From top to bottom: Our reconstructions reprojected on the original images, side view of our reconstructions, reconstructions obtained with Shen09 CTF reprojected on the original images, side view of those reconstructions. For a well-textured surface, the baseline manages to reconstruct fairly large deformations, but is less consistent than our approach, as illustrated for two very similar frames. For a poorly-textured surface, the baseline only manages to reconstruct small deformations, whereas our approach can deal with much larger ones. The rightmost column shows a failure of our method due to an ambiguity in the facet reconstruction and to the use of a coarse mesh.

from the template mesh to illustrate the fact that our approach can perform reconstruction from a single input image. Since no training data is available for these surfaces, we used a single training example consisting of the template mesh with reference image to learn the potential weights. In Fig. 7, we visually compare our reconstructions to those of Shen09. We do not show the results of Salz10, since with the template mesh as single training example, it would always predict the reference shape, and thus perform the same as Shen09. For the well-textured surface, Shen09 manages to reconstruct fairly large deformations. However, as illustrated by the two leftmost columns of the figure for two very similar frames, it is less consistent than our approach. For the poorly-textured surface, the baseline is completely unable to cope with large deformations. Our approach, however, still manages to reconstruct the surface. In the rightmost column of the figure, we show a failure case of our approach, where the facet orientation is ambiguous. Furthermore, the topology of the coarse mesh makes it harder to bend the surface along this diagonal. Note, however, that as opposed to the baseline, we still recover some degree of surface deformation.

5 Conclusion

We have introduced an approach to non-rigid 3D reconstruction of a potentially poorly-textured surface from a single image when no good initialization is available. To this end, we have formulated reconstruction as a structured prediction problem, and have shown that the popular image likelihoods decompose into unary and pairwise potentials, thus making inference algorithms practical for our purpose. We have demonstrated the benefits of our approach over state-of-the-art gradient-based methods in various scenarios, and have shown tremendous improvement over existing baselines. The current main limitation of our technique comes from the computational burden of performing structured prediction with large graphs. However, as research in that field advances, our approach will be applicable to denser and denser meshes. Studying these advances, as well as other image information such as shading, will be the focus of our future work.

References

1. Akhter, I., Sheikh, Y., Khan, S., Kanade, T.: Nonrigid Structure from Motion in Trajectory Space. In: NIPS (2008)
2. Batra, D., Yadollahpour, P., Guzman-Rivera, A., Shakhnarovich, G.: Diverse M-Best Solutions in Markov Random Fields. In: Fitzgibbon, A., Lazebnik, S., Perona, P., Sato, Y., Schmid, C. (eds.) ECCV 2012, Part V. LNCS, vol. 7576, pp. 1–16. Springer, Heidelberg (2012)
3. Blanz, V., Vetter, T.: A Morphable Model for the Synthesis of 3D Faces. In: SIGGRAPH (1999)
4. Bregler, C., Hertzmann, A., Biermann, H.: Recovering Non-Rigid 3D Shape from Image Streams. In: CVPR (2000)
5. Brunet, F., Hartley, R., Bartoli, A., Navab, N., Malgouyres, R.: Monocular Template-Based Reconstruction of Smooth and Inextensible Surfaces. In: Kimmel, R., Klette, R., Sugimoto, A. (eds.) ACCV 2010, Part III. LNCS, vol. 6494, pp. 52–66. Springer, Heidelberg (2011)
6. Cootes, T.F., Edwards, G.J., Taylor, C.J.: Active Appearance Models. In: Burkhardt, H., Neumann, B. (eds.) ECCV 1998. LNCS, vol. 1407, pp. 484–498. Springer, Heidelberg (1998)
7. `http://cvlab.epfl.ch/data/dsr/`
8. Fayad, J., Agapito, L., Del Bue, A.: Piecewise Quadratic Reconstruction of Non-Rigid Surfaces from Monocular Sequences. In: Daniilidis, K., Maragos, P., Paragios, N. (eds.) ECCV 2010, Part IV. LNCS, vol. 6314, pp. 297–310. Springer, Heidelberg (2010)
9. Fromer, M., Globerson, A.: An LP view of the M best problem. In: NIPS (2009)
10. Gumerov, N., Zandifar, A., Duraiswami, R., Davis, L.S.: Structure of Applicable Surfaces from Single Views. In: Pajdla, T., Matas, J. (eds.) ECCV 2004. LNCS, vol. 3023, pp. 482–496. Springer, Heidelberg (2004)
11. Hazan, T., Urtasun, R.: A primal-dual message-passing algorithm for approximated large scale structured prediction. In: NIPS (2010)
12. Hazan, T., Shashua, A.: Norm-Product Belief Propagation: Primal-Dual Message-Passing for LP-Relaxation and Approximate Inference. In: IT (2011)
13. Kass, M., Witkin, A., Terzopoulos, D.: Snakes: Active Contour Models. IJCV (1988)
14. Mcinerney, T., Terzopoulos, D.: A Finite Element Model for 3D Shape Reconstruction and Nonrigid Motion Tracking. In: ICCV (1993)
15. Metaxas, D., Terzopoulos, D.: Constrained Deformable Superquadrics and Nonrigid Motion Tracking. PAMI (1993)

16. Peng, J., Hazan, T., McAllester, D., Urtasun, R.: Convex Max-Product Algorithms for Continuous MRFs with Applications to Protein Folding. In: ICML (2011)
17. Pentland, A., Sclaroff, S.: Closed-Form Solutions for Physically Based Shape Modeling and Recognition. PAMI (1991)
18. Perriollat, M., Hartley, R., Bartoli, A.: Monocular Template-Based Reconstruction of Inextensible Surfaces. IJCV (2010)
19. Russell, C., Fayad, J., Agapito, L.: Energy Based Multiple Model Fitting for Non-Rigid Structure from Motion. In: CVPR (2011)
20. Salzmann, M., Urtasun, R., Fua, P.: Local Deformation Models for Monocular 3D Shape Recovery. In: CVPR (2008)
21. Salzmann, M., Urtasun, R.: Combining Discriminative and Generative Methods for 3D Deformable Surface and Articulated Pose Reconstruction. In: CVPR (2010)
22. Schwing, A., Hazan, T., Pollefeys, M., Urtasun, R.: Distributed Message Passing for Large Scale Graphical Models. In: CVPR (2011)
23. Shen, S., Shi, W., Liu, Y.: Monocular 3D Tracking of Inextensible Deformable Surfaces Under L2-Norm. In: ACCV (2009)
24. Taylor, J., Jepson, A.D., Kutulakos, K.N.: Non-Rigid Structure from Locally-Rigid Motion. In: CVPR (2010)
25. Torresani, L., Hertzmann, A., Bregler, C.: Nonrigid Structure-From-Motion: Estimating Shape and Motion with Hierarchical Priors. PAMI (2008)
26. Varol, A., Shaji, A., Salzmann, M., Fua, P.: Monocular 3D Reconstruction of Locally Textured Surfaces. PAMI (2011)
27. Xiao, J., Kanade, T.: Uncalibrated Perspective Reconstruction of Deformable Structures. In: ICCV (2005)

Learning Spatially-Smooth Mappings in Non-Rigid Structure From Motion

Onur C. Hamsici[1], Paulo F.U. Gotardo[2], and Aleix M. Martinez[2]

[1] Qualcomm Research, San Diego, CA, USA
[2] The Ohio State University, Columbus, OH, USA
ohamsici@qualcomm.com,{gotardop,aleix}@ece.osu.edu

Abstract. Non-rigid structure from motion (NRSFM) is a classical underconstrained problem in computer vision. A common approach to make NRSFM more tractable is to constrain 3D shape deformation to be smooth over time. This constraint has been used to compress the deformation model and reduce the number of unknowns that are estimated. However, temporal smoothness cannot be enforced when the data lacks temporal ordering and its benefits are less evident when objects undergo abrupt deformations. This paper proposes a new NRSFM method that addresses these problems by considering deformations as spatial variations in shape space and then enforcing spatial, rather than temporal, smoothness. This is done by modeling each 3D shape coefficient as a function of its input 2D shape. This mapping is learned in the feature space of a rotation invariant kernel, where spatial smoothness is intrinsically defined by the mapping function. As a result, our model represents shape variations compactly using custom-built coefficient bases learned from the input data, rather than a pre-specified set such as the Discrete Cosine Transform. The resulting kernel-based mapping is a by-product of the NRSFM solution and leads to another fundamental advantage of our approach: for a newly observed 2D shape, its 3D shape is recovered by simply evaluating the learned function.

1 Introduction

Structure from motion (SFM) techniques have seen vast improvements over the past three decades by relying on the assumption of object rigidity [1]. However, computer vision applications often involve the observation of deformable objects such as the human face and body. When the assumption of object rigidity is relaxed, and in the absence of any prior knowledge on 3D shape deformation, computing non-rigid structure from motion (NRSFM) becomes a challenging, underconstrained problem. Given a set of corresponding 2D points, established over multiple images of a deformable object, the goal of NRSFM is to recover the object's 3D shape and 3D pose (relative camera position) in each image [2–15].

To make this largely underconstrained problem more tractable, recent research work has attempted to define new, general constraints for 3D shape deformation. A common approach to NRSFM is the matrix factorization method of [2], which

A. Fitzgibbon et al. (Eds.): ECCV 2012, Part IV, LNCS 7575, pp. 260–273, 2012.

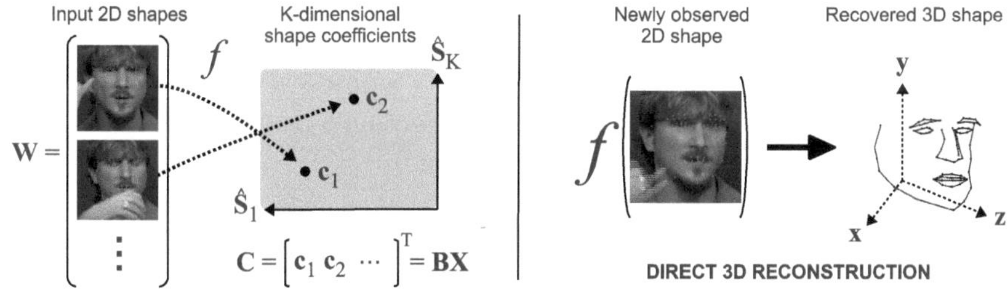

Fig. 1. Before solving NRSFM, a basis **B** is computed as to compactly represent a nonlinear mapping from the input data to the coefficients $\mathbf{C} = \mathbf{BX}$ of the linear shape model: (*left*) **B** is obtained by modeling each coefficient vector as a function $f(\cdot)$ of its input 2D shape; an RIK feature space is used to learn $f(\cdot)$ and **B** based on similarities in these input shapes; (*right*) with $f(\cdot)$ being a by-product of the NRSFM solution, the 3D reconstruction of a newly observed 2D shape is done by simply evaluating $f(\cdot)$.

constrains all 3D shapes to lie within a low-dimensional linear shape space. In addition, many NRSFM techniques also enforce smoothness constraints on camera motion and object deformation, which are assumed to change only gradually over subsequent images [3, 6, 11–13, 15].

The recent Shape Trajectory Approach (STA) of [13], a generalization of [12], demonstrates how gradual 3D shape deformation can be seen as the smooth time-trajectory of a single point (object) within a low-dimensional shape space. As a result, a few low-frequency components of the Discrete Cosine Transform (DCT) can be used as basis vectors to define a compact representation of 3D shape deformation. Because the DCT basis is known *a priori*, the number of unknowns that need to be estimated is greatly reduced. STA has been shown to outperform a number of state-of-the-art NRSFM algorithms when applied to the 3D reconstruction of challenging datasets. However, it was also shown in [13] that sudden (high-frequency) deformations require the use of a large DCT basis, leading to less compact models. In addition, if the input 2D points come from a collection of images for which no temporal relation is known, the smoothness assumption does not hold and there is no gain in using the DCT basis.

This paper presents a novel NRSFM approach that addresses these problems by considering deformations as spatial variations in shape space and then enforcing spatial, rather than temporal, smoothness. Instead of using the DCT basis, we represent the coefficients of the linear shape model compactly using custom-built bases learned from the input data. These bases are obtained by expressing each 3D shape coefficient as a function of its input 2D shape, Fig. 1(left). This smooth function is learned in the feature space of a rotation invariant kernel (RIK) [16], in terms of the input data; more specifically, we learn a compact subspace using kernel principal component analysis (KPCA) [17]. The learned mapping becomes a by-product of our NRSFM solution and leads to another fundamental advantage of our approach: for a newly observed 2D shape, its 3D reconstruction is obtained via the simple evaluation of this function, Fig. 1(right).

Finally, we also propose a novel model fitting algorithm, based on iteratively-reweighted least squares (IRLS) [18], to extract local (sparse) modes of deformation – which are key features in applications that analyze 3D object deformation.

Our NRSFM model is derived in Section 3. Section 4 presents our IRLS-based algorithm, with experimental results in Section 5.

2 Related Work and Basic Formulation

We first summarize the notation used in the following: matrices and column vectors are denoted using upper-case and lower-case bold letters, respectively; $\mathbf{I}_n$ is the $n \times n$ identity matrix; $\mathbf{A} \otimes \mathbf{B}$ is the Kronecker product of two matrices; $\mathbf{A}^\dagger$ denotes the Moore-Penrose pseudo-inverse of $\mathbf{A}$; $\|\mathbf{A}\|_F$ is the Frobenius norm; $\mathbf{z}^*$ is the Hermitian of complex vector $\mathbf{z}$; and $\delta_{i,j}$ is the Kronecker delta.

For a NRSFM problem with T images (cameras), the n input 2D point tracks are given in an input matrix $\mathbf{W} \in \mathbb{R}^{2T \times n}$; $[x_{t,j}, y_{t,j}]^T$ is the 2D projection of the jth 3D point observed on the tth image, $t = 1, 2, \ldots, T$, $j = 1, 2, \ldots, n$. For clarity of presentation, assume for now that: (i) $\mathbf{W}$ is complete, meaning that no 2D points became occluded during tracking; and (ii) its mean column vector $\mathbf{t} \in \mathbb{R}^{2T}$ has been subtracted from all columns, making them zero-mean. With orthographic projection and a world coordinate system centered on the observed 3D object, $\mathbf{t}$ gives the observed 2D camera translations in each image.

The matrix factorization approach of [2] models $\mathbf{W} = \mathbf{MS}$ as a product of two matrix factors of low-rank $3K$, $\mathbf{M} \in \mathbb{R}^{2T \times 3K}$ and $\mathbf{S} \in \mathbb{R}^{3K \times n}$,

$$\underbrace{\begin{bmatrix} x_{1,1} & x_{1,2} & \cdots & x_{1,n} \\ y_{1,1} & y_{1,2} & \cdots & y_{1,n} \\ \vdots & \vdots & \ddots & \vdots \\ x_{T,1} & x_{T,2} & \cdots & x_{T,n} \\ y_{T,1} & y_{T,2} & \cdots & y_{T,n} \end{bmatrix}}_{\mathbf{W}} = \underbrace{\begin{bmatrix} \widehat{\mathbf{R}}_1 & & & \\ & \widehat{\mathbf{R}}_2 & & \\ & & \ddots & \\ & & & \widehat{\mathbf{R}}_T \end{bmatrix}}_{\mathbf{D}} \left(\underbrace{\begin{bmatrix} c_{1,1} & \cdots & c_{1,K} \\ c_{2,1} & \cdots & c_{2,K} \\ \vdots & \ddots & \vdots \\ c_{T,1} & \cdots & c_{T,K} \end{bmatrix}}_{\mathbf{C}} \otimes \mathbf{I}_3 \right) \underbrace{\begin{bmatrix} \widehat{\mathbf{S}}_1 \\ \vdots \\ \widehat{\mathbf{S}}_K \end{bmatrix}}_{\mathbf{S}} \tag{1}$$

Factor $\mathbf{M} = \mathbf{D}\,(\mathbf{C} \otimes \mathbf{I}_3)$ comprises a block-diagonal rotation matrix $\mathbf{D} \in \mathbb{R}^{2T \times 3T}$ and a shape coefficient matrix $\mathbf{C} \in \mathbb{R}^{T \times K}$. Let $\mathbf{c}_t^T$ be the tth row of $\mathbf{C}$. The unknown 3D shape of the tth image is modeled as the matrix function

$$S(\mathbf{c}_t^T) = (\mathbf{c}_t^T \otimes \mathbf{I}_3)\mathbf{S} = \sum_{k=1}^{K} c_{t,k} \widehat{\mathbf{S}}_k, \tag{2}$$

that is, a *linear* combination of K basis shapes $\widehat{\mathbf{S}}_k \in \mathbb{R}^{3 \times n}$ as described by the shape coordinates $c_{t,k}$. The camera orientation (object pose) at image t is given by $\widehat{\mathbf{R}}_t \in \mathbb{R}^{2 \times 3}$, a 3D rotation followed by an orthographic projection to 2D.

The factors $\mathbf{M}$ and $\mathbf{S}$ are computed from the singular value decomposition (SVD) $\mathbf{W} = (\mathbf{U}\mathbf{\Sigma}^{\frac{1}{2}})(\mathbf{\Sigma}^{\frac{1}{2}}\mathbf{V}^T) = \overline{\mathbf{M}}\overline{\mathbf{S}}$, with all but the largest $3K$ singular values in $\mathbf{\Sigma}$ set to zero. This non-unique solution is defined only up to a rank-$3K$ ambiguity matrix $\mathbf{Q} \in \mathbb{R}^{3K \times 3K}$. To recover $\mathbf{D}$ and $\mathbf{C}$, an Euclidean upgrade step [11] finds a corrective $\mathbf{Q}$ for the solution $\mathbf{W} = (\overline{\mathbf{M}}\mathbf{Q})(\mathbf{Q}^{-1}\overline{\mathbf{S}}) = \mathbf{MS}$.

To further constrain the reconstruction process above, many authors assume that the observed 3D shape deformation is only gradual over time $t = 1, \dots, T$ [3,6,12,13]. Here, we summarize STA [13], which is closely related to our new method. STA considers $\mathbf{c}_t^T = c(t)$ as a single K-dimensional point describing a smooth time-trajectory within an unknown linear shape space. This means that each shape coordinate $c_{t,k}$ varies smoothly with t. The shape trajectory is then modeled compactly using a small number d of low-frequency DCT coefficients,

$$\mathbf{C} = \mathbf{\Omega}_d \left[\mathbf{x}_1, \dots, \mathbf{x}_K\right] = \mathbf{\Omega}_d \mathbf{X}, \qquad \mathbf{x}_k \in \mathbb{R}^d. \tag{3}$$

With $d \ll T$, $\mathbf{X} \in \mathbb{R}^{d \times K}$ represents $\mathbf{C} \in \mathbb{R}^{T \times K}$ compactly in the domain of the truncated DCT basis matrix $\mathbf{\Omega}_d \in \mathbb{R}^{T \times d}$. The fth column of $\mathbf{\Omega}_d$ is the fth-frequency cosine wave [12,13]. Because the DCT matrix is known *a priori*, the number of unknowns in $\mathbf{C}$ is significantly reduced with STA.

The optimization stage of STA considers that $\mathbf{S} = \mathbf{M}^\dagger \mathbf{W}$ is a function of $\mathbf{M}$ and $\mathbf{W}$. The goal is then to minimize the 2D reprojection error,

$$e(\mathbf{M}) = \|\mathbf{W} - \mathbf{W}^*\|_F^2, \quad \mathbf{W}^* = \mathbf{M}\mathbf{S} = \mathbf{M}\mathbf{M}^\dagger \mathbf{W}. \tag{4}$$

With $\mathbf{M} = \mathbf{D}(\mathbf{\Omega}_d \mathbf{X} \otimes \mathbf{I}_3)$, a coarse initial deformation model ($\mathbf{X} = \mathbf{I}_K$) [12] is first used to compute $\mathbf{D}$. Then higher-frequency DCT coefficients in $\mathbf{X}$ are estimated using a Gauss-Newton algorithm to minimize (4) in terms of $\mathbf{X}$ only.

3 NRSFM with RIKs

In this section, we propose a new kernel-based solution to NRSFM. Our goal is to derive a function that estimates the coefficient matrix $\mathbf{C}$ and is not restricted to cases of smooth deformations over time. As a result, we will also learn a custom-built basis $\mathbf{B}$ from the input data, providing a compact representation $\mathbf{C} = \mathbf{B}\mathbf{X}$. To this end, we first need to establish a relationship between $\mathbf{C}$ and the observed data in $\mathbf{W}$. More especially, we learn a function $f(\cdot)$ that estimates vector $\mathbf{c}_t^T$ – representing an unknown 3D shape as a point within the shape space – given the corresponding input 2D shape $\mathbf{w}^t \in \mathbb{R}^{2 \times n}$ observed on the tth image,

$$\mathbf{c}_t^T = f(\mathbf{w}^t), \qquad \mathbf{w}^t = \begin{bmatrix} x_{t,1} & x_{t,2} & \cdots & x_{t,n} \\ y_{t,1} & y_{t,2} & \cdots & y_{t,n} \end{bmatrix}. \tag{5}$$

This mapping becomes a by-product of the NRSFM solution and leads to a fundamental advantage of our approach. Given a new image with a previously unseen 2D shape, the estimation of the corresponding 3D shape is readily achieved.

3.1 Defining a Mapping Using the Kernel Trick

Following the well-known kernel trick [17], we first consider a nonlinear mapping of each 2D shape $\mathbf{w}^t$ onto vector $\phi(\mathbf{w}^t)$, located within a high dimensional space where a final linear mapping can be learned. According to the Representer Theorem, the function $f(\cdot)$ that we seek can be expressed as a linear combination of a few representative $\phi(\mathbf{w}^t)$. Thus, we can model the kth coefficient of $\mathbf{c}_t^T$ as

$$c_{t,k} = f_k(\mathbf{w}^t) = \sum_{i=1}^{d} \phi(\mathbf{w}^t)^T \phi(\mathbf{w}_b^i) x_{ik} \tag{6}$$

where x_{ik} are the coefficients of a linear combination of a few 2D basis shapes, $\mathbf{w}_b^i$. The number of basis elements d must be sufficient as to represent the relations between $\mathbf{C}$ and $\mathbf{W}$, as discussed below.

In general, explicitly evaluating the mapping $\phi(\cdot)$ can be computationally expensive or even impossible when the image is a function in an infinite dimensional space. Thus, we perform this mapping only implicitly by embedding it in the computation of a generalized inner product given by a kernel function $\kappa(\cdot,\cdot)$,

$$c_{t,k} = f_k(\mathbf{w}^t) = \sum_{i=1}^{d} \kappa(\mathbf{w}^t, \mathbf{w}_b^i) x_{ik}. \tag{7}$$

The kernel function above must provide a similarity measure for two 2D shapes observed from different points of view (*i.e.*, poses); its proper definition is discussed in Section 3.3. Considering all K coefficients of $\mathbf{c}_t^T$, $\forall t$, from (7) we obtain

$$\mathbf{C} = \mathbf{\Phi}(\mathbf{W})^T \mathbf{\Phi}(\mathbf{W}_b)\mathbf{X} = \mathbf{K}_{\mathbf{W}\mathbf{W}_b}\mathbf{X} \stackrel{\text{def}}{=} \mathbf{B}\mathbf{X}, \tag{8}$$

where $\mathbf{X} \in \mathbb{R}^{d \times K}$ is a coefficient matrix; $\mathbf{B} \stackrel{\text{def}}{=} \mathbf{K}_{\mathbf{W}\mathbf{W}_b} \in \mathbb{R}^{T \times d}$ is a custom-built basis matrix that has the inner product values for all pairings of a 2D shape in $\mathbf{W}$ and a 2D basis shape in $\mathbf{W}_b$.

Unfortunately, selecting the best set of basis shapes with d out of the T observed 2D shapes is an NP-complete problem. We therefore define a simple, alternative solution based on kernel principal component analysis (KPCA) [17]. We first pre-compute a complete kernel matrix $\mathbf{K}_{\mathbf{W}\mathbf{W}} \in \mathbb{R}^{T \times T}$ and its eigenvector matrix $\mathbf{V}$ associated with the d largest eigenvalues in the diagonal matrix $\mathbf{\Lambda}$, *i.e.*, $\mathbf{K}_{\mathbf{W}\mathbf{W}}\mathbf{V} = \mathbf{V}\mathbf{\Lambda}$. In the range space of mapping $\phi(\cdot)$, we have d eigenfunctions given by $\mathbf{\Phi}(\mathbf{W})\mathbf{V}\mathbf{\Lambda}^{-1/2}$. By projecting each observation $\phi(\mathbf{w}^t)$ onto this eigenfunction subspace, we can then define our new basis matrix $\mathbf{B}$ of $\mathbf{C}$ as,

$$\mathbf{C} = \mathbf{\Phi}(\mathbf{W})^T \mathbf{\Phi}(\mathbf{W})\mathbf{V}\mathbf{\Lambda}^{-1/2}\mathbf{X} = \underbrace{\mathbf{K}_{\mathbf{W}\mathbf{W}}\mathbf{V}\mathbf{\Lambda}^{-1/2}}_{\mathbf{B}}\mathbf{X}. \tag{9}$$

The number of eigenfunctions d must be large enough as to provide a subspace that captures a sufficient amount of the variation in the kernel matrix.

Finally, we obtain our new NRSFM model with $\mathbf{M} = \mathbf{D}(\mathbf{B}\mathbf{X} \otimes \mathbf{I}_3)$. A solution is achieved by estimating the rotation matrix $\mathbf{D}$ and the $d \times K$ coefficient matrix $\mathbf{X}$ as to minimize the reprojection error in (4). This optimization procedure is detailed in Section 4. Once the optimal $\mathbf{M}$ and $\mathbf{S} = \mathbf{M}^{\dagger}\mathbf{W}$ have been found, we can use (2) to recover the 3D shape for the tth image as

$$S(\mathbf{c}_t^T) = S(f(\mathbf{w}^t)) = \left(f(\mathbf{w}^t) \otimes \mathbf{I}_3\right)\mathbf{M}^{\dagger}\mathbf{W}, \quad \text{with} \tag{10}$$

$$\mathbf{c}_t^T = f(\mathbf{w}^t) = \boldsymbol{\kappa}(\mathbf{w}^t, \mathbf{W})\mathbf{V}\mathbf{\Lambda}^{-1/2}\mathbf{X}, \quad \text{and} \tag{11}$$

$$\boldsymbol{\kappa}(\mathbf{w}^t, \mathbf{W}) = \left[\ \kappa(\mathbf{w}^t, \mathbf{w}^1)\ \kappa(\mathbf{w}^t, \mathbf{w}^2)\ \ldots\ \kappa(\mathbf{w}^t, \mathbf{w}^T)\ \right]. \tag{12}$$

This new approach is referred to as NRSFM with RIKs.

3.2 Recovering the 3D Shape from a Newly Seen 2D Shape

An important advantage of NRSFM with RIKs is the ability to easily reconstruct the 3D shape from a newly observed image that was not considered in the optimization above; let $\mathbf{w}^\tau$ ($\tau > T$) denote this newly observed 2D shape. Notice from (10) that the 3D shape $S(f(\mathbf{w}^\tau))$ associated with $\mathbf{w}^\tau$ can be easily estimated given $\mathbf{W}$, $\mathbf{M}$, $f(\cdot)$ from the optimization above.

Once the 3D shape has been recovered, the associated rotation (pose) matrix $\widehat{\mathbf{R}}_\tau$ can also be readily estimated by solving two simple systems of linear equations, $\mathbf{w}^\tau = \widehat{\mathbf{R}}_\tau \, S(f(\mathbf{w}^\tau))$, then using the SVD of $\widehat{\mathbf{R}}_\tau$ to enforce orthogonality.

3.3 Rotation Invariant Kernels

The kernel function must provide a similarity measure for two 3D shapes based on their 2D projections, $\mathbf{w}^t$ and $\mathbf{w}^{t'}$, taken from different points of view. One possible choice of the kernel function $\kappa(\cdot,\cdot)$ is the RIK of [16]. This RIK calculates the rotation invariant similarity between two scale-normalized 2D shapes represented in the complex domain, vectors $\mathbf{z}_t$ and $\mathbf{z}_{t'}$ with $\mathbf{z}_t^*\mathbf{z}_t = \mathbf{z}_{t'}^*\mathbf{z}_{t'} = 1$,

$$\kappa(\mathbf{z}_t, \mathbf{z}_{t'}) = \exp\left(\frac{-1 + |\mathbf{z}_t^*\mathbf{z}_{t'}|}{\sigma^2}\right), \quad \mathbf{z}_t = \frac{(\mathbf{w}^t)^T}{\|\mathbf{w}^t\|_F}\begin{bmatrix} 1 \\ \sqrt{-1}\end{bmatrix} \in \mathbb{C}^n. \tag{13}$$

The scale (smoothness) of this RIK is defined by parameter σ. The 2D rotation invariance property ensures that $k(\mathbf{z}_t, \mathbf{z}_{t'}) = k(e^{\theta\sqrt{-1}}\mathbf{z}_t, \mathbf{z}_{t'})$ for any rotation angle θ in the complex plane. This is a property of the inner product in the complex domain. Although the kernel above is not invariant to the 3D orientation of the observed shapes, we can still use it to learn the mapping in (11) because the input 2D shapes are highly correlated with the underlying 3D shapes – we can even use *appearance features* that are correlated with 3D shape [19].

Here we also propose a new kernel dubbed the *affine structure from motion* (aSFM) kernel. The aSFM RIK is defined in terms of the reprojection error $r_{t,t'}^2$ of an affine, rigid SFM solution obtained from the two observations $\mathbf{w}^t$ and $\mathbf{w}^{t'}$,

$$\kappa(\mathbf{w}^t, \mathbf{w}^{t'}) = \exp\left(\frac{-r_{t,t'}^2}{\sigma^2}\right) + \alpha\delta_{t,t'}, \quad r_{t,t'} = \left\| \begin{bmatrix} \mathbf{w}^t \\ \mathbf{w}^{t'} \end{bmatrix} - \begin{bmatrix} \mathbf{A}^t \\ \mathbf{A}^{t'} \end{bmatrix} \mathbf{S}_a \right\|_F \tag{14}$$

where σ is the kernel scale and parameter α regulates how similar the 3D shapes are in general, while also ensuring that the kernel matrix is positive semi-definite. The affine cameras $\mathbf{A}^t$ and $\mathbf{A}^{t'} \in \mathbb{R}^{2\times 3}$ and the affine 3D shape $\mathbf{S}_a \in \mathbb{R}^{3\times n}$ are obtained from a rank-3 approximation to $\mathbf{w}^t$ and $\mathbf{w}^{t'}$ using SVD. If these 2D shapes are projections of two dissimilar 3D shapes, then the rigid SFM solution will provide a large reprojection error and the aSFM kernel value will be small.

3.4 Model Analysis

Parameter Setting: With the rank parameter K assumed to be known, the number of unknowns in $\mathbf{X} \in \mathbb{R}^{d\times K}$ depends on the number of columns d of

$\mathbf{B} \in \mathbb{R}^{T \times d}$. A rank-$3K$ solution $\mathbf{M}$ requires $d \geq K$. If $d = K$, then $\mathbf{X}$ must be full-rank (*i.e.*, $\mathbf{X}^{-1}$ exists) and the non-unique solution $\mathbf{M} = \mathbf{D}(\mathbf{BX} \otimes \mathbf{I}_3)$ has an equivalent form $\overline{\mathbf{M}} = \mathbf{M}(\mathbf{X}^{-1} \otimes \mathbf{I}_3) = \mathbf{D}(\mathbf{BI}_K \otimes \mathbf{I}_3)$, with a constant $\overline{\mathbf{X}} = \mathbf{I}_K$. By assuming $d > K$, we allow the rank-$3K$ solution to consider other important variations in the kernel matrix, leading to better results.

The discussion above suggests a deterministic initialization $\mathbf{X}_0 = [\ \mathbf{I}_K\ \mathbf{0}\ ]^T$ in which the coefficients associated with less important principal components are initially zero. Not surprisingly, the same initialization is used in STA, with high-frequency DCT coefficients set to zero. Note that the DCT and PCA bases are known to be closely related for certain types of random processes.

To select d, a common approach in PCA is to choose a d-dimensional subspace that captures about 99% of the total variance in the dataset, discarding small variations assumed as noise. In NRSFM with RIKs, we note that d is closely related to the RIK scale parameter σ: the larger σ is, the more smoothness is applied to the shape similarity values and the more compact is the KPCA space. Therefore, we consider d as a user-supplied parameter that defines the desired compactness of the model; then σ is easily chosen, automatically, as to yield a d-dimensional KPCA space with about 99% of the data variance. In the aSFM RIK, α is also set automatically as to yield a positive semi-definite kernel matrix.

Comparison to Related Work: There are two main differences between our model above and that of the kernel NRSFM approach in [15]. First, NRSFM with RIK models 3D shapes within a linear space; the approach in [15] defines a non-linear model. Second, in NRSFM with RIK the inputs to the kernel-based mapping are observed 2D shapes; in [15], the inputs are the coefficients of the non-linear model. Nevertheless, the two approaches are complementary: future work can use RIKs to define a mapping from observed 2D shapes onto the coefficients of the non-linear model of [15].

4 Model Fitting

Having obtained the basis matrix $\mathbf{B}$ through an RIK and KPCA, as described above, the next step is to estimate $\mathbf{D}$ and $\mathbf{X}$ in $\mathbf{M} = \mathbf{D}(\mathbf{BX} \otimes \mathbf{I}_3)$ as to minimize the reprojection error in (4). Two alternative algorithms are presented in this section. Here, we will assume that the rotation matrix $\mathbf{D}$ has been estimated by an initialization algorithm (*e.g.*, using rigid SFM if some points are known to remain in a rigid configuration, or using the procedure of STA). Thus, we focus on the iterative process for fitting our new model $\mathbf{C} = \mathbf{BX}$. If necessary, we can later refine $\mathbf{D}$ and $\mathbf{X}$ in an alternated manner, by fixing one of these matrices.

Algorithm 1 (NRSFM with RIK): We first consider an optimization procedure in which the computation of $\mathbf{X}$ is carried out using the iterative Gauss-Newton method proposed in [14], with the DCT basis replaced by our new basis $\mathbf{B}$. This procedure is summarized in Algorithm 1.

Algorithm 2 (Iteratively-Reweighted NRSFM with RIK): With a linear shape model, the 3D shape of a non-rigid object can be seen as comprising two main components: a rigid (average) 3D shape and $K-1$ modes of deformation.

For typical objects, these modes should reflect localized (sparse) deformations involving a small subset of points (sub-shapes). Also, different parts of an object often present different amounts of deformation. For instance, consider facial shapes that present larger deformation for the mouth in comparison to the nose; other shapes may even present points that remain in a rigid configuration.

NRSFM algorithms in general estimate shape deformation using a globally uniform least squares criterion; the objective function is automatically tuned to points with large deformation and is not sensitive to local deformations. Furthermore, the global solution does not allow for the modeling of local deformations with different complexities (ranks). This usually results in an inaccurate extraction of the rigid component and associated modes of deformation.

To address these problems, we propose a new method based on iteratively-reweighted least squares (IRLS) [18]. The algorithm iteratively minimizes the residual error resulting from Algorithm 1 above. The initial step extracts the rigid shape component of the observed object; the following steps are targeted at modeling localized modes of deformation. While IRLS has been used to implement robustness against outliers (whose errors are allowed to remain large), our goal here is to focus on columns that have a similar error pattern, corresponding to a mode of deformation that was not yet reconstructed properly.

More specifically, let $\mathbf{W} \approx \mathbf{M}_1\mathbf{S}_1$ be the output of Algorithm 1 with $K = 1$. The single 3D basis shape recovered in iteration 1 describes the rigid component of the object shape. Next, we calculate the error matrix $\mathbf{E}_1 = \mathbf{W} - \mathbf{M}_1\mathbf{S}_1$ whose columns capture modes of shape deformation. To extract local (sub-shape) deformation, we focus on a subset of the columns of $\mathbf{E}_1$ corresponding to 2D points with similar motion. This is done by specifying a weight matrix that emphasizes columns (points) with a similar pattern of error (deformation). Let $\mathbf{e}_{i,j}$ be the jth column of $\mathbf{E}_i$ (in the ith iteration). We then define a Gaussian weighting mask with nonzero diagonal elements,

$$\mathbf{G}_i(j,j) = \exp\left(-\frac{\|\mathbf{e}_{i,j} - \mathbf{e}_{i,j_{max}}\|_2^2}{\sigma_e^2}\right), \quad j_{max} = \arg\max_j \|\mathbf{e}_{i,j}\|_2 \tag{15}$$

where σ_e^2 is the average distance between $\mathbf{e}_{i,j_{max}}$ and its $0.1n$ (10%) nearest neighbors. This mask $\mathbf{G}_i$ assigns weight 1 to the column with largest error, $\mathbf{e}_{i,j_{max}}$, and slightly smaller weights to other similar columns. It is used to project $\mathbf{E}_i$ onto a subspace of large error, $\widetilde{\mathbf{E}}_1 = \mathbf{E}_1\mathbf{G}_1$.

The following iterations uses Algorithm 1 to factorize $\widetilde{\mathbf{E}}_i \approx \mathbf{M}_{i+1}\mathbf{S}_{i+1}$, always using $K = 1$. The error matrix $\mathbf{E}_i$ is updated and the iterations continue until the error $\|\mathbf{E}_i\|_F$ is sufficiently small. Note that rotation matrix $\mathbf{D}$ remains constant during this iterative process and, therefore, the recovered deformation components are aligned in 3D space. The Iteratively-Reweighted NRSFM with RIK algorithm is summarized in Algorithm 2.

To recover the 3D shape for a new image whose 2D shape $\mathbf{w}^\tau$ has now being detected, we now follow the iterative procedure in Algorithm 3. Each iteration estimates the coefficient $c_{\tau,i} = f_i(\mathbf{w}^\tau)$ associated with the ith 3D basis shape $\mathbf{S}_i$.

Algorithm 1. NRSFM with RIK

Input: 2D shapes in $\mathbf{W}$, basis size d, rank parameter K.
Compute the RIK matrix $\mathbf{K_{WW}}$ with σ^2 and α as described in the text.
Find d-dimensional KPCA subspace with 99% of data variance.
Define basis matrix $\mathbf{B}$ as in Eq.(9).
Estimate rotation matrix $\mathbf{D}$.
Estimate $d \times K$ matrix $\mathbf{X}$ s.t. $\mathbf{M} = \mathbf{D}(\mathbf{BX} \otimes \mathbf{I}_3)$ minimizes Eq.(4).
Refine $\mathbf{D}$ and $\mathbf{X}$ in alternation as to minimize Eq.(4).
Output: $\mathbf{D}$, $\mathbf{B}$, $\mathbf{X}$, and $f(\cdot)$ as in Eq.(11).

Algorithm 2. Iteratively-Reweighted NRSFM with RIK

Input: 2D shapes in $\mathbf{W}$, basis size d, rank parameter $K = 1$, level of accuracy ϵ.
Initialize $i = 0$, $\mathbf{E}_0 = \mathbf{W}$, and $\mathbf{G}_0 = \mathbf{I}_n$.
repeat
  Calculate projected error matrix $\widetilde{\mathbf{E}}_i = \mathbf{E}_i \mathbf{G}_i$.
  Compute the factorization $\widetilde{\mathbf{E}}_i \approx \mathbf{M}_{i+1}\mathbf{S}_{i+1}$ using Algorithm 1.
  Update the error matrix $\mathbf{E}_{i+1} = \mathbf{E}_i - \mathbf{M}_{i+1}\mathbf{S}_{i+1}$.
  Calculate the weighting mask $\mathbf{G}_{i+1}$ as in Eq.(15).
  $i = i + 1$.
until $\|\mathbf{E}_i\|_F < \epsilon$
Compute the final, recovered 3D shapes as $\mathbf{S}_{3D} = \sum_i (\mathbf{B}_i\mathbf{X}_i \otimes \mathbf{I}_3)\,\mathbf{S}_i$.
Output: $\mathbf{S}_{3D}$, $\mathbf{D}$, $\mathbf{B}_i$, $\mathbf{X}_i$, $\mathbf{S}_i$, and $f_i(\cdot)$.

Algorithm 3. Iterative 3D Reconstruction for a newly seen 2D shape

Input: newly observed 2D shape $\mathbf{w}^\tau$.
for $i = \{1, \ldots, N\}$ **do**
  Restore $\mathbf{S}_i$, and $f_i(\cdot)$, as previously computed with Algorithm 2.
  Evaluate $c_{\tau,i} = f_i(\mathbf{w}^\tau) = \boldsymbol{\kappa}_i(\mathbf{w}^\tau\mathbf{G}_i, \widetilde{\mathbf{E}}_i)\mathbf{V}_i\boldsymbol{\Lambda}_i^{-1/2}\mathbf{X}_i$.
  Update the current 3D shape estimate, $S(\mathbf{c}_\tau^T) = \sum_{l \le i} c_{\tau,l}\mathbf{S}_l$
  Update the 3D pose matrix $\mathbf{R}_\tau$ s.t. $\mathbf{w}^\tau \approx \mathbf{R}_\tau S(\mathbf{c}_\tau^T)$.
  Compute the 2D error $\mathbf{w}^\tau = \mathbf{w}^\tau - \mathbf{R}_\tau S(\mathbf{c}_\tau^T)$.
end for
Output: shape coefficients $\mathbf{c}_\tau^T$, 3D pose $\mathbf{R}_\tau$, and 3D shape $S(\mathbf{c}_\tau^T)$.

5 Experimental Results

We evaluate the proposed methods in three different applications. First, we compare the solutions of NRSFM with RIK against those of STA with its fixed DCT basis (see [14] for a comparison of STA against other NRSFM methods). Second, we provide experiments that show the generalization performance of our NRSFM solutions to newly seen 2D shapes. Finally, we illustrate and analyze the local modes of deformation extracted with Algorithm 2. Additional results are also available with the supplementary material at *http://cbcsl.ece.ohio-state.edu.*

We consider a variety of motion capture 3D datasets, with the number of frames and 3D points indicated as (T, n) after the dataset name: *face1* (74,37) [9]; *stretch* (370,41), *pick-up* (357,41), *yoga* (307,41), *dance* (264,75) [12]; and *walking* (260,55) [3]. The input $\mathbf{W}$ is obtained via 2D orthographic projection.

NRSFM with RIK *versus* STA: Temporal smoothness, enforced by STA, does not hold when the observed shape undergoes abrupt deformation, or when the data lacks temporal ordering. NRSFM with RIK does not suffer such limitations because it enforces spatial smoothness of $f(\cdot)$ in the RIK space. From (7),

Table 1. Average 3D error (standard deviation) of NRSFM solutions on temporally ordered and randomly permuted (π) datasets. Parameters (d, K or N) are also shown.

Algorithm	face1	stretch	pick-up	yoga	dance	walking
STA	0.056 (0.037)	0.068 (0.043)	0.228 (0.176)	0.147 (0.119)	0.172 (0.171)	0.105 (0.141)
A1	0.067 (0.041)	0.087 (0.062)	0.229 (0.175)	0.150 (0.120)	0.174 (0.164)	0.133 (0.203)
$A1_{aSFM}$	0.069 (0.049)	0.086 (0.053)	0.231 (0.173)	0.152 (0.120)	0.173 (0.163)	0.104 (0.120)
A2	0.063 (0.050)	0.118 (0.103)	0.231 (0.164)	0.163 (0.129)	0.212 (0.223)	0.180 (0.230)
$A2_{aSFM}$	0.084 (0.059)	0.120 (0.089)	0.223 (0.158)	0.168 (0.125)	0.215 (0.237)	0.177 (0.248)
STA^{π}	0.130 (0.098)	0.384 (0.346)	0.424 (0.281)	0.366 (0.303)	0.396 (0.312)	0.323 (0.445)
$A1^{\pi}$	0.067 (0.041)	0.087 (0.062)	0.229 (0.175)	0.150 (0.120)	0.174 (0.164)	0.133 (0.203)
$A1^{\pi}_{aSFM}$	0.069 (0.049)	0.086 (0.053)	0.231 (0.173)	0.152 (0.120)	0.173 (0.163)	0.104 (0.120)
$A2^{\pi}$	0.063 (0.050)	0.118 (0.103)	0.231 (0.164)	0.163 (0.129)	0.212 (0.223)	0.180 (0.230)
$A2^{\pi}_{aSFM}$	0.084 (0.059)	0.120 (0.089)	0.223 (0.158)	0.168 (0.125)	0.215 (0.237)	0.177 (0.248)
STA (d, K)	$0.3T$, 5	$0.1T$, 8	$0.1T$, 3	$0.1T$, 7	$0.1T$, 7	$0.3T$, 5
A1 (d, K)	$0.3T$, 5	$0.2T$, 8	$0.2T$, 3	$0.2T$, 7	$0.2T$, 7	$0.2T$, 5
$A1_{aSFM}$	$0.3T$, 5	$0.2T$, 8	$0.2T$, 3	$0.2T$, 7	$0.1T$, 7	$0.1T$, 5
A2 (d, N)	$0.4T$, 26	$0.3T$, 26	$0.3T$, 26	$0.3T$, 26	$0.2T$, 26	$0.1T$, 26
$A2_{aSFM}$	$0.3T$, 26	$0.1T$, 26	$0.1T$, 26	$0.1T$, 26	$0.1T$, 26	$0.2T$, 26

Table 2. Average 3D error (standard deviation) of new shapes using cross-validation

Algorithm	face1	stretch	pickup	yoga	dance	walking
A1	0.098 (0.101)	0.090 (0.059)	0.233 (0.174)	0.160 (0.125)	0.179 (0.180)	0.108 (0.123)
A2	0.125 (0.080)	0.126 (0.110)	0.245 (0.166)	0.167 (0.128)	0.216 (0.232)	0.278 (0.299)

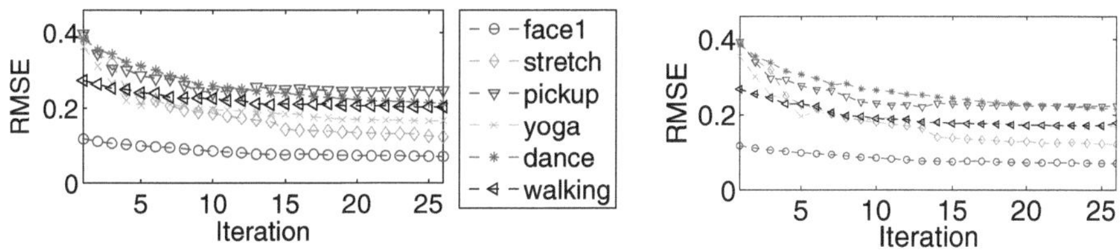

Fig. 2. Reconstruction errors of A2 versus the number of iterations: 2D RIK (left) and aSFM RIK (right). Final reconstructions are obtained with approximately 15 iterations.

note that the same function $f(\cdot)$ can be learned regardless of the temporal order of the input 2D shapes. The following experiment illustrates this property.

STA, Algorithm 1 (A1), and Algorithm 2 (A2) are first used to reconstruct 3D shapes from temporally ordered 2D shapes $\mathbf{w}^t$ in $\mathbf{W}$. Then, 3D reconstructions are computed from an unordered matrix $\mathbf{W}^{\pi}$, obtained with a random permutation $\pi(t)$ of the input 2D shapes. To focus on the evaluation of the different 3D shape models, all algorithms are run with the same rotation matrix, $\mathbf{D}$ or $\mathbf{D}^{\pi}$, obtained from the original $\mathbf{W}$ as in [11].

Table 1 shows the 3D reconstruction error for each algorithm – *i.e.*, average Euclidean distance to the 3D points of the ground truth shapes, normalized by average shape size [13]. Note that the performance of the RIK-based methods is unaffected by permutations in the input data, while the performance of STA decreases significantly. When temporal smoothness holds, the three algorithms show similar performance, with compact solutions (small d). The similar performance presented by the aSFM and the 2D RIK shows that the 2D RIK adequately captures shape variations in the input data. Overall, the aSFM RIK often leads to more compact solutions while the 2D RIK is faster to evaluate. Table 1 shows the best results of STA and A1 with $K = 1, 2, \ldots, 26$. While the results of NRSFM methods in general degenerate as K increases (*i.e.*, as the low-rank constraint is gradually relaxed), the reconstructions obtained with the IRLS-based A2 are less sensitive to the choice of this parameter. Fig. 2 shows that the solutions of A2 on each dataset stabilized after approximately 15 iterations. A2 also computes sparse modes of deformation with more meaningful information to computer vision applications, as discussed later in this section.

Reconstruction of newly observed 2D shapes: Another key advantage of NRSFM with RIKs is the capability of recovering 3D shapes of newly observed 2D shapes using the learned function $f(\cdot)$. Considering this scenario, we illustrate the performance of A1 and A2 using 30-fold cross-validation: the 2D shapes in $\mathbf{W}$ are randomly permuted and divided into 30 validation sets. In each fold, one validation set $\mathcal{S}_{\mathbf{W}}$ with nearly 3% of the 2D shapes is left out of the input data $\mathbf{W}$ and $f(\cdot)$ is learned from the remaining 2D shapes, with $(d, K$ or $N)$ set as in Table 1. Then the 3D reconstruction of each 2D shape $\mathbf{w}^{\tau} \in \mathcal{S}_{\mathbf{W}}$ is obtained using (10) or Algorithm 3. This process is repeated for each validation set. The average 3D error of all these reconstructions is shown in Table 2, for each dataset. These errors are similar to those obtained on the complete datasets (Table 1), indicating that the learned functions correctly reconstructed the new 2D shapes.

We also performed a similar experiment using 2D face shapes of a single person, taken from the real video sequence *ASL* (114,77) of [14]. First, $\mathrm{A1}_{\mathrm{aSFM}}$ $(K = 4, d = 0.3T)$ was used to recover the 3D shapes of all 114 input 2D faces, Fig. 3(left). Then a second 3D reconstruction was computed for each 2D shape, this time using 30-fold cross-validation as above. Comparing these two sets of 3D shapes, we observed a very small average 3D difference of 0.025 (0.034),

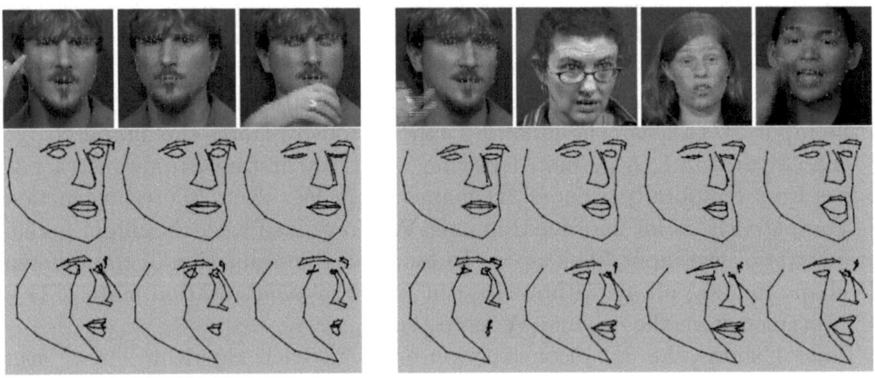

Fig. 3. Using the mapping $f(\cdot)$ learned from a real dataset: (*left*) sample 2D face shapes (green dots) of a same person and NRSFM solution of $\mathrm{A1}_{\mathrm{aSFM}}$, in two views; (*right*) result of evaluating the learned $f(\cdot)$ on newly seen 2D face shapes from different people.

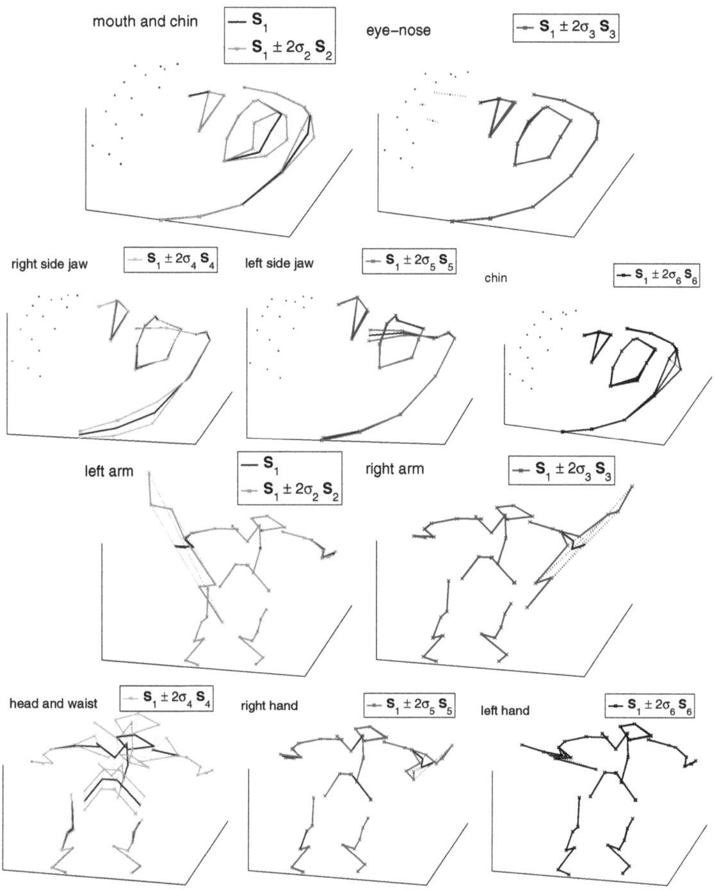

Fig. 4. The 3D shape bases obtained in the first 6 iterations of Algorithm 2 on *face1* and *stretch*. The 3D basis shapes $\mathbf{S}_2, ..., \mathbf{S}_6$ correspond to sub-shape deformations around the rigid shape component $\mathbf{S}_1$ of the first iteration. These deformations are shown as $\mathbf{S}_1 \pm 2\sigma_i \mathbf{S}_i$, with σ_i the standard deviations of the corresponding coefficients. Note that the original motion capture markers on *stretch* were not located along straight lines.

relative to the average face size. As an additional experiment, we also evaluated the learned $f(\cdot)$ on input 2D shapes from a separate dataset with faces of the same person and also faces of other people. This is an example application in transfer of facial expression across subjects, which is very useful in computer graphics and animation. Note that, in cases of occlusion, the kernel is evaluated only on the subset of points that are observed on both 2D shapes being compared. Fig. 3(right) shows that the recovered 3D shapes do capture the learned deformations even when expressed by other people. As expected, the recovered 3D shapes can only express the identity and modes of deformation learned during the NRSFM (training) stage, using the data illustrated in Fig. 3(left). Nevertheless, this is not a limitation of our approach because, with the removal of the temporal smoothness assumption, the NRSFM stage can consider multiple datasets depicting different identities and shape variations (deformations). Naturally, if the newly observed 2D shapes differ considerably from the training shapes, 3D reconstruction may be inaccurate due to the limitations of the shape model when used for extrapolation. Future work will develop this capability further, considering new constraints such as ensuring $\mathbf{c}^T = f(\mathbf{w}^T)$ remains in the vicinity of the training samples within the learned shape space.

Recovered Modes of Local 3D Deformation: A limitation of most kernel methods is the use of a unique parameter σ, defining the smoothness of the estimated function globally. The Gaussian weighting masks $\mathbf{G}_i$ of A2 can be seen as altering (customizing) σ for each column on the input error matrix $\mathbf{E}_i$. This is important in NRSFM because the observed objects often present localized deformations with different spatial smoothness (*e.g.*, mouth shapes of a talking face present larger variations than nose shapes). A2 can model these local deformations by extracting a set of functions that correspond to sub-shape variations. The property described above is illustrated by the extracted modes of deformation shown in Fig. 4. For *face1*, the local deformation $\mathbf{S}_2$ represents mouth opening and closing (correlated with chin movement), $\mathbf{S}_3$ eye-nose distance, $\mathbf{S}_4$ right side jaw, $\mathbf{S}_5$ left side jaw, and $\mathbf{S}_6$ chin movements. For *stretch*, the deformations are: $\mathbf{S}_2$ left arm, $\mathbf{S}_3$ right arm, $\mathbf{S}_4$ head and waist, $\mathbf{S}_5$ right hand, and $\mathbf{S}_6$ left hand movements. In comparison to the standard model in NRSFM, the basis shapes above describe more meaningful, local deformations that can be combined in different ways as to better extrapolate new 3D shapes. Future work on A2 will explore this fact to further improve the generalization of the learned function $f(\cdot)$ to shapes largely different than those seen in the NRSFM stage.

6 Conclusion

We propose a new kernel-based solution to NRSFM that is not restricted to cases of smooth deformations over time. The main idea is to use a spatial, rather than temporal, smoothness constraint. Using a RIK and KPCA, we derive a smooth function that outputs 3D shape coefficients directly from an input 2D shape. As a result, we learn a custom-built basis to model the shape coefficient compactly while solving NRSFM. The learned mapping becomes a by-product of our NRSFM solution and leads to another fundamental advantage of our approach: for a newly observed 2D shape, its 3D reconstruction is obtained via the simple evaluation of this function. Finally, we also propose a novel model fitting algorithm based on IRLS that computes localized modes of deformation carrying meaningful information to computer vision applications.

NRSFM with RIK is a generic new approach that can make use of customized RIKs to build mappings that even exploit correlations between object appearance and 3D shape. Our approach can potentially combine the functionalities of NRSFM and 3D active appearance models with RIKs [19]: while NRSFM is seen as the training stage, “testing” corresponds to the evaluation of the learned mapping with a previously unseen 2D shape. These new capabilities allow for learning deformable models in a studio, reliably (*e.g.*, with known camera positions in $\mathbf{D}$), to reconstruct the 3D shapes of objects observed elsewhere.

Acknowledgements. This research was supported by the National Institutes of Health, grants R01 EY 020834 and R21 DC 011081.

References

1. Hartley, R., Zisserman, A.: Multiple View Geometry in Computer Vision. Cambridge University Press (2003)
2. Bregler, C., Hertzmann, A., Biermann, H.: Recovering non-rigid 3d shape from image streams. In: Proc. IEEE CVPR, vol. 2, pp. 690–696 (2000)
3. Torresani, L., Hertzmann, A., Bregler, C.: Nonrigid structure-from-motion: Estimating shape and motion with hierarchical priors. IEEE Trans. PAMI 30, 878–892 (2008)
4. Bartoli, A., Gay-Bellile, V., Castellani, U., Peyras, J., Olsen, S., Sayd, P.: Coarse-to-fine low-rank structure-from-motion. In: IEEE CVPR, vol. 1, pp. 1–8 (2008)
5. Yan, J., Pollefeys, M.: A factorization-based approach for articulated nonrigid shape, motion and kinematic chain recovery from video. IEEE Trans. PAMI 30, 865–877 (2008)
6. Rabaud, V., Belongie, S.: Rethinking nonrigid structure from motion. In: Proc. IEEE CVPR, vol. 1, pp. 1–8 (2008)
7. Rabaud, V., Belongie, S.: Linear embeddings in non-rigid structure from motion. In: Proc. IEEE CVPR (2009)
8. Del Bue, A., Llado, X., Agapito, L.: Non-rigid metric shape and motion recovery from uncalibrated images using priors. In: Proc. IEEE CVPR, vol. 1, pp. 1191–1198 (2006)
9. Paladini, M., Del Bue, A., Stošić, M., Dodig, M., Xavier, J., Agapito, L.: Factorization for non-rigid and articulated structure using metric projections. In: Proc. IEEE CVPR, pp. 2898–2905 (2009)
10. Fayad, J., Russell, C., Agapito, L.: Automated articulated structure and 3d shape recovery from point correspondences. In: Proc. IEEE ICCV (2011)
11. Akhter, I., Sheikh, Y., Khan, S.: In defense of orthonormality constraints for non-rigid structure from motion. In: Proc. IEEE CVPR, pp. 1534–1541 (2009)
12. Akhter, I., Sheikh, Y.A., Khan, S., Kanade, T.: Trajectory space: A dual representation for nonrigid structure from motion. IEEE Trans. PAMI 33, 1442–1456 (2011)
13. Gotardo, P.F.U., Martinez, A.M.: Computing smooth time-trajectories for camera and deformable shape in structure from motion with occlusion. IEEE Trans. PAMI 33, 2051–2065 (2011)
14. Gotardo, P.F.U., Martinez, A.M.: Non-rigid structure from motion with complementary rank-3 spaces. In: Proc. IEEE CVPR, pp. 3065–3072 (2011)
15. Gotardo, P.F.U., Martinez, A.M.: Kernel non-rigid structure from motion. In: Proc. IEEE ICCV (2011)
16. Hamsici, O.C., Martinez, A.M.: Rotation invariant kernels and their application to shape analysis. IEEE Trans. PAMI 31, 1985–1999 (2009)
17. Scholkopf, B., Smola, A.J.: Learning with Kernels: Support Vector Machines, Regularization, Optimization, and Beyond. MIT Press (2002)
18. Hastie, T., Tibshirani, R., Friedman, J.H.: The elements of statistical learning: data mining, inference, and prediction, 2nd edn. Springer (2008)
19. Hamsici, O.C., Martinez, A.M.: Active appearance models with rotation invariant kernels. In: Proc. IEEE ICCV (2009)

In Defence of RANSAC for Outlier Rejection in Deformable Registration

Quoc-Huy Tran[1], Tat-Jun Chin[1], Gustavo Carneiro[1], Michael S. Brown[2], and David Suter[1]

[1] School of Computer Science, The University of Adelaide, Australia
{huy,tjchin,carneiro,dsuter}@cs.adelaide.edu.au
[2] School of Computing, National University of Singapore, Singapore
brown@comp.nus.edu.sg

Abstract. This paper concerns the robust estimation of non-rigid deformations from feature correspondences. We advance the surprising view that for many realistic physical deformations, the error of the mismatches (outliers) usually dwarfs the effects of the curvature of the manifold on which the correct matches (inliers) lie, to the extent that one can tightly enclose the manifold within the error bounds of a low-dimensional hyperplane for accurate outlier rejection. This justifies a simple RANSAC-driven deformable registration technique that is at least as accurate as other methods based on the optimisation of fully deformable models. We support our ideas with comprehensive experiments on synthetic and real data typical of the deformations examined in the literature.

1 Introduction

The goal of non-rigid registration is to align pixels in two or more images corresponding to an object which can move and deform smoothly, e.g., a beating heart, a waving t-shirt. The task is usually accomplished by estimating the transformation (e.g., a Radial Basic Function - RBF - warp) which maps pixels from one image to another. Representative applications include shape matching, segmentation in medical images, and retexturing of deformable surfaces.

A popular class of methods relies on detecting and matching salient features (keypoints) between the images, which are then used to learn the mapping parameters [1–4]. A critical issue in such *feature-based* methods is the identification and rejection of mismatches which unavoidably arise due to imperfect keypoint detection and matching. If no mismatches exist, estimating the transformation is trivial, e.g., by solving a linear system for a Thin Plate Spline (TPS) warp [5].

Common sense suggests that standard outlier rejection tools like RANSAC [6] are inapplicable, the fundamental obstacle being that the underlying transformation is of *unknown* and *varying* complexity [7, 8], i.e., the size of the minimal subset cannot be determined. It is also widely assumed that many realistic deformations (e.g., bending paper, rippling cloth) are too non-linear to be amenable to simple geometric modelling. Fig. 2(a) depicts such impressions of the data.

This paper advances the surprising view that, in practice, the scale of error of the mismatches are orders of magnitude larger than the effects of the curvature

A. Fitzgibbon et al. (Eds.): ECCV 2012, Part IV, LNCS 7575, pp. 274–287, 2012.

(a) SIFT correspondences between a template and an input image. True matches are in green while incorrect matches are in red.

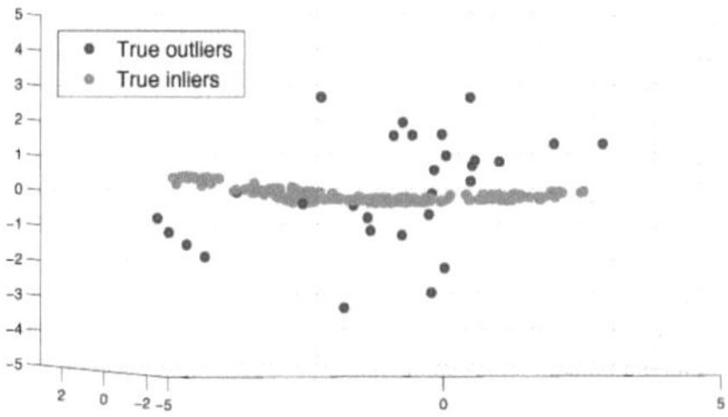

(b) Correspondences from (a) plotted using first-3 principal components.

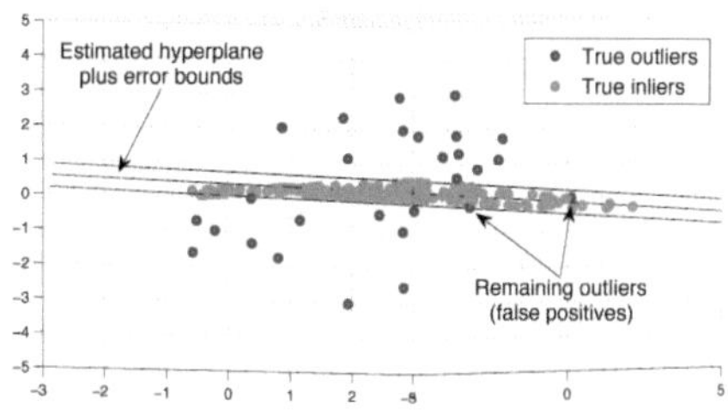

(c) Another view of (b) with the fitted hyperplane shown in its "side view".

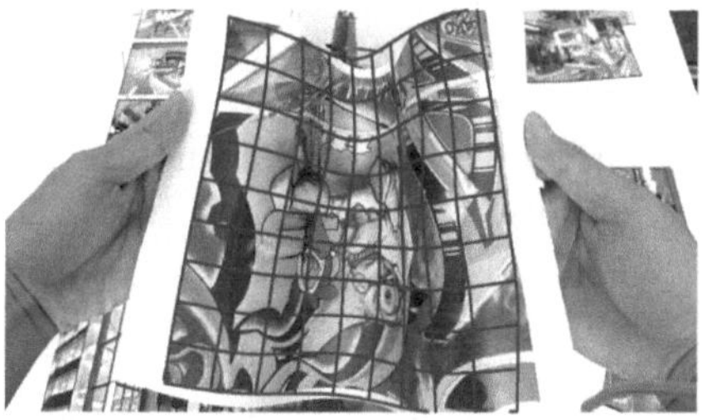

(d) TPS estimated using matches lying within the hyperplane bounds in (c).

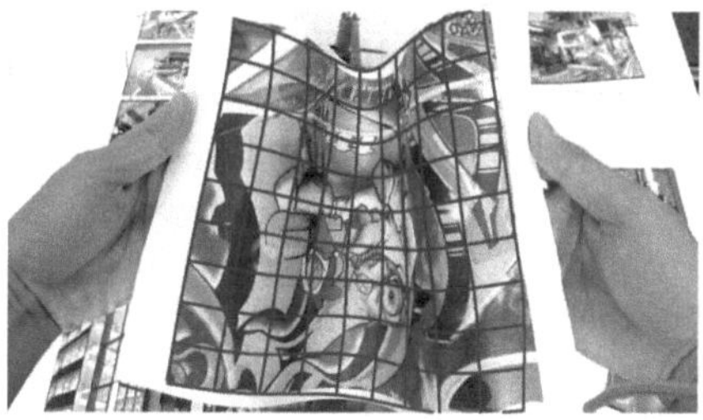

(e) TPS estimated using the true correspondences identified manually.

Fig. 1. Feature-based robust deformable registration using RANSAC

of the manifold containing the correct matches. Fig. 1 illustrates what we mean with images showing a sheet of paper bending — this kind of data is typically used in the literature, e.g., see [1, 8, 9]. SIFT [10] is first invoked to yield a set of correspondences $\mathcal{X} = \{\mathbf{x}_i\}_{i=1}^N$, where each $\mathbf{x}_i = [x_i \ y_i \ x'_i \ y'_i]^T \in \mathbb{R}^4$. Projecting the data onto the first-3 principal components reveals that the correct matches (inliers) are actually distributed compactly on a 2D affine hyperplane, *relative* to the gross error of the mismatches; see Figs 1(b) and 1(c). This means that we can robustly fit a hyperplane onto the data to dichotomise the inliers and outliers; Fig 1(d) shows the TPS warp estimated using the matches returned by RANSAC, which models the underlying warp very well. As we show later, this is characteristic of many of the physical deformations tested in the literature.

Our observation motivates the point that, for many types of deformations, a linear hyperplane is adequate to model the "correspondence manifold" for

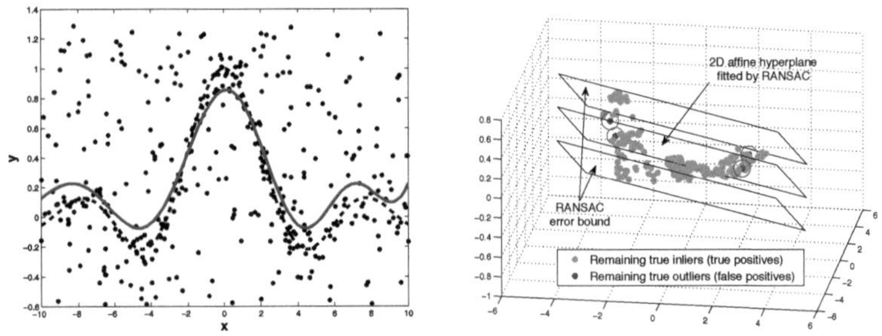

(a) (b)

Fig. 2. (a) The characteristic and level of difficulty of the correspondence manifold targeted in [11]. This figure(a) is taken from [11]. (b) Data remaining after RANSAC, shown in the "local" scale of the manifold.

outlier removal. Any outliers remaining (i.e., false positives) are relatively benign rather than outright mismatches, and can usually be smoothened out by the regulariser of the warp estimator; see Fig. 2(b). Observe that the TPS in Fig. 1(d) is very similar to the "ground truth" TPS in Fig. 1(e) estimated using only the true inliers. It is worth noting that without further pixel-based refinement [9], warps estimated from keypoint matches alone cannot extrapolate well to correspondence-poor or occluded regions; see bottom right of Fig. 1(e).

In a sense our observation is not surprising, since PROSAC [12] - a variant of RANSAC - has been used as preprocessing to remove egregious mismatches or to provide affine initialisations for warp estimation [3, 4] (although it was not used in [1, 2], there are few obstacles to initialise with PROSAC/RANSAC there). However, it has always been assumed that due to the complexity of the inlier distribution, significant outliers will remain and it is vital to further optimise the warp robustly, e.g., by an annealing procedure which jointly identifies outliers and learns deformation parameters [3, 4]. Our aim is to show that such procedures overestimate the difficulty of the data, and basic RANSAC followed directly by (non-robust) warp estimation is sufficient.

Close to our work are recently proposed outlier rejection schemes for deformable registration [13, 11, 9]. In [11], SVM regression is used in conjunction with resampling to learn the correspondence manifold in the presence of outliers. In Section 3 of [9], local smoothness constraints are imposed (via Delaunay triangulation) to enable an iterative deformable outlier rejection scheme. These methods assume that substantial non-linearity of the data precludes the usage of RANSAC, which disagrees with our observation typified by Fig. 1(b). Using synthetic and real datasets, we convincingly show that basic RANSAC is at least as accurate as these approaches.

The rest of the paper is organised as follows: Sec. 1.1 surveys related work to put this paper in the context. Sec. 2 explains how RANSAC can be applied for outlier rejection, as well as presents detailed experiments on synthetic and real data. Sec. 3 investigates and compares the performance of our approach on retexturing of deformable surfaces, using publicly available sequences. We conclude and summarise our work in Sec. 4.

1.1 Related Work

Two major paradigms of image-based deformable registration can be distinguished: feature-based methods which rely on keypoint detection and matching [1–4], and pixel-based methods which operate on pixels directly [14, 15]. Feature-based methods are faster but less accurate, and cannot extrapolate well to correspondence-poor areas. However they are crucial for bootstrapping pixel-based methods which are more accurate but slower [9]. Since feature-based methods can only be relied upon to produce "rough" registration, it is desirable to keep this stage of the pipeline as simple and fast as possible. We argue that, on many datasets, bootstrapping based on RANSAC is sufficient.

More recently, methods capable of outlier rejection in feature-based deformable registration have been proposed ([13, 11], Section 3 of [9]). Li et al. [13, 11] proposed that outlier rejection amounts to robustly learning the "correspondence manifold" which, as depicted in Fig. 2(a), is assumed to be highly non-linear and mixed among uniformly distributed outliers. We show that such an assumption is overly pessimistic, since on many datasets the scale of the matching errors is extreme relative to the non-linearity of the manifold.

A parallel area is non-rigid structure from motion (NRSfM), where the aim is to recover the structure of objects that have deformed between views. A number of works assume the deformation to be piecewise rigid [16, 17], which is equivalent to recognising that the distribution of non-rigid data has low degrees of variation. Our work is different in that, towards the goal of outlier rejection for deformable registration, we propose that a *single and global* affine model (instead of a set of rigid or affine models) is sufficient for most correspondence data.

Note that our work is different to non-rigid point cloud or shape alignment, e.g., [18, 19], where the inputs are two sets of unmatched discrete points or landmarks, usually without accompanying image textures. This requires the joint estimation of the transformation and correspondence, whereas our work focusses on rejecting wrongly matched keypoints before non-rigid registration.

2 Outlier Rejection for Deformable Registration

In this section we describe how RANSAC can be applied to outlier rejection in deformable registration, and present experimental results to examine its efficacy.

2.1 The Correspondence Manifold

RBF warps have been applied extensively to model the deformation of various kinds of objects [5]. For deformations of 2D image features, it is common to use two separate RBF warps that share the same centres $\{\mathbf{c}_k\}_{k=1}^K$

$$\begin{bmatrix} x \\ y \end{bmatrix} \mapsto \begin{bmatrix} x' \\ y' \end{bmatrix} \quad \text{where} \quad \begin{matrix} x' = [x\ y\ 1]^T \mathbf{a}_1 + \mathbf{w}_1^T \boldsymbol{l}(x,y) \\ y' = [x\ y\ 1]^T \mathbf{a}_2 + \mathbf{w}_2^T \boldsymbol{l}(x,y) \end{matrix}, \tag{1}$$

$\boldsymbol{l}(x, y)$ is a non-linear lifting function encapsulating the centres

$$\boldsymbol{l}(x, y) = [\phi(\|[x\ y]^T - \mathbf{c}_1\|_2)\ \dots\ \phi(\|[x\ y]^T - \mathbf{c}_K\|_2)]^T, \tag{2}$$

and $\phi(\cdot)$ is the RBF, e.g., Gaussian or TPS. Given a set of matching features $\mathcal{X} = \{(x_i, y_i), (x'_i, y'_i)\}_{i=1}^N$, the centres are taken as $\{(x_i, y_i)\}_{i=1}^N$. Learning an RBF involves estimating the affine parameters $\mathbf{a}_1, \mathbf{a}_2$ and the coefficients $\mathbf{w}_1, \mathbf{w}_2$ with regularisation to control the warp's bending energy. For TPS warps this can be achieved by solving a linear system [5].

By regarding each correspondence as a point $\mathbf{x}_i = [x_i\ y_i\ x'_i\ y'_i]^T$ in the joint image space $\mathbb{R}^4$, it can be shown that $\mathcal{X} = \{\mathbf{x}_i\}_{i=1}^N$ are samples from a smooth manifold [13]. It is clear that the manifold is two dimensional due to the two degrees of freedom of (x_i, y_i). Assuming that the underlying warp is an RBF warp, we can express each point on the manifold as

$$\mathbf{x}_i = \underbrace{\begin{bmatrix} 1 & 0 \\ 0 & 1 \\ \mathbf{a}_{11} & \mathbf{a}_{21} \\ \mathbf{a}_{12} & \mathbf{a}_{22} \end{bmatrix} \begin{bmatrix} x_i \\ y_i \end{bmatrix} + \begin{bmatrix} 0 \\ 0 \\ \mathbf{a}_{13} \\ \mathbf{a}_{23} \end{bmatrix}}_{\text{2D affine subspace}} + \underbrace{\begin{bmatrix} 0 \\ 0 \\ \mathbf{w}_1^T \boldsymbol{l}(x_i, y_i) \\ \mathbf{w}_2^T \boldsymbol{l}(x_i, y_i) \end{bmatrix}}_{\text{Non-linear deviation}}, \tag{3}$$

where $\mathbf{a}_{pq}$ is the q-th component of the p-th affine parameter vector. In other words, the correspondence manifold "undulates" around a 2D affine subspace, and the deviation of each $\mathbf{x}_i$ from the subspace is due to the data-dependent non-linear terms $\mathbf{w}_p^T \boldsymbol{l}(x_i, y_i)$; see Fig. 2(b).

Given a set of matched keypoints $\mathcal{X}$ containing outliers, our premise is that the effects of the matching errors far outweigh the deviation of the true inliers from the affine component of the correspondence manifold. To illustrate this point, Fig. 3 plots the distribution of the orthogonal distances of the data in Fig. 1(a) to the RANSAC-fitted 2D affine hyperplane in Fig. 1(b). It is apparent that a clear separation exists between the inlier and outlier distribution.

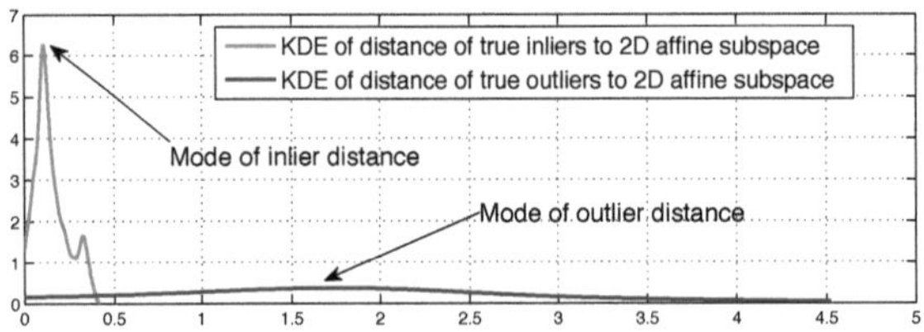

Fig. 3. Distribution of distances to RANSAC-fitted 2D affine hyperplane

2.2 Outlier Rejection and Warp Estimation Using RANSAC

Our observations suggest that RANSAC is sufficient for outlier rejection in deformable registration. The goal is to robustly fit a 2D affine subspace onto $\mathcal{X}$. A minimal solution can be estimated from three data randomly sampled from $\mathcal{X}$ (recall that each datum $\mathbf{x}_i = [x_i\ y_i\ x'_i\ y'_i]^T \in \mathcal{X}$ is a particular correspondence). Let $S = [\mathbf{x}_{s_1}\ \mathbf{x}_{s_2}\ \mathbf{x}_{s_3}] \in \mathbb{R}^{4\times3}$ be a random minimal subset with the data concatenated horizontally. First, the mean of the sample $\boldsymbol{\mu}_S$ is subtracted from each column to yield $\hat{S}$, whose first-two left singular vectors $\mathbf{A}_{\hat{S}} \in \mathbb{R}^{4\times 2}$ are then obtained. The pair $(\boldsymbol{\mu}_S, \mathbf{A}_{\hat{S}})$ is sufficient to characterise the affine subspace. The residual (orthogonal distance) of datum $\mathbf{x}_i$ to the fitted subspace is

$$d(\mathbf{x}_i|\boldsymbol{\mu}_S, \mathbf{A}_{\hat{S}}) = \left\|\mathbf{x}_i - \mathbf{A}_{\hat{S}}\mathbf{A}_{\hat{S}}^T(\mathbf{x}_i - \boldsymbol{\mu}_S) - \boldsymbol{\mu}_S\right\|_2. \tag{4}$$

RANSAC iteratively generates a set of M 2D affine subspace hypotheses, each fitted on a randomly sampled minimal subset. The consensus of a hypothesis is the number of data with residual less than θ from the associated 2D affine subspace, and the hypothesis with the maximum consensus is returned. The inliers of the best hypothesis are then used to estimate the RBF warp.

A crucial parameter is the threshold θ. Firstly, to allow the usage of a constant θ for all datasets, we normalise the data such that the centroid of $\{(x_i, y_i)\}_{i=1}^N$ lies at the origin, and the mean distance of all points to the original is $\sqrt{2}$. The same normalisation is applied on the points $\{(x'_i, y'_i)\}_{i=1}^N$. The threshold parameter is then manually tuned and used for input images. *Note that an equivalent threshold on the error is required in the other methods* [1–4, 13, 11, 9] (e.g., r in [1, 2], σ in [3, 4], ξ in [11], and d_{TH} in [9]).

A second important parameter is the number of hypotheses M. To ensure with probability p that at least one all-inlier minimal subset is retrieved,

$$M = \frac{\log(1-p)}{\log(1-(1-\epsilon)^3)}, \tag{5}$$

where ϵ is the ratio of outliers among $\mathcal{X}$. For example, for $p = 0.99$ and $\epsilon = 0.5$, M is approximately 35. In practice the number of iterations used is several times larger than the predicted M. In our experiments we consistently set $M = 100$ for all datasets; as we show later this is still faster than other methods. Moreover, M can be further reduced by using guided sampling methods [12, 20] or the threshold θ can also be estimated automatically [21, 22], though we do not explore these options in our work.

2.3 Experiments on Synthetic Data

We first test the performance of RANSAC on synthetic data. A rectangular mesh is created with control points (RBF centres) distributed on a grid. Using the control points, a TPS warp is randomly generated following the method proposed in [23]. Inliers are produced by randomly sampling 100 positions on the template mesh and mapped using the synthesised TPS warp. The mapped points are then perturbed with Gaussian noise of std. dev. 5 pixels. We then randomly sample positions on the left and right "image" to form outliers. Fig. 4 shows data generated in this manner, with $\epsilon = 0.33$ (33% outliers). Parameter ν in the random warp generator controls the bending energy of the warp (see [23] for details). The effects of different values of ν are shown also in Fig. 4. Observe that for $\nu = 200$ and 500 the mesh is deformed seriously with self-occlusions.

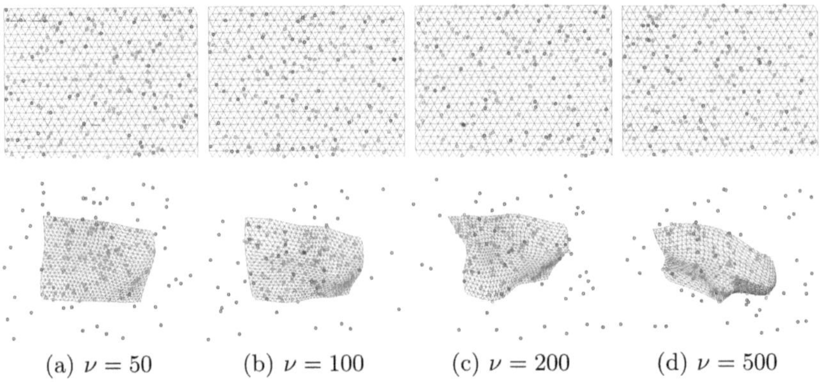

Fig. 4. Top row: Template meshes. Bottom: Meshes warped using randomly generated TPS warps, with bending energy increasing from left to right. Green and red points indicate respectively inliers and outliers (correspondence lines not drawn for clarity).

We benchmark RANSAC against state-of-the-art outlier rejection methods for deformable registration: Iterative local smoothness test [9] (Section 3 of that article) and SVM regression with resampling [11]. We also compare against the class of annealed M-estimation methods [1–4]; since these methods are comparable in accuracy, it is sufficient to compare against [3] which offers the most efficient algorithm. Note that [1–4] can jointly optimise the warp identify outliers; here we concentrate on the aspect of outlier rejection/identification.

The ROC curve of each method is obtained by varying the threshold parameter and recording the resultant true positive rate (number of true inliers recovered over all true inliers) and false positive rate (number of true outliers misidentified as inliers over all true outliers). We set $\nu = 50, 100, 200$ and 500, and for each ν, the outlier rate ϵ is set as 0.33 and 0.5. For each combination of ν and ϵ, 100 random (and distinct) TPS warps are generated, and the ROC curves for each method are averaged over the 100 warps. Fig. 5 presents the results.

An apparent and expected trend is that as ν and ϵ increase, the accuracy of all methods decrease, with the method of [11] deteriorating the fastest, followed by [9]. The other two methods provide very comparable accuracies[1]. The strength of our method, however, lies in its simplicity and efficiency. Table 1 presents the average running time of all methods for $\epsilon = 0.33$ and 0.5, where RANSAC is clearly the fastest[2]. The major factors affecting the speed of RANSAC are the outlier rate ϵ and the size of the minimal subset — since only three data are required for a minimal solution, RANSAC can tolerate large ϵ's without significant sampling effort. On the other hand, the algorithms of [3, 11, 9] are more complicated and the run times scale with the data size.

[1] We were unable to secure the authors' own implementation of the competing algorithms. However the generally good performance of the competing methods implies that our implementation is correct. See code in supplementary material.

[2] Following a reviewer's comment, we have optimised our implementation of [3]. All methods were implemented and run in MATLAB, which makes the results in Table 1 an accurate picture for *relative* comparisons of run time.

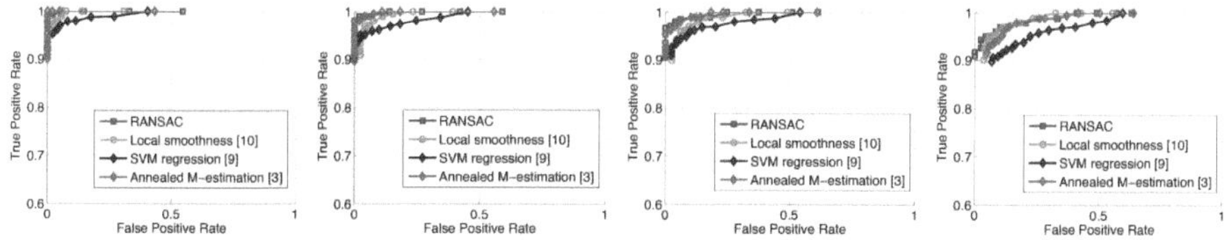

(a) $\nu = 50, \epsilon = 0.33$ (b) $\nu = 100, \epsilon = 0.33$ (c) $\nu = 200, \epsilon = 0.33$ (d) $\nu = 500, \epsilon = 0.33$

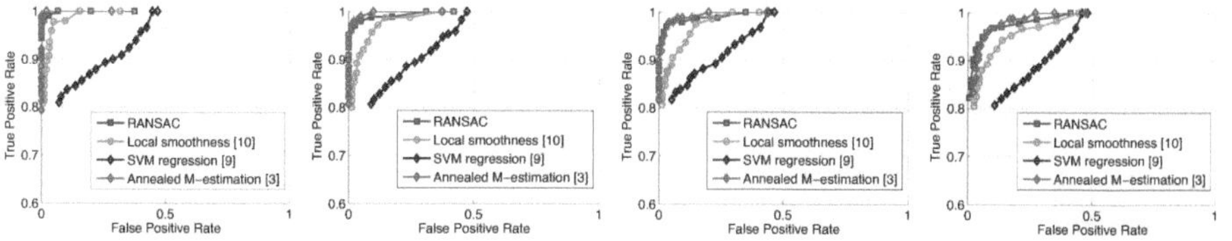

(e) $\nu = 50, \epsilon = 0.5$ (f) $\nu = 100, \epsilon = 0.5$ (g) $\nu = 200, \epsilon = 0.5$ (h) $\nu = 500, \epsilon = 0.5$

Fig. 5. ROC curves for outlier rejection on synthetic data

Table 1. Average run time (in seconds) for outlier rejection on synthetic data

	$\epsilon = 0.33$ (total 150 matches)	$\epsilon = 0.5$ (total 200 matches)
RANSAC	0.04	0.04
Local smoothness [9]	0.26	0.29
SVM regression [11]	0.06	0.09
Annealed M-estimation [3]	1.41	2.92

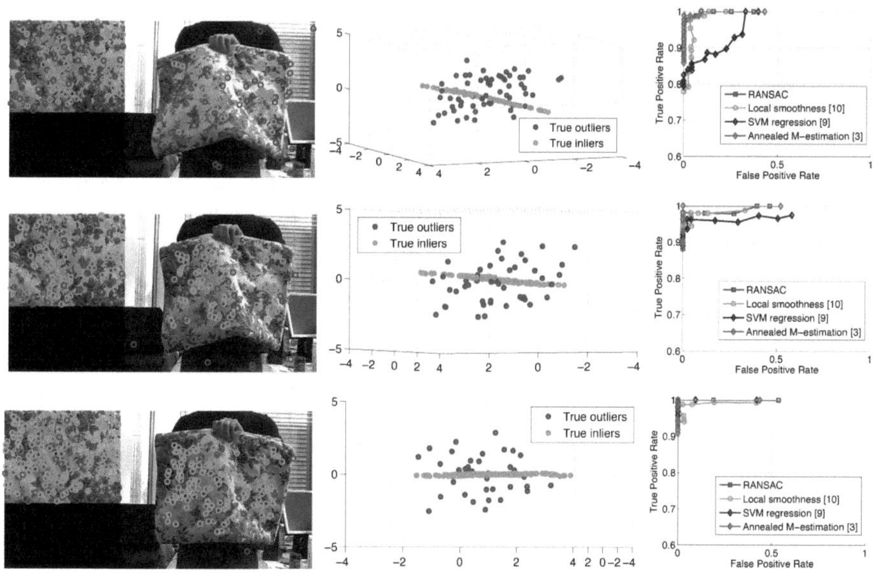

Fig. 6. Results on Frame 140 (145 matches, 41.38% outliers), Frame 160 (152 matches, 31.58% outliers) and Frame 178 (196 matches, 19.90% outliers) from the bedsheet sequence. Col 1: SIFT matches. Col 2: Data after PCA. Col 3: ROC curves.

Table 2. Average run time (in seconds) for outlier rejection on real data

Sequence name	bedsheet			tshirt			cushion		
Frame number	140	160	178	407	720	784	160	175	190
RANSAC	0.04	0.04	0.04	0.04	0.04	0.04	0.04	0.04	0.04
Local smoothness [9]	0.26	0.29	0.28	0.21	0.17	0.19	0.28	0.26	0.22
SVM regression [11]	0.06	0.06	0.08	0.06	0.04	0.05	0.12	0.10	0.06
Annealed M-estimation [3]	1.34	1.52	3.36	1.66	1.40	1.33	3.04	2.30	1.70

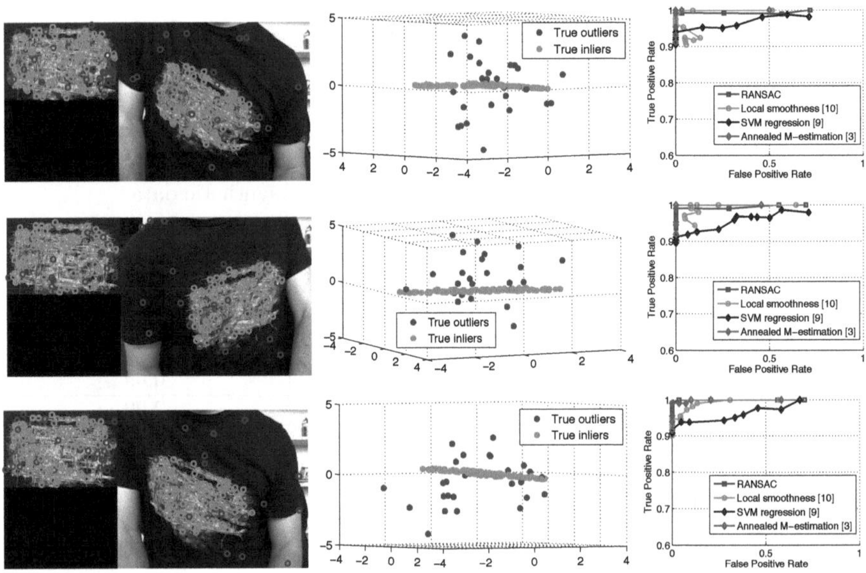

Fig. 7. Results on Frame 407 (154 matches, 19.48% outliers), Frame 720 (127 matches, 18.90% outliers) and Frame 784 (136 matches, 19.85% outliers) from the tshirt sequence. Col 1: SIFT matches. Col 2: Data after PCA. Col 3: ROC curves.

2.4 Experiments on Real Data

We now test our method on real images. We used publicly available[3] image sequences previously used for NRSfM (e.g., see [24]). In this experiment we chose 3 representative frames from the 3 hardest sequences (bedsheet, tshirt and cushion) as input images for outlier rejection. A subimage encapsulating a large portion of the surface was cropped from the first image of each sequence to form the template image. SIFT was invoked to produce keypoint matches, which we then manually categorised as true inliers and outliers. For RANSAC, 100 repetitions were performed on each input image and the average results (ROC curves) are reported. Figs. 6, 7 and 8 illustrate the results.

[3] Obtained from `http://cvlab.epfl.ch/data/dsr/`

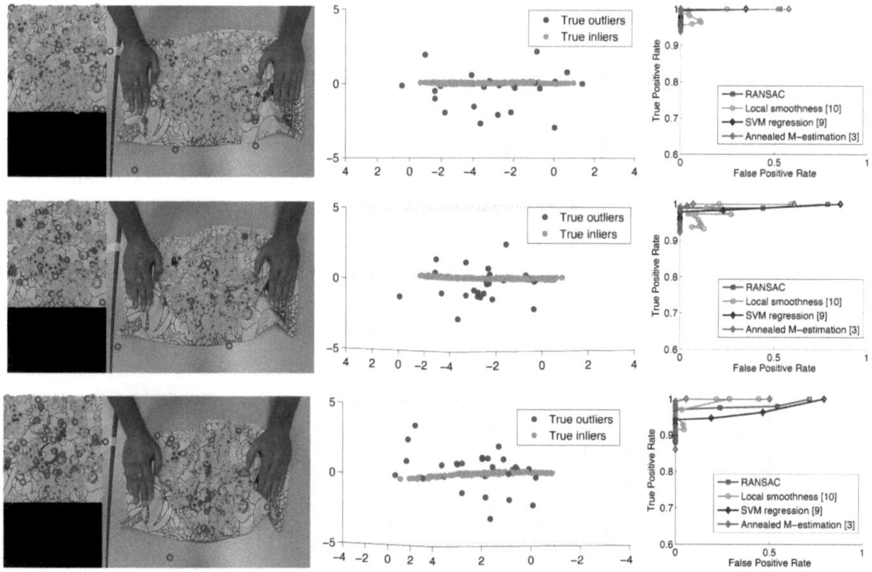

Fig. 8. Results on Frame 160 (234 matches, 10.68% outliers), Frame 175 (205 matches, 13.17% outliers) and Frame 190 (163 matches, 20.25% outliers) from the cushion sequence. Col 1: SIFT matches. Col 2: Data after PCA. Col 3: ROC curves.

Table 3. Number of vertices in warped mesh within 3 pixels away from corresponding vertices in the ground truth mesh

Sequence name	bedsheet			tshirt			cushion		
Frame number	140	160	178	407	720	784	160	175	190
RANSAC	603	728	810	667	660	653	667	666	649
Local smoothness [9]	400	518	675	475	339	217	667	552	645
SVM regression [11]	17	146	702	294	138	220	659	564	473
Annealed M-estimation [3]	648	810	810	667	667	663	667	666	667

The low-dimensional visualisations of all data show that again, relative to the outliers, the inliers are distributed compactly within a 2D affine hyperplane. Based on the ROC curves, a similar conclusion can be made on the accuracy of outlier rejection, i.e., annealed M-estimation [3] and RANSAC are the most accurate, followed by iterative local smoothness test [9] and SVM regression with resampling [11]. The run times of all methods are depicted in Table 2. Again, RANSAC is the fastest method, with constant run times across all images.

The data in which the gap in accuracy between annealed M-estimation [3] and RANSAC is the largest is Frame 190 of cushion (Fig. 8). In the next section we investigate the practical difference due to this disparity in accuracy. *Due to page limits, we provide outlier rejection and warp estimation results on all frames of the sequences (and on other sequences) as supplementary material.*

3 Retexturing Deformable Surfaces

Figs. 9, 10 and 11 provide qualitative comparisons of two best performing outlier rejection methods in Sec. 2.4. The warps for the meshes (for images used in Sec. 2.4) are obtained by first using RANSAC and annealed M-estimation [3] to reject outliers, and then using the remaining matches to estimate a TPS warp. The ground truth warp is obtained by estimating a TPS warp using only true inliers. The threshold value for RANSAC and annealed M-estimation is optimised using the ROC curves in Sec. 2.4. Note that annealed M-estimation can jointly identify outliers and estimate warps, however to yield comparable parameters (a different kind of warp and bending energy are used in [3]) we simply estimate a TPS warp using the inliers returned.

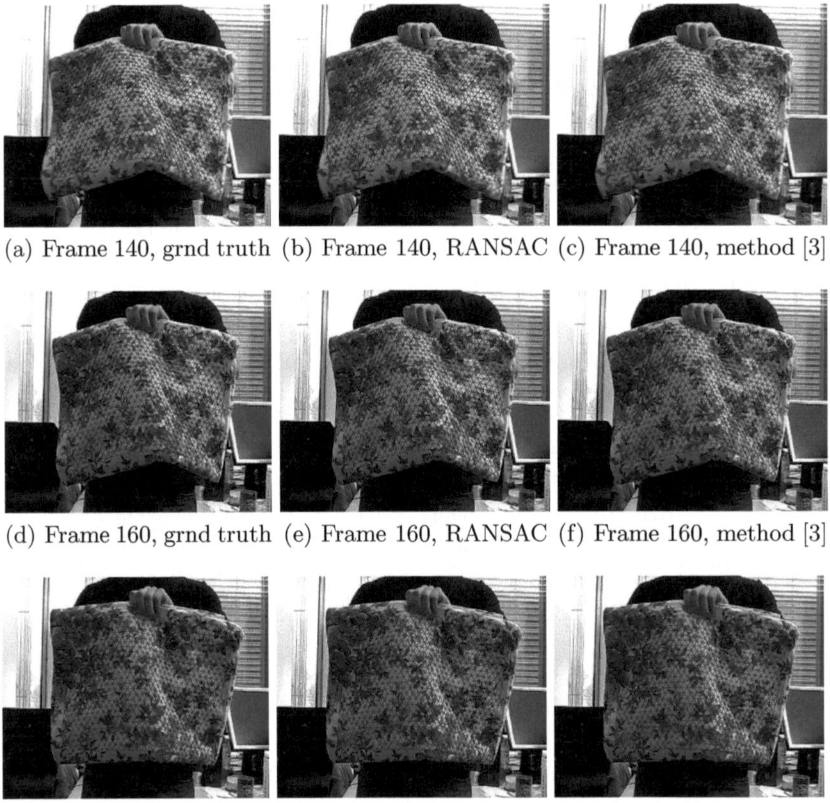

(a) Frame 140, grnd truth (b) Frame 140, RANSAC (c) Frame 140, method [3]

(d) Frame 160, grnd truth (e) Frame 160, RANSAC (f) Frame 160, method [3]

(g) Frame 178, grnd truth (h) Frame 178, RANSAC (i) Frame 178, method [3]

Fig. 9. Retexturing bedsheet images (best viewed on screen)

Both methods yield very close results to the ground truth, including Frame 190 of cushion in which the disparity in outlier rejection accuracy between RANSAC and annealed M-estimation is the largest (see Row 3 of Fig. 8). As mentioned in Sec. 1, false positives produced by RANSAC are normally benign outliers which can be smoothened out by the warp's regulariser.

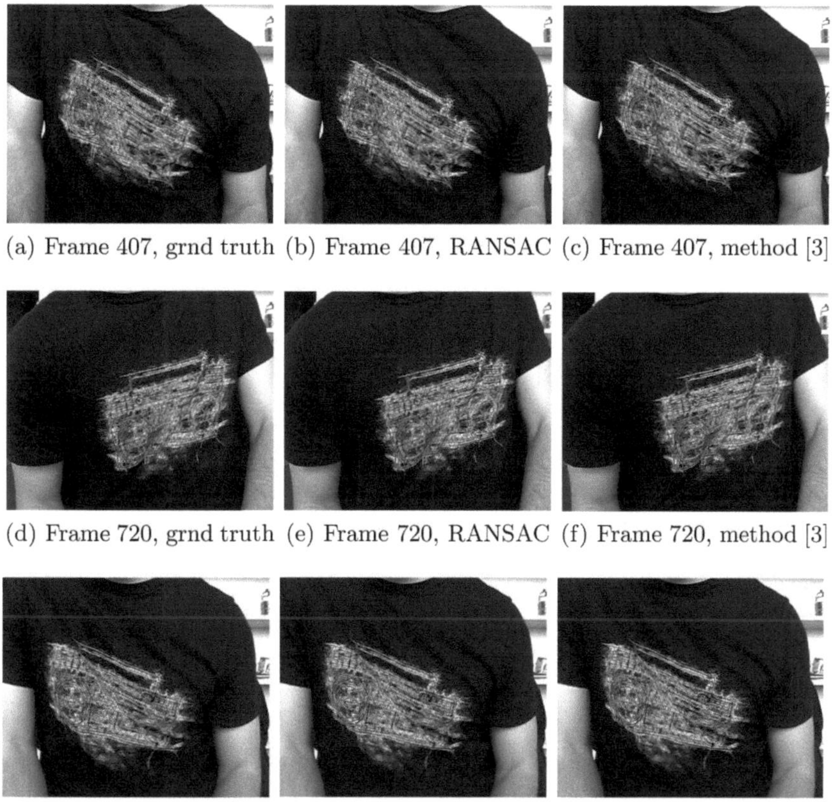

(a) Frame 407, grnd truth (b) Frame 407, RANSAC (c) Frame 407, method [3]

(d) Frame 720, grnd truth (e) Frame 720, RANSAC (f) Frame 720, method [3]

(g) Frame 784, grnd truth (h) Frame 784, RANSAC (i) Frame 784, method [3]

Fig. 10. Retexturing tshirt images (best viewed on screen)

For quantitative benchmarking, we compute the goodness of each estimated warp as the number of vertices in the warped mesh which are within 3 pixels away from the corresponding vertices in the ground truth mesh. The results in Table 3 show that on several images annealed M-estimation is better than RANSAC in this measure — however, [3] imposes local smoothness constraints which help to "pin down" the position of each vertex relative to the others and this is beneficial for the goodness measure. This additional information is not provided to RANSAC. In any case, as shown in Figs. 9, 10 and 11, the practical differences between the two methods are minuscule.

A general problem for feature-based methods however is the lack of correspondences in certain areas of the surface. To deal with this issue, we track and propagate features in an image sequence. First, the template is divided into rectangular regions (e.g., 5×5 grid). If the number of matches in a region between the current frame and the template falls below a threshold, Mean Shift is initiated to track (pre-matched) features from the previous frame. All matches are then vetted by RANSAC before TPS warp estimation. Note that feature

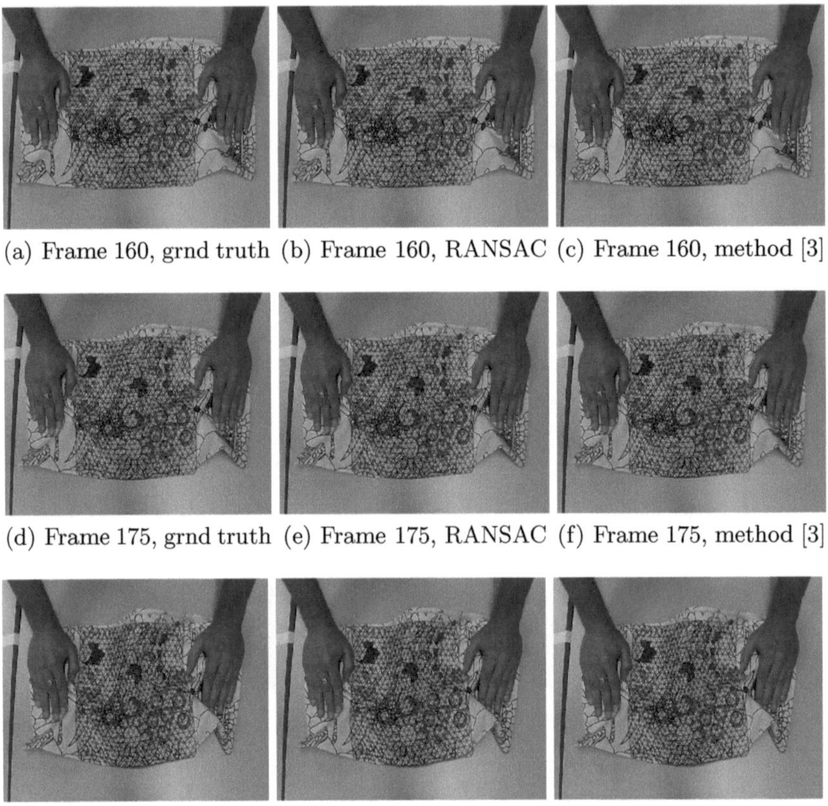

(a) Frame 160, grnd truth (b) Frame 160, RANSAC (c) Frame 160, method [3]

(d) Frame 175, grnd truth (e) Frame 175, RANSAC (f) Frame 175, method [3]

(g) Frame 190, grnd truth (h) Frame 190, RANSAC (i) Frame 190, method [3]

Fig. 11. Retexturing cushion images (best viewed on screen)

tracking and propagation benefit all feature-based methods [1–4, 13, 11, 9] — *See supplementary material for the results.*

4 Concluding Remarks

We have provided in this paper (and supplementary material) extensive results supporting RANSAC as a viable and simple alternative for outlier rejection compared to more sophisticated approaches. Our premise and observation is that, relative to the extreme scale of gross mismatches, the distribution of inliers usually resembles a low-dimensional affine subspace. While we focus here on RANSAC, there are many approaches to robust fitting of linear manifolds. Some may have advantages over RANSAC and, in that regard, an important message of this paper is that the outlier detection issue with non-linear warping, can likely be done with a relatively cheap schemes.

References

1. Pilet, J., Lepetit, V., Fua, P.: Real-time non-rigid surface detection. In: CVPR (2005)
2. Pilet, J., Lepetit, V., Fua, P.: Fast non-rigid surface detection, registration and realistic augmentation. IJCV 76, 109–122 (2008)
3. Zhu, J., Lyu, M.R.: Progressive finite newton approach to real-time nonrigid surface detection. In: CVPR (2007)
4. Zhu, J., Hoi, C.H., Lyu, M.R.: Nonrigid shape recovery by gaussian process registration. In: CVPR (2009)
5. Bookstein, F.L.: Principal warps: thin-plate splines and the decomposition of deformations. IEEE TPAMI 11, 567–585 (1989)
6. Fischler, M.A., Bolles, R.C.: Random sample consensus: a paradigm for model fitting with applications to image analysis and automated cartography. Commun. ACM 24 (1981)
7. Carneiro, G., Jepson, A.D.: Flexible spatial configuration of local image features. IEEE TPAMI 29, 2089–2104 (2007)
8. Bartoli, A.: Maximizing the predictivity of smooth deformable image warps through cross-validation. J. Math. Imaging Vis. 31, 233–244 (2008)
9. Pizarro, D., Bartoli, A.: Feature-based deformable surface detection with self-occlusion reasoning. IJCV (to appear)
10. Lowe, D.G.: Distinctive image features from scale-invariant keypoints. IJCV 60, 91–110 (2004)
11. Li, X., Hu, Z.: Rejecting mismatches by correspondence function. IJCV 89, 1–17 (2010)
12. Chum, O., Matas, J.: Matching with prosac - progressive sample consensus. In: CVPR (2005)
13. Li, X., Li, X., Li, H., Cao, M.: Rejecting outliers based on correspondence manifold. Acta Automatica Sinica 35, 17–22 (2009)
14. Bartoli, A., Zisserman, A.: Direct estimation of non-rigid registrations. In: BMVC (2004)
15. Gay-Bellile, V., Bartoli, A., Sayd, P.: Direct estimation of nonrigid registrations with image-based self-occlusion reasoning. IEEE TPAMI 32, 87–104 (2010)
16. Varol, A., Salzmann, M., Tola, E., Fua, P.: Template-free monocular reconstruction of deformable surfaces. In: ICCV (2009)
17. Taylor, J., Jepson, A., Kutulakos, K.: Non-rigid structure from locally rigid motion. In: CVPR (2010)
18. Belongie, S., Malik, J., Puzicha, J.: Shape matching and object recognition using shape contexts. IEEE TPAMI 24, 509–521 (2002)
19. Chui, H., Rangarajan, A.: A new point matching algorithm for non-rigid registration. CVIU 89, 114–141 (2003)
20. Choi, S., Kim, T., Yu, W.: Performance evaluation of RANSAC family. In: BMVC (2009)
21. Chen, H., Meer, P.: Robust regression with projection based m-estimators. In: ICCV (2003)
22. Rozenfeld, S., Shimshoni, I.: The modified pbm-estimator method and a runtime analysis technique for the ransac family. In: CVPR (2005)
23. Donato, G., Belongie, S.: Approximate Thin Plate Spline Mappings. In: Heyden, A., Sparr, G., Nielsen, M., Johansen, P. (eds.) ECCV 2002, Part III. LNCS, vol. 2352, pp. 21–31. Springer, Heidelberg (2002)
24. Salzmann, M., Fua, P.: Reconstructing sharply folding surfaces: a convex formulation. In: CVPR (2009)

A Tensor Voting Approach for Multi-view 3D Scene Flow Estimation and Refinement

Jaesik Park, Tae Hyun Oh, Jiyoung Jung, Yu-Wing Tai, and In So Kweon

Korea Advanced Institute of Science and Technology, Daejeon, South Korea
{jspark,thoo,jyjung}@rcv.kaist.ac.kr, yuwing@cs.kaist.ac.kr,
iskweon@kaist.ac.kr

Abstract. We introduce a framework to estimate and refine 3D scene flow which connects 3D structures of a scene across different frames. In contrast to previous approaches which compute 3D scene flow that connects depth maps from a stereo image sequence or from a depth camera, our approach takes advantage of full 3D reconstruction which computes the 3D scene flow that connects 3D point clouds from multi-view stereo system. Our approach uses a standard multi-view stereo and optical flow algorithm to compute the initial 3D scene flow. A unique two-stage refinement process regularizes the scene flow direction and magnitude sequentially. The scene flow direction is refined by utilizing 3D neighbor smoothness defined by tensor voting. The magnitude of the scene flow is refined by connecting the implicit surfaces across the consecutive 3D point clouds. Our estimated scene flow is temporally consistent. Our approach is efficient, model free, and it is effective in error corrections and outlier rejections. We tested our approach on both synthetic and real-world datasets. Our experimental results show that our approach outperforms previous algorithms quantitatively on synthetic dataset, and it improves the reconstructed 3D model from the refined 3D point cloud in real-world dataset.

Keywords: Scene Flow, Tensor Voting, Multi-view.

1 Introduction

3D scene flow [1] is a dense 3D motion vector field which describes the non-rigid motion of objects in 3D world. Over the last decade, various approaches [1–11] have been proposed for 3D scene flow estimation. Among the proposed approaches, most of them [2, 3, 5, 6, 8–11] were developed based on stereoscopic inputs such that the estimated 3D scene flow is defined up to the depth map ambiguities [11] where scene flow in occluded areas was undetermined. Also, since depth map provides incomplete information about the 3D world, the estimated scene flow can be easily biased. In this work, we introduce a 3D scene flow algorithm which utilizes the 3D point cloud from multi-view stereo. Our estimated scene flow, thus, describes the full 3D motion vector field of objects' motions in 3D world.

Our approach is built on top of recent advances in 3D multi-view reconstruction and in 2D optical flow estimation. In 3D multi-view reconstruction, recent works such as [12] can reconstruct accurate 3D model with metric error less than

A. Fitzgibbon et al. (Eds.): ECCV 2012, Part IV, LNCS 7575, pp. 288–302, 2012.

1mm in the standard middlebury multi-view stereo dataset [13]. Their techniques are well suited for illumination changes, occlusion and low-textured regions. In optical flow estimation, recent algorithms such as [14] have demonstrated less than 1 pixel average end-point error and less than 5 degree average angular error in the standard middlebury optical flow dataset [15]. However, when combining them together for the scene flow estimation through back projecting the estimated optical flow onto the estimated 3D model [1], the accuracy of the estimated 3D scene flow is far from satisfactory. This is because such a naive approach can easily amplify errors from both the estimated 3D model and the estimated optical flow. In addition, since optical flow is estimated individually in 2D image domain, errors caused by aperture problem, occlusion/disocclusion from certain view point can be easily propagated to the estimated 3D scene flow. There are various approaches [16–18, 4] which jointly estimate the 3D model together with scene flow through mesh deformation and/or 3D points tracking. However, such approaches usually involve complicated data structures to handle deformed meshes or they require rich textures on the reconstructed surface for accurate and dense 3D points tracking. In contrast, our approach computes the scene flow across 3D point clouds which is model free, simple in data representation, and it is computationally efficient.

Our approach starts with an initial scene flow computed by back projecting 2D optical flow from different view points onto the 3D point cloud [1]. Inspired by the work from Wu *et al.* [19] which uses the closed form tensor voting (CFTV) to reject outliers and to estimate surface normals without explicit computation of surface mesh, we modify the CFTV to handle scene flow data. Since CFTV only provides us the scene flow direction, but not the magnitude of the scene flow, we utilize implicit surface representation to estimate the scene flow magnitude by connecting the scene flow of the 3D point cloud at time t with the implicit surface of the 3D point cloud at time $t+1$. One major advantage of our approach is that it can effectively reduce computation and number of parameters by converting the direction and magnitude estimation of the scene flow into a two-stage process that is optimized sequentially. By adopting the CFTV framework in scene flow direction estimation, our scene flow refinement algorithm is structure-aware and we gain the advantage on outlier rejections and error corrections of the 3D point cloud. Our experimental results show that our approach is effective in improving the accuracy of the estimated scene flow from its initialization. Also, our scene flow refinement algorithm is ready to be adopted to other scene flow estimation algorithms as post-processing to further enhance their performances.

2 Related Work

Since the concept of scene flow estimation introduced by Vedula *et al.* [1], various scene flow estimation algorithms have been introduced. In [1], Vedula *et al.* first introduced a scene flow estimation algorithm which projects optical flow onto a known 3D model with photometric consistent constraint from each of the input images to regularize the estimated scene flow. There are other studies on scene flow estimation in multi-view camera setup as well, such as [7, 20]. Zhang *et al.* [7] combine 2D motion from optical flow and stereo view constraint in scene flow estimation. Pons *et al.* [20] estimate scene flow after scene reconstruction by matching images at time t and images at time $t+1$ to refine scene flow over multiple cameras. Wedel *et al.* [6] take stereo image sequences as input. They use stereo matching algorithm to estimate depth map and computes the scene flow across the estimated depth map.

Other approaches use joint estimation framework [3, 5, 9]. These approaches estimate depth map and scene flow simultaneously under different camera configurations. For instance, Huguet *et al.* [3] couples optical flow estimations for each camera with dense stereo matching. Rabe *et al.* [5] present a real time implementation of a variational optical flow algorithm with Kalman filter for temporal smoothness. Basha *et al.* [2] estimates 3D structure and scene flow simultaneously in a unified variational framework. Their approach is based on 3D parameterizations of depth map and 3D scene flow. Vogel *et al.* [8] improves the work from Basha *et al.* [2] by introducing a rigid motion prior into optimization function for scene flow estimation. Wedel *et al.* [11] compute 3D scene flow from hand held video cameras through stereoscopic analysis of video depth to estimate 3D motions of camera and scene flow. Recently, Hadfield *et al.*[10] introduce scene flow particle filter which operate directly on the depth map captured by Xbox Kinect.

Besides optimization based methods, there are methods which rely on deformation and 3D points tracking. In [17], Devernay *et al.* tracks the poses of surfels [21] in video sequence to estimate scene flow. They represent the surfel as a small planar square region. Through analyzing the deformation of surfel in each video frame, they can estimate the translation and rotation parameters of surfel across different frames and hence obtain the scene flow in terms of surfel deformation parameters. Furukawa *et al.* [18] start with a 3D mesh representation, and track the projected motion trajectory of vertex coordinates of the 3D mesh in a scene through tracking the optical flow of feature points. Since 3D topology is known, the scene flow is obtained through computing the deformed mesh which agrees with the projected optical flow.

There are several approaches in scene flow estimation employing various 3D representations that should also be mentioned. Carceroni and Kutulakos [22] represent scene flow as dynamic surfel which encodes the instantaneous local shape, reflectance, and motion of a small region in the scene under known illumination conditions. Wand *et al.* [23] operate on point cloud inputs, but also infer the topology of the point cloud. Courchay *et al.* [24] use animated mesh to simultaneously estimate 3D shape and 3D motion of a dynamic scene from multiple-viewpoint calibrated videos.

Comparing our approach with previous works, our approach also uses regularization to estimate and to refine the scene flow. A major difference between our approach and the previous approaches is that we process our algorithm on the 3D point cloud while many of the previous algorithms are processed on the depth map in 2D image plane. Comparing 3D point clouds with depth maps, 3D point

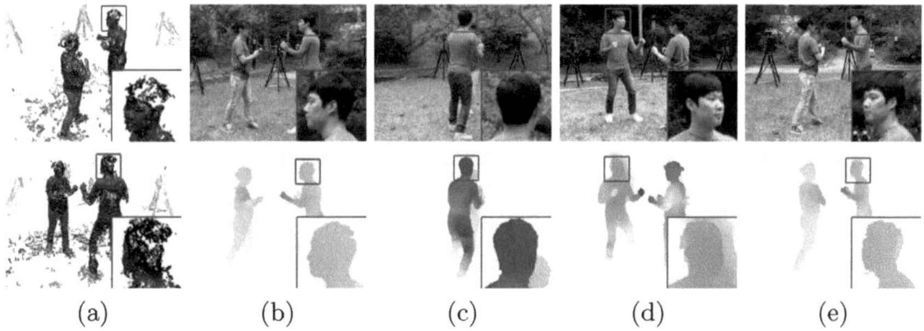

Fig. 1. Initial inputs of our approach. Our data is captured by 20 synchronized cameras which were arranged uniformly around the target objects in an outdoor environment. (a) The 3D point cloud reconstructed by using PMVS [12]. (b) to (e) The estimated optical flow from different cameras by using method in [14]. Note the errors of the 3D point cloud and optical flow around the head area caused by color ambiguity.

clouds are unstructured, and its sampling can be highly non-uniform. These factors cause additional challenges in computing scene flow for 3D point clouds. In addition, neighborhood regularization in 3D point clouds without mesh reconstruction is not as trivial as the neighborhood regularization for scene flow working on depth map where the spatial neighborhood is well defined and well sampled in 2D image domain. For this reason, we adopt the CFTV [19] which defines neighborhood in 3D not only based on the Euclidean distance, but also based on the relative location and normal orientations of 3D points. We choose to work on an unstructured 3D point cloud since this is a model free representation, and it provides the maximum freedom of deformation for scene flow estimation comparing to previous works using surfel/mesh representation. Also, data structure for an unstructured 3D point cloud is simple, and hence it is computationally efficient.

3 Our Approach

3.1 Data Acquisition

Our system for data acquisition consists of 20 cameras uniformly distributed around the target objects. These cameras are calibrated and synchronized with image resolution 1600×1200. Instead of putting our system in a well controlled indoor environment, we capture our data in outdoor environment with uncontrolled lighting and complex background to demonstrate a more general application of our approach. Figure 1 shows the setting and initial inputs of our approach.

3.2 Initial Scene Flow Estimation

Our approach starts with an initial estimation of the scene flow from multi-view stereo and optical flow triangulation. For our convenience, we use the source code from the patch based multi-view stereo (PMVS)[12] to obtain our initial

3D point cloud for each frame individually. We also use the source code provided by Sun *et al.* [14] to compute the optical flow for every image sequence from each camera individually.

We denote by $\mathbf{x} = \{u, v\}$ the image plane coordinates, $\mathbf{X} = \{x, y, z\}$ the 3D world coordinates, $\mathbf{f} = \{f_u, f_v\}$ the optical flow in image plane, $\mathbf{F} = \{F_x, F_y, F_z\}$ the scene flow in 3D world, and $\mathbf{P}$ the 3×4 camera projection matrix. We use subscript index $i \in [1, M]$ to represent the i-th point in the 3D point cloud, subscript index $j \in [1, N]$ to represent the j-th camera in the system setting, and superscript index $t \in [1, T]$ to represent time (the t-th frame) in input image sequences where M is total number of points in the 3D point cloud, $N = 20$ is the total number of cameras, and T is the total number of frames respectively. Hence, $\mathbf{x}^t_{ij} = \mathbf{P}_j \mathbf{X}^t_i$, and $\mathbf{f}^t_{ij} = \mathbf{P}_j \mathbf{F}^t_i$.

In order to obtain the initial scene flow from the 3D point cloud and the 2D optical flow, we utilize the approach from Ruttle *et al.* [16] which minimizes the least square reprojection errors of the scene flow projected onto the image plane from each camera. This is achieved by solving $A_i(\mathbf{X}_i + \mathbf{F}_i) = 0$ for each point in the 3D point cloud individually where A_i is equal to:

$$A_i = \begin{bmatrix} (u_{i1} + f_{u,i1})\mathbf{P}_{3,1} - \mathbf{P}_{1,1} \\ (v_{i1} + f_{v,i1})\mathbf{P}_{3,1} - \mathbf{P}_{2,1} \\ \vdots \\ (u_{iN} + f_{u,iN})\mathbf{P}_{3,N} - \mathbf{P}_{1,N} \\ (v_{iN} + f_{v,iN})\mathbf{P}_{3,N} - \mathbf{P}_{2,N} \end{bmatrix}, \tag{1}$$

where $\{u_{ij}, v_{ij}\}$ is the image coordinate of the i-th point projected on the j-th camera, and $\{f_{u,ij}, f_{v,ij}\}$ is the 2D optical flow of the i-th point on the image plane of the j-th camera. $\mathbf{P}_{1,j}$, $\mathbf{P}_{2,j}$, and $\mathbf{P}_{3,j}$ are the first, the second and the third rows of the j-th camera projection matrix $\mathbf{P}_j$ respectively.

3.3 Closed Form Tensor Voting

Since our approach for scene flow refinement is built on top of the closed form tensor voting (CFTV) framework[25, 19], we briefly review it here. CFTV improves the reconstruction accuracy of Furukawa *et al.*[12] by refining noisy surface normal vectors. The tensor voting field considers normal orientation and minimum curvature connections between local neighborhood in 3D to define the neighborhood connectivity prior.

For each point $\mathbf{X}_i$ in the 3D point cloud, a vote is received from each of its neighborhood points $\mathbf{X}_{\tilde{i}}$ as tensor $\mathbf{T}_{i\tilde{i}}$:

$$\mathbf{T}_{i\tilde{i}} = c_{i\tilde{i}} R_{i\tilde{i}} K_{\tilde{i}} R'_{i\tilde{i}} \tag{2}$$

where $R_{i\tilde{i}} = \mathbf{I} - 2\mathbf{r}_{i\tilde{i}}\mathbf{r}^{\mathsf{T}}_{i\tilde{i}}$, $R'_{i\tilde{i}} = (\mathbf{I} - \frac{1}{2}\mathbf{r}_{i\tilde{i}}\mathbf{r}^{\mathsf{T}}_{i\tilde{i}})R_{i\tilde{i}}$, I is 3×3 identity matrix, $\mathbf{r}_{i\tilde{i}}$ is a unit vector whose direction is the same as $\mathbf{X}_{\tilde{i}} - \mathbf{X}_i$, $K_{\tilde{i}} = \mathbf{n}_{\tilde{i}}\mathbf{n}^{\mathsf{T}}_{\tilde{i}}$ is a kernel function which encodes the most likely normal direction, $\mathbf{n}_i$, of $\mathbf{X}_i$ casted by $\mathbf{X}_{\tilde{i}}$ defined by the osculating arc connecting $\mathbf{X}_i$ and $\mathbf{X}_{\tilde{i}}$, and $c_{i\tilde{i}} = \exp(-\frac{\|\mathbf{X}_i - \mathbf{X}_{\tilde{i}}\|^2}{\sigma_d})$

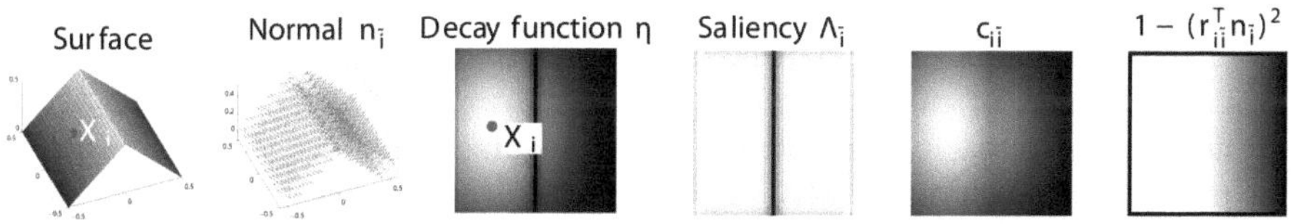

Fig. 2. An example to illustrate the effects of each component (titled with its variable names) in the decay function η in Equation (4). Our decay function combines the surface saliency, Euclidean distance, and normal orientation to evaluate the influence of neighborhood to $\mathbf{X}_i$. A larger weight is given to a point with larger surface saliency, with closer distance, and with better agreement on normal orientations.

is a decay function controlled by a parameter σ_d which penalizes neighborhood points that are further away from $\mathbf{X}_i$.

After collecting votes from neighborhood, the refined normal direction is obtained by using eigen-decomposition to get the eigenvector with the largest eigenvalue. Note that CFTV does not need to reconstruct mesh model in order to estimate and refine normal direction, and this is a major benefit which fits to our problem for scene flow refinement with an unstructured 3D point cloud. In addition, through analyzing the eigenvalue of tensor sum, $\sum_{\bar{i}} \mathbf{T}_{i\bar{i}}$, CFTV rejects outliers which received very limited amount of votes from its neighborhood. It can also be used to correct 3D point location by searching a position along the normal direction of a 3D point which receives the maximum amount of vote from its neighborhood. In our implementation, we adopt CFTV as a second step to improve the accuracy of the 3D point cloud from PMVS before scene flow estimation and refinement.

3.4 Scene Flow Refinement

Scene Flow Direction Refinement. We extend the CFTV framework to handle our scene flow data. The basic idea is to define a "voting field" of scene flow which collects the most likely scene flow direction from neighborhood such that structures of 3D points are considered without explicit mesh reconstruction in order to avoid complicated data structure and to make the scene flow refinement process efficient. Also, by incorporating the scene flow and the normal direction propagation together in CFTV, we can further enhance the outlier rejection and error correction ability of CFTV.

We define our scene flow tensor as follow:

$$\mathbf{S}_{i\bar{i}} = \eta(\mathbf{X}_i, \mathbf{X}_{\bar{i}}, \mathbf{n}_i, \mathbf{n}_{\bar{i}}) \overrightarrow{\mathbf{F}}_{\bar{i}} \overrightarrow{\mathbf{F}}_{\bar{i}}^{\mathsf{T}}, \tag{3}$$

where $\overrightarrow{\mathbf{F}}_{\bar{i}}$ is the normalized scene flow direction of $\mathbf{X}_{\bar{i}}$ and $\eta(\mathbf{X}_i, \mathbf{X}_{\bar{i}}, \mathbf{n}_i, \mathbf{n}_{\bar{i}})$ is a structure aware decay function defined as:

$$\eta(\mathbf{X}_i, \mathbf{X}_{\bar{i}}, \mathbf{n}_i, \mathbf{n}_{\bar{i}}) = c_{i\bar{i}} \left[\Lambda_i (1 - (\mathbf{r}_{i\bar{i}}^{\mathsf{T}} \mathbf{n}_i)^2) + \Lambda_{\bar{i}} (1 - (\mathbf{r}_{i\bar{i}}^{\mathsf{T}} \mathbf{n}_{\bar{i}})^2) \right], \tag{4}$$

where $\Lambda_{\bar{i}} = \lambda_{1,\bar{i}} - \lambda_{2,\bar{i}}$ and $\Lambda_i = \lambda_{1,i} - \lambda_{2,i}$ are the surface saliency of $\mathbf{X}_{\bar{i}}$ and $\mathbf{X}_i$ respectively, $\lambda_{1,i}$ and $\lambda_{2,i}$ are the first and second largest eigenvalues of structure tensor sum $\sum_j \mathbf{T}_{ij}$ in Equation (2), and $1-(\mathbf{r}_{\bar{i}i}^{\mathsf{T}}\mathbf{n}_i)^2$ and $1-(\mathbf{r}_{i\bar{i}}^{\mathsf{T}}\mathbf{n}_{\bar{i}})^2$ measures how likely $\mathbf{X}_i$ and $\mathbf{X}_{\bar{i}}$ are connected to each other given the configurations of normal directions $\mathbf{n}_i$ and $\mathbf{n}_{\bar{i}}$ respectively [25]. Hence, if two points $\mathbf{X}_i$ and $\mathbf{X}_{\bar{i}}$ are physically close to each other but the normal configurations of the two points do not match with each other, $\eta(\mathbf{X}_i, \mathbf{X}_{\bar{i}}, \mathbf{n}_i, \mathbf{n}_{\bar{i}})$ returns a small weight in propagation since $\mathbf{X}_i$ and $\mathbf{X}_{\bar{i}}$ are unlikely to connect with each other on the same surface. On the other hand, we give a large weight to $\mathbf{X}_i$ and $\mathbf{X}_{\bar{i}}$ if they are physically closed and the normal configurations agree with each other. Figure 2 illustrates the effects of $\eta(\mathbf{X}_i, \mathbf{X}_{\bar{i}}, \mathbf{n}_i, \mathbf{n}_{\bar{i}})$ and each individual component of $\eta(\mathbf{X}_i, \mathbf{X}_{\bar{i}}, \mathbf{n}_i, \mathbf{n}_{\bar{i}})$ where $\mathbf{X}_i$ receives a larger weight from a point that lies on the same surface with the same normal direction and smaller weight from a point that lie on another surface with different normal directions.

After we collect the second order moment of the scene flow from neighborhood, we can obtain the scene flow direction through eigen-decomposition to find the direction of eigenvector with the largest eigenvalue. The sign ambiguity is resolved by choosing the sign that provides smaller angular difference between the refined scene flow direction and the initial scene flow direction. The scene flow CFTV can estimate the scene flow direction, but it does not provide the magnitude of scene flow since magnitude of scene flow is not encoded in the second order moment. Although we can also propagate the scene flow magnitude individually similar to the scene flow direction propagation, the estimated scene flow magnitude might not be physically correct. For instance, it does not guarantee that the estimated scene flow will touch the surface of the 3D model in the next frame.

Scene Flow Magnitude Refinement. With the estimated scene flow direction, $\overrightarrow{\mathbf{F}}$, we estimate the scene flow magnitude, $\mathbf{m}$, by exploiting the physical property of the scene flow which connects the surface of the 3D model of the two consecutive frames. The energy function we want to minimize is defined as follow:

$$E(m_i)=\frac{1}{\mathbf{X}_{\sigma,i}^2} \| \mathbf{X}_{\mu,i} - (\mathbf{X}_i + m_i \overrightarrow{\mathbf{F}}_i) \|^2 + \kappa \sum_{\bar{i}} \eta(\mathbf{X}_i, \mathbf{X}_{\bar{i}}, \mathbf{n}_i, \mathbf{n}_{\bar{i}}) \| m_i - m_{\bar{i}} \|^2 \quad (5)$$

where $\mathbf{X}_{\mu,i}$ is the predicted 3D point location of $\mathbf{X}_i$ at time $t+1$ evaluated by the surface saliency of the 3D point cloud at time $t+1$ along the direction $\overrightarrow{\mathbf{F}}_i$ connecting $\mathbf{X}_i$, $\mathbf{X}_{\sigma,i}^2$ is the variance of surface saliency, $\kappa = 0.5$ is the parameter balancing the data term in the first half of Equation (5) and the smoothness term in the second half of Equation (5).

$\mathbf{X}_{\mu,i}$ and $\mathbf{X}_{\sigma,i}^2$ can be estimated by sampling several (7 in our implementation) discrete locations along $\overrightarrow{\mathbf{F}}_i$ to collect votes and to evaluate the variation of surface saliency. A Gaussian distribution is fitted to the evaluated surface saliency and hence $\mathbf{X}_{\mu,i}$ and $\mathbf{X}_{\sigma,i}^2$ correspond to the mean and variance of the fitted Gaussian distribution. Note that the estimation of $\mathbf{X}_{\mu,i}$ and $\mathbf{X}_{\sigma,i}^2$ can be computed individually for each $\mathbf{X}_i$ without explicit surface reconstruction. Equation (5) is then optimized after initial estimation of the scene flow magnitude of all $\mathbf{X}_i$.

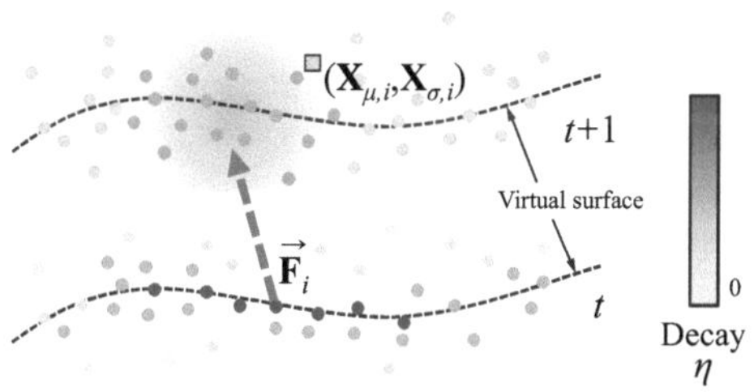

Fig. 3. We estimate the magnitude of the scene flow by utilizing the physical property of the scene flow that connects the 3D structures of the consecutive frames. Since our approach is mesh free, we compute a "virtual surface" by evaluating the variation of the surface saliency by collecting tensor votes along the scene flow direction. The optimal scene flow magnitude is the one which touches the virtual surface at $t+1$ with structure aware neighbor smoothness regularization defined by Equation (5).

Note that we use the same weighting function $\eta(\mathbf{X}_i, \mathbf{X}_{\tilde{i}}, \mathbf{n}_i, \mathbf{n}_{\tilde{i}})$ in Equation (3) to define the neighborhood smoothness term which embeds the normal configuration of $\mathbf{X}_i$ and $\mathbf{X}_{\tilde{i}}$ and the neighborhood smoothness prior defined by CFTV into account. Figure 3 illustrates this process of finding the scene flow magnitude that connects the virtual surface of two point clouds at time t and $t+1$. We can also further reject outliers by evaluating the scene flow saliency collected by Equation (3).

3.5 Temporally Consistent 3D Scene Flow

The above process refines the scene flow of 3D point cloud for each frame individually. In order to fully utilize the correlation between consecutive frames, and to improve the temporal coherency of the estimated scene flow in a long range, we redefine the set of nearest neighbor along the temporal domain for frame $t-1$ and $t+1$. For temporal neighborhood, we can again propagate the scene flow direction, but now we need to modify the voting field such that the voting direction is along the tangential direction of osculating arc defined by the scene flow direction of 3D points at time $t-1$ and $t+1$. Our modified scene flow tensor for temporal neighborhood is defined as follow:

$$\mathcal{S}_{i\tilde{i}^{t+1}} = c_{i\tilde{i}^{t+1}} \mathcal{R}_{i\tilde{i}^{t+1}} \mathcal{K}_{\tilde{i}^{t+1}} \mathcal{R}'_{i\tilde{i}^{t+1}}, \tag{6}$$

where $\tilde{i}^{t+1}$ is the index of 3D point neighbor at time $t+1$, $\mathcal{R}_{i\tilde{i}} = 2\mathbf{r}_{i\tilde{i}}\mathbf{r}_{i\tilde{i}}^{\top}$, $\mathcal{R}'_{i\tilde{i}} = (\frac{1}{2}\mathbf{r}_{i\tilde{i}}\mathbf{r}_{i\tilde{i}}^{\top})\mathcal{R}_{i\tilde{i}}$, and $\mathcal{K}_{\tilde{i}} = \mathbf{F}_{\tilde{i}}\mathbf{F}_{\tilde{i}}^{\top}$ is the kernel function that encodes the most likely scene flow direction, $\mathbf{F}_i^t$, of $\mathbf{X}_i^t$ casted by $\mathbf{X}_{\tilde{i}}^{t+1}$. The scene flow tensor for $\mathcal{S}_{i\tilde{i}^{t-1}}$ is defined similarly. The decay function $c_{i\tilde{i}^{t+1}}$ is same as in Equation (2).

After including temporal neighborhood and the scene flow direction propagation from temporal neighborhood, our estimated scene flow is temporally consistent. At the same time, the scene flow structures/discontinuities can be well preserved in the structure aware scene flow propagation by Equation (3) and Equation (5). In our implementation, we alternate the refinement processes

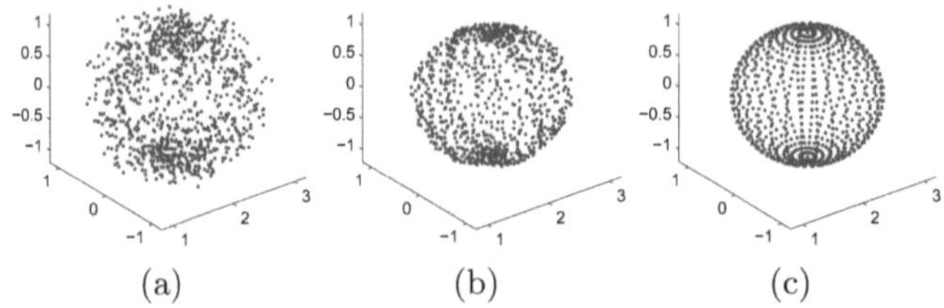

Fig. 4. *Sphere* dataset. The 3D points on the sphere are translated with (a) initial noisy scene flow, (b) our refined scene flow and (c) the ground truth scene flow.

Table 1. Mean square error of Figure 4. Our approach achieves the lowest MSE after magnitude regularization.

	MSE
Noisy 3D scene scene flow	0.239
Ours without magnitude regularization	0.130
Ours with magnitude regularization	**0.077**

described in Section 3.4 and Section 3.5 iteratively. In real world dataset, we observe two iterations are sufficient to converge. From our experiments, we found that including temporal neighborhood from time $t+1$ and $t-1$ is sufficient to guarantee temporal coherence without over smoothing the scene flow structures.

4 Experimental Results

Our first experiments consists of a synthetic dataset, *sphere*, as shown in Figure 4. The radius of the sphere is 1, and the ground truth scene flow is $[1, 0, 0]^\mathsf{T}$ uniformly moving in x-direction. To simulate a noisy scene flow from optical flow projection, we add uniform noise with range [-0.25,0.25] in random directions, but the ground truth locations of 3D points are unaltered. We apply our approach to refine the noisy scene flow. As shown in Figure 4(a) and (b), our approach can successfully refine the noisy scene flow. After shifting the 3D points according to our refined scene flow, the shape of sphere is still preserved. Table 1 shows quantitative evaluation on the mean square error of scene flow comparing to ground truth. It shows that both the direction refinements by scene flow CFTV, and the magnitude refinement by scene flow magnitude regularization are effective.

We compare our results with the results of Huguet *et al.* [3] and Basha *et al.* [2] using *ball* dataset in [2] as shown in Figure 5, which is publicly available with ground truth. This dataset consists of 10 rendered images which represent 5 different view points at time t and $t+1$. The textured sphere and background plane are rotated differently, and the mask for the occluded region and the discontinuity region are provided. In this example, we have also provided an additional baseline comparison to illustrate the relative performance between ours and [18]. Approach in [18] is a mesh deformation approach which refines

Table 2. Quantitative evaluation on the synthetic *ball* dataset. Our results are compared with results from Huguet *et al.* [3] and Basha *et al.* [2]. Ours(Baseline) shows initially estimated scene flow results without any refinement. From left to right are the evaluation metrics for the NRMS errors of the estimated 3D point location ($NRMS_{\mathbf{X}}(\%)$), the NRMS errors of the estimated scene flow ($NRMS_{\mathbf{F}}(\%)$), and the AEE of the estimated scene flow ($AAE_{\mathbf{F}}(deg)$). For each row of each compared methods, the first row and the second row shows the results where the errors in the discontinuities mask (w/o Discontinuities) and occlusion mask (w/o Occlusions) were excluded, the last row shows the results where all pixels are included (All pixels) for evaluation. Best quantitative results were underlined.

Method	Measurement	$NRMS_{\mathbf{X}}(\%)$	$NRMS_{\mathbf{F}}(\%)$	$AAE_{\mathbf{F}}(deg)$
Huguet *et al.* [3]	w/o Discontinuities	9.82	15.96	7.17
	w/o Occlusions	1.19	11.04	6.66
	All pixels	10.43	19.09	9.20
Basha *et al.* [2]	w/o Discontinuities	0.65	$\underline{2.94}$	$\underline{1.32}$
	w/o Occlusions	1.99	5.63	$\underline{2.09}$
	All pixels	4.39	9.71	3.39
Ours (Baseline)	w/o Discontinuities	0.25	6.43	4.74
	w/o Occlusions	0.26	6.99	4.98
	All pixels	1.12	7.89	5.28
Ours (After Refinement)	w/o Discontinuities	$\underline{0.23}$	4.88	2.73
	w/o Occlusions	$\underline{0.24}$	$\underline{5.07}$	2.72
	All pixels	$\underline{0.57}$	$\underline{5.42}$	$\underline{2.83}$

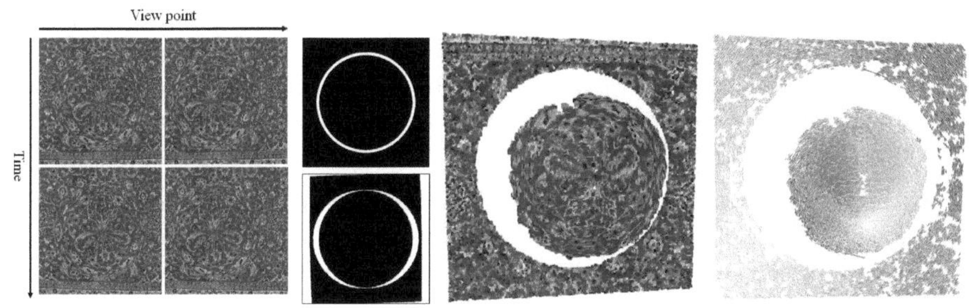

(a) (b) (c) (d)

Fig. 5. Synthetic *ball* dataset from [2]. (a) The synthetic rendered images for inputs. (b) Discontinuity map and occlusion map. (c) Our estimated 3D structure. (d) Our estimated scene flow (color coded for scene flow direction).

the initial mesh from [12] and scene flow through matching the correspondents between time t and $t+1$. In our baseline comparison, we also start with initial 3D point location from [12]. We skip the CFTV refinement of location so that our 3D point location is more closed to the input of [12]. In scene flow refinement, instead of using implicit surface, we found the correspondent at $t+1$ that is closest to the estimated scene flow end-point to get the refined scene flow. We also skip the temporal consistent scene flow refinement described in Section 3.5. We use the evaluation metrics in [2] to measure the quality of our results in term

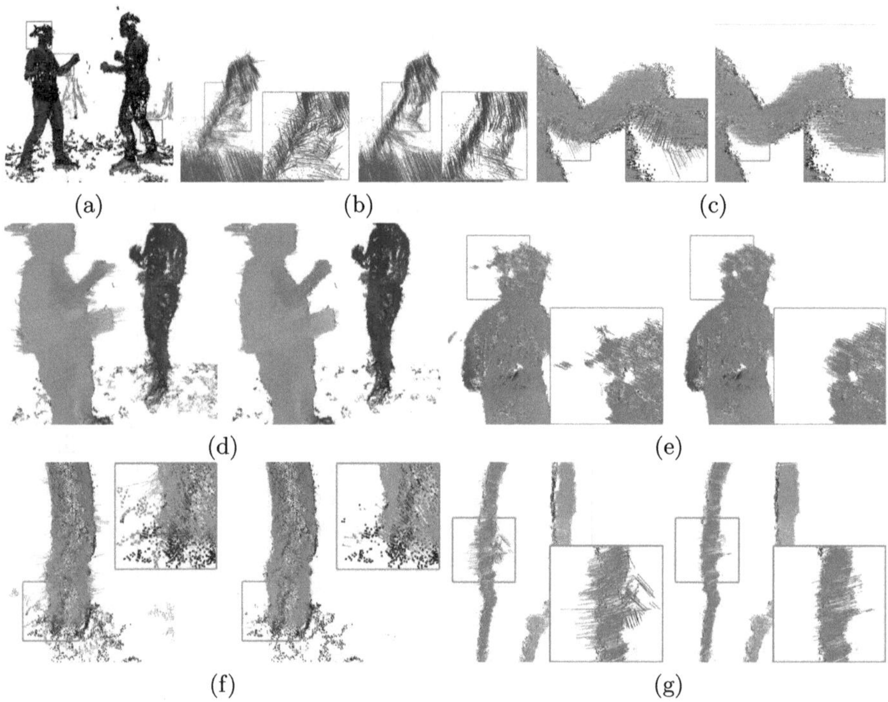

Fig. 6. Scene flow refinement results on *outdoor* dataset. (a) The reconstructed 3D structure at t. For better visualization and evaluation, we zoom-in the scene flow for different body parts: (b) arm part viewed from above, (c) elbow part, (d) back part, (e) head part, (f) ankle part and (g) vertical cross section of human's torso are presented. The scene flow before and after the refinement are shown for comparison.

of the normalized root mean square (NRMS) error for the estimated 3D point locations and for the estimated scene flow, and the absolute angular error (AAE) for the estimated scene flow. Table 2 shows the quantitative comparisons.

Our baseline results in Table 2 is worse than the result of [2]. Comparing the results of ours after refinement with those of our baseline, it is shown that our approach works reasonably and keeps 3D point positions accurately. In addition, the positions of 3D points are further improved by the outlier rejection step of our approach. While the results from [2] show a better performance when the pixels of discontinuity regions are excluded, our approach shows a better performance when all pixels are evaluated due to the usage of CFTV that can handle outliers and discontinuities implicitly in the framework. The result of [2] can be biased due to smoothness assumption on the occlusion region. Also, note that our approach is designed for scene flow refinement for general 3D point clouds, not limited to stereoscopic inputs while both Huguet *et al.* [3] and Basha *et al.* [2] are designed to handle stereoscopic data.

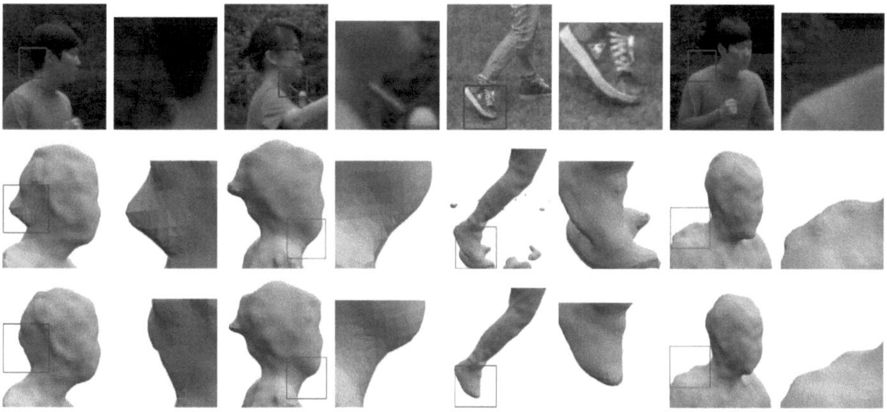

Fig. 7. Our approach improves the 3D reconstruction accuracy. First row: reference input image. Second row: reconstructed 3D model using the 3D point cloud from PMVS [12]. Third row: reconstructed 3D model using our refined 3D point locations of the 3D point cloud.

We evaluate our approach qualitatively on real-world outdoor dataset shown in Figure 1. This dataset consists of around 350,000 points on average per frame. We run our algorithm on a machine with Intel(R) Core (TM) i7 3Ghz PC with 8Ghz RAM memory. The PMVS [12] takes around 2.5 minutes to reconstruct the 3D point cloud per frame, and the optical flow implementation from [14] takes around 15 seconds to compute the optical flow per each image per frame. Our C++ implementation with approximate nearest neighbor data structure [26] (it takes around 5 minutes for initialization and building the ANN data structure) takes around 3 minutes for the direction refinement and around 5 seconds for the magnitude refinement for all points per frame. We use 10 neighbor points in implementation. For each frame of filtered 210,000 points, our un–optimized C++ implementation takes about 250 seconds from Section (3.5) to Section (3.3). Therefore, overall time for temporal consistency takes around 500 seconds.

For better visualization of our results, we show the zoomed-in regions on several parts of the human body in Figure 1. We show the scene flow before and after refinement for comparisons. Our approach is successful in improving the accuracy of scene flow via scene flow direction refinement and scene flow magnitude refinement. Due to the usage of CFTV, our approach can reject outliers and correct locations of 3D points. To visualize the effect of outliers rejection, we show the reconstructed 3D model using Poission surface reconstruction [27] in Figure 7. We have also translated the 3D points at time t to time $t+1$ according to the estimated scene flow in Figure 8. As we can observe in Figure 8, the translated 3D points at t (orange points) match with the 3D points at $t+1$ (cyan points).

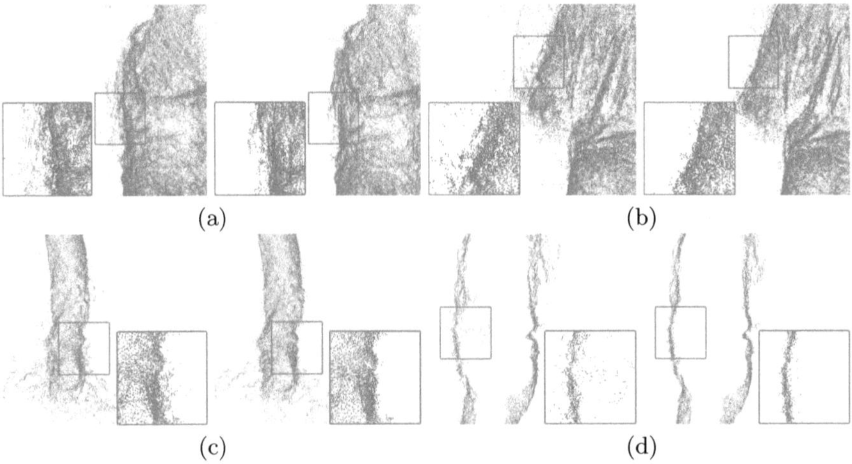

Fig. 8. We translate the point cloud at t (orange points) to match with the point cloud at $t+1$ (cyan points) according to the estimated scene flow. We show the zoom-in regions for: (a) man's back (b) arm part (c) ankle part. (d) Vertical cross section of human's torso. As we can see from the figure, the orange points align well with the cyan points which shows that our estimated scene flow is accurate.

5 Conclusion

In this paper, we have presented a framework to refine the scene flow estimated by multi-view stereo and optical flow back projection from images to 3D points. Our approach extends the CFTV framework to handle scene flow data in addition to the normal estimation problem tackled by the original CFTV framework. To estimate the scene flow magnitude, we exploit the physical property of the scene flow to connect the implicit surface of 3D point clouds in the consecutive frames. We have also introduced the scene flow temporal neighborhood and described how to propagate the scene flow direction from temporal neighborhood. Our approach is model free, and it is robust to handle outliers and noisy scene flow. As part of our future work, we shall study how to include other motion priors, such as rigid motion prior [8], to further enhance the performance of our framework. We will also study how to use the estimated scene flow data for different video editing, segmentation, view synthesis and recognition tasks.

Acknowledgement. This research was supported by the National Research Foundation of Korea(NRF) grant funded by the Korea government(MEST) (No.2012-0000986 and No. 2012-0003359) and partially by Microsoft Research Asia under KAIST-Microsoft Research Collaboration Center(KMCC). We thank ETRI for capturing the multi-view dataset.

References

1. Vedula, S., Baker, S., Rander, P., Collins, R., Kanade, T.: Three-dimensional scene flow. IEEE Trans. on PAMI 27(3), 475–480 (2005)
2. Basha, T., Aviv, T., Moses, Y., Kiryati, N.: Multi-view scene flow estimation: A view centered variational approach. In: CVPR (2010)
3. Huguet, F., Devernay, F.: A variational method for scene flow estimation from stereo sequences. In: ICCV (2007)
4. Neumann, J., Aloimonos, Y.: Spatio-temporal stereo using multi- resolution subdivision surfaces. IJCV 47(1-3), 181–193 (2002)
5. Rabe, C., Müller, T., Wedel, A., Franke, U.: Dense, Robust, and Accurate Motion Field Estimation from Stereo Image Sequences in Real-Time. In: Daniilidis, K., Maragos, P., Paragios, N. (eds.) ECCV 2010, Part IV. LNCS, vol. 6314, pp. 582–595. Springer, Heidelberg (2010)
6. Wedel, A., Rabe, C., Vaudrey, T., Brox, T., Franke, U., Cremers, D.: Efficient Dense Scene Flow from Sparse or Dense Stereo Data. In: Forsyth, D., Torr, P., Zisserman, A. (eds.) ECCV 2008, Part I. LNCS, vol. 5302, pp. 739–751. Springer, Heidelberg (2008)
7. Zhang, Y., Kambhamettu, C.: On 3-d scene flow and structure recovery from multiview image sequences. IEEE Trans. on Sys. Man Cyber. B 33(4), 592–606 (2003)
8. Vogel, C., Schindler, K., Roth, S.: 3D scene flow estimation with a rigid motion prior. In: ICCV (2011)
9. Valgaerts, L., Bruhn, A., Zimmer, H., Weickert, J., Stoll, C., Theobalt, C.: Joint Estimation of Motion, Structure and Geometry from Stereo Sequences. In: Daniilidis, K., Maragos, P., Paragios, N. (eds.) ECCV 2010, Part IV. LNCS, vol. 6314, pp. 568–581. Springer, Heidelberg (2010)
10. Hadfield, S., Bowden, R.: Kinecting the dots: Particle based scene flow from depth sensors. In: ICCV (2011)
11. Wedel, A., Brox, T., Vaudrey, T., Rabe, C., Franke, U., Cremers, D.: Stereoscopic scene flow computation for 3d motion understanding. IJCV 95(1), 29–51 (2011)
12. Furukawa, Y., Ponce, J.: Accurate, dense, and robust multiview stereopsis. IEEE Trans. on PAMI 32(8), 1362–1376 (2010)
13. Seitz, S., Curless, B., Diebel, J., Scharstein, D., Szeliski, R.: A comparison and evaluation of multi-view stereo reconstruction algorithms. In: CVPR (2006)
14. Sun, D., Roth, S., Black, M.J.: Secrets of optical flow estimation and their principles. In: CVPR (2010)
15. Baker, S., Scharstein, D., Lewis, J.P., Roth, S., Black, M.J., Szeliski, R.: A database and evaluation methodology for optical flow. IJCV 92(1), 1–31 (2011)
16. Ruttle, J., Manzke, M., Dahyot, R.: Estimating 3d scene flow from multiple 2d optical flows. In: International Machine Vision and Image Processing Conference, IMVIP 2009 (2009)
17. Devernay, F., Mateus, D., Guilbert, M.: Multi-camera scene flow by tracking 3-d points and surfels. In: CVPR (2006)
18. Furukawa, Y., Ponce, J.: Dense 3D motion capture from synchronized video streams. In: CVPR (2008)
19. Wu, T.P., Yeung, S.K., Jia, J., Tang, C.K.: Quasi-dense 3D reconstruction using tensor-based multiview stereo. In: CVPR (2010)
20. Pons, J., Keriven, R., Faugeras, O.: Multi-view stereo reconstruction and scene flow estimation with a global image-based matching score. IJCV 72(2), 179–193 (2007)

21. Pfister, H., Zwicker, M., van Baar, J., Gross, M.: Surfels: Surface elements as rendering primitives. SIGGRAPH (2000)
22. Carceroni, R., Kutulakos, K.: Multi-view scene capture by surfel sampling: From video streams to non-rigid 3d motion, shape and reflectance. IJCV 49(2-3), 175–214 (2002)
23. Wand, M., Jenke, P., Huang, Q., Bokeloh, M., Guibas, L., Schilling, A.: Reconstruction of deforming geometry from time-varying point clouds. In: Eurographics Symposium on Geometry Processing (2007)
24. Courchay, J., Pons, J.-P., Monasse, P., Keriven, R.: Dense and Accurate Spatio-temporal Multi-view Stereovision. In: Zha, H., Taniguchi, R.-I., Maybank, S. (eds.) ACCV 2009, Part II. LNCS, vol. 5995, pp. 11–22. Springer, Heidelberg (2010)
25. Wu, T.P., Yeung, S.K., Jia, J., Tang, C.K., Medioni, G.: A closed-form solution to tensor voting: Theory and applications. IEEE Trans. on PAMI 34(8), 1482–1495 (2012)
26. Mount, D.M., Arya, S.: ANN: A library for approximate nearest neighbor searching (2010), http://www.cs.umd.edu/~mount/ANN/
27. Michael Kazhdan, M.B., Hoppe, H.: Poission surface reconstruction. In: Eurographics Symposium on Geometry Processing (2006)

Two-View Underwater Structure and Motion for Cameras under Flat Refractive Interfaces

Lai Kang[1,3], Lingda Wu[1,2], and Yee-Hong Yang[3]

[1] College of Information System and Management, National University of Defense Technology, Changsha, China
lkang.vr@gmail.com
[2] The Key Laboratory, Academy of Equipment Command & Technology, Beijing, China
wld@nudt.edu.cn
[3] Department of Computing Science, University of Alberta, Edmonton, Canada
yang@cs.ualberta.ca

Abstract. In an underwater imaging system, a refractive interface is introduced when a camera looks into the water-based environment, resulting in distorted images due to refraction. Simply ignoring the refraction effect or using the lens radial distortion model causes erroneous 3D reconstruction. This paper deals with a general underwater imaging setup using two cameras, of which each camera is placed in a separate waterproof housing with a flat window. The impact of refraction is explicitly modeled in the refractive camera model. Based on two new concepts, namely the Ellipse of Refrax (EoR) and Refractive Depth (RD) of a scene point, we show that provably optimal underwater structure and motion under L_∞-norm can be estimated given known rotation. The constraint of known rotation is further relaxed by incorporating two-view geometry estimation into a new hybrid optimization framework. The experimental results using both synthetic and real images demonstrate that the proposed method can significantly improve the accuracy of camera motion and 3D structure estimation for underwater applications.

1 Introduction

Structure and motion from images is an active research topic in computer vision [1]. While remarkable success has been achieved in the last decade for land-based systems, accurate 3D reconstruction from images captured by underwater cameras, however, has not attracted much attentions in the computer vision community only until recently [2][3]. The key challenge is that the refraction of light occurs when a light ray passing through different media, rendering the perspective camera model invalid.

In early works, the effects of refraction in underwater 3D reconstruction are simply ignored [4] or modeled by approximate methods, such as focal length adjustment [5], lens radial distortion [6] and a combination of the two [7]. Unfortunately, these methods are insufficient since the effect of refraction is known to be highly non-linear and depends on the 3D location of a scene. As shown by

A. Fitzgibbon et al. (Eds.): ECCV 2012, Part IV, LNCS 7575, pp. 303–316, 2012.

Treibitz et al. [8], assuming a single viewpoint (SVP) model can be erroneous for camera calibration in underwater applications.

A more desirable method to compensate for refraction is to use a physically correct refractive camera model. Chari and Sturm [2] analyze using theoretical analysis the underlying multi-view relationships between two cameras when the scene has a single refractive planar surface separating two different media. The authors demonstrate the existence of geometric entities such as the refractive fundamental matrix and the refractive homography matrix. Nevertheless, no practical application of these theoretical results is given in [2]. Chang and Chen [3] study a similar configuration involving multiple views of a scene through a single interface. Refractive distortion is explicitly modeled as a function of depth. In [3], an additional piece of hardware called inertial measurement unit (IMU) is required to provide the roll and pitch angles of the camera. Also, the normal of the refractive interface is assumed to be known. Based on this additional information, the authors derive a linear solution to the relative pose problem and a closed-form solution to the absolute pose problem. More recently, Agrawal et al. [9] show that the underlying refractive geometry corresponds to an axial camera and develop a general theory of calibrating such systems using a planar checkerboard.

Sedlazeck and Koch [10] study the calibration of housing parameters for underwater stereo camera rigs. Rather than minimizing the reprojection error in the image space, the error on the outer interface plane is minimized by deriving the virtual perspective projection [11] for each 3D point. One issue of this method is, as reported in [10], that the optimization process is time consuming (in the order of 3 hours). Compared with [10], our proposed algorithm allows more general configuration of cameras and can minimize the reprojection error in image space efficiently. Another limitation for most existing underwater photography works is that a calibration target with known dimensions is required to perform system calibration [12][11][8].

In this paper, we focus on structure and motion estimation for a general underwater imaging setup consisting of two cameras, of which each camera is placed in a separate waterproof housing with a flat window, without using any calibration object. The main contributions of this paper are: 1) Two new concepts, namely the Ellipse of Refrax (EoR) and the Refractive Depth (RD) of a scene point for the refractive camera model are presented. These two concepts facilitate the derivation of an algorithm which yields globally optimal estimation of relative camera translation, interface distances and 3D structure under L_∞-norm, given known camera rotation and the interface normal; 2) A new hybrid optimization framework is proposed to perform two-view underwater structure and motion. Within this framework, the constraint of known rotation is further relaxed and the reprojection errors in image space are minimized.

2 Refractive Camera Model

This section gives a brief review of the refractive camera model and presents two new concepts to facilitate the recovery of underwater structure and motion.

2.1 Notations and Background

The refractive camera model which consists of a conventional perspective camera model and a refractive interface is shown in Fig. 1(a). This subsection introduces notations used in the refractive camera model, backward projection and forward projection.

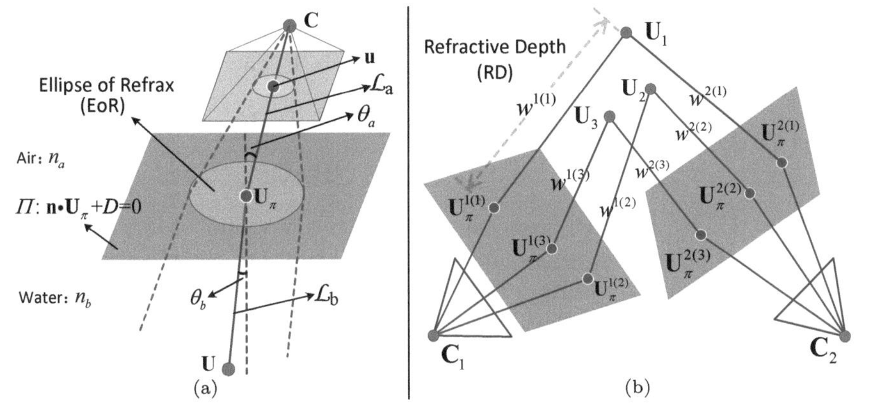

Fig. 1. Illustration of the refractive camera model and two new related concepts. (a) A perspective camera centered at **C** in the air observes a 3D point **U** in water. The light ray is refracted at the refractive interface Π. The Ellipse of Refrax (EoR) of **U** also lies on Π. (b) The Refractive Depth (RD) of 3D point. See text for details.

Back Projection calculates the refracted light ray which originates from the camera center and goes through the corresponding 3D scene point for a given image point. Let the camera projection matrix be of the form $\mathbf{P} = \mathbf{K}[\mathbf{R}|\mathbf{t}]$, where $\mathbf{K}$ is the calibration matrix of the camera, $\mathbf{R}$ the rotation matrix and $\mathbf{t}$ the translation vector. As shown in Fig. 1(a), the corresponding light ray $\mathcal{L}_a$ in the air is determined by the camera center $\mathbf{C}$ and its direction is given by $\mathbf{r}_a = \mathbf{R}^{-1}\mathbf{K}^{-1}\mathbf{u}$, where $\mathbf{u}$ stands for the homogeneous coordinates of the image point. Given $\mathcal{L}_a$, the point $\mathbf{U}_\pi$ (which is called refrax according to [13]) where the refraction occurs can be determined by computing the intersection of $\mathcal{L}_a$ and the refractive interface Π. In order to calculate the direction of the refracted ray $\mathcal{L}_b$, Snell's law is applied, namely $n_a \sin\theta_a = n_b \sin\theta_b$, where n_a and n_b are the refractive indices of air and water, respectively. The direction of $\mathcal{L}_b$ can thus be written as [14]:

$$\mathbf{r}_b = \frac{n_a}{n_b}\frac{\mathbf{r}_a}{\|\mathbf{r}_a\|_2} - \left(\frac{n_a}{n_b}\cos\theta_a - \sqrt{1-\sin^2\theta_b}\right)\mathbf{n}, \tag{1}$$

where $\sin\theta_b$ can be rewritten as a function of $\cos\theta_a = \mathbf{n}\cdot\frac{\mathbf{r}_a}{\|\mathbf{r}_a\|_2}$ and $\mathbf{n}$ is the normal of Π.

Forward Projection calculates the projection of a 3D scene point onto the image plane. The forward projection of a 3D point under the refractive camera model corresponds to solving a 4th degree polynomial. Details on forward projection can be found in [3] and [9].

2.2 Ellipse of Refrax (EoR) and Refractive Depth (RD) of a Scene Point

Let $\underline{\mathbf{u}}$ and $\mathbf{u}$ be the ground truth and the measured homogenous image coordinates (with the 3rd element equals to 1) of a scene point $\mathbf{U}$, respectively. For a perspective camera with camera projection matrix $\mathbf{P}$, the reprojection error is:

$$d(\mathbf{P}, \mathbf{U}, \mathbf{u}) = \|\mathbf{u} - \underline{\mathbf{u}}\|_2 = \frac{\left\| [\mathbf{P}]_1\tilde{\mathbf{U}} - [\mathbf{u}]_1[\mathbf{P}]_3\tilde{\mathbf{U}}, [\mathbf{P}]_2\tilde{\mathbf{U}} - [\mathbf{u}]_2[\mathbf{P}]_3\tilde{\mathbf{U}} \right\|_2}{[\mathbf{P}]_3\tilde{\mathbf{U}}} \tag{2}$$

where $\tilde{\mathbf{U}} = [\mathbf{U}^\top 1]^\top$ and $[\mathbf{P}]_k$ represents the k-th row vector of matrix $\mathbf{P}$. Also, without loss of generality, we assume that $[\mathbf{P}]_3\tilde{\mathbf{U}} > 0$. For the refractive camera model, it is incorrect to use Eq. (2) to calculate the reprojection error. However, since the light ray between the camera center $\mathbf{C}$ and refrax $\mathbf{U}_\pi$ is a straight line (see Fig. 1(a)), we can get a similar equation on $\mathbf{U}_\pi$ by replacing $\mathbf{U}$ with $\mathbf{U}_\pi$ in Eq. (2). In addition, the refrax $\mathbf{U}_\pi$ should lie on the refractive interface, which gives another linear constraint. Given a 3D scene point $\mathbf{U}$ with image point $\mathbf{u}$, we define its Ellipse of Refrax (EoR) as:

$$\mathcal{R}(\mathbf{P}, \mathbf{n}, \mathbf{u}) = \{\mathbf{U}_\pi | d(\mathbf{P}, \mathbf{U}_\pi, \mathbf{u}) \le \gamma, \mathbf{n} \cdot \mathbf{U}_\pi + D = 0, \} \tag{3}$$

where γ is a threshold ($\gamma = 3$ pixels in this paper) specifying the largest reprojection error on image plane. For a camera with projection matrix $\mathbf{P} = \mathbf{K}[\mathbf{R}|\mathbf{t}]$, assume that $\mathbf{K}$ and $\mathbf{R}$ are known, the first constraint of $\mathcal{R}$ can be rewritten as:

$$\|f_1(\mathbf{x}'), f_2(\mathbf{x}')\|_2 \le \gamma f_3(\mathbf{x}'), \tag{4}$$

where f_1, f_2 and f_3 are affine functions with unknown vector $\mathbf{x}' = (\mathbf{t}^\top, \mathbf{U}_\pi^\top)^\top$ and coefficients determined by $\mathbf{K}$, $\mathbf{R}$ and $\mathbf{u}$. For a fixed γ, Eq. (4) is known to be a Second Order Cone (SOC), which is convex [15][16]. Note that $\mathcal{R}$ corresponds to the intersection of a SOC and a plane, which is an ellipse (see Fig. 1(a)). Also, it is easy to see that, by assuming that the normal of the refractive interface $\mathbf{n}$ is known, the second constraint of $\mathcal{R}$ is linear in $\mathbf{x}'' = (\mathbf{U}_\pi^\top, D)^\top$. Based on the above discussion, we conclude that EoR defines a convex set for known $\mathbf{K}$, $\mathbf{R}$, $\mathbf{n}$ and image measurement $\mathbf{u}$.

Since EoR directly imposes constraint on the refrax $\mathbf{U}_\pi$ rather than on scene point, solely using EoR does not make sense for reconstructing a 3D point. Suppose a scene consisting of N 3D points $\mathbf{U}_j (j = 1, \cdots, N)$ is observed by two cameras with camera center $\mathbf{C}_i (i = 1, 2)$, the refrax of the j-th 3D point on the i-th interface is denoted by $\mathbf{U}_\pi^{i(j)}$ (see Fig. 1(b)). According to backward projection, each image measurement (or each refrax) imposes a linear constraint on its corresponding 3D scene point. For instance, the constraint for $\mathbf{U}_\pi^{i(j)}$ is given by:

$$\mathbf{U}_j = \mathbf{U}_\pi^{i(j)} + w^{i(j)}\mathbf{r}_b^{i(j)}, \tag{5}$$

where $\mathbf{r}_b^{i(j)}$ denotes the direction of the refracted ray that corresponds to refrax $\mathbf{U}_\pi^{i(j)}$. As the direction of the refracted ray is uniquely determined by $\mathbf{K}$, $\mathbf{R}$, $\mathbf{n}$ and image measurement $\mathbf{u}$ (see subsection 2.1), Eq. (5) generates three new independent linear constraints on $\mathbf{U}_j, \mathbf{U}_\pi^{i(j)}$ and the coefficient $w^{i(j)}$, which we call the Refractive Depth (RD) of 3D point $\mathbf{U}_j$ with respect to the i-th camera.

3 Underwater Structure and Motion with Known Rotation

In this subsection, we show that the constraints from EoR and RD presented in the aforementioned section can be imposed in a new formulation of the underwater with known rotation problem. In the context of this problem, the term rotation refers to the rotation of the perspective camera and the normal of the refractive interface.

3.1 Underwater Known Rotation Problem with Provably Optimal Solution

The underwater with known rotation problem (UKRP1) is formulated as the following min-max problem:

$$\begin{aligned} \mathsf{UKRP1} \quad & \min \max\nolimits_{ij} d(\mathbf{P}_i, \mathbf{U}_\pi^{i(j)}, \mathbf{u}^{i(j)}) \\ & \text{subject to } \mathbf{n}_i \cdot \mathbf{U}_\pi^{i(j)} + D_i = 0, \\ & \qquad \mathbf{U}_j = \mathbf{U}_\pi^{i(j)} + w^{i(j)} \mathbf{r}_b^{i(j)}, \\ & \qquad \forall i = 1, 2, \\ & \qquad \forall j = 1, \cdots, N. \end{aligned} \tag{6}$$

with unknown vector

$$\mathbf{X} = \left(\mathbf{U}_1^\top, \cdots, \mathbf{U}_N^\top, \mathbf{U}_\pi^{1(1)\top}, \cdots, \mathbf{U}_\pi^{2(N)\top}, w^{1(1)}, \cdots, w^{2(N)}, \mathbf{t}_1^\top, \mathbf{t}_2^\top, D_1, D_2 \right)^\top. \tag{7}$$

The UKRP1 minimizes the L_∞-norm of the vector of reprojection errors on image plane. More conveniently, UKRP1 can be rewritten in its equivalent form:

$$\begin{aligned} \mathsf{UKRP2} \quad & \min \gamma \\ & \text{subject to } d(\mathbf{P}_i, \mathbf{U}_\pi^{i(j)}, \mathbf{u}^{i(j)}) \le \gamma, \\ & \qquad \mathbf{n}_i \cdot \mathbf{U}_\pi^{i(j)} + D_i = 0, \\ & \qquad \mathbf{U}_j = \mathbf{U}_\pi^{i(j)} + w^{i(j)} \mathbf{r}_b^{i(j)}, \\ & \qquad \forall i = 1, 2, \\ & \qquad \forall j = 1, \cdots, N. \end{aligned} \tag{8}$$

The first two constraints in UKRP2 correspond to the EoR and the third constraint corresponds to the RD defined in subsection 2.2. As the constraints in UKRP2 are convex for a fixed γ, the solution to UKRP2 can be found by solving a sequence of feasibility problems within a bisection procedure [16]. In particular, the underwater feasibility problem (UFSBP) is given by:

$$\begin{aligned}
\textsf{UFSBP} \qquad & \text{Given } \gamma \\
& \text{does there exist } \mathbf{X} \\
& \text{subject to } d(\mathbf{P}_i, \mathbf{U}_\pi^{i(j)}, \mathbf{u}^{i(j)}) \le \gamma, \\
& \mathbf{n}_i \cdot \mathbf{U}_\pi^{i(j)} + D_i = 0, \\
& \mathbf{U}_j = \mathbf{U}_\pi^{i(j)} + w^{i(j)} \mathbf{r}_b^{i(j)}, \\
& \forall i = 1, 2, \\
& \forall j = 1, \cdots, N.
\end{aligned} \tag{9}$$

Since a feasibility problem does not have an objective function, we only need to examine whether all the constraints are satisfied for a given γ. Because all the constraints of UFSBP are convex, the feasibility problem UFSBP is also convex and can be solved efficiently using convex optimization [15].

3.2 Robust Formulation of the Underwater Known Rotation Problem

While the algorithm proposed in subsection 3.1 can estimate camera translation, interface distances and scene structure optimally, minimization under the L_∞-norm is known to be particularly sensitive to outliers [16]. In this paper, outliers are handled by introducing auxiliary variables as in [17]. Instead of solving a sequence of convex problems, satisfactory estimation of structure and motion can also be obtained by solving the following single convex optimization problem:

$$\begin{aligned}
\textsf{UKRP3} \qquad & \min \textstyle\sum_{j=1}^{N} s_j \\
& \text{subject to } d(\mathbf{P}_i, \mathbf{U}_\pi^{i(j)}, \mathbf{u}^{i(j)})[\mathbf{P}_i]_3 \mathbf{U}_\pi^{i(j)} \le \gamma [\mathbf{P}_i]_3 \mathbf{U}_\pi^{i(j)} + s_j, \\
& \mathbf{n}_i \cdot \mathbf{U}_\pi^{i(j)} + D_i = 0, \\
& \mathbf{U}_j = \mathbf{U}_\pi^{i(j)} + w^{i(j)} \mathbf{r}_b^{i(j)}, \\
& \forall i = 1, 2, \\
& \forall j = 1, \cdots, N.
\end{aligned} \tag{10}$$

with unknown vector

$$\widetilde{\mathbf{X}} = \left(\mathbf{X}^\top, s_1, \cdots, s_N\right)^\top. \tag{11}$$

Again, for a fixed γ, the UKRP3 is convex and can be solved efficiently. The case $s_j > 0$ in the solution to UKRP3 indicates that the reprojection error of the j-th 3D point is larger than γ in at least one image, and thus can be identified as outlier.

4 Underwater Structure and Motion with Rotation Estimation

For two general underwater cameras, a minimal set of 11 parameters is required to model the two view geometry (intrinsic parameters are assumed to be known).

Since we assume that the image plane of each camera is nearly parallel to its refractive interface, the required number of parameters is reduced to 7, of which 5 are for the relative pose of the two cameras and 2 for the distances between the cameras and their refractive interfaces. From subsection 3.1, we know that the relative translation and the distance between each camera and its refractive interface can be optimally estimated. In this section, the algorithm proposed in subsection 3.1 is incorporated into Differential Evolution (DE), which is one of the most powerful population-based stochastic function minimizer [18], resulting in a new hybrid framework. Consequently, the underwater structure and motion problem is reduced to a small scale optimization problem over the rotation space, which can be concisely parameterized by only 4 parameters using quaternion.

4.1 Two-View Geometry Estimation Using Hybrid Optimization

Similar to many other evolutionary algorithms, DE maintains a population of N_p individuals. N_p new trial vectors are generated from the perturbation (scaled difference between two randomly selected population vectors) of points in the current generation. The trial vector competes against the population vector of the same index, and the vector with a better fitness value will be marked as a member of the next generation. In our problem, each individual $\mathbf{\Theta}$ is a 4-dimensional real-valued trial vector, which corresponds to a possible solution. Each individual in the initial population is randomly selected under uniform distribution in the rotation space. Without loss of generality, the coordinate system of the first camera is chosen to coincide with the world coordinate system. Given a trial vector $\mathbf{\Theta}$, the rotation matrices of the two cameras are given by $\mathbf{R}_1 = \mathbf{I}_{3\times3}$ (3×3 identity matrix) and $\mathbf{R}_2 = R_m(\mathbf{\Theta})$, where $R_m(.)$ transforms a quaternion into its equivalent rotation matrix. The normals of the two interfaces are given by $\mathbf{n}_1 = (0, 0, 1)^\top$ and $\mathbf{n}_2 = R_m^{-1}(\mathbf{\Theta})(0, 0, 1)^\top$.

Our proposed hybrid optimization consists of three stages. In the first stage, we search for the best camera rotation using DE [18]. In this stage, a subset of outlier free image correspondences are used and the individual evaluation for a given trial vector $\mathbf{\Theta}$ is performed as follows: first, retrieve the system parameters (camera rotation and interface normal) specified by the given trial vector; then, estimate the provably optimal structure and motion by solving UKRP2 (see subsection 3.1) and finally calculate the RMS reprojection error of reconstructed 3D scene as the fitness of $\mathbf{\Theta}$. In the second stage, we use all image correspondences (may contain outliers) and the best rotation estimated in the first stage to remove outliers and obtain robust estimates by solving the UKRP3 (see subsection 3.2). In the final stage, both system parameters and 3D structure are further refined by bundle adjustment as shown in the next subsection.

4.2 Sparse and Dense Underwater 3D Reconstruction

Given the rotation parameters and a set of outlier affected image correspondences, the sparse 3D structure and updated motion can be obtained by solving the robust underwater known rotation problem UKRP3. We minimize the following objective function:

$$\mathcal{J} = \sum_{i=1}^{2} \sum_{j=1}^{N} [d'(\mathbf{P}_i, \mathbf{n}_i, D_i, \mathbf{U}_j, \mathbf{u}^{i(j)})]^2, \tag{12}$$

where $d'(\mathbf{P}_i, \mathbf{n}_i, D_i, \mathbf{U}_j, \mathbf{u}^{i(j)})$ is the reprojection error of the j-th 3D point $\mathbf{U}_j$ in the i-th image. The projection of a 3D point can be analytically computed using forward projection [3][9]. The objective function defined in Eq. (12) is a typical non-linear function and its scale can be large for 3D reconstruction problem. In this paper, we adopt a general purpose sparse Levenberg-Marquart (splm) algorithm [19] to improve the efficiency of optimization. For the dense 3D reconstruction, a modified version of the patch-based multi-view stereo (PMVS) algorithm [20][3] is used and it generates a (quasi) dense set of oriented patches covering the surface of scene, which can be converted into a mesh in a post processing stage.

5 Experiments

In order to evaluate the performance of our proposed method, we implemented the algorithms in C++ and carried out extensive experiments using both synthetic data and real images. The academic version of MOSEK [21] was used to solve the convex optimization problems. The refractive index of water is set to 1.33. In order to establish feature correspondences between two images, SIFT image features were detected and matched using the methods proposed in [22]. For the first stage of our proposed hybrid optimization, a subset of outlier free image correspondences are selected manually. The error metrics for quantitative evaluation are defined as follows: 1) the error in the relative camera rotation $\Delta\mathbf{R}$ is measured as the angle (in degrees) in the axis-angle representation of the rotation $\mathbf{R}_{est}\mathbf{R}_{gt}^{\top}$, where $\mathbf{R}_{gt}$ and $\mathbf{R}_{est}$ are the ground truth and the estimated relative camera rotation, respectively; 2) the error in the relative camera translation $\Delta\mathbf{t}$ is measured as the angle (in degrees) between the estimated relative camera translation $\mathbf{T}_{est}$ and the ground truth relative camera translation $\mathbf{T}_{gt}$; and 3) the error in the relative interface distance ΔD is measured as

$$\Delta D = \frac{1}{2}\left(\left| \frac{d_{est1}}{d_{gt1}} \cdot \frac{\|\mathbf{T}_{gt}\|}{\|\mathbf{T}_{est}\|} - 1 \right| + \left| \frac{d_{est2}}{d_{gt2}} \cdot \frac{\|\mathbf{T}_{gt}\|}{\|\mathbf{T}_{est}\|} - 1 \right| \right), \tag{13}$$

where d_{est1}, d_{est2} are the estimated distances between each camera and its refractive interface, and d_{gt1}, d_{gt2} are the corresponding ground truth distances. Since the magnitude of $\mathbf{T}_{est}$ cannot be recovered in metric 3D reconstruction, a scale factor $\frac{\|\mathbf{T}_{gt}\|}{\|\mathbf{T}_{est}\|}$ is used to normalize ΔD.

5.1 Synthetic Data

Our first set of experiments uses synthetic data, where a 3D scene consists of randomly generated 3D points within a unit cube. The two cameras were placed two units away from the center of the cube, looking toward the center of the cube. Both the relative camera rotation and translation were randomly perturbed to generate various setups. The distance between each camera and its interface was randomly chosen from 0.2 units to 1 unit.

First, we evaluate the performance of the globally optimal structure and motion estimation algorithm described in subsection 3.1 using noise free data sets. Examined quantities are $\Delta\mathbf{T}$ and ΔD as defined earlier. Three data sets with a different number of 3D scene points are generated, each of which consists of 500 randomly generated instances. The statistical results using noise free data are shown in Fig. 2(a), which demonstrate that our proposed algorithm can estimate the camera and interface parameters accurately in the absence of noise, and that using more image correspondences improves the accuracy. Note that the accuracy of estimation can be further improved by specifying a smaller error tolerance in the bisection procedure. Next, we study the performance of the globally optimal algorithm under different amounts of noise. In addition to uniformly distributed noise under which it yields provably optimal estimation, the influence of Gaussian noise is also investigated. For each level of noise, 30 instances are analyzed statistically. Shown in Fig. 2(b) and Fig. 2(c) are the results of camera pose and interface parameter estimation under Uniform and Gaussian noise, respectively. Attributed to efficient convex programming solver provided in MOSEK, the running time is stable and increases approximately linearly with respect to the scale of problem. Specifically, it takes approximately 0.1 seconds for the synthetic scene consisting of 16 scene points and 0.5 seconds for 64 3D scene points.

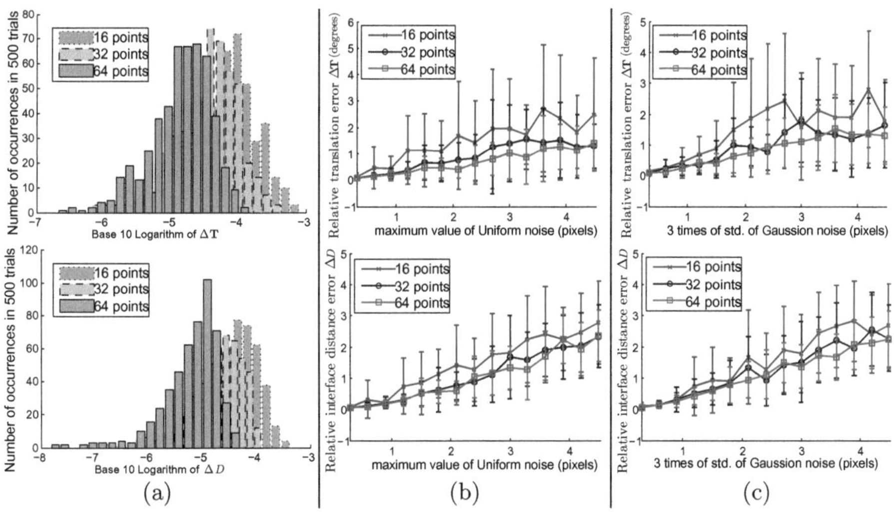

Fig. 2. Accuracy of parameter estimation (solution to UKRP2) (a) using noise free data sets, (b) under Uniform noise and (c) under Gaussian noise with a different number of 3D scene points

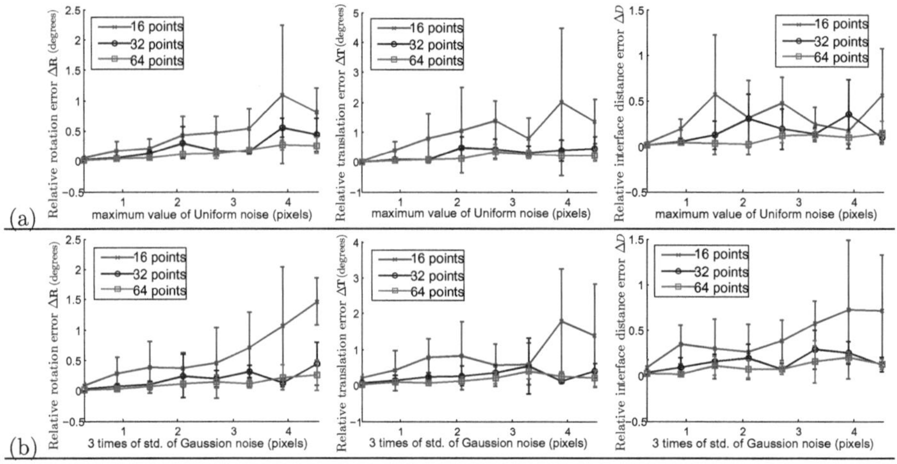

Fig. 3. Accuracy of parameter estimation using hybrid optimization for data sets (a) under Uniform noise and (b) under Gaussian noise

Then, we evaluate the performance of two-view geometry estimation using our proposed hybrid optimization described in subsection 4.1. Statistics over 20 randomly generated instances with a specified number of 3D points under each level of noise are shown in Fig. 3(a) (under Uniform noise) and Fig. 3(b) (under Gaussian noise). The results show that our proposed two-view geometry estimation method can obtain accurate estimation of camera pose and interface parameters. It is noteworthy that even though the solution to UKRP2 (see Fig. 2(b) and Fig. 2(c)) is provably optimal under Uniform noise, the proposed hybrid method can significantly improve the accuracy of camera and interface parameter estimation. The improvements indicate that hybrid optimization is more suitable for the refractive camera model which possesses highly intrinsic non-linearity. In addition, this set of experiments once again confirms that using more image correspondences can improve the accuracy of geometry estimation.

5.2 Synthetically Rendered Images

While subsection 5.1 presents the performance of proposed algorithms statistically, this subsection presents the comparison of results using synthetically rendered images. Since rendered images can be very realistic, they provide an

Table 1. Comparison of the accuracy of camera localization

Method	$\Delta\mathbf{R}$	$\Delta\mathbf{T}$
NDist	3.157	6.123
FAdj	3.044	3.438
RDist	2.236	6.179
FAdj+RDist	2.869	4.985
NEW	0.017	0.051

alternative way to evaluate practical performance of our proposed algorithms. In this experiment, we use POVRay, an publicly available ray tracer, to generate synthetically rendered images. In particular, we create a square water-filled pool of size 1.15×1×0.55 (L×W×H unit). The Stanford bunny model standing on an isosceles right angled prism is placed at the bottom of the pool. Each camera is placed in a glass housing deployed underwater to one side of the pool. The thickness of the glass is set to 0.01 units, the distance between each camera and its refractive interface is set to 0.1 units. The focal length of the camera is 800 pixels and the resolution of the image is 1024×768. Such settings result in a 65° horizontal field of view (FOV) of camera. The setup and two rendered images are shown in Fig. 4(a).

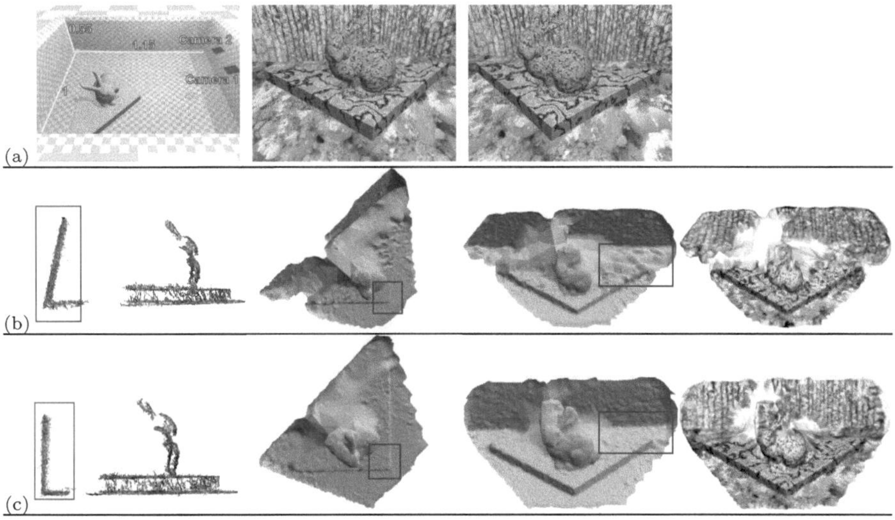

Fig. 4. Experiments with synthetically generated images. Figures in (a) are the simulated setup and two rendered images. Figures in (b) are the results of 3D reconstruction using FAdj+RDist. Figures in (c) are the results of 3D reconstruction using our proposed method. Interested regions are highlighted. Apparent distortion in 3D reconstruction includes: The wall and floor of the pool become non-perpendicular in the first column of (b), the two equal sides of the reconstructed isosceles right angled prism become non-perpendicular in the second column of (b), and the reconstructed scene far from the cameras is noisy in the third column of (b).

The performance of our proposed method (denoted as NEW) are compared with four cases: 1) simply ignore distortion (denoted as NDist); 2) use focal length adjustment (denoted as FAdj); 3) use lens radial distortion (denoted as RDist) and 4) simultaneously adjust focal length and lens radial distortion parameters (denoted as FAdj+RDist). All of the four compared cases are performed with bundler [23]. A comparison of the accuracy of camera localization is shown in Table 1. The results confirm that the conventional image-space distortion models are incapable in compensating for the refraction effect. On the contrary, our proposed method can handle refractive distortion properly.

The presence of the refractive interface not only affect camera localization, but also results in distorted and incomplete 3D reconstruction. In particular, we found that apart from distortion in the reconstructed dense 3D scene, it fails to reconstruct consistent patches for the part of the scene far from the cameras, since the distortion induced by refraction increases as scene depth increases. For qualitative evaluation, the results of dense 3D reconstruction using FAdj+RDist and our proposed method are shown in Fig. 4(b) and Fig. 4(c), respectively.

5.3 Real Images

The practical performance of our proposed method has also been tested on real images. Two Point Grey Research Flea2 cameras were placed behind two planar faces of a large, water-filled tank. The optical axis of each camera was approximately parallel to the normal of its refractive interface and the intrinsic camera parameters were assumed to be known. In this imaging setup, the thickness of glass is about 6 mm, the distance between each camera and its refractive

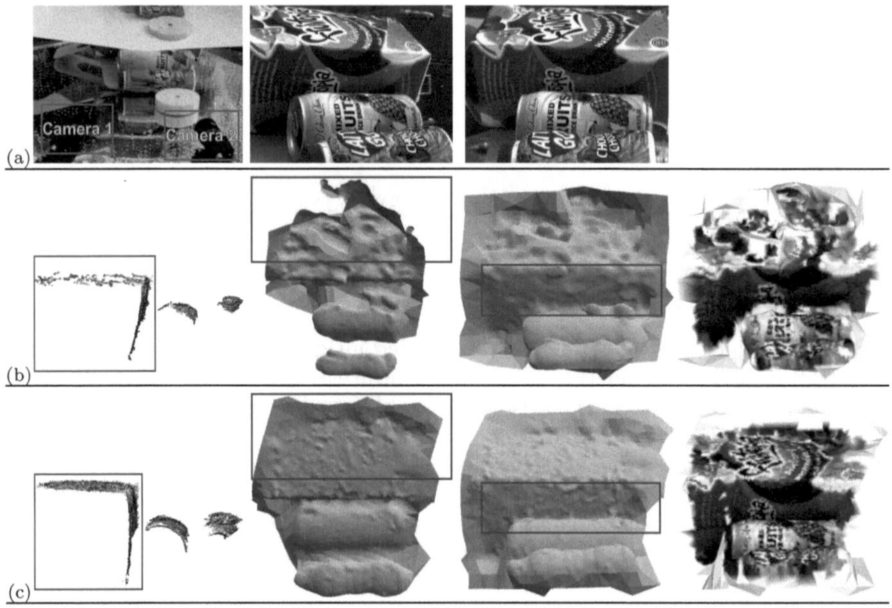

Fig. 5. Experiments with real images. Figures in (a) are the setup constructed in our lab and the two captured images. Figures in (b) are the results of 3D reconstruction using FAdj+RDist. Figures in (c) are the results of 3D reconstruction using our proposed method. Interested regions are highlighted. Apparent distortion in 3D reconstruction includes: The two sides of the box become non-perpendicular in the first column of (b), the reconstructed scene far from the cameras is noisy in the second and the third columns of (b).

interface is about 15 mm. The scene placed about 400 mm away from each camera contains three close together containers leaned on a bracket. The resolution of the captured images is 1032×776 pixels, the focal length of the camera is roughly 1800 pixels, and the horizontal field of view of the camera is about 32°. The experimental setup and captured images are shown in Fig. 5(a).

The results of dense 3D reconstruction using FAdj+RDist and our proposed methods are presented in Fig. 5(b) and Fig. 5(c) for qualitative evaluation. Compared with the results on synthetically rendered images (see Fig. 4), the 3D reconstruction on real images is less accurate due to a large amount noise in image measurements. Nevertheless, more complete and accurate surface has been obtained using our proposed method than that using FAdj+RDist, which demonstrates the superiority of our method.

6 Conclusions and Discussions

This paper proposes a method to perform structure and motion from two images captured by a general underwater imaging setup consisting of two cameras, of which each camera is placed in a separate waterproof housing with a flat window. A new formulation of the underwater known rotation problem for the refractive camera model is proposed based on two new concepts, namely Ellipse of Refrax (EoR) and Refractive Depth (RD). The proposed formulation allows one to obtain provably optimal underwater structure and motion under L_∞-norm given known rotation. The constraint of known rotation is further relaxed in a new hybrid optimization framework. Promising results on synthetic data, synthetically rendered images and real images demonstrate that the proposed method can significantly improve the accuracy of camera motion and 3D structure estimation for underwater applications.

Two simplification of the underwater imaging setup were made in this paper. First, the thickness of refractive was ignored. In fact, as pointed out by Treibitz et al. [8], the thickness of the glass interface results in negligible shift in the image because the thickness of interface is normally small and the refractive indices of glass and water are close. Second, the image plane of each camera was assumed to be nearly parallel to its refractive interface, as in most real underwater imaging system. Thus, both assumptions are reasonable for practical underwater applications. As for future work, it would be interesting to investigate scenarios where the refractive indices of media are unknown.

Acknowledgments. This work was partially supported by the Chinese Scholarship Council (grant no. 2010611068), the Hunan Provincial Innovation Foundation for Postgraduate (grant no. CX2010B025), the Natural Sciences and Engineering Research Council of Canada (NSERC) and the University of Alberta. The authors would like to thank the three anonymous reviewers for their constructive comments.

References

1. Hartley, R., Zisserman, A.: Multiple View Geometry in Computer Vision, 2nd edn. Cambridge University Press, New York (2004)
2. Chari, V., Sturm, P.: Multiple-view geometry of the refractive plane. In: BMVC (2009)
3. Chang, Y., Chen, T.: Multi-view 3d reconstruction for scenes under the refractive plane with known vertical direction. In: ICCV (2011)
4. Queiroz-Neto, J.P., Carceroni, R., Barros, W., Campos, M.: Underwater stereo. In: CGIP, XVII Brazilian Symposium (2004)
5. Ferreira, R., Costeira, J.P., Santos, J.A.: Stereo Reconstruction of a Submerged Scene. In: Marques, J.S., Pérez de la Blanca, N., Pina, P. (eds.) IbPRIA 2005. LNCS, vol. 3522, pp. 102–109. Springer, Heidelberg (2005)
6. Pizarro, O., Eustice, R., Singh, H.: Relative pose estimation for instrumented, calibrated imaging platforms. In: DICTA (2003)
7. Lavest, J.M., Rives, G., Lapresté, J.T.: Underwater Camera Calibration. In: Vernon, D. (ed.) ECCV 2000. LNCS, vol. 1843, pp. 654–668. Springer, Heidelberg (2000)
8. Treibitz, T., Schechner, Y.Y., Singh, H.: Flat refractive geometry. In: CVPR (2008)
9. Agrawal, A., Ramalingam, S., Taguchi, Y., Chari, V.: A theory of multi-layer flat refractive geometry. In: CVPR (2012)
10. Sedlazeck, A., Koch, R.: Calibration of housing parameters for underwater stereo-camera rigs. In: BMVC (2011)
11. Telem, G., Filin, S.: Photogrammetric modeling of underwater environments. ISPRS Journal of Photogrammetry and Remote Sensing 65(5), 433–444 (2010)
12. Kunz, C., Singh, H.: Hemispherical refraction and camera calibration in underwater vision. In: OCEANS (2008)
13. Glaeser, G., Schrocker, H.P.: Reflections on refractions. Journal for Grometry and Graphics 4, 1–18 (2000)
14. Glassner, A.S.: An Introduction to Ray Tracing. Academic Press Ltd., London (1989)
15. Boyd, S., Vandenberghe, L.: Convex Optimization. Cambridge University Press, New York (2004)
16. Kahl, F., Hartley, R., Member, S.: Multiple-view geometry under the L_∞-norm. IEEE TPAMI 30(9), 1603–1617 (2008)
17. Olsson, C., Eriksson, A., Hartley, R.: Outlier removal using duality. In: CVPR (2010)
18. Price, K., Storn, R.M., Lampinen, J.A.: Differential Evolution: A Practical Approach to Global Optimization. Springer-Verlag New York, Inc., Secaucus (2005)
19. Lourakis, M.I.A.: Sparse Non-linear Least Squares Optimization for Geometric Vision. In: Daniilidis, K., Maragos, P., Paragios, N. (eds.) ECCV 2010, Part II. LNCS, vol. 6312, pp. 43–56. Springer, Heidelberg (2010)
20. Furukawa, Y., Ponce, J.: Accurate, dense, and robust multi-view stereopsis. In: CVPR (2007)
21. MOSEK, `http://www.mosek.com/`
22. Lowe, D.G.: Distinctive image features from scale-invariant keypoints. IJCV 60, 91–110 (2004)
23. Snavely, N., Seitz, S.M., Szeliski, R.: Photo tourism: exploring photo collections in 3D. In: ACM SIGGRAPH (2006)

Reading Ancient Coins: Automatically Identifying Denarii Using Obverse Legend Seeded Retrieval

Ognjen Arandjelović

Swansea University, Wales, UK
ognjen.arandjelovic@gmail.com

Abstract. The aim of this paper is to automatically identify a Roman Imperial denarius from a single query photograph of its obverse and reverse. Such functionality has the potential to contribute greatly to various national schemes which encourage laymen to report their finds to local museums. Our work introduces a series of novelties: (i) this is the first paper which describes a method for extracting the legend of an ancient coin from a photograph; (ii) we are also the first to suggest the idea and propose a method for identifying a coin using a series of carefully engineered retrievals, each harnessed for further information using visual or meta-data processing; (iii) we show how in addition to a unique standard reference number for a query coin, the proposed system can be used to extract salient coin information (issuing authority, obverse and reverse descriptions, mint date) and retrieve images of other coins of the same type.

Keywords: Recognition, Text, Image, Reverse, Motif, Inscription.

1 Introduction

The aim of this paper is to automatically identify a Roman Imperial denarius from a single query photograph of its obverse ("front") and reverse ("back"). Specifically, we wish to infer the issuer of the coin (usually the emperor depicted on the obverse), textual descriptions of its obverse and reverse, its reference identifier in the standard reference work "Roman Imperial Coinage" (RIC) [1] and the year it was minted.

Motivation. Our primary motivation comes from the immense value that this functionality would bring to such projects as the "Portable antiquities scheme" [2]. This scheme, pioneered in England and Wales, encourages the general public (primarily metal detectorists) to report their archeological findings to local museums for the sake of obtaining a record of the relevant and potentially valuable details of the find, without confiscating the find. It has been an immense success. In fact, the scheme has been so popular that the major limitation at present is the ability to process the large volume of finds, most of which are coins, and which are individually identified by an expert. Identification by the

A. Fitzgibbon et al. (Eds.): ECCV 2012, Part IV, LNCS 7575, pp. 317–330, 2012.

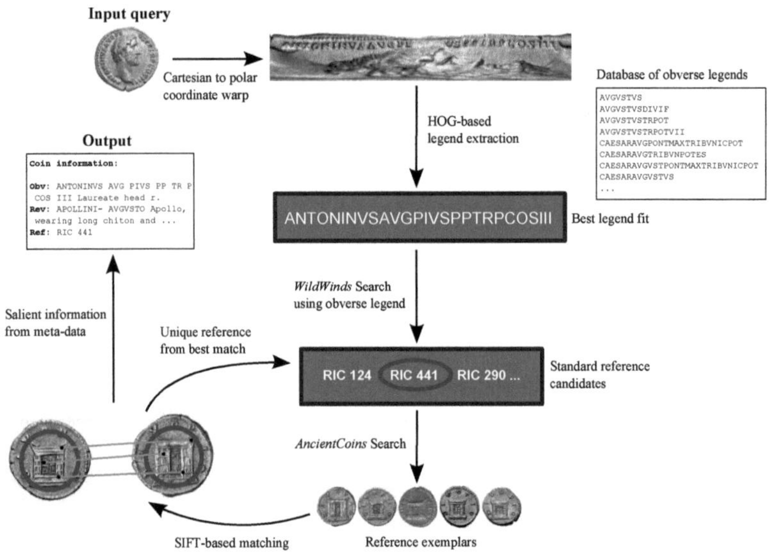

Fig. 1. (i) After the original image of a coin's obverse is mapped from Cartesian to quasi-polar coordinates, the corresponding legend is extracted using a HoG-like descriptor and an exhaustive database of possible legends; (ii) the extracted legend is used in a *WildWinds* search to select potential candidate coin types, whose unique reference IDs are used to retrieve matching images using the *AncientCoins* search; (iii) the correct coin type is determined by SIFT matching the query coin's reverse with the reverses of the retrieved exemplars for each candidate type; (iv) finally, salient coin information is extracted by integrating meta-data of all *AncientCoins* search results for the correct coin type.

finder is unsatisfactory: most of them are laymen, without the necessary expertize or access to specialist literature, and the risk of erroneous data entry would be unacceptably high. Our goal is to develop an automated online system which could process submitted images of coins. Such system would greatly reduce the burden on the experts, while at the same time making the "Portable antiquities scheme" even more widely accessible. Indeed, even a simple Google search readily reveals a plethora of requests to help identify a Roman coin.

Previous Work and Its Limitations. Computer vision work on the analysis of ancient coins is still scarce, with most of the previous work focusing on modern coins instead [3–6]. It is only in recent years that ancient coins in particular have started attracting attention of the community, through collaborations with museums and organizers of programmes such as the "Portable antiquities scheme" described previously. All of the published computer vision work focused on the analysis of ancient coins – by Zaharieva *et al.* [7], Kampel and Zaharieva [8] and Arandjelović [9] – aim to match coins using a variation of SIFT-like local features, the results universally demonstrating the challenge involved in this task. Another similarity, and we argue limitation, of these methods is that they treat the entire area of a coin in exactly the same manner, as an appearance pattern. However, in doing so they fail to optimally exploit what is a characteristically very rich source of information on Roman Imperial coins: the legend (i.e. textual inscription) around the coin edge. The method described in the present paper makes the extraction of the legend its first step, which is followed by a sequence of retrievals, each of which is used to gather further visual or meta-data, until a unique coin type is identified.

Overview of the Proposed Method. Our system starts by extracting the obverse legend of a coin from its image. We select the legend from a database of 1478 legends[1] using a HoG-like descriptor to describe the appearance of an individual letter and a spatial model which constrains the relative locations of neighbouring letters. The extracted legend is used as the initial seed for a sequence of retrievals. The results of each retrieval, some visual some textual (meta-data), are used to further constrain the range of possible coin identities. First, we use the obverse legend to perform a *WildWinds* [10] search which explicitly retrieves all references in RIC with the same legend. Next, a new retrieval for each candidate reference is performed using the *AncientCoins* search [11], which indexes a greater number of entries and coin exemplar images. The correct type is chosen by visually matching the query coin against the retrieved reverse motifs. Finally, the meta-data of the matching type is processed and salient coin information extracted.

2 Method Details

We start with the problem of extracting the legend from an image of the obverse of a coin. As illustrated in Fig. 2 (a), the legend on Roman Imperial coins runs circularly around the edge of the coin. In this example it reads ANTONINVSAVGPI-VSPPTRPCOSIII and it comprises a series of words or abbreviations. There are several features of obverse legends which are important to observe. Firstly, the legend is extraordinarily rich in information. ANTONINVS designates the issuer (here Antoninus Pius), usually depicted on the central part of the obverse; AVG (Augustus), PIVS, PP (father of the country), TR P (tribune of the people) and COS III (consul for the third time) all designate different titles of the issuer which can be used to constrain the coin's mint date. For example, in this case COS III can be used to constrain the mint date to 143-144 AD. Lastly, note the "-" symbol in the string used to describe the legend. It denotes a so-called "legend break" which is a point at which there is a gap in the physical inscription, usually due to a feature of the coin's design. Two inscriptions are usually considered as corresponding to the same legend even if their legend breaks are differently positioned.

2.1 Geometric Normalization

The obverse legend on a coin runs circularly near the coin's edge. This means that the orientation of letters varies across the entire range from 0° to 360°

[1] The database is available for download from `http://mi.eng.cam.ac.uk/~oa214/`

which is not ideal from the point of view of matching efficiency. Instead, we estimate the location $\mathbf{x}_c = (x_c, y_c)$ of the coin's centre and its radius r using the Hough transform as described in [9], and then transform the image from Cartesian to quasi-polar coordinates, as illustrated in Fig. 2. A point at the location $\mathbf{x} = (x, y)$ in the original image J is thus mapped to the point $\mathbf{x}' = (x', y')$ in the geometrically normalized image I:

$$y' = s \cdot \sqrt{(y - y_c)^2 + (x - x_c)^2} \tag{1}$$

$$x' = \begin{cases} s \cdot 2r \ \arccos((y_c - y)/|\mathbf{x} - \mathbf{x}_c|) & x < x_c \\ s \cdot 2r \ (2\pi - \arccos((y_c - y)/|\mathbf{x} - \mathbf{x}_c|) & x \geq x_c \end{cases} \tag{2}$$

The scaling factor s is used to ensure the uniform scale of 942×150 pixels. Lastly, note that the x coordinate in the processed image starts at the line extending from the coin's centre downwards, just as the legend does.

(a) Query obverse (b) Normalized query obverse

Fig. 2. (a) Original image of a query coin's obverse and (b) the corresponding geometrically normalized image we use to extract the legend

2.2 Legend Extraction

We treat the problem of extracting the obverse legend of a coin as one of optimal hypothesis choice, each hypothesis corresponding to a particular legend of n_l legends in our database. Thus we wish to find the index i^* of the hypothesis such that:

$$i^* = \arg \max_{1 \leq i \leq n_l} p(l_1^{(i)}, \ldots, l_{n_i}^{(i)} | I) \tag{3}$$

where n_i is the number of letters in the i-th legend and $l_1^{(i)} \ldots l_{n_i}^{(i)}$ are the corresponding letters in order.

It is certainly not the case that different legends are equally common. Some legends are shared amongst more coin types; certain coin types are also rarer than others. Indeed, RIC provides a rarity guide (C = common, S = scarce, R = rare, R2 = very rare, and R3 = extremely rare), estimated from a range of museum collections. However, we argue that this would not form a good basis for a prior in the present work: museums have biases in their interests and the relative frequencies of different types of coins likely to be submitted by lay users is difficult to predict. Thus we adopt an uninformative prior which makes our choice a maximum likelihood test:

$$i^* = \arg\max_i p(l_1^{(i)}, \ldots, l_{n_i}^{(i)}|I) = \arg\max_i p(I|l_1^{(i)}, \ldots, l_{n_i}^{(i)}) \tag{4}$$

where also:

$$p(I|l_1^{(i)}, \ldots, l_{n_i}^{(i)}) = \max_{\substack{x_1,\ldots,x_{n_i} \\ y_1,\ldots,y_{n_i}}} p(I|l_1^{(i)}, \ldots, l_{n_i}^{(i)}, x_1, \ldots, x_{n_i}, y_1, \ldots, y_{n_i}) \tag{5}$$

The estimation of the likelihood $p(I|l_1^{(i)}, \ldots, l_{n_i}^{(i)})$ is computationally complex in no small part because of the potential presence of legend breaks which can have a range of widths and which can in principle occur between any two consecutive letters. To make the problem tractable, we propose a two stage approach: (i) first, we estimate the optimal placement of the legend letters using only the evidence from the corresponding image patches and a spatial constraint on consecutive letters, and then (ii) evaluate the likelihood for the entire image strip of the legend, taking into account how well the appearance of legend breaks is explained too. Thus, to find the optimal placement of letters $(x_1, y_2), \ldots, (x_{n_i}, y_{n_i})$ we maximize the following likelihood:

$$\hat{P}(x_1, \ldots, x_{n_i}, y_1, \ldots, y_{n_i}) = p(I_{x_1,y_1}|l_1^{(i)}) \prod_{j=1}^{n_i-1} p(I_{x_{j+1},y_{j+1}}|l_{j+1}^{(i)})\ p(x_{j+1}, y_{j+1}|x_j, y_j) \tag{6}$$

where I_{x_j,y_j} is a letter-sized image patch centred at (x_j, y_j). Our spatial prior on the locations of consecutive letters is given by:

$$p(x_{j+1}, y_{j+1}|x_j, y_j) \propto \begin{cases} 1 & t_{x1} < x_{j+1} - x_j < t_{x2} \text{ and } |y_{j+1} - y_j| < t_y \\ 0 & \text{otherwise} \end{cases} \tag{7}$$

The primary function of the the thresholds t_{x1} and t_y is to eliminate implausible relative letter placements. In contrast, the threshold t_{x2} is chiefly used for computational reasons, i.e. to restrict the image search area. We set t_{x1} to 80% of the letter width, t_y to 20% of the letter height and t_{x2} to six times the letter width. Our appearance model used to estimate individual letter likelihoods $p(I_{x_j,y_j}|l_j^{(i)})$ is explained next.

Letter Appearance Model. The appearance of a particular letter in a legend can exhibit great variability. Firstly, legend letters are small features which were manually engraved without the use of any magnifying instruments. This means that both their shape and orientation can change significantly from instance to instance. Letter appearance is also affected by illumination, wear, strike in the minting process etc. We experimented with a number of possible representations including raw and filtered appearance, and wavelet based features, with limited success. An approach based on HoG features [12] was found to be the most successful one and it is what we adopt henceforth.

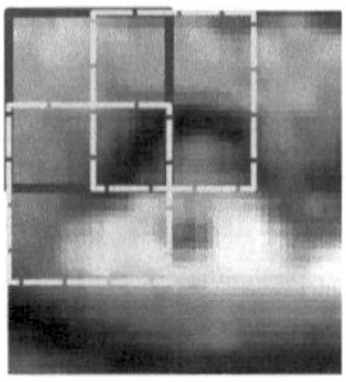

(a) Patch sub-regions

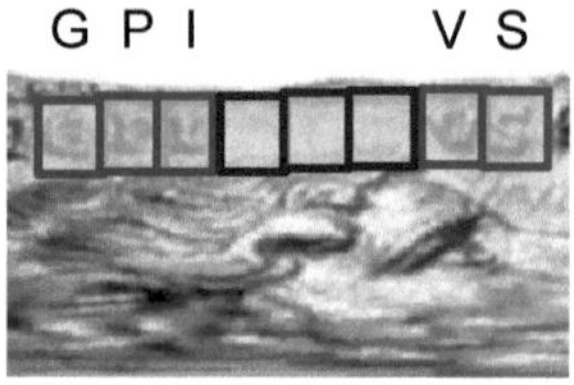

(b) Legend matching

Fig. 3. (a) Letter sized patch is divided into nine overlapping sub-regions each covering a quarter of the area of the entire patch. Shown is a sub-region (red) and two horizontally and vertically adjacent sub-regions. (b) Initially, the optimal placement of the letters for a particular hypothesized legend is determined using image evidence corresponding to letter regions only (shown in red). The likelihood of the hypothesis is subsequently estimated using evidence both from letter image regions as well as legend breaks found between letters (shown in blue). Thus a legend hypothesis which explains letter regions well but produces gaps which do not look like actual breaks, does not result in a high likelihood value.

We represent each patch as a feature vector obtained by concatenating nine weighted histograms corresponding to different sub-regions of the patch. Each histogram comprises nine bins (gradient directions) over 180°, gradients at 180° from one another contributing to the same bin. We make each patch sub-region half as wide as the entire patch, with two vertically or horizontally adjacent sub-regions sharing a 50% overlap, as shown in Fig. 3 (a). That gives three possible vertical and horizontal displacement and hence $3 \times 3 = 9$ sub-regions and a $9 \times 9 = 81$ dimensions for the concatenated descriptor.

In comparison to the original descriptor proposed by Dalal and Triggs, our descriptor contains several modifications which make it more suitable for the problem at hand. Firstly, we do not weight gradient contributions in proportion to their magnitude. We found that due to small irregularities on the coin's surface and the small physical size of the surface represented by a patch, gradients of small magnitude can build up and obscure the main features in the patch that we seek to describe. Instead, we use weights obtained by transforming gradient magnitudes using a sigmoid function of the following form:

$$\hat{g} = \frac{1}{1 + \exp\{-0.5(g - 0.5g_{max})\}} \tag{8}$$

where g_{max} is the maximal gradient magnitude of the entire patch (not a specific sub-region), g the original gradient magnitude and $\hat{g}$ the transformed value used to weight bin contributions. Another difference introduced here is that unlike Dalal and Triggs, we do not normalize histograms of different sub-regions. Rather, sub-region histograms are concatenated in their raw form. We found that this produced superior results on our problem.

Using a manually annotated corpus of 30 images of coins with the associated legends, we learn the range of variation of each letter's descriptor as a multivariate Gaussian distribution. The distribution is over an 81D space in which we take the first 5 eigenvector directions as the basis of the principal subspace. The corresponding largest eigenvalues (variances) are left unchanged. Since the remaining eigenvalues are assumed to come from random noise sampling they are averaged, thus ensuring that the Kullback-Leibler divergence between the true distribution and its estimate is minimized [13]. The likelihood $p(I_{x_j,y_j}|l_j^{(i)})$ is then evaluated by first computing the HoG-like descriptor of the image patch I_{x_j,y_j} and then the corresponding value of the Gaussian representing letter $l_j^{(i)}$. For each locus (x_j, y_j) we compute the likelihood at three scales (letter heights of 18, 22 and 26 pixels) and assign the largest of these to (x_j, y_j).

Inferring Optimal Letter Placement. Using the introduced appearance and spatial models, the maximum likelihood solution to Equation 6 can be computed exactly and efficiently using dynamic programming. If $L_{k+1}^{(i)}(x, y)$ the maximum likelihood of the i partial legend up to its $(k + 1)$-st letter:

$$k = 0 \; : \; L_{k+1}^{(i)}(x, y) = p(I_{x_1,y_1}|l_1^{(i)}) \tag{9}$$

$$k > 0 \; : \; L_{k+1}^{(i)}(x, y) = \max_{\substack{x_1,\ldots,x_k \\ y_1,\ldots,y_k}} p(I_{x_1,y_1}|l_1^{(i)}) \; p(I_{x,y}|l_{k+1}^{(i)}) \; p(x, y|x_k, y_k) \times \tag{10}$$

$$\times \prod_{j=1}^{k-1} p(I_{x_{j+1},y_{j+1}}|l_{j+1}^{(i)}) \; p(x_{j+1}, y_{j+1}|x_j, y_j) \tag{11}$$

then the following recurrence holds:

$$k = 0 \; : \; L_1^{(i)}(x, y) = p(I_{x,y}|l_1^{(i)}) \tag{12}$$

$$k > 0 \; : \; L_{k+1}^{(i)}(x, y) = p(I_{x,y}|l_{k+1}^{(i)}) \times \tag{13}$$

$$\times \max_{\Delta x, \Delta y} L_k^{(i)}(x - \Delta x, y - \Delta y) p(x, y|x - \Delta x, y - \Delta y) \tag{14}$$

In other words, the maximal likelihood of a partial legend which places its last letter at a particular location in the image can be computed by scanning the area of possible loci for the preceding letter, and updating the corresponding maximal likelihood value.

Estimating Legend Likelihood. The proposed dynamic programming based approach to estimating the likelihood in Equation 6 accounts only for evidence of image patches which correspond to the loci of the legend letters, as illustrated by red rectangles in Fig. 3 (b). There are two key reasons why this likelihood is not a good approximation to the likelihood in Equation 5 and thus not a good criterion for selecting the best fitting legend:

- generally it tends to penalize legends with a greater number of letters, and
- it fails to account for the appearance of spaces between letters, which should look as legend breaks.

Consequently, out approach continues as follows. After the optimal letter placements of a legend are estimated using Equation 6, we fill any significant gaps between consecutive letters (greater than 80% of the letter width) with letter sized patches, as illustrated with blue rectangles in Fig. 3 (b). These should contain the appearance of legend breaks. Unlike in the case of letters, we do not learn the appearance model for the legend break because we know that in the idealized coin specimen they should be blank. In other words, considering that we do not perform the block normalization of Dalal and Triggs, all of the entries in the corresponding HoG-like feature should be close to zero. This observation allows us to compute the likelihood of a hypothesized legend break patch $I_{x,y}$ at (x, y) using a zero mean isotropic Gaussian whose covariance we estimate as the mean noise covariance across the distributions representing individual letters. The likelihood of a particular legend thus becomes:

$$P(x_1, \ldots, x_{n_i}, y_1, \ldots, y_{n_i}) = \hat{P}(x_1, \ldots, x_{n_i}, y_1, \ldots, y_{n_i}) \prod_{j=1}^{\hat{n}_i} p_b(I_{\hat{x}_j, \hat{y}_j}) \qquad (15)$$

where $\hat{n}_i$ is the number of breaks in the i-th legend (note that $n_i + \hat{n}_i = \text{const.}$), p_b the likelihood of a break corresponding to a letter sized patch, and $I_{\hat{x}_j, \hat{y}_j}$ a letter sized patch at a hypothesized legend break location $(\hat{x}_j, \hat{y}_j)$.

2.3 Making a Shortlist of RIC Identifiers

The free *WildWinds* coin search engine allows the user to retrieve RIC identifiers of coin types that match a particular legend fragment, disregarding the positions of legend breaks. This means that a search using the legend ANTONINVSAVGPIVSPPTRPCOSIII (see Fig. 2) correctly finds the types RIC 70, RIC 612, RIC 660 and RIC 716, all which have the correct query legend at the obverse. However, it also finds the type RIC 415 with the legend ANTONINVSAVGPIVSPPTRPCOSIIII (note the extra "I", signifying the fourth consulship year). To overcome this limitation of the search engine, we perform retrieval using multiple queries. First, we use the extracted legend as the query and obtain the set of possible matches, $\mathbb{S}_0$. In addition we also search using each of the d_{i^*} entries in our legends database which contain the extracted legend as a sub-string, obtaining further sets of matches, $\mathbb{S}_1, \ldots \mathbb{S}_{d_{i^*}}$ say. These results allow us to infer the correct shortlist of identifiers as the set difference $\mathbb{S}^* = \mathbb{S}_0 \setminus \cup_{j=1}^{d_{i^*}} \mathbb{S}_j$.

2.4 Visual Sifting by Matching Reverse Motifs

As we explained earlier, the obverse legend of a Roman coin is typically very rich in information content. However, it is also seldom sufficient to uniquely identify a coin. Indeed, a particular legend is usually found on many different types; the legend ANTONINVSAVGPIVSPPTRPCOSIIII, for example, occurs on over twenty.

A coin type is characterized by particular obverse and reverse legends and central motifs. Two coins which match in these features are considered to be of the same type. The obverse motif on Roman denarii and aureii is universally a portrait of the coin's issuer, shown in profile, and it provides little additional information over the corresponding legend regarding the coin's type[2]. Thus, we

[2] A more detailed treatment of this issue is out of scope of the present paper.

Fig. 4. A random sample of six reverses retrieved in an *AncientCoins* search using the automatically generated query `Antoninus Pius ("RIC 441" "R.I.C. 441")`. The reverse motif of the query coin is matched against the set of retrieved reverses. The overall matching score of the query coin with the type is estimated as the highest of the corresponding individual matching scores.

focus on the content shown on the reverse to disambiguate the matching of our query coin against the shortlist $\mathbb{S}^*$ of its possible types. Specifically, we match reverse motifs, disregarding the reverse legend. Unlike in the case of obverse legends, the list of possible reverse legends is far greater and to the best of the knowledge of these authors, no such list has been compiled, which prohibits us from applying the approach described in Sec. 2.2.

To obtain exemplars of reverses of a particular coin type we employ the free *AncientCoins* search engine [11], which retrieves coins from a wide range of coin dealers' web sites and past auctions by matching a textual query with the text associated with each coin. Using this search engine with a simple query comprising the name of the coin's issuer (determined from the obverse legend, as explained in Sec. 2.2) and a particular RIC reference from the shortlist $\mathbb{S}^*$ we retrieve exemplar images of coins of the corresponding type. An example of six retrieved reverses is illustrated in Fig. 4. Note the variability in both the style and positioning of the legend, as well as the central motif (an altar in this case).

Registration. Our approach to matching the reverse of our query coin with each of the retrieved reverses comprises two stages. First, we register the motifs of the two reverses which are being compared. This is necessary because the precise positioning of the motif can very significantly across different dies of the same type, as can be readily observed in Fig. 4. We use Euclidean registration and estimate its two parameters by matching SIFT descriptors. Following Lowe's recommendation [14], we accept a SIFT keypoint match in the query reverse with its closest (in terms of feature similarity) keypoint in a retrieved reverse, if the distance of the second closest keypoint is at least 1.5 greater. We apply this keypoint matching in a RANSAC framework so as to eliminate the effects of spurious matches and pool the estimates of correctly matched keypoints to achieve more robust registration.

Appearance Matching. After the two reverses are registered and their reverse motifs aligned, they are compared in appearance. Here too we employ SIFT features. We try to match each detected feature in the query coin's reverse with a feature detected in the reverse of the coin it is compared with, subject to appearance and spatial criteria. First, we require that the similarity of two features (as a normalized dot product of the corresponding feature vectors) exceeds a threshold. Also, we require that the two features are within a specific distance from each other (in our implementation the maximal distance is set to 20 pixels), and in agreement in scale (within 20%) and direction (within 30°). The similarity of two reverses is then measured by the number of matched feature pairs.

After each of the reverses retrieved using a search for a particular RIC type is compared against the query reverse, we compute the overall matching confidence for the type as the maximum of all the computed similarities. Finally, the correct RIC type match is chosen as the one with the highest matching confidence.

2.5 Extraction of Salient Coin Information from Textual Meta-data

The first aim of the present paper was to uniquely identify the query coin's reference in RIC. To a proficient numismatist, this reference contains sufficient information which can be used to look up further relevant details, such as the coin's mint date. However, there are several reasons why it is advantageous to do this automatically, which we set out to do here. First, it saves time needed to look up a reference and then manually enter relevant detail. It also gives immediate and more readily understandable feedback which can be used to check for the correctness of the result. Lastly, it provides the lay user, who may be submitting his/her find online, a more satisfying and meaningful description of the find.

We specifically seek to extract textual descriptions of the obverse and reverse motifs, as well as the mint date of the coin. For this we use textual meta-data associated with the coins already retrieved using the *AncientCoins* search with the correct RIC reference. Any retrieved text which is not in English, we translate into English using Google's automatic translator and replace various delimiters by "white space". Examples include hyphens, which are used to denote legend breaks, and square brackets which signify that the enclosed part of the legend is missing, for example because it has been damaged or because it is off the flan of the coin.

Obverse and reverse descriptions are localized in text using explicit rules which reflect a number of standard conventions used in describing ancient coins. For example, the obverse description may be located as the sentence which contains the obverse legend extracted in Sec. 2.2, or the sentence which follows the word "obverse", its abbreviation "obv" or indeed "av", the abbreviation for obverse used in German and French (for "avers") and which is not automatically translated by Google. A description of the obverse and reverse thus may be extracted from every retrieved coin record. However, some of these may be incorrect as the search string comprising the RIC type of the query coin may in some instances occur even in records of coins of a different type. For example this may be because a coin is in some sense compared with the query coin type (rarer, similar, and so on). Thus, we wish to choose the best of extracted descriptions. We achieve this by creating a histogram of words across the corpus of all extracted descriptions after eliminating undiscriminative words (e.g. "in", "left", "emperor", "head", "bust"), and then selecting the best fitting legend as the one with the words of the highest average frequency in the corpus.

The manner in which we obtain the mint date (or more generally, mint period) of the coin involves a different strategy. There are two key problems that we had to address here. The first is that some records contain incorrect mint dates. The second is that some coin records do not contain the most precise (narrowest) mint period found in specialist literature, but a broader one. For example, some entries will simply have the entire period of the issuer's reign as the mint period (e.g. 138-161 AD). We solve both of the aforementioned problems as follows. Initializing the algorithm with the issuer's rule period, each time a candidate period is extracted from a coin record we fragment the range of possible periods, so that each fragment begins and ends at the beginning or the end of an extracted period. Then, we choose the fragment with the most votes (most overlapping periods extracted from coin records), as the correct one.

3 Results

The coin identification system described in this paper was evaluated on 25 coins. These coins were identified by an expert. Relevant ground truth information – the coin's issuer, its obverse and reverse legends, the descriptions of its obverse and reverse motifs and the minting date – was obtained from RIC.

3.1 Legend Extraction

We first examined the performance of our method for extracting the obverse legend, described in Sec. 2.2. For all but one coin, the correct legend was inferred. The one incorrect result was caused by a particularly challenging relative placements of two letters. Specifically, the letter I representing the Roman numeral one, was engraved unusually close to the preceding letter. Consequently, the appearance of the preceding letter contributed to the feature vector extracted from a letter sized patch centred at I, producing a low likelihood score at that location for all letters. Since there is a valid legend identical to the correct one in all respects except that it does not contain the problematic I (i.e. the same form of the legend for the previous consulship year), this legend was selected as the highest likelihood one.

3.2 RIC Types Shortlisting

Providing that the correct obverse legend was extracted in the previous stage of the algorithm and that the correct RIC type is not so rare as to be absent from the *WildWinds* database, our method of creating a shortlist of possible types is guaranteed to include the correct type. Thus, as expected, for the 24 test coins for which the obverse legend was correctly extracted, the ground truth RIC type was amongst the shortlisted ones. Equally, the correct type of the coin for which the legend was not correctly extracted, was not amongst the shortlisted types.

3.3 Visual Sifting by Matching Reverse Motifs

Of the 24 coins for which the obverse legend extraction and shortlisting produced correct results, 22 were matched with the correct RIC type based on the appearance of the reverse motif. A few representative examples are shown in Fig. 6. An example of an incorrect match is shown in Fig. 5. It can be readily seen that the matched motifs, although not the same, bear a high degree of resemblance – both feature a standing figure, holding a small object (patera and wand respectively) in the extended right arm and a long stick-like object in the left (spear and sceptre), with a further object at feet (altar and globe). It is equally interesting to notice that the two types are readily differentiated from one another by their reverse legends. While the query reverse legend reads RESTITVTOR VRBIS, that of the incorrectly matched type is PROVID AVGG.

(a) RIC 166 (b) RIC 167

Fig. 5. An example of an incorrect type match. Shown is (a) the correct type RIC 166 and (b) the incorrect type RIC 167 that the query coin was matched to instead

Considering that the correct RIC type was not in the shortlist of possible types for the one coin whose obverse legend was not correctly extracted, the end type it was matched to could not be correct. However, the coin was matched to the correct reverse motif, which means that in every respect except for the one missing letter of the obverse legend, our method was successful. Indeed, the obverse and reverse motifs were commonly repeated across different consulship years, which means that in most cases in which the obverse legend extraction fails due to unintelligibility of Roman numerals, a nearly identical if not entirely correct type will be found. This is highly comforting as it is reasonable to expect that most errors in our legend extraction algorithm will be caused precisely in the matching of numerals because the contextual constraints are much looser in comparison with, say, the name of the emperor in the legend.

3.4 Meta-data Parsing

Examples of automatically extracted textual descriptions of the key coin facts can be see in the central column of Fig. 6. In all cases, the extracted information correctly matched the identified coin type. The only problem we observed with this stage of our system pertains to limitations of Google's automatic translator when dealing with words which are rarely used in everyday speech but are

Query	Description	Example specimen
	Issuer: Antoninus Pius Obverse: DIVVS ANTONINVS Bare head of Antoninus Pius to right. Reverse: CONSECRATIO Altar with two closed doors. Minted: 161 AD Reference: RIC 441	
	Issuer: Septimius Severus Obverse: SEVERVS PIVS AVG, bust right belorbeerte. Reverse: PM TRP XVII COS III PP, Jupiter stands left between two children. Minted 209 AD Reference: RIC 226	
	Issuer: Faustina I Obverse: DIVA FAVSTINA, bust draped right. Reverse: AETERNITAS, draped and veiled female figure standing right, head left, raising right hand and holding scepter in left. Minted 141 AD Reference: RIC 344	

Fig. 6. Examples of typical end results of our system. The left-hand column shows query coins, the central column its RIC type and automatically extracted obverse and reverse descriptions, and the right-hand column a further example of the same type obtained using the free *AncientCoins* search engine.

frequent in numismatics. For example, note the German word "belorbeerte" (laureate) which was not translated in the description of the obverse of the second coin in Fig. 6. That happens if the coin entries of a specific type are predominantly in a foreign language – an untranslated word may feature in the majority of extracted descriptions and thus be included in the description which best matches the entirety of the retrieved meta-data.

4 Conclusions and Future Work

This paper introduced the first automatic system which can identify a Roman denarius from a single photograph. The system comprises a cascade of steps, each aimed at extracting additional information which allows the range of possible coin types to be reduced further. The extraction of the obverse legend, a problem also addressed here for the first time, is crucial as the legend is used to initiate a series of public search engine retrievals, each of which is used to harness new information. The first search is used to create a shortlist of possible types based on the obverse legend alone. The second search is used to obtain images of exemplar coins for each type. The reverse motifs of these coins are matched with the reverse of the query coin, the best matching type eventually being selected as the correct match. The associated textual meta-data is further used to extract salient coin information: descriptions of its obverse and reverse motifs, and mint date period.

Our experiments demonstrated highly encouraging results and highlighted the most promising directions for further improvement. We first aim to investigate different letter appearance representations, which would allow to extract not only the obverse legend but also the highly discriminative reverse legend too. This would also allow us to extend our statistical model used to match obverse legends to handle more robustly partially damaged legends, which the method proposed in this paper does not do. Lastly, the occasional failure of our approach in matching reverse motifs and its sensitivity to the precise coin specimens retrieved, add to the corpus of evidence of previous research that the development of features more specific to the particular problem at hand, rather than generic SIFT features, is another promising research avenue.

References

1. Webb, P.H. (vol. I), Mattingly, H., Sydenham, A., Sutherland, C.H.V. (vol. II-III), Sutherland, C.H.V., Carson, R.A.G. (vol. VI-IX), Carson, R.A.G., Kent, J.P.C., Burnett, A.M. (vol. X) (eds.): Roman Imperial Coinage, vol. I–X. Spink, London (1923-1994)
2. The portable antiquities scheme, `http://finds.org.uk/` (last accessed July 2012)
3. Davidsson, P.: Coin classification using a novel technique for learning characteristic decision trees by controlling the degree of generalization. In: Proc. IEA/AIE, pp. 403–412 (1996)
4. Mitsukura, Y., Fukumi, M., Akamatsu, N.: Design and evaluation of neural networks for coin recognition by using GA and SA. In: Proc. IJCNN, vol. 5, pp. 178–183 (2000)
5. Huber, R., Ramoser, H., Mayer, K., Penz, H., Rubik, M.: Classification of coins using an eigenspace approach. Pattern Recognition Letters 26(1), 61–75 (2005)
6. van der Maaten, L., Boon, P.: COIN-O-MATIC: A fast system for reliable coin classification. In: Proc. MUSCLE CIS Coin Recognition Competition Workshop, pp. 7–18 (2006)
7. Zaharieva, M., Kampel, M., Zambanini, S.: Image Based Recognition of Ancient Coins. In: Kropatsch, W.G., Kampel, M., Hanbury, A. (eds.) CAIP 2007. LNCS, vol. 4673, pp. 547–554. Springer, Heidelberg (2007)
8. Kampel, M., Zaharieva, M.: Recognizing Ancient Coins Based on Local Features. In: Bebis, G., Boyle, R., Parvin, B., Koracin, D., Remagnino, P., Porikli, F., Peters, J., Klosowski, J., Arns, L., Chun, Y.K., Rhyne, T.-M., Monroe, L. (eds.) ISVC 2008, Part I. LNCS, vol. 5358, pp. 11–22. Springer, Heidelberg (2008)
9. Arandjelović, O.: Automatic attribution of ancient Roman imperial coins. In: Proc. CVPR, pp. 1728–1734 (2010)
10. WildWinds graphical partial legend search engine, `http://www.wildwinds.com/coins/findstr.html` (last accessed July 2012)
11. Ancient coins search engine, `http://www.acsearch.info/` (last accessed July 2012)
12. Dalai, N., Triggs, B.: Histograms of oriented gradients for human detection. In: Proc. CVPR, vol. 1, pp. 886–893 (2005)
13. Tipping, M.E., Bishop, C.M.: Probabilistic principal component analysis. Journal of the Royal Statistical Society 61(3), 611–622 (1999)
14. Lowe, D.G.: Distinctive image features from scale-invariant keypoints. IJCV 60(2), 91–110 (2003)

Robust and Practical Face Recognition via Structured Sparsity

Kui Jia[1], Tsung-Han Chan[1], and Yi Ma[2,3]

[1] Advanced Digital Sciences Center, Singapore
[2] Microsoft Research Asia, Beijing, China
[3] Dept. Elec. and Comp. Eng., University of Illinois at Urbana-Champaign

Abstract. Sparse representation based classification (SRC) methods have recently drawn much attention in face recognition, due to their good performance and robustness against misalignment, illumination variation, and occlusion. They assume the errors caused by image variations can be modeled as pixel-wisely sparse. However, in many practical scenarios these errors are not truly pixel-wisely sparse but rather sparsely distributed with structures, i.e., they constitute contiguous regions distributed at different face positions. In this paper, we introduce a class of structured sparsity-inducing norms into the SRC framework, to model various corruptions in face images caused by misalignment, shadow (due to illumination change), and occlusion. For practical face recognition, we develop an automatic face alignment method based on minimizing the structured sparsity norm. Experiments on benchmark face datasets show improved performance over SRC and other alternative methods.

1 Introduction

Face recognition is a long-standing problem in computer vision. It has broad applications ranging from less-demanding ones such as family photo album organization (e.g., Apple iPhoto), to the most challenging applications of mass surveillance and terrorist watchlist that require high recognition performance but good training images are difficult to be obtained. In this work, we consider an application scenario that falls between these two extremes, where high recognition performance is desired but a rich set of training face images can be pre-captured in controlled conditions. Notable applications of this kind are access control for secure facilities, computer systems, automobiles, etc. Among face recognition methods targeting for this scenario, the classical subspace methods such as Eigenfaces [1], Fisherfaces [2] and nearest subspace (NS) [7] have been extensively studied. They generally work well in laboratory conditions. Under practical working or testing conditions their performance is very sensitive to illumination change, occlusion, or misalignment (due to scale or pose changes).

Recently, sparse representation based classification (SRC) methods have been proposed [3,13,11] and shown their promise in handling these variabilities in face recognition. In particular, Wright *et al.* [3] proposed to use an extended ℓ_1-norm minimization for robust face recognition. Assuming access to a face

A. Fitzgibbon et al. (Eds.): ECCV 2012, Part IV, LNCS 7575, pp. 331–344, 2012.

database with each subject having multiple registered training images taken under varying illuminations, [3] casts face recognition as the problem of finding a sparse representation of a test image in terms of the training ones, plus a sparse error image compensating for possible occlusion or corruption. Denote the set of training images as $\{\mathbf{A}_k\}_{k=1}^K$ for K subjects. $\mathbf{A}_k \in \mathbb{R}^{m \times n_k}$ contains images of subject k, with each image being concatenated as a column vector of $\mathbf{A}_k$. We can put images of all subjects together to form a large matrix $\mathbf{A} = [\mathbf{A}_1, \mathbf{A}_2, \ldots, \mathbf{A}_K] \in \mathbb{R}^{m \times n}$. The sparse representation $\mathbf{x}$ and sparse error $\mathbf{e}$ are recovered in [3] by solving the extended ℓ_1-norm minimization problem

$$(\ell_1\text{-}\ell_1): \qquad \min_{\mathbf{x},\mathbf{e}} \|\mathbf{x}\|_1 + \|\mathbf{e}\|_1 \quad \text{s.t.} \quad \mathbf{y} = \mathbf{A}\mathbf{x} + \mathbf{e}, \tag{1}$$

where $\mathbf{y} \in \mathbb{R}^m$ is the given test face image. A key component in their method leading to the above robustness is to enforce sparsity by ℓ_1-norm on the residual or error image $\mathbf{e}$. By leveraging the same sparsity assumption using ℓ_1-norm minimization, an automatic face alignment algorithm was developed in [13]. Suppose $\mathbf{y}'$ is an observed test face that is not in register with the training images $\{\mathbf{A}_k\}_{k=1}^K$. To recover a well aligned image $\mathbf{y} = \mathbf{y}' \circ \tau$ so that it can be readily used for robust face recognition, where τ represents some transformation acting on the image domain (e.g., 2D similarity transformation), [13] proposed to solve the following optimization problem to seek the correct transformation τ and sparse error $\mathbf{e}$

$$\min_{\mathbf{e},\tau_k,\mathbf{x}_k} \|\mathbf{e}\|_1 \quad \text{s.t.} \quad \mathbf{y}' \circ \tau_k = \mathbf{A}_k\mathbf{x}_k + \mathbf{e}, \tag{2}$$

where $\mathbf{y}'$ is sequentially aligned to each subject $\mathbf{A}_k$ instead of the whole training set $\mathbf{A}$, mainly due to the difficulty of optimization associated with the later case, as discussed in [13]. [13] demonstrates the state-of-the-art face recognition performance in a practical access control setting. The success of SRC methods has also inspired many following works [14,15].

In the context of statistical signal processing, it is well known that when using ℓ_1-norm to promote the sparsity in the errors $\mathbf{e}$, it assumes that each pixel is independently corrupted. However, for many practical face variations such as occlusion, disguise, or shadow caused by illumination change, errors due to these variations are typically spatially contiguous. It becomes inappropriate to model these variations using ℓ_1-norm minimization, as did in [3,13,14].

The theory of compressed sensing suggests that given contiguous structures, it is possible to recover sparse signals with fewer measurements [12]. This means that from a fixed number of measurements (pixels), we should expect to correct a larger fraction of errors and subsequently obtain improved recognition performance if the structural prior knowledge of the corruption can be properly harnessed. In particular, [11] has used a Markov Random Fields (MRF) model to estimate a contiguous error support from the obtained $\mathbf{e}$, and has demonstrated significantly improved performance over [3] for contiguous occlusion. However, the performance of the MRF model [11] drops drastically when test images are subject to slight misalignment. To handle misalignment [13] still resorts to promoting the sparsity on $\mathbf{e}$ with ℓ_1-norm.

In this paper we introduce a new class of norms that can promote error sparsity patterns with the properties of contiguity and spatial locality. Our motivation follows the recent development of new sparsity-inducing norms that are capable of encoding prior knowledge about the expected structured sparsity patterns. While ℓ_1-norm can only promote independent sparsity [16], one can partition variables into disjoint groups and promote group sparsity using the so called group Lasso regularization [17]. To induce more sophisticated structured sparsity patterns, it becomes essential to use structured sparsity-inducing norms built on overlapping groups of variables [20,19]. In this paper, we consider to use a hierarchical tree-structured sparsity-inducing norm [20,22] on the error $\mathbf{e}$ of a test face, as shown in Figure 1, where overlapping groups of pixels are from local patches of varying size and each group corresponds to a node of the tree. As shown in our experiments in Section 4, without knowing explicitly the number, locations, sizes, and shapes of contiguous errors caused by various face variations, our method performs better than [3] in terms of handling spatially contiguous errors. When test images are not well aligned with training images, unlike the MRF based method, we can effectively bring the images in alignment via minimizing the structured sparsity norm, by simply replacing the ℓ_1-norm in equation (2). In fact, experiments show that our method performs better than using the ℓ_1-norm for alignment and recognition [13], especially in cases when only partial face is visible due to occlusion or disguise.

To solve the corresponding optimization problems, we develop efficient algorithms based on the Augmented Lagrange Multiplier (ALM) method [23], in which a proximal problem associated with structured sparsity norm regularization can be efficiently solved using techniques given in [21,22]. The better error correction capability of structured sparsity translates readily into improved face recognition performance. Experiments on benchmark face databases show that our methods achieve the state-of-the-art recognition results, and outperform other SRC-based methods in simultaneously handling illumination change, occlusion, and misalignment in the test face image.

2 Modeling Using Structured Sparsity-Inducing Norms

In this section, we discuss how we could systematically develop sparsity-inducing norms that can incorporate prior structures on the support of the errors such as spatial continuity. We hope that such structures can better model corruptions in practical face images due to shadows, occlusion or disguise, and misalignment.

In this broader context, the work of [3] essentially considers a special case to the following problem

$$\min_{\mathbf{x},\mathbf{e}} \|\mathbf{x}\|_1 + \psi(\mathbf{e}) \quad s.t. \quad \mathbf{y} = \mathbf{A}\mathbf{x} + \mathbf{e} \tag{3}$$

with the regularizer $\psi(\cdot)$ on $\mathbf{e}$ chosen to be $\|\mathbf{e}\|_1$. The geometry of how ℓ_1-norm penalizing sparse errors is illustrated in Figure 2-(a), i.e., the unit ball of ℓ_1-norm. Clearly, the ℓ_1-norm regularization treats each entry (pixel) in $\mathbf{e}$ independently. It does not take into account any specific structures or possible

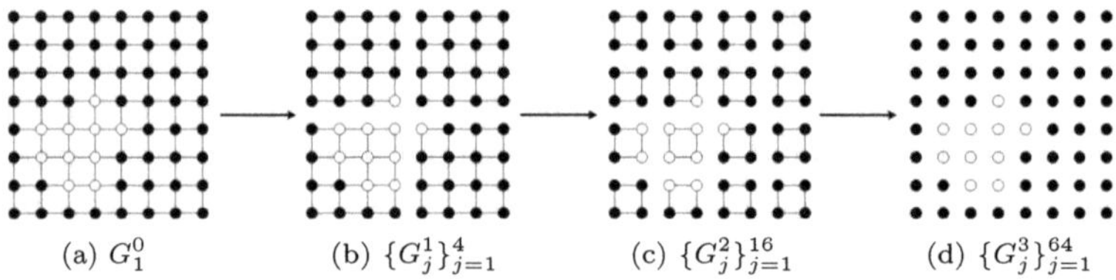

Fig. 1. Illustration of a four-level hierarchical tree group structure defined on the error image. Each circle represents a pixel, and connected circles represent a node/group in the tree. The 8×8 image in (a) is divided into 4 sub-images in (b) according to spatial locality, and each sub-image can be viewed as a child node of (a). The similar relation goes from (b) to (c), and from (c) to (d). Each group of connected black circles represents a node forced to zero, and white circles show the induced sparsity pattern by the tree-structured norm (4).

relations among subsets of the entries. While in face recognition scenarios, shadows caused by illumination change, occlusion, misalignment, or even pose and expression changes normally have the structural properties of spatial contiguity and locality. Indeed, as reported in [3], SRC based on ℓ_1-norm performs better in case of random pixel corruption than contiguous occlusion. Unfortunately the later case is actually closer to practical situations in face recognition.

To encode prior knowledge, researchers have proposed to partition variables into disjoint groups, and use the so called group Lasso penalty [17] to promote sparsity on the group level. Given $\mathbf{e} \in \mathbb{R}^m$, the variables with indices $\{1, \ldots, m\}$ can be partitioned into a disjoint set of groups, denoted as $\mathcal{G}$, with each group $G \in \mathcal{G}$ containing a subset of these indices. A group Lasso norm used in [17] is defined as $\psi(\mathbf{e}) = \sum_{G \in \mathcal{G}} \|\mathbf{e}_G\|_2$. As expected, a regularized solution by this norm has the property that variables in the same group are prone to be zero or nonzero simultaneously. Figure 2-(d) shows a geometric interpretation. Applied to the face error image $\mathbf{e}$, it corresponds to divide $\mathbf{e}$ into non-overlapping local patches. However, the error patterns in $\mathbf{e}$ corresponding to various face variations could have arbitrary shapes, with unknown sizes and number. It is impossible to pre-design disjoint group structures in order to promote error patterns precisely matching corruptions in actual face images.

To induce more diverse and sophisticated sparse error patterns, we consider structured sparsity-inducing norms that involve overlapping groups of variables, motivated by recent advances in structured sparsity [20,19]. Although it still assumes pre-defined group structures, the overlapping patterns of groups and the norms associated with the groups of variables allow to encode much richer classes of structured sparsity. Figure 2-(d) and -(e) give a geometric comparison between overlapping and non-overlapping group norms for a 3-dimensional vector. In this work, we consider a tree-structured sparsity-inducing norm. It involves a hierarchical partition of the m variables in $\mathbf{e}$ into groups, as shown in Figure 1. The tree is defined in a way that leaf nodes are singleton groups corresponding to individual pixels, and internal nodes/groups correspond to local patches of varying size. Thus each parent node contains a hierarchy of child nodes that

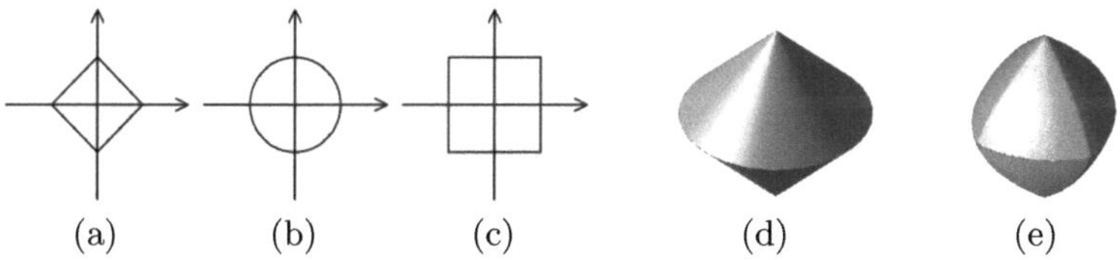

Fig. 2. Unit balls of different norms. (a), (b), and (c) are respectively for ℓ_1-norm, ℓ_2-norm, and ℓ_∞-norm in 2-dimensional space. (d) is for a non-overlapping group Lasso norm in 3-dimensional space: $\psi(\mathbf{e}) = \|\mathbf{e}_{\{1,2\}}\|_2 + |\mathbf{e}_3|$. (e) is for a structured sparsity norm with overlapping groups in 3-dimensional space: $\psi(\mathbf{e}) = \|\mathbf{e}_{\{1,2,3\}}\|_2 + \|\mathbf{e}_{\{1,2\}}\|_2 + |\mathbf{e}_1| + |\mathbf{e}_2| + |\mathbf{e}_3|$. Singular points appearing on these balls characterize the sparsity-inducing behavior of the underlying norms.

are spatially adjacent to each other and constitute a local part in the face error image $\mathbf{e}$. As illustrated in Figure 1, when a parent node goes to zero all its descendents in the tree must go to zero. Consequently, the nonzero or support patterns are formed by removing those nodes forced to zero. This is exactly the desired effect of structured error patterns of spatial locality and contiguity.

To put formally, denote $\mathcal{G}$ as a set of groups from the power set of the index set $\{1, \ldots, m\}$, with each group $G \in \mathcal{G}$ containing a subset of these indices. The tree-structured groups used in this paper are defined as follows: A set of groups $\mathcal{G}$ is said to be *tree-structured* in $\{1, \ldots, m\}$ if $\mathcal{G} = \{\ldots, G_1^i, G_2^i, \ldots, G_{b_i}^i, \ldots\}$ where $i = 0, 1, 2, \ldots, d$, d is the depth of the tree, $b_0 = 1$ and $G_1^0 = \{1, 2, \ldots, m\}$, $b_d = m$ and correspondingly $\{G_j^d\}_{j=1}^m$ are singleton groups. Let G_j^i be the parent node of a node $G_{j'}^{i+1}$ in the tree, we have $G_{j'}^{i+1} \subseteq G_j^i$. For any $1 \leq j, k \leq b_i$, $j \neq k$, we also have $G_j^i \cap G_k^i = \emptyset$.

Similar group structures are also considered in [20,22]. With the above notation, a general tree-structured sparsity-inducing norm can be written as

$$\psi(\mathbf{e}) = \sum_{i=0}^{d} \sum_{j=1}^{b_i} w_j^i \|\mathbf{e}_{G_j^i}\|_p, \tag{4}$$

where $\mathbf{e}_{G_j^i}$ is a vector with entries equal to those of $\mathbf{e}$ for the indices in G_j^i and 0 otherwise. w_j^i are positive weights for groups G_j^i. It is commonly chosen as $w_j^i = 1$. $\|\cdot\|_p$ denotes ℓ_p-norm with $p \geq 1$, and popular choices of p are $\{2, \infty\}$. Note that support patterns in the error image $\mathbf{e}$ corresponding to practical face variations are usually spatially localized and continuous, such as occlusion or shadow caused by illumination change. Pixels inside each of such error regions may have similarly large magnitude. When applying the sparsity-inducing norm $\|\cdot\|_p$ to $\mathbf{e}_{G_j^i}$, i.e., a group of pixels in a local patch, we expect similar errors in magnitude can be induced. For the ℓ_∞-norm, it is the maximum value of pixels in a group that decides if the group is set to nonzero or not, and it does encourage the rest of the pixels to take arbitrary (hence close to the maximum) values. Thus, in this paper we choose $p = \infty$ in the tree-structured norm (4). Figure 2-(b) and -(c) compares the unit balls of ℓ_∞ and ℓ_2 norms. The effectiveness of this choice is also corroborated with empirical evidences. The so defined norm (4) promotes sparse error patterns more consistent to practical face variations than standard ℓ_1-norm. Figure 3 shows such an advantage by comparing with [3] on recovering a clean face from occlusion.

3 Robust Face Recognition via Structured Sparsity

In this section, we use the so defined structured sparsity-inducing norm to replace the ℓ_1-norm for modeling the error $\mathbf{e}$ in robust face recognition. Thus, the (ℓ_1-ℓ_1) objective function in the optimization program (1) is modified to the following

$$(\ell_1\text{-}\ell_{struct}): \qquad \min_{\mathbf{x},\mathbf{e}} \|\mathbf{x}\|_1 + \lambda \sum_{i=0}^{d} \sum_{j=1}^{b_i} w_j^i \|\mathbf{e}_{G_j^i}\|_\infty \quad \text{s.t.} \quad \mathbf{y} = \mathbf{A}\mathbf{x} + \mathbf{e}, \qquad (5)$$

where the sparse vector $\mathbf{x}$ induced by ℓ_1-norm is naturally discriminative and encodes the identity of the test sample $\mathbf{y}$. λ is a parameter controlling the trade-off between sparsity of $\mathbf{x}$ and structured sparsity of $\mathbf{e}$.

A drawback of formulation (5) is that $\mathbf{y}$ could be linearly represented by training samples of multiple subjects. As a consequence, the induced error $\mathbf{e}$ contains both within-class variation and between-class difference. On the other hand, identification of within-class variation is essential for face recognition since misclassification is mainly due to these variations. We thus propose another subject-wise face recognition method that involves solving

$$(\ell_{struct}): \qquad \min_{\mathbf{e}_k,\mathbf{x}_k} \sum_{i=0}^{d} \sum_{j=1}^{b_i} w_j^i \|\mathbf{e}_{k,G_j^i}\|_\infty \quad \text{s.t.} \quad \mathbf{y} = \mathbf{A}_k\mathbf{x}_k + \mathbf{e}_k, \qquad (6)$$

w.r.t. each subject k of all the K subjects. If $\mathbf{y}$ belongs to subject k, solving (6) makes it possible to identify face regions of $\mathbf{y}$ that correspond to within-class variations. By discarding those regions a clean face image well-approximated by $\mathbf{A}_k$ can be recovered. The formulation (6) is thus a good approach to measure the capabilities of different methods for identifying within-class variations of test images. In this paper, we compare (6) with ℓ_1-norm variant of (6), which was considered in [11], in these settings. When optimizing (6) w.r.t. each subject, ideally the optimal $\mathbf{e}_k^*$ with the true subject would be smallest if based on some properly defined measure. (6) thus suggests new classification criteria which will be introduced shortly.

Both (5) and (6) are convex programs. To solve them we have developed algorithms based on Augmented Lagrange Multiplier (ALM) methods [23]. ALM has demonstrated its good balance between efficiency and accuracy in related sparse representation based face recognition methods [4,13]. The notable difference here is that in our ALM framework, a subproblem concerns with a proximal problem associated with structured sparsity-inducing norm regularization. A few recently proposed techniques can be exploited to efficiently solve the proximal problems of such kind [21,22,20]. For the case of ℓ_∞-norm applied to overlapping groups considered in this paper, solutions can be found by solving a quadratic min-cost flow problem [21]. Please refer to the supplemental material[1] for details of our developed algorithms for solving (5) and (6).

3.1 Alternative Classification Criteria

Given a test image $\mathbf{y}$, solving (5) enables us to obtain the optimal sparse vectors $\mathbf{x}^*$ and $\mathbf{e}^*$. When $\mathbf{y}$ is a face image from one of the K classes in the training set, we use the method in [3] for face classification. Denote $\delta_k(\mathbf{x})$ as a function to select coefficients from $\mathbf{x}$ corresponding to training samples of subject k, $\mathbf{y}$ can be classified as the class that minimizes the residuals

$$\text{identity}(\mathbf{y}) = \arg\min_k r_k(\mathbf{y}), \quad r_k(\mathbf{y}) = \|\mathbf{y} - \mathbf{A}_k \delta_k(\mathbf{x}^*)\|_2. \tag{7}$$

Solving (6) w.r.t. each subject gives the optimal vectors $\{\mathbf{e}_k^*\}_{k=1}^K$ and $\{\mathbf{x}_k^*\}_{k=1}^K$. Since $\{\mathbf{x}_k^*\}_{k=1}^K$ are computed locally w.r.t. each subject, it is no longer available to use the criteria as above. Instead, it is natural to compare $\mathbf{e}_k^*$, $k = 1, \ldots, K$, to classify $\mathbf{y}$ if $\mathbf{y}$ is from one of the K training subjects. In this paper, we choose to classify $\mathbf{y}$ to the class that minimizes the structured group sparsity norms

$$\text{identity}(\mathbf{y}) = \arg\min_k \psi(\mathbf{e}_k^*),\ \psi(\mathbf{e}_k^*) = \sum_{i=0}^{d} \sum_{j=1}^{b_i} w_j^i \|\mathbf{e}_{k,G_j^i}^*\|_\infty. \tag{8}$$

This criteria outperforms the conventional ℓ_1-norm alternative, as reported in our experiments in Section 4.

The so obtained $\{\mathbf{e}_k^*\}_{k=1}^K$ provide information for identifying the regions of $\mathbf{y}$ that correspond to either within-class variation or between-class difference[2]. Intuitively, the size of support regions for within-class variation should be smaller than that for between-class difference. This suggests a new classification criteria based on support regions of $\mathbf{e}_k^*$ for $k = 1, \ldots, K$. To identify the support regions, [11] adopted a non-convex formulation based on a Markov random field model. Instead, we here consider a simple thresholding scheme in order to show the superiority of structured sparsity for identification of different face variations. In particular, we can normalize the range of entry values of each $\mathbf{e}_k^*$ to $[0, 1]$. Denote $0 < \tau < 1$ as a threshold parameter, and $\mathbf{s}_k \in \{0, 1\}^m$ as a support vector for each $\mathbf{e}_k^*$. $\mathbf{s}_k$ can be computed by setting $\mathbf{s}_k[i] = 0$ when $\mathbf{e}_k^*[i] \le \tau$ and $\mathbf{s}_k[i] = 1$ otherwise. With the above notations the new classification criteria based on the sizes of support regions of $\{\mathbf{e}_k^*\}_{k=1}^K$ is defined as

$$\text{identity}(\mathbf{y}) = \arg\min_k \frac{\|\hat{\mathbf{e}}_k^*\|_1}{|\{i|\mathbf{s}_k[i] = 0\}|} \frac{1}{|\{i|\mathbf{s}_k[i] = 0\}|}, \tag{9}$$

where $\hat{\mathbf{e}}_k^*$ is a subvector of $\mathbf{e}_k^*$ with entries of indices corresponding to $\{i|\mathbf{s}_k[i] = 1\}$ removed. Thus the first part in (9) computes the averaged error value for each entry of $\hat{\mathbf{e}}_k^*$, and the introduction of the second part in (9) make this criteria favor $\mathbf{e}_k^*$ with smaller support regions.

---

[1] `http://web.adsc.com.sg/perception/publications.html`

[2] Usually entries of $\mathbf{e}_k^*$ will be very small in magnitude rather than exactly zero. And support regions of $\mathbf{e}_k^*$ cannot be directly obtained.

3.2 Robust Face Alignment via Structured Sparsity

So far we have assumed that the test image $\mathbf{y}$ is well aligned with the training images $\mathbf{A} = [\mathbf{A}_1, \mathbf{A}_2, \ldots, \mathbf{A}_K]$. Precise alignment is crucial for success of sparse representation based face recognition methods – in fact, good alignment is important for any recognition tasks. However, practically observed test image $\mathbf{y}'$ could be subject to some pose change or misalignment, so that the above assumed linear model $\mathbf{y}' = \mathbf{A}_k\mathbf{x}_k + \mathbf{e}_k$ no longer holds for any k. In the context of practical face recognition, $\mathbf{y}'$ can be related to $\mathbf{y}$ by $\mathbf{y} = \mathbf{y}' \circ \tau$, where τ stands for some transformation in the image domain (e.g., 2D similarity transformation for correcting misalignment, or 2D projective transformation for handling some pose change). The objective thus becomes to find the correct τ so that after transformation the obtained $\mathbf{y}$ from $\mathbf{y}'$ can be represented linearly by the training images.

As suggested in [13], the assumption of sparsity itself provides a strong cue for finding the deformation τ. As an extension to the problem (6), based on our structured sparisty, we formulate the alignment problem as the following optimization objective

$$\tau_k^* = \arg \min_{\tau_k, \mathbf{e}_k, \mathbf{x}_k} \sum_{i=0}^{d} \sum_{j=1}^{b_i} w_j^i \|\mathbf{e}_{k,G_j^i}\|_\infty \quad \text{s.t.} \quad \mathbf{y}' \circ \tau_k = \mathbf{A}_k\mathbf{x}_k + \mathbf{e}_k, \tag{10}$$

for $k = 1, \ldots, K$. The problem (10) is a difficult, nonconvex optimization problem over the deformation τ_k, error $\mathbf{e}_k$ and coefficient vector $\mathbf{x}_k$. Fortunately, in practice a good initialization of τ_k can be obtained from the output of an automatic face detector [8]. To solve (10), we follow the strategy of [13] by repeatedly linearizing about the current estimate of τ_k, and seeking a deformation step $\Delta\tau_k$ via the following minimization problem

$$\Delta\tau_k^* = \arg \min_{\Delta\tau_k, \mathbf{e}_k, \mathbf{x}_k} \sum_{i=0}^{d} \sum_{j=1}^{b_i} w_j^i \|\mathbf{e}_{k,G_j^i}\|_\infty \quad \text{s.t.} \quad \mathbf{y}' \circ \tau_k + J\Delta\tau_k = \mathbf{A}_k\mathbf{x}_k + \mathbf{e}_k, \tag{11}$$

where $J = \frac{\partial}{\partial \tau_k}\mathbf{y}' \circ \tau_k$ is the Jacobian of $\mathbf{y}' \circ \tau_k$ w.r.t. the transformation parameters τ_k. The notable difference of model (11) from that considered in [13] is the sparsity-inducing norm enforced on error $\mathbf{e}_k$: here we use structured group sparsity norm while ℓ_1-norm was used in [13]. We empirically observe that when $\mathbf{y}'$ contains large variations such as occlusion or disguise, our model is much better than that in [13] for face alignment and recognition, as reported in our experiments in Section 4. For solving (11), we have again developed an algorithm based on ALM. Please refer to the supplemental material for details of our algorithm. Similar to [13], it is important to normalize the warped image $\mathbf{y}' \circ \tau_k$ in optimization of (11), by replacing the linearization of $\mathbf{y}' \circ \tau_k$ with a linearization of the normalized version $\frac{\mathbf{y}' \circ \tau_k}{\|\mathbf{y}' \circ \tau_k\|_2}$.

After solving (10) w.r.t. all K subjects, the optimal $\{\tau_k^*\}_{k=1}^K$ and $\{\mathbf{e}_k^*\}_{k=1}^K$ can be obtained. The per-subject alignment residuals $\{\mathbf{e}_k^*\}_{k=1}^K$ can be naturally used

Algorithm 1. Robust face alignment and classification via structured sparsity

input : A test image $\mathbf{y}' \in \mathbb{R}^m$, initial transformations $\{\tau_k^0\}_{k=1}^K$, a matrix of well-aligned and normalized training samples of K subjects $\mathbf{A} = [\mathbf{A}_1, \mathbf{A}_2, \ldots, \mathbf{A}_K] \in \mathbb{R}^{m \times n}$, a set of pre-defined tree-structured groups $\mathcal{G} = \{G_j^i\}$ with $i = 0, 1, \ldots, d$ and $j = 1, \ldots, b_i$, the weight $w_j^i \geq 0$ for each G_j^i, and a regularization parameter $\lambda > 0$.

for *each subject* k **do**
  let $\tau_k = \tau_k^0$,
  while *not converged* **do**
    compute an optimal step $\Delta\tau_k^*$ by solving (11): $\Delta\tau_k^* =$
    $\arg\min_{\Delta\tau_k, \mathbf{e}_k, \mathbf{x}_k} \sum_{i=0}^{d} \sum_{j=1}^{b_i} w_j^i \|\mathbf{e}_{k,G_j^i}\|_\infty \quad s.t. \quad \mathbf{y}' \circ \tau_k + J\Delta\tau_k = \mathbf{A}_k\mathbf{x}_k + \mathbf{e}_k$,
    update $\tau_k \leftarrow \tau_k + \Delta\tau_k^*$.
  end
end
keep the indices of top S candidates $c_1, \ldots, c_S$ among $\{1, \ldots, K\}$ with the smallest structured group sparsity norm $\psi(\mathbf{e}_k) = \sum_{i=0}^{d} \sum_{j=1}^{b_i} w_j^i \|\mathbf{e}_{k,G_j^i}\|_\infty$.
set $\tilde{\mathbf{A}} \leftarrow [\mathbf{A}_{c_1} \circ \tau_{c_1}^{*-1}, \ldots, \mathbf{A}_{c_S} \circ \tau_{c_S}^{*-1}]$.
compute an optimal $\tilde{\mathbf{x}}^*$ via solving
$\tilde{\mathbf{x}}^* = \arg\min_{\tilde{\mathbf{x}}, \mathbf{e}} \|\tilde{\mathbf{x}}\|_1 + \lambda \sum_{i=0}^{d} \sum_{j=1}^{b_i} w_j^i \|\mathbf{e}_{G_j^i}\|_\infty \quad s.t. \quad \mathbf{y}' = \tilde{\mathbf{A}}\tilde{\mathbf{x}} + \mathbf{e}$.
compute the residuals $r_k(\mathbf{y}') = \|\mathbf{y}' - \tilde{\mathbf{A}}_k\delta_k(\tilde{\mathbf{x}}^*)\|_2$ for $k = c_1, \ldots, c_S$.
output : identity$(\mathbf{y}') = \arg\min_k r_k(\mathbf{y}')$.

for robust face recognition. For example, we can use (8) to classify the test image $\mathbf{y}'$ to one of the K subjects. To further improve the recognition performance, a global sparse representation problem (5) can be solved by aligning training samples of each $\mathbf{A}_k$ to $\mathbf{y}'$ using the computed τ_k^*. We thus get a discriminative representation $\mathbf{x}^*$ in terms of the entire training set, and (7) can be used as the criteria for face classification. The complete procedure of our robust face classification with automatic alignment is summarized as Algorithm 1, where the parameter S is used to reduce the number of subjects used in the global sparse representation problem (5), leaving a much smaller problem to solve.

4 Experiments

In this section, we conduct experiments to test the effectiveness of enforcing structured sparsity on the error $\mathbf{e}$ for robust and practical face recognition. We use three publicly available databases including the Extended Yale B [5,7], AR [10] and Multi-Pie [9] databases. We compare our method with those closely related sparse representation based face recognition methods [3,11,13], and also with other baseline classifiers such as Nearest Neighbor (NN), Nearest Subspace (NS), and Support Vector Machine (SVM). We will first present how different methods perform when both training and test images are well aligned, and then present experiments of practical face recognition by automatic face alignment.

4.1 Robust Face Recognition with Well Aligned Face Images

Recognition with Synthetic Block Occlusion. We use Extended Yale B database to test the robustness of our method against illumination change and

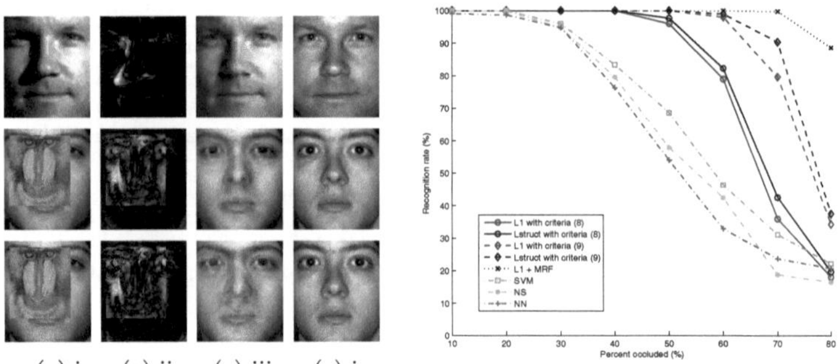

(a)-i (a)-ii (a)-iii (a)-iv

(a) (b)

Fig. 3. Recognition on the Extended Yale B database (*better view the electronic version*). (a) shows example results for test images under extreme illumination condition or with large fraction of occlusion: (a)-i test images; (a)-ii estimated error images; (a)-iii recovered images; (a)-iv training images with frontal illumination. Top row in (a) is the result by our method ℓ_1-ℓ_{struct} on a test image under extreme illumination condition. Middle and bottom rows in (a) compare our method with the method ℓ_1-ℓ_1 [3] on a test image with 60% occlusion. (b) plots recognition results of our method ℓ_{struct} and its ℓ_1 variant under classification criteria (8) and (9), and compares with NN, NS, SVM, and the method $\ell_1 +$ MRF [11].

contiguous occlusion. There are 1238 frontal face images of 38 subjects captured under varying laboratory lighting conditions in Subsets 1, 2, and 3 of the Extended Yale B database. Subsets 1, 2, and 3 contain face images under mild, moderate, and extreme illumination conditions respectively. We choose four illuminations from Subset 1, two from Subset 2, and two from Subset 3 for testing, and the rest of the images are used for training. The total number of training and test images are respectively 935 and 303. All images are manually aligned and cropped to the size of 96×84. In our experiments we simulate various levels of contiguous block occlusion from 10% to 80%, by replacing a randomly located block of each test image with an unrelated image, where locations of the occlusion are unknown to the computer. We test both of our recognition methods, namely ℓ_1-ℓ_{struct} for equation (5) and ℓ_{struct} for equation (6). For ℓ_1-ℓ_{struct}, we set $\lambda = 1$, which is chosen to seek a balanced sparsity between $\mathbf{x}$ and $\mathbf{e}$. We compare our methods with NN, NS, SVM, and especially with related sparse representation based methods, dubbed ℓ_1-ℓ_1 for [3] and $\ell_1 +$ MRF for [11].

Figure 3-(a) shows example results using our method ℓ_1-ℓ_{struct}. For the case of no occlusion shown in the first row of Figure 3-(a), the obtained error image by our method compensates well for the shadow around nose, which is due to a violation of the assumed linear subspace model. Correspondingly a clean face without dark shadow is recovered. The second and third rows of Figure 3-(a) show results of our method and the method ℓ_1-ℓ_1 for an example test image with 60% occlusion. This is a difficult recognition task even for humans. Careful comparison between the second and third rows of Figure 3-(a) shows that our method performs better in terms of recovering the clean face with no occlusion.

Table 1. Recognition results of our method $\ell_1\_\ell_{struct}$ and the method $\ell_1\_\ell_1$ [3] on the Extended Yale B database with varying levels of synthetic block occlusion

Percent occluded	10%	20%	30%	40%	50%	60%	70%	80%
$\ell_1\_\ell_1$ [3]	**100%**	**100%**	**100%**	99.7%	98.0%	68.4%	44.1%	22.4%
$\ell_1\_\ell_{struct}$	**100%**	**100%**	**100%**	**100%**	**99.3%**	**73.7%**	**47.0%**	**24.1%**

We quantitatively compare the recognition performance of different methods in Table 1 and Figure 3-(b). We can see from Table 1 that up to 50% occlusion, our method $\ell_1\_\ell_{struct}$ performs almost perfectly, and it consistently outperforms the method $\ell_1\_\ell_1$ up to 80% occlusion. For our method ℓ_{struct} (problem (6)), we report results in Figure 3-(b) by comparing with a variant of (6), dubbed "ℓ_1"[3], under classification criteria (8) and (9), where τ is set as 0.1 for criteria (9). Under criteria (8), enforcing structured sparsity by ℓ_{struct} gives better results than the ℓ_1 variant does. Under criteria (9), we also compare with NN, NS, SVM, and the method $\ell_1 +$ MRF [11]. $\ell_1 +$ MRF uses the ℓ_1 variant of (6) as initialization, and a complicated non-convex optimization method based on MRF to specifically address occlusion. Results by our method based on simple thresholding (cf. Section 3.1) are comparable with those from $\ell_1 +$ MRF up to 70% occlusion, and also consistently better than those from NN, NS, SVM, and the thresholding based ℓ_1 variant. It should be noted that $\ell_1 +$ MRF can only address the case that test images are well aligned, while our method is able to automatically align test images, as will be reported shortly. For the well aligned case, our method is also possible to be integrated with MRF to specifically address occlusion, as did by $\ell_1 +$ MRF [11]. Nevertheless, results in Table 1 and Figure 3 clearly demonstrate that structured sparsity-inducing norm is a better choice for robust face recognition.

Recognition with Disguise. We test our method's ability to cope with real disguises using a subset of the AR database. The training set consists of 799 unoccluded face images of 100 subjects with different facial expressions[4]. We consider two separate test sets, each of which contains 200 face images. In the first test set are images of subjects wearing sunglasses, which occlude about 30% of each image. In the second test set are images of subjects wearing a scarf, which occludes roughly half of each image. All training and test images are resized to 83×60. Table 2-Left compares our method $\ell_1\_\ell_{struct}$ with NN, NS, SVM, and $\ell_1\_\ell_1$ [3], where we again set $\lambda = 1$ for $\ell_1\_\ell_{struct}$. Table 2-Right compares our method ℓ_{struct} with its ℓ_1 variant under the classification criteria (9) (τ is set as 0.1 for both ℓ_{struct} and its ℓ_1 variant), and also with the method $\ell_1 +$ MRF [11]. Table 2 shows that $\ell_1 +$ MRF achieves the best performance for the case of

[3] The ℓ_1 variant of (6) solves the problem: $\min_{\mathbf{e}_k,\mathbf{x}_k} \|\mathbf{e}_k\|_1 \; s.t. \; \mathbf{y} = \mathbf{A}_k\mathbf{x}_k + \mathbf{e}_k$, w.r.t. each subject k of all the K subjects.

[4] We use image IDs $\{1-4\}$ and $\{14-17\}$ for each subject in the AR database, except one corrupted image.

Table 2. Recognition results of different methods on the AR database with disguises

	NN	NS	SVM	ℓ_1-ℓ_1	ℓ_1-ℓ_{struct}	ℓ_1((9))	ℓ_{struct}((9))	ℓ_1+MRF
sunglasses	60.5%	59.0%	66.5%	91.0%	**92.5%**	99.0%	**99.5%**	**99.5%**
scarf	14.0%	15.0%	16.5%	64.0%	**69.0%**	84.0%	87.5%	**97.5%**

occlusion by scarf. Since the scarf used in AR database [10] occludes half (the lower part) of each test image, and it happens to be with dark color and resembles some bearded men in the database, when pursuing sparse representation, there could be a degenerate solution that considers the scarf as the correct signal and the remainder of the face as error. In this case, the non-convex MRF approach in [11] is helpful in iteratively guiding the identification of error support into the scarf region, and hence getting improved performance. However, Table 2 also shows that our method ℓ_1-ℓ_{struct} outperforms ℓ_1-ℓ_1, and our method ℓ_{struct} outperforms its ℓ_1 variant, for both cases of sunglasses and scarf. It demonstrates that promoting structured sparsity on the error image is generally better than promoting standard sparsity using ℓ_1-norm in coping with real disguises.

4.2 Robust Face Recognition with Automatic Alignment

In this subsection, we test the effectiveness of our Algorithm 1 for automatic and robust face alignment and recognition, using the CMU Multi-Pie database. The CMU Multi-Pie database contains face images of 337 subjects captured in four sessions with simultaneous variations in illumination, pose, and expression. Of these 337 subjects, we use all the 249 subjects present in Session 1 as training subjects. For each of the 249 subjects we choose frontal images of 7 illuminations[5] with neutral facial expression as training images. As suggested in [13], these 7 extreme illuminations of frontal view are chosen in order to linearly represent other frontal illuminations well. We manually click outer eye corners in all the training images and crop them to the size of 80×60. The distance between the two outer eye corners is normalized to be 50 pixels. We start with experiments on region of attraction to verify the effectiveness of our alignment algorithm, and then present face recognition experiments with automatic alignment.

Experiments on Region of Attraction. In the CMU Multi-Pie database, we use frontal images of illumination 10 with neutral expression from Session 2 as our test images. We manually align these images in the same way as for training images, to provide ground truth for our region of attraction experiments. We introduce artificial deformation of translation, rotation, or scaling to these test images. To measure success of alignment, we use the structured sparsity norm on error $\mathbf{e}$, i.e., $\psi(\mathbf{e})$ defined in (4), as the alignment error. More specifically, let r_0 be the alignment error obtained by aligning a test image without any artificial perturbation, and r be the error for the case with perturbation. We consider the alignment as successful if $|r - r_0| < 0.01 r_0$. Region of attraction results for

[5] They are illuminations $\{0, 1, 7, 13, 14, 16, 18\}$ of the total 20 illuminations.

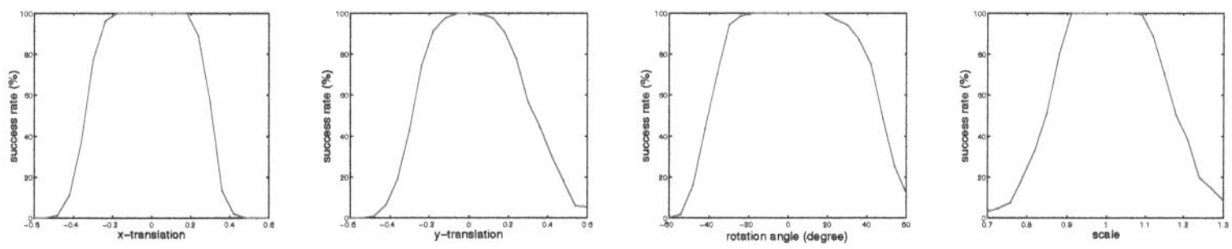

Fig. 4. Experiments on Region of Attraction. The amount of translation is defined as a fraction of the distance between the outer eye corners. From left to right: translation in x direction, translation in y direction, in-plane rotation, and scale change.

Table 3. Accuracy of recognition with automatic alignment on the Multi-Pie database. Left table shows recognition results for test images from Session 1 under varying levels of synthetic block occlusion. Right table shows recognition results for test images from Sessions 2 - 4.

occlusion %	10%	20%	30%	40%	50%	Session 2	Session 3	Session 4
[13],$S = 1$	99.2%	94.4%	76.7%	44.2%	18.5%	90.7%	89.6%	87.5%
Alg.1,$S = 1$	**100%**	95.6%	81.1%	48.6%	20.9%	92.1%	90.6%	88.4%
[13]	99.2%	95.2%	79.1%	48.2%	21.1%	93.9%	93.8%	92.3%
Alg.1	**100%**	**96.8%**	**85.5%**	**52.6%**	**24.5%**	**95.7%**	**94.9%**	**93.7%**

different kinds of deformation are plotted in Figure 4. Figure 4 shows that our algorithm works well when translation is below 20% of the eye corner distance (or 10 pixels) in both x- and y-directions, when in-plane rotation is below 30 degrees, or when change in scale is below 10%. As discussed in [13], outputs from Viola and Jones' face detector [8] fall safely inside this region of attraction.

Experiments on Face Alignment and Recognition. We first test the robustness of our method against misalignment, illumination change, and contiguous occlusion. We use frontal images of illumination 10 from Session 1 (the same session used for training) of the Multi-Pie database as our test images. This choice is deliberate in order to remove other types of occlusion such as hair-style change across sessions. We simulate various levels of contiguous block occlusion from 10% to 50%, by replacing a randomly located block of each test image with an unrelated image. We compare our method with the closely related method [13], which is based on ℓ_1-norm minimization for alignment and recognition. For both methods, outputs from Viola and Jones' face detector [8] are used as initialization of the alignment process. Table 3-Left shows that our method performs reasonably well up to 30% of occlusion, and consistently outperforms [13] for both cases of $S = 1$ and $S = 10$ in Algorithm 1. These results show that enforcing structured sparsity on the error $\mathbf{e}$ is a better choice in simultaneously handling misalignment, illumination change, and contiguous occlusion.

We also test our method on frontal images of all the 20 illuminations from Sessions $2-4$ of the Multi-Pie database. Table 3-Right reports our results, and compares with those from [13]. Again, our method achieves better results.

Acknowledgments. This study is supported by the research grant for the Human Sixth Sense Programme at the Advanced Digital Sciences Center from Singapores Agency for Science, Technology and Research (A*STAR), and the funding of ONR N00014-09-1-0230, NSF CCF 09-64215, NSF IIS 11-16012, and DARPA KECoM 10036- 100471.

References

1. Turk, M., Pentland, A.: Eigenfaces for recognition. In: CVPR (1991)
2. Belhumeur, P., Hespanda, J., Kriegman, D.: Eigenfaces vs. Fisherfaces: recognition using class specific linear projection. PAMI 19(7), 711–720 (1997)
3. Wright, J., Yang, A., Ganesh, A., Sastry, S., Ma, Y.: Robust face recognition via sparse representation. PAMI 31(2), 210–227 (2009)
4. Yang, A. Y., Ganesh, A., Zhou, Z., Sastry, S., Ma, Y.: A review of fast ℓ_1-minimization algorithms for robust face recognition (2010) (preprint)
5. Georghiades, A., Belhumeur, P., Kriegman, D.: From few to many: Illumination cone models for face recognition under variable lighting and pose. PAMI (2001)
6. Basri, R., Jacobs, D.: Lambertian reflectance and linear subspaces. PAMI (2003)
7. Lee, K., Ho, J., Kriegman, D.: Acquiring linear subspaces for face recognition under variable lighting. PAMI 27(5), 684–698 (2005)
8. Viola, P., Jones, M.J.: Robust real-time face detection. IJCV (2004)
9. Gross, R., Matthews, I., Cohn, J., Kanade, T., Baker, S.: Multi-PIE. In: FG (2008)
10. Martinez, A., Benavente, R.: The AR face database. CVC T.R., No. 24 (1998)
11. Zhou, Z., Wagner, A., Wright, J., Mobahi, H., Ma, Y.: Face recognition with contiguous occlusion using markov random fields. In: ICCV (2009)
12. Cevher, V., Duarte, M.F., Hegde, C., Baraniuk, R.G.: Sparse signal recovery using markov random fields. In: NIPS (2008)
13. Wagner, A., Wright, J., Ganesh, A., Zhou, Z., Mobahi, H., Ma, Y.: Towards a practical face recognition system: robust alignment and illumination by sparse representation. PAMI (2011)
14. Elhamifar, E., Vidal, R.: Robust classification using structured sparse representation. In: CVPR (2011)
15. Zhang, L., Yang, M., Feng, X.C.: Sparse representation or collaborative representation which helps face recognition? In: ICCV (2011)
16. Tibshirani, R.: Regression shrinkage and selection via the Lasso. Journal of the Royal Stat. Soc., Series B, 267–288 (1996)
17. Yuan, M., Lin, Y.: Model selection and estimation in regression with grouped variables. Journal of the Royal Stat. Soc., Series B 68(1), 49–67 (2006)
18. Beck, A., Teboulle, M.: A fast iterative shrinkage-thresholding algorithm for linear inverse problems. SIAM Journal on Imaging Sci. 2(1), 183–202 (2009)
19. Jenatton, R., Audibert, J.-Y., Bach, F.: Structured variable selection with sparsity-inducing morms. JMLR 12, 2777–2824 (2011)
20. Zhao, P., Rocha, G., Yu, B.: The composite absolute penalties family for grouped and hierarchical variable selection. Annals of Statistics 37(6A), 3468–3497 (2009)
21. Mairal, J., Jenatton, R., Obozinski, G., Bach, F.: Network flow algorithms for structured sparsity. In: NIPS (2010)
22. Liu, J., Ye, J.: Moreau-Yosida regularization for grouped tree structure learning. In: NIPS (2010)
23. Bertsekas, D.: Constrained optimization and Lagrange multiplier methods. Academic Press (1982)

Recognizing Materials from Virtual Examples

Wenbin Li and Mario Fritz

Max Planck Institute for Informatics, Saarbrucken, Germany
{wenbinli,mfritz}@mpi-inf.mpg.de

Abstract. Due to the strong impact of machine learning methods on visual recognition, performance on many perception task is driven by the availability of sufficient training data. A promising direction which has gained new relevance in recent years is the generation of virtual training examples by means of computer graphics methods in order to provide richer training sets for recognition and detection on real data. Success stories of this paradigm have been mostly reported for the synthesis of shape features and 3D depth maps. Therefore we investigate in this paper if and how appearance descriptors can be transferred from the virtual world to real examples. We study two popular appearance descriptors on the task of material categorization as it is a pure appearance-driven task. Beyond this initial study, we also investigate different approach of combining and adapting virtual and real data in order to bridge the gap between rendered and real-data. Our study is carried out using a new database of virtual materials VIPS that complements the existing KTH-TIPS material database.

1 Introduction

The recognition of materials is a key visual competence which humans perform with ease. It enables us to make predictions about the world and chose our actions with care. Will I slip when I walk on this slope? Will I get stuck in this ground? How do I acquire a stable grasp of an object? Can I lift the object? Will I break or scratch the object? All these questions relate to materials around us as well as their associated properties. Naturally, we want to equip robotic systems with the same capabilities so that they can act appropriately and successfully generalize to new scenarios.

Recognition of materials by the appearance has received significant attention in the vision community. Most importantly, generalization across instances has been studied which is a key factor in the scenarios described above. However, this setting requires several example instances at training time recorded under different conditions in order to present the intra-class variation to the learning algorithm. Current studies are limited to a maximum of about 10 material classes which seems largely insufficient to address real-world scenarios. One of the main problems we see in the rather tedious acquisition of such datasets for learning.

This problem is common to many areas of visual recognition and has stimulated research in how to tap into more resourceful ways to acquire training data.

A. Fitzgibbon et al. (Eds.): ECCV 2012, Part IV, LNCS 7575, pp. 345–358, 2012.

While grabbing large databases from the internet has been a promising direction pursued in recent years, it often comes with a bias and is less appropriate for domains for which there is an underlying parametric structure that should be learnt. Therefore we have seen increased interest in approaches that render training data from 3D models. Probably one of the biggest success stories in this field is the body pose estimation model from the Kinect that strongly leveraged rendered depth maps for generating millions of training examples [1].

However we realize that most successful applications of this data acquisition paradigm rely on 2D and/or 3D shape information and applications to appearance-based descriptions has been limited. One possible explanation is that despite rendering engines have become more and more powerful and appealing to the human eye, the generated statistics are still different to real-world images. The focus on features and application domains that rely on shape information mask the problem that there is an underlying unsolved problem.

Therefore we study in this paper the problem of appearance transfer from rendered materials to real ones. In contrast to object or scene recognition we have to entirely rely on appearance descriptors. We investigate different method of combining real and virtual examples and formulating the mismatch of the two data sources as an alignment or domain adaptation problem. Our approach proposes a roadmap to scalable acquisition of rich models of material appearances, as a large library of material shaders are available from companies that supply the computer graphics domain or even for free from hobbyist and enthusiast.

Contributions: We present the first study on leveraging rendered materials for the recognition of real materials. We show recognition from virtual data only as well as improved performance by combining virtual and real data. We analyze how well different appearance descriptors can cope with this domain shift. Beyond this, we also investigate the applicability of recent metric learning and domain adaptation method to this problem which is the first principled approach to deal with the discrepancies between rendered and real data examples. Our study is based on a new database of virtual materials called MPI-VIPS which complements the existing material database KTH-TIPS. The new database is available at `http://www.d2.mpi-inf.mpg.de/mpi-vips`.

2 Related Work

There is a long tradition of analyzing the visual appearance of texture and deriving good representations for this task [2,3]. While earlier studies often looked at single material instances as facilitated by the Curet database [4] the focus shifted more towards recognizing whole material classes [5,6], e.g. based on the KTH-TIPS database. In order to even further increase intra class variance, a web-based material recognition challenges has recently proposed [7,8]. While previous investigation have looked at a pure appearance based recognition challenge, this new database images whole objects and therefore investigates the question how material recognition can be performed in context.

Recently, the generation of virtual training data has gained a lot of attention. We distinguish two main threads: recombination and rendering. Recombination methods leverage real examples and recombine aspects of them by certain model assumption in order to form new ones. Examples include invariant support vector machines [9] that expand the support vector set by applying transformations to them which are know to maintain class membership, generative pedestrian models that can re-mix shape, appearance and backgrounds [10,11].Also synthesizing new views from real material samples has been investigated to expand the training set [12]. On the other hand, rendering method generate genuinely new examples from a model-based description. Probably the most prominent approach is the recently presented approach to robust pose estimation from 3D data that strongly leveraged rendered depth maps to attain the desired performance [1]. A similar approach has been taken for object recognition in range data by leveraging 3D model from google warehouse [13,14]. Other applications include 3D car models for learning edge-based shape representations of cars [15] and scene matching from 3D city models [16] .

As alluded to before, leveraging virtual training data tends to introduce some discrepancy between the statistics of the real and the synthesized data. Distribution mismatch between training and test time is a problem that relates to the concept of domain shift. One of the first investigation in object recognition has only been conducted quite recently [17,18]. They employ metric learning [19] in order to adapt data from the web to be more suitable for in situ recognition task. Another example is the adaptation of rendered data to real examples [13] where the domain adaptation approaches were used to adapt synthesized depth maps from 3D google warehouse data for recognition in LIDAR scans. In contrast, this paper conducts the first study on purely appearance-based descriptors for the task of material recognition utilizing virtual examples.

3 Method

First, we describe our main recognition architecture and review the employed feature descriptors. Then we explain the acquisition of virtual material examples and present the new database (MPI-VIPS) on which our study is based on. Lastly, we describe the approaches we investigate in order to mitigate the discrepancies between virtual data and real data. We propose an alignment procedures tailored to the material recognition task. In addition we recap the "Frustratingly Easy Domain Adaptation" approach [20] as well as a metric learning approach [19] which we consider as generic machine learning approaches to this problem.

3.1 Material Recognition

Our main material recognition pipeline is based on a kernel classifier combined with appearance features LBP and SIFT. Our choice of classifier and feature is motivated by [5,6,8]. We continue with a brief review of the employed features descriptors as well as the recognition architecture and choice of kernel.

Multi-scale LBP. The LBP descriptor [21] has shown to be a powerful description of image texture. They key idea is to compute for each pixel a set of differences to pixels in a local neighborhood. Depending on the sign of those differences, the pixel is assigned a distinct pattern id. The final descriptor is a histogram of the occurrences of such pattern id on an image patch of interest.

The most prominent limitation of the LBP operator has been its small spatial support area. Features calculated in a small local neighborhood cannot capture large-scale structures that may be the dominant features of some textures. Several extensions have been introduced to overcome its limitations. We use rotationally invariant, uniform LBP descriptor at 4 scales. Studies on the KTH-TIPS2 database [5,6] have shown strong performance for this descriptor on the task of material classification.

Color. Color is an important attribute of surfaces and can be a cue for material recognition. Although color alone sometimes may be misleading, significant boost have been reported (e.g. [8]) when combined with other descriptors. In our experiment, we follow their scheme and extract color features from 5x5 pixel patches.

Dense SIFT. SIFT features have been widely used in scene and object recognition to characterize the spatial and orientational distribution of local gradients and it also has been shown to work well for material recognition task [8,22]. In our experiment, we again follow the setup of [8] and use dense SIFT.

Classification. We use a Support-Vector-Machine (SVM) classifier. As previous studies [6] and our own investigations have shown the described histogram-based descriptors tend to show superior performance when used in combination with an exponential-χ^2 kernel [23]:

$$K(x,y) = \exp\{-\alpha\chi^2(x,y)\}$$
$$\chi^2(x,y) = \sum_i \frac{|x_i - y_i|^2}{|x_i + y_i|}$$

Histograms were normalized to unit length and the kernel parameter α was found by cross-validation on the training set.

3.2 Rendering

Bidirectional Reflection Functions (BRDF) give a full account on how light interacts with a surface. Therefore they are a rich source to truthfully recreate the appearance of material that carries discriminative information for classification [24,25]. This would make them the ideal source for synthesizing a virtual data set.

However their acquisition is tedious and time consuming – even more than the generation of image datasets that we aim to circumvent. But the widespread use of computer graphics rendering engines among professionals and hobbyists has lead to large libraries of material shaders that seek to capture the appearance of materials in sufficient quality to yield photorealistic synthesis as well as provide a computational efficient form to ensure fast rendering. 1000s of such material shaders are available form commercial (e.g. DOSCH design) and free e.g. `http://www.vray-materials.de`) online sources. Being able to tab into those vast resources would boost scalability of material recognition by up to two orders of magnitude.

Consequently, we propose to use approximative models as they are widely used in the material shaders in most of the available rendering packages. In particular we consider such material shaders that provide us with the following 3 informations:

Phong-type Shading Model. We recollect that the basic Phong shading equations is a combination of a ambient, a diffuse and a specular term. Therefore the light intensity $L_r(\hat{v}_r;\lambda)$ observed in view direction $\hat{v}_r$ at wavelength λ is given by:

$$\begin{aligned} L_r(\hat{v}_r;\lambda) = k_a(\lambda)L_a(\lambda) + \\ k_d(\lambda)\sum_i L_i(\lambda) < \hat{v}_i, \hat{n} >^+ + \\ k_s(\lambda)\sum_i L_i(\lambda)(< \hat{v}_r, \hat{s}_i >)^{k_e} \end{aligned}$$

where k_a, k_d, k_s are the reflection distribution of the ambient, diffuse and specular part respectively (color of the object), L_a is the wavelength distribution of the ambient illumination and L_i is the wavelength distribution of the i-th light source. The diffuse part is further governed by the angle between the surface normal $\hat{n}$ and the lighting direction $\hat{v}_i$ of light source i and the specular part by the angle between viewing direction and the specular reflection direction s_i. A parameter k_e controls the peakedness of the specular reflection.

Bump Map. As 3D texture induced by the local micro structure of the material is one very important effect which complicates robust classification [2], we require our material shaders to provide a bump map. The method stores local variations in geometry as a height map which is in turn used to compute a local normal. This normal map is then used to modulates the original surface normal in order to recreate shading effects of local 3D structure of the material.

Texture Map. All our materials also come with a texture map that basically encode the local and diffuse color of the material k_d and also any other residual effects. It is worth noting that for many material shaders available commercially or online a visual appealing appearance is the prime modeling target and not necessarily physical realism.

3.3 MPI-VIPS Database of Rendered Materials

We use the shader model described above to generate a new database of rendered materials which we call MPI-VIPS (Virtual texture under varying Illumination, Pose and Scales). One of our motivation is the availability of material shaders from commercial suppliers to the computer graphics community as well as internet resources. We therefore collect a set of shaders that match the material classes from the KTH-TIPS2 database in order to facilitate a systematic study. To obtain the virtual data, we use Autodesk 3ds Max to do the rendering and follow the scene setting in the KTH-TIPS2 database. In details, we vary the distance from the rendered patch to camera to simulate the changes in scales and apply directional light and ambient light to simulate the lighting condition in the original database. Note all operations to change the scene settings can be done precisely and easily with MAXScript in contrast to manually collection of real world data. Fig 3 shows the rendered patches for the 11 material classes. Next to them we also display the texture and bump maps included in the shader information. While some of them show strong visual similarity to the true materials (e.g. bread (2nd row), cork (4th row), there are also significant variations in style, color and detail. Several of the cloth samples show different color and design patterns on them which make them very distinct from the examples in the KTH-TIPS database. The same holds true for the level of realism. While the above mentioned materials look quite realistic, examples with more complex light interactions (e.g. aluminum foil (1st row), lettuce leaf (7th row)) look artificial. We consider these properties to be an inherent characteristic of this setting and consider this mix between good and bad matches as quite typical and therefore well suited for our study.

3.4 Manifold Alignment

One concern when using rendered data is a mismatch in appearance when compared to real examples. From a statistics point of view, we have one manifold which is formed by the real examples and one which is formed by the rendered ones. We would like to bring them to a coarse alignment by appropriate choice of such rendering parameters. As we know the normal of the patch we are rendering and we also use a rotation invariant descriptor, view point and rotation are less concerning. However, we don't get any notion of absolute scale from the shader models. Therefore propose an alignment strategy that matches the scale of our rendered examples to the real ones.

In details, there are 9 scales equally spaced logarithmically over two octaves, 3 different poses and 4 illumination conditions for each instance in the original KTH-TIPS dataset. We choose a set of samples for each category with the same pose, illumination conditions and placed at the 9 logarithmically equally spaced scales$\{y_1, ..., y_9\}$, generate a series of N scales equally spaced logarithmically $\{x_1, x_2, ..., x_N\}$ as a pool of samples, and treat each consecutive 9 scales starting from x_i as one candidate alignment$\{x_i, x_i + 1, ..., x_i + 8\}$. We compute descriptor d on both samples and the candidates as $\{d(y_1), ..., d(y_9)\}$ and $\{d(x_i), ...d(x_i + 8)\}$, then measure the accumulated difference between the two sets as $\sum_{j=1}^{n} \Delta(d(x_i - 1 + j), d(y_j))$, where Δ denotes for the difference between the descriptors computed from the two sets, can be either $L1$ and $L2$ distance. We then choose $i = \underset{i}{\operatorname{argmin}} \sum_{j=1}^{n} \Delta(d(x_i - 1 + j), d(y_j))$.

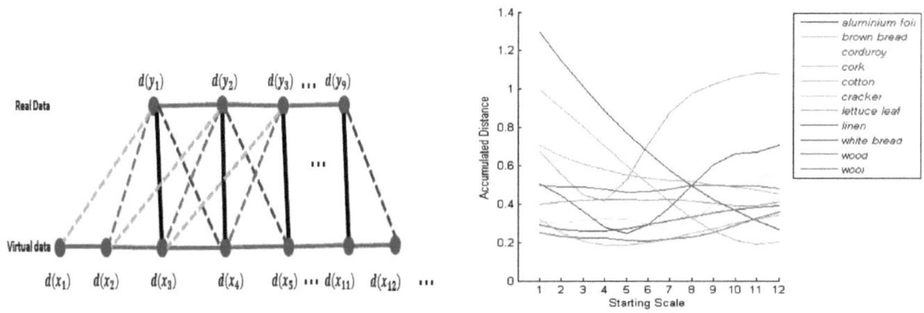

Fig. 1. (Left) Illustration of our aligment approach. Nodes denote descriptors in different scales, and lines with different colors denote different alignment of scales between the baseline real samples and the candidate alignments. (Right) Coarse alignment with scales. x-axis denotes different candidate scales and y-axis denotes accumulated differences between candidates and baseline samples.

Figure 3.4 shows the resulting scores for different choices of alignment scales. We see that most of the materials have a distinct minimum which – on visual inspection – also corresponded to the correct scale. Two materials could not be aligned with this procedure due to lack of a minimum. For those we had to pick the scale manually. As we will show in our results, such an alignment step is crucial for successfully utilizing rendered data.

3.5 Learning Approaches

While the previous section proposed a method of providing a first coarse alignment of the appearance manifolds, there are more subtle changes that differentiate rendered and real examples. The challenge we face here is that we don't have a good handle how to parameterize those changes or even pin point the exact discrepancies. Therefore we investigate metric learning and domain adaptation approaches that follow an exemplar-based paradigm. As we do have corresponding material patches in rough alignment, we can use them in such a machine learning approach to learn a transformed space that is more robust to the changes introduced by the two domains.

Metric Learning: Information theoretic metric learning (ITML.) ITML [19] optimizes the Mahalanobis distance between each point pair $x_i, x_j \in R^d$

$$d_a(x_i, x_j) = (x_i - x_j)^T A (x_i - x_j)$$

It reduces to simple euclidean distance when $A = I$. To learn the metric matrix A, the algorithm apply iterative procedures to minimizes the logdet divergence between the current metric A and the initial matrix A_0 with respect to pairwise similarity constraints:

$$\begin{aligned} \underset{A}{\text{minimize}} \quad & D_{ld}(A, A_0) \\ \text{subject to} \quad & d_A(x_i, x_j) \leq b_u,\ (i,j) \in S \\ & d_A(x_i, x_j) \geq b_l,\ (i,j) \in D \end{aligned}$$

where b_u and b_l are upper and lower bound of similarity and dissimilarity constraints. S and D are sets of similarity and dissimilarity constraints based on the labeled data, namely pairs in the same categories are set with similarity constraints, otherwise with dissimilarity constraints. The optimization is done by repeated Bregman projections of a single constraint per iteration. It is also convenient to extend the framework to a kernelized version that can also learn non-linear deformations of the original space. In our experiment, we use the kernel matrix instead of raw data and subsample $^1/_4$ of the full constraints to reduce computational cost.

Frustratingly Easy Domain Adaptation. Daume III [20] has introduced the "frustratingly easy domain adaptation" by feature augmentation. In our experiment, since we use $\exp -\chi^2$ kernel for classification, we use a kernelized version of it. For which, we define mapping

$$\Phi^s = <\Phi(x), \Phi(x), 0> \tag{1}$$

$$\Phi^t = <\Phi(x), 0, \Phi(x)> \tag{2}$$

where $0 =< 0, ..., 0 >$ is the zero vector, $\Phi(x)$ denotes the feature mapping in the original space. This leads to the new kernel function:

$$K'(x, x') = \begin{cases} 2K(x, x') & \text{if } x, x' \text{ are in the same domain} \\ K(x, x') & \text{if } x, x' \text{ are in different domains} \end{cases}$$

4 Experiments

In the experimental section we investigate how rendered materials can be utilized to recognize real ones. Our investigation also evaluates methods that support the transfer of appearance-based descriptors from the virtual to the real domain. We report average accuracies over 4 trials by randomly splitting training and testing data, while we always insure that we use different material instances in training and test.

4.1 Datasets

We use two publicly available datasets in our experiments: the Flickr Material Database and KTH-TIPS2 database. In addition we use our new database of virtual materials MPI-VIPS (Virtual texture under varying Illumination, Pose and Scale) which is intended to complement the KTH-TIPS (Texture under varying Illumination, Pose and Scale) [5] database. Therefore it provides a test bed for studying the transfer of appearance from rendered to real materials.

Table 1. Results. The classification rate with different sets of features for the Flickr database.

Method	Feature	Classification Rate (%)
aLDA	Best Feature Comb.	44.6
	SIFT	35.2
Ours	MLBP + Color	48.1
	MLBP	37.4

The Flickr Material Database. The database is collected using Flickr photos [7]. This includes 1000 images in 10 common material categories, ranging from fabric, paper, and plastic, to wood, stone, and metal. State-of-the-art results were obtained by exploring a large set of heterogeneous features and a Latent Dirichlet Allocation (LDA) model [8]. We use this database in order to establish reference for our recognition architecture to other recent approaches on material recognition. Table 1 shows our results on the Flickr dataset and their combinations. In our experiments on Flickr, we use kernelized SVM instead of aLDA model but use the same experimental setting in order to stay comparable, and we do four trials and report the average accuracies. The mlbp descriptor does slightly better than any of the single features tested there (35%). By combing color and mlbp, our test accuracy is 48.1% – higher than the reported one in [8] (45%) and on par with most recent findings in [26] (48.2%). The competitive performance shows the validity of our recognition approach for this task.

We chose to not further study material recognition on this dataset as it convolutes the problem with object level biases. While we agree that this might be intended in many applications, we want to restrict our study on pure appearance aspects in the material recognition setting. Therefore the remaining part focuses on the KTH TIPS database and its rendered counterpart MPI-VIPS.

KTH-TIPS2 Database. The KTH-TIPS2 database [5] was designed to study material recognition with a special focus on generalization to novel instances of material. It includes 4608 images from 11 material categories, and each category has 4 different instances. All the instances are imaged from varying viewing angles (frontal, rotated 22.5° left and 22.5°), lighting conditions (from the front, from the side at 45°, from the top at 45°, and ambient light) and scales (9 scales equally spaced logarithmically over two octaves), which gives a total of $3 \times 4 \times 9 = 108$ images per instance. We show examples of all the materials with all their instances in Fig 3. Note the challenge posed by the intra-class variation of the materials.

The first block in Table 2 shows results of our recognition pipeline in the standard setting. Each line represents a different of the 4 available material instances into training and test. Our performance is on par with results shown previously in this setup [5]. Best performance of 73.1% is obtained for 3 training instances and Color+MLBP feature.

Table 2. Results on KTH TIPS and the new VIPS database

train on real – test on real			
Setting	Dense SIFT	MLBP	Color+MLBP
1 real train + 3 real test	45.5(±3.6)	59.1(±3.7)	61.4(±2.8)
2 real train + 2 real test	52.3(±2.3)	65.8(±1.4)	70.4(±0.7)
3 real train + 1 real test	56.4(±2.6)	70.7(±3.2)	73.1(±4.6)
train on **unaligned** virtual – test on real			
Setting	Dense SIFT	MLBP	Color+MLBP
1 virtuall train + 3 real test	26.7(±1.2)	31.9(±1.6)	31.3(±2.5)
train on **aligned** virtual – test on real			
Setting	Dense SIFT	MLBP	Color+MLBP
1 virtual train + 3 real test	33.1(±1.2)	43.7(±2.1)	40.3(±2.7)
train on **mix** of **unaligned** virtual and real – test on real **(kernel-SVM)**			
Setting	Dense SIFT	MLBP	Color+MLBP
1 virtual train + 1 real train + 3 real test	42.4(±1.8)	59.3(±4.0)	59.9(±1.8)
1 virtual train + 2 real train + 2 real test	53.6(±1.3)	67.1(±2.5)	66.8(±3.4)
1 virtual train + 3 real train + 1 real test	52.4(±1.1)	70.0(±1.4)	73.2(±4.7)
train on **mix** of **aligned** virtual and real – test on real **(kernel-SVM)**			
Setting	Dense SIFT	MLBP	Color+MLBP
1 virtual train + 1 real train + 3 real test	45.1(±2.3)	62.2(±2.7)	63.8(±1.4)
1 virtual train + 2 real train + 2 real test	51.8(±2.5)	69.2(±1.2)	68.2(±1.8)
1 virtual train + 3 real train + 1 real test	54.4(±2.9)	72.5(±4.1)	80.2(±4.5)
train on **mix** of **aligned** virtual and real – test on real **(metric learning)**			
Setting	DenseSift	MLBP	Color+MLBP
1 virtual train + 1 real train + 3 real test	43.2(±2.3)	62.4(±4.0)	64.1(±2.0)
1 virtual train + 2 real train + 2 real test	46.7(±2.5)	65.7(±1.3)	68.7(±2.6)
1 virtual train + 3 real train + 1 real test	50.9(±2.9)	71.8(±1.5)	74.7(±2.4)
train on **mix** of **aligned** virtual and real – test on real **(FE domain adaption)**			
Setting	Dense SIFT	MLBP	Color+MLBP
1 virtual train + 1 real train + 3 real test	47.8(±2.5)	59.3(±3.7)	59.8(±1.3)
1 virtual train + 2 real train + 2 real test	52.8(±2.4)	66.1(±1.9)	65.3(±1.0)
1 virtual train + 3 real train + 1 real test	55.2(±2.4)	70.9(±3.2)	72.8(±2.5)

4.2 Can We Recognize Real Materials from Rendered Examples?

The second and third block in Table 2 present our results training only on rendered examples from the VIPS database and evaluating on the real examples of the KTH TIPS database. The difference between the two is that the third block is using the described manifold alignment procedure. We can see that the alignment procedure increases the performance up to 11%. Overall, we observe that the MLBP features seems to cope better with this domain shift than the dense SIFT feature, leading to a performance of 43.7%. We hypothesize that the

Table 3. Example images of the new material database (VIPS) of rendered examples from material shaders on the left and corresponding examples from the KTH TIPS database on the right. Please note that these are only the canonical view points and both databases incorporate variations in scale, viewpoint and lighting.

New MPI-VIPS database of virtual materials			KTH-TIPS material database
texture	bump map	rendered sample	real samples

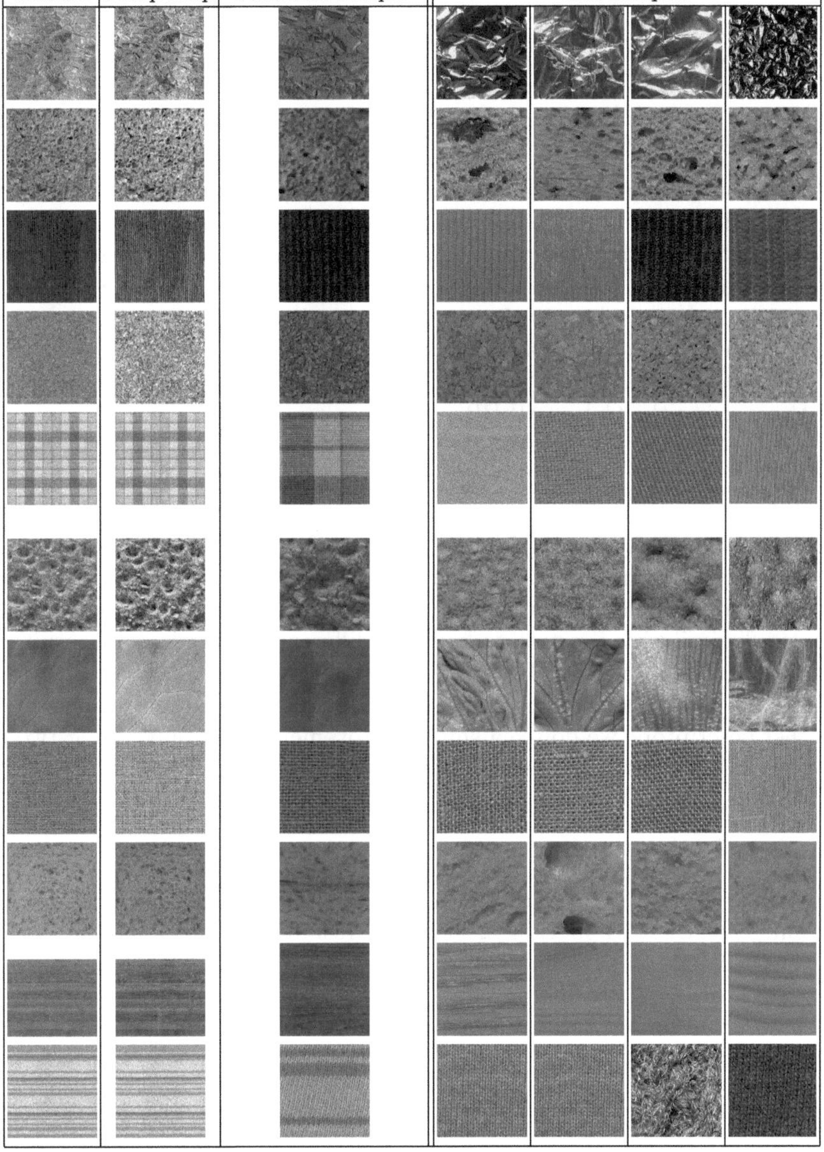

binary feature are more reliable to extract than the gradient values in the SIFT that might be easily effected by unrealistic reproduction of the materials. Adding color information degrades performance in this setting which calls for another alignment procedure to minimize those discrepancies between the domains which we leave for future work.

According the results, the conclusion must be that it is possible to recognize real materials from rendered ones. However, we realize that there is still a significant performance gap between the information we get from a real instance and a virtual one. The alignment step has proven critical to improve performance.

4.3 Mixing Real and Rendered Examples

In the rest of the experimental section we ask the questions if there are ways to combine real and rendered data in order to boost the performance. The 4th and 5th block of Table 2 show the results for a mixed training set of real and rendered examples – again with and without the alignment procedure. While the results without alignment either stay the same compared to training without rendered data or even decrease, we observe up to 7% improvement after alignment. The best performance of 80.2% is obtained for training on 1 rendered example and 3 real ones using the Color+MLBP.

4.4 Metric Learning

We also apply metric learning in an attempt to further bridge the gap between the virtual and real materials. Therefore we build on top aligned data. Similarity constraints are generated between the virtual and real materials of the same class and also dissimilarity constraints between different materials. The results are presented in the 6th block of Table 2. Again, the dense SIFT descriptor performs consistently worse and the metric learning doesn't provide improvements. On the other descriptors, we do see a small improvement when only one or two real materials are observed at training time.

4.5 Domain Adaptation

Lastly, we apply the "frustratingly easy" domain adaptation technique to this problem. The last block in Table 2 shows the results. The previous result is kind of reversed. While this method shows marginally increased performance for the dense SIFT descriptor when only one or two examples are available, no effect can be observed for the other two features.

5 Conclusions

We have presented a new database MPI-VIPS of rendered materials that allows to study the challenges when learning the appearance of real materials from or supported by rendered materials. We have shown the feasibility and present results indicating that LBP based features are more suited to this task as SIFT based representations. We further evaluate different approaches to deal with the appearance mismatch ranging from mixed training sets, data alignment, metric learning and domain adaptation. Our results suggest that an alignment of the two data sources is crucial and in combination with a kernel classifier trained on mixed real and rendered data we obtain a significant performance improvement of 7%.

Acknowledgments. Wenbin Li was supported by the scholarship from the Saarbrücken Graduate School of Computer Science, Saarland University.

References

1. Shotton, J., Fitzgibbon, A., Cook, M., Sharp, T., Finocchio, M., Moore, R., Kipmanand, A., Blake, A.: Real-time human pose recognition in parts from a single depth image. In: CVPR (2011)
2. Leung, T., Malik, J.: Representing and recognizing the visual appearance of materials using three-dimensional textons. IJCV 43, 29–44 (2001)
3. Varma, M., Zisserman, A.: A statistical approach to texture classification from single images. Int. J. Comput. Vision 62, 61–81 (2005)
4. Dana, K., van Ginneken, B.: Reflectance and texture of real-world surfaces. In: CVPR (1997)
5. Hayman, E., Caputo, B., Fritz, M., Eklundh, J.-O.: On the Significance of Real-World Conditions for Material Classification. In: Pajdla, T., Matas, J. (eds.) ECCV 2004. LNCS, vol. 3024, pp. 253–266. Springer, Heidelberg (2004)
6. Caputo, B., Hayman, E., Mallikarjuna, P.: Class-specific material categorisation. In: ICCV (2005)
7. Sharan, L., Rosenholtz, R., Adelson, E.H.: Material perception: What can you see in a brief glance? Journal of Vision (2009)
8. Liu, C., Sharan, L., Adelson, E.H., Rosenholtz, R.: Exploring features in a bayesian framework for material recognition. In: CVPR (2010)
9. Decoste, D., Schölkopf, B.: Training invariant support vector machines. Mach. Learn. 46, 161–190 (2002)
10. Enzweiler, M., Gavrila, D.M.: A mixed generative-discriminative framework for pedestrian classification. In: CVPR (2008)
11. Pishchulin, L., Jain, A., Wojek, C., Andriluka, M., Thormaehlen, T., Schiele, B.: Learning people detection models from few training samples. In: CVPR (2011)
12. Targhi, A.T., Geusebroek, J.M., Zisserman, A.: Texture classification with minimal training images. In: IEEE International Conference on Pattern Recognition (2008)
13. Lai, K., Fox, D.: 3D laser scan classification using web data and domain adaptation. In: Proceedings of Robotics: Science and Systems (2009)
14. Wohlkinger, W., Vincze, M.: 3D object classification for mobile robots in home-environments using web-data. In: International Conference on Cognitive Systems, CogSys (2010)
15. Stark, M., Goesele, M., Schiele, B.: Back to the future: Learning shape models from 3D cad data. In: BMVC (2010)
16. Kaneva, B., Torralba, A., Freeman, W.: Evaluation of image features using a photorealistic virtual world. In: ICCV (2011)

17. Saenko, K., Kulis, B., Fritz, M., Darrell, T.: Adapting Visual Category Models to New Domains. In: Daniilidis, K., Maragos, P., Paragios, N. (eds.) ECCV 2010, Part IV. LNCS, vol. 6314, pp. 213–226. Springer, Heidelberg (2010)
18. Kulis, B., Saenko, K., Darrell, T.: What you saw is not what you get: Domain adaptation using asymmetric kernel transforms. In: CVPR (2011)
19. Davis, J., Kulis, B., Jain, P., Sra, S., Dhillon, I.: Information-theoretic metric learning. In: ICML (2007)
20. Daumé III, H.: Frustratingly easy domain adaptation. In: Conference of the Association for Computational Linguistics, ACL (2007)
21. Ojala, T., Pietikäinen, M., Harwood, D.: A comparative study of texture measures with classification based on featured distributions. Pattern Recognition 29, 51–59 (1996)
22. Zhang, J., Marszałek, M., Lazebnik, S., Schmid, C.: Local features and kernels for classification of texture and object categories: a comprehensive study. IJCV 73, 213–238 (2007)
23. Chapelle, O., Haffner, P., Vapnik, V.: Svms for histogram-based image classification. IEEE Transactions on Neural Networks (1999)
24. Nillius, P., Eklundh, J.-O.: Classifying Materials from Their Reflectance Properties. In: Pajdla, T., Matas, J. (eds.) ECCV 2004. LNCS, vol. 3024, pp. 366–376. Springer, Heidelberg (2004)
25. Wang, O., Gunawardane, P., Scher, S., Davis, J.: Material classification using brdf slices. In: CVPR (2009)
26. Liu, L., Fieguth, P., Kuang, G., Zha, H.: Sorted random projections for robust texture classification. In: ICCV (2011)

Scene Recognition on the Semantic Manifold

Roland Kwitt[1], Nuno Vasconcelos[2], and Nikhil Rasiwasia[3]

[1] Kitware Inc., Carrboro, NC, USA
[2] Department of Electrical and Computer Engineering, UC San Diego, USA
[3] Yahoo Labs! Bangalore, India

Abstract. A new architecture, denoted *spatial pyramid matching on the semantic manifold* (SPMSM), is proposed for scene recognition. SPMSM is based on a recent image representation on a semantic probability simplex, which is now augmented with a rough encoding of spatial information. A connection between the semantic simplex and a Riemmanian manifold is established, so as to equip the architecture with a similarity measure that respects the manifold structure of the semantic space. It is then argued that the closed-form geodesic distance between two manifold points is a natural measure of similarity between images. This leads to a conditionally positive definite kernel that can be used with any SVM classifier. An approximation of the geodesic distance reveals connections to the well-known Bhattacharyya kernel, and is explored to derive an explicit feature embedding for this kernel, by simple square-rooting. This enables a low-complexity SVM implementation, using a linear SVM on the embedded features. Several experiments are reported, comparing SPMSM to state-of-the-art recognition methods. SPMSM is shown to achieve the best recognition rates in the literature for two large datasets (MIT Indoor and SUN) and rates equivalent or superior to the state-of-the-art on a number of smaller datasets. In all cases, the resulting SVM also has much smaller dimensionality and requires much fewer support vectors than previous classifiers. This guarantees much smaller complexity and suggests improved generalization beyond the datasets considered.

1 Introduction

The ability of humans to assign semantic labels (i.e., scene categories) to images, even at modest levels of attention [1], has motivated significant recent interest in image classification in computer vision (e.g., [2–7]). A popular image representation for this problem is the *bag-of-visual-features (BoF)*, an orderless collection of features extracted from the image at the nodes of an evenly-spaced grid [3]. This is used to learn a mid-level *theme* representation, which provides an image description at a higher level of abstraction. In many works [4, 8, 9], the mid-level representation consists of a codebook of *visual words*, learned in a fully unsupervised manner. The quantization of the BoF with this codebook produces a *bag-of-visual-words (BoW)* histogram, which is fed to a discriminant classifier, typically a variant of the support vector machine (SVM), for image classification. It has been shown that augmenting the BoW representation with a rough

A. Fitzgibbon et al. (Eds.): ECCV 2012, Part IV, LNCS 7575, pp. 359–372, 2012.

encoding of spatial information [4] and a non-linear kernel [10] can substantially boost recognition performance.

An alternative to the unsupervised theme space is to rely on *predefined* semantic themes. A set of themes is defined, a classifier trained for the detection of each theme, and each image fed to all theme classifiers. The image is finally represented by the vector of resulting classification labels. These could be binary, denoting presence/absence of the theme in the image, or graded, denoting the posterior probability of the theme given the image [11]. Since the graded representation contains all information necessary to derive the binary labels, it is the only one considered in this work. When compared to BoW, these approaches have several advantages. First, they produce a *semantic* theme space, i.e., a theme space whose coordinate axes correspond to semantic concepts. This space is usually denoted the *semantic space* (cf. [12]). It has been argued that relying on representations close to human scene understanding is as important as pure recognition accuracy [13]. Second, since the dimensionality of the semantic space is linear in the number of themes, this representation is much more compact than the high dimensional histograms required by BoW. Finally, while it has been argued that BoW lacks discriminative power [14], theme models are by definition discriminant. Hence, besides being more compact, semantic themes usually enable a more discriminative encoding of image content. When compared to BoW, the main limitation of the semantic theme representation is that theme models can lack generalization ability. This follows from the limited number of training images available per theme, much smaller than total training set size. The problem has been addressed in the literature, where different strategies have been suggested to tackle the discrimination vs. generalization trade-off, by adapting a general *background* model to the characteristics of each theme [15, 7]. A second limitation is that the theme-based representation has not been explored as extensively as the BoW. Although it could potentially benefit from the extensions developed for the latter, such as spatial information encoding and non-linear kernels, these have so far not been explored extensively. In some cases, e.g., kernel design, they are not straightforward, due to the fact that the semantic space is a *probability simplex*.

Besides classification accuracy, the computational complexity of image representations has been deemed increasingly important for image classification in the recent past. This is partly due to the emergence of large-scale benchmark datasets, such as *MIT Indoor* [5] or *SUN* [16]. In BoW methods, where recognition performance tends to increase with codebook size [17, 18], codebook generation quickly becomes a computational bottleneck. This is compounded by the need to train a kernelized classifier from a vast number of high dimensional BoW histograms. Finally, by multiplying the dimensionality of the BoW feature space by the number of spatial pyramid cells, the addition of the spatial pyramid structure of [4] can render the classification problem computationally intractable. Although the semantic space representation is much more compact than BoW, its combination with spatial encoding mechanisms and large theme vocabularies can also lead to large-scale learning problems. While in the BoW literature some authors have proposed explicit data embedding strategies [19, 20], which enable the replacement of non-linear by linear SVMs, greatly reducing computation, such embeddings are not yet available for theme-based representations.

Contribution. In this work, we address several of the current limitations of the semantic theme representation by *proposing extensions of spatial information encoding, kernel design, and data embeddings compatible with image representation on a probability simplex*. This is done through the following contributions. In Section 3.1, we introduce the probability simplex as a statistical manifold and leverage principles of information geometry to derive a novel non-linear kernel on that manifold. We then adapt the spatial pyramid structure of [4] to the semantic space. Following [4], we refer to this architecture, i.e., the combination of the new kernel and the underlying semantic theme representation, as *spatial pyramid matching on the semantic manifold (SPMSM)*. In Section 3.2, we further show that the Bhattacharyya kernel is an approximation to the geodesic distance on this manifold. This leads to an explicit feature embedding, which enables the use of linear SVMs on large-scale problems. Extensive experiments, reported in Section 4, demonstrate that image classification based on the proposed SPMSM has state-of-the-art performance on a number of datasets.

2 Mid-Level Theme Representation

We start by briefly reviewing the representation of [11]. This is based on a predefined collection $\mathcal{T}$ of M themes (e.g., *sky, grass, street*). Learning is weakly supervised from a training set of images I_j, each augmented by a binary caption vector $\boldsymbol{c}^j$. Weak supervision implies that a non-zero entry at the i-th position of $\boldsymbol{c}^j$ indicates that theme i is present in image j, but a zero entry does not necessarily imply that it is absent. Images are labeled with one or more themes, which could be drawn from the set of scene category labels $\mathcal{T}$ or from another label set (e.g., scene attributes). When theme labels are the image labels, $\boldsymbol{c}^j$ contains a single non-zero entry.

As in BoW, an image I_j is represented as a collection of visual features, in some feature space $\mathcal{X}$, i.e., $I_j = \{\boldsymbol{x}_i^j\}_{i=1}^N$. These features are extracted from N localized image patches P_i^j, $\boldsymbol{x}_i^j = f(P_i^j)$. The generative model that maps an image to the semantic space is shown in the *inference* part of Fig. 1: visual features are drawn independently from themes, and themes are drawn from a multinomial random variable of parameter vector $\boldsymbol{s}^j \in [0,1]^M$. The theme occurrences of image I_j are summarized in the theme occurrence vector $(o_1^j, \ldots, o_M^j)'$. The mutinomial parameters in $\boldsymbol{s}^j$ are inferred from $\{\boldsymbol{x}_i^j\}_{i=1}^N$ as follows (the image index j is omitted for brevity). First, the theme of largest posterior probability is found per $\boldsymbol{x}_i$, i.e., $t_i^* = q_b(\boldsymbol{x}_i)$ with

$$q_b(\boldsymbol{x}_i) = \arg\max_{t\in\mathcal{T}} P_{T|\mathbf{X}}(t|\boldsymbol{x}_i) = \arg\max_{t\in\mathcal{T}} \frac{P_{\mathbf{X}|T}(\boldsymbol{x}_i|t)}{\sum_w P_{\mathbf{X}|T}(\boldsymbol{x}_i|w)} \quad . \tag{1}$$

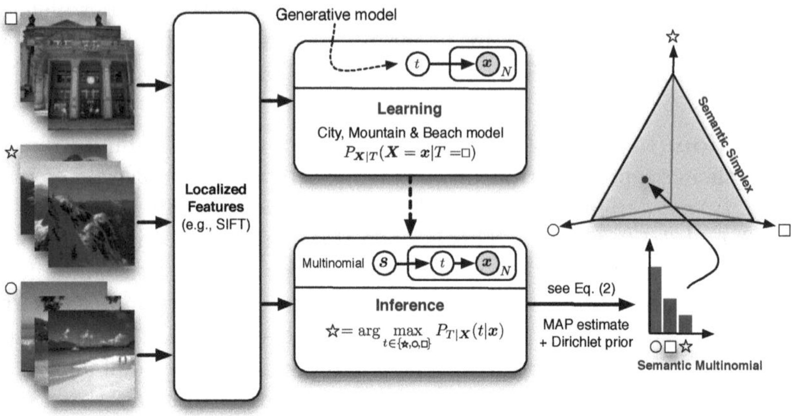

Fig. 1. Mapping of database images, represented by collections of visual features, to points on the semantic simplex (here $\mathbb{P}^2$)

This assumes equal prior probability for all themes, but could be easily extended for a non-uniform prior. The mapping $q_b : \mathcal{X} \to \mathcal{T}$ *quantizes* features into themes in a Bayesian, *minimum probability-of-error*, fashion. The occurrences $o_t = |\{i : t_i^* = t\}|$ of each theme t are then tallied to obtain the empirical theme occurrence vector. Finally, the MAP estimate of $\boldsymbol{s}$, for a Dirichlet prior of parameter α, is

$$\hat{\boldsymbol{s}} = \left(\frac{o_1 + \alpha - 1}{\sum_w (o_w + \alpha - 1)}, \ldots, \frac{o_M + \alpha - 1}{\sum_w (o_w + \alpha - 1)}\right)' \tag{2}$$

where α acts as a regularization parameter. In the terminology of [11], $\hat{\boldsymbol{s}}$ is denoted the *semantic multinomial (SMN)* of image I. This establishes the desired mapping $\Pi : \mathcal{X}^N \to \mathbb{P}^{M-1}$, $I \mapsto \boldsymbol{s}$ from an image represented in feature space to an image represented as a point on the *semantic (probability) simplex* $\mathbb{P}^{M-1}$.

Learning the mapping Π requires estimates of the theme-conditional distributions $P_{\boldsymbol{X}|T}(\boldsymbol{x}|t)$ from the available weakly-labeled image data. Since the theme label of *each* visual feature is not known, this is done with resort to multiple instance learning, based on the image formation model shown in the *learning* part of Fig. 1: visual features extracted from all images labeled with theme t are pooled into dataset $\mathcal{D}_t = \{\boldsymbol{x}_i^j | \boldsymbol{c}_t^j = 1\}$, which is then used to estimate $P_{\boldsymbol{X}|T}(\boldsymbol{x}|t)$. The intuition is that visual features representative of the semantic theme are more likely to occur in the training set and dominate the probability estimates. In multiple instance learning terminology, $\mathcal{D}_t$ is the *bag of positive examples* for theme t. Fig. 1 illustrates learning and inference on a three-category toy problem. Note that $\mathbb{P}^{M-1}$ serves as a new feature space for training a discriminant classifier.

3 Spatial Pyramid Matching on the Semantic Manifold

In this section we 1) introduce a statistical (semantic) manifold for image representation, 2) derive a suitable image matching kernel from the principles of information geometry and 3) augment the theme representation of the previous section with a commonly used encoding of spatial information.

3.1 The Semantic Manifold

To design a kernel for the SMN representation, one pragmatic strategy would be to choose a kernel which computes l_2 distances in feature space [18, 9], e.g., the classic RBF kernel. This, however, implicitly assumes a flat Euclidean geometry and ignores the actual geometry of the SMN data on the semantic simplex. One alternative that achieves better classification performance for BoW is the spatial pyramid match kernel (SPMK) of [10, 4], which replaces the l_2 norm by the histogram intersection (HI) metric. This, and the introduction of computationally efficient approximations [19], have made SPMK the prevalent kernel for the BoW representation.

To design a kernel suited for the SMN representation, we study the semantic simplex $\mathbb{P}^{M-1}$ in more detail. Since SMNs are parameter vectors of multinomial distributions, we equate similarity between two SMNs as the *distance* among the two associated multinomial distributions. From information geometry, it is known that $\mathbb{P}^{M-1}$ is a *Riemannian manifold*[1] if endowed with the Fisher information metric $\mathcal{I}$ (cf. [21, 22]). Hence, the distance among two SMNs $\boldsymbol{s}$ and $\boldsymbol{s}^*$ can be computed as the geodesic distance $d_{\mathcal{I}}(\boldsymbol{s}, \boldsymbol{s}^*)$ on this multinomial manifold. Although geodesics are in general hard to compute, it is possible to exploit the isomorphism $F : \mathbb{P}^{M-1} \to \mathbb{S}_+^{M-1}, \quad \boldsymbol{s} \mapsto 2\sqrt{\boldsymbol{s}}$ between the manifolds $(\mathbb{P}^{M-1}, \mathcal{I})$ and $(\mathbb{S}_+^{M-1}, \delta)$, where $\mathbb{S}_+^{M-1}$ is the positive portion of a sphere of radius two and δ denotes the Euclidean metric inherited from embedding $\mathbb{S}_+^{M-1}$ in $\mathbb{R}^M$. The isometry enables the computation of $d_{\mathcal{I}}$ as the arc on the great-circle connecting $F(\boldsymbol{s})$ and $F(\boldsymbol{s}^*)$ on the sphere, i.e.,

$$d_{\mathcal{I}}(\boldsymbol{s}, \boldsymbol{s}^*) = d_{\delta}(F(\boldsymbol{s}), F(\boldsymbol{s}^*)) = 2 \arccos(\langle \sqrt{\boldsymbol{s}}, \sqrt{\boldsymbol{s}^*} \rangle) \ . \tag{3}$$

Since $\mathbb{P}^{M-1}$ is denoted the semantic simplex, we refer to $(\mathbb{P}^{M-1}, \mathcal{I})$ as the associated *semantic manifold*. It is worth mentioning that the Hellinger distance $d_H(\boldsymbol{s}, \boldsymbol{s}^*) = 2\sin(d_{\mathcal{I}}(\boldsymbol{s}, \boldsymbol{s}^*)/4)$ and the Kullback-Leibler (KL) divergence are identical to $d_{\mathcal{I}}$ up to second order as $\boldsymbol{s} \to \boldsymbol{s}^*$ [23]. The KL divergence was previously used as a similarity measure between SMNs, in a retrieval context [12], but without exploring the connections to information geometry.

These connections are particularly important for kernel design, where the metric determines the properties of the kernel. For example, the KL divergence is not symmetric and does not guarantee a positive definite kernel [24]. On

[1] A technical issue is to ensure, by (2), that SMN components are positive to guarantee that $\mathbb{P}^{M-1}$ is actually a manifold [21].

the other hand, it is known that 1) the negative of the geodesic distance $-d_{\mathcal{I}}$ satisfies all properties of a *conditionally positive definite (cpd)* kernel [22], and 2) cpd kernels can be used in any SVM classifier [25]. Consequently, we define the *semantic kernel* on the semantic manifold as

$$k(\boldsymbol{s}, \boldsymbol{s}^*) := -d_{\mathcal{I}}(\boldsymbol{s}, \boldsymbol{s}^*) \quad \boldsymbol{s}, \boldsymbol{s}^* \in \mathbb{P}^{M-1}. \tag{4}$$

As a matter of fact, the *information-diffusion kernel* of [26], specialized to the multinomial family, is an exponential (squared) variant, i.e., $\exp(-d_{\mathcal{I}}^2)$, of (4). Given a smooth-parametrization of (4), we could also leverage the work of [27], where the authors propose an adaption to SVM learning that optimizes smoothly-parametrized kernels on the simplex. While the semantic kernel might potentially benefit from those advances, we have not explored that direction in this work.

Spatial Pyramid Encoding. It is now well established that augmenting the BoW representations with a rough encoding of spatial information, by means of a *spatial pyramid* [4, 28, 9], leads to significant gains in image classification. The extension of this idea to the SMN representation is quite straightforward. It suffices to compute a SMN for each of the spatial pyramid cells. Note that this introduces a *localized* semantic representation, which captures many attributes of human scene understanding. More precisely, the global SMN at pyramid level 0 captures the semantic *gist* of the image, e.g., "mostly about grass, sky, and mountains", while SMNs at higher levels *localize* this description to each spatial pyramid cell, e.g., "mostly grass in bottom cells, mostly sky in upper cells, mostly mountains in between". In this way, spatial cells at finer grid resolutions are more informative of local semantics and exhibit less ambiguity (cf. [13]). The structure of the SMN representation and the procedure used to estimate SMNs also enable the computation of the pyramid cell SMNs in a very efficient manner. In fact, it suffices to compute the SMNs of the pyramid cells at the finest grid resolution. The SMN of index n at the overlying pyramid level l can then be directly inferred from its four child-cell SMNs $\{\boldsymbol{s}_{l+1,4n+i}\}_{i=0}^3$, at level $l+1$, by computing the convex combination $\boldsymbol{s}_{l,n} = 1/4 \cdot (\boldsymbol{s}_{l+1,4n} + \cdots + \boldsymbol{s}_{l+1,4n+3})$. In other words, the SMN of one spatial pyramid cell at level l lies in the *convex hull* spanned by its four child-cell SMNs at the next finer level. In total, there are $1/3 \cdot (4^L - 1)$ SMNs per image, for a spatial pyramid with L levels.

In order to incorporate spatial constraints in the classification, it is possible to combine the semantic kernel with the spatial pyramid structure, in a way similar to [4]. This consists of 1) assigning more weight to matches at finer pyramid resolutions and 2) normalizing the geodesic distances at one pyramid level by the number of grid cells at that level. Given two images I_a and I_b, represented by their concatenated SMNs $\boldsymbol{\alpha}$ and $\boldsymbol{\beta}$, the *semantic spatial pyramid match kernel (SSPMK)* is defined as

$$k(\boldsymbol{\alpha}, \boldsymbol{\beta}) = -\sum_{l=0}^{L-1} w_l \sum_{n=0}^{4^l} d_{\mathcal{I}}(\varphi_{l,n}(\boldsymbol{\alpha}), \varphi_{l,n}(\boldsymbol{\beta})) \tag{5}$$

with $w_l := \tilde{w}_l \bar{w}_l$, where $\tilde{w}_l = {}^1\!/_{4^l}$ denotes the *normalization* weight at level l and $\bar{w}_l = 2^{-(L+l)}$ denotes the corresponding *matching* weight. Note that we used $\varphi_{l,n}(\boldsymbol{\alpha}) = \boldsymbol{s}_{l,n}$ to denote the extraction of $\boldsymbol{s}_{l,n}$ from a concatenated SMN vector $\boldsymbol{\alpha}$. Since (5) is a weighted sum of semantic kernels, and the closure property for weighted sums of positive definite kernels extends to the family of cpd kernels [25], the SSPMK is a cpd kernel.

3.2 Data Embedding

Given the SMN representation, it remains to train an SVM classifier. For small-scale datasets, it is feasible to learn a non-linear SVM, albeit the training complexity is somewhere between quadratic and cubic [20]. In general, however, non-linear SVMs do not scale well with training set size. On large-scale problems, linear SVMs are overwhelmingly preferred due to their efficient (i.e., linear-time) training algorithms. The question is how to rely on a linear SVM, but still somehow exploit the power of the SSPMK. Ideally, it would be possible to derive an explicit SMN embedding that preserves the advantages of the geodesic distance. The training of a non-linear SVM for SMN classification could then be reduced to training a linear SVM on the embedded features. Unfortunately, exact embeddings are rarely available. Although approximations are possible, these usually entail a loss in recognition performance.

While a popular embedding exists for the HI kernel [19], it exploits the additivity property of the kernel. Since the semantic kernel of (4) is not additive, neither the embedding of [19], nor the embedding learning method of [20] are feasible. One alternative, that we explore, is to replace the arccos term by a first-order Taylor series around 0, i.e., $\arccos(x) \approx {}^{\pi}\!/_{2} - x + \mathcal{O}(x)^2$. This leads to the approximation of (4) by

$$k(\boldsymbol{s}, \boldsymbol{s}^*) \approx -\pi + \langle \sqrt{\boldsymbol{s}}, \sqrt{\boldsymbol{s}^*} \rangle \quad \boldsymbol{s}, \boldsymbol{s}^* \in \mathbb{P}^{M-1} \ . \tag{6}$$

Notably, the dot-product on the right-hand side is the additive Bhattacharyya kernel of [20]. Although, a linear approximation can be coarse, the ability to immediately read the explicit data embedding $\phi(x) = \sqrt{x}$ is appealing, since it entails almost no computational cost. Finally, taking the spatial pyramid structure into account, the extended embedding for the n-th SMN at pyramid level l can be written as

$$\phi(\boldsymbol{s}_{n,l}) = \sqrt{w_l \boldsymbol{s}_{n,l}} \ . \tag{7}$$

While the Bhattacharyya kernel has previously been used in image classification (cf. [29]), its practical success now has another principled justification due to the close relationship with the geodesic distance.

4 Experiments

In this section, we report on a number of experiments designed to evaluate the classification accuracy of the proposed SPMSM architecture, i.e., the combination of the SMN representation of (2) and the SSMPK of (5).

4.1 Datasets and Implementation

Three popular, yet rather small, benchmark datasets and two recent mid- to large-scale datasets were used in our recognition experiments. The smaller ones are the *LabelMe* [2], UIUC *Sports* [30] and *15 Scenes (N15)* [3, 4] datasets. For mid- to large-scale experiments, we used the *MIT Indoor* [5] scenes and the *SUN* [16] dataset. We use the prevalent training/testing configurations in the literature. Recognition rates on *LabelMe*, *Sports* and *N15* were averaged over three test runs with random training/testing splits. In the case of *MIT Indoor* and *SUN*, the training/testing configurations are provided by the original authors. All images were converted to grayscale and resized to have maximum dimension of 256 pixels (while maintaining the aspect ratio).

The appearance representation was based on SIFT[2] descriptors [31], computed on an evenly-spaced 4×4 pixel grid. 128-component Gaussian mixtures of diagonal covariance were used to model theme distributions, and mixture parameters estimated with the EM algorithm (initialized by K-Means++). We chose a directed mixture parameter estimation approach in contrast to the hierarchical estimation procedure employed in [12, 11]. All experiments involving spatial pyramids relied on three pyramid levels. Further refinements did not produce improvements, confirming the findings of [4]. For the tests on *LabelMe*, *Sports*, *N15* and *MIT Indoor*, we used the LIBSVM [32] implementation of a C-SVM and a 1-vs-1 multi-class classification strategy. On feature embedding experiments, we relied on LIBLINEAR [33] to train a linear SVM and switched from 1-vs-1 to 1-vs-all multi-class classification, for performance reasons. The SVM cost factor C was determined by three-fold cross-validation on the training data, evaluated at 20 linearly spaced positions of $\log C \in [-2, 4]$.

4.2 Evaluation

Semantic Kernel. The first set of experiments was designed to evaluate the semantic kernel of (4). In all cases, the image representation was the SMN of (2). We started with a comparison to two popular kernels in the literature: HI (k_{HI}), and χ^2 (k_{χ^2}). The kernel definitions are given in Table 1 for two input vectors $\boldsymbol{x}, \boldsymbol{y} \in [0, 1]^M$. It is worth noting that SVM training with one of these kernels only requires tuning of the cost factor C, whereas RBF variants require tuning of the kernel width as well. The table presents the recognition accuracies obtained on *Sports*, *LabelMe* and *N15*. The semantic kernel achieves the highest average rate on all datasets. This illustrates the benefits of adopting a kernel which is tailored to the manifold structure of the semantic space.

Spatial Pyramid Encoding. We next considered the full SPMSM architecture, by augmenting the semantic kernel with SPM. This was compared to the standard implementation of SPM with the kernels of the previous experiment. Results are listed in Table 1. Two conclusions are possible from the table. First,

[2] LEAR impl.: `http://lear.inrialpes.fr/people/dorko/downloads.html`

Table 1. Comparison of the semantic kernel to the HI (k_{HI}) and the χ^2 kernel (k_{χ^2}) *without* and *with* SPM

Kernel Type	**without** SPM			**with** SPM		
	Sports	*LabelMe*	*N15*	*Sports*	*Labelme*	*N15*
Proposed, see (4), (5)	**79.1**	**84.7**	**79.1**	**83.0**	**87.5**	**82.3**
$k_{\chi^2}, \sum_i \frac{x_i y_i}{(x_i+y_i)}$	78.6	84.6	78.9	81.6	86.2	81.0
$k_{HI}, \sum_i \min(x_i, y_i)$	77.8	84.1	78.6	81.8	87.0	82.0

the addition of the spatial pyramid structure does not change the relative performances of the kernels: the gap in recognition performance between SPM with k_{HI} and SPMSM is similar to that between the HI (k_{HI}) and the semantic kernel when omitting SPM. Second, the results are consistent with previous reports on the benefits of spatial information encoding [4]. Comparing the results *with* and *without* SPM shows that, for the SSPMK, this gain is around three to four percentage points. In addition, we remark that training with a RBF kernel, optimizing the cost factor and kernel width on a 2-D grid, exhibits performance similar to the worst result per kernel on each database of Table 1 (with and without SPM). This underpins the assertion (cf. [34, 27]) that kernels which are effective in Euclidean space (like RBF) are not necessarily effective in another space, such as the semantic manifold.

Data Embedding. Finally, we evaluated the semantic kernel approximation of Section 3.2 and the square-root embedding of (6). This was compared to the popular HI kernel embedding of [19] and to a linear SVM *without* any embedding, i.e., applied directly to the SMNs. The comparison to [19] was performed against the sparse ϕ_2 embedding[3] (denoted as ϕ_2^s in the original work) with ten discrete levels. Table 2 lists the recognition rates on all datasets, without spatial pyramid matching. A few conclusions are possible from the table. First, the advantages of using the kernel+embedding combination are not very significant for small datasets. In fact, [19] underperformed the linear SVM without embedding on semantic space, on all three small datasets. While the square-root embedding outperformed the latter, the gains were relatively small. Second, a different picture emerges for the large datasets, where both embeddings outperformed the SVM without embedding. Again, the square-root embedding achieved the best performance, now with non-trivial gains over the two other approaches. Third, the square-root embedding outperformed the embedding of [19], preserving the advantages of the semantic kernel on all datasets. Finally, although there is a drop in recognition rate when compared to Table 1, this drop is small (about one to two percentage points). We believe that the computational savings associated with a linear SVM far outweigh this slight loss in recognition performance.

Comparing to Bag-of-Words. This set of experiments was designed to compare SPMSM to the combination of BoW and SPM, which can be considered a

[3] Available from `http://www.cs.berkeley.edu/~smaji/projects/add-models/`

Table 2. Comparison (*without* SPM) of the proposed feature embedding to that of [19] and no embedding

Dataset	Embedding Variant		
	Maji & Berg [19]	Proposed	Without
Sports	76.9	**77.8**	77.1
LabelMe	83.0	**84.3**	84.0
N15	76.8	**77.3**	77.0
MIT Indoor	32.2	**33.7**	31.9
SUN	23.1	**24.3**	22.0

de-facto standard for image classification. However, the comparison turned out not to be straightforward. For example, it is well known that the performance of BoW methods increases with codebook size. This is, in significant part, due to the associated increase in the dimensionality of the SVM that ultimately classifies the images. In general, the performance of an SVM improves with the dimensionality of its input, as long as the latter remains in a reasonable range. The problem is that SPMSM and BoW+SPM can have very different SVM dimensionalities.

Without the spatial pyramid structure, this dimensionality equals the number of themes, for SMN, and the number of codewords, for BoW. With the spatial pyramid, these numbers are multiplied by the number of spatial pyramid cells, which is 21 for three pyramid levels. Since there are as many themes as scene category labels, SPMSM has a fixed SVM dimensionality. On the other hand, it is always possible to increase the codebook size of BoW. While this suggests using SPMSM as a reference, its dimensionality is usually too low for BoW+SPM, which performs quite poorly for codebook cardinalities equivalent to the number of scene categories. An alternative would be to increase the dimensionality of SPMSM, e.g., by replacing the hard assignment of (1) with a histogram of the posterior probabilities $P_{T|\mathbf{X}}(t|\boldsymbol{x}_i)$ for each theme t.

We have not considered such possibilities, simply measuring the recognition rate of BoW+SPM for various values of the codebook size. The recognition rates are shown in Table 3. Rates higher than those achieved by SPMSM are marked in bold, whereas rates at *equivalent dimensionality* are underlined. It is clear that BoW+SPM requires a much higher dimensionality than SPMSM, for equivalent performance. For the datasets considered, the ratio of dimensionalities is ≈ 30. While this may not be a problem for the small corpora that are commonly used in the literature, e.g., the eight category *LabelMe* or *Sports* datatsets, it can be much more problematic for richer corpora, such as *MIT Indoor* or *SUN*. Even on the modestly sized *N15* dataset, SPM+BoW requires a codebook of size 512 to guarantee a minor gain over SPMSM. This corresponds to a SVM of $512 \times 21 = 10,752$ dimensional input, as opposed to the $15 \times 21 = 315$ dimensions of SPMSM. From the trend in Table 3, the aforementioned threshold would likely occur at $43,008$ dimensions for *MIT Indoor*. Since this exceeds the capacity of

Table 3. Recognition rate of BoW+SPM, for varying codebook sizes. Results higher than those achieved by SPMSM (shown at the bottom) are marked bold; results at *equal SVM dimensionality* are underlined. Numbers in parentheses denote the percentage of the training examples selected as support vectors.

Codebook	Dataset			
	LabelMe	*Sports*	*N15*	*MIT Indoor*
8	<u>74.0</u> (74)	<u>64.8</u> (87)	63.0 (89)	19.1 (98)
16	78.8 (75)	69.3 (88)	<u>69.7</u> (89)	25.3 (98)
32	82.9 (75)	77.7 (88)	73.6 (89)	32.6 (98)
64	85.9 (75)	80.4 (89)	77.9 (89)	<u>36.2</u> (99)
128	87.4 (77)	81.4 (90)	80.8 (90)	38.8 (99)
256	**88.0** (79)	**83.6** (91)	81.7 (91)	41.0 (99)
512	**88.6** (82)	**84.7** (92)	**83.1** (93)	43.6 (99)
SPMSM	87.5(57)	83.0 (67)	82.3 (74)	**44.0**(95)

the SVM package that we have used in these experiments we could not even confirm if BoW+SPM can actually outperform SPMSM (dimensionality 1,407) on this dataset.

Another factor that confounds the comparison of the two approaches is the type of support vectors that they produce. In fact, the percentage of examples that an SVM chooses as support vectors is a well known measure of the difficulty of the classification, and the degree to which the classifier is "overfitting to the dataset", i.e., modeling the intricacies of the particular dataset where performance is evaluated, rather than learning a truly generic decision rule. The numbers in parenthesis in Table 3 show the support vector percentages of BoW+SPM, for various codebook sizes, and SPMSM. Note that the percentages are indeed higher for the datasets of lower recognition rate. It is also clear that, on the harder datasets, the BoW+SPM SVM considers virtually every training example a support vector. The fact that the SPMSM SVM achieves near equivalent recognition rates with much smaller support vector percentages indicates that the classification is much *easier* on the semantic manifold. Hence, SPMSM is likely to generalize much better if applied to data collected from other sources.

In summary, on the large datasets considered, SPMSM has state-of-the-art performance. On the remaining, its performance is superior to that of BoW+SPM, by a large margin, for SVMs of equivalent dimensionality. On all datasets, it took BoW+SPM a 30-fold increase in dimensionality to achieve results similar to those of SPMSM, if at all. The percentages of examples selected as support vectors also suggest that classification is much simpler on the semantic manifold, and that SPMSM is likely to generalize better to unseen datasets. Computationally, since SVM complexity is linear on the *product* of the number of support vectors and dimensionality, the SPMSM SVM is significantly less challenging to implement.

Comparing to the State-of-the-Art. Finally, we compare SPMSM to the state-of-the-art in the literature. An overview of the recognition rates of various methods is given in Table 4. Note that a direct comparison of the different

Table 4. Comparison to the state-of-the-art

Dataset	State-of-the-Art	Rate [%]
	Li & Fei-Fei [30]	73.4
Sports	**Proposed**	83.0
	Wu & Rehg [28]	**84.3**
	Wang et al. [35]	76.0
LabelMe	Dixit et al. [7]	86.9
	Proposed	**87.5**
	Lazebnik et al. [4]	81.2
N15	**Proposed**	82.3
	Dixit et al. [7]	**85.4**
	Quattoni & Torralba [5]	25.0
MIT Indoor	Pandey & Lazebnik [36]	43.1
	Proposed	**44.0**
SUN	Xiao et al. [16]	27.2
	Proposed	**28.9**

dentaloffice 42.9 57.1 **(14.2)**
stairscase 30.0 35.0 **(5)**
children_room 5.6 44.4 **(38.8)**
hospital_room 35.0 35.0 (0)
closet 38.9 77.8 **(38.9)**
bar 22.2 38.9 **(16.7)**
warehouse 9.5 33.3 **(23.8)**
grocerystore 38.1 42.9 **(4.8)**
buffet 55.0 65.0 **(10)**
classroom 50.0 50.0 (0)
inside_subway 23.8 71.4 **(47.6)**
corridor 38.1 57.1 **(19)**
jewelleryshop 0.0 27.3 **(27.3)**
prisoncell 10.0 45.0 **(35)**
operating_room 10.5 31.6 **(21.1)**
pool_inside 25.0 50.0 **(25)**
hairsalon 9.5 33.3 **(23.8)**
locker_room 38.1 38.1 (0)
elevator 61.9 66.7 **(4.8)**
concert_hall 45.0 55.0 **(10)**
restaurant_kitchen 4.3 30.4 **(26.1)**
gameroom 25.0 30.0 **(5)**

bookstore 20.0 55.0 **(35)**
inside_bus 39.1 60.9 **(21.8)**
auditorium 55.6 55.6 (0)
kindergarden 5.0 55.0 **(50)**
lobby 10.0 25.0 **(15)**
deli 21.1 15.8 (-5.3)
computerroom 44.4 50.0 **(5.6)**
videostore 27.3 36.4 **(9.1)**
movietheater 15.0 45.0 **(30)**
trainstation 35.0 75.0 **(40)**
museum 4.3 21.7 **(17.4)**
clothingstore 22.2 44.4 **(22.2)**
mall 0.0 20.0 **(20)**
kitchen 23.8 47.6 **(23.8)**
dining_room 16.7 27.8 **(11.1)**
bathroom 33.3 33.3 (0)
church_inside 63.2 68.4 **(5.2)**
meeting_room 9.1 31.8 **(22.7)**
restaurant 5.0 30.0 **(25)**
nursery 35.0 47.4 **(12.4)**
toystore 13.6 40.9 **(27.3)**
shoeshop 5.3 21.1 **(15.8)**
pantry 25.0 65.0 **(40)**

livingroom 15.0 10.0 (-5)
bowling 45.0 75.0 **(30)**
tv_studio 27.8 50.0 **(22.2)**
library 40.0 50.0 **(10)**
bakery 15.8 31.6 **(15.8)**
studiomusic 36.8 36.8 (0)
florist 36.8 73.7 **(36.9)**
gym 27.8 22.2 (-5.6)
cloister 45.0 80.0 **(35)**
greenhouse 50.0 70.0 **(20)**
waitingroom 19.0 19.0 (0)
bedroom 14.3 47.6 **(33.3)**
laboratorywet 0.0 40.9 **(40.9)**
winecellar 23.8 28.6 **(4.8)**
casino 21.1 57.9 **(36.8)**
office 0.0 38.1 **(38.1)**
fastfood_restaurant 23.5 64.7 **(41.2)**
airport_inside 10.0 10.0 (0)
laundromat 31.8 40.9 **(9.1)**
artstudio 10.0 25.0 **(15)**
subway 9.5 42.9 **(33.4)**
garage 27.8 55.6 **(27.8)**

Fig. 2. Detailed comparison of the recognition performance of SPMSM and the baseline of [5] on *MIT Indoor*. The difference is given in parentheses. Scenes where SPMSM performs worse are marked red (best viewed in color).

methods is not totally fair, since they differ along many dimensions, not just the kernel. In fact, many of the BoW enhancements at the core of these methods could be applied to the SPMSM. Nevertheless, the results of SPMSM classification are excellent: to the best of our knowledge, the proposed classifier has the highest published rates on the large- and mid-scale datasets (*SUN* and *MIT Indoor*), and one of the small-scale ones (*LabelMe*). On *MIT Indoor*, it substantially outperforms the baseline of [5], and does slightly better than the previous best approach of [36]. A detailed comparison to [5] is shown in Fig. 2. The improvements are distributed across all indoor scene categories: there are only 11 classes where SPMSM performs at a similar or worse level. With respect to the remaining datasets, *Sports* and *N15*, SPMSM outperforms the baseline and achieves results competitive with the best in both cases. Note, for example, that the best method on *N15* [7] specifically addresses the generalization ability of theme models, through model adaptation techniques. Since these techniques could equally be used to improve the theme models of SPMSM, the two methods are *complementary,* not competitors. We plan to include model adaptation in SPMSM in future work.

Acknowledgements. This work was supported, in part, by the NIH/NIBIB grant "National Alliance of Medical Image Computing" (1U54EB005149), the NIH/NCI grant "Image Registration for Ultrasound-Based Neurosurgical Navigation" (1R01CA138419) and the NSF award CCF-0830535.

References

1. Fei-Fei, L., Van Rullen, R., Koch, C., Perona, P.: Rapid natural scene categorization in the near absence of attention. PNAS 99, 9566–9601 (1999)
2. Olivia, A., Torralba, A.: Modeling the shape of a scene: A holistic representation of the spatial envelope. IJCV 42, 145–175 (2001)
3. Fei-Fei, L., Perona, P.: A bayesian hierarchical model for learning natural scene categories. In: CVPR (2005)
4. Lazebnik, S., Schmid, C., Ponce, J.: Beyond bags of features: Spatial pyramid matching for recognizing scene categories. In: CVPR (2006)
5. Quattoni, A., Torralba, A.: Recognizing indoor scenes. In: CVPR (2009)
6. Li, L.J., Su, H., Xing, E., Fei-Fei, L.: Object bank: A high-level image representation for scene classification & semantic feature sparsification. In: NIPS (2010)
7. Dixit, M., Rasiwasia, N., Vasconcelos, N.: Adapted gaussian mixtures for image classification. In: CVPR (2011)
8. Bosch, A., Zisserman, A., Munoz, X.: Image classification with random forests and ferns. In: ICCV (2007)
9. Wu, J., Rehg, J.: CENTRIST: A visual descriptor for scene categorization. PAMI 33, 1489–1501 (2011)
10. Grauman, K., Darrell, T.: Pyramid match kernels: Discriminative classification with sets of image features. In: ICCV (2005)
11. Rasiwasia, N., Vasconcelos, N.: Scene classification with low-dimensional semantic spaces and weak supervision. In: CVPR (2008)
12. Rasiwasia, N., Moreno, P., Vasconcelos, N.: Bridging the gap: Query by semantic example. IEEE Trans. Multimedia 9, 923–938 (2007)
13. Schwaninger, A., Vogel, J., Hofer, F., Schiele, B.: A psychophysically plausible model for typicality ranking of natural scenes. ACM Trans. Appl. Percept. 3, 333–353 (2006)
14. Boiman, O., Shechtman, E., Irani, M.: In defense of nearest-neighbor based image classification. In: CVPR (2008)
15. Perronnin, F.: Universal and adapted vocabularies for generic visual categorization. PAMI 30, 1243–1256 (2008)
16. Xiao, J., Hayes, J., Ehringer, K., Olivia, A., Torralba, A.: SUN database: Large-scale scene recognition from Abbey to Zoo. In: CVPR (2010)

17. Nowak, E., Jurie, F., Triggs, B.: Sampling Strategies for Bag-of-Features Image Classification. In: Leonardis, A., Bischof, H., Pinz, A. (eds.) ECCV 2006, Part IV. LNCS, vol. 3954, pp. 490–503. Springer, Heidelberg (2006)
18. Csurka, G., Dance, C., Fan, L., Willamowski, J., Bray, C.: Visual categorization with bags of keypoints. In: Proceedings of the International Workshop on Statistical Learning in Computer Vision (2004)
19. Maji, S., Berg, A.: Max-margin additive classifiers for detection. In: ICCV (2009)
20. Perronnin, F.: Large-scale image categorization with explicit data embedding. In: CVPR (2010)
21. Lebanon, G.: Riemannian Geometry and Statistical Machine Learning. PhD thesis, Carnegie Mellon University (2005)
22. Zhang, D., Chen, X., Lee, W.: Text classification with kernels on the multinomial manifold. In: ACM SIGIR (2005)
23. Kaas, R.: The geometry of asymptotic inference. Stat. Sci. 4, 188–219 (1989)
24. Moreno, P., Ho, P., Vasconcelos, N.: A Kullback-Leibler divergence based kernel for SVM classification in multimedia applications. In: NIPS (2003)
25. Schölkopf, B., Smola, A.: Learning with Kernels: Support Vector Machines, Regularization, Optimization, and Beyond. MIT Press, Cambridge (2001)
26. Lafferty, J., Lebanon, G.: Diffusion kernels on statistical manifolds. JMLR 6, 129–163 (2005)
27. Ablavsky, V., Sclaroff, S.: Learning parameterized histogram kernels on the simplex manifold for image and action classification. In: ICCV (2011)
28. Wu, J., Rehg, J.: Beyond the euclidean distance: Creating effective visual codebooks using the histogram intersection kernel. In: ICCV (2009)
29. Zhou, X., Yu, K., Zhang, T., Huang, T.S.: Image Classification Using Super-Vector Coding of Local Image Descriptors. In: Daniilidis, K., Maragos, P., Paragios, N. (eds.) ECCV 2010, Part V. LNCS, vol. 6315, pp. 141–154. Springer, Heidelberg (2010)
30. Li, L.J., Fei-Fei, L.: What, where and who? classifying events by scene and object recognition. In: ICCV (2007)
31. Lowe, D.: Distinctive image features from scale-invariant keypoints. IJCV 60, 91–110 (2004)
32. Chang, C.C., Lin, C.J.: LIBSVM: A library for support vector machines. ACM TIST 2, 1–27 (2011)
33. Fan, R.E., Chang, K.W., Hsieh, C.J., Wang, X.R., Lin, C.J.: LIBLINEAR: A library for large linear classification. JMLR 9, 1871–1874 (2008)
34. Chapelle, O., Haffner, P., Vapnik, V.: Support vector machines for histogram-based image classification. IEEE Trans. Neural Netw. 10, 1055–1064 (1999)
35. Wang, C., Blei, D., Fei-Fei, L.: Simultaneous image classification and annotation. In: CVPR (2009)
36. Pandey, M., Lazebnik, S.: Scene recognition and weakly supervised object localization with deformable part-based models. In: ICCV (2011)

Unsupervised Temporal Commonality Discovery

Wen-Sheng Chu, Feng Zhou, and Fernando De la Torre

Robotics Institute, Carnegie Mellon University

Abstract. Unsupervised discovery of commonalities in images has recently attracted much interest due to the need to find correspondences in large amounts of visual data. A natural extension, and a relatively unexplored problem, is how to discover common semantic temporal patterns in videos. That is, given two or more videos, find the subsequences that contain similar visual content in an unsupervised manner. We call this problem Temporal Commonality Discovery (TCD). The naive exhaustive search approach to solve the TCD problem has a computational complexity quadratic with the length of each sequence, making it impractical for regular-length sequences. This paper proposes an efficient branch and bound (B&B) algorithm to tackle the TCD problem. We derive tight bounds for classical distances between temporal bag of words of two segments, including ℓ_1, intersection and χ^2. Using these bounds the B&B algorithm can efficiently find the global optimal solution. Our algorithm is general, and it can be applied to any feature that has been quantified into histograms. Experiments on finding common facial actions in video and human actions in motion capture data demonstrate the benefits of our approach. To the best of our knowledge, this is the first work that addresses unsupervised discovery of common events in videos.

Keywords: Temporal bag of words, branch and bound, temporal commonality discovery.

1 Introduction

Unsupervised discovery of visual patterns in images has been a long standing computer vision problem driven by applications to cosegmentation [8,15,20], learning grammars of images [34], detecting irregularity [6] and automatic tagging [23]. Although recently there has been several work on unsupervised discovery of visual patterns in images, a relatively unexplored problem in computer vision is to discover common temporal patterns among video sequences. For instance, given two or more videos, finding the segments that contain common human actions. Fig. 1 illustrates the main problem addressed in this paper. Given two videos from "*As Good As It Gets*" and "*Indiana Jones And The Last Crusade*", this paper proposes an unsupervised method to find multiple subsequences that share similar semantic contents (*e.g.*, *Kissing* or *Handshake*). Through the paper, we will refer to this problem as Temporally Commonality Discovery (TCD).

A. Fitzgibbon et al. (Eds.): ECCV 2012, Part IV, LNCS 7575, pp. 373–387, 2012.

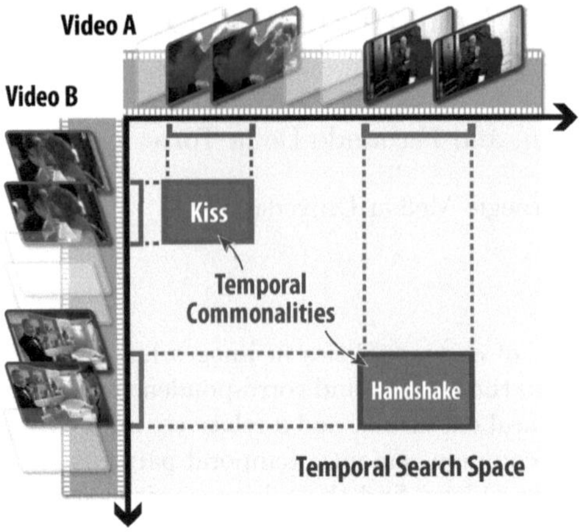

Fig. 1. Temporal Commonality Discovery (TCD). Given two videos from the movies "*As Good As It Gets*" (top) and "*Indiana Jones And The Last Crusade*" (left), how to discover in an unsupervised manner the common actions between them? In this case our algorithm found segments of *Kissing* and *Handshaking* as common actions between both videos. Note that the common segments can have different lengths.

Recall that TCD is a fully unsupervised problem, so no prior knowledge is provided—we do not know what the commonalities are, how many there are and where they start and end. A naive method to find desired pair(s) of common subsequences would be the *sliding window* approach, *i.e.*, exhaustively search all possible pairs of subsequences and select the pair(s) with the highest score(s). However, the complexity of this approach scales quadratically with the length of both sequences, $\mathcal{O}(m^2n^2)$, for two sequences of length m and n. For instance, in the case of two sequences with 200 and 300 frames, there are more than *three billion* possible matchings that need to be computed at different lengths and locations. Therefore, the naive approach is computationally prohibitive for reasonable length sequences.

Inspired by [13,32] that used the branch and bound (B&B) algorithm to efficiently search for optimal image patches or video volumes, we propose to adopt B&B for searching simultaneously over all possible segments in each video sequence (see Fig. 1). Two are the main contributions of this study: (1) Introduce the new problem of unsupervised TCD. While there exist studies that address commonality discovery in images [8,15,20,30], to the best of our knowledge there is little work that tackles unsupervised search of commonalities in video sequences. Also, note that there are several studies that address the problem of event detection or sequence labeling of human actions in video (*e.g.*, [12,27,32]). However, unlike TCD, those studies require learning a set of classifiers from training data. (2) Formulate the TCD as an integer optimization problem and propose an efficient B&B algorithm that finds the globally optimal solution. We derive new tight bounds for ℓ_1, intersection and χ^2 distances between histograms, allowing the B&B scheme to discard large portion of the search space. Experimental validation on standard datasets for finding similar facial expressions in video and human actions in motion capture data illustrates the benefits of our approach.

2 Related Work

Our work is inspired by recent success on using B&B with Support Vector Machines (SVM) for efficient template matching. Lampert *et al.* [13] proposed Efficient Subwindow Search (ESS) to find the optimal subimage that maximizes the prediction score of a pre-trained SVM classifier. Hoai *et al.* [12] combined a multiclass SVM with Dynamic programming for efficient temporal classification and segmentation. Yuan *et al.* [32] generalized Lampert's 4-D search to the 6-D Spatio-Temporal Branch-and-Bound (STBB) by incorporating time, to search for spatio-temporal volumes. However, unlike TCD, these approaches are supervised and require a training stage.

Recently, there have been interests in temporal clustering algorithms for unsupervised discovery of human actions. Wang *et al.* [30] exploited deformable template matching of shape and context in static images to discover action classes. Si *et al.* [25] learned an event grammar by clustering event co-occurrence into a dictionary of atomic actions. Zhou *et al.* [33] combined spectral clustering and dynamic time warping to cluster time series, and applied it to learn taxonomies of facial expressions. Turaga *et al.* [28] used extensions of switching linear dynamical systems for clustering human actions in video sequences. However, if we cluster two sequences that only have one segment in common, previous methods for clustering time series will likely need many clusters to find the common segments. In our case, TCD discovers only similar segments and avoids the need for clustering all the video that is computationally expensive and prone to local minima. Another unsupervised technique related to TCD is motif detection [18,19]. Time series motif algorithms find repeated patterns within a single sequence. Minnen *et al.* [18] discovered motifs as high-density regions in the space of all subsequences. Mueen and Keogh [19] further improved the motif discovery problem using an online technique, maintaining the exact motifs in real-time performance. Nevertheless, these work detects motifs within only one sequence, but TCD considers two (or more) sequences. Moreover, it is unclear how these technique can be robust to noise.

The longest common subsequence (LCS) [10,17,21] is also related to TCD. The LCS problem consists on finding the longest subsequence that is common within a set of sequences (often just two) [21,31]. Closer to our work is the algorithm for longest consecutive common subsequence (LCCS) [31] that finds the longest contiguous part of original sequences (*e.g.*, videos). However, different from TCD, these approaches have a major limitation in that they find only identical subsequences, and hence are not robust to noise that is typical in realistic videos.

3 Unsupervised TCD

3.1 Problem Formulation

In the following, we will assume that at least one commonality exists among a pair of time series (*e.g.*, two video sequences), represented as matrices

$\mathbf{A} = [\mathbf{a}_1, \ldots, \mathbf{a}_m]$ and $\mathbf{B} = [\mathbf{b}_1, \ldots, \mathbf{b}_n]$ (see notation[1]). We formulate the TCD problem as the integer programming over two integer intervals $[b_1, e_1] \subseteq [1, m]$ and $[b_2, e_2] \subseteq [1, n]$:

$$\begin{aligned} \min_{b_1,e_1,b_2,e_2} \quad & d\left(\varphi_{\mathbf{A}[b_1,e_1]}, \varphi_{\mathbf{B}[b_2,e_2]}\right), \\ \text{s.t.} \quad & e_i - b_i \geq \ell, \forall i \in \{1,2\}, \end{aligned} \tag{1}$$

where $\mathbf{A}[b_1, e_1] = [\mathbf{a}_{b_1}, \ldots, \mathbf{a}_{e_1}]$ denotes the subsequence of $\mathbf{A}$ that begins from frame b_1 and ends in frame e_1 (similar for $\mathbf{B}[b_2, e_2]$). $\varphi_{\mathbf{x}}$ is a feature mapping for a sequence $\mathbf{x}$ (see Sec. 3.3 for details), $d(\mathbf{y}, \mathbf{z})$ is a distance measurement between two feature vectors $\mathbf{y}$ and $\mathbf{z}$, and ℓ controls the minimal length for each subsequence to avoid the trivial solution of both lengths being zero.

Given a sequence pair $\mathbf{A}$ and $\mathbf{B}$, the goal of TCD is to find the two most common intervals $[b_1, e_1]$ and $[b_2, e_2]$, such that problem (1) is minimized. Note that, as illustrated in Fig. 1, the discovered sequences $\mathbf{A}[b_1, e_1]$ and $\mathbf{B}[b_2, e_2]$ can have different lengths, thus we don't assume a fixed length for discovered sequences. A naive approach for solving (1) is to search over all possible locations for (b_1, e_1, b_2, e_2). However, it leads to an algorithm with computational complexity $\mathcal{O}(m^2 n^2)$, which is prohibitive for regular videos with hundreds or thousands of frames. To cope with this problem, this paper proposes a B&B algorithm to efficiently find the global optimal solution to (1).

3.2 Optimization by Branch and Bound (B&B)

With a proper bounding function, the B&B framework is significantly more efficient than exhaustive approaches. In this section, we leverage B&B to efficiently find the global solution for problem (1).

Problem Interpretation: To have a better understanding of the search space, we first re-formulate the problem (1) as the problem of searching over two sequence's timelines (as illustrated in Fig. 1). A rectangle r in the search space indicates one candidate solution (b_1, e_1, b_2, e_2) for (1). This candidate solution would match a segment in video $\mathbf{A}$ beginning at b_1 and ending at e_1 with another segment in video $\mathbf{B}$ beginning at b_2 and ending at e_2. To allow a more efficient representation for searching, we parameterize each step as searching over sets of candidate solutions. That is, we search over intervals instead of individual value for each parameter. Each parameter interval corresponds to a rectangle set in the search space, *i.e.*, $\mathcal{R} = [B_1, E_1, B_2, E_2]$, where $B_i = [b_i^{lo}, b_i^{hi}]$ and $E_i = [e_i^{lo}, e_i^{hi}]$ (i=1 and 2) indicate tuples of parameters ranging from frame lo to frame hi.

The B&B Algorithm: Algorithm 1 summarizes the proposed TCD procedure. We use a priority queue $\mathcal{Q}$ to maintain the search process. Each state in $\mathcal{Q}$ contains a rectangle set $\mathcal{R}$, its upper bound $u(\mathcal{R})$ and lower bound $l(\mathcal{R})$.

[1] Bold capital letters denote a matrix $\mathbf{X}$, bold lower-case letters a column vector $\mathbf{x}$. $\mathbf{x}_i$ represents the ith column of the matrix $\mathbf{X}$. All non-bold letters represent scalars.

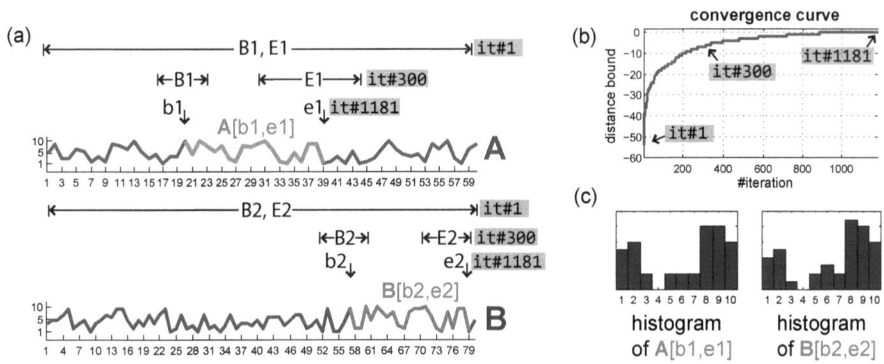

Fig. 2. An example of TCD for two synthetic 1-D time series (best viewed in color). Note that in this case when $\ell = 20$, a naive sliding window approach needs more than *5 million* evaluations while the proposed B&B method takes only 1181 to converge. (a) Search ranges at iterations (`it`) #1, #300 and #1181 over sequences **A** and **B**. Commonalities $\mathbf{A}[b_1, e_1]$ and $\mathbf{B}[b_2, e_2]$ are discovered at convergence (#1811). (b) Convergence curve of the lower bound. (c) Histograms of the discovered commonalities.

Each iteration starts by selecting the rectangle set $\mathcal{R}$ from the top state, which is defined as the state containing the maximal lower bound (recall that lower bounds can be negative; see Sec. 3.3 for details of the bounds). Then in the *branch step*, each rectangle set is split by its largest interval into two disjoint subsets. For example, suppose E_2 is the largest interval, then $\mathcal{R} \to \mathcal{R}' \cup \mathcal{R}''$ where $E_2' := [e_2^{lo}, \lfloor \frac{e_2^{lo}+e_2^{hi}}{2} \rfloor]$ and $E_2'' := [\lfloor \frac{e_2^{lo}+e_2^{hi}}{2} \rfloor + 1, e_2^{hi}]$. In the *bound step*, we calculate the bounds for the lowest dissimilarity for each rectangle set, and then update new rectangle sets and bounds into $\mathcal{Q}$. The algorithm terminates when $\mathcal{R}$ contains a unique entry. Fig. 2 shows an example of TCD for discovering commonality between two 1-D sequences. Despite that in the worst case the complexity of B&B can be still $\mathcal{O}(m^2n^2)$, we will experimentally show that in general B&B is much more efficient than the naive search.

Note that the optimal discovered sequences can be of length greater than ℓ. To show an example, consider two 1-D sequences $\mathbf{A} = [1, 2, 2, 1]$ and $\mathbf{B} = [1, 1, 3]$. Suppose we use ℓ_1 distance, set the minimal length $\ell = 3$, and represent their 3-bin histograms as $\varphi_{\mathbf{A}[1,4]} = [2, 2, 0]$, $\varphi_{\mathbf{A}[1,3]} = [1, 2, 0]$ and $\varphi_{\mathbf{B}} = [2, 0, 1]$. Hereby we can conclude by showing the distances: $d_{\ell_1}(\varphi_{\mathbf{A}[1,4]}, \varphi_{\mathbf{B}}) = 3 < 4 = d_{\ell_1}(\varphi_{\mathbf{A}[1,3]}, \varphi_{\mathbf{B}})$.

Differences from ESS [13] and STBB [32]: Although the proposed B&B algorithm is in spirit similar to ESS and STBB, it has three essential differences from these methods: (1) Different search space. ESS and STBB search over spatial coordinates of an image or spatio-temporal volumes in a video, while TCD

Algorithm 1. Temporal Commonality Discovery

input : Feature lists for a sequence pair $\mathbf{A}, \mathbf{B}$; minimal length ℓ
output: Optimal rectangle r^* in the temporal search space

Initialize $\mathcal{Q} \leftarrow$empty priority queue;
Initialize $\mathcal{R} \leftarrow [1,m] \times [1,m] \times [1,n] \times [1,n]$;
while *Size of* $\mathcal{R}$ *is not 1* **do**
  Split one interval into two disjoint sets $\mathcal{R} \rightarrow \mathcal{R}' \cup \mathcal{R}''$ (*branch step*);
  Compute bounds in Sec. 3.3 for two new intervals $\mathcal{R}'$ and $\mathcal{R}''$ (*bound step*);
  Push both $\mathcal{R}'$ and $\mathcal{R}''$ into $\mathcal{Q}$, ordered by bounds;
  Pop the top state $\mathcal{R}$ from $\mathcal{Q}$;
end
Assign the optimal rectangle $r^* \leftarrow \mathcal{R}$;

searches over beginning and ending positions of the segments in two sequences. (2) ESS and STBB are supervised techniques and seek for highly confident regions according to a pre-trained SVM classifier; TCD is unsupervised. (3) We introduce new bounding functions for the B&B framework that guarantee efficiency and optimality for the TCD problem. Moreover, ESS and STBB consider only upper bounds, while TCD incorporates both upper and lower bounds and hence is able to prune the priority queue for accelerating the search.

3.3 Construction of a Bounding Function

Representation of Signals: Throughout the paper we will use the Bag of Temporal Words (BoTW) model [26,32] to represent video segments. Observe, that any features that can be discretized into histograms can fit into our framework. In BoTW the codebook is built using a clustering method (*e.g.*, k-means) to group similar feature vectors. Each frame is then quantized according to the k-entry dictionary. The histogram for a given sequence is then built by accumulating individual frame histograms. We represent the feature mapping $\varphi_{\mathbf{A}[b_1,e_1]}$ in (1) as the histogram of temporal words for the subsequence in the interval $[b_1, e_1]$. Another notable benefit of the histogram representation is that it allows for fast recursive computation using the concept of *integral image* [29]. That is, for frame t, we accumulate the sum of $\varphi_{\mathbf{A}[1,t]}$ of the histograms up to t. Using this structure, we can efficiently compute the histogram for any subsequence $\mathbf{A}[t_1, t_2]$ as $\varphi_{\mathbf{A}[t_1,t_2]} = \varphi_{\mathbf{A}[1,t_2]} - \varphi_{\mathbf{A}[1,t_1-1]}$.

Properties of Bounding Functions: Recall that $\mathcal{R}$ is a rectangle set and $r \equiv (b_1, e_1, b_2, e_2)$ a rectangle in the temporal search space representing two subsequences $\mathbf{A}[b_1, e_1]$ and $\mathbf{B}[b_2, e_2]$. We denote $d(r) = d(\varphi_{\mathbf{A}}, \varphi_{\mathbf{B}})$ as the distance between their histograms $\varphi_{\mathbf{A}}$ and $\varphi_{\mathbf{B}}$. The smaller the value of $d(\varphi_{\mathbf{A}}, \varphi_{\mathbf{B}})$, the more likely the sequences share commonalities. To harness the B&B framework, we need to find an upper bound $u(\mathcal{R})$ and a lower bound $l(\mathcal{R})$ that satisfy the three properties:

(a) $u(\mathcal{R}) \geq \max_{r\in\mathcal{R}} d(r)$,
(b) $l(\mathcal{R}) \leq \min_{r\in\mathcal{R}} d(r)$,
(c) $u(\mathcal{R}) = d(r) = l(\mathcal{R})$, if r is the only element in $\mathcal{R}$.

Properties (a) and (b) ensure that $u(\mathcal{R})$ and $l(\mathcal{R})$ appropriately bound all candidate solutions in $\mathcal{R}$ from above and from below, whereas (c) guarantees the algorithm to converge to the optimal solution. As shown in problem (1) our goal is to minimize a distance function. Hence $u(\mathcal{R})$ in this case is not relevant for the minimization. However, we can use $u(\mathcal{R})$ to prune the priority queue for speeding our search, *i.e.*, eliminate any state $\mathcal{S}$ that satisfies $l(\mathcal{S}) > u(\mathcal{R})$ [3].

Bounding Individual Histogram Bins: Suppose $\mathbf{A}^+$ and $\mathbf{A}^-$ are the longest possible and shortest possible subsequence of $\mathbf{A}$ for a given rectangle set $\mathcal{R}$. We denote their K-bin *unnormalized* histograms as $\varphi_{\mathbf{A}^+} = \{h_1^+, \ldots, h_K^+\}$ and $\varphi_{\mathbf{A}^-} = \{h_1^-, \ldots, h_K^-\}$. Let $r \in \mathcal{R}$ be a rectangle in the search space representing two subsequences $\mathbf{A}[b_1, e_1]$ and $\mathbf{B}[b_2, e_2]$ with histograms $\{h_1, \ldots, h_K\}$ and $\{k_1, \ldots, k_K\}$. Considering both histograms of $\mathbf{A}^+, \mathbf{A}^-$ and $\mathbf{B}^+, \mathbf{B}^-$, we can represent the range for the bth histogram bins as

$$0 \leq h_b^- \leq h_b \leq h_b^+, \; 0 \leq k_b^- \leq k_b \leq k_b^+. \tag{2}$$

For *normalized* histograms, we use the fact that $|\mathbf{A}^-| < |\mathbf{A}[b_1, e_1]| < |\mathbf{A}^+|$ and $|\mathbf{B}^-| < |\mathbf{B}[b_2, e_2]| < |\mathbf{B}^+|$, where $|\mathbf{X}| = \sum_{b=1}^{K} \varphi_{\mathbf{X}b}$ is summation over histogram bins of a sequence $\mathbf{X}$. Then we can rewrite (2) for the ranges of normalized bins $\widehat{h}_b = h_b/|\mathbf{A}[b_1, e_1]|$ and $\widehat{k}_b = k_b/|\mathbf{B}[b_2, e_2]|$:

$$0 \leq \frac{h_b^-}{|\mathbf{A}^+|} \leq \widehat{h}_b \leq \frac{h_b^+}{|\mathbf{A}^-|}, \; 0 \leq \frac{k_b^-}{|\mathbf{B}^+|} \leq \widehat{k}_b \leq \frac{k_b^+}{|\mathbf{B}^-|}. \tag{3}$$

Bounding Distance between Histograms: With the per-bin bounds, we show in the following exemplar constructions of bounds between histograms, *i.e.*, ℓ_1, intersection, and χ^2 distance, which have been widely applied to many tasks such as objection recognition [9,13] and action recognition [7,11,14,16,22].

1) Bounding ℓ_1 Distance: Applying the operators min/max on (2), we get

$$\begin{aligned} \min(h_b^-, k_b^-) &\leq \min(h_b, k_b) \leq \min(h_b^+, k_b^+), \\ \max(h_b^-, k_b^-) &\leq \max(h_b, k_b) \leq \max(h_b^+, k_b^+). \end{aligned} \tag{4}$$

Reordering both the above inequalities, we obtain the upper bound u_b and lower bound l_b for the bth histogram bin:

$$\begin{aligned} l_b &= \max(h_b^-, k_b^-) - \min(h_b^+, k_b^+) \\ &\leq \max(h_b, k_b) - \min(h_b, k_b) = |h_b - k_b| \\ &\leq \max(h_b^+, k_b^+) - \min(h_b^-, k_b^-) = u_b. \end{aligned} \tag{5}$$

Summing all the histogram bins, we obtain the bounds of the ℓ_1 distance for two unnormalized histograms $\varphi_{\mathbf{A}}, \varphi_{\mathbf{B}}$:

$$l_{\ell_1}(\mathcal{R}) = \sum_{b=1}^{K} l_b \leq \underbrace{\sum_{b=1}^{K} |h_b - k_b|}_{d_{\ell_1}(\varphi_{\mathbf{A}}, \varphi_{\mathbf{B}})} \leq \sum_{b=1}^{K} u_b = u_{\ell_1}(\mathcal{R}). \tag{6}$$

Similarly, we can obtain the bounds for normalized histograms $\widehat{\varphi}_{\mathbf{A}}, \widehat{\varphi}_{\mathbf{B}}$ by the same operations as (4) and (5):

$$\widehat{l}_{\ell_1}(\mathcal{R}) = \sum_{b=1}^{K} \widehat{l}_b \leq d_{\ell_1}(\widehat{\varphi}_{\mathbf{A}}, \widehat{\varphi}_{\mathbf{B}}) \leq \sum_{b=1}^{K} \widehat{u}_b = \widehat{u}_{\ell_1}(\mathcal{R}), \tag{7}$$

where

$$\widehat{l}_b = \max(\frac{h_b^-}{|\mathbf{A}^+|}, \frac{k_b^-}{|\mathbf{B}^+|}) - \min(\frac{h_b^+}{|\mathbf{A}^-|}, \frac{k_b^+}{|\mathbf{B}^-|}), \tag{8}$$

$$\text{and } \widehat{u}_b = \max(\frac{h_b^+}{|\mathbf{A}^-|}, \frac{k_b^+}{|\mathbf{B}^-|}) - \min(\frac{h_b^-}{|\mathbf{A}^+|}, \frac{k_b^-}{|\mathbf{B}^+|}). \tag{9}$$

2) Bounding Intersection Distance: Given two normalized histograms $\widehat{\varphi}_{\mathbf{A}} = \{\widehat{h}_1, \ldots, \widehat{h}_K\}$ and $\widehat{\varphi}_{\mathbf{B}} = \{\widehat{k}_1, \ldots, \widehat{k}_K\}$, we define their intersection distance by the Hilbert space representation [24]:

$$d_{\cap}(\widehat{\varphi}_{\mathbf{A}}, \widehat{\varphi}_{\mathbf{B}}) = -\sum_{b=1}^{K} \min(\widehat{h}_b, \widehat{k}_b). \tag{10}$$

By (3) and (4), we can find its lower bound and upper bound:

$$l_{\cap}(\mathcal{R}) = -\sum_{b=1}^{K} \min(\frac{h_b^+}{|\mathbf{A}^-|}, \frac{k_b^+}{|\mathbf{B}^-|}) \text{ and } u_{\cap}(\mathcal{R}) = -\sum_{b=1}^{K} \min(\frac{h_b^-}{|\mathbf{A}^+|}, \frac{k_b^-}{|\mathbf{B}^+|}). \tag{11}$$

3) Bounding χ^2 Distance: The χ^2 distance has been proven to be a good metric to measure distance between two histograms for TCD due to its simplicity and efficiency. The χ^2 distance is defined as

$$d_{\chi^2}(\widehat{\varphi}_{\mathbf{A}}, \widehat{\varphi}_{\mathbf{B}}) = \sum_{b=1}^{K} \frac{(\widehat{h}_b - \widehat{k}_b)^2}{\widehat{h}_b + \widehat{k}_b}. \tag{12}$$

Incorporating the bounds $\widehat{l}_b$ and $\widehat{u}_b$ for normalized histograms in (8) and the inequalities in (3), we obtain the lower bound and upper bound for d_{χ^2} by summing throughout all histogram bins:

$$l_{\chi^2}(\mathcal{R}) = \sum_{b=1}^{K} \frac{(\max(0, \widehat{l}_b))^2}{h_b^+/|\mathbf{A}^-| + k_b^+/|\mathbf{B}^-|} \text{ and } u_{\chi^2}(\mathcal{R}) = \sum_{b=1}^{K} \frac{\widehat{u}_b^2}{h_b^-/|\mathbf{A}^+| + k_b^-/|\mathbf{B}^+|}. \tag{13}$$

The derived lower and upper bounds clearly satisfy the bounding properties (a) and (b). To show how property (c) holds, one can consider the case that $\mathcal{R}$ contains only one rectangle r. Take the d_{ℓ_1} for example, when $r \in \mathcal{R}$ is the unique rectangle, we have $h_b^+ = h_b = h_b^-$ and $k_b^+ = k_b = k_b^-$, and thus Eq. (5) becomes $u_b = |h_b - k_b| = l_b$. Hereby we obtain $l_{\ell_1}(\mathcal{R}) = d_{\ell_1}(\varphi_{\mathbf{A}}, \varphi_{\mathbf{B}}) = u_{\ell_1}(\mathcal{R})$. One can show property (c) holds for other distances in a similar manner.

4 Extensions to Multiple TCD and Video Indexing

In the following we show how a simple modification of our proposed algorithm can be applied to multiple TCD and video indexing.

Discover Multiple Commonalities: For realistic sequences that often contain more than one commonality, we can discover multiple commonalties by applying Algorithm 1 repeatedly. Every time Algorithm 1 returns an optimal rectangle in the temporal search space that represents the best match. Once a commonality is found, we remove the corresponding rectangle from the search space and then begin over the search process to find the next best. The process continues until a desired number of rectangles have been retrieved or the returned matching distance $d(\cdot, \cdot)$ is greater than some threshold, which depends on the desire of applications.

Note that our implementation is different from the conventional multiple-object detection tasks [13]. In object detection, the whole spatial region is removed to search for the next object. In our case, we can not remove all the time-segments for both time sequences because we might miss some commonality at the same location. Instead, we position those rectangles to the bottom of the priority queue by imposing a large penalty to their scores. Using this strategy, we are able to handle *many-to-many* mapping, *i.e.*, $\mathbf{A}[b_1, e_1]$ can match multiple subsequences in $\mathbf{B}$ and vice versa.

Video Indexing: A simple modification of the proposed B&B algorithm could be useful for efficient searching for a video with similar content. That is, given a query video, how to efficiently search for common subsequences in a longer video. Let $\mathbf{Q}$ be the query sequence we want to find in the target video $\mathbf{T}$. We can modify (1) by fixing one of the pairwise sequences:

$$\min_{b_t, e_t} \quad d\left(\varphi_{\mathbf{T}[b_t, e_t]}, \varphi_{\mathbf{Q}}\right) \quad \text{s.t.} \quad e_t - b_t \geq \ell. \tag{14}$$

The problem now becomes simpler but it still is an integer programming. Nevertheless, Algorithm 1 can be applied again to find the optimal match efficiently. Searching for multiple segments can also be done as discussed above. Note that we do not claim that this indexing algorithm is state-of-the-art. We just want to illustrate the versatility of our approach.

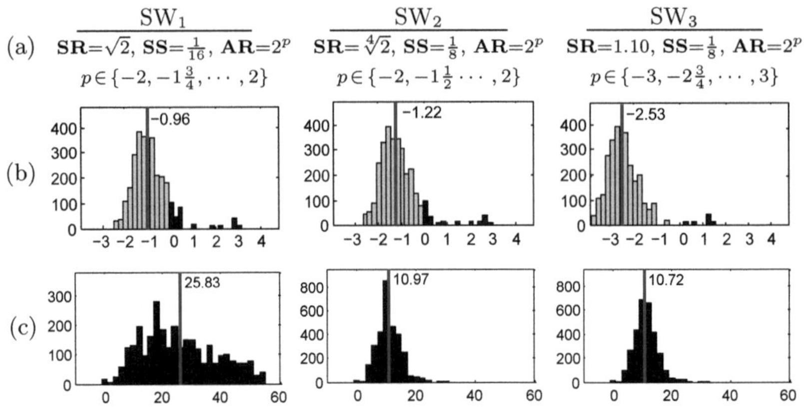

Fig. 3. Efficiency comparison between TCD and the naive sliding window (SW) approach. (a) Parameters for each SW$_i$: size-ratio (**SR**), stepsize (**SS**), and aspect ratios (**AR**) as 2^p. (b) Histograms ratio of the number of evaluation $\log \frac{n^{\mathrm{TCD}}}{n^{\mathrm{SW}_i}}$. (c) Histograms of difference between resulting distances $d(r^{\mathrm{SW}}) - d(r^{\mathrm{TCD}})$.

5 Experimental Results

We evaluated our approach on two experiments. First, we discovered common facial events in the RU-FACS database [5]. Second, we found multiple common human actions in CMU-Mocap dataset [1]. The code is available at `http://www.humansensing.cs.cmu.edu/software/tcd.html`.

5.1 Common Facial Events Discovery

This experiment evaluates the capability of our algorithm to find similar facial events in the RU-FACS database [5]. The RU-FACS database consists of digitized video and manual coding of 34 young adults. They were recorded during an interview of approximately 2 minutes duration in which they lied or told the truth in response to an interviewer's questions. Pose orientation was mostly frontal with moderate out-of-plane head motions. We selected the Action Unit (AU) 12 (*i.e.*, smile) from 15 subjects that had most occurrence of this facial AU. We collected 100 segments containing one AU-12 and other AUs, resulting in 4,950 video sequence pairs with different subjects.

We represented features as the distances between the height of lips and teeth, angles for mouth corners and SIFT descriptors in the points tracked by Active Appearance Models (AAM) [33] (see Fig. 4(a) for an illustration). We built a 1,000-entry codebook on a random subset of 50,000 feature vectors (see Sec. 3.3).

Efficiency Comparison with the Naive Sliding Window: This experiment evaluates the increase in speed in comparison with the naive sliding window (SW)

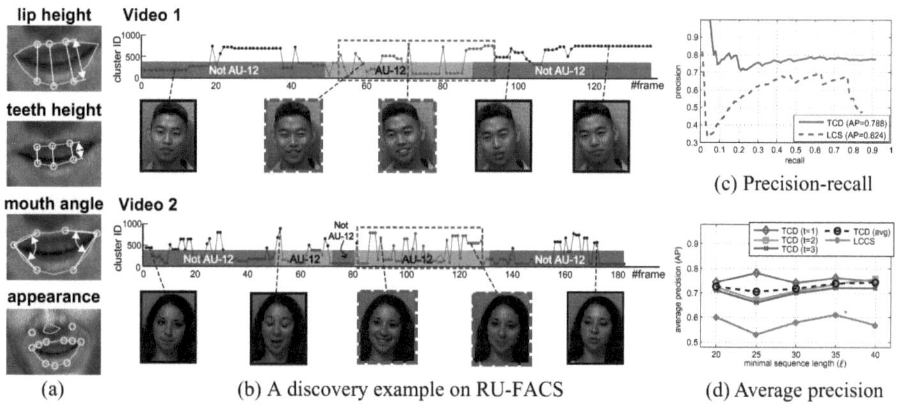

Fig. 4. (a) Facial features extracted from the tracked points as in [33]. (b) An example of common discovered facial events (indicated by dashed-line rectangles). (c)(d) Accuracy evaluation on precision-recall and average precision (AP).

approach. In the standard SW approach there are three parameter settings to improve efficiency [29]. We denote the parameters as SW_i $(i=1,2,3)$; see Fig. 3(a) for detailed settings. The size-ratio (**SR**) refers to the window scaling factors, the stepsize (**SS**) is the window offset, and the ratio of the window width to its height is the aspect ratio (**AR**). We refer to [29] for more details about the parameters. Recall the lengths of two sequences are m,n and the minimal length for each sequence is ℓ. We fixed the maximal and the minimal rectangle sizes for SW to be $(m \times n)$ and $(\ell\sqrt{\mathbf{AR}} \times \frac{\ell}{\sqrt{\mathbf{AR}}})$, respectively.

To be independent of a particular implementation, we measured the *discovery speed* as the number of evaluations that TCD and SW need to compute the bounding functions. The number of evaluations are referred as n^{TCD} and n^{SW_i} $(i=1,2,3)$. Fig. 3(b) shows the histograms of the log ratio for $n^{\text{TCD}}/n^{\text{SW}_i}$. Light green bars show that TCD requires less evaluations than SW, while dark blue bars indicate the opposite. Red vertical line indicates the average ratio. The smaller the ratio value, the less times TCD has to evaluate the distance bounds. Although SW was parameterized by standard settings [13,29] to search only a subset of the search space, TCD searches the entire space yet still performs on average 6.18 times less evaluations than SW.

In order to evaluate the *discovery quality*, we also compared the difference between the distances measured by TCD and SW, *i.e.*, $d(r^{\text{SW}}) - d(r^{\text{TCD}})$. The larger the difference the worse results SW got. Fig. 3(c) shows the histograms of these differences. One can observe that the differences are always greater than or equal to zero. This is because our method always finds the global optimum. Recall that SW, depending on the parameter settings, only does a partial search, hence it is not surprising that it often performs worse than our method.

Accuracy Evaluation: Because the problem of TCD is relatively new in computer vision, to the best of our knowledge there are no baselines we could compare to. Hence, for a baseline comparison, we selected the state-of-the-art method in longest common consecutive subsequence matching (LCCS) [31]. Observe that when the feature representation for each frame was quantized into a temporal word, the unsupervised TCD problem can be naturally interpreted as an LCCS. For fair comparisons with the LCCS that uses a 0-1 distance, in this experiment we used ℓ_1 distance. The minimal subsequence length ℓ was fixed to the same value for both LCCS and TCD. To evaluate the performance, we measured the *overlap score* between the ground truth and the discovered segments, as usually used in object detection tasks [9]: overlap$(r, g) = \frac{\text{area}(r \cap g)}{\text{area}(r \cup g)}$, where r is the rectangle in the search space representing a discovered commonality, and g is the ground true rectangle indicating the correct match. The higher the overlap score, the better the algorithm discovered the commonality. We consider that a rectangle is correct if the overlap score is greater than a threshold ε (here $\varepsilon = 0.5$). Fig. 4(b) shows an example of a correct discovery. We evaluated the event-level accuracy as precision and recall.

Fig. 4(c) plots the precision-recall curves for the first output result of TCD and LCCS. We computed the average precision (AP) [9] and found TCD outperforms LCCS by 15%. Compared to LCCS that finds identical subsequences, TCD considers a histogram appearing in two sequence, it is more robust to deal with uncertainty in noisy signals such as videos. Fig. 4(d) shows the average precision of our approach under different parameters. We varied the minimal sequence length ℓ in $\{20, 25, \ldots, 40\}$, and examined the AP of the tth result individually. As can be observed from the averaged AP (black dashed line), our method is more robust across different settings of ℓ and t. As a result, TCD performed on average 16% better than LCCS in discovering the common AU-12.

5.2 Multiple Common Motions Discovery in Motion Capture Data

In the second experiment we used the CMU-Mocap dataset [1] to demonstrate the ability to discover *multiple* common actions (as discussed in Sec. 4). We selected Subject 86 that contains 15 long sequences. Each sequence contains thousands of frames and up to 10 actions (out of a total of 25 human actions) such as walking, jumping, punching, etc. See Fig. 5(a) for an example. Each sequence ranges from 100 to 300 frames each action. Then we randomly selected 45 pairs of sequences (each having up to 10 actions) and discovered common actions among each pair. We downsampled each sequence by a factor of 4 to make it 30 fps, resulting in a set of sequences with 1,200~2,600 frames. Note that this experiment is much more challenging than the previous one due to longer sequences and more complicated actions. In this case, we excluded SW for comparison because it needs 10^{12} evaluations which is impractical.

Each human motion was represented as the root position, orientation, and 29 relative joint angles. In order to provide a continuous representation, the 3-D Euler angles were transformed to 3-D quaternions. Following [4], we represented 10 joints as a 30-dimensional feature vector of 3-D quaternions for each frame.

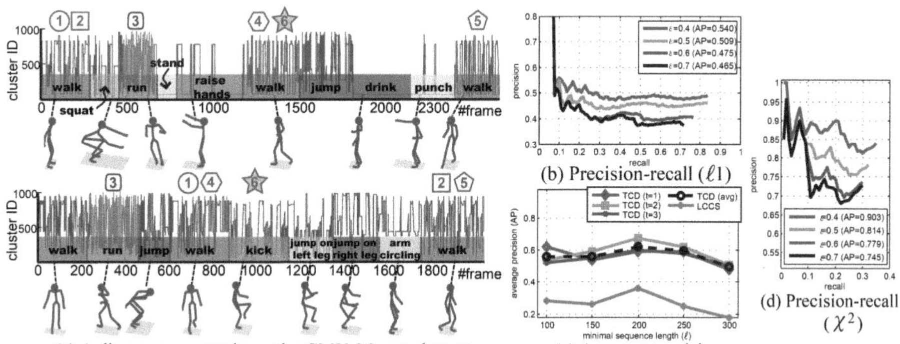

(a) A discovery example on the CMU-Mocap dataset (b) Precision-recall ($\ell 1$) (c) Average precision (d) Precision-recall (χ^2)

Fig. 5. (a) An example of the top six discovered common motions. The numbers indicate discovered commonalities. Note that we shaded the star (number 6) to indicate an incorrect discovery that matched *walk* and *kick*. (b)(c) Precision-recall and average precision on ℓ_1 distance. (d) Precision-recall on χ^2 distance.

We determined a correct discovery if its overlap score is greater than a threshold ε. Fig. 5(a) illustrates the first six common motions discovered by TCD. A failure discovery is shown in the shaded number 6. Fig. 5(b) shows the precision-recall curve for different values of ε. Using the naive ℓ_1 distance, the curve decreases about 10% AP when the overlap score ε raises from 0.4 to 0.7, which implies that we can obtain higher quality results without losing too much precision. For comparison with the baseline LCCS approach, Fig. 5(c) shows their APs over various ℓ on the nth discovered result. LCCS performed poorly to obtain long common subsequences since in this experiment human motions have more variability than just one facial event (*e.g.*, AU-12). On the other hand, TCD utilized histogram representation, and thus allowed more tolerance in analogy with BoW in the context of object recognition. One can observe that AP drops with increasing ℓ since the common actions in this database can have very short distance, *e.g.*, *jump* and *squad*. Moreover, to demonstrate the generalization performance of our method, we also evaluated the χ^2 distance and plotted the precision-recall curve in Fig. 5(d). The bounds for χ^2 distance were discussed in Sec. 3.3. Although the Mocap dataset is very challenging in terms of various motions and diverse sequence lengths, our approach with χ^2 performed 30% better than ℓ_1 and LCCS. It shows χ^2 is a more powerful measurement for histograms than ℓ_1. Overall, using the χ^2 measurement and $\varepsilon = 0.5$, our algorithm achieved 81% precision.

6 Discussion and Future Work

This paper introduced the new problem of TCD, to find temporal commonalities between sequences in an unsupervised manner. We have shown that the proposed B&B algorithm can efficiently find a global optimal solution for TCD. We presented results in discovering common facial events and human actions.

It is important to observe that our method can be applied to any features that can be quantified into histograms. Although this work has shown better performance than baseline methods, more research can be done to speed up the search process, *e.g.*, [2]. Currently, we are also looking to derive tight bounds for other metrics between temporal segments such as dynamic time warping.

Acknowledgements. This work was supported by the National Science Foundation (NSF) under Grant No. RI-1116583 and CPS-0931999. Any opinions, findings, and conclusions or recommendations expressed in this material are those of the author(s) and do not necessarily reflect the views of the NSF.

References

1. `http://mocap.cs.cmu.edu/`
2. An, S., Peursum, P., Liu, W., Venkatesh, S.: Efficient subwindow search with submodular score functions. In: CVPR (2011)
3. Balakrishnan, V., Boyd, S., Balemi, S.: Branch and bound algorithm for computing the minimum stability degree of parameter-dependent linear systems. International Journal of Robust and Nonlinear Control 1(4), 295–317 (1991)
4. Barbič, J., Safonova, A., Pan, J.Y., Faloutsos, C., Hodgins, J.K., Pollard, N.S.: Segmenting motion capture data into distinct behaviors. In: Proc. of Graphics Interface (2004)
5. Bartlett, M.S., Littlewort, G.C., Frank, M.G., Lainscsek, C., Fasel, I.R., Movellan, J.R.: Automatic recognition of facial actions in spontaneous expressions. Journal of Multimedia 1(6), 22–35 (2006)
6. Boiman, O., Irani, M.: Detecting irregularities in images and in video. In: ICCV (2005)
7. Brendel, W., Todorovic, S.: Learning spatiotemporal graphs of human activities. In: ICCV (2011)
8. Chu, W.-S., Chen, C.-P., Chen, C.-S.: MOMI-Cosegmentation: Simultaneous Segmentation of Multiple Objects among Multiple Images. In: Kimmel, R., Klette, R., Sugimoto, A. (eds.) ACCV 2010, Part I. LNCS, vol. 6492, pp. 355–368. Springer, Heidelberg (2011)
9. Everingham, M., Zisserman, A., Williams, C.I., Van Gool, L.: The PASCAL visual object classes challenge 2006 results. In: 2th PASCAL Challenge (2006)
10. Gusfield, D.: Algorithms on strings, trees, and sequences: computer science and computational biology. Cambridge Univ. Press (1997)
11. Han, D., Bo, L., Sminchisescu, C.: Selection and Context for Action Recognition. In: ICCV (2009)
12. Hoai, M., Zhong Lan, Z., De la Torre, F.: Joint segmentation and classification of human actions in video. In: CVPR (2011)
13. Lampert, C., Blaschko, M., Hofmann, T.: Efficient subwindow search: A branch and bound framework for object localization. PAMI 31(12), 2129–2142 (2009)
14. Laptev, I., Marszalek, M., Schmid, C., Rozenfeld, B.: Learning realistic human actions from movies. In: CVPR (2008)
15. Liu, H., Yan, S.: Common visual pattern discovery via spatially coherent correspondences. In: CVPR (2010)
16. Liu, J., Shah, M., Kuipers, B., Savarese, S.: Cross-view action recognition via view knowledge transfer. In: CVPR (2011)

17. Maier, D.: The complexity of some problems on subsequences and supersequences. Journal of the ACM 25(2), 322–336 (1978)
18. Minnen, D., Isbell, C., Essa, I., Starner, T.: Discovering multivariate motifs using subsequence density estimation. In: AAAI (2007)
19. Mueen, A., Keogh, E.: Online discovery and maintenance of time series motifs. In: KDD (2010)
20. Mukherjee, L., Singh, V., Peng, J.: Scale invariant cosegmentation for image groups. In: CVPR (2011)
21. Paterson, M., Dančík, V.: Longest common subsequences. Mathematical Foundations of Computer Science 841, 127–142 (1994)
22. Sadanand, S., Corso, J.J.: Action bank: A high-level representation of activity in video. In: CVPR (2012)
23. Schindler, G., Krishnamurthy, P., Lublinerman, R., Liu, Y., Dellaert, F.: Detecting and matching repeated patterns for automatic geo-tagging in urban environments. In: CVPR (2008)
24. Scholkopf, B.: The kernel trick for distances. In: NIPS (2001)
25. Si, Z., Pei, M., Yao, B., Zhu, S.: Unsupervised learning of event and-or grammar and semantics from video. In: ICCV (2011)
26. Sivic, J., Zisserman, A.: Video Google: A text retrieval approach to object matching in videos. In: ICCV (2003)
27. Tang, K., Fei-Fei, L., Koller, D.: Learning latent temporal structure for complex event detection. In: CVPR (2012)
28. Turaga, P., Veeraraghavan, A., Chellappa, R.: Unsupervised view and rate invariant clustering of video sequences. CVIU 113(3), 353–371 (2009)
29. Viola, P., Jones, M.: Robust real-time face detection. International Journal of Computer Vision 57(2), 137–154 (2004)
30. Wang, Y., Jiang, H., Drew, M.S., Li, Z., Mori, G.: Unsupervised discovery of action classes. In: CVPR (2006)
31. Wang, Y., Velipasalar, S.: Frame-level temporal calibration of unsynchronized cameras by using Longest Consecutive Common Subsequence. In: ICASSP (2009)
32. Yuan, J., Liu, Z., Wu, Y.: Discriminative video pattern search for efficient action detection. PAMI 33(9), 1728–1743 (2011)
33. Zhou, F., De la Torre, F., Cohn, J.F.: Unsupervised discovery of facial events. In: CVPR (2010)
34. Zhu, S., Mumford, D.: A stochastic grammar of images. Foundations and Trends in Computer Graphics and Vision 2(4), 259–362 (2006)

Finding People Using Scale, Rotation and Articulation Invariant Matching

Hao Jiang

Computer Science Department, Boston College, Chestnut Hill, MA 02467, USA

Abstract. A scale, rotation and articulation invariant method is proposed to match human subjects in images. Different from the widely used pictorial structure scheme, the proposed method directly matches body parts to image regions which are obtained from object independent proposals and successively merged superpixels. Body part region matching is formulated as a graph matching problem. We globally assign a body part candidate to each node on the model graph so that the overall configuration satisfies the spatial layout of a human body plan, part regions have small overlap, and the part coverage follows proper area ratios. The proposed graph model is non-tree and contains high order hyper-edges. We propose an efficient method that finds global optimal solution to the matching problem with a sequence of branch and bound procedures. The experiments show that the proposed method is able to handle arbitrary scale, rotation, articulation and match human subjects in cluttered images.

Keywords: Human pose, scale and rotation invariant matching, global optimization.

1 Introduction

Finding human subjects in cluttered images is a challenging task and it has many important potential applications. In this paper, we match a human subject in images and label the body part regions such as torso, arms and legs. The target object may have different scales and rotations. Most current pictorial structure approaches quantize the scale and rotation and optimize on the discrete cases. As the scaling range increases, searching through a huge number of discrete cases soon becomes impractical. The question is whether it is possible to efficiently match a human target without enumerating the quantized scales and rotations. In this paper, we address this problem and propose an efficient global optimization method that is able to match human subjects in images with unknown scale and rotation.

In contrast to the cardboard model that uses rectangle or polygon body parts, we match region candidates in images so that the combination of these regions forms a valid human body layout. The region candidates are from object independent proposals [19] and successively merged superpixels [18]. The proposed method assembles candidate regions and labels them as arm, leg and torso. Different from pictorial structure methods [9, 2], the proposed method does not

A. Fitzgibbon et al. (Eds.): ECCV 2012, Part IV, LNCS 7575, pp. 388–401, 2012.

Fig. 1. We label human part regions in images by matching a graph model to the target human subject. The arm regions are red, legs are green and torsos are blue. The proposed matching method is scale, rotation and articulation invariant.

detect bar structures or obtain them from region candidates; instead it directly optimizes the region assembly. By directly working on part region candidates, our method is efficient and when properly constructed it is invariant to scale, rotation and object articulation. Fig. 1 illustrates matching human part regions using the proposed method.

Finding human poses in images has been intensively studied. If object foreground segmentation is available, poses can be estimated using regression and machine learning approaches [5]. In [22], object foreground proposals and latent structured models are used to find human poses. Other top-down methods detect poses by matching exemplars in databases [6–8]. These top-down pose estimation methods work best when poses are in a small domain. If poses are unconstrained, the performance of these methods degrades. Methods that reply on object foreground segmentation are also limited by the quality of figure-ground separation, which itself is a hard problem especially for segmenting human subjects.

Bottom-up pose estimation methods detect body parts and then assemble them into a human-shaped object. Pictorial structure model is widely used, in which arms, legs, torso and head are represented as rectangle or polygon patches. The coupling body parts form a graph model. Different methods have been proposed to optimize the body part assembly. Tree structure models [1–3, 17] allow efficient inference using dynamic programming. Non-tree models that include more constraints among body parts have also been intensively studied [10, 11, 4].

Part based methods also benefit from image segmentation. Object foreground segmentation helps part detection and pose verification [9]. In [4], part assembly is optimized as a max-cover to the object foreground. Even rough foreground estimation is found useful to improve pose estimation [17]. In [13, 12], part candidates (the parallel bars) are extracted from superpixel boundaries and then grouped into a stick figure. Superpixels have also been used in [14] to improve the pictorial structure methods. Joint foreground segmentation and pose estimation for pedestrians have been studied in [16, 20]. In [21], object segmentation and graph matching are optimized together to achieve reliable unconstrained pose estimation.

The key obstacle for the pictorial structure methods is that it is hard to make the model adapt to the unknown scale of target objects. The body part assembly has to be optimized for each quantized scale and sometimes each rotation. This would be a slow process if we have to enumerate many discrete cases. Fitting rectangle structures to superpixel boundaries is able to make pose estimation scale invariant [13]; however, this procedure may lose detection of body parts. Apart from rectangle body parts, rectangle image patches (poselets) have also been used to match human subjects [23]. Poselet is not scale and rotation invariant. In this paper, we propose a method that directly matches regions. The body part regions are assembled so that the overall configuration fits a human body model. Such a scheme is scale, rotation and articulation invariant when properly constructed.

Grouping regions into a human shape is not a new concept. The jigsaw puzzle problem has been studied in [15], where the over-segmented superpixels are grouped together to fit a human model. Since superpixels are not able to group regions with different colors or textures, body parts with non-uniform appearance are often split into multiple superpixels. A parse tree method is proposed to merge superpixels in [15]. The parse tree may become huge and hard to process. As a compromise, a sequential procedure is applied: legs are first detected and then the torso is predicted from the leg detection using polygon matching. In [24], accurate body part region labeling has been achieved for pedestrians. This method replies on the shape priors of pedestrians and pedestrian detectors; it is thus hard to extend to matching people with arbitrary poses. Grouping a set of regions into a human shape and labeling the part regions is still an open problem.

The contribution of this paper is that we propose a global optimization method to match human body part regions. Our method groups superpixels [18] and region proposals [19] so that their spatial correlations and region ratios fit a human model. Our method is able to handle arbitrary human poses. It is scale and rotation invariant and can be globally optimized using a fast branch and bound approach.

2 Method

We treat human part matching as an assignment problem. We assign a candidate region to each body part so that the configuration follows the model constraints. Here the body part candidates are segments from successive superpixel merging and object independent region proposals.

The body part model is shown in Fig. 2. The corresponding graph model has five nodes that represent torso, arms and legs. The hyper-edges linking the nodes indicate the torso-arms, torso-legs and arms-legs constraints. These constraints enforce the spatial layout, overlapping area, symmetry, size ratio, and overall region coverage. Given a set of candidate regions, we optimize the body part assignment on the graph model: each graph node selects a candidate region so that the following energy function is minimized.

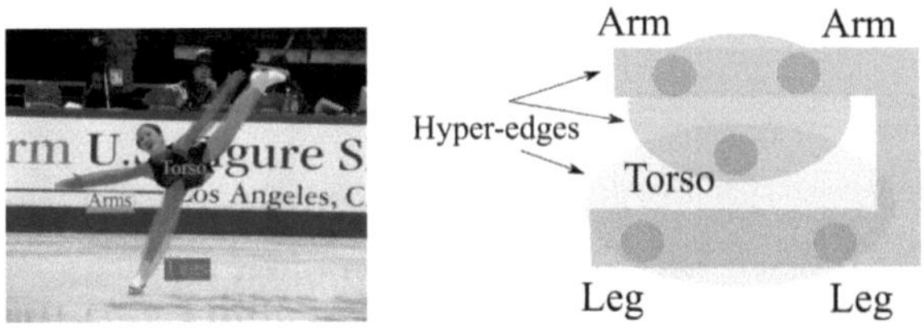

Fig. 2. Left: The 5-part body model. Right: The interaction of body parts in a graph. The graph includes five nodes and three hyper-edges among them.

$$\min_{L,s}\{\mathcal{U}(L)+\alpha\mathcal{D}(L)+\beta\mathcal{P}(L)+\eta\mathcal{R}(L)+\gamma\mathcal{S}(L)+\mu\mathcal{W}(L,s)\} \quad (1)$$
$$\text{s.t. } L \text{ is a valid part assignment, and } s \text{ is the scale estimation.}$$

where $\mathcal{U}(.)$ is the unary assignment cost, which is small if part candidate regions have similar shape to the corresponding part templates. $\mathcal{D}(.), \mathcal{P}(.), \mathcal{R}(.)$ and $\mathcal{S}(.)$ are tri-part terms, which are small if the labeling of arms-torso combination and the legs-torso combination satisfies specific constraints. $\mathcal{D}(.)$ quantifies the distance between specific body parts. $\mathcal{P}(.)$ penalizes selecting region candidates that are overlapping. $\mathcal{R}(.)$ enforces the relative sizes among body parts. $\mathcal{S}(L)$ encourages selecting regions with symmetrical appearance for arms or legs. $\mathcal{W}(.)$ is used to control the interaction among arms and legs, and encourages the overall coverage of arms and legs to fit a target size, i.e., the arms and legs do not overlap much and the overall area approaches a predicted value. During the body part region labeling, we estimate the scale s simultaneously. The coefficients of $\alpha, \beta, \eta, \gamma$ and μ control the weight among different terms. In this paper, we set $\eta = 0.1$, $\alpha = \gamma = 0.01$ and $\beta = \mu = 0.001$. The energy function is invariant to the scale, rotation and object articulation. Due to the loopy structure and high order terms, finding optimal body part region assignment is a challenging problem. In the following, we propose an efficient global optimal solution to this problem.

2.1 Finding Body Part Candidates

Before optimizing the body part configuration, we first find candidate regions for each body part. Different from the approach in [15], we do not merge small regions during the optimization, instead we select parts from a large set of candidate regions to form a human body assembly. The proposed method assumes that "correct" body part segments are in the candidate set. It is not necessary that separate arms or legs are detected; we allow merging of arms or legs into a single region. At first sight, this setting seems limited. However, we can almost always obtain roughly correct body part segments from object independent region proposals and progressively merged superpixels. Object independent region proposals [19] provide thousands of region candidates in an image by segmentation with randomly selected seed points and region pruning by object priors.

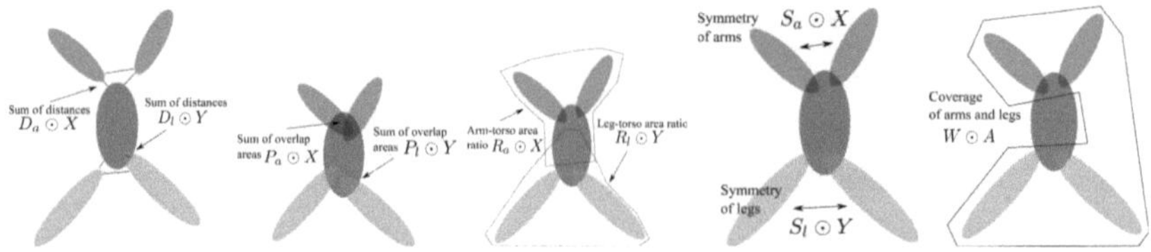

(a) Distance (b) Overlap (c) Area Ratio (d) Symmetry (e) Coverage

Fig. 3. The constraints on body parts and their notations

This method works well to identify part regions on a human subject even when they are composed of sub-regions with different appearance. To further improve the chance of obtaining parts such as arms or legs, we also include candidate regions generated by progressively merging over-segmented superpixels. The merging process starts from fine superpixels [18] and then successively merges two neighboring superpixels with the most similar color histogram and the weakest boundary. With the object independent region proposals and successively merged superpixels, there is a high chance that the true body part segments are included in the candidate sets. Note that we do not require accurate part candidates; our method is robust when handling region merging and inaccurate candidates.

Given the region candidates, we solve a combinatorial search problem to assemble regions so that the overall configuration resembles a human subject. Naive exhaustive search is not feasible. We propose an efficient global optimization method.

2.2 The Formulation

We formulate the optimization in this section. The basic idea is to construct the optimization so that it can be linearized for fast solution.

We introduce some notations. We define an arm assignment tensor X and a leg assignment tensor Y. The arm tensor $X = [x_{i,j,k}]$ whose element $x_{i,j,k}$ indicates the assignment of region candidate i to arm one, region candidate j to arm two and candidate k to torso. And, similarly we define the leg tensor $Y = [y_{i,j,k}]$ to indicate the assignment of parts i, j, and k to leg one, leg two and torso respectively. The elements of X and Y are indicator variables whose values are either 0 or 1. In X or Y there is a single 1 element and every other element is 0. We also define a torso assignment vector $Z = [z_i]$, where $z_i = 1$ if torso selects candidate i, and otherwise $z_i = 0$.

The Unary Term: Each region candidate has a cost when assigned to a body part. We measure the shape similarity of each candidate region to the template. We use the inner distance [25] histogram to quantify the shape of a segment. The shape descriptor is the histogram of the distance between each pair of points in a region. It can be efficiently computed using dynamic programming in $O(n^3)$ time, where n is the number of points in the region. The histogram has 20 bins in the range from 0 to the longest pairwise distance. We further normalize the histogram by the number of point pairs. The normalized inner distance histogram is scale and rotation invariant and roughly articulation invariant.

For each part p, e.g., arm, leg or torso, we have a set of exemplars $\{e_1, e_2, ...e_{k_p}\}$ in which e_i is the inner distance histogram of the ith template shape. The cost of the assignment of a candidate whose shape descriptor is h is defined as $\min_i ||h - e_i||$ where $||.||$ is the Euclidean distance. We build assignment cost tensor $U = [u_{i,j,k}]$ and $V = [v_{i,j,k}]$, where $u_{i,j,k} = a(i) + a(j)$ and $a(.)$ is the arm assignment cost for a candidate, $v_{i,j,k} = l(i) + l(j)$ and $l(.)$ is the leg assignment cost. The torso assignment cost vector is denoted as $T = [t_i]$, where t_i is the assignment cost of torso candidate i. In this paper, we keep the top 100 candidates for arm, leg and torso based on their local matching costs. The overall unary part assignment cost is

$$\mathcal{U} = U \odot X + V \odot Y + Z \odot T, \tag{2}$$

where $\odot$ is the operator to sum the product of corresponding tensor elements.

Distance Term: A valid body configuration requires that the chosen arm candidates and leg candidates should be adjacent to the selected torso candidate. Arms or legs also tend to be close to each other. The distance term is

$$\mathcal{D} = D_a \odot X + D_l \odot Y, \tag{3}$$

where D_a and D_l are distance tensors for arms and legs. $D_a = [d_{i,j,k}]$ where $d_{i,j,k} = d_{i,j} + d_{i,k} + d_{j,k}$, and we define $d_{i,j}$ as the distance between the closest points on the boundaries of arm candidate regions i and j, $d_{i,k}$ and $d_{j,k}$ are distances from arm candidates i and j to torso candidate k. Tensor D_l is similarly defined for legs. The shortest distances between region contours can be efficiently computed using the distance transform. The notations for the distance term are illustrated in Fig. 3(a).

Overlap Term: Simply minimizing the boundary distances among part regions does not guarantee a correct body part layout, since overlapping regions also have small boundary distances. We minimize the overlap between arms, legs, and torso:

$$\mathcal{P} = P_a \odot X + P_l \odot Y, \tag{4}$$

in which $P_a = [p_{i,j,k}]$ is an arm overlap tensor whose element $p_{i,j,k} = p_{i,j} + p_{i,k} + p_{j,k}$; $p_{i,j}$ is the overlapping area between arm candidate regions i and j, $p_{i,k}$ and $p_{j,k}$ are the overlapping areas of arm candidate regions i and j with torso region k. The leg overlap tensor P_l is similarly defined to penalize the overlap between legs, and between legs and torsos. The notations are illustrated in Fig. 3(b).

Size Ratio Term: A valid matching also should maintain correct size ratio between parts. The size ratio is also important for distinguishing arms and legs. We enforce that the arm-torso ratio, leg-torso ratio, arm-arm ratio and leg-leg ratio conform to the priors. The ratio term is

$$\mathcal{R} = |R_{at} \odot X - r_{at}| + |R_{lt} \odot Y - r_{lt}| + |R_{aa} \odot X - r_{aa}| + |R_{ll} \odot Y - r_{ll}|, \tag{5}$$

where r_{at}, r_{aa}, r_{lt} and r_{ll} are the arm-torso, arm-arm, leg-torso and leg-leg region ratio priors, and $r_{aa} = r_{ll} = 1$. $R_{at} = [r^{(at)}_{i,j,k}]$ is the arm-torso ratio tensor and $r^{(at)}_{i,j,k} = (b_i + b_j)/b_k$ where b_i and b_j are the areas of arm candidates i and j, and b_k is the area of torso candidate k. The arm-arm ratio tensor $R_{aa} = [r^{(aa)}_{i,j,k}]$, where $r^{(aa)}_{i,j,k} = b_i/b_j$. The leg-torso ratio tensor R_{lt} and leg-leg ratio tensor R_{ll} are similarly defined. The notations are illustrated in Fig. 3(c). We use the L1 norm here so that we can linearize the ratio term by introducing auxiliary variables.

Symmetry Term: The arms and legs are symmetrical parts that usually have similar appearance. We minimize their histogram difference:

$$\mathcal{S} = S_a \odot X + S_l \odot Y, \tag{6}$$

where S_a and S_l are the symmetry tensors for arms and legs. We have $S_a = [s_{i,j,k}]$, $s_{i,j,k} = ||H_i - H_j||$, where H_i and H_j are the normalized color histograms of arm candidate regions i and j. S_l is similarly defined for the legs. When minimizing the symmetry term, we prefer to select arms and legs with similar appearance as shown in Fig. 3(d).

The Overall Coverage of Arms and Legs: The above terms do not explicitly constrain the layout of arms and legs. Without further constraints, the legs and arms may choose closely overlapping region candidates. Here we control their overall region coverage so that they should occupy a preferred region size. To this end, we find a set of "finer" segments so that all the region candidates can be represented as the union of these small units. In this paper, we use over-segmented superpixels as the unit regions. Let w_n be a variable to indicate whether unit region n is part of the object region and let $W = [w_n], n = 1..N$, where N is the number of unit regions. Let a be the total area of the template arm and leg regions and A be the vector of the areas of the unit regions, we minimize

$$\mathcal{W} = |sW \odot A - a| \tag{7}$$

Subject to:

$$\begin{aligned} &w_n \leq 1, \;\; w_n \leq F_n \odot X + G_n \odot Y, \; n = 1..N \\ &w_n \geq x_{i,j,k}, \; \forall f^{(n)}_{i,j,k} = 1, \; n = 1..N \\ &w_n \geq y_{i,j,k}, \; \forall g^{(n)}_{i,j,k} = 1, \; n = 1..N \end{aligned}$$

where F_n and G_n are 0-1 arm and leg mask tensors for unit region n. We define $F_n = [f^{(n)}_{i,j,k}]$ where $f^{(n)}_{i,j,k} = 1$ if arm candidate region i or region j covers unit region n; G_n is defined similarly. In such a setting, if an arm or a leg region covers unit region n, $w_n = 1$ and otherwise $w_n = 0$. Therefore, $W \odot A$ equals the total area of the region covered by the arms and legs. The coverage is scaled by s for scale invariance. Notations are illustrated in Fig. 3(e).

2.3 Linearization and Branch and Bound

Combining all the terms, we have a complete minimization problem. However, this optimization is still hard to solve due to huge number of variables and constraints. We decompose the optimization into slave linear programs corresponding to each torso candidate. Each of the sub-problems becomes much simpler and can be quickly solved. For a 3D tensor M whose last dimension is k, we denote $M^{(k)}$ as the kth slice of tensor M. For instance, $X^{(k)}$ and $Y^{(k)}$ indicate the arm and leg assignment given the torso selection k. We use such a notation for all the matrices including U, V, D, P, S, R, F and G. We also estimate the scale s by computing the ratio between the model torso area and the area of current torso candidate k; the scale estimation is denoted as $\hat{s}_k$. The linear optimization corresponding to torso region k is written as follows:

$$\begin{aligned}&\min\{(U^{(k)} + \alpha D_a^{(k)} + \beta P_a^{(k)} + \gamma S_a^{(k)}) \odot X^{(k)} + (V^{(k)} + \alpha D_l^{(k)} + \\ &\beta P_l^{(k)} + \gamma S_l^{(k)}) \odot Y^{(k)} + t_k + \eta(q_{aa} + q_{ll} + q_{at} + q_{lt}) + \mu(w^+ + w^-)\}\end{aligned} \quad (8)$$

Subject to:

$$\begin{aligned}
&|X^{(k)}| = 1,\ |Y^{(k)}| = 1\\
&-q_{aa} \le R_{aa}^{(k)} \odot X^{(k)} - 1 \le q_{aa},\ -q_{ll} \le R_{ll}^{(k)} \odot Y^{(k)} - 1 \le q_{ll}\\
&-q_{at} \le R_{at}^{(k)} \odot X^{(k)} - r_{at} \le q_{at},\ -q_{lt} \le R_{lt}^{(k)} \odot Y^{(k)} - r_{lt} \le q_{lt}\\
&\hat{s}_k W \odot A - a = w^+ - w^-\\
&w_n \le 1,\ \ w_n \le F_n^{(k)} \odot X^{(k)} + G_n^{(k)} \odot Y^{(k)},\ n = 1..N\\
&w_n \ge x_{i,j,k},\ \forall f_{i,j,k}^{(n)} = 1,\ n = 1..N\\
&w_n \ge y_{i,j,k},\ \forall g_{i,j,k}^{(n)} = 1,\ n = 1..N
\end{aligned}$$

All the variables are non-negative, X and Y are binary.

Here $|X^{(k)}|$ and $|Y^{(k)}|$ denote the summation of all the elements in a matrix. t_k is the unary cost of torso candidate k. The nonnegative auxiliary variables q_{aa}, q_{ll}, q_{at}, q_{lt} equal the absolute value terms $|R_{aa}^{(k)} \odot X^{(k)} - 1|$, $|R_{ll}^{(k)} \odot Y^{(k)} - 1|$, $|R_{at}^{(k)} \odot X^{(k)} - r_{at}|$, $|R_{lt}^{(k)} \odot Y^{(k)} - r_{lt}|$ and $w^+ + w^-$ equals $|\hat{s}_k W \odot A - a|$, when the objective function is minimized. There are K slave mixed integer linear programs, each of which has K^2 arm and leg pairwise variables and N unit superpixel variables. In this paper $K = 100$ and and N is around 1000. We notice that when the torso selection is fixed, the only coupling between the arms and legs is the region overlapping constraints, which implies that each slave program can be solved quite efficiently.

We use branch and bound method to obtain the integer solution to each mixed integer slave program. Each slave program has the format $\min cu : Du = d$, where u includes the binary X and Y variables, and continuous w, q variables. We compute the lower bound by solving the relaxed linear program in which the binary constraints on X and Y variables are discarded. Any feasible integer solution provides an upper bound, which can be initialized using the local best part matching.

New search tree branches are generated on the node with the smallest lower bound. We introduce integer cuts on the most fractional variable (the variable closest to 0.5). For the node with the lowest lower bound, a new cut $u_i = 0$ or $u_i = 1$ where u_i is either an X variable or a Y variable is included in the linear program. We do not have to solve each linear program from scratch, since there is only one more new constraint included in each branch and cut iteration. By introducing slack variables, $u_i = 0$ or equivalent $u_i \leq 0$ becomes $u_i + v_{i,0} = 0$, and $u_i = 1$ or equivalent $u_i \geq 1$ becomes $u_i - v_{i,1} = 1$ where $v_{i,0} \geq 0, v_{i,1} \geq 0$. u_i is a basic variable and its right hand side is a fractional number in the final simplex tabular. For the $u_i = 0$ branch, we subtract the original u_i row from $u_i + v_{i,0} = 0$, and for the $u_i = 1$ branch, we subtract $u_i - v_{i,1} = 1$ from the u_i row. In either case, we turn $v_{i,0}$ or $v_{i,1}$ into a basic variable that is not feasible because it has negative value on the right hand side. The dual-simplex method is then applied in pivoting and usually it takes very few steps to regain the optimal solution. We discard the branch whose linear program solution is infeasible or is greater than the current upper bound. Most of the branches are pruned quickly.

We keep track of the upper bound B_u and lower bound B_l of the solution. B_l is the lowest lower bound of all the active search tree nodes. Branch and bound can be terminated prematurely when the tolerance gap $\delta = \frac{2(B_u - B_l)}{(B_u + B_l)}$ is reached, and the objective is upper bounded by $(\delta + 2)/(2 - \delta)$ times the global minimum. In this paper, we terminate the iteration when $\delta \leq 10^{-3}$. After solving each slave program, the optimal solution of the original problem is the minimum of all the slave programs.

3 Experiment

An Example: Fig. 4 shows the example of matching a human subject using the proposed method. In this example, we generate about 1000 candidate regions. The local matching costs for the torso, leg and arm are shown in Fig. 4(b), (c) and (d), where brighter color indicates that a region is more likely to be a specific body part. The unary part cost is computed by matching the normalized inner distance histograms of the region candidates to those of the template shapes. Local matching is noisy and as shown in Fig. 4(e) a simple greedy method that selects the best match for each part does not give satisfactory result. The proposed method constructs a mixed integer program corresponding to each torso candidate. Here we keep the top 100 candidates for the torso, arm and leg. Our optimization yields much better result. The top 5 matching results are shown in Fig. 4 (f)-(j). The optimal matching accurately localizes the body parts in this example. The proposed method is also efficient; the optimization takes less than 10 seconds on a 2.8GHZ machine.

Fig. 4. A matching example using the proposed method. (a) Input image. (b), (c) and (d) show the local matching costs of the candidate regions to the torso, leg and arm templates (the brighter a segment, the more likely it is a corresponding body part). (f)-(j) show the top 5 matching results using the proposed method. (red, green and blue indicate arm, leg and torso regions respectively).

Fig. 5. Object foreground is not always in the region candidates. The odd number images show the closest region candidates to the object foreground. The proposed method uses smaller part candidates and is able to match the target reliably, as shown in the even number images.

Proposal Regions and Object Foreground Segmentation: The region candidates from the object independent proposals and successively merged superpixels are not always able to give the overall human subject foreground. The sample test images in Fig. 5 are from the 305-image human pose dataset [2]. To make the matching problem more general, we resize the height of each image to 480 pixels so that the human subjects have different scales, and we rotate each image by 90 degrees. The best overall body segmentation from region candidates can be quite far from the ground truth as shown in the odd number images in Fig. 5. The proposed method is able to localize the target by using smaller part regions which are much easier to detect as shown in the even number images in Fig. 5.

Comparison with Competing Methods on Pose Dataset: We further compare the proposed method with competing methods. We first compare the proposed method with a greedy method that assigns the lowest cost candidate to the corresponding body part. The comparison is on the 305-image human pose dataset [2]. The images are scaled so that the height is 480 pixels. The scale factor is not determined due to a variety of image sizes in the dataset. Without

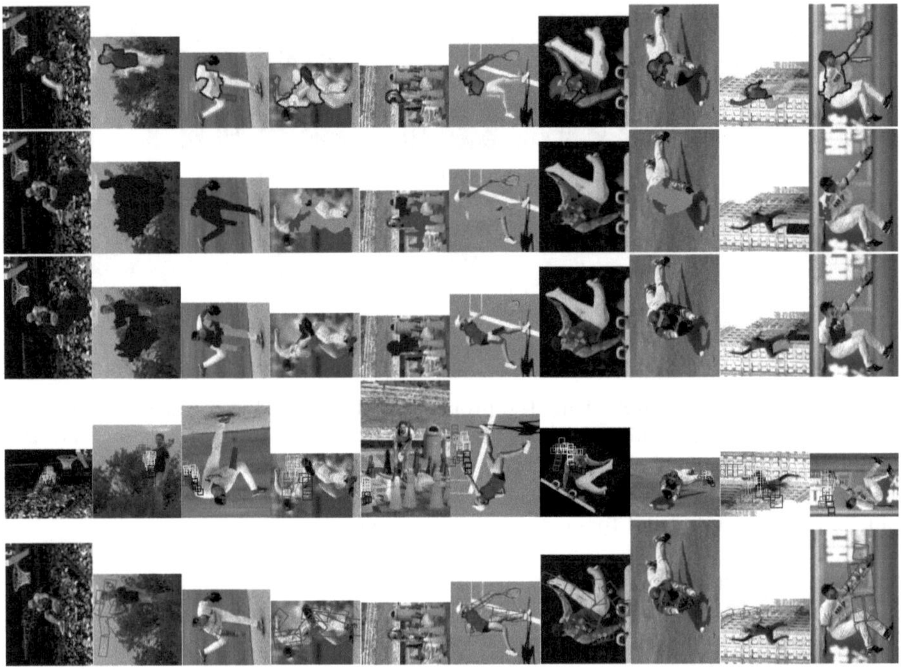

Fig. 6. Sample matching results of the proposed method (row 1), greedy method (row 2), Hough Transform based deformable matching (row 3), a recent people detector [2] (row 4) and 10-part pictorial structure method with strong part detector [3] (row 5)

loosing generality, we rotate all the images by 90 degrees and we assume that all the testing methods do not know the rotation angle. Due to the noisy local matching costs and lack of constraints among body parts, the simple greedy approach gives poor results. Fig. 6 row 1 shows sample results of the proposed method, and Fig. 6 row 2 shows the matching results of the greedy method. The proposed method yields much better results. The quantitative comparison on all the images in the dataset is shown in Fig. 7. We define the matching score for a part as $|T \cap G|/|T \cup G|$, where T is the target part region, G is the ground truth region of the corresponding part, and $|.|$ computes the area of a region. In this paper, the ground truth regions are obtained from the ground truth joint labeling and by fitting a bar with suitable width to each body part segment. We compute the matching scores for the torso, arms and legs. The matching score is in $[0, 1]$ and the higher the matching score the better the matching; a perfect matching has the score of 1. The proposed method has much higher matching scores than the greedy method.

We compare the proposed method with a Hough Transform based method. In this method, we use a star structure model constrained by the global scale and rotation. The whole model is thus non-tree. The energy function is the linear combination of the unary matching cost, the pairwise matching cost, and the global scale and rotation consistency cost. The pairwise cost enforces the vector

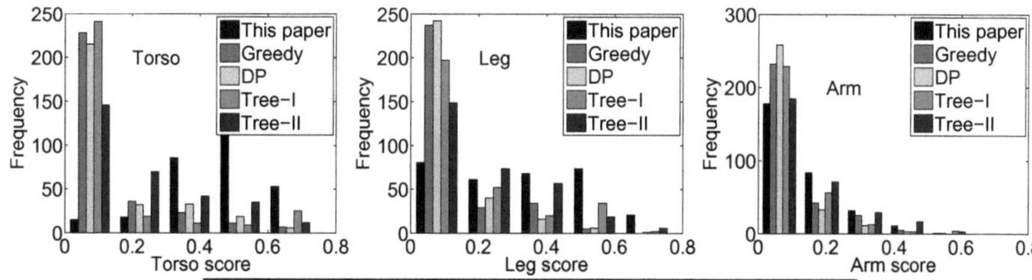

	This paper	Greedy	DP	Tree-I [2]	Tree-II [3]
Torso	0.4612	0.0979	0.1240	0.1058	0.2025
Leg	0.3205	0.0865	0.0788	0.1444	0.1954
Arm	0.1159	0.0728	0.0497	0.0764	0.1208

Fig. 7. Comparison with competing methods on the 305-image pose dataset [2]. Row 1 shows matching score distributions for torso, leg and arm. Row 2 gives average matching scores of different methods. Higher scores indicate better results.

from the center of one part to the center of its neighbor part to conform to the model under some unknown rotation and scaling, and it also enforces that the area ratio of the part pairs follows the model. By quantizing scales and rotations, the optimization of the deformable matching turns into a sequence of dynamic programming on each scale and rotation. This matching method is essentially the extended Hough Transform in which the torso position is voted from all the part candidates. The final result is the matching with the lowest energy. We choose a stretch-out pose as the model spatial layout. As shown in Fig. 6 the dynamic programming (DP) approach gives results worse than the proposed method. The average matching scores and the matching score distributions shown in Fig. 7 confirm the advantage of the proposed method. The DP matching method is not able to handle large object articulations and therefore yields poor results for this dataset.

We compare the proposed method with a recent human detector [2] and a pictorial structure method using strong part detectors [3]. The method in [2] is not rotation invariant. We thus rotate each input image from 0 to 360 degrees with 24 steps, and we select the result with the best matching score. Fig. 6 row 4 shows sample matching results of the people detector. The proposed method greatly improves the result. Generating the foreground part segmentation by connecting joint detections of the pictorial structure method [2] and thickening the lines, we can use the region ratio metric to quantitatively measure the matching performance. The ratio of line thickening uses the same scheme as the one in ground truth region generation, i.e., a perfect matching would give a score of 1 for each part. Fig. 7 compares the matching scores between the proposed method and [2]. The proposed method has much better performance. Another pictorial structure method [3] that uses strong local part detectors is further compared with the proposed method. This method operates on discrete scales from 1 to 5 with 10 steps and 24 rotation angles. The pictorial structure method takes about 20 minutes to process each image, while the proposed method takes

Fig. 8. Sample results of the proposed methods on the human pose dataset [2]. Arm regions are red, legs are green and torsos are blue. The test images are scaled from 1 to 5 and rotated by 90 degrees. The results are rotated back to the normal position and rescaled.

about 10 seconds in the optimization (the candidate region generation takes about 60 seconds per image). The comparison is shown in Fig. 6 and Fig. 7. The proposed method has much higher detection scores for the torso and legs than [3] and the arm detection score is comparable with [3]. More sample results of the proposed methods are shown in Fig. 8.

4 Conclusion

We propose an efficient method to localize human subject in images by matching body part region proposals. The proposed linearization scheme and branch and bound approach are able to give global optimal result efficiently. The proposed method is scale, rotation and articulation invariant. It has a clear advantage over competing methods when the target human subject has unknown scale and rotation. The proposed method will be useful for many different applications including human detection, tracking and action recognition.

Acknowledgments. This research is supported by US NSF grant 1018641.

References

1. Ramanan, D.: Learning to Parse Images of Articulated Objects. In: NIPS (2006)
2. Yang, Y., Ramanan, D.: Articulated Pose Estimation Using Flexible Mixtures of Parts. In: CVPR (2011)
3. Andriluka, M., Roth, S., Schiele, B.: Pictorial Structures Revisited: People Detection and Articulated Pose Estimation. In: CVPR (2009)
4. Jiang, H.: Human Pose Estimation Using Consistent Max-Covering. In: ICCV (2009)
5. Rosales, R., Sclaroff, S.: Inferring Body Pose without Tracking Body Parts. In: CVPR (2000)
6. Mori, G., Malik, J.: Estimating Human Body Configurations Using Shape Context Matching. In: Heyden, A., Sparr, G., Nielsen, M., Johansen, P. (eds.) ECCV 2002, Part III. LNCS, vol. 2352, pp. 666–680. Springer, Heidelberg (2002)
7. Gavrila, D.M.: A Bayesian, Exemplar-based Approach to Hierarchical Shape Matching. TPAMI 29(8) (2007)
8. Shakhnarovich, G., Viola, P., Darrell, T.: Fast Pose Estimation with Parameter Sensitive Hashing. In: ICCV (2003)
9. Felzenszwalb, P.F., Huttenlocher, D.P.: Pictorial Structures for Object Recognition. IJCV 61(1) (January 2005)
10. Sigal, L., Black, M.J.: Measure Locally, Reason Globally: Occlusion Sensitive Articulated Pose Estimation. In: CVPR (2006)
11. Tian, T.P., Sclaroff, S.: Fast Globally Optimal 2D Human Detection with Loopy Graph Models. In: CVPR (2010)
12. Mori, G.: Guiding Model Search Using Segmentation. In: ICCV (2005)
13. Ren, X.F., Berg, A.C., Malik, J.: Recovering Human Body Configurations Using Pairwise Constraints between Parts. In: ICCV 2005, vol. 1, pp. 824–831 (2005)
14. Sapp, B., Jordan, C., Taskar, B.: Adaptive Pose Priors for Pictorial Structures. In: CVPR (2011)
15. Cour, T., Shi, J.: Recognizing Objects by Piecing Together The Segmentation Puzzle. In: CVPR (2007)
16. Kohli, P., Rihan, J., Bray, M., Torr, P.H.S.: Simultaneous Segmentation and Pose Estimation of Humans Using Dynamic Graph Cuts. IJCV 79(3), 285–298 (2008)
17. Ferrari, V., Manuel, M., Zisserman, A.: Pose Search: Retrieving People Using Their Pose. In: CVPR (2008)
18. Felzenszwalb, P.F., Huttenlocher, D.P.: Efficient Graph-based Image Segmentation. IJCV 59(2) (2004)
19. Endres, I., Hoiem, D.: Category Independent Object Proposals. In: Daniilidis, K., Maragos, P., Paragios, N. (eds.) ECCV 2010, Part V. LNCS, vol. 6315, pp. 575–588. Springer, Heidelberg (2010)
20. Chen, C., Fan, G.: Hybrid Body Representation for Integrated Pose Recognition, Localization and Segmentation. In: CVPR (2008)
21. Wang, H., Koller, D.: Multi-Level Inference by Relaxed Dual Decomposition for Human Pose Segmentation. In: CVPR (2011)
22. Ionescu, C., Li, F., Sminchisescu, C.: Latent Structured Models for Human Pose Estimation. In: ICCV (2011)
23. Bourdev, L., Maji, S., Brox, T., Malik, J.: Detecting People Using Mutually Consistent Poselet Activations. In: Daniilidis, K., Maragos, P., Paragios, N. (eds.) ECCV 2010, Part VI. LNCS, vol. 6316, pp. 168–181. Springer, Heidelberg (2010)
24. Bo, Y., Fowlkes, C.: Shape-based Pedestrian Parsing. In: CVPR (2011)
25. Ling, H., Jacobs, D.W.: Shape Classification Using the Inner-Distance. IEEE Trans. on Pattern Anal. and Mach. Intell. 29(2), 286–299 (2007)

Measuring Image Distances via Embedding in a Semantic Manifold

Chen Fang and Lorenzo Torresani

Dartmouth College, Computer Science Department
Hanover, NH, USA
http://vlg.cs.dartmouth.edu

Abstract. In this work we introduce novel image metrics that can be used with distance-based classifiers or directly to decide whether two input images belong to the same class. While most prior image distances rely purely on comparisons of low-level features extracted from the inputs, our metrics use a large database of labeled photos as auxiliary data to draw semantic relationships between the two images, beyond those computable from simple visual features. In a preprocessing stage our approach derives a semantic image graph from the labeled dataset, where the nodes are the labeled images and the edges connect pictures with related labels. The graph can be viewed as modeling a semantic image manifold, and it enables the use of graph distances to approximate semantic distances. Thus, we reformulate the task of measuring the semantic distance between two *unlabeled* pictures as the problem of embedding the two input images in the semantic graph. We propose and evaluate several embedding schemes and graph distance metrics. Our results on Caltech101, Caltech256 and ImageNet show that our distances consistently match or outperform the state-of-the-art in this field.

1 Introduction

Psychological studies have shown that humans can easily determine whether two visual examples belong to the same basic category, even when that class is new and has never been seen before [1]. This suggests that to address this problem our brain employs a general semantic distance metric valid across all classes. In this work we are interested in investigating computational models that can tackle the same problem: our objective is to design distance functions providing a measure of whether two input photos belong to the same basic class, regardless of what that class may be. Image metrics implementing such semantic notions of similarity promise to enable a wide array of computer vision applications, and have been used in the past in image retrieval [2,3], object classification [4], as well as semantic segmentation and annotation of photos [5].

Most prior image metrics rely solely on comparisons of low-level features extracted from the two input images [2,4,6]. While directly comparing visual features may be sufficient to assess simple notions of similarity, such as near-duplicate or object-instance similarity, we argue for the need of auxiliary labeled

A. Fitzgibbon et al. (Eds.): ECCV 2012, Part IV, LNCS 7575, pp. 402–415, 2012.

data to provide accurate estimates of semantic relatedness and membership to the same object class. In a sense, our proposed use of this background knowledge is akin to the way children exploit past observations of many examples of different classes in order to learn to recognize instances of a new category [7].

At a high-level, our approach operates as follows. During an offline preprocessing stage, our method uses the auxiliary dataset of images with class labels to compute an image graph. The nodes of the graph are the labeled pictures and the edges link images that are semantically similar, as determined by the class labels. The shortest path distance between two nodes of the graph can then be viewed as a measure of their semantic relatedness. The shortest path distances are approximations of the geodesic distances of the unknown semantic manifold of images. This idea has been previously used for many tasks including dimensionality reduction [8], and semi-supervised learning [9]. While the graph per se provides estimates of semantic distance only for the labeled image nodes, we propose to extend its use also for unlabeled pictures, by embedding these photos in the graph. For each unlabeled input photo, this requires first determining its position in the graph, using only visual features. Once the input is embedded in the graph, we can compute its semantic distance to all the other pictures in the graph. Similarly, given two unlabeled images, we can embed them both in the graph in order to measure their semantic distance.

In this paper we propose several schemes to embed unlabeled pictures in the semantic graph. Our methods perform the embedding by using a visual distance (i.e., a metric based on low-level image features) to compare the input photo to the images in the graph. While this may appear to defeat the purpose of side-stepping visual distances to measure semantic relationships between images, we argue that our embedding task is far easier than the problem of directly computing semantic distances from low-level descriptors, for the following reasons:

1. Embedding the input images requires only selecting the most semantically-related photos. As shown by studies in human perception [10] and in computer vision [11], the most semantically similar pictures to a given input photo tend to be those most visually similar to it. Thus, these images are easy to identify even with distances based on low-level image descriptors.
2. We can simplify the task by using a large-scale database of labeled photos. It has been shown [12] that making the database larger will increase the probability that the top images retrieved according to a visual metric will also be semantically close to the input image, even when using simple low-level features to calculate visual distances. We exploit this property by using a database of 10M images (the ImageNet dataset [13]) to build our graph.
3. It is possible to exploit the structure of the graph to improve the embedding results: while the visual distances are brittle and may produce a set of candidate nodes including some outliers (i.e., images not semantically related to the input photo), this candidate set can then be refined (or denoised) to identify related nodes that lie close to each other in the graph. In other words, it is possible to enforce coherence of labels among the selected nodes to make the embedding more accurate and robust.

2 Related Work

Most object categorization systems require some form of similarity function to compare examples, such as the distance metric used by the nearest neighbor (NN) classifier or the kernels in SVMs. Most recent approaches to defining image metrics are based on learning methods which train the distance function using a set of labeled examples, typically consisting of images annotated with class labels. This problem is often referred to as metric learning. Within the wide range of proposed approaches in this area we can identify two main categories: techniques to learn "global" metrics versus methods computing "local" distances.

Algorithms in the former category operate by learning a single parametric transformation mapping the inputs to a new target space, such that a predefined metric (most typically the Euclidean distance) in this space satisfies certain desired properties [14,15]. Similarly to these approaches, our method uses labeled examples to map images to a new target space – in our case, the semantic graph. However, rather than computing a parametric transformation and employing a predefined distance in the target space, our method uses the examples non-parametrically both to compute the mapping and also to define a distance metric expressed in terms of the entire labeled set.

The second strand of related work involves methods to compute "local" distances, i.e., metrics that vary across the space of examples (see [6] for a comprehensive survey). A simple form of local distance is one that changes for each individual training example [2,4]. Alternatively, a local distance can be learned for each category to recognize [16] or by grouping together classes that can share effectively the same metric [17]. Our approach can be viewed also as implementing a local metric, since the semantic graph can be complex and anisotropic: our distance will vary depending on the embedding point of the test example. In a sense, our metric is closely related to algorithms that learn a different metric for each *test* example by using as training points its closest neighbors [18,19]. However, unlike these prior systems, we exploit label information associated to the training examples, so as to suppress the effect of outliers present in the visual neighbors and to obtain a distance that is optimized for class recognition. Furthermore, while prior local metrics have been trained for a predefined set of classes (with the only exception of [17] which demonstrates good generalization to novel classes), our aim is to define a general distance that can be used to compare images of arbitrary classes, even categories not present in the labeled graph. Indeed, nearly all our experiments are carried out with this setup.

Our approach is inspired by the recent work of Deselaers and Ferrari [11], who have also proposed to compute image distances through comparisons to an auxiliary labeled dataset. They named their metric the "ImageNet distance", as it relies on the ImageNet database to infer the semantic relation between the input photos. For each input image, their method computes the distribution of class labels associated to its ImageNet neighbors; the distance between two input images is then calculated by comparing their class-label histograms. A related idea is presented in [3] where the distance between two images is computed by comparing their membership probabilities to a set of 103 Flickr groups, estimated using a set of SVM classifiers.

As in [11], we also exploit ImageNet as the auxiliary source of labeled images. However, we argue that our graph-based representation of this data provides several advantages over the system of [11]. First, it enables semantic filtering: while the ImageNet distance uses the labels of *visual* neighbors to measure similarity between two images, our embedding methods exploit the graph structure to find target nodes that are not only visually similar to the input but also *semantically* coherent. In our experiments we demonstrate that this refinement improves the results. Furthermore, the graph allows us to measure indirect semantic relations: while the ImageNet distance measures the number of *exactly matching* class labels between the two neighbor sets, the graph allows us to take into account indirect semantic relations between the neighbors, even when their class labels do not match exactly.

3 Approach Overview

Our approach consists of an offline preprocessing stage, during which the semantic graph is built from a dataset of labeled images, and a test stage in which the graph is used to measure the distance between any two new unlabeled images.

Let us denote with $\mathcal{D} = \{(\mathbf{x}_1, y_1), \ldots, (\mathbf{x}_N, y_N)\}$ the labeled dataset of N images that we use to build the semantic graph, where $\mathbf{x}_i$ is the descriptor of the i-th image in the database and y_i is a label indicating the category of the object present in the i-th image. While our approach can be used with any arbitrary image descriptor, our experiments use two different feature vectors: the first is the GIST descriptor [20], which is a low-level image representation capturing the spatial layout in the picture; the second is the "classeme" feature vector [21], which is a higher-level descriptor containing the output of 2659 predefined classifiers evaluated on the image. We chose these two descriptors for several reasons: they are compact in size and thus well suited to large-scale databases; both descriptors have been shown to capture categorical information; finally, they allow us to understand the pros and cons of using a low-level as opposed to a high-level representation with our approach.

The final goal of our system is to compute the distance between any two unlabeled images $\mathbf{x}, \mathbf{x}'$. While sections 4,5 describe formally the method, here we explain the intuition behind the two stages of our approach, schematically illustrated in figure 1.

Offline Stage: Construction of the Semantic Graph. The aim of this stage is to reorganize the auxiliary dataset $\mathcal{D}$ in the form of a graph. The nodes in the graph represent the labeled images and the edges link pictures that are detected to be highly similar, *both visually as well semantically.* The semantic relation between the labeled images is determined by comparing their annotations, while their visual similarity is computed using image-content features. The edges in the graph are supplemented with weights, corresponding to the visual distance

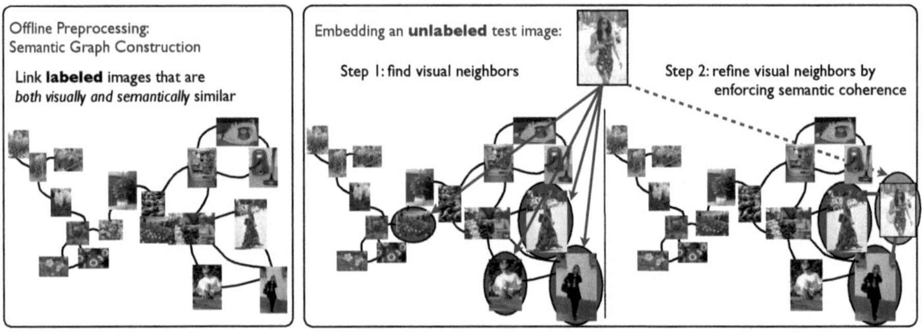

Fig. 1. Conceptual illustration of our embedding method. During an offline stage a semantic image graph is constructed using a labeled database: links are created between images that satisfy the joint conditions of being visually close and having related class labels. At test time, the unlabeled photo is embedded in the graph via a two-step process: first, visual neighbors are found; then, the position of the test images in the graph is computed by finding visual neighbors that are semantically coherent.

between the two nodes connected by the edge. The high-level idea is that for images that are closely related, the visual distance provides a reliable estimate of their similarity. For two images that are not directly linked via an edge, their similarity can be measured through their shortest connecting path within the graph. Thus, the graph embodies a form of semantic manifold where geodesics provide measures of semantic relatedness between images.

Test Time: Embedding Unlabeled Images in the Graph. The semantic distance between two unlabeled images is computed by embedding independently both images in the graph so as to measure their distance in the semantic manifold. As illustrated in figure 1, this is done via the following two steps:

- *Step 1: find visual neighbors in the graph.* For each of the two input examples, the m closest database images are found according to the visual distance.
- *Step 2: embed the points by enforcing semantic coherence.* While the initial selection of the m candidate nodes ensures that these images are visually similar to the input, in this step we impose semantic coherence among these nodes to compute the final positions of the inputs in the graph.

After embedding, the distance between the inputs is calculated by comparing their positions inside the semantic graph.

4 Semantic Graph Construction

As previously discussed, we construct our semantic graph from the large-scale ImageNet dataset [13], which consists of roughly 10M images encompassing over 15000 categories. The ImageNet categories are structured according to the semantic hierarchy of WordNet [22]: each class is described by a set of synonyms, called a *synset*, and the children of a synset represent more specialized synsets of that visual category (e.g., the children of synset "plant" are "tree", "flower" and "vegetable"). For each synset, on average, the dataset includes 632 manually-validated images illustrating that visual concept.

We exploit the hierarchy of ImageNet to build the semantic graph, as discussed below. In order to maintain the computational and storage costs manageable in spite of the large database size, we propose to construct a sparse graph, where each image is connected only to a small number of other photos.

For each database image $\mathbf{x}_i$, we define $\mathcal{S}_i$ to be the set of synsets comprising the synset of $\mathbf{x}_i$ and the children of the synsets of $\mathbf{x}_i$. We refer to $\mathcal{S}_i$ as the "extended synset" of $\mathbf{x}_i$. Then, the graph is constructed by creating an undirected edge between each image $\mathbf{x}_i$ and its k-closest neighbors within its extended synset $\mathcal{S}_i$, computed using the L2 distance between image descriptors. To each edge connecting node i to node j, we associate weight $w_{ij} \equiv ||\mathbf{x}_i - \mathbf{x}_j||$. Note that this strategy achieves two fundamental goals: on one hand, by linking each image only to nodes within its extended synset we establish semantically-consistent edges; on the other hand, by letting edges to be created across the original WordNet synsets, we avoid ending up with a myriad of disconnected graph components.

One issue, however, is that the root node in the ImageNet hierarchy has no associated images. This would cause the subtrees of the top-layer synsets to be disconnected components in the graph. To avoid this problem, we establish edges between the image pairs with the 1000 smallest visual distances among all pictures in the top synsets. After this operation, 99.36% of all images belong to the largest connected component of the graph. Thus, we simply discard the images outside the largest component, since this is a tiny subset of the database.

5 Embedding Unlabeled Images in the Graph

We now present different strategies to embed an unlabeled image $\mathbf{x}$ in the graph. The initial step for all methods involves selecting a set of candidate neighbors in the graph using the visual distance: we indicate with $\mathcal{R} \subset \{1, \ldots, N\}$ the indices of the m-nearest neighbors of $\mathbf{x}$ in the graph, computed according to the L2 distance between image descriptors. In practice, the set $\mathcal{R}$ will include images semantically related to $\mathbf{x}$ but also some outliers. The methods described below enforce semantic coherence to improve the embedding.

Semantic Energy Optimization (SEO). This embedding method operates by connecting the input to a subset of n nodes $\mathcal{T}$, which we name the *target nodes*. The subset $\mathcal{T}$ is chosen from the set of visual neighbors $\mathcal{R}$ by imposing semantic coherence via an energy optimization approach. While the parameter n could be set a-priori to be equal to k, in practice we found beneficial to tune n via cross validation. We represent the subset $\mathcal{T} \subset \mathcal{R}$ by introducing binary variables $z_i \in \{0, 1\}$ for the nodes $i \in \mathcal{R}$: we use $z_i = 1$ to indicate that $i \in \mathcal{T}$ (i.e., the node is selected as a target node), while $z_i = 0$ denotes that $i \notin \mathcal{T}$. We indicate with

$\mathbf{z}$ the $|\mathcal{R}|$-dimensional binary-valued vector obtained by concatenating these binary variables, i.e., $\mathbf{z} = (z_i \mid i \in \mathcal{R})$. An intuitive idea is to determine the subset $\mathcal{T}$ by minimizing the following energy function:

$$E(\mathbf{z}) = \sum_{i \in \mathcal{R}} \theta_i z_i + \lambda \sum_{i,j \in \mathcal{R}} \theta_{ij} z_i z_j \tag{1}$$

subject to constraint $\sum_{i \in \mathcal{R}} z_i = n$, where

$$\theta_i = ||\mathbf{x} - \mathbf{x}_i|| \tag{2}$$

$$\theta_{ij} = \begin{cases} d^{SPD}(\mathbf{x}_i, \mathbf{x}_j) & \text{if } d^{SPD}(\mathbf{x}_i, \mathbf{x}_j) < \tau \\ \tau & \text{otherwise} \end{cases} \tag{3}$$

with $d^{SPD}(\mathbf{x}_i, \mathbf{x}_j)$ denoting the shortest path distance in the semantic graph between $\mathbf{x}_i$ and $\mathbf{x}_j$. Intuitively, the unary terms of eq. 1 encode our preference for choosing nodes that are visually similar to $\mathbf{x}$, while the pairwise terms encourage selection of neighbors that are close to each other in the semantic graph. The threshold τ is used to avoid penalizing excessively selection of nodes that are far apart in the graph: this makes the model more robust to outliers. It can be shown that the constrained discrete optimization defined by eq. 1 is NP-hard in general [23]. Nevertheless, we have tried to minimize this energy by reformulating the optimization as a mixed integer program (MIP) expressed in term of auxiliary variables $t_{ij} \in [0, 1]$ bounding the pairwise interactions $z_i z_j$ via constraints $t_{ij} \leq z_i$, $t_{ij} \leq z_j$, $t_{ij} \geq z_i + z_j - 1$ for all $i, j \in \mathcal{R}$. We obtained good optimization results by minimizing the resulting MIP with the state-of-the-art Gurobi solver [24], which in practice globally optimizes 26% of our problems.

However, even when the optimal $\mathcal{T}$ could be found, the resulting embedding did not perform well in our tests. Through experimental investigation, we discovered that the energy model of eq. 1 is simply too strict as it wants *all* target neighbors to be close to each other. In practice, for many images this is an unreasonable assumption. Consider for example the photo of a group of children playing soccer in the street: the picture should be linked to nodes of synset "soccer, association football" but possibly also to nodes of synset "city, metropolis, urban center". Based on this observation we designed a "softer" version of our semantic energy that forces each selected node to be close to at least l other target nodes, where $l < n$. In other words, we encourage each selected neighbor to be near a few other target nodes, but not necessarily to *all* nodes in $\mathcal{T}$. This soft constraint is implemented by optimizing the following energy:

$$E(\mathbf{z}, \mathbf{t}) = \sum_{i \in \mathcal{R}} \theta_i z_i + \lambda \sum_{i,j \in \mathcal{R}} \theta_{ij} t_{ij} \tag{4}$$

subject to $\sum_{i \in \mathcal{R}} z_i = n$, and to constraints:

$$z_i \in \{0, 1\},\ t_{ij} \in \{0, 1\},\ t_{ij} \leq z_i, t_{ij} \leq z_j\ \forall i, j \in \mathcal{R} \tag{5}$$

$$\sum_{j \in \mathcal{R}} t_{ij} \geq l z_i\ \forall i \in \mathcal{R} \tag{6}$$

where θ_i, θ_{ij} are defined as above. These constraints ensure that for each target node i, only the l smallest pairwise terms θ_{ij} between i and other selected nodes are included in the objective. We found that this optimization is also much easier to solve: the Gurobi solver was able to globally optimize *all* of our test cases. We refer to minimization of eq. 4 as Semantic Energy Optimization (SEO).

Random Walk (RW). The high-level idea of this embedding method is to find the nodes that are most likely to be reached by a Markov random walk [25] inside the graph starting from the initial candidate nodes $\mathcal{R}$. We use random walks to denoise the initial set $\mathcal{R}$ by finding nodes that are "close" to the majority of these initial vertices, while suppressing the effect of the outliers in $\mathcal{R}$. In order to perform the random walk, for each graph edge linking i to j we define the one-step transition probability from i to j in terms of the weights w_{ij} (we remind the reader that the weights w_{ij} are the visual distances computed during the graph construction). Specifically, for each edge (i, j) we define the probability of transitioning from node i at time t to node j at time $t+1$ to be

$$P_{t+1|t}(j|i) = \frac{1/w_{ij}}{\sum_k 1/w_{ik}} \tag{7}$$

so that the probabilities out of node i sum up to 1 (this probability is set to 0 for nodes not directly connected by an edge). Note that for nodes linked by an edge $P_{t+1|t}(j|i)$ is inversely proportional to the visual distance between $\mathbf{x}_i$ and $\mathbf{x}_j$. This implies that at each time the walk is likely to progress into a node that is highly similar to the current one. The random walk is initiated from a starting distribution $\mathbf{q} \in \mathbb{R}^N$ computed from the candidate nodes $\mathcal{R}$ as follows:

$$q_i = \begin{cases} \frac{1/||\mathbf{x}-\mathbf{x}_i||}{\sum_{k\in\mathcal{R}} 1/||\mathbf{x}-\mathbf{x}_k||} & \text{if } i \in \mathcal{R} \\ 0 & \text{otherwise} \end{cases} \tag{8}$$

If we store the one-step probabilities into a matrix A whose (i, j)-th entry is set equal to $P_{t+1|t}(j|i)$, then we can calculate the distribution $\mathbf{r}$ of nodes reached from $\mathbf{q}$ after t steps of random walk as $\mathbf{r}^T = \mathbf{q}^T A^t$. This can be more efficiently calculated by means of t matrix-vector products, i.e., $\mathbf{r} = (((\mathbf{q}^T A)A)\ldots A)$. The resulting vector $\mathbf{r}$ can be shown [26] to measure the "volume" of paths leading to the individual nodes in the graph from the initial configuration $\mathbf{q}$. Intuitively, the random walk will tend to suppress paths originating from outlier nodes in $\mathcal{R}$, while paths starting from nearby nodes in $\mathcal{R}$ will tend to reinforce each other.

In principle, we could select as target nodes $\mathcal{T}$ the vertices that correspond to the n largest entries in $\mathbf{r}$, i.e., the ones that are more likely to be reached from the initial configuration. However, we found this strategy to produce relatively poor results. Instead we have had more success by directly using the random walk probabilities r_i to calculate semantic distances as follows. Let $\mathbf{r}$ and $\mathbf{r}'$ be the node distributions obtained via t steps of random walk for two input images $\mathbf{x}$ and $\mathbf{x}'$. Note that $\mathbf{r}$ can be viewed as a new semantic representation for image $\mathbf{x}$, encoding the relation of the image to the entire graph. Based on this intuition, we define the random walk distance to be $d^{RW}(\mathbf{x}, \mathbf{x}') = d^{\chi^2}(\mathbf{r}, \mathbf{r}')$, which measures the χ^2 distance between the two images in this semantic space.

6 Discussion of Computational Costs

In this section we discuss the computational costs of our approach and possible strategies to reduce them. We factor out from this discussion the creation of the graph, since this is done only once during an offline stage and it can be reused for all inputs, regardless of their class. The graph is represented as a sparse matrix which occupies little space in memory. At test time the most expensive operation is computing the visual distances from the input to all nodes. Without any optimization, this operation takes about 2 minutes per input. However, this runtime can be greatly reduced by adopting efficient NN search methods: for example, the system in [27] runs in a couple of seconds on a database of 10M images by using product quantization on classeme vectors to speed up the search with little loss in accuracy. The RW embedding takes on average 99 seconds per input when using $t = 25$ steps, but also this operation could be made much faster by reformulating the walk in terms of powers of eigenvectors of the matrix A, as discussed in [25]. The SEO optimization on average runs in 48 seconds per example on a standard budget PC using $m = 400, n = 100, l = 4$.

7 Experiments

We now describe experimental evaluations of our distance metrics on the following datasets: Caltech101, Caltech256 [28] and the ILSVRC2010 database [29]. Unless otherwise noted, all results are based on a graph constructed from the 10M ImageNet dataset using connectivity $k = 10$ (see [30] for our study of the sensitivity to the size of the auxiliary dataset N and the graph connectivity k).

7.1 Evaluation of Metrics for "Same or Different Class" Recognition

We begin by presenting results on the Caltech101 dataset. While this image database is known to be simple for the recognition standards of modern categorization systems, it was the dataset used in [11] to compare different image metrics. We follow the experimental setup used in [11]: we use the same set of 1020 photos (10 samples for each of the 102 classes); the set is split in two subsets of 51 classes; each subset is used in turn as training and testing set, so as to tune the parameters with two-fold cross validation. The final result is presented as the average cross-validation error. In each cross validation set, there are 129,795 distinct image pairs: in 2295 of these pairs the two images contain an object of the same class, while in the remaining pairs the two images belong to different category. In this experiment the value of distance is directly used to make a classification decision on whether the two samples contain the same object. As in [11], the result is presented in terms of Area Under the Curve (AUC) computed from the ROC curve.

We consider in our evaluation our two proposed embedding methods – **SEO** and **RW**. In addition, we include the simple embedding obtained by connecting

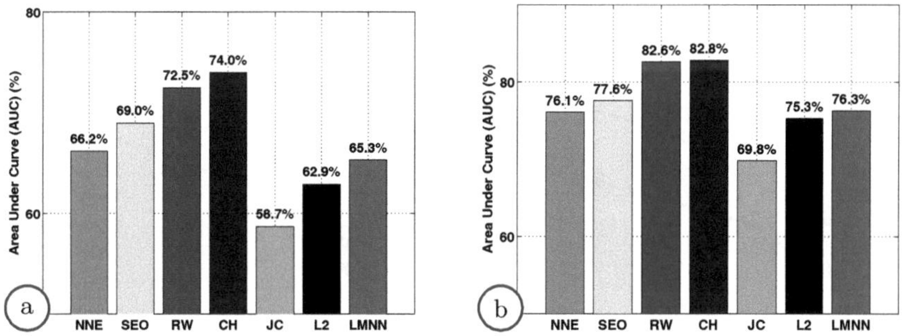

Fig. 2. Performance of distance metrics on Caltech101 using (a) GIST and (b) classeme features. Our metrics based on embedding in the graph are: NNE, SEO, RW. The ImageNet metrics proposed in [11] are CH and JC. The visual distances are L2 (the Euclidean metric) and LMNN (learned using the method of [16]).

each test image to its n closest visual neighbors in the graph, and denote this embedding method as Nearest-Neighbor Embedding (**NNE**). For NNE and SEO, the final semantic distance is computed as the shortest path distance between the two embedded nodes. As discussed in section 5, for the RW embedding we compute the semantic metric as the χ^2 distance between the random walk probability vectors. In addition to these metrics, we include the two distances proposed in [11]: **CH** is the "ImageNet" category histogram metric, while **JC** is the distance inspired by the Jiang-Conrath semantic similarity [31]. All parameters were optimized individually for each method by considering the following values: $m \in \{100, 200, 400, 800\}, n \in \{5, 10, 100, 200\}, l \in \{1, 2, 4, 6\}$. We also present results for two baseline metrics that do not use the auxiliary ImageNet database: **L2** denotes the L2 distance between the feature vectors of the two input images; **LMNN** indicates the distance learned using the large-margin nearest-neighbor approach described in [16]. Even for LMNN, we trained and tested the metric by using two-fold cross validation (i.e, the training and test sets involve two sets of disjoint classes), with 10 samples per class. To train this metric we used the software provided by the authors and as recommended in the manual we preprocessed the feature vectors via PCA, tuning the PCA target dimensionality for the best possible accuracy.

The performances of the different metrics are shown in figure 2. We can see that SEO, RW and CH perform considerably better than the visual distances (L2 and LMNN), with RW and CH nearly tied as the best metrics. The use of the auxiliary labeled data enables these distances to infer additional semantic connections yielding large improvements over LMNN, which has been previously shown to be one of the best metric learning methods (see, e.g., evaluations in [16,6,11]). It is also interesting to notice that both SEO and RW perform much better than the naïve NNE strategy which directly links the test images to their visual neighbors: this suggests that the semantic coherence enforced by SEO and RW produces a beneficial refinement of the initial set of visual neighbors.

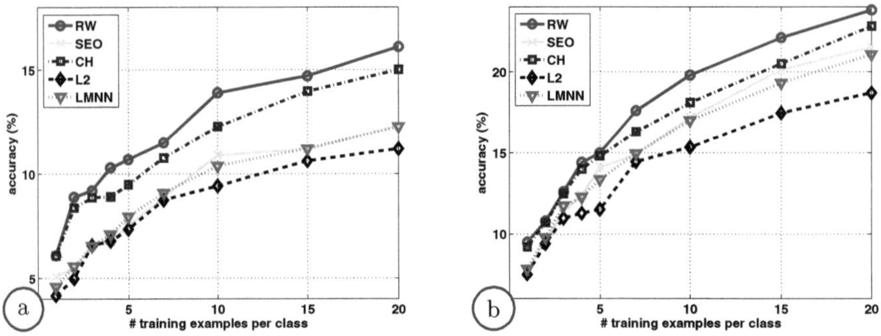

Fig. 3. Caltech256 multiclass recognition using a NN classifier based on different image metrics using (a) GIST and (b) classeme descriptors. Our RW metric gives consistently the best results: it even outperforms the LMNN metric, which in this experiment has been advantageously trained on the test categories.

7.2 Using Semantic Distances for Multiclass Object Categorization

In this section we demonstrate the use of semantic distances to perform multiclass object recognition using two different classification models – the NN classifier and a SVM trained with kernels defined by our metrics.

Nearest-Neighbor Classification with Semantic Metrics. We begin by presenting an evaluation on the Caltech256 dataset. The test set was obtained by sampling 10 images from each of the 256 classes. The training set size is varied from a minimum of 1 to a maximum of 20 examples per class. We use the NN classifier to perform multiclass recognition as follows: for each test image, we compute its distance to the training examples of all 256 classes and then pick the class most voted among the K nearest neighbors, where K is an integer optimized individually for each distance metric. Note that the embedding of the training images in the graph is done without exploiting the textual tags of the Caltech256 classes. We report the NN classification accuracy obtained with the RW, SEO, CH, L2 and LMNN metrics (we omit NNE and JC as they produce much poorer results). Here the LMNN metric was learned from a separate training set of 10 images for each of the 256 classes: thus the LMNN method here is given the significant advantage of training on the test classes. Figure 3 shows the recognition accuracy as a function of the number of training examples for (a) GIST and (b) classeme features. We see that on this task RW outperforms all distances, including CH as well as the LMNN metric trained in highly favorable conditions. The SEO metric performs better than the L2 distance but not as well as the RW and CH metrics.

We now describe NN multiclass recognition on a subset of the ILSVRC2010 dataset. This is a difficult test: the ILSVRC2010 images are more challenging than those in the Caltech sets as they often contain multiple objects, and exhibit a much wider within-class variance. However, the downside of this test is that the

ILSVRC2010 classes are present as synsets in the ImageNet dataset (although the two sets of images are, of course, disjoint). This means that the test categories are also included in the manifold. For this experiment, we sample 5 images from 500 randomly selected categories. We then partition the dataset into 5 subsets, each containing one example of each class. We use this partition to evaluate the 5-fold cross validation error of the NN classifier using different metrics. The recognition accuracies using classeme features are **6.04%, 5.08%, 2.92%** for RW, CH, and L2, respectively. Note that while the absolute accuracy rates are low due to the small number of training examples per class (only 4 for each validation run) and the large number of classes, the RW metric provides a relative improvement of 18% over the accuracy obtained using the state-of-the-art CH distance.

Nonlinear SVM Classification with Semantic Kernels. We conclude by presenting experiments demonstrating that our metrics can be used to construct powerful kernels for nonlinear Support Vector Machines (SVM). We compare kernels built from our distances to popular hand-defined kernels for categorization and show that in all cases our RW metric provides superior results.

Most kernels for SVMs are defined so that the kernel distance is close to 1 when the input vectors are similar and near to 0 when the inputs are highly different. In order to achieve this desired behavior with our metrics, we apply the "exp" function to the negative values of the distances, i.e., we define the kernel as $k(\mathbf{x}, \mathbf{x}') = \exp(-d(\mathbf{x}, \mathbf{x}')/\gamma)$, where d is the semantic distance and γ is a hyperparameter. We denote with expRW, expSEO, and expCH the kernels built by using as distance d the metrics RW, SEO and CH, respectively. Note that expRW and expCH are obtained by applying the exponential function to negative χ^2-distances, which always yields a Mercer kernel [32]. Instead, expSEO may produce a kernel matrix that is not Mercer. When this happens, we follow the common practice of thresholding the negative eigenvalues of the distance matrix to zero in order to yield a proper kernel matrix [33]. Finally, we include as baselines the exponential kernel (expL2) and the Gaussian kernel (Gaussian), both built by applying the exponential function to distances between visual descriptors: $k^{\text{expL2}}(\mathbf{x}, \mathbf{x}') = \exp(-||\mathbf{x} - \mathbf{x}'||/\gamma)$ and $k^{\text{Gaussian}}(\mathbf{x}, \mathbf{x}') = \exp(-||\mathbf{x} - \mathbf{x}'||^2/\gamma)$. These two kernels are commonly used for image classification.

We evaluate this set of kernels on the Caltech256 dataset, using 15 training examples per class. With the Gram matrix of each kernel, we train a nonlinear one-vs-the-rest SVM by optimizing the dual objective. The SVM regularization parameter C and the kernel hyperparameter γ are selected individually for each method via 5-fold cross validation. We evaluate the resulting SVMs on a test set of 10 images per class as in the previous subsection. We include in this comparison also the dot-product kernel $k^{\text{linear}}(\mathbf{x}, \mathbf{x}') = \mathbf{x}^T\mathbf{x}'$, which produces a linear SVM. The results are shown in fig. 4 for both (a) GIST and (b) classeme features. From this plot we see that the kernels defined by our RW distance yield much higher accuracy than the traditional hand-defined nonlinear kernels considered here. As in all our previous experiments, even in this evaluation our RW metric matches or outperforms the CH distance proposed in [11].

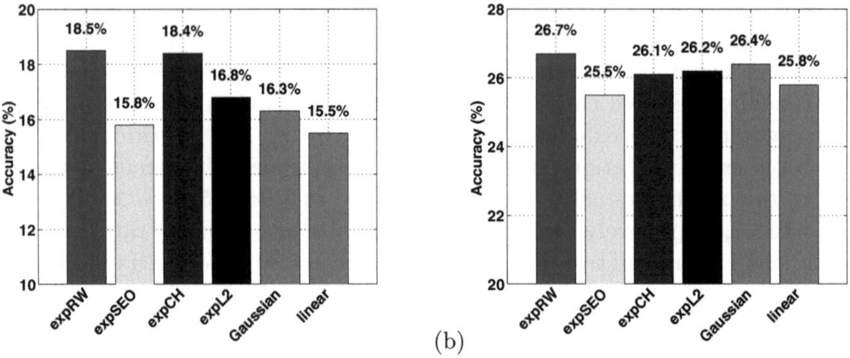

Fig. 4. Caltech256 performance of nonlinear SVMs trained with different kernels using (a) GIST and (b) classeme features: expRW and expSEO denote kernels constructed from our RW and SEO distances; expCH is the kernel induced by the CH distance of Deselaers and Ferrari [11]; exp-L2 and Gaussian are the exponential and Gaussian kernels computed from the L2 visual distances; linear indicates the linear SVM learned using the dot-product kernel. The training set consists of 15 examples per class.

8 Conclusions

We have presented new image metrics for categorization. Our distances are computed by embedding the photos in a semantic image manifold. This allows our methods to infer semantic relations that cannot be captured by directly comparing the two input images. We have shown that this yields results matching or outperforming the state-of-the-art on three different datasets. Our current embedding methods require calculating distances to all nodes in the graph. To reduce this cost in the future we are interested in learning parametric embedding models. Our graphs and image embedding software may be obtained from [30].

Acknowledgments. We are grateful to S. Nowozin and C. Rother for useful discussion on strategies to optimize our SEO energy and to T. Deselaers and V. Ferrari for sharing data. Thanks to A. Bergamo for help with the experiments.

References

1. Carey, S., Bartlett, E.: Acquiring a single new word. In: The Stanford Child Language Conference (1978)
2. Frome, A., Singer, Y., Sha, F., Malik, J.: Learning globally-consistent local distance functions for shape-based image retrieval and classification. In: ICCV (2007)
3. Wang, G., Hoiem, D., Forsyth, D.: Learning image similarity from flickr using stochastic intersection kernel machines. In: Intl. Conf. Computer Vision (2009)
4. Malisiewicz, T., Efros, A.A.: Recognition by association via learning per-exemplar distances. In: CVPR (2008)
5. Liu, C., Yuen, J., Torralba, A.: Nonparametric scene parsing: Label transfer via dense scene alignment. In: CVPR (2009)
6. Ramanan, D., Baker, S.: Local distance functions: A taxonomy, new algorithms, and an evaluation. IEEE Trans. Pattern Anal. Mach. Intell. 33, 794–806 (2011)

7. Tenenbaum, J.B., Kemp, C., Griffiths, T.L., Goodman, N.D.: How to Grow a Mind: Statistics, Structure, and Abstraction. Science 331, 1279–1285 (2011)
8. Tenenbaum, J.B., Silva, V., Langford, J.C.: A Global Geometric Framework for Nonlinear Dimensionality Reduction. Science 290, 2319–2323 (2000)
9. Belkin, M., Niyogi, P., Sindhwani, V.: Manifold regularization: A geometric framework for learning from labeled and unlabeled examples. JMLR (2006)
10. Rosch, E.: Cognitive representations of semantic categories. J. of Experimental Psychology: General (1975)
11. Deselaers, T., Ferrari, V.: Visual and semantic similarity in ImageNet. In: CVPR, pp. 1777–1784 (2011)
12. Torralba, A., Fergus, R., Freeman, W.T.: 80 million tiny images: A large data set for nonparametric object and scene recognition. IEEE Trans. PAMI (2008)
13. Deng, J., Dong, W., Socher, R., Li, L.J., Li, K., Li, F.F.: Imagenet: A large-scale hierarchical image database. In: CVPR, pp. 248–255 (2009)
14. Goldberger, J., Roweis, S., Hinton, G., Salakhutdinov, R.: Neighbourhood components analysis. In: NIPS (2004)
15. Torresani, L., Lee, K.C.: Large margin component analysis. In: NIPS (2006)
16. Weinberger, K.Q., Saul, L.K.: Distance metric learning for large margin nearest neighbor classification. Journal of Machine Learning Research 10, 207–244 (2009)
17. Babenko, B., Branson, S., Belongie, S.: Similarity metrics for categorization: From monolithic to category specific. In: ICCV, pp. 293–300 (2009)
18. Hastie, T., Tibshirani, R.: Discriminant adaptive nearest neighbor classification. IEEE Trans. PAMI (1996)
19. Domeniconi, C., Peng, J., Gunopulos, D.: Locally adaptive metric nearest-neighbor classification. IEEE Trans. Pattern Anal. Mach. Intell. 24, 1281–1285 (2002)
20. Oliva, A., Torralba, A.: Building the gist of a scene: The role of global image features in recognition. Visual Perception, Progress in Brain Research 155 (2006)
21. Torresani, L., Szummer, M., Fitzgibbon, A.: Efficient Object Category Recognition Using Classemes. In: Daniilidis, K., Maragos, P., Paragios, N. (eds.) ECCV 2010, Part I. LNCS, vol. 6311, pp. 776–789. Springer, Heidelberg (2010)
22. Miller, G.A., Beckwith, R., Fellbaum, C., Gross, D., Miller, K.: WordNet: An online lexical database. International Journal of Lexicography 3, 235–244 (1990)
23. Lim, Y., Jung, K., Kohli, P.: Energy Minimization under Constraints on Label Counts. In: Daniilidis, K., Maragos, P., Paragios, N. (eds.) ECCV 2010, Part II. LNCS, vol. 6312, pp. 535–551. Springer, Heidelberg (2010)
24. http://www.gurobi.com/
25. Craswell, N., Szummer, M.: Random walks on the click graph. In: SIGIR (2007)
26. Szummer, M., Jaakkola, T.: Partially labeled classification with markov random walks. In: NIPS (2001)
27. Rastegari, M., Fang, C., Torresani, L.: Scalable object-class retrieval with approximate and top-k ranking. In: ICCV, pp. 2659–2666 (2011)
28. Griffin, G., Holub, A., Perona, P.: Caltech-256 object category dataset. Technical Report 7694, Caltech (2007)
29. Berg, A., Deng, J., Fei-Fei, L.: Large scale visual recognition challenge (2010), http://www.image-net.org/challenges/LSVRC/2010/
30. http://vlg.cs.dartmouth.edu/semanticembedding
31. Jiang, J.J., Conrath, D.W.: Semantic similarity based on corpus statistics and lexical taxonomy. CoRR (1997)
32. Bishop, C.M.: Pattern Recognition and Machine Learning. Springer (2006)
33. Duchenne, O., Joulin, A., Ponce, J.: A graph-matching kernel for object categorization. In: ICCV, pp. 1792–1799 (2011)

Efficient Point-to-Subspace Query in ℓ^1 with Application to Robust Face Recognition

Ju Sun, Yuqian Zhang, and John Wright

Department of Electrical Engineering, Columbia University, New York, USA
{jusun,yuqianzhang,johnwright}@ee.columbia.edu

Abstract. Motivated by vision tasks such as robust face and object recognition, we consider the following general problem: given a collection of low-dimensional linear subspaces in a high-dimensional ambient (image) space, and a query point (image), efficiently determine the nearest subspace to the query in ℓ^1 distance. We show in theory this problem can be solved with a simple two-stage algorithm: (1) random Cauchy projection of query and subspaces into low-dimensional spaces followed by efficient distance evaluation (ℓ^1 regression); (2) getting back to the high-dimensional space with very few candidates and performing exhaustive search. We present preliminary experiments on robust face recognition to corroborate our theory.

Keywords: ℓ^1 point-to-subspace distance, nearest subspace search, Cauchy projection, face recognition, subspace modeling.

1 Introduction

Although visual data reside in very high-dimensional spaces, they often exhibit much lower-dimensional intrinsic structure. Modeling and exploiting this low-dimensional structure is a central goal in computer vision, with impact on applications from low-level tasks such as signal acquistion and denoising to higher-level tasks such as object detection and recognition.

In face and object recognition alone, many popular, effective techniques can be viewed as searching for the low-dimensional model which best matches the query (test) image. To each object $\mathcal{O}$ of interest, we may associate a low-dimensional subset $\mathcal{M} \subset \mathbb{R}^D$, which approximates the set of images of $\mathcal{O}$ that can be generated under different physical conditions – say, varying pose or illumination. Given n objects $\mathcal{O}_i$, the recognition problem becomes one of finding the nearest low-dimensional structure: $\min_i d(\mathbf{q}, \mathcal{M}_i)$, where $\mathbf{q} \in \mathbb{R}^D$ is the test image, and $d(\cdot,\cdot)$ is some metric.

This paradigm is broad enough to encompass very classical work in face recognition [1] and object instance recognition [2], as well as more recent developments [3,4,5]. In situations in which sufficient training data is available to accurately fit the $\mathcal{M}_i$, it can achieve high recognition rates [6]. In applying it to a particular scenario, however, at least three critical questions must be answered:

A. Fitzgibbon et al. (Eds.): ECCV 2012, Part IV, LNCS 7575, pp. 416–429, 2012.

First, *what is the most appropriate class of low-dimensional models* $\mathcal{M}_i$*?* The proper class of models may depend on the properties of the object $\mathcal{O}$, as well as the types of nusiance variations that may be encountered. For example, variations in illumination may be well-captured using low-dimensional *linear* models [7,8], whereas variations in pose or alignment are highly nonlinear [9].

Second, *how should we measure the distance between* $\mathbf{q}$ *and* $\mathcal{M}_i$*?* Typically, one adopts a metric $d(\cdot,\cdot)$ on $\mathbb{R}^D$, and then sets $d(\mathbf{q},\mathcal{M}_i) = \min_{\mathbf{v}\in\mathcal{M}_i} d(\mathbf{q},\mathbf{v})$. Here, again, the appropriate choice metric d depends on our prior knowledge. For example, if the observation $\mathbf{q}$ is known to be perturbed by i.i.d. Gaussian noise, minimizing the ℓ^2 norm $d(\mathbf{q},\mathbf{v}) = \|\mathbf{q}-\mathbf{v}\|_2$ yields a maximum likelihood estimator. However, in practice other norms may be more appropriate: for example, in situations where the data may have errors due to occlusions, shadows, specularities, the ℓ^1 norm is a more robust alternative [5].

Finally, given an appropriate model and error distance, *how can we efficiently determine the nearest model to a given input query?* That is to say, we would like to solve

$$\min_i \min_{\mathbf{v}\in\mathcal{M}_i} d(\mathbf{q},\mathbf{v}) \tag{1}$$

using computational resources that depend as gracefully as possible on the ambient dimension D (typically number of pixels in the image) and the number of models n. In practical applications, both of these quantities could be very large.

This paper. In this paper, we consider the case when the low-dimensional models $\mathcal{M}_i$ are *linear subspaces.* As mentioned above, subspace models are well-justified for modeling illumination variations [7,8] (say, in near-frontal face recognition), and also form a basic building block for modeling and computing with more general, nonlinear sets [10,11].

Our methodology pertains to distances $d(\mathbf{q},\mathbf{v})$ induced by the ℓ^p norm $\|\mathbf{q}-\mathbf{v}\|_p$, with $p\in(0,2]$. We focus here on the ℓ^1 norm, $\|\mathbf{q}-\mathbf{v}\|_1 = \sum_i |q_i - v_i|$. The ℓ^1 norm is a natural and well-justified choice when the test image contains pixels that do not fit the model – say, due to moderate occlusion, cast shadows, or specularities [5]. For $p\in(0,2]$, the ℓ^p norm with $p=1$ strikes a unique compromise between computational tractability (convexity) and robustness to gross errors.

With this choice of models and distance, at recognition time we are left with the following computational task:

Problem 1. Given n linear subspaces $\mathcal{S}_1,\dots,\mathcal{S}_n$ of $\mathbb{R}^D$ of dimension r and a query point $\mathbf{q}\in\mathbb{R}^D$, determine the nearest $\mathcal{S}_i$ to $\mathbf{q}$ in ℓ^1 norm.

This problem has a straightforward solution: solve a sequence of n ℓ^1 regression problems:

$$\min_{\mathbf{v}\in\mathcal{S}_i} \|\mathbf{q}-\mathbf{v}\|_1, \tag{2}$$

and choose the i with the smallest optimal objective value. The total cost is $O(n\cdot T_{\ell^1}(D,r))$, where $T_{\ell^1}(D,r)$ is the time required to solve the linear program (2). For example, for interior point methods [12], we have $T_{\ell^1}(D,r) = O(D^{3.5})$.

There exist more scalable first-order methods [13,14,15,16], which improve on the dependence on D at the expense of higher iteration complexity. The best known complexity guarantees for each of these methods are again superlinear in D, although linear runtimes may be achievable when the residual $\mathbf{q} - \mathbf{v}_\star$ is very sparse [17] or the problem is otherwise well-structured [18]. Even in the best case, however, the aforementioned algorithms have complexity $\Omega(nD)$.[1] When both terms are large, this dependence is prohibitive: *Although Problem 1 is simple to state and easy to solve in polynomial time, achieving real-time performance or scaling massive databases of objects appears to require a more careful study.*

In this paper, we present a very simple, practical approach to Problem 1, with much improved computational complexity, and reasonably strong theoretical guarantees. Rather than working directly in the high-dimensional space $\mathbb{R}^D$, we randomly embed the query $\mathbf{q}$ and subspaces $\mathcal{S}_i$ into $\mathbb{R}^d$, with $d \ll D$. The random embedding is given by a $d \times D$ matrix $\mathbf{P}$ whose entries are iid standard Cauchy random variables. That is to say, instead of solving (2), we solve

$$\min_{\mathbf{v} \in \mathcal{S}_i} \|\mathbf{Pq} - \mathbf{Pv}\|_1. \tag{3}$$

We prove that if the embedded dimension d is sufficiently large – say $d = \mathrm{poly}(r \log n)$, then with constant probability the model $\mathcal{S}_i$ obtained from (3) is the same as the one obtained from the original optimization (2).

The required dimension d does not depend in any way on the ambient dimension D, and is often significantly smaller: e.g., $d = 25$ vs. $D = 32,000$ for one typical example of face recognition. The resulting (small) ℓ^1 regression problems can be solved very efficiently using customized interior point solvers (e.g., [19]). These methods are numerically reliable, and can yield a speedup of several orders of magnitude over the naive approach (2).

The price paid for this improved computational profile is a small increase in the probability of failure of the recognition algorithm, due to the use of a randomized embedding. Our theory quantifies how large d needs to be to render this probability of error under control. Repeated trials with independent projections $\mathbf{P}$ can then be used to make the probability of failure as small as desired. Because ℓ^1 regression is so much cheaper in the low-dimensional space $\mathbb{R}^d$, these repeated trials are affordable.

The end result is a simple, practical algorithm that guarantees to maintain the good properties of ℓ^1 regression, with substantially improved computational complexity. We demonstrate this on model problems in subspace-based face and digit recognition (in supplementary material). In addition to improved complexity in theory, we observe remarkable improvements on real data examples, suggesting that point-to-subspace query in ℓ^1 could become a practical strategy (or basic building block) for face and object recognition tasks involving large databases, or small databases and hard time constraints.

[1] On a more technical level, when the $\mathcal{S}_i$ are fit to sample data, the aforementioned first-order methods may require tuning for optimal performance.

Relationship to existing work. Problem 1 is an example of a *subspace search* problem. For 0-dimensional affine subspaces in ℓ^2 (i.e., points), this problem coincides with the nearest neighbor problem. Its approximate version can be solved in time *sublinear* in n, the number of points, using randomized techniques such as locality sensitive hashing [20]. When the dimension r is larger than zero, the problem becomes significantly more challenging. For the case of $r = 1$, sublinear time algorithms exist, although they are more complicated [21].

Recently two groups have proposed approaches to tackling larger r. Basri et. al. [22] lift subspaces into a higher dimensional vector space (identifying the subspace with its $D \times D$ orthoprojector) and then apply point-based near neighbor search. Jain et. al. give several random hash functions for the case when the $\mathcal{S}_i$ are hyperplanes [23]. Both of these approaches pertain to ℓ^2 only. Both perform well on numerical examples, but have limitations in theory, as neither is known to yield an algorithm with provably sublinear complexity for all inputs. Results in theoretical computer science suggest that these limitations may be intrinsic to the problem: a sublinear time algorithm for approximate nearest hyperplane search would refute the strong version of the "exponential time hypothesis", which conjectures that general boolean satisfiability problems cannot be solved in time $O(2^{cn})$ for any $c < 1$ [24].

The above algorithms exploit special properties of the ℓ^2 version of Problem 1, and do not apply to its ℓ^1 variant. However, the ℓ^1 variant retains the aforementioned difficulties, suggesting that an algorithm for ℓ^1 near subspace search with sublinear dependence on n is unlikely as well.[2] This motivates us to focus on ameliorating the dependence on D. Our approach is very simple and very natural: Cauchy projections are chosen because the Cauchy is the unique 1-stable distribution, a property which has been widely exploited in previous algorithmic work [20,26,27].

However, on a technical level, it is not obvious that Cauchy embedding should succeed for this problem. The Cauchy is a heavy tailed distribution, and because of this it does not yield embeddings that very tightly preserve distances between points, as in the Johnson-Lindenstrauss lemma. In fact, for ℓ^1, there exist lower bounds showing that certain point sets in ℓ^1 cannot be embedded in significantly lower-dimensional spaces without incurring non-negligble distortion [28]. For a single subspace, embedding results exist – most notably due to Soehler and Woodruff [27], but the distortion incurred is so large as to render them inapplicable to Problem 1. Nevertheless, several elegant technical ideas in the proof of [27] turn out to be useful for analyzing Problem 1 as well.

The problem studied here is also related to recent work on sparse modeling and sparse error correction. Indeed, one of the strongest technical motivations for using the ℓ^1 norm is its provable good performance in sparse error correction [29,30]. These results give conditions under which it is possible to recover a vector $\mathbf{x}$ from grossly corrupted observations $\mathbf{q} = \mathbf{v} + \mathbf{e}$, with $\mathbf{v} \in \mathcal{S}$ and the sparse error $\mathbf{e}$ unknown. These results are quite strong: they imply exact recovery, even

[2] Although it could be possible if we are willing to accept time and space complexity exponential in r or D, ala [25].

if the error $\mathbf{e}$ has nonnegligible fractions of nonzero entries, of arbitrary size. For example, [29] proves that under technical conditions, ℓ^1 minimization

$$\min \|\mathbf{e}\|_1 \quad \text{s.t.} \quad \mathbf{q} - \mathbf{e} \in \mathcal{S} \tag{4}$$

exactly recovers $\mathbf{e}$. [30] presents similar theory for the case when $\mathcal{S}$ is union of subspaces solved by a variant of optimization in (4).

On the other hand, exact recovery may be stronger than what is needed for recognition. For recognition, as formulated in this work, we only need to know which subspace minimizes the distance $d(\mathbf{q}, \mathcal{S}_i)$ – we do not need to precisely estimate the difference vector itself. The distinction is important: while [5] shows that significant dimensionality reduction is possible if there are no gross errors $\mathbf{e}$, when errors are present, the cardinality of the error vector gives a hard lower bound on the number of observations required for correct recovery. In contrast, for the simpler problem of finding the nearest model, it is possible to give an algorithm that uses very small d, and is agnostic to the properties of $\mathbf{q}$ and $\mathcal{S}_1 \ldots \mathcal{S}_n$.

2 Our Algorithm and Main Results

The core of our algorithm is summarized as follows.

Input: n subspaces $\mathcal{S}_1, \cdots, \mathcal{S}_n$ of dimension r and query $\mathbf{q}$
Output: Identity of the closest subspace $\mathcal{S}_\star$ to $\mathbf{q}$

Preprocessing: Generate $\mathbf{P} \in \mathbb{R}^{d \times D}$ with iid Cauchy RV's ($d \ll D$) and Compute the projections $\mathbf{P}\mathcal{S}_1, \cdots, \mathbf{P}\mathcal{S}_n$
Test: Compute the projection $\mathbf{Pq}$, and compute its ℓ^1 distance to each of $\mathbf{P}\mathcal{S}_i$

Our main theoretical result states that if d is chosen appropriately, with at least constant probability, the subspace $\mathcal{S}_{i_\star}$ selected will be the original closest subspace $\mathcal{S}_\star$:

Theorem 1. *Suppose we are given n linear subspaces $\{\mathcal{S}_1, \cdots, \mathcal{S}_n\}$ of dimension r in $\mathbb{R}^D$ and any query point $\mathbf{q}$, and that the ℓ^1 distances of $\mathbf{q}$ to each of $\{\mathcal{S}_1, \cdots, \mathcal{S}_n\}$ are $\xi_{1'} \le \cdots \le \xi_{n'}$ when arranged in ascending order, with $\xi_{2'}/\xi_{1'} \ge \eta > 1$. For any fixed $\alpha < 1 - 1/\eta$, there exists $d \sim O\left[(r \log n)^{1/\alpha}\right]$ (assuming $n > r$), if $\mathbf{P} \in \mathbb{R}^{d \times D}$ is iid Cauchy, we have*

$$\arg\min_{i \in [n]} d_{\ell^1}(\mathbf{Pq}, \mathbf{P}\mathcal{S}_i) = \arg\min_{i \in [n]} d_{\ell^1}(\mathbf{q}, \mathcal{S}_i) \tag{5}$$

with (nonzero) constant probability.

The condition in Theorem 1 depends on several factors. Perhaps the most interesting is the relative gap η between the closest subspace distance and the second closest subspace distance. Notice that $\eta \in [1, \infty)$, and that the exponent $1/\alpha$

becomes large as η approaches one. This suggests that our dimensionality reduction will be most effective when the relative gap is nonnegligible. For example, when $\eta = 1/2$ the required dimension is proportional to r^2.

Notice also that d depends on the number of models n only through its logarithm. This rather weak dependence is a strong point, and, interestingly, mirrors the Johnson-Lindenstrauss lemma for dimensionality reduction in ℓ^2, even though JL-syle embeddings are impossible for ℓ^1.

Before stating our overall algorithm, we suggest two additional practical implications of Theorem 1. First, Theorem 1 only guarantees success with constant probability. This probability is easily amplified by taking T independent trials. Because the probability of failure drops exponentially in T, it usually suffices to keep T rather small. Each of these T trials generates one or more candidate subspaces $\mathbf{S}_i$. We can then perform ℓ^1 regression in $\mathbb{R}^D$ to determine which of these candidates is actually nearest to the query. Note that it may also be possible to perform this second step in $\mathbb{R}^{d'}$, where $d < d' \ll D$; we save this for future work.

Second, the importance of the gap η suggests another means of controlling the resources demanded by the algorithm. Namely, if we have reason to believe that η will be especially small, we may instead set d according to the gap between $\xi_{1'}$ and $\xi_{k'}$, for some $k' > 2$. With this choice, Theorem 1 implies that with constant probability the desired subspace is amongst the $k'-1$ nearest to the query. Again, all of these $k'-1$ subspaces need to be retained for further examination. However, if $k' \ll n$, this is still a significant saving over the naive approach.

3 A Sketch of the Analysis

In this section, we sketch the analysis leading to Theorem 1. The basic rationale for using Cauchy projection is that the Cauchy distribution is the unique *stable* distribution for the ℓ^1 norm: if $\mathbf{v} \in \mathbb{R}^D$ is any fixed vector, and $\mathbf{P} \in \mathbb{R}^{d \times D}$ is a matrix with iid Cauchy entries, then the vector $\mathbf{Pv} \equiv_d \|\mathbf{v}\|_1 \times \mathbf{z}$, where $\mathbf{z}$ is again an iid Cauchy vector, and $\equiv_d$ denotes equality in distribution. So, $\|\mathbf{Pv}\|_1 \equiv_d \|\mathbf{v}\|_1 \|\mathbf{z}\|_1 = \|\mathbf{v}\|_1 \sum_i |z_i|$. The random variables $|z_i|$ are iid *half-Cauchy*, with probability density function

$$f_{\mathcal{HC}}(x) = \frac{2}{\pi} \frac{1}{1+x^2} \quad \text{if } x \geq 0, \tag{6}$$

and $f_{\mathcal{HC}}(x) = 0$ for $x < 0$.

In point-to-subspace query, we need to understand how $\mathbf{P}$ acts on many vectors $\mathbf{v}$ simultaneously – including the query $\mathbf{q}$ and all of the subspaces $\mathcal{S}_1 \ldots \mathcal{S}_n$. Here, we encounter a challenge: although the Cauchy is the unambiguously correct distribution for estimating ℓ^1 norms, it is rather ill-behaved: its mean and variance do not exist, and the sample averages $\frac{1}{n} \sum_i |z_i|$ do not obey the classical Central Limit Theorem.

Figure 1 shows how this behavior affects the point-to-subspace distance $d_{\ell^1}(\mathbf{q}, \mathcal{S})$. The figure shows a histogram of the random variable $\psi = d_{\ell^1}(\mathbf{Pq}, \mathbf{P}\mathcal{S})$, over randomly generated Cauchy matrices $\mathbf{P}$, for two different configurations of query $\mathbf{q}$ and subspace $\mathcal{S}$. Two properties are especially noteworthy. First, the upper tail of the distribution can be quite heavy: with non-negligible probability, ψ may significantly exceed its median. On the other hand, the lower tail is much better behaved: with very high probability, ψ is not significantly smaller than its median. This inhomogeneous behavior (in particular, the heavy upper tail)

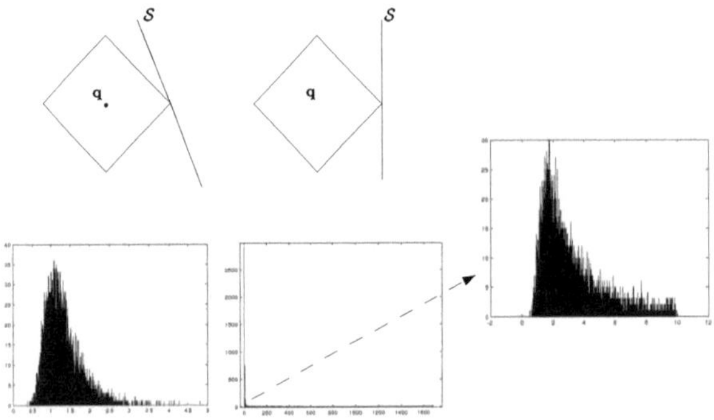

Fig. 1. Statistics of ℓ^1 distance ratios (after vs. before) by random projections over 10000 trials. The subspaces are randomly-oriented (1st column) and axis-aligned (2nd column), respectively. Here $r = 10$, $D = 10000$, $d = 35$, and $d_{\ell^1}(q, \mathcal{S}) = 1$.

precludes very tight distance-preserving embeddings using the Cauchy. However, our goal is *not* to find an embedding of the data, per se, but rather to find the nearest subspace, $\mathcal{S}_\star$, to the query. In fact, for nearest subspace search, this inhomogeneous behavior is much less of an obstacle. To guarantee to find $\mathcal{S}_\star$, we need to ensure that

- (i) $\mathbf{P}$ does not increase the distance from $\mathbf{q}$ to $\mathcal{S}_\star$ too much, and,
- (ii) $\mathbf{P}$ does not shrink the distance from $\mathbf{q}$ to any of the other subspaces $\mathcal{S}_i$ too much.

The first property, (i), holds with constant probability: although the tail of ψ is heavy, with probability at least $1/2$, $\psi \leq \text{median}(\psi)$. For the second event, (ii), $\mathbf{P}$ needs to be well-behaved on $n-1$ subspaces simultaneously. Notice, however, that for the bad subspaces $\mathcal{S}_i$, the lower tail in Figure 1 is most important. If projection happens to significantly increase the distance between $\mathbf{q}$ and $\mathcal{S}_i$, this will not cause an error (and may even help!). Since the lower tail is sharp, we *can* guarantee that if d is chosen correctly, $\mathbf{Pq}$ will not be significantly closer to any of the $\mathbf{P}\mathcal{S}_i$.

Below we describe some of the technical manipulations needed to carry this argument through rigorously, and state key lemmas for each part. Sec. 3.1 elaborates on property (i), while Sec. 3.2 describes the arguments needed to establish property (ii). Theorem 1 follows directly from the results in Secs. 3.1 and 3.2. This argument, as well as proofs of several routine or technical lemmas are deferred to the supplementary material.

3.1 Bounded Expansion for the Good Subspace

Let $\mathbf{v}_\star \in \mathcal{S}_\star$ be a closest point to $\mathbf{q}$ in ℓ^1 norm, before projection:

$$\mathbf{v}_\star \in \arg\min_{\mathbf{v} \in \mathcal{S}_\star} \|\mathbf{q} - \mathbf{v}\|_1.$$

Such a point $\mathbf{v}_\star$ may not be unique, but always exists. After projection, $\mathbf{P}\mathbf{v}_\star$ might no longer be the closest point to $\mathbf{P}\mathbf{q}$. However, the distance $\|\mathbf{P}\mathbf{q}-\mathbf{P}\mathbf{v}_\star\|_1$ *does* upper bound the distance from $\mathbf{P}\mathbf{q}$ to $\mathbf{P}\mathcal{S}_\star$:

$$d_{\ell^1}(\mathbf{P}\mathbf{q}, \mathbf{P}\mathcal{S}_\star) = \min_{\mathbf{h}\in\mathbf{P}\mathcal{S}_\star} \|\mathbf{P}\mathbf{q}-\mathbf{h}\|_1 \le \|\mathbf{P}\mathbf{q}-\mathbf{P}\mathbf{v}_\star\|_1 = \|\mathbf{P}(\mathbf{q}-\mathbf{v}_\star)\|_1.$$

Hence, it is enough to show that $\mathbf{P}$ preserves the norm of the particular vector $\mathbf{w}=\mathbf{q}-\mathbf{v}_\star$. We use the following lemma for this purpose:

Lemma 1. *There exists numerical constant $c\in(0,1)$ with the following property. If $\mathbf{w}\in\mathbb{R}^D$ be any fixed vector, and suppose that $\mathbf{P}\in\mathbb{R}^{d\times D}$ is a matrix with iid standard Cauchy entries. Then for any $\rho>1$,*

$$\mathbb{P}\left[\|\mathbf{P}\mathbf{w}\|_1 > \rho\frac{2}{\pi}d\log d\,\|\mathbf{w}\|_1\right] < c+\frac{1-c}{\rho} < 1. \tag{7}$$

3.2 Bounded Contraction for the Bad Subspaces

For the "bad" subspaces $\mathcal{S}_2\ldots\mathcal{S}_n$, our task is more complicated, since we have to show that under projection $\mathbf{P}$, *no* point in $\mathcal{S}_i$ comes close to $\mathbf{q}$. In fact, we will show something slightly stronger: for appropriate γ, with high probability the following holds for any i:

$$\forall\, \mathbf{w}\in\mathcal{S}_i\oplus\mathrm{span}(\mathbf{q}),\quad \|\mathbf{P}\mathbf{w}\|_1 \ge \gamma\|\mathbf{w}\|_1. \tag{8}$$

Above, $\oplus$ denotes the direct sum of subspaces, so $\tilde{\mathcal{S}}_i=\mathcal{S}_i\oplus\mathrm{span}(\mathbf{q})$ is the linear span of $\mathcal{S}_i$ and the query together. Since for any $\mathbf{v}\in\mathcal{S}_i$, $\mathbf{q}-\mathbf{v}\in\tilde{\mathcal{S}}_i$, whenever (8) holds, we have

$$\begin{aligned} d_{\ell^1}(\mathbf{P}\mathbf{q},\mathbf{P}\mathcal{S}_i) &= \min_{\mathbf{v}\in\mathcal{S}_i}\|\mathbf{P}\mathbf{q}-\mathbf{P}\mathbf{v}\|_1 \ \ge\ \min_{\mathbf{v}\in\mathcal{S}_i}\|\mathbf{P}(\mathbf{q}-\mathbf{v})\|_1 \\ &\ge \min_{\mathbf{v}\in\mathcal{S}_i}\gamma\|\mathbf{q}-\mathbf{v}\|_1 \ =\ \gamma\, d_{\ell^1}(\mathbf{q},\mathcal{S}_i), \end{aligned} \tag{9}$$

and the distance to any "bad" subspace $\mathcal{S}_i$ contracts by at most a factor of γ.

To show (8), we use a discretization argument. Let Γ denote the intersection of the unit ℓ^1 "sphere" with the expanded subspace $\tilde{\mathcal{S}}_i$:

$$\Gamma=\{\mathbf{w}\mid\|\mathbf{w}\|_1=1\}\cap\tilde{\mathcal{S}}_i.$$

Recall that for any set Γ, an *ε-net* is a subset N_i such that for every $\mathbf{w}\in\Gamma$, $\|\mathbf{w}-\mathbf{w}'\|_1\le\epsilon$ for some $\mathbf{w}'\in N$. Standard arguments (see [31]) show that for any $\epsilon>0$, there exists an ϵ net N_i for Γ of size at most $(3/\epsilon)^{d+1}$.

Consider the following two events:
- (ii.a) $\min_{\mathbf{w}'\in N}\|\mathbf{P}\mathbf{w}'\|_1\ge\beta$, and
- (ii.b) For all $\mathbf{w}\in\tilde{\mathcal{S}}_i$, $\|\mathbf{P}\mathbf{w}\|_1 \le L\|\mathbf{w}\|_1$.

When both hold, we have for any $\mathbf{w}\in\Gamma$ (with associated closest point $\mathbf{w}'\in N_i$)

$$\|\mathbf{P}\mathbf{w}\|_1\ge\|\mathbf{P}\mathbf{w}'+\mathbf{P}(\mathbf{w}-\mathbf{w}')\|_1 \ge \|\mathbf{P}\mathbf{w}'\|_1-\|\mathbf{P}(\mathbf{w}-\mathbf{w}')\|_1 \ge \beta-L\epsilon. \tag{10}$$

Moreover, since for any $\mathbf{w}\in\tilde{\mathcal{S}}_i$, $\mathbf{w}/\|\mathbf{w}\|_1\in\Gamma$, we have that

$$\forall\,\mathbf{w}\in\tilde{\mathcal{S}}_i,\quad \|\mathbf{P}\mathbf{w}\|_1\ge(\beta-L\epsilon)\|\mathbf{w}\|_1,$$

and we may set $\gamma=\beta-L\epsilon$. So, it is left to establish items (ii.a) and (ii.b) above.

Establishing (ii.a). We use the following tail bound:

Lemma 2 (Concentration in Lower Tail). *Let* $\mathbf{P} \in \mathbb{R}^{d \times D}$ *be an iid Cauchy matrix. Then for any fixed vector* $\mathbf{w} \in \mathbb{R}^D$ *and* $\alpha, \delta \in (0,1)$,

$$\mathbb{P}\left[\|\mathbf{Pw}\|_1 < (1-\alpha)(1-\delta)\frac{2}{\pi}d\log d\,\|\mathbf{w}\|_1\right] < d^{1-\alpha}\exp\left(-\frac{\delta^2}{2\pi}d^\alpha\right). \quad (11)$$

This estimate gives the optimal power, d^α, in the exponent. The proof is straightforward, and is deferred to the supplementary material.

This bound is sharp enough to allow us to simultaneously lower bound $\|\mathbf{Pw}'\|_1$ over all $\mathbf{w}' \in N_i$. Set

$$\beta_{\alpha,\delta} = (1-\alpha)(1-\delta)\tfrac{2}{\pi}d\log d,$$

and let $\mathcal{E}_{\mathrm{net},i}$ denote the event that there exists $\mathbf{w}' \in N_i$ with $\|\mathbf{Pw}'\|_1 < \beta_{\alpha,\delta}\|\mathbf{w}'\|_1$.

$$\mathbb{P}\left[\mathcal{E}_{\mathrm{net},i}\right] < |N_i|\, d^{1-\alpha}\exp\left(-\tfrac{\delta^2}{2\pi}d^\alpha\right). \quad (12)$$

Establishing (ii.b). In bounding the Lipschitz constant L in (ii.b), we have to cope with the heavy tails of the Cauchy, and simple arguments like the above argument for β are insufficient. Rather, we borrow an elegant argument of Sohler and Woodruff [27]. The rough idea is to work with a certain special basis for $\tilde{\mathcal{S}}_i$, which can be considered an ℓ^1 analogue of an orthonormal basis. Just as an orthonormal basis preserves the ℓ^2 norm, an ℓ^1 *well-conditioned basis* approximately preserves the ℓ^1 norm, up to distortion $(r+1)$. The argument then controls the action of $\mathbf{P}$ on the elements of this basis. Due to space limitations, we defer further discussion of this idea to the supplementary material, and instead simply state the resulting bound:

Lemma 3. *Let* $\mathbf{P} \in \mathbb{R}^{d \times D}$ *be an iid Cauchy matrix, and* $\mathcal{S}$ *a fixed subspace of dimension* $r+1$. *Set* $L = \sup_{\mathbf{w} \in \mathcal{S}\setminus\{\mathbf{0}\}} \|\mathbf{Pw}\|_1/\|\mathbf{w}\|_1$. *Then for any* $B > 0$, *we have*

$$\mathbb{P}\left[L > t\,(r+1)\right] \le \frac{2d(r+1)}{\pi B} + \frac{2d(r+1)}{\pi t}\log\sqrt{1+B^2}. \quad (13)$$

The proof of Theorem 1 follows from Lemmas 1-3 above, by choosing appropriate values of the parameters B, t, δ and ϵ. We give the detailed calculation in the supplementary material.

4 Experiments

We present two experiments[3] to corroborate our theoretical result and demonstrate its particular relevance to subspace/manifold-based instance recognition.

[3] The second one on digit recognition is presented in the supplementary material.

4.1 Note on Implementation

Projection Matrices and Subspaces. Our main theorem is for any fixed set of subspaces and any fixed query point. Of course, if we fix $\mathbf{P}$ and consider many different $\mathbf{q}$, the success or failure will be dependent random variables. This suggests sampling a new matrix $\mathbf{P}$ for each test image, which would then require that we re-project each of the subspaces $\mathcal{S}_i$. In practice, it is more efficient to maintain a pool of k Cauchy projection matrices[4] $\mathbf{P}_j$ and store $\mathbf{P}_j\mathcal{S}_i$ for each i and j. During testing, we randomly sample a combination of N_{rep} (for repetition) matrices and corresponding projected subspaces and also apply these projections to the query. This sampling strategy from a finite pool does not generate independent projections for different query points, but it allows economic implementation and empirically still yields impressive performance. We fix $k = 20$ and normally set $N_{rep} = 3$ throughout.

Solvers for ℓ^1 Regression. We perform high-dimensional NS search in ℓ^1 (HDS) as baseline. Due to the large scale, we employ an Augmented Lagrange Method (ALM) numerical solver for the regression. All the other instances of ℓ^1 regression are in low dimensions and can be handled by interior point method (IPM) solvers. We will report typical running times, with the caveat that direct comparison may not be fair: the ALM solver is built for moderate accuracy with high scalability and subject to careful tuning of optimization parameters, while IPM solvers are meant for high accuracy. Despite this, our algorithm is often significantly faster.

4.2 Robust Face Recognition on Extended Yale B

Face images of one person taken with fixed pose and varying illumination are known to lie very close to a nine-dimensional linear subspace [8]. Because physical phenomena such as occlusions and specularities on faces may violate the linear model, we formulate the recognition problem as one of finding the closest subspace to $\mathbf{q}$ in ℓ^1 norm [5][5].

The Extended Yale B face dataset [7] (EYB, cropped version) contains cropped, well-aligned frontal face images (168×192) of 38 subjects under 64 illuminations (2,432 images in total, the 18 corrupted during acquisition not used here). For each subject, we took half of the images for training (1205 in total) and the others for testing (1209 in total). To better illustrate the behavior of our algorithm, we strategically divided the test set into two subsets: moderately illuminated (909, **Subset M**) and extremely illuminated (300, **Subset E**). The division is

[4] The standard Cauchy projection matrix $\mathbf{P}$ generated as $\mathbf{A}./\mathbf{B}$, where both $\mathbf{A}$ and $\mathbf{B}$ are iid standard normal and "./" denotes elementwise matrix division.

[5] In other words, we formulate the problem as ℓ^1 nearest subspace (ℓ^1 NS) search. This is different from the idea of sparse representation in SRC [5] for face recognition. Since our focus here is not to propose a new or optimal face recognition algorithm (although ℓ^1 NS method happens to be new for the task), we prefer to save detailed discussions in this line for future work. Nevertheless, our preliminary results indeed suggest ℓ^1 NS is as competitive as SRC for typical robust face recognition benchmarks.

based on the light source direction (*wrt.* the camera axis): images taken with either azimuth angle greater than 90° or elevation angle greater than 60° would be classified as extremely illuminated.

Recognition with Original Images. Fig. 2 presents the evolution of recognition rate on **Subset M** as the projection dimension (d) grows *with only one repetition of the projection* ($N_{rep} = 1$). Our experiment shows the HDS achieves

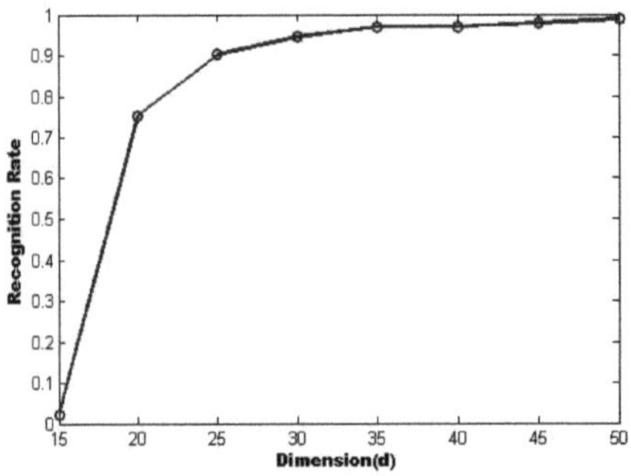

Fig. 2. Recognition rate versus projection dimension (d) *with one repetition* on **Subset M** face images of EYB. The recognition rate stays stable above 95% with $d \geq 25$. The high-dimensional NS in ℓ^1 achieves perfect (100%) recognition. Note the ambient dimension in this case is $D = 168 \times 192 = 32256$.

perfect recognition (100%) on this subset, implying recognition in this subset corresponds perfectly to NS search in ℓ^1. So Fig. 2 actually represents the evolution of "average" success probability for *one repetition* over the subset. Suppose the distance gap is significant such that $1/\alpha \to 1$, our theorem suggests that one needs to set roughly $d = r \log n = 9 * \log 38 \approx 33$ to achieve a constant probability of success. Our result is consistent with this theoretical prediction and the probability is already stable above 0.9 for $d \geq 25$. With 3 repetitions and $d = 25$, the overall recognition rate is 99.56% (4 errors out of 909), nearly perfect. Fig. 3 presents the failing cases. They either contain significant artifacts

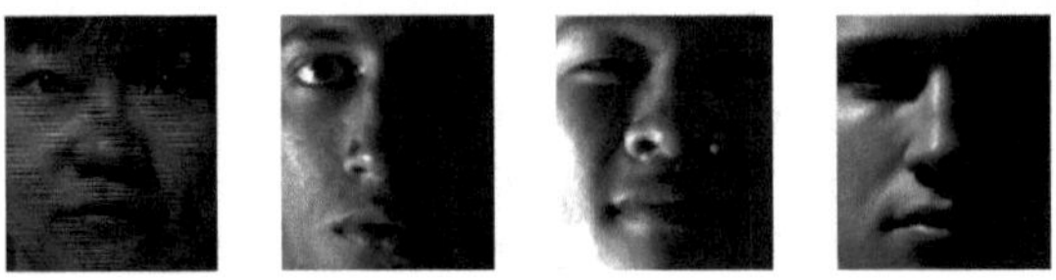

Fig. 3. Failing cases of our method on **Subset M** of EYB

or approach the extremely illuminated cases, the failing mechanism and remedy of which are explained below.

For extremely illuminated face images, the ℓ^1 distance gap between the first and second nearest subspaces is much less significant (one example shown in Fig. 4). Our theory suggests d should be increased to compensate for the weak gap (because the exponent $1/\alpha$ becomes significant). Our experimental results confirm this prediction. Specifically, the HDS achieves 94.7% accuracy while our method achieves only 79.3% when $d = 25$ and $N_{back} = 5$ (N_{back} is the number of

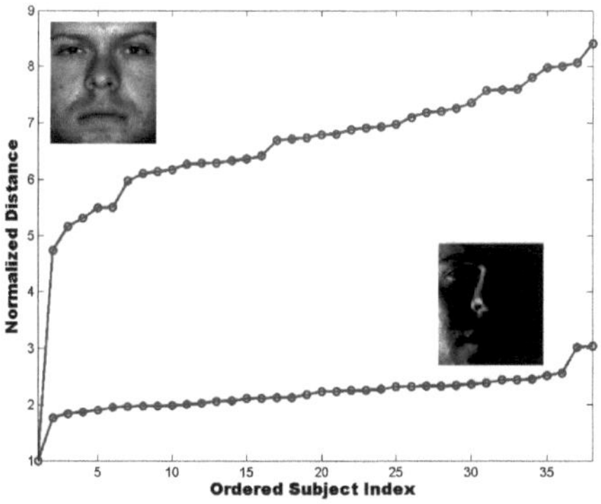

Fig. 4. Samples of moderately/extremely illuminated face images and their ℓ^1 distances to other subject subspaces. The subjects have been ordered in ascending order of ℓ^1 distance from the sample and the distances are normalized such that the first distance is 1. Note that for the moderately illuminated sample, a distance gap of about 4.8 is observed while this is only about 1.8 for the extremely illuminated sample.

back-research in high dimensions). The recognition rate is boosted significantly when we increase d, or increase N_{back} (this is another way of amplifying the success probability), as evident from Table 1.

Table 1. Recognition Rate on **Subset E** of EYB with varying d and N_{back}

	HDS	$d = 25$	$d = 50$	$d = 70$
$r = 15, N_{back} = 5$	94.7%	79.3%	87.7%	92.3%
$r = 15, N_{back} = 10$	94.7%	87.3%	92.0%	94.0%

Recognition on Artificially Corrupted Images. In order to illustrate the robustness of ℓ^1 NS approach for recognition and particularly the capability of our method to preserve such property of ℓ^1, we corrupted each original test image with (1) randomly-distributed sparse corruptions, and (2) structured occlusions. For the first setting, we replaced, respectively, 5%, 10%, 15%, and 20% of randomly chosen pixels with iid uniform noise in $[0, 255]$[6]. For the second, the *lena* image of fixed size (i.e. depending on the desired percentage of occlusion) was randomly placed on each test image. Fig. 5 shows some typical samples of both cases, and also the effect of corruptions on distance gaps - corruptions significantly weaken the gaps. Therefore we set d to 50 and 70 in this experiment for comparison. Table 2 summarizes the recognition performances for each setting. Our method exhibits comparable level of performance with the HDS for corruptions less than 10% and observable performance lag beyond. This is a reasonable price to pay as we insist on working in low dimensions for efficiency.

Running Time. In our Matlab implementation, the typical time required for solving one instance of HDS is 8.3s (with ALM solver), and that for our method is only about 1.2s (ℓ^1-magic interior point solver) which is mostly consumed by the back search in high dimensions. There is no observable difference in timing with or without the corruptions.

[6] In other words, any valid pixel value for 8-bit gray-scaled image. Note also that our training is still half of all the samples as in last part, in contrast to the setting in [5], where only those moderately illuminated are considered.

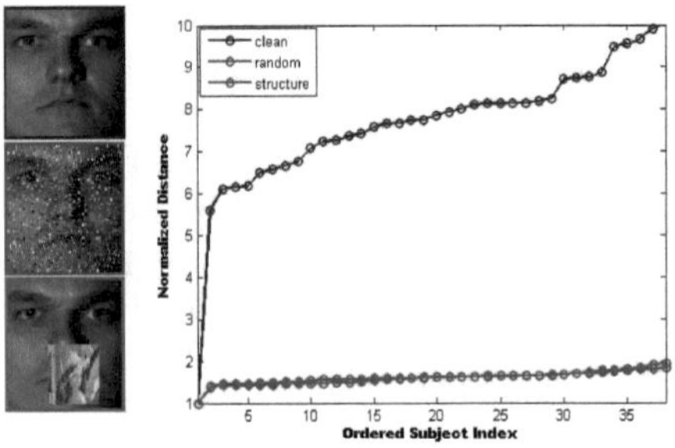

Fig. 5. Left: Sample of original images and the corrupted versions. In both corrupted images 20% of the pixels are contaminated. Right: Comparison of the ordered original ℓ^1 distances to other subspaces and that of after introducing the artificial corruptions. This distance gap is significantly suppressed due to the corruptions.

Table 2. Recognition Rate under Corruptions for all Test Samples on EYB. ($r = 15$)

Occlusion	Occluded Pixels	HDS	$d = 50$	$d = 70$
Random	5%	98.8%	96.2%	97.2%
	10%	98.6%	93.7%	95.2%
	15%	99.2%	89.2%	91.9%
	20%	99.2%	85.4%	87.8%
Structured	5%	98.7%	95.7%	96.7%
	10%	97.8%	91.3%	94.7%
	15%	95.9%	87.3%	91.6%
	20%	93.5%	82.7%	84.6%

Acknowledgments. JS was supported by the Wei Family Private Foundation Fellowship.

References

1. Turk, M., Pentland, A.: Eigenfaces for recognition. In: CVPR (1991)
2. Murase, H., Nayar, S.: Visual learning and recognition of 3D objects from appearance. IJCV 14(1), 5–24 (1995)
3. Cootes, T., Edwards, G., Taylor, C.: Active appearance models. IEEE Trans. PAMI 23(6), 681–685 (2001)
4. Blanz, V., Vetter, T.: Face recognition based on fitting a 3D morphable model. IEEE Trans. PAMI 25(9), 1063–1074 (2003)
5. Wright, J., Yang, A., Ganesh, A., Sastry, S., Ma, Y.: Robust face recognition via sparse representation. IEEE Trans. PAMI 31(2), 210–227 (2009)
6. Wagner, A., Wright, J., Ganesh, A., Zhou, Z., Mobahi, H., Ma, Y.: Towards a practical automatic face recognition system: Robust alignment and illumination by sparse representation. IEEE Trans. PAMI 34(2), 372–386 (2012)
7. Georghiades, A., Belhumeur, P., Kriegman, D.: From few to many: Illumination cone models for face recognition under variable lighting and pose. IEEE Trans. PAMI 23(6), 643–660 (2001)
8. Basri, R., Jacobs, D.: Lambertian reflectance and linear subspaces. IEEE Trans. PAMI 25(2), 218–233 (2003)
9. Donoho, D., Grimes, C.: Image manifolds which are isometric to Euclidean space. J. of Math. Imag. and Vis. 23(1), 5–24 (2005)

10. Simard, P.Y., LeCun, Y.A., Denker, J.S., Victorri, B.: Transformation Invariance in Pattern Recognition - Tangent Distance and Tangent Propagation. In: Orr, G.B., Müller, K.-R. (eds.) Neural Networks: Tricks of the Trade. LNCS, vol. 1524, pp. 239–274. Springer, Heidelberg (1998)
11. Roweis, S., Saul, L.: Nonlinear dimensionality reduction by locally linear embedding. Science 290, 2323–2326 (2000)
12. Boyd, S., Vandenberghe, L.: Convex Optimization. Cambridge University Press (2004)
13. Efron, B., Hastie, T., Johnstone, I., Tibshirani, R.: Least angle regression. Annals of Statistics 32, 407–499 (2004)
14. Beck, A., Teboulle, M.: A fast iterative shrinkage-thresholding algorithm for linear inverse problems. SIAM J. on Imag. Sci. 2(1), 183–202 (2009)
15. Yin, W., Osher, S., Goldfarb, D., Darbon, J.: Bregman iterative algorithms for ℓ^1-minimization with applications to compressed sensing. SIAM J. Imag. Sci 1(1), 143–168
16. Yang, A., Ganesh, A., Ma, Y., Sastry, S.: Fast ℓ^1-minimization algorithms and an application in robust face recognition: A review. In: ICIP (2010)
17. Donoho, D., Tsaig, Y.: Fast solution of ℓ^1-norm minimization problems when the solution may be sparse. IEEE Trans. IT 54(11), 4789–4812 (2008)
18. Agarwal, A., Negahban, S., Wainwright, M.: Fast global convergence of gradient methods for high-dimensional statistical recovery. In: NIPS (2011)
19. Mattingley, J., Boyd, S.: CVXGEN: A code generator for embedded convex optimization. Optimization and Engineering 13(1), 1–27 (2012)
20. Datar, M., Indyk, P.: Locality-sensitive hashing scheme based on p-stable distributions. In: SCG, pp. 253–262. ACM Press (2004)
21. Andoni, A., Indyk, P., Krauthgamer, R., Nguyen, H.: Approximate line nearest neighbor in high dimensions. In: SODA (2009)
22. Basri, R., Hassner, T., Zelnik-Manor, L.: Approximate nearest subspace search. IEEE Trans. PAMI 33(2), 266–278 (2011)
23. Jain, P., Vijayanarasimhan, S., Grauman, K.: Hashing hyperplane queries to near points with applications to large-scale active learning. In: NIPS (2010)
24. Williams, R.: A new algorithm for optimal 2-constraint satisfaction and its implications. Theo. Comp. Sci. 348, 357–365 (2005)
25. Magen, A., Zouzias, A.: Near Optimal Dimensionality Reductions That Preserve Volumes. In: Goel, A., Jansen, K., Rolim, J.D.P., Rubinfeld, R. (eds.) APPROX and RANDOM 2008. LNCS, vol. 5171, pp. 523–534. Springer, Heidelberg (2008)
26. Li, P., Hastie, T., Church, K.: Nonlinear estimators and tail bounds for dimension reduction in ℓ^1 using cauchy random projections. JMLR 8, 2497–2532 (2007)
27. Sohler, C., Woodruff, D.: Subspace embeddings for the ℓ_1-norm with applications. In: STOC (2011)
28. Brinkman, B., Charikar, M.: On the impossibility of dimension reduction in ℓ^1. J. ACM 52, 766–788 (2005)
29. Candés, E., Tao, T.: Decoding by linear programming. IEEE Trans. IT 51(12), 4203–4215 (2005)
30. Wright, J., Ma, Y.: Dense error correction via ℓ^1-minimization. IEEE Trans. IT 56(7), 3540–3560 (2010)
31. Ledoux, M.: The Concentration of Measure Phenomenon. AMS (2001)

Recognizing Complex Events Using Large Margin Joint Low-Level Event Model

Hamid Izadinia and Mubarak Shah

Computer Vision Lab, University of Central Florida, Orlando, Florida
{izadinia,shah}@eecs.ucf.edu

Abstract. In this paper we address the challenging problem of complex event recognition by using low-level events. In this problem, each complex event is captured by a long video in which several low-level events happen. The dataset contains several videos and due to the large number of videos and complexity of the events, the available annotation for the low-level events is very noisy which makes the detection task even more challenging. To tackle these problems we model the joint relationship between the low-level events in a graph where we consider a node for each low-level event and whenever there is a correlation between two low-level events the graph has an edge between the corresponding nodes. In addition, for decreasing the effect of weak and/or irrelevant low-level event detectors we consider the presence/absence of low-level events as hidden variables and learn a discriminative model by using latent SVM formulation. Using our learned model for the complex event recognition, we can also apply it for improving the detection of the low-level events in video clips which enables us to discover a conceptual description of the video. Thus our model can do complex event recognition and explain a video in terms of low-level events in a single framework. We have evaluated our proposed method over the most challenging multimedia event detection dataset. The experimental results reveals that the proposed method performs well compared to the baseline method. Further, our results of conceptual description of video shows that our model is learned quite well to handle the noisy annotation and surpass the low-level event detectors which are directly trained on the raw features.

1 Introduction

The majority of current human action recognition work deals with the classification of short video clips (e.g. 3-10 sec) which contain some simple and well-defined actions such as running, biking, diving, etc, and the main challenges are how to deal with low resolution, arbitrary camera motion, occlusion and clutter in the scene. However, real lifetime videos are of longer length which contain complex events happening at specific place and time such as birthday party and wedding ceremony; such videos may depict complex scenes and involve a number of human actions in which people interact with each other and/or with objects. For example a video of *birthday party* event can be described by the objects (*cake, candle*), scene (*indoor, outdoor*), actions (*person singing, laughing*) and

A. Fitzgibbon et al. (Eds.): ECCV 2012, Part IV, LNCS 7575, pp. 430–444, 2012.

Fig. 1. Examples from complex video event categories: (from left to right, column wise) *boarding trick, feeding animal, landing fish, wedding, woodworking project, birthday party, changing tire, flash mob, vehicle unstuck, grooming animal, making sandwich, parade, parkour, repairing appliance, sewing project.*

surrounding voices (*music, cheering*) that happen in it. Therefore, it is apparent that classifying a complex realistic event is a much more challenging task than just recognizing a set of motion discriminative actions (low level events) in standard datasets (such as KTH [1], UCF-Sports [2], UCF50 [3], and HMDB [4]). Some example video frames from complex event categories considered in this paper are shown in Fig. 1.

Recently, the bag-of-words (BoW) approach has achieved impressive results in many recognition problems including action recognition [5, 6]. However, this approach has innate limitations in representation and semantic description of the underlying data as it jumps directly from low level features to the very high level class labels. Therefore, the methods which are based on BoW approach cannot easily provide any semantic intermediate description of the data.

For recognizing complex events, we argue that it is crucial to learn the low-level events along with their relationships to the event categories. For example, for *Birthday party* event, low-level events may include: *person cheering, person singing, person blowing candles, person taking pictures*, etc. For each low-level event we use a collection of various features to learn its model. We then use the learned low-level event detectors to train a discriminative model for recognizing complex events. To this end, we model the joint relations between the low-level events by a latent graphical model. In our model, we have a node for each low-level event and the edges between the nodes represent the correlations between the low-level events. Since, the number of all possible co-occurrence of these low-level events is very large, we take the advantage of the fact that a large portion of possible co-occurrences is rather unlikely to happen and exploit only those which have high rate of coincidence. We consider the presence or absence of low-level events as latent variables and learn their correlations in a latent SVM framework, which simultaneously alleviate the problem of noisy low-level event detectors and improves the accuracy of high-level event recognition.

The overview of the proposed method is summarized in Fig. 2. At the first stage the raw features extracted from the training videos along with the information obtained by low-level event annotation are used to train the low-level event detectors. The graph of low-level event co-occurrence is also constructed using annotations. In addition, high level event detectors are trained using raw features

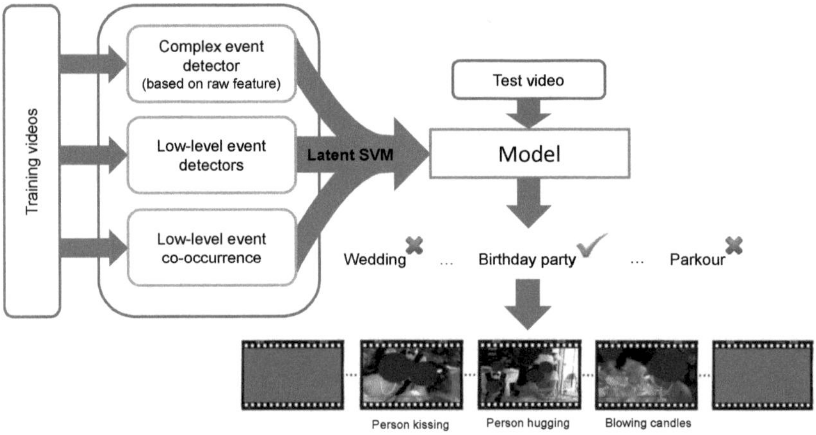

Fig. 2. Given the training videos and low-level event annotation, we train low-level event detectors and high-level event detector using raw feature. Then we employ co-occurrence of low-level events along with the individual low-level event detector outputs in latent SVM framework to detect the high-level event label. We also use the latent parameter vector for describing an unseen test video in terms of low-level events. For example, the given video of birthday party is described by the sequence of low-level events: *person kissing, person hugging and blowing candles.*

directly. The final model is generated using the low-level events, co-occurrence graph and high-level event detectors. Our training data includes long sequences of each of 15 complex events which are divided into short clips of typically 10 seconds. Each short clip potentially contains one of 62 low-level events. Each clip is assigned to one of the 62 low-level event labels by human annotators, which are only used for training the detectors. At the testing time, we need to predict the category of a given complex event video. Thus, we use a latent SVM model in which the low-level event are treated as latent variables. Also, in our latent SVM framework, we learn the co-occurrence pattern of the low-level events for further improvement of the recognition performance. As an example, a given test video could be a short movie of a wedding ceremony that contains low-level events such as *kissing, hugging, dancing, taking picture*, at different temporal locations in a video. Using trained low-level event detectors, we can compute the confidence scores for the presence of the low-level events in all the 10 second clips of the test video. With our trained latent SVM model and the obtained confidence scores, we can accurately describe each video.

The key contributions of our work are as follows: First, our proposed model shows that learning low-level events can improve the recognition rate of complex events. Here, we model low-level events in a latent graphical model where for discovering the joint relations between low-level event a latent SVM is trained. Second, our model provides a flexible framework for using the combination of various types of low-level features for modeling contextual information, local appearance, motion patterns and audio properties. Third, using trained latent

SVM model, we can provide a semantic description of a given video which can be used in problems like video retrieval, where the aim is to detect the presence or absence of a semantic concept in video.

2 Related Work

The explosive growth of digital videos on the Internet has made an urgent necessity for having efficient methods for video analysis. Amongst all, high level video event classification and recognition is one of the most critical problems that should be solved to this end. While the action recognition problem, which can be considered as low-level event recognition, is widely explored, the problem of event recognition is not much explored [7–9]. The challenging nature of event recognition problem lies in the fact that simple actions are the building blocks of events while the action recognition problem is itself one of the most challenging recognition problems to date. Thus, we argue that it is very logical to treat the action recognition as an intermediate step in recognizing complex events.

On the other hand, the use of different attributes for the recognition task has recently been explored in different computer vision applications such as object classification [10–13], image ranking and retrieval [14] and human action recognition [15]. Some of the attributes that has been used in these methods have semantic meaning while some of them are data driven attributes[15]. The data driven attributes are extracted from training data based on raw features. These attributes can only increase the performance of the recognition but do not provide any conceptual description about the content of the video.

Our notion of low-level events is similar to the attributes in the sense that both are used as a source of intermediate information for recognition of a more complex task. However, in the literature, an attribute refers to an atomic part of a more general category while each of our low-level events is itself a general category. Thus, the general notion of attribute stands at a smaller granularity than our low-level events. For example in the object recognition a set of possible attributes for recognizing objects can be (furry, leg, metallic surfaces, 3D boxy) [10] and in action recognition can be (up-down motion, torso motion, twist) [15]. Whereas, some of our low-level events are (Person dancing, people marching, animal eating). The other main difference of our approach with the attribute based methods is that, in the attribute based methods, the presence/absence of the attributes is used to improve the recognition task, but there is no concrete representation for each of the attributes and thus the attribute detection is not that informative. Whereas, each of our low-level events refer to a certain clip and our method learns the low-level event for both event recognition and temporal video description. Recently, [16–18] modeled the temporal structure of the video. However, they anchor a predefined number of low-level events/actions in temporal domain and attempt to find the best discriminative temporal model for each high-level event/action. In our work we do not impose any constraint on the temporal location of each low-level event but instead we learn the co-occurrence pattern of the low-level events for further improvement of the recognition performance. Thus, we are not limited by any kind of prior information about the temporal locations of low-level events and learn the co-occurrence via a latent SVM framework.

3 Complex Event Recognition Using Low-Level Events

For classifying videos we start by considering each video as a collection of low-level events. Each low-level event can either refer to a simple action that is performed by one or more actors such as *person walking*, a complex action that takes place while interacting with other objects (*person petting*) or a particular behavior that is performed by a group of people (*people dancing*). Thus, for solving the video classification we propose to learn low-level events along with their correlations by analyzing the video sequence temporally and using a set of diverse features: ISA (independent subspace analysis) [5], STIP (spatio-temporal interest point descriptor) [19], Dollar [20], GIST [21], SIFT [22] and MFCC (Mel-frequency cepstral coefficients) [23] for describing each low-level event. The correlations between low-level events are then learned in latent SVM framework.

For learning the low-level events we have manually annotated the training videos, as is typically done in human action recognition work. Of course, we assume these labels are considered not to be available at the test time. For each of these low-level events a classifier is trained based on the low-level features.

Using the low-level event detectors, we then compute a feature vector for each event video and use it for training high level event detectors. To this end, we need to compute the confidence scores of different low-level event detectors for the clips of each video. The low-level events are of different temporal length, since the videos contain real world events. Thus, we compute the confidence score of the low level detectors on overlapping clips of the video in a hierarchical fashion. At the first level of the hierarchy the confidence scores are computed using fixed length overlapping clips, then at each higher level the confidence score for two adjacent clips of the lower level is computed. After computing all the confidence feature vectors, the final high-level feature vector for the video is computed by max pooling over all confidence vectors.

3.1 Large Margin Learning Based on Underlying Latent Structure

In this section, we address the problem of learning a model for labeled and structured data. For the high level event recognition problem considered in this paper, we explore the underlying structure based on a joint relation graph which is constructed using the co-occurrence of the low-level events.

Each training sample is represented by (x, z, y) in which x is a video and $y \in \mathcal{Y}$ denotes its class label. And the low-level event representation of a video is defined by a C-dimensional binary vector $z = (z_1, ..., z_C)$ where each dimension shows the presence/absence of a specific low-level event in a video. For instance, if the ith video belongs to the *Birthday party* event and the cth dimension corresponds to the *Person lighting candle* low-level event, z_c would probably be equal to 1.

We consider a training set that consists of n input/output pairs $(x_1, y_1), ...,$ $(x_n, y_n) \in \mathcal{X} \times \mathcal{Y}$. Given the training data, we are interested in learning a discriminative function $\mathcal{F}_\theta : \mathcal{X} \times \mathcal{Y} \rightarrow \mathbb{R}$ over the feature vector of a video and its event class label. Here $\mathcal{F}$ is parameterized by θ. During testing, we can predict the class label of a high-level event video using Eq. (1);

$$y^* = \underset{y \in \mathcal{Y}}{\text{argmax}}\, \mathcal{F}_\theta(x, y). \tag{1}$$

Since we consider latent low-level event representation for each video, the discriminative function $\mathcal{F}$ scores based on the latent variable which is computed by $\mathcal{F}_\theta(x, y) = \max_z \; \Theta^\top \Phi(x, z, y)$. Here $\Theta^\top \Phi(x, z, y)$ depends on global event potential, unary low-level event potential and joint low-level event potential:

$$\Theta^\top \Phi(x, z, y) = \theta_y^\top \phi(x) + \sum_{j \in \mathcal{V}} (\theta_{z_j}^\top \varphi(x) + \beta_{(y,j)}) + \sum_{(j,k) \in \mathcal{E}} \theta_{(j,k)}^\top \psi(z_j, z_k), \tag{2}$$

in which $\Theta = (\theta_y, \theta_{z_j}, \theta_{(j,k)})$ is the parameter (weight) vector of $\mathcal{F}$. The potentials are defined in the following.

Global Event Potential: The global potential $\theta_y^\top \phi(x)$ represents a linear discriminative model for event detection without considering low-level events, where each video x is represented by a feature vector $\phi(x)$. In order to speed up the training process we pre-train a classifiers for each event and incorporate θ_y to regularize the confidence score of the event classifiers. Thus, without loss of generality $\phi(x)$ refers to the confidence score of the corresponding event classifier for the input video x. However, as we use different feature types (i.e. image, video and audio), we need to pre-train a classifier for each feature type so the score of each event classifier is weighted by θ_y that is a k dimensional vector for k different feature types.

Unary Low-Level Event Potential: The low-level event potential $(\theta_{z_j}^\top \varphi(x) + \beta_{(y,j)})$ determines the occurrence of each low-level event in a video. We can use the raw feature vector and then train a large parameter vector for recognizing each low-level event, but similar to the global potential, we use a pre-trained binary classifier for each low-level event. Therefore, the unary potential for each low-level event is the confidence score produced by each low-level event detector and $\beta_{(y,j)}$, which represents the occurrence of each low-level event in each event class.

Joint Low-Level Event Potential: There is a meaningful relationship in the co-occurrence of more than one low-level event in a video. For example, there are a certain number of low-level event e.g. *person kissing, taking picture, person dancing* which frequently occur in a particular event such as *wedding ceremony*, while it is very unlikely that some other low-level events like *person hammering* may occur in the same event. The joint potential $\theta_{(j,k)}^\top \psi(z_j, z_k)$ incorporates the co-occurrence of low-level events in training the classifier. Since we only consider presence and absence of low-level events as the latent variable, we have four possible joint potentials $\{(0,0), (0,1), (1,0), (1,1)\}$ between any two low-level events.

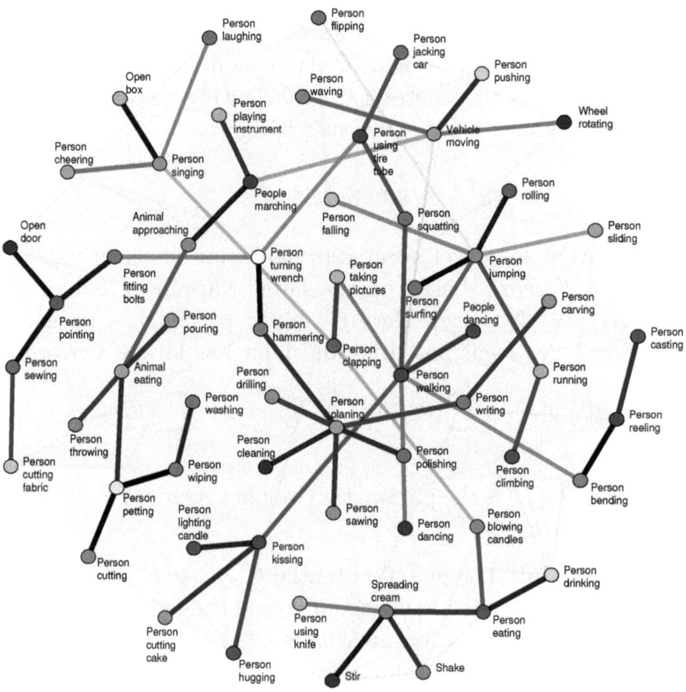

Fig. 3. The low-level events joint relation model computed by running maximum spanning tree on the complete co-occurrence graph. The weight of edges express the normalized co-occurrence between the vertices. The darker edges show stronger correlation between the low-level events.

In practice, some low-level event pairs may have rather weak correlations, including both in their presence or absence. For example, the low-level event pairs (*person dancing* and *person using tire tube*), or (*person jumping*, *person drinking*) indeed do not have too much correlations, that is to say, the presence/absence of one low-level event will not contribute to that of another (i.e., their occurrence are independent of each other). Based on this observation, we remove the weaker relations and only consider the strongly correlated pairs. The selection of low-level events can be manually determined by experts or automatically selected by some data-driven approaches. In this paper, we measure the correlations of low-level event pair using the normalized co-occurrence defined by $\frac{\mathcal{N}(z_j,z_k)}{\mathcal{N}(z_j)\mathcal{N}(z_k)}$ in which $\mathcal{N}(.)$ and $\mathcal{N}(.,.)$ respectively count the number of occurrences and co-occurrences in the entire training set using annotations. Once we compute the concept pair co-occurrence, we construct the correlation graph in which the low-level events represent vertices and the weight of edges are the normalized co-occurrences. We cannot find the optimum low-level event representation over complete correlation graph without enumerating the entire set of combinations which is exponential in cardinality of each node (i.e. $|\{0,1\}| = 2$ and for 62 low-level events is 2^{62}). To eliminate this problem, we compute the maximum spanning tree to find a co-occurrence tree so that only the most correlated pairs are adjacent. In this case, the inference problem becomes tractable and can be solved by dynamic programming. Fig. 3 shows the maximum spanning tree obtained for 62 low-level events. As shown in this figure, the connection between low-level event pairs are meaningful. For instance, *person surfing, person jumping and person sliding* are connected which are usually co-occur in *boarding trick* event. Another example is *person throwing* and *animal eating* which are usually co-occur in *feeding animal event* videos.

3.2 Large Margin Learning

We train a binary classifier for each complex event class. Each classifier scores an example x using Eq. 1, so we must learn the parameter vector Θ from the set of positive and negative samples. The parameter vector Θ for each event class is trained iteratively by minimizing the objective function

$$f(\Theta) = \frac{\lambda}{2}\|\Theta\|^2 + \sum_{i=1}^{n} R_i(\Theta), \tag{3}$$

where λ makes trade-off between generalization and the data fitting. The risk function R_i is computed based on the optimum latent variable z^* and the predicted class label y^* for each training sample. We define inference function $\mathcal{G}(x, z, y, \Theta) = \Theta^\top \Phi(x, z, y)$ which finds the optimum latent variables z^* based on the model parameter Θ using

$$z_y^* = \operatorname*{argmax}_{z \in \mathcal{Z}} \mathcal{G}(x, z, y, \Theta) \quad \forall y \in \{-1, 1\}. \tag{4}$$

Then we use optimum latent variable z_y^* and find the predicted label for the ith video y^* by

$$y^* = \operatorname*{argmax}_{y \in \{-1,1\}} (\mathcal{G}(x_i, z_y^*, y, \Theta) + \Delta(y, y_i)), \tag{5}$$

where y_i is the ground truth label and $\Delta(y, y_i)$ is the loss function. A variety of loss functions have been used in the literature, here we use 0/1 loss function which is $\Delta(y, y_i) = 1$ if $y \neq y_i$, and $\Delta(y, y_i) = 0$ otherwise. Once the y^* is computed for the ith sample, the risk is computed by

$$R_i = \mathcal{G}(x_i, z_{y^*}^*, y^*, \Theta) + \Delta(y^*, y_i) - \mathcal{G}(x_i, z_{y_i}^*, y_i, \Theta). \tag{6}$$

Apparently, the risk function is non-zero if $y^* \neq y_i$. We minimize the objective function $f(\Theta)$ using non-convex regularized bundle method [24]. This method relies on the cutting plane technique, where a cutting plane in defined using the sub-gradient of objective function $f(\Theta)$ by

$$\delta_\Theta f = \lambda\Theta + \sum_{i=1}^{n} \left(\Phi(x_i, z_{y^*}^*, y^*) - \Phi(x_i, z_{y_i}^*, y_i)\right). \tag{7}$$

Table 1. The Average Precision of low-level event detection using different features

Low-level event	ISA	STIP	Dollar	SIFT	GIST	MFCC	Low-level event	ISA	STIP	Dollar	SIFT	GIST	MFCC
Person surfing	61.6	37.9	2.3	40.7	25.8	2.4	Person laughing	2.8	3.0	1.2	11.8	1.1	1.8
People marching	48.4	55.4	23.7	53.4	25.5	25.3	Lighting candle	11.1	0.4	0.3	0.3	0.3	0.2
Person carving	49.6	43.2	8.8	45.6	18.7	53.3	Person squatting	2.5	1.5	1.4	7.3	2.0	10.8
Person sewing	49.9	19.4	24.7	19.6	12.2	23.8	Person hugging	5.2	8.9	3.6	10.8	1.4	1.8
Vehicle moving	42.3	47.6	14.3	29.0	26.9	15.3	Wheel rotating	2.4	10.4	1.4	10.7	1.0	1.0
Animal eating	24.4	23.8	11.2	44.7	7.0	16.7	Using tire tube	10.4	5.3	4.0	7.5	4.0	4.9
People dancing	31.2	42.7	13.2	34.3	7.9	3.7	Person drilling	6.3	5.7	1.6	7.8	10.3	1.1
Person singing	30.8	34.8	7.8	34.7	6.0	40.2	Person falling	6.8	9.8	3.0	6.6	3.2	4.3
Person washing	38.8	21.7	5.0	40.0	10.9	8.2	Person running	9.4	7.5	1.5	3.2	1.3	3.3
Person pointing	22.5	7.9	7.4	7.7	1.5	30.0	Person waving	5.8	3.2	2.3	8.7	1.6	2.5
Person kissing	29.0	12.7	6.3	8.2	1.9	10.3	Taking pictures	4.1	8.1	6.3	5.0	2.2	3.0
Person sliding	26.7	14.9	4.6	18.9	16.0	3.0	Blowing candles	4.7	7.0	2.0	7.6	1.6	1.9
Open door	26.6	18.8	10.3	18.8	3.1	8.2	Person clapping	4.9	3.5	2.7	7.2	2.2	3.9
Turning wrench	23.1	17.9	4.7	26.1	5.3	13.5	Person casting	6.3	2.8	1.0	3.8	0.7	0.9
Person reeling	25.1	10.6	2.2	14.7	12.3	2.2	Person petting	6.0	1.4	0.7	1.8	0.7	3.8
Person planing	16.8	14.7	9.2	22.8	15.8	8.2	Person wiping	5.7	0.6	0.4	1.8	0.3	0.8
Person jumping	17.7	20.5	12.3	21.6	11.1	21.1	Person bending	5.4	2.8	1.8	5.4	1.9	2.2
Person flipping	18.1	21.4	7.1	21.1	14.7	8.1	Person rolling	0.7	2.0	0.7	4.6	0.3	2.6
Person walking	13.5	19.2	10.5	21.1	9.9	6.0	Person climbing	3.6	4.0	1.8	1.8	0.8	2.0
Person cutting	9.1	3.4	2.9	20.6	2.1	3.1	Shake	3.7	0.3	0.5	0.6	0.3	0.4
Person dancing	8.9	18.0	3.4	19.6	4.5	3.4	Playing instrument	0.5	2.8	0.4	1.4	0.3	0.5
Spreading cream	19.0	16.1	3.7	8.5	2.5	5.4	Stir	2.0	2.7	0.4	0.4	0.3	1.3
Person eating	5.7	4.8	3.5	16.6	2.2	3.7	Person jacking car	1.6	2.7	1.1	1.5	0.6	0.7
Open box	1.0	6.6	0.3	16.1	0.3	0.7	Person cheering	0.8	1.6	0.6	1.5	0.7	2.6
Person throwing	15.5	5.5	1.7	9.5	0.9	2.4	Person cutting cake	2.2	0.8	1.1	0.9	0.4	0.6
Person hammering	4.0	12.2	8.6	15.2	6.4	4.8	Person pushing	1.4	1.0	0.8	2.1	0.8	0.7
Person using knife	11.8	14.7	11.4	7.6	2.1	5.1	Person polishing	1.9	1.3	1.0	1.2	0.6	1.7
Person sawing	7.1	2.9	4.0	5.7	6.0	14.5	Animal approaching	1.1	1.3	0.7	1.8	0.9	0.9
Fitting bolts	13.8	13.2	2.7	14.3	5.1	14.1	Person cleaning	1.5	0.8	0.9	1.5	0.4	0.7
Cutting fabric	13.8	1.2	3.2	11.4	0.7	10.6	Person drinking	1.3	0.7	0.9	0.5	0.4	0.5
Person writing	11.9	9.0	4.1	12.4	6.5	6.6	Person pouring	0.6	0.5	0.6	0.8	0.5	0.8

Table 2. The mean average precision value using different features

Feature	ISA	STIP	Dollar	SIFT	GIST	MFCC
mean AP	13.56	11.24	4.54	13.04	5.08	7.07

The bundle method iteratively builds an increasingly accurate piecewise quadratic lower bound of the objective function by selecting the most violated sample and building the bundle using the sub-gradient at that point. Such a cutting plane is a linear lower bound of the risk function $R(\Theta)$ and is a quadratic lower bound of the objective function $f(\Theta)$.

4 Experiments

To evaluate the performance of the proposed method, we present results for event recognition on the TRECVID11-MED event kit [25] which is the most challenging multimedia event dataset. This dataset contains 2,061 multimedia videos (i.e., video clips including both video and audio) collected from Internet. The videos are divided into 15 different events: *Boarding trick, Feeding animal, Landing fish, Wedding, Wood working project, Birthday party, Changing tire, Flash mob, Vehicle unstuck, Grooming animal, Making sandwich, Parade, Parkour, Repairing appliance*, and *Sewing project*. As the dataset contains plenty of videos, we randomly split the videos of each class in the dataset into 70% videos for training and 30% for testing and report the recognition rate using the precision criteria. For quantitative comparison we use Average Precision (AP) which is used in PASCAL VOC challenge [26]. The AP summarizes the characteristic of precision/recall curve, and is defined as the mean precision at a set of equally spaced recall levels $[0, 0.1, ..., 1]$. For a given class, the precision/recall curve is computed using the output confidence scores.

4.1 Feature Representation

We use six different feature types: ISA, Dollar and STIP as motion features; SIFT and GIST for local and global image appearance features, respectively. We also use MFCC along with its first and second derivatives as audio features. For ISA feature we use pre-trained convolutional ISA network which is provided in released package[1]. The Dollar descriptors are extracted around spatio-temporal interest points where a predefined space-time filter has significant response. For STIP feature we use 3D Harris corner detector and combination of HoG-HoF is used as a descriptor. For extracting SIFT and GIST features, we uniformly sample every K frame of each video and extract 128-D SIFT and 960-D GIST descriptors from each of those key frames. We also use a standard set of short-term MFCC features from down-sampled audio signal to 16kHz. We extract MFCC features from each frame of 25 ms with 10 ms overlap, and retain 21 coefficients as audio features.

4.2 Low-Level Event Detection

Table 1 shows the performance of our low-level event detectors using different types of features. This figure shows that for some of the low-level events the performance is very low which is due to lack of sufficient training samples and diverse patterns of low-level events appearing in the training video clips.

In addition, the average performance using each feature is summarized in Table 2. Although this table shows that ISA and SIFT had the highest average performance, Table 1 shows that each of the above features has the highest performance for some of the low-level events, when used separately. For example, the *MFCC* features obtains the highest average precision compared to other features in *singing* and *Person carving* low-level events, where the audio contains discriminative information. Whereas in motion dominant low-level events like *People marching* and *People dancing* the STIP features have higher accuracy. Thus, the need for using different feature types in a unified framework is obvious.

4.3 Complex Event Recognition

Fig. 4 demonstrates the unary part of the trained parameter vector θ_{z_j}. This figure shows the importance of individual low-level event detectors and that the relevant low-level event have higher weights. For example, in the *making sandwich* event, *person eating*, *person using knife* and *spreading cream* have the highest weights. Fig. 5 demonstrates the learned underlying structure for the *Birthday party* event. The edges are bolder whenever the corresponding learned

[1] `http://ai.stanford.edu/~wzou/`

pairwise correlation is of more importance. As expected, the latent learning procedure was successfully able to assign larger weights for (*open box*, *person singing*) and (*blowing candle*, *person eating*) edges, which quite frequently happen in a birthday party. While, the rarely co-occurring low-level event pairs like *person walking* and *person bending* are assigned low weights. On the other hand, a low pairwise weight is assigned to the low-level event *person cutting cake* which usually takes place in a *birthday party*. This is due to the noisy patterns of the *cutting cake* in the training videos and low performance of the *person cutting cake* detector. This reveals that the latent model could compensate the effect of noisy low-level event detectors by assigning a small value to the corresponding pairwise weights.

The classification results of our proposed method compared to the state of the art methods are summarized in Table 3. The best performance of the bag of words is obtained by using ISA features which is 55.87%. By fusing output of low-level event detectors with high-level event detectors for all feature types the performance is increased up to 62.63%. While co-occurrence of low-level events help remove the effect of noisy low-level event detectors and resulted in 64.25% average precision. Our proposed latent model using both low-level event and high-level event detectors has gained the highest performance i.e. 66.10%. Table 3 shows the comparison of classifier performance for each individual event. As can be observed, the precision of the latent event detector is higher than the other methods in most of the events. This is mostly visible in the *Flash mob*, *Birthday party* and *Parade* events which is due to their well performing low-level event detectors such as *People dancing*, *Person singing* and *People marching*.

Table 3. The average precision of our approach compared with the baseline methods. The first 6 columns show the results obtained using bag of words approach employing individual features. The next column shows the results obtained by training a linear SVM on the confidences of low-level and high-level event detectors, mean AP is better than the ones obtained by using any individual features. Following that under Joint LL event column we show the results obtained by joint relationship of LL using latent SVM, the performance is further improved here. Finally, in the last column we show results obtained using both high-level and low-level event detectors joint model trained using latent SVM, which provides the best results

High-level event	ISA	STIP	Dollar	SIFT	GIST	MFCC	Linear SVM ensemble	Joint (LL event)	Joint (HL+LL)
Flash mob	62.7	60.7	80.8	78.3	72.9	78.5	85.9	88.8	91.9
Repairing appliance	77.6	63.2	63.8	57.9	49.0	70.2	80.8	73.5	78.2
Birthday party	63.2	28.2	47.6	35.3	20.2	59.0	70.9	76.0	78.2
Boarding trick	49.4	58.1	52.4	54.3	54.8	65.3	75.6	68.8	75.7
Landing fish	29.1	46.2	69.8	39.8	36.0	64.6	74.1	71.6	72.2
Parade	42.3	36.7	46.3	45.2	36.0	42.2	65.7	71.0	72.4
Vehicle unstuck	35.3	39.5	48.2	48.2	39.5	44.1	66.1	67.8	69.1
Parkour	27.1	34.1	67.8	35.4	43.8	62.0	53.4	65.3	66.4
Wedding	53.4	52.1	66.3	63.2	62.2	66.5	66.5	64.4	67.5
Woodworking project	45.8	24.1	47.3	31.9	30.8	55.9	57.6	64.8	65.3
Feeding animal	34.3	28.6	39.1	27.5	30.1	51.4	58.2	57.8	56.5
Sewing project	37.8	20.6	35.1	32.7	23.0	55.3	56.9	56.4	57.5
Grooming animal	24.9	27.7	36.2	28.8	28.3	49.7	45.7	48.0	51.0
Changing tire	20.3	7.6	29.5	19.1	17.4	45.0	46.5	48.1	47.7
Making sandwich	25.4	21.9	32.5	19.0	19.6	28.5	35.6	41.5	41.9
mean AP	55.87	37.57	41.12	50.85	36.63	41.90	62.63	**64.25**	**66.10**

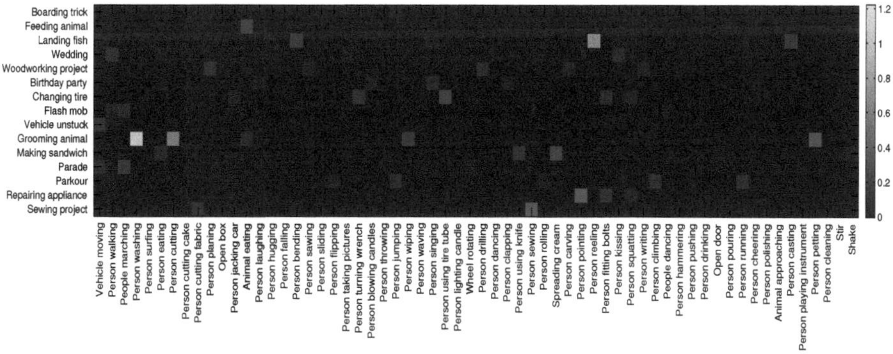

Fig. 4. The visualization of unary model parameters in terms of low-level events for the trained latent model of all events. The higher value shows more influence of low-level events in complex event recognition.

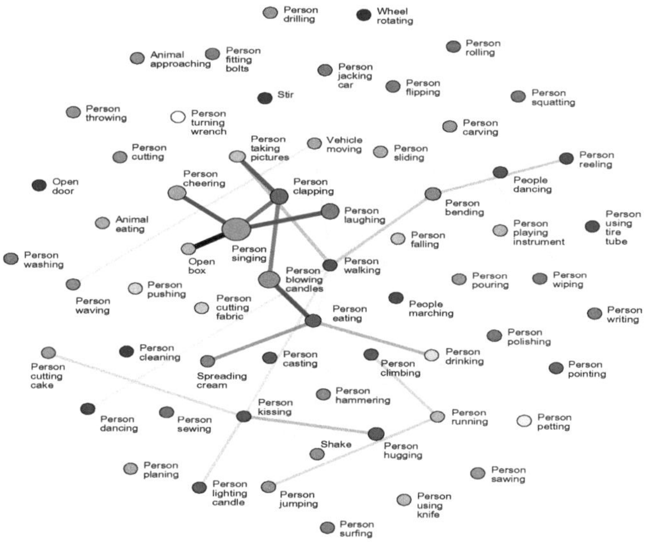

Fig. 5. The low-level event joint model trained by proposed latent method for *Birthday party*. The darker edge shows more discriminative joint for classifying this specific event.

4.4 Describing Video in Terms of Low-Level Events

We want to label each clip (10 sec) of a given video with one of our low-level events. One simple approach for doing this is to directly use the output of low-level event detectors. However, as shown in Fig. 6 the low-level event detectors are too noisy due to errors in the human annotations. However, as shown in Fig. 4 our unary term parameter vector θ_z that are trained in the latent training

Fig. 6. Temporal description of our method compared with the confidence score of low-level event detectors (LL confidence score) for two sample event videos. We sort the confidence score of all low-level events for each 10-second clip and show top five low-level events for each clip. The irrelevant low-level events with high confidence score are shown in bold.

procedure, can filter out irrelevant low-level events by assigning smaller weights to them. Therefore, for labeling each clip of a given video, we compute its confidence scores for all the low-level events. Having the vector of confidence scores, we simply compute $\theta_z^\top \varphi(x)$ and report the first five low-level events with highest $\theta_z^\top \varphi(x)$ value. The results obtained by this approach are shown in Fig. 6 for two sample videos. The caption of the videos contains the results obtained by the direct use of low-level event confidence scores and our approach.

5 Conclusion

In this paper we presented an event detection method based on latent low-level event model. Our proposed model learns a set of low-level event detectors and gets help from the low-level event co-occurrence in a latent SVM training procedure. Our model has the ability to filter out the noisy output of low-level event detectors and thus gains a good generalization for detecting low-level events. Additionally, our proposed method has the flexibility to get the benefits of using a set of different features in a unified framework. We evaluated the performance of our proposed method on the very challenging dataset and obtained impressive results on both event recognition and low-level event description.

Acknowledgements. The research presented in this paper is supported by the Intelligence Advanced Research Projects Activity (IARPA) via Department of Interior National Business Center contract number D11PC20071. The U.S.

Government is authorized to reproduce and distribute reprints for Governmental purposes notwithstanding any copyright annotation thereon. The views and conclusions contained herein are those of the authors and should not be interpreted as necessarily representing the official policies or endorsements, either expressed or implied, of IARPA, DoI/NBC, or the U.S. Government.

References

1. Schuldt, C., Laptev, I., Caputo, B.: Recognizing human actions: a local svm approach. In: ICPR (2004)
2. Rodriguez, M., Ahmed, J., Shah, M.: Action mach a spatio-temporal maximum average correlation height filter for action recognition. In: CVPR (2008)
3. Ucf50 action dataset, `http://vision.eecs.ucf.edu/data/UCF50.rar`
4. Kuehne, H., Jhuang, H., Garrote, E., Poggio, T., Serre, T.: HMDB: a large video database for human motion recognition. In: ICCV (2011)
5. Le, Q., Zou, W., Yeung, S., Ng, A.: Learning hierarchical invariant spatio-temporal features for action recognition with independent subspace analysis. In: CVPR (2011)
6. Wang, H., Kläser, A., Schmid, C., Cheng-Lin, L.: Action recognition by dense trajectories. In: CVPR (2011)
7. Jiang, Y.G., Yang, J., Ngo, C.W., Hauptmann, A.G.: Representations of keypoint-based semantic concept detection: A comprehensive study. IEEE Trans. Multimedia 12(1), 42–53 (2010)
8. Merler, M., Huang, B., Xie, L., Hua, G., Natsev, A.: Semantic model vectors for complex video event recognition. IEEE Trans. Multimedia 14(1), 88–101 (2012)
9. Natarajan, P., et al.: Bbn viser trecvid 2011 multimedia event detection system. In: NIST TRECVID Workshop (2011)
10. Farhadi, A., Endres, I., Hoiem, D., Forsyth, D.: Describing objects by their attributes. In: CVPR (2009)
11. Ferrari, V., Zisserman, A.: Learning visual attributes. In: NIPS (2007)
12. Wang, Y., Mori, G.: A Discriminative Latent Model of Object Classes and Attributes. In: Daniilidis, K., Maragos, P., Paragios, N. (eds.) ECCV 2010, Part V. LNCS, vol. 6315, pp. 155–168. Springer, Heidelberg (2010)
13. Lampert, C., Nickisch, H., Harmeling, S.: Learning to detect unseen object classes by between-class attribute transfer. In: CVPR (2009)
14. Siddiquie, B., Feris, R., Davis, L.: Image ranking and retrieval based on multi-attribute queries. In: CVPR (2011)
15. Liu, J., Kuipers, B., Savarese, S.: Recognizing human actions by attributes. In: CVPR (2011)
16. Gaidon, A., Harchaoui, Z., Schmid, C.: Actom sequence models for efficient action detection. In: CVPR (2011)
17. Niebles, J.C., Chen, C.-W., Fei-Fei, L.: Modeling Temporal Structure of Decomposable Motion Segments for Activity Classification. In: Daniilidis, K., Maragos, P., Paragios, N. (eds.) ECCV 2010, Part II. LNCS, vol. 6312, pp. 392–405. Springer, Heidelberg (2010)
18. Tang, K., Fei-Fei, L., Koller, D.: Learning latent temporal structure for complex event detection. In: CVPR (2012)
19. Laptev, I.: On space time interest points. IJCV 64 (2005)

20. Dollar, P., Rabaud, V., Cottrell, G., Belongie, S.: Behavior recognition via sparse spatio-temporal features. In: IEEE International Workshop on VS-PETS (2005)
21. Oliva, A., Torralba, A.: Modeling the shape of the scene: A holistic representation of the spatial envelope. IJCV 42, 145–175 (2001)
22. Lowe, D.G.: Distinctive image features from scale-invariant keypoints. IJCV 60(2) (2004)
23. Rabiner, L., Juang, B.H.: Fundamentals of Speech Recognition. Prentice Hall (1993)
24. Do, T.M.T., Artières, T.: Large margin training for hidden markov models with partially observed states. In: ICML (2009)
25. Trecvid multimedia event detection track (2011), `http://www.nist.gov/itl/iad/mig/med11.cfm`
26. Everingham, M., Gool, L., Williams, C.K., Winn, J., Zisserman, A.: The pascal visual object classes (voc) challenge. IJCV 88, 303–338 (2010)

Multi-component Models for Object Detection

Chunhui Gu[1], Pablo Arbeláez[2], Yuanqing Lin[3], Kai Yu[4], and Jitendra Malik[2]

[1] Google Inc., Mountain View, CA, USA
chunhui@google.com
[2] UC Berkeley, Berkeley, CA, USA
{arbelaez,malik}@eecs.berkeley.edu
[3] NEC Labs America, Cupertino, CA, USA
ylin@sv.nec-labs.com
[4] Baidu Inc., Beijing, China
yukai@baidu.com

Abstract. In this paper, we propose a multi-component approach for object detection. Rather than attempting to represent an object category with a monolithic model, or pre-defining a reduced set of aspects, we form visual clusters from the data that are tight in appearance and configuration spaces. We train individual classifiers for each component, and then learn a second classifier that operates at the category level by aggregating responses from multiple components. In order to reduce computation cost during detection, we adopt the idea of object window selection, and our segmentation-based selection mechanism produces fewer than 500 windows per image while preserving high object recall. When compared to the leading methods in the challenging VOC PASCAL 2010 dataset, our multi-component approach obtains highly competitive results. Furthermore, unlike monolithic detection methods, our approach allows the transfer of finer-grained semantic information from the components, such as keypoint location and segmentation masks.

1 Introduction

Consider the object in the center of Figure 1. Although its appearance is very different from any of the surrounding instances, they all belong to the same semantic category "aeroplane". The main causes of intra-class variations in recognition are pose and viewpoint changes, as well as the presence of visually heterogeneous subcategories. For instance, aeroplanes look quite different from side to 45-degree views, and their appearance also changes significantly among the three main subcategories: wide-body passenger jets, fighter jets and propeller aeroplanes. We refer to such visual clusters as *components*.

In this paper, we propose an approach that models each component independently, which we show is easier and more accurate than attempting to characterize all components in a monolithic model. Another significant advantage of our approach over monolithic models is that it enables tasks that are finer-grained than bounding box prediction. Objects in the same component are tight in configuration space, and thus inference on the object keypoint locations and

A. Fitzgibbon et al. (Eds.): ECCV 2012, Part IV, LNCS 7575, pp. 445–458, 2012.

Fig. 1. One key challenge of object categorization is intra-class variations induced by pose changes, subcategories, etc. Since objects belonging to the same category form clusters in the appearance and configuration spaces, it is natural to construct individual models for each cluster and combine them later at the category level. We refer to such a cluster as *component*.

segmentation masks becomes feasible. The keypoints and mask of an object can be predicted from those of its most likely component.

While monolithic models are still common in the literature [7,21], there have been several influential approaches modeling multiple components of objects [10,12,5,17]. Nevertheless, each of these methods has it own limitations. Felzenszwalb et al.[10] learn global and part components jointly, but the number of components is pre-defined and not inferred from data. Gu and Ren[12] focus on modeling only viewpoint variations of objects and ignore other sources of intra-class variations such as subcategories. Bourdev et al.[5] use keypoints to align objects but their poselet models typically characterize parts rather than global objects. Malisiewicz et al.[17] is most similar to our work. However, that approach uses only one positive instance for training, which significantly reduces the generalization capacity of each component model and therefore compromises categorization performance. Last but not least, all these methods use expensive multi-scale window scanning for object detection, which sets a limit on the number of components as well as on the ability to apply more sophisticated features and more powerful classifiers for better accuracy.

To reduce the computation cost during detection, we adopt the popular idea of object candidate selection [11,1,8,14,21], but implement our own bounding box generation scheme based on bottom-up segmentation. Our scheme produces fewer than 500 bounding boxes per image on the VOC2010 dataset, drastically reducing the search space when compared to exhaustive multiscale window scanning, while maintaining high recall of objects over all 20 categories. Furthermore, since this scheme does not rely on category-specific knowledge, the number of candidate windows is independent of the number of categories and thereby scalable to large data.

Overall, this paper presents three distinct contributions that, when combined, provide competitive performance on the PASCAL detection challenge while

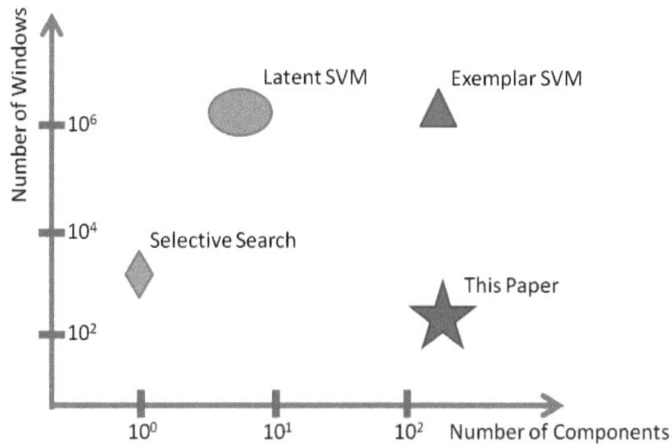

Fig. 2. Comparison of our approach with related previous methods (Latent SVM by [10], Exemplar SVM by [17], and Selective Search by [21]) in 2D space where the two axes represent the number of components and the number of window candidates per image. Our approach is distinct from others by combining multi-component models and selective window candidates.

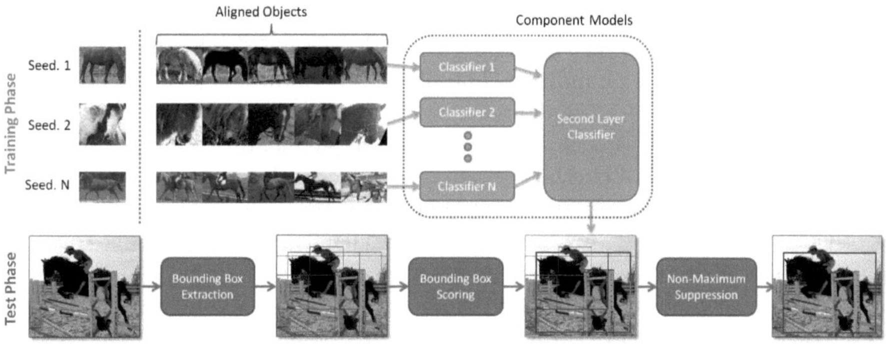

Fig. 3. An overview of our detection pipeline. In the training phase (top row), we pick a seed object from training data, and align the rest of the objects with the seed based on keypoint and mask annotations. The top aligned objects are then used as positive set for learning a single-component classifier. Given N seeds, we have N such classifiers. A second-layer classifier takes the outputs of these component classifiers as input, and produces a final category-level classification score. In the test phase (bottom row), we generate a small number of bounding boxes using bottom-up segmentation cues to avoid exhaustive window scanning. Each candidate box is then scored by our learned two-layer classifiers. Finally, a non-maximum suppression is applied to generate final detection results.

enabling finer-grained tasks than bounding box prediction: (1) global and generic multi-component models characterizing intra-class variation; (2) a category level classifier aggregating responses from multiple components; (3) a simple yet effective algorithm allowing prediction of object keypoint locations and masks. Figure 2 depicts various detection methods in a 2D plot that characterizes the number of components of an object model and the number of scanned windows per image, respectively. This work is, to the best of our knowledge, the first one addressing the combination of multi-component models and selective window candidates.

Figure 3 gives an overview of our detection framework. In the training phase, a two-layer model is learned to capture and aggregate the components of an object category from data. Each first-layer model is a binary classifier trained with a seed and a list of aligned objects. In the detection phase, a small number of candidate bounding boxes are generated for each image using our selection scheme. After scoring these boxes with our two-layer model, a non-maximum suppression is applied to produce final detection results.

The rest of the paper is organized as follows. In Section 2, we describe our bounding box generation scheme. Sections 3 and 4 show how to find and train a component model. Section 5 describes the mechanism of combining component model outputs into a final category-level classifier. We discuss the experiments in Section 6 and conclude in Section 7.

2 Bounding Box Generation

Exhaustive window scanning is computationally expensive when the number of components scales up to hundreds. Therefore, a bounding box selection scheme is necessary to prune out windows in an early stage that do not contain any object. In this paper, we start by applying the segmentation algorithm of [3] which produces a pool of overlaid segments over scales for an input image. Since the algorithm uses *gPb* contour signals as input which recovers almost full recall of object boundaries at a low threshold, the output segments encode the sizes and shapes of objects in the input image quite precisely.

Next, each segment in the pool proposes a bounding box which is the smallest rectangle containing it. This proposal gives us the same number of bounding box candidates as the number of segments in the pool. Some candidates are identical, even though their original segments are different. After duplicate removal, we end up with on average fewer than 500 candidate boxes per image on the PASCAL VOC 2010 training set. Figure 4 shows for each category the recall of objects

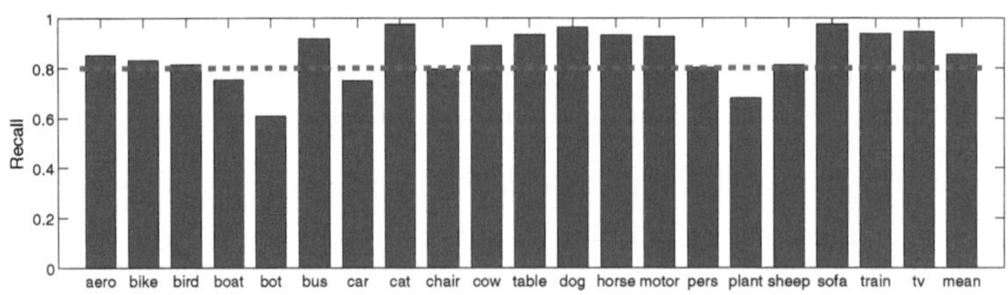

Fig. 4. Percentage of actual objects found by our bounding box generation on all 20 PASCAL VOC categories. We obtain a recall of 80% or higher among 16/20 categories.

whose ground truth bounding boxes overlap more than 50% with at least one of our proposed boxes. In 16/20 categories, we have a recall rate of 80% or higher.

Our object candidate selection scheme proposes bounding boxes efficiently and category-independently, thus avoiding unnecessary redundancies both in the image space and across categories. It provides a huge saving of computation during detection.

3 Finding Components

Clustering of all training data of an object category seems to be a natural strategy for finding the components of that category, since objects belonging to the same component, by definition, have smaller appearance and configuration distances to each other. However, in practice, this strategy does not work well. One main reason is that the components that are less common are very difficult to discover because they are easily absorbed by the components of common poses or dominant subcategories. Furthermore, objects within a cluster are, in many cases, not tight enough to build a robust component model because no global alignment is enforced among them during clustering.

Therefore, we apply a different two-step strategy to construct each of our components:

- A "seed" object is picked from the training data which characterizes a component.
- The rest of the training objects of the category are aligned to the seed through a global transformation using the keypoint and mask annotations. The top aligned objects constitute the positive set of the component.

We use the annotation data from [6] for keypoints and masks of training objects. These annotations are crowdsourced from Amazon Mechanic Turk. For each category, 10 to 20 semantically meaningful keypoints (e.g. head, tail, wing tips, wing bases, and stabilizer tip for aeroplane) are marked on the objects. Invisible keypoints are not labeled and thus excluded in the global transform step. In addition, object masks are also labeled using a polygon approximation.

With these additional annotations in hand, we recover a similarity transformation between two objects and use it to align one object to the other. Precisely, let I and J be two objects that need to be aligned, and p_I, p_J, M_I, M_J be their keypoints and masks, respectively. The transformation matrix $\mathbb{T}$ has a close-form solution when the objective is to minimize the Procrustes distance between two sets of keypoints p_I and p_J. The quality of the alignment can be measured by the following distance function:

$$d_{quality} = (1 - \lambda) \cdot d_{procrustes} + \lambda \cdot (1 - d_{overlap})$$

where $d_{procrustes} = \sum_{i \in I} (\mathbb{T}(p_J^i) - p_I^i)^2$ is the Procrustes distance, and

$$d_{overlap} = \frac{Area(M_I \cap \mathbb{T}(M_J))}{Area(M_I \cup \mathbb{T}(M_J))}$$

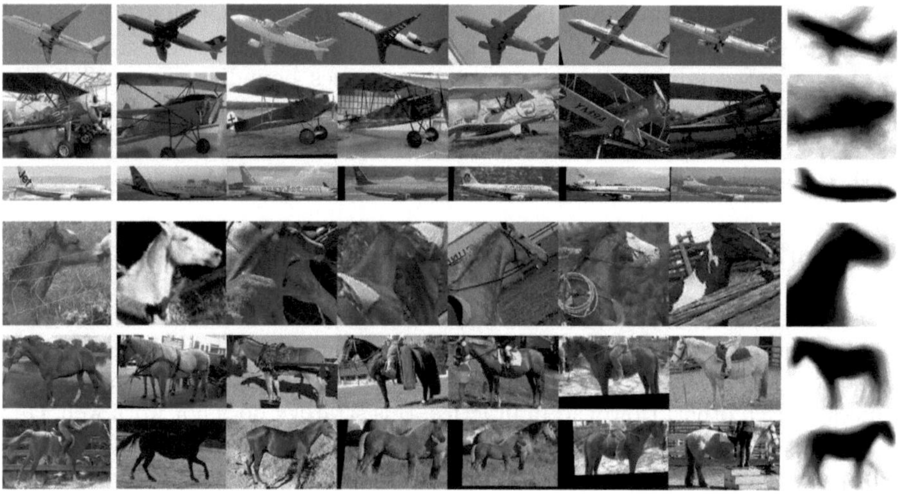

Fig. 5. Visualization of some of our components for aeroplane (top) and horse (bottom) categories. Each row corresponds to a component. The left-most images are seeds; the middle six images are top aligned objects for each seed; and the right-most images are averaged mask of top 32 aligned objects. Note that, due to our global alignment strategy, objects within each component are tight in configuration space.

is the intersection-over-union score between the seed mask and the transformed object mask. The parameter λ controls the relative weight between the two terms. In our experiments, we observe that even $\lambda = 1$(only the mask scores count) gives reasonable alignment results. Finally, we sort all aligned objects for a given seed based on the quality distances defined above, and pick top 32 as positive instances of the component model. In the PASCAL VOC 2010 data, 32 is an empirical choice that is small enough to exclude degraded object alignment for most components of categories, and big enough to make the model generalizable.

With one component model set up, we can easily extend this two-step scheme and construct a set of component models by picking multiple distinct seeds from the training data. Again, our strategy prevents less-common components from being absorbed by common ones. Objects within each component are tight in configuration space after global alignment which enables us to train strong classifiers. Figure 5 shows our alignment results on the aeroplane and horse categories with three components each. Each component model is a binary classifier and we will describe the training framework in the next section.

4 Training Components

Each of our component models is a binary classifier characterizing a particular category component. Given the set of aligned objects obtained from the previous section, we conduct the following two-step strategy to complete component training process:

- We construct a negative set from all bounding box candidates extracted from negative training images for each component.
- We learn an Intersection Kernel Support Vector Machine (IKSVM[16,22]) based on the positive and negative sets for each component, and the model is bootstrapped once by data-mining hard negatives. The SVM scores are then converted to probabilities through a sigmoid function whose parameters are also learned from data.

We use four types of features to describe our bounding boxes, three of them using a spatial pyramid pooling, and the last one using object-centric pooling. Each component model learns all the feature types separately. Our second layer classifier, which we will describe in the next section, aggregates the outputs of all components of all feature types.

4.1 Spatial Pyramid of Vector Quantized SIFT

We implement a spatial pyramid of vector quantized SIFT[13] in the standard way: interest points are extracted from an image in a grid basis. A set of three-scale opponent-SIFT[20] descriptors are computed and concatenated to form a vector at each interest point. These vectors are then quantized to codewords based on a class-specific codebook. The size of our codebook is 400. Next, we divide each bounding box into 2×2 cells and count the frequencies of the codewords within each cell where interest points lie. The final descriptor of the bounding box is the concatenated histograms of codewords within each cell.

4.2 Spatial Pyramid of Poselet Activations

The implementation of this feature is similar to that of the vector quantized SIFT, except that we replace the SIFT-based codewords by poselet activations. Poselets[4] have been shown powerful in describing shapes for characteristic parts of objects. Compared to SIFT features, poselet activations are more sparse, informative, and discriminative. Each poselet fires only twice per image on average on the VOC dataset, and provides both strength and rectangular support of the activation. Each poselet model is trained with a highly discriminative classifier. We use pre-trained models of [5]. A typical number of poselets per category is 100 to 200. We apply a "soft count" strategy to aggregate poselet activations within an image cell. Denote $H(C, w)$ as the bin value for poselet index i in the histogram of image cell C.

$$H(C,i) = \sum_{a\in A} S(a) \times \frac{Area(B(a) \cap B(C))}{Area(B(a))} \times \mathbf{1}(I(a) = i)$$

where $I(a)$, $S(a)$ and $B(a)$ are the index, strength, and support of the activation a, and $B(C)$ is the support of C. Note that we soft count the strength of an activation by the fraction of overlap between the support of the activation and the image cell. It proves essential to smooth out the spatial quantization noise caused by the activation location with respect to image cells.

4.3 Spatial Pyramid of Local Coordinate Coding with HOG

The work in [15] demonstrates a state-of-the-art image classification system using spatial pyramid of local coordinate coding (LCC) on local descriptors. Here we implement a similar feature representation. We sample HOG descriptors[7] on a dense grid with step size of four pixels. Then each HOG descriptor is coded using local coordinate coding [23] with codebook size of 8192. Finally, the coding results are max-pooled with a spatial pyramid representation of 1×1 and 3×3 cells.

4.4 Object-Centric Spatial Pooling

The work in [19] demonstrates that object-centric spatial pooling (OCP) is more effective than traditional spatial pyramid matching(SPM) based pooling for bounding box classification. Given a bounding box, OCP pools separately the foreground and background regions to form a bounding box representation. In contrast to traditional SPM that only performs pooling on foreground, OCP includes pooling on background and is able to provide more accurate localization. This is because the learned object detector with OCP will prevent the leakage of parts of a object into background.

For each candidate bounding box, we generate its feature representation using object-centric pooling. The way to generate the feature is the same as in Section 4.3 except that the SPM pooling was replaced by OCP.

5 Second-Layer Classifier and Non-Maximum Suppression

We leverage our learned component classifiers for the task of categorical prediction through learning a second-layer classifier, taking all component outputs of a bounding box into an input vector, and outputting a single probability score for that box during detection. Same as the design of component classifiers, our second-layer is a binary Intersectional Kernel SVM for each category, enabling the importance of components to be reflected by its learned weights. In order to avoid overfitting, we use a validation set, separated from the training set that we use for learning component classifiers, for cross-validating the parameter choices of our second-layer classifier.

We notice that the choices of positive and negative bounding boxes have a large impact on the detection performance during second-layer training. Table 1 shows various design choices on the aeroplane category and compares their detection performance. On the positive data side, enriching the positive set through adding near-duplicates of positive boxes improves the overall performance. Since

Table 1. Design choices of second-layer classifier on the aeroplane category of VOC 2010 val dataset using the spatial pyramid of poselet activation features. We notice that including only hard boxes for negative data and having up to 4 near-duplicates as positive data both improve the detection performance (mean Average Precision).

Negative Set		Positive Set		
All Boxes	Hard Boxes	No Duplicate	up to 2 Dup	up to 4 Dup
.302	.420	.382	.407	.420

Table 2. Detection results on VOC 2010 **val**: In order to better understand the power of each individual feature and their combinations, we run control experiments on the validation set of VOC 2010 and compare performance using different types of features. Note that features contribute differently to different categories, and feature combination is essential for improved performance. S,P,L,O stands for VQ'ed SIFT, VQ'ed poselet, LCC HOG, and Object-centric features, respectively.

	aer	bik	bir	boa	bot	bus	car	cat	cha	cow	din	dog	hor	mot	per	pot	she	sof	tra	tvm
S	.373	.348	.092	.061	.171	.411	.297	.251	.043	.133	.093	.152	.314	.322	.177	.061	.217	.169	.178	.300
P	.420	.361	.167	.108	.171	.585	.321	.266	.117	.218	.193	.272	.325	.433	.255	.150	.308	.260	.350	.422
L	.352	.443	.139	.094	.194	.537	.375	.356	.137	.292	.191	.273	.378	.490	.194	.170	.317	.230	.361	.372
O	.529	.294	.108	.103	.081	.469	.248	.451	.036	.102	.186	.284	.201	.386	.220	.048	.193	.198	.320	.374
SP	.454	.415	.174	.112	.216	.548	.356	.335	.111	.217	.179	.252	.392	.430	.289	.138	.337	.277	.348	.428
SPL	.457	.469	.215	.113	.242	.602	.421	.397	.153	.352	.242	.350	.466	.532	.289	.183	.414	.310	.412	.478
SPLO	.568	.434	.248	.164	.234	.635	.384	.568	.134	.298	.302	.430	.425	.514	.332	.163	.411	.381	.472	.482

some positive objects may correspond to a large number of bounding boxes, we apply a multiple-instance-learning[2] framework to automatically pick best set of near-duplicate boxes for those objects. On the negative data side, we choose to only include boxes where at least one component classifier fires (we call them "hard boxes") in the negative set. This choice enables component selection, as bad components usually fire everywhere and can be easily identified by this reduced set.

After all proposed bounding boxes are scored by our two layer classifiers, we apply non-maximum suppression on these boxes to generate detection results. The bounding boxes are sorted by their detection scores, and we greedily select the highest scoring ones while removing those that are sufficiently covered by a previously selected bounding box. We use 30% as the coverage threshold based on cross-validation results.

6 Experiments

6.1 Object Detection on PASCAL VOC

We use the standard PASCAL VOC [9] platform to benchmark our detection framework. Each of our component models is trained on VOC 2010 train data, and evaluated on 2010 val. We use all but no more than 500 objects from training data as seed objects. In addition, each seed and its aligned objects are mirrored

Table 3. Detection Results on VOC 2010 **test**: This table compares our full system with other leading approaches on VOC 2010 test data. For each category, the winner is shown in **bold** font and the runner-up in *italics*. The performance of our approach is highly competitive.

	aer	bik	bir	boa	bot	bus	car	cat	cha	cow	din	dog	hor	mot	per	pot	she	sof	tra	tvm
[5]	.332	.519	.085	.082	*.348*	.390	*.488*	.222	-	.206	-	.185	.482	.441	**.485**	.091	.280	.130	.225	.330
[10]	.524	*.543*	.130	.156	**.351**	.542	**.491**	.318	.155	.262	.135	.215	.454	.516	*.475*	.091	.351	.194	.466	.380
[21]	**.582**	.419	**.192**	.140	.143	.448	.367	**.488**	.129	.281	**.287**	**.394**	.441	.525	.258	**.141**	**.388**	**.342**	.431	**.426**
NLPR	.533	**.553**	**.192**	**.210**	.300	*.544*	.467	.412	**.200**	**.315**	.207	.303	*.486*	*.553*	.465	.102	.344	.265	**.503**	.403
[24]	*.542*	.485	.157	*.192*	.292	**.555**	.435	.417	.169	.285	.267	.309	.483	.550	.417	.097	*.358*	*.308*	.472	*.408*
NUS	.491	.524	.178	.120	.306	.535	.328	.373	*.177*	*.306*	*.277*	.295	**.519**	**.563**	.442	.096	.148	.279	*.495*	.384
Ours	.537	.429	.181	.165	.235	.481	.421	*.454*	.067	.234	*.277*	*.352*	.407	.490	.320	*.116*	.346	.287	.433	.392

Table 4. Detection Results on VOC 2007 **test**: This table compares the results on VOC 2007 test set between our multi-component(MC) model and the monolithic(MN) model using the same feature set and training data. Note the improvement of multi-component model over monolithic model on almost every category. In addition, our model also outperforms [17] that trains each component model using only one positive instance.

	aer	bik	bir	boa	bot	bus	car	cat	cha	cow	din	dog	hor	mot	per	pot	she	sof	tra	tvm	avg
MN	.248	.268	.059	.109	.092	.381	.375	.228	.097	.163	**.236**	.147	.252	.260	.177	.104	.197	.211	.210	.358	.209
MC	**.334**	.370	**.150**	**.150**	**.226**	**.431**	**.493**	**.328**	.115	**.358**	.178	**.163**	.436	.382	**.298**	**.116**	**.333**	**.235**	.302	**.396**	**.290**
[17]	.208	**.480**	.077	.143	.131	.397	.411	.052	**.116**	.186	.111	.031	**.447**	**.394**	.169	.112	.226	.170	**.369**	.300	.227

to produce a left-right symmetric model. These design choices end up with 400 to 1000 components, depending on the category.

Table 2 illustrates the power of individual features and their combinations. The mean average precisions(mAP) of all categories on VOC 2010 val are shown. Note that features play different roles in different object categories. Furthermore, feature combination significantly improves performance on all categories.

Table 3 compares the results of our full system with leading approaches on the VOC 2010 test set. Our results are highly competitive to the leading performance on this benchmark.

6.2 Multi-Component vs. Monolithic vs. Per Exemplar Models

In addition to knowing where our approach stands in the detection field, we are also interested in knowing how much we benefit from our multi-component scheme. Table 4 illustrates control experiments that compare our multi-component model with a monolithic model using the same set of features (SIFT and poselet activations) as well as training data (the positive set of the monolithic model is the set of all positive data used in the component models). We conclude from the table that our multi-component model handles intra-class variations better than the monolithic model and therefore yields much improved results for all PASCAL categories.

On the other hand, our results are significantly better than [17] which uses a single object per component as positive set. This illustrates the generalization power of our component models through global object alignment.

Fig. 6. Visualization of our detection results on PASCAL VOC dataset. Red bounding boxes indicate detection. Figures on the left show correct detection, while figures on the right show some failure cases. Many are due to heavy occlusion/trancation, poor localization, and confusion between similar categories.

6.3 Keypoints and Mask Transfer via Component Models

Like [11,17], our multi-component models provide more information than just bounding boxes in the object detection framework. The output scores of the first-layer component classifiers imply the most similar component in appearance and configuration to a detected object. We refer to the one assigning the highest score to a detection as the "matching" component of that detection. See Figure 7 for some examples. Since training objects are tight within a component, a projection of the keypoints and mask of the seed object onto the test image based on the transformation between the seed and the detection windows provides reasonable estimates of the keypoint locations and the mask of the detected object. This is a straight-forward yet useful application which is difficult to obtain from most previous related work.

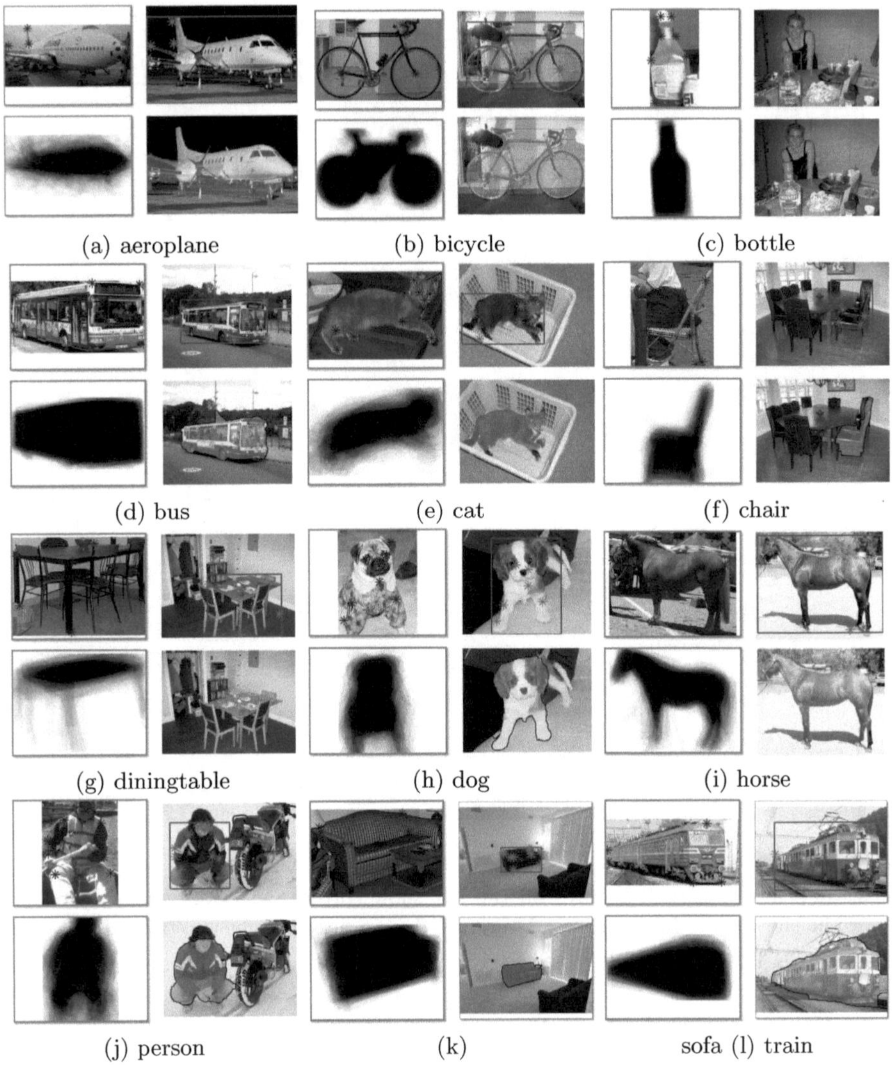

Fig. 7. Our multi-component models enable fine-grained visual recognition applications such as keypoint prediction and segmentation, as shown in the figures above. Each detected object in the test image (shown in the top-right of each category) is associated with a "matching" component that assigns the highest detection score to the object. The two figures on the left of each category depict the seed object (with its keypoints marked in blue) and the average mask of the "matching" component. Inference on keypoint locations and mask of the test object is obtained through a transformation between the bounding box of the seed and that of the test object, as well as bottom-up segmentation cues. The two figures on the right of each category show our results, where estimated keypoint locations are marked in pink, and segmentation mask in red.

In fact, further improvement on object mask prediction can be achieved through two modifications on the projection pipeline. First, the average mask of all aligned objects of the component is a more robust measurement of component mask than that of the seed. Second, the bottom-up image segmentation cues can be used to refine our results. Suppose that the final object mask is a selected union of the image segments, our objective is to maximize the amount of overlap of the final object mask to the transformed mask of the matching component. We use a greedy selection solution to approximate the result. Starting with the single best segment among the pool that overlaps with the transformed mask, we pick a segment from the pool at each iteration and merge it with the current mask so that it maximizes the intersection-over-union score. The iteration continues until the score starts to decrease. In practice, this approximation works very well, and Figure 7 highlights our mask prediction results.

7 Conclusion

This paper presents a novel multi-component model that, combined with object window selection, achieves highly competitive results for object detection. Each component characterizes a pose or subcategory of an object category, and objects within each component are tight in appearance and configuration. Therefore, component models are both easy to learn and highly discriminative. A second layer classifier is learned to aggregate the outputs of component models into final scores. We also illustrate applications of our multi-component models beyond detection, e.g., object keypoint and mask prediction.

Acknowledgments. We thank ONR MURI N00014-10-10933 for their support to this work. This research was conducted as part of Chunhui Gu"s Phd thesis at UC Berkeley.

References

1. Alexe, B., Deselaers, T., Ferrari, V.: What is an Object? In: Computer Vision and Pattern Recognition (2010)
2. Andrews, S., Tsochantaridis, I., Hofmann, T.: Support Vector Machines for Multiple-instance Learning. In: Neural Information Processing Systems (2002)
3. Arbeláez, P., Hariharan, B., Gu, C., Gupta, S., Bourdev, L., Malik, J.: Semantic Segmentation Using Regions and Parts. In: Computer Vision and Pattern Recognition (2012)
4. Bourdev, L., Malik, J.: Poselets: Body Part Detectors Trained Using 3D Human Pose Annotations. In: International Conference on Computer Vision (2009)
5. Bourdev, L., Maji, S., Brox, T., Malik, J.: Detecting People Using Mutually Consistent Poselet Activations. In: Daniilidis, K., Maragos, P., Paragios, N. (eds.) ECCV 2010, Part VI. LNCS, vol. 6316, pp. 168–181. Springer, Heidelberg (2010)
6. Brox, T., Bourdev, L., Maji, S., Malik, J.: Object Segmentation by Alignment of Poselet Activations to Image Contours. In: Computer Vision and Pattern Recognition (2011)

7. Dalal, N., Triggs, B.: Histograms of Oriented Gradients for Human Detection. In: Computer Vision and Pattern Recognition (2005)
8. Endres, I., Hoiem, D.: Category Independent Object Proposals. In: Daniilidis, K., Maragos, P., Paragios, N. (eds.) ECCV 2010, Part V. LNCS, vol. 6315, pp. 575–588. Springer, Heidelberg (2010)
9. Everingham, M., Van Gool, L., Williams, C., Winn, J., Zisserman, A.: The Pascal Visual Object Classes (VOC) Challenge. International Journal of Computer Vision 88(2), 303–338 (2010)
10. Felzenszwalb, P., Girshick, R., McAllester, D., Ramanan, D.: Object Detection with Discriminatively Trained Part Based Models. Transactions on Pattern Analysis and Machine Intelligence 32(9), 1627–1645 (2010)
11. Gu, C., Lim, J., Arbeláez, P., Malik, J.: Recognition Using Regions. In: Computer Vision and Pattern Recognition (2009)
12. Gu, C., Ren, X.: Discriminative Mixture-of-Templates for Viewpoint Classification. In: Daniilidis, K., Maragos, P., Paragios, N. (eds.) ECCV 2010, Part V. LNCS, vol. 6315, pp. 408–421. Springer, Heidelberg (2010)
13. Lazebnik, S., Schmid, C., Ponce, J.: Beyond Bags of Features: Spatial Pyramid Matching for Recognizing Natural Scene Categories. In: Computer Vision and Pattern Recognition (2006)
14. Li, F., Carreira, J., Sminchisescu, C.: Object Recognition as Ranking Holistic Figure-Ground Hypotheses. In: Computer Vision and Pattern Recognition (2010)
15. Lin, Y., Cao, L., Lv, F., Zhu, S., Yang, M., Cour, T., Yu, K., Huang, T.: Large-scale Image Classification: Fast Feature Extraction and SVM Training. In: Computer Vision and Pattern Recognition (2011)
16. Maji, S., Berg, A., Malik, J.: Classification Using Intersection Kernel Support Vector Machines is Efficient. In: Computer Vision and Pattern Recognition (2008)
17. Malisiewicz, T., Gupta, A., Efros, A.: Ensemble of Exemplar-SVMs for Object Detection and Beyond. In: International Conference on Computer Vision (2011)
18. Parkhi, O., Vedaldi, A., Jawahar, C., Zisserman, A.: The Truth About Cats and Dogs. In: International Conference on Computer Vision (2011)
19. Russakovsky, O., Lin, Y., Yu, K., Fei-Fei, L.: Object-Centric Spatial Pooling for Image Classification. In: Fitzgibbon, A., Lazebnik, S., Perona, P., Sato, Y., Schmid, C. (eds.) ECCV 2012, Part II. LNCS, vol. 7573, pp. 1–15. Springer, Heidelberg (2012)
20. van de Sande, K., Gevers, T., Snoek, C.: Evaluating Color Descriptors for Object and Scene Recognition. Transactions on Pattern Analysis and Machine Intelligence 32(9), 1582–1596 (2010)
21. van de Sande, K., Uijlings, J., Gevers, T., Smeulders, A.: Segmentation as Selective Search for Object Recognition. In: International Conference on Computer Vision (2011)
22. Vedaldi, A., Fulkerson, B.: VLFeat: An Open and Portable Library of Computer Vision Algorithms (2008), `http://www.vlfeat.org/`
23. Yu, K., Zhang, T., Gong, Y.: Nonlinear Learning Using Local Coordinate Coding. In: Neural Information Processing Systems (2009)
24. Zhu, L., Chen, Y., Yuille, A., Freeman, W.: Latent Hierarchical Structural Learning for Object Detection. In: Computer Vision and Pattern Recognition (2010)

Discriminative Decorrelation for Clustering and Classification*

Bharath Hariharan[1], Jitendra Malik[1], and Deva Ramanan[2]

[1] Univerisity of California at Berkeley, Berkeley, CA, USA
{bharath2,malik}@cs.berkeley.edu
[2] University of California at Irvine, Irvine, CA, USA
dramanan@ics.uci.edu

Abstract. Object detection has over the past few years converged on using linear SVMs over HOG features. Training linear SVMs however is quite expensive, and can become intractable as the number of categories increase. In this work we revisit a much older technique, viz. Linear Discriminant Analysis, and show that LDA models can be trained almost trivially, and with little or no loss in performance. The covariance matrices we estimate capture properties of natural images. Whitening HOG features with these covariances thus removes naturally occuring correlations between the HOG features. We show that these whitened features (which we call WHO) are considerably better than the original HOG features for computing similarities, and prove their usefulness in clustering. Finally, we use our findings to produce an object detection system that is competitive on PASCAL VOC 2007 while being considerably easier to train and test.

1 Introduction

Over the last decade, object detection approaches have converged on a single dominant paradigm: that of using HOG features and linear SVMs. HOG features were first introduced by Dalal and Triggs [1] for the task of pedestrian detection. More contemporary approaches build on top of these HOG features by allowing for parts and small deformations [2], training separate HOG detectors for separate poses and parts [3] or even training separate HOG detectors for each training exemplar [4].

Figure 1(a) shows an example image patch of a bicycle, and a visualization of the corresponding HOG feature vector. Note that while the HOG feature vector does capture the gradients of the bicycle, it is dominated by the strong contours of the fence in the background. Figure 1(b) shows an SVM trained using just this image patch as a positive, and large numbers of background patches as negative [4]. As is clear from the figure, the SVM learns that the gradients of the fence are unimportant, while the gradients of the bicycle are important.

* This work was funded by ONR-MURI Grant N00014-10-1-0933 and NSF Grant 0954083.

A. Fitzgibbon et al. (Eds.): ECCV 2012, Part IV, LNCS 7575, pp. 459–472, 2012.

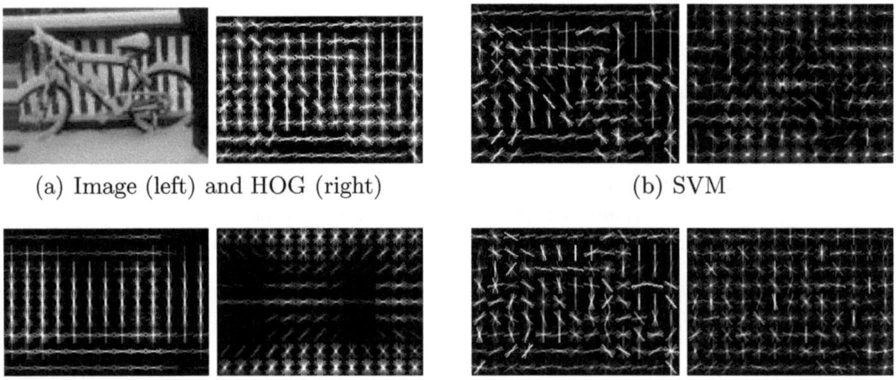

(a) Image (left) and HOG (right) (b) SVM (c) PCA (d) LDA

Fig. 1. Object detection systems typically use HOG features, as in (a). HOG features however are often swamped out by background gradients. A linear SVM learns to stress the object contours and suppress background gradients, as in (b), but requires extensive training. An LDA model, shown in (d), has a similar effect but with negligible training. PCA on the other hand completely kills discriminative gradients, (c). The PCA, LDA and SVM visualizations show the positive and negative components separately, with the positive components on the left and negative on the right.

However, training linear SVMs is expensive. Training involves expensive bootstrapping rounds where the detector is run in a scanning window over multiple negative images to collect "hard negative" examples. While this is feasible for training detectors for a few tens of categories, it will be challenging when the number of object categories is of the order of tens of thousands, which is the scale in which humans operate.

However, linear SVMs aren't the only linear classifiers around. Indeed, Fisher proposed his linear discriminant as far back as 1936 [5]. Fisher discriminant analysis tries to find the direction that maximizes the ratio of the between-class variance to the within-class variance. Linear discriminant analysis (LDA) is a generative model for classification that is equivalent to Fisher's discriminant analysis if the class covariances are assumed to be equal. Textbook accounts of LDA can be found, for example, in [6,7]. Given a training dataset of positive and negative features (x, y) with $y \in \{0, 1\}$, LDA models the data x as generated from class-conditional Gaussians:

$$P(x, y) = P(x|y)P(y) \quad \text{where} \quad P(y = 1) = \pi \quad \text{and} \quad P(x|y) = N(x; \mu_y, \Sigma)$$

where means μ_y are class-dependent but the covariance matrix Σ is class-independent. A novel feature x is classified as a positive if $P(y = 1|x) > P(y = 0|x)$, which is equivalent to a linear classifier with weights given by $w = \Sigma^{-1}(\mu_1 - \mu_0)$. Figure 1(d) shows the LDA model trained with the bicycle image patch as positive and generic image patches as background. Clearly, like the SVM, the LDA model suppresses the contours of the background, while enhancing the gradients of the bicycle. LDA has been used before in computer vision, one of the earliest and most popular appications being face recognition [8].

Training an LDA model requires figuring out the means μ_y and Σ. However, unlike an SVM which has to be trained from scratch for every object category, we show that μ_0 (corresponding to the background class) and Σ can be estimated just once, and reused for all object categories, making training almost trivial. Intuitively, LDA computes the average positive feature μ_1, centers it with μ_0, and "whitens" it with Σ^{-1} to remove correlations. The matrix Σ acts as a model of HOG patches of natural images. For instance, as we show in section 2, this matrix captures the fact that adjacent HOG cells are highly correlated owing to curvilinear continuity. Thus, not all of the strong vertical gradients in the HOG cells of Figure 1(a) are important: many of them merely reflect the continuity of contours. Removing these correlations therefore leaves behind just the discriminative gradients.

The LDA model is just the difference of means in a space that has been whitened using the covariance matrix Σ. This suggests that this whitened space might be significant outside of just training HOG classifiers. In fact, we find that dot products in this whitened space are more indicative of visual similarity than dot products in HOG space. Consequently, clustering whitened HOG feature vectors (which we call WHO for Whitened Histogram of Orientations) gives more coherent and often semantically meaningful clusters.

Principal components analysis (PCA) is a related method that has been explored for tasks such as face recognition [9] and tools for dimensionality reduction in object recognition [10]. In particular, Ke and Sukthankar [11] and Schwartz et al [12] examine (linear) low-dimensional projections of oriented gradient features. In PCA, the data is projected onto the directions of the most variation, and the directions of least variation are ignored. However, for our purposes, the directions that are ignored are often those that are the most discriminative. Figure 1(c) shows the result of projecting the data down to the top 30 principal components. Clearly, this is even worse than the original HOG space: contours of the bicycle are more or less completely discarded. Our observations mirror those of Belhumeur et al [8] who showed that in the context of face recognition, the directions retained by PCA often correspond to variations in illumination and viewing direction, rather than variations that would be discriminative of the identity of the face. [8] conclude that Fisher's discriminant analysis outperforms PCA on face recognition tasks. In section 4 we show concretely that the low dimensional subspace chosen by PCA is significantly worse than whitened HOG as far as computing similarity is concerned.

Our aim in this paper is therefore to explore the advantages provided by whitened HOG features for clustering and classification. In section 2 we go into the details of our LDA models, describing how we obtain our covariance matrix, and the properties of the matrix. Section 3 describes our first set of experiments on the INRIA pedestrian detection task, showing that LDA models can be competitive with linear SVMs. Section 4 outlines how WHO features can be used for clustering exemplars. We then use these clusters to train detectors, and evaluate the performance of the LDA model vis-a-vis SVMs and other choices in section 5. In section 6 we tie it all together to produce a final object detection system that performs competitively on the PASCAL VOC 2007 dataset, while being orders-of-magnitude faster to train (due to our LDA classifiers) and orders-of-magnitude faster to test (due to our clustered representations).

2 Linear Discriminant Analysis

In this section, we describe our model of image gradients based on LDA. For our HOG implementation, we use the augmented HOG features of [2]. Briefly, given an image window of fixed size, the window is divided into a grid of 8×8 cells. From each cell we extract a feature vector x_{ij} of gradient orientations of dimensionality $d = 31$. We write $x = [x_{ij}]$ for the final window descriptor obtained by concatenating features across all locations within the window. If there are N cells in the window, the feature vector has dimensionality Nd.

The LDA model is a linear classifier over x with weights given by $w = \Sigma^{-1}(\mu_1 - \mu_0)$. Here Σ is an $Nd \times Nd$ matrix, and a naive approach would require us to estimate this matrix again for every value of N and also for every object category. In what follows we describe a simple procedure that allows us to learn a Σ and a μ_0 (corresponding to the background) once, and then reuse it for every window size N and for every object category. Given a new object category, we need only a set of positive features which are averaged, centered, and whitened to compute the final linear classifier.

2.1 Estimating μ_0 and Σ

Object-Independent Backgrounds: Consider the task of learning K 1-vs-all LDA models from a multi-class training set spanning K objects and background windows. One can show that the maximum likelihood estimate of Σ is the sample covariance estimated across the entire training set, ignoring class labels. If we assume that the number of instances of any one object is small compared to the total number of windows, we can similarly define a generic μ_0 that is independent of object type. This means that we can learn a generic μ_0 and Σ from *unlabeled* windows, and this need not be done anew for every object category.

Marginalization: We are now left with the task of estimating a μ_0 and Σ for every value of the window size N. However, note that the statistics of smaller-size windows can be obtained by marginalizing out statistics of larger-size windows. Gaussian distributions can be marginalized by simply dropping the marginalized variables from μ_0 and Σ. This means that we can learn a single μ_0 and Σ for the largest possible window of N_0 cells, and generate means and covariances for smaller window sizes "on-the-fly" by selecting subpartitions of μ_0 and Σ. This reduces the number of parameters to be estimated to an $N_0 d$ dimensional μ_0 and an $N_0 d \times N_0 d$ matrix Σ.

Scale and Translation Invariance: Image statistics are largely scale and translation invariant [13]. We achieve such invariance by including training windows extracted from different scales and translations. We can further exploit translation invariance, or stationarity in statistical terms, to reduce the number of model parameters. To encode a stationary μ_0, we compute the mean HOG feature $\mu = E[x_{ij}]$, averaged over all features x and cell locations (i, j). μ_0 is just μ replicated over all N_0 cells.

Write Σ as a block matrix with blocks $\Sigma_{(ij),(lk)} = E[x_{ij}x_{lk}^T]$. We then incorporate assumptions of translation invariance by modeling Σ with a *spatial autocorrelation function* [14]:

$$\Sigma_{(ij),(lk)} = \Gamma_{(i-l),(j-k)} = E[x_{uv}x_{(u+i-l),(v+j-k)}^T] \tag{1}$$

where the expectation is over cell locations (u, v) and gradient features x. In other words, we assume that $\Sigma_{(ij),(kl)}$ depends only on the relative offsets $(i-k)$ and $(j-l)$. Thus instead of estimating an $N_0 d \times N_0 d$ matrix Σ, we only have to estimate the $d \times d$ matrices $\Gamma_{s,t}$ for every offset (s, t). For a spatial window with N_0 cells, there exist only N_0 distinct relative offsets. Thus we only need to estimate $O(N_0 d^2)$ parameters.

We now estimate μ and the matrices $\Gamma_{s,t}$ from *all* subwindows extracted from a large set of unlabeled, 10,000 natural images (the PASCAL VOC 2010 dataset). This computation can be done once and for all, and the resulting μ and Γ stored. Then, given a new object category, μ_0 can be reconstructed by replicating μ over all the cells in the window and Σ can be reconstructed from Γ using (1).

Regularization: Even given this large training set and our $O(N)$ parametrization, we found Σ to be low-rank and non-invertible. This implies that it would be even more difficult to learn a separate covariance matrix for each positive class because we have much fewer positive examples, further motivating a single-covariance assumption. In general, it is difficult to learn high-dimensional covariance matrices [14]. For typical-size N values, Σ can grow to a $10,000 \times 10,000$ matrix. One solution is to enforce conditional independence assumptions with a Gaussian Markov random field; we discuss this further below. In practice, we regularized the sample covariance by adding a small value ($\lambda = .01$) to its diagonal, corresponding to an isotropic prior on Σ.

2.2 Properties of the Covariance Matrix

WHO: We define a whitened histograms of orientations (WHO) descriptor as $\hat{x} = \Sigma^{-1/2}(x - \mu_0)$. The transformed feature vector $\hat{x}$ then has an isotropic covariance matrix. An alternative interpretation of the linear discriminant is that w computes the difference between the average positive and negative features in WHO space. Such descriptors maybe useful for clustering because euclidean distances are more meaningful in this space. We explore this further in section 4. We use a cholesky decomposition $RR^T = \Sigma$ and Gaussian elimination (Matlab's blackslash) to efficiently compute this whitening transformation.

Analysis: We examine the structure of Σ in Fig.2. Intuitively, Σ encodes generic spatial statistics about oriented gradients. For example, due to curvilinear continuity, we expect a strong horizontal gradient response to be correlated with a strong response at a horizontally-adjacent location. Multiplying gradient features by Σ^{-1} subtracts off such correlated measurements. Because Σ^{-1} is sparse, features need only be de-correlated with adjacent or nearby spatial locations. This in turn suggests that image gradients can be fit will with a 3rd or 4th-order spatial Markov model, which may make for easier estimation and faster computations. A spatial Markov assumption makes intuitive sense; given we see a strong horizontal gradient at a particular location, we expect to see a strong gradient to its right regardless of the statistics to its left. We experimented with such sparse models [15], but found an unrestricted Σ to work well and simpler to implement.

Implications: Our statistical model, though quite simple, has several implications for scanning-window templates. (1) One should learn templates of larger spatial extent than the object. For example, a 2nd-order spatial Markov model implies that one should score gradient features two cells away from the object border in order to de-correlate features. Intuitively, this makes sense; a pedestrian template wants to find vertical edges at the side of the face, but if it also finds vertical edges above the face, then this evidence maybe better explained by the vertical contour of a tree or doorway. Dalal and Triggs actually made the empirical observation that larger templates perform better, but attributed this to local context [1]; our analysis suggests that decorrelation may be a better explanation. (2) Current strategies for modeling occlusion/truncation by "zero"ing regions of a template may not suffice [16,17]. Rather, our model allows us to properly marginalize out such regions from μ and Σ. The resulting template w will not be equivalent to a zero-ed out version of the original template, because the de-correlation operation must change for gradient features near the occluded/truncated regions.

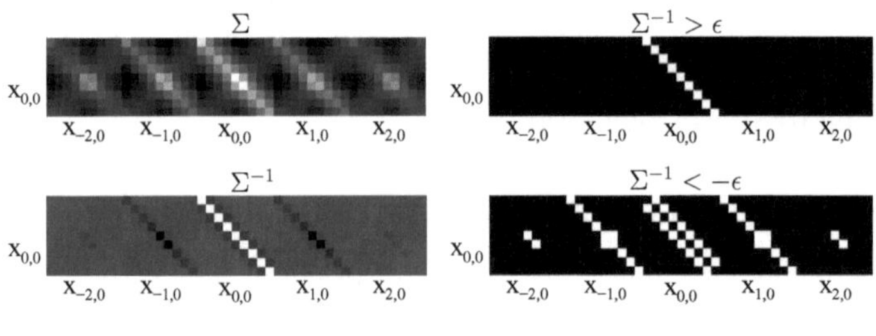

Fig. 2. We visualize correlations between 9 orientation features in horizontally-adjacent HOG cells as concatenated set of 9×9 matrices. Light pixels are positive while dark pixels are negative. We plot the covariance and precision matrix on the **left**, and the positive and negative values of the precision matrix on the **right**. Multiplying a HOG vector with Σ^{-1} decorrelates it, subtracting off gradient measurements from adjacent orientations and locations. The sparsity pattern of Σ^{-1} suggests that one needs to decorrelate features only a few cells away, indicating that gradients maybe well-modeled by a low-order spatial Markov model.

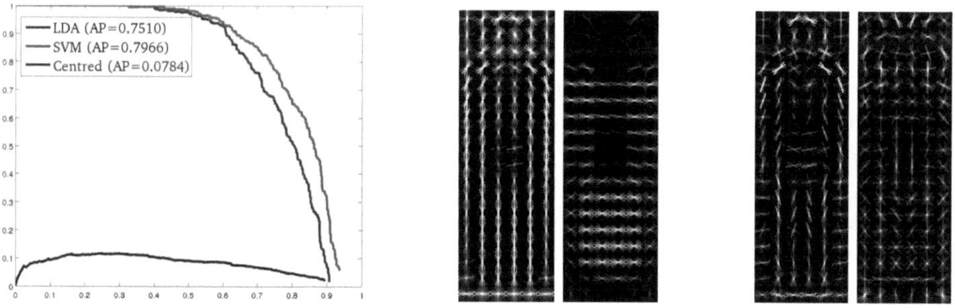

(a) AP (b) Centered (c) LDA

Fig. 3. The performance (AP) of the LDA model and the centered model (LDA without whitening) vis-a-vis a standard linear SVM on HOG features. We also show the detectors for the centered model and the LDA model.

3 Pedestrian Detection

HOG feature vectors were first described in detail in [1], where they were shown to significantly outperform other competing features in the task of pedestrian detection. This is a relatively easy detection task, since pedestrians don't vary significantly in pose. Our local implementation of the Dalal-Triggs detector achieves an average precision (AP) of 79.66% on the INRIA dataset, outperforming the original AP of 76.2% reported in Dalal's thesis [18]. We think this difference is due to our SVM solver, which implements multiple passes of data-mining for hard negatives. We choose this task as our first test bed for WHO features.

We use our LDA model to train a detector and evaluate its performance. Figure 3 shows our performance compared to that of a standard linear SVM on HOG features. We achieve an AP of 75.10%. This is slightly lower than the SVM performance, but nearly equivalent to the original performance of [18]. However, note that compared to the SVM model, the LDA model is estimated only from a few positive image patches and neither requires access to large pools of negative images nor involves any costly bootstrapping steps. Given this overwhelmingly reduced computation, this performance is impressive.

Constructing our LDA model from HOG feature vectors involves two steps, i.e, subtracting μ_0 (centering) and multiplying by Σ^{-1} (whitening). To tease out the contribution of whitening, we also evaluate the performance when the whitening step is removed. In other words, we consider the detector formed by simply taking the mean of the centered positive feature vectors. We call this the "centered model", and its performance is indicated by the black curve in Figure 3. It achieves an AP of less than 10%, indicating that whitening is crucial to performance. We also show the detectors in Figure 3, and it can be clearly seen that the LDA model does a better job of identifying the discriminative contours (the characteristic shape of the head and shoulders) compared to simple centering.

4 Clustering in WHO Space

Owing to large intra-class variations in pose and appearance, a single linear classifier over HOG feature vectors can hardly be expected to do well for generic object detection. Hence many state of the art methods train multiple "mixture components", multiple "parts" or both [3,2]. These mixture components and parts are either determined based on extra annotations [3], or inferred as latent variables during training [2]. [4] consider an extreme approach and consider each positive example as its own mixture component, training a separate HOG detector for each example.

In this section we consider a cheaper and simpler strategy of producing components by simply clustering the feature vectors. As a test bed we use the PASCAL VOC 2007 object detection dataset (train+val) [19]. We first cluster the exemplars of a category using kmeans on aspect ratio. Then for each cluster, we resize the exemplars in that cluster to a common aspect ratio, compute feature vectors on the resulting image patches and finally subdivide the clusters using recursive normalized cuts [20]. The affinity we use for N-cuts is the exponential of the cosine of the angle between the two feature vectors.

We can either cluster using HOG feature vectors or using WHO feature vectors ($\hat{x} = \Sigma^{-1/2}(x - \mu_0)$, see section 2). Alternatively, we can use PCA to project HOG features down to a low dimensional space (we use 30 dimensions), and cluster in that space. Figure 4 shows an example cluster obtained in each case for the 'bus' category. The cluster based on WHO features is in fact semantically meaningful, capturing buses in a particular pose. HOG based clustering produces less coherent results, and the cluster becomes significantly worse when performed in the dimensionality-reduced space. This is because as Figure 1 shows, HOG overstresses background, whereas whitening removes the correlations common in natural images, leaving behind only discriminative gradients. PCA goes the opposite way and in fact *removes* discriminative directions, making matters worse. Figure 5 shows some more examples of HOG-based clusters and WHO-based clusters. Clearly, the WHO-based clusters are significantly more coherent.

5 Training Each Cluster

We now turn to the task of training detectors for each cluster. Following our experiments in section 3, we have several choices:

1. Train a linear SVM for each cluster, using the images of the cluster as positives, and image patches from other categories/background as negatives (SVM on cluster).
2. Train an LDA model on the cluster, i.e, use $w = \Sigma^{-1}(x_{mean} - \mu_0)$ (LDA on cluster).
3. Take the mean of the centered HOG features of the patches in the cluster, i.e use $w = x_{mean} - \mu_0$ ("centered model" on cluster).

[4] treat each exemplar separately, and get their boost from training to discriminate each exemplar from the background. On the other hand we believe that

(a) HOG

(b) PCA

(c) WHO

Fig. 4. Clusters obtained using N-cuts using HOG feature vectors, HOG vectors projected to a PCA basis and WHO feature vectors. Observe that while all clusters make mistakes, the HOG-based cluster is much less coherent than the WHO-based cluster. The PCA cluster is even less coherent than the HOG-based cluster.

we can get bigger potential gains by averaging over multiple positive examples. In order to evaluate this, we also consider the following choices:

4. Train an LDA model on just the medoid, i.e $w = \Sigma^{-1}(x_{medoid} - \mu_0)$ (LDA on the medoid).
5. Take the medoid of the cluster and train a linear SVM, using the medoid as positive and image patches from other categories/background as negative.

We take the clusters obtained as described in the previous section for three categories : horse, motorbike and bus. For each cluster we train detectors according to the five schemes above. We then run each detector on the test set of PASCAL VOC 2007, and compute its AP. The ground truth for each cluster consists of all objects of that category.

Table 1 shows a summary comparison of the five schemes, and Figure 6 compares the performance of the LDA model with the other four schemes in more detail. First note that both single-example schemes perform worse than the LDA model. Indeed, for all but 6 of the 77 clusters tested, the LDA model achieves a higher AP than a single SVM trained using the medoid. This clearly shows that simple averaging over similar positive examples helps more than explicitly training to discriminate single exemplars from the background. This also provides an indirect validation of our clustering step, since it indicates that each cluster is coherent enough to be better than any single individual example. In our experimental results, we further quantitatively evaluate our clusters by demonstrating that they perform similarly to "brute-force" methods that train a separate exemplar template for every member of every cluster [4]. Our clustered representation performs similarly while being faster to evaluate.

Secondly, observe that on average the performance of the LDA model is very similar to the performance of a linear SVM, and is also highly correlated with

(a) horse

(b) aeroplane

Fig. 5. Examples of clusters obtained for aeroplane and horse using HOG feature vectors (left) and WHO feature vectors (right). Note how the clusters based on WHO are significantly more coherent than the clusters based on HOG.

it. This reiterates our observations on the pedestrian detection task in section 3. This also indicates that our LDA model can be used in place of SVMs for HOG based detectors with little or no loss in performance, at a fraction of the computational cost and with very little training data.

Finally, the performance of the centered model without whitening is much lower than the LDA model, and is in fact significantly worse than even the single-example models. This again shows that decorrelation, and not just centering, is crucial for performance.

6 Combining across Clusters

In this section we attempt to tie the previous two sections together to produce a full object detection system. We compare here to the approach of [4], who show competitive performance on PASCAL VOC 2007 by simply training one linear SVM per exemplar. This performance is impressive given that they use only HOG features and do not have any parts [2,3].

Table 1. Mean and median AP (in %) of the different models

	LDA on cluster	SVM on cluster	LDA on medoid	SVM on medoid	Centered
Mean AP	7.59 ± 4.86	6.75 ± 4.80	4.84 ± 4.13	4.05 ± 4.12	0.74 ± 2.02
Median AP	9.25 ± 3.86	9.16 ± 4.04	4.65 ± 3.71	2 ± 3.6	0.06 ± 0.7

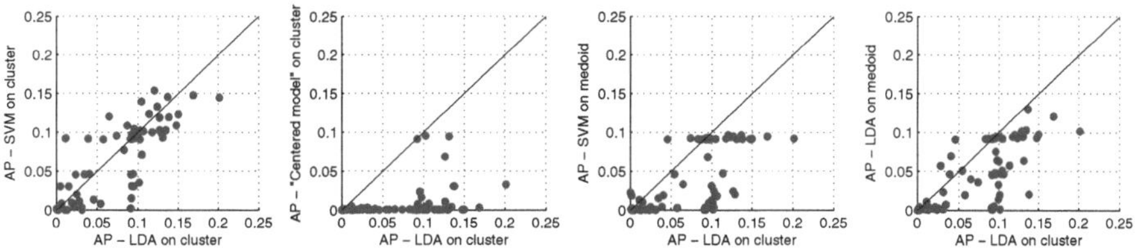

Fig. 6. Performance (AP) of the LDA model compared to (from left to right) an SVM trained on the cluster, the centered model trained on the cluster, an SVM trained on the medoid and an LDA model trained on the medoid. The blue line is the $y = x$ line. The LDA performs significantly better than both the single-example approaches and is comparable to an SVM trained on the cluster.

We agree with them on the fact that using multiple components instead of single monolithic detectors is necessary for handling the large intra-class variation. However, training a separate SVM for each positive example entails a huge computational complexity. Because the negative class for each model is essentially the background, one would ideally learn background statistics just once, and simply plug it in for each model.

LDA allows us to do precisely that. Background statistics in the form of Σ and μ are computed just once, and training only involves computing the mean of the positive examples. This reduces the computational complexity drastically: using LDA we can train all exemplar models of a particular category on a single machine in a few minutes. Table 2 shows how exemplar-LDA models compare to exemplar-SVMs [4]. As can be seen, there is little or no drop in performance.

Replacing SVMs by LDA significantly reduces the complexity at train time. However at test time, the computational complexity is still high because one has to run a very large number of detectors over the image. We can reduce this computational complexity considerably by first clustering the positive examples as described in Section 4. We then train one detector for each cluster, resulting in far fewer detectors. For instance, the 'horse' category has 403 exemplars but only 29 clusters.

To build a full object detection system, we need to combine these cluster detector outputs in a sensible way. Following [4], we train a set of rescoring functions that rescore the detections of each detector. Note that only detections that score above a threshold are rescored, while the rest are discarded.

We train a separate rescoring function for each cluster. For each detection, we construct two kinds of features. The first set of features considers the dot

Table 2. Our performance on VOC 2007, reported as AP in %. We compare with ESVM+Calibr and ESVM+Co-occ [4]. "ELDA+Calibr" constructs exemplar models using LDA, followed by a simple calibration step [4]. The last three columns show the performance using our clusters instead of individual exemplars. "Ours-only 1" is our performance using only the "sibling" features, while "Ours- only 2" is our performance using only the context features. Clearly both sets of features give us a boost. Our full model performs similarly to [4], but is much faster to train and test.

	ESVM +Calibr	ESVM +Co-occ	ELDA +Calibr	Ours-only 1	Ours-only 2	Ours-full
aeroplane	20.4	20.8	18.4	17.4	22.1	23.3
bicycle	40.7	48.0	39.9	35.5	37.4	41.0
bird	9.3	7.7	9.6	9.7	9.8	9.9
boat	10.0	14.3	10.0	10.9	11.1	11.0
bottle	10.3	13.1	11.3	15.4	14.0	17.0
bus	31.0	39.7	39.6	17.2	18.0	37.8
car	40.1	41.1	42.1	40.3	36.8	38.4
cat	9.6	5.2	10.7	10.6	6.5	11.5
chair	10.4	11.6	6.1	10.3	11.2	11.8
cow	14.7	18.6	12.1	14.3	13.5	14.5
diningtable	2.3	11.1	3	4.1	12.1	12.2
dog	9.7	3.1	10.6	1.8	10.5	10.2
horse	38.4	44.7	38.1	39.7	43.1	44.8
motorbike	32.0	39.4	30.7	26.0	25.8	27.9
person	19.2	16.9	18.2	23.1	21.3	22.4
pottedplant	9.6	11.2	1.4	4.9	5.1	3.1
sheep	16.7	22.6	12.2	14.1	13.8	16.3
sofa	11.0	17.0	11.1	8.7	12.2	8.9
train	29.1	36.9	27.6	22.1	30.6	30.3
tvmonitor	31.5	30.0	30.2	15.2	12.8	28.8
Mean	19.8	22.6	19.1	17.0	18.3	21.0

product of the WHO feature vector of the detection window with the WHO feature vector of every exemplar in the cluster. This gives us as many features as there are examples in the cluster. These features encode the similarity of the detection window with the purported "siblings" of the detection window, namely the exemplars in the cluster.

The second set of features is similar to context features as described in [4,3]. We consider every other cluster and record its highest scoring detection that overlaps by more than 50% with this detection window. These features record the similarity of the detection window to other clusters and allow us to boost scores of similar clusters and suppress scores of dissimilar clusters.

These features together with the original score given by the detector form the feature vector for the detection window. We then train a linear SVM to predict which detection windows are indeed true positives, and fit a logistic to the SVM scores. At test time the detections of each cluster detector are rescored using these second-level classifiers, and then standard non-max suppression is

Fig. 7. Detection and appearance transfer. The top row shows detections while in the bottom row the detected objects have been replaced by the most similar exemplars.

performed to produce the final, sparse set of detections. Note that this second level rescoring is relatively cheap since only detection windows that score above a threshold are rescored. Indeed, our cluster detectors can be thought of as the first step of a cascade, and significantly more sophisticated methods can be used to rescore these detection windows.

As shown in Table 2, our performance is very close to the performance of the Exemplar SVMs. This is in spite of the fact that our first-stage detectors require no training at all, and our second stage rescoring functions have an order of magnitude fewer parameters than ESVM+Co-occ [4] (for instance, for the horse category, in the second stage we have fewer than 2000 parameters, while ESVM+Co-occ has more than 100000). Although our performance is lower than part-based models [2], one could combine such approaches and possibly train parts with LDA.

Finally, each detection of ours is associated with a cluster of training exemplars. We can go further and associate each detection to the closest exemplar in the cluster, where distance is defined as cosine distance in WHO space. This allows us to match each detection to an exemplar, as in [4]. Figure 7 shows examples of detections and the training exemplars they are associated with. As can be seen, the detections are matched to very similar and semantically related exemplars.

7 Conclusion

Correlations are naturally present in features used in object detection, and we have shown that significant advantages can be derived by accounting for these correlations. In particular, LDA models trained using these correlations can be used as a highly efficient alternative to SVMs, without sacrificing performance. Decorrelated features can also be used for clustering examples, and we have shown that the combination of these two ideas allows us to build a competitive object detection system that is significantly faster not just at train time but also at run time. Our work can be built upon to produce state-of-the-art object detection systems, mirroring the developments in SVM-based approaches [2,3].

Our statistical models also suggest that natural image statistics, largely ignored in the field of object detection, are worth (re)visiting. For example, gradient statistics may be better modeled with heavy-tailed distributions instead of our Gaussian models [13]. However, the ideas expressed here are quite general, and as we have shown, can also be applied to tasks other than object detection, such as clustering.

References

1. Dalal, N., Triggs, B.: Histograms of oriented gradients for human detection. In: CVPR (2005)
2. Felzenszwalb, P., Girshick, R., McAllester, D., Ramanan, D.: Object detection with discriminatively trained part-based models. TPAMI 32 (2010)
3. Bourdev, L., Malik, J.: Poselets: Body part detectors trained using 3D human pose annotations. In: ICCV (2009)
4. Malisiewicz, T., Gupta, A., Efros, A.A.: Ensemble of exemplar-svms for object detection and beyond. In: ICCV (2011)
5. Fisher, R.: The use of multiple measurements in taxonomic problems. Annals of Human Genetics (1936)
6. Hastie, T., Tibshirani, R., Friedman, J.J.H.: The elements of statistical learning. Springer (2009)
7. Duda, R., Hart, P.: Pattern recognition and scene analysis (1973)
8. Belhumeur, P., Hespanha, J., Kriegman, D.: Eigenfaces vs. fisherfaces: Recognition using class specific linear projection. TPAMI 19 (1997)
9. Turk, M., Pentland, A.: Eigenfaces for recognition. Journal of Cognitive Neuroscience (1991)
10. Murase, H., Nayar, S.: Visual learning and recognition of 3-D objects from appearance. IJCV 14 (1995)
11. Ke, Y., Sukthankar, R.: Pca-sift: A more distinctive representation for local image descriptors. In: CVPR (2004)
12. Schwartz, W., Kembhavi, A., Harwood, D., Davis, L.: Human detection using partial least squares analysis. In: ICCV (2009)
13. Hyvärinen, A., Hurri, J., Hoyer, P.: Natural Image Statistics: A probabilistic approach to early computational vision (2009)
14. Rue, H., Held, L.: Gaussian Markov random fields: theory and applications (2005)
15. Marlin, B., Schmidt, M., Murphy, K.: Group sparse priors for covariance estimation. In: UAI (2009)
16. Vedaldi, A., Zisserman, A.: Structured output regression for detection with partial truncation. In: NIPS (2009)
17. Gao, T., Packer, B., Koller, D.: A segmentation-aware object detection model with occlusion handling. In: CVPR (2011)
18. Dalal, N.: Finding people in Images and Videos. PhD thesis, INRIA (2006)
19. Everingham, M., Van Gool, L., Williams, C.K.I., Winn, J., Zisserman, A.: The PASCAL Visual Object Classes Challenge 2007 (VOC2007) Results, `http://www.pascal-network.org/challenges/VOC/voc2007/workshop/index.html`
20. Shi, J., Malik, J.: Normalized cuts and image segmentation. TPAMI 22 (2000)

Beyond Spatial Pyramids: A New Feature Extraction Framework with Dense Spatial Sampling for Image Classification

Shengye Yan[1], Xinxing Xu[1], Dong Xu[1], Stephen Lin[2], and Xuelong Li[3]

[1] School of Computer Engineering, Nanyang Technological University
[2] Microsoft Research Asia
[3] OPTIMAL, State Key Laboratory of Transient Optics and Photonics, Xi'an Institute of Optics and Precision Mechanics, Chinese Academy of Sciences
{syyan,xuxi0006,dongxu}@ntu.edu.sg,
stevelin@microsoft.com, xuelong_li@opt.ac.cn

Abstract. We introduce a new framework for image classification that extends beyond the window sampling of fixed spatial pyramids to include a comprehensive set of windows densely sampled over location, size and aspect ratio. To effectively deal with this large set of windows, we derive a concise high-level image feature using a two-level extraction method. At the first level, window-based features are computed from local descriptors (e.g., SIFT, spatial HOG, LBP) in a process similar to standard feature extractors. Then at the second level, the new image feature is determined from the window-based features in a manner analogous to the first level. This higher level of abstraction offers both efficient handling of dense samples and reduced sensitivity to misalignment. More importantly, our simple yet effective framework can readily accommodate a large number of existing pooling/coding methods, allowing them to extract features beyond the spatial pyramid representation.

To effectively fuse the second level feature with a standard first level image feature for classification, we additionally propose a new learning algorithm, called Generalized Adaptive ℓ_p-norm Multiple Kernel Learning (GA-MKL), to learn an adapted robust classifier based on multiple base kernels constructed from image features and multiple sets of pre-learned classifiers of all the classes. Extensive evaluation on the object recognition (Caltech256) and scene recognition (15Scenes) benchmark datasets demonstrates that the proposed method outperforms state-of-the-art image classification algorithms under a broad range of settings.

Keywords: Image Classification, Spatial Pyramid, Sliding Window, Multiple Kernel Learning, Adapted Classifier.

1 Introduction

A well-established approach to image classification was introduced in [1], where an image is subdivided into increasingly finer regions according to a spatial pyramid representation (SPR), and then a Bag-of-Features (BoF) [2, 3] is computed

A. Fitzgibbon et al. (Eds.): ECCV 2012, Part IV, LNCS 7575, pp. 473–487, 2012.

within each of the subregions. In the past few years, many sophisticated feature extraction techniques have been extended from this framework [4–10].

While the spatial pyramid representation has become widely used in image classification, the grid cells within a pyramid correspond to a rather limited set of spatial regions where features are defined: the cells have a fixed aspect ratio; their areas vary only by multiples of four; and their locations must align with a grid. Many of the possible spatial regions are excluded, though some of them may provide important discriminative information.

Motivated by the success of sliding windows in object detection [11], we seek in this paper a general framework for image classification that accounts for a comprehensive set of windows densely sampled with respect to location, size, and aspect ratio, while allowing existing methods for encoding and pooling to be incorporated. However, two important issues arise from a direct approach. One is that the feature vector would become extremely large, since it is formed as a concatenation of features from each of the windows. Such large feature vectors would make image classification computationally very inefficient. The other issue that seriously impairs this approach is that different images are often not aligned with each other in image classification scenarios. Feature vectors with a strong spatial structure can therefore be detrimental when corresponding features do not coincide in image position.[1]

To avoid these issues, we propose a simple but effective image feature derived from densely sampled windows that is relatively compact and less sensitive to misalignment. This feature represents an image-level abstraction of the window-based features used in [1]. It is obtained via a two-level feature extraction method in which the first level computes window-based features from local descriptors (e.g., SIFT, spatial HOG, LBP), and the second level repeats the encoding and pooling procedure on the window-based features to acquire the new image feature. Feature pooling over the image yields a feature vector with the same number of elements as the codebook. Moreover, as in window-based features [1], exact positional information within the image is left out of the image feature in the same manner. This image feature implicitly captures useful spatial information, and will be shown to enhance classification performance when added to SPR. Furthermore, various pooling/coding techniques [6–10, 12] which extract features only from fixed spatial pyramids can be easily extended to go beyond the spatial pyramid representation within our proposed feature extraction framework.

For SVM classification, we propose a new learning method called Generalized Adaptive ℓ_p-norm Multiple Kernel Learning (GA-MKL), which is motivated by the recent success of MKL methods for various vision applications, such as object categorization [13, 14] and action recognition [15]. GA-MKL allows for different features such as our new second level feature and the standard first level feature to be effectively combined for classification. Moreover, GA-MKL takes advantage of pre-learned classifiers of other classes, based on the intuition that some classes

[1] We note that certain image categories tend to share a common spatial arrangement, such as people located in the middle of images, which works to the benefit of features based on SPR.

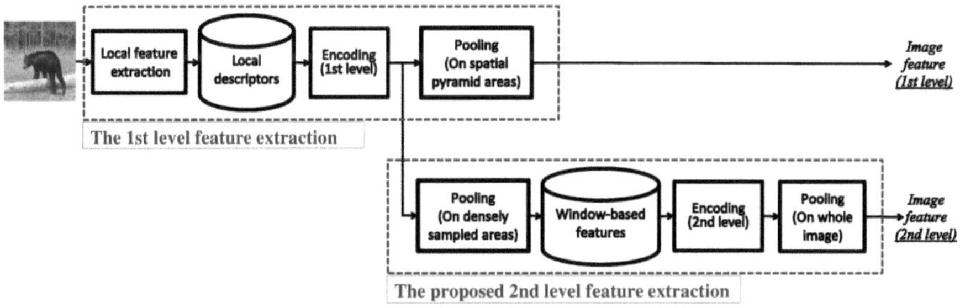

Fig. 1. Overview of the proposed two-level feature extraction framework

may share common information that can benefit each other. For example, classes like "Swan", "Duck" and "Goose" may share the same background of "Water" and similar components like beaks. Therefore it may be beneficial to train an adapted classifier for "Swan" that leverages on pre-learned classifiers for "Duck" and "Goose". GA-MKL takes advantage of this by learning an adapted classifier using multiple sets of base kernels and multiple sets of pre-learned SVM classifiers from other classes.

This work provides the first practical unsupervised feature extraction framework for going beyond spatial pyramids with densely sampled windows in image classification, in a general manner that easily accommodates existing encoding and pooling schemes. Through extensive experiments conducted on two widely-used benchmarks – Caltech256 [16] and 15Scenes [1, 17, 18] – we demonstrate the effectiveness of our feature extraction framework based on the second level feature and leveraging pre-learned classifiers from other classes through GA-MKL. These results show that our work consistently outperforms the state-of-the-art over a broad range of test cases.

2 Related Work

Different variants of the spatial pyramid representation have been employed for image classification. Though the original work of [1] found no performance improvement with pyramids expanded beyond the conventional three levels, others have reported better classification when a fourth level is included [14, 19]. In [20], adding overlapping spatial areas to the non-overlapped grid for the second and third levels was shown to capture more spatial information. The novel spatial pyramid layout used by the winner of VOC 2007 [21] has been adopted by many recent state-of-the-art methods [22–24]. In [25], fan-shaped areas are used in place of rectangular spatial areas in SPR. In contrast to these aforementioned methods, our work effectively and efficiently processes a complete set of rectangular windows, instead of a handcrafted subset.

In feature extraction, spatial information has been accounted for on two levels: in the local descriptor (such as the SIFT feature) and in the code of the local descriptor (as done in SPR). Kulkarni et al. [26] used affine SIFT to handle pose and viewpoint variance. Boureau et al. [4] proposed a mid-level feature based on sparse coding on local groups of SIFT features, instead of individual ones. They also presented a pooling scheme that can effectively handle large codebooks [12]. Feng et al. [10] proposed geometric ℓ_p pooling that places different importance on different geometric positions. Yang et al. [5] took advantage of spatial pyramid co-occurrence for overhead aerial imagery. For object recognition, Bosch et al. [27] utilized a region of interest detection procedure before applying BoW feature extraction. Our method differs from these techniques by introducing a higher level of feature that accounts for densely sampled windows of any location, size and aspect ratio.

The work in [28, 29] proposed to extract new types of higher level feature representations to exploit spatial or spatial-temporal co-occurrences beyond local descriptors. In both works, for final classification, their proposed features are pooled to obtain a global histogram for the whole image (i.e., a 1x1 spatial pyramid). In contrast, our method goes beyond spatial pyramids such that the final feature is extracted from windows densely sampled over location, size and aspect ratio. Jia et al. [30] also presented a method to go beyond spatial pyramids, by learning optimal pooling parameters for an over-complete set of receptive field candidates.

Another stream of research takes advantage of attribute or object level classifiers to extract high level features directly [31, 32] or use them indirectly for visual word disambiguation [33]. All these methods involve supervised learning of attribute classifiers using an extra training set collected from Google search or other sources. By contrast, our feature extraction framework does not use any extra training set, and the entire feature extraction process is unsupervised.

Several feature extraction techniques have been presented for purposes other than image classification. Duchenne et al. [34] proposed a graph-matching method that matches corresponding object points in different images for object classification. Boiman et al. [35] applied the nearest-neighbor classifier directly on different categories of SIFT features. Gehler et al. [36] combined different kinds of features and showed high performance with multiple kernel combinations. Bo et al. [37] framed image recognition as an image matching problem and solved it by kernel matching.

Recent work [15, 38] demonstrated that it is generally beneficial to utilize the pre-learned classifiers from other classes for event/action recognition. In contrast to the ℓ_1-norm constraint used in existing methods like [15, 38], in GA-MKL, we utilize the more general ℓ_p-norm constraint (*e.g.*, $p = 2$ in this work) which can preserve *complementary and orthogonal information* [39]. This is particularly important when base kernels contain complementary information as in our two level feature extraction framework. Furthermore, GA-MKL also learns the weights for multiple sets of pre-learned classifiers. Using the pre-learned classifiers for other classes also distinguishes GA-MKL from the existing ℓ_p-MKL technique.

3 Two-Level Feature Extraction

3.1 First Level Image Feature

For the first level, we employ BoF image feature extraction, which consists of four key components – local feature extraction, dictionary learning, feature encoding and feature pooling – which are illustrated in the upper part of Fig. 1. This is performed using the SPR framework of [1]. First, local descriptors such as SIFT are extracted from image patches. A visual word dictionary is then generated from these local features via clustering. This visual dictionary thereafter is used to encode each local feature into a coded vector by soft assignment [9]. Next, max pooling [6] is performed on the coded vectors in each window of the spatial pyramid. We note that other advanced encoding [6–9] or pooling [10, 12] methods can be readily used in our framework to improve classification performance. In this work, we take soft assignment [9] and max pooling [6] as an example to illustrate our framework because of their efficiency and reasonable effectiveness.

A spatial pyramid subdivides the input image into a sequence of grids with incrementally finer non-overlapping regions of the same size. As illustrated at the left of Fig. 2, the grid at level l has 2^l cells along each dimension, for a total of $D = 2^l \times 2^l$ cells. The vectors generated for each window by max pooling are all concatenated to form the first level image feature. This feature extraction procedure is the same as that used in [9].

3.2 Second Level Image Feature

Dense Sampling of Spatial Areas. The conventional spatial pyramid representation can greatly boost the performance of image classification, and with our second level image feature we aim to go beyond SPR by transplanting the idea of sliding windows [11] into image classification. Towards this end, we sample the spatial areas densely with respect to location, aspect ratio and size. This is achieved as follows. Suppose each spatial area is denoted by $Area(x, y, w, h)$, where (x, y) denotes the image position of the upper-left corner of the window, and (w, h) denotes the window width and height. All 4-tuples of $Area(x, y, w, h)$ are enumerated to obtain a comprehensive set of spatial areas.

The dense sampling procedure is illustrated in the right part of Fig. 2. For each window size $(\hat{w}, \hat{h})$, each image position $(\hat{x}, \hat{y})$ is scanned as shown by the red arrows. The window is iteratively shifted from left to right (X-direction), and from top to bottom (Y-direction). Sampling of different window widths and heights is illustrated along the black horizontal and vertical axes, respectively. The size and aspect ratio of windows are shown at the top-left of each image.

By dense sampling, windows that tightly bound an object or other potentially meaningful image patch are captured. This is shown by yellow rectangles in Fig. 2 for the bear's head and leg, and also a log on the ground.

In practice, we do not exhaustively sample the spatial areas pixel by pixel. Our implementation uses a step size of 30 pixels for x, y, w, h.

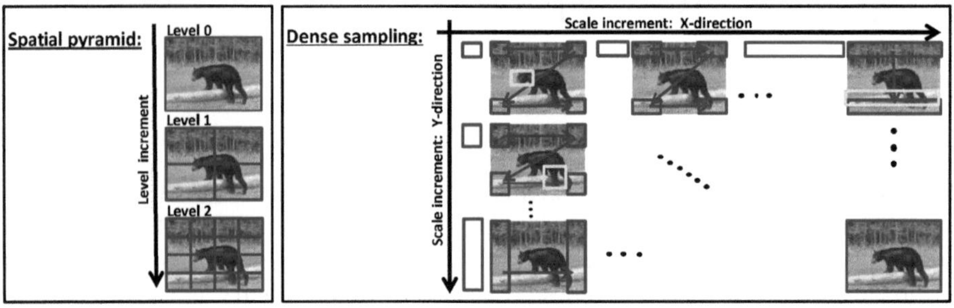

Fig. 2. Illustration of dense spatial sampling. The left side shows spatial pyramid sampling in [1]. The right side shows dense sampling as done in our proposed framework.

Second Level Coding and Pooling. We now have a set of spatial areas from dense sampling. Feature pooling is then performed on each spatial area to produce a feature vector which we refer to as a window-based feature. From the window-based features (one per spatial area), we compute an image feature vector that is the final output of feature extraction.

To go from window-based features to the final image feature, we propose to do a second level of feature extraction. This second level differs from the first level in that clustering is carried out on the window-based features instead of local SIFT descriptors. The secondary codebook learned in this clustering step is used to encode the window-based features. Finally, pooling of the encoded window-based features is done over the entire image to determine the image feature vector, which contains the same number of elements as the secondary codebook. As mentioned previously, we use soft assignment [9] and max pooling [6] in this work, but any encoding and pooling methods may be used instead.

Similar to the way the first level image feature relates each pyramid window to SIFT codewords, the second level feature relates the entire image to window-based codewords. The window-based codewords essentially represent a set of "window clusters" that each have similar first level feature content. These "window clusters" can be considered as a form of higher level SIFT-based feature defined over larger areas. We will later show in the experiments that this higher level abstraction of standard window descriptors provides a useful complement to first level image features.

3.3 Extension to Multiple Local Descriptors

The two-level feature extraction framework offers the generality to incorporate any kind of local descriptor, such as SIFT [40], Spatial HOG [41, 42] and LBP [43]. Two-level feature extraction for spatial HOG follows the exact same procedure as for SIFT. For LBP, histograms are extracted at the first level feature extraction, then LBP histograms are further processed by the proposed second level feature extraction.

4 Generalized Adaptive ℓ_p-norm Multiple Kernel Learning

In the following, we define the ℓ_p-norm of the M dimensional vector $\mathbf{d}$ as $||\mathbf{d}||_p = (\sum_{m=1}^{M} d_m^p)^{1/p}$, and specially denote the ℓ_2-norm of $\mathbf{d}$ simply as $||\mathbf{d}||$ for brevity. We also use the superscript $'$ to signify the transpose of a vector, and denote the element-wise product between two vectors $\boldsymbol{\alpha}$ and $\mathbf{y}$ as $\boldsymbol{\alpha} \odot \mathbf{y} = [\alpha_1 \mathrm{y}_1, \cdots, \alpha_l \mathrm{y}_l]'$. Moreover, $\mathbf{1} \in \mathbb{R}^l$ denotes an l dimensional vector with all elements of 1, and the inequality $\mathbf{d} = [d_1, \ldots, d_M]' \geqslant 0$ indicates that $d_m \geqslant 0$ for $m = 1, \ldots, M$.

Multiple Kernel Learning (MKL) has been widely utilized to fuse different types of visual features. The traditional ℓ_1-norm MKL selects a very sparse set of base kernels, which may discard some useful information. The recent ℓ_p-norm Multiple Kernel Learning (ℓ_p-MKL) [39] utilizes the more general ℓ_p-norm constraint (*e.g.*, $p = 2$ in this work) for the kernel coefficients, which can preserve *complementary and orthogonal information* [39] in contrast to ℓ_1-norm MKL.

In our work, we wish to additionally take advantage of existing SVM classifiers trained from different types of visual features for different classes. Our intuition is that different classes may share some common information that benefits others. We thus propose a new learning method called Generalized Adaptive ℓ_p-norm Multiple Kernel Learning (GA-MKL) to learn a robust adapted classifier that not only fuses different types of visual features (*e.g.* first and second level image features) but also incorporates pre-learned classifiers trained on different types of features for all of the classes.

We consider one-versus-rest classification in this work. For any given class, let us denote the training set as $\{(\mathbf{x}_i, \mathrm{y}_i)|_{i=1}^{l}\}$ where $\mathbf{x}_i$ is the ith training image with $\mathrm{y}_i \in \{+1, -1\}$ being the corresponding label. Suppose that we have a total number of H classes and S sets of pre-learned classifiers $\{f_s^1(\mathbf{x}), \cdots, f_s^H(\mathbf{x})\}|_{s=1}^{S}$, each set of which can be learned from some kind of image representation (In this work, different representations are coming from different types of visual features). Motivated by [38], we assume that the decision function for the new classifier is a linear combination of all the pre-learned classifiers with a perturbation function modeled by using the original visual feature, and define the decision function as

$$f(\mathbf{x}) = \sum_{s=1}^{S} \boldsymbol{\beta}_s' \boldsymbol{f}_s(\mathbf{x}) + \Delta f(\mathbf{x}), \qquad (1)$$

where $\boldsymbol{f}_s(\mathbf{x}) = [f_s^1(\mathbf{x}), \cdots, f_s^H(\mathbf{x})]'$ is the sth decision value vector for the input image $\mathbf{x}$ from the pre-learned classifiers, $\boldsymbol{\beta}_s = [\beta_s^1, \cdots, \beta_s^H]'$ is the corresponding weight vector to be optimized, and $\Delta f(\mathbf{x})$ can be any perturbation function from the original visual feature space. If we utilize the decision function of Multiple Kernel Learning as the perturbation function, and assume that a total number of M base kernels are used, then $\Delta f(\mathbf{x}) = \sum_{m=1}^{M} d_m \mathbf{w}_m' \varphi_m(\mathbf{x}) + b$, where $\varphi_m(\cdot)$ is the mapping of the mth base kernel, $\mathbf{d} = [d_1, \ldots, d_M]'$ is the vector of base kernel coefficients, and $\mathbf{d}, \mathbf{w}_m|_{m=1}^{M}, b$ are the variables of the MKL.

The new adapted classifier $f(\mathbf{x})$ can be learned by minimizing the following objective function:

$$\min_{d_m,\mu_s} \min_{\mathbf{v}_m,b,\xi_i,\boldsymbol{\beta}_s} \frac{1}{2}\sum_{s=1}^{S}\frac{\|\boldsymbol{\beta}_s\|^2}{\mu_s} + \frac{\lambda}{2}\sum_{s=1}^{S}\mu_s^2 + \underbrace{\frac{1}{2}\sum_{m=1}^{M}\frac{\|\mathbf{v}_m\|^2}{d_m} + C\sum_{i=1}^{l}\xi_i}_{\mathbf{J}(\Delta f)} \tag{2}$$

$$\text{s.t. } \mathrm{y}_i\left(\sum_{s=1}^{S}\boldsymbol{\beta}_s'\boldsymbol{f}_s(\mathbf{x}_i) + \sum_{m=1}^{M}\mathbf{v}_m'\varphi_m(\mathbf{x}_i) + b\right) \geqslant 1-\xi_i, \xi_i \geqslant 0, i = 1,\cdots,l,$$
$$\mathbf{d} \geqslant 0, ||\mathbf{d}||_p^2 \leqslant 1, \boldsymbol{\mu} \geqslant 0,$$

where $C > 0$ is the MKL regularization parameter, $\mathbf{v}_m = d_m\mathbf{w}_m$, $\mathbf{J}(\Delta f)$ is the MKL structural risk functional, and $p \geqslant 1$ is the norm parameter for the base kernel coefficients introduced in ℓ_p-MKL [39]. Besides the structural risk term $\mathbf{J}(\Delta f)$ for standard MKL, the coefficients $\boldsymbol{\beta}_s|_{s=1}^S$ for the pre-learned classifiers are also penalized as $\|\boldsymbol{\beta}_s\|^2|_{s=1}^S$. Considering that the pre-learned classifiers from different visual features have different classification capacity, we further introduce an intermediate vector $\boldsymbol{\mu} = [\mu_1, \cdots, \mu_S]'$ to control the contributions of the penalty terms from different pre-learned classifier sets. The regularization term $\frac{\lambda}{2}\sum_{s=1}^S \mu_s^2$ with regularization parameter $\lambda > 0$ is included to avoid a trivial solution for $\boldsymbol{\mu}$. In this way, we not only fuse different types of visual features but also utilize the pre-learned classifiers of all the classes.

Since the optimization problem in (2) is convex w.r.t. $\mathbf{v}_m, b, \xi_i, \boldsymbol{\beta}_s, \mathbf{d}, \boldsymbol{\mu}$, the global optimum can be obtained by using the block-wise coordinate descent algorithm [39]. We thus alternatively optimize these variables with the following two steps.

Optimize $\mathbf{v}_m, b, \xi_i, \boldsymbol{\beta}_s$ with Fixed $\mathbf{d}, \boldsymbol{\mu}$: With fixed $\mathbf{d}, \boldsymbol{\mu}$, the problem in (2) is a convex problem w.r.t. $\mathbf{v}_m, b, \xi_i$ and $\boldsymbol{\beta}_s$. By introducing the non-negative Lagrangian multipliers $\alpha_i|_{i=1}^l$, the dual can be derived as follows:

$$\max_{\boldsymbol{\alpha}} \boldsymbol{\alpha}'\mathbf{1} - \frac{1}{2}(\boldsymbol{\alpha}\odot\mathbf{y})'\left(\sum_{m=1}^{M} d_m\mathbf{K}_m + \sum_{s=1}^{S}\mu_s\mathbf{F}_s\right)(\boldsymbol{\alpha}\odot\mathbf{y}) \tag{3}$$
$$\text{s.t. } \boldsymbol{\alpha}'\mathbf{y} = 0, 0 \leqslant \boldsymbol{\alpha} \leqslant C,$$

where $\boldsymbol{\alpha} = [\alpha_1, \ldots, \alpha_l]'$, $\mathbf{y} = [\mathrm{y}_1, \ldots, \mathrm{y}_l]'$, $\mathbf{K}_m(\mathbf{x}_i, \mathbf{x}_j) = \varphi_m(\mathbf{x}_i)'\varphi_m(\mathbf{x}_j)$ and $\mathbf{F}_s(\mathbf{x}_i, \mathbf{x}_j) = \boldsymbol{f}_s(\mathbf{x}_i)'\boldsymbol{f}_s(\mathbf{x}_j)$. It can be seen that (3) is in a standard form of the SVM dual problem with the kernel $\mathbf{K} = \sum_{m=1}^M d_m\mathbf{K}_m + \sum_{s=1}^S \mu_s\mathbf{F}_s$. Therefore, it can be solved via existing SVM solvers such as libsvm [44].

With the optimum $\boldsymbol{\alpha}$ obtained from problem (3), we can recover the primal variables $\mathbf{v}_m, \boldsymbol{\beta}_s$ accordingly:

$$\mathbf{v}_m = d_m\sum_{i=1}^{l}\alpha_i\mathrm{y}_i\varphi_m(\mathbf{x}_i),\ m = 1,\ldots,M, \tag{4}$$

$$\boldsymbol{\beta}_s = \mu_s\sum_{i=1}^{l}\alpha_i\mathrm{y}_i\boldsymbol{f}_s(\mathbf{x}_i),\ s = 1,\ldots,S. \tag{5}$$

Algorithm 1. Block-wise coordinate descent algorithm for GA-MKL.

1: Initialize $\mathbf{d}^1$ and $\boldsymbol{\mu}^1$; set $t = 1$.
2: **repeat**
3: Obtain $\boldsymbol{\alpha}^t$ by solving (3) using the SVM solver with $\mathbf{d}^t$ and $\boldsymbol{\mu}^t$.
4: Calculate $\|\mathbf{v}_m^t\|^2$ by using (4) and solve for $\mathbf{d}^{t+1}$ by using (7).
5: Calculate $\|\boldsymbol{\beta}_s^t\|^2$ by using (5) and solve for $\boldsymbol{\mu}^{t+1}$ by using (8).
6: $t = t + 1$.
7: **until** The convergence criterion is reached.

Optimize $\mathbf{d}, \boldsymbol{\mu}$ with Fixed $\mathbf{v}_m, b, \xi_i, \boldsymbol{\beta}_s$: With fixed $\mathbf{v}_m, b, \xi_i, \boldsymbol{\beta}_s$, the problem in (2) reduces to the following constrained convex minimization problem:

$$\min_{d_m,\mu_s} \frac{1}{2}\sum_{s=1}^{S}\frac{\|\boldsymbol{\beta}_s\|^2}{\mu_s} + \frac{\lambda}{2}\sum_{s=1}^{S}\mu_s^2 + \frac{1}{2}\sum_{m=1}^{M}\frac{\|\mathbf{v}_m\|^2}{d_m} \tag{6}$$
$$\text{s.t. } \mathbf{d} \geqslant 0, ||\mathbf{d}||_p^2 \leqslant 1, \boldsymbol{\mu} \geqslant 0.$$

Similar to the derivations in [39], we obtain the closed-form solutions as follows:

$$d_m = \frac{||\mathbf{v}_m||^{\frac{2}{p+1}}}{(\sum_{r=1}^{M}||\mathbf{v}_r||^{\frac{2p}{p+1}})^{1/p}}, \; m = 1, \ldots, M, \tag{7}$$

$$\mu_s = \sqrt[3]{\frac{||\boldsymbol{\beta}_s||^2}{2\lambda}}, \; s = 1, \ldots, S, \tag{8}$$

where $\|\mathbf{v}_m\|^2$ and $\|\boldsymbol{\beta}_s\|^2$ can be calculated by using (4) and (5), respectively.

The entire optimization procedure is summarized in Algorithm 1. After obtaining the optimal $\mathbf{d}$, $\boldsymbol{\mu}$ and $\boldsymbol{\alpha}$ using Algorithm 1, the final classifier for the test images can be expressed as

$$f(\mathbf{x}) = \sum_{i=1}^{l}\alpha_i y_i \left(\sum_{s=1}^{S}\mu_s \boldsymbol{f}_s(\mathbf{x})'\boldsymbol{f}_s(\mathbf{x}_i)\right) + \sum_{i=1}^{l}\alpha_i y_i \left(\sum_{m=1}^{M} d_m \mathbf{K}_m(\mathbf{x}, \mathbf{x}_i)\right) + b.$$

5 Experiments

In this section, we evaluate the proposed two-level feature extraction framework and GA-MKL on two broadly recognized image databases for object and scene classification: Caltech256 [16] and 15Scenes [1, 17, 18].

5.1 Experimental Setup

Local Descriptor Extraction: Three types of local descriptors – dense SIFT [40], spatial HOG [42] and LBP [43] – are used in our experiments. SIFT is extracted from densely located patches centered at every 4 pixels in the image, with a patch size of 16×16 pixels. For spatial HOG, the HOG descriptors are extracted from densely located patches centered at every 8 pixels in the image, with a patch size of 8×8 pixels. Then the spatial HOG descriptor is formed by stacking together 2×2 neighboring local HOG descriptors. For LBP, the uniform LBP as described in [43] is adopted.

Dictionary Learning: K-means clustering is employed for both levels of feature extraction. The dictionary size for all second level feature extractions is set to 4,096. The dictionary size for the first level SIFT feature extraction is set to 4,096 as well. All other dictionary sizes are set to 1,024.

Encoding: Localized soft assignment [9] is used for both levels of encoding.

Pooling: The first level feature extraction of LBP is pooled by average pooling. In all other cases, the codes are pooled via max pooling. A three level spatial pyramid of 1×1, 2×2 and 4×4 is used.

Feature Normalization and Designation: The first level image features of the LBP local descriptor are normalized with the ℓ_1-norm equal to 1. The other types of image features are each normalized with the ℓ_2-norm equal to 1.

The first level image feature is referred to as a Spatial Pyramid Representation (SPR) feature. The first level feature together with the second level feature is referred to as the Beyond Spatial Pyramid Representation (BSPR) feature.

Kernel Learning: ℓ_p-MKL and GA-MKL are implemented using the libsvm software package [44]. Linear kernels with C set to 10 are used throughout the experiments. In ℓ_p-MKL and GA-MKL, we fix p to 2. In GA-MKL, we empirically set λ to 10 for both datasets. For the pre-learned classifiers in GA-MKL, there are six sets in total, with each set learned by using each type of BSPR feature. From the six sets of pre-learned classifiers and the six linear kernels generated by the six kinds of BSPR features, the GA-MKL classifier is learned.

All experiments on each dataset are repeated five times with different randomly selected training images and the same experimental settings. The results are reported in terms of the mean and standard deviation from all five runs.

5.2 Results on the Caltech256 Dataset

Caltech256 [16] provides challenging data for object recognition. It consists of 30,608 images with 256 object categories and 80 to 827 images per category. In our series of experiments on Caltech256, we take 30, 45 and 60 images from each category for training and use the rest as test samples.

Performance comparisons with the baseline method are listed in the upper part of Table 1. From it, one can see that the classification accuracy with BSPR features consistently yields better results than the one with SPR features in all three of the training scenarios. With ℓ_p-norm MKL, the improvements of the BSPR feature over the SPR feature are 2.03%, 2.38% and 2.73% respectively. This demonstrates that the proposed second level features provide additional information which is complementary to the SPR with the first level features. Also,

Table 1. Classification accuracy (%) on the Caltech256 dataset. SPR feature (ℓ_p-MKL) is the baseline method implemented in this paper. BSPR feature (ℓ_p-MKL) and BSPR feature (GA-MKL) correspond to our proposed BSPR feature learned with ℓ_p-MKL and our proposed GA-MKL. Note: - indicates unavailability of results.

Method	30 training	45 training	60 training
SPR feature (ℓ_p-MKL)	43.75 ± 0.20	47.23 ± 0.23	48.92 ± 0.31
BSPR feature (ℓ_p-MKL)	45.78 ± 0.18	49.61 ± 0.16	51.65 ± 0.35
BSPR feature (GA-MKL)	**46.82 ± 0.23**	**50.69 ± 0.15**	**52.91 ± 0.59**
Sparse coding [6]	34.02 ± 0.35	37.46 ± 0.55	40.14 ± 0.91
Improved Fisher Kernel [24]	40.80 ± 0.10	45.00 ± 0.20	47.90 ± 0.40
Efficient Match Kernel [37]	30.50 ± 0.40	34.40 ± 0.40	37.60 ± 0.50
Affine sparse codes [26]	45.83	49.30	51.36
Locality-constrained linear coding [7]	41.19	45.31	47.68
Geometric ℓ_p-norm Feature Pooling [10]	43.17	47.32	-
Nearest-neighbor [35]	42.70	-	-
Random Forest [27]	44.00	-	-
Graph-matching kernel [34]	38.10 ± 0.60	-	-
Multi-way local pooling [12]	41.70 ± 0.80	-	-

it is shown in the table that the results using the BSPR feature and our proposed GA-MKL are better than those using BSPR and ℓ_p-MKL by 1.04%, 1.08% and 1.26%, which indicates that it is beneficial to learn an adapted classifier that leverages on pre-learned classifiers from other classes. This is consisted with the previous work [15, 38, 45]. In total, the proposed BSPR feature and GA-MKL improves upon the baseline method by 3.07%, 3.46% and 3.99% respectively.

After learning the adapted classifiers, we observe that similar concepts have higher weights than dissimilar ones. Taking for instance the concepts of "Swan" and "Gorilla", the two largest β values are as follows: Swan($\beta_{duck} = 0.092$, $\beta_{goose} = 0.078$), Gorilla($\beta_{chimp} = 0.195$, $\beta_{raccoon} = 0.106$). These learned values also reflect the benefit of leveraging pre-learned classifiers of other classes.

Comparisons with State-of-the-Art: In the lower part of Table 1, comparisons with state-of-the-art methods are provided. The listed methods include the most recently reported techniques as well as the highest achieving methods from the past. Our method is seen to outperform all the existing methods with various numbers of training samples. To be exact, Our method exceeds the existing best results [26] (underlined in Table 1) by 0.99%, 1.39% and 1.55% for 30, 45 and 60 training samples, respectively.

5.3 Results on the 15Scenes Dataset

The 15Scenes dataset is composed of 15 classes of scenes and contains 4,485 images in total, reported in [1, 17, 18]. Following the common evaluation protocol on this dataset, we randomly select 100 images from each class as training samples and use the rest as test samples. Table 2 presents performance comparisons.

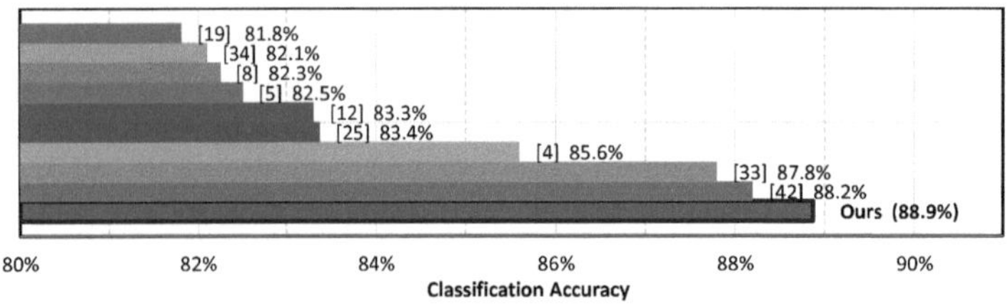

Fig. 3. Comparison with state-of-the-art results on 15Scenes

Table 2. Classification accuracy (%) on 15Scenes with 100 training images

Method	Classification Accuracy
SPR feature (ℓ_p-MKL)	86.60 ± 0.66
BSPR feature (ℓ_p-MKL)	88.32 ± 0.72
BSPR feature (GA-MKL)	**88.87 ± 0.56**

Using ℓ_p-MKL, classification accuracy with the BSPR features exceeds that of the baseline method with SPR features, which again demonstrates the effectiveness of our proposed two level feature extraction framework. The result using the BSPR feature and GA-MKL is also better than that from the BSPR feature and ℓ_p-MKL, which validates the effectiveness of GA-MKL in leveraging pre-learned classifiers from other classes. In total, our proposed BSPR feature with our GA-MKL brings an overall improvement in classification accuracy of 2.27% over the baseline.

Performance of Individual Features: For individual BSPR features, the results are 83.2%, 84.6% and 70.4% (resp. 75.8%, 69.8%, 69.5%) using SIFT, SHOG and LBP features at the first (resp. second) level. Note that the result after combining all three first level features (86.6%) is better than the results from each individual feature at the first level, which shows the effectiveness of ℓ_p-MKL. Though the individual results at the second level are not as good as those corresponding to the first level, they are complementary to the first level features, and the combination of two levels of features using ℓ_p-MKL leads to a better result (i.e., 88.32% vs. 86.6% in Table 2).

Comparisons with State-of-the-Art: In Fig. 3, comparisons with state-of-the-art methods are provided. The listed methods include the latest techniques and top performers. Our method still achieves the best results on this dataset.

5.4 Computation Time

The proposed two-level feature extraction framework involves a second round of encoding and pooling that adds to the computation time. Processing speed additionally depends on the codebook sizes in the first level and second level feature extraction, the number of local descriptors in the first level, and the number of windows in the second level. For the methods and settings used in this work, with the SIFT descriptor as an example, the CPU times for the first level (5,184 SIFT descriptors with the feature dimension of 128) and second level (3,025 windows with the window-based feature dimension of 4,096) feature extraction are about 10s and 15s on a 300×300 image for Caltech256, with an IBM workstation (3.33GHz CPU with 18GB RAM) and Matlab implementation.

6 Conclusion

We presented two technical contributions for image classification. The first is a novel feature extraction framework that generalizes window-based features to the image level in a manner that efficiently accounts for densely sampled windows and allows for existing encoding and pooling techniques to be used. Secondly, we proposed Generalized Adaptive ℓ_p-norm Multiple Kernel Learning (GA-MKL) to incorporate the two different levels of features and to leverage multiple sets of pre-learned classifiers from other classes. Our extensive experimental results on benchmark datasets show that our work outperforms the state-of-the-art.

Acknowledgement. This research is supported by the Singapore National Research Foundation under its Interactive & Digital Media (IDM) Public Sector R&D Funding Initiative and administered by the IDM Programme Office. This research is also supported by the National Natural Science Foundation of China (Grant No: 61125106).

References

1. Lazebnik, S., Schmid, C., Poncer, J.: Beyond bags of features: Spatial pyramid matching for recognizing natural scene categories. In: CVPR (2006)
2. Sivic, J., Zisserman, A.: Video google: A text retrieval approach to object matching in videos. In: ICCV (2003)
3. Csurka, G., Dance, C., Fan, L., Willamowski, J., Bray, C.: Visual categorization with bags of keypoints. In: Workshop on Statistical Learning in Computer Vision, ECCV (2004)
4. Boureau, Y.L., Bach, F., LeCun, Y., Ponce, J.: Learning mid-level features for recognition. In: CVPR (2010)
5. Yang, Y., Newsam, S.: Spatial pyramid co-occurrence for image classification. In: ICCV (2011)
6. Yang, J., Yu, K., Gong, Y., Huang, T.S.: Linear spatial pyramid matching using sparse coding for image classification. In: CVPR (2009)
7. Wang, J., Yang, J., Yu, K., Lv, F., Huang, T.S., Gong, Y.: Locality-constrained linear coding for image classification. In: CVPR (2010)
8. Huang, Y., Huang, K., Yu, Y., Tan, T.: Salient coding for image classification. In: CVPR (2011)
9. Liu, L., Wang, L., Liu, X.: In defense of soft-assignment coding. In: ICCV (2011)
10. Feng, J., Ni, B., Tian, Q., Yan, S.: Geometric ℓ_p-norm feature pooling for image classification. In: CVPR (2011)

11. Yan, S., Shan, S., Chen, X., Gao, W., Chen, J.: Locally assembled binary (lab) feature with feature-centric cascade for fast and accurate face detection. In: CVPR (2008)
12. Boureau, Y.L., Roux, N.L., Bach, F.: Ask the locals: Multi-way local pooling for image recognition. In: ICCV (2011)
13. Varma, M., Ray, D.: Learning the discriminative power-invariance trade-off. In: ICCV (2007)
14. Yang, J., Li, Y., Tian, Y., Duan, L., Gao, W.: Group-sensitive multiple kernel learning for object categorization. In: ICCV (2009)
15. Wu, X., Xu, D., Duan, L., Luo, J.: Action recognition using context and appearance distribution features. In: CVPR (2011)
16. Griffin, G., Holub, A., Perona, P.: Caltech-256 object category dataset. Technical report, California Institute of Technology (2007)
17. Oliva, A., Torraba, A.: Modeling the shape of the scene: A holistic representation of the spatial envelop. IJCV (2001)
18. Li, F.F., Fergus, R., Perona, P.: Learning generative visual models from few training examples: An incremental bayesian approach tested on 101 object categories. In: CVPR (2004)
19. Harada, T., Ushiku, Y., Yamashita, Y., Kuniyoshi, Y.: Discriminative spatial pyramid. In: CVPR (2011)
20. Wu, J., Rehg, J.M.: Beyond the euclidean distance: Creating effective visual codebooks using the histogram intersection kernel. In: ICCV (2009)
21. Marszałek, M., Schmid, C., Harzallah, H., Van De Weijer, J.: Learning object representations for visual object class recognition. In: ICCV, Visual Recognition Challenge Workshop (2007)
22. Zhou, X., Yu, K., Zhang, T., Huang, T.S.: Image Classification Using Super-Vector Coding of Local Image Descriptors. In: Daniilidis, K., Maragos, P., Paragios, N. (eds.) ECCV 2010, Part V. LNCS, vol. 6315, pp. 141–154. Springer, Heidelberg (2010)
23. Yang, J., Yu, K., Huang, T.: Efficient Highly Over-Complete Sparse Coding Using a Mixture Model. In: Daniilidis, K., Maragos, P., Paragios, N. (eds.) ECCV 2010, Part V. LNCS, vol. 6315, pp. 113–126. Springer, Heidelberg (2010)
24. Perronnin, F., Sánchez, J., Mensink, T.: Improving the Fisher Kernel for Large-Scale Image Classification. In: Daniilidis, K., Maragos, P., Paragios, N. (eds.) ECCV 2010, Part IV. LNCS, vol. 6314, pp. 143–156. Springer, Heidelberg (2010)
25. Wang, X., Bai, X., Liu, W., Latecki, L.J.: Feature context for image classification and object detection. In: CVPR (2011)
26. Kulkarni, N., Li, B.: Discriminative affine sparse codes for image classification. In: CVPR (2011)
27. Bosch, A., Zisserman, A., Munoz, X.: Image classification using random forests and ferns. In: ICCV (2007)
28. Agarwal, A., Triggs, B.: Multilevel image coding with hyperfeatures. IJCV (2008)
29. Kovashka, A., Grauman, K.: Learning a hierarchy of discriminative space-time neighborhood features for human action recognition. In: CVPR (2010)
30. Jia, Y., Huang, C., Darrell, T.: Beyond spatial pyramids: Receptive field learning for pooling image features. In: CVPR (2012)
31. Li, L.J., Su, H., Xing, E.P., Fei-Fei, L.: Object bank: A high-level image representation for scene classification & semantic feature sparsification. In: NIPS (2010)
32. Torresani, L., Szummer, M., Fitzgibbon, A.: Efficient Object Category Recognition Using Classemes. In: Daniilidis, K., Maragos, P., Paragios, N. (eds.) ECCV 2010, Part I. LNCS, vol. 6311, pp. 776–789. Springer, Heidelberg (2010)

33. Su, Y., Jurie, F.: Visualword disambiguation by semantic contexts. In: ICCV (2011)
34. Duchenne, O., Joulin, A., Ponce, J.: A graph-matching kernel for object categorization. In: ICCV (2011)
35. Boiman, O., Shechtman, E., Irani, M.: In defense of nearest-neighbor based image classification. In: CVPR (2008)
36. Gehler, P., Nowozin, S.: On feature combination for multiclass object classification. In: ICCV (2009)
37. Bo, L., Sminchisescu, C.: Efficient match kernels between sets of features for visual recognition. In: NIPS (2009)
38. Duan, L., Xu, D., Tsang, I.W.H., Luo, J.: Visual event recognition in videos by learning from web data. TPAMI (2012)
39. Kloft, M., Brefeld, U., Sonnenburg, S., Zien, A.: ℓ_p-norm multiple kernel learning. JMLR (2011)
40. Lowe, D.: Distinctive image features from scale-invariant keypoints. IJCV (2004)
41. Xiao, J., Hays, J., Ehinger, K.A., Oliva, A., Torralba, A.: Sun database: Large-scale scene recognition from abbey to zoo. In: CVPR (2010)
42. Dalal, N., Triggs, B.: Histograms of oriented gradients for human detection. In: CVPR (2005)
43. Ojala, T., Pietikainen, M., Maenpaa, T.: Multiresolution gray-scale and rotation invariant texture classification with local binary patterns. TPAMI (2002)
44. Chang, C.C., Lin, C.J.: Libsvm: A library for support vector machines. ACM TIST (2011)
45. Chen, L., Xu, D., Tsang, I.W.H., Luo, J.: Tag-based image retrieval improved by augmented features and group-based refinement. IEEE Trans. on Multimedia (2012)

Subspace Learning in Krein Spaces: Complete Kernel Fisher Discriminant Analysis with Indefinite Kernels

Stefanos Zafeiriou*

Department of Computing, Imperial College London
London SW7 2AZ, U.K.
s.zafeiriou@imperial.ac.uk
http://ibug.doc.ic.ac.uk/people/szafeiriou

Abstract. Positive definite kernels, such as Gaussian Radial Basis Functions (GRBF), have been widely used in computer vision for designing feature extraction and classification algorithms. In many cases non-positive definite (npd) kernels and non metric similarity/dissimilarity measures naturally arise (e.g., Hausdorff distance, Kullback Leibler Divergences and Compact Support (CS) Kernels). Hence, there is a practical and theoretical need to properly handle npd kernels within feature extraction and classification frameworks. Recently, classifiers such as Support Vector Machines (SVMs) with npd kernels, Indefinite Kernel Fisher Discriminant Analysis (IKFDA) and Indefinite Kernel Quadratic Analysis (IKQA) were proposed. In this paper we propose feature extraction methods using indefinite kernels. In particular, first we propose an Indefinite Kernel Principal Component Analysis (IKPCA). Then, we properly define optimization problems that find discriminant projections with indefinite kernels and propose a Complete Indefinite Kernel Fisher Discriminant Analysis (CIKFDA) that solves the proposed problems. We show the power of the proposed frameworks in a fully automatic face recognition scenario.

Keywords: subspace learning, indefinite kernels, face recognition.

1 Introduction

In many computer vision applications we encounter the following problem. Given a high dimensional visual representation of objects we wish to find a condensed representation that captures their underlying, possibly non-linear, structure. The aforementioned problem is usually tackled by the application of linear and non-linear dimensionality reduction techniques, also referred to as subspace learning techniques. Research on subspace learning mainly revolves around two main interrelated directions, that is (a) subspace learning using kernels [1–4, 7–9] and (b) manifold learning [10, 11].

* This work was funded by Junior Research Fellowship of Imperial College London.

A. Fitzgibbon et al. (Eds.): ECCV 2012, Part IV, LNCS 7575, pp. 488–501, 2012.

Linear dimensionality reduction is usually performed by finding a set of projections bases while low-dimensional feature extraction is performed by applying these learned bases onto a vector representation of the data. Kernel-based subspace learning methods mainly extend their linear counterparts using (conditionally) positive definite (pd) functions as kernels [1–4, 7–9]. A pd kernel is interpreted as an inner product in a Hilbert space [12]. Kernel-based subspace learning algorithms perform an implicit mapping of the input data into a high-dimensional Hilbert space (also referred to as feature space) and use the reproducing properties of pd kernels to express the projections as a linear combination of the data in the feature space. Dimensionality reduction is then performed by projecting the data in the feature space using the learned bases. All computations are efficiently performed via the inner product of the feature space (the so-called kernel trick).

Notable kernel-based methods include the Kernel Principal Component Analysis (KPCA) [1] and Kernel Fisher Discriminant Analysis (KDA) [2, 7–9]. KDA finds a set of projection bases by maximizing the trace of between-class scatter matrix while minimizing the trace within-class scatter matrix of low-dimensional space. The solution of the KDA optimization problem has resulted in a wealth of research works dealing with the problem of how the range and the useful null space of the within-class scatter matrix can be used for discovering projection bases. The most popular methods discard discriminative information, either in one space or the other [3, 7–9]. A complete framework which extracts features from both spaces was proposed in [2].

The above noted kernel subspace-learning techniques are applicable only in the case of pd kernels. This imposes limitations to their applicability, since many non-pd (npd) kernels arise as similarity measures. For example, in [13–15] the authors tried to incorporate invariance or robustness into the measure. Another family of useful npd kernels are the compact support (cs) kernels [16]. Popular non-Euclidean (nonmetric) similarities/dissimilarities, such as Hausdorff distances [17] and Kullback-Leibler divergence between probability distributions, can be used to define npd kernels [18, 19]. Hence, there is both practical and theoretical need to properly handle all these measures and npd kernels in order to extract discriminant features using an KDA framework with npd kernels. One way to deal with this is to approximate the npd kernel with a positive definite (pd) one and use this kernel instead [6].

The need to properly handle npd kernels, instead of approximating them with pd ones, has initiated a number of studies on the proper design of classification algorithms [20]. In particular in [21] a geometrical interpretation of learning a large margin classifier with indefinite kernels has been discussed. In [21] classification frameworks based on two-class Kernel Fisher Discriminant Analysis (KFDA) and in [18] Kernel Quadratic Discriminant (KQD) analysis with indefinite kernels were proposed. In this paper we study feature extraction with npd (or simple indefinite) kernels. We first formulate Indefinite Kernel Principal Component Analysis (IKPCA) in Krein spaces. A Krein space is a vector space $\mathcal{K}$

equipped with an indefinite inner product[1]. The npd kernel is interpreted as the indefinite inner product of the Krein space. Furthermore, we define optimization problems for extracting discriminant projections in Krein spaces. In particular, we formulate a Complete Indefinite Kernel Discriminant Analysis (CIKDA) in Krein spaces.

We would like to highlight that in [5, 18, 21] only classifiers based on quadratic discriminant functions and two class classifier based on IKFDA in Krein spaces were proposed. Our paper takes a different direction. That is, we propose subspace learning algorithms in Krein Spaces for feature extraction and object representation. To the best of our knowledge this is the first time that discriminant feature extraction is performed in Krein spaces. Summarizing the contributions of this paper are: (a) an Indefinite Kernel Principal Component Analysis in Krein Spaces[2] (b) a Complete Indefinite Kernel Fisher Discriminant Analysis (ICKFDA) in Krein spaces. We furthermore propose npd kernels that contrary to [18] achieve state-of-the-art performance in fully automatic face recognition.

2 Krein Spaces

Krein spaces are important as they provide feature-space representations of dissimilarities and provide us with insights on the geometry of classifiers defined with non-positive kernels [18, 21].

An abstract space $\mathcal{K}$ is a Krein space over reals $\Re$ if there exists an (indefinite) inner product $\langle .,. \rangle_{\mathcal{K}} : \mathcal{K} \times \mathcal{K} \rightarrow \Re$ with the following properties [22]:

$$\begin{aligned} \langle \mathbf{x}, \mathbf{y} \rangle_{\mathcal{K}} &= \langle \mathbf{y}, \mathbf{x} \rangle_{\mathcal{K}} \\ \langle c_1\mathbf{x} + c_2\mathbf{z}, \mathbf{y} \rangle_{\mathcal{K}} &= c_1 \langle \mathbf{x}, \mathbf{y} \rangle_{\mathcal{K}} + c_2 \langle \mathbf{z}, \mathbf{y} \rangle_{\mathcal{K}} \end{aligned} \tag{1}$$

for all $\mathbf{x}, \mathbf{y}, \mathbf{z} \in \mathcal{K}$ and $c_1, c_2 \in \Re$. $\mathcal{K}$ is composed of two vector spaces, such that $\mathcal{K} = \mathcal{K}_+ \oplus \mathcal{K}_-$. $\mathcal{K}_+$ and $\mathcal{K}_-$ describe two Hilbert spaces over $\Re$. We denote their corresponding positive definite inner products as $\langle .,. \rangle_{\mathcal{K}_+}$ and $\langle .,. \rangle_{\mathcal{K}_-}$, respectively. The decomposition of $\mathcal{K}$ into two such subspaces defines two orthogonal projections: $\mathbf{P}_+$ onto $\mathcal{K}_+$ and $\mathbf{P}_-$ onto $\mathcal{K}_-$, known as fundamental projections of $\mathcal{K}$. Using these projections, $\mathbf{x} \in \mathcal{K}$ can be represented as $\mathbf{x} = \mathbf{P}_+\mathbf{x} + \mathbf{P}_-\mathbf{x}$. The identity matrix in $\mathcal{K}$ is given by $\mathbf{I}_{\mathcal{K}} = \mathbf{P}_+ + \mathbf{P}_-$.

Let us denote by $\mathbf{x}_+ \in \mathcal{K}_+$ and $\mathbf{x}_- \in \mathcal{K}_-$, the projections onto the subspaces $\mathbf{P}_+\mathbf{x}$ and $\mathbf{P}_-\mathbf{x}$, respectively. Then, $\langle \mathbf{x}_+, \mathbf{y}_- \rangle_{\mathcal{K}} = 0$ for all $\mathbf{x}, \mathbf{y} \in \mathcal{K}$. Moreover, $\langle \mathbf{x}_+, \mathbf{y}_+ \rangle_{\mathcal{K}} > 0$ and $\langle \mathbf{x}_-, \mathbf{y}_- \rangle_{\mathcal{K}} < 0$ for any non-zero vectors $\mathbf{x}$ and $\mathbf{y}$ in $\mathcal{K}$. Therefore, $\mathcal{K}_+$ is a positive subspace, while $\mathcal{K}_-$ is a negative subspace. The inner product of $\mathcal{K}$ is defined as the difference of $\langle .,. \rangle_{\mathcal{K}_+}$ and $\langle .,. \rangle_{\mathcal{K}_-}$, *i.e.* for all $\mathbf{x}, \mathbf{y} \in \mathcal{K}$:

$$\langle \mathbf{x}, \mathbf{y} \rangle_{\mathcal{K}} = \langle \mathbf{x}_+, \mathbf{y}_+ \rangle_{\mathcal{K}_+} - \langle \mathbf{x}_-, \mathbf{y}_- \rangle_{\mathcal{K}_-} \tag{2}$$

[1] For more information regarding Krein spaces the interested reader can refer to [22].

[2] Although, methods similar to the proposed IKPCA were implied in previous works [18, 19] and in Chapter 6 of the PhD thesis [35] a complete formulation of IKPCA in Krein spaces has not been proposed before.

A Krein space $\mathcal{K}$ has an associated Hilbert space $|\mathcal{K}|$ which can be found *via* the linear operator $\mathbf{J} = \mathbf{P}_+ - \mathbf{P}_-$, called the fundamental symmetry. This symmetry satisfies $\mathbf{J} = \mathbf{J}^{-1} = \mathbf{J}^T$ and describes the basic properties of a Krein space. Its connection to the original Krein space can be written in terms of a "conjugate" by using (2) and $\mathbf{J}$, as

$$\mathbf{x}^*\mathbf{y} \triangleq \langle \mathbf{x}, \mathbf{y} \rangle_{\mathcal{K}} = \mathbf{x}^T\mathbf{J}\mathbf{y} = \langle \mathbf{J}\mathbf{x}, \mathbf{y} \rangle_{|\mathcal{K}|}. \tag{3}$$

That is, $\mathcal{K}$ can be turned into its associated Hilbert space $|\mathcal{K}|$ by using the positive definite inner product of the associated Hilbert space,$\langle .,. \rangle_{|\mathcal{K}|}$, as $\langle \mathbf{x}, \mathbf{y} \rangle_{|\mathcal{K}|} = \langle \mathbf{x}, \mathbf{J}\mathbf{y} \rangle_{\mathcal{K}}$.

In the following we are particularly interested in finite dimensional Krein spaces where $\mathcal{K}_+$ is isomorphic to $\Re^p$ and $\mathcal{K}_-$ is isomorphic to $\Re^q$. Such a Krein space describes a pseudo-Euclidean space and is characterized by its so-called signature, $(p, q) \in \mathbb{N}^2$, which indicates the dimensionality, p and q, of the positive and negative subspaces, respectively [18]. The fundamental symmetry is

$$\mathbf{J} = \begin{bmatrix} \mathbf{I}_p & \mathbf{0} \\ \mathbf{0} & -\mathbf{I}_q \end{bmatrix} \tag{4}$$

where $\mathbf{I}_z$ is the identity matrix in $\Re^{z \times z}$ and $\mathbf{0}$ implies zero padding.

A non-positive definite (npd) kernel k defines an implicit mapping $\psi : \Re^d \to \mathcal{K}$ into a (in)finite dimensional Krein space. Analogously to Hilbert space, our kernel is equivalent to the dot-product in feature space, *i.e.* $k(\mathbf{x}_i, \mathbf{x}_j) = \langle \psi(\mathbf{x}_i), \psi(\mathbf{x}_j) \rangle_{\mathcal{K}}$. The squared distance in feature space is given by

$$\begin{aligned} l^2(\mathbf{x}_i, \mathbf{x}_j) &= (\psi(\mathbf{x}_i) - \psi(\mathbf{x}_j))^*(\psi(\mathbf{x}_i) - \psi(\mathbf{x}_j)) \\ &= k(\mathbf{x}_i, \mathbf{x}_i) - 2k(\mathbf{x}_i, \mathbf{x}_j) + k(\mathbf{x}_j, \mathbf{x}_j). \end{aligned} \tag{5}$$

Also a non-negative dissimilarity measure $l^2(\mathbf{x}_i, \mathbf{x}_j)$ that satisfies the following properties (1) $l^2(\mathbf{x}_i, \mathbf{x}_i) = 0$, (2) $l^2(\mathbf{x}_i, \mathbf{x}_j) > 0$, $\forall\, \mathbf{x}_i \neq \mathbf{x}_j$ and (3) $l^2(\mathbf{x}_i, \mathbf{x}_j) = l^2(\mathbf{x}_j, \mathbf{x}_i)$ and does not satisfy the triangular inequality can define an npf kernel.

3 KPCA in Krein Spaces

Let $\mathbf{X} = [\mathbf{x}_1 \cdots \mathbf{x}_N] \in \Re^{d \times N}$ be a set of given samples and $\mathbf{X}_\psi = [\psi(\mathbf{x}_1) \cdots \psi(\mathbf{x}_N)]$ be their implicit mapping. Motivated by KPCA and pseudo-Euclidean embedding [18, 23], we formulate KPCA with Krein spaces.

Let us define the mean $\mathbf{m}^{\mathcal{K}}$, and the centralized matrix $\tilde{\mathbf{X}}_\psi$ as

$$\mathbf{m}^{\mathcal{K}} = \tfrac{1}{N}\mathbf{X}_\psi \mathbf{1}_N \quad \tilde{\mathbf{X}}_\psi = \mathbf{X}_\psi \mathbf{L} \tag{6}$$

where $\mathbf{L} \triangleq \mathbf{I}_N - \frac{1}{N}\mathbf{1}_N\mathbf{1}_N^T$ and $\mathbf{1}_N$ is an N-dimensional vector containing only ones [18]. We then define the total scatter matrix in $\mathcal{K}$ as

$$\mathbf{S}_t^{\mathcal{K}} \triangleq \tfrac{1}{N}\textstyle\sum_{i=1}^N (\psi(\mathbf{x}_i) - \mathbf{m}^{\mathcal{K}})(\psi(\mathbf{x}_i) - \mathbf{m}^{\mathcal{K}})^* = \tfrac{1}{N}\tilde{\mathbf{X}}_\psi\tilde{\mathbf{X}}_\psi^* = \tfrac{1}{N}\tilde{\mathbf{X}}_\psi\tilde{\mathbf{X}}_\psi^T\mathbf{J} = \mathbf{S}_{|\mathcal{K}|}\mathbf{J} \tag{7}$$

where $\mathbf{S}_{|\mathcal{K}|}$ is the total scatter matrix in the associated Hilbert space $|\mathcal{K}|$.

In a similar way to that of KPCA in Hilbert space, we generalize KPCA in Krein space as follows. We wish to compute a set of projections $\mathbf{U}_o = [\mathbf{u}_1 \cdots, \mathbf{u}_N]$ with $\mathbf{u}_i \in \mathcal{K}$ such that[3]

$$\mathbf{U}_o = \arg\max_{\mathbf{U}} \mathrm{tr}\left(\mathbf{U}^*\mathbf{S}_t^{\mathcal{K}}\mathbf{U}\right) \text{ s.t.} \mathbf{U}^*\mathbf{U} = \mathbf{J}. \tag{8}$$

We write the set of projections as a linear combination of samples as $\mathbf{U} = \tilde{\mathbf{X}}_\psi \mathbf{Q}$, and (8) becomes:

$$\begin{aligned}\mathbf{Q}_o &= \arg\max_{\mathbf{Q}} \mathrm{tr}\left(\mathbf{Q}^T\tilde{\mathbf{X}}_\psi^T\mathbf{J}\tilde{\mathbf{X}}_\psi\tilde{\mathbf{X}}_\psi^T\mathbf{J}\tilde{\mathbf{X}}_\psi\mathbf{Q}\right) \\ &= \arg\max_{\mathbf{Q}} \mathrm{tr}\left(\mathbf{Q}^T\tilde{\mathbf{K}}\tilde{\mathbf{K}}\mathbf{Q}\right)\end{aligned} \quad \text{s.t. } \mathbf{Q}^T\tilde{\mathbf{X}}_\psi^T\mathbf{J}\tilde{\mathbf{X}}_\psi\mathbf{Q} = \mathbf{Q}^T\mathbf{K}\mathbf{Q} = \mathbf{J} \tag{9}$$

where $\tilde{\mathbf{K}} = \tilde{\mathbf{X}}_\psi^*\tilde{\mathbf{X}}_\psi$ is the centralized kernel matrix. The eigendecomposition of $\tilde{\mathbf{K}}$ then yields the solution of the above

$$\tilde{\mathbf{K}} = \mathbf{V}\mathbf{\Lambda}\mathbf{V}^T = \mathbf{V}|\mathbf{\Lambda}|^{\frac{1}{2}}\mathbf{J}|\mathbf{\Lambda}|^{\frac{1}{2}}\mathbf{V}^T \tag{10}$$

where $\mathbf{\Lambda}$ is a diagonal matrix whose main diagonal consists of p positive and q negative eigenvalues ($p+q \leq N$) in the following order: first, positive eigenvalues with decreasing values, then negative ones with decreasing absolute values and finally zero values. Matrix $|\mathbf{\Lambda}|$ is the diagonal matrix containing the absolute values of the eigenvalues. The fundamental symmetry, matrix $\mathbf{J}$, is defined as in (4), and (p, q) is the pseudo-Euclidian space's signature. Consequently, we obtain the optimal solution of (9) from $\mathbf{Q}_o = \mathbf{V}_{p+q}|\mathbf{\Lambda}_{p+q}|^{-\frac{1}{2}}$ and the optimal projection matrix from $\mathbf{U}_o = \tilde{\mathbf{X}}_\psi\mathbf{V}_{p+q}|\mathbf{\Lambda}_{p+q}|^{-\frac{1}{2}}$, where $\mathbf{\Lambda}_{p+q}$ contains the non-zero eigenvalues and $\mathbf{V}_{p+q}$ denotes the corresponding eigenvectors.

Let $\mathbf{y} \in \mathbb{C}^d$ be a new sample, and $\acute{\mathbf{y}} = \psi(\mathbf{y}) \in \mathcal{K}$ denotes its mapping. Then, the part of $\acute{\mathbf{y}}$ which belongs to the positive subspace $\Re^p$ is given by:

$$\begin{aligned}\acute{\mathbf{y}}_+ &= |\mathbf{\Lambda}_p|^{-\frac{1}{2}}\mathbf{V}_p^T\mathbf{M}^T\mathbf{X}_\psi^*\psi(\mathbf{y}) \\ &= |\mathbf{\Lambda}_p|^{-\frac{1}{2}}\mathbf{V}_p^T\mathbf{M}^T\begin{bmatrix}\langle\psi(\mathbf{x}_1),\psi(\mathbf{y})\rangle_{\mathcal{K}} \\ \cdots \\ \langle\psi(\mathbf{x}_N),\psi(\mathbf{y})\rangle_{\mathcal{K}}\end{bmatrix} = |\mathbf{\Lambda}_p|^{-\frac{1}{2}}\mathbf{V}_p^T\mathbf{M}^T\begin{bmatrix}k(\mathbf{x}_1,\mathbf{y}) \\ \cdots \\ k(\mathbf{x}_N,\mathbf{y})\end{bmatrix}\end{aligned} \tag{11}$$

where $\mathbf{\Lambda_p}$ contains only the positive eigenvalues, and $\mathbf{V}_p$ denotes the corresponding eigenvectors. Similarly, we can compute the features $\acute{\mathbf{y}}_- \in \Re^q$ using

$$\acute{\mathbf{y}}_- = |\mathbf{\Lambda}_q|^{-\frac{1}{2}}\mathbf{V}_q^T\mathbf{M}^T\mathbf{X}_\psi^*\psi(\mathbf{y}) \tag{12}$$

where $\mathbf{\Lambda}_q$ and $\mathbf{V}_q$ corresponds to the negative eigenvalues. Furthermore, we can verify that the inner product of $\acute{\mathbf{x}}, \acute{\mathbf{y}} \in \mathcal{K}$ is equal to the kernel value as follows

$$\begin{aligned}\langle\acute{\mathbf{x}},\acute{\mathbf{y}}\rangle_{\mathcal{K}} &= \acute{\mathbf{x}}^*\acute{\mathbf{y}} = \acute{\mathbf{x}}^T\mathbf{J}\acute{\mathbf{y}} = \psi(\mathbf{x})^*\tilde{\mathbf{X}}_\psi\mathbf{V}|\mathbf{\Lambda}|^{-\frac{1}{2}}\mathbf{J}|\mathbf{\Lambda}|^{-\frac{1}{2}}\mathbf{V}^T\tilde{\mathbf{X}}_\psi^*\psi(\mathbf{y}) \\ &= \psi(\mathbf{x})^T\mathbf{J}\mathbf{U}^*\mathbf{U}\mathbf{J}\psi(\mathbf{y}) = \psi(\mathbf{x})^T\mathbf{J}\psi(\mathbf{y}) = \langle\psi(\mathbf{x}),\psi(\mathbf{y})\rangle_{\mathcal{K}} = k(\mathbf{x},\mathbf{y}).\end{aligned} \tag{13}$$

[3] Although pseudo-euclidean embedding has been proposed [19] the actual formulation of KPCA in Krein Spaces has not been previously proposed.

In order to establish a dimensionality reduction strategy, we can start by expanding the objective function of the optimization problem (8) as

$$\begin{aligned}\operatorname{tr}(\mathbf{U}^*\mathbf{S}_{\mathcal{K}}\mathbf{U}) &= \operatorname{tr}\left(\mathbf{Q}^T\tilde{\mathbf{K}}\tilde{\mathbf{K}}\mathbf{Q}\right) = \operatorname{tr}\left(|\mathbf{\Lambda}|^{-\frac{1}{2}}\mathbf{V}^T\mathbf{V}\mathbf{\Lambda}\mathbf{V}^T\mathbf{V}\mathbf{\Lambda}\mathbf{V}^T\mathbf{V}|\mathbf{\Lambda}|^{-\frac{1}{2}}\right)\\ &= \operatorname{tr}(|\mathbf{\Lambda}|) = \textstyle\sum_{i=1}^{N}|\lambda_i|.\end{aligned} \tag{14}$$

As it can be observed, the actual functional to be minimized is based on the absolute eigenvalues, $|\lambda_i|$. Hence, the dimensionality reduction may be performed by removing the eigenvectors that correspond to the smallest in terms of magnitude eigenvalues. The signature of the reduced Krein space is then given by (p_1, q_1) with $p_1 \leq p$ and $q_1 \leq q$.

4 Discriminant Learning in Krein Spaces

Kernel Discriminant Analysis (KDA) in Hilbert spaces with positive definite (pd) kernels aims at finding discriminant projection bases by exploiting class-label information in the feature space. In the following we will formulate discriminant subspace learning algorithms by defining optimization problems based on the traces of the projected within and between class scatter matrices. We assume that our training set consists of C classes $\mathcal{C}_1, \cdots, \mathcal{C}_C$. N_c denotes the cardinality of set $\mathcal{C}_c$. We define the between-class, within-class and total scatter matrices $\mathbf{S}_b^{\mathcal{K}}$, $\mathbf{S}_w^{\mathcal{K}}$ and $\mathbf{S}_t^{\mathcal{K}}$ in $\mathcal{K}$ as

$$\mathbf{S}_b^{\mathcal{K}} \triangleq \sum_{c=1}^{C} N_c(\mathbf{m}_c^{\mathcal{K}} - \mathbf{m}^{\mathcal{K}})(\mathbf{m}_c^{\mathcal{K}} - \mathbf{m}^{\mathcal{K}})^* \tag{15}$$

$$\mathbf{S}_w^{\mathcal{K}} \triangleq \sum_{c=1}^{K} \sum_{\mathbf{x}_i \in \mathcal{C}_c} (\psi(\mathbf{x}_i) - \mathbf{m}_c^{\mathcal{K}})(\psi(\mathbf{x}_i) - \mathbf{m}_c^{\mathcal{K}})^* \tag{16}$$

where $\mathbf{m}_c^{\mathcal{K}} = \frac{1}{N_c}\sum_{\mathbf{x}_i \in \mathcal{C}_c} \psi(\mathbf{x}_i)$ is the mean vector of each class.

In Hilbert spaces with pd kernels the main optimization problem for finding the discriminant projection is

- the one that maximizes the trace of the projected between class scatter matrix subject to having a projected orthogonal within-class scatter matrix [2, 9, 24]
- maximizes the trace of the projected between class scatter matrix subject to the useful null-space of within-class scatter matrix [2, 3, 25].

Using the theory developed in the previous Section, we formulate the optimization problems that find the discriminant projections with npf kernels in Krein spaces. That is, we aim at finding a set of projections $\mathbf{U}_1 = [\mathbf{u}_1^1|\cdots|\mathbf{u}_p^1]$ with every column $\mathbf{u}_1^j \in \mathcal{K}$

$$\mathbf{U}_1 = \max_{\mathbf{U}} \ \operatorname{tr}\left[\mathbf{U}^*\mathbf{S}_b^{\mathcal{K}}\mathbf{U}\right] \ \text{s.t}\ \mathbf{U}^*\mathbf{S}_w^{\mathcal{K}}\mathbf{U} = \mathbf{I}, \tag{17}$$

and $\mathbf{U}_2 = [\mathbf{u}_1^2|\cdots|\mathbf{u}_p^2]$ with every column $\mathbf{u}_j^1 \in \mathcal{K}$

$$\mathbf{U}_2 = \max_{\mathbf{U}} \ \mathrm{tr}\left[\mathbf{U}^*\mathbf{S}_b^{\mathcal{K}}\mathbf{U}\right] \ \text{s.t } \mathbf{U}^*\mathbf{S}_w^{\mathcal{K}}\mathbf{U} = \mathbf{0}. \tag{18}$$

The equivalent optimization problem (17) in Hilbert spaces was solved in [2, 9, 24], while approaches to solve optimization problem (18) were proposed in [2, 3, 25]. The Complete Kernel Fisher Discriminant (CKF) framework [2] solves the equivalent optimization problems (17) and (18) simultaneously by projecting the within-class scatter matrix onto the non-null space of total scatter matrix. The CKFD framework is not applicable in our case, since the developed theoretical framework in [2] can be only applied for the case of pd kernels. To alleviate this problem, in the following section, we propose the Complete Fisher Discriminant with Indefinite Kernels (CFDIK) in Krein spaces. To the best of our knowledge this is the first time discriminant subspace algorithms are proposed in Krein spaces with npd kernels.

5 Solving the Optimization Problems

In the following we will show how optimization problems (17) and (18) can be solved. Let us first define the block $\mathbf{M}_c \triangleq \frac{1}{N_c}\mathbf{1}_{N_c}\mathbf{1}_{N_c}^T$ and the block diagonal matrix $\mathbf{M}$ as:

$$\mathbf{M} \triangleq \mathrm{diag}[\mathbf{M}_1, \mathbf{M}_2, \ldots, \mathbf{M}_C]. \tag{19}$$

The useful properties of $\mathbf{M}$ are: (1) $\mathbf{M}$ is idempotent, i.e. $\mathbf{M}^n = \mathbf{M}$ with $n \neq 0$, (2) $\mathbf{I} - \mathbf{M}$ is idempotent, (3) $\mathbf{M}$ has C eigenvectors corresponding to C non-zero eigenvalues, (4) $\mathbf{I} - \mathbf{M}$ has $N - C$ eigenvectors corresponding to $N - C$ non-zero eigenvalues (5) for a full ranked symmetric matrix $\mathbf{A} \in \Re^{N\times N}$ matrices $\mathbf{AMA}$ and $\mathbf{A}(\mathbf{I} - \mathbf{M})\mathbf{A}$[4] have C and $N - C$ N eigenvectors corresponding to C and $N - C$ non-zero (positive) eigenvalues, respectively.

Using $\mathbf{M}$ and the fact that $\mathbf{S}_w^{\mathcal{K}} = \mathbf{S}_t^{\mathcal{K}} - \mathbf{S}_b^{\mathcal{K}}$, $\mathbf{S}_w^{\mathcal{K}}$ we write

$$\mathbf{S}_b^{\mathcal{K}} = \tilde{\mathbf{X}}_\psi \mathbf{M} \tilde{\mathbf{X}}_\psi^*, \ \mathbf{S}_w^{\mathcal{K}} = \tilde{\mathbf{X}}_\psi (\mathbf{I} - \mathbf{M}) \tilde{\mathbf{X}}_\psi^* \tag{20}$$

5.1 Solving the Optimization Problem (17)

In this section, we present how to diagonalize the within-class scatter matrix $\mathbf{S}_w^{\mathcal{K}}$ in the Krein feature space. Before proceeding we need the following Theorem I.

Theorem I: Define matrices $\mathbf{A}$ and $\mathbf{B}$ such that $\mathbf{A} = \mathbf{\Phi}\mathbf{\Phi}^*$ and $\mathbf{B} = \mathbf{\Phi}^*\mathbf{\Phi}$. Let $\mathbf{U}_B$ be the eigenvectors corresponding to the non-zero eigenvalues $\mathbf{\Lambda}_B$ of $\mathbf{B}$. Then, $\mathbf{U}_A = \mathbf{\Phi}\mathbf{U}_B|\mathbf{\Lambda}_B|^{-1}$ diagonalizes $\mathbf{\Phi}\mathbf{\Phi}^*$,

The proof is omitted due to lack of space.

Using the fact that $\mathbf{I} - \mathbf{M}$ is idempotent, $\mathbf{S}_w^{\mathcal{H}}$ can be written as

$$\mathbf{S}_w^{\mathcal{K}} = \tilde{\mathbf{X}}_\psi (\mathbf{I} - \mathbf{M})(\tilde{\mathbf{X}}_\psi)^* = \left(\tilde{\mathbf{X}}_\psi (\mathbf{I} - \mathbf{M})\right)\left(\tilde{\mathbf{X}}_\psi (\mathbf{I} - \mathbf{M})\right)^*. \tag{21}$$

[4] $\forall$ symmetric real matrices $\mathbf{A}$ matrices $\mathbf{AMA} = (\mathbf{MA})^T\mathbf{MA}$ and $\mathbf{A}(\mathbf{I} - \mathbf{M})\mathbf{A} = ((\mathbf{I} - \mathbf{M})\mathbf{A})^T(\mathbf{I} - \mathbf{M})\mathbf{A}$ are positive semi definite by construction.

By Theorem I, in order to diagonalize $\mathbf{S}_w^{\mathcal{K}}$ we need to apply eigen-analysis to $\mathbf{K}_w$

$$\mathbf{K}_w = \left(\tilde{\mathbf{X}}_\psi(\mathbf{I}-\mathbf{M})\right)^* \left(\tilde{\mathbf{X}}_\psi(\mathbf{I}-\mathbf{M})\right) = (\mathbf{I}-\mathbf{M})\tilde{\mathbf{K}}(\mathbf{I}-\mathbf{M}). \tag{22}$$

Since, $\tilde{\mathbf{K}}$ is npd so is $\mathbf{K}_w$ hence it admits an eigendecomposition as

$$\mathbf{K}_w = \mathbf{Q}_w|\mathbf{\Lambda}_w|^{\frac{1}{2}}\mathbf{J}|\mathbf{\Lambda}_w|^{\frac{1}{2}}\mathbf{Q}_n^T. \tag{23}$$

Now we seek an optimal solution that can be written as a linear combination of matrix $\tilde{\mathbf{X}}_\psi(\mathbf{I}-\mathbf{M})\mathbf{Q}_w|\mathbf{\Lambda}_w|^{-1}$ which diagonalizes $\mathbf{S}_w^{\mathcal{K}}$, i.e.

$$\mathbf{U} = \tilde{\mathbf{X}}_\psi(\mathbf{I}-\mathbf{M})\mathbf{Q}_w|\mathbf{\Lambda}_w|^{-1}\mathbf{A}. \tag{24}$$

where $\mathbf{A} \in \Re^{(N-C)\times C}$. Using $\mathbf{U}$ the objective matrix $\mathbf{U}^*\mathbf{S}_b^{\mathcal{K}}\mathbf{U}$ is reformulated as

$$\begin{aligned}\mathbf{U}^*\mathbf{S}_b^{\mathcal{K}}\mathbf{U} &= \mathbf{A}^T|\mathbf{\Lambda}_w|^{-1}\mathbf{Q}_w^T(\mathbf{I}-\mathbf{M})\tilde{\mathbf{X}}_\psi^*\tilde{\mathbf{X}}_\psi\mathbf{M}\tilde{\mathbf{X}}_\psi^*\tilde{\mathbf{X}}_\psi(\mathbf{I}-\mathbf{M})\mathbf{Q}_w|\mathbf{\Lambda}_w|^{-1}\mathbf{A} \\ &= \mathbf{A}^T|\mathbf{\Lambda}_w|^{-1}\mathbf{Q}_w^T(\mathbf{I}-\mathbf{M})\tilde{\mathbf{K}}\mathbf{M}\tilde{\mathbf{K}}(\mathbf{I}-\mathbf{M})\mathbf{Q}_w|\mathbf{\Lambda}_w|^{-1}\mathbf{A} \\ &= \mathbf{A}^T\left(\mathbf{M}\tilde{\mathbf{K}}(\mathbf{I}-\mathbf{M})\mathbf{Q}_w|\mathbf{\Lambda}_w|^{-1}\right)^T\left(\mathbf{M}\tilde{\mathbf{K}}(\mathbf{I}-\mathbf{M})\mathbf{Q}_w|\mathbf{\Lambda}_w|^{-1}\right)\mathbf{A}\end{aligned} \tag{25}$$

$\mathbf{K}_b = |\mathbf{\Lambda}_w|^{-1}\mathbf{Q}_w^T(\mathbf{I}-\mathbf{M})\tilde{\mathbf{K}}\mathbf{M}\tilde{\mathbf{K}}(\mathbf{I}-\mathbf{M})\mathbf{Q}_w|\mathbf{\Lambda}_w|^{-1}$ is positive semi-definite by definition. Then, optimization problem (17) is reformulated as

$$\mathbf{A}_o = \max_{\mathbf{A}} \ \mathrm{tr}\left[\mathbf{A}^T\mathbf{K}_b\mathbf{A}\right] \ \text{s.t } \mathbf{A}^T\mathbf{A} = \mathbf{I}, \tag{26}$$

which is solved by the choosing $\mathbf{A}_o$ to contain as columns the $C-1$ eigenvectors of $\mathbf{K}_b$ that correspond to non-zero eigenvalues.

5.2 Solving Optimization Problem (18)

We cannot solve the optimization problem (18) by writing the solution $\mathbf{U}_l$ as a linear combination of $\tilde{\mathbf{X}}_\psi(\mathbf{I}-\mathbf{M})\mathbf{Q}_l$ where $\mathbf{Q}_l$ is the complementary subspace of $\mathbf{Q}_w$ (i.e., the eigenvectors of $(\mathbf{I}-\mathbf{M})\tilde{\mathbf{K}}(\mathbf{I}-\mathbf{M})$ that correspond to null eigenvalues). Such a solution should be written as $\mathbf{U}_l = \tilde{\mathbf{X}}_\psi(\mathbf{I}-\mathbf{M})\mathbf{Q}_l\mathbf{A}$. We have

$$\mathbf{U}_l^*\mathbf{U}_l = \mathbf{A}^T{\mathbf{Q}_l}^T(\mathbf{I}-\mathbf{M})(\tilde{\mathbf{X}}_\psi)^*\tilde{\mathbf{X}}_\psi(\mathbf{I}-\mathbf{M})\mathbf{Q}_l\mathbf{A} = \mathbf{0}, \tag{27}$$

which further gives $\mathbf{U}_l = \mathbf{0}$.

To find $\mathbf{U}_l$, we write $\mathbf{U}_l = \tilde{\mathbf{X}}_\psi\Xi_l\mathbf{A}$, $\Xi_l \in \Re^{N\times C}$, $\mathbf{A} \in \Re^{C\times(C-1)}$. Additionally, $\mathbf{U}_l$ satisfies

$$\mathbf{U}_l{}^*\mathbf{S}_w^{\mathcal{K}}\mathbf{U}_l = \mathbf{A}^T\Xi_l^T\tilde{\mathbf{K}}(\mathbf{I}-\mathbf{M})\tilde{\mathbf{K}}\Xi_l\mathbf{A} = \mathbf{0}. \tag{28}$$

From the properties of matrices $\mathbf{I}-\mathbf{M}$, $\tilde{\mathbf{K}}$, $(\tilde{\mathbf{K}}^T = \tilde{\mathbf{K}})$ has $N-C$ non-zero eigenvalues. The constraint (28) can be satisfied by choosing Ξ_l from performing eigenanalysis of $\tilde{\mathbf{K}}(\mathbf{I}-\mathbf{M})\tilde{\mathbf{K}}$ and keeping the C eigenvectors which correspond to the zero eigenvalues.

Using $\mathbf{U}_l$, $\mathbf{U}_l^* \mathbf{S}_b^{\mathcal{K}} \mathbf{U}_l$ is reformulated as

$$\begin{aligned}\mathbf{U}_l^* \mathbf{S}_b^{\mathcal{K}} \mathbf{U}_l &= \mathbf{A}^T \Xi_l^T \tilde{\mathbf{X}}_\psi^* \tilde{\mathbf{X}}_\psi \mathbf{M} \tilde{\mathbf{X}}_\psi^* \tilde{\mathbf{X}}_\psi \Xi_l \mathbf{A} = \mathbf{A}^T \Xi_l^T \tilde{\mathbf{K}} \mathbf{M} \tilde{\mathbf{K}} \Xi_l \mathbf{A} \\ &= \mathbf{A}^T \left(\mathbf{M}\tilde{\mathbf{K}}\Xi_l\right)^T \left(\mathbf{M}\tilde{\mathbf{K}}\Xi_l\right) \mathbf{A}\end{aligned} \tag{29}$$

$\mathbf{K}_{b,2} = \Xi_l^T \tilde{\mathbf{K}} \mathbf{M} \tilde{\mathbf{K}} \Xi_l$ is positive semi-definite by construction. Using the above equation optimization problem (18) is reformulated as

$$\mathbf{A}_o = \max_{\mathbf{A}} \ \mathrm{tr}\left[\mathbf{A}^T \mathbf{K}_{b,2} \mathbf{A}\right], \ \text{s.t} \ \ \mathbf{A}^T \mathbf{A} = \mathbf{I}, \tag{30}$$

which is solved by the eigenanalysis of $\mathbf{K}_b$ and keeping the $C-1$ eigenvectors that correspond to the $C-1$ non-zero eigenvalues. Finally we prove that the projections $\mathbf{U}_w$ and $\mathbf{U}_l$ derived from the optimization problems (17) and (18) are orthogonal ($\mathbf{U}_l^* \mathbf{U}_w = \mathbf{0}$) (the proof is omitted due to lack of space).

6 Comparison with the Methods in [18],[21],[26],[27]

The literature regarding learning with indefinite kernels mainly revolves around the design of classifiers [18, 21, 27]. In particular in [21] an geometrical interpretation of learning a large margin classifier with indefinite kernels has been given. The most closely related works are the classification frameworks proposed in [18] and [21] for two class problems.

In this problem we have two classes $\mathcal{C}_1$ and $\mathcal{C}_2$. We define matrices $\mathbf{S}_b^{\mathcal{K}}$ and $\mathbf{S}_w^{\mathcal{K}}$ as in (15) and in (16), respectively, for the two class problem. Then, the methods in [18, 21] find a vector $\mathbf{w} \in \mathcal{K}$ and a scalar b such that

$$\mathbf{w}_o = \arg\max_{\mathbf{w}} \frac{\mathbf{w}^* \mathbf{S}_b^{\mathcal{K}} \mathbf{w}}{\mathbf{w}^* \mathbf{S}_w^{\mathcal{K}} \mathbf{w}}. \tag{31}$$

In order to solve the above optimization problem $\mathbf{w}$ was written as a linear combination of the training samples as $\mathbf{w} = \sum_{i=1}^n \mathbf{a}_i \psi(\mathbf{x}_i) = \mathbf{X}_\psi \mathbf{a}$ then optimization problem (31) can be written as

$$\mathbf{a}_o = \arg\max_{\mathbf{a}} \frac{\mathbf{a}^T \mathbf{K}\mathbf{M}\mathbf{K}\mathbf{a}}{\mathbf{a}^T \mathbf{K}(\mathbf{I}-\mathbf{M})\mathbf{K}\mathbf{a}}, \tag{32}$$

since matrices $\mathbf{N} = \mathbf{KMK}$ and $\mathbf{C} = \mathbf{K}(\mathbf{I}-\mathbf{M})\mathbf{K}$ are positive semi-definite by construction, the solution is given by keeping the eigenvector that corresponds to the largest eigenvalues of $\mathbf{C}^{-1}\mathbf{N}$. The matrix $\mathbf{C}$ is not invertible since it contains only one eigenvector that corresponds to non-zero eigenvalues. In [18, 21] a standard heuristic approach was applied, i.e. $\mathbf{a}$ was found by performing eigenanalysis to $(\mathbf{C}+\beta\mathbf{I})^{-1}\mathbf{N}$ where β is a small positive constant arbitrarily chosen. Unfortunately, this is not the solution to the optimization problem (31). Since, for two-class data both optimization problems (31) and (17) we can readily find the optimal $\mathbf{w}$ that optimizes both (31) by applying the methodology proposed in Section 5.

7 Experimental Results

We tested the proposed IKPCA and CKFDA approaches in the face recognition problem. The first indefinite kernel we used is the CS kernel used in [16] (also widely referred to as a mollifier)

$$k(\mathbf{x}, \mathbf{y}) = \exp\left(\frac{1}{||\mathbf{x}-\mathbf{y}||^2-\gamma}\right) H(\alpha - ||\mathbf{x}-\mathbf{y}||^2) \tag{33}$$

where $H(r)$ is the usual heaviside function. The CS kernels are of great importance in robust statistics since they are less influenced by outliers. In our experiments we used as distance $||\mathbf{x}-\mathbf{y}||^2$ the weighted distance $||\mathbf{x}-\mathbf{y}||^2_{\mathbf{W}} = (\mathbf{x}-\mathbf{y})^T\mathbf{W}(\mathbf{x}-\mathbf{y})$ proposed in [28] where $\mathbf{W}$ is sum of the power spectrum of the filters used and $\mathbf{x}$ and $\mathbf{y}$ are the vectorized Fourier responses of the images. As filters we used a Gabor filter bank of 8 orientations and 5 scales.

The second class of indefinite kernels we used are defined as the minimum of the correlation surface of image registration algorithms [29]

$$k(I_i, I_j) = \min(\min \mathrm{cor}(I_i, I_j), \min \mathrm{cor}(I_j, I_i)) \tag{34}$$

where $\mathrm{cor}(I_i, I_j)$ is the correlation surface between two images I_i and I_j of the matching algorithm [29]. We chose this particular kernel in order to illustrate the applicability of the proposed feature extraction methods in fully automatic face recognition schemes.

All the reported results were acquired using $C-1$ features produced from the optimization problem (17) and $C-1$ features from the optimization problem (18). For the IKPCA algorithm the reported results were acquired using $N-1$ features produced by the algorithm presented in Section 3. The classifier used was a simple nearest neighbor classifier using as distance the normalized correlation or the projected features.

7.1 Face Recognition Experiments in Yale B Database

The extended Yale B database [30] contains 16128 images of 38 subjects under 9 poses and 64 illumination conditions. We used a subset that consists of 64 near frontal images for each subject. For training, we randomly selected a subset with 5, 10 and 20 images per subject. The training set was also further split into training and validation to find the optimal parameters of the kernels used (i.e., γ and α). For testing, we used the remaining images. Finally, we performed 20 different random realizations of the training/test sets.

For comparison reasons we used the the pd Gaussian RBF (GRBF) kernel using the same distances $||\mathbf{x}-\mathbf{y}||^2_{\mathbf{W}}$ as $k(\mathbf{x}, \mathbf{y}) = \exp\left(-\frac{1}{\sigma^2}||\mathbf{x}-\mathbf{y}||^2_{\mathbf{W}}\right)$. Using the GRBF kernel the IKPCA and the proposed CIKDFA framework collapse to the KPCA and CKFDA [2] frameworks, respectively. Table I summarizes the obtained results. As we can see the proposed IKPCA and CIKFDA with the proposed npd kernel outperforms all other algorithms.

Table 1. Average recognition rates and standard deviations on the Extended YALE B database

5—10—20	Proposed Kernel (33)			GRBF		
IKPCA	80.5(1.12)	93.5(0.89)	96.6(0.25)	78.8(1.02)	90.8(0.83)	93.4(0.75)
CIKFDA (17)	77.2(1.12)	93.1(0.82)	97.8 (0.25)	76.8(1.67)	90.4(1.01)	95.9(0.88)
CIKFDA (18)	74.6(1.8)	92.7(0.76)	97.1 (0.3)	75.4(1.63)	89.1(1.21)	95.0(0.73)

Face Recognition Experiments in a Subset of FERET. In order to simulate results acquired using a fully automatic system, we used directly the faces returned from a face detector (both training and testing)[5]. The kernel in (34) was used for matching the faces provided by the face detector. To the best of our knowledge there are very few works reporting results in such a difficult setting with the most recent one the work published in [31].

In this experiment, we attempted to combine the experimental setting suggested in [2, 4] with facial images obtained directly from the face detector. We did so in order to show the power of the proposed CIKFDA when more than one images are available for training. In particular, we randomly selected 600 facial images corresponding to 200 subjects, such that each subject has three images (taken form FA, FB, DupI and DupII). We randomly chose two out of three images for training and then used the third image for testing.

Table 2 summarizes the recognition rates. We also report recently proposed state-of-the-art methods for face recognition [33] in manually aligned facial images (aligned according to the eye coordinates), for comparison reasons. We also compared our method with LBPs using both manually aligned images and detector extracted images. We achieved a recognition rate of 95% which demonstrates that the proposed scheme can be efficiently combined with fully automatic methods for face detection and matching. We also significantly outperform (by 7%) state-of-the-art methods that used **manually** aligned data.

Table 2. Recognition rates in the subset of FERET. SRC represents the results acquired using the method in [33] with manual alignment. LBP-d represents the results of Local Binary Patterns using detector extracted images and LBP-m represents the results with images after manual alignment.

Methods	SRC [33]	LBP-d	LBP-m	IKPCA	CIKFDA (17)	CIKFDA (17)
RR	87	35	89	90	95	93.5

7.2 Face Recognition with the XM2VTS Database

We carried out face verification experiments on the test set of Configuration I of the XM2VTS database. The training set contained 200 subjects with three images per subject which enabled us to apply our kernel combined with the

[5] In particular we used the publicly available face detector implemented in OpenCV

proposed discriminant analysis. The evaluation set contained three images per client for genuine claims and 25 evaluation impostors with eight images per impostor. The testing set contained two images per client and 70 impostors with eight images per impostor. For additional details on the XM2VTS database and the protocol used, the interested reader may refer to [34].

A face detector was also used to provide the faces. The applied kernel combined with the proposed kernel discriminant analysis on the samples of the face detector achieved a TER (Total Error Rate)[6] equal to 1.92%. Table 3 summarizes the best results of each competition in fully automatic facial image registration scenarios, as well as, the performance of of some recent algorithms tested under automatic alignment by using the eye coordinates. Our method, which is applied directly on the results of the detector, achieved a TER which is the best reported for the XM2VTS database according to the best of our knowledge. The results reported with the SRC method in [33] were achieved using manually aligned data.

Table 3. Best Results in XM2VTS database under automatic image alignment

Methods	Best of [36]	Best of [37]	Best of [38]	[39]	SRC [33]	Proposed Approach
TER%	13.10	3.86	2.14	2.3	4	**1.92**

8 Conclusions

In this paper we presented a theoretical framework for discriminant feature extraction in Krein spaces. In particular we proposed a Complete Indefinite Kernel Fisher Discriminant Analysis (CIKFDA) which discovers discriminant projections both in the range and null spaces of the within-class-scatter matrix in the Krein space. We demonstrated the superiority of the proposed approach in fully automatic face recognition scenarios where state-of-the-art results were achieved using the output images acquired from a face detector.

References

1. Scholkopf, B., Smola, A., Müller, K.R.: Nonlinear component analysis as a kernel eigenvalue problem. Neural Computation 10, 1299–1319 (1998)
2. Yang, J., Frangi, A.F., Yang, J., Zhang, D., Jin, Z.: KPCA plus LDA: A complete kernel Fisher discriminant framework for feature extraction and recognition. IEEE Transactions on Pattern Analysis and Machine Intelligence 27, 230–244 (2005)
3. Cevikalp, H., Neamtu, M., Wilkes, M.: Discriminative common vector method with kernels. IEEE Transactions on Neural Networks 17 (2006)
4. Chengjun, L.: Capitalize on dimensionality increasing techniques for improving face recognition grand challenge performance. IEEE Transactions on Pattern Analysis and Machine Intelligence 28, 725–737 (2006)

[6] For more details regarding the TER refer to [34].

5. Ong, C.S., Mary, X., Canu, S., Smola, A.J.: Learning with non-positive kernels. In: ICML, pp. 81–88 (2004)
6. Chen, Y., Gupta, M.R., Recht, B.: Learning kernels from indefinite similarities. In: ICML, pp. 145–152 (2009)
7. Lu, J., Plataniotis, K.N., Venetsanopoulos, A.N.: Face recognition using kernel direct discriminant analysis algorithms. IEEE Transactions on Neural Networks 14, 117–126 (2003)
8. Yang, M.: Kernel eigenfaces vs. kernel fisherfaces: Face recognition using kernel methods. In: FG, pp. 215–220 (2002)
9. Baudat, G., Anouar, F.: Generalized discriminant analysis using a kernel approach. Neural Computation 12, 2385–2404 (2000)
10. Roweis, S., Saul, L.: Nonlinear dimensionality reduction by locally linear embedding. Science 290 (2000)
11. Tenenbaum, J.B., De Silva, V., Langford, J.C.: A global geometric framework for nonlinear dimensionality reduction. Science 290 (2000)
12. Scholkopf, B., Smola, A.: Learning with Kernels. MIT Press, Cambridge (2002)
13. Simard, P., LeCun, Y., Denker, J., Victorri, B.: Transformation invariance in pattern recognition: Tangent distance and propagation. IJIST 11, 181–197 (2000)
14. Haasdonk, B., Burkhardt, H.: Invariant kernel functions for pattern analysis and machine learning. Machine Learning 68, 35–61 (2007)
15. Jacobs, D., Weinshall, D., Gdalyahu, Y.: Class representation and image retrieval with non-metric distances. IEEE Transactions on Pattern Analysis and Machine Intelligence 22 (2000)
16. Jamshidi, A., Kirby, M.: Examples of compactly supported functions for radial basis approximations. In: ICML, pp. 155–160 (2006)
17. Dubuisson, M., Jain, A.: A modified hausdorff distance for object matching. In: ICPR, vol. 1, pp. 566–568 (1994)
18. Pekalska, E., Haasdonk, B.: Kernel discriminant analysis for positive definite and indefinite kernels. IEEE Transactions on Pattern Analysis and Machine Intelligence 31 (2009)
19. Pekalska, E., Paclik, P., Duin, R.P.W.: A generalized kernel approach to dissimilarity-based classification. Journal of Machine Learning Research 2, 175–211 (2002)
20. Woznica, A., Kalousis, A., Hilario, M.: Distances and (indefinite) kernels for sets of objects. In: ICDM, pp. 1151–1156 (2006)
21. Haasdonk, B., Pekalska, E.: Indefinite kernel fisher discriminant. In: ICPR (2008)
22. Hassibi, B., Sayed, A.H., Kailath, T.: Linear estimation in Krein spaces. I. Theory. IEEE Transactions on Automatic Control 41, 18–33 (1996)
23. Pekalska, E., Duin, R.: The dissimilarity representation for pattern recognition: foundations and applications. World Scientific Pub. Co. Inc. (2005)
24. Liu, C.: Capitalize on dimensionality increasing techniques for improving face recognition grand challenge performance. IEEE Transactions on Pattern Analysis and Machine Intelligence 28, 725–737 (2006)
25. Cevikalp, H., Neamtu, M., Wilkes, M., Barkana, A.: Discriminative common vectors for face recognition. IEEE Transactions on Pattern Analysis and Machine Intelligence 27, 4–13 (2005)
26. Haasdonk, B., Pekalska, E.: Indefinite kernel discriminant analysis. In: COMPSTAT (2010)
27. Haasdonk, B.: Feature space interpretation of SVMs with indefinite kernels. IEEE Transactions on Pattern Analysis and Machine Intelligence 27, 482–492 (2005)

28. Ashraf, A., Lucey, S., Chen, T.: Re-interpreting the application of gabor filters as a manipulation of the margin in linear support vector machines. IEEE Transactions on Pattern Analysis and Machine Intelligence, 1335–1341 (2010)
29. Tzimiropoulos, G., Argyriou, V., Zafeiriou, S., Stathaki, T.: Robust fft-based scale-invariant image registration with image gradients. IEEE Transactions on Pattern Analysis and Machine Intelligence 32, 1899–1906 (2010)
30. Lee, K., Ho, J., Kriegman, D.J.: Acquiring linear subspaces for face recognition under variable lighting. IEEE Transactions on Pattern Analysis and Machine Intelligence, 684–698 (2005)
31. Wagner, A., Wright, J., Ganesh, A., Zhou, Z., Ma, Y.: Toward a practical face recognition system: Robust alignment and illumination by sparse representation. IEEE Transactions on Pattern Analysis and Machine Intelligence 34, 372–386 (2012)
32. Phillips, P.J., Moon, H., Rizvi, S.A., Rauss, P.J.: The FERET evaluation methodology for face recognition algorithms. IEEE Transactions on Pattern Analysis and Machine Intelligence 22, 1090–1104 (2000)
33. Wright, J., Yang, A.Y., Ganesh, A., Sastry, S.S., Ma, Y.: Robust face recognition via sparse representation. IEEE Transactions on Pattern Analysis and Machine Intelligence, 210–227 (2009)
34. Messer, K., Matas, J., Kittler, J., Luettin, J., Maitre, G.: XM2VTSDB: The extended M2VTS database. In: AVBPA, pp. 72–77 (1999)
35. Ong, C.S.: Kernels: Regularization and Optimization. PhD thesis, The Australian National University (2005)
36. Matas, J., et al.: Comparison of face verification results on the XM2VTS database. In: ICPR, pp. 858–863 (2000)
37. Messer, K., et al.: Face Verification Competition on the XM2VTS Database. In: Kittler, J., Nixon, M.S. (eds.) AVBPA 2003. LNCS, vol. 2688, pp. 964–974. Springer, Heidelberg (2003)
38. Messer, K., Kittler, J., Short, J., Heusch, G., Cardinaux, F., Marcel, S., Rodriguez, Y., Shan, S., Su, Y., Gao, W., Chen, X.: Performance Characterisation of Face Recognition Algorithms and Their Sensitivity to Severe Illumination Changes. In: Zhang, D., Jain, A.K. (eds.) ICB 2005. LNCS, vol. 3832, pp. 1–11. Springer, Heidelberg (2005)
39. González-Jiménez, D., Alba-Castro, J.: Shape-driven Gabor jets for face description and authentication. IEEE Transactions on Information Forensics and Security 2, 769–780 (2007)

A Novel Material-Aware Feature Descriptor for Volumetric Image Registration in Diffusion Tensor Space

Shuai Li[1,*], Qinping Zhao[1], Shengfa Wang[3], Tingbo Hou[2], Aimin Hao[1], and Hong Qin[2]

[1] State Key Laboratory of Virtual Reality Technology and Systems, Beihang University, Beijing, China
[2] Stony Brook University, Stony Brook, New York, USA
[3] Dalian University of Technology, Dalian, China

Abstract. This paper advocates a novel material-aware feature descriptor for volumetric image registration. We rigorously formulate a novel probability density function (PDF) based distance metric to devise a compact local feature descriptor supporting invariance of full 3D orientation and isometric deformation. The central idea is to employ anisotropic heat diffusion to characterize the detected local volumetric features. It is achieved by the elegant unification of diffusion tensor (DT) space construction based on local Hessian eigen-system, multi-scale feature extraction based on DT-weighted dyadic wavelet transform, and local distance definition based on PDF formulated in DT space. The diffusion, intrinsic structure-aware nature makes our volumetric feature descriptor more robust to noise. With volumetric images registration as verifiable application, various experiments on different volumetric images demonstrate the superiority of our descriptor.

1 Introduction and Motivation

With the rapid advancement of various volumetric imaging modalities, we have been witnessing the urgent need for automatic feature detection and the discriminative feature description of complex volumetric dataset in image registration, object recognition, video event detection, image retrieval, etc. To achieve this, some recent works have tried to extend 2D SIFT-like methods to 3D versions, for example, Scovanner et al. [1] created a 3D SIFT descriptor for video action recognition, Flitton et al. [2] extended the SIFT approach to 3D rigid recognition, and other applications include rigid registration of medical images [3, 4] and panoramic medical image stitching [5, 6].

Despite the limited success, certain difficulties still prevail and need to be resolved. The challenges are prompted by the facts that volumetric images typically have much more spatial flexibility, and are frequently accompanied by

* This research is supported in part by National Natural Science Foundation of China (No.61190120, No.61190121 and No.61190125) and NSF grants IIS-0949467, IIS-1047715, and IIS-1049448.

A. Fitzgibbon et al. (Eds.): ECCV 2012, Part IV, LNCS 7575, pp. 502–515, 2012.

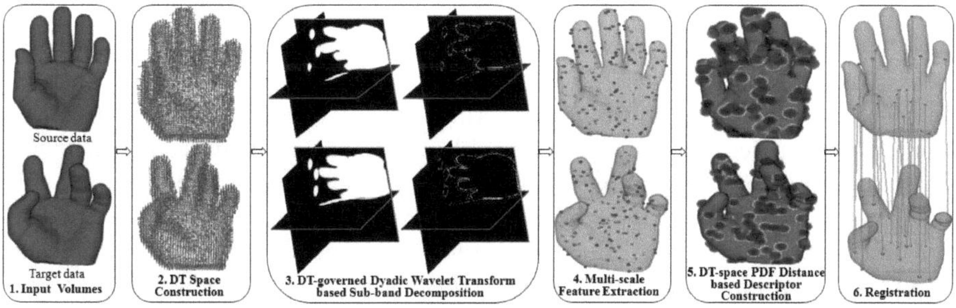

Fig. 1. The algorithmic pipeline of our method

non-rigid deformation with higher degrees of freedom. As for non-rigid registration, although some intensity/information entropy based methods can easily achieved this goal by integrating global energy optimization and deformable templates, however, a typical global approach tends not to consider local deformable feature-driven information and non-affine distortion. It remains hard for localized, feature-centric registration methods, since this requires the feature descriptor to be intrinsic, concise, informative, and discriminative. Simple statistics on local properties in intensity and gradient domain won't work, we should resort to the intrinsically physical laws underlying the embedded manifold space. Specially, the main challenges are documented as follows.

First, due to the complex topological degrees of freedom inside the volume dataset, multi-scale feature extraction based on Difference-of-Gaussian (DoG) convolution analysis frequently obtain a large number of less salient or false alarm candidates. Especially, ambiguities are unavoidable for the ones with low contrast or being poorly localized nearby an edge. More material-aware convolution kernels, which can respect the local geometry structure and its orientations, still need to be further explored for multi-scale feature extraction.

Second, most of the 3D descriptors simply imitated from 2D SIFT can only partially satisfy the rotational invariance. Although Allaire et al. [3] achieves the full rigid orientation invariance by taking 3-angle orientation (azimuth, elevation, and tilt) into account, the descriptor dimensionality is up to 16,384. From the application's viewpoint, this is less efficient and far from practical.

Third, analogous to the analysis for shape descriptor in [7], and besides the rigid transformation, the feature descriptor should take deformation into account as much as possible. However, this typically requires certain kind of mapping by parameterizing local volumetric structure with intrinsic metric over certain canonical domain, which may cause even more severe deformation effects. Thus, intrinsic metrics supporting deformation-invariant volumetric feature description are yet to be systematically explored.

To tackle the aforementioned challenges, we systematically articulate a novel material-aware feature descriptor for volumetric images. Towards the ambitious goal of isometric invariance, our observation is that, the diffusion process is intrinsically relevant to the diffusion distance metric design and the probability of random walk, which are informative for the description of local intrinsic structure. Meanwhile, naively using the popular isotropic diffusion process (e.g., Gaussian kernel) will naturally give rise to the smooth transition between nearby regions without respecting evident clues on edges and ridges. One feasible strategy to combat this problem is to replace Gaussian kernel with the structure-aware anisotropic DT-weighted kernel during convolution. Thus, we formulate a novel descriptor by combining random walk with probability density functions in DT space. Fig. 1 illustrates the pipeline of our approach, and highlights its application in automatic registration of volumetric features (undergoing quasi-isometric deformation). The salient contributions of this paper include:

- We formulate a local diffusion tensor based on Hessian eigen-system, which can fully grasp the second order differential properties, encode the directional curvatures of local structure, intrinsically reveal the material continuity, and control the diffusion in anisotropic way.
- We devise a data-specific kernel by integrating diffusion tensor with bilateral filter, which can be employed to conduct dyadic-wavelet based direction-aware decomposition for structure-respected multi-scale feature extraction.
- We design a random walk based feature descriptor, which depicts the local material property by measuring the difference among probability density functions defined in DT space. Inherited from heat diffusion, it is robust to noise, supports isometric deformation invariance, and can better reveal the underlying material distribution statistics.

2 Related Work

2.1 Feature Descriptor Design

Existing descriptors can be roughly divided in two classes according to their level of invariance. Rigid transformation has been accommodated rather easily in different descriptors, such as phase-based descriptor, spin images, gradient location and orientation histogram [3], automated learning based descriptor [8], and combined method of logarithmic sampling with Fourier analysis [9]. As for non-rigid deformation, to our best knowledge, only in the field of surface shape analysis, some deformation-invariant descriptors have been proposed in [10–12]. Of which, most advanced approaches are the ones based upon Laplacian spectrum analysis [13], however, the required global eigen-decomposition of such methods cannot be afforded by volumetric images. Thus, analogous intrinsic feature descriptors of volumetric images still need to be systematically explored in a local and efficient way.

2.2 Image Structure Analysis

Tensor space method has great superiority in structure-respected image analysis. The structure tensor, as a measurement for edges and their orientations, has been widely used in texture analysis. For Example, Malcolm et al. [14] generalized the tensor method to segment images by taking the Riemannian geometry of the tensor space into account. However, the structure tensor used in [14] only reflects the orientation information at a single scale and fails to discriminate textures which are varying across different scales. Most recently, the multi-scale structure tensor proposed in [15] has demonstrated successful applications in image fusion. Besides, Brox et al. [16] argued that if the local orientation is not homogeneous, the local neighborhood induced by the Gaussian filter will integrate ambiguous structure information. Thus, Bazán and Blomgren [17] proposed to perform image smoothing and edge detection by combining anisotropic diffusion and bilateral filtering. As an extension to this, Bazán et al. [18] also successfully used this technique to enhance the structure of electron tomography. Therefore, it is necessary to introduce certain tensor distance metric to govern multi-scale feature extraction.

2.3 Intrinsic Distance Metrics

Geodesic distance can measure the shortest path between two points over the curved surface, which has been widely used in graphics tasks. However, as noted in [19], the geodesic is not shape-aware, and sensitive to topological noise. Another popular metric is the diffusion distance, which has been widely employed in texture synthesis, gradient approximation, and shape matching [20]. In essence, the diffusion distance relates to diffusion time and a number of random walks in Brownian motion. The integration of diffusion distance along time [21], named commute-time distance, is also adopted on graphs. It measures the average time of the heat diffusion between two points, and relates to the Green's function of the Laplacian. As an improvement, Lipman et al. [19] proposed the bi-harmonic distance derived from the Green's function of the bi-harmonic operator. The bi-harmonic distance is locally isotropic, globally shape-aware, and isometry-invariant. However, it fails to handle local/partial shape analysis, because the Green's function is globally defined. For other distance metrics, please refer to the comprehensive survey [22]. Inspired by these, it is a robust way to devise intrinsic volumetric feature descriptor by measuring local material distribution with the help of diffusion-like distance metric.

3 Diffusion Tensor Space Construction

As already demonstrated in many previous works, the proper definition of tensor space over a scalar image will be a key to local material structure analysis and subsequent image processing. The rich differential geometry theory offers an elegant method to achieve this by treating an image as a differentiable manifold [23].

As the simplest tensor, structure tensor (Fig.2A) is derived from first-order differential analysis, which can locally characterize the predominant directions of material changes and how those directions are related to each other. However,

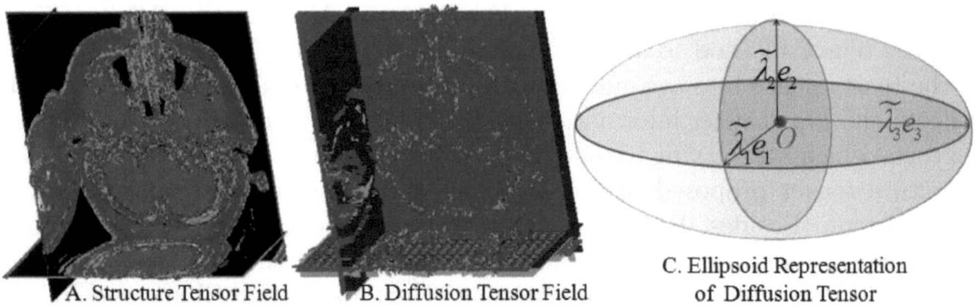

Fig. 2. Illustration of structure tensor, diffusion tensor and its physical meaning

first-order derivatives cannot fully grasp the local geometric differential property. Thus, we employ Hessian eigen-system to define the local diffusion tensor, which facilitates to the description of the second-order structure and intuitively depicts how the surface normal changes.

Hessian matrix **H** is a symmetric matrix consisting of second-order partial derivatives, and has real-valued eigenvalues (λ_1, λ_2, λ_3) and corresponding eigenvectors. The directions corresponding to the maximal eigenvalue of **H** should represent the most direct change from one material to adjacent neighboring material, while the direction corresponding to the minimal eigenvalue shows the material interface and how such material flows along the interface. To suppress the diffusion when cutting across sharp material boundaries, we formulate an anisotropic diffusion tensor by a spectral representation as:

$$\mathbf{D}(p) = \widetilde{\lambda}_1 \mathbf{e}_1 \mathbf{e}_1^T + \widetilde{\lambda}_2 \mathbf{e}_2 \mathbf{e}_2^T + \widetilde{\lambda}_3 \mathbf{e}_3 \mathbf{e}_3^T, \quad (1)$$

$$\widetilde{\lambda}_i = \exp\Big(- \frac{\lambda_i}{\sigma_d} \Big), i = 1, 2, 3, \quad (2)$$

with diffusion parameter σ_d that controls the diffusion velocities. As shown in Fig.2C, in fact we construct an ellipsoid that encodes the direction and velocity of diffusion. According to the theory of Rayleigh quotient, the diffusion velocity from voxel p along $\mathbf{e}$ can be viewed as the length of the vector projection onto the ellipsoid, which is expressed as

$$vel(p, \mathbf{e}) = \frac{\mathbf{e}^T \mathbf{D}(p) \mathbf{e}}{\mathbf{e}^T \mathbf{e}}. \quad (3)$$

Therefore, for a voxel inside a blob, all of its diffusion directions are principal diffusion directions. For a voxel on a boundary surface, all the directions aligning with its tangent plane are principal diffusion directions. For a voxel on a sharp edge, the direction along the edge is principal diffusion direction. For an isolated noise voxel, it will have no principal diffusion directions, as the velocities along all the directions are extremely small.

4 Multi-scale Feature Extraction

With the constructed anisotropic diffusion tensor field governing the diffusion direction and velocity, we extract multi-scale point features founded upon dyadic wavelet transform based decomposition, which comprises two steps: anisotropic wavelet kernel construction, multi-scale analysis and feature extraction.

4.1 Anisotropic Wavelet Kernel Construction

The visual perception research has indicated that the cells having directional selectivity are found in the retinas and visual cortices of the entire major vertebrate classes, thus naively using the anisotropic kernel will naturally give rise to directional information loss without having evident clues on material structure.

In order to respect the direction information embedded in the local structure during multi-scale analysis, our anisotropic wavelet kernel (AWK) is derived from the diffusion tensor and bilateral filter. AWK determines the convolution weights by considering both the directional continuity of material structures and the photometric similarity, which prefers nearby values to distant values in both spatial and material metric domain (DT space). Given two neighboring voxels located at p and q, we first define their diffusion tensor space distance as

$$d_D(p,q) = exp(-(p-q)^T(w_{pq}(\mathbf{D}(p)+\mathbf{D}(q))^{-1}(p-q)), \quad (4)$$

w_{pq} is introduced to amend the gradient, which changes in response to the intensity change of neighboring voxels. In fact, $\mathbf{D}(p)+\mathbf{D}(q)$ describes the diffusivity and controls the diffusion directions and velocities, and w_{pq} respects the intensity variance between neighboring voxels. Therefore, we can define the AWK as

$$\Psi(p) = \frac{1}{W_p}\sum_{q\in N(p)} G_{\sigma_s}(p-q)G_{\sigma_k}(d_D(p,q))I(q). \quad (5)$$

where W_p is a normalization factor, $G_\sigma(x) = \exp(-x^2/\sigma^2)$ is the Gaussian kernel function, and σ_k is a control parameter being set to the inverse of the maximal eigenvalues of diffusion matrices $\mathbf{D}(p)$ and $\mathbf{D}(q)$.

4.2 AWK Based Multi-scale Feature Extraction

With the built-in capability to faithfully respect material structure, and also inspired by the wavelet decomposition nature of DOG operation in the SIFT framework, we can use the proposed AWK to decompose a volumetric image into an approximation sub-band and a detail sub-band. However, only one-level decomposition is not enough to extract the feature information since images may be noisy and objects inherently comprise different details changing as a function of the observation scale. Thus, we adopt the dyadic wavelet transform to define the multi-scale form of AWK as

$$I^{n+1}(p,\sigma_s) = \frac{1}{W_p}\sum_{q\in N(q)} \omega^n(p-q,\sigma_s)G_{\sigma_k}(d^n_D(p,q))I^n(q), \quad (6)$$

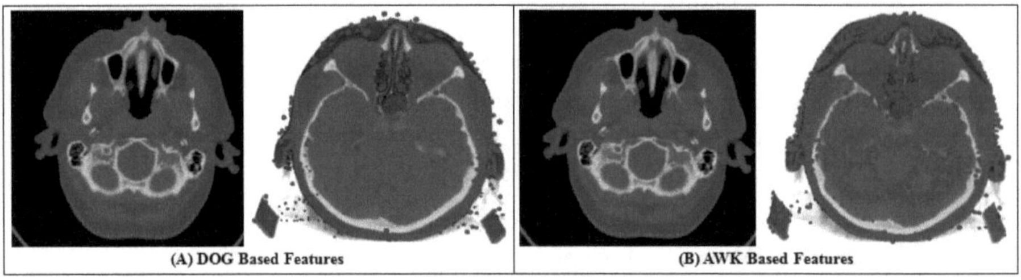

Fig. 3. Illustration of features respectively extracted by DOG and AWK operators

$$\omega^n(x, \sigma_s) = \begin{cases} G_{\sigma_s}(||\frac{x}{2^n}||) & \text{if } \frac{x}{2^n} \in Z^3 \text{ and } ||\frac{x}{2^n}|| < m \\ 0 & \text{otherwise} \end{cases} \tag{7}$$

n represents the n-th level of the decomposition, W_p has the same meaning as Eq. (5), m is a threshold to control the size of neighboring region.

In implementation, it is iterated over the approximate sub-bands according to Eq. (6) and only the one-ring neighbors of each voxel are considered in each iteration. After $k + 1$ iterations, the approximate sub-band corresponding to a certain scale can be obtained, and k detail sub-bands are respectively the difference between the neighboring approximate sub-bands as

$$I(p, k\sigma) = I^{k+1}(p, \sigma) - I^k(p, \sigma). \tag{8}$$

Since point features are usually defined as local extrema of some quantities related to geometry, texture, or other information, and our multi-scale sub-band decomposition is exactly an anisotropic approximation to the Laplacian, the multi-scale point features can be obtained by extracting local minima/maxima from the detail sub-bands across scales, where a voxel will be accepted as feature if and only if all of its 80 neighbors approve that it is the brightest/darkest one respectively. Fig. 3 shows the comparison of DOG based features and AWK based features. In Fig. 3 and the other experiment figures, larger point corresponds to larger scale feature. AWK operator proves to be more informative, since the resulted features intrinsically respect sharp structures and suppress the unstable features which are poorly localized near the low contrast regions.

5 Invariant Feature Descriptor Based on PDF Distances

5.1 DT-Space PDF Distance Metrics

Inside the diffusion tensor space, the behavior of anisotropic heat diffusion can be determined by its graph Laplacian. Consider volumetric image I as an undirected graph $G = (V, E)$, the anisotropic diffusion operator $\mathbf{T}$ can be defined as

$$\mathbf{T}(v_i, v_j) = \mathbf{S}(v_i) - \mathbf{L}(v_i, v_j), \tag{9}$$

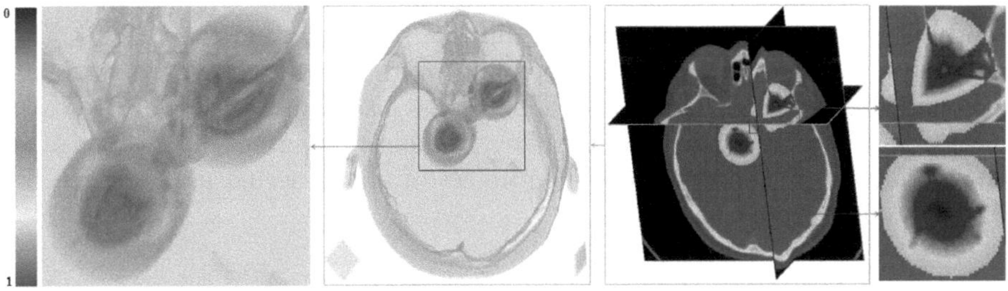

Fig. 4. Illustration of unnormalized PDFs for two feature points inside head volume

where $\mathbf{L}$ denotes the graph Laplacian operator over G, $\mathbf{L}(v_i, v_j)$ equals to $d_D(v_i, v_j)$ (Eq. (4)), and $\mathbf{S}(v_i) = \sum_{v_j \in N_i} \mathbf{L}(v_i, v_j)$. Since $\mathbf{L}$ is self-adjoint, the operator $\mathbf{T}$ is self-adjoint with all non-negative entries.

From the perspective of probability in Brownian motion, $\mathbf{T}$ is a random walk matrix with non-zero entries along the main diagonal, which allows one-step walk from a point to itself. Each entry $\mathbf{T}(v_i, v_j)$ stands for the probability of the Brownian motion moving from v_i to v_j in one step. Thus, the power $\mathbf{T}^n$ encodes the probability of a Brownian motion from one point to another in n steps, which naturally gives rise to the random walk based probability density functions (PDF) after approximation and normalization. We formulate the PDF $\mathbf{P}_{v_i}(v_j)$ of voxel v_i as

$$\mathbf{P}_{v_i}(v_j) = \frac{\mathbf{T}^n(v_i, v_j)}{\|\mathbf{T}^n(v_i, v_k)\|_2}, \tag{10}$$

where the denominator serves for the normalization purpose, thus $||\mathbf{P}_{v_i}(v_j)||_2 = 1$ and $\mathbf{P}_{v_i}(v_j) > 0$. The number of random walks n is a positive integer. For fast computation, we select n from the dyadic powers 2^j. It allows to compute the matrix power $\mathbf{T}^n$ through matrix multiplication in numerics. Since we are particularly interested in measuring the local geometry structure of volumetric image, the number of random walks n is empirically set to 2^4. Fig. 4 illustrates the unnormalized PDFs for two feature points (the central red point). It states that PDF can efficiently reflect the material continuity, for example, the voxels belonging to the same kind of material as that of feature point have high probability, which appear red.

Consider a family of PDFs $\{\mathbf{P}_v\}_{v \in V}$ in I, if $\forall v_x, v_y \in V$, $v_x \neq v_y$, and there $\exists v_z \in V$, satisfies $\mathbf{P}_{v_x}(v_z) \neq \mathbf{P}_{v_y}(v_z)$, then $\{\mathbf{P}_v\}_{v \in V}$ is called *generic*, which means that no two PDFs are completely the same in a generic family of PDFs. We use the *2-norm* distance between two PDFs in $\{\mathbf{P}_v\}_{v \in V}$ as PDF metrics (PDFM):

$$d_P(v_x, v_y) = \|\mathbf{P}_{v_x}(v_z) - \mathbf{P}_{v_y}(v_z)\|_2. \tag{11}$$

Eq. (11) can also use L_p ($p > 0$) norm. Since $\mathbf{P}$ is a vector, the range of $d_P(v_x, v_y)$ is $[0, 2^{1/p}]$. Thus it is $[0, \sqrt{2}]$ here.

In essence, PDFM describes the intrinsic material relationship, which has many attractive properties. First, inheriting from the anisotropic Laplacian operator, it is isometry-invariant. Second, it is locally supported, since the power series $\mathbf{T}^n$ span a scaling space in the diffusion wavelets, and the PDF $\mathbf{P}_{v_i}(v_j)$ is purely determined by a local sub-volume with v_i as a center, whose range is bounded by steps n. Third, according to the probability theory of Brownian motion and Markov chain, it is insensitive to noise, because small local changes do not have much influence to the entire set of all connected paths, hence the distribution of probabilities.

5.2 Feature Descriptor Design

PDFM is a metric naturally based on heat diffusion, and it is defined in DT space, so if the underlying material undergoes isometric deformation, the PDFM distribution in the vicinity of feature points is expected to have little or no change. We define our feature descriptor as a 2D shape context histograms comprising PDFM and the normalized image density (or gradient norm) of the volumetric image with the closest scale to that of each feature point.

We select a sub-volume centered around each feature point and compute the PDFM for all voxels in this sub-volume, and the radius is set to be the length of 8 voxels in our experiments. According to the value range of PDFM, we create 15 bins from 0 to $\sqrt{2}$ with step internal 0.1. For each bin, we take statistics of the normalized intensity (or gradient norm) of the voxels whose PDFM distance to the feature point is in current bin. Then, we create 17 intensity bins from 0 to 255 with step internal 15 or 10 gradient norm bins from 0 to 1 with step internal 0.1.

Compared with [3], which can only support rigid transformation/rotation invariance and whose descriptor dimensionality is up to 16,384, our feature descriptor is much more effective and compact (we at most need a 255-dimensional feature descriptor for each feature point).

6 Applications and Experimental Results

Our prototype system is implemented using C++, and some Matlab functions are invoked to perform sparse matrix multiplication. We conduct experiments on a laptop with Intel Core (TM) i7 CPU (1.6GHz, 4 cores) and 4G RAM. Table 1 documents the time performance (in seconds) and some other experimental statistics, including Hessian matrix computation, DT construction (DTC), subband decomposition (SD), feature extraction (FE), number of feature points, descriptor construction (DC) and registration.

First, in order to verify the full orientation invariance with ground truth, we create various rotated volumetric images from the original one. In the interest of visual clearness, only half of the registration lines are shown in Fig. 5 (The exact number of the matching pairs is documented at the bottom of each subfigure). During feature registration, the matching is determined by *Distance Ratio*, which is computed by comparing the distance of the closest candidate to that of second-closest candidate, we set the *Distance Ratio* to be 0.8. A match

Table 1. Time performance (in seconds) of our experiments

Dataset	Volume Size	Hessian	DTC	SD	FE	Feature #	DC	Registration
Fig.1	$128^2 \times 128$	40.9	95.3	12.7	224.6	357	220.7	14.6
Fig.5	$256^2 \times 73$	152.4	121.8	27.8	515.4	459	296.4	51.2
Fig.6	$256^2 \times 62$	150.1	105.8	24.9	567.7	559	469.3	83.2
Fig.7	$256^2 \times 64$	96.7	111.7	19.2	373.5	126	106.3	4.2
Fig.8	$128^2 \times 115$	38.9	65.5	12.1	279.4	570	480.9	88.7

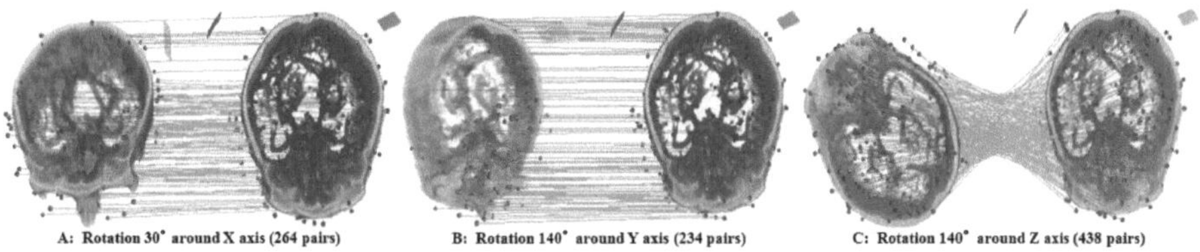

Fig. 5. Rigid registration with full 3D orientation of head volumetric images

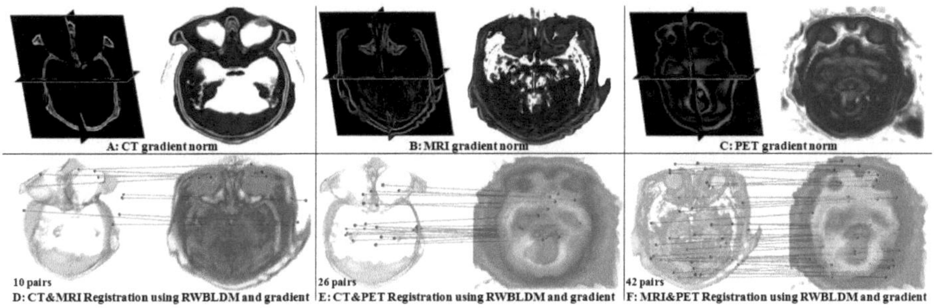

Fig. 6. Multi-modality registration of Monkey head volumetric images

is deemed true when the counterpart lies within 2 voxel diagonal length of the ground truth position, the results in Fig. 5 quantitatively prove that our method can well (average 98% accuracy) support full orientation invariance.

Second, to test the capacity of our method in multi-modality volumetric image registration, we use datasets downloaded from the Laboratory of Neuro Imaging of UCLA, which have already been registered, thus offering the ground truth. Here, we compute our feature descriptor with gradient norm bin, because the gradient norm is more informative than intensity among different modality images. Fig. 6 (A-C) respectively illustrates the volumetric gradient norm of original datasets. Since the CT dataset includes less structure information than the MRI and PET datasets, the corresponding number of the matched pairs in Fig. 6 (D-E) is a bit less than that of Fig. 6 (F). In this group of experiments, we can achieve the average registration accuracy of more than 95 percents for multi-modality images.

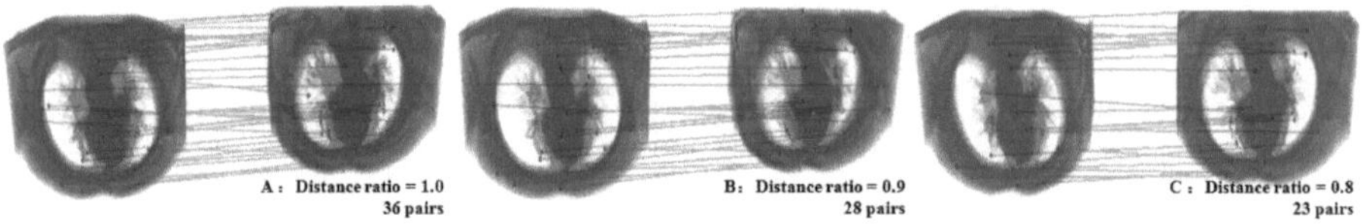

Fig. 7. Feature-based nonrigid registration of thorax MRI volumes

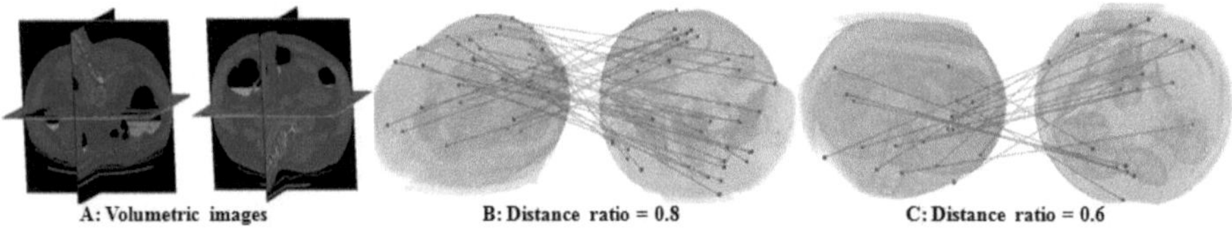

Fig. 8. Feature-based nonrigid registration of abdomen CT volumes

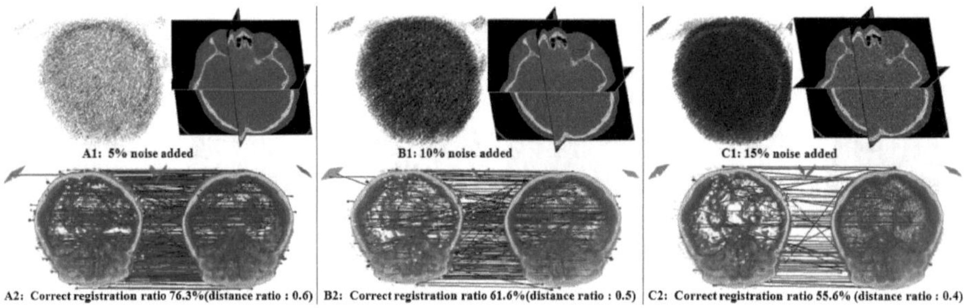

Fig. 9. Noise-perturbed datasets of head MRI volume and the registration results

Third, as for volumetric images with quasi-isometric deformation (far beyond isometric deformation), we use two experiments to qualitatively verify the isometric deformation invariance of our feature descriptor. Fig. 7 shows the nonrigid registration results of human MRI thorax volumes which are obtained from the same person before and after breathing. Although the shape of the heart and blood vessel deforms drastically, with the *Distance Ratio* reducing from 1.0 to 0.8, the mismatched pairs gradually disappear, and almost all the feature points in Fig. 7 (C) can be accepted as true. Fig. 8 shows the non-rigid registration results of two abdomen CT volumes respectively scanned in supine and prone orientations. All the matched lines in Fig. 8 (B-C) are roughly forming a cross shape, which well aligns with the orientation change (from supine to prone). When the *Distance Ratio* is set to be 0.6, most of the features located at muscle, stomach and spine can be retrieved as correct ones. It proves the superiority of our descriptor in feature-based registration with isometric deformation.

Fourth, to further examine the robustness, we respectively add 5%, 10% and 15% (of average intensity) random noise to the original volumetric images at

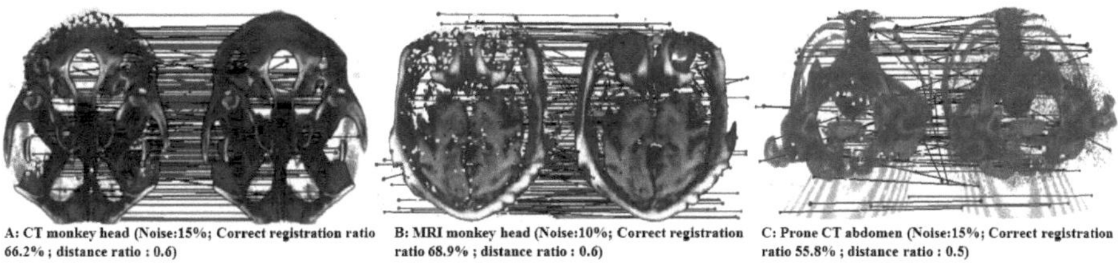

Fig. 10. More registration results for noise-perturbed datasets

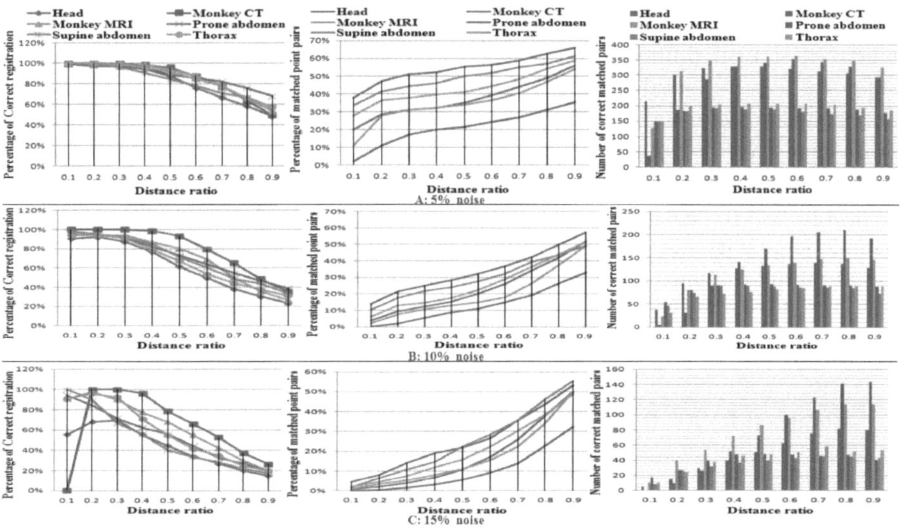

Fig. 11. The performance analysis

randomly-sampled locations. The top row of Fig. 9 shows the noise effects overlaid onto the original MRI head volume. We use the original dataset as source image and the noise-perturbed dataset as target image for feature registration. The *match ratio* is defined as the percentage of the matched pairs to the total detected feature points. As we have the ground truth, we accept the matched pair as correct ones if the distance between source point and target point is less than two voxels. For each registration result in Fig. 9, we document the *correct registration ratio* and the corresponding *Distance Ratio*. More results are also shown in Fig. 10 and our supplementary video, where red lines denote correct registration, blue lines denote incorrect registration, and feature points in yellow are the ones that cannot be matched.

Finally, we use correct registration ratios, feature matching ratios, and number of correctly-matched feature pairs to conduct quantitative evaluation. The left, middle, and right subgraph of Fig. 11 respectively reveals the relationship between the above indicators and the parameter *Distance Ratio*. For example, the head dataset can achieve better registration performance when the *Distance Ratio* is around 0.5, since it will have both higher correct registration ratios and enough correctly-matched feature pairs even though the match ratios are not very high. As for other datasets, focusing on each type of curves, we can observe similar trends despite different noise perturbation levels and data types.

7 Conclusion

We have detailed a comprehensive feature extraction and description method for volumetric images with intrinsic properties of being material-aware. The technical originality is centered in the integration of diffusion tensor weighted dyadic wavelet transform for multi-scale analysis and the PDF distance based metric design in diffusion tensor space. At the application level, our method supports feature-based volumetric registration with full orientation invariance and isometric deformation invariance. Extensive experiments and comprehensive evaluation have demonstrated the effectiveness and robustness of our method.

For our ongoing efforts, we will continue to conduct comprehensive evaluation, and to broaden the application scope. Applications of immediate interest include local parametric representation, solid recognition, similar shapes clustering, material distance embedded meshless physical simulation, and etc.

References

1. Scovanner, P., Ali, S., Shah, M.: A 3-dimensional SIFT descriptor and its application to action recognition. In: Proceedings of International Conference on Multimedia, pp. 357–360 (2007)
2. Flitton, G., Breckon, T., Megherbi, B.N.: Object recognition using 3D SIFT in complex CT volumes. In: Proceedings of Britich Machine Vision Conference, pp. 11.1–11.12 (2010)
3. Allaire, S., Kim, J., Breen, S., Jaffray, D., Pekar, V.: Full orientation invariance and improved feature selectivity of 3D SIFT with application to medical image analysis. In: Proceedings of CVPR Workshops, pp. 1–8 (2008)
4. Niemeijer, M., Garvin, M.K., Lee, K., Ginneken, B.V., Abrámoff, M.D., Sonka, M.: Registration of 3D spectral OCT volumes using 3D SIFT feature point matching. In: Proceedings of SPIE Medical Imaging, pp. 72591I.1–72591I.8 (2009)
5. Dalvi, R., Hacihaliloglu, I., Abugharbieh, R.: 3D ultrasound volume stitching using phase symmetry and harris corner detection for orthopaedic applications. In: Proceedings of SPIE Medical Imaging, pp. 762330.1–762330.8 (2010)
6. Ni, D., Chui, Y., Qu, Y., Yang, X., Qin, J., Wong, T., Ho, S., Heng, P.: Reconstruction of volumetric ultrasound panorama based on improved 3D SIFT. Comp. Med. Imag. and Graph. 33(7), 559–566 (2009)
7. Bronstein, M.M., Kokkinos, I.: Scale-invariant heat kernel signatures for non-rigid shape recognition. In: Proceedings of CVPR, pp. 1704–1711 (2010)
8. Winder, S.A.J., Brown, M.: Learning local image descriptors. In: Proceedings of CVPR, pp. 1–8 (2007)
9. Kokkinos, I., Yuille, A.L.: Scale invariance without scale selection. In: Proceedings of CVPR, pp. 1–8 (2008)

10. Bronstein, A.M., Bronstein, M.M., Bruckstein, A.M., Kimmel, R.: Analysis of two-dimensional non-rigid shapes. Int. J. Comput. Vision 78(1), 67–88 (2008)
11. Lipman, Y., Funkhouser, T.: Möbius voting for surface correspondence. ACM Trans. Graph. 28(3), 72.1–72.12 (2009)
12. Reuter, M., Biasotti, S., Giorgi, D., Patané, G., Spagnuolo, M.: Discrete laplace-beltrami operators for shape analysis and segmentation. Computers and Graphics 33(3), 381–390 (2009)
13. Aubry, M., Schlickewei, U., Cremers, D.: The wave kernel signature: A quantum mechanical approach to shape analysis. In: Proceedings of ICCV Workshops, pp. 1626–1633 (2011)
14. Malcolm, J., Rathi, Y., Tannenbaum, A.: A graph cut approach to image segmentation in tensor space. In: Proceedings of CVPR, pp. 18–25 (2007)
15. Han, S., Tao, W., Wang, D., Tai, X.C., Wu, X.: Image segmentation based on grabcut framework integrating multiscale nonlinear structure tensor. Trans. Img. Proc. 18(10), 2289–2302 (2009)
16. Brox, T., van den Boomgaard, R., Lauze, F., van de Weijer, J., Weickert, J., Mrázek, P., Kornprobst, P.: Adaptive structure tensors and their applications. In: Weickert, J., Hagen, H. (eds.) Visualization and Processing of Tensor Fields, vol. 1, pp. 17–47. Springer, Berlin (2006)
17. Bazán, C., Blomgren, P.: Image smoothing and edge detection by nonlinear diffusion and bilateral filter. Technical Report CSRCR2007-21, San Diego State University (2007)
18. Bazán, C., Miller, M., Blomgren, P.: Structure enhancement diffusion and contour extraction for electron tomography of mitochondria. J. Struct. Biol. 166(2), 144–155 (2009)
19. Lipman, Y., Rustamov, R.M., Funkhouser, T.A.: Biharmonic distance. ACM Trans. Graph. 29(3), 27.1–27.11 (2010)
20. Bronstein, A.M., Bronstein, M.M., Kimmel, R., Mahmoudi, M., Sapiro, G.: A gromov-hausdorff framework with diffusion geometry for topological-robust non-rigid shape matching. Int. J. Comput. Vision 89(2-3), 266–286 (2010)
21. Yen, L., Fouss, F., Decaestecker, C., Francq, P., Saerens, M.: Graph Nodes Clustering Based on the Commute-Time Kernel. In: Zhou, Z.-H., Li, H., Yang, Q. (eds.) PAKDD 2007. LNCS (LNAI), vol. 4426, pp. 1037–1045. Springer, Heidelberg (2007)
22. Cha, S.H.: Comprehensive survey on distance/similarity measures between probability density functions. International Journal of Mathematical Models and Methods in Applied Sciences 1(4), 300–307 (2007)
23. Zhang, J., Zheng, J., Cai, J.: A diffusion approach to seeded image segmentation. In: Proceedings of CVPR, pp. 2125–2132 (2010)

Efficient Closed-Form Solution to Generalized Boundary Detection

Marius Leordeanu[1], Rahul Sukthankar[3,4], and Cristian Sminchisescu[2,1]

[1] Institute of Mathematics of the Romanian Academy
[2] Faculty of Mathematics and Natural Science, University of Bonn
[3] Google Research
[4] Carnegie Mellon University

Abstract. Boundary detection is essential for a variety of computer vision tasks such as segmentation and recognition. We propose a unified formulation for boundary detection, with closed-form solution, which is applicable to the localization of different types of boundaries, such as intensity edges and occlusion boundaries from video and RGB-D cameras. Our algorithm simultaneously combines low- and mid-level image representations, in a single eigenvalue problem, and we solve over an infinite set of putative boundary orientations. Moreover, our method achieves state of the art results at a significantly lower computational cost than current methods. We also propose a novel method for soft-segmentation that can be used in conjunction with our boundary detection algorithm and improve its accuracy at a negligible extra computational cost.

1 Introduction

Boundary detection is a fundamental task in computer vision, with broad applicability in areas such as feature extraction, object recognition and image segmentation. The majority of papers on edge detection have focused on using only low-level cues, such as pixel intensity or color [1–5]. Recent work has started exploring the problem of boundary detection based on higher-level representations of the image, such as motion, surface and depth cues [6–8], segmentation [9], as well as category specific information [10, 11].

In this paper we propose a general formulation for boundary detection that can be applied, in principle, to the identification of any type of boundaries, such as general edges from low-level static cues (Figure 6), and occlusion boundaries from motion and depth cues (Figures 1, 7, 8). We generalize the classical view of boundaries from sudden signal changes on the original low-level image input [1–4, 12–14], to a locally linear (planar or step-wise) model on multiple layers of the input, over a relatively large image region. The layers can be interpretations of the image at different levels of visual processing, which could be low-level (e.g., color or grey level intensity), mid-level (e.g., segmentation, optical flow), or high-level (e.g., object category segmentation).

Despite the abundance of research on boundary detection, there is no general formulation of this problem. In this paper, we make the popular but implicit

A. Fitzgibbon et al. (Eds.): ECCV 2012, Part IV, LNCS 7575, pp. 516–529, 2012.

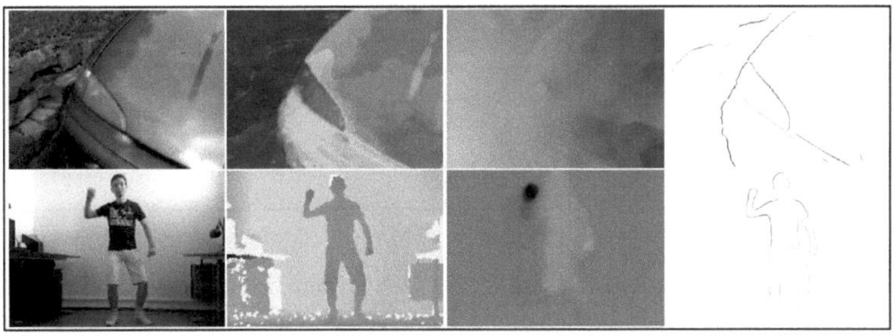

Fig. 1. Our method (Gb) combines, in a unified formulation, different types of information (first three columns) to find boundaries (right column). Top row: Gb uses color, soft-segmentation and optical flow. Bottom row: Gb uses color, depth and optical flow.

intuition of boundaries explicit: boundary pixels mark the transition from one relatively constant property region to another, in appropriate interpretations of the image. We can summarize our assumptions as follows:

1. A boundary separates different image regions, which in the absence of noise are almost constant, at some level of image interpretation or processing. For example, at the lowest level, a region could have constant intensity. At a higher-level, it could be a region delimiting an object category, in which case the output of a category-specific classifier would be constant.
2. For a given image, boundaries in one layer often coincide, in terms of position and orientation, with boundaries in other layers. For example, discontinuities in intensity are typically correlated with discontinuities in optical flow, texture or other cues. Moreover, the boundaries that align across multiple layers typically correspond to the semantic boundaries that interest humans.

Based on these observations, we develop a unified model that can simultaneously consider both lower-level and higher-level information.

Classical vector-valued techniques on multi-images [12,13,15] can be simultaneously applied to several image channels, but differ from the proposed approach in a fundamental way: they are specifically designed for low-level input, by using first or second-order derivatives of the image channels, with edge models limited to very small neighborhoods, as needed for approximating the derivatives. Derivatives are very often noisy and usually do not have sufficient spatial support to indicate true object boundaries with high confidence. Moreover, even though edges from one layer coincide with those from a different layer, their location may not match perfectly — an assumption implicitly made by the use of derivatives. We argue that in order to confidently classify boundary pixels and combine multiple layers of information, one must go beyond a few pixels, to much larger neighborhoods, in line with more recent methods [5,9,16,17].

The main advantage of our approach over current methods is the efficient estimation of boundary strength and orientation in a single closed-form computation. The idea behind Pb and its variants [9,16] is to classify each possible

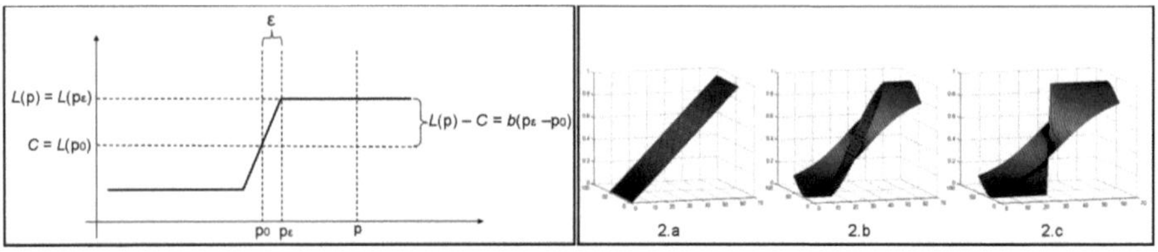

Fig. 2. Left: 1D view of our model. Right: 2D view of our boundary model with different values of ϵ relative to the window size W: 2.a) $\epsilon > W$; 2.b) $\epsilon = W/2$; 2.c) $\epsilon = W/1000$. For small ϵ the model is a step, along the normal passing through the window center.

boundary pixel based on the histogram difference in color and texture information between the two half disks on each side of a putative orientation, for a fixed number of candidate angles. The separate computation for each orientation considerably increases the computational cost and limits orientation estimates to a particular angular quantization, thus affecting the estimated probability of boundary.

We summarize our contributions as follows: **1)** we present a novel boundary model with an efficient closed-form solution for generalized boundary detection; **2)** we recover exact boundary normals through direct estimation rather than evaluating coarsely sampled orientation candidates as in [16]; **3)** we optimize simultaneously over both low and mid-levels of image processing, and can easily incorporate outputs from new image interpretation methods. This is in contrast to current approaches [6, 7, 9] that process low and mid-level layers separately and combine them in different ways to detect different types of boundaries. **4)** we only learn a small set of parameters, enabling efficient training with limited data. Our approach essentially bridges the gap between model fitting methods such as [18, 19], and recent learning-based boundary detectors.

2 Generalized Boundary Model

Given a $N_x \times N_y$ image I, let its k-th layer L_k be some real-valued array, of the same size, whose boundaries are relevant to our task. For example, L_k could contain, at each pixel, values from a color channel, filter responses, optical flow, or the output of a patch-based binary classifier trained to detect a specific color distribution, texture or a certain object category.[1] Thus, L_k could consist of relatively constant regions separated by boundaries.

We expect that boundaries in different layers may not precisely align. Given a set of layers, each corresponding to a particular interpretation of the image, we wish to identify the most consistent boundaries across these layers. The output of our method for each point $\mathbf{p}$ on the $N_x \times N_y$ image grid is a real-valued probability

[1] The output of a discrete-valued multi-class classifier can be encoded as multiple input layers, where each layer represents a given label.

that $\mathbf{p}$ lies on a boundary, given the information in all image interpretations L_k centered at $\mathbf{p}$.

We model a boundary point in layer L_k as a transition, either sudden or gradual, in the corresponding values of L_k along the normal to the boundary. If several K such layers are available, let $\mathbf{L}$ be a three-dimensional array of size $N_x \times N_y \times K$, such that $\mathbf{L}(x, y, k) = L_k(x, y)$, for each k. Thus, $\mathbf{L}$ contains all the information available for the current boundary detection problem, given multiple interpretations of the image. Figure 1 illustrates how we perform boundary detection by combining different layers, such as color, depth, soft-segmentation and optical flow.

Let $\mathbf{p}_0$ be the center of a window $W(\mathbf{p}_0)$ of size $\sqrt{N_W} \times \sqrt{N_W}$, where N_W is the number of pixels in the window. For each image location $\mathbf{p}_0$ we want to evaluate the probability of boundary using the information in $\mathbf{L}$, restricted to that particular window. For any $\mathbf{p}$ within the window, we model the boundary with the following locally linear approximation:

$$L_k(\mathbf{p}) \approx C_k(\mathbf{p}_0) + b_k(\mathbf{p}_0)(\hat{\mathbf{p}}_\epsilon - \mathbf{p}_0)^\top \mathbf{n}(\mathbf{p}_0). \tag{1}$$

Here b_k is nonnegative and corresponds to the boundary "height" for layer k at location $\mathbf{p}_0$; $\hat{\mathbf{p}}_\epsilon$ is the closest point to $\mathbf{p}$ (projection of $\mathbf{p}$) on the disk of radius ϵ centered at $\mathbf{p}_0$; $\mathbf{n}(\mathbf{p}_0)$ is the normal to the boundary and $C_k(\mathbf{p}_0)$ is a constant over the window $W(\mathbf{p}_0)$. Note that if we set $C_k(\mathbf{p}_0) = L_k(\mathbf{p}_0)$ and use a sufficiently large ϵ such that $\hat{\mathbf{p}}_\epsilon = \mathbf{p}$, our model reduces to the first-order Taylor expansion of $L_k(\mathbf{p})$ around the current $\mathbf{p}_0$.

As shown in Figure 2, ϵ controls the steepness of the boundary, going from completely planar when ϵ is large to a sharp step-wise discontinuity through the window center $\mathbf{p}_0$, as ϵ approaches zero. When ϵ is very small we have a step along the normal through the window center, and a sigmoid that flattens as we move farther away from the center, along the boundary normal. As ϵ increases, the model flattens to become a perfect plane for any ϵ greater than the window radius. In 2D, our model is not an ideal ramp (see Figure 2), which enables it to handle corners as well as edges. The idea of ramp edges has been explored in the literature before, albeit very differently [20].

When the window is far from any boundary, the value of b_k will be near zero, since the only variation in the layer values is due to noise. If we are close to a boundary, then b_k becomes large. The term $(\hat{\mathbf{p}}_\epsilon - \mathbf{p}_0)^\top \mathbf{n}(\mathbf{p}_0)$ approximates the sign indicating the side of the boundary: it does not matter on which side we are, as long as a sign change occurs when the boundary is crossed. When a true boundary is present within several layers at the same position ($b_k(\mathbf{p}_0)$ is non-zero and possibly different, for several k) the normal to the boundary should be consistent. Thus, we model the boundary normal $\mathbf{n}$ as common across all layers.

We can now write the above equation in matrix form for all layers, with the same window size and location as follows: let $\mathbf{X}$ be a $N_W \times K$ matrix with a row i for each location $\mathbf{p}_i$ of the window and a column for each layer k, such that $X_{i;k} = L_k(\mathbf{p}_i)$. Similarly, we define $N_W \times 2$ position matrix $\mathbf{P}$: on its i-th row we store the x and y components of $\hat{\mathbf{p}}_\epsilon - \mathbf{p}_0$ for the i-th point of the window.

Let $\mathbf{n} = [n_x, n_y]$ denote the boundary normal and $\mathbf{b} = [b_1, b_2, \ldots, b_K]$ the step sizes for layers $1, 2, \ldots, K$. Also, let us define the rank-1 $2 \times K$ matrix $\mathbf{J} = \mathbf{n}^\top \mathbf{b}$. We also define matrix $\mathbf{C}$ of the same size as $\mathbf{X}$, with each column k constant and equal to $C_k(\mathbf{p}_0)$. We rewrite Equation 1 (dropping the dependency on $\mathbf{p}_0$ for notational simplicity), with unknowns $\mathbf{J}$ and $\mathbf{C}$:

$$\mathbf{X} \approx \mathbf{C} + \mathbf{PJ}. \tag{2}$$

Since $\mathbf{C}$ is a matrix with constant columns, and each column of $\mathbf{P}$ sums to 0, we have $\mathbf{P}^\top \mathbf{C} = \mathbf{0}$. Thus, by multiplying both sides of the equation above by $\mathbf{P}^\top$, we eliminate the unknown $\mathbf{C}$. Moreover, it can be easily shown that $\mathbf{P}^\top \mathbf{P} = \alpha \mathbf{I}$, i.e., the identity matrix scaled by a factor α, which can be computed since $\mathbf{P}$ is known. We finally obtain a simple expression for the unknown $\mathbf{J}$ (since both $\mathbf{P}$ and $\mathbf{X}$ are known):

$$\mathbf{J} \approx \frac{1}{\alpha} \mathbf{P}^\top \mathbf{X}. \tag{3}$$

Since $\mathbf{J} = \mathbf{n}^\top \mathbf{b}$ it follows that $\mathbf{J}\mathbf{J}^\top = \|\mathbf{b}\|^2 \mathbf{n}^\top \mathbf{n}$ is symmetric and has rank 1. Then $\mathbf{n}$ can be estimated as the principal eigenvector of $\mathbf{M} = \mathbf{J}\mathbf{J}^\top$ and $\|\mathbf{b}\|$ as the square root of its largest eigenvalue. $\|\mathbf{b}\|$ is the norm of the boundary step vector $\mathbf{b} = [b_1, b_2, ..., b_K]$ and captures the overall strength of boundaries from all layers simultaneously. If layers are properly scaled, then $\|\mathbf{b}\|$ could be used as a measure of boundary strength. Once we identify $\|\mathbf{b}\|$, we pass it through a one-dimensional logistic model to obtain the probability of boundary, similarly to recent methods [9,16]. The parameters of the logistic model are learned using standard procedures, explained in Section 3.2. The normal to the boundary $\mathbf{n}$ is then used for non-maxima suppression. Note that $\|\mathbf{b}\|$ is different from the gradient of multi-images [12,13] that is computed from local derivatives, which could be noisy and lack sufficient spatial support. We compute the boundary strength by fitting a model, which, by controlling the window size and ϵ, can vary from a small to a large patch and from planar to step-wise.

Additionally, we propose to weigh the importance of each pixel in a window by an isotropic 2D Gaussian located at the window center $\mathbf{p_0}$. This puts more weight on model fitting errors from data points that are closer to the window center. The idea is implemented by multiplying each row of both $\mathbf{X}$ and $\mathbf{P}$ with the Gaussian weight corresponding to that particular location. We mention that the introduction of Gaussian weighting does not change the model (Equation 2), but only the contributions of data points to the model fitting process: $C_k(\mathbf{p_0})$, with its rows also multiplied by the corresponding Gaussian weights, still cancels out and the final Equation 3 remains valid. As seen in the middle plot of Figure 3, the performance is significantly influenced by the choice of Gaussian standard deviation σ_G, which confirms our assumption that points closer to the boundary should constrain the model parameters more.

In our experiments we used a window radius equal to 2% of the image diagonal, $\epsilon = 1$ pixel, and Gaussian σ_G equal to half of the window radius. These parameters produced the best F-measure on the BSDS300 training set [16] and

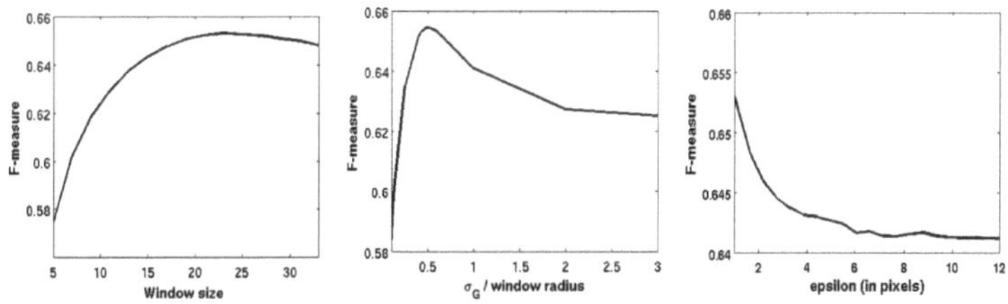

Fig. 3. Evaluation on BSDS300 test set by varying the window size (in pixels), σ_G of the Gaussian weighting (relative to window radius) and ϵ. One parameter is varied, while the others are set to their optimum (learned from training images). Left: windows with large spatial support give a significantly better accuracy. Middle: points closer to the boundary should contribute more to the model, as evidenced by the best $\sigma_G \approx$ half of the window radius. Right: small ϵ leads to better performance, confirming the usefulness of our step-wise model.

were also near-optimal on the test set, as shown in Figure 3. We draw the following conclusions about our model: 1) a large window size leads to significantly better performance as more evidence can be used in reasoning about boundaries. Note that when the window size is small our model becomes similar to methods based on local approximation of derivatives [4,12,13,15]. 2) the usage of a small ϵ produces boundaries with significantly better localization and strength. It strongly suggests that boundary transitions in natural images tend to be sudden, not gradual. 3) the Gaussian weighting is justified: the model is better fitted if more weight is placed on points closer to the boundary.

3 Algorithm

Before applying the main algorithm we scale each layer in $\mathbf{L}$ according to its importance, which may be problem dependent. We learn the scaling of layers from training data using a direct search method [21] to optimize the F-measure (Section 3.2). Algorithm 1 (termed Gb) summarizes the proposed approach.

The pseudo-code presented in Algorithm 1 gives a description of Gb that directly relates to our boundary model. Upon closer inspection we observe that elements of $\mathbf{M}$ can also be computed exactly by convolving each layer L_k twice, using two different kernels: $H_x(x-x_0, y-y_0) \propto g(x-x_0, y-y_0)^2(x_\epsilon - x_0)$ and $H_y(x-x_0, y-y_0) \propto g(x-x_0, y-y_0)^2(y_\epsilon - y_0)$, and then combining the results. Here $g(x-x_0, y-y_0)$ is the Gaussian weight applied at location $(x-x_0, y-y_0)$ and $(x_\epsilon, y_\epsilon) = \mathbf{p}_\epsilon$. This observation leads to a straightforward implementation.[2] Note the analytic difference between our filters and Derivative of Gaussian filters (i.e., $G_x(x-x_0, y-y_0) \propto g(x-x_0, y-y_0)(x-x_0)$), which could be used for computing the gradient of multi-images [13]. While Gaussian derivatives have the computational advantage of being separable, when used for computing the gradient of multi-images they produce boundaries of inferior quality (see Table 2).

[2] Code available online at: `http://www.imar.ro/clvp/code/Gb`

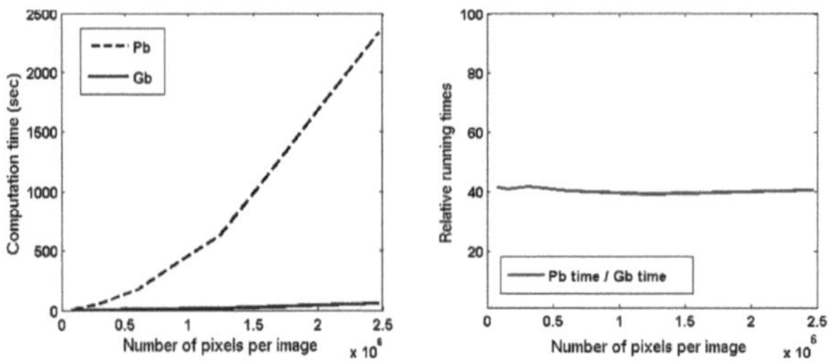

Fig. 4. Left: Edge detection run times on a 3.2 GHz desktop for our MATLAB implementation of Gb vs. the publicly available code of Pb [16]. Right: ratio of run time of Pb to run time of Gb. Each algorithm runs over a single scale and uses the same window size, which is a constant fraction of the image size. Here, Gb is 40× faster.

Algorithm 1. Gb: Generalized Boundary Detection

Initialize $\mathbf{L}$, scaled appropriately.
Initialize w_0 and w_1.
Pre-compute matrix $\mathbf{P}$
for all pixels $\mathbf{p}$ **do**
  $\mathbf{M} \leftarrow (\mathbf{P}^\top \mathbf{X_p})(\mathbf{P}^\top \mathbf{X_p})^\top$
  $(\mathbf{v}, \lambda) \leftarrow$ principal eigenpair of $\mathbf{M}$
  $b_\mathbf{p} \leftarrow \frac{1}{1+\exp(w_0 + w_1 \sqrt{\lambda})}$
  $\theta_\mathbf{p} \leftarrow \text{atan2}(v_y, v_x)$
end for
return $\mathbf{b}, \theta$

3.1 Computational Complexity

The overall complexity of Gb is straightforward to derive. For each pixel $\mathbf{p}$, the most expensive step is computing the matrix $\mathbf{M}$, which has $O((N_W + 2)K)$ complexity, where N_W denotes the number of pixels in the window and K the number of layers. $\mathbf{M}$ is a 2×2 matrix, so computing its eigenpair $(\mathbf{v}, \lambda)$ is a closed-form operation, with small fixed cost. Thus, for a fixed N_W and a total of N pixels per image the overall complexity is $O(KN_WN)$. If N_W is a fraction f of N, then complexity becomes $O(fKN^2)$.

The running time of Gb compares favorably to that of Pb [9, 16]. Pb in its exact form has complexity $O(fKN_oN^2)$, where N_o is a discrete number of candidate orientations. Both Gb and Pb are quadratic in the number of image pixels. However, Pb has a significantly larger fixed cost per pixel as it requires the computation of histograms for each individual image channel and orientation. In Figure 4, we show the run times for Gb and Pb (publicly available code) on a 3.2GHz desktop in MATLAB, on the same images, using the same window size and a single scale. While Gb produces boundaries of similar quality (see Table 2), it is consistently faster than Pb (about 40×), independent of the image size (Figure 4, right plot). For example, on 0.15 MP images the times are: 19.4 sec for Pb vs. 0.48 sec for Gb; to process 2.5 MP images, Pb takes 38 min while Gb only 57 sec.

A fast parallel implementation of gPb [9] is proposed in [22]. The authors implement the method directly on the high-performance Nvidia GTX 280 graphics card with a high degree of parallelism (30 multiprocessors). Local Pb is computed at three different scales. The authors offer two implementations for local cues: one for the exact computation and the other for a faster approximate computation that uses integral images and is linear in the number of image pixels. The approximation has $O(fKN_oN_bN)$ time complexity, where N_b is the number of histogram bins for the different image channels and N_o is the number of candidate orientations. Note that N_oN_b is large in practice and affects the overall running time considerably. It requires computing (and possibly storing) a large number of integral images, one for each combination of (histogram bin, image channel, orientation). The actual number is not explicitly stated in [22], but we estimate that it is in the order of one thousand per input image (4 channels × 8 orientations × 32 histogram bins = 1024). The approximation also requires special processing for the rotated integral images of texton labels, to minimize interpolation artifacts. The authors propose a solution based on Bresenham lines, which further affects the discretization of the rotation angle. In Table 1 we present run time comparisons with Pb's local cues computation from [22]. Our exact implementation of Gb (using 3 color layers) in MATLAB is 8 times faster than the exact parallel computation of Pb over 3 scales on GTX 280.

Table 1. Run times: Gb implementation in MATLAB on a 3.2 Ghz desktop vs. Catanzaro et al.'s parallel computation of local cues on Nvidia GTX 280 [22]

Algorithm	Gb (exact)	[22] (exact)	[22] (approx.)
Run time (sec.)	0.473	4.0	0.569

3.2 Learning

Our model uses a small number of parameters. Only two parameters (w_0, w_1) are needed for the logisic function that models the probability of boundary (Algorithm 1). For layer scaling the maximum number of parameters needed is equal to the number of layers. We reduce this number by tying the scaling for layers of the same type: 1) for color (in CIELAB space) we fix the scale of L to 1 and learn a single scaling for both channels a and b; 2) for soft-segmentation (Section 4) we learn a single scaling for all 8 segmentation layers; 3) for optical flow (Section 5.2) we learn one parameter for the 2 flow channels, another for the 2 channels of the unit normalized flow, and a third for the flow magnitude; 4) for RGB-D images (Section 5.3) we need one additional scaling for depth.

Fig. 5. Soft-segmentation results from our method. The first 3 dimensions of the soft-segmentations are shown on the RGB channels. Computation time for soft-segmentation is less than 2 seconds per 0.15 MP image in MATLAB.

Learning the weights of layers is based on the observation that the matrix $\mathbf{M}$ can be written as a linear combination of matrices $\mathbf{M}_i$ computed for each scaling s_i separately:

$$\mathbf{M} = \sum_i s_i^2 \mathbf{M}_i, \tag{4}$$

where $\mathbf{M}_i \leftarrow (\mathbf{P}^\top \mathbf{X}_i)(\mathbf{P}^\top \mathbf{X}_i)^\top$ and $\mathbf{X}_i$ is the submatrix of $\mathbf{X}$, with the same number of rows as $\mathbf{X}$ and with columns corresponding only to those layers that are scaled by s_i. It follows that the largest eigenvalue of $\mathbf{M}$, $\lambda = \frac{1}{2}(\text{tr}(\mathbf{M}) + \sqrt{\text{tr}(\mathbf{M})^2 - \det(\mathbf{M})/4})$, can be computed from s_i's and the elements of $\mathbf{M}_i$'s. Thus, the F-measure, which depends on (w_0, w_1) and λ, can also be computed over the training data as a function of the parameters (w_0, w_1) and s_i, which have to be learned. To optimize the F-measure, we use the direct search method of Lagarias et al. [21], since it does not require an analytic form of the cost and can be easily applied in MATLAB by using the `fminsearch` function. In our experiments, the positive and negative training edges were sampled at equally spaced locations on the output of Gb using only color, with all channels equally scaled (after non-maxima suppression applied directly on the raw $\sqrt{\lambda}$). Positive samples are the ones sufficiently close (less than 3 pixels) to the human-labeled ground truth boundaries.

4 An Efficient Soft-Segmentation Method

In this section we present a novel method to rapidly generate soft image segmentations. Its continuous output is similar to the eigenvectors computed by Ncuts [23], but its computational cost is significantly lower: under 2 sec (3.2 GHz CPU) vs. over 150 sec required for Ncuts (2.66 GHz CPU [22]) per 0.15MP image in MATLAB. We briefly describe it here because it serves as a fast mid-level representation of the image that significantly improves the boundary detection accuracy over raw color alone. While we describe this method in the context of color, we emphasize that it is general enough to integrate a variety of other image features, such as texture.

The method is motivated by the observation that regions of semantic interest (such as objects) can often be modeled with a certain, potentially complex, color distribution: each possible color has a certain probability of occurrence, given the region. Specifically, we assume that the colors of any image patch are generated from a distribution that is a linear combination of a finite number of color probability distributions belonging to the regions of interest in the image.

Let $\mathbf{c}$ be an indicator vector associated with some patch from the image, such that $c_i = 1$ if color i is present in the patch and 0 otherwise. If we assume that the image is formed by a composition of regions with colors generated from a few color distributions, then we can consider $\mathbf{c}$ to be a multi-dimensional random variable drawn from a mixture of distributions $\mathbf{h}_i$: $\mathbf{c} \sim \sum_i \pi_i \mathbf{h}_i$. The linear subspace of these distributions can be automatically learned by PCA applied to a the set of indicator vectors $\mathbf{c}$, sampled uniformly from the image. Once the subspace is discovered, for any patch P sampled from the image and its associated indicator vector $\mathbf{c}$, its generating distribution (considered to be the distribution of the foreground) can be obtained by PCA reconstruction: $\mathbf{h_F}(\mathbf{c}) \approx \mathbf{h}_0 + \sum_i (\mathbf{c} - \mathbf{h}_0)^\top \mathbf{v}_i$. The distribution of the background is also obtained from the PCA model using the same coefficients, but with opposite sign: thus we obtain a background distribution that is as far as possible (in the subspace) from the foreground: $\mathbf{h_B}(\mathbf{c}) \approx \mathbf{h}_0 - \sum_i (\mathbf{c} - \mathbf{h}_0)^\top \mathbf{v}_i$.

Having computed the figure/ground distributions, we classify whether each location in the image belongs to the same region as the current patch P. If we perform the same classification procedure for n_s (≈ 150) patches uniformly sampled on the image grid, we obtain n_s figure/ground segmentations for the same image. At a final step, we again perform PCA on vectors collected from all pixels in the image; each vector is of dimension n_s and corresponds to a certain image pixel, such that its i-th element is equal to the value at that pixel in the i-th figure/ground segmentation. Finally we use, for each image pixel, the coefficients of the first 8 principal dimensions to obtain a set of 8 soft-segmentations which represent a compressed version of the entire set of n_s segmentations. These soft-segmentations are used as input layers to our boundary detection method, and are similar in spirit to the normalized cuts eigenvectors computed for *gPb* [9]. In Figure 5 we show examples of the first three such soft-segmentations on the RGB color channels.

5 Experiments

To evaluate the generality of our proposed method, we conduct experiments on detecting boundaries in image, video and RGB-D data. First, we show results on static images using only color. Second, we perform experiments on occlusion boundary detection in short video clips. Multiple frames, closely spaced in time, provide significantly more information about dynamic scenes and make occlusion boundary detection possible, as shown in recent work [6–8, 24]. Third, we

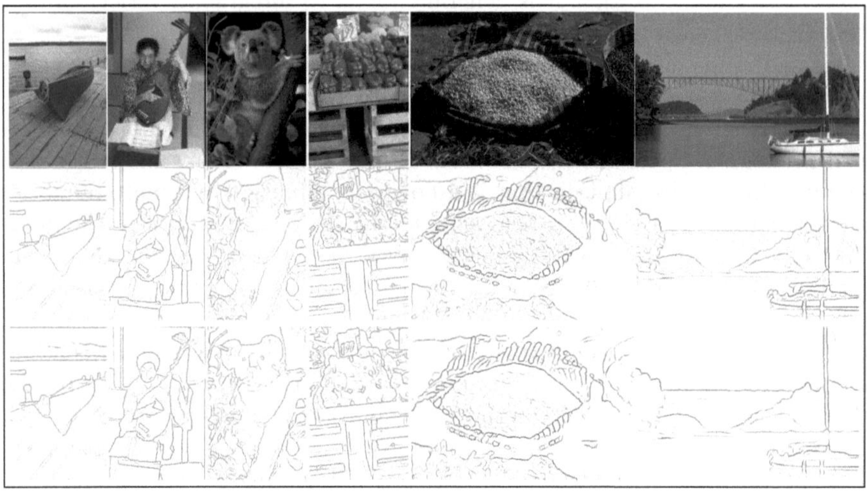

Fig. 6. Top row: input images from BSDS300 dataset. Middle row: output of Gb using only color layers. Bottom row: output of Gb using both color and our soft-segmentation.

experiment with RGB-D video frames and show that depth can be effectively combined with color and optical flow to detect moving occlusion boundaries.

5.1 Boundaries in Static Color Images

We evaluate Gb on the well-known BSDS300 dataset [16] (Figure 6). We compare the accuracy and computational time of Gb with Pb [16], Gaussian derivatives (GD) for the gradient of multi-images [15], and Canny [4] edge detectors (Table 2). Canny uses brightness information, Gb and GD use brightness and color, whereas Pb uses brightness, color and texture information. Gb and GD use the same window size and Gaussian scale. For Gb we present two results, one using color (C), and the other using both color and soft-segmentation based on color (C+S). The total time reported for Gb (C+S) includes all processing: computing soft-segmentations and boundary detection. Even though Pb does not use segmentation we believe that our comparison is fair, since the total time for Gb (C+S) is more than 6 times faster than Pb in MATLAB. Also, Pb has the advantage of using learned textons, whereas Gb (C+S) uses only color. To test our model's robustness to overfitting we performed 30 different learning experiments for Gb (C+S) using 30 images randomly sampled from BSDS300 training set and obtained the same F-measure on the 100 images test set (measured $\sigma < 0.1\%$). The method of [17] obtains a higher F-measure of 0.68 on this dataset by combining the output of Pb at three scales, but the same multi-scale method could use Gb instead. The state of the art global Pb [9,22] achieves an F-measure of 0.70 by using Ncuts soft-segmentations. Our formulation is general and could easily incorporate better soft-segmentations as extra layers for

Fig. 7. Example boundary detection results on the CMU Motion Dataset

Table 2. Comparison of accuracy (F-measure) and total running time on BSDS. For Gb (C+S), the running time includes the computation of soft-segmentations.

Algorithm	Gb (C+S)	Gb (C)	Pb [16]	GD [15]	Canny [4]
F-measure	**0.67**	0.65	0.65	0.62	0.58
Total time (sec.)	3.0	0.5	19.5	0.3	0.1

improved performance. In fact, given a pool of figure/ground segments using CPMC [25], we obtained higher quality soft-segmentations by applying the same PCA reconstruction procedure from Section 4. This raised Gb's F-measure to 0.70 [26].

5.2 Occlusion Boundaries in Video

State-of-the-art techniques for occlusion boundary detection in video are based on combining, in various ways, the outputs of existing boundary detectors for static color images with optical flow, followed by a global processing phase [6–8, 24]. Table 3 compares Gb against reported results on the CMU Motion Dataset [6] We use, as one of our layers, the flow computed using Sun et al.'s public code [27]. Additionally, Gb uses color and soft segmentation (Section 4). In contrast to the other methods [6–8, 24], which require significant time for processing and optimization, we require less than 1.6 seconds on average to process 230×320 images from the CMU dataset (excluding Sun et al.'s flow computation). Figure 7 shows qualitative results.

5.3 Occlusion Boundaries in RGB-D Video

The third set of experiments uses RGB-D video of a moving person. We combine low-level color and depth input with large-displacement optical flow [28].

Fig. 8. Detecting occlusion boundaries in RGB-D by combining color, depth and flow

Table 3. Occlusion boundary detection on the CMU Motion Dataset

Algorithm	Gb	Sundberg et al. [7]	He & Yuille [8]	Sargin et al. [24]	Stein et al. [6]
F-measure	**0.62**	0.61	0.47	0.57	0.48

Figures 1 shows an example of the input layers and the output of our method. We learned the parameters of our model from only 3 images of human-labeled silhouettes. Figure 8 shows qualitative results. Note that in a single formulation, Gb detects the moving occlusion boundaries and successfully learns to ignore most of the other ones.

6 Conclusions

We present Gb, a novel model and algorithm for generalized boundary detection. Our method effectively combines multiple low-level and mid-level interpretation layers of an input image in a principled manner to achieve competitive results on standard datasets at a significantly lower computational cost than current methods. Gb's broad real-world applicability is demonstrated through qualitative and quantitative results on detecting boundaries in natural images, occlusion boundaries in video and moving object boundaries in RGB-D data.

Acknowledgements. This work was supported by CNCS-UEFICSDI, under PNII RU-RC-2/2009, PCE-2011-3-0438, and CT-ERC-2012-1.

References

1. Roberts, L.: Machine perception of three-dimensional solids. In: Optical and Electro-Optical Information Processing, pp. 159–197. MIT Press (1965)
2. Prewitt, J.: Object enhancement and extraction. In: Picture Processing and Psychopictorics, pp. 75–149. Academic Press, New York (1970)
3. Marr, D., Hildtreth, E.: Theory of edge detection. Proc. Royal Society (1980)

4. Canny, J.: A computational approach to edge detection. PAMI 8, 679–698 (1986)
5. Ruzon, M., Tomasi, C.: Edge, junction, and corner detection using color distributions. PAMI 23 (2001)
6. Stein, A., Hebert, M.: Occlusion boundaries from motion: Low-level detection and mid-level reasoning. IJCV 82 (2009)
7. Sundberg, P., Brox, T., Maire, M., Arbelaez, P., Malik, J.: Occlusion boundary detection and figure/ground assignment from optical flow. In: CVPR (2011)
8. He, X., Yuille, A.: Occlusion Boundary Detection Using Pseudo-depth. In: Daniilidis, K., Maragos, P., Paragios, N. (eds.) ECCV 2010, Part IV. LNCS, vol. 6314, pp. 539–552. Springer, Heidelberg (2010)
9. Arbelaez, P., Maire, M., Fowlkes, C., Malik, J.: Contour detection and hierarchical image segmentation. PAMI 33 (2011)
10. Mairal, J., Leordeanu, M., Bach, F., Hebert, M., Ponce, J.: Discriminative Sparse Image Models for Class-Specific Edge Detection and Image Interpretation. In: Forsyth, D., Torr, P., Zisserman, A. (eds.) ECCV 2008, Part III. LNCS, vol. 5304, pp. 43–56. Springer, Heidelberg (2008)
11. Hariharan, B., Arbelaez, P., Bourdev, L., Maji, S., Malik, J.: Semantic contours from inverse detectors. In: ICCV (2011)
12. Kanade, T.: Image understanding research at CMU. In: DARPA IUW (1987)
13. Di Senzo, S.: A note on the gradient of a multi-image. CVGIP 33 (1986)
14. Cumani, A.: Edge detection in multispectral images. CVGIP 53 (1991)
15. Koschan, M., Abidi, M.: Detection and classification of edges in color images. Signal Processing Magazine, Special Issue on Color Image Processing 22 (2005)
16. Martin, D., Fawlkes, C., Malik, J.: Learning to detect natural image boundaries using local brightness, color, and texture cues. PAMI 26 (2004)
17. Ren, X.: Multi-scale Improves Boundary Detection in Natural Images. In: Forsyth, D., Torr, P., Zisserman, A. (eds.) ECCV 2008, Part III. LNCS, vol. 5304, pp. 533–545. Springer, Heidelberg (2008)
18. Meer, P., Georgescu, B.: Edge detection with embedded confidence. PAMI 23 (2001)
19. Baker, S., Nayar, S.K., Murase, H.: Parametric feature detection. In: DARPA Image Understanding Workshop (1997)
20. Petrou, M., Kittler, J.: Optimal edge detectors for ramp edges. PAMI 13 (1991)
21. Lagarias, J., Reeds, J.A., Wright, M.H., Wright, P.E.: Convergence properties of the Nelder-Mead simplex method in low dimensions. SIAM Optimization 9 (1998)
22. Catanzaro, B., Su, B.Y., Sundaram, N., Lee, Y., Murphy, M., Keutzer, K.: Efficient, high-quality image contour detection. In: ICCV (2009)
23. Shi, J., Malik, J.: Normalized cuts and image segmentation. PAMI 22 (2000)
24. Sargin, M., Bertelli, L., Manjunath, B., Rose, K.: Probabilistic occlusion boundary detection on spatio-temporal lattices. In: ICCV (2009)
25. Carreira, J., Sminchisescu, C.: Constrained parametric min-cuts for automatic object segmentation. In: CVPR (2010)
26. Leordeanu, M., Sukthankar, R., Sminchisescu, C.: Generalized boundaries from multiple image interpretations. Techincal Report, Institute of Mathematics of the Romanian Academy (August 2012)
27. Sun, D., Roth, S., Black, M.: Secrets of optical flow estimation and their principles. In: CVPR (2010)
28. Brox, T., Bregler, C., Malik, J.: Large displacement optical flow. In: CVPR (2009)

Attribute Learning for Understanding Unstructured Social Activity

Yanwei Fu, Timothy M. Hospedales, Tao Xiang, and Shaogang Gong

School of EECS, Queen Mary University of London, UK
{yanwei.fu,tmh,txiang,sgg}@eecs.qmul.ac.uk

Abstract. The rapid development of social video sharing platforms has created a huge demand for automatic video classification and annotation techniques, in particular for videos containing social activities of a group of people (e.g. YouTube video of a wedding reception). Recently, attribute learning has emerged as a promising paradigm for transferring learning to sparsely labelled classes in object or single-object short action classification. In contrast to existing work, this paper for the first time, tackles the problem of attribute learning for understanding group social activities with sparse labels. This problem is more challenging because of the complex multi-object nature of social activities, and the unstructured nature of the activity context. To solve this problem, we (1) contribute an unstructured social activity attribute (USAA) dataset with both visual and audio attributes, (2) introduce the concept of semi-latent attribute space and (3) propose a novel model for learning the latent attributes which alleviate the dependence of existing models on exact and exhaustive manual specification of the attribute-space. We show that our framework is able to exploit latent attributes to outperform contemporary approaches for addressing a variety of realistic multi-media sparse data learning tasks including: multi-task learning, N-shot transfer learning, learning with label noise and importantly zero-shot learning.

1 Introduction

With the rapid development of digital and mobile phone cameras and proliferation of social media sharing, billions of unedited and unstructured videos produced by consumers are uploaded to the social media websites (e.g. YouTube) but few of them are labelled. Obtaining exhaustive annotation is impractically expensive. This huge volume of data thus demands effective methods for automatic video classification and annotation, ideally with minimised supervision. A solution to these problems would have huge application potential, e.g., content-based recognition and indexing, and hence content-based search, retrieval, filtering and recommendation of multi-media..

In the paper, we tackle the problem of *automatic classification and annotation of unstructured group social activity*. Specifically, we are interested in home videos of social occassions such graduation ceremony, birthday party, and wedding reception which feature activities of group of people ranging anything

A. Fitzgibbon et al. (Eds.): ECCV 2012, Part IV, LNCS 7575, pp. 530–543, 2012.

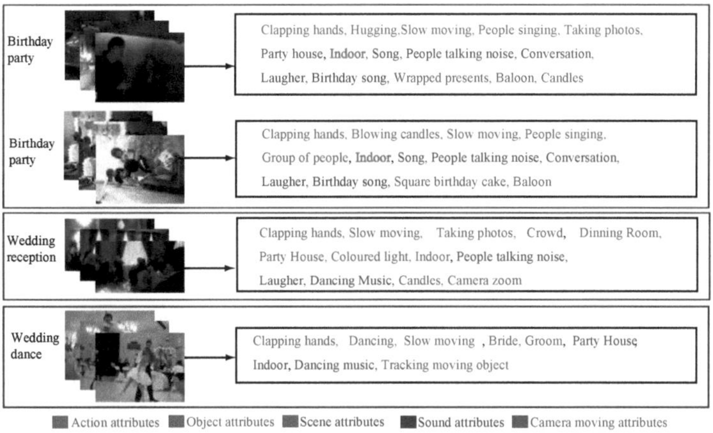

Fig. 1. Examples in social activity attribute video dataset. Different types of attributes of both visual and audio modalities are shown in different colour.

between a handful to hundreds (Fig. 1). By classification, we aim to categorise each video into a class; and by annotation we aim to predict what are present in the video. This implies a wide range of multi-modal annotation types including object (e.g. group of people, cake, balloon), action (e.g. clapping hands, hugging, taking photos), scene (e.g. indoor, garden, street), and sound (e.g. birthday song, dancing music). We consider that the problem of classification and annotation are inter-related and should be tackled together. There have been extensive works on image classification and annotation [1]. However, little effort has been taken on video data, especially on unstructured group social activity video.

We propose to solve the problem using an attribute learning framework, where annotation becomes the problem of attribute prediction and video classification is helped by a learned attribute model. Attributes describe the characterisitics that embody an instance or a class. Recently, attribute-based learning [2,3,4,5,6] has emerged as a powerful approach for image and video understanding. Essentially attributes answer the question of *describing* a class or instance in contrast to the typical (classification) question of *naming* an instance [2,3]. The attribute description of an instance or category is useful as a semantically meaningful intermediate representation to bridge the gap between low level features and high level classes [6]. Attributes thus facilitate transfer and zero-shot learning [6] to alleviate issues of the lack of labelled training data, by expressing classes in terms of well known attributes.

We contribute a new benchmarking multi-modal attribute dataset for social activity video classification and annotation: *unstructured social activity attribute* (USAA) dataset[1]. It comprises of 8 classes (around 1500 videos totally) and the visual and audio content of each video is manually annotated using 69 multi-modal binary attributes. Figure 1 shows examples of videos with annotated

[1] Downloadable from `http://www.eecs.qmul.ac.uk/~yf300/USAA/download/`

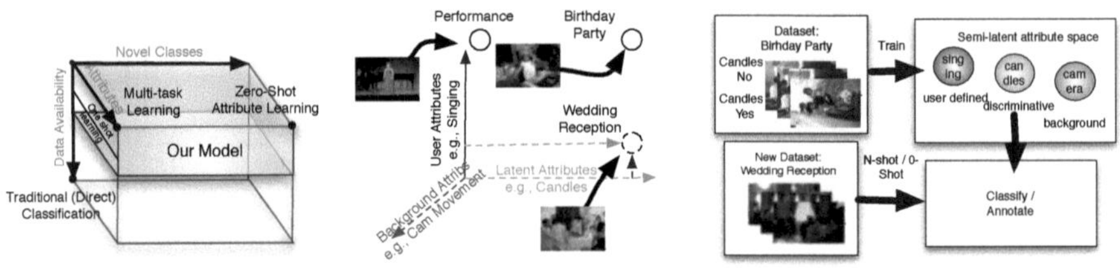

(a) Problem Context (b) Semi-latent Attribute Space (c) Model Overview

Fig. 2. (a) Our approach to semi-latent attribute space learning can be applied in various problem contexts. (b) Representing data in terms of a semi-latent attribute space partially defined by the user (solid axes), and partially learned by the model (dashed axes). A novel class (dashed circle) may be defined in terms of both user and latent attributes. (c) Model overview. New classes are learned via expression in terms of learned semi-latent attribute-space from (b).

attributes. Learning these attributes can support a wide range of studies including object recognition, scene classification, action recognition and audio event recognition. There are a number of unique characters and challenges of this dataset which can be beneficial to the wide community: (1) The data is weakly labelled (each attribute annotation does not tell which part of the video contribute to that attribute). (2) Different instances of one social activity video class (Fig. 1) typically cover a wide variety of attributes (e.g., birthday party class may or may not exhibit candles). One thus cannot make the assumption that a class can be uniquely determined by a deterministic vector of binary attributes [2]. (3) Even with 69 attributes, one cannot assume that the user-defined space of attributes is perfectly and exhaustively defined due to limited annotation, and subjectiveness of manual annotation. (4) The most semantically salient attributes may not be the most discriminative and most discriminative attributes may not correspond to semantic concept and thus can never be manually defined. Discovering and learning those discriminative yet latent attributes thus becomes the key.

To this end, in this paper we introduce the novel concept of semi-latent attribute space. As illustrated in Fig. 1(b), this attribute space consists of three types of attributes: user-defined (UD) attributes, class-conditional (CC) discriminative latent attributes and background non-discriminative (BN) latent attributes. Among the two types of latent attributes, the CC attributes are discriminative attributes which are predictive of class, whilst the BN attributes are uncorrelated to class of interest and should thus be ignored as background data, e.g. random camera or background object movements which are common characteristics of most unstructured social activity videos. It is crucial that these three types of attributes should be learned jointly so that the CC attributes do not repeat the user-defined attributes (UD attributes often are also discriminative), and are separated explicitly from background attributes which explain away irrelevant dimension of the data [7].

To learn this semi-latent attribute space, we present a new approach to attribute learning based on a probabilistic topic model [8,9]. A topic model is chosen because it provides an intuitive mechanism for modelling latent attributes using latent topics. We consider the attribute/topic learning process as *semantic feature reduction* [6] from the raw data to a lower dimensional attribute space (where the axes are the attribute/topic set) (Fig. 1(b)). Classification is then performed in this semantic feature space. To learn the three types of attributes: UD, CC, and BN, the topic model learns three types of topics, namely UD topics, CC topics and BN topics. Among them the UD topics are learned supervised using the labelled use-defined attributes, whilst the learning of CC is supervised by the class label available during training, and the BN topics are learned unsupervised. An important advantage of this approach is that it can seamlessly bridge the gap between context where the attribute space is completely and precisely specified by the user; and scenarios where the attribute space is completely unknown (Fig. 1(a)). This means that unlike existing approaches, our approach is robust to the amount of domain knowledge / annotation budget possessed by the user. Specifically, if the relevant attribute space is exhaustively and correctly specified, we create a topic or set of topics for each attribute, and learn a topic model where the topics for each instance are constrained to not violate the instance-attribute labels. However, if the attribute space is only partially known, we complete the semantic space using *latent* attributes by learning two additional types of topics: CC topics to discover unique attributes of each known class [9]; and BN topics to segment out background non-discriminative attributes [7]. At the extreme, if the relevant attribute space is completely unknown, the latent attributes alone can discover a discriminative and transferrable intermediate representation. Figure 1(c) gives an overview of the process.

2 Related Work

Learning attribute-based semantic representations of data has recently been topical for images [2,5,10,4,11]. The primary contribution of attribute-based representations has been to enable transfer learning (via attribute classifiers) to learn classes with few or zero instances. However, most of these studies [2,5,4,11] assume that an exhaustive space of attributes has been manually specified. Moreover, it is also assumed that each class is simple enough to be determined by a single list of attributes. In practice a complete space of relevant attributes is unlikely to be available a priori since human labelling is limited and the space of classes is unbounded. Furthermore, semantically obvious attributes for humans do not necessarily correspond to the space of useful and computable discriminative attributes [12] (Fig. 1(b)).

A few studies ([3] for object and [13] for action) have considered augmenting user-defined (UD) attributes with data-driven attributes which correspond to our definition of class-conditional (CC) attributes. However these do not span the full spectrum between unspecified and fully specified attribute-spaces as cleanly as our model. Notably, they learn UD attributes and CC attributes separately.

This means that the learned CC attributes are not necessarily complementary to user-defined ones (i.e., they may be redundant). Additionally, some data-driven attributes may be irrelevant to other discriminative tasks, and should thus be ignored. This may not be a problem for annotating an object bounding box [3] and a single object action without people interaction [13] where background information does not present a big issue for learning discriminative foreground attributes. It is however a problem for unstructured social activity video where shared characteristics (therefore attributes) across classes may not be relevant for either classification or annotation. In our approach, by jointly learning user-defined, class-conditional and background non-discriminative (BN) attributes, we ensure that the latent attribute space is both complementary and discriminative.

Probabilistic topic models [8] have been used quie extensively in modelling images [1] and video [14,15,9,7]. However, the topic spaces in those models are used for completely unsupervised dimensionality reduction. Here, we focus on an attribute learning interpretation to learn a semantically meaningful semi-latent topic-space, which leverages as much from any given prior knowledge, either in the form of sparely labelled either class or user-defined attributes.

User-defined video attribute learning is related to the video concept detection (video ontology) work in the multimedia community [16,17,18,19,20,21,22,23] which has defined top-down shared visual concepts, in order to recognise them in video. There are several TRECVID challenges about video ontologies, e.g. in TRECVID Multimedia Event Detection [2]. However, these studies generally consider strongly labelled data and prescriptive ontologies and do not leverage discriminative latent attributes for classification.

This paper makes the following specific contributions: (i) To study the issue of unstructured group social activity video classification and annotation, we present a multi-modal social activity attribute dataset to be made available to the community. (ii) We propose a new topic-model based approach for attribute learning. By learning a unified semi-latent space of user-defined and two types of latent-attributes, we are able to learn a complete and discriminative attribute-space in a way that is robust to any amount of user prior-knowledge. (iii) We show how these properties improve a variety of tasks in the sparse data domain including multi-task learning, N-shot and 0-shot transfer learning. (iv) Our unified framework enables us to leverage latent attributes even in zero-shot learning which has not been attempted before.

3 Methods

3.1 Formalisation

Context. Prior work on detection or classification typically takes the approach of learning a classifier $F : \mathcal{X}^d \rightarrow \mathcal{Z}$ mapping d-dimensional raw data $\mathcal{X}$ to label

[2] `http://www.nist.gov/itl/iad/mig/med12.cfm`

$\mathcal{Z}$ from training data $D = \{(\mathbf{x}_i, z_i)\}_{i=1}^n$. A variant of the standard approach considers a composition of two mappings:

$$F = S(L(\cdot)),\ L : \mathcal{X}^d \to \mathcal{Y}^p,\ S : \mathcal{Y}^p \to \mathcal{Z}, \tag{1}$$

where L maps the raw data to an intermediate representation $\mathcal{Y}^a$ (typically with $a < d$) and then S maps the intermediate representation to the final class $\mathcal{Z}$. Examples of this approach include dimensionality-reduction via PCA [24] (where L is learned to explain the variance of $\mathbf{x}$) or linear discriminants and multi-layer neural networks (where L is learned to predict $\mathcal{Z}$).

Attribute learning [2,6] exploits the idea of manually defining $\mathcal{Y}$ as a *semantic feature* or *attribute* space. L is then learned by direct supervision with pairs of instances and attribute vectors $D = \{(\mathbf{x}_{i,}\mathbf{y}_i)_{i=1}^n\}$. A key feature of this approach is that it permits practical zero-shot learning: the recognition of novel classes without training examples $F : X^d \to \mathcal{Z}^*$ $(\mathcal{Z}^* \notin \mathcal{Z})$ via the learned attribute mapping L and a manually specified template $S^*$of the novel class. Attribute learning can also assist general multi-task and N-shot transfer learning, where we learn a second "target" dataset $D^* = \{(\mathbf{x}_i, z_i^*)\}_{i=1}^m$but $m \ll n$. Here, the attribute mapping L is learned from the large "source" dataset, and is transferred to the target task, leaving only parameters of S to be learned. Most prior attribute-learning work, however, assumes the semantic space $\mathcal{Y}^a$ is completely defined in advance, an assumption we would like to relax.

Semi-latent Attributes. We aim to define an attribute-learning model L which can learn an attribute-space $\mathcal{Y}^a$ from training data D where $|\mathbf{y}| = a_{ud}$, $0 \leq a_{ud} \leq a$. That is, only an a_{ud} sized subset of the attribute dimensions are labeled, and a_{la} other relevant latent dimensions are discovered automatically. The attribute-space is partitioned into observed and latent subspaces: $\mathcal{Y}^a = \mathcal{Y}_{ud}^{a_{ud}} \times \mathcal{Y}_{la}^{a_{la}}$ with $a = a_{ud} + a_{la}$. To support a full spectrum of applications, we should permit $a = a_u$ (traditional attribute learning), and $a = a_l$ (unsupervised latent space).

3.2 Semi-latent Attribute Space Topic Model

LDA. To learn a suitably flexible model for L (Eq. (1)), we generalize LDA[8], modeling each attribute as a topic. LDA provides a generative model for a discrete dataset $D = \{\mathbf{x}_i\}$ in terms of a latent topic y_{ij} for each word x_{ij} given prior topic concentration α and word-topic parameters β. Assuming vector topic proportions α we have

$$p(D|\alpha,\beta) = \prod_i \int \left(\prod_j \sum_{y_{ij}} p(x_{ij}|y_{ij},\beta)p(y_{ij}|\theta_i) \right) p(\theta_i|\alpha)d\theta_i, \tag{2}$$

where j indexes individual words, $\theta_i|\alpha$ is the Dirichlet topic prior for instance i, $x_{ij}|y_{ij}$ and $y_{ij}|\theta_i$ are discrete with parameters $\beta_{y_{ij}}$ and θ_i.

Variational inference for LDA approximates the intractable posterior $p(\theta_i, \mathbf{y}_i|\mathbf{x}_i, \alpha, \beta)$ in terms of a factored variational distribution: $q(\theta_i, \mathbf{y}_i|\gamma_i, \phi_i) = q(\theta_i|\gamma_i)\prod_j q(y_{ij}|\phi_{ij})$ resulting in the updates:

$$\phi_{ijk} \propto \beta_{x_{ij}k} \exp(\Psi(\gamma_{ik})), \quad \gamma_{ik} = \alpha_{ik} + \sum_j \phi_{ijk}. \tag{3}$$

Semi-Latent Attribute Space (SLAS). With no user defined attributes ($a = a_{la}, a_{ud} = 0$), an a-topic LDA model provides a mapping L from raw data $\mathbf{x}$ to an a-dimensional latent space by way of the variational posterior $q(\theta|\gamma)$. This is a discrete analogy to the common use of PCA to reduce the dimension of continuous data. However, to (i) support user-defined attributes when available and (ii) ensure the latent representation is discriminative, we add constraints.

User defined attributes are typically provided in terms of size a^{ud} binary vectors $\mathbf{v}_z^{ud}$ specifying which are present in class z [2,6] We cannot use $\mathbf{v}$ to directly determine or constrain the LDA topic vector $\mathbf{y}^{ud}$. This is because LDA associates each word x_{ij} with a topic y_{ij}, and we don't know word-attribute correspondence. We only know whether each attribute is present in each instance. To enforce this type of constraint, we define a *per instance* prior $\alpha_i = [\alpha_i^{ud}, \alpha_i^{la}]$, setting $\alpha_{i,k}^{ud} = 0$ whenever $v_{z(i),k}^{ud} = 0$. That is, enforcing that instances i of class z lacking an attribute k can never use that attribute the explain the data; but otherwise leaving the inference algorithm to infer attribute proportions and word correspondence. Interestingly, in contrast to other methods, this allows our approach to reason about how strongly each attribute is exhibited in each instance instead of only modeling binary presence and absence.

To learn the latent portion of the attribute-space, we could simply leave the remaining portion α^{la} of the prior unconstrained; however while resulting latent topics/attributes will explain the data, they are not necessarily discriminative. Instead, inspired by [9,7], we split the prior into two components $\alpha_i^{la} = [\alpha_i^{cc}, \alpha^{bn}]$. The first, $\alpha_i^{cc} = \{\alpha_{i,z}\}_{z=1}^{N_z}$, is a series of "class conditional" subsets $a_{i,z}$ corresponding to classes z. For an instance i with label z_i, all the other components $\alpha_{i,z\neq z_i}^{cc}$ are constrained to zero. This enforces that only instances with class z can allocate topics y_z^{cc} and hence that these topics are discriminative for class z. The second component of the latent space prior, α^{bg} is left unconstrained, meaning that in contrast to the CC topics, these "background" topics are shared between all classes. When learned jointly with the CC topics, BN topics are therefore likely to represent common non-discriminative background information [9,7] and thus should be ignored for classification. This is supported by our experiments where we show that better CC topics are learned when BN topics are present.

Classification. Defining the mapping L in Eq. (2) as the posterior statistic γ in SLAS (Eq. (3)), the remaining component to define is the attribute-class mapping S. Importantly, for our complex data, this mapping is not deterministic and 1:1 as is often assumed [2,6]. Like [13], we therefore use standard classifiers to learn this mapping from the γ_is obtained from our SLAS attribute learner.

Zero-Shot Learning (ZSL) with Latent Attributes. To recognize novel classes $\mathcal{Z}^*$, we define the mapping S manually. Existing attribute-learning approaches [2,6] define a simple deterministic prototype $\mathbf{v}_{z^*}^{ud} \in \mathcal{Y}^u$ for class z^*, and classify by NN matching of data to prototype templates. For realistic unstructured video data, huge intra-class variability means that a single prototype is a very poor model of a class, so zero-shot classification will be poor. Counter-intuitively, but significantly more interestingly, *we can actually leverage the latent portion of the attribute-space even without training data for novel class* z^* (so long as there is at least one UD attribute, $a^u \geq 1$) with the following self-training algorithm:

1. Infer attributes γ^* for novel test data X^* (Eq. (3))
2. NN matching in the user-defined space $\gamma^{ud,*}$ against prototypes $\mathbf{v}_{z^*}^{ud}$
3. For each novel class z^*:
   (a) Find top-K most confident test-set matches $\{\gamma_{l,z^*}\}_{l=1}^{K}$
   (b) Self train a new prototype in the full attribute-space: $\mathbf{v}_{z^*} = \frac{1}{K}\sum_l \gamma_{l,z^*}$.
4. NN matching in the full attribute space of γ^* against prototypes $\mathbf{v}_{z^*}$.

Previous ZSL studies are constrained to UD attributes, thus being critically dependent on the completeness of the user attribute-space. In contrast, our approach uniquely leverages a potentially much larger body of latent attributes via even a loose manual definition of a novel class. We will show later this approach can significantly improve zero-shot learning performance.

4 Experiments

In this section we first introduce our new dataset, and then describe the quantitative results obtained for four types of problems: Multi-task classification; learning with label noise; N-shot learning and ZSL. For each reported experiment, we report test set performance averaged over 5 cross-validation folds with different random selections of instances, classes, or attributes held out as appropriate. We compare the following models:

Direct: Direct KNN or SVM classification on raw data without attributes. SVM is used for experiments with > 10 instances and KNN otherwise.[3].

SVM-UD+LR: SVM attribute classifiers learn available UD attributes. A logistic regression (LR) classifier then learns classes given the probability mapped attribute classifier outputs.[4] This is the obvious generalisation of Direct Attribute Prediction (DAP) [2] to non-deterministic attributes.

SLAS+LR: Our SLAS is learned, then a LR classifier learns classes based on the UD and CC topic profile.

[3] Our experiments show that KNN performed consistently better than SVM until #Instance > 10.

[4] LR was chosen over SVM because it is more robust to sparse data.

For all experiments, we cross-validate the regularisation parameters for SVM and LR. For all SVM models, we use the χ^2 kernel. For SLAS, in each experiment, we keep the complexity fixed at 85 topics, up to 69 of which are UD attributes, and the others equally divided between CC and BN latent attributes. The UD part of the SLAS topic profile is estimating the same thing as the SVM attribute classifiers, however the latter are slightly more reliable due to being discriminatively optimised. As input to LR, we therefore actually use the SVM attribute classifier outputs in conjunction with the latent part of our topic profile.

4.1 Unstructured Social Activity Attribute (USAA) Dataset: Classes and Attributes

A new benchmark attribute dataset for social activity video classification and annotation is introduced. We manually annotate the groundtruth attributes for 8 semantic class videos of CCV dataset [16], and select 100 videos per-class for training and testing respectively. These classes were selected as the most complex social group activities. As shown in Fig. 1, a wide variety of attributes have been annotated. The 69 attributes can be broken down into five broad classes: actions, objects, scenes, sounds, and camera movement. We tried our best to exhaustively define every conceivable attribute for this dataset, to make a benchmark for unstructured social video classification and annotation. Of course, real-world video will not contain such extensive tagging. However, this exhaustive annotation gives the freedom to hold out various subsets and learn on the others in order to quantify the effect of annotation density and biases on a given algorithm. These eight classes are birthday party, graduation party, music performance, non-music performance, parade, wedding ceremony, wedding dance and wedding reception (shown in Fig. 3). Each class has a strict semantic definition in the CCV video ontology. Directly using the ground-truth attributes (average annotation density 11 attributes per video) as input to a SVM, the videos can be classified with 86.9% accuracy. This illustrates the challenge of this data: while the attributes are informative, there is sufficient intra-class variability in the attribute-space, that even perfect knowledge of the attributes in an instance is insufficient for perfect classification. The SIFT, STIP and MFCC features for all these videos are extracted according to [16], and included in the dataset. We report the baseline accuracy of SVM-attribute classifiers learned on the whole test set in Fig. 4. Clearly some can be detected almost perfectly, and others cannot be detected given the available features.

4.2 Multi-task Learning

The main advantage of attribute-centric learning when all classes are known in advance is exploiting feature sharing [25]. The statistical strength of data supporting a given attribute can be aggregated across its occurrences in all classes. This treats classification like a multi-task learning problem where the class models share parameters, rather than each class being modelled independently.

Fig. 3. Example frames from the eight class unstructured social activity dataset

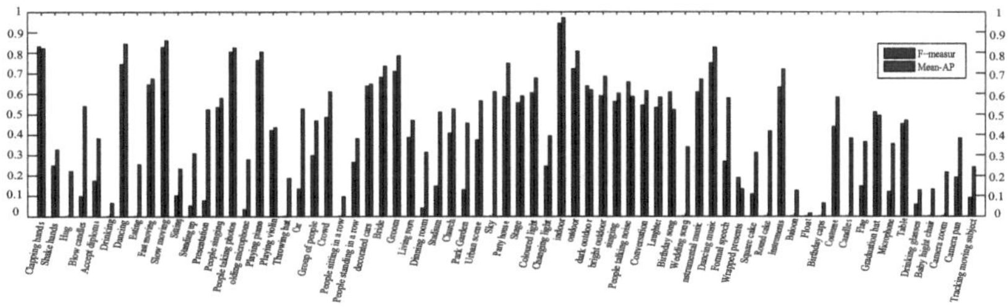

Fig. 4. Attribute-classification accuracy using SVM

Table 1 summarises our results. We first consider the simplest classification scenario where the data is plentiful and the attributes are exhaustively defined. In this case all the models perform similarly. Next, we consider a sparse data variant, with only 10 instances per class to learn from. Here Direct KNN performs poorly due to insufficient data. The attribute models perform better due to leveraging statistical strength across the classes. To the most realistic case of a sparsely defined attribute space, we next limit the attributes to a randomly selected seven every trial, rather than the exhaustively defined 69. In this challenging case SVM+LR performance drops 10% while our SLAS continues to perform similarly, now outperforming the others by a large margin. It is able to share statistical strength among attributes (unlike Direct KNN) and able to fill out the partially-defined attribute space with latent attributes (unlike SVM+LR). Finally, the other challenge in learning from real-world sources of unstructured social video is that the attribute annotations are likely to be very noisy. To

Table 1. Multi-task classification performance (%). (8 classes, chance = 12.5%).

	Direct	SVM+LR	SLAS+LR
100 Inst, 69 UD	**66**	65	65
10 Inst, 69 UD	29	37	**40**
10 Inst, 7 UD	29	27	**36**
10 Inst, 7 UD, attribute noise	27	23	**36**

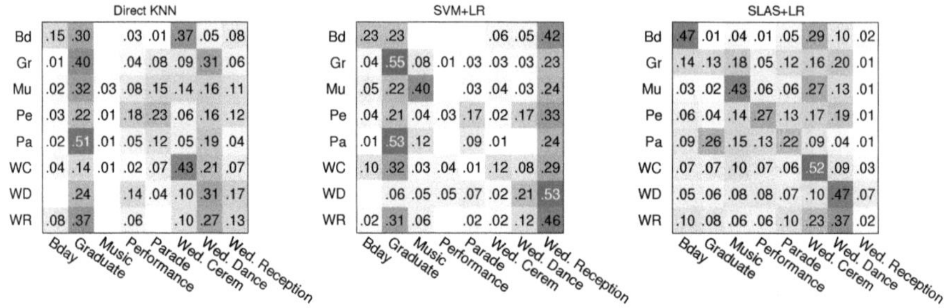

Fig. 5. Confusion matrices for multi-task classification with 10 instances per class

simulate this, we repeated the previous experiment, but randomly changed 50% of attribute bits on 50% of the training videos (so 25% wrong attribute annotations). In this case, performance of the traditional attribute-learning approach is further reduced, while the that of our model is unchanged. This is because our model learns and leverages a whole space of latent attributes to produce a robust representation which can compensate for noise in the UD attributes.

Fig. 5 shows the confusion matrices for the 10 instance, 7 attribute task. The matricies for the traditional Direct KNN and SVM attribute classification have vertical bands indicating consistent misclassifications. Our SLAS has the clearest diagonal structure with little banding, indicating no consistent errors.

4.3 N-Shot Transfer Learning

In transfer learning, one assumes ample examples of a set of source classes, and sparse examples of a *disjoint* set of target classes. To test this scenario, in each trial we randomly split our 8 classes into two disjoint groups of four source and target classes. We use all the data from the source task to train our attribute learning models (SLAS and SVM), and then use these to obtain the attribute profiles of the target task. Using the target task attribute profiles we perform N-shot learning, with the results summarised by Table 6. Importantly, traditional attribute learning approaches cannot deal with zero attribute situations. Our SLAS performs comparably or better than both Direct-KNN and SVM+LR for zero, seven and 34 attributes.This illustrates the robustness of our model to the density of the attribute-space definition. Importantly, standard attribute-learning (SVM+LR) cannot function with zero attributes, but our attribute model maintains a significant margin over Direct KNN in this case.

4.4 Zero-Shot Learning

One of the most interesting capabilities of attribute-learning approaches is zero-shot learning. Like N-shot learning, the task is to learn transferrable attribute knowledge from a source dataset for use on a disjoint target dataset. However, no training examples of the target are available. Instead, user manually specifies the definition of each novel class in the semantic attribute space. Zero-shot learning

	1-shot			5-shot		
	Direct KNN	SVM+LR	SLAS+LR	Direct KNN	SVM+LR	SLAS+LR
0 UD	30	-	**34**	34	-	**42**
7 UD	30	32	**33**	34	43	**44**
34 UD	30	**37**	35	34	47	**48**

Fig. 6. N-shot classification performance (%). (4 classes, chance = 25%)

is often evaluated in simple situations where classes have unique 1:1 definitions in the attribute-space [2]. For our unstructured social data, strong intra-class variability violates this assumption, making evaluation slightly more subtle. We compare two approaches: "continuous" prototypes, where a novel class definition is given by continuous values in attribute-space, and "binary" prototypes, where the novel class is defined as a binary attribute vector. These correspond to two models of human provided semantic knowledge: continuous or thresholded probability that a new class has a particular attribute. E.g., saying that cakes and candles are definite attributes of a birthday party vs saying they might occur with 90% and 80% probability respectively. To simulate these two processes of prior knowledge generation, we take the mean and the thresholded mean (as in [13,10]) of the attribute profiles for each instance.

Our results are summarised in Table 2. Using latent attributes to support the user-defined attributes (Sec. 3.2) allows our SLAS model to improve on the conventional user-defined attribute only approach to zero-shot learning. Interestingly, continuous definition of class prototypes is a significantly more powerful approach for both methods (Table 2, Continuous vs Binary). To illustrate the value of our other contribution, we also show the performance of our model when learned without free background topics (SLAS (NF)). The latent attribute approach is still able to improve on using pure user-defined attribute, but by a smaller margin. The BN topics generally improve performance by segmenting the less discriminative dimensions of the latent attribute space and allowing them to be ignored by the classifier.

Table 2. Zero-shot classification performance (%). (4 classes, chance = 25%).

Continuous			Binary		
UD	UD+Latent		UD	UD+Latent	
SVM-DAP	SLAS	SLAS (NF)	SVM-DAP	SLAS	SLAS (NF)
38	**45**	41	31	**36**	31

5 Conclusions

Summary. In this paper we have considered attribute learning for the challenging task of understanding unstructured multi-party social activity video. To promote study of this topical issue, we introduced a new multi-modal dataset with extensive detailed annotations. In this context, a serious practical issue is the limited availability of annotation relative to the number and complexity of relevant concept classes. We introduced a novel semi-latent attribute-learning technique which is able to: (i) flexibly learn a full semantic-attribute space when attribute space is exhaustively defined, or completely unavailable, available in a small subspace (i.e., present but sparse), or available but noisy; (ii) perform conventional and N-shot while leveraging latent attributes and (iii) go significantly beyond existing zero-shot learning approaches (which only use defined attributes), in leveraging latent attributes.. In contrast, standard approaches of direct classification or regular attribute-learning fall down in some portion of the contexts above (Section 4).

Future Work. There are a variety of important related open questions for future study. Thus far, our attribute-learner does not consider inter-attribute correlation explicitly (like most other attribute learners with the exception of [13]). This can be addressed relatively straightforwardly by generalising the correlated topic model (CTM) [26] for our task instead of regular LDA [8]. A correlated attribute model should produce commensurate gains in performance to those observed elsewhere [13].

We have made no explicit model [27] of the different modalities of observations in our data. However explicit exploitation of the different statistics and noise-processes of the different modalities is an important potential source of improved performance and future study (e.g., learning modality-attribute correlations and inter-modality correlations via attributes).

The complexity of our model was fixed to a reasonable value throughout (i.e., the size of the semi-latent attribute/topic-space), and we focused on learning with attribute-constraints on some sub-set of the topics. More desirable would be a non-parametric framework which could infer the appropriate dimensionality of the latent attribute-space automatically. Moreover, we ware able to broadly separate foreground and "background" topics via the different constraints imposed; however it is not guaranteed that background topics are irrelevant, so not using them in classification may be sub-optimal. A more systematic way (e.g., [7]) to automatically segment discriminative "foreground" and distracting "background" attributes would be desirable.

References

1. Wang, C., Blei, D., Li, F.F.: Simultaneous image classification and annotation. In: Proc. CVPR (2009)
2. Lampert, C.H., Nickisch, H., Harmeling, S.: Learning to detect unseen object classes by between-class attribute transfer. In: CVPR, pp. 951–958 (2009)
3. Farhadi, A., Endres, I., Hoiem, D., Forsyth, D.: Describing objects by their attributes. In: Proc. CVPR (2009)
4. Farhadi, A., Endres, I., Hoiem, D.: Attribute-centric recognition for cross-category generalization. In: CVPR (2010)
5. Parikh, D., Grauman, K.: Relative attributes. In: Proc. ICCV (2011)
6. Palatucci, M., Hinton, G., Pomerleau, D., Mitchell, T.M.: Zero-shot learning with semantic output codes. In: Proc. NIPS (2009)

7. Hospedales, T., Gong, S., Xiang, T.: Learning tags from unsegmented videos of multiple human actions. In: Proc. ICDM (2011)
8. Blei, D.M., Ng, A.Y., Jordan, M.I.: Latent dirichlet allocation. Journal of Machine Learning Research 3, 993–1022 (2003)
9. Hospedales, T., Li, J., Gong, S., Xiang, T.: Identifying rare and subtle behaviours: A weakly supervised joint topic model. PAMI (2011)
10. Farhadi, A., Endres, I., Hoiem, D., Forsyth, D.: Describing objects by their attributes. In: Proc. CVPR (2009)
11. Mahajan, D., Sellamanickam, S., Nair, V.: A joint learning framework for attribute models and object descriptions. In: Proc. ICCV (2011)
12. Parikh, D., Grauman, K.: Interactively building a discriminative vocabulary of nameable attributes. In: CVPR (2011)
13. Liu, J., Kuipers, B., Savarese, S.: Recognizing human actions by attributes. In: Proc. CVPR (2011)
14. Wang, Y., Mori, G.: Human action recognition by semilatent topic models. TPAMI 31, 1762–1774 (2009)
15. Niebles, J.C., Wang, H., Fei-Fei, L.: Unsupervised learning of human action categories using spatial-temporal words. IJCV 79, 299–318 (2008)
16. Jiang, Y.G., Ye, G., Chang, S.F., Ellis, D., Loui, A.C.: Consumer video understanding: A benchmark database and an evaluation of human and machine performance. In: ICMR (2011)
17. Yanagawa, A., Loui, E.C., Luo, J., Chang, S.F., Ellis, D., Jiang, W., Kennedy, L.: Kodak consumer video benchmark data set: concept definition and annotation. In: Proc. ACM MIR (2007)
18. Gupta, A., Srinivasan, P., Shi, J., Davis, L.S.: Understanding videos, constructing plots learning a visually grounded storyline model from annotated videos (2009)
19. Wang, M., Hua, X.S., Hong, R., Tang, J., Qi, G.J., Song, Y.: Unified video annotation via multigraph learning. IEEE Trans. Cir. and Sys. for Video Technol. (2009)
20. Tang, J., Yan, S., Hong, R., Qi, G.J., Chua, T.S.: Inferring semantic concepts from community-contributed images and noisy tags. In: Proc. ACM MM (2009)
21. Tang, J., Hua, X.S., Qi, G.J., Song, Y., Wu, X.: Video annotation based on kernel linear neighborhood propagation. IEEE Transactions on Multimedia (2008)
22. Snoek, C.G.M., Worring, M.: Concept-based video retrieval. Foundations and Trends in Information Retrieval 4, 215–322 (2009)
23. Snoek, C.G.M., Huurnink, B., Hollink, L., de Rijke, M., Schreiber, G., Worring, M.: Adding semantics to detectors for video retrieval. IEEE Transactions on Multimedia 9, 975–986 (2007)
24. Dollar, P., Rabaud, V., Cottrell, G., Belongie, S.: Behavior recognition via sparse spatio-temporal features. In: VS-PETS, pp. 65–72 (2005)
25. Salakhutdinov, R., Torralba, A., Tenenbaum, J.: Learning to share visual appearance for multiclass object detecti. In: Proc. CVPR (2011)
26. Blei, D., Lafferty, J.: A correlated topic model of science. Annals of Applied Statistics 1, 17–35 (2007)
27. Putthividhy, D., Attias, H.T., Nagarajan, S.S.: Topic regression multi-modal latent dirichlet allocation for image annotation. In: Proc. CVPR, pp. 3408–3415 (2010)

Statistical Inference of Motion in the Invisible

Haroon Idrees, Imran Saleemi, and Mubarak Shah

Computer Vision Lab, University of Central Florida, Orlando, USA
{haroon,imran,shah}@eecs.ucf.edu

Abstract. This paper focuses on the unexplored problem of inferring motion of objects that are invisible to all cameras in a multiple camera setup. As opposed to methods for learning relationships between disjoint cameras, we take the next step to actually infer the exact spatiotemporal behavior of objects while they are invisible. Given object trajectories within disjoint cameras' FOVs (field-of-view), we introduce constraints on the behavior of objects as they travel through the unobservable areas that lie in between. These constraints include vehicle following (the trajectories of vehicles adjacent to each other at entry and exit are time-shifted relative to each other), collision avoidance (no two trajectories pass through the same location at the same time) and temporal smoothness (restricts the allowable movements of vehicles based on physical limits). The constraints are embedded in a generalized, global cost function for the entire scene, incorporating influences of all objects, followed by a bounded minimization using an interior point algorithm, to obtain trajectory representations of objects that define their exact dynamics and behavior while invisible. Finally, a statistical representation of motion in the entire scene is estimated to obtain a probabilistic distribution representing individual behaviors, such as turns, constant velocity motion, deceleration to a stop, and acceleration from rest for evaluation and visualization. Experiments are reported on real world videos from multiple disjoint cameras in NGSIM data set, and qualitative as well as quantitative analysis confirms the validity of our approach.

1 Introduction

The proliferation of large camera networks in recent past has ushered research in multiple camera analysis, and several methods have been proposed to address the problems of calibration, tracking and activity analysis with some degree of reliability [1,2,3,4,5,6,7]. However, despite significant efforts in this area, the majority of literature has been confined to solution of problems like object correspondence and activity correlation between visible objects, while estimation and inference of object behaviors in *unobservable regions* between disjoint cameras has mainly remained unexplored. Such invisible regions between disjoint cameras are always present as visual sensor networks have an inherent inability to provide exhaustive coverage of all areas of interest, while failure of a sensor is always a possibility which can result in loss of coverage of a particular area that was previously being observed. Besides the issue of coverage, there are several other applications that justify research into such inference: improving object correspondences across cameras; estimating patterns of motion and scene structure; aiding

A. Fitzgibbon et al. (Eds.): ECCV 2012, Part IV, LNCS 7575, pp. 544–557, 2012.

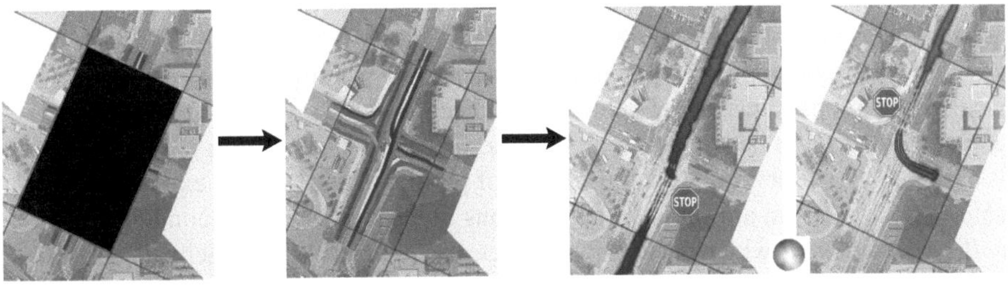

Fig. 1. The first image depicts the input to our method - correspondences across multiple disjoint cameras. In this case, there are five cameras, the FOV of cameras are shown with different colors whereas invisible region is represented by black. Given the input, we reconstruct individual trajectories using constraints introduced in this paper. Next, reconstructed trajectories are used to infer expected behavior at each location in the scene, shown as thick color regions, where the direction of motion is shown by HSV color wheel. We also infer different behaviors such as stopping and turning from the reconstructed trajectories.

expensive operations for PTZ camera focusing by precise localization of unobservable objects; and generalized scene understanding, etc.

In this paper, we pose the question of what information can be inferred about objects while they are not observable in any camera, given tracking and object correspondence information in a multiple camera setup? This is an under-constrained problem, for instance, the correspondence provides two sets of constraints (position, velocity), but if the object is invisible for a hundred time steps, then we have to solve for a hundred variables. For instance, in the scenario shown in Fig. 1, the knowledge that an object exits a camera's FOV on the top, and enters another's on the right is of little use in guessing what its behavior was while invisible. The best we can do it to assume that object moved with the constant velocity through the invisible region. But, this is a rather strong assumption, since the object may have stopped at some unknown locations for unknown amounts of time, or may have taken an indirect path between exit and re-entry into the camera network. Such behavior is influenced by scene structure (such as allowable paths), obstacle avoidance, collision avoidance with other objects, and if the object is a vehicle, it may further be influenced by dynamic aspects of the invisible scene such as traffic signals. Besides being an assumption that is not always true, constant velocity does not provide with any useful information about motion of object or the invisible region itself. The question then becomes, can we do better than constant velocity? If we assume absolutely no information about the invisible region and treat objects independently, the answer is no. But, if we have correspondences for multiple objects available, then the fact that motion of an object is dependent on proximal objects can be used to constrain its movement to a certain degree. The idea of using object-specific contextual constraints has been used as social force models for tracking [8] and simulation, and for describing vehicular motion in transportation theory [9,10,11]. But, these models differ in application from the problem addressed in his paper, in that they assume object positions are known with certainty, we on the other hand, use these constraints as costs which we minimize to obtain positions at each time instant. This is further complicated by the fact that, each object affects motion of its nearby objects and thus, circular inter-dependencies exist between objects. This requires some form of precedence mechanism where some objects receive priority in the solution over others.

In the proposed approach, given object trajectories within disjoint cameras' FOVs, we introduce constraints on the behavior of objects as they travel through the unobservable areas that lie in between. The first of these constraints is *vehicle following*, which is based on the observation that trajectories of proximal vehicles that exit a camera and enter another camera are time-shifted versions of each other. The second constraint is *collision avoidance*, which ensures that vehicles do not collide with each other. The next constraint *temporal smoothness* restricts the allowable movements of vehicles based on physical limits. The last constraint *behavior localization* bounds the cost introduced by collision avoidance ensuring that solution is non-trivial. The constraints are embedded in a generalized, global cost function for the entire scene, incorporating influences of all objects, followed by a minimization to obtain trajectory representations of objects that define their exact dynamics and behavior while invisible. Finally, a statistical representation of motion in the entire scene is estimated to obtain a probabilistic distribution representing individual behaviors, such as turns, constant velocity motion, deceleration to a stop, and acceleration from rest, for evaluation and visualization.

To the best of our knowledge, there are currently no methods in literature that attempt to infer any salient properties for unobservable areas (trajectories, motion patterns, static and dynamic behavior of objects). In addition to the applications listed earlier, such inference will allow economically viable deployment of large sensor networks without the need to cover all possible regions of interest, and learning of patterns of activity for an invisible region will allow detection of anomalous behavior without directly observing it. To summarize our contributions, the proposed framework has the ability to infer the following about an *invisible* scene without any observations:

- Estimation of object trajectories in (x, y, t) as they travel through the unobservable area,
- Inference of static and dynamic aspects of the scene such as positions where objects generally stop and traffic lights without direct observation, and
- Completely unsupervised discovery and statistical representation of salient object patterns of motion for the entire scene including large invisible regions.

The organization of the rest of the paper follows. We briefly review relevant literature in §2, followed by detailed problem formulation and solution in §3, inference of static and dynamic scene structure in §4 and presentation of experimental evaluation in §5.

2 Related Work

The literature involving multi-camera scenarios contains techniques proposed for object tracking as well as scene and activity modeling and understanding [12,13,14]. In particular, many methods have been proposed specifically for analysis of disjoint, or non-overlapping multiple cameras [4,6,5,15]. The objective of modeling camera relationships is to use these models to solve for hand-off between cameras, but the patterns are modeled only for motion within the field of views of cameras. Dockstader and Tekalp [16] use Bayesian networks for tracking and occlusion reasoning across calibrated overlapping cameras while in a series of papers [17,18,19], authors employ Kalman Consensus Filter for tracking in multiple camera networks.

In terms of inference of topological relationships between multiple disjoint cameras, Makris et al. [3] determined the topology of a camera network by linking entry and exit zones using co-occurrence relationships between them, while Tieu et al. [20] avoid explicit feature matching by computing the statistical dependence between observations in different cameras to infer network topology. Stauffer [21] proposed an improved linking method to handle cases where exit-entry events may be correlated, but the correlation is not due to valid object transitions. Another interesting area of research is the focus of work by Loy et al. [7], where instead of assuming feature correspondences across cameras, or availability of any tracking data, regions of locally homogenous motion are first discovered in all camera views using correlation of object dynamics. A canonical cross correlation analysis is then performed to discover and quantify the time delayed correlations of regional activities observed within and across multiple cameras in a common reference space.

For our purpose of behavior inference in unobservable regions, avoidance of object collision in structured scenes is one of the most important cues. In this respect, research in transportation theory has attempted to perform collision prediction and detection in the visual domain. Atev et al. [22] propose a collision prediction algorithm using object trajectories, and van den Berg et al. [23] solve the problem of collision avoidance for independently moving robots that can observe each other. In our proposed framework, however, it is essentially assumed that no collisions took place in the unobservable region, and the goal is to infer unobserved object behavior given this assumption. Notice that although some of the proposed constraints bear similarity to 'motion planning' algorithms in robotics [24], some of the significant differences include the fact that for path planning the obstacles are directly observable and the length of time taken to reach the destination is unconstrained. Our method essentially deals with the reverse problem of path planning, i.e., inferring the path that has already been traversed. We therefore propose a solution to a previously unexplored problem. In the following, we formally define the problem and discuss our approach to solve it.

3 Problem Formulation and Solution

Given a set of trajectories (for only observable areas) that have been transformed to a global frame-of-reference, we focus on the difficult and interesting scenario when the unobservable region contains traffic intersections even though the solution we propose in this paper can handle simpler situations such as straight roads as well. The input variables of the problem are the correspondences, i.e., a vehicle's position, velocity, and time when it enters and exits the invisible region (or equivalently exits a camera's field of view and enters another's).

Let p_i^t, v_i^t, and a_i^t denote the position, velocity and acceleration respectively, of the ith vehicle at time t while traveling through the invisible region and η_i and χ_i be the time instants it enters and exits the invisible region. Thus, given the pair of triplets for entry (p^η, v^η, η) and exit (p^χ, v^χ, χ), our goal is to find p_i^t for all $t \in [\eta_i, \chi_i]$, for each vehicle which correspondingly determines v_i^t and a_i^t.

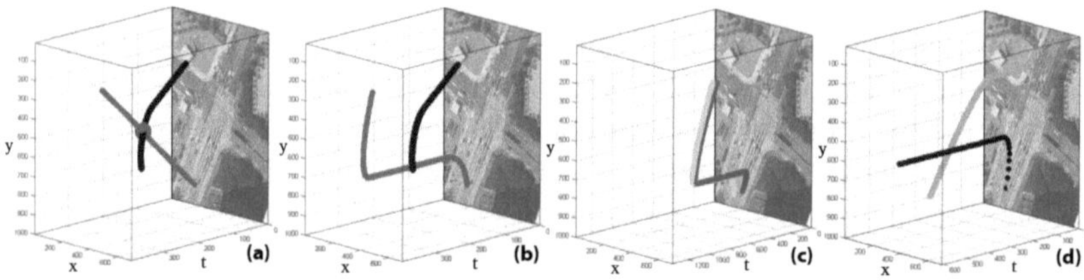

Fig. 2. Depiction of constraints using vehicle trajectories in (x, y, t): (a) The point of collision between green and black trajectories shown with a red sphere, whereas collision is avoided in (b). (c) shows an example of vehicle-follwing behavior where vehicle in yellow trajectory follows the one in red. In (d) the orange trajectory does not violate smoothness constraint but the one in black does (abrupt deceleration).

A path $\mathcal{P}_i$ is a set of 2d locations traversed by a vehicle i and is obtained by connecting p^η with p^χ such that derivative of $\mathcal{P}_i$ is computable at all points i.e. there are no sudden turns or bends. The path so obtained does not contain any information about time. Associating each location in $\mathcal{P}_i$ with time gives us the trajectory $\{p_i^t\}$. Two vehicles i and j have the same path i.e., $\mathcal{P}_i \equiv \mathcal{P}_j$, if $\|p_i^{\eta_i} - p_j^{\eta_j}\|$ and $\|p_i^{\chi_i} - p_j^{\chi_j}\|$ are less than threshold T, and they have temporal overlap $\mathcal{O}(i, j) = 1$, if $\eta_i < \chi_j \wedge \eta_j < \chi_i$. Moreover, their paths intersect, i.e., $i \perp j$, if $\mathcal{P}_i$ obtained by joining $p_i^{\eta_i}$ to $p_i^{\chi_i}$, intersects with $\mathcal{P}_j$.

Since inference of motion in invisible regions in a severely under-constrained problem, we impose some priors over the motion of vehicles as they travel through the region. These priors in §3.1-3.4 below, are used as constraints that will later allow us to reconstruct complete trajectories in the invisible region. The first two constraints (collision avoidance and vehicle following) essentially capture the context of spatially and temporally proximal vehicles while third constraint (smoothness of trajectories) establishes physical limits on the mobility of vehicles as they travel through the region. Using these constraints, we propose an algorithm to reconstruct trajectories in §3.6.

3.1 Collision Avoidance

The first prior we exploit is the fact that vehicles are driven by intelligent drivers who tend to avoid collisions with each other. The probability that a vehicle will occupy a location at particular time becomes low if the same location is occupied by another vehicle at that same time. This effectively reduces the possible space of the solution, leaving only those solutions that have low probability of collisions. Consider the two vehicle trajectories shown in Fig. 2(a) where black trajectory shows a vehicle making a left-turn while vehicle with green trajectory moves straight. The corresponding 2d paths, $\mathcal{P}$ intersect at the point marked with a red sphere. A collision implies that a single point in (x, y, t) is occupied by more than one object. Collision avoidance, thus, enforces that no two trajectories pass though the same (x, y, t) point. In Fig. 2(b), the collision is avoided by a change in shape of the green trajectory. Note that, collision avoidance doesn't necessarily mean that vehicles change paths in space, but that they don't occupy the same spatial location at the same time. Formally, let τ be the time when vehicles with intersecting paths are closest to each other in (x, y, t), then the collision cost for vehicle i given by:

$$C_i^{\alpha} = \sum_j \exp\left(\omega^{\alpha} \cdot \frac{v_i^{\tau}.v_j^{\tau}}{\|p_i^{\tau} - p_j^{\tau}\|}\right), \text{ where } \tau = \underset{t}{\text{argmin}} \left\|p_i^t - p_j^t\right\|, \tag{1}$$

$\forall j | i \perp j \wedge \mathcal{O}(i,j) = 1$, ω^{α} being the weight. The above equation captures the cost due to motion at the point of closest approach from all vehicles with respect to the vehicle under consideration. The exponentiation softens the impact of collision to nearby points in (x, y, t), thus forcing vehicles to not only avoid the same point but avoid close proximity as well. Two proximal vehicles both moving with a high velocity will have a high cost, however, if at least one vehicle is stationary, this cost will be low.

3.2 Vehicle Following

Like collision avoidance, this constraint reduces the solution space by making sure that relative positions of adjacent and nearby vehicles remain consistent throughout their travel in the invisible region. It is inspired from transportation theory, where vehicle following models describe the relationship between vehicles as they move on the roadway [9,10,11]. Many of them are sophisticated functions of distance, relative velocity and acceleration of vehicles and have several parameters such as desired velocity based on speed limit, desired spacing between vehicles and comfortable braking distance.

We, on the other hand, use vehicle following to define a spatial constraint between leading and following vehicles. The leader $\mathfrak{l}$ and follower $\mathfrak{f}$ are given by the pair:

$$\begin{aligned}(\mathfrak{l}, \mathfrak{f}) = \big\{&(i,j) | \mathcal{P}_i = \mathcal{P}_j, \mathcal{O}(i,j) = 1 \wedge \eta_i < \eta_j, \\ &\chi_i < \chi_j \wedge \nexists k | \eta_i < \eta_k < \eta_j \vee \chi_i < \chi_k < \chi_j\big\}.\end{aligned} \tag{2}$$

We use the relationship between leader and follower to constrain the possible movement of follower by forcing it to remain behind its leader throughout its travel through the invisible region. This also caters for the correct stopping position of follower since it must stop behind the leader and not occupy the same spot, an event which is highly likely if we only take into account cost from collision. The vehicle-following cost for follower given the leader is written as:

$$C_i^{\beta} = exp\left(\omega^{\beta} \sum_t \|p_j^t - p_i^t\|_+\right), \tag{3}$$

where $\|p_j^t - p_i^t\|_+ = \|p_j^t - p_i^t\|$, if $\|p_j^t - p_j^{\chi_j}\| < \|p_i^t - p_j^{\chi_j}\|$ and 0 otherwise; ω^{β} is the weight associated to this cost.

Vehicle-following constraint enforces the condition that trajectories of vehicles adjacent to each other following the same path are time-shifted versions of each other, as can be seen in Fig. 2(c) where red and yellow trajectories belong to the leading and following vehicles respectively.

3.3 Smoothness of Trajectory

The smoothness constraint restricts the allowable movements of vehicles based on physical limits as it happens in real life. It prevents the solution from having abrupt acceleration or deceleration as well as sudden stops. This is an object-centric constraint and is computed as:

$$C_i^\gamma = exp\left(\omega^\gamma \sum_t \left(1 - \sqrt{\frac{\pi}{2}} \mathcal{N}(\frac{v_i^t}{v_i^{t-1}}; 1, \sigma^\gamma)\right)\right), \tag{4}$$

where ω^γ is the weight, and $\mathcal{N}$ is the normal distribution with $\sigma^\gamma = 0.25$ variance.

The above equation ensures that distance in space-time volume between any two adjacent points in a single trajectory is a small multiple of the other. In Fig. 2(d), the orange trajectory is has low smoothness cost whereas black trajectory has higher cost due to abrupt deceleration in the beginning.

3.4 Stopping Behavior Localization

The above three constraints do not completely specify the solution because trivial solutions with high values of acceleration and deceleration can exist. This is possible when a vehicle is made to stop with high deceleration i.e. near $p_i^{\eta_i}$, stays there as long as possible before leaving the invisible region with high acceleration while satisfying the smoothness constraint. This *afraid-of-collision* solution for a vehicle is not only incorrect, it also will result in wrong results for all of the following vehicles. The following additional cost will rectify this problem avoiding such solution,

$$C_i^\delta = exp\left(\omega^\delta \left\| x_{i,j} - p_i^{t_\varphi} \right\|\right), j | i \bot j \wedge \mathcal{O}(i,j) = 1, \tag{5}$$

where ω^δ is the associated weight, $x_{i,j}$ is the spatial point where vehicle paths intersect and t_φ is the time when vehicle stops. This constraint dictates that stopping point for a vehicle cannot be arbitrarily away from the possible collision locations, essentially localizing the move-stop-move events in space and time.

3.5 Trajectory Parametrization

As mentioned earlier, given entry and exit locations, each trajectory is represented by a 2D path, $\mathcal{P}$ by joining the two locations in a way that allows for bends as they happen in the case of turns. Parameterizing the curve by placing $\chi - \eta$ equidistant points for a vehicle gives us a trajectory that represents motion with constant velocity. Parameterizing in this way reduces the number of variables to one-half (from 2D to 1D). Our goal then becomes to find the temporal parametrization of the trajectory that minimizes cost from the constraints. But, given that we might be dealing with thousands of vehicles, each invisible for hundreds of time units, the extremely large variable space ($\sim 10^6$) makes the problem intractable.

In order to make the problem tractable, we reduce the parameters defining a trajectory to three: deceleration (ϕ), duration of stopping time (φ) and acceleration (ψ).

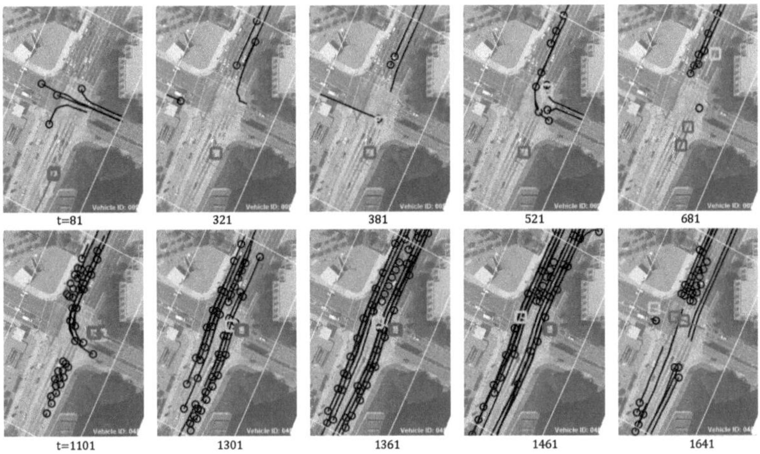

Fig. 3. Each row is an example of trajectory reconstruction. Vehicle under consideration is shown with squares, yellow depicts constant velocity, red is from proposed method and green square marks the ground truth. Rest of the vehicles are shown in black. In first row, reconstruction with constant velocity causes collisions at $t = 381$ and 521, and in the second row, between $t = 1200$ and 1500. On the other hand, proposed method and ground truth allow the vehicles to pass without any collision.

The constant velocity case corresponds to $\phi = \varphi = \psi = 0$. Thus, we can model all cases between constant velocity to complete stopping by varying values of these variables. However, since the exact duration of invisibility and end-point velocities are known, we have only two-degrees of freedom making one of the variables dependent on the other two. We choose ϕ and φ to represent the trajectory, while ψ is determined based on time and velocity constraints. Thus, the parametrization results in constant or zero acceleration and deceleration while satisfying entry and exit velocities.

3.6 Optimization for Motion Inference

Considering each vehicle individually, given the time it enters and exits the region, the best estimate for its motion is constant velocity. However, since an invisible region (in our case, an intersection) may involve vehicles traveling in from all directions, each vehicle influences the motion of other vehicles. A constant velocity prediction for each vehicle will result in collisions even though it may satisfy the constraints of vehicle-following and smoothness.

Given entry and exit triplets of position, velocity and time for each vehicle, our goal is to find the parameters ϕ and φ for all vehicles that pass though the invisible region. Since each vehicle's position at every time instant is conditionally dependent on all other vehicles that also pass through the invisible region, this information is exploited in the form of four constraints. The proposed solution iteratively minimizes the local cost of each vehicle by making sure it satisfies the constraints, fixing its parameters and then moving onto other vehicles.

Algorithm 1. Algorithm to infer motion of vehicles given $[p^\eta, v^\eta, \eta]$ and $[p^\chi, v^\chi, \chi]$ for vehicles $1:n$

procedure INVISIBLEINFERENCE
  Prioritize vehicles using Eq. 6
  for all $i \leftarrow 1, n$ as per Θ_i **do**
    Identify $j|\mathcal{O}(i,j) = 1$ and $i \perp j$
    $\phi_i, \varphi_i \leftarrow \underset{\phi,\varphi}{\operatorname{argmin}}\ C_i^\alpha + C_i^\beta + C_i^\gamma + C_i^\delta$
    Parameterize trajectory i according to ϕ_i, φ_i
  end for
end procedure

We impose a prioritizing function on the trajectories, which is a linear function of entry and exit times:

$$\Theta_i = \omega^\chi \chi_i + \omega^\eta \eta_i. \tag{6}$$

If we set $\omega^\chi = 1$ and $\omega^\eta = -1$, the criteria becomes *shortest duration first*, on the other hand, if $\omega^\chi = 1$ and $\omega^\eta = 0$, the criteria becomes *earlier exit first*. The former biases the solution towards high priority vehicles putting very strong constraints on vehicles that spend longer times in the invisible region. We used the latter which makes more intuitive sense also since vehicles will yield way to the a vehicle that exits before them.

The cost for each vehicle is the sum of costs due to collision, vehicle-following, and smoothness including penalty for trivial solution. The parameters are bounded so that -20 ft/s$^2 < \phi < 0$, and $0 < \varphi < \chi - \eta$, and the cost is minimized through an Interior Point Algorithm with initialization provided by uniform grid search over the parameter space. The summary for this simple algorithm is provided in Alg. 1 while Fig. 3 shows the results on real examples.

4 Inference of Scene Structure

After obtaining trajectories using the method and constraints described in the previous section, we now propose methods to statistically represent motion in the invisible region (§4.1), followed by extracting some key features of the scene such as locations of stopping points (static) and timings of traffic signals (dynamic) in §4.2.

4.1 Statistical Representation of Motion

Given the inferred trajectory representations for objects in invisible region, we compute the features, $(x_i^t, y_i^t, u_i^t, v_i^t, t)$, for each point on the ith trajectory derived from $\mathcal{P}_i$, ϕ_i, φ_i, and ψ_i, where $u^t = x^t - x^{t-1}$, and $v^t = y^t - y^{t-1}$. To obtain a probabilistic distribution that represent individual behaviors, such as turns, constant velocity motion, deceleration to a stop, and acceleration from rest, we first cluster feature points using the k-means algorithm, and then treat the clusters as components of a 4d Gaussian mixture model, B for each leg of traffic. A feature point $\mathbf{x}$ induced by B is given as,

$$\mathbf{x} \sim \sum_{k=1}^{N_B} \omega_k \mathcal{N}\left(\cdot \middle| \mu_k, \mathbf{\Sigma}_k\right), \tag{7}$$

where the mixture contains N_B Gaussian components, each with parameters μ, $\mathbf{\Sigma}$, and mixing proportion ω. This representation serves as a generative model that summarizes the spatiotemporal dynamics of objects induced by each behavior, and is potentially useful for scene understanding, anomaly detection, tracking and data association, as well as visualization of results of the proposed inference framework. For visualization, we compute the per-pixel expected motion vectors conditioned on the pixel location along each leg, i.e., $\mathrm{E}_B\left[\sqrt{u^2+v^2}, \tan^{-1}(v/u)|x, y\right]$, to obtain expected magnitude and orientation of motion at each pixel for each behavior, and depict them using the HSV colormap as is done for motion patterns [25].

4.2 Scene Structure and Status Inference

Given the exact motion and behavior of objects in the invisible regions, we propose to estimate some key aspects of the scene structure and status to, show the importance and usefulness of our framework, and allow evaluation. We briefly explain our methods for finding the locations where vehicles exhibit the stopping behavior (equivalent to stopping positions), and the times at which such behaviors occur (equivalent to status of traffic signals) for each path in the invisible region.

We use the locations, $p_i^{t_\varphi}$, for $i|v_i < T$, to vote for regions corresponding to stop positions. Specifically, given n vehicles, we compute the following kernel density estimate of the 2d surface, Γ, representing probability of a pixel, p, belonging to stopping location:

$$\Gamma(\mathrm{p}) = \frac{1}{n}|\mathbf{H}|^{-\frac{1}{2}} \sum_{i=1}^{n} K\left(\mathbf{H}^{-\frac{1}{2}}\left(\mathrm{p} - p_i^{t_\varphi}\right)\right), \tag{8}$$

where K is a 2d Gaussian kernel with a symmetric, positive, diagonal bandwidth matrix, $\mathbf{H}$, of fixed horizontal and vertical variances, set to 10 pixels. Fig. 8(a,b) shows an example of the distribution reflecting probabilities of pixels being stopping positions. The proposed framework therefore estimates salient scene structure in a statistical manner, without making a single observation within the scene.

Secondly, given the representation of behaviors learned earlier which divides the scene into possibly overlapping segments corresponding to traffic intersection legs, by thresholding $\int\int \mathrm{Pr}_B du dv$, we can effectively estimate the signal status for each leg. We use the following simple process: at a given time t, the inferred status (red, green) of a traffic signal for a leg, l, is $\sum_i \|p_i^{t+1} - p_i^t\|$, if i belongs to l and $t > t_\varphi$. Therefore, if any vehicle traveling on leg l has a non-negligible velocity at its stopping positions, it votes for the green signal for that leg at that time. The results of signal status and transitions for all legs of traffic (blue), compared to the results obtained by applying the same process to ground truth trajectories (black), are shown in Fig.8(c).

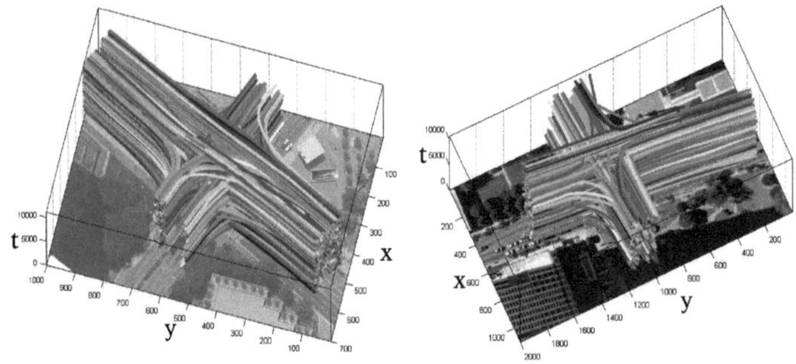

Fig. 4. All trajectories inferred for each dataset shown in 3D. Left and right images are inferred trajectories from Lankershim and Peachtree datasets respectively.

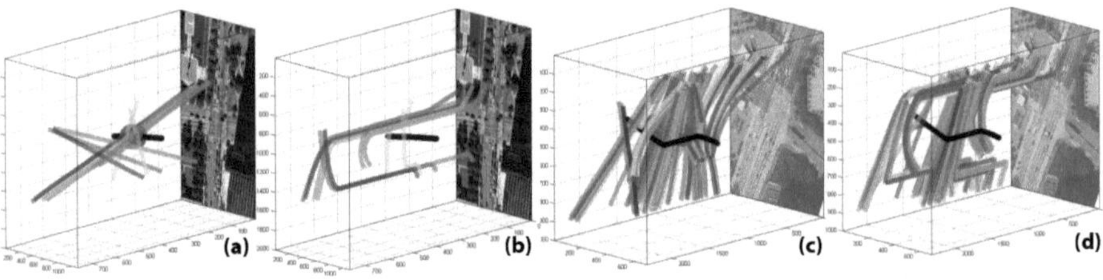

Fig. 5. Trajectories in (a) and (c) represent constant velocity while (b) and (d) show output of proposed method. Collisions due to constant velocity prediction are marked with red spheres in (a) and (c), but this does not occur in (b) and (d), which are the results of proposed trajectory inference.

5 Experiments

We ran our experiments on two datasets from NGSIM (see [26] for details). The first invisible region was from Lankershim 8:30am - 8:45am located at the intersection of Lankershim/Universal Hollywood Dr. (LA) with a total of 1211 vehicles passing through the region. The second invisible region was from Peachtree 4:00pm to 4:15pm located at the intersection of Peachtree/10th Street NE (Atlanta) with 657 vehicles passing through the region. Both intersections were typical four-legged with three possible paths that could be taken by a vehicle entering a particular leg, thus, resulting in 12 total paths. Fig. 4 shows the trajectories that were output by Alg. 1 for both the datasets.

We next analyze the performance of motion inference employing the different constraints, followed by results for motion behaviors and scene structure. Figure 5 provides qualitative results for motion inference where the (a,b) is from Peachtree and (c,d) from Lankershim dataset. The black trajectory corresponds to the vehicle under consideration while proximal vehicles which it could possibly collide with are shown in colors. In both (a) and (c), the trajectories are drawn assuming constant velocity for each vehicle. In (a), the vehicle collides with one of the vehicles whereas in (c), vehicle under consideration collides with six different vehicles. The locations of collision are shown with red spheres partially invisible due to other vehicles. Notice the change in shape in

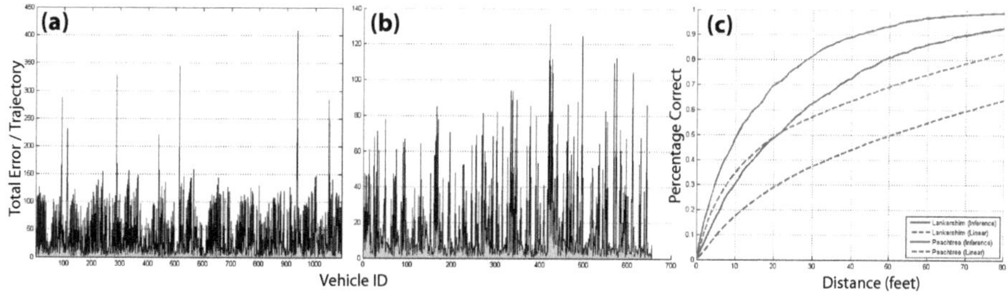

Fig. 6. (a,b) Error profile for our method (yellow) vs. constant velocity (black) for both datasets. As can be seen, our method has lower error (it has smaller magnitude), thus provides more accurate inference. (c) ROC curves for our method (solid) vs. constant velocity (dashed) for the Lankershim (red) and Peachtree (green). The x-axis is the distance threshold in feet while y-axis gives the percentage of points that lie within that threshold distance of the ground-truth.

(b) and (d) after inferring motion for all trajectories with the outcome that none of the trajectories collides with the black trajectory. Both vehicle-following and smoothness constraints are also visibly in effect in both the examples.

Fig. 6(a,b) gives a per-trajectory comparison of error with and without motion inference. These graphs for Lankershim and Peachtree respectively were obtained by computing total error (in feet) for each trajectory by computing Euclidean distance of each point to the groundtruth. The yellow bars correspond to motion inference whereas black bars represent the case of using constant velocity only. Fig. 6(c) gives the ROC curves for the two datasets. On the x-axis is the threshold distance in feet, on y-axis are the percentage of points in all invisible trajectories that lie within that threshold. Using inference, we get an improvement of at least 20% over the baseline in both datasets. After obtaining the inferred trajectories, we statistically represented the motion in the invisible region using the method described in §4.1. Fig. 7 shows MoG for three different legs where three columns represent constant velocity, proposed method and ground truth.

Figures 8 give results for some of the salient features of the invisible region using §4.2. Fig. 8(a) shows the probability map superimposed on the image of invisible region for locations where vehicles stop using only the inferred trajectories from Lankershim whereas Fig. 8(b) shows the same probability map for Peachtree. It can be seen that all of the locations are correct, just before the intersection due to collision avoidance and extend beyond due to vehicle following constraint when vehicles queue up at intersection. Figure 8(c) gives the probability of which traffic light was green at each time instant using the proposed method (blue) and the results are also compared against groundtruth (black). In this figure, we show traffic light behavior over time for 8 of the 12 paths as right turns do not get subjected to signals. Below each blue graph which is obtained using inferred trajectories, is the black graph showing probability of that light being green using groundtruth. The results show little difference, validating the performance and quality of inference.

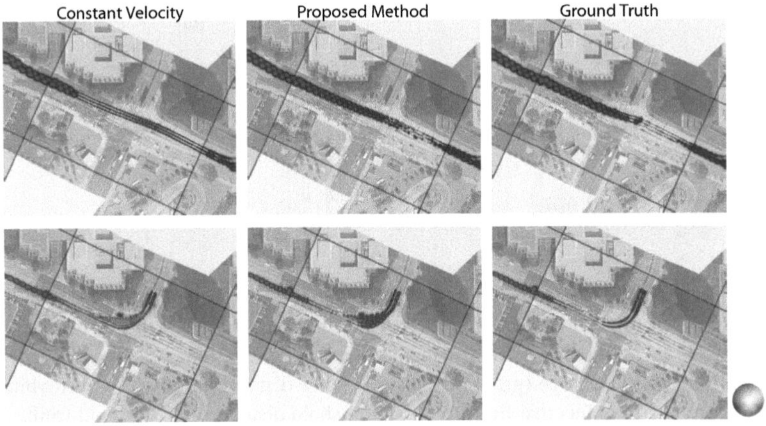

Fig. 7. Each row is the Mixture of Gaussians representation for a particular path using constant velocity, proposed method and ground truth. The patterns in the second and third column are similar and capture acceleration, deceleration, start and stop behaviors whereas in first column, all Gaussians have the same variance due to constant velocity.

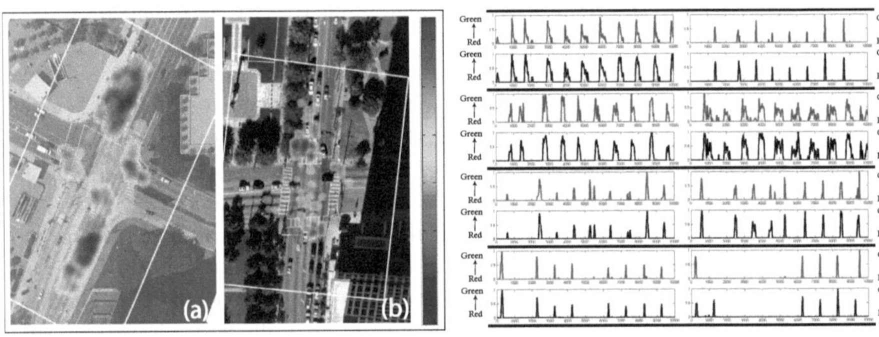

Fig. 8. Left (a,b): The probability map for stopping positions as inferred from Eq. 8 for both datasets which are correct as vehicles in reality stop and queue before the signal. Right: Probability of green signal for each of eight possible legs. The x-axis is time and y-axis in each graph is the *probability* from our method (blue) and groundtruth (black), which are evidently, perfectly aligned in time.

6 Conclusion and Future Work

We presented the novel idea of understanding motion behavior of objects while they are in the invisible region of multiple proximal cameras. The solution used three constraints, two of which employ contextual information of neighboring objects to infer correct motion of object under consideration. Though, an interesting proposal from the perspective of scene and motion understanding, the idea has several potential applications in video surveillance. Possible extensions include handling situations where correspondences are missing or incorrect in some cases and to humans where social force models can be leveraged in addition to current constraints.

References

1. Stauffer, C., Tieu, K.: Automated multi-camera planar tracking correspondence modeling. In: CVPR (2003)
2. Khan, S., Shah, M.: Consistent labeling of tracked objects in multiple cameras with overlapping fields of view. IEEE PAMI 25 (2003)
3. Makris, D., Ellis, T., Black, J.: Bridging the gaps between cameras. In: CVPR (2004)
4. Gheissari, N., Sebastian, T., Hartley, R.: Person reidentification using spatiotemporal appearance. In: CVPR, vol. 2 (2006)
5. Hu, W., Hu, M., Zhou, X., Tan, T., Lou, J., Maybank, S.: Principal axis-based correspondence between multiple cameras for people tracking. IEEE PAMI 28(4) (2006)
6. Gray, D., Tao, H.: Viewpoint Invariant Pedestrian Recognition with an Ensemble of Localized Features. In: Forsyth, D., Torr, P., Zisserman, A. (eds.) ECCV 2008, Part I. LNCS, vol. 5302, pp. 262–275. Springer, Heidelberg (2008)
7. Loy, C.C., Xiang, T., Gong, S.: Multi-camera activity correlation analysis. In: CVPR (2009)
8. Pellegrini, S., Ess, A., Schindler, K., van Gool, L.: You'll never walk alone: Modeling social behavior for multi-target tracking. In: ICCV (2009)
9. Kikuchi, S., Chakroborty, P.: Car following model based on fuzzy inference system. Transport. Res. Record (1992)
10. Nagel, K., Schreckenberg, M.: A cellular automaton model for freeway traffic. J. Phys. I France 2(12) (1992)
11. Newell, G.: Nonlinear effects in the dynamics of car following. Ops. Res. 9(2) (1961)
12. Javed, O., Shafique, K., Rasheed, Z., Shah, M.: Modeling inter-camera space-time and appearance relationships for tracking across non-overlapping views. CVIU 109 (2008)
13. Huang, T., Russell, S.: Object identification in a bayesian context. In: IJCAI (1997)
14. Kettnaker, V., Zabih, R.: Bayesian multi-camera surveillance. In: CVPR (1999)
15. Prosser, B., Gong, S., Xiang, T.: Multi-camera matching using bi-directional cumulative brightness transfer functions. In: BMVC (2008)
16. Dockstader, S., Tekalp, A.: Multiple camera fusion for multi-object tracking. In: IEEE WMOT (2001)
17. Soto, C., Song, B., Roy-Chowdhury, A.: Distributed multi-target tracking in a self-configuring camera network. In: CVPR (2009)
18. Song, B., Kamal, A., Soto, C., Ding, C., Farrell, J., Roy-Chowdhury, A.: Tracking and activity recognition through consensus in distributed camera networks. In: IEEE TIP (2010)
19. Kamal, A., Ding, C., Song, B., Farrell, J.A., Roy-Chowdhury, A.: A generalized kalman consensus filter for wide area video networks. In: IEEE CDC (2011)
20. Tieu, K., Dalley, G., Grimson, W.: Inference of non-overlapping camera network topology by measuring statistical dependence. In: ICCV (2005)
21. Stauffer, C.: Learning to track objects through unobserved regions. In: WMVC (2005)
22. Atev, S., Arumugam, H., Masoud, O., Janardan, R., Papanikolopoulos, N.: A vision-based approach to collision prediction at traffic intersections. IEEE TIT Systems 6(4) (2005)
23. van den Berg, J., Guy, S., Lin, M., Manocha, D.: Reciprocal n-body collision avoidance 70, 3–19 (2011)
24. LaValle, S.M.: Planning Algorithms. Cambridge University Press (2006)
25. Saleemi, I., Hartung, L., Shah, M.: Scene understanding by statistical modeling of motion patterns. In: CVPR (2010)
26. Next Generation Simulation (NGSIM) dataset, `http://www.ngsim.fhwa.dot.gov/`

Going with the Flow: Pedestrian Efficiency in Crowded Scenes

Louis Kratz and Ko Nishino

Department of Computer Science
Drexel University, Philadelphia, PA 19104, USA
{lak24,kon}@drexel.edu

Abstract. Video analysis of crowded scenes is challenging due to the complex motion of individual people in the scene. The collective motion of pedestrians form a crowd flow, but individuals often largely deviate from it as they anticipate and react to each other. Deviations from the crowd decreases the pedestrian's *efficiency*: a sociological concept that measures the difference of actual motion from the intended speed and direction. In this paper, we derive a novel method for estimating pedestrian efficiency from videos. We first introduce a novel crowd motion model that encodes the temporal evolution of local motion patterns represented with directional statistics distributions. This model is then used to estimate the intended motion of pedestrians at every space-time location, which enables visual measurement of the pedestrian efficiency. We demonstrate the use of this pedestrian efficiency to detect unusual events and to track individuals in crowded scenes. Experimental results show that the use of pedestrian efficiency leads to state-of-the-art accuracy in these critical applications.

1 Introduction

A key challenge to video analysis of crowded scenes is the complex motion introduced by the intricate interactions between individual pedestrians. The large number of people and their aggregated motion give rise to coherent motion that form the crowd flow. Individuals in the crowd, however, constantly anticipate and react to others surrounding them, causing pauses or changes in direction and speed. These subtle variations of individual motion result in often large deviations from the crowd flow. These deviations are the main source of difficulty for video analysis as they make individual tracking challenging for a microscopic approach and reduces the accuracy of crowd motion models in a macroscopic approach.

Often pedestrians deviating from crowd flow are reacting to an interruption (e.g., someone cutting them off) or congestion. In such cases, the individual avoids collision by deviating from their intended motion. *Efficiency* is a well studied measure in sociology [1] that quantifies the difference between the actual pedestrian motion and his/her intended speed and direction. Helbing et al. [2] define and measure efficiency in physical space (i.e., meters and seconds measured in the 3D world), and show its direct relationship to crowd stability. To our knowledge, despite the possible applications to visual crowd analysis, efficiency has not been addressed by the vision community.

A. Fitzgibbon et al. (Eds.): ECCV 2012, Part IV, LNCS 7575, pp. 558–572, 2012.

To compute pedestrian efficiency the intended motion of each individual must be known. Although it is impossible to know each individual's intention, pedestrians form emergent behaviors (e.g., lanes or clusters) that reveal clues to their intended directions. Still [3] notes that emergent behaviors form because it is easier "to follow immediately behind someone who is already moving in your direction." In other words, the emergent behaviors formed by pedestrians suggest where they intend to move. Such behaviors depend on the scene and vary temporally [4], but tend to repeat [2], forming an underlying space-time structure in the collective motion of the crowd. By learning this structure the intended motion of pedestrians can be estimated and used to estimate efficiency.

In this paper, we present a novel method for estimating pedestrian efficiency from videos and use it for video analysis of crowded scenes. Our key insight is that we may estimate the intended motion of individual pedestrians by modeling the crowd motion. First, we introduce a space-time model that captures the latent structure induced by the motion of the crowd. For this, we use a collection of hidden Markov models over directional statistics distributions of optical flow. By training this model on a short video of the scene, we encode the temporally varying multi-modal flows in the image space resulting from the emergent behaviors of the people in the crowd. Second, we use this model to anticipate the motion at each space-time location of the video. These predicted local motions can then be used to estimate the intended motion of individuals passing through each of those space-time regions. We then compare this estimate to the actual motion represented by the instantaneous optical flow to compute pedestrian efficiency over the entire video volume. By doing so, we measure efficiency within the scene without identifying each individual pedestrian.

We use our pedestrian efficiency estimate to robustly detect local and global unusual activities and to dynamically adjust motion priors for tracking individuals in videos of crowded scenes. The experimental results on a number of videos of real-world crowded scenes show that our method enables the accurate computation of pedestrian efficiency which in turn leads to better predictions of scene motions. As a result, the use of pedestrian efficiency achieves state-of-the-art accuracy in these two fundamental tasks in video analysis that are especially challenging in crowded scenes.

2 Related Work

Macroscopic approaches to video analysis of crowded scenes view the crowd as a collection of individuals obeying a set of analytical rules. Moore et al. [5] present a hydrodynamics model, treating each pedestrian as a particle in a fluid. As noted by Still [3], however, emergent behaviors such as lane formations or clustering do not occur in fluids. Particles are affected only by the external forces around them, but pedestrian motion is a result of both external forces and reactions to other pedestrians. Efficiency decreases when pedestrians react to one another, and is inversely related to the deviation from the crowd motion. As such, automatically estimating pedestrian efficiency enables a better understanding of how individuals interact with the crowd, and can be used to more accurately predict their behaviors in the scene.

Mehran et al. [6] use a social force model but do not measure the full influence of the crowd on the individual. They represent intended velocity using instantaneous optical

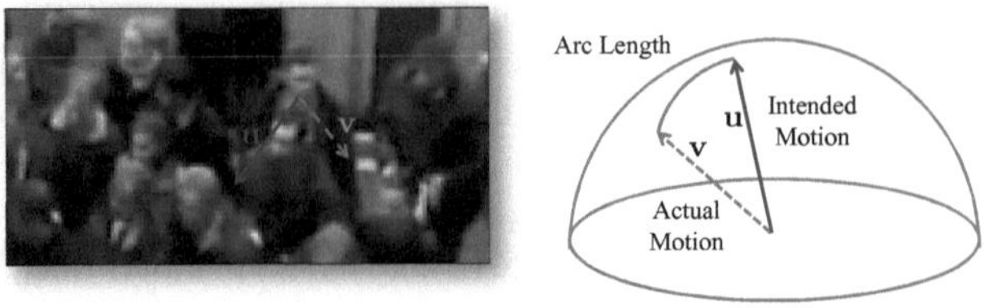

Fig. 1. Pedestrian efficiency in videos can be defined by the difference between the intended and actual motions represented with 3D optical flow vectors. Left: The intended direction $\mathbf{u}$ of an individual may be inhibited causing them to move in a different direction $\mathbf{v}$. Right: We measure the difference between these motions with arc-length on the unit sphere, which is inversely proportional to efficiency.

flow, and the average optical flow as the pedestrian's actual velocity. This assumption is not valid in congested scenes: if an area is highly dense and pedestrians are moving slowly, then the averaged (and instantaneous) optical flow has a low velocity and thus their "interaction force" will not reflect the influence of the crowd on the pedestrian's speed. In addition, pedestrians tend to sway when their motion is restricted [7, 8], suggesting that the instantaneous optical flow does not indicate their intended motion. As we show in Sec. 7, by using a model of the crowd motion our method more accurately estimates the intended motion, and can measure efficiency in high-density scenes.

Tracking and anomaly detection methods often degrade when pedestrian motion largely deviates from the crowd motion. Minor, usual deviations appear as noise to anomaly detection, and are often addressed by complex motion descriptors such as distributions of space-time gradients [9] or dynamic textures [10]. Tracking methods designed for crowds [11–13] lose the target when they deviate from the learned model. Other methods based on motion patterns [14] also assume that objects follow dominant flows. Efficiency indicates the severity of the deviation from the learned model, which we can use to detect unusual crowd activities and track pedestrians with a greater robustness to those deviations as we demonstrate.

3 Efficiency

Individuals move through public areas according to their personal goals and with walking speeds they feel comfortable. As shown in the left image in Fig. 1, they have an intended speed and direction, which may be inhibited by surrounding pedestrians. Helbing and Vicsek [1] define the influence of surrounding pedestrians on an individual as the *interaction rate*, and show it is inversely related to efficiency. Rather than computing efficiency for each pedestrian, we estimate efficiency at each space-time pixel location in the video. By doing so, we may analyze the scene without having to detect and track each pedestrian.

Let t denote time and $\mathbf{p} = [x, y]^T$ a 2D pixel location in the video. We denote the intended motion of the pedestrian occupying pixel $\mathbf{p}$ at time t by

$$\mathbf{u}_t(\mathbf{p}) = [\Delta x, \Delta y, \Delta t]^T \ , \tag{1}$$

where Δx, Δy, and Δt is the change (movement) in the horizontal, vertical, and temporal dimensions, respectively, and $|\mathbf{u}_t(\mathbf{p})| = 1$. The 2D optical flow $\tilde{\mathbf{u}}_t(\mathbf{p})$ induced by this indented motion is computed by temporally normalizing this 3D optical flow vector: $\tilde{\mathbf{u}}_t(\mathbf{p}) = [\Delta x/\Delta t, \Delta y/\Delta t]$. Similarly, let $\mathbf{v}_t(\mathbf{p})$ be the 3D instantaneous optical flow observed in the video.

We derive an image-space equivalent of the physical efficiency from Helbing et al. [2]

$$\frac{\tilde{\mathbf{u}}_t(\mathbf{p}) \cdot \tilde{\mathbf{v}}_t(\mathbf{p})}{|\tilde{\mathbf{u}}_t(\mathbf{p})|^2} . \tag{2}$$

The bounds of Eq. 2, however, are not well defined. For example, if pedestrians move faster than their intended speed (e.g., in a panic situation), then it is unbounded. As illustrated on the right in Fig. 1, we compute the efficiency using the great-circle distance

$$e_t(\mathbf{p}) = 1 - \frac{\arccos\left(\mathbf{u}_t(\mathbf{p})^T \mathbf{v}_t(\mathbf{p})\right)}{\pi} \tag{3}$$

that is bounded by $[1, 0]$. Since we represent motion using 3D optical flow vectors, Eq. 3 captures both differences in direction (longitudinal variations across the unit sphere) and speed (latitudinal variations). To compute efficiency, however, we need the intended motion $\mathbf{u}_t(\mathbf{p})$. Next, we describe our crowd model which we use to estimate $\mathbf{u}_t(\mathbf{p})$.

4 Directional Statistics Crowd Motion Model

In the absence of other pedestrians, individuals move in straight lines towards their destinations. In higher densities, however, they naturally form organized structures (i.e., emergent behaviors) to utilize the available space and achieve a higher flow [15]. These behaviors vary temporally [4] but tend to repeat [2]. We model this structured crowd motion by training a collection of hidden Markov models (HMMs), one for each spatial location in the frame. Our previous work [12, 9] also use a collection of HMMs but retains appearance information in the form of spatial gradients. In this work, we train the HMMs on directional statistics distributions of optical flow resulting in a more compact and accurate representation. It is worth pointing out that other methods [13, 11] do not retain the temporal dynamics of crowd flow.

As shown in Fig. 2(a), we subsample the video using a regular grid and represent the motion in each sub-volume, or "cuboid." Let ∇I_i be a 3D vector containing the image gradient estimated in the horizontal, vertical, and temporal directions, respectively, and $\{\nabla I_i \,|\, i = 1, \ldots, N\}$ be a set of N space-time gradients within a cuboid. When a cuboid contains motion in a single direction, the space-time gradients lie on a plane orthogonal [16] to the 3D optical flow $\mathbf{q}$. Thus $\mathbf{q}$ can be estimated by solving [16]

$$\left[\frac{1}{N}\sum_{i}^{N} \nabla I_i \nabla I_i^T\right] \mathbf{q} = \mathbf{0} . \tag{4}$$

Note that we can use any optical flow estimation algorithm, for instance, those tailored to large displacements [17], if necessary. In this work, we found our gradient-based method sufficient and significantly faster than such dense estimation methods.

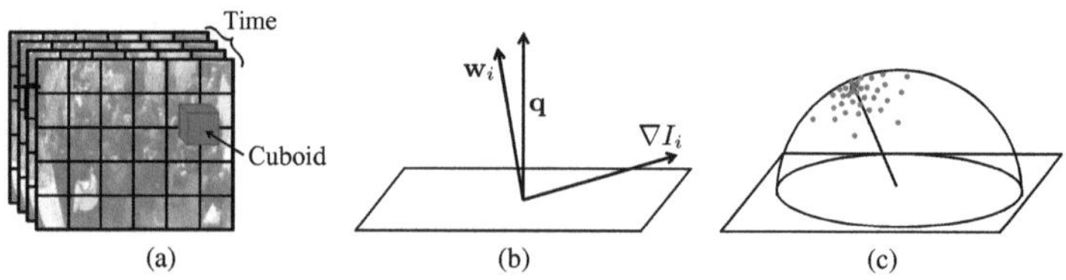

Fig. 2. (a) We subdivide the video into space-time cuboids. (b) The 3D optical flow $\mathbf{q}$ estimated from the cuboid is orthogonal to a plane in spatio-temporal gradient space. A gradient ∇I_i that does not lie on the plane represents uncertainty in the flow, and is orthogonal to another possible flow vector $\mathbf{w}_i$. (c) The set of these possible flow vectors forms a directional distribution on the upper-hemisphere.

Cuboids containing motion in a single direction have gradients that are coplanar, while those containing multiple moving objects have gradients that are not. As illustrated in Fig. 2(b), a space-time gradient ∇I_i that does not lie on the plane suggests motion in another direction $\mathbf{w}_i$ orthogonal to ∇I_i. The vector $\mathbf{w}_i$ is a 3D flow vector

$$\mathbf{w}_i = \frac{\nabla I_i \times \mathbf{q} \times \nabla I_i}{|\nabla I_i \times \mathbf{q} \times \nabla I_i|}, \tag{5}$$

where $\times$ is the cross-product.

As shown in Fig. 2(c), the distribution $\{\mathbf{w}_i \mid i=1,\ldots,N\}$ exists on the upper hemisphere of $\mathbf{q}$. It's shape characterizes the motion in the cuboid: narrow distributions represent motion in a specific direction, and wide distributions represent motion in multiple directions. A natural representation is the von Mises-Fisher distribution [18]

$$\mathrm{p}(\mathbf{x}) = \frac{1}{c(\kappa)} \exp\left\{\kappa \boldsymbol{\mu}^T \mathbf{x}\right\}, \tag{6}$$

where $\boldsymbol{\mu}$ is the mean direction, $c(\kappa)$ is a normalization constant, and κ is the concentration parameter.

We train an HMM on the von Mises-Fisher distributions observed at each spatial grid location. HMMs are defined by J hidden states, a $J{\times}1$ initial probability vector $\boldsymbol{\pi}$, a $J{\times}J$ transition matrix $\mathbf{A}$, and a set of J emissions densities $\{\mathrm{p}(O|s=j) \mid j=1,\ldots,J\}$. In our model, each observation $O=\{\boldsymbol{\mu},\kappa\}$ describes the motion within a specific cuboid. Although κ is not necessary to estimate the intended motion, we include it for tracking in Sec. 6.2. We consider $\boldsymbol{\mu}$ and κ to be statistically independent and define the emission densities analytically

$$\mathrm{p}(O|s=j) = \mathrm{p}(\boldsymbol{\mu}|s=j)\mathrm{p}(\kappa|s=j), \tag{7}$$

where $\mathrm{p}(\kappa|s=j)$ is a Gamma distribution, and $\mathrm{p}(\boldsymbol{\mu}|s=j)$ a von-Mises Fisher distribution (i.e., the conjugate prior on $\boldsymbol{\mu}$ [19]). We train the HMMs on a sample video of the target scene using the Baum-Welch algorithm [20].

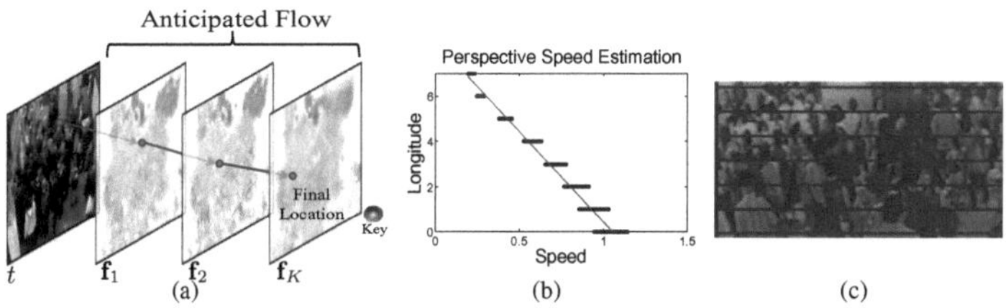

Fig. 3. We estimate the intended direction by advancing each pixel location through a 3D flow field (a) (color indicates speed and direction) that we predict from the HMMs. To estimate the intended speed in scenes captured with a perspective projection, we fit a line to the top 5% of speed measurements (b) at each longitudinal location of the frame (c).

5 Estimation of Intended Motion

Next, we use the trained HMMs to estimate the intended motion at each space-time location in a different video of the same scene. We discuss direction and speed separately, and combine them to compute the intended motion $\mathbf{u}_t(\mathbf{p})$.

5.1 Intended Direction

Given the observed video up to time t and an HMM trained at spatial location $\mathbf{p}$, we compute $\mathbf{z}_k(\mathbf{p})$ as a $1 \times J$ vector representing the likelihood of being in state j at time $t+k$

$$\mathbf{z}_k(\mathbf{p}) = \boldsymbol{\alpha}_t \mathbf{A}^k , \tag{8}$$

where $\mathbf{A}$ is the state transition matrix from the HMM, and $\boldsymbol{\alpha}_t$ is the scaled forward message from the forwards-backwards algorithm [20]. As $k \to \infty$, Eq. 8 approaches the stationary distribution of the Markov process (if it exists).

We use the set $\{\mathbf{z}_k(\mathbf{p}) | k = 1, \ldots, K\}$ to compute the optical flow after time t. We select K large enough to approach the stationary distribution. Let $\mathbf{f}_k(\mathbf{p})$ be the flow predicted from $\mathbf{z}_k(\mathbf{p})$

$$\mathbf{f}_k(\mathbf{p}) = \sum_{j=1}^{J} \mathbf{z}_{k,j}(\mathbf{p}) \mathbb{E}\left[\mathrm{p}(\boldsymbol{\mu} | s{=}j)\right] , \tag{9}$$

where $\mathrm{p}(\boldsymbol{\mu}|s{=}j)$ is the emission density from Eq. 7. The resulting flow field (i.e., $\mathbf{f}_k(\mathbf{p})$ for all spatial locations and values of k) represent the anticipated flow of the crowd.

As shown in Fig. 3(a), we estimate the future location of each point $\mathbf{p}$ by advancing it through the anticipated flow field. Let $\tilde{\mathbf{f}}_k(\mathbf{p})$ be the 2D optical flow computed from $\mathbf{f}_k(\mathbf{p})$, and $\hat{\mathbf{p}}_k$ the location of $\mathbf{p}$ at time $k+t$. The next location $\hat{\mathbf{p}}_{k+1}$ is computed by following the predicted flow at the previous point

$$\hat{\mathbf{p}}_{k+1} = \hat{\mathbf{p}}_k + \tilde{\mathbf{f}}_k(\hat{\mathbf{p}}_k) . \tag{10}$$

Eq. 10 is initialized with $\hat{\mathbf{p}}_0 = \mathbf{p}$. The final location $\hat{\mathbf{p}}_K$ indicates, according the crowd motion, the intended location of the pedestrian occupying $\mathbf{p}$. The intended direction is the difference of this point from the current location

$$\bar{\mathbf{u}}_t(\mathbf{p}) = \frac{1}{Z}(\hat{\mathbf{p}}_K - \mathbf{p}), \tag{11}$$

where Z is a normalization term such that $|\bar{\mathbf{u}}_t(\mathbf{p})| = 1$.

5.2 Intended Speed

The walking speed of pedestrians has been well studied and is near constant if there is no congestion. Zip's [21] least-effort principle implies that pedestrians minimize metabolic energy when walking at roughly 1.33 meters per second [22], which has been verified in observational studies [23, 24]. For scenes recorded at a distance, we may assume orthographic camera projection and thus a constant intended speed can be estimated for all pedestrians. We approximate the intended speed as the maximum observed speed in the training video. Intuitively, we are identifying the few instances where pedestrians can move freely due to lulls in traffic or less-crowded areas. To address unreliable or erroneous flow estimates, we use Chauvenet's criterion [25] to remove outliers.

For near field views that exhibit perspective distortion, as shown in Fig. 3(b), we estimate the intended speed by observing the relationship between each longitudinal frame location. First, we identify the fastest 5% of speed measurements from each longitudinal frame location. Due to the perspective projection, the speeds across the frame have near-linear relationship. We find a least-squares line fit to the speed measurements to estimate the desired speed over the entire image. Outliers are also removed using Chauvenet's criterion.

Finally, given intended speed $s(\mathbf{p})$ and direction $\bar{\mathbf{u}}_t(\mathbf{p})$, we may compute the intended motion

$$\mathbf{u}_t(\mathbf{p}) = \left[\bar{\mathbf{u}}_t(\mathbf{p})^T, s(\mathbf{p})\right]^T, \tag{12}$$

and normalize such that $|\mathbf{u}_t(\mathbf{p})| = 1$.

6 Applications

The pedestrian efficiency computed for each frame of the video can be used to analyze the scene despite the crowd. In this paper, we demonstrate its use in two critical video analysis tasks that are particularly challenging for crowded scenes: anomaly detection and pedestrian tracking.

6.1 Anomaly Detection

Low pedestrian efficiency is an indicator of unusual activities. Atypical motions decrease efficiency in local areas, and crowd disasters contain people moving irrationally.

We can identify *global* anomalies, i.e., affecting a large portion if not the entire crowd, as frames that have low average efficiency values

$$\bar{e}_t = \frac{1}{|\mathcal{P}|} \sum_{\mathbf{p} \in \mathcal{P}} e_t(\mathbf{p}) \,,$$

where $\mathcal{P}$ is the set of 2D pixel locations.

We may also detect *local* anomalies, such as individuals moving against the crowd flow. Such offenders will exhibit low efficiency (since the training data lacks their intended motion) and decrease the efficiency in their immediate vicinity (as surrounding pedestrians must avoid them). We identify local unusual events as space-time regions with low efficiency. Since many scenes naturally contain low efficiency (a congested train station, for example), we normalize the efficiency $\tilde{e}_t(\mathbf{p}) = \frac{e_t(\mathbf{p})}{Z(\mathbf{p})}$, where $Z(\mathbf{p})$ is the average efficiency at spatial location $\mathbf{p}$ of the training data.

We identify the space-time locations with low efficiency using a space-time Markov random field. Details are omitted for limited space, but this can be achieved with binary latent variables indicating whether the scene point exhibits usual activities or not. The latent variables can be computed through energy minimization of an error function consisting of a data term that returns the efficiency value if the scene point contains unusual activity together with an Ising model smoothing term. This energy minimization can be efficiently solved with graph-cuts [26, 27].

6.2 Tracking

Efficiency indicates how much an individual is conforming to the flow of the crowd. As such, we may use it as a dynamic prior on the individual's motion to probabilistically track pedestrians in crowded scenes.

Let $\mathbf{x}_t$ be the 2D pixel location at time t of a pedestrian being tracked. Object-centric methods [28, 29] assume pedestrians exhibit smooth motion and impose (often first order) stochastic dynamics to update the location

$$\mathbf{x}_{t+1} = \mathbf{x}_t + \mathbf{h}_t + \boldsymbol{\epsilon} \,, \tag{13}$$

where $\mathbf{h}_t$ is a 2D flow vector and $\boldsymbol{\epsilon}$ is (typically Gaussian) noise. Crowd methods [12, 13, 11] use a learned model of the crowd

$$\mathbf{x}_{t+1} = \mathbf{x}_t + c(\mathbf{x}_t) + \boldsymbol{\epsilon} \,, \tag{14}$$

where $c(\mathbf{x}_t)$ is the flow of the crowd at location $\mathbf{x}_t$. Using our model, $c(\mathbf{x}_t)$ is the predicted von Mises-Fisher distribution ($\boldsymbol{\mu}$ and κ) from the HMM at location $\mathbf{x}_t$.

Macroscopic approaches assume the crowd motion model yields an accurate prediction, and do not perform well when pedestrians deviate from the crowd (i.e., areas of low efficiency). Microscopic (object-centric) approaches that rely on individual motion models, such as a linear model, struggle in areas without visible backgrounds (often high efficiency). We use pedestrian efficiency as an indicator of how much to trust the crowd motion model and dynamically weight the two motion models

$$\mathbf{x}_{t+1} = \mathbf{x}_t + e_t(\mathbf{x}_t) c_t(\mathbf{x}_t) + [1 - e_t(\mathbf{x}_t)]\, \mathbf{h}_t + \boldsymbol{\epsilon} \,. \tag{15}$$

(a) (b) (c) (d) (e) (f)

Fig. 4. Frames from six videos on which we evaluate our method. The concourse (a) [12], street (b) [6], and sidewalk (c) [30] scenes contain pedestrians moving in many different directions. The platform (d), escalator (f) (both from [31]), and intersection (e) [30] contain more obvious emergent behaviors such as lane formation.

For the individual's motion $\mathbf{h}_t$ we use the expected vector of a von Mises-Fisher distribution fitted to the previous flow observations. Intuitively, we are switching between the crowd motion model and a simple individual motion model that maintains the momentum at that location based on the pedestrian efficiency; when the pedestrian efficiency is high go with the crowd flow and otherwise let the individual maintain its own previous motion. Our final state-transition density is a von Mises-Fisher distribution computed by weighting the expected directions and variances.

7 Experimental Results

Fig. 4 shows frames from six videos of crowded scenes that we use to evaluate our method. For each scene, we train the HMMs on a sample video sequence, and use them to compute the efficiency in a video of the same scene recorded at a different time. The concourse (4(a) from [12]), sidewalk (4(c) from [30]), and street (4(b) from [6]) scenes have few physical obstacles and contain many interactions. The platform (d) and escalator (f) (both from [31]) scenes contain low efficiency due to bottlenecks. The intersection ((e) from [30]) contains pedestrians avoiding each other as they intersect in the middle of the frame. Many of the videos are available from the respective authors.

Fig. 5 shows examples of pedestrians moving inefficiently. The left most example shows an individual changing direction due to congestion. His intended direction is to the left, and efficiency drops when moving around other pedestrians. The middle example shows pedestrians avoiding an oncoming individual (video from [6]). Their intended direction is vertical, and efficiency decreases as they move to the side. The

Fig. 5. Low efficiency (red=low efficiency, blue=high) due to congestion (left), pedestrians avoiding an individual (middle), and a lack of motion (right). The yellow solid arrow is the intended motion, and the green dashed arrow depicts the actual motion (optical flow).

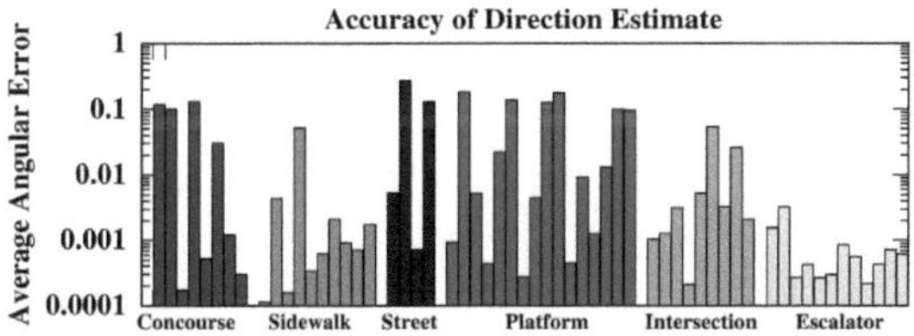

Average Error

Scene	Ours	Mehran et al. [6]
Concourse	0.042	0.458
Street	0.086	0.860
Sidewalk	0.006	0.260
Platform	0.051	0.729
Intersection	0.010	0.207
Escalator	0.001	0.258

Fig. 6. The accuracy of our estimate of future directions for a number of pedestrians (left), along with averages compared with Mehran et al. [6] (right)

pedestrians in the right most example are standing still and exhibit lower efficiency than those moving in the lower left of the image.

Since it is impossible to know a pedestrian's intentions, we cannot directly measure the accuracy of our estimated intended motion. We can, however, assume that pedestrians move in their intended direction over time. Let $\{\hat{\mathbf{x}}_t | t=1,\ldots,T\}$ be a sequence of ground-truth tracking locations for a specific pedestrian. We measure the error

$$\frac{1}{T}\sum_{t=1}^{T} \arccos\left(\frac{\bar{\mathbf{u}}_t(\hat{\mathbf{x}}_t)^T\left[\hat{\mathbf{x}}_{t+w}-\hat{\mathbf{x}}_t\right]}{|\hat{\mathbf{x}}_{t+w}-\hat{\mathbf{x}}_t|}\right), \tag{16}$$

where $\bar{\mathbf{u}}_t$ is the estimated intended direction from Eq. 11, and w is a window size that depends on the subject (typically the duration the subject is in the scene).

The left graph in Fig. 6 shows the estimation error for a number of subjects from different scenes. For almost all of the subjects the estimation error is below 0.1 (about $6°$). None of the error rates exceed 0.2 which is small given the resolution of the video. The theoretical maximum error is π, and thus at most the error is $0.2/\pi \approx 6\%$. The right table in Fig. 6 shows the average error for all scenes, and the error using the optical flow for the intended motion as suggested by Mehran et al. [6]. Scenes with less structure, such as the concourse and street, have higher errors due to the larger number of directions that pedestrians move. Compared with Mehran et al. [6], our method achieves consistently lower errors.

7.1 Anomaly Detection

First, we detect global anomalies as frames with low average efficiency on the University of Minnesota Crowd Dataset [32]. The dataset contains a number of usual and unusual video segments from 3 different scenes. For each scene, we train the HMMs on a usual sequence, and estimate efficiency on the remaining sequences. A frame is considered unusual if its average efficiency is below a specific threshold that is selected empirically. Fig. 7(a) shows visualizations of the efficiency for usual (top) and unusual activities (bottom) for the first scene. The pedestrians in the unusual frame (bottom) exhibit lower efficiency than those in the usual frame (top).

(a) (b) (c) (d)

Fig. 7. The efficiency on frames from the UMN data set (a) is high in usual scenes (top) and low in unusual scenes (bottom). Pedestrians that move against the crowd exhibit low efficiency (b). We detect such anomalies (c) with higher accuracy than our previous method [9] (d) (top) and Mahadevan et al. [10] (bottom). The color indicates the detection results: blue are true positives, red are false negatives, and pink are false positives.

The left graph in Fig. 8 shows the average efficiency plotted over time for a specific scene in the UMN data set. The red and green points are the average efficiency from clips of usual and unusual activities, respectively. The average efficiency drops during all six clips of unusual activities. We vary the threshold to compute an ROC curve. The area under the ROC curve was 0.92, which compares favorably with 0.96 in [6] and 0.99 in [33]. Our slightly poorer performance is due to the higher efficiency at the beginning and end of each unusual sequence (where pedestrians are moving normally) as shown in the left graph in Fig. 8.

We evaluate our local anomaly detection method on the UCSD Anomaly Detection Dataset [34] from [10] and videos of two train station scenes from [9]. We measure detection accuracy by the average of the true positive rates and true negative rates. The UCSD data set provides ground truth for some sequences. We hand-labeled the ground-truth for the remaining sequences and those of the train station.

Fig. 7 shows example frames of local anomalies detected in both datasets. The intended motion of pedestrians moving against the crowd cannot be determined, and thus such individuals exhibit low efficiency as shown in Fig. 7(b). We successfully detect such pedestrians as shown in Fig. 7(c). As shown in Fig. 7(d), efficiency is less sensitive to minor deviations than our previous method [9] and that of Mahadevan et al. [10].

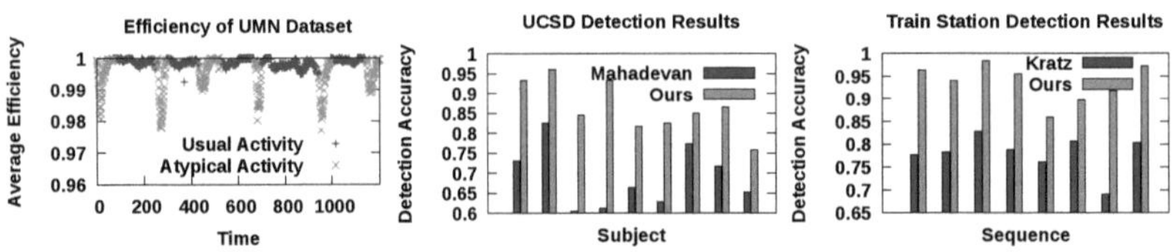

Fig. 8. Left: Efficiency drops when crowds in the UMN data set enter unusual states, as shown by the green points in the graph. Middle: Accuracy of local anomaly detection for 9 sequences in the UCSD Crowd Dataset [34] compared with [10]. Right: Accuracy of 8 sequences from two train station scenes compared with our previous method [9]. Using efficiency achieves higher accuracy for all sequences compared with other approaches.

Table 1. Tracking errors averaged over multiple subjects for the different scenes using estimated pedestrian efficiency compared with our previous crowd motion model approach [12] and that of Rodriguez et al. [11]. Using efficiency achieves lowest error on almost all scenes. On the concourse scene we achieve comparable results to our previous method [12].

	Concourse	Street	Platform	Escalator	Intersection	Sidewalk
Ours	8.7	**3.3**	**2.8**	**8.5**	**3.1**	**7.4**
Kratz and Nishino [12]	**6.8**	47.6	17.3	24.8	3.56	9.9
Rodriguez et al. [11]	24.7	14.8	29.9	60.4	25.9	11.9

The middle graph in Fig. 8 shows the detection accuracy of our method on 9 sequences compared with that of Mahadevan et al. [10], and the right graph in Fig. 8 compares the results on 8 sequences with our previous method [9]. We use the results of Mahadevan et al. [10] posted on the web for comparison. The use of pedestrian efficiency achieves consistently higher accuracy in both cases.

7.2 Tracking

We quantitatively evaluated our tracking method using hand-labeled ground truth of targets. Given a ground-truth location $\hat{\mathbf{x}}_t$ and tracking result $\mathbf{x}_t$, the tracking error $|\hat{\mathbf{x}}_t - \mathbf{x}_t|$ is averaged over all frames $\{t=1,\ldots,T\}$. Table 1 shows the tracking errors (average over multiple subjects for each sequence) using the estimated pedestrian efficiency compared with our previous method [12] and that of Rodriguez et al. [11]. Using pedestrian efficiency achieves superior results on all scenes but one, and significantly lower errors on the platform, escalator, and street scenes where pedestrians move with lower efficiency due to higher density.

Pedestrians that deviate from the flow of the crowd present challenges to tracking. Since such pedestrians naturally have low efficiency, our method is able to reliably track them by gracefully switching to simple individual motion models as defined in Eq. 15. The left most four images in Fig. 9 shows two tracking results using our method and just the crowd motion model (Eq. 14). In both cases, the pedestrian is moving against the crowd: the first is moving left to right, and the second is moving towards the bottom of the frame. As shown in green, the crowd model assumes pedestrians are moving with the crowd, drifts, and loses the target. Our method, shown in red, is able to compensate for the anomaly and accurately track the targets. The middle graph in Fig. 9 shows the tracking errors for 16 anomalous targets using both methods. Using pedestrian efficiency achieves a consistently lower error.

The right graph in Fig. 9 shows the ratio of our tracking error to the tracking error using just the crowd model for different subjects. High ratios (i.e., 1) indicate that our method performs similar to using just the crowd motion model, while a low ratio indicates improvement by our method. The downward trend of the points show the advantage of using pedestrian efficiency: our method vastly improves tracking in crowds when pedestrians are moving inefficiently, and performs similarly to crowd motion models when pedestrians are moving with the flow.

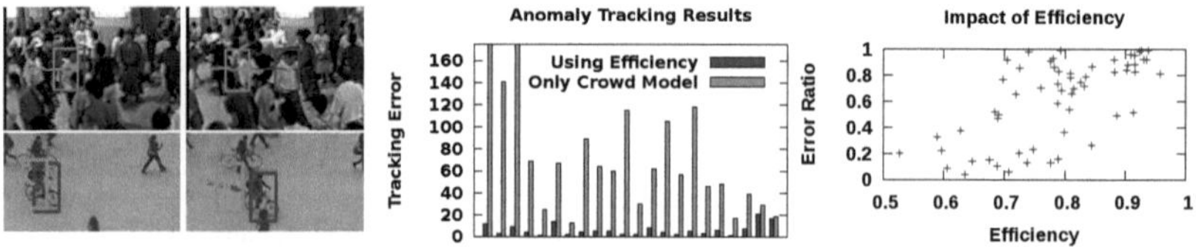

Fig. 9. Left: Tracking results of pedestrians deviating from the general crowd flow in the concourse (top row) and UCSD dataset (bottom row) using our method (red) and just a crowd motion model (green). The crowd motion model assumes that the pedestrians are moving with the crowd causing the tracker to drift (left column) or lose the target (right column). Middle: Since such anomalous pedestrians naturally have low efficiency, our method achieves a lower tracking error for all the tested subjects. Right: Pedestrians moving inefficiently have a low ratio (close to 0) and the downward trend indicates crowd motion models are only accurate when pedestrians are moving efficiently.

8 Conclusion

In this paper, we introduced the use of pedestrian efficiency for video analysis of crowded scenes. We showed that the pedestrian efficiency can be computed from a video without detecting and tracking individuals. The computed pedestrian efficiency can be used to reliably identify global and local anomalous activities, and robustly track individuals through crowded scenes regardless of whether they are conforming to the crowd flow or not. The experimental results show that the computation and use of pedestrian efficiency can indeed enable more reliable video analysis of crowded scenes. We believe that measuring efficiency is but the first step to recognizing the impact of individuality on crowds, and provides new means to further study the complex interactions between pedestrians in videos of crowded scenes.

Acknowledgments. This work was supported in part by National Science Foundation grants IIS-0746717 and Nippon Telegraph and Telephone Corporation. The authors thank Nippon Telegraph and Telephone Corporation for providing the train station videos.

References

1. Helbing, D., Vicsek, T.: Optimal Self-Organization. New Journal of Physics 13 (1999)
2. Helbing, D., Moln, P., Farkas, I.J., Bolay, K.: Self-Organizing Pedestrian Movement. Environment and Planning B: Planning and Design 28, 361–383 (2001)
3. Still, K.: Crowd Dynamics. PhD thesis, University of Warwick (2000)
4. Schadschneider, A., Klingsch, W., Kluepfel, H., Kretz, T., Rogsch, C., Seyfried, A.: Evacuation Dynamics: Empirical Results, Modeling and Applications. In: Encyclopedia of Complexity and Systems Science, pp. 3142–3176 (2009)
5. Moore, B.E., Ali, S., Mehran, R., Shah, M.: Visual Crowd Surveillance Through a Hydrodynamics Lens. Comm. of ACM 54, 64–73 (2011)
6. Mehran, R., Oyama, A., Shah, M.: Abnormal Crowd Behavior Detection using Social Force Model. In: Proc. of IEEE CVPR (2009)

7. Krausz, B., Bauckhage, C.: Analyzing Pedestrian Behavior in Crowds for Automatic Detection of Congestions. In: Proc. of IEEE Workshop on MSVLC (2011)
8. Hoogendoorn, S.P., Daamen, W.: Pedestrian Behavior at Bottlenecks. Transportation Science 39 (2005)
9. Kratz, L., Nishino, K.: Anomaly Detection in Extremely Crowded Scenes Using Spatio-Temporal Motion Pattern Models. In: Proc. of IEEE CVPR, pp. 1446–1453 (2009)
10. Mahadevan, V., Li, W., Bhalodia, V., Vasconcelos, N.: Anomaly Detection in Crowded Scenes. In: Proc. of IEEE CVPR, pp. 1975–1981 (2010)
11. Rodriguez, M., Ali, S., Kanade, T.: Tracking in Unstructured Crowded Scenes. In: Proc. of IEEE ICCV (2009)
12. Kratz, L., Nishino, K.: Tracking Pedestrians using Local Spatio-Temporal Motion Patterns in Extremely Crowded Scenes. IEEE TPAMI 34, 987–1002 (2012)
13. Ali, S., Shah, M.: Floor Fields for Tracking in High Density Crowd Scenes. In: Forsyth, D., Torr, P., Zisserman, A. (eds.) ECCV 2008, Part II. LNCS, vol. 5303, pp. 1–14. Springer, Heidelberg (2008)
14. Yu, Q., Medioni, G.: Motion pattern interpretation and detection for tracking moving vehicles in airborne video. In: Proc. of IEEE CVPR, pp. 2671–2678 (2009)
15. Kretz, T., Grunebohm, A., Kaufman, M., Mazur, F., Schreckenberg, M.: Experimental Study of Pedestrian Counterflow in a Corridor. JSTAT 2006, P10001 (2006)
16. Wright, J., Pless, R.: Analysis of Persistent Motion Patterns Using the 3D Structure Tensor. In: IEEE WACV, pp. 14–19 (2005)
17. Brox, T., Malik, J.: Large Displacement Optical Flow: Descriptor Matching in Variational Motion Estimation. IEEE TPAMI 33, 500–513 (2011)
18. Mardia, K.V., Jupp, P.: Directional Statistics. John Wiley and Sons Ltd. (1999)
19. Mardia, A., El-Atoum, S.: Bayesian Inference for The Von Mises-Fisher Distribution Miscellanea. Biometrika 63, 203–206 (1976)
20. Bishop, C.M.: Pattern Recognition and Machine Learning. Springer (2007)
21. Zipf, G.: Human Behavior and the Principle of Least Effort. Addison-Wesley Press (1949)
22. Guy, S., Chhugani, J., Curtis, S., Dubey, P., Lin, M., Manocha, D.: PLEdestrians: A Least-Effort Approach to Crowd Simulation. In: Proc. of ACM/EG SCA, pp. 119–128 (2010)
23. Teknomo, K.: Microscopic Pedestrian Flow Characteristics: Development of an Image Processing Data Collection and Simulation Model. PhD thesis, Tohoku University (2002)
24. Henderson, L.F.: The Statistics of Crowd Fluids. Nature 229 (1971)
25. Chauvenet, W.: In: A Manual of Spherical and Practical Astronomy, 5th edn., pp. 474–566. Adamant Media Corporation (1891)
26. Boykov, Y., Kolmogorov, V.: An Experimental Comparison of Min-Cut/Max-Flow Algorithms for Energy Minimization in Vision. IEEE TPAMI 26, 1124–1137 (2004)
27. Szeliski, R., Zabih, R., Scharstein, D., Veksler, O., Kolmogorov, V., Agarwala, A., Tappen, M., Rother, C.: A Comparative Study of Energy Minimization Methods for Markov Random Fields. In: Leonardis, A., Bischof, H., Pinz, A. (eds.) ECCV 2006. LNCS, vol. 3952, pp. 16–29. Springer, Heidelberg (2006)
28. Pérez, P., Hue, C., Vermaak, J., Gangnet, M.: Color-Based Probabilistic Tracking. In: Heyden, A., Sparr, G., Nielsen, M., Johansen, P. (eds.) ECCV 2002, Part I. LNCS, vol. 2350, pp. 661–675. Springer, Heidelberg (2002)
29. Isard, M., Blake, A.: CONDENSATION-Conditional Density Propagation for Visual Tracking. IJCV 29, 5–28 (1998)
30. Ali, S., Shah, M.: A Lagrangian Particle Dynamics Approach for Crowd Flow Segmentation and Stability Analysis. In: Proc. of IEEE CVPR, pp. 1–6 (2007)

31. Cheriyadat, A., Radke, R.: Detecting Dominant Motions in Dense Crowds. IEEE Journal of Selected Topics in Signal Processing 2, 568–581 (2008)
32. University of Minnesota: Unusual Crowd Activity Dataset (2006), http://mha.cs.umn.edu/Movies/Crowd-Activity-All.avi
33. Raghavendra, R., Bue, A.D., Cristani, M., Murino, V.: Optimizing Interaction Force for Global Anomaly Detection in Crowded Scenes. In: Proc. of IEEE ICCV, pp. 136–143 (2011)
34. University of California San Diego: Anomaly Detection Dataset (2010), http://www.svcl.ucsd.edu/projects/anomaly/

Reconstructing 3D Human Pose from 2D Image Landmarks

Varun Ramakrishna, Takeo Kanade, and Yaser Sheikh

Robotics Institute, Carnegie Mellon University
{vramakri,tk,yaser}@cs.cmu.edu

Abstract. Reconstructing an arbitrary configuration of 3D points from their projection in an image is an ill-posed problem. When the points hold semantic meaning, such as anatomical landmarks on a body, human observers can often infer a plausible 3D configuration, drawing on extensive visual memory. We present an *activity-independent* method to recover the 3D configuration of a human figure from 2D locations of anatomical landmarks in a single image, leveraging a large motion capture corpus as a proxy for visual memory. Our method solves for anthropometrically regular body pose and explicitly estimates the camera via a matching pursuit algorithm operating on the image projections. Anthropometric regularity (i.e., that limbs obey known proportions) is a highly informative prior, but directly applying such constraints is intractable. Instead, we enforce a necessary condition on the sum of squared limb-lengths that can be solved for in closed form to discourage implausible configurations in 3D. We evaluate performance on a wide variety of human poses captured from different viewpoints and show generalization to novel 3D configurations and robustness to missing data.

1 Introduction

Figure 1(a) shows the 2D projection of a 3D body configuration. From this 2D projection alone, human observers are able to effortlessly organize the anatomical landmarks in three-dimensions and guess the relative position of the camera. Geometrically, the problem of estimating the 3D configuration of points from their 2D projections is ill-posed, even when fitting a known 3D skeleton[1]. With human observers, the ambiguity is likely resolved by leveraging vast memories of likely 3D configurations of humans [2]. A reasonable proxy for such experience is available in the form of motion capture libraries [3], which contain millions of 3D configurations. The computational challenge is to tractably generalize from the configurations spanned in the corpus, ensuring anthropometric plausibility while discouraging impossible configurations.

[1] As noted in [1], each 2D end-point of a limb subtends a ray in 3D space. A sphere of radius equal to the length of the limb centered at any location on one of these rays intersects the other ray at two points (in general) producing a tuple of possible 3D limb configurations for each location on the ray.

A. Fitzgibbon et al. (Eds.): ECCV 2012, Part IV, LNCS 7575, pp. 573–586, 2012.

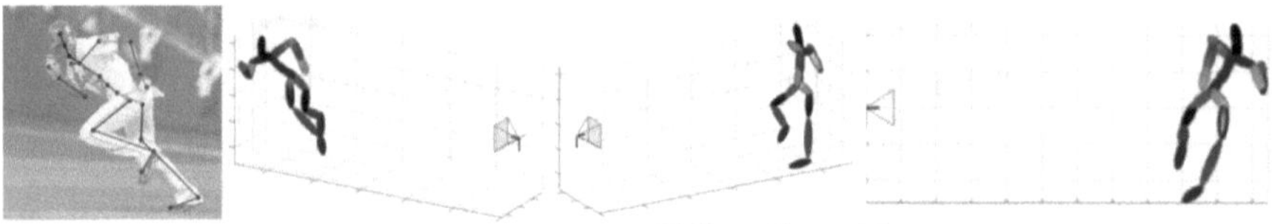

Fig. 1. Given the 2D location of anatomical landmarks on an image, we estimate the 3D configuration of the human as well as the relative pose of the camera

Kinematic representations of human pose are high-dimensional and difficult to estimate directly. Allowing only statistically plausible configurations leads to compact representations that can be estimated from data. Linear dimensionality reduction (such as PCA) is attractive as it yields tractable and optimal estimation methods. It has been successfully applied to constrained deformable objects, such as faces [4] and action-specific body reconstruction, such as walking, [5]. However, as we add poses from varied actions, the complexity of the distribution of poses increases and, consequently, the dimensionality of the reduced model needs to be increased (see Figure 2). If we expand the dimensionality, linear models increasingly allow configurations that violate anthropometric constraints such as limb proportions, yet yield a projection in 2D that is plausible. The goal is therefore to develop an activity-independent model while ensuring anthropometric regularity.

In this paper, we present a method to reconstruct 3D human pose while maintaining compaction, anthropometric regularity, and tractability. To achieve compaction, we separate camera pose variability from the intrinsic deformability of the human body (because combining both leads to an approximately six-fold increase in the number of parameters [6]). To compactly model the intrinsic deformability across multiple actions, we use a sparse linear representation in an overcomplete dictionary. We estimate the parameters of this sparse linear representation with a matching pursuit algorithm. Enforcing anthropometric regularity through strict limb length constraints is intractable because satisfying multiple quadratic equality constraints on a least squares system is nonconvex [7]. Instead, we encourage anthropometric regularity by enforcing a necessary condition (i.e., an equality constraint on the sum of squared lengths) as a constraint that is applied in closed form [8]. We solve for the model coefficients and camera pose within the matching pursuit iterations, decreasing the reprojection error objective in each iteration.

Our core contributions are: (1) a new activity-independent representation of 3D human pose variability as a sparse embedding in an overcomplete dictionary, and (2) an algorithm, Projected Matching Pursuit, to estimate the sparse model from only 2D projections while encouraging anthropometric regularity. Within the matching pursuit iterations, we explicitly estimate both the 3D camera pose and the 3D body configuration. We evaluate our method to test generalization, and robustness to noise and missing landmarks. We compare against a standard linear dimensionality reduction baseline and a nearest neighbor baseline.

2 Related Work

For the single image pose recovery task, some of the earliest work is by Lee and Chen [1] who assumed known limb lengths and recovered pose by pruning a binary interpretation tree that enumerates the entire set of configurations for an articulated body using physical and structural pruning rules and user input. Taylor's approach [9] used known skeletal sizes to recover 3D pose up to a weak perspective scale; this method required human input to resolve the depth ambiguities at each joint. Jiang [10] used Taylor's method [9] to generate hypotheses followed by a nearest neighbor approach to prune the hypotheses. Parameswaran and Chellappa [11] used a strong prior on skeletal size and employed 3D model based invariants to recover the joint angle configuration but made restrictive assumptions on the 3D configurations possible. Other approaches, such as Barron and Kakadiaris [12], estimated anthropometry and pose using strong anthropometric priors on limb lengths by generating a set of plausible poses based on geometric constraints followed by a nonlinear minimization.

Discriminative approaches [13–16] have attempted to directly learn a mapping from 2D image measurements to 3D pose. Several approaches have recovered 3D pose from silhouettes. Elgammal and Lee [17] learned view-based activity manifolds from 2D silhouette data. Rosales and Sclaroff [18] described a method to learn the inverse mapping from silhouette to pose. Salzmann and Urtasun [13] proposed a method to impose physical constraints on the output of a discriminative predictor. Discriminative methods, in general, require large amounts of training data from varied viewpoints and deformations to be able to recover pose reliably and do not generalize well to data that is not represented by the training set.

Enforcing structural constraints optimally is usually intractable. In the context of deformable mesh reconstruction, Salzmann and Fua [19, 20] derived a convex formulation for constraining the solution space of possible 3D configurations by imposing convex inequality constraints on the relative distance between reconstructed points. Wei and Chai [21] and Valmadre and Lucey [22] describe deterministic algorithms to simultaneously estimate limb lengths and reconstruct human pose. These methods require multiple images and manual resolution of depth ambiguities at several joints.

In this paper, we present an automatic algorithm for recovering 3D body pose from 2D landmarks in a single image. To achieve this, we develop a statistical model of human pose variability that can describe a wide variety of actions, and an algorithm that simultaneously estimates 3D camera and body pose while enforcing anthropometric regularity.

3 Sparse Representation of 3D Human Pose

A 3D configuration of P points can be represented by $\mathbf{X} = \left(\mathbf{X}_1^T, \ldots, \mathbf{X}_P^T\right)^T \in \mathbb{R}^{3P\times 1}$ of stacked 3D coordinates. Under weak perspective projection, the 2D coordinates of the points in the image are given by

$$\mathbf{x} = \left(\mathbf{I}_{P\times P} \otimes \begin{bmatrix} s_x & 0 \\ 0 & s_y \end{bmatrix} \begin{bmatrix} 1 & 0 & 0 \\ 0 & 1 & 0 \end{bmatrix} \mathbf{R}\right) \mathbf{X} + \mathbf{t} \otimes \mathbf{1}_{P\times 1}, \tag{1}$$

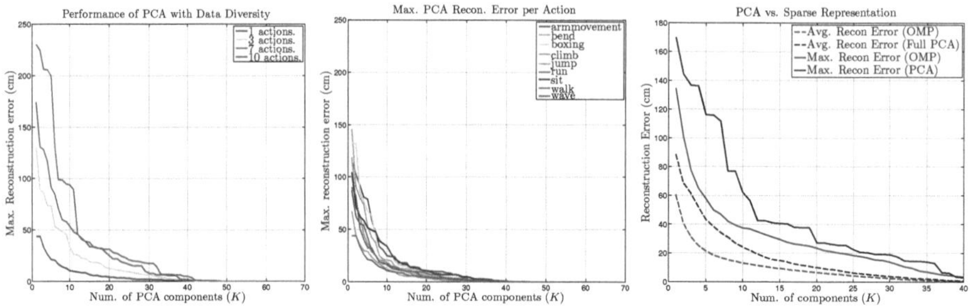

(a) (b) (c)

Fig. 2. Data Complexity. (a) As more actions and, consequently, diverse poses are added to the training corpus, the maximum reconstruction error incurred by a linear dimensionality reduction model increases. (b) Maximum reconstruction error for each action separately using PCA. Each action can be compactly modeled with a linear basis. (c) Using a sparse representation in an overcomplete dictionary estimated using Orthogonal Matching Pursuit (OMP) achieves lower reconstruction error for 3D pose.

where $\mathbf{x} \in \mathbb{R}^{2P \times 1}$, $\otimes$ denotes the Kronecker product, $\mathbf{s} \in \mathbb{R}^{2 \times 2}$ is a diagonal scale matrix with s_x and s_y being the scales in the x and y directions , $\mathbf{R} \in SO(3)$ and $\mathbf{t} \in \mathbb{R}^{2 \times 1}$ denote the rotation and translation parameters of the weak perspective camera that we collectively denote as $\mathcal{C}$. We assume the camera intrinsic parameters are known. Estimating $\mathbf{X}$ and $\mathcal{C}$ from only the image evidence $\mathbf{x}$ is, fundamentally, an ill-posed problem. We see from Equation 1 we have $3P + 7$ parameters that we need to estimate from only $2P$ equations.

If the points form a semantic group that deform in a structured way, such as anatomical landmarks on a human body, we can reduce the number of parameters that need to be estimated using dimensionality reduction methods that learn the correlations between the points [23]. Linear dimensionality reduction methods (e.g., Principal Component Analysis (PCA)) can be used to represent the points as a linear combination of a small number of basis poses,

$$\mathbf{X} = \boldsymbol{\mu} + \sum_{i=1}^{K} \mathbf{b}_i \omega_i, \tag{2}$$

where K is the number of basis poses, $\mathbf{b}_i$ are the basis poses, ω_i are the coefficients, and $\boldsymbol{\mu} \in \mathbb{R}^{3P \times 1}$ is the mean pose computed from training data. Under this model, we now have to estimate only $K+7$ parameters instead of the original $3P + 7$ parameters.

A direct application of PCA to all the poses contained in the corpus[2] raises difficulties as shown in Figure 2(a). For a single action, PCA performs well. As the diversity in actions in the data increases, the number of PCA components required for accurate reconstruction increases, and the assumption of a

[2] We use the Carnegie Mellon Motion Capture Database [3] to obtain a large corpus of 3D human poses.

low dimensional linear subspace becomes strained. In particular, the *maximum* reconstruction error increases as the diversity in the data is increased because PCA inherits the occurrence statistics of poses in the corpus and not just the extent of variability.

3.1 Sparse Representation in an Overcomplete Dictionary

In Figure 2(b) we see that each individual action is compactly representable by a linear basis. Therefore, an arbitrary pose can be compactly represented by some subset of the set of all bases,

$$\begin{aligned} \mathbf{X} = \quad & \boldsymbol{\mu} + \textstyle\sum_{i=1}^{K} \mathbf{b}_i \omega_i, \\ & \{\mathbf{b}_i\}_{i \in I_{\mathbf{B}^*}} \in \mathbf{B}^* \subset \mathcal{B}, \end{aligned} \tag{3}$$

where $\boldsymbol{\mu}$ is the mean pose, $\mathcal{B} \in \mathbb{R}^{3P \times (\sum_{i=1}^{N_a} N_b^i)}$ is an overcomplete dictionary of basis components created by concatenating N_b^i bases computed from N_a different actions, $\mathbf{B}^*$ is an optimal subset of $\mathcal{B}$, and $I_{\mathbf{B}^*}$ are the indices of the optimal basis $\mathbf{B}^*$ in $\mathcal{B}$. We validate this observation in Figure 2(c) by using Orthogonal Matching Pursuit (OMP) [24, 25] to select a sparse set of basis vectors to reconstruct each 3D pose in a test corpus. The sparse representation is able to achieve lower reconstruction error with higher compaction on the test set than using a full PCA model. It is instructive to note the behavior in Figure 2(c) of the maximum reconstruction error, which usually correspond to atypical poses. For human poses, we conclude that the sparse representation demonstrates greater generalization ability than full PCA.

3.2 Anthropometric Regularity

Linear models allow cases where the 2D projection appears to be valid (i.e., the reprojection error is minimized), but the configuration in 3D violates anthropometric quantities such as the proportions of limbs. Enforcing anthropometric regularity (i.e., that limb lengths follow known proportions) would discourage such implausible configurations. For a limb[3] between the ith and j^{th} landmark locations, we denote the normalized limb length as l_{ij}. The normalized limb lengths are set by normalizing with respect to the longest limb of the mean pose ($\boldsymbol{\mu}$). For a 3D pose $\mathbf{X}$, we can ensure anthropometric regularity by enforcing

$$\begin{aligned} \|\mathbf{X}_i - \mathbf{X}_j\|_2 = l_{ij}, \\ \forall (i,j) \in \mathcal{L} \end{aligned} \tag{4}$$

where $\mathcal{L} = \{(i,j)\}_{i=1}^{N_l}$ is the set of pairs of joints between which a limb exists and N_l is the total number of limbs in the model. Unfortunately, applying quadratic

3 We loosely define a limb to be a rigid length between two consecutive anatomical landmarks in the tree.

equality constraints on a linear least squares system is nonconvex. A *necessary* condition for anthropometric regularity is

$$\sum_{\forall(i,j)\in\mathcal{L}} \|\mathbf{X}_i - \mathbf{X}_j\|_2^2 = \sum_{\forall(i,j)\in\mathcal{L}} l_{ij}^2. \tag{5}$$

This constraint limits the sum of the squared distances between valid landmarks to be equal to the sum of squares of the limb lengths[4]. The feasible set of the constraint in Equation 5 contains the feasible set of the constraints in Equation 4. The necessary condition on the sum of squared limb lengths is therefore a relaxation of the constraints in Equation 4. As shown in [8], this necessary condition can be applied in closed form.

4 Projected Matching Pursuit

We solve for the pose and camera by minimizing the reprojection error in the image. The resulting optimization problem can be stated as follows

$$\begin{aligned} \min_{\boldsymbol{\Omega},\mathcal{C},I_{\mathbf{B}^*}} \quad & \|\mathbf{x} - (\mathbf{I}\otimes \mathbf{sR})\,(\mathbf{B}^*\boldsymbol{\Omega} + \boldsymbol{\mu}) - \mathbf{t}\otimes\mathbf{1}\|_2 \\ \text{s.t.} \quad & \sum_{\forall(i,j)\in\mathcal{L}} \|\mathbf{X}_i - \mathbf{X}_j\|_2^2 = \sum_{\forall(i,j)\in\mathcal{L}} l_{ij}^2, \\ & \mathbf{B}^* \subset \mathcal{B}. \end{aligned} \tag{6}$$

Although the problem is non-linear, non-convex, and combinatorial, it has the following useful property in the set of arguments $(\mathcal{C}, \boldsymbol{\Omega}, I_{\mathbf{B}^*})$: we can solve optimally, or near-optimally, for each subset of the arguments given the rest. This property suggests a coordinate descent-style algorithm. Algorithm 1 describes a matching pursuit algorithm we refer to as *Projected Matching Pursuit* for coordinate descent on the reprojection error objective.

4.1 Algorithm

The combinatorial challenge of picking the optimal set of basis vectors from an overcomplete dictionary to represent a given signal is NP-hard. However, techniques exist to solve the sparse representation problem approximately with guarantees [25, 26]. Greedy approaches such as orthogonal matching pursuit (OMP) [27, 25] reconstruct a signal $\mathbf{v}$ with a sparse linear combination of basis vectors from an overcomplete dictionary $\mathcal{B}$. It proceeds in a greedy fashion by choosing, at each iteration, the basis vector from $\mathcal{B}$ that is most aligned with the residual $\mathbf{r}$ (the residual is set equal to $\mathbf{v}$ in the first iteration). The new estimate of the signal $\hat{\mathbf{v}}$ is computed by reconstructing using the basis vectors selected at the current iteration and the new residual ($\mathbf{r} = \mathbf{v} - \hat{\mathbf{v}}$) is computed. The iterations proceed on the residual until K basis vectors are chosen or a tolerance on the residual error is reached.

[4] Note that since we are using normalized limb-lengths, these constraints become constraints on limb proportions rather than on limb lengths.

Algorithm 1. Projected Matching Pursuit

1. Initialize $\mathbf{r}_0 = \mathbf{x} - (\mathbf{I} \otimes \mathbf{sR})\,\boldsymbol{\mu} - \mathbf{t} \otimes \mathbf{1}$
2. While $(\|\mathbf{r}_t\| \geq tol)$
   3. $i_{\max} = \arg\max_{\mathrm{i}} \langle \mathbf{r}_t,\ (\mathbf{I} \otimes \mathbf{s}_t\mathbf{R}_t)\,\mathbf{B}_i \rangle$
   4. $\mathbf{B}^* = [\mathbf{B}^*\ \mathbf{B}_{i_{\max}}]$
   5. Solve: $\{\mathcal{C}^*, \boldsymbol{\Omega}^*\} = \arg\min \|\hat{\mathbf{x}} - (\mathbf{I} \otimes \mathbf{sR})\,\mathbf{B}^*\boldsymbol{\Omega}\|_2$
      subject to constraints in Equation (8) using Section 4.2 & Section 4.3
   6. Recompute residual $\mathbf{r}_{t+1} = \mathbf{x} - (\mathbf{I} \otimes \mathbf{s}^*\mathbf{R}^*)\,(\mathbf{B}^*\boldsymbol{\Omega}^* + \boldsymbol{\mu}) - \mathbf{t}^* \otimes \mathbf{1}$
   7. Set $\boldsymbol{\Omega}_{t+1} = \boldsymbol{\Omega}^*$
8. Return $\{\mathcal{C}^*, \boldsymbol{\Omega}^*, \mathbf{B}^*\}$

In our scenario, we do not have access to the signal of interest, namely the 3D pose $\mathbf{X}$. Instead, we are only given the projection of the original 3D pose in the image $\mathbf{x}$. We present a matching pursuit algorithm for reconstructing a signal from its projection and an overcomplete dictionary. At each iteration of our algorithm, the optimal basis set $\mathbf{B}^*$ is augmented by matching the image residual with basis vectors projected under the current camera estimate and adding the basis vector which maximizes the inner product to the optimal set. Given the current optimal basis set $\mathbf{B}^*$, the pose and camera parameters are re-estimated as outlined in Section 4.2 and Section 4.3. The algorithm terminates when the optimal basis set has reached a predefined size or the image residual is smaller than a tolerance value. The procedure is summarized in Algorithm 1. We have an intuitive and feasible initialization in the mean 3D pose computed from the training corpus.

4.2 Estimating Basis Coefficients with Anthropometric Regularization

To encourage anthropometric regularity we enforce the necessary constraint from Equation 5 which limits the sum of squared limb lengths. We can write each 3D landmark $\mathbf{X}_i = \mathbf{E}_i\mathbf{X}$, where $\mathbf{E}_i = [\cdots\ \mathbf{0}\ \mathbf{I}_{3\times3}\ \mathbf{0}\ \cdots]$ is a $3 \times 3P$ matrix that selects out the ith landmark.

We can write $\mathbf{E}_{ij} = \mathbf{E}_i - \mathbf{E}_j$, and express each limb length as $\|\mathbf{E}_{ij}\mathbf{X}\| = l_{ij}$. Equation 5 can now be rewritten in matrix form as:

$$\|\mathbf{CX}\|_2^2 = \sum_{\forall(i,j)\in\mathcal{L}} l_{ij}^2, \tag{7}$$

where $\mathbf{C}$ is a $3N_l \times 3P$ matrix of the N_l stacked $\mathbf{E}_{ij}$ matrices. Where N_l is the number of limbs.

Given the optimal basis set $\mathbf{B}^*$ and the camera $\mathcal{C}$, solving for the coefficients of the linear model $\boldsymbol{\Omega}$ can now be formulated as the following optimization problem:

$$\begin{aligned} \min_{\boldsymbol{\Omega}} \quad & \|\hat{\mathbf{x}} - \mathbf{sR} \otimes \mathbf{I}_{P\times P}\mathbf{B}^*\boldsymbol{\Omega}\|_2 \\ \text{s.t.} \quad & \|\mathbf{CB}^*\boldsymbol{\Omega} - \mathbf{C}\boldsymbol{\mu}\|_2^2 = \sum_{\forall(i,j)\in\mathcal{L}} l_{ij}^2, \end{aligned} \tag{8}$$

where $\hat{\mathbf{x}} = \mathbf{x} - \mathbf{sR} \otimes \mathbf{I}_{P \times P}\boldsymbol{\mu} - \mathbf{t} \otimes \mathbf{1}_{P \times 1}$. The above problem is a linear least squares problem with a single quadratic equality constraint that can be solved optimally in closed form as shown in [8].

There also exists a natural lower bound on the length of the limb between the estimated joint locations, $\mathbf{X}_i^*$ and $\mathbf{X}_j^*$, in terms of the image projections $\mathbf{x}_i$ and $\mathbf{x}_j$. Using the triangle inequality we can show that

$$\|\mathbf{X}_i^* - \mathbf{X}_j^*\| \geq \|\mathbf{s}^{-1}(\mathbf{x}_i - \mathbf{x}_j)\|. \tag{9}$$

The above inequality shows that the estimated limb lengths are bounded by the length of the limbs in the image. Thus we can guarantee that the estimated limb length will not collapse to zeros as long as the limb has finite length in the image.

4.3 Estimating Camera Parameters

Given the pose $\mathbf{X} = \mathbf{B}^*\boldsymbol{\Omega} + \boldsymbol{\mu}$, and the image projections $\mathbf{x}$, we need to recover the weak perspective camera parameters $\mathcal{C}$. We solve this as an instance of the Orthogonal Procrustes problem [28]. We first write $\mathbf{x}$ and $\mathbf{X}$ in matrix form as $x \in \mathbb{R}^{2 \times P}$ and $\mathcal{X} \in \mathbb{R}^{3 \times P}$ respectively. We denote the mean-centered image projections as $\hat{x} = \mathbf{sR}\mathcal{X}$. Using the singular value decomposition, we can write

$$\mathbf{M} = \hat{x}\mathcal{X}^T(\mathcal{X}\mathcal{X}^T)^{-1} = \mathbf{UDV}^T. \tag{10}$$

We obtain the scale $\mathbf{s}$ by taking the first 2×2 section of the matrix $\mathbf{D}$ and the rotation by setting $\mathbf{R} = \mathbf{UV}^T$.

5 Evaluation

We perform quantitative and qualitative evaluation of our method. We use the Carnegie Mellon motion capture database for quantitative tests and compare our results against using a representation baseline (direct PCA on the entire corpus) and a non-parametric nearest neighbor method.

For all experiments, an overcomplete shape basis dictionary was constructed by concatenating the shape bases learnt for a set of human actions. We use a model with 23 anatomical landmarks. Each pose in the motion capture corpus was aligned by procrustes analysis to a reference pose. Shape bases were then learnt for the following motion categories- *'running'*, *'waving'*, *'arm movement'*, *'walking'*, *'jumping'*, *'jumping jacks'*, *'run'*, *'sit'*, *'boxing'*, *'bend'* by collecting sequences from the CMU Motion Capture Dataset and concatenating PCA components which retained 99% of the energy from each motion category.

5.1 Quantitative Evaluation

Optical Motion Capture. To evaluate our methods we test our algorithm on a sequence of mixed activities from the CMU motion capture database. We take care to ensure that the motion capture frames come from sequences that were

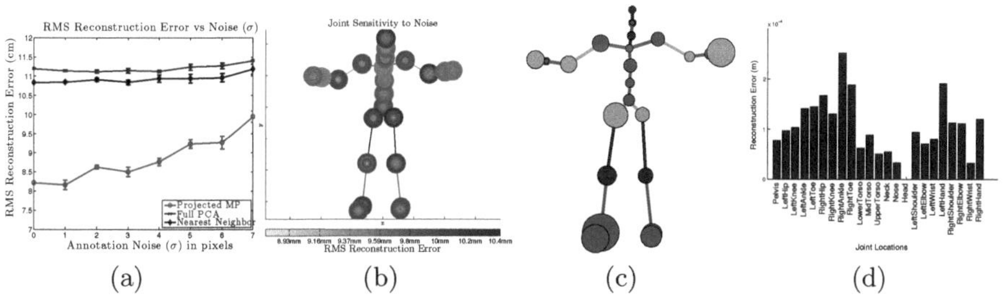

Fig. 3. Quantitative evaluation on optical motion capture. (a) We compare our method against two model baselines - a nearest neighbor approach and a linear model that uses PCA on the entire corpus. Reconstruction error is reported against annotation noise σ on a test corpus. (b) We evaluate the sensitivity of the reconstruction to each anatomical landmark annotation. (c) We show the sensitivity in reconstruction to missing landmarks. The radius of each circle indicates the relative magnitude of error in 3D incurred when the landmark is missing (d) The additional reconstruction incurred when the landmark is missing.

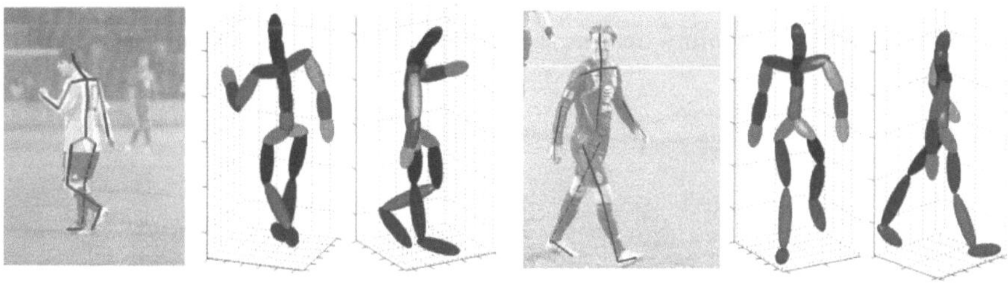

Fig. 4. Our method is able to handle missing data. We show examples of reconstruction with missing annotations. The missing limbs are marked with dotted lines. We are able to reconstruct the pose and impute the missing landmarks in 3D.

not used in the training of the shape bases. We project 30 frames of motion capture of diverse poses into 4 synthetically generated camera views. We then run our algorithm on the 2D projections of the joint locations to obtain the camera location and the pose of the human. We report 3D joint position error with increasing annotation noise σ in Figure 3(a).

We compare our method against two baselines. The first baseline uses as a linear model, a basis computed by performing PCA on the entire training corpus. Anthropometric constraints are enforced as in Section 4.2. The second baseline uses a non-parametric, nearest neighbor approach that retains all the training data. The 2D projections in each test example are matched to every 3D pose in the corpus by estimating the best-fit camera using the method in Section 4.3. The 3D pose that has the least reprojection error under the best-fit camera estimate is returned. The results are reported in Figure 3. We find that our method that used Projected Matching Pursuit achieves the lowest RMS reconstruction error. We also tested the effect of imposing an equality constraint on the sum-of-squared limb length ratios and find that we deviate from the ground truth on our test set by 13.1% on average.

We evaluate the comparative importance of the anatomical landmarks by performing two experiments:

Joint Sensitivity. We test the sensitivity of the reconstruction to each landmark individually. Each pose in the testing corpus is projected into 2D with synthetically generated cameras and each landmark is perturbed with Gaussian noise independently. Figure 3(b) shows the sensitivity of the reconstruction to each landmark. The maximum length of a limb in the image is 200 pixels, the minimum limb length is 20 pixels, and the average length of a limb in the image is 94.5. pixels The noise is varied to about 10% of the average limb length in the image.

Missing Data. An advantage of our formulation is the ability to handle missing data. In Figure 4 we show examples of reconstructions obtained with incomplete annotations. We perform an ablative analysis of the joint annotations by removing each annotation in turn and measure the increase in the reconstruction error. We plot our results in Figure 3(d). The radius of each circle is indicative of the error incurred when the annotation corresponding to that joint is missing. We find that the extremal joints are most informative and help in constraining the reconstruction.

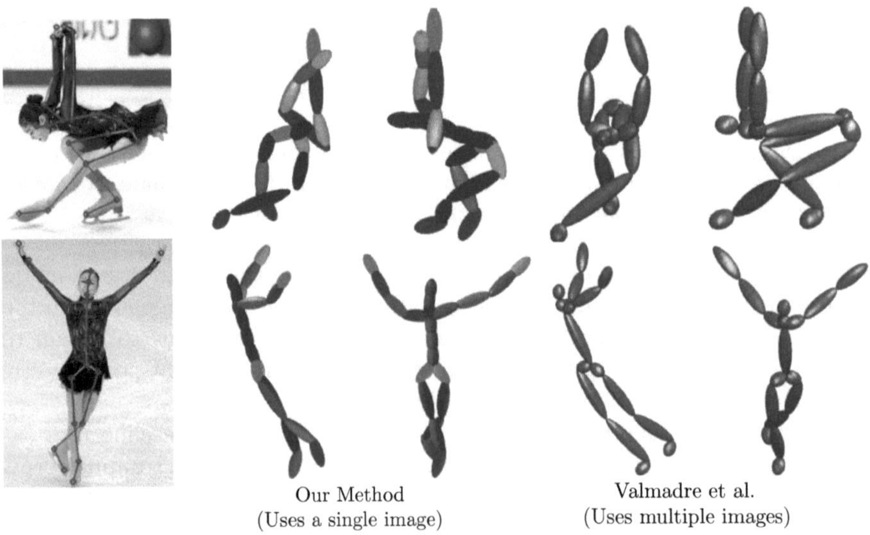

Fig. 5. Comparsion with recent work. Valmadre et al., estimate human pose using multiple images and requires additional annotation to resolve ambiguities. Our method achieves realistic results operating on a single image and does not require additional annotation

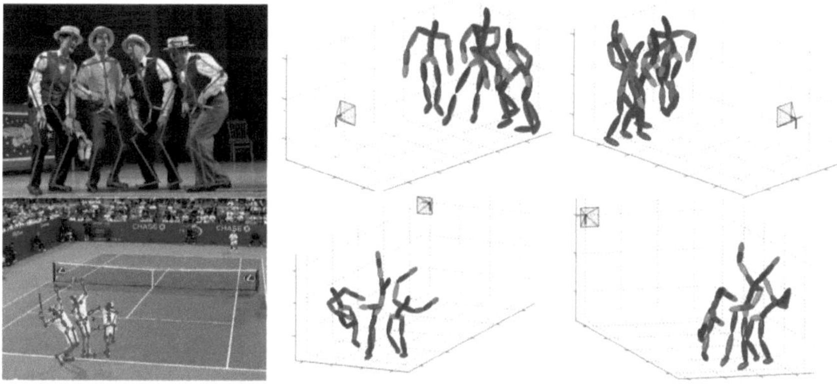

Fig. 6. Reconstruction with multiple people in the same view. The camera estimation is accurate as the people are placed consistently.

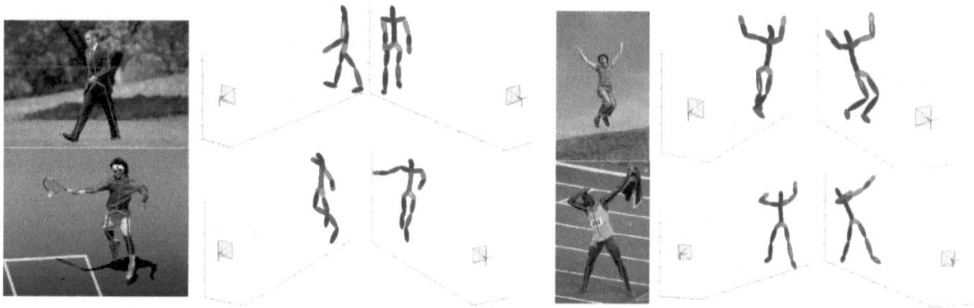

(a) Reconstruction of people in arbitrary poses from internet images.

(b) Reconstruction of people viewed from varied viewpoints.

(c) Our algorithm applied to four frames of an annotated video.

Fig. 7. We acheive realistic reconstructions for people in (a) arbitrary poses, (b) captured from varied viewpoints and (c) monocular video streams

Fig. 8. Failure Cases. The method does not recover the correct pose when there are strong perspective effects and if the mean pose is not a good initialization.

5.2 Qualitative Evaluation

Comparison with Recent Work. We compare reconstructions obtained by our method to recent work by Valmadre et al. [22]. Their method requires multiple images of the same person and requires a human annotator to resolve depth ambiguities. We present our comparative results in Figure 5. Our method is applied per frame to images of the ice skater Yu-Na Kim and compared to the reconstructions obtained by Valmadre et al. We can see in Figure 5 that we are able to obtain good reconstructions per image, without the requirement of a human annotator resolving the depth ambiguities.

Internet Images. We downloaded images of people in a variety of poses from the internet. The 2D joint locations were manually annotated. We present the results in Figures 7(a) and 6. In Figure 6 we first obtained individual camera and pose estimates for each of the annotated human figures. We then fixed the camera upright at an arbitrary location and placed the human figures using the estimated relative rigid pose. It can be seen that the camera estimates are consistent as the actors are placed in their correct locations.

Non-standard Viewpoints. We also test our method on images taken from non-standard viewpoints. We reconstruct the pose and relative camera from photographs downloaded from the internet taken from viewpoints that have generally been considered difficult for pose estimation algorithms. We are able to recover the pose and the viewpoint of the algorithm for such examples as shown in Figure 7(b).

Monocular Video. We demonstrate our algorithm on a set of key frames extracted from monocular video in Figure 7(c). The relative camera estimates are aligned to a single view-point to obtain a sequence of the person performing an action. Note that we are able to estimate the relative pose between the camera and the human correctly resulting in a realistic reconstruction of the sequence.

6 Discussion

We presented a new representation for human pose as a sparse linear embedding in an overcomplete dictionary. We develop a matching pursuit algorithm for estimating the sparse representation of 3D pose and the relative camera from only 2D image evidence while simultaneously maintaining anthropometric regularity. Every step in the matching pursuit iterations is computed in closed form, therefore the algorithm is efficient and takes on average 5 seconds per image to converge. We are able to achieve good generalization to a large range of poses and viewpoints. A case where the algorithm does not result in good reconstructions are in images with strong perspective effects where the weak perspective assumptions on the camera model are violated and in poses where the mean pose is not a reasonable initialization (See Figure 8).

Acknowledgements. This research was funded (in part) by the Intel Science and Technology Center on Embedded Computing, NSF CRI-0855163, and DARPA's Mind's Eye Program. We also thank Daniel Huber and Tomas Simon for providing valuable feedback on the manuscript.

References

1. Lee, H.J., Chen, Z.: Determination of 3D Human Body Postures from a Single View. Computer Vision, Graphics, and Image Processing 30, 148–168 (1985)
2. Peelen, M.V., Downing, P.E.: The Neural Basis of Visual Body Perception. Nature Reviews Neuroscience (8), 636–648
3. MoCap: Carnegie Mellon University Graphics Lab Motion Capture Database, `http://mocap.cs.cmu.edu`
4. Matthews, I., Baker, S.: Active Appearance Models Revisited. International Journal of Computer Vision 60, 135–164 (2003)
5. Safonova, A., Hodgins, J.K., Pollard, N.S.: Synthesizing physically realistic human motion in low-dimensional, behavior-specific spaces. ACM Transactions on Graphics (SIGGRAPH 2004) 23 (2004)
6. Xiao, J., Baker, S., Matthews, I., Kanade, T.: Real-Time Combined 2D+3D Active Appearance Models. In: CVPR, pp. 535–542. IEEE (2004)
7. Boyd, S., Vandenberghe, L.: Convex Optimization. Cambridge University Press (2004)
8. Gander, W.: Least Squares with a Quadratic Constraint. Numerische Mathematik (1981)
9. Taylor, C.: Reconstruction of Articulated Objects from Point Correspondences in a Single Uncalibrated Image. CVIU, 349–363 (2000)
10. Jiang, H.: 3D Human Pose Reconstruction Using Millions of Exemplars. In: ICPR, pp. 1674–1677. IEEE (2010)
11. Parameswaran, V., Chellappa, R.: View Independent Human Body Pose Estimation from a Single Perspective Image. In: CVPR, pp. 16–22. IEEE (2006)
12. Barron, C., Kakadiaris, I.A.: Estimating Anthropometry and Pose from a Single Uncalibrated Image. CVIU, 269–284 (2001)
13. Salzmann, M., Urtasun, R.: Implicitly Constrained Gaussian Process Regression for Monocular Non-Rigid Pose Estimation. In: Advances in Neural Information Processing Systems, pp. 2065–2073 (2010)
14. Agarwal, A., Triggs, B.: 3D Human Pose from Silhouettes by Relevance Vector Regression. In: CVPR, pp. 882–888. IEEE (2004)
15. Mori, G., Malik, J.: Recovering 3D Human Body Configurations using Shape Contexts. PAMI 28, 1052–1062 (2006)

16. Shakhnarovich, G., Viola, P., Darrell, T.: Fast Pose Estimation with Parameter-Sensitive Hashing. In: ICCV, p. 750. IEEE (2003)
17. Elgammal, A., Lee, C.S.: Inferring 3D Body Pose from Silhouettes using Activity Manifold Learning. In: CVPR, pp. 681–688. IEEE (2004)
18. Rosales, R., Sclaroff, S.: Specialized Mappings and the Estimation of Human Body Pose from a Single Image. In: Proceedings of the Workshop on Human Motion, pp. 19–24 (2000)
19. Salzmann, M., Fua, P.: Reconstructing Sharply Folding Surfaces: A Convex Formulation. In: CVPR, pp. 1054–1061. IEEE (2009)
20. Moreno-Noguer, F., Porta, J.M., Fua, P.: Exploring Ambiguities for Monocular Non-Rigid Shape Estimation. In: Daniilidis, K., Maragos, P., Paragios, N. (eds.) ECCV 2010, Part III. LNCS, vol. 6313, pp. 370–383. Springer, Heidelberg (2010)
21. Wei, X.K., Chai, J.: Modeling 3D Human Poses from Uncalibrated Monocular Images. In: ICCV, pp. 1873–1880. IEEE (2009)
22. Valmadre, J., Lucey, S.: Deterministic 3D Human Pose Estimation using Rigid Structure. In: Daniilidis, K. (ed.) ECCV 2010, Part III. LNCS, vol. 6313, pp. 467–480. Springer, Heidelberg (2010)
23. Cootes, T., Edwards, G., Taylor, C.: Active Appearance Models. IEEE Transactions on Pattern Analysis and Machine Intelligence 23, 681–685 (2001)
24. Pati, Y., Rezaiifar, R., Krishnaprasad, P.: Orthogonal Matching Pursuit: Recursive Function Approximation with Applications to Wavelet Decomposition. In: 1993 Conference Record of The Twenty-Seventh Asilomar Conference on Signals, Systems and Computers, vol. 1, pp. 40–44 (1993)
25. Tropp, J.A., Gilbert, A.C.: Signal Recovery from Random Measurements via Orthogonal Matching Pursuit. IEEE Transactions on Information Theory 53, 4655–4666 (2007)
26. Tropp, J.: Greed is Good: Algorithmic Results for Sparse Approximation. IEEE Transactions on Information Theory 50, 2231–2242 (2004)
27. Mallat, S., Zhang, Z.: Matching Pursuits with Time-Frequency Dictionaries. IEEE Transactions on Signal Processing 41, 3397–3415 (1993)
28. Schnemann, P.: A Generalized Solution of the Orthogonal Procrustes Problem. Psychometrika 31, 1–10 (1966) doi:10.1007/BF02289451

Fast Tiered Labeling with Topological Priors

Ying Zheng, Steve Gu, and Carlo Tomasi

Duke University, U.S.A.
{yuanqi,steve,tomasi}@cs.duke.edu

Abstract. We consider labeling an image with multiple tiers. Tiers, one on top of another, enforce a strict vertical order among objects (e.g. sky is above the ground). Two new ideas are explored: First, under a simplification of the general tiered labeling framework proposed by Felzenszwalb and Veksler [1], we design an efficient $O(KN)$ algorithm for the approximate optimal labeling of an image of N pixels with K tiers. Our algorithm runs in over 100 frames per second on images of VGA resolutions when K is less than 6. When $K = 3$, our solution overlaps with the globally optimal one by Felzenszwalb and Veksler in over 99% of all pixels but runs 1000 times faster. Second, we define a topological prior that specifies the number of local extrema in the tier boundaries, and give an $O(NM)$ algorithm to find a single, optimal tier boundary with exactly M local maxima and minima. These two extensions enrich the general tiered labeling framework and enable fast computation. The proposed topological prior further improves the accuracy in labeling details.

1 Introduction

We consider labeling an image with multiple tiers. Tiers, one on top of another, enforce a strict vertical order among objects. For example, the sky is above the ground and bottles are placed on top of a table. For indoor images, the ceiling is above the wall above the floor. In general, ordering may come from physical laws like gravity or typical object arrangements, and is commonly seen in daily life pictures. Figure 1 illustrates the setting for tiered labeling.

Other than the strict order among objects, we often have certain prior knowledge that is useful for object labeling. One important prior is the *regularity* of the shape of an object. A commonly used measure is the total variation of a boundary curve, which only guarantees that a curve is locally smooth. We define instead the *topological smoothness*, which bounds and specifies the number of local extrema of a shape boundary, and is useful for enforcing that a curve is globally smooth and has a given number of peaks or valleys (Figure 2). We explore this novel, topological prior in the multi-tier labeling framework.

1.1 Literature Review

Scene labeling assigns to each pixel a semantic label and has been widely studied [2–7, 1, 8]. Let $f : \Omega \to \mathcal{L}$ be a labeling function mapping from the image grid

A. Fitzgibbon et al. (Eds.): ECCV 2012, Part IV, LNCS 7575, pp. 587–601, 2012.

Fig. 1. The tiered labeling problem partitions an input image (left) into multiple tiers (right). Each tier (6 in total) is displayed with a different color. The labeling takes less than 0.01 seconds on an image of resolution 640 × 480.

Ω to the label space $\mathcal{L}$. Let f_p be the label of pixel p. Labeling can often be modeled as minimizing an energy function in the form of a Markov Random Field (MRF)[2]:

$$\min_f \left\{ \sum_{p\in\Omega} \underbrace{D_p(f_p)}_{\text{data cost}} + \lambda \sum_{(p,q)\in\mathcal{N}} \underbrace{V(f_p, f_q)}_{\text{label inconsistency}} \right\} \tag{1}$$

where $D_p(f_p)$ is the data cost of assigning label f_p to pixel p and $V(f_p, f_q)$ is the label inconsistency cost. $\mathcal{N}$ is a neighborhood system: $(p,q) \in \mathcal{N}$ means p and q are neighbors. Finally, λ is a regularization parameter that balances the two costs. Clearly, the role of the label inconsistency cost V is to enhance the robustness of the labeling when the data cost D_p is insufficient.

The optimization in Equation (1) is known to be NP-hard [3], except when special assumptions and constraints are applied [9, 4, 10, 7, 1, 8]. Of particular interest is the work by Felzenszwalb and Veksler [1] who describe an $O(N^{1.5})$ algorithm for the globally optimal labeling of a three-tiered structure. In that three-tiered structure, each tier is further allowed to be vertically decomposed into an arbitrary number of segments. Here and throughout this paper N refers to the number of image pixels. Unfortunately their algorithm would be too slow for labeling scenes of more than three tiers because of its exponential dependency on the number of tiers. Most recently Strekalovskiy and Cremers [8] extend the

Fig. 2. Although these three pictures differ in scale and perspective, the boundary that separates the sky from the rest has three distinguishable peaks in each image. In this example, the number of local extrema of a boundary curve is a reliable prior that conveys useful domain knowledge.

computation to multi-tiered labeling using a relaxation of the integer convex program, but with an even greater time complexity. Their algorithm is also approximate due to randomized rounding.

Total variation is the conventional measure of smoothness used to regularize the shape of a tier boundary. However, this measure only encourages a tier boundary to be smooth locally rather than globally. We think that the number of extrema of a boundary curve is a useful topological measure of the degree of global smoothness of a curve. Moreover, the number of extrema of a boundary curve can be used as a prior in tiered labeling and in scene label transfer [11]. This topological measure has been studied in the context of topological persistence and simplification of a triangulated surface [12, 13] and recently as a soft prior for one dimensional signal de-noising [14]. To the best of our knowledge this measure has rarely been considered in MRF optimization or in scene label transfer.

1.2 Our Contributions

First, under a restricted cost model, we develop an $O(KN)$ approximation algorithm to solve the K-tier labeling problem. We find that our algorithm works well in practice and runs in over 100 frames per second on images of resolution 640×480 when K is less than 6. When $K = 3$, our solution overlaps with the globally optimal one [1] in over 99% of the pixels but runs 1000 times faster.

Second, we propose to use the number of extrema to regularize the smoothness of a boundary curve and show that this improves the accuracy of tiered labeling, particularly for indoor scene labeling where the number of local extrema of each boundary curve is known *a priori* (e.g. the ceiling-wall boundary has one local maximum and the wall-floor boundary has one local minimum). We give an efficient $O(MN)$ algorithm to find an optimal tier boundary with exactly M local extrema using dynamic programming, and demonstrate improved labeling results in detail on a benchmark data set.

1.3 Organization

Section 2 presents the general framework of tiered labeling, our chosen restricted cost model, and our linear time approximation algorithm for multi-tiered labeling. Section 3 defines the concept of topological smoothness and presents a linear time algorithm to compute a binary labeling with the boundary curve containing a given number of local maxima and minima. Section 4 tests our algorithm on a selected indoor image data set and compares it to the baseline algorithm of [1] in terms of quality and speed. We show that without sacrificing the quality of the tiered-labeling, our algorithm yields running time improvement of several orders of magnitude. Section 5 concludes.

2 Tiered Labeling

The three tiered labeling framework was first studied by Felzenszwalb and Veksler [1]. At a high level, it divides an image into regions of top, middle, and bottom. The middle region is further decomposed into a series of vertical stripes, each with a unique label. We generalize this definition to include multiple tiers. A formal definition is this: Let $\Omega = [1, \cdots, R] \times [1, \cdots, C]$ be an image grid of R rows and C columns. Given a Directed Acyclic Graph (DAG) $\langle \mathcal{L}, \prec \rangle$ where $\mathcal{L}$ is a set of labels and $\prec$ is a partial ordering relation defined in $\mathcal{L}$, we have:

Definition 1 (Tiered Labeling). *A labeling function $f : \Omega \to \mathcal{L}$ is a tiered labeling with respect to $\prec$ if either $f(r,c) = f(r+1,c)$ or $f(r,c) \prec f(r+1,c)$ for each column $1 \leq c \leq C$ and each row $1 \leq r \leq R-1$.*

The relation graph can be further decomposed to a set of tiers if we run Breadth-first Search (BFS) on the DAG and group labels that have the same depth from the root into tiers. Note that labels within each tier have no particular ordering between them. In this section we give an approximate labeling algorithm for the K-tiered labeling problem. We first show that 1D tiered labeling can be solved optimally in linear time with respect to the array size, multiplied by the size of relation graph, using dynamic programming. We then solve the 2D tiered labeling using 1D tiered labeling as submodules for cost approximation.

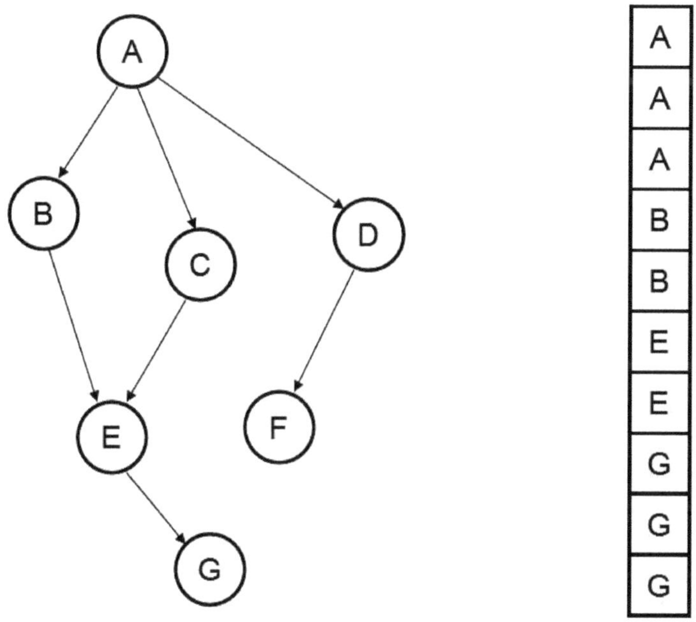

Fig. 3. Left: the "above" relation $\prec$ organized in a directed acyclic graph. Right: one possible tiered labeling in a one dimensional array.

2.1 1D Tiered Labeling

We first show that 1D tiered labeling can be *optimally* solved in $O(EN)$ time on a one dimensional array of size N where E is the number of edges in the relation DAG $\langle \mathcal{L}, \prec \rangle$. The problem is to assign each pixel $1 \leq i \leq N$ a label f_i so that either $f_i = f_{i+1}$ or $f_i \prec f_{i+1}$ for $1 \leq i \leq N-1$. The relation $\prec$ can be understood as "above" and is imposed *a priori*. Figure 3 illustrates the setting.

We show how to solve the global optimization of Equation (1) using dynamic programming. Let $F(i, l)$ be the optimal cost when position i is labeled l. Without loss of generality, l takes positive integer values. We then have the following recursive state equation:

$$F(i, l) = \min_{l' : l' \prec l} \left\{ \underbrace{F(i-1, l') +}_{\text{recursion}} \quad \underbrace{V(l', l)}_{\text{label inconsistency}} \quad + \underbrace{D_i(l)}_{\text{data cost}} \right\} \tag{2}$$

Dynamic programming computes $F(i, l)$ for each $1 \leq i \leq N$ and each $1 \leq l \leq K$. Since each edge is visited once at each i, the overall time complexity is $O(EN)$. For the boundary conditions we specify: $F(1, l) = D_1(l)$ for each $l \in \mathcal{L}$.

We point out that for 1D tiered labeling, both the data cost D and the pairwise potential V are allowed to take arbitrary forms.

2.2 2D Tiered Labeling

While the 1D tiered labeling problem can be optimally solved efficiently for arbitrary number of tiers, the 2D tiered labeling is far more difficult. In fact, it is NP-hard to compute the general 2D tiered labeling problem as it is as difficult as solving the general 2D MRF. We look for approximation algorithms instead.

Three simplifications are made for efficient computation. First, as a preprocessing step we aggregate the cost of multiple labels within a single tier into a *single* cost function. Let D^k be the aggregate cost of tier k. The set of object labels in tier k is denoted $\mathcal{L}_k$, a subset of $\mathcal{L}$. We define for each pixel p:

$$D^k(p) = \min_{l \in \mathcal{L}_k} D_p(l) \; . \tag{3}$$

Then, the modified relation graph $\mathcal{L}$ is reduced to K tiers, each with a single label. In other words, the modified relation graph has K nodes and $K-1$ edges, organized as a linear chain. We argue that this way of compressing the relation graph does not cause serious problems as after assigning the tiered labels under the modified relation graph, one can unfold the collapsed labels in each tier.

In the second simplification, we divide the K-tier labeling to a series of $K-1$ *binary* labeling problems. Each binary labeling problem can be solved in $O(N)$ time. First, we use the 1D tiered labeling algorithm to compute the cumulative cost F_c for each column c. $F_c(i,k)$ is therefore the optimal cost of labeling position i as k at column c, and can be computed using Equation (2). Since the modified relation graph is a linear chain, we label each tier as $1, 2, \cdots, K$ from top to bottom. We start from the bottom tier and separate it from the rest of the tiers.

In the third simplification, we restrict the pairwise potential V. Specifically, $V(f_p, f_q)$ can be arbitrary for $(p,q) \in \mathcal{N}$ in the same column. However, when $(p,q) \in \mathcal{N}$ are in the same row, we take:

$$V(f_p, f_q) = \begin{cases} 1 \text{ if } f_p \neq f_q \\ 0 \text{ otherwise} \end{cases} \; . \tag{4}$$

In other words, the pairwise potential is allowed to take an arbitrary form along columns and takes the form of a Potts model along rows. Combining the second and the third simplifications, the binary labeling problem is equivalent to finding a single path $\{x_c\}_{c=1}^{C}$ of row indices for each column. This path separates the bottom tier from the one above it. The problem formulation is therefore:

$$\min_{x_1, \cdots, x_C} \left\{ \sum_{c=1}^{C} \mu_c(x_c) + \lambda \underbrace{\sum_{c=1}^{C-1} |x_{c+1} - x_c|}_{\text{label inconsistency}} \right\} \tag{5}$$

where

$$\mu_c(x_c) \triangleq F_c(x_c, k-1) + \sum_{r=x_c+1}^{R} D^k(r,c) \tag{6}$$

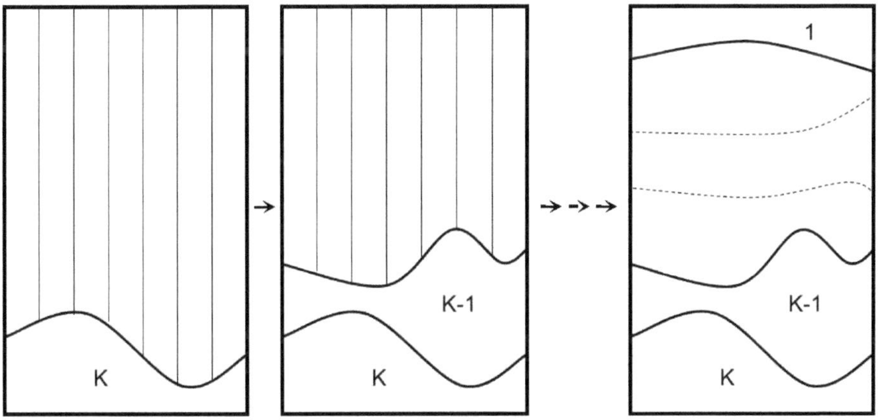

Fig. 4. Decomposing a K-tiered labeling to a series of $K-1$ binary labeling

stands for the data cost and can be evaluated in $O(1)$ time if an integral image is pre-computed for D^k. Let $E_c(x_c)$ be the optimal cost up to column c at pixel x_c. The recursive state equation for the global minimization is:

$$E_c(x_c) = \mu_c(x_c) + \min_{1 \leq x_{c-1} \leq R} \{E_{c-1}(x_{c-1}) + \lambda |x_c - x_{c-1}|\} \ . \tag{7}$$

Thanks to the generalized distance transform [15], Equation (7) can be evaluated in $O(R)$ time. Since this dynamic program takes C steps, the overall time complexity is $O(RC)$ or $O(N)$. Once tier k is separated, we proceed to tier $k-1$ and separate it from the tiers above it in a similar way. Since each time the binary labeling takes $O(N)$ time, the overall time complexity is $O(KN)$. Figure 4 illustrates this greedy construction.

The first simplification compresses the labeling graph into a linear chain. Once the tiered labeling is done, one can further decompose each tier into vertical bands to uncover possible multiple labels (Figure 5). This is essentially a one dimensional problem because each column within each tier can only have one label. Consider tier t and its label set $\mathcal{L}_t$. Let $C(i,l)$ be the optimal cost of labeling column i as label l. Let $D(i,l)$ be the data cost of labeling column i as l. The state equation for recovering the labels within tier t is:

$$C(i,l) = \min \left\{ \lambda + \min_{l' \in \mathcal{L}_t, l' \neq l} C(i-1,l'), C(i-1,l) \right\} + D(i,l) \ . \tag{8}$$

The time complexity for the dynamic program above is linear with respect to the number of columns, multiplied by the square of the number of labels within a tier. Since the number of labels is typically much smaller than the number of rows of an image, the complexity can be safely neglected compared to the main $O(KN)$ algorithm.

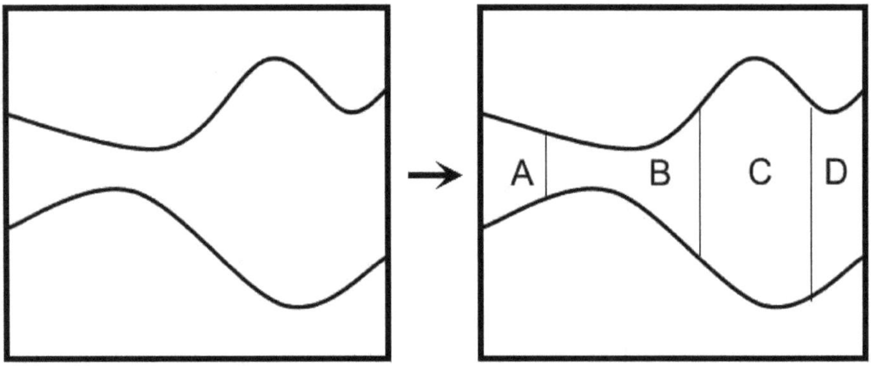

Fig. 5. Unfolding object labels by vertical decomposition

Because of the three simplifications made, our algorithm does not minimize the exact MRF energy function in Equation (1). However, our algorithm guarantees that the solution is a tiered labeling by construction. The advantages of our algorithm lie in its practical efficiency of $O(NK)$ complexity, the ability to label multiple tiers beyond three, and good performance on par with other methods of greater complexity. For instance, although the algorithm given in [1] is globally optimal when $K = 3$, our solution differs from the globally optimal one in less than 1% of the total pixels and runs over 1000 times faster than the $O(N^{1.5})$ algorithm in [1] in our experiments.

3 Topological Smoothness

In the discussion above we use the label inconsistency cost of Equation (4). While this penalty function works generally well in practice, it induces a large penalty for sharp transitions (Figure 6). Moreover, the total variation only quantifies the local smoothness of a curve. Many scenes have tier boundaries that are globally smooth in the sense that the borders contain only one or two local extrema. For instance, in the work of [7], a scene is decomposed into top, left, right, bottom and middle and the top and bottom tier boundaries have only one local minimum and one local maximum respectively due to their polygonal representation.

We propose to use the number of extrema of a path to quantify its topological smoothness. Our algorithm finds a minimal cost path with exactly M local extrema, which is useful for the binary labeling problem described in the previous section. Note that the new prior cannot be modeled appropriately in an MRF formulation. Our algorithm can also be modified to find a path with at most M local extrema or M local maxima, all with the same asymptotic complexity. Let $F_c(x_c)$ be the total data cost of column c if the path passes through x_c.

Here one can simply evaluate $F_c(x_c)$ in $O(1)$ time using a pre-computed integral image representation. The objective under the topological smoothness prior is:

$$\begin{aligned} &\min_{x_1,\cdots,x_C} \sum_{c=1}^{C} F_c(x_c) \\ &\text{subject to: path } \{x_c\}_{c=1}^{C} \text{ has } M \text{ local extrema} \end{aligned} \tag{9}$$

In this constrained optimization, we omit the label inconsistency cost because we expect to use the number of extrema of the path to automatically enhance its regularity. However, including the pairwise smoothness term: $\lambda \sum_{c=1}^{C-1} |x_{c+1} - x_c|$ does not increase the computational complexity of our algorithm thanks again to the generalized distance transform. For ease of description we omit this term in the rest of the discussion. The notion of a local maximum or minimum is this:

Definition 2 (Local Extrema). *An interval $[I, J]$ is said to be a local maximum of $\{x_c\}_{c=1}^{C}$ if $x_{I-1} < x_I = x_{I+1} = \cdots = x_J > x_{J+1}$. The interval $[I, J]$ is said to be a local minimum of $\{x_c\}_{c=1}^{C}$ if it is a local maximum of $\{-x_c\}_{c=1}^{C}$.*

Let $C(r, c, m, \uparrow)$ be the optimal cumulative cost of the path that contains m local extrema before reaching pixel (r, c) through an ascending direction. Similarly, let $C(r, c, m, \downarrow)$ be the optimal cumulative cost of the path that contains m local extrema before reaching pixel (r, c) though a descending direction. We have the following alternating state equations for dynamic programming:

$$C(r, c, m, \uparrow) = F_c(r) + \min \left\{ \min_{r' \geq r} C(r', c-1, m, \uparrow), \min_{r' > r} C(r', c-1, m-1, \downarrow) \right\} \tag{10}$$

$$C(r, c, m, \downarrow) = F_c(r) + \min \left\{ \min_{r' \leq r} C(r', c-1, m, \downarrow), \min_{r' < r} C(r', c-1, m-1, \uparrow) \right\} \tag{11}$$

These state equations utilize the fact that a local maximum is created by an ascending path followed by a descending path and a local minimum is created by a descending path followed by an ascending path. The use of relation symbols $\geq$ and $\leq$ include the equality relations so that the path is allowed to move in the same row across adjacent columns.

The boundary conditions need to be posed carefully. First, when $c = 0$, we have for each $1 \leq r \leq R$ and $1 \leq m \leq M$ the following boundary condition:

$$C(r, 0, m, \uparrow) = C(r, 0, m, \downarrow) = +\infty \tag{12}$$

Second, when $k = 0$, we pre-compute the data cost:

$$B(r, c) = \begin{cases} F_c(r) \text{ if } c = 0 \\ B(r, c-1) + F_c(r) \text{ otherwise} \end{cases} . \tag{13}$$

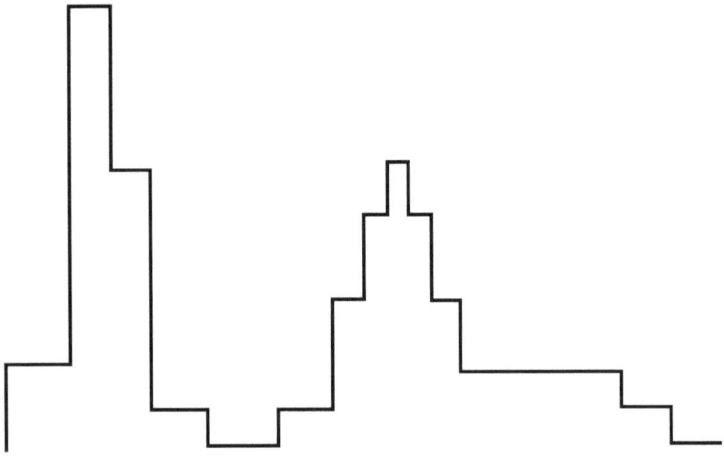

Fig. 6. A cartoon city skyline. This tier boundary induces a large label inconsistency by Equation (4) due to sharp transitions. However, the cost is low by the standard of topological smoothness as the skyline contains only two local maxima. The number of local maxima is a topological quantity that tolerates significant sharp transitions.

The boundary conditions for C are:

$$C(r,c,0,\uparrow) = F_c(r) + \min\left\{\min_{r'\geq r} C(r',c-1,0,\uparrow), \min_{r'>r} B(r,c-1)\right\} \quad (14)$$

$$C(r,c,0,\downarrow) = F_c(r) + \min\left\{\min_{r'\leq r} C(r',c-1,0,\downarrow), \min_{r'<r} B(r,c-1)\right\} \quad (15)$$

The boundary conditions rule out the case that a constant level curve followed by an ascending or descending path may accidentally induce a local maximum or minimum. The correctness of the dynamic programming then follows easily by induction. The overall time complexity is $O(MN)$ by following the state equation and using a simple book-keeping method for updating the running min in a sequential way.

4 Experiments

We demonstrate applications of multi-tier labeling with and without the topological smoothness constraint. We compare our approximation algorithm to the $O(N^{1.5})$ algorithm by Felzenszwalb and Veksler [1] on labeling a three-tiered structure. Although their algorithm is globally optimal in terms of solving Equation (1), we show that our greedy construction achieves similar results but runs much faster in practice. We collect 60 images from two benchmark data sets [16, 17] and annotate the ground truth of a three tiered labeling.

Table 1. Average accuracy over 60 images. "+Topology" refers to our tiered labeling under the topological smoothness constraint: the top tier boundary has one local minimum and the bottom tier boundary has one local maximum. Global accuracy is calculated on the whole image. Detail accuracy is counted on the cropped image. See also Figure 8 for detailed visual comparison.

	naive	DP [1]	Ours	+Topology
Global Accuracy	0.80	0.96	0.96	**0.97**
Detail Accuracy	0.76	0.90	0.91	**0.94**
Timing (seconds)	–	10.1	< 0.01	< 0.01
Overlap with [1]	–	1	> 0.99	–

For fair comparison, both algorithms use the same feature costs. All the data set and our C++/MATLAB implementation are available at authors' website: `http://www.cs.duke.edu/~yuanqi`.

We generate the pixel costs as follows: Let T, O, B be the collection of sampled 3D color vectors associated to the top, middle and bottom tier. Let $d(p)$ be the color vector at pixel p. We compute the ratio:

$$\gamma(p) = \frac{\min_{d \in T} \|d(p) - d\|}{\min_{d \in O \bigcup B} \|d(p) - d\|} \tag{16}$$

and we assign the cost associated to T based on the ratio:

$$f_T(p) = \begin{cases} +1 & \text{if } \gamma(p) > \frac{3}{2} \\ -1 & \text{if } \gamma(p) < \frac{2}{3} \\ +\frac{1}{2} & \text{otherwise} \end{cases} . \tag{17}$$

The rationale behind the cost design is that the closer the feature resembles T's features relative to the background features of O and B, the lower the cost. Ambiguous features would receive a cost that is positive. $f_O(p)$ and $f_B(p)$ are generated similarly under cyclic permutation of T, O, B. Since each tier is composed of a single object, there is no need to invoke the step for recovering multiple objects within a tier.

Figure 7 displays sample results and Table 1 shows numerical comparisons. In summary, our algorithm runs 1000 times faster than [1] on test images and differs from the optimal solution in less than 1% of all the pixels. Accuracy is further improved under the topological prior. This improvement is not obvious if tested on the whole image due to the fact that boundaries are thin. To magnify this advantage we crop the boundary regions and test accuracy on this smaller area (Figure 8). We achieve 4% improvement over Felzenszwalb and Veksler [1] in details. Figure 9 shows that the topological prior tolerates sharp transitions while traditional smoothness priors may fail.

Fig. 7. Each row shows 4 out of 60 test images. From top to bottom: Input image, ground truth, generated cost, tiered labeling of [1], our result, our result under topological smoothness constraint. Best viewed when enlarged and in color.

Fig. 8. Left to right: the cropped image, result by [1], and our labeling with topological constraints (1 local extremum allowed)

Fig. 9. Traditional prior such as total variation misses the sharp transition (left). Our topological prior respects sharp transitions (right).

5 Conclusions

We present an $O(KN)$ greedy algorithm for the K-tier labeling of an image of N pixels. In addition, we propose to use a novel topological prior to regularize the tier boundaries and present an $O(MN)$ algorithm for finding a minimal-cost binary labeling with exactly M local extrema on the border. Our algorithm for multi-tier scene labeling runs much faster than the previous method without sacrificing the labeling accuracy. The accuracy is further improved under the topological prior, which is simple in concept and equally efficient in implementation. One interesting question is whether our algorithm has a non-trivial theoretical approximation bound relative to the globally optimal solution.

Acknowledgement: This work is supported by the Army Research Office under Grant No. $W911NF$-10-1-0387 and by the National Science Foundation under Grant IIS-10-17017.

References

1. Felzenszwalb, P., Veksler, O.: Tiered scene labeling with dynamic programming. In: IEEE CVPR, pp. 3097–3104 (2010)
2. Li, S.: Markov random field modeling in computer vision. Computer science workbench. Springer (1995)
3. Boykov, Y., Veksler, O., Zabih, R.: Fast approximate energy minimization via graph cuts. IEEE PAMI 23, 1222–1239 (2001)
4. Ishikawa, H.: Exact optimization for markov random fields with convex priors. IEEE PAMI 25, 1333–1336 (2003)
5. Winn, J., Shotton, J.: The layout consistent random field for recognizing and segmenting partially occluded objects. In: IEEE CVPR, pp. 37–44 (2006)
6. Kohli, P., Ladicky, L., Torr, P.: Robust higher order potentials for enforcing label consistency. IJCV 82, 302–324 (2009)
7. Liu, X., Veksler, O., Samarabandu, J.: Order-preserving moves for graph-cut-based optimization. IEEE PAMI 32, 1182–1196 (2010)
8. Strekalovskiy, E., Cremers, D.: Generalized ordering constraints for multilabel optimization. In: ICCV (2011)
9. Greig, D., Porteous, B., Seheult, A.: Exact maximum a posteriori estimation for binary images. Journal of the Royal Statistical Society 51(2), 271–279 (1989)
10. Kolmogorov, V., Rother, C.: Minimizing nonsubmodular functions with graph cuts-a review. IEEE PAMI 29, 1274–1279 (2007)
11. Liu, C., Yuen, J., Torralba, A.: Sift flow: Dense correspondence across scenes and its applications. IEEE PAMI 33, 978–994 (2011)
12. Edelsbrunner, H., Letscher, D., Zomorodian, A.: Topological persistence and simplification. Discrete & Computational Geometry 28, 511–533 (2002)
13. Edelsbrunner, H., Harer, J., Zomorodian, A.: Hierarchical morse-smale complexes for piecewise linear 2-manifolds. Discrete & Computational Geometry 30, 87–107 (2003)
14. Gu, S., Zheng, Y., Tomasi, C.: Oscillation regularization. In: The 37th International Conference on Acoustics, Speech, and Signal Processing (2012)

15. Felzenszwalb, P., Huttenlocher, D.: Distance transforms of sampled functions. Technical Report TR2004-1963, Cornell Computing and Information Science (2004)
16. Oliva, A., Torralba, A.: Modeling the shape of the scene: A holistic representation of the spatial envelope. IJCV 42, 145–175 (2001)
17. Quattoni, A., Torralba, A.: Recognizing indoor scenes. In: IEEE CVPR, pp. 413–420 (2009)

TreeCANN - k-d Tree Coherence Approximate Nearest Neighbor Algorithm

Igor Olonetsky and Shai Avidan

Dept. of Electrical Engineering,
Tel Aviv University
igor.olonetsky@gmail.com, avidan@eng.tau.ac.il

Abstract. TreeCANN is a fast algorithm for approximately matching all patches between two images. It does so by following the established convention of finding an initial set of matching patch candidates between the two images and then propagating good matches to neighboring patches in the image plane. TreeCANN accelerates each of these components substantially leading to an algorithm that is $\times 3$ to $\times 5$ faster than existing methods. Seed matching is achieved using a properly tuned k-d tree on a sparse grid of patches. In particular, we show that a sequence of key design decisions can make k-d trees run as fast as recently proposed state-of-the-art methods, and because of image coherency it is enough to consider only a sparse grid of patches across the image plane. We then develop a novel propagation step that is based on the integral image, which drastically reduces the computational load that is dominated by the need to repeatedly measure similarity between pairs of patches. As a by-product we give an *optimal* algorithm for **exact** matching that is based on the integral image. The proposed exact algorithm is faster than previously reported results and depends only on the size of the images and not on the size of the patches. We report results on large and varied data sets and show that TreeCANN is orders of magnitude faster than exact NN search yet produces matches that are within 1% error, compared to the exact NN search.

Keywords: Approximate nearest neighbor search, patch matching.

1 Introduction

Patch-based methods are at the heart of many applications such as texture synthesis [1], image de-noising [2] and image editing [3], to name a few. These methods can often be reduced to Nearest Neighbor Field (NNF) estimation, where the goal is to find, for each patch in one image, the most similar patch in the other image.

The number of patches in an image is roughly equal to the number of pixels and can be in the millions for high-resolution images. Therefore, NNF calculation is a time consuming task that is usually performed using approximation methods. Previous approximation approaches were mostly based on hierarchical-tree

A. Fitzgibbon et al. (Eds.): ECCV 2012, Part IV, LNCS 7575, pp. 602–615, 2012.

structures, such as k-d trees [4], coupled with dimensionality reduction methods (e.g. PCA). This works quite well in practice but is too slow to be used in interactive editing tools, or so it was believed.

Recently, a novel method was introduced, termed PatchMatch [5], that follows a different strategy for estimating the NNF. It achieves a substantial speedup (compared to k-d trees) by exploiting the coherency of NNF. PatchMatch works in rounds where in each round patches are assigned a random match and good matches are propagated to their neighbors in the image plane. This achieves good results even after a small number of iterations. The downside is that PatchMatch is not accurate enough in its recommended configuration (5 iterations), compared to the ground truth error, which is measured as the result of an exact NN search. Moreover, when the coherency assumption does not apply, PatchMatch might fail and lead to many mismatches, which severely degrade the mapping quality. Therefore, applications that require accurate NNF might prefer k-d trees that are slower but more accurate. The random search of PatchMatch was replaced with Locality Sensitive Hashing (LSH) in [6] that showed this to improve both accuracy and speed.

We show that a sequence of design decisions lets us accelerate the use of k-d tree for seed initialization and a novel use of the integral image (II) lets us accelerate the propagation step.

For seed initialization we use an extremely aggressive dimensionality reduction coupled with relaxed k-d tree search. Relaxed search means that we only traverse the tree from root to leaf and do not perform boundary tests to determine if the closest point might in fact be in a nearby branch of the tree. The loss of accuracy is partially compensated by the k-nn retrieval, as we retrieve the k top neighbors from the tree and revaluate all of them. These design decisions accelerate k-d tree search by an order of magnitude. Further acceleration is achieved by working only on a sparse grid of patches.

In the propagation step we make novel use of the II. Specifically, consider a region, in the source image, consisting of 3×3 overlapping patches and suppose we wish to match it to the corresponding region in the target image, based on the current assignment of the central patch. Clearly, we can compute 8 patch similarities to determine if to propagate the patch assignment from the central patch to any of its 8 neighbors. But because the patches overlap we can save considerable amount of time by calculating the difference image between the two regions and constructing an II based on it. Computing patch similarity becomes constant in the size of the patch. And since each patch participates in 9 such region-to-region comparisons we obtain, in effect, a propagation step at a fraction of the computational cost.

This propagation step leads naturally to a novel algorithm for *exact* NNF estimation over the entire image. This is done by shifting the source image across all locations of the target image, taking the difference image and computing the II on it. Patch similarity can now be computed in constant time, regardless of patch size. The overall complexity of this algorithm depends only on the size of the images and is independent of the size of patches.

We have extensively tested the TreeCANN algorithm on the recently presented database [6]. Our experiments indicate that TreeCANN outperforms PatchMatch and CSH, sometimes by up to an order of magnitude speedup, for the same accuracy levels. In addition, TreeCANN can be tuned to reach nearly ground-truth accuracy levels (less than 1% error), presenting more than $\times 100$ speedup compared to exact NN search.

2 Related Work

Patch-based sampling methods have become a popular tool for a wide variety of computer vision and graphics applications.

In practice, most of these applications rely on the process of NNF calculation, which is defined as follows: given two images (or regions) S and T, for every patch in S find the NN (in terms of appearance) in T under a certain metric (usually L_2). When trying to deal with this task in a naive, brute-force way, the computational time complexity of the algorithm is $O(mM^2)$ (where m is the patch size and M is the number of patches in the image), denying it practical use. Over the years more sophisticated techniques have been developed for exact NN matching. For example, it was shown in [7], that the m factor can be eliminated from the time complexity by exploiting the sequential overlap between patches. This brings the overall cost to $O(M^2)$. Other exact methods are mostly based on various hierarchical-tree structures.

Since exact NN methods are not fast enough, another group, known as Approximate NN algorithms, has been developed. All the hierarchical-tree based techniques, such as TSVQ [8], FLANN [9] and the most commonly used k-d tree [4] (frequently coupled with PCA dimensionality reduction technique), have been successfully used.

In parallel with the development of the tree-based techniques, several algorithms employed a different strategy, based on the coherent structure of images. Ashikhmin [10] was the first to introduce an algorithm, which used a *local propagation* technique during the texture synthesis process. This was shortly after extended by Tong et al. [11], who presented the *k-coherence.*

The local propagation methods exploited the natural structure of images and reduced memory foot print, relative to the tree-based algorithms, but failed to define a general framework and have been implemented only for the specific task of texture synthesis. However, this situation changed with the introduction of PatchMatch [5], which is also the one that inspired our work. PatchMatch and its generalized version [12] outperformed previous tree-structured techniques (specifically ANN+PCA) by up to an order of magnitude, and provided interactive performance rates for a wide range of patch-based image editing applications. The PatchMatch algorithm starts with an *initialization stage*, that performs a random assignment of every patch in the source image S to a patch in the target image T. Then it proceeds with a propagation of the good matches to the neighboring patches in the image plane. This is followed by another random assignment step, which prevents the algorithm from being stuck in local minima. The propagation and the random search stages is performed in an iterative manner, and the algorithm usually converges after a small number of iterations.

Recently, a new algorithm, called Coherency Sensitive Hashing (CSH) [6], was introduced. In CSH the *random search* stage of PatchMatch was replaced by a much more efficient process, based on the LSH [13] technique. As a result, CSH is more accurate, as well as 2-3 times faster than PatchMatch.

TreeCANN share the overall structure with CSH. They both use an established ANN method to seed the propagation step, but there are several important distinctions. First, we carefully choose the k-d tree parameters and show empirically that they can bring k-d tree to perform on par with PatchMatch and CSH. We then show that working on a sparse grid is enough to establish the initial matches quickly. Finally, we proposes a novel use of the II to speed up the propagation step. Aa a result, our propagation step requires just a single iteration. TreeCANN is faster, more accurate and with suitable parameter tuning approaches the accuracy of exact NN while being orders of magnitude faster.

3 The TreeCANN Algorithm

Given source image S and target image T we define the NNF problem as a function $f : \mathbb{Z}^2 \mapsto \mathbb{Z}^2$ of values, defined over all possible patch coordinates (the locations of patches' upper-left corners). We assume that both images are of equal size, denoted M. The size of a patch edge is denoted by r, and $m = cr^2$ denotes the total number of values of a patch where c is the number of channels in an image. We take the distance metric $dist(s, t)$, between patches s and t to be the L_2 distance, where s and t are the locations of these patches in images S and T, respectively.

Following the convention of [5,6] our algorithm consists of two main phases. An initial guess (search) step that finds an initial mapping and a propagation step that propagates good matches to neighboring patches. Because our initial step is so effective we make do with a single propagation step.

The estimation of the TreeCANN algorithm's performance is mostly accomplished by observations of the error measure, which is defined as a ratio between the results' errors , obtained by our algorithm, and the ground truth error levels, calculated using an exact NN algorithm.

3.1 ANN Search

We make a number of design decisions to accelerate the performance of k-d trees, and test them extensively, to make the best choice possible.

Aggressive Dimensionality Reduction: We evaluated a large number of target dimensions and found that aggressive dimensionality reduction provides the best trade off between accuracy and speed. Specifically, we define the target dimension, $dim(r)$, of a patch of size r to be a simple linear equation: $dim(r) = 3 + r/2$. For example, an 8×8 RGB patch will be reduced from $192 = 8 * 8 * 3$ to only $7 = 3 + 8/2$ dimensions. This is the first design decision.

We achieve dimensionality reduction by means of PCA and use a very small set of patches to compute it. In all our experiments we use $L = 100$ random patches (randomly selected from both S and T) to compute leading principal components. This is the first design decision we make. We also evaluated the use of the Walsh-Hadamard kernels, as suggested in [6] and found that they accelerate the dimensionality reduction step but hurt the k-d tree retrieval and overall give comparable results. Therefore, we only focus of the use of PCA for dimensionality reduction.

Relaxed ANN Search: k-d tree is extremely fast when the database contains good matches to the query point. In this case k-d tree simply traverse the tree from root to leaf and returns the nearest point encountered along the way. This simple procedure is complicated because of boundary problems, where the search must visit nearby branches of the tree to make sure that they do not contain a closer point to the query. To address this, we relax k-d tree to retrieve points which are within a factor of $1+e$ of the true closest point, for a certain $e \geq 0$ [4]. This technique enables a substantial reduction of the number of leaf cells that are visited, results in at least 3 fold improvement of the overall running-time, while causing only a slight degradation of the accuracy levels. In our experiments we found that $e = 3$ constitutes a good compromise between the speed and the accuracy of our algorithm. This is the second design decision of our algorithm.

***k*-NN Retrieval:** An aggressive dimensionality reduction, combined with a relaxed ANN search hurts accuracy and to combat that we retrieve k nearest neighbors and then choose the nearest patch out of the k based on measuring distance between the retrieved patches and the query patch in the original image space. This is the third design decision we make.

We show the results of our design decisions in figure 1. The figure compares several combinations of dimensionality reduction and k values. We show only the case of $r = 8$ (i.e., RGB patches of size 8×8 pixels) on image of size $M = 0.4$ mega-pixels, and compare target dimensions of $5, 7$ and 9. Results are averaged over the data set of [6]. In all cases we use a relaxed k-d tree search. The graph shows retrieval speed compared to retrieval error, where error is measured as the ratio between the retrieved NN and the ground truth NN as computed by exact NN search. As expected, increasing the target dimension reduces error but increases retrieval time. We also include the PatchMatch curve for comparison. For $k = 1$ the error obtained by a k-d tree, is much higher than the error obtained by PatchMatch, and this is also to be expected. Nevertheless, as k grows, the error levels drop sharply (for instance, for $dim(8) = 5\, or\, 7$ the error drops by a factor of 3, while the run-time increases only by a factor of 1.5). We found that the value of $k = 4$ offers a good tradeoff between speed and accuracy and, consequently, use this value in all our experiments.

Somewhat surprisingly, k-d tree alone, through a sequence of judicious design decisions, outperforms PatchMatch in many points along the accuracy-speed curve. We hope that highlighting these design decisions can benefit other applications that rely on ANN.

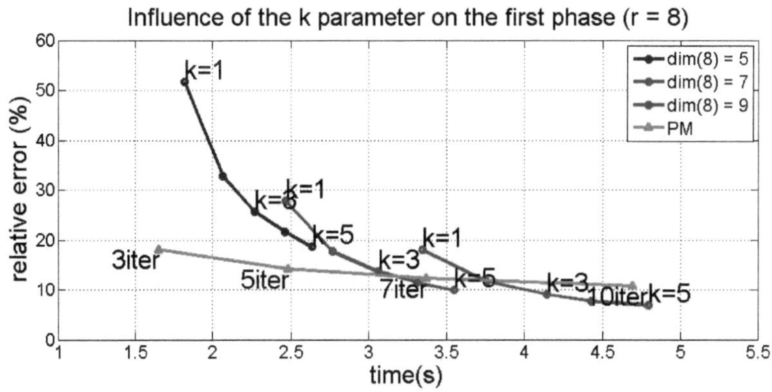

Fig. 1. The performance, obtained by our algorithm, when only its first phase is activated, for different k values. The results of the PatchMatch algorithm are added as a reference.

Working on a Sparse Grid: We further accelerate seed assignment, and reduce memory footprint, by working on a sparse grid of patches. Specifically, we define a sampling grid g_S, g_T on images S and T, respectively. For $g_T = 1$ we use all patches in the image T in the k-d tree search. When setting $g_T = 2$, then we use only a quarter of the patches, which leads to much faster ANN search.

Likewise, for $g_S = 1$ we use all patches in S to query the k-d tree, while for $g_S > 1$ we use less patches for query. The run-time of the TreeCANN algorithm is roughly inversely proportional to the g_S^2 parameter, as it directly influences the second phase and the k-d tree search stage.

When increasing g_S, we create *passive* (non-grid) patches, which passively obtain their final mapping from the active grid patches, without participating in the propagation process.

3.2 The Propagation Phase

Applying approximate NN search methods in conjunction with such an aggressive PCA reduction would inevitably degrade the accuracy of the results (in comparison to the earlier methods). Therefore, it is quite obvious that the results of the first phase of the algorithm are not enough and that additional processing is required in order to achieve the performance levels, which can compete with the earlier methods.

The key observation here is that evaluating patch similarity is the most time consuming part of both PatchMatch and CSH. Therefore, PatchMatch uses early termination to quickly discard bad patch matches and CSH relies on Walsh-Hadamard kernels as a fast approximation of the true Euclidean distance between patches. We, on the other hand, compute the *exact* distance between patches and use the II to speed up the process. This is a crucial ingredient of our algorithm.

Specifically, consider a region, in the source image, consisting of 3×3 overlapping patches. For example, for patches of size 8×8 pixels this will correspond to a region of size 10×10 pixels. Now let the central patch s of the region match some patch t in the target image and take a similar region around patch t.

In order to propagate good matches we wish to compute the similarity between each of the 9 patches in the source region to their corresponding patches in the target region. Naively doing so will require 9 patch similarity comparisons. But because the patches overlap we can reduce the computational cost considerably using the II.

To do so we take the difference between the source and target regions and compute its II. Now we can compute the patch similarity for every patch in that region in constant time, using the II.

This approach relies on the assumption that NNF is coherent so if patch s is mapped to patch t, then the neighbor of patch s will match, with high probability, to the corresponding neighbor of patch t.

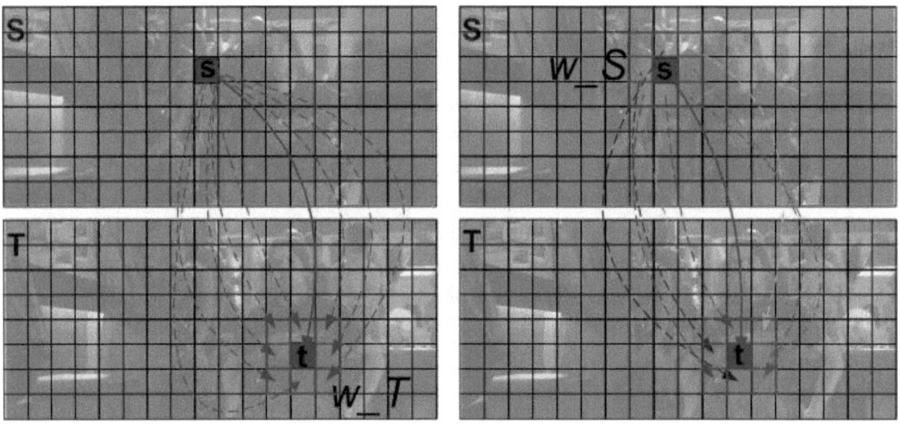

Fig. 2. *Left:* Exploiting the piece-wise constant property of the T image. All the red patches in the T image compose a window attributed to w_T parameter (in this case $w_T = 3$). *Right:* Exploiting the coherency of the S image. All the red patches in image S compose a window, attributed to the w_S parameter (in this case $w_S = 3$). *Both:* Squares on the image represent pixel (and correspond to the upper-left corner of patches). The full arrow represents an initial mapping, while the dotted ones represent all the additional distances calculation.

But there is another assumption that is often made and it is that images are piece-wise constant. This means that if patch $s \in S$ was matched to patch $t \in T$, then because image T is piece-wise constant, there is a high probability that s will also match one of the 8 neighbors of T (see Figure 2). In the experimental section we show empirically (see Table 1) that the first assignment stage, using k-d tree alone, brings about 50% of the patches in the source image to within a distance of up to two pixels, in the image plane, from their optimal location in the target image.

This motivates us to perform the II based matching between a region centered around patch s and regions centered around each of the 8 neighbors of patch t, in addition to the matching between regions centered around t. This means that, in total, each patch in the source image is matched against $81 = 9*9$ patch locations.

As a concrete example, in case of patch size $r = 8$ the use of the II brings to more than $\times 5$ speed up of the propagation phase ($15mM$ instead of $81mM$ operations), and about a factor of 2 speed up for the overall algorithm.

4 An Exact NNF Algorithm

Ignoring the k-d tree initialization step and taking the II based propagation step to the extreme we derive a novel exact NNF algorithm. Specifically, we shift the source image over the target image, compute the integral difference image for each such shift and store the patch similarity score (if smaller than current minimum) of this shift for every patch in the source image. This leads to an algorithm with complexity of $O(M^2)$ instead of $O(mM^2)$. Kumar at al. [14] pointed out that finding the exact NN for all 21×21 patches between two images, that are about 800×600 pixels each, would take over 250 hours. Our exact NNF approach takes less than 20 minutes. We are also faster than the method of Xiao at al. [7] because the constants of our algorithm are smaller.

5 Experiments and Results analysis

We use the efficient ANN (Approximate-k-Nearest-Neighbors) package of Mount and Arya [15], coupled with a Matlab wrapper[1]. Our code is available online. We profiled our code and found that running time is dominated by propagation (about 40% of the time) and k-d tree search (about 30% of the time).

5.1 Choosing Database and Test-Setup

We compare TreeCANN with PatchMatch and CSH on a number of data sets and report results in Figure 3. The first is the recently released database presented in [6], that contain pairs of non-consecutive video frames, taken from the same video scene (the distance between the images of one pair can vary from few to several dozen frames). The second dataset consists of the Caltech-256[2] object recognition data set, where we divide this experiment into two tests. One where both source and target images come from the same object class and another experiment where the source and target images come from different classes. Finally, we also evaluate our algorithm on the stereo[3] database.

[1] `www.wisdom.weizmann.ac.il/~bagon/matlab.html`
[2] `http://www.vision.caltech.edu/Image_Datasets/Caltech256/`
[3] `http://vision.middlebury.edu/stereo/data/scenes2006/`

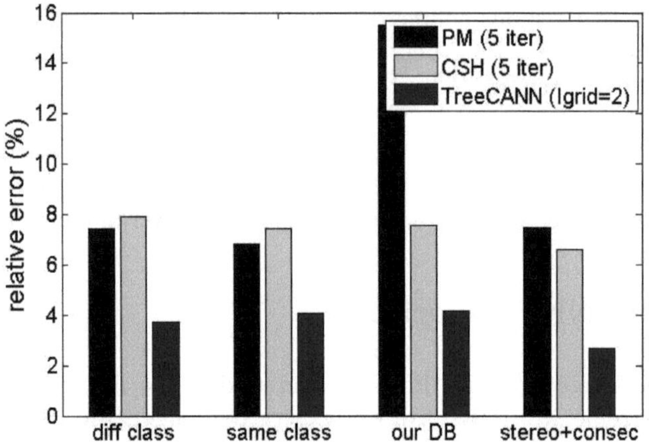

Fig. 3. The results, obtained by the PatchMatch, CSH and TreeCANN algorithms for four different types of image pairs ($r = 8, M = 1.6MB$) : *diff class* - random images from the caltech-256; *same class* - random images from the same classes in the caltech-256; *our DB* - images from database presented in [6]; *stereo+consec* - consists of consecutive frames and stereo image pairs.

There are a number of interesting observations to be made. First, we observe that PatchMatch achieved its higher error rates on the dataset of [6]. This can be explained by the fact that textured scenes are abundantly found in real-world images (such as movie frames), and often cover a large part of these images. These scenes usually contain similar repetitive patterns, which may cause the PatchMatch algorithm to be stuck in local minima for a large number of image regions, due to its mostly local nature. It is also worth noting that there is very little difference in the performance of within vs. between Caltech-256 evaluation. This suggests that variation within and between classes is quite similar.

We have performed a wide range of tests on the database of [6]. Our image samples range from 0.1MB to 1.6MB size (all the image samples were produced by the means of an under-sampling process of the same database), while the chosen patch sizes are 4, 8 and 16. For all the cases an exact NN computation was performed in order to obtain ground truth error levels. All the critical parts of our algorithm were implemented in C++, while Matlab provided the required code flow encapsulation. We use the PatchMatch and CSH code provided by the authors of the respective papers. All our experiments were executed on a single core configuration on a i5 750 (2.66 GHz) machine with 4GB of RAM memory.

5.2 Sparse Grid Acceleration

Our experiments show that we can significantly compensate for the performance degradation when using $g_S > 1$ with larger regions, denoted w_S, and set $w_S = 2g_S + 1$ in all our experiments. This ensures that w_S will be just the right size to cover all the eight neighboring grid-patches, relative to one particular grid-patch, but not more than that, in order to avoid unnecessary computations.

The grid approach also favorably affects the overall memory consumption of the algorithm, as it equals to $O(\frac{dim(r)}{g_I^2}M)$ (since equivalent values of g_S and g_T are used in all our experiments, we substitute them with the g_I parameter).

5.3 Performance Comparison

The main objective of our experiments was to perform a reliable comparison between the PatchMatch, CSH and TreeCANN algorithms on various set ups. Unlike previous methods, which presented an absolute error (an averaged L_2 distance between the matching patches of a source and a target image), we produce our graphs with a relative (to the ground-truth calculation) error, which allows a true understanding of the algorithm's accuracy.

The results of our test runs on the dataset of [6] are shown in Figure 4. It shows, for example, that at the error level reached by PatchMatch after 5 iterations (5 is the number of iteration that was suggested in [5] as the most cost-efficient point in the average case), our algorithm is five times faster (on average) than PatchMatch and about two to three times faster than CSH. If we examine a more specific set-up, like $[r = 4, M = 1.6MB]$, the speed up is almost an order of magnitude. More importantly, it appears that the biggest improvement occurs in the most challenging (from the runtime perspective) case, i.e. in the large image sizes. In this scenario, PatchMatch and CSH could not provide reasonable run-times (and low error levels) for interactive applications.

In general, we can determine that while the minimal error level, which can be achieved by the PatchMatch and the CSH algorithms, degrades as the image size increases, our algorithm maintains almost identical accuracy results. Furthermore, when comparing the runtime performances for lower error levels (for example, $g_I = 3$), the gap between the algorithms increases dramatically. Finally, PatchMatch and CSH can not compete in the range of the lowest error rates ($g_I = 2\, or\, 1$), obtained by TreeCANN algorithm.

In addition, TreeCANN approaches the absolute ground-truth, which was previously accomplished only by exceedingly slow LSH and k-d tree algorithms. For small patch sizes we are only 3% less accurate than the ground-truth, and the accuracy improves for larger patch sizes. And, as already noted, these performance levels can be reached in a very reasonable time (less than 10 PatchMatch iterations). Moreover, if the error rates are all that matters, one can slightly tune several parameters of the algorithm, so that the distance to the ground-truth will be reduced even further. For instance, changing the dimensionality reduction function $dim(r)$, and lowering the e parameter to $e = 2$, will result in additional reduction of the already very low error rates, reaching accuracy levels lower than 1% for all the patch sizes as shown if Figure 5.

In table 1 we explore another characteristic of the TreeCANN algorithm and show the average mapping distance between the TreeCANN algorithm and the Ground Truth. That is, we measure the distance, in the image plane, between

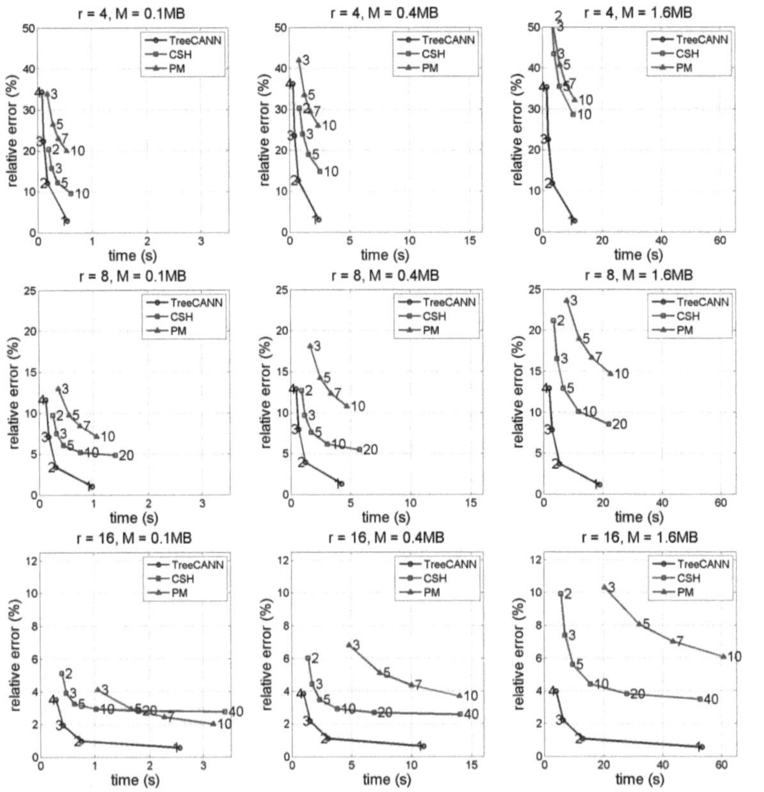

Fig. 4. The relative error performance comparison between the PatchMatch, CSH and the TreeCANN algorithms, versus the absolute run-time for different image sizes and patch sizes. The numbers on the TreeCANN line indicate the values of the g_i parameter (i.e., how sparse is the grid that TreeCANN operate on), while those on the PatchMatch and the CSH lines represent the number of iterations.

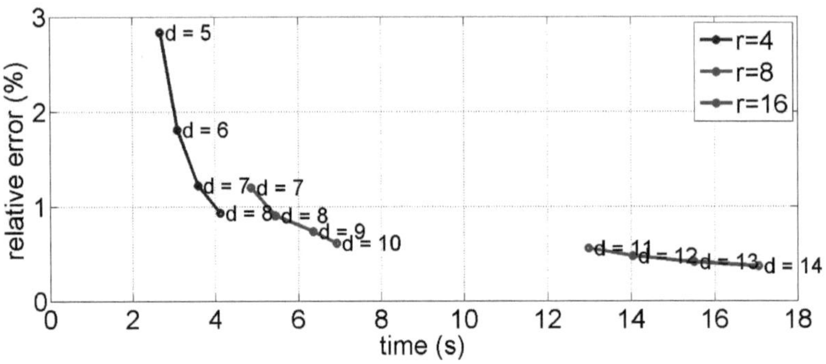

Fig. 5. Further reduction of the minimal error levels that can be obtained by TreeCANN algorithm ($M = 0.4MB$)

Table 1. The mapping distance error results for $r = 8$, $M = 0.4MB$ and $g_I = 1$. After the k-d tree search, roughly 50% of the patches are matched to patches that are at most two pixels away from the Ground Truth (GT) location. After the propagation step this number grows to almost 83%.

dist to GT →	0	1	2	>2
Only k-d tree	28.5%	17.7%	4.0%	49.8%
k-d tree+prop.	81.6%	0.9%	0.4%	17.1%

the mapping suggested by TreeCANN and the mapping found by an exact NN search. As can be seen, already after the k-d tree phase more than 50% of the patches obtain either their optimal matching or one in a very close proximity to the optimal location ($dist \leq 2$ pixels). Furthermore, after the Propagation phase the TreeCANN algorithm finds the optimal mapping for almost 82% of the patches (Figure 6 depicts these results visually for a specific pair of images). Additionally, for a particular image pair we show error images (in inverse colors) which represent the (scaled) difference between the original image S and the reconstructed images of the three algorithms. If examined closely it becomes evident that smaller mapping errors eventually translate to smaller reconstruction errors, as TreeCANN algorithm presents the best results.

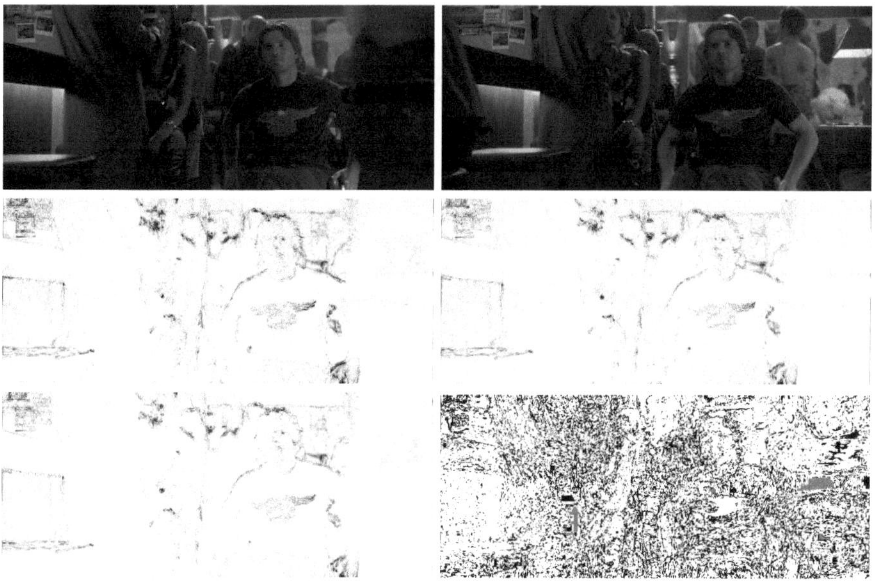

Fig. 6. From top-left to bottom-right: Image S, Image T, PM error, CSH error, TreeCANN error and accuracy map. Error images shown in inverse color (brighter color represents smaller error). The white pixels in the accuracy map indicate that the optimal mapping was found for that specific patch.

5.4 Exact NNF Performance

We have tested the performance of our exact NNF against those of [7] who performed an extensive compassion between various exact NN methods. As can be seen in Figure 7, our algorithm, which is not software optimized or hardware accelerated, is more than four times faster compared to the *N column CPU* method of [7], and is on par with their *N column GPU* approach.

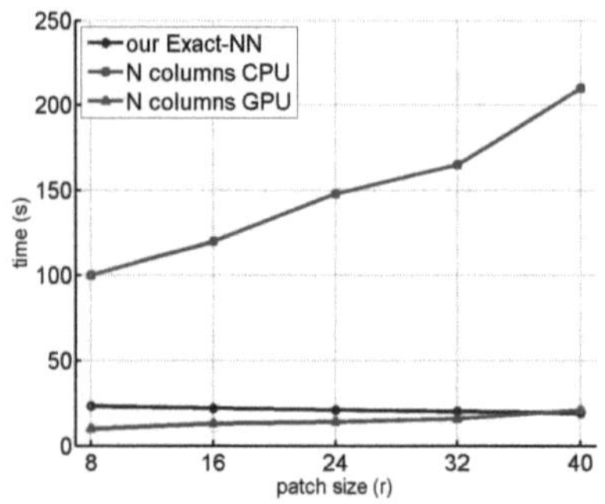

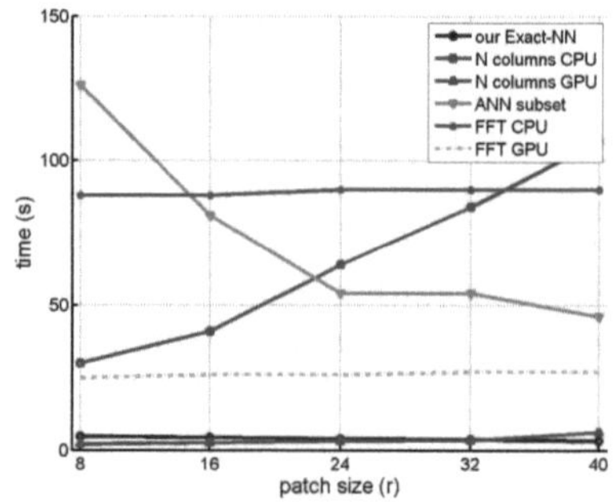

Fig. 7. Exact NNF. Comparing our method to that of [7]. *Left:* The results of [7] (fig. 3a) with our results (denoted our Exact-NN). (the size of the S image is 256x256, and the size of the T image is 278x278). *Right:* The results of the various methods reported in [7] (fig. 9a), with our results overlaid for comparison (the size of the S image is 256x256, and the size of the T image is 128x128).

6 Discussions and Future Work

TreeCANN is the fastest algorithm for NNF estimation reported to date. It does so by properly combining existing techniques at their optimal cost-effective point. We show that k-d tree can perform as fast as other methods simply by properly tuning its parameters. And the novel use of the II makes it possible to match multiple patches at once, leading to large improvement in the speed of the propagation step. Taken to the extreme the integral image can be used in an optimal algorithm for *exact* NNF that is faster than previously reported results.

A wide group of applications, such as object detection, de-noising, and symmetry detection, require the NN patch matching algorithm, which finds several closest matches rather than a single match. Thus, a simple functionality extension of our algorithm would be a detection of k nearest neighbors. With respect to the TreeCANN's performance, one of the obvious and probably the most significant speedup improvements of our algorithm would be an implementation of its multi-threaded and GPU versions.

Acknowledgments. This work was supported in part by an Israel Science Foundation grant 1556/10.

References

1. Efros, A.A., Leung, T.K.: Texture synthesis by non-parametric sampling. In: ICCV, vol. 2, pp. 1033–1038 (1999)
2. Buades, A., Coll, B., Morel, J.: A non-local algorithm for image denoising. In: CVPR, vol. 2, pp. 60–65 (2005)
3. Simakov, D., Caspi, Y., Shechtman, E., Iran, M.: Summarizing visual data using bidirectional similarity. In: CVPR, pp. 1–8 (2008)
4. Arya, S., Mount, D., Netanyahu, N., Silverman, R., Wu, A.: An optimal algorithm for approximate nearest neighbor searching. ACM 45, 891–923 (1998)
5. Barnes, C., Shechtman, E., Finkelstein, A., Goldman, D.: PatchMatch: a randomized correspondence algorithm for structural image editing. ACM Transactions on Graphics (Proc. SIGGRAPH) 28 (2009)
6. Korman, S., Avidan, S.: Coherency sensitive hashing. In: ICCV, pp. 1607–1614 (2011)
7. Xiao, C., Liu, M., Nie, Y., Dong, Z.: Fast exact nearest patch matching for patch-based image editing and processing. IEEE Trans. Vis. Comput. Graph. 17, 1122–1134 (2011)
8. Wei, L.-Y., Levoy, M.: Fast texture synthesis using tree-structured vector quantization. In: SIGGRAPH, pp. 479–488 (2000)
9. Muja, M., Lowe, D.G.: Fast approximate nearest neighbors with automatic algorithm configuration. In: VISSAPP, pp. 331–340 (2009)
10. Ashikhmin, M.: Synthesizing natural textures. In: Proc. Symposium on Interactive 3D Graphics, pp. 217–226 (2001)
11. Tong, X., Zhang, J., Liu, L., Wang, X., Guo, B., Shum, H.: Synthesis of bidirectional texture functions on arbitrary surfaces. ACM Trans. on Graphics 21, 665–672 (2002)
12. Barnes, C., Shechtman, E., Goldman, D.B., Finkelstein, A.: The Generalized PatchMatch Correspondence Algorithm. In: Daniilidis, K. (ed.) ECCV 2010, Part III. LNCS, vol. 6313, pp. 29–43. Springer, Heidelberg (2010)
13. Indyk, P., Motwani, R.: Approximate nearest neighbors: towards removing the curse of dimensionality. In: Symposium on Theory of Computing, pp. 604–613 (1998)
14. Kumar, N., Zhang, L., Nayar, S.: What Is a Good Nearest Neighbors Algorithm for Finding Similar Patches in Images? In: Forsyth, D., Torr, P., Zisserman, A. (eds.) ECCV 2008, Part II. LNCS, vol. 5303, pp. 364–378. Springer, Heidelberg (2008)
15. Mount, D. M., Arya, S.: Ann: A library for approximate nearest neighbor searching (2006), `http://www.cs.umd.edu/~mount/ANN/`

Robust Regression

Dong Huang, Ricardo Silveira Cabral, and Fernando De la Torre

Robotics Institute, Carnegie Mellon University

Abstract. Discriminative methods (*e.g.*, kernel regression, SVM) have been extensively used to solve problems such as object recognition, image alignment and pose estimation from images. Regression methods typically map image features ($\mathbf{X}$) to continuous (*e.g.*, pose) or discrete (*e.g.*, object category) values. A major drawback of existing regression methods is that samples are directly projected onto a subspace and hence fail to account for outliers which are common in realistic training sets due to occlusion, specular reflections or noise. It is important to notice that in existing regression methods, and discriminative methods in general, the regressor variables $\mathbf{X}$ are assumed to be noise free. Due to this assumption, discriminative methods experience significant degrades in performance when gross outliers are present.

Despite its obvious importance, the problem of robust discriminative learning has been relatively unexplored in computer vision. This paper develops the theory of Robust Regression (RR) and presents an effective convex approach that uses recent advances on rank minimization. The framework applies to a variety of problems in computer vision including robust linear discriminant analysis, multi-label classification and head pose estimation from images. Several synthetic and real world examples are used to illustrate the benefits of RR.

Keywords: Robust methods, errors in variables, intra-sample outliers.

1 Introduction

Discriminative methods (*e.g.*, kernel regression, SVM) have been successfully applied to many computer vision problems. Unlike generative approaches that produce a probability density over all variables, discriminative approaches provide a direct attempt to compute the input to output mappings for classification or regression. Typically, discriminative models achieve better performance in classification tasks, especially when large amounts of training data is available.

Linear and non-linear regression have been applied to solve a number of computer vision problems (e.g., classification [1], pose estimation [2]). Although widely used, a major drawback of existing regression approaches is their lack of robustness to outliers and noise, that are common in realistic training sets due to occlusion, specular reflections or image noise. To better understand the

A. Fitzgibbon et al. (Eds.): ECCV 2012, Part IV, LNCS 7575, pp. 616–630, 2012.

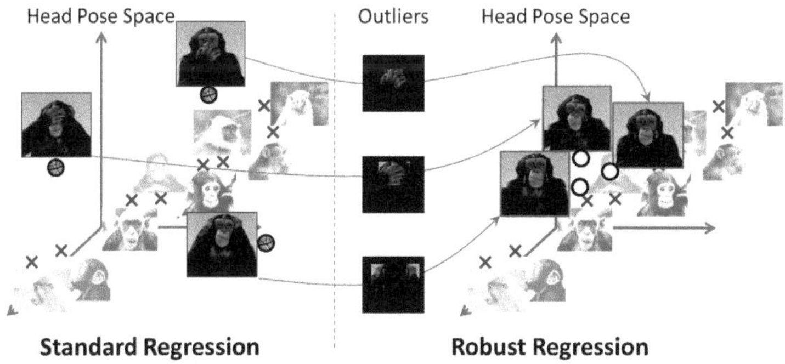

Fig. 1. The goal is to predict the yaw angle of the monkey head from image features. Note the image features (image) contains outliers (hands of the monkey). (Left) Standard regression: projects the partially occluded frontal face images *directly* onto the head pose subspace and fails to estimate the correct pose; (Right) Robust regression removes the intra-sample outliers and projects only the cleaned input images without biasing the pose estimation.

lack of robustness, let us consider the problem of learning a linear regressor from image features $\mathbf{X}$ to pose angles $\mathbf{Y}$ (see Fig. 1) by minimizing (See notation[1])

$$\min_{\mathbf{T}} \|\mathbf{Y} - \mathbf{TX}\|_F^2. \tag{1}$$

In the training stage, we learn the mapping $\mathbf{T}$, and in testing we estimate the pose by projecting the image features of the test image, $\mathbf{Tx}_{test}$. It is important to notice that in training and testing, we assume $\mathbf{X}$ to be noise free. A single outlier can bias the projection because we project the data *directly* onto the subspace of $\mathbf{T}$. For instance, $\mathbf{Tx}_{test}$, the dot product of $\mathbf{x}_{test}$ with each row of $\mathbf{T}$, can be largely biased by only one outlier. For this reason, existing discriminative methods lack robustness to outliers.

Standard regression, Eq. (1), is optimal under the assumption that the error, $\mathbf{E} = \mathbf{Y} - \mathbf{TX}$, is normally distributed. However, it is well known that a small number of gross outliers can arbitrarily bias the estimation of the model's parameters. This is a thoroughly studied problem in statistics, and the last decades have witnessed the fast paced development of the so-called robust methods [3–5]. However, all these traditional robust approaches for regression are different from the problem addressed in this paper. There are two main differences: (1) these approaches

[1] Bold uppercase letters denote matrices ($\mathbf{D}$), bold lowercase letters denote column vectors (*e.g.*, $\mathbf{d}$). $\mathbf{d}_j$ represents the jth column of the matrix $\mathbf{D}$. Non-bold letters represent scalar variables. $\|\mathbf{A}\|_F^2$ designates the Frobenius norm of matrix $\mathbf{A}$. $\|\mathbf{A}\|_*$ is the Nuclear Norm (sum of singular values) of $\mathbf{A}$. ℓ_0 of $\mathbf{A}$, $\|\mathbf{A}\|_0$, denotes the number of non-zero coefficients in $\mathbf{A}$. $\mathbf{I}_k \in \Re^{k\times k}$ denotes the identity matrix. $\mathbf{1}_n \in \Re^n$ is a vector of all 1s. $\mathbf{0}_{k\times n} \in \Re^{k\times n}$ is a matrix of zeros. $\langle \mathbf{A}, \mathbf{B} \rangle$ denotes the inner product between two matrices $\mathbf{A}$ and $\mathbf{B}$. $\mathcal{S}_b(a) = \text{sgn}(a)\max(|a| - b, 0)$ denotes the shrinkage operator. $\mathcal{D}_\alpha(\mathbf{A})$ is the Singular Value Thresholding (SVT) operator.

do not model the error in $\mathbf{X}$ but in $\mathbf{Y}-\mathbf{TX}$, (2) they mostly consider sample-outliers (the whole image is an outlier). This work proposes an intra-sample RR method that explicitly accounts for outliers in $\mathbf{X}$. Our work is related to errors in variables (EIV) models (e.g., [6–8]). However, unlike existing EIV models, RR does not need to have a prior estimate of the noise and all parameters are automatically estimated. We illustrate the power of RR in several computer vision tasks including head pose estimation from images and robust lda for multi-label image classification.

2 Related Work

There exist extensive literature on robust methods for regression. Huber [3] introduced M-estimation for regression, providing robustness to sample outliers. Rousseeuw and Leroy proposed Least Trimmed Squares [4], which explicitly finds a data subset that minimizes the squared residual sum. Parallel to developments in the statistics community, the idea of subset selection has also flourished in many computer vision applications. Consensus approaches such as RANSAC [9] (and its ML and M-estimator variants [10, 11]) randomly subsample input data to construct a tentative model. Model parameters are updated when a new configuration produces smaller inlier error than its predecessors. However, these methods rely on the assumption that the computation of the model parameters of a subset is inexpensive and can only remove sample outliers.

To deal with noise in the variables, Error-In-Variable (EIV) approaches [7] were proposed. However, existing EIV approaches rely on strong parametric assumptions for the errors. For instance, orthogonal regression assumes that the variance of errors in the input and response variables are identical [12] or their ratio is known [13]. Under these assumptions, orthogonal regression can minimize the gaussian error orthogonal to the learned regression vectors. Grouping-based methods [14] assume that errors are respectively i.i.d. among the input and respond variables, so that one can split the data into groups and suppress the errors by computing difference of the group sum, geometric means or instrument variables. Moment-based methods [15] learn the regression by estimating the high-order statistics, *i.e.*, moments, from the data of i.i.d. likelihood-based methods [8] learn a reliable regression when the input and respond variables follow a joint, normal and identical distribution. Total Least Square (TLS) [7] and its nonlinear generalization [16], solve for additive/multiple terms that enforce the correlation between the input and respond variables. TLS-based methods relax the assumption in previous methods to allow correlated and non-identical distributed errors. Nevertheless, they still rely on parametric assumptions on the error. Unfortunately, in typical computer vision applications, errors caused by occlusion, shadow and edges seldom fit such distributions.

Independent of the work on EIV for regression, several authors have addressed the issue of robust classification. On one hand, several authors have proposed robust extension of LDA, where the empirical estimation of the class mean vectors and covariance matrices are replaced by their robust counterparts (e.g., [17]).

In machine learning, several authors [18, 19] have proposed a worst-case FDA/LDA by minimizing the upper bound of the LDA cost function to increase the separation ability between classes under unbalanced sampling. However, these methods are only robust to sample-outliers.

Our work is more related to recent work in computer vision. Fidler and Leonardis [20] robustify LDA for intra-sample outliers. In the training stage, [20] computed PCA on the training data, replaced the minor PCA components by a robustly estimated basis, and combined the two basis into a new one. Then the data is projected into the combined basis and LDA is computed. During testing, [20] first estimates the coefficients of a test data on the recombined basis by sub-sampling the data elements using [21]. Finally, the class label of the test data is determined by applying learned LDA on the estimated coefficients. Although outliers outside of the PCA subspace can be suppressed, [20] do not address the problem of learning LDA with outliers in the PCA subspace of the training data. Zhu and Martinez [22] proposed learning a SVM with missing data and robust to outliers. However, [22] requires that the location of the outliers to be known. In contrast to previous works, our RR enjoys several advantages: (1) it is a convex approach; (2) no assumptions, aside from sparsity, are imposed on the outliers, which makes our method general; (3) it automatically cleans the intra-sample outliers in the training data while learning a classifier.

Our work is inspired by existing work in robust PCA [23] and its recent advances due to rank minimization procedures [24, 25]. These methods model data as the sum of a low-rank clean data component with an arbitrary large and sparse outlier matrix. De La Torre and Black [23] increased PCA robustness by replacing the least-square metric with a robust function, and re-weighted the influences of each component in each sample based on a given influence function (derivative of the robust function). [24, 25] separated a low-rank data matrix from an assumed sparse corruption, despite its arbitrarily large magnitude and unknown pattern. A major advantage of this approach is the convex formulation. This approach has been extended to other problems such as background modeling and shadow removal [25], image tagging and segmentation [26], texture unwrapping [27] or segmentation [28]. These algorithms, however, were originally devised with tasks such as dimensionality reduction or matrix completion in mind, which are unsupervised in nature. In this paper, we will further extend the approach to detect intra-sample outliers in robust regression, and illustrate several applications in computer vision.

3 Robust Regression (RR)

Let $\mathbf{X} \in \Re^{d \times n}$ be a matrix containing n d-dimensional samples possibly corrupted by outliers. Formally, $\mathbf{X} = \mathbf{D} + \mathbf{E}$, where $\mathbf{D}$ is the underlying noise-free component and $\mathbf{E}$ contains the outliers. In regression problems, one learns a mapping $\mathbf{T}$ from $\mathbf{X}$ to an output $\mathbf{Y} \in \Re^{d_y \times n}$. The outliers or the noise-free component $\mathbf{D}$ are unknown, so existing methods use $\mathbf{X}$ in the estimation of $\mathbf{T}$.

In presence of outliers, this results in a biased estimation of **T**. Our RR solves this problem by explicitly factorizing **X** into **D** plus **E**, and only computing **T** using the clean free data **D**. RR solves the following optimization problem

$$\min_{\mathbf{T},\mathbf{D},\mathbf{E}} \frac{\eta}{2} \|\mathbf{W}(\mathbf{Y}-\mathbf{TDH})\|_F^2 + \text{rank}(\mathbf{D}) + \lambda\|\mathbf{E}\|_0 \quad s.t. \quad \mathbf{X}=\mathbf{D}+\mathbf{E}, \qquad (2)$$

where $\mathbf{W} \in \Re^{d_y \times d_y}$ weights the output dimensions, **T** is the regression matrix and $\mathbf{H} = \left(\mathbf{I}_n - \mathbf{1}\mathbf{1}^T/n\right)$ is a centering matrix. RR explicitly avoids projecting the outlier matrix **E** to the output space by learning the regression **T** only from the centered noise-free data **DH**. The second and third terms of (2) are similar to RPCA [25] in that they respectively constrain **D** to a low dimensional subspace and encourages **E** to be sparse. RR is different from RPCA plus regression since it decomposes the input data $\mathbf{X} = \mathbf{D} + \mathbf{E}$ in a supervised manner; that is, the clean data **D** will preserve the subspace of **X** that correlates with **Y**. For this reason, the outlier component **E** computed by RR is able to correct outliers both inside and outside the subspace spanned by **D** (see Section 4.1).

The original form of RR, Eq. (2), is cumbersome to solve as the rank and cardinality operators are neither convex or differentiable. Following the techniques in [25], these operators are respectively relaxed to their convex envelopes: the nuclear norm and the ℓ_1-norm. The cost function (2) is rewritten as

$$\min_{\mathbf{T},\mathbf{D},\mathbf{E}} \frac{\eta}{2} \|\mathbf{W}(\mathbf{Y}-\mathbf{TDH})\|_F^2 + \|\mathbf{D}\|_* + \lambda\|\mathbf{E}\|_1 \quad s.t. \quad \mathbf{X}=\mathbf{D}+\mathbf{E},$$

which can be efficiently optimized using an Augmented Lagrange Muliplier (ALM) technique. Let $\hat{\mathbf{D}} = \mathbf{DH}$, we rewrite (3) as

$$\begin{aligned}\min_{\mathbf{T},\mathbf{D},\hat{\mathbf{D}},\mathbf{E}} \quad & \frac{\eta}{2} \left\|\mathbf{W}(\mathbf{Y}-\mathbf{T}\hat{\mathbf{D}})\right\|_F^2 + \|\mathbf{D}\|_* + \lambda\|\mathbf{E}\|_1 + \langle \Gamma_1, \mathbf{X}-\mathbf{D}-\mathbf{E}\rangle \\ & + \frac{\mu_1}{2}\|\mathbf{X}-\mathbf{D}-\mathbf{E}\|_F^2 + \langle \Gamma_2, \hat{\mathbf{D}}-\mathbf{DH}\rangle + \frac{\mu_2}{2}\|\hat{\mathbf{D}}-\mathbf{DH}\|_F^2, \qquad (3)\end{aligned}$$

where $\Gamma_1 \in \Re^{d\times n}$ and $\Gamma_2 \in \Re^{d\times n}$ are Lagrange multiplier matrices, and μ_1 and μ_2 are the penalty parameters. The resulting algorithm is summarized in Alg .1.

3.1 Robust LDA: An Extension of RR for Classification

Classification problems can be cast as a particular case of binary regression, where each sample in **X** belongs to one of c classes. The goal is then to learn a mapping from **X** to labels indicating the class membership of the data points. LDA learns a linear transformation that maximizes inter-class separation while minimizing intra-class variance, and typical solutions are based on solving a generalized eigenvalue problem. However, when learning from high-dimensional data such as images ($n < d$), LDA typically suffers from the small sample size problem. One possible solution for this is formulating LDA as a least-squares

Algorithm 1. ALM algorithm for solving RR (3)

Input: $\mathbf{X}$, $\mathbf{Y}$, parameters η, λ, ρ, γ

Initialization: $\mathbf{T}^{(0)} = \mathbf{Y}\mathbf{X}^T(\mathbf{X}\mathbf{X}^{\mathbf{T}} + \gamma\mathbf{I}_{d_x})$,$\hat{\mathbf{D}}^{(0)} = \mathbf{T}^{(0)+}\mathbf{Y}$, $\mathbf{E}^{(0)} = \mathbf{X} - \mathbf{D}^{(0)}$,

Lagrange Multiplier Initialization:$\Gamma_1^{(0)} = \frac{\mathbf{X}}{\|\mathbf{X}\|_2}$,$\Gamma_2^{(0)} = \frac{\mathbf{D}^{(0)}}{\|\mathbf{D}^{(0)}\|_2}$,$\mu_1^{(0)} = \frac{dn}{4}\|\mathbf{X}\|_1$, $\mu_2^{(0)} = \frac{dn}{4}\|\mathbf{D}^{(0)}\|_1$.

while $\frac{\left\|\mathbf{X}-\mathbf{D}^{(k)}-\mathbf{E}^{(k)}\right\|_F}{\|\mathbf{X}\|_F} > 10^{-8}$, $\frac{\left\|\hat{\mathbf{D}}^{(k)}-\mathbf{D}^{(k)}\mathbf{H}\right\|_F}{\left\|\hat{\mathbf{D}}^{(k)}\right\|_F} > 10^{-8}$ **do**

- Update $\mathbf{T}$ (assuming $\mathbf{W} = diag\{w_{ii}\}$) :
$\mathbf{T}^{(k+1)} = [\mathbf{t}_1, \mathbf{t}_2, \cdots, \mathbf{t}_c]$, where $\mathbf{t}_i^\top = w_{ii}^2\mathbf{y}_i\hat{\mathbf{D}}^T(w_{ii}^2\hat{\mathbf{D}}^{(k+1)}(\hat{\mathbf{D}}^{(k+1)})^T + \gamma\mathbf{I}_d)^{-1}$
and γ regularizes the scale of $\mathbf{t}_i$.
- Update $\hat{\mathbf{D}}$: $\hat{\mathbf{D}}^{(k+1)} = \left[\eta(\mathbf{T}^{(k)})^T\mathbf{W}^T\mathbf{W}\mathbf{T}^{(k)} + \mu_2^{(k)}\mathbf{I}_d\right]^{-1}\left[\eta(\mathbf{T}^{(k)})^T\mathbf{W}\mathbf{Y} - \Gamma_2^{(k)} + \mu_2^{(k)}\mathbf{D}^{(k)}\mathbf{H}\right]$;
- Update $\mathbf{D}$: $\mathbf{D}^{(k+1)} = \mathcal{D}_{1/\beta}(\mathbf{Z}^{(k+1)})$, $\mathbf{Z}^{(k+1)} = \mathbf{D}^{(k+1)} - \frac{1}{\beta} - \Gamma_1^{(k)} + \mu_1^{(k)}\left[\mathbf{D}^{(k)} - (\mathbf{X} - \mathbf{E}^{(k)})\right] - \Gamma_2^{(k)}\mathbf{H}^T + \mu_2^{(k)}\left[\mathbf{D}^{(k)}\mathbf{H}^{(k)} - \hat{\mathbf{D}}^{(k)}\right]\mathbf{H}^{\mathbf{T}}$, and $\beta \geq \|\mu_1^{(k)}\mathbf{I} + \mu_2^{(k)}\mathbf{H}\mathbf{H}^T\|_F$;
- Update $\mathbf{E}$: $\mathbf{E}^{(k+1)} = \mathcal{S}_{\lambda/\mu_1^{(k)}}\left(\mathbf{X} - \mathbf{D}^{(k)} + \Gamma_1^{(k)}/\mu_1^{(k)}\right)$;
- Update $\Gamma_1^{(k+1)} = \Gamma_1^{(k)} + \mu_1^{(k+1)}(\mathbf{X} - \mathbf{D}^{(k+1)} - \mathbf{E}^{(k+1)})$, $\Gamma_2^{(k+1)} = \Gamma_2^{(k)} + \mu_2^{(k+1)}(\hat{\mathbf{D}}^{(k+1)} - \mathbf{D}^{(k+1)}\mathbf{H})$, $\mu_1^{(k+1)} = \rho\mu_1^{(k)}$, $\mu_2^{(k+1)} = \rho\mu_2^{(k)}$;

end while

Output: $\mathbf{T}$, $\mathbf{D}$, $\mathbf{E}$

(LS) problem [29]. LS-LDA [29] directly maps $\mathbf{X}$ to the class labels represented by an indicator matrix. LS-LDA minimizes

$$\min_{\mathbf{T}} \left\|(\mathbf{Y}\mathbf{Y}^T)^{-1/2}(\mathbf{Y} - \mathbf{T}\mathbf{X})\right\|_F^2, \tag{4}$$

where $\mathbf{Y} \in \Re^{c\times n}$ is a binary indicator matrix, such that $y_{ij} = 1$ if $\mathbf{x}_i$ belongs to class j and $y_{ij} = 0$ otherwise. The normalization factor $\mathbf{W} = (\mathbf{Y}\mathbf{Y}^T)^{-1/2}$ compensates for different number of samples per class. $\mathbf{T} \in \Re^{c\times d}$ is a reduced rank regression matrix (which has rank $c-1$ if the data is centered). After $\mathbf{T}$ is learned, a test data $\mathbf{x}_{test} \in \Re^{d\times 1}$ is projected by $\mathbf{T}$ onto the c dimensional output space spanned by $\mathbf{TX}$, then the class label of the test data $\mathbf{x}_{test}$ is assigned using k-NN.

When $\mathbf{X}$ is corrupted by outliers, Eq. (4) suffers from the same bias problem as standard regression. RR, Eq. (3), can be directly applied to Eq. (4), yielding

$$\min_{\mathbf{T},\mathbf{D},\mathbf{E}} \frac{\eta}{2}\left\|(\mathbf{Y}\mathbf{Y}^T)^{-1/2}(\mathbf{Y} - \mathbf{T}\mathbf{D}\mathbf{H})\right\|_F^2 + \|\mathbf{D}\|_* + \lambda\|\mathbf{E}\|_1 \quad s.t. \quad \mathbf{X} = \mathbf{D} + \mathbf{E},$$

a Robust LDA formulation which can be easily solved as a special case of RR.

3.2 Testing for New Data Points

To remove outliers in a new testing sample $\mathbf{X}_t$, we minimize

$$\min_{\mathbf{Q}_t,\mathbf{E}_t} \frac{\eta\|\mathbf{W}\mathbf{T}\|_F^2}{2}\left\|\mathbf{X}_t - (\mathbf{D}\mathbf{1}\mathbf{1}^T/n + \mathbf{U}\mathbf{Q}_t) - \mathbf{E}_t\right\|_F^2 + \lambda\|\mathbf{E}_t\|_1, \tag{5}$$

where $\mathbf{U}$ contains the principal components of the clean data $\mathbf{D}$ (preserving 99.99% energy), $\mathbf{Q}_t$ are the coefficients such that a linear combination of $\mathbf{U}$ can reconstruct the clean part of the data $\mathbf{X}_t$. η and λ are the same parameters used during training. After solving (5), the regression or classification for $\mathbf{X}_t$ is computed as $\mathbf{Y}_t = \mathbf{T}\mathbf{U}\mathbf{Q}_t$.

4 Experimental Results

This section compares our RR methods against state-of-the-art approaches on regression and classification. The first experiment uses synthetic data to illustrate the ability of RR to remove in-subspace outliers that existing methods can not detect. The second experiment illustrates the application of RR to the problem of head pose estimation from corrupted images. The final experiments report comparisons of our RR against state-of-the-art multi-label classification algorithms on the MSRC, Mediamill and TRECVID2011 databases.

4.1 Synthetic Data

This section illustrates the benefits of RR in a synthetic example. We have generated 200 three dimensional samples, where the first two components are generated from a uniform distribution between $[0, 6]$, and the third dimension is 0. In Matlab notation, $\mathbf{D} = [6 * rand(2, 200); \mathbf{0}^T]$, $\mathbf{X} = \mathbf{D} + \mathbf{E}$, $\mathbf{Y} = \mathbf{T}_*\mathbf{D}$, where $\mathbf{D} \in \Re^{3\times 200}$ is the clean data. The error term, $\mathbf{E} \in \Re^{3\times 200}$, is generated as follows: for 20 random samples, we added random Gaussian noise ($\sim \mathcal{N}(0, 1)$) in the second dimension, this simulates in-subspace noise. Similarly, for another 20 random samples, we added random Gaussian noise ($\sim \mathcal{N}(0, 1)$) in the third dimension, this simulates noise outside the subspace. $\mathbf{T}_* \in \Re^{3\times 3}$ is randomly generated and used as the true regression matrix. The output data matrix is generated as $\mathbf{Y} = \mathbf{T}_*\mathbf{D} \in \Re^{3\times 200}$. Fig. 2 (a) shows the clean data $\mathbf{D}$ with blue "o"s, and the corrupted data $\mathbf{X}$ with black "×"s. For easiness of visualization, we have only shown 100 randomly selected samples. The black line segments connect the same samples before ($\mathbf{D}$) and after corruption ($\mathbf{X}$). The line segments along the vertical direction are the out-of-subspace component of $\mathbf{E} = \mathbf{X} - \mathbf{D}$, while the horizontal line segments represent the in-subspace component of $\mathbf{E} = \mathbf{X} - \mathbf{D}$.

We compared our RR with five state-of-the-art methods: (1) Standard least-squares regression (LSR), (2) GroupLasso (GLasso) [30], (3) RANSAC [9], (4) Total Least Square (TLS) [31] that assumes the error in the data is additive and follow a gaussian distribution, (5) RPCA+LSR, which consist on first performing RPCA [24] on the input data, and then learn the regression on the cleaned data using standard LSR. The LSR learns directly the regression matrix $\mathbf{T}$ using the data $\mathbf{X}$. The other methods (2)-(5) re-weight the data or select a subset of the samples input data $\mathbf{X}$ before learning the regression. We randomly select 100 samples for training and the remaining 100 data points for testing. Both the training and testing sets contain half of the corrupted samples.

Fig. 2(b-f) visualizes the results of the regression for the different methods. Fig. 2(b) shows the results of $\mathbf{TX}$, once $\mathbf{T}$ is learned with GLasso. GLasso learns a sparse regression matrix that re-weights the input data along dimensions, but it is unable to handle within sample outliers. Observe how the samples are far away from the original clean samples. Fig. 2(c) shows the subset of $\mathbf{X}$ selected by RANSAC. Although we selected RANSAC parameters to obtain the best testing error, many of the corrupted data points are still identified as inliers. Fig. 2(d) shows results obtained by TLS, where TLS only partially cleaned the corrupted

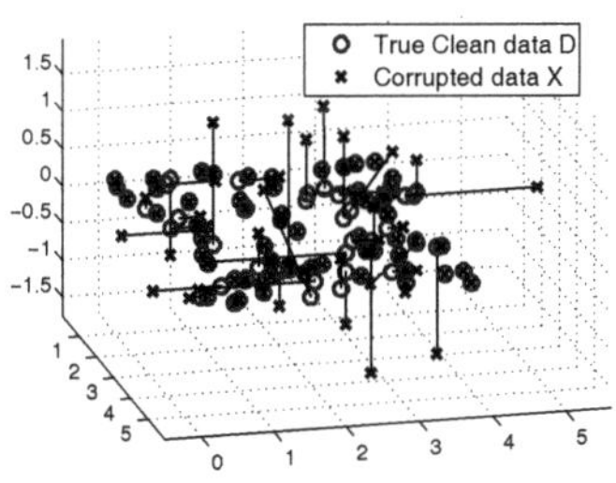

(a) Clean and Corrupted Data

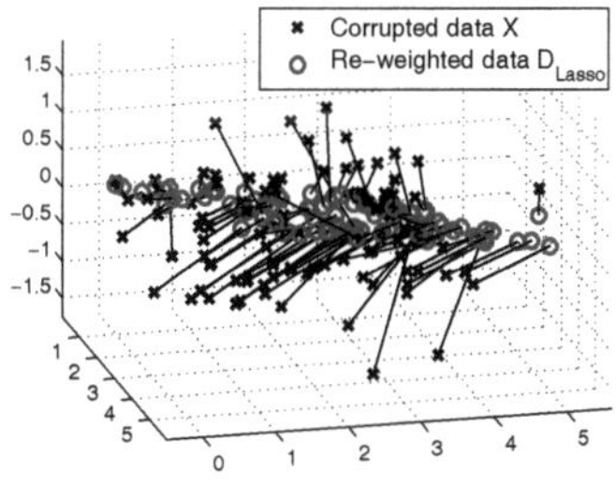

(b) Group Lasso (axis re-weighting)

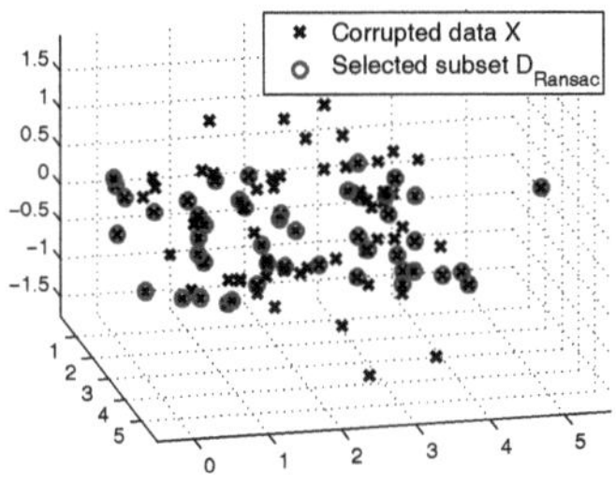

(c) RANSAC (subset selection)

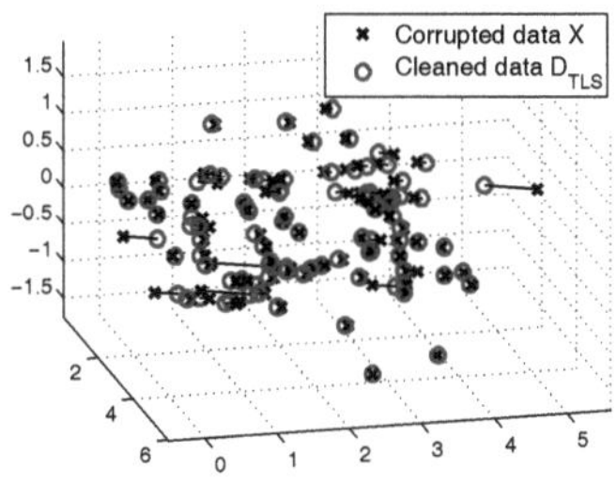

(d) Total Least Square (TLS)

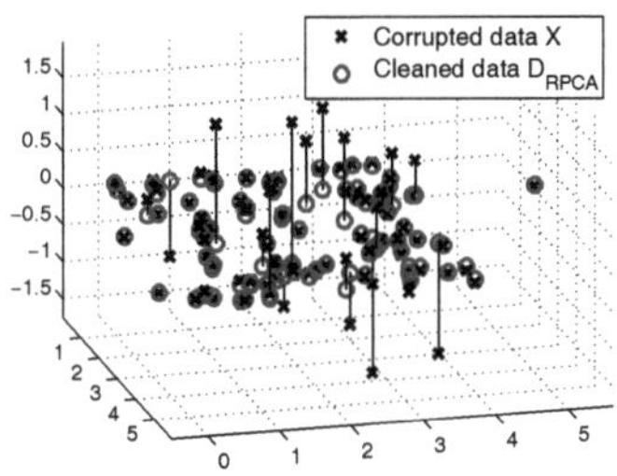

(e) RPCA+LSR

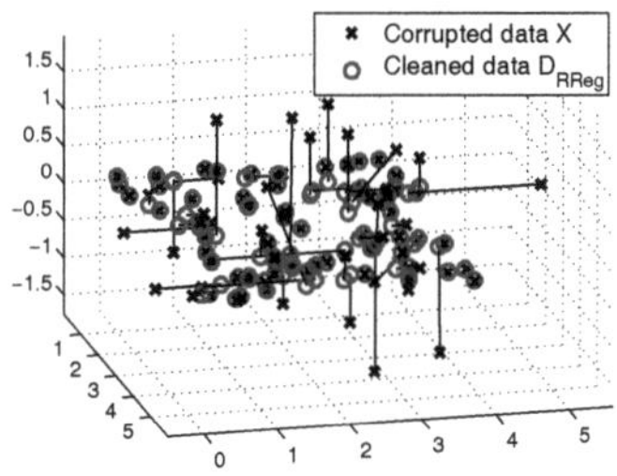

(f) Robust Regression (RR)

Fig. 2. (a) Original and corrupted 3D synthetic dataset. Black lines connect data points before (**D**) and after corruption (**X**). (b)-(e) show the input data processed by several baselines, and (f) shows that RR removes the in-subspace outliers.

data because the synthesized error cannot be modeled by a gaussian distribution of equal error. Fig. 2(e) shows results obtained by the method RPCA+LSR, that first computes RPCA to clean the data and then LSR. The data cleaned by RPCA [24], $\mathbf{D}_{RPCA}$, is displayed with red "o"s. Because $\mathbf{D}_{RPCA}$ is computed in an unsupervised manner, only the out-of-subspace error (the vertical lines) can be discarded, while the in-subspace outliers can not be corrected. Finally, Fig. 2 (f) shows the result of RR. The clean data $\mathbf{D}_{RR}$ is denoted by red"o"s. Observe that our approach is able to clean both the in-subspace outliers (the horizontal lines) and out-of-subspace (the vertical lines). This is because our method computes jointly the regression and the subspace estimation.

We also computed the error for the regression matrix $\mathbf{T}_*$ (the first two columns) and the testing error for $\mathbf{Y}_t$ on the 100 test samples. Table 1 compares the mean regression error measured by the Relative Absolute Error (RAE) between the true labels $\mathbf{Y}_t \in \Re^{3\times 100}$ and the estimated labels $\widetilde{\mathbf{Y}}_t$. $RAE_{\mathbf{T}} = \frac{\|\widetilde{\mathbf{T}}(:,1:2)-\mathbf{T}_*(:,1:2)\|_F}{\|\mathbf{T}_*(:,1:2)\|_F}$ and $RAE_{\mathbf{Y}} = \frac{\|\widetilde{\mathbf{Y}}_t-\mathbf{Y}_t\|_F}{\|\mathbf{Y}_t\|_F}$. The information in the third column of $\mathbf{T}_*$ is excluded in generating $\mathbf{Y} = \mathbf{TD}$. Therefore, we dismiss this column when evaluating $RAE_{\mathbf{T}}$. As shown in Table 1, RR produces the smallest estimation error for both $\mathbf{T}_*$ and $\mathbf{Y}_t$ among the five compared methods, while GroupLasso, RANSAC and RPCA+LSR produce small improvements over standard LSR due to their limitation to deal with both the in-subspace and out-of-subspace corruptions.

Table 1. RAE error for **Y** and **T** for different methods

	LSR	GLasso	RANSAC	TLS	RPCA+LSR	**RR**
$RAE_{\mathbf{T}}$	0.078	0.078	0.070	0.052	0.074	**0.005**
$RAE_{\mathbf{Y}}$	0.0272	0.0274	0.0263	0.0261	0.0262	**0.011**

4.2 Pose Estimation from Images

This section illustrates the benefit of RR in the problem of head pose estimation from corrupted images. We used a subset of CMU Multi-PIE database [32] that contains 3707 face images of all 337 subjects from all 4 sessions. For each subject, we used images taken under 11 head poses with yaw angle [$-90°$, $-75°$, $-60°$, $-45°$, $-15°$, $0°$, $15°$, $45°$, $60°$, $75°$, $90°$]. Each image is cropped around the face region and resized to 50×60. We vectorized the images into a vector of 3000 dimensions in the matrix $\mathbf{X} \in \Re^{3000\times 3707}$ and the yaw angles of the images are gathered as the output data $\mathbf{Y} \in \Re^{1\times 3707}$. To evaluate the robustness of the compared methods, we simulate structured occlusions by adding white blocks (0.1 times the image width) at 5 random locations (see Fig. 3a for examples of corrupted images).

Table 2. Yaw angle error for different methods and corruption percentages

% of corruption	0%	20%	40%	80%
LSR	12.3°	14.5°	15.1°	17.3°
GLasso	16.0°	17.8°	20.2°	21.1°
RANSAC	12.2°	14.1°	14.9°	17.8°
RPCA+LSR	13, 3°	15.4°	18.3°	20.4°
RR	**12.1°**	**13.0°**	**13.7°**	**15.2°**

Similar to the previous section, we have compared RR with four methods to learn a regression from the image **X** to the yaw angle **Y**: (1) LSR, (2) GLasso [30], (3) RANSAC [9], (4) RPCA+LSR. For a fair comparison, we randomly divided the 3707 images into 10 folds and performed 10-fold cross-validation in methods (2)-(4) to compute parameters of interest. The performance of the compared methods is measured with the mean deviations of angle error on all test folders.

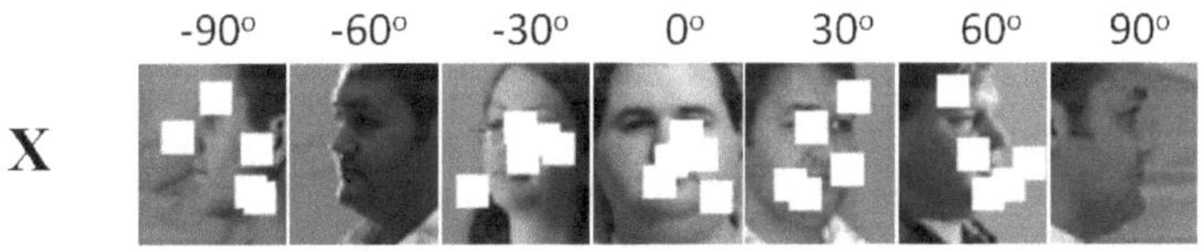

(a) Examples of partially corrupted input images $\mathbf{X}$

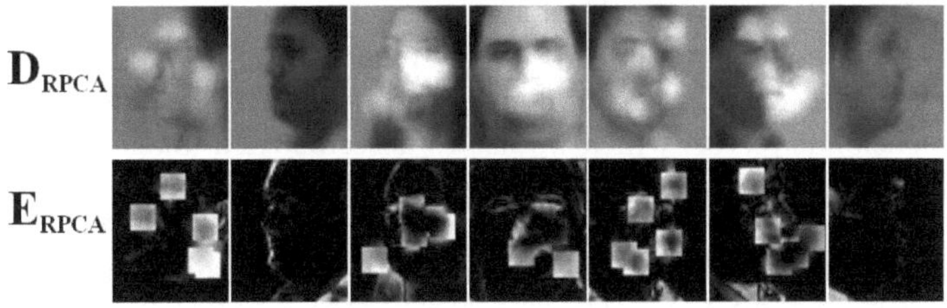

(b) Decomposition of images in (a) as $\mathbf{X} = \mathbf{D}_{RPCA} + \mathbf{E}_{RPCA}$ by RPCA

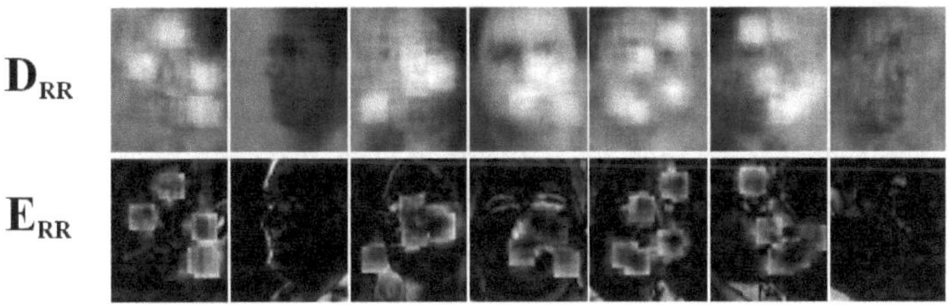

(c) Decomposition of images in (a) as $\mathbf{X} = \mathbf{D}_{RR} + \mathbf{E}_{RR}$ by RR.

Fig. 3. Decomposition of input images in (a) by RPCA (b) and RR (c)

Table 2 summarizes the results of methods (1)-(4) and RR when 0%, 20%, 40%, 80% of the images are corrupted in both the training and testing folders. As expected, the LSR method produced larger angle error with the increasing percentage of outliers. RANSAC produced comparable error as standard LSR indicating that RANSAC is unable to select a subset of "inliers" to robustly estimate the regression matrix. RPCA+LSR produced relatively larger yaw angle error. This is because RPCA is unsupervised and lack the ability to preserve the discriminative information in $\mathbf{X}$ that correlates with the angles $\mathbf{Y}$. RR got the smallest error and it is stable w.r.t. the percentage of corruption.

To further illustrate how RR differs from RPCA+LSR, Fig. 3 visualizes the decomposition done by RR, *i.e.*, $\mathbf{X} = \mathbf{D}_{RR} + \mathbf{E}_{RR}$ an by RPCA, *i.e.*, $\mathbf{X} = \mathbf{D}_{RPCA} + \mathbf{E}_{RPCA}$, for the same input images. Images under all pose angles (except $-60°$ and $90°$) are corrupted with white blocks (see Fig. 3(a)). Fig. 3(b)-(c) show that both RPCA and RR are able to remove most of the white blocks. However RR preserves much less personal facial details in $\mathbf{D}_{RR}$ than RPCA in $\mathbf{D}_{RPCA}$ (especially images under pose $-60°$ and $90°$). With less facial details and more dominant profiles, the regression trained on $\mathbf{D}_{RR}$ (as in RR) is able to model higher correlation with the pose angles than using $\mathbf{D}_{RPCA}$. This is why RR tends to be more robust than the RPCA in estimating the pose angles.

4.3 Robust LDA

This section evaluates our Robust LDA (RLDA) method on two multi-label and one multi-class classification tasks: object categorization on the MSRC dataset, action recognition in the MediaMill dataset and event video indexing on the TRECVID 2011 dataset. Each dataset corpus and features is described below:

MSRC Dataset (Multi-label)[2] has 591 photographs (see Fig. 4(a)) distributed among 21 classes, with an average of 3 classes per image. We mimic [1] and divide each image into an 8×8 grid and calculate the first and second order moments for each color channel on each grid in the RGB space. This results in a 384 dimensional vector, which we use to describe each image.

Mediamill Dataset (Multi-label) [33] consists of 43907 sub-shots divided in 101 classes. We follow [1] and eliminate classes containing less than 1000 samples, leaving 27 classes. Then, we randomly select 2609 sub-shots such that each class has at least 100 labeled data points. Each image is therefore characterized by a 120-dimensional feature vector, as described in [33].

TRECVID 2011 Dataset (Multi-class)[3] consists of video data in MED 2010 and the development data of MED 2011, totaling 9822 video clips belonging exclusively to one of 18 classes. We first detect 100 shots for each video and then use their center frames as keyframes. We describe each keyframe using dense SIFT descriptors. From these, we learn a 4096 dimension Bag-of-Words dictionary. Each video is represented by a normalized histogram of all of its feature points. We used a 300 core cluster to extract the SIFT features, which took about 2687 CPU hours in total. In the experiment, we randomly split the dataset into two subsets, with 3122 entries for training and 6678 for testing.

(a)

(b)

Fig. 4. Multi-label datasets for object recognition and action classification. Example images in MSRC (a) and example keyframes in Mediamill (b).

We compared RLDA to the state of the art approach for Multi-Label LDA (MLDA) [1], and to Robust PCA [24] followed by traditional LDA (RPCA+LDA). For control, we also compare to LDA, PCA+LDA (preserving 99.9% of energy) and a linear one-*vs.*-all SVM.

[2] `http://research.microsoft.com/en-us/projects/ObjectClassRecognition/`

[3] `http://www-nlpir.nist.gov/projects/tv2011/`

For the classic LDA-based testing procedure, one first projects the test points using the learned **T** from training; then for each projected test sample, find k-nearest-neighbor (kNN) from the training samples projected by **T**; finally select the class label from the class labels of k-neighbors by majority voting. However, this procedure is not appropriate in our evaluation for two reasons (1) it's not fair to use a fixed k for classes with different number of samples, *e.g.*, samples per class are in $[19, 200]$ for MSRC, $[100, 2013]$ for Mediamill; (2) kNN introduces nonlinearity to the LDA-based classifiers, which is unfair to linear SVM. For these reasons, we use Area Under Receiver Operating Characteristic (AUROC) as our evaluation metric. AUROC summarizes the cost/benifit ratio over all possible classification thresholds. We report the average AUROC (over 5-fold Cross Validation) for each method under their best parameters in Table 3. In the MSRC dataset results in Table 3, LDA performs the worst since it's most sensitive to the noise in data. SVM performs better than PCA+LDA and RPCA+LDA. Our method (RLDA) leads to significant improvements over the others due to its joint classification and data cleaning (for both gaussian and sparse noise in the input). For Mediamill, LDA is just slightly worse than PCA+LDA and RPCA+LDA due to the low noise level in the data. In this case, RLDA does not "over-clean" the data, and performs similar to PCA+LDA and RPCA+LDA.

Table 3. AUROC for Multi-label Object (MSRC) and Action (Mediamill) classification. *Higher* value indicates better performance. Best results are in bold.

Database	LDA	SVM	PCA+LDA	MLDA	RPCA+LDA	RLDA
MSRC	0.6463	0.7863	0.7585	0.6313	0.7480	**0.8170**
Mediamill	0.7667	0.6230	0.7702	0.6658	0.7704	**0.7710**

To test our method in a large scale dataset, we run experiments on the TREC2011 dataset. We used the Minimum Normalized Detection Cost (MinNDC), the evaluation criteria for MED 2010 and MED 2011 challenges suggested by NIST. Fig. 5 shows that RLDA achieved the best class-wise MinNDC for 8 out of 18 classes over other linear methods, *i.e.*, LDA/MLDA, SVM and RPCA+LDA. Note for the class-wise cases LDA and MLDA are identical. SVM is heavily affected by outliers for the "Wedding Ceremony", "Getting a vehicle unstuck" and "Making a sandwich" cases. For some classes, LDA and RPCA+LDA are similar or better than RLDA. Nevertheless, among all linear algorithms, our method (RLDA) obtains the best average MinNDC. In addition, to show how nonlinearity affects the performances, we compared the kernelized version of the LDA, RPCA+LDA and RLDA. Here we apply the homogeneous kernel maps technique [34] to obtain a three order approximation of the χ^2 kernel. Other more accurate approximations are possible [35]. Fig. 5 shows that KRLDA still obtain a better results, 13 out of 18 best class-wise MinNDC and best average MinNDC over all classes.

Event Description \ Methods	LDA/MLDA	SVM	RPCA+LDA	RLDA	KLDA	KRPCA+KLDA	KRLDA
Maling a cake	1.0027	1.0038	0.999	**0.9091**	0.9819	1.0019	**0.929**
Batting a run	**0.6987**	1.0019	0.9498	0.8552	0.7413	0.929	**0.6832**
Assembling a shelter	0.9989	1.0152	1.0026	**0.9787**	1.0038	1.0019	**0.9744**
Attempting a board trick	**1.0019**	**1.0018**	1.0057	**1.0019**	**0.9494**	0.979	0.9513
Feeding an animal	1.0038	**0.9899**	1.0038	1.0019	**0.9889**	0.995	0.9992
Landing a fish	0.9605	1.0019	0.9169	**0.9056**	0.8937	0.9399	**0.872**
Wedding ceremony	0.9967	12.4498	**0.9789**	0.9923	0.8048	0.8741	**0.7675**
Woodworking project	1.0051	**0.8588**	1.0038	1.0057	1.0032	1.0038	**0.9975**
Birthday party	0.9862	0.9561	**0.9368**	0.9881	0.9654	0.9695	**0.9595**
Changing a vehicle tire	0.9856	0.9842	1.0019	**0.9549**	**0.923**	0.9572	**0.923**
Flash mob gathering	0.8384	0.9675	0.8933	**0.8189**	0.7905	0.7786	**0.734**
Getting a vehicle unstuck	0.9848	11.6719	**0.9659**	0.9867	0.9524	0.9581	**0.9468**
Grooming an animal	**0.9691**	1.0019	0.9868	1.0094	**0.9918**	1.0019	1.0006
Making a sandwich	1.0019	4.0583	1.0132	**0.981**	0.9936	**0.9917**	**0.9917**
Parade	0.9931	**0.9723**	0.9931	0.9805	1.0006	**0.9949**	0.9987
Parkour	0.9837	1.0019	**0.9336**	1.0019	0.8412	0.8211	**0.8203**
Repairing an appliance	0.9369	**0.5998**	1.0075	0.9344	**0.9312**	0.9652	0.9419
Working on a sewing project	1.0057	1.0056	1.0025	**0.9192**	0.9349	0.9544	**0.9054**
Average Score	0.9641	2.3635	0.9775	**0.9571**	0.9273	0.951	**0.9109**

Fig. 5. MinNDC results for Media Event Detection on TREC2011. *Lower* value indicates better performance. Best results are in bold.

5 Conclusion

This paper addressed the problem of robust discriminative learning, and presents a convex formulation for RR. Our robust approach jointly learns a regression, while removing the outliers that are not correlated with labels or regression outputs. We illustrated the benefits of RR in several computer vision problems ranging from RR for pose estimation, robust LDA to multi-labeled image classification. Experiments show that by removing outliers, our methods consistently learn better representations and outperform state-of-the-art methods, in both the linear and kernel spaces (using homogeneous kernel maps). Finally, our approach is general and can be easily applied to robustify other subspace methods such as partial least square or canonical correlation analysis.

Acknowledgments. The second author was supported by the Portuguese Foundation for Science and Technology through the CMU-Portugal program under the project FCT/CMU/P11. The authors would like to thank Francisco Vicente for the assistance with the experiment on the TRECVID 2011 Dataset.

References

1. Wang, H., Ding, C., Huang, H.: Multi-label Linear Discriminant Analysis. In: Daniilidis, K., Maragos, P., Paragios, N. (eds.) ECCV 2010, Part VI. LNCS, vol. 6316, pp. 126–139. Springer, Heidelberg (2010)
2. Huang, D., Storer, M., De la Torre, F., Bischof, H.: Supervised local subspace learning for continuous head pose estimation. In: CVPR (2011)

3. Huber, P.: Robust Statistics. Wiley and Sons (1981)
4. Rousseeuw, P., Leroy, A.: Robust Regression and Outlier Detection. Wiley (2003)
5. Meer, P.: Robust Techniques for computer vision. In: Medioni, G., Kang, S. (eds.) Emerging Topics in Computer Vision. Prentice Hall (2004)
6. Gillard, J.: An Historical Overview of Linear Regression with Errors in both variables. Cardiff University, School of Mathematics, TR (2006)
7. Huffel, S.V., Vandewalle, J.: The Total Least Squares Problem: Computational Aspects and Analysis. SIAM (1991)
8. Lindley, D.: Regression lines and the linear functional relationship. Suppl. J. Roy. Statist. Soc. 9, 218–244 (1947)
9. Fischler, M., Bolles, R.: Random sample consensus: A paradigm for model fitting with applications to image analysis and automated cartography. Comm. of the ACM 24, 381–395 (1981)
10. Torr, P., Zisserman, A.: Mlesac: A new robust estimator with application to estimating image geometry. CVIU 78, 138–156 (2000)
11. Choi, S., Kim, T., Yu, W.: Performance Evaluation of RANSAC Family. In: BMVC (2009)
12. Adcock, R.: A problem in least squares. Analyst. 5, 53–54 (1878)
13. Kummel, C.: Reduction of observed equations which contain more than one observed quantity. Analyst. 6, 97–105 (1879)
14. Wald, A.: The fitting of straight lines if both variables are subject to error. Ann. Math. Statistics 11, 285–300 (1940)
15. Gillard, J., Iles, T.: Method of moments estimation in linear regression with errors in both variables. Cardiff University, School of Mathematics, TR (2005)
16. Matei, B., Meer, P.: Estimation of nonlinear errors-in-variables models for computer vision applications. IEEE Trans. PAMI 28, 1537–1552 (2006)
17. Croux, C., Dehon, C.: Robust linear discriminant analysis using s-estimators. Canadian Journal of Statistics 29 (2001)
18. Kim, S., Magnani, A., Boyd, S.: Robust FDA. In: NIPS (2005)
19. Zhang, Y., Yeung, D.Y.: Worst-case linear discriminant analysis. In: NIPS (2010)
20. Fidler, S., Skocaj, D., Leonardis, A.: Combining reconstructive and discriminative subspace methods for robust classification and regression by subsampling. PAMI 28, 337–350 (2006)
21. Leonardis, A., Bischof, H.: Robust recognition using eigenimages. CVIU 78, 99–118 (2000)
22. Jia, H., Martinez, A.: Support vector machines in face recognition with occlusions. In: CVPR (2009)
23. De la Torre, F., Black, M.: A framework for robust subspace learning. International Journal on Computer Vision 54, 117–142 (2003)
24. Candès, E., Li, X., Ma, Y., Wright, J.: Robust principal component analysis? Journal of the ACM 58 (2011)
25. Wright, J., Ganesh, A., Rao, S., Peng, Y., Ma, Y.: Robust principal component analysis: Exact recovery of corrupted low-rank matrices via convex optimization. In: NIPS (2009)
26. Cabral, R., De la Torre, F., Costeira, J.P., Bernardino, A.: Matrix completion for multi-label image classification. In: NIPS (2011)
27. Zhang, Z., Liang, X., Ma, Y.: Unwrapping low-rank textures on generalized cylindrical surfaces. In: ICCV (2011)
28. Cheng, B., Liu, G., Wang, J., Huang, Z., Yan, S.: Multi-task low-rank affinity pursuit for image segmentation. In: ICCV (2011)

29. De la Torre, F.: A least-squares framework for component analysis. IEEE Trans. PAMI 34, 1041–1055 (2012)
30. Yuan, M., Lin, Y.: Model selection and estimation in regression with grouped variables. Journal of the Royal Statistical Society, Series B 68, 49–67 (2007)
31. Golub, G., Loan, C.V.: Regression lines and the linear functional relationship. SIAM J. Numer. Anal. 17, 883–893 (1980)
32. Gross, R., Matthews, I., Cohn, J.F., Kanade, T., Baker, S.: The cmu multi-pose, illumination, and expression (multi-pie) face database. Technical report, CMU Robotics Institute.TR-07-08 (2007)
33. Snoek, C., Worring, M., Gemert, J., Geusebroek, J.M., Smeulders, A.: The challenge problem for automated detection of 101 semantic concepts in multimedia. In: ACM MM (2006)
34. Vedaldi, A., Zisserman, A.: Efficient additive kernels via explicit feature maps. IEEE Trans. PAMI 34, 480–492 (2012)
35. Li, F., Lebanon, G., Sminchisescu, C.: Chebyshev Approximations to the Histogram χ^2 Kernel. In: CVPR (2012)

Domain Adaptive Dictionary Learning

Qiang Qiu[1], Vishal M. Patel[1], Pavan Turaga[2], and Rama Chellappa[1]

[1] Center for Automation Research, UMIACS, University of Maryland, College Park
[2] Arts Media and Engineering, Arizona State University
qiu@cs.umd.edu, {pvishalm,rama}@umiacs.umd.edu, pturaga@asu.edu

Abstract. Many recent efforts have shown the effectiveness of dictionary learning methods in solving several computer vision problems. However, when designing dictionaries, training and testing domains may be different, due to different view points and illumination conditions. In this paper, we present a function learning framework for the task of transforming a dictionary learned from one visual domain to the other, while maintaining a domain-invariant sparse representation of a signal. Domain dictionaries are modeled by a linear or non-linear parametric function. The dictionary function parameters and domain-invariant sparse codes are then jointly learned by solving an optimization problem. Experiments on real datasets demonstrate the effectiveness of our approach for applications such as face recognition, pose alignment and pose estimation.

1 Introduction

In recent years, sparse and redundant modeling of signals has received a lot of attention from the vision community [1]. This is mainly due to the fact that signals or images of interest are sparse or compressible in some dictionary. In other words, they can be well approximated by a linear combination of a few elements (also known as atoms) of a redundant dictionary. This dictionary can either be an analytic dictionary such as wavelets or it can be directly trained from data. It has been observed that dictionaries learned directly from data provide better representation and hence can improve the performance of many applications such as image restoration and classification [2].

When designing dictionaries for image classification tasks, we are often confronted with situations where conditions in the training set are different from those present during testing. For example, in the case of face recognition, more than one familiar view may be available for training. Such training faces may be obtained from a live or recorded video sequences, where a range of views are observed. However, the test images can contain conditions that are not necessarily presented in the training images such as a face in a different pose. The problem of transforming a dictionary trained from one visual domain to another without changing signal sparse representations can be viewed as a problem of domain adaptation [3] and transfer learning [4].

Given the same set of signals observed in different visual domains, our goal is to learn a dictionary for the new domain without corresponding observations. We formulate this problem of dictionary transformation in a function learning

A. Fitzgibbon et al. (Eds.): ECCV 2012, Part IV, LNCS 7575, pp. 631–645, 2012.

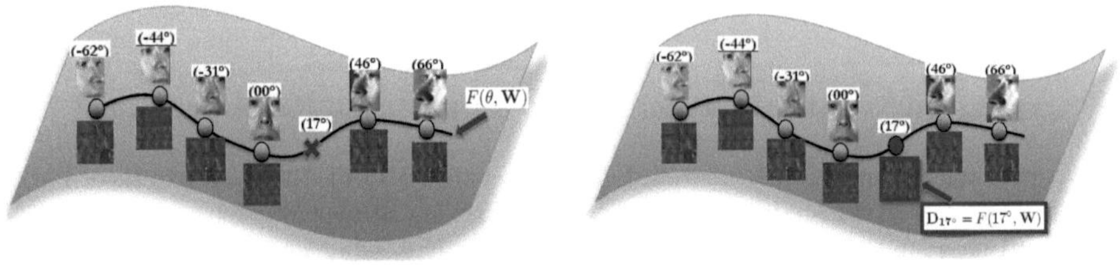

(a) Example dictionaries learned at known poses with observations.

(b) Domain adapted dictionary at a pose ($\theta = 17°$) associated with no observations.

Fig. 1. Overview of our approach. Consider example dictionaries corresponding to faces at different azimuths. (a) shows a depiction of example dictionaries over a curve on a dictionary manifold which will be discussed later. Given example dictionaries, our approach learns the underlying dictionary function $F(\theta, \mathbf{W})$. In (b), the dictionary corresponding to a domain associated with observations is obtained by evaluating the learned dictionary function at corresponding domain parameters.

framework, i.e., dictionaries across different domains are modeled by a parametric function. The dictionary function parameters and domain-invariant sparse codes are then jointly learned by solving an optimization problem. As shown in Figure 1, given a learned dictionary function, a dictionary adapted to a new domain is obtained by evaluating such a dictionary function at the corresponding domain parameters, e.g., pose angles.

For the case of pose variations, linear interpolation methods have been discussed in [5] to predict intermediate views of faces given a frontal and profile views. These methods essentially apply linear regression on the PCA coefficients corresponding to two different views. In [6], Vetter and Poggio present a method for learning linear transformations from a basis set of prototypical views. Their approach is based on the linear class property which essentially states that if a 3D view of an object can be represented as the weighted sum of views of other objects, its rotated view is a linear combination of the rotated views of the other objects with the same weights [6], [7], [8]. Note that our method is more general than the above mentioned methods in that it is applicable to visual domains other than pose. Second, our method is designed to maintain consistent sparse coefficients for the same signal observed in different domains. Furthermore, our method is based on the recent dictionary learning methods and is able to learn dictionaries that are more general than the ones resulting from PCA.

This paper makes the following contributions

- A general continuous function learning framework is presented for the task of dictionary transformations across domains.
- A simple and efficient optimization procedure is presented that learns dictionary function parameters and domain-invariant sparse codes simultaneously.
- Experiments for various applications, including pose alignment, pose and illumination estimation and face recognition across pose, are presented.

2 Overall Approach

We consider the problem of dictionary transformations in a learning framework, where we are provided with a few examples of dictionaries $\mathbf{D}_i$ with corresponding domain parameter θ_i. Let the parameter space be denoted by Θ, i.e. $\theta_i \in \Theta$. Let the *dictionary space* be denoted $\mathcal{D}$. The problem then boils down to constructing a mapping function $F : \Theta \mapsto \mathcal{D}$. In the simple case where $\Theta = \mathbb{R}$ and $\mathcal{D} = \mathbb{R}^n$, the problem of fitting a function can be solved efficiently using curve fitting techniques [9]. A dictionary of d atoms in $\mathbb{R}^n$ is often considered as an $n \times d$ real matrix or equivalently a point in $\mathbb{R}^{n\times d}$. However, often times there are additional constraints on dictionaries that make the identification with $\mathbb{R}^{n\times d}$ not well-motivated. We present below a few such constraints:

– Subspaces: For the special case of under-complete dictionaries where the matrix is full-rank and thus represents a choice of basis vectors for a d-dimensional subspace in $\mathbb{R}^n$, the dictionary space is naturally considered as a Grassmann manifold $\mathcal{G}_{n,d}$ [10]. The geometry of the Grassmann manifold is studied either as a quotient-space of the special orthogonal group or in terms of full-rank projection matrices, both of which result in non-Euclidean geometric structures.
– Products of subspaces: In many cases, it is convenient to think of the dictionary as a union of subspaces, e.g. a line and a plane. This structure has been utilized in many applications such as generalized PCA (GPCA), sparse subspace clustering [11] etc. In this case, the dictionary-space becomes a subset of the product space of Grassmann manifolds.
– Overcomplete dictionaries: In the most general case one considers an overcomplete set of basis vectors, where each basis vector has unit-norm, i.e. each basis vector is a point on the hypershere $\mathbb{S}^{n-1}$. In this case, the dictionary space becomes a subset of the product-space $\mathbb{S}^{(n-1)\times d}$.

To extend classic multi-variate function fitting to manifolds such as the ones above, one needs additional differential geometric tools. In our case, we propose extrinsic approaches that rely on embedding the manifold into an ambient vector space, perform function/curve fitting in the ambient space, and project the results back to the manifold of interest. This is conceptually simpler, and we find in our experiments that this approach works very well for the problems under consideration. The choice of embedding is in general not unique. We describe below the embedding and the corresponding projection operations for the manifolds of interest describe above.

– Subspaces: Each point in $\mathcal{G}_{n,d}$ corresponds to a d-dimensional subspace of $\mathbb{R}^n$. Given a choice of orthonormal basis vectors for the subspace $\mathbb{Y}$, the $n \times n$ projection matrix given by $\mathbf{P} = \mathbb{Y}\mathbb{Y}^T$ is a unique representation for the subspace. The projection matrix represntation can then be embedded into the ambient vector-space $\mathbb{R}^{n\times n}$. The projection operation $\mathbf{\Pi}$ is given by $\mathbf{\Pi}(\mathbf{M}) = \mathbf{U}\mathbf{U}^\mathbf{T}$, where $\mathbf{M} = \mathbf{U}\mathbf{\Sigma}\mathbf{V}^\mathbf{T}$ is a rank-d SVD of $\mathbf{M}$ [12].
– Products of subspaces: Following the procedure above, each component of the product space can be embedded into a different vector-space and the projected back to the manifold using the corresponding projection operation.

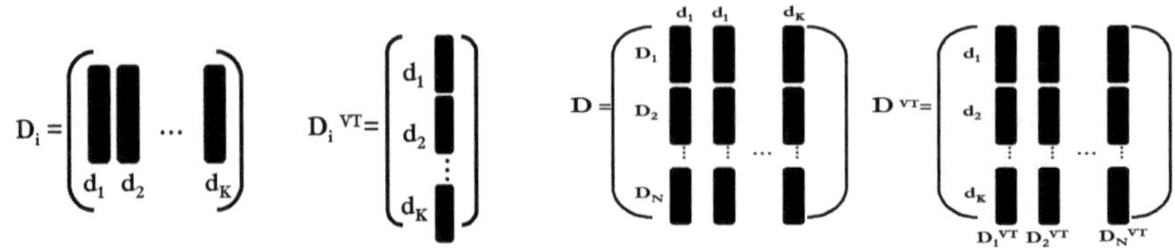

(a) $\mathbf{D_i}$ vs. $\mathbf{D_i}^{VT}$ (b) $\mathbf{D}$ vs. $\mathbf{D}^{VT}$

Fig. 2. The vector transpose (VT) operator over dictionaries

- Overcomplete dictionaries: The embedding from $\mathbb{S}^{n-1}$ to $\mathbb{R}^n$ is given by a vectorial representation with unit-norm. The projection $\mathbf{\Pi} : \mathbb{R}^n \mapsto \mathbb{S}^{n-1}$ is given by $\mathbf{\Pi}(\mathbf{V}) = \frac{\mathbf{V}}{\|\mathbf{V}\|}$, where $\|.\|$ is the standard Euclidean norm. A similar operation on the product-space $\mathbb{S}^{(n-1)\times d}$ can be defined by component-wise projection operations.

In specific examples in the paper, we consider the case of over-complete dictionaries. We adopt the embedding and projection approach described above as a means to exploit the wealth of function-fitting techniques available for vector-spaces. Next, we describe the technique we adopt.

2.1 Problem Formulation

We denote the same set of P signals observed in N different domains as $\{\mathbf{Y_1}, ..., \mathbf{Y_N}\}$, where $\mathbf{Y_i} = [\mathbf{y_{i1}}, ..., \mathbf{y_{iP}}]$, $\mathbf{y_{ip}} \in \mathbb{R}^n$. Thus, $\mathbf{y_{ip}}$ denotes the pth signal observed in the ith domain. In the following, we will use $\mathbf{D_i}$ as the vector-space embedded dictionary. Let $\mathbf{D_i}$ denote the dictionary for the ith domain, where $\mathbf{D_i} = [\mathbf{d_{i1}} ... \mathbf{d_{iK}}]$, $\mathbf{d_{ik}} \in \mathbb{R}^n$. We define a *vector transpose* (VT) operation over dictionaries as illustrated in Figure 2. The VT operator treats each individual dictionary atom as a value and then perform the typical matrix transpose operation. Let $\mathbf{D}$ denote the stack dictionary shown in Figure 2b over all N domains. It is noted that $\mathbf{D} = [\mathbf{D^{VT}}]^{\mathbf{VT}}$.

The domain dictionary learning problem can be formulated as (1). Let $\mathbf{X} = [\mathbf{x_1}, ..., \mathbf{x_P}]$, $\mathbf{x_p} \in \mathbb{R}^K$, be the sparse code matrix. The set of domain dictionary $\{\mathbf{D_i}\}_i^N$ learned through (1) enables the same sparse codes $\mathbf{x_p}$ for a signal $\mathbf{y_p}$ observed across N different domains to achieve domain adaptation.

$$\arg \min_{\{\mathbf{D_i}\}_\mathbf{i}^\mathbf{N}, \mathbf{X}} \sum_i^N \|\mathbf{Y_i} - \mathbf{D_i X}\|_F^2 \quad s.t. \; \forall p \; \|\mathbf{x}_p\|_o \leq T, \tag{1}$$

where $\|\mathbf{x}\|_o$ counts the number of non-zero values in $\mathbf{x}$. T is a sparsity constant.

We propose to model domain dictionaries $\mathbf{D_i}$ through a parametric function in (2), where $\boldsymbol{\theta_i}$ denotes a vector of domain parameters, e.g., view point angles, illumination conditions, etc., and $\mathbf{W}$ denotes the dictionary function parameters.

$$\mathbf{D_i} = F(\boldsymbol{\theta}_i, \mathbf{W}) \tag{2}$$

Applying (2) to (1), we formulate the domain dictionary function learning as (3).

$$\arg\min_{\mathbf{W},\mathbf{X}} \sum_{i}^{N} \|\mathbf{Y_i} - F(\boldsymbol{\theta_i}, \mathbf{W})\mathbf{X}\|_F^2 \quad s.t.\ \forall p\ \|\mathbf{x}_p\|_o \le T. \tag{3}$$

Once a dictionary is estimated it is projected back to the dictionary-space by the projection operation described earlier.

2.2 Domain Dictionary Function Learning

We first adopt power polynomials to model $\mathbf{D_i^{VT}}$ in Figure 2a through the following dictionary function $F(\boldsymbol{\theta_i}, \mathbf{W})$,

$$F(\boldsymbol{\theta_i}, \mathbf{W}) = w_0 + \sum_{s=1}^{S} w_{1s}\theta_{is} + ... + \sum_{s=1}^{S} w_{ms}\theta_{is}^m \tag{4}$$

where we assume S-dimensional domain parameter vectors and an mth-degree polynomial model. For example, given $\boldsymbol{\theta_i}$ a 2-dimensional domain parameter vector, a quadratic dictionary function is defined as,

$$F(\boldsymbol{\theta_i}, \mathbf{W}) = w_0 + w_{11}\theta_{i1} + w_{12}\theta_{i2} + w_{21}\theta_{i1}^2 + w_{22}\theta_{i2}^2$$

Given $\mathbf{D_i}$ contains K atoms and each dictionary atom is in the $\mathbb{R}^n$ space, as $\mathbf{D_i^{VT}} = F(\boldsymbol{\theta_i}, \mathbf{W})$, it can be noted from Figure 2 that w_{ms} is a nK-sized vector. We define the function parameter matrix $\mathbf{W}$ and the domain parameter matrix $\boldsymbol{\Theta}$ as

$$\mathbf{W} = \begin{bmatrix} w_0^{(1)} & w_0^{(2)} & w_0^{(3)} & ... & w_0^{(nK)} \\ w_{11}^{(1)} & w_{11}^{(2)} & w_{11}^{(3)} & ... & w_{11}^{(nK)} \\ & & & \vdots & \\ w_{mS}^{(1)} & w_{mS}^{(2)} & w_{mS}^{(3)} & ... & w_{mS}^{(nK)} \end{bmatrix} \qquad \boldsymbol{\Theta} = \begin{bmatrix} 1 & 1 & 1 & ... & 1 \\ \theta_{11} & \theta_{21} & \theta_{31} & ... & \theta_{N1} \\ & & & \vdots & \\ \theta_{1S}^m & \theta_{2S}^m & \theta_{3S}^m & ... & \theta_{NS}^m \end{bmatrix}$$

Each row of $\mathbf{W}$ corresponds to the nK-sized w_{ms}^T, and $\mathbf{W} \in \mathbb{R}^{(mS+1)\times nK}$. N different domains are assumed and $\boldsymbol{\Theta} \in \mathbb{R}^{(mS+1)\times N}$. With the matrix $\mathbf{W}$ and $\boldsymbol{\Theta}$, (4) can be written as,

$$\mathbf{D^{VT}} = \mathbf{W^T}\boldsymbol{\Theta} \tag{5}$$

where $\mathbf{D^{VT}}$ is defined in Figure 2b. Now dictionary function learning formulated in (3) can be written as,

$$\arg\min_{\mathbf{W},\mathbf{X}} \|\mathbf{Y} - [\mathbf{W^T}\boldsymbol{\Theta}]^{\mathbf{VT}}\mathbf{X}\|_F^2 \quad s.t.\ \forall p\ \|\mathbf{x}_p\|_o \le T \tag{6}$$

where $\mathbf{Y}$ is the stacked training signals observed in different domains as illustrated in Figure 3. With the objective function defined in (6), the dictionary function learning can be performed as described below:

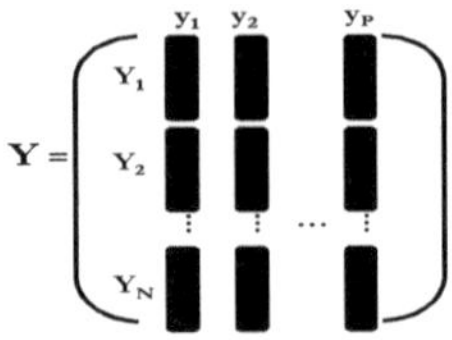

Fig. 3. The stack P training signals observed in N different domains

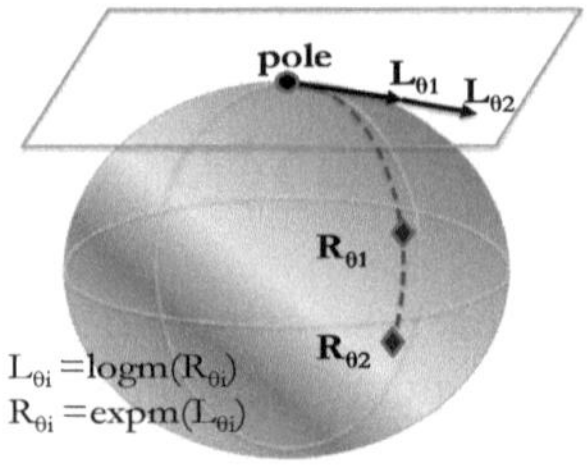

Fig. 4. Illustration of exponential maps *expm* and inverse exponential maps *logm* [12]

Step 1: Obtain the sparse coefficients X and $[\mathbf{W}^{\mathbf{T}}\boldsymbol{\Theta}]^{\mathbf{VT}}$ via any dictionary learning method, e.g., K-SVD [13].
Step 2: Given the domain parameter matrix $\boldsymbol{\Theta}$, the optimal dictionary function can be obtained as [14],

$$\mathbf{W} = [\boldsymbol{\Theta}\boldsymbol{\Theta}^{\mathbf{T}}]^{-1}\boldsymbol{\Theta}[[[\mathbf{W}^{\mathbf{T}}\boldsymbol{\Theta}]^{\mathbf{VT}}]^{\mathbf{VT}}]^{\mathbf{T}}. \tag{7}$$

Step 3: Sample the dictionary function at desired parameters values, and project it to the dictionary-space using an appropriate projection operation.

2.3 Non-linear Dictionary Function Models

Till now, we only assume power polynomials for the dictionary model. In this section, we discuss non-linear dictionary functions. We only focus on linearizeable functions, and a general Newton's method based approach to learn a non-linear dictionary function is presented in Algorithm 2 in Appendix A.

Linearizeable Models. There are several well-known linearizeable models, such as the Cobb-Douglass model, the logistic model, etc. We use the Cobb-Douglass model as the example to discuss in detail how dictionary function learning can be performed over these linearizable models.

The Cobb-Douglass model is written as,

$$\mathbf{D}_{\mathbf{i}}^{\mathbf{VT}} = F(\boldsymbol{\theta}_i, \mathbf{W}) = w_0 \exp(\sum_{s=1}^{S} w_{1s}\theta_{is} + ... + \sum_{s=1}^{S} w_{ms}\theta_{is}^m) \tag{8}$$

The logarithmic transformation yields,

$$\log(\mathbf{D}_{\mathbf{i}}^{\mathbf{VT}}) = \log(w_0) + \sum_{s=1}^{S} w_{1s}\theta_{is} + ... + \sum_{s=1}^{S} w_{ms}\theta_{is}^m$$

As the right side of (8) is in the same linear form as (4), we can define the corresponding function parameter matrix $\mathbf{W}$ and the domain parameter matrix $\boldsymbol{\Theta}$ as discussed. The dictionary function learning is written as,

$$\arg\min_{\mathbf{W},\mathbf{X}} \|\mathbf{Y} - [\exp(\mathbf{W}^{\mathbf{T}}\boldsymbol{\Theta})]^{\mathbf{VT}}\mathbf{X}\|_F^2 \;\; s.t. \; \forall p \; \|\mathbf{x}_p\|_o \leq T.$$

Through any dictionary learning methods, we obtain $[[\exp(\mathbf{W}^{\mathbf{T}}\mathbf{\Theta})]^{\mathbf{T}}]^{\mathbf{VT}}$ and $\mathbf{X}$. Then, the dictionary function is obtained as,

$$\mathbf{W} = [\mathbf{\Theta}\mathbf{\Theta}^{\mathbf{T}}]^{-1}\mathbf{\Theta}[\log([[\exp(\mathbf{W}^{\mathbf{T}}\mathbf{\Theta})]^{\mathbf{VT}}]^{\mathbf{VT}})]^{\mathbf{T}}.$$

2.4 Domain Parameter Estimation

Given a learned dictionary function $F(\boldsymbol{\theta}, \mathbf{W})$, the domain parameters $\boldsymbol{\theta_y}$ associated with an unknown image $\mathbf{y}$, e.g., pose (azimuth, altitude) or light source directions (azimuth, altitude), can be estimated using Algorithm 1.

It is noted that we adopt the following strategy to represent the domain parameter vector $\boldsymbol{\theta}$ for each pose in a linear space: we first obtain the rotation matrix $\mathbf{R}_\theta$ from the azimuth and altitude of a pose; we then compute the inverse

Input: a dictionary function $F(\theta, \mathbf{W})$, an image $\mathbf{y}$, domain parameter matrix $\mathbf{\Theta}$
Output: an S-dimensional domain parameter vector $\boldsymbol{\theta_y}$ associated with $\mathbf{y}$
begin
  1. Initialize with mean domain parameter vector: $\boldsymbol{\theta_y} = \text{mean}(\mathbf{\Theta})$;
  2. Estimate $\theta^{(s)}$, the sth value in $\boldsymbol{\theta_y}$;
  for $s \leftarrow 1$ **to** S **do**
    3. Obtain the value range to estimate $\theta^{(s)}$
      $\theta^{(s)}_{min} = \min$ (s^{th} row of $\mathbf{\Theta}$) ;
      $\theta^{(s)}_{max} = \max$ (s^{th} row of $\mathbf{\Theta}$) ;
      $\theta^{(s)}_{mid} = (\theta^{(s)}_{min} + \theta^{(s)}_{max})/2$;
    4. Estimate $\theta^{(s)}$ via a search for the parameters to best represent $\mathbf{y}$.
    repeat
      $\boldsymbol{\theta_{min}} \leftarrow$ replace the sth value of $\boldsymbol{\theta_y}$ with $\theta^{(s)}_{min}$;
      $\boldsymbol{\theta_{max}} \leftarrow$ replace the sth value of $\boldsymbol{\theta_y}$ with $\theta^{(s)}_{max}$;
      $\mathbf{x}_{\mathbf{min}} \leftarrow \min_{\mathbf{x}} |\mathbf{y} - F(\boldsymbol{\theta_{min}}, \mathbf{W})|^2_2, \quad s.t. |\mathbf{x}|_o \leq$ t (sparsity) ;
      $\mathbf{x}_{\mathbf{max}} \leftarrow \min_{\mathbf{x}} |\mathbf{y} - F(\boldsymbol{\theta_{max}}, \mathbf{W})|^2_2, \quad s.t. |\mathbf{x}|_o \leq$ t (sparsity) ;
      $\mathbf{r}_{\mathbf{min}} \leftarrow \mathbf{y} - F(\boldsymbol{\theta_{min}}, \mathbf{W})\mathbf{x}_{\mathbf{min}}$;
      $\mathbf{r}_{\mathbf{max}} \leftarrow \mathbf{y} - F(\boldsymbol{\theta_{max}}, \mathbf{W})\mathbf{x}_{\mathbf{max}}$;
      if $\mathbf{r}_{\mathbf{min}} \leq \mathbf{r}_{\mathbf{max}}$ **then**
        $\theta^{(s)}_{max} = \theta^{(s)}_{mid}$;
      else
        $\theta^{(s)}_{min} = \theta^{(s)}_{mid}$;
      end
      $\theta^{(s)}_{mid} = (\theta^{(s)}_{min} + \theta^{(s)}_{max})/2$;
    until $|\theta^{(s)}_{max} - \theta^{(s)}_{min}| \leq$ *threshold*;
    $\theta^{(s)} \leftarrow \theta^{(s)}_{mid}$;
  end
  7. return $\boldsymbol{\theta_y}$;
end

Algorithm 1. Domain parameters estimation

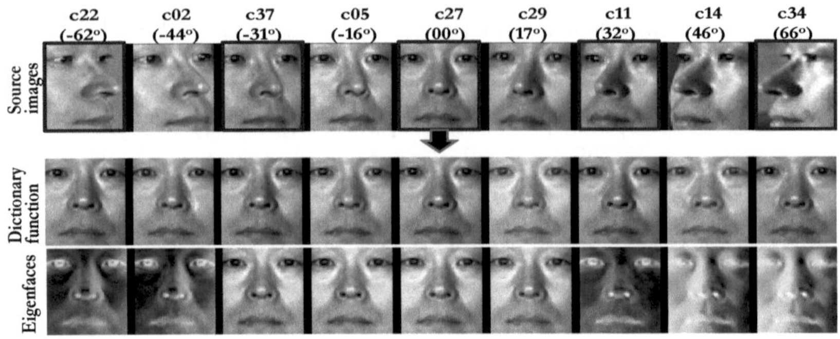

Fig. 5. Frontal face alignment. For the first row of source images, pose azimuths are shown below the camera numbers. Poses highlighted in blue are known poses to learn a linear dictionary function (m=4), and the remaining are unknown poses. The second and third rows show the aligned face to each corresponding source image using the linear dictionary function and Eigenfaces respectively.

exponential map of the rotation matrix logm($\mathbf{R}_\theta$) as shown in Figure 4. We denote $\boldsymbol{\theta}$ using the upper triangular part of the resulting skew-symmetric matrix [12]. The exponential map operation in Figure 4 is used to recover the azimuth and altitude from the estimated domain parameters. We represent light source directions in the same way.

3 Experimental Evaluation

We conduct our experiments using two public face datasets: the CMU PIE dataset [15] and the Extended YaleB dataset [16]. The CMU PIE dataset consists of 68 subjects in 13 poses and 21 lighting conditions. In our experiments we use 9 poses which have approximately the same camera altitude, as shown in the first row of Figure 5. The Extended YaleB dataset consists of 38 subjects in 64 lighting conditions. All images are in 64×48 size. We will first evaluate the basic behaviors of dictionary functions through pose alignment. Then we will demonstrate the effectiveness of dictionary functions in face recognition and domain estimation.

3.1 Dictionary Functions for Pose Alignment

Frontal Face Alignment In Figure 5, we align different face poses to the frontal view. We learn for each subject in the PIE dataset a linear dictionary function $F(\boldsymbol{\theta}, \mathbf{W})$ (m=4) using 5 out of 9 poses. The training poses are highlighted in blue in the first row of Figure 5. Given a source image $\mathbf{y_s}$, we first estimate the domain parameters $\boldsymbol{\theta_s}$, i.e., the pose azimuth here, by following Algorithm 1. We then obtain the sparse representation $\mathbf{x_s}$ of the source image as $\min_{\mathbf{x_s}} \|\mathbf{y_s} - F(\boldsymbol{\theta_s}, \mathbf{W})\mathbf{x_s}\|_2^2$, *s.t.* $\|\mathbf{x_s}\|_o \leq T$ (sparsity level) using any pursuit methods such as OMP [17]. We specify the fontal pose azimuth (00°) as the

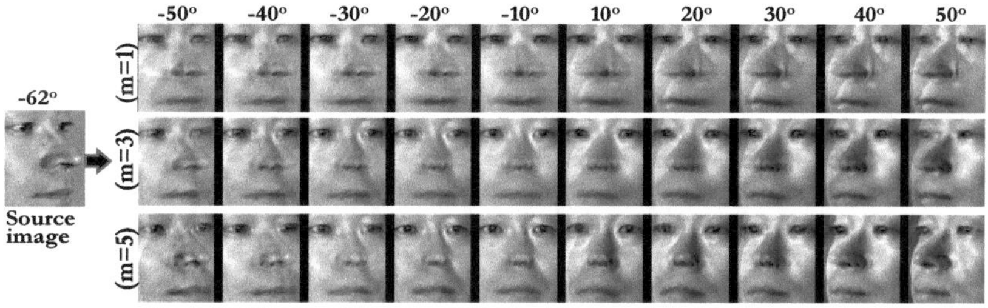

(a) Pose synthesis using a linear dictionary function

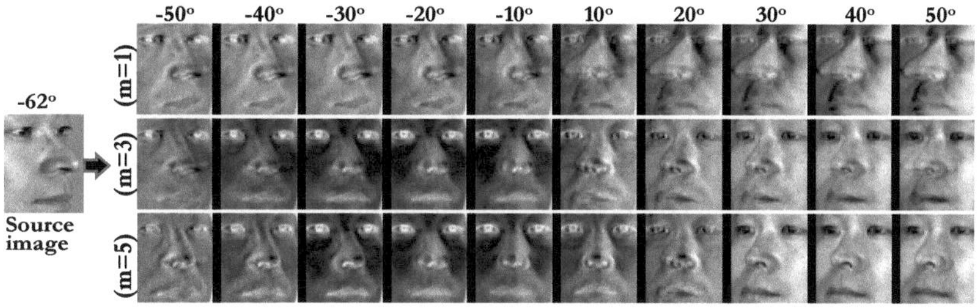

(b) Pose synthesis using Eigenfaces

Fig. 6. Pose synthesis using various degrees of dictionary polynomials. All the synthesized poses are unknown to learned dictionary functions and associated with no actual observations. m is the degree of a dictionary polynomial in (4).

parameter for the target domain $\boldsymbol{\theta_t}$, and obtain the frontal view image $\mathbf{y_t}$ as $\mathbf{y_t} = F(\boldsymbol{\theta_t}, \mathbf{W})\mathbf{x_s}$. The second row of Figure 5 shows the aligned frontal view images to the respective poses in the first row. These aligned frontal faces are close to the actual image, i.e., c27 in the first row. It is noted that images with poses c02, c05, c29 and c14 are unknown poses to the learned dictionary function.

For comparison, we learn Eigenfaces for each of the 5 training poses and obtain adapted Eigenfaces at 4 unknown poses using the same function fitting method in our framework. We then project each source image (mean-subtracted) on the respective eignefaces and use frontal Eigenfaces to reconstruct the aligned image shown in the third row of Figure 5. Our method of jointly learning the dictionary function parameters and domain-invariant sparse codes in (6) significantly outperforms the Eigenfaces approach, which fails for large pose variations.

Pose Synthesis. In Figure 6, we synthesize new poses at any given pose azimuth. We learn for each subject in the PIE dataset a linear dictionary function $F(\boldsymbol{\theta}, \mathbf{W})$ using all 9 poses. In Figure 6a, given a source image $\mathbf{y_s}$ in a profile pose (-62°), we first estimate the domain parameters $\boldsymbol{\theta_s}$ for the source image, and sparsely decompose it over $F(\boldsymbol{\theta_s}, \mathbf{W})$ for its sparse representation $\mathbf{x_s}$. We specify every 10° pose azimuth in $[-50^o, 50^o]$ as parameters for the target domain $\boldsymbol{\theta_t}$, and obtain a synthesized pose image $\mathbf{y_t}$ as $\mathbf{y_t} = F(\boldsymbol{\theta_t}, \mathbf{W})\mathbf{x_s}$. It is noted that none of the target poses are associated with actual observations. As shown in Figure 6a, we obtain reasonable synthesized images at poses with no observations. We observe improved synthesis performance by increasing the value of

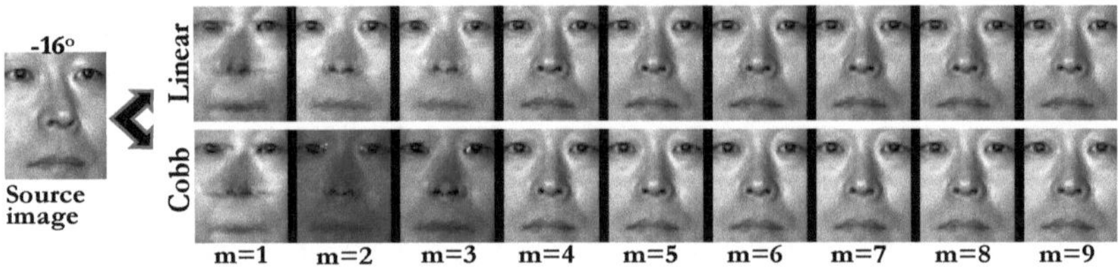

(a) Pose c05 frontal alignment

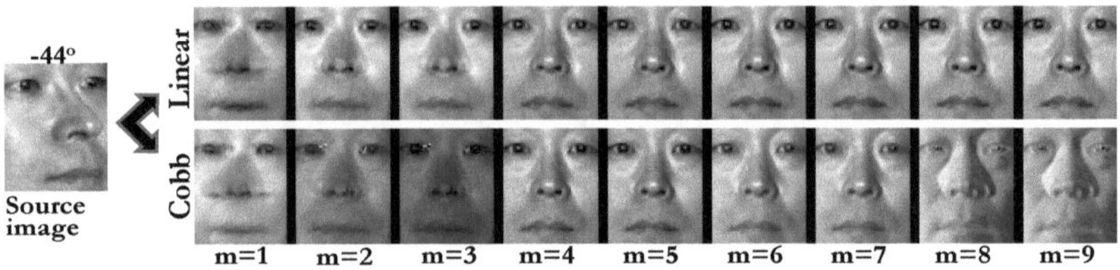

(b) Pose c02 frontal alignment

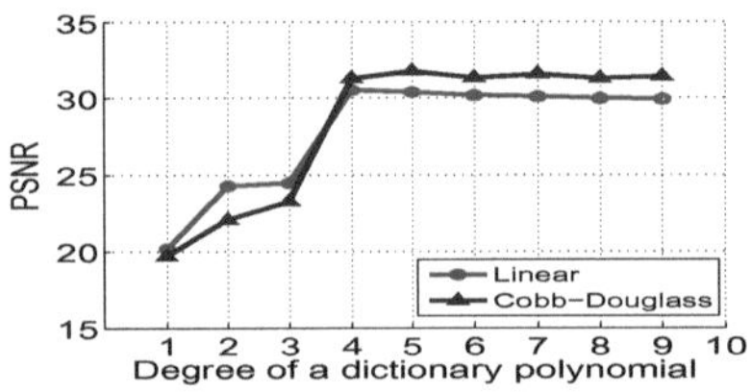

(c) Pose c05 alignment PSNR

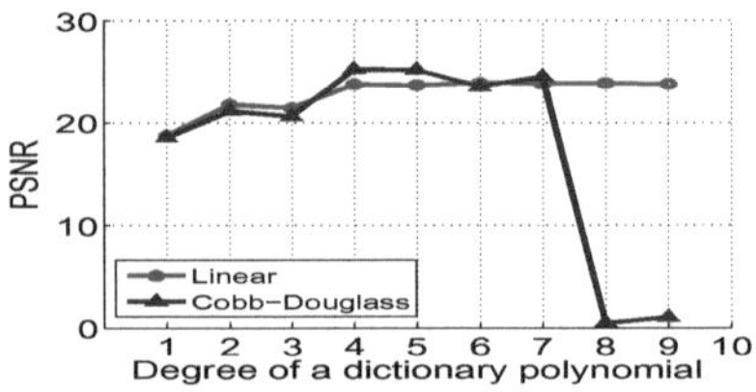

(d) Pose c02 frontal PSNR

Fig. 7. Linear vs. non-linear dictionary functions. m is the degree of a dictionary polynomial in (4) and (8).

m, i.e., the degree of a dictionary polynomial. In Figure 6b, we perform curve fitting over Eigenfaces as discussed. The proposed dictionary function learning framework exhibits better synthesis performance.

Linear vs. Non-linear. In Figure 7, we conduct the same frontal face alignment experiments discussed above. Now we learn for each subject both a linear and a nonlinear Cobb-Douglass dictionary function discussed in Section 2.3. As a Cobb-Douglass function is linearizeable, various degrees of polynomials are experimented for both linear and nonlinear dictionary function learning. As shown in Figure 7a and Figure 7c, the nonlinear Cobb-Douglass dictionary function exhibits better reconstruction while aligning pose c05, which is also indicated by the higher PSNR values. However, in Figure 7b and 7d, we notice that the Cobb-Douglass dictionary function exhibits better alignment performance only when $m \leq 7$, and then the performance drops dramatically. Therefore, a linear dictionary function is a more robust choice over a nonlinear Cobb-Douglass dictionary function; however, at proper configurations, a nonlinear Cobb-Douglass dictionary function outperforms a linear dictionary function.

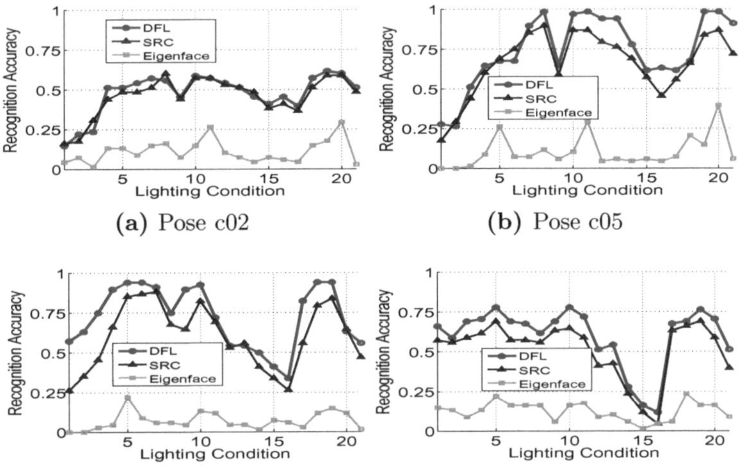

(a) Pose c02 (b) Pose c05

(c) Pose c29 (d) Pose c14

Fig. 8. Face recognition accuracy on the CMU PIE dataset. The proposed method is denoted as DFL in color red.

3.2 Dictionary Functions for Classification

Two face recognition methods are adopted for comparisons: Eigenfaces [18] and SRC [19]. Eigenfaces is a benchmark algorithm for face recognition. SRC is a state of the art method to use sparse representation for face recognition. We denote our method as the Dictionary Function Learning (DFL) method. For a fair comparison, we adopt exactly the same configurations for all three methods, i.e., we use 68 subjects in 5 poses c22, c37, c27, c11 and c34 in the PIE dataset for training, and the remaining 4 poses for testing.

For the SRC method, we form a dictionary from the training data for each pose of a subject. For the proposed DFL method, we learn from the training data a dictionary function across pose for each subject. In SRC and DFL, a testing image is classified using the subject label associated with the dictionary or the dictionary function respectively that gives the minimal reconstruction error. In Eigenfaces, a nearest neighbor classifier is used. In Figure 8, we present the face recognition accuracy on the PIE dataset for different testing poses under each lighting condition. The proposed DFL method outperforms both Eigenfaces and SRC methods for all testing poses.

3.3 Dictionary Functions for Domain Estimation

Pose Estimation. As described in Algorithm 1, given a dictionary function, we can estimate the domain parameters associated with an unknown image, e.g., view point or illumination. It can be observed from the face recognition experiments discussed above that the SRC and eigenfaces methods can also estimate the domain parameters based on the domain associated with each dictionary

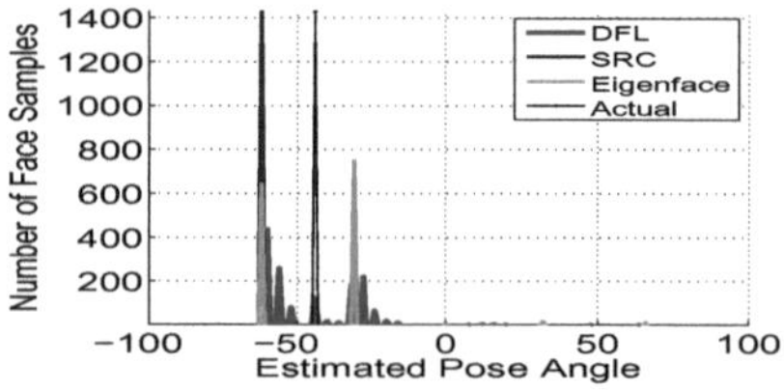

(a) Pose c02 (-44°)

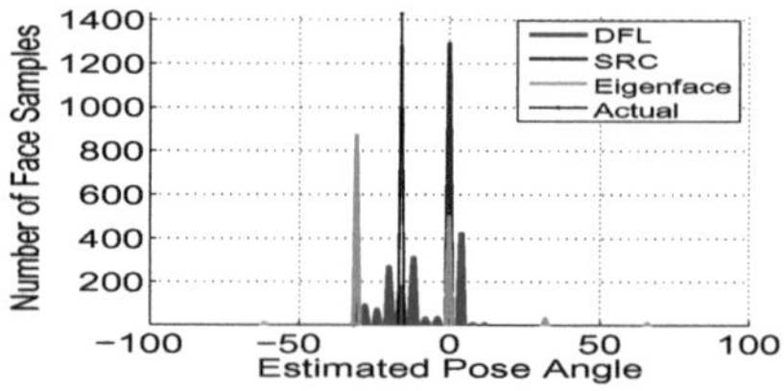

(b) Pose c05 (-16°)

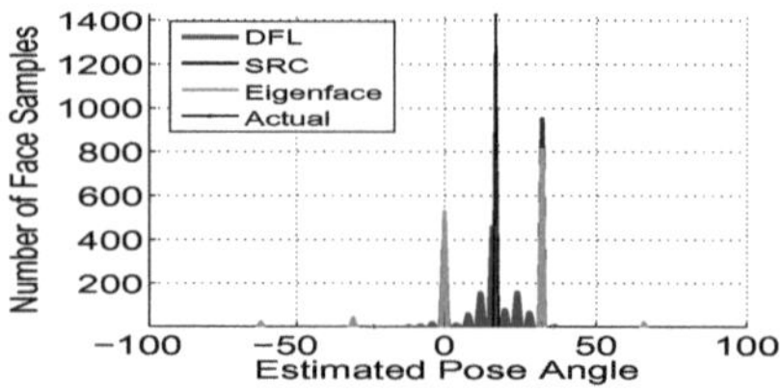

(c) Pose c29 (17°)

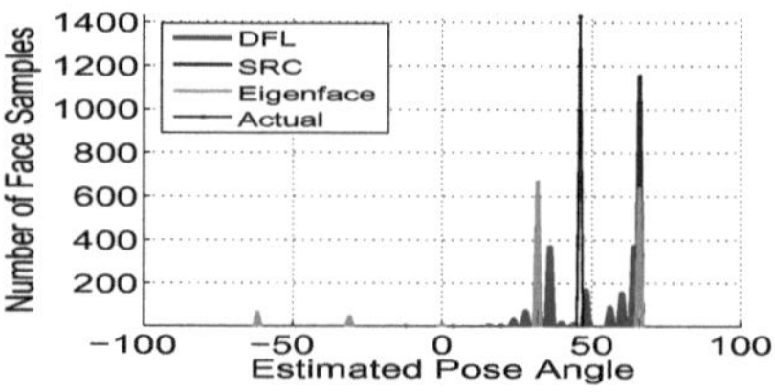

(d) Pose c14 (46°)

Fig. 9. Pose azimuth estimation histogram (*known* subjects). Azimuths estimated using the proposed dictionary functions (red) spread around the true values (black).

or each training sample. However, the domain estimation accuracy using such recognition methods is limited by the domain discretization steps present in the training data. We perform pose estimation along with the classification experiments above. We have 4 testing poses and each pose contains 1428 images (68 subjects in 21 lighting conditions). Figure 9 shows the histogram of pose azimuth estimation. We notice that poses estimated from Eigenfaces and SRC methods are limited to one of the 5 training pose azimuths, i.e., -62° (c22), -31° (c37), 00° (c27), 32° (c11) and 66° (c34). As shown in Figure 9, the proposed DFL method enables a more accurate pose estimation, and poses estimated through the DFL method are distributed in a continuous region around the true pose.

To demonstrate that a dictionary function can be used for domain estimation for unknown subjects, we use the first 34 subjects in 5 poses c22, c37, c27, c11 and c34 in the PIE dataset for training, and the remaining 34 subjects in the rest 4 poses for testing. We learn from the training data a dictionary function across pose over the first 34 subjects. As shown in Figure 10, the proposed DFL method provides a more accurate continuous pose estimation.

Illumination Estimation. In this set of experiments, given a face image in the Extended YaleB dataset, we estimate the azimuth and elevation of the single light source direction. We randomly select 50% (32) of the lighting conditions in the Extended YaleB dataset to learn a dictionary function across illumination over all 34 subjects. The remaining 32 lighting conditions are used for testing. For the SRC method and for each training illumination condition, we form a dictionary from the training data using all 34 subjects. We perform illumination estimation in a similar way as pose estimation. Figure 11a, 11b, and 11c show the illumination estimation for several example lighting conditions. The proposed DFL method provides reasonable estimation to the actual light source directions.

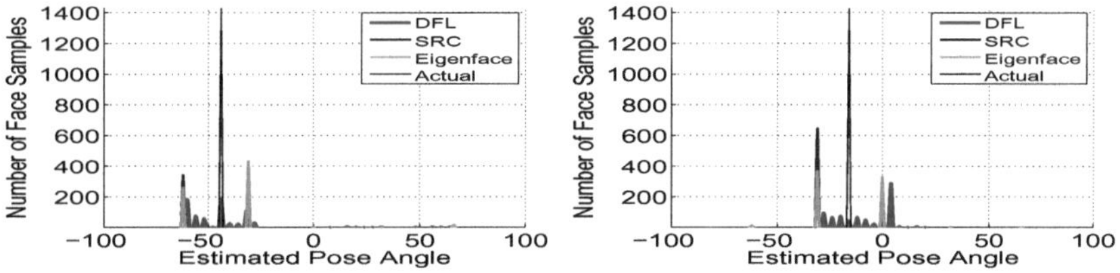

(a) Pose c02 (-44°) **(b)** Pose c05 (-16°)

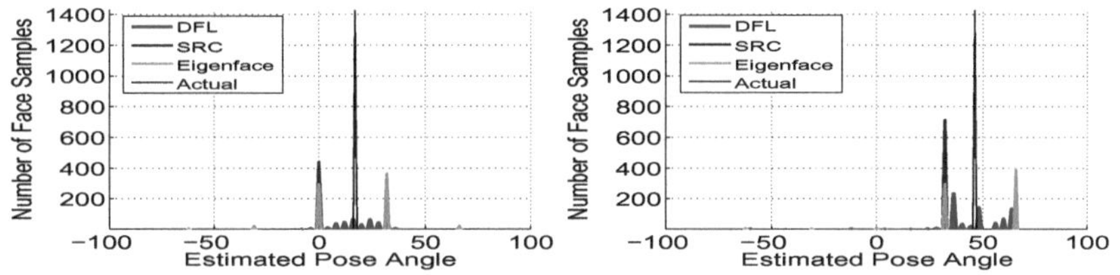

(c) Pose c29 (17°) **(d)** Pose c14 (46°)

Fig. 10. Pose azimuth estimation histogram (*unknown* subjects). Azimuths estimated using the proposed dictionary functions (red) spread around the true values (black).

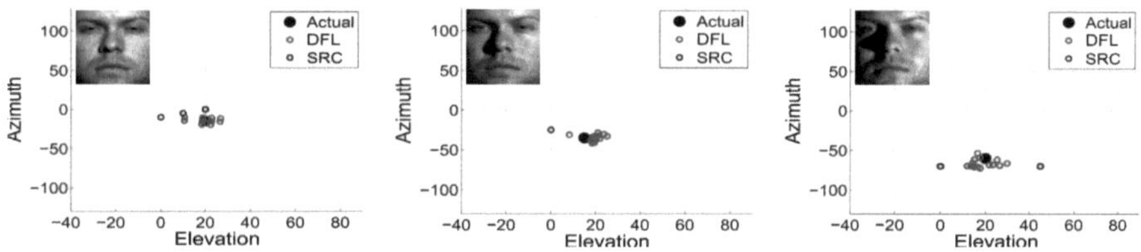

(a) Lighting condition f40 **(b)** Lighting condition f45 **(c)** Lighting condition f51

Fig. 11. Illumination estimation in the Extended YaleB face dataset

4 Conclusion

We have presented a general dictionary function learning framework to transform a dictionary learned from one domain to the other. Domain dictionaries are modeled by a parametric function. The dictionary function parameters and domain-invariant sparse codes are then jointly learned by solving an optimization problem with a sparsity constraint. Extensive experiments on real datasets demonstrate the effectiveness of our approach on applications such as pose alignment, pose and illumination estimation and face recognition. The proposed framework can be generalized for non-linearizeable dictionary functions, however, further experimental evaluations are to be performed.

Acknowledgment. This work was supported by a MURI grant N00014-10-1-0934 from the Office of Naval Research.

A A Nonlinear Dictionary Function Learning Algorithm

Input: signals in N different domains $\{\mathbf{Y_i}\}_{i=1}^{N}$, domain parameter matrix $\mathbf{\Theta}$
Output: dictionary function $\mathbf{W}$
begin
  Initialization:
  1. Create the stack signal $\mathbf{Y}$ and initialize $\mathbf{D}$ from $\mathbf{Y}$ using K-SVD;
  2. Initialize $\mathbf{W}$ with random values ;
  repeat
    3. Compute current residuals: $\mathbf{R} \leftarrow \mathbf{D} - \mathbf{F}(\mathbf{\Theta}, \mathbf{W})$;
    4. Compute the row vector of derivatives w.r.t. $\mathbf{W}$ evaluated at $\mathbf{\Theta}$ $\mathbf{P} \leftarrow \nabla\mathbf{F}(\mathbf{\Theta}, \mathbf{W})$;
    5. Learn the linear dictionary function $\mathbf{B}$ using $\mathbf{R} = \mathbf{PB}$
    6. Update the dictionary function parameters: $\mathbf{W} \leftarrow \mathbf{W} + \lambda\mathbf{B}$
  until *convergence*;
  7. return $\mathbf{W}$;
end

Algorithm 2. A general method for nonlinear dictionary function learning

References

1. Wright, J., Ma, Y., Mairal, J., Sapiro, G., Huang, T., Yan, S.: Sparse representation for computer vision and pattern recognition. Proceedings of the IEEE 98, 1031–1044 (2010)
2. Rubinstein, R., Bruckstein, A., Elad, M.: Dictionaries for sparse representation modeling. Proceedings of the IEEE 98, 1045–1057 (2010)
3. Ben-David, S., Blitzer, J., Crammer, K., Kulesza, A., Pereira, F., Vaughan, J.: A theory of learning fromdifferent domains. Machine Learning 79, 151–175 (2010)
4. Pan, S.J., Yang, Q.: A survey on transfer learning. IEEE Trans. Knowledge and Data Engineering 22, 1345–1359 (2010)
5. Gong, S., McKenna, S.J., Psarrou, A.: Dynamic vision from images to face recognition. Imperial College Press (2000)
6. Vetter, T., Poggio, T.: Linear object classes and image synthesis from a single example image. PAMI 19, 733–742 (1997)
7. Beymer, D., Shashua, A., Poggio, T.: Example-based image analysis and synthesis. Artificial Intelligence Laboratory A.I. Memo No. 1431 19 (1993)
8. Beymer, D., Poggio, T.: Face recognition from one example view. Artificial Intelligence Laboratory A.I. Memo No. 1536 19 (1995)
9. Lancaster, P., Salkauskas, K.: Curve and surface fitting (1990)
10. Edelman, A., Arias, T.A., Smith, S.T.: The geometry of algorithms with orthogonality constraints. SIAM J. Matrix Analysis and Applications 20, 303–353 (1999)
11. Elhamifar, E., Vidal, R.: Sparse subspace clustering. In: CVPR (2009)
12. Turaga, P., Veeraraghavan, A., Srivastava, A., Chellappa, R.: Statistical Analysis on Manifolds and its Applications to Video Analysis. In: Schonfeld, D., Shan, C., Tao, D., Wang, L. (eds.) Video Search and Mining. SCI, vol. 287, pp. 115–144. Springer, Heidelberg (2010)

13. Aharon, M., Elad, M., Bruckstein, A.: k-SVD: An algorithm for designing overcomplete dictionaries for sparse representation. IEEE Trans. on Signal Process. 54, 4311–4322 (2006)
14. Machado, L., Leite, F.S.: Fitting smooth paths on riemannian manifolds. Int. J. Appl. Math. Stat. 4, 25–53 (2006)
15. Sim, T., Baker, S., Bsat, M.: The CMU pose, illumination, and expression (PIE) database. PAMI 25, 1615–1618 (2003)
16. Georghiades, A.S., Belhumeur, P.N., Kriegman, D.J.: From few to many: Illumination cone models for face recognition under variable lighting and pose. PAMI 23, 643–660 (2001)
17. Pati, Y.C., Rezaiifar, R., Krishnaprasad, P.S.: Orthogonal matching pursuit: Recursive function approximation with applications to wavelet decomposition. In: Asilomar Conf. on Signals, Systems, and Computers (1993)
18. Turk, M., Pentland, A.: Face recognition using eigenfaces. In: CVPR (1991)
19. Wright, J., Yang, A., Ganesh, A., Sastry, S., Ma, Y.: Robust face recognition via sparse representation. PAMI 31, 210–227 (2009)

A Robust and Efficient Doubly Regularized Metric Learning Approach

Meizhu Liu* and Baba C. Vemuri

Siemens Corporate Research & Technology, Princeton, NJ, 08540
CISE, University of Florida, Gainesville, FL, 32611

Abstract. A proper distance metric is fundamental in many computer vision and pattern recognition applications such as classification, image retrieval, face recognition and so on. However, it is usually not clear what metric is appropriate for specific applications, therefore it becomes more reliable to learn a task oriented metric. Over the years, many metric learning approaches have been reported in literature. A typical one is to learn a Mahalanobis distance which is parameterized by a positive semidefinite (PSD) matrix **M**. An efficient method of estimating **M** is to treat **M** as a linear combination of rank-one matrices that can be learned using a boosting type approach. However, such approaches have two main drawbacks. First, the weight change across the training samples may be non-smooth. Second, the learned rank-one matrices might be redundant. In this paper, we propose a doubly regularized metric learning algorithm, termed by DRMetric, which imposes two regularizations on the conventional metric learning method. First, a regularization is applied on the weight of the training examples, which prevents unstable change of the weights and also prevents outlier examples from being weighed too much. Besides, a regularization is applied on the rank-one matrices to make them independent. This greatly reduces the redundancy of the rank-one matrices. We present experiments depicting the performance of the proposed method on a variety of datasets for various applications.

Keywords: Regularized metric learning, boosting, PSD matrix.

1 Introduction

The choice of an appropriate distance or similarity measure over the input space is critical to many computer vision and pattern recognition applications, including but not limited to clustering and classification [1], image retrieval [2], shape detection [3], face recognition [4–9], tracking [10]. There are many commonly used distance metrics, e.g. Euclidean distance, L_1-norm distance, χ^2 distance, and Mahalanobis distance etc. However, it is usually very hard to predict which

* This work was done when Meizhu Liu was studying for her PhD degree at University of Florida. This research was in part supported by the NIH grant EB007082 to Vemuri.

A. Fitzgibbon et al. (Eds.): ECCV 2012, Part IV, LNCS 7575, pp. 646–659, 2012.

distance measure is appropriate for a certain application with specific inputs. Therefore, it is more apt to develop a task-dependent metric based on the available knowledge of the inputs. It was shown [1, 9] that a properly designed distance metric, compared with the standard distances, can significantly improve the performance for many applications.

There are a lot of metric learning algorithms in the literature. A good metric learning algorithm should be able to learn a metric that can amplify informative dimensions (feature) and squash non-informative dimensions. This is unlike Euclidean distance, which treats every dimension equally and does not consider the correlation between them.

In most cases, metric learning algorithms are derived from the labeled training datasets, and the goal of the algorithm is to learn a metric which can separate the instances of different classes apart, and bring together the instances belonging to the same class. To be specific, the labeling of the inputs can be provided mainly in three ways. First, the input constraint is $(\mathbf{x}_i, y_i)$ where $\mathbf{x}_i \in \mathbb{R}^D$ is an instance and y_i is its label. Second, the input constraint is $((\mathbf{x}_i, \mathbf{x}_j), y_{ij})$ where y_{ij} indicates whether $\mathbf{x}_i$ and $\mathbf{x}_j$ are "similar" or "dissimilar" [11]. An even weaker representation often used in information retrieval [12] is the proximity relationship over triplets (i, j, k), meaning that $\mathbf{x}_i$ is closer to $\mathbf{x}_j$ than to $\mathbf{x}_k$. Proximity relationships are the most natural constraint for learning a metric, and are of the weakest representation because proximity triplets can be derived from the other kinds of constraints, but not vice versa.

In this paper, we propose a doubly regularized metric learning algorithm, termed by DRMetric. Our goal is to learn a Mahalanobis distance metric which tries to preserve the proximity relationships over the input. Mahalanobis distance metric is parameterized by a positive semidefinite (PSD) matrix [13, 14][1]. It has been well studied and advantages were shown over some other metrics such as multidimensional scaling (MDS) [15], ISOMAP [16], and locally linear embedding (LLE) [17].

Several aspects of our DRMetric are novel. First, we use the total Kullbak-Leibler (tKL) divergence [18] to regularize the evolution of the weights on the training triplets. tKL is a recently proposed divergence which has been proved to be statistically robust [18]. The regularization automatically ensures that the weight of the examples is upper bounded, therefore, the weight can not be extremely large for outliers. Note that without regularization, the weight of an outlier example will keep increasing, which may lead to serious problems such as overfitting and inefficiency. Furthermore, for some noisy examples, their weight may depict severe oscillations. This not only hampers the convergence rate of the metric learning algorithm, but also leads to overfitting, and lowers the accuracy. Second, we regularize the rank-one PSD matrices to minimize the dependence between them. This regularization makes the rank-one matrices least correlated,

[1] Strictly speaking, this matrix should be symmetric positive definite (SPD) in order for it to be a metric. However, we relax the requirement and allow two different instances to have zero distance.

and therefore least redundant, which greatly decreases the number of rank-one matrices needed and improves the efficiency.

The rest of the paper is organized as follows. In Section 2, we briefly review the metric learning literature. In Section 3, we present the doubly regularized linear programming metric learning algorithm, termed by DLMetric. In Section 4, we investigate DLMetric empirically by evaluating our algorithm on a number of datasets for various applications. We also compare our method with the state-of-the-art metric learning and other algorithms. Finally, we conclude the paper in Section 5.

2 Literature Review

A good task dependent metric has attracted extensive attention recently. The machine learning community has done many researches to automatically learn a distance function from available knowledge of the dataset [13, 19, 20, 11]. Most existing works assume the metrics to be Mahalanobis distance, which are parameterized by PSD matrices.

Various techniques have been proposed to learn a PSD matrix from the dataset. Some techniques force the negative eigenvalues in the learned symmetric matrix to be zero as in [11]. Some others set the matrix to be the inverse of the covariance matrix of the centered data points in small subsets of points with known relevant information [13]. In [20], the matrix exponential gradient update was used which preserves symmetry and positive definiteness due to the fact that the matrix exponential of a symmetric matrix is always an SPD matrix. In [21], Iwasawa factorization was used to ensure the positive definiteness [21]. Most of these techniques are limited from a scalability or a computational complexity view point.

More recently, some researchers [1, 12] adapted the boosting technique to metric learning. This kind of metric learning is based on an important theorem that a PSD matrix with trace one can always be represented as a convex combination of multiple rank-one PSD matrices. This is a generalization of boosting [22] in the sense that the weak learner in these metric learning algorithms is a rank-one matrix instead of a classifier. The main idea behind these boosting-based metric learning algorithms is that at each iteration, they will learn a rank-one matrix from the training examples that follow a distribution. The weighted rank-one matrix is then added to the PSD matrix. This weight is typically related to the rank-one matrix's ability to discriminate the examples from different classes. The higher the discriminatory power, the larger the weight, and vise versa. After learning the rank-one matrix, the distribution of the examples is updated. The examples are reweighted according to the rule that misclassified examples tend to gain weight and correctly classified examples tend to lose weight. Therefore, the rank-one matrices to be learned will be focused more on the examples that were misclassified previously.

However, these methods are not statistically robust i.e., the learning process is sensitive to noisy data and outliers [23, 24]. The reason is that the weight of noisy examples might switch between severe increase and severe decrease frequently, which seriously slows down the convergence of the learning process. Furthermore, the weight of outliers might keep increasing, which largely affects the metric to be learned. To avoid these issues and inspired by the regularized boosting [23, 24] techniques, we propose a regularized metric learning algorithm, which regularizes the weight updating process involved in the training stage. Furthermore, in order to reduce the redundancy of the learned rank-one matrices, we add another regularization term to make the dependence between the learned rank-one matrices as small as possible. In this way, we can use much fewer number of rank-one matrices (i.e. much fewer number of iterations) to form the PSD matrix which parameterizes a suitable metric. Experimental results illustrate that for a dataset of D dimensions, DRMetric is able to learn a relatively good metric in D iterations.

3 Proposed Method

Given a dataset $\mathbf{X} = \{\mathbf{x}_i\}$, with $\mathbf{x}_i \in \mathbb{R}^D$, and its associated triplet set $\mathcal{T} = \{(i, j, k)\}$, with (i, j, k) meaning that $\mathbf{x}_i$ is more similar to $\mathbf{x}_j$ than to $\mathbf{x}_k$. Let $N = |\mathcal{T}|$ denote the number of triplets in $\mathcal{T}$. The goal is to learn a Mahalanobis distance which preserves the relationship in $\mathcal{T}$.

A Mahalanobis distance is parameterized by a PSD matrix $\mathbf{M} \in \mathbb{R}^{D\times D}$. The Mahalanobis distance between $\mathbf{x}_i \in \mathbf{X}$ and $\mathbf{x}_j \in \mathbf{X}$ based on $\mathbf{M}$ is

$$d_{\mathbf{M}}(\mathbf{x}_i, \mathbf{x}_j) = (\mathbf{x}_i - \mathbf{x}_j)^T \mathbf{M} (\mathbf{x}_i - \mathbf{x}_j) \tag{1}$$

To remove the scalability effect of the distance resulting from $\mathbf{M}$, we require $tr(\mathbf{M}) = 1$. Since any trace-one PSD matrix can be decomposed as a convex combination of rank-one trace-one PSD matrices, i.e.,

$$\mathbf{M} = \sum_{l=1}^{D} w_l \mathbf{u}_l \mathbf{u}_l^T, \mathbf{u}_l \in \mathbb{R}^D, \|\mathbf{u}_l\| = 1, \mathbf{w} \in \Delta_D . \tag{2}$$

To avoid notation clutter in later computations, we introduce a vector $\mathbf{v}_n = [v_{nl}]$, where v_{nl} corresponds to $\mathbf{u}_l$ and the nth triplet (i, j, k), and is defined as

$$v_{nl} = (\mathbf{x}_i - \mathbf{x}_k)^T \mathbf{u}_l \mathbf{u}_l^T (\mathbf{x}_i - \mathbf{x}_k) - (\mathbf{x}_i - \mathbf{x}_j)^T \mathbf{u}_l \mathbf{u}_l^T (\mathbf{x}_i - \mathbf{x}_j). \tag{3}$$

A potentially appropriate $\mathbf{M}$ should be able to maximize the soft margin defined in the following linear programming,

$$\begin{aligned} &\max_{\mathbf{w},\rho,\zeta} \rho - \alpha \sum_{n=1}^{N} \zeta_n \\ &\text{s.t.} \sum_{l=1}^{t} w_l v_{nl} \geq \rho - \zeta_n , \, n = 1, \cdots , N, \\ &\mathbf{w} \in \Delta_t, \, \zeta \geq \mathbf{0} , \end{aligned} \tag{4}$$

where ζ_n is the slack variable, and α is a constant factor which penalizes the slack variables.

The Lagrangian dual problem of (4) is

$$\max_{\mathbf{d},c,\mathbf{q}} \min_{\mathbf{w},\rho,\zeta} \mathcal{L}(\mathbf{w},\rho,\zeta,\mathbf{d},c,\mathbf{q}) = -\rho+\alpha\sum_{n=1}^{N}\zeta_n-\sum_{n=1}^{N}d_n(\sum_{l=1}^{t}w_l v_{nl}-\rho+\zeta_n)+c(\mathbf{1}^T\mathbf{w}-1)-\mathbf{q}^T\zeta, \tag{5}$$

where $\mathbf{d}$, c, and $\mathbf{q}$ are non-negative regularizers. After some simple algebraic manipulation we arrive at the dual problem of (4) given by,

$$\min_{\mathbf{d}\in\Delta_N,\mathbf{d}\leq\alpha\mathbf{1}} \max_{l=1,\cdots,t} \sum_{n=1}^{N} d_n v_{nl}. \tag{6}$$

3.1 Regularization on d

The regularization on $\mathbf{d}$ is very important because for the non-regularized metric learning algorithm, the weight of the training examples might change very severely, i.e., the weight of a training example might oscillate significantly when it is misclassified or correctly classified by the weak learners (rank-one matrices) as shown in Fig. 1. This instability will seriously affect the learning efficiency, accuracy, and also lead to overfitting. With regularization, severe oscillations and instabilities can be prevented, which makes the algorithm converge faster, i.e. need fewer number of rank-1 PSD matrices. Fig. 1 depicts that, using regularization, the resulting weight change of the training data is stable.

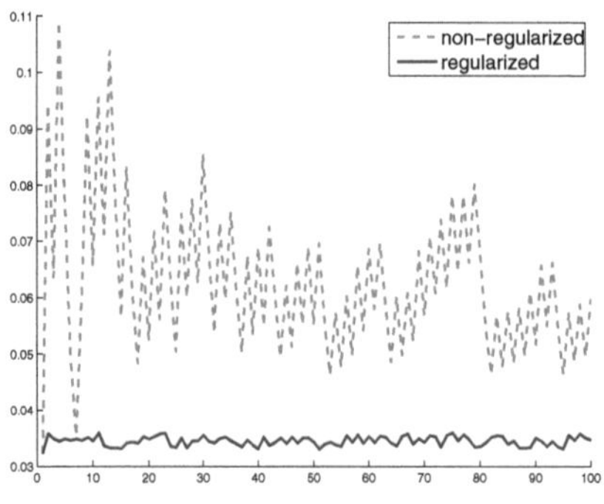

Fig. 1. Change in the weight of a training example in the Heart disease dataset from the UCI repository, under metric learning without regularization and with regularization

To overcome the aforementioned instabilities, we add a regularization term to the update of $\mathbf{d}$ in (6), i.e.,

$$\min_{\mathbf{d}\in\Delta_N,\mathbf{d}\leq\alpha\mathbf{1}} \max_{l=1,\cdots,t} \sum_{n=1}^{N} d_n v_{nl} + \eta\delta(\mathbf{d},\hat{\mathbf{d}}), \tag{7}$$

where η is the regularization coefficient that balances the margin and the smoothness. η is set to be a fixed number[2] as in [23] to make the number of iterations upper bounded by a constant without hurting the accuracy. $\delta(\mathbf{d}, \hat{\mathbf{d}})$ is the tKL divergence [23, 25], and

$$\delta(\mathbf{d}, \hat{\mathbf{d}}) = \frac{\sum_{n=1}^{N} d_n \log \frac{d_n}{\hat{d}_n}}{\sqrt{1 + \sum_{j=1}^{N} \hat{d}_j (1 + \log \hat{d}_j)^2}}. \tag{8}$$

Note that the regularization term $\delta(\mathbf{d}, \hat{\mathbf{d}})$ ensures that the evolution of $\mathbf{d}$ is smooth.

Here, $\hat{\mathbf{d}}$ can be chosen in different ways. In this paper, we set $\hat{\mathbf{d}} = \mathbf{d}^0$, where $\mathbf{d}^0$ is the initialized distribution, this means $\mathbf{d}$ should not be far away from the initialized distribution. Since $\mathbf{d}^0$ is user defined, it is usually set according to the application problem and the data. One tends to initialize larger weight on the examples with more importance, so we use $\delta(\mathbf{d}, \mathbf{d}^0)$ as the regularizer. Note that the d_n is upper bounded by α as in (6), therefore the weight of the noisy examples and outliers is prevented from being too large leading to possible domination in the learning[3].

To directly compute $\mathbf{d}^t$ from (7) is complicated, instead, we will first find its Lagrangian and use it to compute $\mathbf{d}^t$. To find the Lagrangian, we rewrite (7) into the following form

$$\begin{aligned} &\min_{\beta, \mathbf{d}} \; \beta + \eta \delta(\mathbf{d}, \mathbf{d}^0) \\ &\text{s.t.} \; \sum_{n=1}^{N} d_n v_{nl} \le \beta, \; l = 1, \cdots, t \\ &\quad\; \mathbf{d} \in \Delta_N, \; \mathbf{d} \le \alpha \mathbf{1}\,. \end{aligned} \tag{9}$$

The Lagrangian Ψ of (9) is given by,

$$\Psi(\mathbf{d}, \beta, \mathbf{w}, \xi, \gamma) = \beta + \eta \delta(\mathbf{d}, \mathbf{d}^0) + \sum_{l=1}^{t} w_l (\sum_{n=1}^{N} d_n v_{nl} - \beta) + \sum_{n=1}^{N} \xi_n (d_n - \alpha) + \gamma(\mathbf{d} \cdot \mathbf{1} - 1) \tag{10}$$

where, w_l, $l = 1, \cdots, t$, ξ_n, $n = 1, \cdots, N$ and γ are non-negative regularizers. Using some simple calculus and the KKT condition [26], we can simplify (10) and get the partial Lagrangian

$$\Psi(\mathbf{d}, \mathbf{w}) = \eta \delta(\mathbf{d}, \mathbf{d}^t) + \sum_{l=1}^{t} w_l \sum_{n=1}^{N} d_n v_{nl}\,. \tag{11}$$

[2] $\eta = \frac{\epsilon \sqrt{1 + (\log N - 1)^2}}{2 \log(ND)}$, where N is the number of training samples, D is the dimension of each training sample, and ϵ is the error tolerance of the margin between different classes based on the learned metric [23].

[3] To make such a $\mathbf{d}$ exist, we should require $\alpha \ge 1/N$. It was shown in [24] that $\alpha = 1/s$, and $s \in \{1, \cdots, N\}$ is a favorable choice.

Now differentiating Ψ with respect to $\mathbf{d}$, setting it to 0, and normalizing $\mathbf{d}$, we get,

$$d_n^t = \frac{d_n^0 \exp\left(-c\sum_{l=1}^t w_l v_{nl}\right)}{Z_t}, \text{ where } c = \frac{1}{\eta}\sqrt{1+\sum_{n=1}^N d_n^0(1+\log d_n^0)^2}, \quad (12)$$

and Z_t is the normalization parameter to make $\sum_{n=1}^N d_n^t = 1$. Here if $d_n^t > \alpha$, then we manually set $d_n^t = \alpha$.

3.2 Regularization on u

We put two constraints on $\mathbf{u}$. First, we want it to maximize the margin. Second, we require $\mathbf{u}$ to be independent of the previously learned $\mathbf{u}_l$, $l = 1, 2, \cdots, t$, so that the learned $\{\mathbf{u}\}$ will not be redundant. Therefore, the number of rank-one matrices needed to form a good metric is reduced. The dependence between $\mathbf{u}$ and $\mathbf{u}_l$ is measured by $\|\mathbf{u}^T\mathbf{u}_l\|^2 \in [0,1]$. The larger $\|\mathbf{u}^T\mathbf{u}_l\|^2$ is, the more dependent they are. When $\|\mathbf{u}^T\mathbf{u}_l\|^2 = 0$, $\mathbf{u}$ and $\mathbf{u}_l$ are independent.

The two constraints on $\mathbf{u}$ are described as

$$\max_{\mathbf{u}} \sum_{n=1}^N d_n^t[(\mathbf{x}_i-\mathbf{x}_k)^T\mathbf{u}\mathbf{u}^T(\mathbf{x}_i-\mathbf{x}_k) - (\mathbf{x}_i-\mathbf{x}_j)^T\mathbf{u}\mathbf{u}^T(\mathbf{x}_i-\mathbf{x}_j)] - \lambda\sum_{l=1}^{t-1}\|\mathbf{u}^T\mathbf{u}_l\|^2, \quad (13)$$

where λ is the regularization coefficient to penalize the dependence. (13) can be rewritten as

$$\max_{\mathbf{u}} \mathbf{u}^T\{\sum_{n=1}^N d_n^t[(\mathbf{x}_i-\mathbf{x}_k)(\mathbf{x}_i-\mathbf{x}_k)^T - (\mathbf{x}_i-\mathbf{x}_j)(\mathbf{x}_i-\mathbf{x}_j)^T] - \lambda\sum_{l=1}^t \mathbf{u}_l\mathbf{u}_l\}\mathbf{u}^T \quad (14)$$

Let matrix $\mathbf{A}^t = \sum_{n=1}^N d_n^t[(\mathbf{x}_i-\mathbf{x}_k)(\mathbf{x}_i-\mathbf{x}_k)^T-(\mathbf{x}_i-\mathbf{x}_j)(\mathbf{x}_i-\mathbf{x}_j)^T]-\lambda\sum_{l=1}^t \mathbf{u}_l\mathbf{u}_l^T$, then $\mathbf{u}_{t+1}$ is the eigenvector corresponding to the largest eigenvalue of $\mathbf{A}^t$.

The weight vector $\mathbf{w}$ for the rank-one matrices should satisfy the linear programming problem (4) which can be solved using column generation [27] or a gradient based method.

3.3 Building the Triplets

For each $\mathbf{x}_i \in \mathbf{X}$, we first find the a instances $\{\mathbf{x}_j\}_{j=1}^a$ which are in the same category as $\mathbf{x}_i$ but are most different from $\mathbf{x}_i$. After that, we find the a nearest neighbors $\{\mathbf{x}_k\}_{k=1}^a$ in a different category, then (i,j,k) will form a triplet. If the size of $\mathbf{X}$ is small, we will use a larger a, otherwise, we will use a smaller a. Furthermore, if the number of triplets is very large, we will randomly select $10 \sim 50\%$ of the triplets for training.

As a summary, the algorithm for the proposed DRMetric is presented in Algorithm 1. The proof of the convergence is very similar to the proof from Schapire and Singer [28].

Algorithm 1. Doubly Regularized Metric Learning

Input: Dataset $\mathbf{X} = \{\mathbf{x}_i\}$, $\mathbf{x}_i \in \mathbb{R}^D$
Triplet set $\mathcal{T} = \{(i,j,k) \mid \mathbf{x}_i$ is closer to $\mathbf{x}_j$ than to $\mathbf{x}_k\}$. $N = |\mathcal{T}|$, the number of triplets in $\mathcal{T}$.
Output: $\mathbf{M} = \sum_{l=1}^{t} w_l \mathbf{u}_l \mathbf{u}_l^T$, $\mathbf{u}_l \in \mathbb{R}^D$, $\|\mathbf{u}_l\| = 1$, $\mathbf{w} \in \Delta_t$, t is the number of iterations.
Initialization: Initialize d_n^0, the weight of the nth triplet, $n = 1, \cdots, N$, according to the importance, or set $d_n^0 = 1/N$ by default.
for $l = 1$ to t **do**
  Find the optimal $\mathbf{u}_l$ according to (13);
  Update the distribution $\mathbf{d}$ according to (12);
  Update the weight $\mathbf{w}$ according to (4)
end for
Return $\mathbf{M} = \sum_{l=1}^{t} w_l \mathbf{u}_l \mathbf{u}_l^T$.

4 Experimental Results

The proposed algorithm is evaluated on a number of public domain datasets for a variety of applications. We use the UCI machine learning repository [29] for classification, use the COREL image dataset for content based image retrieval, and use the Labeled Faces in the Wild (LFW) [30] dataset for face recognition. We compare our method with many state-of-the-art metric learning and other techniques. The results show that our proposed metric learning method is very promising for many applications.

4.1 Classification

The classification experiments are performed on the UCI machine learning repository [29], which is a collection of datasets that have been extensively used for analyzing machine learning techniques. The repository contains a large variety of datasets, including very noisy datasets (e.g. the Optical Recognition of Handwritten Digits dataset, the wine dataset) as well as relatively clean datasets, which is optimal for testing the robustness and accuracy of classification algorithms. We selected 9 datasets from the UCI repository. The selected datasets include noisy and clean datasets, cover small size to large size datasets in terms of number of instances in the datasets, and range from low dimension to high dimension in terms of number of attributes per instance of the datasets. The description of the selected datasets is shown in Table 1.

We use 5-fold cross validation to evaluate the proposed algorithm. The regularization parameters α, η and λ are determined during the training and validation stage, and they are set to be the numbers which maximize the performance on the training dataset. The final result is the average of the results obtained over the 5 runs. The proposed DRMetric is compared with many other non-metric learning and metric learning algorithms, including Euclidean distance, L_1-norm

Table 1. Description of the selected UCI datasets

dataset	♯ instances	♯ attributes
Heart disease	303	74
Australian sign	6650	14
Blood transfusion service center	748	5
Artificial characters	6000	7
Glass identification dataset	214	10
Adult dataset	48842	14
Handwritten digits	5620	64
Wine dataset	178	13

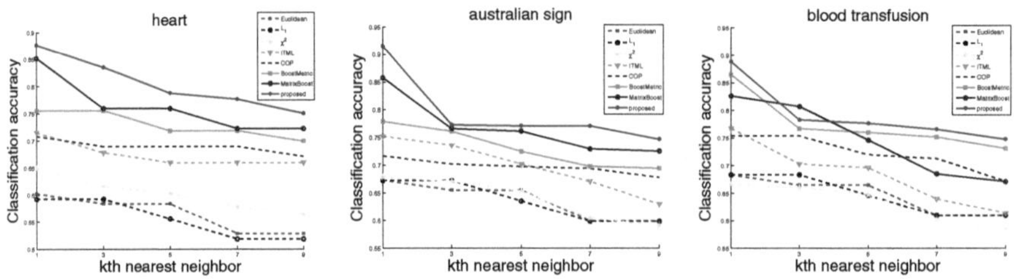

Fig. 2. The neighbor accuracy curves from different metrics on the Heart disease, Australian sign and Blood transfusion service center datasets in the UCI repository

distance, χ^2 distance, BoostMetric [9], MatrixBoost [1], ITML [14], and COP [11]. The code for metric learning methods is obtained directly from the corresponding authors or downloaded from the authors' webpage. The classification performance is measured based on neighbor accuracy curves. The neighbor accuracy measures the percentage of correctly classified instances based on the kth ($k = 1, 3, 5, 7, 9$) nearest neighbor. The average neighbor accuracy is shown in Fig. 2. The comparison depicts that in general DRMetric yields higher classification accuracy.

We also evaluate the 3-nearest-neighbor voting classification accuracy on several UCI datasets including the Glass Identification dataset, the Adult dataset, the Optical Recognition of Handwritten Digits dataset, and the Wine dataset. The classification results are shown in Table 2, which reflects that the proposed method outperforms the other methods.

Besides, for DRMetric, we examined the relationship between the classification accuracy change and the number of iterations. The results are shown in Fig. 3, which implies that when the number of iterations is less than D (the dimension of the dataset), the classification accuracy increases at a higher rate. However, when the number of iterations is larger than D, the classification accuracy improves very slowly. This means that, using our method, D rank-one matrices can form a relatively high quality Mahalanobis distance.

Table 2. Classification accuracy using different metrics on selected datasets from the UCI repository

dataset	Euclidean	L_1	χ^2	ITML	COP	BoostMetric	MatrixBoost	proposed
Characters	0.7235	0.7452	0.7651	0.9114	0.8889	0.9147	0.9049	0.9288
Glass	0.6114	0.6404	0.6479	0.7975	0.7850	0.8135	0.7991	0.8204
Adult	0.6017	0.6249	0.6284	0.7760	0.7752	0.7981	0.7894	0.8075
Digits	0.6865	0.7107	0.7284	0.7352	0.7473	0.8014	0.8148	0.8290
Wine	0.7240	0.7261	0.7602	0.8625	0.8958	0.9074	0.9152	0.9161

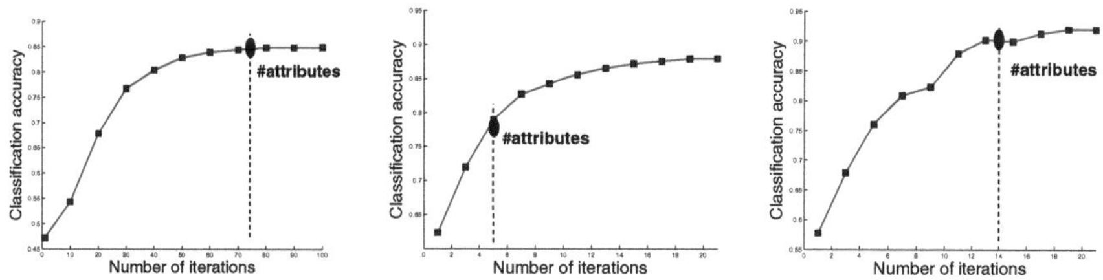

Fig. 3. The change of classification accuracy with related to the number of iterations using DRMetric on the Heart disease (left), Australian sign (middle), and Blood transfusion service center (right) datasets. The black disk corresponds the classification accuracy when the number of iterations equals to the number of attributes.

4.2 Content Based Image Retrieval

The task for image retrieval is that given one image in a category, find the images in the same category. We use the COREL image database [31] to evaluate our method on content based image retrieval. The database contains 3400 real-world images with 34 different categories, and 100 images per category.

Each image is represented as a 33 dimensional feature vector, which is a combination of low level features including color features, edge features and texture features. For color features, we first represent the images in the HSV color space, and then compute the mean, variance, skewness of the HSV color to get a 9 dimensional feature vector. For edge features, the Canny edge detector [32] is first applied to images to detect the edges, and the histogram for edge direction was quantized into 9 bins of every 40 degrees, which resulted in 9 different edge features. For texture features, we use the multi-resolution simultaneous autoregressive (MASAR) model [33] to get 15 features. In total, there are 33 features for each image.

We use 10-fold cross validation to evaluate the proposed algorithm, i.e., 90% images are used to learn the metric, and 10% images are used for evaluation. We use every image in the test dataset as a query, if the retrieved image belongs to the same category as the query image, the retrieval is correct. We measure the retrieval performance based on the neighbor accuracy curves. Neighbor accuracy measures the percentage of correctly retrieved images in the kth nearest neighbors of the query images ($k = 1, \cdots, 40$ in our experiments).

We compared our method to many algorithms, including Euclidean distance, L_1-norm distance, χ^2 distance, BoostMetric [9], MatrixBoost [1], ITML [14], and COP [11]. The retrieval results are shown in Fig. 4. The results illustrate that our proposed method achieves a higher neighbor accuracy when using 1st $\sim$ 25th and 34th $\sim$ 40th nearest neighbors. However, it's a little worse than MatrixBoost when using the 26th $\sim$ 33rd nearest neighbors.

We compare the computational time of BoostMetric [9], MatrixBoost [1], and DRMetric to learn the distance metric on the COREL database. All algorithms are run on a laptop with Intel(R) Core(TM)2 CPU L7500 @1.6GHz, 4GB memory, GNU Linux and MATLAB (Version R2011a). The average CPU time taken to converge for our algorithm is 167.68s, while BoostMetric takes 244.81s, and MatrixBoost takes 239.28s.

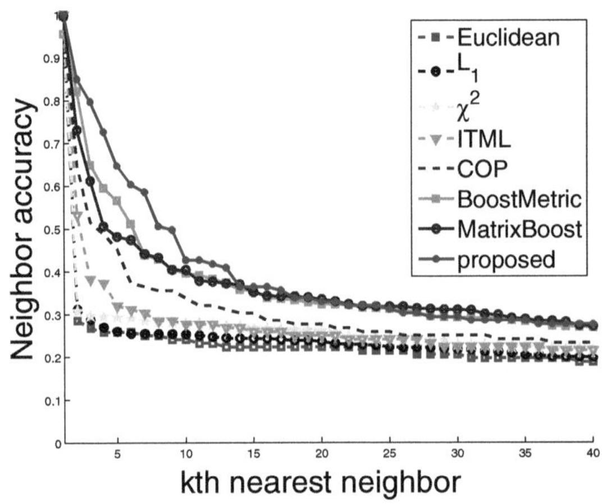

Fig. 4. Comparison of using different metric learning methods for content based image retrieval on the COREL dataset

4.3 Face Recognition

In this scenario, the goal for face recognition is to do pair matching: given two face images, determine if these two images belong to the same person. We use the Labeled Faces in the Wild (LFW) [30] dataset. This is a fairly difficult dataset for face recognition, because it has a large range of the variation (varying pose: straight, left, right, up; expression: neutral, happy, sad, angry; eyes: wearing glasses or not; clothes: wearing different clothes; size: small, medium or large) seen in real life. It includes 13233 images of 5749 people collected from news articles on the Internet. The number of images per person ranges from 1 to 530, and 1680 people have two or more distinct images in the dataset. This is a popular dataset which has been used by many researchers [4, 6, 34, 8, 35] to evaluate their face recognition frameworks.

In this experiment, we have compared the proposed DRMetric to the state-of-the-art methods for the task of face pair-matching problem. To ensure fairness, we used the same features as used in the literature [4–9, 36]. Features of face images are extracted by computing the 3-scale, 128-dimensional SIFT descriptors [37], centered on 9 points of facial features extracted by a facial feature descriptor, as described in [5]. In this way, we get $3 \times 128 \times 9 = 3456$ features in total for each image. PCA is then performed on the feature vectors to reduce the dimension to 400 (because the result in [9] showed that dimension 400 is a good compromise between performance and efficiency) for training. The triplets are built according to Section 3.3. The number of generated triplets is 44794, out of which, we use 20% (i.e. 8960) for training. We compared our method with LDML funneled [38], Hybrid aligned [36], V1-like funneled [8], Simile [6], Attribute + Simile [6], Background sample [39] Multiple LE + comp [4], and FrobMetric [9]. All these methods except FrobMetric are more complicated than our method, because they either use additional information, hybrid descriptors or combination of classifiers. The performance is described using an ROC curve[4] on which each point represents the average over the 10 runs of (false positive rate, true positive rate) for a fixed distance threshold. The results from all other techniques were taken from their latest published results. The comparison is shown in Fig. 5, which depicts that our method is only slightly worse than the two leading techniques (Attribute + Simile [6] and Background sample [39]) that are much more complicated. Furthermore, our method is comparable to or better than other state-of-the-art techniques on face recognition.

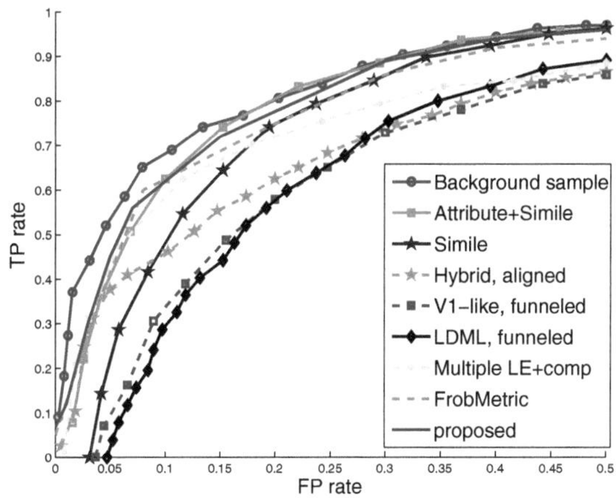

Fig. 5. False positive (FP) rate versus true positive (TP) rate on face recognition using different metric learning methods on the LFW dataset

[4] If the distance, based on the learned metric, is above some threshold, the two images will be declared as not belonging to the same person, and vice versa. For each threshold, we get the corresponding FP/TPrate. By changing the thresholds, we get a set of {FP/TPrate}, which forms the ROC curve. Using ROC curve to evaluate face recognition methods is widely used in literature [38, 36, 6, 39, 8].

5 Conclusions

We proposed an efficient and robust doubly regularized metric learning algorithm DRMetric. It has two regularization parts. First, we use tKL to regularize the update of the weight of the training examples. This avoids instabilities in the weight change, and consequently avoids overfitting and make it more robust to noisy data as well as outliers. Second, we add a regularization to the rank-one matrices enforcing them to be as independent as possible. In this way, the redundancy of the learned rank-one matrices as well as the number of necessary rank-one matrices are significantly reduced, which leads to higher efficiency. Furthermore, DRMetric is robust and capable of handling a variety of datasets for different applications. Though the idea behind DRMetric seems simple, its robustness and applicability can not be undervalued.

References

1. Bi, J., et al.: AdaBoost on low-rank PSD matrices for metric learning with applications in Computer Aided Diagnosis. In: IEEE CVPR, pp. 1049–1056 (2011)
2. Yang, L., et al.: A Boosting framework for visuality-preserving distance metric learning and its application to medical image retrieval. TPAMI, 30–44 (2010)
3. Ong, E., Bowden, R.: A boosted classifier tree for hand shape detection. In: IEEE Int. Conf. Automatic Face & Gesture Recogn., pp. 889–894 (2004)
4. Cao, Z., Yin, Q., Tang, X., Sun, J.: Face recognition with learning-based descriptor. In: IEEE CVPR, pp. 2707–2714 (2010)
5. Guillaumin, M., Verbeek, J., Schmid, C.: Multimodal semi-supervised learning for image classification. In: IEEE CVPR, pp. 902–909 (2010)
6. Kumar, N., Berg, A.C., Belhumeur, P.N., Nayar, S.K.: Attribute and simile classifiers for face verification. In: IEEE ICCV, pp. 365–372 (2009)
7. Nowak, E., Jurie, F.: Learning visual similarity measures for comparing never seen objects. In: IEEE CVPR (2007)
8. Pinto, N., DiCarlo, J.J., Cox, D.D.: How far can you get with a modern face recognition test set using only simple features? In: IEEE CVPR (2009)
9. Shen, C., Kim, J., Wang, L.: A scalable dual approach to semidefinite metric learning. In: IEEE CVPR, pp. 2601–2608 (2011)
10. Jiang, N., Liu, W., Wu, Y.: Adaptive and Discriminative Metric Differential Tracking. In: IEEE CVPR (2011)
11. Xing, E., Ng, A., Jordan, M., Russell, S.: Distance metric learning, with application to clustering with side-information. NIPS 15, 505–512 (2002)
12. Shen, C., Kim, J., Wang, L., van den Hengel, A.: Positive semidefinite metric learning with boosting. In: NIPS (2009)
13. Bar-Hillel, A., Hertz, T., Shental, N., Weinshall, D.: Learning a mahalanobis metric from equivalence constraints. JMLR 6, 937–965 (2005)
14. Davis, J., Kulis, B., Jain, P., Sra, S., Dhillon, I.S.: Information-theoretic metric learning. In: ICML, pp. 209–216 (2007)
15. Cox, M., Cox, T.: Multidimensional Scaling. In: Handbooks Comp. Statistics, pp. 315–347. Springer (2008)
16. Tenenbaum, J., Silva, V., Langford, J.: A Global Geometric Framework for Nonlinear Dimensionality Reduction. Science 290, 2319–2323 (2000)

17. Roweis, S., Saul, L.: Nonlinear dimensionality reduction by locally linear embedding. Science 290, 2323–2326 (2000)
18. Vemuri, B.C., Liu, M., Amari, S.I., Nielsen, F.: Total Bregman divergence and its applications to DTI analysis. IEEE TMI 30, 475–483 (2011)
19. Shalev-Shwartz, S., Singer, Y., Ng, A.Y.: Online and batch learning of pseudo-metrics. In: ICML (2004)
20. Tsuda, K., Rsch, G., Warmuth, M.K.: Matrix exponentiated gradient updates for on-line learning and bregman projection. JMLR 6, 995–1018 (2005)
21. Jian, B., Vemuri, B.C.: Metric learning using iwasawa decomposition. In: IEEE ICCV, pp. 1–6 (2007)
22. Saberian, M.J., Vasconcelos, N.: Multiclass Boosting: Theory and Algorithms. In: NIPS (2011)
23. Liu, M., Vemuri, B.C.: Robust and efficient regularized boosting using total bregman divergence. In: IEEE CVPR, pp. 2897–2902 (2011)
24. Warmuth, M.K., Glocer, K.A., Vishwanathan, S.V.: Entropy regularized LPBoost. In: Int. Conf. Alg. Learn. Theory, pp. 256–271 (2008)
25. Liu, M., , Vemuri, B.C., Amari, S., Nielsen, F.: Shape retrieval using hierarchical total bregman soft clustering. IEEE TPAMI (2012)
26. Boyd, S., Vandenberghe, L.: Convex optimization. Cambridge University Press, Cambridge (2004)
27. Demiriz, A., Bennett, K.P., Shawe-Taylor, J.: Linear programming boosting via column generation. Mach. Learn. 46, 225–254 (2002)
28. Schapire, R., Singer, Y.: Improved boosting algorithms using confidence-rated predictions. Mach. Learn. 37, 297–336 (1999)
29. Frank, A., Asuncion, A.: UCI machine learning repository (2010)
30. Huang, G.B., Ramesh, M., Berg, T., Learned-Miller, E.: Labeled faces in the wild: A database for studying face recognition in unconstrained environments. In: ECCV (2008)
31. French, J., Watson, J., Jin, X., Martin, W.: An exogenous approach for adding multiple image representations to content-based image retrieval systems. In: Int. Sym. Signal Processing App., vol. 1, pp. 201–204 (2003)
32. Canny, J.: A computational approach to edge detection. IEEE TPAMI 8, 679–698 (1986)
33. Manjunath, B.S., Ma, W.: Texture features for browsing and retrieval of image data. IEEE TPAMI 18, 837–842 (1996)
34. Nguyen, H.V., Bai, L.: Cosine Similarity Metric Learning for Face Verification. In: Kimmel, R., Klette, R., Sugimoto, A. (eds.) ACCV 2010, Part II. LNCS, vol. 6493, pp. 709–720. Springer, Heidelberg (2011)
35. Yin, Q., Tang, X., Sun, J.: An Associate-Predict Model for Face Recognition. In: IEEE CVPR, pp. 497–504 (2011)
36. Taigman, Y., Wolf, L., Hassner, T., Tel-Aviv, I.: Multiple One-Shots for utilizing class label information. In: BMVC (2009)
37. Lowe, D.G.: Distinctive image features from scale-invariant keypoints. IJCV 60, 91–110 (2004)
38. Guillaumin, M., Verbeek, J., Schmid, C.: Is that you? metric learning approaches for face identification. In: IEEE ICCV, pp. 498–505 (2009)
39. Wolf, L., Hassner, T., Taigman, Y.: Similarity Scores Based on Background Samples. In: Zha, H., Taniguchi, R.-I., Maybank, S. (eds.) ACCV 2009, Part II. LNCS, vol. 5995, pp. 88–97. Springer, Heidelberg (2010)

A Discriminative Data-Dependent Mixture-Model Approach for Multiple Instance Learning in Image Classification

Qifan Wang, Luo Si, and Dan Zhang

Department of Computer Science
Purdue University
West Lafayette, IN, USA, 47907-2107
{wang868,lsi,zhang168}@purdue.edu

Abstract. Multiple Instance Learning (MIL) has been widely used in various applications including image classification. However, existing MIL methods do not explicitly address the multi-target problem where the distributions of positive instances are likely to be multi-modal. This strongly limits the performance of multiple instance learning in many real world applications. To address this problem, this paper proposes a novel discriminative data-dependent mixture-model method for multiple instance learning (MM-MIL) approach in image classification. The new method explicitly handles the multi-target problem by introducing a data-dependent mixture model, which allows positive instances to come from different clusters in a flexible manner. Furthermore, the kernelized representation of the proposed model allows effective and efficient learning in high dimensional feature space. An extensive set of experimental results demonstrate that the proposed new MM-MIL approach substantially outperforms several state-of-art MIL algorithms on benchmark datasets.

1 Introduction

With the pervasion of digital images, automatic image classification has become increasingly important. Multiple-instance learning (MIL) [2] is a useful technique in machine learning that addresses the classification problem of a bag of data instances. In multiple instance learning, each bag is composed of multiple data instances associated with input features. The purpose of MIL is to accurately predict bag level labels based on all the instances in each bag with the assumption that a bag is labeled positive if at least one of its instances is positive, whereas a negative bag only contains negative instances. In the case of image classification, each image is treated as a bag and different regions inside the image are viewed as individual data instances [15].

The advantage of MIL ascribes to the fact that in training it only requires the label information of a bag instead of individual instances in the bag. However, due to the label ambiguity in the instances, traditional supervised classification methods may not be directly applied to MIL framework. Existing methods in solving MIL problem fall into two categories. The first category is generative model based algorithms, such as axis parallel hyper-rectangles [2], Diverse Density (DD) [9] and Expectation Maximization

A. Fitzgibbon et al. (Eds.): ECCV 2012, Part IV, LNCS 7575, pp. 660–673, 2012.

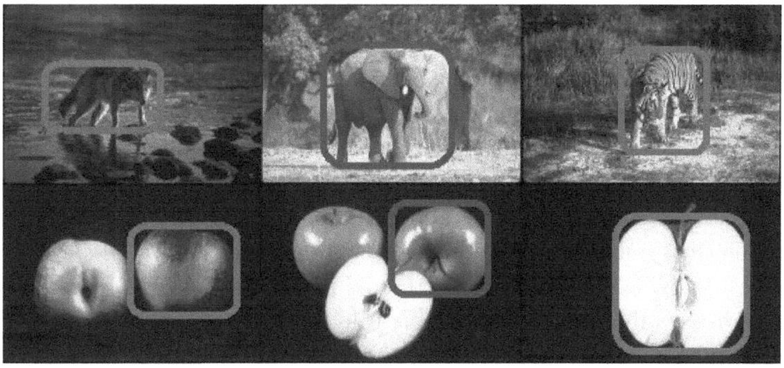

Fig. 1. Six images from COREL dataset. The top three images have a common concept 'animal'. The bottom three images form a concept 'apple'. Different colors represent different clusters the instances lie in.

DD (EM-DD) [10]. For example, EM-DD generates data instances in bags with their labels in a joint manner. The second category is discriminative model based methods including DD-SVM [7], MI-SVM [1], MILES [8], etc. These methods model the labels of bags and data instances by the input features of data instances or bags. For example, some methods based on SVM map features into a high dimensional feature space, with a non-linear function, and then apply the standard kernelized large-margin SVM framework to train a classifier from the constructed new features. These large margin discriminative methods often generate more robust results compared to the generative algorithms.

However, most existing multiple instance learning algorithms do not explicitly address the multi-target problem, where positive instances often tend to have multi-modal distributions or lie in different clusters in many real word applications. Two examples are provided as follows. In the first example the concept is 'animal'. There are various kinds of animals in the training samples like fox, elephant and tiger (top row in Fig.1). Different species have different characteristics in terms of color, size, shape, etc. Therefore, the positive instances come from distinct clusters and form a multi-modal distribution in the feature space. Even if the concept is relatively 'small', the instances could still form several compact clusters. In another scenario, the concept is 'apple'. The images in the bottom row in Fig.1 show three training examples. All the three images contain the concept 'apple'. However, the positive targets in the pictures are different as red apple, green apple and half-apple, which form different clusters. Please note that the multi-target problem of multiple instance learning is different from multi-class multiple instance learning since no specific class information is available for the diversified representation of positive instances and all positive bags are labeled in the same manner.

To address this problem, this paper proposes a novel data-dependent Mixture-Model MIL (MM-MIL) approach in the discriminative learning framework to handle the multi-modal distributions of positive data instances for image classification with multiple instance learning. In particular, a set of latent variables are introduced to represent the clusters associated with each data instance based on a multinomial logit model. Within each cluster, a logistic regression model is utilized to generate labels given the input features of individual data instances. These two models are integrated together for representing the assumption of multiple instance learning as each positive bag contains at least one positive data instance and each negative bag does not contain any positive instance. Furthermore, a kernelized presentation of the new method is proposed to allow effective and efficient learning in high-dimensional space. An efficient inference algorithm is derived for the proposed method based on a combination of Expectation and Maximization (EM) method and gradient descent optimization.

To our best knowledge, the MM-MIL model is the first concrete research work that explicitly addresses the multi-target problem in multiple instance learning. The main contributions of this paper are: First, the proposed MM-MIL model introduces a data-dependent mixture model that effectively captures the multi-modal distributions among the instances and formalizes the problem into a regularization framework. Second, we introduce an efficient inference algorithm to solve the optimization problem by combining the EM method and gradient descent scheme. Third, a kernelization framework is proposed to allow effective and efficient learning, especially for large scale image dataset.

The rest of the paper is organized as follows. Section 2 discusses the related work on MIL-based image classification. Section 3 proposes the novel MM-MIL method, which includes the problem formulation, the inference algorithm and the kernelization framework. We will also discuss the relationship between MM-MIL and some other existing MIL algorithms. Section 4 presents an extensive set of experimental results on different datasets for comparing the MM-MIL method with several state-of-the-art MIL algorithms. Section 5 concludes and points out some possible future research directions.

2 Related Work

Image classification algorithms based on multi-instance learning (MIL) model the relationship between labels and regions [2,10,7,8]. An image is treated as a bag consisting of multiple instances, ie, regions. Existing MIL algorithms can be divided into two categories, generative models and discriminative models. Generative model methods, like EM-DD [10], try to learn a single target distribution to generate instances/bags and their labels in a joint manner. Discriminative models focuses on modeling data/bag labels given features of data instances, which include MI-SVM [1] and MILES [8] based on kernelized support vector machine.

Many generative algorithms try to predict bag labels by first inferring the hidden labels of individual instances. The Diverse Density (DD) [9] approach uses a scaling and gradient search algorithm to find the prototype points in the instance space with the maximal DD value. Zhang and Goldman [10] combined the idea of Expectation-Maximization (EM) with DD and developed an algorithm, EM-DD, to search for the most likely concept. These methods are quite efficient in learning, but they are based on the assumption that that all positive instances form a tight cluster in the feature space [3], which is not realistic in applications with diversified positive instances. The research work in [9] briefly mentioned that it is possible to model multiple concepts within a generative model, but no concrete prior research work has been conducted for this. We also designed the first concrete generative multiple instance learning algorithm for multiple concepts in this paper. But the empirical results and discussions in section 4 show that our discriminative data-dependent mixture-model outperforms the generative model for multiple instance learning with multiple concepts.

Most discriminative methods attempt to directly predict bag labels in a large margin framework. DD-SVM [7] selects a set of instances using the DD function, and then a SVM is trained based on the bag-level features summarized by these selected instances. In MI-SVM [1], Andrews *et al* formulated MIL as a mixed integer quadratic programming problem. Integer variables are used to select a positive instance from each positive bag. A standard SVM framework is introduced to tune the variables. In the work of MILES [8], bags are embedded into a feature space defined by all the instances. 1-norm SVM is applied to train the bag-level classifiers. Some methods based on instance-level information were also proposed. Yang *et al* [11] proposed an Asymmetric Support Vector Machine-based MIL algorithm (ASVM-MIL) by defining an asymmetric loss function to exploit instance labels. Ray *et al* [17] extended the DD framework by using a Logistic Regression algorithm to estimate the equivalent probability for an instance and a $softmax$ function is used to combine the instance-level information to predict the bag label. Boosting methods such as MILBoost [13] translated MIL into an AdaBoost framework, where the combination function (eg, Integrated Segmentation and Recognition (ISR) or noisy-or) is applied to combine instance labels into bag label. Fu *et al* [3] proposed an instance selection MIL approach which aims to handle large scale data. A kernel density estimator is first learned from all the negative instances in negative bags to reduce the number of positive candidates. One instance per positive bag is selected to represent the concept. Standard SVM is then applied to train the classifier based on constructed bag-level features. Discriminative methods are often more robust and achieve improved performance compared to the generative approaches.

Recently, several MIL methods [23,27] has been used for online visual tracking. A discriminative classifier is trained in an online manner to separate the object from the background. Qi *et al* [6] explicitly modeled the inter-dependencies between instances by using concurrent tensors to better capture images' inherent semantics. Rank-1 tensor factorization is applied to obtain the label of each instance. A kernelization framework is then used for learning. In the work [25,32], Random Forest methods have been proposed to dealing with the multi-class/multi-label problem in MIL. Hidden class labels are defined inside bags as random variables. These random variables are optimized by training random forests and using a fast iterative homotopy method for solving the non-convex optimization problem. The multi-label issue is also addressed in work [5,26], where multi-label MIL algorithms are introduced to simultaneously captures both the connections between semantic labels and regions and the correlations among the labels based on hidden conditional random fields. Most recently, Dan *et al* [29,30] introduce the un-supervised learning methods under the maximum margin principle for multiple instance clustering, where bag labels are not utilized in training. A semi-supervised MIL approach [28] is also proposed by him in learning structured data. Multiple instance active learning for localized content based image retrieval is proposed in [32].

However, none of existing works in multiple instance learning addresses the multi-target problem where positive instances may lie in different clusters in the feature space.

To address this issue, we propose the MM-MIL algorithm, which will be described in the next section.

3 Mixture Model Multiple Instance Learning

This section presents the novel MM-MIL model that explicitly addresses the multi-target problem in multiple instance learning. We first introduce some notations. Let bag set $B = \{B_i\}, i = 1, 2, \ldots, N$. Let $L = \{l_i\}$ denotes the bag labels. $l_i = 1$ or 0 indicates B_i is a positive or negative bag. Let $B_i = \{B_{ij}\}, j = 1, 2, \ldots, N_i$ where B_{ij} is the jth instance in bag B_i. Let $y_i = P(+|B_i)$ denotes the probability of B_i being a positive bag and $y_{ij} = P(+|B_{ij})$ denotes the probability of B_{ij} being a positive instance.

3.1 Problem Formulation

Given B and L, our goal is to maximize the following conditional probability:

$$P(L|B) = \prod_{i=1}^{N} P(l_i|B_i) = \prod_{i=1}^{N} P(+|B_i)^{l_i}(1 - P(+|B_i))^{1-l_i} \tag{1}$$

In our method, we make a similar choice like many existing multiple instance learning works, eg, IS-MIL [3], for modeling $P(+|B_i)$ as follows:

$$P(+|B_i) = \max_j P(+|B_{ij}) \tag{2}$$

which means we select the instance with the maximum probability to be positive to represent the bag. This is also consistent with the MIL assumption. It is also possible to make other choices like a $softmax$ [17] to combine instance labels.

As we discussed in section 2, traditional MIL algorithms do not explicitly address the multi-target problem when modeling the probability of an instance being positive, ie, $P(+|B_{ij})$. For example, say the concept is 'animal' (Fig.1), the positive instance could lie in a cluster that stands for 'tiger' where the bag should be labeled as positive. It is also possible that the instance comes from an 'elephant' cluster which also indicates the bag positive. In order to capture the multi-modal distribution, we encode a data-dependent mixture model on $P(+|B_{ij})$ assuming that there are M clusters that represent the M targets in the feature space. A latent variable z_m is introduced to denote the mth cluster that the instance lies in. Then the probability of an instance to be positive can be written as:

$$P(+|B_{ij}) = \sum_{m=1}^{M} P(+|z_m, B_{ij})P(z_m|B_{ij}) \tag{3}$$

The first term $P(+|z_m, B_{ij})$ indicates the probability of B_{ij} being positive within cluster z_m. We use a logistic regression model for the purpose, which is similar with the logistic function chosen in [13] and [19]:

$$P(+|z_m, B_{ij}) = \frac{1}{1 + \exp(-t_m^T B_{ij})} \tag{4}$$

where t_m is the model parameter in the mth cluster. The second term, $P(z_m|B_{ij})$, in Eqn.3 indicates the probability that instance B_{ij} lies in the cluster z_m , which is actually a multi-class distribution and we apply a multinomial logit model to capture the underlying probability:

$$P(z_m|B_{ij}) = \frac{\exp(w_m^T B_{ij})}{\sum_{r=1}^{M} \exp(w_r^T B_{ij})} \tag{5}$$

where w_m is the model parameter. Both two parts in the mixture model are dependent on the data instance B_{ij}, which is more flexible to capture the dependencies among instances. Let $y_{ijm} = P(+|z_m, B_{ij})$, $\theta_{ijm} = P(z_m|B_{ij})$. Note that $\sum_m \theta_{ijm} = 1$ for every instance. Substituting Eqn. 2,3,4 and 5 into Eqn.1 and taking the negative logarithm on both sides we have:

$$E = -\sum_{i=1}^{N} \left((l_i \ln(\max_j \sum_{m=1}^{M} y_{ijm}\theta_{ijm}) + (1 - l_i) \ln(1 - \max_j \sum_{m=1}^{M} y_{ijm}\theta_{ijm}) \right) \tag{6}$$

Maximizing the probability in Eqn.1 is equivalent to minimize Eqn.6. In order to avoid overfitting, a regularizer is introduced on the model parameters, w_m and t_m. Then we obtain the following optimization problem:

$$\begin{aligned} \min_{w,t} \quad & -\sum_{i=1}^{N} \left((l_i \ln(\max_j \sum_{m=1}^{M} y_{ijm}\theta_{ijm}) + (1 - l_i) \ln(1 - \max_j \sum_{m=1}^{M} y_{ijm}\theta_{ijm}) \right) \\ & + \lambda \sum_{m=1}^{M} ||w_m||^2 + \beta \sum_{m=1}^{M} ||t_m||^2 \end{aligned} \tag{7}$$

where λ and β are weight parameters. We now describe an iterative EM and gradient descent algorithm for solving the above optimization problem.

3.2 Inference Algorithm

Directly minimizing Eqn.7 is intractable, as many terms are coupled together and a max function makes it non-differentiable. The EM framework is a powerful tool in learning mixture models [16]. In this section, we first derive an upper bound for Eqn.7 and then an iterative EM scheme is developed to solve the optimization problem.

Inspired by IS-MIL [3] and MI regression [21], in the E-step of each iteration, we remove the max function in Eqn.6 by choosing one instance per bag which has the maximum probability to be positive based on the previous w and t as follows:

$$j^* = arg \max_j \sum_{m=1}^{M} y_{ijm}\theta_{ijm} \tag{8}$$

Denote $y_{im} = y_{ij^*m}$, $\theta_{im} = \theta_{ij^*m}$ since j^* is fixed during the current iteration. Using the fact $\sum_m \theta_{im} = 1$, we can obtain $1 - \sum_{m=1}^{M} y_{im}\theta_{im} = \sum_{m=1}^{M} \theta_{im}(1 - y_{im})$. Then Eqn.6 can be written as:

$$\begin{aligned} E &= -\sum_{i=1}^{N}\left(l_i \ln(\sum_{m=1}^{M} y_{im}\theta_{im}) + (1-l_i)\ln(1-\sum_{m=1}^{M} y_{im}\theta_{im})\right) \\ &= -\sum_{i=1}^{N}\left(l_i \ln(\sum_{m=1}^{M} \theta_{im}y_{im}) + (1-l_i)\ln(\sum_{m=1}^{M} \theta_{im}(1-y_{im}))\right) \end{aligned} \tag{9}$$

We now establish an upper bound of Eqn. 9 with Jensen's inequality by observing that logarithm function is a concave function and $\sum_m \theta_{im} = 1$.

$$E \leq -\sum_{i=1}^{N}\sum_{m=1}^{M} \theta_{im}(l_i \ln y_{im} + (1-l_i)\ln(1-y_{im})) \tag{10}$$

Denote $\gamma_{im} = l_i \ln y_{im} + (1-l_i)\ln(1-y_{im})$. In M-step, using a similar divide-and-conquer strategy in [24], we minimize the above upper bound plus regularization terms by splitting it into two slightly simpler sub-problems. The idea is that we first fix $\theta_{im} = \theta_{im}^p$ that is obtained from the previous iteration, and then find t which optimize the following sub-problem:

$$SP1: \quad -\sum_{i=1}^{N}\sum_{m=1}^{M} \theta_{im}^p \gamma_{im} + \beta\sum_{m=1}^{M} ||t_m||^2 \tag{11}$$

Furthermore, we can fix $y_{im} = y_{im}^p$ that gives us γ_{im}^p and solve for the following optimization problem for γ:

$$SP2: \quad -\sum_{i=1}^{N}\sum_{m=1}^{M} \theta_{im}\gamma_{im}^p + \lambda\sum_{m=1}^{M} ||w_m||^2 \tag{12}$$

$SP1$ is essentially a combination of weighted logistic regression and $SP2$ can be viewed as a multi-class logistic regression. A direct gradient descent scheme could be applied for solving these two sub-problems. We refer to chapter 4.3 in [22] for full details. By solving $SP1$ and $SP2$ iteratively in the M-step, the obtained optimal solutions of w_m^* and t_m^* are then substituted into Eqn.8 to update the instance chosen from each bag.

3.3 Kernelization Framework

In this section, we will seek for optimal functions defined over the feature space on the basis of a kernelized representation of two sub-problems, $SP1$ and $SP2$. Consider $SP1$ first, since the objective function is point-wise, which only defines on the value of $t_m^T B_{ij}$ at the instances $\{B_{ij^*} : 1 <= i <= N\}$, based on the generalized representer theorem [20], the minimizer exists and has a representation of the form:

$$t_m^T B_{i'r} = \sum_{i=1}^{N} \alpha_{mi}^t k(B_{i'r}, B_{ij^*}) = \boldsymbol{k}_{B_{i'r}}^T \boldsymbol{\alpha_m^t} \tag{13}$$

where $k(B_{i'r}, B_{ij})$ is a kernel function defined on the feature space of instance. A Gaussian Kernel is defined as $k(B_{i'r}, B_{ij}) = exp(-\frac{||B_{i'r} - B_{ij}||^2}{2\sigma^2})$, σ^2 is the radius parameter. Substituting Eqn.13 into $SP1$, we obtain:

$$SP1_{ker} : -\sum_{m=1}^{M}((\boldsymbol{\theta l})_{\boldsymbol{m}}^{\boldsymbol{T}}\boldsymbol{K}\boldsymbol{\alpha}_{\boldsymbol{m}}^{\boldsymbol{t}} - \boldsymbol{\theta}_{\boldsymbol{m}}^{\boldsymbol{T}}\ln(1+\exp(\boldsymbol{K}\boldsymbol{\alpha}_{\boldsymbol{m}}^{\boldsymbol{t}}))) + \beta\sum_{m=1}^{M}(\boldsymbol{\alpha}_{\boldsymbol{m}}^{\boldsymbol{t}})^{\boldsymbol{T}}\boldsymbol{K}\boldsymbol{\alpha}_{\boldsymbol{m}}^{\boldsymbol{t}} \quad (14)$$

where $\boldsymbol{\theta}_{\boldsymbol{m}}^{\boldsymbol{T}} = [\theta_{1m}^p, \ldots, \theta_{Nm}^p]$, $(\boldsymbol{\alpha}_{\boldsymbol{m}}^{\boldsymbol{t}})^{\boldsymbol{T}} = [\alpha_{m1}^t, \ldots, \alpha_{mN}^t]$, $(\boldsymbol{\theta l})_{\boldsymbol{m}}^{\boldsymbol{T}} = [\theta_{1m}^p l_1, \ldots, \theta_{Nm}^p l_N]$ and $\boldsymbol{K}$ is the Gram matrix with the kernel function defined above. To solve $SP1_{ker}$, we derive the partial derivative w.r.t. $\boldsymbol{\alpha}_{\boldsymbol{m}}^{\boldsymbol{t}}$:

$$\frac{\partial SP1_{ker}}{\boldsymbol{\alpha}_{\boldsymbol{m}}^{\boldsymbol{t}}} = -(\boldsymbol{\theta l})_{\boldsymbol{m}}^{\boldsymbol{T}}\boldsymbol{K} + \boldsymbol{\theta}_{\boldsymbol{m}}{}^{\boldsymbol{T}}\frac{\exp(\boldsymbol{K}\boldsymbol{\alpha}_{\boldsymbol{m}}^{\boldsymbol{t}})}{1+\exp(\boldsymbol{K}\boldsymbol{\alpha}_{\boldsymbol{m}}^{\boldsymbol{t}})}\boldsymbol{K} + 2\beta(\boldsymbol{\alpha}_{\boldsymbol{m}}^{\boldsymbol{t}})^{\boldsymbol{T}}\boldsymbol{K} \quad (15)$$

With this obtained gradient, L-BFGS quasi-Newton method [18] is applied to solve this optimization problem. Similar to the work [12] and [4], the minimizer of $SP2$ has a form:

$$w_m^T B_{i'r} = \sum_{i=1}^{N}\alpha_{mi}^w k(B_{i'r}, B_{ij^*}) = \boldsymbol{k}_{B_{i'r}}^T\boldsymbol{\alpha}_{\boldsymbol{m}}^{\boldsymbol{w}} \quad (16)$$

Substituting Eqn.16 into $SP2$, we obtain:

$$SP2_{ker} : -\sum_{i=1}^{N}\sum_{m=1}^{M}\gamma_{im}^p\frac{\exp(\boldsymbol{k}_{\boldsymbol{B}_{\boldsymbol{ij*}}^{\boldsymbol{T}}}\boldsymbol{\alpha}_{\boldsymbol{m}}^{\boldsymbol{w}})}{\sum_r\exp(\boldsymbol{k}_{\boldsymbol{B}_{\boldsymbol{ij*}}^{\boldsymbol{T}}}\boldsymbol{\alpha}_{\boldsymbol{r}}^{\boldsymbol{w}})} + \lambda\sum_{m=1}^{M}(\boldsymbol{\alpha}_{\boldsymbol{m}}^{\boldsymbol{w}})^{\boldsymbol{T}}\boldsymbol{K}\boldsymbol{\alpha}_{\boldsymbol{m}}^{\boldsymbol{w}} \quad (17)$$

The scheme for solve $SP2_{ker}$ is contained in [12], we refer to section 5 in [12] for details on the optimization algorithm of the above multi-class kernel logistic regression. The complete kernelization framework for MM-MIL is shown in Table 1. Note that in the kernelization framework, the parameters are $\boldsymbol{\alpha}^{\boldsymbol{t}}$ and $\boldsymbol{\alpha}^{\boldsymbol{w}}$, which are updated in the M-step and are fixed and utilized to calculate y_{ijm} and θ_{ijm} in the E-step.

3.4 Discussion

In the novel MM-MIL model, M is the number of latent clusters formed by the instances. Different M will have different behavior. When M equals 1, which means we assume all instance comes from one cluster, then Eqn.9 becomes:

$$E = -\sum_{i=1}^{N}(l_i \ln y_i + (1-l_i)\ln(1-y_i)) \quad (18)$$

Now we discuss the relationship between our MM-MIL and some previous methods when $M = 1$. If choosing $\ln y_i$ to be a quadratic loss function, Eqn.18 is exactly the EM-DD model. When modeling $\ln y_i$ by a logistic loss function, the above model turns out to be MI-Regression in work [21]. If putting a hinge loss function on $\ln y_i$, then Eqn.18 could be optimized using a standard SVM framework in a similar way to MI-SVM [1] and MILES [8]. With a value of M larger than 1, ie, the latent number of

Table 1. Our full kernelized MM-MIL inference framework

Initialize M,λ,β,σ and $\boldsymbol{K}$
Initialize parameters $\boldsymbol{\alpha^t}$ and $\boldsymbol{\alpha^w}$
Start EM iterations
E-step:
Calculate y_{ijm} based on Eqns.4 and 13
Calculate θ_{ijm} based on Eqns.5 and 16
Select one instance per bag from Eqn.8
M-step:
Obtain $\boldsymbol{\alpha^t}$ by solving $SP1_{ker}$
Obtain $\boldsymbol{\alpha^w}$ by solving $SP2_{ker}$
Update θ_{im} and γ_{im} by Eqns.4,5,13 and 16
Repeat the above three steps until convergence
Update $\boldsymbol{\alpha^t}$ and $\boldsymbol{\alpha^w}$ repeat EM iteration until convergence

clusters increase, which makes our model more flexible in modeling the dependencies between the instances. The desired value of M can be obtained by cross-validation or utilizing some model selection criterions like the Bayesian Information Criterion. This work uses cross validation and the empirical studies in section 4 show that robust classification results can often be obtained with a reasonably wide range of M values.

4 Experimental Results

In this section, the MM-MIL is evaluated with three configurations of experiments. First, MM-MIL is evaluated on several multi-target datasets to show the advantage of data-dependent mixture model against several existing algorithms in this setting. Second, MM-MIL is compared with existing MIL approaches in image classification on the commonly used COREL and SIVAL benchmark datasets. Third, we provide more experimental results to study the choice of M in terms of classification accuracy.

Each image is a bag and segments are instances. A set of low-level features is extracted from each segment to represent an instance, including color correlogram, color moment, region size, wavelet texture and shape. Some model parameters in our experiment are Gaussian Kernel radius σ^2, and the weight parameters λ and β. We apply a twofold cross-validation on the training set to obtain the optimal values. σ^2 is chosen from 1 to 15 where λ and β are selected from $0.01, 0.1, 1, 10, 100$. The number of hidden clusters M is picked in the same manner from 1 to 15. During each experiment, images are randomly partitioned into two halves to form the training and the testing sets. Each experiment is repeated 10 times and the average results are calculated.

4.1 Evaluation on Multi-Target Datasets

In order to illustrate the ability of MM-MIL in capturing the multi-modal concepts, we merge several categories that form similar concepts together into a lager dataset. Within our experiment, we construct three such merged data sets. The first merged data set, we refer to MergeData1, is collected from the *Tiger*, *Fox* and *Elephant* data set [1] which

Fig. 2. Examples of positive instances selected from different clusters (three different colors). The left three columns are from MergeData2 and the right three columns are from MergeData3. The first and third row contains twelve original images and the second and fourth row shows the corresponding segmented regions.

form a general concept 'animal'. The are 600 images in MergeData1 with 300 positive images and 300 negative ones. The second data set, MergeData2, is mixed from three SIVAL categories, ie, *DataMiningBook*, *RapBook* and *StripedNotebook*, containing a common concept 'book'. MergeData3 is combined by another three classes, *CardboardBox*, *FabricSoftenerBox* and *GreenTeaBox*, from SIVAL data set, where 'box' is the ideal concept. Both MergeData2 and MergeData3 contain 360 images with half positive images and half negative images, where the negative ones are randomly chosen from other categories.

Various measurements can be applied for evaluating the performance. In our experiments we will use AUC (area under the ROC curve), which is a widely used metric in multi-instance learning tasks. The ROC curve shows the relationship between the true positive rate and the false positive rate, and AUC measures the probability that a randomly chosen positive image will be ranked higher than a randomly chosen negative image [6].

We compare our MM-MIL with EM-DD, MI-SVM, mi-SVM, DD-SVM, MILES, IS-MIL and MIForest. In order to obtain a full comparison, we also implement a generative multiple instance learning algorithm MC-EMDD for multiple concepts within the EM-DD framework as we mentioned in section 2. In MC-EMDD, y_{ij} is modeled by $P(+|B_{ij}) = \max_t P(+_t|B_{ij})$ where $+_t$ is the tth disjunctive concept [9]. The results are given in Table 2, which show that MM-MIL achieves the best results among the key MIL methods on all three merged datasets. This is because all these merged data sets strongly reflect the multi-target problem, and MM-MIL can effectively model this underlying pattern with a data-dependent mixture. Although MC-EMDD also considers multi-modal concepts, the results of MM-MIL are substantially better. Our hypothesis is that MM-MIL benefits from both the smaller asymptotic error rate as a discriminative model and the data-dependent mixture modeling, while MC-EMDD is a generative model and can be shown to use data-independent mixtures. Different from previous methods, the proposed MM-MIL can not only label the regions (instances), but also tell which cluster a positive instance lies in by computing the *posterior* probability $P(z_m|B_{ij},+)$. Figures 1 and 2 show several examples of positive instances selected from different bags. As illustrated, the new MM-MIL algorithm successfully localizes the target regions from each image and explicitly identifies the latent cluster the target belongs to.

Table 2. Average AUC for merged datasets and benchmark datasets by different algorithms

Algorithms	MergeData1	MergeData2	MergeData3	COREL	SIVAL
EM-DD [10]	0.543	0.643	0.661	0.564	0.687
MC-EMDD	0.602	0.694	0.718	0.616	0.691
MI-SVM [1]	0.536	0.628	0.652	0.535	0.698
mi-SVM [1]	0.542	0.614	0.674	0.557	0.683
DD-SVM [7]	0.568	0.671	0.704	0.675	0.762
MILES [8]	0.574	0.682	0.726	0.683	0.814
MIForest [25]	0.669	0.675	0.731	0.671	0.784
IS-MIL [3]	0.661	0.745	0.768	0.697	0.805
MM-MIL	**0.713**	**0.815**	**0.854**	**0.790**	**0.819**

4.2 Evaluation on Benchmark Datasets

The COREL dataset contains 2000 images from 20 different categories, with 100 images in each category and the SIVAL benchmark includes 25 different image categories with 60 images in each. COREL images contain various scenes and objects, eg, building, bus and elephant, where the target is typically close-ups and centered in the image. SIVAL consists of images of single objects photographed under different backgrounds, where objects may occur anywhere spatially in the image and also may be photographed at a wide-angle or close up. These two benchmarks were used extensively in the previous MIL researches [7,8,6,5,14]. The COREL dataset contains diversified positive instances while SIVAL dataset generally contains images with a single object in each category.

MM-MIL is compared with EM-DD, MI-SVM, mi-SVM, DD-SVM, MILES, IS-MIL and MIForest on these two benchmark datasets. M is chosen by cross-validation as in section 4.1. The average AUC results are reported in Table 2 and it shows that MM-MIL outperforms other methods on both COREL and SIVAL datasets. The AUC difference between MM-MIL and previous methods on SIVAL is relative small, whereas the difference on COREL is larger. The reason is that for one category, the targets from COREL images have very different features. For example, the 'Dinosaur' category consists of various kinds of dinosaurs. While in SIVAL dataset, each category contains one identical object with different backgrounds. Therefore, the AUC gap between MM-MIL and existing method is larger on COREL than that on SIVAL images. The superior performance of our method against existing discriminative MIL methods is mainly because: traditional MIL approaches are trying to learn one classifier for all instances/bags based on SVM framework, while our method first learn to separate instances into different clusters, and then a classifier is trained inside each cluster. Therefore, our MM-MIL method is more powerful in capturing the underlying patterns of the distribution of instances.

4.3 Experiments with Different Number of Hidden Mixtures

Figure 3 illustrates how the performance of MM-MIL varies with different values of M as the number of clusters. We plot the average AUC of MergeData1, MergeData2, MergeData3, COREL and SIVAL against the number of clusters from 1 to 10. When M equals 1, our proposed method degrades to a logistic regression model and has almost the same power as existing discriminative algorithms. With increases of M, up to a certain value, the performance saturates, which represents the true underlying pattern in the dataset. As illustrated in Figure 3, the saturated M in MergeData1, MergeData2 and MergeData3 is around 3 which capture the true clusters in these datasets. The AUC curve of COREL keeps increasing till M approaches 6, while the SIVAL curve is almost flat since there is a single target in SIVAL dataset from each category. It can be seen from Figure 3 that MM-MIL generates accurate results with a reasonably wide range of M values.

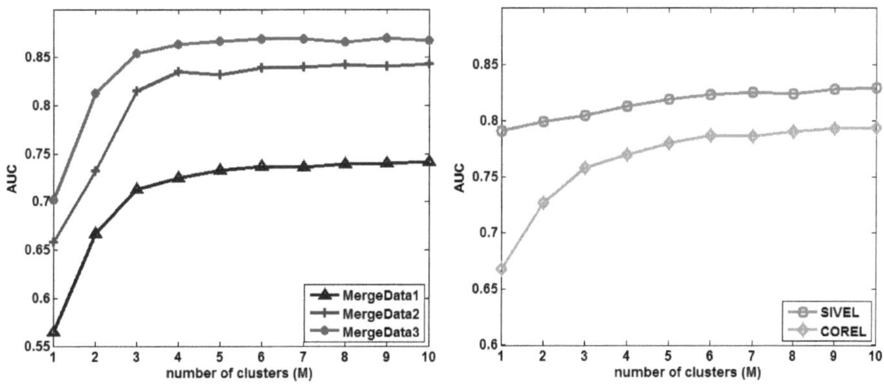

Fig. 3. AUC curves on different number of clusters for MergeData, COREL and SIVAL

5 Conclusions

Multiple instance learning is an important research topic with many applications such as image classification. Existing MIL methods do not explicitly address the multi-target problem where the distributions of positive instances are likely to be multi-modal in many practical applications. This paper presents a novel data-dependent mixture-model approach in the discriminative framework for multiple instance learning, which explicitly addresses the multi-target problem. Furthermore, a kernelized framework is proposed to allow efficient modeling within high dimensional feature space. Empirical results in image classification have shown that the new method outperforms several existing MIL algorithms on several datasets with multi-target positive instances and is consistently better than existing algorithms on benchmark datasets.

There are several possibilities to extend the research in this paper. For example, we plan to investigate different methods of combining instance labels to bag labels. We also plan to study the behavior of different types of kernels used in the classification. Furthermore, we plan to explore a non-parametric Bayesian method for modeling mixtures.

Acknowledgments. This work is partially supported by NSF research grants IIS-0746830, CNS-1012208 and IIS-1017837. This work also partially supported by the Center for Science of Information (CSoI), an NSF Science and Technology Center, under grant agreement CCF-0939370.

References

1. Andrews, S., Tsochantaridis, I., Hofmann, T.: Support Vector Machines for Multiple-Instance Learning. In: NIPS, pp. 561–568 (2002)
2. Dietterich, T.G., Lathrop, R.H., Lozano-Pérez, T.: Solving the Multiple Instance Problem with Axis-Parallel Rectangles. Artif. Intell. 89(1-2), 31–71 (1997)
3. Fu, Z., Robles-Kelly, A.: An Instance Selection Approach to Multiple Instance Learning. In: CVPR (2009)
4. Hu, Y., Li, M., Yu, N.: Multiple-Instance Ranking: Learning to Rank Images for Image Retrieval. In: CVPR (2008)
5. Zha, Z., Hua, X., Mei, T., Wang, J., Qi, G., Wang, Z.: Joint Multi-Label Multi-Instance Learning for Image Classification. In: CVPR (2008)
6. Qi, G., Hua, X., Rui, Y., Mei, T., Tang, J., Zhang, H.: Concurrent Multiple Instance Learning for Image Categorization. In: CVPR (2007)
7. Chen, Y., Wang, J.Z.: Image Categorization by Learning and Reasoning with Regions. Journal of Machine Learning Research (5), 913–939 (2004)
8. Chen, Y., Bi, J., Wang, J.Z.: MILES: Multiple-Instance Learning via Embedded Instance Selection. IEEE Trans. Pattern Anal. Mach. Intell. 28(12), 1931–1947 (2006)
9. Maron, O., Lozano-Pérez, T.: A Framework for Multiple-Instance Learning. In: NIPS (1997)
10. Zhang, Q., Goldman, S.A.: EM-DD: An Improved Multiple-Instance Learning Technique. In: NIPS (2001)
11. Yang, C., Dong, M., Hua, J.: Region-based Image Annotation using Asymmetrical Support Vector Machine-based Multiple-Instance Learning. In: CVPR (2006)
12. Zhu, J., Hastie, T.: Kernel logistic regression and the import vector machine. Journal of Computational and Graphical Statistics 14(1), 185–205 (2005)
13. Viola, P.A., Platt, J.C., Zhang, C.: Multiple Instance Boosting for Object Detection. In: NIPS (2005)
14. Rahmani, R., Goldman, S.A.: MISSL: Multiple-Instance Semi-supervised Learning. In: ICML (2006)
15. Maron, O., Ratan, A.L.: Multiple-Instance Learning for Natural Scene Classification. In: ICML (1998)
16. Si, L., Jin, R.: Flexible Mixture Model for Collaborative Filtering. In: ICML, pp. 704–711 (2003)
17. Ray, S., Craven, M.: Supervised Versus Multiple Instance Learning: An Empirical Comparison. In: ICML (2005)

18. Liu, D.C., Nocedal, J.: On the limited memory BFGS method for large scale optimization. Mathematical Programming 45(1-3), 503–528 (1989)
19. Lin, Z., Hua, G., Davis, L.S.: Multiple Instance Feature for Robust Part-based Object Detection. In: CVPR (2009)
20. Schölkopf, B., Herbrich, R., Smola, A.J.: A Generalized Representer Theorem. In: Helmbold, D.P., Williamson, B. (eds.) COLT/ EuroCOLT 2001. LNCS (LNAI), vol. 2111, pp. 416–426. Springer, Heidelberg (2001)
21. Ray, S., Page, D.: Multiple Instance Regression. In: ICML, pp. 425–432 (2001)
22. Bishop, C.M.: Pattern Recognition and Machine Learning. Springer Science, Business Media, LLC (2006)
23. Babenko, B., Yang, M.-H., Belongie, S.J.: Visual tracking with online Multiple Instance Learning. In: CVPR (2009)
24. Wang, Q., Tao, L., Di, H.: A Globally Optimal Approach for 3D Elastic Motion Estimation from Stereo Sequences. In: Daniilidis, K., Maragos, P., Paragios, N. (eds.) ECCV 2010, Part IV. LNCS, vol. 6314, pp. 525–538. Springer, Heidelberg (2010)
25. Leistner, C., Saffari, A., Bischof, H.: MIForests: Multiple-Instance Learning with Randomized Trees. In: Daniilidis, K., Maragos, P., Paragios, N. (eds.) ECCV 2010, Part VI. LNCS, vol. 6316, pp. 29–42. Springer, Heidelberg (2010)
26. Xue, X., Zhang, W., Zhang, J., Wu, B., Fan, J., Lu, Y.: Correlative Multi-Label Multi-Instance Image Annotation. In: ICCV (2011)
27. Zeisl, B., Leistner, C., Saffari, A., Bischof, H.: On-line Semi-supervised mMultiple-instance Boosting. In: CVPR (2010)
28. Zhang, D., Liu, Y., Si, L., Zhang, J., Lawrence, R.D.: Multiple Instance Learning on Structred Data. In: NIPS (2011)
29. Zhang, D., Wang, F., Si, L., Li, T.: M3IC: Maximum Margin Multiple Instance Clustering. In: IJCAI (2009)
30. Zhang, D., Wang, F., Si, L., Li, T.: Maximum Margin Multiple Instance Clustering With Applications to Image and Text Clustering. IEEE Transactions on Neural Networks 22(5), 739–751 (2011)
31. Vezhnevets, A., Buhmann, J.M.: Towards Weakly Supervised Semantic Segmentation by Means of Multiple Instance and Multitask learning. In: CVPR (2010)
32. Zhang, D., Wang, F., Shi, Z., Zhang, C.: Interactive Localized Content-Based Image Retrieval with Multiple Instance Active Learning. Pattern Recognition 43(2), 478–484 (2010)

No Bias Left behind: Covariate Shift Adaptation for Discriminative 3D Pose Estimation

Makoto Yamada[1], Leonid Sigal[2], and Michalis Raptis[2]

[1] NTT Communication Science Laboratories
[2] Disney Research Pittsburgh
yamada@sg.cs.titech.ac.jp, {lsigal,mraptis}@disneyresearch.com

Abstract. Discriminative, or (structured) prediction, methods have proved effective for variety of problems in computer vision; a notable example is 3D monocular pose estimation. All methods to date, however, relied on an assumption that training (source) and test (target) data come from the same underlying joint distribution. In many real cases, including standard datasets, this assumption is flawed. In presence of training set bias, the learning results in a biased model whose performance degrades on the (target) test set. Under the assumption of covariate shift we propose an unsupervised domain adaptation approach to address this problem. The approach takes the form of training instance re-weighting, where the weights are assigned based on the ratio of training and test marginals evaluated at the samples. Learning with the resulting *weighted* training samples, alleviates the bias in the learned models. We show the efficacy of our approach by proposing weighted variants of Kernel Regression (KR) and Twin Gaussian Processes (TGP). We show that our weighted variants outperform their un-weighted counterparts and improve on the state-of-the-art performance in the public (HumanEva) dataset.

1 Introduction

Many problems in computer vision can be expressed in the form of (structured) predictions of real-valued multivariate output, $\boldsymbol{y} \in \mathbb{R}^{d_y}$, from a high-dimensional multivariate input, $\boldsymbol{x} \in \mathbb{R}^{d_x}$. In this paper, we focus on such models in the context of articulated 3D pose estimation.

Articulated 3D pose estimation, particularly from monocular images and/or video, is a challenging problem due to variability in person appearance, pose, body shape, lighting, and motion. Despite these challenges, discriminative methods, have proved to be effective in recovering the 3D pose [1–17] in variety of scenarios. In these methods the goal is to learn a direct (and often multi-modal) mapping, $f : \mathbb{R}^{d_x} \rightarrow \mathbb{R}^{d_y}$, from image features (e.g., bag-of-words of HoG or SIFT descriptors) $\boldsymbol{x} \in \mathbb{R}^{d_x}$ to 3D poses $\boldsymbol{y} \in \mathbb{R}^{d_y}$, typically expressed as joint positions or angles. Probabilistic formulations do so by learning the conditional distribution $p(\boldsymbol{y}|\boldsymbol{x})$ based on the training dataset of n_{tr} image-pose pairs – $\{(\boldsymbol{x}_i^{\text{tr}}, \boldsymbol{y}_i^{\text{tr}})\}_{i=1}^{n_{\text{tr}}}$ (assumed to be independent and identically distributed (i.i.d.) samples from the underlying joint density $p_{\text{tr}}(\boldsymbol{x}, \boldsymbol{y})$). A number of methods

A. Fitzgibbon et al. (Eds.): ECCV 2012, Part IV, LNCS 7575, pp. 674–687, 2012.

[1–17] of this form have been proposed over the last decade that explore a gamut of models, image features and learning architectures. However, in *all* cases it has been assumed that the training and test distributions are one and the same, i.e., $p_{\text{tr}}(\boldsymbol{x}, \boldsymbol{y}) = p_{\text{te}}(\boldsymbol{x}, \boldsymbol{y})$, and hence the model learned using the training feature-pose pairs can be directly applied to the test image features, $\boldsymbol{x}^{\text{te}}$, to infer the output 3D pose $\boldsymbol{y}^{\text{te}}$.

The problem of *dataset bias* is starting to emerge as very prominent issue in object categorization [18–22], where even large datasets (e.g., LabelMe or ImageNet) have shown to exhibit significant (and often unexpected) biases [22] in the form of lighting, object appearance and viewpoint to name a few. We argue that similar issues exist in 3D pose estimation and need to be addressed if one is to build a system that works outside of well calibrated laboratory setups and datasets. The issues of dataset bias and overfitting to the training set, in 3D pose estimation, are evident from poor generalization that one often sees when applying such models to novel data. In addition, we argue that *within* dataset bias is, at least in certain cases, as prevalent as the *between* dataset bias. While in dataset creation an effort is typically made to make the training and test sets as similar as possible, this is difficult to achieve precisely. For example, Urtasun and Darrell in [16] show that performance decreases dramatically (to as low as 25% of the baseline) when training and test sequences are disjoint[1]. Note that this is despite the fact that, even in the disjoint case, training and test sequences were captured by the same static cameras and with no appreciable difference in subject appearance and lighting. Similar degradation of performance is often observed when a subject is not included in the training set, or when training data comes from multiple subjects (and/or motions) and at the test time only a single subject (and/or motion) is observed [5].

Unfortunately, the domain adaptation approaches proposed in [18–21] are not adequate for addressing the bias in this case. First, they typically assume categorical classification, as opposed to multi-valued (structured) predictions. Second, and more importantly, they are supervised and assume existence of one or more labeled instances from the test set to allow the transfer learning to fine tune the source model to a target test set. In many scenarios, such as, 3D pose estimation, obtaining 3D pose for a test image is infeasible. To this end, we formulate a novel training instance re-weighting mechanism for addressing the bias in (structured) prediction problems under the assumption of a *covariate shift* [24] in an unsupervised manner; where we assume that $p(\boldsymbol{y}|\boldsymbol{x}) = p_{\text{tr}}(\boldsymbol{y}|\boldsymbol{x}) = p_{\text{te}}(\boldsymbol{y}|\boldsymbol{x})$, but the marginals are different ($p_{\text{tr}}(\boldsymbol{x}) \neq p_{\text{te}}(\boldsymbol{x})$).

Contributions: The key contributions of this work is to shed some light on the potential issues of dataset bias in the structured prediction problems, mainly, 3D pose estimation, and to propose a simple, yet effective, solution for handling such bias through training instance re-weighting in a covariate shift adaptation formulation. We illustrate the efficacy of our approach by proposing weighted

[1] The baseline sampled training/test sets on per-frame bases from the full HumanEva-I [23] dataset.

variants of Kernel Regression and Twin Gaussian Processes and showing that they outperform their non-weighted counterparts in various setups and with different image features. As a consequence we achieve state-of-the-art performance on HumanEva-I dataset. The proposed training instance re-weighting, however, is general and is amenable to most popular formulations (e.g., Linear Regression, Mixture of Experts, GPLVM, Kernel Information Embeddings), as well as to other (structured) prediction problems in computer vision.

2 Related Work

Discriminative models are popular in vision for various tasks, including 3D human pose [1–17], human shape [25], hand pose [26, 27] and face pose [28] estimation. The focus of this paper is on 3D pose estimation which we discuss next; we also discuss transfer learning techniques that motivated our approach.

A variety of (structured) prediction methods have been proposed for 3D pose estimation in the literature, including Nearest Neighbor regression (NN) [13], linear Locally-Weighted Regression (LWR) [13], Linear Regression (LR) [2], Relevance Vector Regression (RVR) [2], Kernel Regression (KR) [13] and Gaussian Process Regression (GPR) [17]. The observation that the mapping from image features to 3D pose is typically multi-modal, due to inherent imaging ambiguities, has led to introduction of multi-modal alternatives and mixture models, including Mixture of Linear Regressors (MoLR) [1], conditional Bayesian Mixture of Experts (cMoE) [4, 8, 14, 15], Local GP Regression (LGPR) [16] and Twin Gaussian Processes (TGP) [5], to name a few. Mixture models, such as MoLR and cMoE, can produce multiple solutions (one for each expert) with the hope that ambiguities can be resolved by an oracle [4, 8] or over time [14]; alternatively, optimization can be used to ascend to the most prominent mode of the conditional distribution [5]. We leverage these prior methods and propose an Importance Weighted Twin Gaussian Processes (IWTGP) model, based on TGP [5], where importance weights adopt the model to the test data at hand in an un-supervised fashion.

The methods outlined above differ significantly in learning and inference. The issue of learning from large datasets was addressed in [4] using a forward feature selection and bound optimization, allowing training of cMoE models from upward of 100,000 input-output samples. A competing issue of learning from small datasets has also received much attention, with most methods converging on intermediate shared low-dimensional latent representations (e.g., shared GPLVM (sGPLVM) [6, 9] or shared Kernel Information Embeddings (sKIE) [12]) to address overfitting with few input-output samples; some formulations were shown to be amenable semi-supervised learning settings [8, 9, 12] where a large number of *unpaired* marginal samples, which are drawn from the training distribution (not test distribution), are available. We deal with training from large datasets, as in [16] and [5], by first selecting an active set of input-output pairs (k Nearest Neighbors to the test input feature vector $\boldsymbol{x}$) and then learning an IWTGP model for this reduced set. This results in a fixed model and inference complexity regardless of training set size (apart from the initial kNN lookup).

Our method is also motivated by recent works that study effects of dataset biases in vision. The issue of dataset bias has recently emerged as a serious problem in object categorization, with Torralba and Efros [22] showing that significant biases exist in all current datasets. As a result, techniques for *domain adaptation* in object categorization are starting to emerge [18–21]. However, unlike our method, the focus of such techniques, so far, has been on a supervised setting where one or more labeled examples are available at test time (in the target domain). This allows the source models, obtained using training data, to be adopted to the target test domain explicitly. A more recent variant by Kulis *et al.* [19] introduces a method for doing this in a cross-domain setting, where the representation of the features at train and test time may in itself be different. Our setting, here, is substantially different, however, as we assume that no labeled instances are present at test time. This makes the problem more challenging, but at the same time more realistic for our target application, as it is unreasonable to assume that accurate 3D pose can be annotated for monocular test images. This setting is a special case of domain adaptation known as *covariate shift* [24], where the training distribution $p_{\mathrm{tr}}(\boldsymbol{x})$ and test distribution $p_{\mathrm{te}}(\boldsymbol{x})$ over the inputs are different (i.e., $p_{\mathrm{tr}}(\boldsymbol{x}) \neq p_{\mathrm{te}}(\boldsymbol{x})$) but the conditional distribution of output values, $p(\boldsymbol{y}|\boldsymbol{x})$, remains same.

The influence of the covariate shift could be mitigated by re-weighting of the log likelihood terms according to their importance within the test set. Since the importance is generally unknown, the key issue of covariate shift adaptation is to estimate these importance weights accurately. Following this idea, several direct importance weight estimation methods have been recently proposed [29–32]. In this paper, we adopt a novel importance weight estimation method called *relative unconstrained least-squares importance fitting* (RuLSIF) [32], since it holds practical advantage over competing methods. Mainly, it is computationally efficient and can naturally control the *adaptiveness* to the test distribution. In contrast to [32], however, we adopt RuLSIF for (structured) real-valued predictions and illustrate it's efficacy on a real-world vision problem.

3 Covariate Shift in 3D Pose Estimation

At first glance, it may not be evident why dataset bias plays a role in discriminative models, considering that discriminative methods are trying to model the conditional distribution $p(\boldsymbol{y}|\boldsymbol{x})$ and it seems reasonable to assume that $p(\boldsymbol{y}|\boldsymbol{x}) = p_{\mathrm{tr}}(\boldsymbol{y}|\boldsymbol{x}) = p_{\mathrm{te}}(\boldsymbol{y}|\boldsymbol{x})$ (even if $p_{\mathrm{tr}}(\boldsymbol{x}, \boldsymbol{y}) \neq p_{\mathrm{te}}(\boldsymbol{x}, \boldsymbol{y})$). In other words, how can the fact that $p_{\mathrm{tr}}(\boldsymbol{x}) \neq p_{\mathrm{te}}(\boldsymbol{x})$ effect the conditional distribution? The issue is that the conditional models assume a certain functional form and typically choose the optimal parameters (within this functional form) by minimizing the average regression error (i.e., average discrepancy between the predicted and true values on the *training* set). Intuitively this means that the learned model performs more accurately in the denser regions than in the sparser regions of $p_{\mathrm{tr}}(\boldsymbol{x})$, because the denser regions dominate the average regression error. Hence, if $p_{\mathrm{tr}}(\boldsymbol{x}) \neq p_{\mathrm{te}}(\boldsymbol{x})$, the learned model may no longer be *optimal* for the test set.

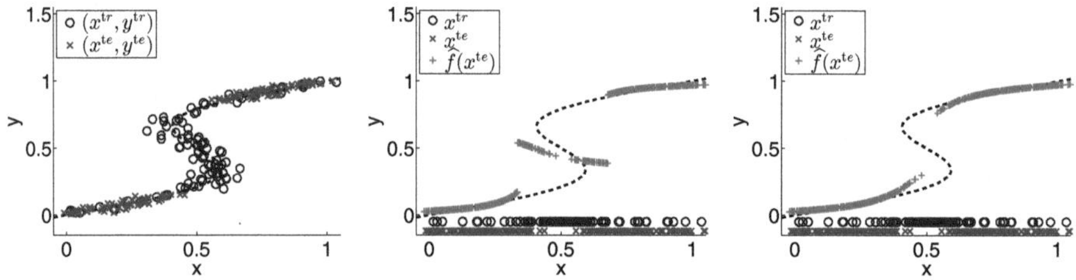

(a) Data samples (b) TGP (MSE=0.038) (c) IWTGP (MSE=0.002)

Fig. 1. Predicted outputs y by TGP (b) and IWTGP (c) under covariate shift in green. (a) Samples from the model $x = y + 0.3\sin(2\pi y) + e$ where $e \sim \mathcal{N}(0, 0.05^2)$; $\circ$ and $\times$ are training and test samples respectively (for clarity we also illustrate marginals $p_{\mathrm{tr}}(\boldsymbol{x})$ and $p_{\mathrm{te}}(\boldsymbol{x})$ in (b) and (c) bottom). Note that the input-output test samples are not used in the training of TGP and the output test samples are not used in the training of IWTGP, they are plotted in the figure for illustration purposes.

The formulation outlined in the previous paragraph is known in the transfer learning community as one of *covariate shift* [24]. Under covariate shift setup it is assumed that labeled training image-pose pairs $\{(\boldsymbol{x}_i^{\mathrm{tr}}, \boldsymbol{y}_i^{\mathrm{tr}})\}_{i=1}^{n_{\mathrm{tr}}}$ drawn i.i.d. from $p(\boldsymbol{y}|\boldsymbol{x})p_{\mathrm{tr}}(\boldsymbol{x})$ and unlabeled test image features $\{\boldsymbol{x}_j^{\mathrm{te}}\}_{j=1}^{n_{\mathrm{te}}}$ drawn i.i.d. from $p_{\mathrm{te}}(\boldsymbol{x})$ (which is usually different from $p_{\mathrm{tr}}(\boldsymbol{x})$) are available. The goal of (structured) prediction is to learn a mapping, $\boldsymbol{f} : \mathbb{R}^{d_{\mathrm{x}}} \to \mathbb{R}^{d_{\mathrm{y}}}$, which in the most general form can be expressed as:

$$\boldsymbol{y} = \boldsymbol{f}(\boldsymbol{x}) + \boldsymbol{e}, \tag{1}$$

where $\boldsymbol{e} \in \mathbb{R}^{d_{\mathrm{y}}}$ is the noise. Under covariate shift this mapping is learned based on a *weighted* set of training image-pose pairs $\{(w_i, \boldsymbol{x}_i^{\mathrm{tr}}, \boldsymbol{y}_i^{\mathrm{tr}})\}_{i=1}^{n_{\mathrm{tr}}}$. Re-weighting each training instances by the ratio (a.k.a., importance weight), $w_i = w_1(\boldsymbol{x}_i^{\mathrm{tr}}; \boldsymbol{\theta}) = \frac{p_{\mathrm{te}}(\boldsymbol{x}_i^{\mathrm{tr}})}{p_{\mathrm{tr}}(\boldsymbol{x}_i^{\mathrm{tr}})}$, removes the training set bias producing an unbiased model under assumption of covariate shift [24]. Note $\{\boldsymbol{x}_j^{\mathrm{te}}\}_{j=1}^{n_{\mathrm{te}}}$ are necessary to estimate the numerator. The main challenge, however, is estimation of the importance weight; we discuss this in detail in Section 4.

Before proceeding, however, we would like to illustrate the effect of *covariate shift* on a synthetic toy example. In Figure 1, we illustrate the efficacy of our reweighting scheme under covariate shift by incorporating it into Twin Gaussian Process (TGP); for details see Section 5.2. As can be seen, Importance Weighted TGP (IWTGP) can predict the true test output well, while standard TGP fails to predict the true test output, in particular, around $x = 0.5$. Note that in this specific case the mean squared error (MSE) is improved by a large margin (from 0.038 to 0.002) by incorporating the importance weight into the learning.

4 Importance Weight Estimation

The importance weight may be computed by separately estimating densities $p_{\mathrm{tr}}(\boldsymbol{x})$ and $p_{\mathrm{te}}(\boldsymbol{x})$ from training and test feature vectors and then taking their ratio. However, density estimation is known to be a hard problem and taking the ratio of estimated densities tends to increase the estimation error [30]. Thus, this two step approach is not appropriate in practice. We adopt a method that allows us to directly learn the importance weight function without going through density estimation. The method is called the *relative unconstrained least-squares importance fitting* (RuLSIF) [32].

Let us first define the *relative importance weight* [32]:

$$w_\alpha(\boldsymbol{x}) = \frac{p_{\mathrm{te}}(\boldsymbol{x})}{(1-\alpha)p_{\mathrm{te}}(\boldsymbol{x}) + \alpha p_{\mathrm{tr}}(\boldsymbol{x})}, \quad 0 \leq \alpha \leq 1, \tag{2}$$

where α is the tuning parameter to control the *adaptiveness* to the test distribution. If $\alpha = 0$ (i.e., $w_0(\boldsymbol{x}) = 1$) gives no adaptation, while $\alpha = 1$ (i.e., $w_1(\boldsymbol{x}) = \frac{p_{\mathrm{te}}(\boldsymbol{x})}{p_{\mathrm{tr}}(\boldsymbol{x})}$) gives the full adaptation from $p_{\mathrm{tr}}(\boldsymbol{x})$ to $p_{\mathrm{te}}(\boldsymbol{x})$; $0 < \alpha < 1$ will give an intermediate estimator[2].

Let $\mathcal{X}^{\mathrm{tr}}(\subseteq \mathbb{R}^{d_{\mathrm{x}}})$ be the domain of training image feature vector $\boldsymbol{x}^{\mathrm{tr}}$ and $\mathcal{X}^{\mathrm{te}}(\subseteq \mathbb{R}^{d_{\mathrm{y}}})$ be the domain of test image feature vector $\boldsymbol{x}^{\mathrm{te}}$. Suppose we are given n_{tr} and n_{te} i.i.d. training and test image feature vectors, $\{\boldsymbol{x}_i^{\mathrm{tr}} \mid \boldsymbol{x}_i^{\mathrm{tr}} \in \mathcal{X}^{\mathrm{tr}},\ i = 1, \ldots, n_{\mathrm{tr}}\}$, $\{\boldsymbol{x}_j^{\mathrm{te}} \mid \boldsymbol{x}_j^{\mathrm{te}} \in \mathcal{X}^{\mathrm{te}},\ j = 1, \ldots, n_{\mathrm{te}}\}$, drawn from distributions with densities $p_{\mathrm{tr}}(\boldsymbol{x})$ and $p_{\mathrm{te}}(\boldsymbol{x})$, respectively.

The final goal of relative importance weight estimation is to estimate the relative importance weight based on the training and test image features. Let us model the relative importance weight $w_\alpha(\boldsymbol{x})$ by the following kernel model:

$$w_\alpha(\boldsymbol{x}; \boldsymbol{\theta}) = \sum_{\ell=1}^{n_{\mathrm{te}}} \theta_\ell\ \kappa(\boldsymbol{x}, \boldsymbol{x}_\ell^{\mathrm{te}}) = \sum_{\ell=1}^{n_{\mathrm{te}}} \theta_\ell \exp\left(-\frac{\|\boldsymbol{x} - \boldsymbol{x}_\ell^{\mathrm{te}}\|^2}{2\tau^2}\right), \tag{3}$$

where $\boldsymbol{\theta} = (\theta_1, \ldots, \theta_{n_{\mathrm{te}}})^\top$ are parameters to be learned from data samples, $^\top$ denotes the transpose, $\kappa(\cdot,\cdot)$ is the Gaussian kernel and τ (> 0) is the kernel bandwidth.

The parameters $\boldsymbol{\theta}$ in the model $w_\alpha(\boldsymbol{x}; \boldsymbol{\theta})$ are determined so that the following expected squared-error J is minimized:

$$\begin{aligned} J(\boldsymbol{\theta}) &= \frac{1}{2}\mathbb{E}_{q_\alpha(\boldsymbol{x})}\left[(w_\alpha(\boldsymbol{x};\boldsymbol{\theta}) - w_\alpha(\boldsymbol{x}))^2\right] \\ &= \frac{(1-\alpha)}{2}\mathbb{E}_{p_{\mathrm{te}}(\boldsymbol{x})}\left[w_\alpha(\boldsymbol{x};\boldsymbol{\theta})^2\right] + \frac{\alpha}{2}\mathbb{E}_{p_{\mathrm{tr}}(\boldsymbol{x})}\left[w_\alpha(\boldsymbol{x};\boldsymbol{\theta})^2\right] - \mathbb{E}_{p_{\mathrm{te}}(\boldsymbol{x})}[w_\alpha(\boldsymbol{x};\boldsymbol{\theta})] + \mathrm{Const.}, \end{aligned}$$

where $q_\alpha(\boldsymbol{x}) = (1-\alpha)p_{\mathrm{te}}(\boldsymbol{x}) + \alpha p_{\mathrm{tr}}(\boldsymbol{x})$, and we used $w_\alpha(\boldsymbol{x})q_\alpha(\boldsymbol{x}) = p_{\mathrm{te}}(\boldsymbol{x})$ in the third term (see supplemental materials for derivation[3]).

[2] $\alpha = 1$ (i.e., $w_1(\boldsymbol{x}) = \frac{p_{\mathrm{te}}(\boldsymbol{x})}{p_{\mathrm{tr}}(\boldsymbol{x})}$) gives the full adaptation from $p_{\mathrm{tr}}(\boldsymbol{x})$ to $p_{\mathrm{te}}(\boldsymbol{x})$. However, since the importance weight $w_1(\boldsymbol{x}) = \frac{p_{\mathrm{te}}(\boldsymbol{x})}{p_{\mathrm{tr}}(\boldsymbol{x})}$ can diverge to infinity under a rather simple setting, e.g., when the ratio of two Gaussian function is considered [33], the estimation of $w_1(\boldsymbol{x}) = \frac{p_{\mathrm{te}}(\boldsymbol{x})}{p_{\mathrm{tr}}(\boldsymbol{x})}$ is unstable and the covariate shift adaptation tends to be unstable [24]. To cope with this instability issue, setting α to $0 < \alpha < 1$ is practically useful for stabilizing the covariate shift adaptation, even though it cannot give an unbiased model under covariate shift [32].

[3] `http://www.cs.brown.edu/~ls/Publications/eccv2012_supplemental.pdf`

Approximating the expectations by empirical averages, we obtain the following optimization problem:

$$\widehat{\boldsymbol{\theta}} = \underset{\boldsymbol{\theta} \in \mathbb{R}^{n_{\mathrm{te}}}}{\operatorname{argmin}} \left[\frac{1}{2} \boldsymbol{\theta}^\top \widehat{\boldsymbol{H}} \boldsymbol{\theta} - \widehat{\boldsymbol{h}}^\top \boldsymbol{\theta} + \frac{\nu}{2} \boldsymbol{\theta}^\top \boldsymbol{\theta} \right], \tag{4}$$

where $\nu \boldsymbol{\theta}^\top \boldsymbol{\theta}/2$ is included to avoid overfitting, and ν (≥ 0) denotes the regularization parameter. $\widehat{\boldsymbol{H}}$ is the $n_{\mathrm{te}} \times n_{\mathrm{te}}$ matrix with the (ℓ, ℓ')-th element

$$\widehat{H}_{\ell,\ell'} = \frac{(1-\alpha)}{n_{\mathrm{te}}} \sum_{i=1}^{n_{\mathrm{te}}} \kappa(\boldsymbol{x}_i^{\mathrm{te}}, \boldsymbol{x}_\ell^{\mathrm{te}}) \kappa(\boldsymbol{x}_i^{\mathrm{te}}, \boldsymbol{x}_{\ell'}^{\mathrm{te}}) + \frac{\alpha}{n_{\mathrm{tr}}} \sum_{j=1}^{n_{\mathrm{tr}}} \kappa(\boldsymbol{x}_j^{\mathrm{tr}}, \boldsymbol{x}_\ell^{\mathrm{te}}) \kappa(\boldsymbol{x}_j^{\mathrm{tr}}, \boldsymbol{x}_{\ell'}^{\mathrm{te}});$$

$\widehat{\boldsymbol{h}}$ is the n_{te}-dimensional vector with the ℓ-th element $\widehat{h}_\ell = \frac{1}{n_{\mathrm{te}}} \sum_{i=1}^{n_{\mathrm{te}}} \kappa(\boldsymbol{x}_i^{\mathrm{te}}, \boldsymbol{x}_\ell^{\mathrm{te}})$. Then the solution to Eq. (4) can be *analytically* obtained as

$$\widehat{\boldsymbol{\theta}} = (\widehat{\boldsymbol{H}} + \nu \boldsymbol{I})^{-1} \widehat{\boldsymbol{h}}, \tag{5}$$

where $\boldsymbol{I}$ is the $n_{\mathrm{te}} \times n_{\mathrm{te}}$-dimensional identity matrix.

The performance of RuLSIF depends on the choice of the kernel bandwidth τ and the regularization parameter ν. Model selection of RuLSIF is possible based on cross-validation with respect to the squared-error criterion J [32].

Computational Complexity: Learning RuLSIF has complexity $O(n_{\mathrm{te}}^3)$ due to the matrix inversion. However, when the number of test data is large, we may reduce the number of kernels in Eq.(3) to $b_{\mathrm{te}} (< n_{\mathrm{te}})$. Then, the inverse matrix in Eq.(5) can be efficiently computed with complexity $O(b_{\mathrm{te}}^3)$.

5 Importance Weighted 3D Human Pose Estimation

Given the derivation of the importance weight estimator, in previous section, we now formulate two regression-based methods that take these weights into account. We start by formulating Importance Weighted Kernel Regression (IWKR), which has a particularly simple form and allows learning of non-linear mapping between the image features and the 3D pose. IWKR, similar to standard KR, is well suited for unimodal predictions. However, in 3D pose estimation, the mapping from image features to 3D pose has been shown to be multi-modal, due to the inherent imaging ambiguities [14]. To address this, we also introduce an Importance Weighted Twin Gaussian Process model, based on [5], which in addition imposes structure on the output 3D poses. As a result, IWTGP is able to estimate the most prominent mode, corresponding to the most likely 3D pose, as opposed to averaging across modes as is the case with KR and IWKR.

5.1 Importance Weighted Kernel Regression

In kernel regression vector-valued regression function $\boldsymbol{f}$, in Eq.(1), takes the following form:

$$\boldsymbol{f}(\boldsymbol{x}; \boldsymbol{A}) = \boldsymbol{A}^\top \boldsymbol{k}(\boldsymbol{x}), \tag{6}$$

where $\boldsymbol{A} = [\boldsymbol{\alpha}_1, \ldots, \boldsymbol{\alpha}_{d_y}] \in \mathbb{R}^{(n_{\mathrm{tr}}+1)\times d_y}$ is a model parameter, d_y is the dimensionality of pose $\boldsymbol{y}$, $\boldsymbol{k}(\boldsymbol{x}) = [1, K(\boldsymbol{x}, \boldsymbol{x}_1^{\mathrm{tr}}), K(\boldsymbol{x}, \boldsymbol{x}_2^{\mathrm{tr}}), \ldots, K(\boldsymbol{x}, \boldsymbol{x}_{n_{\mathrm{tr}}}^{\mathrm{tr}})]^\top$, and $K(\boldsymbol{x}, \boldsymbol{x}')$ is a kernel function. We use the Gaussian kernel [34] in our experiments: $K(\boldsymbol{x}, \boldsymbol{x}') = \exp\left(-\frac{\|\boldsymbol{x}-\boldsymbol{x}'\|^2}{2\rho_x^2}\right)$, where ρ_x is the kernel bandwidth.

Under covariate shift setup, the use of *relative importance weighted* risk minimization was shown to be useful for adaptation from $p_{\mathrm{tr}}(\boldsymbol{x})$ to $p_{\mathrm{te}}(\boldsymbol{x})$ [32]:

$$\min_{\boldsymbol{A}} \left[\sum_{i=1}^{n_{\mathrm{tr}}} w_\alpha(\boldsymbol{x}_i^{\mathrm{tr}}) \|\boldsymbol{y}_i^{\mathrm{tr}} - \boldsymbol{A}^\top \boldsymbol{k}(\boldsymbol{x}_i^{\mathrm{tr}})\|^2 + \frac{\gamma}{2} \sum_{j=1}^{d_y} \|\boldsymbol{\alpha}_j\|^2 \right], \tag{7}$$

where $w_\alpha(\boldsymbol{x})$ is the *relative importance weight* in Eq.(2), α is the tuning parameter to control the *adaptiveness* to the test distribution, and $\gamma \geq 0$ is the regularization parameter; we call this *importance weighted kernel regression* (IWKR).

The solution to Eq.(7) can be obtained analytically by

$$\widehat{\boldsymbol{A}} = (\widetilde{\boldsymbol{K}}^{\mathrm{tr}} \boldsymbol{W} (\widetilde{\boldsymbol{K}}^{\mathrm{tr}})^\top + \gamma \boldsymbol{I}) \widetilde{\boldsymbol{K}}^{\mathrm{tr}} \boldsymbol{W} (\boldsymbol{Y}^{\mathrm{tr}})^\top, \tag{8}$$

where $\widetilde{\boldsymbol{K}}^{\mathrm{tr}} = [\boldsymbol{k}(\boldsymbol{x}_1^{\mathrm{tr}}), \ldots, \boldsymbol{k}(\boldsymbol{x}_{n_{\mathrm{tr}}}^{\mathrm{tr}})] \in \mathbb{R}^{(n_{\mathrm{tr}}+1)\times n_{\mathrm{tr}}}$, $\boldsymbol{Y}^{tr} = [\boldsymbol{y}_1^{\mathrm{tr}}, \ldots, \boldsymbol{y}_{n_{\mathrm{tr}}}^{\mathrm{tr}}] \in \mathbb{R}^{d_y \times n_{\mathrm{tr}}}$, and $\boldsymbol{W}$ is the $n_{\mathrm{tr}} \times n_{\mathrm{tr}}$-dimensional diagonal matrix with (i,i)-th diagonal element defined by $\boldsymbol{W}_{i,i} = w_\alpha(\boldsymbol{x}_i^{\mathrm{tr}})$.

The above IWKR method includes two tuning parameters: kernel parameter ρ and the regularization parameter γ. These parameters can be selected using importance-weighted variant of cross-validation (IWCV) [35].

Computational Complexity: Learning IWKR has complexity $O((n_{\mathrm{tr}}+1)^3)$. Similar to RuLSIF, when the number of training data is large, we may reduce the number of kernels in Eq.(6) to $b_{\mathrm{tr}}(< n_{\mathrm{tr}}+1)$. Then, the inverse matrix in Eq.(8) can be efficiently computed with complexity $O(b_{\mathrm{tr}}^3)$. Since IWKR also includes the estimation of relative importance weight and its complexity is $O(b_{\mathrm{te}}^3)$. Thus, the complexity of IWKR is $O(b_{\mathrm{tr}}^3) + O(b_{\mathrm{te}}^3)$.

5.2 Importance Weighted Twin Gaussian Process

We now propose the importance-weighted variant of twin Gaussian processes [5] called IWTGP. The benefit of IWTGP over IWKR is that it can naturally take into account the multi-modality present in the human pose estimation, by incorporating structure over the output poses into the regression.

The Gaussian Process (GP) regression assumes a linear model in the function space with Gaussian noise for the k-th dimension (e.g., joint position):

$$y_k = f_k(\boldsymbol{x}) + e_k,\ e_k \sim \mathcal{N}(0, \sigma^2), \qquad f_k(\boldsymbol{x}) = \boldsymbol{\beta}_k^\top \boldsymbol{\phi}(\boldsymbol{x}), \tag{9}$$

where there is a zero mean Gaussian prior over the parameters $\boldsymbol{\beta}_k \sim \mathcal{N}(\boldsymbol{0}_p, \boldsymbol{\Sigma}_p)$; $\boldsymbol{0}_p$ is the p-dimensional zero vector and $\boldsymbol{\Sigma}_p$ is the p-dimensional covariance matrix, $\boldsymbol{\phi}(\boldsymbol{x})$ is the function which maps a d_x dimensional input vector $\boldsymbol{x}$ into an p dimensional feature space. To make prediction for the test sample, one needs to average over all possible parameter values, weighted by their posterior, resulting in a Gaussian predictive distribution. GP has similar problems with multi-modality as KR. To address this limitation, TGP encodes the relations between both inputs and outputs using GP priors. This is achieved by minimizing the Kullback-Leibler divergence between the marginal GP of outputs (poses) and observations (features); we refer the reader to [5] for derivation.

As a result, the estimated pose in TGP is given as the solution of the following optimization problem [5]:

$$\widehat{\boldsymbol{y}}=\operatorname*{argmin}_{\boldsymbol{y}\in\mathbb{R}^{d_{\mathrm{y}}}}\left[L(\boldsymbol{y},\boldsymbol{y})-2\boldsymbol{l}(\boldsymbol{y})^\top\boldsymbol{u}-\eta\log\left[L(\boldsymbol{y},\boldsymbol{y})-\boldsymbol{l}(\boldsymbol{y})^\top(\boldsymbol{L}+\lambda_{\mathrm{y}}\boldsymbol{I})^{-1}\boldsymbol{l}(\boldsymbol{y})\right]\right], \quad (10)$$

where $\boldsymbol{u} = (\boldsymbol{K} + \lambda_{\mathrm{x}}\boldsymbol{I})^{-1}\boldsymbol{k}(\boldsymbol{x})$, $\eta = K(\boldsymbol{x},\boldsymbol{x}) - \boldsymbol{k}(\boldsymbol{x})^\top\boldsymbol{u}$, $K(\boldsymbol{x},\boldsymbol{x}') = \exp\left(-\frac{\|\boldsymbol{x}-\boldsymbol{x}'\|^2}{2\rho_{\mathrm{x}}^2}\right)$ and $L(\boldsymbol{y},\boldsymbol{y}') = \exp\left(-\frac{\|\boldsymbol{y}-\boldsymbol{y}'\|^2}{2\rho_{\mathrm{y}}^2}\right)$ are the Gaussian kernel function for image feature vector $\boldsymbol{x}$ and pose feature vector $\boldsymbol{y}$, ρ_{x} and ρ_{y} are the kernel bandwidth, $\boldsymbol{l}(\boldsymbol{y}) = [L(\boldsymbol{y},\boldsymbol{y}_1),\ldots,L(\boldsymbol{y},\boldsymbol{y}_{n_{\mathrm{tr}}})]^\top$, $\boldsymbol{k}(\boldsymbol{x}) = [K(\boldsymbol{x},\boldsymbol{x}_1),\ldots,K(\boldsymbol{x},\boldsymbol{x}_{n_{\mathrm{tr}}})]^\top$, and λ_{y} and λ_{x} are regularization parameters to avoid overfitting. This optimization problem can be solved using a second order, BFGS quasi-Newton optimizer with cubic polynomial line search for optimal step size selection [5].

Under covariate shift, the likelihood of Gaussian Process can be given as [24]

$$\prod_{i=1}^{n_{\mathrm{tr}}} p(y_i^{tr}|\boldsymbol{x}_i^{\mathrm{tr}},\boldsymbol{\beta})^{w_\alpha(\boldsymbol{x}_i^{\mathrm{tr}})} \propto \prod_{i=1}^{n_{\mathrm{tr}}} \frac{1}{\sqrt{2\pi}\sigma}\exp\left(-\frac{\|w_\alpha^{\frac{1}{2}}(\boldsymbol{x}_i^{\mathrm{tr}})y_i^{tr} - w_\alpha^{\frac{1}{2}}(\boldsymbol{x}_i^{\mathrm{tr}})\boldsymbol{\phi}(\boldsymbol{x}_i^{\mathrm{tr}})^\top\boldsymbol{\beta}\|^2}{2\sigma^2}\right), \quad (11)$$

where $w_\alpha(\boldsymbol{x})$ is the relative importance weight function. Note, if we consider the MAP estimate for Eq. (11) with a prior distribution over $\boldsymbol{\beta}$, then we can show that IWKR and Eq. (11) are one and the same.

Thus, the GP regression model under covariate shift can be represented by

$$w_\alpha^{\frac{1}{2}}(\boldsymbol{x})y_k = w_\alpha^{\frac{1}{2}}(\boldsymbol{x})\boldsymbol{\phi}(\boldsymbol{x})^\top\boldsymbol{\beta}_k + e_k,\ e_k \sim \mathcal{N}(0,\sigma^2). \quad (12)$$

That is, to achieve covariate shift adaptation in TGP, we need to simply re-weight each input and output by $w_\alpha^{\frac{1}{2}}(\boldsymbol{x})$. Therefore, the output of the importance weighted TGP (IWTGP) is given by

$$\begin{aligned}\widehat{\boldsymbol{y}} = \operatorname*{argmin}_{\boldsymbol{y}\in\mathbb{R}^{d_{\mathrm{y}}}} \Big[& L(\boldsymbol{y},\boldsymbol{y}) - 2\boldsymbol{l}(\boldsymbol{y})^\top\boldsymbol{u}_w \\ & -\eta_w\log\left[L(\boldsymbol{y},\boldsymbol{y})-\boldsymbol{l}(\boldsymbol{y})^\top\boldsymbol{W}^{\frac{1}{2}}(\boldsymbol{W}^{\frac{1}{2}}\boldsymbol{L}\boldsymbol{W}^{\frac{1}{2}}+\lambda_{\mathrm{y}}\boldsymbol{I})^{-1}\boldsymbol{W}^{\frac{1}{2}}\boldsymbol{l}(\boldsymbol{y})\right]\Big], \end{aligned} \quad (13)$$

where $\boldsymbol{u}_w = \boldsymbol{W}^{\frac{1}{2}}(\boldsymbol{W}^{\frac{1}{2}}\boldsymbol{K}\boldsymbol{W}^{\frac{1}{2}} + \lambda_{\mathrm{x}}\boldsymbol{I})^{-1}\boldsymbol{W}^{\frac{1}{2}}\boldsymbol{k}(\boldsymbol{x})$, $\eta_w = K(\boldsymbol{x},\boldsymbol{x}) - \boldsymbol{k}(\boldsymbol{x})^\top\boldsymbol{u}_w$. IWTGP can also be solved using a second order, BFGS quasi-Newton optimizer with cubic polynomial line search for optimal step size selection. We ignore the weighting for certain terms that are independent of $\boldsymbol{y}$, and hence do not effect the optimization, for simplicity.

Computational Complexity: IWTGP requires matrix inversions of $n_{\text{tr}} \times n_{\text{tr}}$ matrices, the complexity of solving Eq.(13) is $O(n_{\text{tr}}^3)$, which is impractical when n_{tr} is large. To deal with this issue, we first find the M nearest neighbors of a test input and estimate IWTGP on the reduced set of training paired samples. Then, the inverse matrix in Eq.(13) can be efficiently computed with complexity $O(M^3)$. IWTGP also includes the estimation of relative importance weight, thus the total complexity of IWTGP is $O(M^3) + O(b_{\text{te}}^3)$.

5.3 Importance Weighting for Other Methods

The proposed weighting methodology is amenable to most popular formulations (e.g., Linear Regression, Mixture of Experts (MoE), GPLVM, KIE), as well as to other (structured) prediction problems in computer vision. For example, in Linear Regression importance weighting can be incorporate via Weighted Linear Regression. Incorporating importance weighting into MoE would amount to secondary weighting on top of expert assignment; for MoE models with soft expert assignments this would require very minor changes to the learning procedure. Latent variants like GPLVM and KIE can also make use of the importance weighting, for example, in KIE the importance weighted version of Mutual Information can be used to learn an IWKIE model.

6 Experiments

We compare the performance of the proposed methods IWKR and IWTGP with their un-weighted counterparts, KR [1] and TGP (we use public implementation from [5]), and weighted k-Nearest Neighbors approach (WkNN) [13]. We report performance on two publicly available datasets: Poser [2] and HumanEva-I [23].

Parameters: For Poser dataset, we experimentally (through grid search) set the TGP and IWTGP parameters to $\lambda_{\text{x}} = \lambda_{\text{y}} = 10^{-4}$, $2\rho_{\text{x}}^2 = 5$, and $2\rho_{\text{y}}^2 = 5000$. For HumanEva-I dataset, we used the original parameter setting of [5]: $\lambda_{\text{x}} = \lambda_{\text{y}} = 10^{-3}$, $2\rho_{\text{x}}^2 = 5$, and $2\rho_{\text{y}}^2 = 5 \times 10^5$. The number of M nearest neighbors in TGP and IWTGP is set to $min(800, n_{\text{tr}})$. In RuLSIF, we set the $\alpha = 0.5$ and $b_{\text{te}} = \min(500, n_{\text{te}})$. For KR and IWKR, we set $b_{\text{tr}} = \min(500, n_{\text{tr}})$, and all the parameters are chosen by cross-validation (CV) and importance weighted CV; in WkNN we set the number of nearest neighbors to 25. In addition, instead of using the entire test set to adopt the model, we use a temporal window of 20 frames (feature vectors) around the current test sample to compute the importance weight for IWTGP and IWKR. This is more efficient and is also more realistic, as one will typically not see the full set of test examples all at once.

Computational Speed: The overhead for importance weighting is small compared to the base methods; for example, IWTGP is about 4% slower than TGP when entire training set is used. Moreover, experimentally we observed that IWTGP can be faster than TGP with few samples (see supplemental materials). We attribute this to the fact that weighting in TGP can lead to an easier optimization problem, offsetting the coast of the weight estimation itself.

Table 1. Performance of IWKR and IWTGP on Poser dataset

	IWTGP	TGP	**IWKR**	KR	NN [12]	GPLVM [6]	sKIE [12]
Error (deg)	**5.75**	5.83	**5.72**	6.04	6.87	6.50	5.77/5.95

6.1 Poser Dataset

Poser dataset [2] consists of 1927 training and 418 test images, which are synthetically generated, using Poser software package, from motion capture (Mocap) data (54 joint angles per frame). The image features, corresponding to bag-of-words representation with silhouette-based shape context features, and error metric are provided with the dataset [2]. Since the Poser data is synthetically generated and was tuned to unimodal predictions [2], there exists only a small bias between training and test images/features.

Error Metric: The proposed error measure amounts to the root mean square error (in degrees), averaged over all joints angles, and is given by: $Error_{pose}(\widehat{\boldsymbol{y}}, \boldsymbol{y}^*) = \frac{1}{54}\sum_{m=1}^{54} \|(\widehat{\boldsymbol{y}}^{(m)} - \boldsymbol{y}^{*(m)}) \bmod 360°\|$, where $\widehat{\boldsymbol{y}} \in \mathbb{R}^{54}$ is an estimated pose vector, and $\boldsymbol{y}^* \in \mathbb{R}^{54}$ is a true pose vector.

Performance: Table 1 shows the pose estimation result averaged across the test set. Proposed IWKR and IWTGP outperform their un-weighted counterparts, reducing error by 5% and 2% respectively. IWKR and IWTGP also compare favorably with other existing methods reported elsewhere. It is worth mentioning that Shared KIE required a local model computed using a small neighborhood of 25 training samples to achieve comparable performance (with the global model the performance drops from 5.77 to 5.95 degrees on average). In contrast, the IWKR and IWTGP models are more global, since IWTGP takes 800 neighbors into account and IWKR uses all the training data[4].

6.2 HumanEva-I Dataset

HumanEva-I contains synchronized multi-view video and Mocap data. It consists of 3 subjects performing multiple activities: walking, jogging, boxing, throw and catch, and gesturing. We use the histogram of oriented gradient (HoG) features ($\in \mathbb{R}^{270}$) proposed in [5] (we refer to [5] for details[5]). We use training and validations sub-sets of HumanEva-I and only utilize data from 3 color cameras with a total of 9630 image-pose frames for each camera. This is consistent with experiments in [5]. We use half of the data (4815 frames) for training and half (4815 frames) for testing; the test and training data is disjoint. Where fewer, e.g., $n_{\text{tr}} = 500$, training samples are necessary (as in Figure 2) we randomly subsample n_{tr} from the full training set; to alleviate the sampling bias we sample 10 times and average the resulting errors.

The bias in pose estimation can come in (at least) two forms: (1) the training data may simply be biased and, for example, not contain the subject present in

[4] While all the data is used it is dynamically re-weighed based on the importance weight so not all of it is *active* at all times.

[5] We thank the authors for making their features publicly available.

Table 2. Performance on the entire HumanEva-I dataset averaged over all motions

Transfer Type	Subject Train	Subject Test	**IWTGP**	TGP	**IWKR**	KR	WkNN
Selection Bias (C1)	S1,S2,S3	S1	**54.2**	55.1	**71.1**	80.1	70.2
	S1,S2,S3	S2	**52.5**	53.2	**67.6**	75.5	71.5
	S1,S2,S3	S3	**57.5**	57.9	**75.1**	86.0	72.5
Selection Bias (C1-3)	S1,S2,S3	S1	**81.9**	83.9	**101.9**	119.9	94.3
	S1,S2,S3	S2	**72.7**	75.1	**102.7**	120.0	100.7
	S1,S2,S3	S3	**77.2**	86.1	**111.7**	134.8	110.4
Subject Transfer (C1)	S2,S3	S1	**126.2**	126.9	**137.3**	168.4	128.2
	S1,S3	S2	116.7	**116.6**	**130.5**	141.5	130.6
	S1,S2	S3	**140.0**	159.7	**168.4**	209.1	145.5

the test set (we call this *subject transfer*), or (2) the training data may contain data from variety of subjects, motions and cameras, where as at test time only a sub-set of that data is presented at any given time (we call this *selection bias*). To evaluate our methods under such scenarios we propose 3 experiments of interest:

Selection bias (C1): Only camera 1 data is used for training and testing.
Selection bias (C1-3): All camera data is used for training and testing ($3 \times 4815 = 14445$ frames of training and 14445 frames of test data).
Subject transfer (C1): Test subject is not included in training phase.

Error metric: In HumanEva-I pose is encoded by (20) 3D joint markers defined relative to the 'torsoDistal' joint in camera-centric coordinate frame, so $\boldsymbol{y} = [\boldsymbol{y}^{(1)}, \ldots, \boldsymbol{y}^{(20)}]^\top \in \mathbb{R}^{60}$ and $\boldsymbol{y}^{(i)} \in \mathbb{R}^3$. Error (in mm) for each pose is measured as average Euclidean distance: $Error_{pose}(\widehat{\boldsymbol{y}}, \boldsymbol{y}^*) = \frac{1}{20}\sum_{m=1}^{20} \|\widehat{\boldsymbol{y}}^{(m)} - \boldsymbol{y}^{*(m)}\|$, where $\widehat{\boldsymbol{y}}$ is an estimated pose vector, and $\boldsymbol{y}^*$ is a true pose vector.

Performance: Figure 2 shows the average mean pose estimation error as a function of training set size (averaged over all motions and 10 runs). The graphs clearly show that IWTGP and IWKR outperform their un-weighted counterparts. Moreover, IWTGP overall compares favorably with existing methods in terms of the overall performance. Table 2 shows performance using the entire training set. IWTGP tends to have smaller error compared to all other methods. Note that both the weighted and their un-weighted counterparts use the same parameters and inference procedures; the key difference is in the interest weighting that alters the learning. Moreover, paired t-tests were conducted for all experiments, we observe that about 80% cases the importance weighted methods, IWTGP and IWKR, statistically outperform their non-weighted counterparts at p=0.05 (5%) significance. In certain settings, we see more drastic improvements, e.g., 14% reduction in error in subject transfer with S3 using IWTGP (and 19% using IWKR), or over 10% reduction in error in selection bias (C1-3) with S3. We also see significant improvements on certain specific motions (see supplementary material), where, for example, on gesture motion under selection bias we observe improvement by 22.6 mm (reducing error by 20%) or under subject transfer by 64.5 mm (reducing error by 33%).

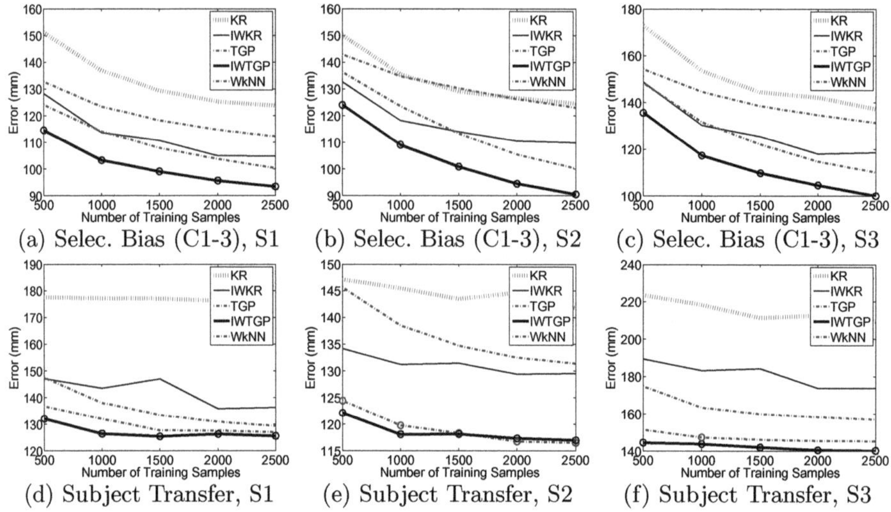

(a) Selec. Bias (C1-3), S1 (b) Selec. Bias (C1-3), S2 (c) Selec. Bias (C1-3), S3

(d) Subject Transfer, S1 (e) Subject Transfer, S2 (f) Subject Transfer, S3

Fig. 2. Performance on HumanEva-I dataset illustrated as a function of the number of training samples; we averaged the error over all motions for each subject. Comparable methods according to the paired *t-test* at the significance level 5% are specified by '∘'.

Conclusions: We propose a simple, yet effective, unsupervised method for addressing training set bias through covariate shift adaptation in (structured) prediction problems. As part of our formulation, we also introduce importance weighted variants of kernel regression (IWKR) and twin Gaussian processes (IWTGP) which produce state-of-the-art 3D pose estimation performance on standard datasets (HumanEva-I and Poser [2]). We view our approach as the first step towards eliminating bias in structured prediction problems in vision.

References

1. Agarwal, A., Triggs, B.: Monocular human motion capture with a mixture of regressors. In: CVPR Workshop. (2005)
2. Agarwal, A., B.Triggs: Recovering 3D human pose from monocular images. IEEE Trans. on PAMI **28** (2006) 44—58
3. Bissacco, A., Yang, M., Soatto, S.: Fast human pose estimation using appearance and motion via multi-dimensional boosting regression. In: CVPR. (2007) 1–8
4. Bo, L., Sminchisescu, C., Kanaujia, A., Metaxas, D.: Fast algorithms for large scale conditional 3d prediction. In: CVPR. (2008)
5. Bo, L., Sminchisescu, C.: Twin gaussian processes for structured prediction. Int. J. Comput. Vision **87** (2010) 28–52
6. Ek, C., Torr, P., Lawrence, N.: Gaussian process latent variable models for human pose estimation. In: Workshp on ML for Mult. Inter. Volume 4892., LNCS (2007)
7. Ionescu, C., Bo, L., Sminchisescu, C.: Structural svm for visual localization and continuous state estimation. In: ICCV. (2009)
8. Kanaujia, A., Sminchisescu, C., Metaxas, D.: Semi-supervised hierarchical models for 3d human pose reconstruction. In: CVPR. (2007)

9. Navaratnam, R., Fitzgibbon, A., Cipolla, R.: The joint manifold model for semi-supervised multi-valued regression. In: ICCV. (2007)
10. Rosales, R., S.Sclaroff: Learning body pose via specialized maps. In: NIPS. (2002)
11. Salzmann, M., Ek, C.H., Urtasun, R., Darrell, T.: Factorized orthogonal latent spaces. In: AISTATS. (2010)
12. Sigal, L., Memisevic, R., Fleet, D.: Shared kernel information embedding for discriminative inference. In: CVPR. (2009)
13. Shakhnarovich, G., Viola, P., Darrell, T.: Fast pose estimation with parameter-sensitive hashing. In: ICCV. Volume 2. (2003) 750—757
14. Sminchisescu, C., Kanaujia, A., Li, Z., Metaxas, D.: Discriminative density propagation for 3d human motion estimation. In: CVPR. (2005)
15. Sminchisescu, C., Kanaujia, A., Metaxas, D.: Learning joint top-down and bottom-up processes for 3d visual inference. In: CVPR. (2006)
16. Urtasun, R., Darrell, T.: Sparse probabilistic regression for activity-independent human pose inference. In: CVPR. (2008)
17. Zhao, X., Ning, H., Liu, Y., Huang, T.S.: Discriminative estimation of 3d human pose using gaussian processes. In: CVPR. (2008)
18. Aytar, Y., Zisserman, A.: Tabula rasa: Model transfer for object category detection. In: ICCV. (2011)
19. Kulis, B., Saenko, K., Darrell, T.: What you saw is not what you get: Domain adaptation using asymmetric kernel transforms. In: CVPR. (2011)
20. Saenko, K., Kulis, B., Fritz, M., Darrell, T.: Adapting visual category models to new domains. In: ECCV. (2010)
21. Stark, M., Goesele, M., Schiele, B.: A shape-based object class model for knowledge transfer. In: ICCV. (2009)
22. Torralba, A., Efros, A.: Ubiased look at dataset bias. In: CVPR. (2011)
23. Sigal, L., Black, M.J.: Humaneva: Synchronized video and motion capture dataset for evaluation of articulated human motion. In: TR CS-06-08, Brown Univ. (2006)
24. Shimodaira, H.: Improving predictive inference under covariate shift by weighting the log-likelihood function. Journal of Statistical Planning and Inference **90** (2000)
25. Sigal, L., Balan, A., Black, M.: Combined discriminative and generative articulated pose and non-rigid shape estimation. (2007)
26. de Campos, T., Murray, D.: Regression-based hand pose estimation from multiple cameras. In: CVPR. Volume 1. (2006) 782–789
27. Rosales, R., Athitsos, V., Sigal, L., Scarloff, S.: 3d hand pose reconstruction using specialized mappings. In: ICCV. Volume 1. (2001) 378–385
28. Fanelli, G., Gall, J., Gool, L.V.: Real time head pose estimation with random regression forests. In: CVPR. (2011)
29. Huang, J., Smola, A.J., Gretton, A., Borgwardt, K.M., B. Schölkopf, B.: Correcting sample selection bias by unlabeled data. In: NIPS. (2007)
30. Sugiyama, M., Nakajima, S., Kashima, H., Buenau, P.V., Kawanabe, M.: Direct importance estimation with model selection and its application to covariate shift adaptation. In: NIPS. (2008)
31. Kanamori, T., Hido, S., Sugiyama, M.: A least-squares approach to direct importance estimation. JMLR **10** (2009) 1391–1445
32. Yamada, M., Suzuki, T., Kanamori, T., Hachiya, H., Sugiyama, M.: Relative density-ratio estimation for robust distribution comparison. In: NIPS. (2011)
33. Cortes, C., Mansour, Y., Mohri, M.: Learning bounds for importance weighting. In: NIPS. (2010)
34. Schölkopf, B., Smola, A.J.: Learning with Kernels. MIT Press (2002)
35. Sugiyama, M., Krauledat, M., Müller, K.R.: Covariate shift adaptation by importance weighted cross validation. JMLR **8** (2007) 985–1005

Labeling Images by Integrating Sparse Multiple Distance Learning and Semantic Context Modeling

Chuanjun Ji[1], Xiangdong Zhou[1], Lan Lin[2], and Weidong Yang[1]

[1] School of Computer Science, Fudan University, China
{10210240023,xdzhou,wdyang}@fudan.edu.cn
[2] School of Electronics and Information, Tongji University, China
linlan@tongji.edu.cn

Abstract. Recent progress on Automatic Image Annotation (AIA) is achieved by either exploiting low level visual features or high level semantic context. Integrating these two paradigms to further leverage the performance of AIA is promising. However, very few previous works have studied this issue in a unified framework. In this paper, we propose a unified model based on Conditional Random Fields (CRF), which establishes tight interaction between visual features and semantic context. In particular, Kernelized Logistic Regression (KLR) with multiple visual distance learning is embedded into the CRF framework. We introduce L_1 and L_2 regularization terms into the unified learning process for the distance learning and the parameters penalty respectively. The experiments are conducted on two benchmarks: Corel and TRECVID-2005 data sets for evaluation. The experimental results show that, compared with the state-of-the-art methods, the unified model achieves significant improvement on annotation performance and shows more robustness with increasing number of various visual features.

Keywords: Automatic Image Annotation, multiple distance learning, semantic context, alternating optimization.

1 Introduction

Automatic Image Annotation (AIA) has been an appealing research topic for almost a decade. The challenge originates from the so called "semantic gap", namely the mismatch between image semantics and visual perception. A great deal of research efforts have been devoted to bridge the semantic gap. Both low level visual features and high level semantics are explored in previous literatures [1–10].

In recent years, most impressive works of AIA can be categorized into two general classes. The first class is exploring visual feature learning techniques, such as feature selection [11], which combines multiple visual features to enhance annotation performance. TagProp [12] obtains competitive result by using multiple similarity measurements learning. The second class is the semantic context

A. Fitzgibbon et al. (Eds.): ECCV 2012, Part IV, LNCS 7575, pp. 688–701, 2012.

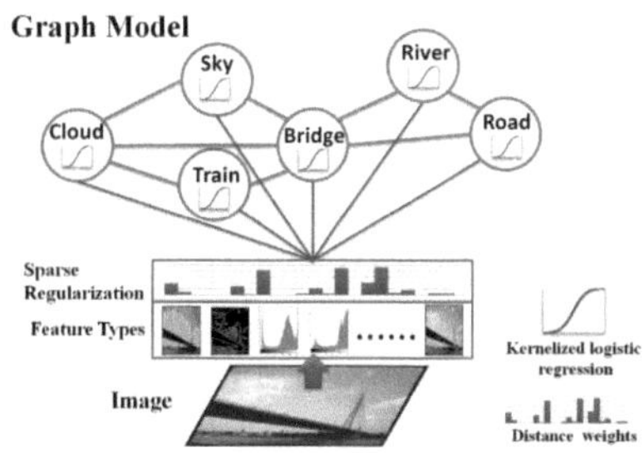

Fig. 1. Illustrative images with annotations for semantic context from Corel dataset

Fig. 2. Framework of the proposed Kernelized Conditional Random Fields

modeling technique [13–16]. In the scenario of AIA, semantic context refers to contextual relationships between concepts that co-occur frequently. For example, "bridge" and "water" often appear in the same image. Intuitively, for images annotated with "bridge", it is more likely to observe "water". Some illustrative images with human annotated keywords from [1] are presented in Figure 1. Probabilistic graphical model is adopted for semantic context modeling to boost the performance of AIA [13]. Integrating these two paradigms to further leverage the performance of AIA seems very promising. However, very few previous works have studied this issue in a unified framework.

In this paper, we propose the Kernelized Conditional Random Fields (KCRF), a unified model that integrates semantic context modeling and sparse multiple distance learning with tight interaction between them. To the best of our knowledge, our work is the first attempt to integrate these two paradigms in a unified framework for AIA. Within the unified framework, semantic contextual information is directly utilized in learning the optimal multiple feature combination, while at the same time the visual feature combination yields powerful support for modeling the semantic context.

Our KCRF model is built on semantic level to capture the relationships between semantic keywords. Figure 2 illustrates the graph structure and framework of our model. In the graph model, sites (nodes) represent concepts and edges refer to the interactions between them. To explore multiple visual feature learning, we introduce KLR [17] into the site potential. Our kernel function is based on a weighted sum of distances of multiple visual features. The parameter set of our unified model is made up of distance weights (visual parameters) and CRF parameters (semantic context parameters). Different from previous layered approaches [11, 18] that separate feature learning from image labeling, our multiple distance learning and CRF parameter estimation are conducted simultaneously subjecting to one unified object function, resulting in close interactions between the two paradigms. A pairwise L_1 and L_2 regularization term is introduced into the unified object function. Specifically, we impose L_1 regularization on the distance weight vector to obtain sparse distance combination, which makes our model more robust when dealing with increasing number of visual features. On the other hand, the semantic context parameters are penalized by L_2

regularization. We use an alternating optimization approach to estimate the optimal distance weights and CRF parameters iteratively.

To evaluate our model, we conduct experiments on Corel [1] and TRECVID-2005 datasets. Comparing with the state-of-the-art approaches, such as non-contextual methods and semantic context modeling methods, our model achieves the best performance on these two datasets with significant improvement over the others. Particularly, the experimental results show that, with increasing number of visual features, our model is more robust.

The rest of the paper is organized as follows: Section 2 reviews some related work. Section 3 presents the model setting. Section 4 and Section 5 detail the alternating parameter estimation and model inference respectively. Section 6 presents the experiment setup, and Section 7 provides the experimental results. Section 8 concludes the paper.

2 Related Work

Most of the previous AIA work[19, 2, 3] can be considered as propagating semantic concepts from training images to unlabeled images based on visual similarity. This idea is further developed by JEC [11] and TagProp [12]. Both methods focus on exploring optimal combination of multiple distances based on K-nearest neighbor (KNN) technique. In [11], the authors also tried to introduce L_1 regularization for feature selection in logistic regression. However, due to the separation of feature learning from image labeling, the logistic regression model does not outperform the JEC model using equally weighted combination of various distances. Subsequently, TagProp [12] adopts metric learning in KNN and gives out more competitive result.

Another remarkable technique is semantic context modeling. Feng and Manmatha [15] use Markov Random Fields (MRF) and propose a framework for image and video retrieval using discrete image features. Xiang et al. [13] adapted MRF for semantic context modeling in AIA. Song et al. [16] propose the Contextualized Support Vector Machine, which employs contextual information to adjust the classification hyperplane.

Considering the effectiveness of semantic context modeling technique and optimal combination of visual features, it is a rational attempt to integrate them into one consistent framework to achieve better performance. MMCRF [18] tries to make use of multiple visual features under Conditional Random Fields framework, but the feature weights are learned independently from the image labeling. Wang et al. [20] propose a Bi-relational Graph (BG) that combines the data graph connecting images and the label graph connecting concepts through label assignments. Different from previous work, our model integrates semantic context modeling and sparse multiple distance learning by using Kernel Logistic Regression in CRF framework. Rather than resorting to a layered approach as in [11], our sparse multiple distance learning and CRF parameter estimation are conducted simultaneously subjecting to one unified object function.

3 Kernelized Conditional Random Fields

In this section we present our Kernelized Conditional Random Fields model. Detailed description of the kernelized site potential and edge potential is described subsequently.

3.1 General Conditional Random Fields

Conditional Random Fields (CRF) [21] uses discriminative models for the nodes and the interactions between nodes. Let $G = (S, E)$ be a graph with site set $S = \{1, 2, ..., m\}$ and edge set E. Let $\mathbf{y} = \{y_1, y_2, ..., y_m\}$ be a set of random variables indexed by S, and $\mathbf{x} \in \chi$ be the feature vector of observed data. Then $(\mathbf{y}, \mathbf{x})$ is said to be a conditional random field if, when conditioned on $\mathbf{x}$, the random variable y_i obey the Markov property with respect to the graph: $P(y_i|\mathbf{x}, \mathbf{y}_{S-\{i\}}) = P(y_i|\mathbf{x}, \mathbf{y}_{\mathcal{N}_i})$, where $S - \{i\}$ is the set of all nodes in G except node i, $\mathcal{N}_i$ is the set of neighbors of node i in G, and $\mathbf{y}_\Omega$ represents the set of labels on nodes in the set Ω. The conditional distribution over the labels $\mathbf{y}$ given $\mathbf{x}$ is defined as,

$$P(\mathbf{y}|\mathbf{x}) = \frac{1}{Z} exp\Big(\sum_{i \in S} A(y_i, \mathbf{x}) + \sum_{i \in S} \sum_{j \in N_i} I(y_i, y_j, \mathbf{x})\Big), \tag{1}$$

where Z is a normalizing constant called the partition function, and -A and -I are the site potential and edge potential respectively. Notice that in this paper we only consider cliques of order up to two.

3.2 Kernelized Site Potential

AIA can be considered as a binary classification problem on each site of the CRF model, i.e., $y_i \in \{-1, +1\}$ represents the absence/presence of the ith concept. Hence we model site potential using a local discriminative classifier which outputs the probability of label y_i conditioned on the observation $\mathbf{x}$ on site i ignoring its neighboring sites. In order to facilitate the use of multiple image features within the context modeling framework, we employ kernelized logistic regression (KLR) [17], the nonlinear kernelized variant of logistic regression, to model the local class posterior. Given training set $\mathcal{T} = \{(\mathbf{x}^n, \mathbf{y}^n)\}_{n=1}^N$, the posterior of label y_i is defined as,

$$P(y_i|\mathbf{x}, \boldsymbol{\alpha}_i) = \frac{1}{1 + exp(-y_i f(\mathbf{x}, \boldsymbol{\alpha}_i))}, \tag{2}$$

where

$$f(\mathbf{x}, \boldsymbol{\alpha}_i) = \sum_{m=1}^{N} \alpha_i^m K(\mathbf{x}, \mathbf{x}^m), \tag{3}$$

N is the number of training images, $\boldsymbol{\alpha}_i = (\alpha_i^1, \alpha_i^2, ..., \alpha_i^N)^T$ is the parameter for site i and kernel K is the dot product matrix in a feature space. The construction of kernel will be explained in section 3.4. Finally the site potential is modeled as,

$$A(y_i, \mathbf{x}) = u_i log(P(y_i|\mathbf{x}, \boldsymbol{\alpha}_i)) = u_i log(\frac{1}{1 + exp(-y_i f(\mathbf{x}, \boldsymbol{\alpha}_i))}), \quad (4)$$

where u_i is the parameter controlling the contribution of site potential to the overall conditional distribution. Larger value of u_i indicates stronger effect of site potential. We use a spherical Gaussian prior with expectation value 1 for u_i, which will be described later. Note that the logarithm transformation ensures that our model degenerates into KLR if $u_i = 1$ and the edge potential in Eq.1 is set to zero.

3.3 Edge Potential

Using a linear discriminative model, we define edge potential as,

$$I(y_i, y_j, \mathbf{x}) = v_{ij} y_i y_j P(y_j|\mathbf{x}), \quad (5)$$

where v_{ij} is the parameter on edge (i, j) to be estimated, and $P(y_j|\mathbf{x})$ is the conditional probability of label y_j given observation $\mathbf{x}$. The edge potential is designed to favor identical labels at a pair of sites. When $v_{ij} > 0$, equal values of y_i and y_j will raise the conditional probability Eq.1 with confidence $P(y_j|\mathbf{x})$, while different value will cause punishment. In our experiment we use kernel logistic regression [17] described in Section 3.2 to generate $P(y_j|\mathbf{x})$ before the training procedure of our model. For each label $y_j (j = 1, ..., m)$, a KLR model is learned and then used to obtain $P(y_j|\mathbf{x})$. Hence, $P(y_j|\mathbf{x})$ can be regarded as a constant in Eq.5.

3.4 Kernel Construction

Through the use of Kernel our model is able to utilize multiple visual features yielding stronger support to capture semantics. Specifically, a Gaussian radial basis kernel is used on distance metric,

$$K(\mathbf{x}, \mathbf{x}') = exp(-d_{\mathbf{w}}(\mathbf{x}, \mathbf{x}')/2\sigma^2), \quad (6)$$

where σ is the width of the Gaussian kernel. The distance metric $d_w(\mathbf{x}, \mathbf{x}')$ is defined as a weighted sum of distances of image $\mathbf{x}$ and $\mathbf{x}'$ on different features,

$$d_{\mathbf{w}}(\mathbf{x}, \mathbf{x}') = \sum_{t=1}^{T} w_t d_t(\mathbf{x}, \mathbf{x}'), \quad (7)$$

where T denotes the number of features, $d_t(\mathbf{x}, \mathbf{x}')$ is the distance on the tth feature, and $\mathbf{w} = (w_1, w_2, ..., w_T)$ is the feature weight vector. A larger value of w_t indicates higher importance of the corresponding feature, whereas a non-relevant feature will be assigned with zero value. As a result, the whole parameter set of our unified model consists of two parts, i.e., the conventional CRF parameters $\{(\boldsymbol{\alpha}_i, u_i, v_{ij})_{j \in N_i}\}_{i \in S}$ on sites and edges, and the feature weight vector $\mathbf{w}$.

3.5 Concept Graph

The concept graph of our model is constructed based on concept co-occurrence in the training set $\mathcal{T} = \{(\mathbf{x}^n, \mathbf{y}^n)\}_{n=1}^N$, where $\mathbf{x}^n$ denotes the nth image, $\mathbf{y}^n = (y_1^n, y_2^n, ..., y_m^n)$ is the corresponding label vector with $y_i^n \in \{-1, +1\}$ indicating the absence or presence of the ith concept, and N is the size of the training set. If two keywords appear in the same training image, they are treated as associated, and an edge between them is added to the graph $G = (S, E)$. Accordingly, the neighborhood of site i is defined as $\mathcal{N}_i = \{j | j \in S \wedge (i, j) \in E\}$. We extract a subgraph from G for every site to capture the semantic relationship more precisely. The subgraph contains only the site in concern and its neighboring sites as well as all the edges connecting them.

4 Alternating Parameter Estimation

Maximum likelihood is a widely used approach for CRF parameter estimation. But the computation of the partition function in Eq.1 is a generally NP-hard problem. To avoid this, we resort to the pseudo-likelihood scheme, which uses a factored approximation on every site such that

$$P(\mathbf{y}|\mathbf{x}) \approx \prod_{i \in S} P(y_i | \mathbf{y}_{\mathcal{N}_i}, \mathbf{x}) = \prod_{i \in S} \frac{1}{Z_i} exp\Big(A(y_i, \mathbf{x}) + \sum_{j \in \mathcal{N}_i} I(y_i, y_j, \mathbf{x}) \Big). \quad (8)$$

Then the negative log pseudo-likelihood on the training set $\mathcal{T}$ is defined as,

$$L = -\sum_{n=1}^{N} \sum_{i \in S} \Big\{ u_i F(y_i^n, \mathbf{x}^n, \boldsymbol{\alpha}_i) + \sum_{j \in \mathcal{N}_i} v_{ij} y_i^n y_j^n P(y_j^n | \mathbf{x}^n) - log Z_i^n \Big\} + R_{CRF} + R_{\mathbf{w}}, \quad (9)$$

where $F(y_i^n, \mathbf{x}^n, \boldsymbol{\alpha}_i)$ is defined as,

$$F(y_i^n, \mathbf{x}^n, \boldsymbol{\alpha}_i) = log(1/\{1 + exp(-f(\mathbf{x}^n, \boldsymbol{\alpha}_i) y_i^n)\}), \quad (10)$$

where $f(\mathbf{x}^n, \boldsymbol{\alpha}_i)$ is defined in Eq.3. The partition function for site i on the nth observation is,

$$Z_i^n = \sum_{y_i^n} z(y_i^n, \mathbf{x}^n, \boldsymbol{\alpha}_i), \quad (11)$$

where $z(y_i^n, \mathbf{x}^n, \boldsymbol{\alpha}_i)$ is defined as

$$z(y_i^n, \mathbf{x}^n, \boldsymbol{\alpha}_i) = exp\{u_i F(y_i^n, \mathbf{x}^n, \boldsymbol{\alpha}_i) + \sum_{j \in \mathcal{N}_i} v_{ij} y_i^n y_j^n P(y_j^n | \mathbf{x}^n)\}. \quad (12)$$

$R_{\mathbf{w}}$ and R_{CRF} are pairwise regularization terms on feature weight $\mathbf{w}$ and the CRF parameters $\{(\boldsymbol{\alpha}_i, u_i, v_{ij})_{j \in \mathcal{N}_i}\}_{i \in S}$ respectively. As these two parts of parameters have different effect on our model, we impose different kinds of penalty on them. Specifically, to prevent our AIA model from overfitting, we use L_2 regularization for R_{CRF}. L_1 regularization is adopted for $R_{\mathbf{w}}$ to perform sparse multiple distance learning, which encourages non-relevant feature's weight to be zero.

4.1 Alternating Parameter Estimation Procedure

An alternating procedure is proposed for parameter estimation. In CRF parameter estimation stage, the algorithm fixes $\mathbf{w}$ and optimizes $(\boldsymbol{\alpha}_i, u_i, v_{ij})_{j\in N_i}$, while in the sparse multiple distance learning stage, with fixed $(\boldsymbol{\alpha}_i, u_i, v_{ij})_{j\in N_i}$, it searches for the optimal $\mathbf{w}$. At each stage of the algorithm, the regularization term of fixed parameters is omitted, as it remains constant through the optimization process. Consequently, the object functions of each stage differ slightly with regularization terms. Detailed description of the object functions will be given in subsequent sections. Before the training process, for each site i, we build a training set $T_i = \{(\mathbf{x}^n, \mathbf{y}^n)\}_{n=1}^{N_i}$ from the original training set T by randomly selecting more balanced positive and negative samples. In our experiments the parameter estimation procedure converge rapidly after two or three times of parameters update alternations.

4.2 CRF Parameter Estimation

To optimize $\{(\boldsymbol{\alpha}_i, u_i, v_{ij})_{j\in N_i}\}_{i\in S}$, we fix $\mathbf{w}$ and omit the corresponding regularization. The estimation task is then reduced to the same problem as learning CRF parameters. Since there are no shared parameters among all sites, $(\boldsymbol{\alpha}_i, u_i, v_{ij})_{j\in N_i}$ can be trained per site. The negative log pseudo-likelihood of site i is,

$$L_i = -\sum_{n=1}^{N}\left\{u_i F(y_i^n, \mathbf{x}^n, \boldsymbol{\alpha}_i) + \sum_{j\in\mathcal{N}_i} v_{ij} y_i^n y_j^n P(y_j^n|\mathbf{x}^n) - logZ_i^n\right\} + R_{CRF}^i. \quad (13)$$

In practice, edge parameters tend to be overestimated that we need to penalize them more. Hence we introduce piecewise L_2 regularization terms on $\boldsymbol{\alpha}_i$, u_i and v_{ij} respectively,

$$R_{CRF}^i = \frac{\lambda_1}{2}\boldsymbol{\alpha}_i^T K\boldsymbol{\alpha}_i + \frac{\lambda_2}{2}\|u_i - 1\|^2 + \frac{\lambda_3}{2}\sum_{j\in\mathcal{N}_i}\|v_{ij}\|^2, \quad (14)$$

where K is the kernel matrix calculated using Eq.6 on the Training set T, λ_1, λ_2 and λ_3 are constants controlling the strength of the penalty, which are chosen empirically. Notice that the regularization term on $\boldsymbol{\alpha}_i$ is the same as KLR. The regularization for u_i forces it to stay around 1. The derivatives of Eq.13 with respect to $\boldsymbol{\alpha}_i$ equals to

$$\frac{\partial L_i}{\partial \boldsymbol{\alpha}_i} = -u_i K\mathbf{M}_i + \lambda_1 K\boldsymbol{\alpha}_i, \quad (15)$$

where $\mathbf{M}_i = (M_i^1, M_i^2, ..., M_i^N)^T$ is a coefficient vector with each of its component defined as

$$M_i^n = \frac{y_i^n}{1 + exp(y_i^n f(\mathbf{x}^n, \boldsymbol{\alpha}_i))} - \frac{1}{Z_i^n}\sum_{y_i^n} z(y_i^n, \mathbf{x}^n, \boldsymbol{\alpha}_i)\frac{y_i^n}{1 + exp(y_i^n f(\mathbf{x}^n, \boldsymbol{\alpha}_i))}. \quad (16)$$

The derivatives of Eq.13 with respect to u_i is

$$\frac{\partial L_i}{\partial u_i} = -\sum_{n=1}^{N}\left\{F(y_i^n, \mathbf{x}^n, \boldsymbol{\alpha}_i) - \frac{1}{Z_i^n}\sum_{y_i^n} z(y_i^n, \mathbf{x}^n, \boldsymbol{\alpha}_i)F(y_i^n, \mathbf{x}^n, \boldsymbol{\alpha}_i)\right\} + \lambda_2(u_i - 1). \tag{17}$$

By differentiating Eq.13 with respect to v_{ij}, we will get

$$\frac{\partial L_i}{\partial v_{ij}} = -\sum_{n=1}^{N}\left\{y_j^n P(y_j^n, \mathbf{x}^n)(y_i^n - \frac{1}{Z_i^n}\sum_{y_i^n} y_i^n z(y_i^n, \mathbf{x}^n, \boldsymbol{\alpha}_i))\right\} + \lambda_3 v_{ij}. \tag{18}$$

To minimize Eq.13 we set its derivatives Eq.15, Eq.17 and Eq.18 to zero. Eq.13 is concave when λ_1, λ_2 and λ_3 are given and can be easily minimized using a projected gradient algorithm.

4.3 Sparse Multiple Distance Learning

At this stage we fix the CRF parameters and optimize the feature weight vector $\mathbf{w}$. Regularization term on CRF parameters is left out. We penalize $\mathbf{w}$ with L_1 regularization. The object function becomes,

$$L_{\mathbf{w}} = -\sum_{n=1}^{N}\sum_{i\in S}\left\{u_i F(y_i^n, \mathbf{x}^n, \boldsymbol{\alpha}_i) + \sum_{j\in\mathcal{N}_i} v_{ij} y_i^n y_j^n P(y_j^n|\mathbf{x}^n) - log Z_i^n\right\} + C\sum_{t=1}^{T}|w_t|, \tag{19}$$

where C is the coefficient controlling the level of sparsity of $\mathbf{w}$. In practice it is chosen empirically. As the absolute value function is not differentiable at the zero value point, solving optimization problem Eq.19 is harder than solving differentiable optimization problems. Here we take the sub-gradient [22] of the second term in Eq.19 with respect to w_t at zero,

$$\frac{\partial L_{\mathbf{w}}}{\partial w_t} = -\sum_{n=1}^{N}\sum_{i\in S}\left\{u_i \frac{y_i^n g(\mathbf{x}^n, \boldsymbol{\alpha}_i)}{1 + exp(y_i^n f(\mathbf{x}^n, \boldsymbol{\alpha}_i))} - \frac{1}{Z_i^n}\frac{\partial Z_i^n}{\partial w_t}\right\} + C\text{sign}(w_t), \tag{20}$$

where $\text{sign}(w_t) = 1$ if $w_t > 0$, $\text{sign}(w_t) = -1$ if $w_t < 0$, and $\text{sign}(w_t) = 0$ if $w_t = 0$, and $g(\mathbf{x}^n, \boldsymbol{\alpha}_i)$ is defined as,

$$g(\mathbf{x}^n, \boldsymbol{\alpha}_i) = \sum_{m=1}^{N} \alpha_i^m K(\mathbf{x}^n, \mathbf{x}^m)(-d_t(\mathbf{x}^n, \mathbf{x}^m)/2\sigma^2), \tag{21}$$

and the derivative of Z_i^n in Eq.20 is,

$$\frac{\partial Z_i^n}{\partial w_t} = \sum_{y_i^n} z(y_i^n, \mathbf{x}^n, \boldsymbol{\alpha}_i) u_i g(\mathbf{x}^n, \boldsymbol{\alpha}_i)(y_i^n - \frac{1}{1 + exp(-y_i^n f(\mathbf{x}^n, \boldsymbol{\alpha}_i))}). \tag{22}$$

Using the method in [22], we compute the pseudo-gradient of the L1 penalty to the extent that it does not change its sign. The limited memory BFGS algorithm is adopted to obtain the optimization of the weight parameters.

5 Model Inference

The inference problem of KCRF is to find the optimal label configuration $\mathbf{y}$ given an image $\mathbf{x}$:

$$\mathbf{y}^* \leftarrow \arg\max_{\mathbf{y}} P(\mathbf{y}|\mathbf{x}), \tag{23}$$

where $P(\mathbf{y}|\mathbf{x})$ is defined in Eq.1. The iterative conditional modes (ICM) algorithm is employed in our model. In the $(k+1)^{th}$ iteration, given the observation $\mathbf{x}$ and labels on neighboring sites $y_{\mathcal{N}_i}^{(k)}$ obtained in the last iteration, the algorithm sequentially updates each $y_i^{(k)}$ to $y_i^{(k+1)}$ that yields maximal conditional probability $P(y_i|\mathbf{y}_{\mathcal{N}_i}^{(k)}, \mathbf{x})$ defined in Eq.8. The update rule can be written as follows

$$y_i^{(k+1)} = \begin{cases} +1, \text{ if } P(y_i = 1|\mathbf{y}_{\mathcal{N}_i}^{(k)}, \mathbf{x}) > P(y_i = -1|\mathbf{y}_{\mathcal{N}_i}^{(k)}, \mathbf{x}) \\ -1, \text{ otherwise.} \end{cases} \tag{24}$$

The ICM algorithm starts with the initial configuration that all labels are set to be -1 and runs until convergence when two label vectors of consecutive iterations are the same. If it does not converge after 10 iterations, the process will be stopped. Ultimately it outputs the approximate result of the most probable label configuration of the observation.

6 Experiment Setup

6.1 Experimental Datasets

Our experiments are conducted on two commonly used datasets: **Corel 5k Dataset:** [1] is an important benchmark for AIA performance evaluation. It contains 5000 images, where 500 of them are used for testing and the rest for training. The whole vocabulary consists of 260 unique words with each image annotated with 1-5 keywords; **TRECVID-2005 Dataset** contains about 108 hours broadcast news, which can well represents the real world scenario. A total of 69,901 keyframes are extracted from these videos. It consists of 39 keywords. For computational efficiency, we select training images from 90 videos and testing images from the other 47 videos. For each keyword (concept), no more than 500 and 100 positive samples for training and testing respectively are included. Finally 6,657 keyframes are used for training and 1,748 keyframes for testing.

6.2 Feature Extraction

22 visual features are utilized in the experiments, where 15 feature provided by [12] are included. Apart from these features, we also extract Texture Co-occurrence, Scalable Color, HarrWavelet, Edge Histogram, Color Moments, Color Layout, and Color Correlogram according to MPEG7. All features except Gist [23] are L1-normalized. Following previous work on distance calculation, we use L2 metric for Gist, L1 for color histograms and $\chi 2$ for the rest.

6.3 Evaluation Measurements

For AIA performance evaluation, we use recall, precision and F1 measure. For a given query word w, let $|W_G|$ be the number of images with label w in the test set, $|W_M|$ be the number of annotated images by our model with the same label, then recall, precision and F1 are defined as $recall = \frac{|W_G \bigcap W_M|}{|W_G|}$, $precision = \frac{|W_C \bigcap W_M|}{|W_M|}$ and $F1 = \frac{2 \times recall \times precision}{recall + precision}$. We compute recall and precision for each keyword and then average them to measure the overall annotation performance. $F1$ is calculated with the derived mean recall and precision.

7 Experimental Results and Discussions

7.1 Performance Evaluation on Corel

In this section we evaluate the annotation performance of our method. TagProp [12] is chosen for comparison due to its state-of-the-art performance and adopting a metric learning approach. The code we use is provided by the authors. Different from TagProp, KCRF's multiple distance learning is embedded with semantic context, thus the resulted distance combination is expected to capture semantics more precisely. We conduct 9 rounds of experiments, where we start with 14 visual features and add 1 new feature incrementally in each subsequent round until all the 22 features are used in the last round. The F1 of all the 9 round experiments are given in Figure 3.

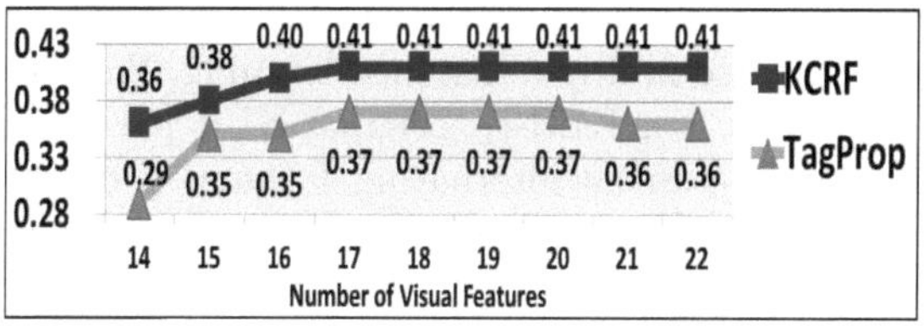

Fig. 3. F1 measure comparisons between KCRF and TagProp on Corel

It shows that KCRF outperforms TagProp in all cases, achieving the highest improvement of 24.1% in F1 score when 14 features are used, where KCRF gets 0.36 while TagProp gets 0.29. Annotation accuracy increases from 14 features to 17 features are observed for both models, while KCRF is more stable producing a smoother F1 score line. KCRF reaches the best F1 score of 0.41 with 17 features, leading to an improvement of 10.8% over TagProp, which also reaches its best F1 score of 0.37. F1 of KCRF remains the same afterward. But for TagProp model, performance decrease occurs when more than 20 features are used. The reason is that, the optimality of the distance weights is not guaranteed in TagProp, because it directly sets negative weight value to 0 to derive non-negative weight vector [12]. Unlike TagProp, KCRF introduces L_1 regularization to ensures sparsity of weight vector. Thus KCRF has higher stability with increasing number of features.

Table 1. Performance comparisons between KCRF and TagProp on Corel dataset. N+, Length, Recall, Precision, F1 and Zero-weight denote the number of keywords with non-zero recall value, average annotation length, average recall, average precision, f1 score and number of features with zero weight respectively.

Models	TagProp-14	KCRF-14	TagProp-18	KCRF-18	TagProp-22	KCRF-22
N+	140	183	160	190	158	189
Length	5	5.2	5	4.9	5	5.0
Recall	0.33	0.41	0.42	0.47	0.42	**0.48**
Precision	0.26	0.33	0.33	0.36	0.32	**0.36**
F1	0.29	0.36	0.37	0.41	0.36	**0.41**
Zero-weight	2	6	9	9	10	10

We present some detailed statistics of 3 rounds of experiments in Table 1. For the limit of page space, we cannot give out all results. Note that in Table 1, the suffixes "-14", "-18" and "-22" in the model name denote the number of features it uses. "KCRF-22" gives out the highest precision of 0.48 and the highest recall of 0.36.

7.2 Evaluation of the Unified Model

In this experiment we will clarify that, the performance improvements of KCRF given in previous sections are brought by integration of context modeling and multiple distance learning, rather than by either one of them individually. Thus we compare KCRF to these two separate methods: First, the candidate for multiple distance learning is obtained by removing context modeling from KCRF. Specifically, we set the edge potentials to 0 and it becomes Kernel Logistic Regression (KLR) with sparse multiple distance learning. We use KLR-l_1 to refer to it in following sections. For KLR-l_1, original KLR parameters and distance weights are also estimated in an alternating fashion. Second, sparse multiple distance learning is removed from our model, and we get the conventional Conditional Random Fields (CRF) as a representative for context modeling. The only difference between CRF and KCRF is the absence of multiple distance learning. Distances of different features are combined with equal weight one for CRF. The same distance metrics and kernel function are used for KCRF, KLR-l_1 and CRF. Experiment is conducted on the Corel dataset. Here all the 22 features are used. The annotation length of KLR-l_1 is fixed to be 5, while CRF and KCRF can decide the length automatically.

Experimental results are shown in Table 2. It can be observed that KCRF gives out significant performance superiority over KLR-l_1 and CRF. Specifically, the recall, precision and F1 for our unified model are 0.48, 0.36 and 0.41 respectively. It outperforms KLR-l_1 by 24% and CRF by 13.9% in F1. We also provide comparisons between distance weights of 22 features learned by KCRF and KLR-l_1 in Figure 4. From the figure, KCRF generates more sparse weight vector than KLR-l_1 and achieves better performance. It well demonstrates that the proposed unified model is able to find the optimal distances combination and

Table 2. Performance comparison with KLR-l_1 and CRF on Corel dataset

Models	KLR-l_1	CRF	KCRF
N+	157	166	**189**
Length	5	5.6	5.0
Recall	0.37	0.41	**0.48**
Precision	0.31	0.32	**0.36**
F1	0.33	0.36	**0.41**
zero-weight	6	0	10

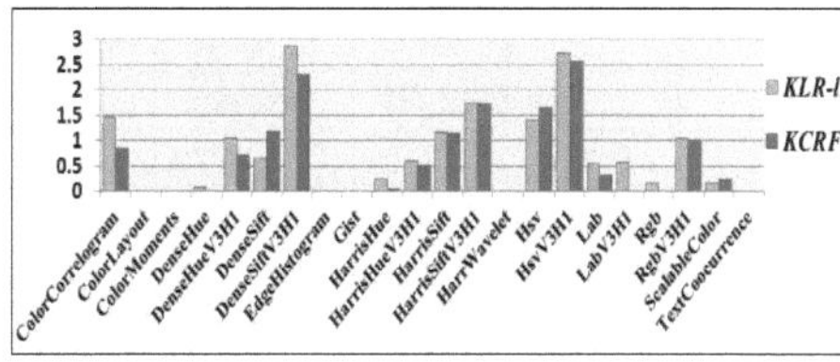

Fig. 4. Feature Weights of 22 Features Produced by KCRF and KLR-l_1

achieves better performance, which is not obtainable when using only the sparse multiple distance learning. Hence, the integration of sparse multiple distance learning and context modeling has significant advantages over the separated methods.

7.3 Performance Comparison on Corel

To further evaluate KCRF, we compare it to the TagProp [12], the semantic context modeling MRFA [13], and the other AIA methods such as MBRM [19], the supervised multi-class labeling (SML) [2], and the Nearest Spanning Chain (NSC) [3]. These models are representative techniques, and some of them achieve the stat-of-the-art performance so far. Figure 5(a) gives out the experimental results.

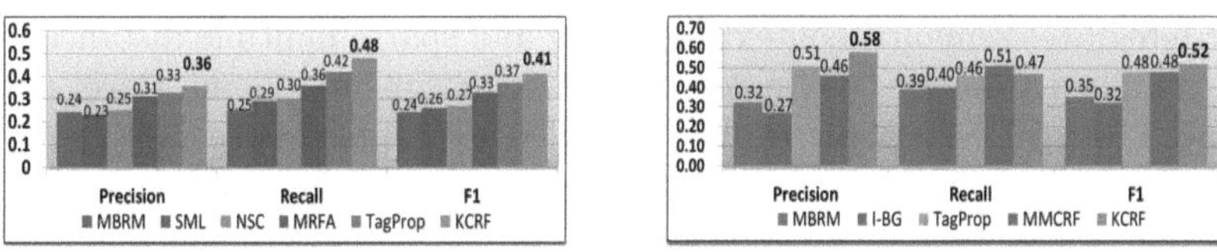

(a) Corel (b) Trecvid

Fig. 5. Performance Comparison with Other Methods on Corel and Trecvid Datasets

It shows that our KCRF model has the best performance with significant improvement over the others. Specifically, the average recall, precision and F1 score of KCRF are 0.48, 0.36, and 0.41, realizing improvements in F1 score of 10.8% and 24.2% over TagProp and MRFA, which give out the second and the third highest F1 of 0.37 and 0.33, respectively. Figure 6 gives some examples of annotation results generated by KCRF and the corresponding ground-truth. It shows that the annotations of our model captures the semantics of images precisely.

7.4 Performance Comparison on TRECVID-2005

As MMCRF [18] also employs multiple visual features in CRF and achieves very competitive result on this dataset, we choose it for comparison. Besides,

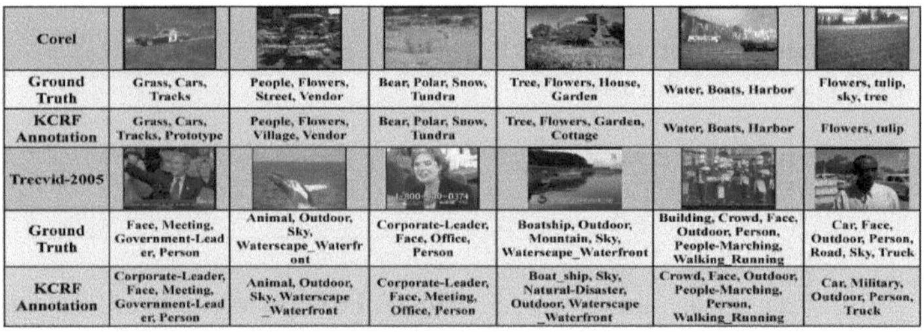

Fig. 6. Comparisons of KCRF annotation results with ground-truth annotations on Corel dataset and TRECVID-2005 dataset

MBRM [19], Tagprop [12] and the newly proposed BG model [20] are also included for comparison. Experimental result is given in Figure 5(b). It shows that our model also outperforms all the other methods with significant improvement. Specifically, KCRF gives out the highest F1 score of 0.52, realizing an improvement of 8.3% over TagProp and MMCRF, whose F1 scores are both 0.48. KCRF also achieves the highest precision of 0.58. Some annotation examples of KCRF are given in Figure 6 compared to the ground-truth. Specially, perfect match is reported in the second keyframes.

8 Conclusion

We propose a novel Kernelized Conditional Random Fields model for AIA problem. It integrates semantic context modeling and sparse multiple distance learning in a unified framework. We conduct the experiments on the Corel dataset and the TRECVID-2005 for evaluation. The experimental results show that through integrated learning of "visual" parameters and "semantic" parameters, our model is able to leverage the annotation performance significantly. Compared to the state-of-the-art metric learning based AIA work, KCRF is more robust and achieves higher annotation accuracy, especially with a bigger feature set.

Acknowledgments. This work was supported by the Natural Science Foundation of China under Grant No.61073002 and No.60773077.

References

1. Duygulu, P., Barnard, K., de Freitas, J.F.G., Forsyth, D.: Object Recognition as Machine Translation: Learning a Lexicon for a Fixed Image Vocabulary. In: Heyden, A., Sparr, G., Nielsen, M., Johansen, P. (eds.) ECCV 2002, Part IV. LNCS, vol. 2353, pp. 97–112. Springer, Heidelberg (2002)
2. Carneiro, G., Chan, A., Moreno, P., Vasconcelos, N.: Supervised learning of semantic classes for image annotation and retrieval. IEEE PAMI 29 (2007)
3. Liu, J., Li, M., Ma, W., Liu, Q., Lu, H.: An adaptive graph model for automatic image annotation. In: ACM Workshop on Multimedia Information Retrieval (2006)

4. Wang, Y., Mori, G.: Max-margin latent dirichlet allocation for image classification and annotation. In: 22nd British Machine Vision Conference, BMVC (2011)
5. Zhou, X., Wang, M., Zhang, J., Zhang, Q., Shi, B.: Automatic image annotation by an iterative approach: Incorporating keyword correlations and region matching. In: ACM Int'l Conf. Image and Video Retrieval, CIVR (2007)
6. Li, L., Li, F.: What, where and who? classifying events by scene and object recognition. In: CVPR (2007)
7. Deng, J., Dong, W., Socher, R., Li, L., Li, K., Li, F.: Imagenet: A large-scale hierarchical image database. In: CVPR (2009)
8. Tang, J., Hong, R., Yan, S., Chua, T.S., Qi, G.J., Jain, R.: Image annotation by knn-sparse graph-based label propagation over noisily-tagged web images. ACM Transactions on Intelligent Systems and Technology 2 (2011)
9. Qi, G., Hua, X., Rui, Y., Tang, J., Mei, T., Zhang, H.: Correlative multi-label video annotation. In: ACM SIGMM (2007)
10. Jiang, Y.G., Dai, Q., Wang, J., Ngo, C.W., Xue, X., Chang, S.F.: Fast semantic diffusion for large-scale context-based image and video annotation. IEEE Transactions on Image Processing 21 (2012)
11. Makadia, A., Pavlovic, V., Kumar, S.: A New Baseline for Image Annotation. In: Forsyth, D., Torr, P., Zisserman, A. (eds.) ECCV 2008, Part III. LNCS, vol. 5304, pp. 316–329. Springer, Heidelberg (2008)
12. Guillaumin, M., Mensink, T., Verbeek, J., Schmid, C.: Tagprop: Discriminative metric learning in nearest neighbor models for image auto-annotation. In: ICCV (2009)
13. Xiang, Y., Zhou, X., Chua, T., Ngo, C.: A revisit of generative model for automatic image annotation using markov random fields. In: CVPR (2009)
14. Rasiwasia, N., Vasconcelos, N.: Holistic context modeling using semantic co-occurences. In: CVPR (2009)
15. Feng, S., Manmatha, R.: A discrete direct retrieval model for image and video retrieval. In: CIVR (2008)
16. Song, Z., Chen, Q., Huang, Z., Hua, Y., Yan, S.: Contextualizing object detection and classification. In: CVPR (2011)
17. Roth, V.: Probabilistic Discriminative Kernel Classifiers for Multi-class Problems. In: Radig, B., Florczyk, S. (eds.) DAGM 2001. LNCS, vol. 2191, pp. 246–253. Springer, Heidelberg (2001)
18. Xiang, Y., Zhou, X., Liu, Z., Chua, T., Ngo, C.: Semantic context modeling with maximal margin conditional random fields for automatic image annotation. In: CVPR (2010)
19. Feng, S., Manmatha, R., Lavrenko, V.: Multiple bernoulli relevance models for image and video annotation. In: CVPR (2004)
20. Wang, H., Huang, H., Ding, C.: Image annotation using bi-relational graph of images and semantic labels. In: CVPR (2011)
21. Lafferty, J., McCallum, A., Pereira, F.: Conditonal random fields: Probabilistic models for segmenting and labeling sequence data. In: ICML (2001)
22. Andrew, G., Gao, J.: Scalable training of l1-regularized log-linear models. In: ICML (2007)
23. Oliva, A., Torralba, A.: The role of context in object recognition. Trends in Cognitive Sciences 11(12), 520–527 (2007)

Exploiting the Circulant Structure of Tracking-by-Detection with Kernels

João F. Henriques, Rui Caseiro, Pedro Martins, and Jorge Batista

Institute of Systems and Robotics, University of Coimbra
{henriques,ruicaseiro,pedromartins,batista}@isr.uc.pt

Abstract. Recent years have seen greater interest in the use of discriminative classifiers in tracking systems, owing to their success in object detection. They are trained online with samples collected during tracking. Unfortunately, the potentially large number of samples becomes a computational burden, which directly conflicts with real-time requirements. On the other hand, limiting the samples may sacrifice performance.

Interestingly, we observed that, as we add more and more samples, the problem acquires circulant structure. Using the well-established theory of Circulant matrices, we provide a link to Fourier analysis that opens up the possibility of extremely fast learning and detection with the Fast Fourier Transform. This can be done in the dual space of kernel machines as fast as with linear classifiers. We derive closed-form solutions for training and detection with several types of kernels, including the popular Gaussian and polynomial kernels. The resulting tracker achieves performance competitive with the state-of-the-art, can be implemented with only a few lines of code and runs at hundreds of frames-per-second. MATLAB code is provided in the paper (see Algorithm 1).

1 Introduction

Tracking is a fundamental problem in computer vision, with applications in video surveillance, human-machine interfaces and robot perception. Even though some settings allow for strong assumptions about the target [1, 2], sometimes it is desirable to track an object with little a-priori knowledge. Model-less tracking consists of learning and adapting a representation of the target online.

A very successful approach has been tracking-by-detection [3–7]. This stems directly from the development of powerful discriminative methods in machine learning, and their application to detection with offline training. Many of these algorithms can be adapted for online training, where each successful detection provides more information about the target.

Almost all of the proposed methods have one thing in common: a sparse sampling strategy [3, 5–7]. In each frame, several samples are collected in the target's neighborhood, where typically each sample characterizes a subwindow the same size as the target (illustrated in Table 1). Clearly, there is a lot of redundancy, since most of the samples have a large amount of overlap. This underlying structure is usually ignored. Instead, most methods simply collect a small number of samples, because the cost of not doing so would be prohibitive.

A. Fitzgibbon et al. (Eds.): ECCV 2012, Part IV, LNCS 7575, pp. 702–715, 2012.

Table 1. Overview of the main differences between standard tracking-by-detection and the proposed approach. The speed is for a 64×64 window region. See text for details.

		Storage	**Bottleneck**	**Speed**
Random Sampling (p random subwindows)		Features from p subwindows	Learning algorithm (Struct. SVM [4], Boost [3, 6]...)	10 - 25 FPS
Dense Sampling (all subwindows, proposed method)		Features from one image	Fast Fourier Transform	320 FPS

The fact that the training data has so much redundancy means that we are probably not exploiting its structure efficiently. We propose a new theoretical framework to address this. We show that the process of taking subwindows of an image induces *circulant structure*. We then establish links to Fourier analysis that allows the use of the Fast Fourier Transform (FFT) to quickly incorporate information from all subwindows, without iterating over them.

These developments enable new learning algorithms that can be orders of magnitude faster than the standard approach. We also show that classification on non-linear feature spaces with the Kernel Trick can be done as efficiently as in the original image space.

1.1 Previous Work

We will briefly discuss tracking-by-detection, but also other works that are relevant to our specific approach.

The literature on visual object tracking is extensive, and a full survey is outside the scope of this paper.[1] Like other works in tracking-by-detection, our contributions are focused on the appearance model, as opposed to the motion model and search strategy. Many use established learning algorithms such as Boosting [6, 3], Support Vector Machines (SVM) [5], or Random Forests [7], and adapt them to online training. Recent works have focused increasingly on problems specific to tracking, such as uncertainty in the training labels. Some notable examples use Semi-Supervised Learning [6] and Multiple Instance Learning [3] (MILTrack) to handle this. Going even further, Hare et al. [4] propose Struck, an online version of Structured Output SVM. This is closer to our work, since the framework allows sample selection over the possible subwindows (argmax step). However, in practice, the number of samples is still limited.

The idea of exploring subwindow redundancy has been noted before, but mostly in the context of detection, not training. Lampert et al. [10] use branch-and-bound optimization to find the maximum of a classifier's response without necessarily evaluating it at all locations. Alexe et al. [11] propose a method that can efficiently find the most similar subwindows between two images, which is

[1] We refer the reader to 2 reviews: [8] is more in-depth, while [9, Sec. 3] is more recent.

a related problem. Although they are useful and provide interesting insights, it may still be desirable to compute the responses at many locations, for example to allow more robust mode seeking or to evaluate the quality of the response [12]. An alternative is to use linear classification in a first stage, and then non-linear classification on promising locations [13, 14], but the results can be suboptimal.

Also closely related are adaptive correlation filters, rooted on classical signal processing [15, 12]. Their response can be evaluated quickly at all subwindows using the Fast Fourier Transform (FFT). It's possible to perform training on the Fourier domain as well, minimizing the error of the filter's response at all subwindows of the training images. The crucial detail is that they never actually iterate over the subwindows. The Minimum Output Sum of Squared Error (MOSSE) filter [12] has been shown to be competitive with the methods outlined before, but at a fraction of the complexity, and runs at impressive speeds.

Because they can be interpreted as linear classifiers, there is the question of whether correlation filters can take advantage of the Kernel Trick to classify on richer non-linear feature spaces. Patnaik and Casasent [16] investigate this problem, and show that, given the Fourier representation of an image, many classical filters cannot be kernelized. Instead, they propose a kernelized filter that is trained with a single subwindow (called Kernel SDF). An ideal solution would implicitly train with all subwindows.

We believe that the method we propose achieves this goal. We are able to devise Kernel classifiers with the same characteristics as correlation filters, namely their ability to be trained and evaluated quickly with the FFT.

1.2 Contributions

The contributions of this paper are as follows:

1. A theoretical framework to study generic classifiers that are trained with all subwindows (of fixed size) of an image. We call this approach *dense sampling*.
2. Proof that the kernel matrix in this case has circulant structure, for unitarily invariant kernels (Theorem 1).
3. Closed-form, fast and exact solutions (all running in $\mathcal{O}(n^2 \log n)$ for $n \times n$ images) for:
   (a) Kernel Regularized Least Squares with dense sampling (Section 2.4).
   (b) Detection at all subwindows with generic Kernel classifiers (Section 2.5).
   (c) Computation of a variety of kernels at all subwindows, including the popular Gaussian and polynomial kernels (Section 3).
4. Finally, we propose a tracker based on these ideas. We show it is competitive with state-of-the-art trackers, but has a simpler implementation and runs many times faster. Source code is provided.

2 Learning with Dense Sampling

The core component in tracking-by-detection is a classifier. Each frame, a set of samples is collected around the estimated position of the target; samples close

Fig. 1. Example results for `coke` and `surfer` sequences, best viewed in color. High values in the response map are red/opaque, low values are blue/transparent. Notice the highly localized responses, except when the target is under occlusion.

to the target are labeled positive and the ones further away are labeled negative. Updating the classifier with these samples allows it to adapt over time. Due to computational constraints, only a handful of random samples are collected [3–7].

We propose a radically different approach. We intend to train a classifier with *all* samples: we call this *dense sampling*. Counter to intuition, this allows a more efficient training. The reason is that the kernel matrix in this case becomes highly structured, and we can exploit it to our advantage.

2.1 Regularized Risk Minimization

We start with a general formulation, mostly to introduce notation. Given a set of training patterns and labels $(\mathbf{x}_1, y_1), \ldots, (\mathbf{x}_m, y_m)$, a classifier $f(\mathbf{x})$ is trained by finding the parameters that minimize the regularized risk. A linear classifier has the form $f(\mathbf{x}) = \langle \mathbf{w}, \mathbf{x} \rangle + b$, where $\langle \cdot, \cdot \rangle$ is the dot product, and the minimization problem is

$$\min_{\mathbf{w},b} \sum_{i=1}^{m} L\left(y_i, f(\mathbf{x}_i)\right) + \lambda \left\|\mathbf{w}\right\|^2, \tag{1}$$

where $L(y, f(\mathbf{x}))$ is a loss function, and λ controls the amount of regularization[2].

This framework includes the popular Support Vector Machine (SVM), which uses the hinge loss $L(y, f(\mathbf{x})) = \max(0, 1 - yf(\mathbf{x}))$. An alternative is Regularized Least Squares (RLS), also known as Ridge Regression, which uses the quadratic loss $L(y, f(\mathbf{x})) = (y - f(\mathbf{x}))^2$. It has been shown that, in many practical problems, RLS offers equivalent classification performance to SVM [17].

It is well known that the Kernel Trick [18] can improve performance further, by allowing classification on a rich high-dimensional feature space. The inputs are mapped to the feature space using $\varphi(\mathbf{x})$, defined by the kernel $\kappa(\mathbf{x}, \mathbf{x}') = \langle \varphi(\mathbf{x}), \varphi(\mathbf{x}') \rangle$. The Representer Theorem [18, p. 89] then states that a solution can be expanded as a linear combination of the inputs: $\mathbf{w} = \sum_i \alpha_i \varphi(\mathbf{x}_i)$.

Then, RLS with Kernels (KRLS) has the simple closed form solution [17]

$$\boldsymbol{\alpha} = (K + \lambda I)^{-1} \mathbf{y}, \tag{2}$$

where K is the kernel matrix with elements $K_{ij} = \kappa(\mathbf{x}_i, \mathbf{x}_j)$, I is the identity matrix, and the vector $\mathbf{y}$ has elements y_i. The solution $\mathbf{w}$ is implicitly represented

[2] The bias term b is not important in practice, when finding the maximum response.

by the vector $\boldsymbol{\alpha}$, whose elements are the coefficients α_i. We will show that the matrix inversion in Eq. 2 can be avoided entirely for our purposes.

2.2 Circulant Matrices

The main observation that will allow efficient learning is that, under suitable conditions, the kernel matrix becomes *circulant.* An $n \times n$ circulant matrix $C(\mathbf{u})$ is obtained from the $n \times 1$ vector $\mathbf{u}$ by concatenating all possible cyclic shifts of $\mathbf{u}$:

$$C(\mathbf{u}) = \begin{bmatrix} u_0 & u_1 & u_2 & \cdots & u_{n-1} \\ u_{n-1} & u_0 & u_1 & \cdots & u_{n-2} \\ u_{n-2} & u_{n-1} & u_0 & \cdots & u_{n-3} \\ \vdots & \vdots & \vdots & \ddots & \vdots \\ u_1 & u_2 & u_3 & \cdots & u_0 \end{bmatrix} . \tag{3}$$

The first row is vector $\mathbf{u}$, the second row is $\mathbf{u}$ shifted one element to the right (the last element wraps around), and so on.

The motivation behind circulant matrices is that they encode the convolution of vectors, which is conceptually close to what we do when evaluating a classifier at many different subwindows. Since the product $C(\mathbf{u})\mathbf{v}$ represents convolution of vectors $\mathbf{u}$ and $\mathbf{v}$ [19], it can be computed in the Fourier domain, using

$$C(\mathbf{u})\mathbf{v} = \mathcal{F}^{-1}\left(\mathcal{F}(\mathbf{u}) \odot \mathcal{F}(\mathbf{v})\right), \tag{4}$$

where $\odot$ is the element-wise product, while $\mathcal{F}$ and $\mathcal{F}^{-1}$ denote the Fourier transform and its inverse, respectively.

The properties of circulant matrices make them particularly amenable to manipulation, since their sums, products and inverses are also circulant [19]. We never have to explicitly compute and store a circulant matrix $C(\mathbf{u})$, because it is defined by $\mathbf{u}$. These operations often involve the Fourier Transform of $\mathbf{u}$.

There are a couple of different definitions of $C(\mathbf{u})$ that we will find useful [19]. One is that the row i of $C(\mathbf{u})$ is given by $P^i\mathbf{u}$, where P is the permutation matrix that cyclically shifts $\mathbf{u}$ by one element. The matrix power in P^i applies the permutation i times, resulting in i cyclic shifts.

Alternatively, the elements of $C(\mathbf{u})$ can be defined as $c_{ij} = u_{(j-i) \bmod n}$. That is, a matrix is circulant if its elements only depend on $(j-i) \bmod n$, where mod is the modulus operation (remainder of division by n). To make some derivations easier, all indexes are zero-based.

2.3 The Kernel Matrix with Dense Sampling

We introduce the concept of dense sampling. For a matter of clarity, we start with one-dimensional images with a single feature (ie., the pixel value). This allows more intuitive proofs with simpler notation. However, they are readily transferable to the case of 2D images with multiple channels, such as RGB images, and dense SIFT or HOG descriptors. Appendix A.3 presents more details.

Given a single image $\mathbf{x}$, expressed as a $n \times 1$ vector, the samples are defined as

$$\mathbf{x}_i = P^i \mathbf{x}, \quad \forall i = 0, \ldots, n-1 \tag{5}$$

with P the permutation matrix that cyclically shifts vectors by one element, as defined earlier. Intuitively, the samples are all possible translated versions of $\mathbf{x}$ (except at the boundaries, discussed in Section 4.1). We will now prove that the resulting kernel matrix is circulant, and show under what conditions.

Theorem 1. *The matrix K with elements $K_{ij} = \kappa(P^i \mathbf{x},\ P^j \mathbf{x})$ is circulant if κ is a unitarily invariant kernel.*

Proof. A kernel κ is unitarily invariant if $\kappa(\mathbf{x}, \mathbf{x}') = \kappa(U\mathbf{x}, U\mathbf{x}')$ for any unitary matrix U. Since permutation matrices are unitary, $K_{ij} = \kappa(P^i \mathbf{x},\ P^j \mathbf{x}) = \kappa(P^{-i} P^i \mathbf{x},\ P^{-i} P^j \mathbf{x}) = \kappa(\mathbf{x},\ P^{j-i} \mathbf{x})$. Because K_{ij} depends only on $(j-i) \bmod n$, K is circulant.

Corollary 1. *K as defined above is circulant for dot-product and radial basis function kernels. Particular examples are the polynomial and Gaussian kernels.*

This is an important property that allows the creation of efficient learning algorithms. We will now focus on applying this knowledge to KRLS.

2.4 Efficient Kernel Regularized Least Squares solution

Theorem 1 is readily applicable to KRLS. We will define vector $\mathbf{k}$ with elements

$$k_i = \kappa(\mathbf{x},\ P^i \mathbf{x}), \quad \forall i = 0, \ldots, n-1 \tag{6}$$

which compactly represents the kernel matrix $K = C(\mathbf{k})$. Notice that $\mathbf{k}$ is only $n \times 1$, while the full K would be $n \times n$.

Some operations on matrices of the form $C(\mathbf{u})$, like multiplication and inversion, can be done element-wise on the vectors $\mathbf{u}$, if they are transformed to the Fourier domain [19].

By applying these properties to Eq. 2 and Eq. 6, we obtain the KRLS solution:

$$\boldsymbol{\alpha} = \mathcal{F}^{-1}\left(\frac{\mathcal{F}(\mathbf{y})}{\mathcal{F}(\mathbf{k}) + \lambda}\right), \tag{7}$$

where the division is performed element-wise. A detailed proof is in Appendix A.1.

Note that the vector $\boldsymbol{\alpha}$ contains all the α_i coefficients. This closed-form solution is very efficient: it uses only Fast Fourier Transform (FFT) and element-wise operations. We'll see in Sec. 3 that $\mathbf{k}$ can also be computed quickly with the FFT.

For $n \times n$ images, the proposed algorithm has a complexity of only $\mathcal{O}(n^2 \log n)$, while a naive KRLS implementation would take $\mathcal{O}(n^4)$ operations. This is done without reducing the number of samples, which would sacrifice performance.

2.5 Fast Detection

The general formula for computing the classifier response for a single input $\mathbf{z}$ is

$$y' = \sum_i \alpha_i \kappa(\mathbf{x}_i, \mathbf{z}). \tag{8}$$

This formula is typically evaluated at all subwindows, in a sliding-window manner. However, we can exploit the circulant structure to compute all the responses simultaneously and efficiently. Using the properties discussed earlier, the vector with the responses at *all* positions is given by

$$\hat{\mathbf{y}} = \mathcal{F}^{-1}\left(\mathcal{F}(\bar{\mathbf{k}}) \odot \mathcal{F}(\boldsymbol{\alpha})\right), \tag{9}$$

where $\bar{\mathbf{k}}$ is the vector with elements $\bar{k}_i = \kappa(\mathbf{z},\, P^i\mathbf{x})$. We provide an extended proof in Appendix A.2. Just like the formula for KRLS training, the complexity is bound by the FFT operations and is only $\mathcal{O}(n^2 \log n)$ for 2D images.

3 Fast Computation of Non-linear Kernels

The proposed training procedure is fast, but the question of how to evaluate non-linear kernels quickly for all subwindows (ie., compute $\mathbf{k}$ and $\bar{\mathbf{k}}$) still remains. As of this writing, this is a topic of active research [10, 11, 16].

Linear kernels are usually preferred in time-critical problems such as tracking, because the weights vector $\mathbf{w}$ can be computed explicitly. Non-linear kernels require iterating over all samples (or support vectors). The work that comes closest to the goal of efficiently computing non-linear kernels at all locations is by Patnaik [20]. Unfortunately, it requires inputs that have unit norm, and the normalization may discard important information.

In this work, we propose closed-form solutions to compute a variety of kernels at all image locations, in an efficient manner that fully exploits the problem structure. The formulas are exact, and simple to compute.

3.1 Dot-Product Kernels

Dot-product kernels have the form $\kappa(\mathbf{x}, \mathbf{x}') = g(\langle \mathbf{x}, \mathbf{x}' \rangle)$, for some function g. In this case, the compact representation $\mathbf{k}$ of the kernel matrix (Eq. 6) will be denoted by $\mathbf{k}^{\mathrm{dp}}$. Each element of $\mathbf{k}^{\mathrm{dp}}$ is given by

$$k_i^{\mathrm{dp}} = \kappa(\mathbf{x},\, P^i\mathbf{x}') = g\big(\mathbf{x}^T P^i \mathbf{x}'\big)\,. \tag{10}$$

With slight abuse of notation, we will say that g can also be applied element-wise to an input vector, so $\mathbf{k}^{\mathrm{dp}}$ can be written as $\mathbf{k}^{\mathrm{dp}} = g\big(C^T(\mathbf{x})\,\mathbf{x}'\big)$.

Since $C^T(\mathbf{u}) = C(\mathcal{F}^{-1}(\mathcal{F}^*(\mathbf{u})))$, with * denoting the complex-conjugate, and using the convolution property from Eq. 4, we obtain the solution

$$\mathbf{k}^{\mathrm{dp}} = g\big(\mathcal{F}^{-1}\left(\mathcal{F}(\mathbf{x}) \odot \mathcal{F}^*(\mathbf{x}')\right)\big)\,. \tag{11}$$

Eq. 11 means that a dot-product kernel can be quickly evaluated at all image locations, using only a few FFT and element-wise operations. In particular, for a polynomial kernel,

$$\mathbf{k}^{\text{poly}} = \left(\mathcal{F}^{-1}\left(\mathcal{F}(\mathbf{x}) \odot \mathcal{F}^*(\mathbf{x}')\right) + c\right)^d . \tag{12}$$

3.2 Radial Basis Function Kernels

RBF kernels have the form $\kappa(\mathbf{x}, \mathbf{x}') = h(\|\mathbf{x} - \mathbf{x}'\|^2)$, for some function h. The corresponding $\mathbf{k}$ from Eq. 6 will be denoted by $\mathbf{k}^{\text{rbf}}$.

$$k_i^{\text{rbf}} = \kappa(\mathbf{x},\, P^i\mathbf{x}') = h\left(\left\|\mathbf{x} - P^i\mathbf{x}'\right\|^2\right) \tag{13}$$

We can expand the norm, obtaining

$$k_i^{\text{rbf}} = h\left(\|\mathbf{x}\|^2 + \|\mathbf{x}'\|^2 - 2\mathbf{x}^T P^i \mathbf{x}'\right) . \tag{14}$$

The permutation P^i doesn't affect the norm of $\mathbf{x}'$ due to Parseval's identity.

Since $\|\mathbf{x}\|^2$ and $\|\mathbf{x}'\|^2$ are constant w.r.t. i, Eq. 14 is in the same form as for dot-product kernels. Following the same derivation as in Section 3.1, we arrive at the general solution for RBF kernels

$$\mathbf{k}^{\text{rbf}} = h\left(\|\mathbf{x}\|^2 + \|\mathbf{x}'\|^2 - 2\mathcal{F}^{-1}\left(\mathcal{F}(\mathbf{x}) \odot \mathcal{F}^*(\mathbf{x}')\right)\right) . \tag{15}$$

In particular, we have, for the Gaussian kernel,

$$\mathbf{k}^{\text{gauss}} = \exp\left(-\frac{1}{\sigma^2}\left(\|\mathbf{x}\|^2 + \|\mathbf{x}'\|^2 - 2\mathcal{F}^{-1}\left(\mathcal{F}(\mathbf{x}) \odot \mathcal{F}^*(\mathbf{x}')\right)\right)\right) . \tag{16}$$

For an $n \times n$ image, direct kernel computation at n^2 locations would take $\mathcal{O}(n^4)$ operations, however the corresponding frequency-domain solution brings this complexity down to only $\mathcal{O}(n^2 \log n)$.

The generic formulas we derived for each kernel will quickly compute the $\mathbf{k}$ and $\bar{\mathbf{k}}$ terms in KRLS training (Eq. 7) and detection (Eq. 9). We expect them to be of general interest, however, and be useful for other kernel methods.

3.3 The Linear Case

The simplest kernel function, $\kappa(\mathbf{x}, \mathbf{x}') = \langle \mathbf{x}, \mathbf{x}' \rangle$, which is just the dot-product in the original space, is worth investigating. It produces a linear classifier that does not make use of the Kernel Trick, so we can compute $\mathbf{w}$ explicitly, instead of implicitly as $\boldsymbol{\alpha}$. Plugging it into the KRLS equations, we obtain:

$$\mathbf{w} = \mathcal{F}^{-1}\left(\frac{\mathcal{F}(\mathbf{x}) \odot \mathcal{F}^*(\mathbf{y})}{\mathcal{F}(\mathbf{x}) \odot \mathcal{F}^*(\mathbf{x}) + \lambda}\right) . \tag{17}$$

This is a kind of correlation filter that has been proposed recently, called Minimum Output Sum of Squared Error (MOSSE) [12, 15], with a single training image. It is remarkably powerful despite its simplicity.

Table 2. Tracker precisions at a threshold of 20 (percentage of frames where the predicted location is within 20 pixels of the ground truth). This threshold was used by Babenko et al. [3]. The best precision for each sequence is highlighted in bold.

	MILTrack	Struck	MOSSE	MOSSE^2	Proposed method
`coke11`	0.61	0.97	0.71	0.71	**1.00**
`faceocc`	0.46	0.96	0.21	**1.00**	**1.00**
`faceocc2`	0.69	0.95	0.53	0.93	**1.00**
`surfer`	0.98	0.97	0.37	**0.99**	**0.99**
`sylvester`	0.90	0.95	0.78	0.90	**1.00**
`tiger1`	0.83	**0.94**	0.26	0.30	0.61
`tiger2`	**0.93**	0.91	0.25	0.22	0.63
`dollar`	0.82	0.96	0.39	**1.00**	**1.00**
`girl`	0.31	0.95	0.83	**0.99**	0.59
`david`	0.56	**0.92**	0.77	0.34	0.49
`cliffbar`	0.89	0.44	0.37	0.56	**0.97**
`twinings`	0.98	**1.00**	0.20	**1.00**	0.93

Note, however, that correlation filters are obtained with classical signal processing techniques, directly in the Fourier domain. As we have shown, Circulant matrices are the key enabling factor to extend them with the Kernel Trick.

4 Experiments

We used the techniques described above to implement a simple tracking system. Many obvious improvements, like failure detection, motion and uncertainty models (eg., particle filter), or feature extraction, were deliberately left out. This was done to reduce the confounding factors to a minimum, and provide an accurate validation of the learning algorithm.

From now on, we will assume two-dimensional images. A thorough proof is given in Appendix A.3. In practice it means that the 2D Fourier transform can replace the 1D FT in all the previous equations.

4.1 Pre-processing

The proposed method can operate directly on the pixel values, with no feature extraction. However, since the Fourier transform is periodic, it does not respect the image boundaries. The large discontinuity between opposite edges of a non-periodic image will result in a noisy Fourier representation. A common solution is to band the original $n \times n$ image (x^{raw}) with a cosine (or sine) window:

$$x_{ij} = \left(x_{ij}^{\text{raw}} - 0.5\right) \sin(\pi i/n) \sin(\pi j/n), \quad \forall i, j = 0, \ldots, n-1 \qquad (18)$$

Values near the borders will be weighted to zero, eliminating discontinuities.

4.2 Training Outputs

During training, we must assign a label to each sample. In tracking-by-detection, samples near the target center are positive and others are negative. But since the square loss of KRLS allows for continuous values, we don't need to limit ourselves to binary labels. The line between classification (binary output) and regression (continuous output) is essentially blurred.

Given the choice of a continuous training output, we will use a Gaussian function, which is known to minimize ringing in the Fourier domain [21]. The output will be 1 near the target location (i', j'), and decay to 0 as the distance increases, with a bandwidth of s:

$$y_{ij} = \exp\left(-\left((i-i')^2 + (j-j')^2\right)/s^2\right), \quad \forall i,j = 0,\ldots,n-1 \tag{19}$$

The continuous labeling yields spatially smooth classifier responses, which results in more accurate position estimates than binary labeling (Table 2).

4.3 Overview

The tracker follows a simple pipeline. A window of a fixed size (double the target size) is cropped from the input image, at the estimated target location. No feature extraction is performed, other than a cosine window on the raw pixel values (Eq. 18). The target is located by evaluating Eq. 9 and finding the maximum response. Eq. 7 is then used to train a new model ($\boldsymbol{\alpha}$ and $\mathbf{x}$).

To provide some memory, the new model is integrated by linearly interpolating the new parameters with the ones from the previous frame. We found that this scheme, adapted from the work of Bolme et al. [12], is enough for our purposes. Future work will explore other ways to aggregate samples over time.

4.4 Evaluation

We compared the proposed method with several state-of-the-art trackers, on 12 challenging videos. We used available ground truth data to compute precisions.

The best way to evaluate trackers is still a debatable subject. Averaged measures like mean center location error or average bounding box overlap can yield unintuitive results, for example penalizing an accurate tracker that fails for a small amount of time more than an inaccurate tracker.

Babenko et al. [3] argue for the use of precision plots. The plots show, for a range of distance thresholds, the percentage of frames that the tracker is within that distance of the ground truth. These plots are easy to interpret. More accurate trackers have high precision at lower thresholds, and if a tracker fails it will never reach a precision of 1 for a large range. They are shown in Fig. 2.

The parameters are *fixed for all videos* to prevent overfitting. We tested our tracker with a Gaussian kernel. A polynomial kernel with appropriate parameters gives similar results, but the Gaussian kernel is easier to adjust, since it has only one parameter with an intuitive meaning. The bandwidth of the Gaussian kernel

Algorithm 1 . MATLAB code for our tracker, using a Gaussian kernel
It is possible to reuse some values, reducing the number of FFT calls. An implementation with GUI is available at: `http://www.isr.uc.pt/~henriques/`

```
% Training image x(current frame) and test image z(next frame)
% must be pre-processed with a cosine window. y has a Gaussian
% shape centered on the target. x, y and z are M-by-N matrices.
% All FFT operations are standard in MATLAB.

function alphaf = training(x, y, sigma, lambda)        % Eq. 7
  k = dgk(x, x, sigma);
  alphaf = fft2(y) ./ (fft2(k) + lambda);
end

function responses = detection(alphaf, x, z, sigma)    % Eq. 9
  k = dgk(z, x, sigma);
  responses = real(ifft2(alphaf .* fft2(k)));
end

function k = dgk(x1, x2, sigma)                        % Eq. 16
  c = fftshift(ifft2(fft2(x1) .* conj(fft2(x2))));
  d = x1(:)'*x1(:) + x2(:)'*x2(:) - 2*c;
  k = exp(-1 / sigma^2 * abs(d) / numel(x1));
end
```

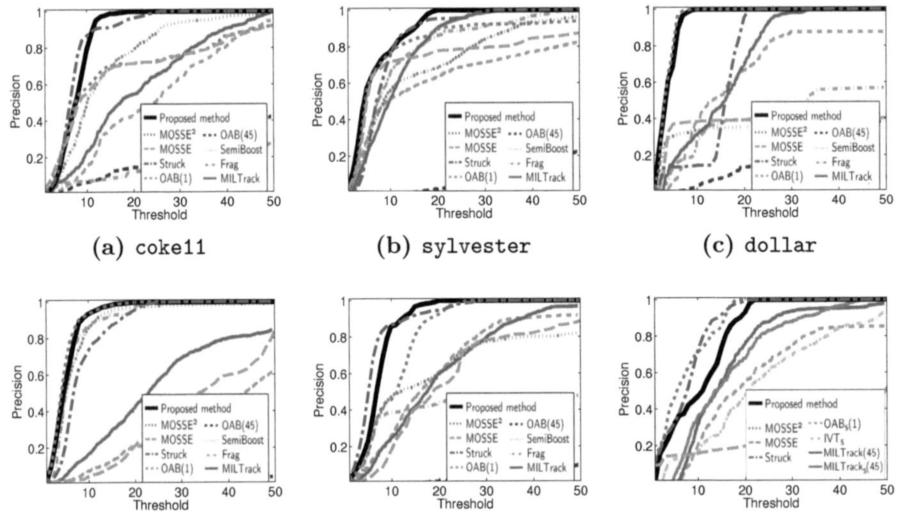

(a) coke11 (b) sylvester (c) dollar

(d) faceocc (e) faceocc2 (f) twinings

Fig. 2. Precisions plots for 6 sequences (percentage of frames where the predicted location is within the threshold of the ground truth). Best viewed in color. See the supplemental material for plots of the remaining sequences.

is $\sigma = 0.2$, spatial bandwidth is $s = \sqrt{mn}/16$ for an $m \times n$ target, regularization is $\lambda = 10^{-2}$, and the interpolation factor for adaptation is 0.075.

We found that MOSSE [12] is tuned only for 64×64 images. However, to provide a fair comparison, we made some improvements: regularization $\lambda = 10^{-4}$, spatial bandwidth proportional to target size ($s = \sqrt{mn}/16$), no failure detection and no randomized initial samples. This is essentially our system with a linear kernel (Sec. 3.3). We called it MOSSE^2. All other parameters are the same as with the Gaussian kernel. It has high accuracy on many sequences, but ours shows equal or greater accuracy in 10 of the 12 sequences (see Table 2).

For non-deterministic trackers, we take the median of the precisions over 5 runs. The sequences `twinings` and `cliffbar` have large scale changes, so we compare with versions of MILTrack [3], Online Ada-Boost (OAB) [3, Sec. 4] and IVT [22] that track through scale. Even without a notion of scale, the proposed method works well in these videos, as shown in Table 2.

Struck [4] achieves very good results (over 0.9 in most sequences), and outperforms other trackers like MILTrack, OAB, SemiBoost [6] and FragTrack [23]. Still, it has lower accuracy than the proposed method because it optimizes bounding box overlap. The proposed tracker is especially geared for high localization, because circulant matrix theory allows it to encode samples from all locations. This includes, as negative samples, both distant distractors and small displacements of the true target. The frequency-domain representation also allows us to minimize ringing (Sec. 4.2), resulting in spatially smooth responses (Fig. 1). This is not possible with unstructured random sampling.

Please note that the goal is *not* merely to show higher precisions. Indeed, every tracker fails in at least one video. However, we can achieve very competitive results with a much simpler and faster tracker. Most recent trackers rely on heavy optimization methods, and manage budgets of support vectors or similar. Our algorithm has only a few lines of code (Algorithm 1) and runs at hundreds of frames-per-second. We also hope our theoretical analysis is of interest in itself.

5 Conclusion

We presented a theoretical framework to analyze and explore the consequences of dense sampling in tracking-by-detection. The result is a collection of closed-form, fast and exact solutions for online training, detection, and computation of non-linear kernels. We expect this last contribution to find useful applications outside of tracking. We also hope to have shown that some structures that occur naturally in computer vision, such as Circulants, are still relatively unexplored.

Acknowledgments. The authors thank Sam Hare and Boris Babenko, for providing their results. They also acknowledge the FCT project PTDC/EEA-CRO/122812/2010, grants SFRH/BD75459/2010, SFRH/BD74152/2010, and SFRH/BD45178/2008.

References

1. Henriques, J.F., Caseiro, R., Batista, J.: Globally optimal solution to multi-object tracking with merged measurements. In: ICCV (2011)

2. Zamir, A.R., Dehghan, A., Shah, M.: GMCP-Tracker: Global Multi-object Tracking Using Generalized Minimum Clique Graphs. In: Fitzgibbon, A., Lazebnik, S., Perona, P., Sato, Y., Schmid, C. (eds.) ECCV 2012, Part II. LNCS, vol. 7573, pp. 343–356. Springer, Heidelberg (2012)
3. Babenko, B., Yang, M.-H., Belongie, S.: Robust object tracking with online multiple instance learning. TPAMI 33(8), 1619–1632 (2011)
4. Hare, S., Saffari, A., Torr, P.: Struck: Structured output tracking with kernels. In: ICCV (2011)
5. Avidan, S.: Support vector tracking. TPAMI 26(8), 1064–1072 (2004)
6. Grabner, H., Leistner, C., Bischof, H.: Semi-supervised On-Line Boosting for Robust Tracking. In: Forsyth, D., Torr, P., Zisserman, A. (eds.) ECCV 2008, Part I. LNCS, vol. 5302, pp. 234–247. Springer, Heidelberg (2008)
7. Saffari, A., Leistner, C., Santner, J., Godec, M., Bischof, H.: On-line random forests. In: 3rd IEEE ICCV Workshop on On-line Computer Vision (2009)
8. Yilmaz, A., Javed, O., Shah, M.: Object tracking: A survey. ACM Computing Surveys 38(4), 13–58 (2006)
9. Yang, H., Shao, L., Zheng, F., Wang, L., Song, Z.: Recent advances and trends in visual tracking: A review. Neurocomputing 74(18), 3823–3831 (2011)
10. Lampert, C.H., Blaschko, M.B., Hofmann, T.: Beyond sliding windows: Object localization by efficient subwindow search. In: CVPR (2008)
11. Alexe, B., Petrescu, V., Ferrari, V.: Exploiting spatial overlap to efficiently compute appearance distances between image windows. In: NIPS (2011)
12. Bolme, D.S., Beveridge, J.R., Draper, B.A., Lui, Y.M.: Visual object tracking using adaptive correlation filters. In: CVPR (2010)
13. Vedaldi, A., Gulshan, V., Varma, M., Zisserman, A.: Multiple kernels for object detection. In: ICCV (2009)
14. Harzallah, H., Jurie, F., Schmid, C.: Combining efficient object localization and image classification. In: ICCV (2009)
15. Bolme, D.S., Draper, B.A., Beveridge, J.R.: Average of synthetic exact filters. In: CVPR (2009)
16. Patnaik, R., Casasent, D.: Fast FFT-based distortion-invariant kernel filters for general object recognition. In: Proceedings of SPIE, vol. 7252 (2009)
17. Rifkin, R., Yeo, G., Poggio, T.: Regularized least-squares classification. Nato Science Series Sub Series III: Computer and Systems Sciences 190, 131–154 (2003)
18. Schölkopf, B., Smola, A.J.: Learning with kernels: Support vector machines, regularization, optimization, and beyond. MIT Press (2002)
19. Gray, R.M.: Toeplitz and Circulant Matrices: A Review. Now Publishers (2006)
20. Patnaik, R.: Distortion-invariant kernel correlation filters for general object recognition. PhD thesis, Carnegie Mellon University (2009)
21. González, R.C., Woods, R.E.: Digital image processing. Prentice Hall (2008)
22. Ross, D.A., Lim, J., Lin, R.-S., Yang, M.-H.: Incremental learning for robust visual tracking. IJCV 77(1-3), 125–141 (2007)
23. Adam, A., Rivlin, E., Shimshoni, I.: Robust fragments-based tracking using the integral histogram. In: CVPR (2006)

Appendix A.1: Dense Sampling KRLS Derivation

We will use the fact that K is circulant, replacing Eq. 6 in the generic KRLS solution of Eq. 2. Observing that any identity matrix I is circulant, $I = C(\boldsymbol{\delta})$ with $\boldsymbol{\delta} = [1, 0, 0, \ldots, 0]^T$, Eq. 2 becomes

$$\boldsymbol{\alpha} = \left(C(\mathbf{k}) + \lambda C(\boldsymbol{\delta})\right)^{-1} \mathbf{y} = \left(C(\mathbf{k} + \lambda \boldsymbol{\delta})\right)^{-1} \mathbf{y}. \tag{20}$$

The properties of circulant matrices allow element-wise multiplication and inversion in the Fourier domain [19]. Making use of these properties, and the fact that $\mathcal{F}(\boldsymbol{\delta}) = \mathbb{1}$, where $\mathbb{1}$ is an $n \times 1$ vector of ones,

$$\boldsymbol{\alpha} = \left(C\left(\mathcal{F}^{-1}\left(\mathcal{F}(\mathbf{k}) + \lambda\mathbb{1}\right)\right)\right)^{-1}\mathbf{y} = C\left(\mathcal{F}^{-1}\left(\frac{1}{\mathcal{F}(\mathbf{k}) + \lambda}\right)\right)\mathbf{y}. \tag{21}$$

The division is performed element-wise. Using Eq. 4, we finally obtain

$$\boldsymbol{\alpha} = \mathcal{F}^{-1}\left(\frac{\mathcal{F}(\mathbf{y})}{\mathcal{F}(\mathbf{k}) + \lambda}\right). \tag{22}$$

Appendix A.2: Derivation of Fast Detection Formula

If we denote the test image by $\mathbf{z}$, detection amounts to classifying all the shifted test images $\mathbf{z}_i = P^i\mathbf{z}$. Each response is then given by

$$\hat{y}_i = \sum_j \alpha_j \kappa(P^i\mathbf{z},\, P^j\mathbf{x}), \tag{23}$$

since the training samples are $\mathbf{x}_i = P^i\mathbf{x}$ (Eq. 5). Rewriting it in matrix notation, the vector of all classifier responses is $\hat{\mathbf{y}} = C(\bar{\mathbf{k}})\boldsymbol{\alpha}$, where $\bar{\mathbf{k}}$ is the vector with elements $\bar{k}_i = \kappa(\mathbf{z},\, P^i\mathbf{x})$. We can now apply the convolution property (Eq. 4):

$$\hat{\mathbf{y}} = \mathcal{F}^{-1}\left(\mathcal{F}(\bar{\mathbf{k}}) \odot \mathcal{F}(\boldsymbol{\alpha})\right). \tag{24}$$

Appendix A.3: Generalization of Circulant Forms

For a matter of clarity, all of our derivations have assumed that the images are one-dimensional. The 2D case, despite its usefulness, is also more difficult to analyze. The reason is that the 2D generalization of a circulant matrix, related to the 2D Fourier Transform, is a Block-Circulant Circulant Matrix (BCCM, ie., a matrix that is circulant at the block level, composed of blocks themselves circulant). All of the properties we used for circulant matrices have BCCM equivalents.

We will now generalize Theorem 1. A 1D image $\mathbf{x}$ can be shifted by i with $P^i\mathbf{x}$. With a 2D image X, we can shift both its rows by i and its columns by i' with $P^iXP^{i'}$. Additionally, in an $n^2 \times n^2$ matrix M composed of $n \times n$ blocks, we will index the element $i'j'$ of the block ij as $M_{(ii'),(jj')}$.

Theorem 2. *The block matrix K with elements $K_{(ii'),(jj')} = \kappa(P^iXP^{i'},\, P^jXP^{j'})$ is a BCCM if κ is a unitarily invariant kernel.*

Proof. Because κ is unitarily invariant, we have $K_{(ii'),(jj')} = \kappa(X,\, P^{j-i}XP^{j'-i'})$. Since $K_{(ii'),(jj')}$ depends only on $(j-i) \bmod n$ and $(j'-i') \bmod n$, K is BCCM.

K can now be constructed as $C(K')$, where the $n \times n$ matrix K' has elements $k_{ii'} = \kappa(X,\, P^iXP^{i'})$, and $C(\cdot)$ constructs a BCCM. The relevant solutions can then be re-derived with the 2D FT in place of the 1D FT.

Online Spatio-temporal Structural Context Learning for Visual Tracking

Longyin Wen, Zhaowei Cai, Zhen Lei, Dong Yi, and Stan Z. Li*

CBSR & NLPR, Institute of Automation, Chinese Academy of Sciences
95 Zhongguancun Donglu Beijing 100190, China
{lywen,zwcai,zlei,dyi,szli}@cbsr.ia.ac.cn
http://www.cbsr.ia.ac.cn

Abstract. Visual tracking is a challenging problem, because the target frequently change its appearance, randomly move its location and get occluded by other objects in unconstrained environments. The state changes of the target are temporally and spatially continuous, in this paper therefore, a robust Spatio-Temporal structural context based Tracker (STT) is presented to complete the tracking task in unconstrained environments. The temporal context capture the historical appearance information of the target to prevent the tracker from drifting to the background in a long term tracking. The spatial context model integrates contributors, which are the key-points automatically discovered around the target, to build a supporting field. The supporting field provides much more information than appearance of the target itself so that the location of the target will be predicted more precisely. Extensive experiments on various challenging databases demonstrate the superiority of our proposed tracker over other state-of-the-art trackers.

Keywords: Spatio-temporal, context constraint, subspaces learning, multiple instance boosting, unconstrained environments.

1 Introduction

Visual tracking attracts lots of attentions due to its core status in applications, *e.g.* human-computer interaction, video surveillance, virtual reality, etc. For most of these applications, trackers are demanded to work for a long time in unconstrained environments, which greatly challenges the robustness of the trackers. To overcome this difficulty, numerous complex models are designed, but most of them still focus on the appearance of target itself (*e.g.* color, edge responses, texture and shape cues) [1,2] or the difference between the target and background [3,4,5,6,7].

In real-world, the temporal and spatial information is important and necessary in tracking task. In continuous frames, the target appearance changes gradually, and all of the historical appearance variations in pose, scale and illumination have more or less influences and constraints on the next appearance state. For example, no matter what appearance changes happen to a panda, it is still a panda and the tracker should not recognize it as another animal. Meanwhile, the target moves gradually from one location to another location, rather than abruptly and discretely jumps. In another words,

* Corresponding author.

A. Fitzgibbon et al. (Eds.): ECCV 2012, Part IV, LNCS 7575, pp. 716–729, 2012.

the spatial context presents strong or weak spatial correlation between the target and the background. For example, if two similar pandas walk together, it is easy to jump from one panda to another for the trackers which only focus on appearance features. However, if the spatial context constraints are considered, the skip problem will be circumvented because the surroundings around the two pandas are different. Unfortunately, the spatio-temporal context information has not been paid enough attention in the previous tracking strategies. In this paper, we propose a novel tracking framework based on the spatio-temporal structural context to precisely predict the location of the target, which is expected to be more robust than the previous methods.

1.1 Related Works

In recent decades, numerous tracking strategies have been proposed in literatures, which perform well in some specific conditions. To better represent the target features, some methods [1,2,8,9,10] model the appearance of the target in a generative way. Fragment-based tracker [2] represents the target with histograms of local patches, which takes structural information of the target itself and handles partial occlusion very well. However, its template is not updated over time and the correlation of target and surroundings is not constructed. In [1], an Incremental Visual Tracker (IVT) adaptively updates its appearance model with the historical and sequential appearance variations. While IVT performs well in deformable motion and illumination variation, the lack of spatial information results in drift problem because the accumulated errors decrease the accuracy of appearance model.

Some discriminative model [11,5,12] formulate the tracking task as a classification problem which focuses on the difference between the target and the background. However, these trackers discard the historical separating function during updating which leads the insufficient temporal information to predict next state. Yu et al. [4] combined the generative model and discriminative model to describe different views of the target. Experimentally, the combined tracker achieves more stable performances than single generative or discriminative tracker as the result of mutual supervision. Nevertheless, the tracker in [4] just incorporated the background information as negative samples for training the classifier, and no semantic context is considered. Recently, tracking-by-detection methods [3,7,6] are very popular and reliable in long term surveillance sequences, because the appearance model will be corrected by detector over time and the target will be re-located even if it has been out of view. However, these detection based trackers are easily distracted by other objects that have similar appearance with the target, which is the result of lacking strong spatio-temporal constraints.

For long-term tracking task in unconstrained environment, merely learning the descriptive or discriminative features of the target cannot ensure the robustness of the system. Yang et al. constructed a context-aware tracker (CAT) [13] to track random field around the target instead of the target itself. The introduction of auxiliary objects that are suitable for tracking and have consistent motion correlations to the target greatly prevents the tracker from being trapped into drifting problem. Amir Saffari et. al [14] proposed a novel multi-class LPBoost algorithm to handle the tracking task. They treated the tracking task as a multi-class classification problem where background patterns become virtual classes. The proposed method performs well in constrained environments, but it fails to handle the complex environments, *e.g.* occlusion, background clutter and illumination variations. Similar as [13], in [15], Gu and Tomasi considered the spatial relation between the similar target and track these similar targets simultaneously. However, the method ignores the temporary information of the target which causes its sensitiveness to target appearance changes and it may collapse when motion blur occurs due to the utilization of SIFT descriptors. Grabner et al. [16] introduced the definition of supporters which are useful features to predict the target location. The tracker in [16] utilizes strong motion coupling constraints to locate the target even when the target is invisible, with the help of some other available related context information. However, its detecting and matching all of the local features are expensive and the motion of the object of the view is not easily predicted. To further expand the theory of supporter, Dinh et al. developed a new context framework based on distracters and supporters [17]. The distracters are the regions that have similar appearance as the target and the supporters are the local key-points around the target which have the motion correlation with the target in a short time span. Although the introduction of context in these trackers expands the available information we can get from the scene, the motion correlation between the target and the context is hard to define.

1.2 Our Approach

The novel spatio-temporal structural context based tracker (STT) we build here greatly differs from the previous published models. For temporal context part, a new incremental subspace model is constructed to represent the gist of target with low dimensionality feature vectors, in which several sequential positive samples are packed into one subspace to update the model. Most of the appearance information of the target, including pose, scale, and illumination are efficiently incorporated into the model to help predict the next state of the target, as shown in the left side of Fig. 1. For the spatial context part, we introduce the contributors that are the regions having the same size and consistent motion correlation with the target. The positions of these contributors are produced by the key-point detection method SURF [18], which represent more information than those non-key-points. Based on the success of Fragment Tracker [2], we also decompose the target and the contributors into several small blocks. In another words, the intra-structural information and the inter-structural features are incorporated. In unconstrained environment, it is not easy to dig out the strong contextual contributors to help locate the target. Instead, numerous weak contextual contributors around the target can be combined together into a strong supporting field, as shown in the right side of Fig. 1. The representative features within the strong supporting field are optimally selected by boosting method [5] from the weak features pool. The contributions and the differences of our algorithm from other previous methods are as follows:

- The global temporal context model is constructed by the linear subspace method, which is updated with continuous positive samples and the correlation between them is considered.
- The appearance information of contributors is also considered in our model, and the pairwise features are produced by the difference between target and contributors to describe the spatial correlations.

Fig. 1. The instruction of the temporal context constraint and the spatial context constraint of tracking task

- The target and contributors are decomposed into small blocks, hence the intra- and inter- structural information is described.
- Instead of building complex motion models to represent the correlation between the target and contributors, our approach efficiently utilizes boosting method to select the most representative weak relations to construct a strong supporting field.

2 MAP Spatio-temporal Structure Context Based Tracker

The tracking task is formulated as a state estimation problem and the motion process is assumed to be a Markovian state transition process. Let $O_{1:i} = \{O_1, \cdots, O_i\}$ represent the observation data set up to time i. Z_i is the state of the target at time i, which contains the position and size information of the target. In our tracker, the state vector Z_i is composed by the position of the target centered at $l_t = (x_t, y_t)$, target width w_t, target height h_t, which is defined as $Z_t = (x_t, y_t, w_t, h_t)$. The posterior probability is estimated as the recursive equation:

$$p(Z_t|O_{1:t}) \propto p(O_t|Z_t) \int p(Z_t|Z_{t-1})p(Z_{t-1}|O_{1:t-1})dZ_{t-1} \quad (1)$$

where $p(O_t|Z_t)$ is the likelihood of the candidate samples provided by our spatio-temporal structural context constraint. $p(Z_t|Z_{t-1})$ is the state transition probability and $p(Z_{t-1}|O_{1:t-1})$ is the state estimation probability given all observations up to time $t-1$. Similar as [5], we adopt the simplest greedy Maximum A Posteriori probability (MAP) strategy to solve the above equation, where the motion model is specified as:

$$p(l_t|l_{t-1}) = \begin{cases} 1 & \|l_t - l_{t-1}\|_2 < r \\ 0 & \|l_t - l_{t-1}\|_2 \geq r \end{cases} \quad (2)$$

where l_t is the position of the target at time t, r is the search radius. The scale of the target is similarly handled as the strategy utilized in [5].

Assume there are K contributors of the target of state s, which is represented as $f(s) = \{f_1(s), \cdots, f_K(s)\}$. The appearance model of the target in Equ. 1 is defined based on the global temporal context and the local spatial context:

$$Z_t^* = \arg\max_{Z_t} p(O_t|Z_t) = \arg\max_{Z_t}\{e^{-(1-\alpha)U(Z_t) - \alpha U(Z_t|f(Z_t))}\} \quad (3)$$

where Z_t^* is the optimal state at time t, $\alpha \in (0, 1)$ is the coherence parameter to balance the global temporal context constraint and the local spatial context constraint. The energy function mentioned above consists of two terms: the global temporal context constraint energy function $U(Z_t)$ and local spatial context constraint energy function $U(Z_t|f(Z_t))$. In order to avoid the unreliable updating, we set the predefined thresholds θ_s and θ_t to decide whether the spatial and temporal context models will be updated. The algorithm of the proposed tracker is summarized in Algorithm 1 and the temporal and spatial context models are detailed in the following sections.

Algorithm 1. Spatio-Temporal Structural Context based Tracker

```
Initialize target T, extract the contributors f(·).
Initialize the global temporal context model M_t and the local spatial context model M_s.
while run do
    Sample the image to get the Candidates.
    for all Candidates do
        Calculate the global temporal context constraint energy U(Z_t);
        Calculate the local spatial context constraint energy U(Z_t|f(Z_t));
        Combine them to get the energy of the Candidates (Eq. 3)
    end for
    Find the MAP solution of the Candidates to get the minimum energy state Z_t^* (Eq. 3).
    if U(Z_t^*|f(Z_t^*)) < θ_s and U(Z_t^*) < θ_t then
        Update contributors around of the target state Z_t^*.
        Update the global temporal context model M_t with the optimal target state Z_t^*.
        Update the local spatial context model M_s with the generated contributors.
    end if
end while
```

3 Global Temporal Context with Incremental Subspace Model

Target tracking is a physically and psychologically continuous process, hence all of the prior information will be used to predict the next state of the target. The following appearances of the target have more or less correlation to the previous appearance information. For example, a man cannot abruptly change into a monkey based on historical appearances. Under this premise, global temporal context exploits historical appearance variations as an extra source of global constraints to estimate the configuration of the target. Murphy et al. [19] exploit context features using a scene 'gist', which influences priors of the object existence and state, and the work of Torralba et al. [20] shows 'gist' is sufficient to provide a useful prior for what types of objects may appear in the image. This opens our mind that we also can use object 'gist' to constrain the following states of the target. Here, we define the 'gist' as the feature vector that summarizes the target. A newly proposed incremental linear subspace method is used to reduce the high dimensionality of the feature space, so that more historical information will be stored and used efficiently.

Unlike the Hall's subspace learning method [21] and its variant [1], the newly proposed subspace learning strategy updates the energy dissipation of subspace dimension reduction in the updating process (Algorithm 2), which acquires the target features more accurately. Meanwhile, it utilizes the combined samples in adjacent frames rather than individual ones for updating. The proposed method is called Incremental Multiple Instance Subspace Learning (IMISL), which can eliminate the homogeneous noise in sequential samples effectively. An observed instance $O_t \in \mathbb{R}^d$ is a vectorized image patch corresponding to the state Z_t and d is the feature dimension of the observations. Let $\Omega_t = (\mu_t, V_t, \Lambda_t, n_t)$, where μ_t, V_t, Λ_t and n_t represent the mean vector, the eigenvectors, the eigenvalues and the number of samples of the subspace at time t respectively. Let $\Lambda_t = (\lambda_{1,t}, \cdots, \lambda_{q,t})$. To evaluate the probability of a candidate belonging to the subspace, similar to [22], the following equation is utilized:

$$U(Z_t) = \frac{\varepsilon(O_t)^2}{2\sigma_t^2} + (d-q)\log\sigma_t + \sum_{i=1}^{q}\left(\frac{G_{i,t}^2}{2\lambda_{i,t}} + \frac{1}{2}\log\lambda_{i,t}\right) \tag{4}$$

where q is the reduction dimension of the subspace, $\varepsilon(O_t) = \|O_t - VV^T O_t\|_2$ is the projection error of the candidate sample, σ_t is the energy dissipation in dimension reduction of covariance matrix at time t and $G_t = (G_{1,t}, \cdots, G_{q,t}) = V_t^T(O_t - \mu_t)$.

The core problem in incremental subspace learning is the updating strategy. Our proposed strategy utilizes the subspaces for updating instead of single samples, namely merges the two subspaces into one subspace. We first compress D updating instances into a local subspace. The subspace construction process can be completed by Eigenvalue Decomposition (EVD) or the efficient Expectation Maximization (EM) algorithm proposed in [23]. A η-truncation is utilized to decide the reduction dimension of the subspace to maintain the energy, that is $q = \arg\min_i(\frac{\sum_i \lambda_i}{tr(\Lambda)} \geq \eta)$. We derive from the basic equations of the mean value and covariance matrix of the training data, that are: $\mu^{(k)} = \frac{1}{k}\sum_{i=1}^{k}\mathcal{I}_i$, $S^{(k)} = \frac{1}{k}\sum_{i=1}^{k}(\mathcal{I}_i - \mu^{(k)})(\mathcal{I}_i - \mu^{(k)})^T$, where $S^{(k)}$ represents the covariance matrix of the subspace, $\mathcal{I}_i$ is the updating sample and $\mu^{(k)}$ is the mean value of the samples. We get the covariance matrix of the merged subspace:

$$S^{(k+l)} = \frac{k}{k+l}S^{(k)} + \frac{l}{k+l}S^{(l)} + yy^T \tag{5}$$

where $y = \sqrt{\frac{k\cdot l}{(k+l)^2}}(\mu^{(k)} - \mu^{(l)})$. Furthermore, the covariance matrix can be decomposed as the following: $S^{(k)} = \sigma_k^2 I + \sum_{i=1}^{q_k}(\lambda_{i,k} - \sigma_k^2)v_{i,k}v_{i,k}^T$, where $\sigma_k^2 = \frac{1}{d_k - q_k}\sum_{q_k+1}^{d_k}\lambda_{i,k}$, and q_k is the reduction dimension. Then plug the equation to (5):

$$S^{(k+l)} = \frac{k\sigma_k^2 + l\sigma_l^2}{k+l}I + \frac{k}{k+l}\sum_{i=1}^{q_k}(\lambda_{i,k} - \sigma_k^2)v_{i,k}v_{i,k}^T + \frac{l}{k+l}\sum_{i=1}^{q_l}(\lambda_{i,l} - \sigma_l^2)v_{i,l}v_{i,l}^T + yy^T \tag{6}$$

where $v_{i,k}$, $\lambda_{i,k}$, σ_k and $v_{i,l}$ $\lambda_{i,l}$, σ_l are the ith eigenvector, i^{th} eigenvalue, energy dissipation in dimension reduction of the covariance matrix $S^{(k)}$ and $S^{(l)}$ respectively. We reformulate the Equ. 6 to get:

$$S^{(k+l)} = \frac{k\sigma_k^2 + l\sigma_l^2}{k+l}I + LL^T \tag{7}$$

where $L = [\sqrt{\rho(\lambda_{1,k} - \sigma_k^2)}v_{1,k}, \cdots, \sqrt{\rho(\lambda_{q_k,k} - \sigma_k^2)}v_{q_k,k}, \sqrt{(1-\rho)(\lambda_{1,l} - \sigma_l^2)}v_{1,l}, \cdots, \sqrt{(1-\rho)(\lambda_{q_l,l} - \sigma_l^2)}v_{q_l,l}, y]$ and $\rho = \frac{k}{k+l}$.

Due to the computation complexity of decomposing matrix LL^T directly, we decompose $L^T L$ instead, to get the decomposition of matrix $S^{(k+l)}$. Let $Q = L^T L$. The size of matrix Q is $q \times q$, where $q = q_k + q_l + 1$. We utilize the partitioned matrix to represent the matrix $Q = \begin{pmatrix} \Sigma & \beta \\ \beta^T & \alpha \end{pmatrix}$, where $\Sigma = \begin{pmatrix} \Sigma_1 & A \\ A^T & \Sigma_2 \end{pmatrix}$,$\alpha = y^T y$ and

$$\beta_i = \begin{cases} \sqrt{\rho(\lambda_{i,k} - \sigma_k^2)}v_{i,k}^T y & 1 \le i \le q_k \\ \sqrt{(1-\rho)(\lambda_{i,l} - \sigma_l^2)}v_{i,l}^T y & q_k < i < q \end{cases}$$

$$A(i,j) = \sqrt{\rho(1-\rho)(\lambda_{i,k} - \sigma_k^2)(\lambda_{j,l} - \sigma_l^2)}v_{i,k}^T v_{j,l}$$

$$\Sigma_1 = diag\{\rho(\lambda_{1,k} - \sigma_k^2), \cdots, \rho(\lambda_{q_k,k} - \sigma_k^2)\}$$

$$\Sigma_2 = diag\{(1-\rho)(\lambda_{1,l} - \sigma_l^2), \cdots, (1-\rho)(\lambda_{q_l,l} - \sigma_l^2)\}$$

Then the subspace updating process can be done efficiently by decomposing the matrix $L^T L$ and the process is detailed in Algorithm 2. In this way, the 'gist' features of the target can be captured efficiently and be utilized to predict the state of the target in the following frames.

Algorithm 2. The Subspace Updating Algorithm

1: Update the mean value of the subspaces, $\mu^{(k+l)} = \frac{k}{k+l}\mu^{(k)} + \frac{l}{k+l}\mu^{(l)}$.
2: Set $\rho = \frac{k}{k+l}$. Get the observation covariance matrix $S^{(k+l)} = (\rho\sigma_k^2 + (1-\rho)\sigma_l^2)I + LL^T$
3: Set $Q = L^T L = \begin{pmatrix} \Sigma & \beta \\ \beta^T & \alpha \end{pmatrix}$, the size of matrix Q is $(q+1) \times (q+1)$. Decompose Q as: $Q = U\Gamma U^T$, where $\Gamma = diag\{\xi_1, \xi_2, \cdots, \xi_{q+1}\}$, $U^T U = I$. Then $V_{q_k+q_l+1} = LU\Gamma^{-\frac{1}{2}}$, where matrix $V_{q_k+q_l+1} = [v_{1,k+l}, \cdots, v_{q_k+q_l+1,k+l}]$ is composed by the first $q_k + q_l + 1$ eigenvectors of the covariance matrix $S^{(k+l)}$.
4: The observation covariance matrix is represented as: $S^{(k+l)} = (\rho\sigma_k^2 + (1-\rho)\sigma_l^2)I + \sum_{i=1}^{q_k+q_l+1} \xi_i v_{i,k+l} v_{i,k+l}^T$. The first $q_k + q_l + 1$ eigenvalues of the covariance matrix can be updated as $\lambda_{i,k+l} = \sigma^{(k+l)^2} + \xi_i$, and the sigma value is updated as $\sigma_{k+l}^2 = \frac{1}{d-q_{k+l}}(\sum_{i=q_{k+l}+1}^{q_k+q_l+1} \lambda_{i,k+l} + (d - q_k - q_l - 1)\sigma^{(k+l)^2})$, then $\sigma^{(k+l)^2} = \rho\sigma_k^2 + (1-\rho)\sigma_l^2$, and $q_{k+l} = \arg\min_i(\frac{\sum_i \lambda_{i,k+l}}{\sum_{j=1}^{q_k+q_l+1} \xi_j} \ge \eta)$.

4 Local Spatial Context with Contributors

As discussed in Section 1.2, local spatial context information is derived from the area that surrounds the target to track (here we use surrounding patches as local context information, as shown in the left side of Fig. 1). The role of local context has been studied in psychology for the task of object detection [24,25], The study in [24] has proved the effectiveness of local context for object detection, and Sinha et al. [25] found that the inclusion of local contextual regions such as facial bounding contour substantially improves face detection performance. Besides, the works in [13,16,17] show that the local context information including supporters and distracters will enforce the robustness of the tracker, even when the target is partially invisible. However, different from [13] which constructs complex relative motion model between the target and auxiliary objects and [17] which statistically counts the matched supporters around the target, our proposed strategy focuses on the weak correlation between every contributor and the target, and then combines them to construct a strong classifier to locate the target. Multiple instance boosting is exploited to efficiently select the most representative contributors and combines them together to build the supporting field.

For multiple instance boosting, each selected weak classifier corresponds to a weak correlation, and the correlations are combined together to vote the score (namely the spatial energy item in Equ. 3) of a candidate sample. The vote is expressed as:

$$U(Z_t|f(Z_t)) \propto -\sum_i h_t^i \tag{8}$$

where h_t^i is the ith selected weak classifier at time t. Please refer to [5,26] for more details about multiple instance boosting algorithm.

Contributor Selection. For the contributor, similar to [17], we defines it as the key point around the target that can help to locate the target. Here, SURF descriptor is employed to find the contributors around the target which is generated by the fast Hessian algorithm. When updating, the SURF descriptor is generated in the rectangle around the center of the target with the width $r_d \cdot w$ and height $r_d \cdot h$, where r_d is the enlargement factor and we set $r_d \in [0.1, 0.6]$ in our experiments, w and h are the width and height of the target in the current frame respectively. If the extracted candidate contributors are more than the required ones, we randomly select some of them to be the final contributors. On the other hand, if they are inadequate, we randomly generate some more points to supplement them.

Feature Construction. In order to incorporate the structure information of the target, we try to partition the target and contributors into a few blocks, and the structure information is constructed with the relationships between each blocks. The structure information comes from two parts: one is the mutual-pairwise features between the blocks of the target and the contributors, and the other one is the self-pairwise features of inner blocks of the target itself. Then, these numerous relations are collected to build a feature pool. For simplicity, the structure features are produced by the difference between the sums of pixel values in each block. Certainly, other relation expression strategy can be considered, *e.g.*, Normalized Cross-Correlation (NCC). The structure features between the target and contributors deliver the holistic and detailed information of the supporting field.

Separately divide the target and contributors into $N = n_1 \times n_2$ blocks (we set $n_1 = 5, n_2 = 5$ in our experiments), $I(x, y)$ represents the pixel value of the image at position (x, y), and $P_i(s)$ represents the ith block of the target or contributors corresponding to the target state s. Here we define the distance function $d(P_m(s_1), P_n(s_2))$ of two blocks:

$$d(P_m(s_1), P_n(s_2)) = \sum_{(i,j)\in P_m(s_1)} I(i,j) - \sum_{(i,j)\in P_n(s_2)} I(i,j) \tag{9}$$

Next, we collect all these weak relations to construct the feature pool. As defined in Section 2, the contributors of the target of the state s are $f(s) = \{f_1(s), \cdots, f_K(s)\}$. The pairwise feature pool $\mathcal{F}$ is constructed from two parts, the self-pairwise feature pool $\mathcal{F}_{sp}$ and the mutual-pairwise feature pool $\mathcal{F}_{mp}$, that is $\mathcal{F} = \mathcal{F}_{sp} \cup \mathcal{F}_{mp}$. The self-pairwise feature pool of the target itself is constructed as

$$\mathcal{F}_{sp} = \{d(P_i(s), P_j(s)) | i = 1, \cdots, N; j = 1, \cdots, N; i \neq j\} \quad (10)$$

The mutual-pairwise feature pool of the target and its contributors is constructed as

$$\mathcal{F}_{mp} = \{d(P_i(s), P_j(f_k(s))) | i = 1, \cdots, N; j = 1, \cdots, N; k = 1, \cdots, K\} \quad (11)$$

Then the multiple instance boosting algorithm is utilized to select some of the most representative relations to construct the supporting field. In this paper, the weak classifier is adopted as in [11,5].

5 Experiments

5.1 Experimental Setup

We conduct some experiments to evaluate the performance of our spatial-temporal structural context based tracker. Our tracker is implemented in C++ code and runs on the standard PC platform. The tracker is evaluated on 10 publicly available sequences which contains different challenging conditions, and these sequences have been issued in previous works [5,27,7,6], which can be found in their own websites. Our tracker is initialized with the first frame and it outputs the trajectory of the target. The quantitative comparison results of IVT[1], FragTrack[2], SemiBoost[3], CoGD[4], MIL[5], PROST[6], VTD[27], TLD[7], ContextT[17] and our tracker are shown in Fig. 2, Table 1 and Table 2. More results can be found in the supplementary materials.

Parameters. The search radius r of the tracker is set in the interval $[20, 50]$. For the global temporal context model, every 5 frames are combined together to update the subspace model and the parameter $\eta = 0.99$ of η-truncation in subspace construction. For the local spatial context model, $K = 12$ contributors are generated to construct the supporting field and each of them are partitioned into 5×5 blocks. About 350 weak relations are combined together to construct the supporting field. For the positive bags, the samples are collected from the circle with the radius 8 and about 45 of the collected samples are packaged. For the negative bags, 50 samples are collected from the ring of the radius interval $[12, 40]$. The conservative updating threshold in our experiments are set as $\theta_s \in [-20, -10]$ and $\theta_t \in [10, 20]$. For the experimental results of other trackers we cite here, we utilize the default parameters which are provided in public available codes and choose the best one of 5 runs, or take the results directly from the published papers. Specifically, we reproduce the CoGD tracker in C++ code and adopt the parameters as described in [4].

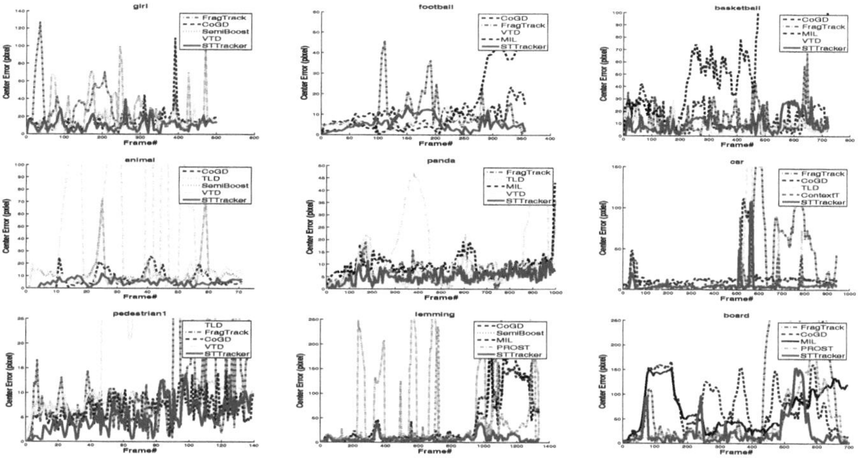

Fig. 2. Tracking results of our tracker, FragTrack[2], SemiBoost[3], CoGD[4], MIL[5], PROST[6], TLD[7], VTD[27] and Context tracker[17]. The results of five trackers with relatively better results are displayed.

5.2 Comparison with Other Trackers

Heavy Occlusion. The targets in sequence *car* and *occlude2* undergo long-term heavy occlusion for several times, and IVT which uses holistic appearances without any consideration of spatial information fails to track the target precisely. Relatively, TLD and Context Tracker perform very well in these two sequences, because the detection based trackers will re-locate the target after the occlusion, even though they lose the target during occlusion. Since the spatio-temporal context increases the possibility of our tracker to find the real target, our tracker also has good performance. A similar object usually confuses the trackers and finally misleads the trackers when it occludes the target, just like what happens in sequence *girl*. As shown in Fig. 3, approximately at the frame 463, TLD and MIL drift away for the fully occlusion of the man's face, whereas the context around the target and efficient temporal constraint provide our tracker strong discriminative ability to recognize the target.

Abrupt Motion and Motion Blur. The robustness of many trackers will be challenged by the abrupt motion resulting from hand-hold camera in sequence *pedestrian1*. The spatio-temporal context information provides enough information to ensure the robustness of the tracker. Another great challenge for the trackers is the motion blur. The loss of appearance features attributing to motion blur in the sequence *animal* and *lemming* finally results in the inaccuracy of FragTrack, SemiBoost, and TLD. However, since our temporal constraint model represents the target with low dimensionality 'gist' and the context information that can be clearly captured helps to locate the target, our tracker still has the best performance.

Cluttered Background. The cluttered background in sequence *animal* and *football* actually confuses the tracker a lot, as shown in Figure 3. Lacking spatial constraints, MIL are easily hijacked by other objects that have similar appearance with the target.

Table 1. Comparison results of average error center location in pixel

Seq.	STT	IVT	CoGD	Semi	MIL	Frag	PROST	VTD	TLD	ContextT
girl	**10.4**	40.4	14.1	22.8	31.6	25.4	19.0	12.5	35.7	18.6
occlude2	9.39	19.7	13.3	25.2	14.2	21.5	17.2	9.40	14.9	**9.25**
animal	**5.20**	226	7.38	12.3	80.3	71.4	-	9.68	50.7	81.2
basketball	**10.5**	95.4	13.8	153	93.3	12.7	-	11	158	159
football	**6.15**	17.2	9.16	102	12.7	9.92	-	6.25	13.0	51.2
pedestrian1	**5.14**	109	6.75	30.3	40.3	11.5	-	62.6	8.75	61.5
panda	**5.20**	58.2	64.5	41.7	9.42	6.85	-	6.33	17.7	77.5
car	6.26	56.9	16.6	46.4	80.7	28.6	-	51.8	11.8	**5.47**
lemming	**8.45**	128	39.8	99.8	40.5	82.8	25.1	98	167	182
board	**23.9**	169	74.5	389	69.2	90.1	39.0	70.1	134	103

Table 2. Tracking results. The numbers indicate the count of successful tracking frames based on the evaluation metric of PASCAL VOC object detection[28] in which the overlap ratio larger than 0.5 is regarded as successfully detected.

Seq.	Frames	STT	IVT	CoGD	Semi	MIL	Frag	PROST	VTD	TLD	ContextT
girl	**502**	497	353	482	388	378	378	447	502	219	328
occlude2	**812**	797	583	767	548	807	618	665	792	712	687
animal	**71**	71	3	62	56	5	13	-	66	43	48
basketball	**725**	715	75	335	90	175	630	-	601	15	50
football	**362**	346	246	292	65	272	302	-	357	272	55
pedestrian1	**140**	113	4	135	35	71	92	-	45	80	27
panda	**1000**	580	120	175	375	195	465	-	510	315	300
car	**945**	915	414	804	504	101	644	-	571	878	896
lemming	**1336**	1246	284	907	733	882	733	942	471	234	40
board	**698**	583	30	279	105	354	474	524	274	95	60

Although TLD considers positive and negative constraints and Context Tracker incorporates semantic context, they still frequently skip to other objects because they depend too much on detectors. The complex background in sequence *board* and *lemming* significantly increases the difficulty in tracking task. This is also the reason why many trackers which ignore background information including FragTrack, IVT and VTD perform bad in these sequences. Although CoGD, MIL, and PROST take the background into account, their performances are not as accurate as ours.

Large Variation of Pose and Scale. Some trackers such as FragTrack does not update their model effectively and easily lose the target when 3D pose of the target changes dramatically, as seen in sequence *girl*, *board*, and *lemming*. IVT, CoGD, and VTD adopt online updating mechanism to learn the different appearances of the target, but the large pose variation still drives them to drift away and they cannot recover. TLD and Context Tracker are good at long term surveillance sequence, but they cannot track the target precisely once large pose variation happens. When non-rigid motion happens in sequence *panda* and *basketball*, IVT and SemiBoost perform bad. Some other trackers such as CoGD, MIL and TLD have relatively good tracking results, but they do not succeed all the time. Since VTD combines multiple basic models with different features of the target, it performs well in these two sequences. Nevertheless, it does not consider the surrounding information, thus its tracking performances are not satisfactory as ours, as described in Table 1 and Table 2.

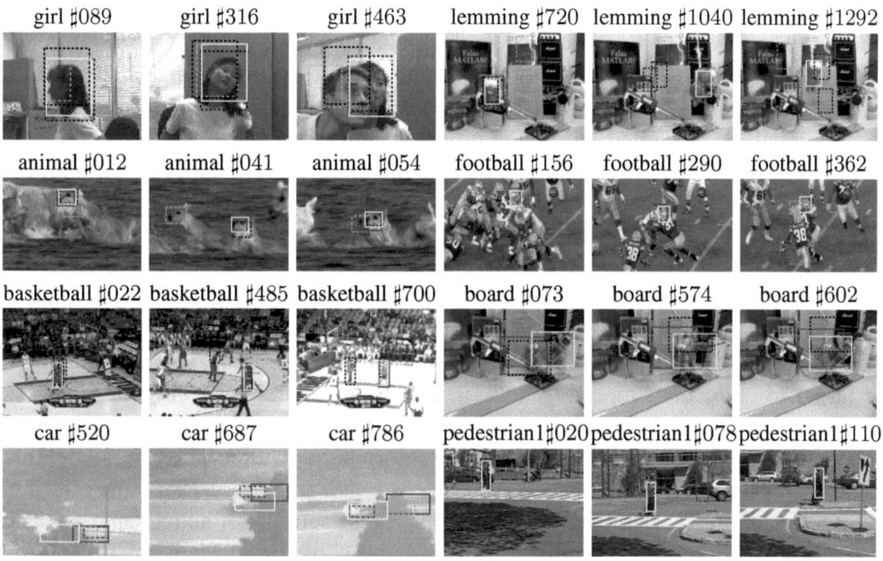

Fig. 3. Tracking results. The results of our tracker, CoGD[4], MIL[5], PROST[6], TLD[7], VTD[27] and ContextT[17] are depicted as yellow, blue, black, light green, cyan, red and purple rectangles respectively. Only the trackers with relatively better performances of each sequences are displayed.

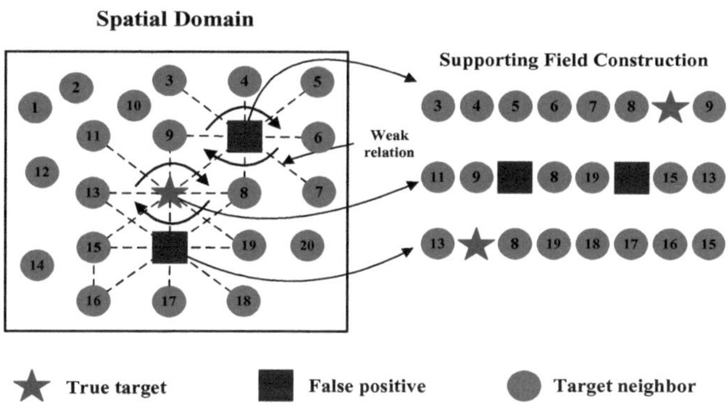

Fig. 4. The red pentagram represents the true target position, the blue triangle represents the false positive in the background and the magenta circle represents other surrounding patches. The relation between the target and its surroundings can greatly enhance the discriminability of the tracker.

5.3 Analysis

In these sequences, our proposed spatio-temporal structural context based tracker outperforms some of the state-of-the-art trackers [1,2,3,4,5,6,7,27,17]. The reason why our

STT is so stable is the introduction of global and local constraints, namely temporal and spatial context. The linear subspace (the global temporal context constraint) represents the historical appearance variations of the target with low dimensionality feature vectors. Only the gist of the object will be preserved and other noise and valueless information will be discarded during the process of subspace construction. Therefore, it is easy to explain why STT is able to handle illumination variation, motion blur, and appearance changes, because these annoying factors nearly will not influence the accuracy of our temporal context model. Particularly, we also can notice that STT is very good at dealing with the distraction by other objects which is similar to the target. As depicted in Fig. 4, when there exists a false positive near the target, while the appearances of the target and the false positive are highly similar, the surroundings of these two objects are totally varied. Once we incorporate the surrounding information around the target to build the supporting field, it is easy to differentiate the target from the false positive. Someone may doubt that STT will be drifted away by the surroundings if it keeps being updated with the surrounding information. Unlike TLD, Semiboot, and Context Tracker which utilize detectors to correct their trackers, STT is supervised by the temporal context which only focuses the target itself. The mutual supervision of spatio-temporal context ensures the long term stability of our STT.

6 Conclusion

In this paper, a spatio-temporal structural context based tracker is proposed. The appearance of target is described by the global temporal context information and the local spatial context information. The structured spatial context model automatically discovers the contributors around the target, and incorporates them to build a supporting field. In order to prevent our tracker from being drifted away by the surroundings, a strong temporal constraint model is included, which represents the target with low dimensionality feature vectors. Experimental comparison with the state-of-the-art tracking strategies demonstrates the superiority of our proposed tracker. Our future work includes the introduction of the adaptive balance coefficient between the global temporal context constraint and the local spatial context constraint, which will provide more robustness.

Acknowledgments. This work was supported by the Chinese National Natural Science Foundation Project #61070146, #61105023, #61103156, #61105037, National IoT R&D Project #2150510, Chinese Academy of Sciences Project No. KGZD-EW-102-2, European Union FP7 Project #257289 (TABULA RASA http://www.tabularasa-euproject.org), and AuthenMetric R&D Funds.

References

1. Lim, J., Ross, D.A., Lin, R.S., Yang, M.H.: Incremental learning for visual tracking. In: NIPS (2004)
2. Adam, A., Rivlin, E., Shimshoni, I.: Robust fragments-based tracking using the integral histogram. In: CVPR, pp. 798–805 (2006)

3. Grabner, H., Leistner, C., Bischof, H.: Semi-supervised On-Line Boosting for Robust Tracking. In: Forsyth, D., Torr, P., Zisserman, A. (eds.) ECCV 2008, Part I. LNCS, vol. 5302, pp. 234–247. Springer, Heidelberg (2008)
4. Yu, Q., Dinh, T.B., Medioni, G.G.: Online Tracking and Reacquisition Using Co-trained Generative and Discriminative Trackers. In: Forsyth, D., Torr, P., Zisserman, A. (eds.) ECCV 2008, Part II. LNCS, vol. 5303, pp. 678–691. Springer, Heidelberg (2008)
5. Babenko, B., Yang, M.H., Belongie, S.J.: Visual tracking with online multiple instance learning. In: CVPR, pp. 983–990 (2009)
6. Santner, J., Leistner, C., Saffari, A., Pock, T., Bischof, H.: PROST: Parallel robust online simple tracking. In: CVPR, pp. 723–730 (2010)
7. Kalal, Z., Matas, J., Mikolajczyk, K.: P-N learning: Bootstrapping binary classifiers by structural constraints. In: CVPR, pp. 49–56 (2010)
8. Mei, X., Zhou, S.K., Porikli, F.: Probabilistic visual tracking via robust template matching and incremental subspace update. In: ICME, pp. 1818–1821 (2007)
9. Ross, D.A., Lim, J., Lin, R.S., Yang, M.H.: Incremental learning for robust visual tracking. International Journal of Computer Vision 77, 125–141 (2008)
10. Liu, B., Huang, J., Yang, L., Kulikowski, C.A.: Robust tracking using local sparse appearance model and k-selection. In: CVPR, pp. 1313–1320 (2011)
11. Grabner, H., Bischof, H.: On-line boosting and vision. In: CVPR, pp. 260–267 (2006)
12. Wang, S., Lu, H., Yang, F., Yang, M.H.: Superpixel tracking. In: ICCV, pp. 1323–1330 (2011)
13. Yang, M., Wu, Y., Hua, G.: Context-aware visual tracking. IEEE Trans. Pattern Anal. Mach. Intell. 31, 1195–1209 (2009)
14. Saffari, A., Godec, M., Pock, T., Leistner, C., Bischof, H.: Online multi-class lpboost. In: CVPR, pp. 3570–3577 (2010)
15. Gu, S., Tomasi, C.: Branch and track. In: CVPR, pp. 1169–1174 (2011)
16. Grabner, H., Matas, J., Van Gool, L.J., Cattin, P.C.: Tracking the invisible: Learning where the object might be. In: CVPR, pp. 1285–1292 (2010)
17. Dinh, T.B., Vo, N., Medioni, G.G.: Context tracker: Exploring supporters and distracters in unconstrained environments. In: CVPR, pp. 1177–1184 (2011)
18. Bay, H., Ess, A., Tuytelaars, T., Van Gool, L.J.: SURF: Speeded-up robust features. Computer Vision and Image Understanding 110, 346–359 (2008)
19. Murphy, K., Torralba, A., Freeman, W.T.: Using the forest to see the trees: A graphical model relating features, objects, and scenes. In: NIPS (2003)
20. Torralba, A.: Contextual priming for object detection. International Journal of Computer Vision 53, 169–191 (2003)
21. Hall, P.M., Marshall, A.D., Martin, R.R.: Adding and subtracting eigenspaces with eigenvalue decomposition and singular value decomposition. Image Vision Comput. 20, 1009–1016 (2002)
22. Moghaddam, B., Pentland, A.: Probabilistic visual learning for object representation. IEEE Trans. Pattern Anal. Mach. Intell. 19, 696–710 (1997)
23. Tipping, M., Bishop, C.: Probabilistic principal component analysis. J. Royal Statistical Soc. Series B 61, 611–622 (1999)
24. Palmer, S.: The effects of contextual scenes on the identification of objects. Memory & Cognition 3, 519–526 (1975)
25. Torralba, A., Sinha, P.: Detecting faces in impoverished images. Journal of Vision 2 (2002)
26. Viola, P.A., Platt, J.C., Zhang, C.: Multiple instance boosting for object detection. In: NIPS (2005)
27. Kwon, J., Lee, K.M.: Visual tracking decomposition. In: CVPR, pp. 1269–1276 (2010)
28. Everingham, M., Van Gool, L.J., Williams, C.K.I., Winn, J.M., Zisserman, A.: The pascal visual object classes (voc) challenge. International Journal of Computer Vision 88, 303–338 (2010)

Automatic Tracking of a Large Number of Moving Targets in 3D

Ye Liu, Hui Li, and Yan Qiu Chen

School of Computer Science, Fudan University, Shanghai, China
{yeliu,hui_li,chenyq}@fudan.edu.cn

Abstract. This paper addresses the problem of tracking a large number of targets moving in 3D space using multiple calibrated video cameras. Most visual details of the targets are lost in the captured images because of limited image resolution, and the remainder can be easily corrupted due to frequent occlusion, which makes it difficult to determine both across-view and temporal correspondences. We propose a fully automatic tracking system that is capable of detecting and tracking a large number of flying targets in a 3D volume. The system includes a 3D tracking method in the framework of particle filter. Different from previous 2D tracking methods, the proposed method models the 3D attributes of targets and furthest collects weak visual information from multiple views, which makes the tracker robust against occlusion and distraction. The ambiguities in stereo matching when initializing trackers are handled by an effective multiple hypothesis generation and verification mechanism. The whole system is fully automatic in dealing with variable number of targets and robust against detection and matching errors. Our system has successfully been used by biologists to recover the 3D trajectories of hundreds of fruit flies flying freely in a 3D volume.

1 Introduction

Tracking targets in video sequence captured by a single camera has been studied for many years, there has however not been much research attention paid to the problem of recovering 3D trajectories of a large group of moving objects. Such phenomena is very common in nature, examples include bird flocks, insect swarms and fish schools. Scientists are interested in their motion trajectories because they give detailed information not only about the behavior of each individual but also about the collective behavior of the community.

Recovering the 3D trajectory of target from single-view video is difficult unless some strong assumptions are made [1]. Perhaps the most feasible way is to use multiple synchronized cameras. Even with this setup, it is still challenging to reconstruct the trajectories of a large number (sometimes hundreds) of targets, which involves determining both across-view correspondences (stereo matching) and temporal correspondences (visual tracking). The targets (fruit flies in our experiment for example) may well resemble each other in appearance and one target may be frequently occluded by other targets, all these challenges make it difficult for traditional stereo matching and 2D tracking methods to cope with.

A. Fitzgibbon et al. (Eds.): ECCV 2012, Part IV, LNCS 7575, pp. 730–742, 2012.

Most stereo matching methods use the photometric consistency cue to find correspondences between image pair of different views [2]. However in our case, photometric consistency becomes hardly useful, because 1) the targets may look alike which causes ambiguity in matching. 2) The targets are sometimes so small that slight viewpoint change may result in great appearance variation. 3) Occlusion happens frequently. Du *et al* [3] proposed a method that uses a motion cue and the epipolar constraint instead of photo consistency to find correspondences. They made an assumption that the 2D motion of the points to be matched in both views is reliably obtainable which is also not valid in the problem here.

Tracking in each single-view video in our case also faces challenges. In our imaging condition, temporal coherency in target appearance which is a crucial cue in most 2D trackers becomes weak. The nearly identical appearances of the targets may result in ambiguities and 2D trackers may be distracted by other targets in the scene. Besides, as the targets are moving in 3D space, occlusion happens frequently which makes the problem even more severe.

Aiming at overcoming these challenges discussed above, we design a tracking system that is capable of reconstruct the 3D trajectories for hundreds of flying animals (fruit flies) automatically. Although temporal visual coherency are weak and vulnerable, we show in our system that if the target is properly modeled in their native 3D space and multiple visual cues from multiple views are utilized carefully, we are able to overcome several major challenges such as frequent occlusion and make accurate estimation. Ambiguities in stereo matching are better handled by a multiple hypothesis generation and verification mechanism. The key idea of this mechanism is that whenever matching ambiguity occurs, instead of making decisions right away, multiple hypotheses are maintained and will be verified in later tracking stage where more evidence will be collected. Thus the chance of making false decision has been greatly reduced.

2 Related Work

Particle filters (PF) have been successfully applied and extended to various tracking problems ever since it was first introduced in visual tracking [4], because of their simplicity and the capability to handle nonlinearity and non-Gaussianity. Many researchers have extended particle filter to multi-target tracking [5–8]. As for single-view multi-target tracking, numerous approaches have been proposed including multiple hypothesis tracking (MHT) [9], JPDAF [10] and greedy assignment [11]. Okuma *et al* [6] proposed a particle filter based tracking method for tracking hokey players using the color histogram as observation model, when a player newly enters the scene, it is detected and a tracker is started for it. Khan *et al* [8] proposed a particle filter based method to track multiple targets that frequently interact with each other. They used MCMC to sample the resulted high-dimensional state space.

Some efforts have been made towards 3D tracking of multiple humans with multiple cameras [12–14]. Human bodies are highly deformable and their motion is complex but usually restricted on the ground plane, the targets we track are tiny with little visual details in captured images, the population size is much larger and they are likely to freely fly to any area of a 3D volume. Compared with human tracking, occlusion in our problem happens much more frequently but each occlusion event lasts for shorter period.

Some previous works have attempted to track similar tiny targets in 3D. Du *et al* [3] tracked particles using simply the nearest-neighbor strategy which first produce 2D trajectory segments, and then these segments are matched across different views using the epipolar constraint. Although some good stereo matching results were reported, trajectories were broken into many segments which is undesirable for many applications. Zou *et al* [15] proposed an off-line tracking algorithm which sought to minimize a global energy function via dynamic programming. Wu *et al* [16] proposed a method that linked the trajectory segments generated from 2D tracking. Their methods involve multiple high-cost linear assignment steps. The one to one assumption of linear assignment makes the trajectories prone to breaking up because if a detected object has been assigned to one tracker it cannot be assigned to another tracker which is invalid when occlusion occurs. This constraint was relaxed in [17]. All these methods highly depend on detection results.

3 Problem and Method

3.1 The 3D Multi-target Tracking Problem

Given video sequences from multiple cameras which have been geometrically calibrated and temporally synchronized, our goal is to retrieve the 3D locations at each time step for each target. Like other tracking problem, for each target in the scene we can define a state space at t as s_t and the data available up to t as $z_{1:t}$, then the tracking problem becomes estimation of the posterior probability density function $p(s_t|z_{1:t})$. The state sequence $\{s_t \mid t \in \mathbb{N}\}$ is assumed to be a first-order Markov process $p(s_t|s_{1:t-1}) = p(s_t|s_{t-1})$. Under this basic probabilistic framework, the task is now to build appropriate models that take advantage of the information from multiple views.

3.2 State Space and Transition Model

Most single-view tracking methods consider intuitively the position of target in image as state space. In fact, 2D image is the projection of 3D scene, occlusion and distraction in 2D image may not actually have existed in 3D space. So the first term we incorporated into the state space is the 3D location $X = (x, y, z)$. But 3D location alone only models translation in 3D space, a full rigid transform has 6 degrees of freedom (with another three rotation angles $A = (\theta_x, \theta_y, \theta_z)$). If we ignore the non-rigid deformation of the target, we can model the full motion as $R = (X, A)$. We define the state at time t as $s_t = (R_t, R_{t-1})^T$. And a transition model is defined as

$$s_t = Bs_{t-1} + v_{t-1}, \tag{1}$$

where B is a 12×12 state transition matrix, and $v_{t-1} \sim \mathcal{N}(0, \Sigma)$ is Gaussian noise. This transition model translates from previous state to current state which is physically more meaningful if 3D attributes have been modeled, and thus it is more likely to achieve accurate estimation.

3.3 Observation Model

Background Modeling. Our goal is to build an automatic tracking system, which is able to first of all find the targets from cluttered scene. We adopt a simple background modeling method which outputs for each frame a probabilistic map, the pixel value of which indicates the probability of each pixel belonging to the foreground. Particularly, let I_t^i denote frame t of view i, we calculate the background B_t^i as the median image of the previous p frames up to t

$$B_t^i = median(I_{t-p+1}^i, \dots, I_t^i). \tag{2}$$

Then the probabilistic map is

$$F_t^i \propto |I_t^i - B_t^i|. \tag{3}$$

By thresholding F_t^i and finding the barycenters of resulted connected regions, we are able to detect most of the moving targets in the scene.

Although simple, the above method works effectively for the detection of tiny moving targets. We do not expect to detect all the targets in one detection, because detection miss is inevitable due to occlusion. But as the detection procedure is carried out in every frame, the missed target is more likely to be detected in later frames when occlusion disappears. The probabilistic map obtained here is not just used for detection it also serves as one of the cues in the observation model which will be discussed below.

Appearance. We have explained that in our case little visual details of the targets can be captured. A majority of the features that have been commonly used in state-of-the-art tracking algorithms are invalid here, for example, color, texture, edge *etc.* Even so, we found that calculating simple image metric such as sum of square differences (SSD) and normalized-cross-correlation (NCC) between two image patches work effectively in most of the cases. We think the reason is that although each target may take up only a few pixels in image, these pixels jointly encode a discriminative feature which is the combined product of target intrinsic appearance, depth, orientation, background and illumination. These factors may vary among different targets, but for one target during a period of sufficiently long, they are approximately invariant. We choose NCC because it is more robust under slight occlusion and illumination change.

If we have a 3D model of the target with texture mapped, we can project it onto any image plane, get the predicted image and then check the appearance consistency of predicted and captured image. But it is infeasible because such textured 3D model is difficult to obtain. Therefore, we adopt a simplified strategy: consider a target at time t_0, its current state is $s_{t_0} = (X_{t_0}, A_{t_0})$, X_{t_0} is

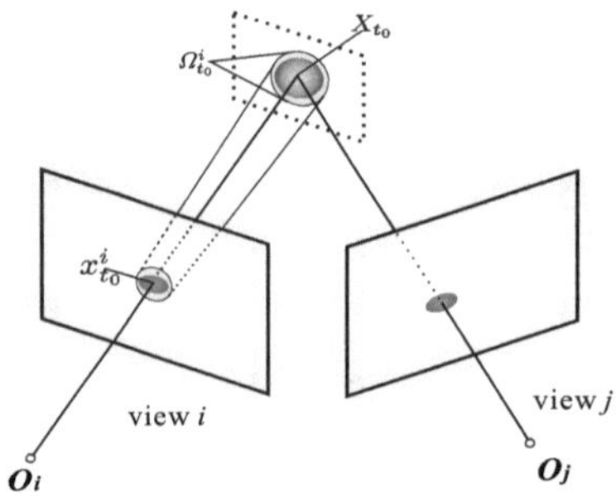

(a) Appearance cue

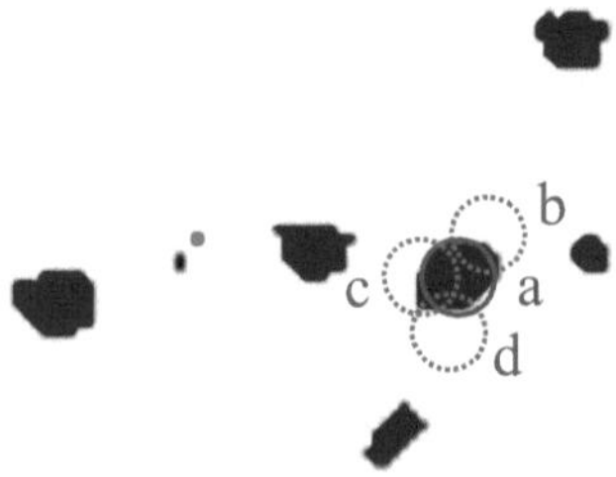

(b) silhouette cue

Fig. 1. (a) At t_0, a circular window at $x^i_{t_0}$ is back-projected onto a plane that is parallel to the image plane. The back-projected sample points then move with the target and their pixel values are also kept as reference. (b) a, b, c and d indicate four different states, and the four circles are their projected regions on image. State a has a higher silhouette score than the other three, because its proportion of area belonging to the foreground is the highest.

its 3D position, $x^i_{t_0}$ is the projected position on the ith camera (see Fig 1(a)). A circular window around the $x^i_{t_0}$ is selected, and then the pixel values in this window are kept in r_i which is a vector whose length n is the number of pixels in the window. The pixel positions in the window are back-projected onto a plane in 3D space which is parallel to the image plane (see Fig 1(a)), the back-projected point set is termed $\Omega^i_{t_0}$. At time t, the target is in state $s_t = (X_t, A_t)$, we can compute a 3D rigid transform T^i_t with the difference between s_{t_0} and s_t. The 3D points in $\Omega^i_{t_0}$ are transformed with T^i_t and obtain a new 3D point set $\Omega^i_t = \{T^i_t X \mid X \in \Omega^i_{t_0}\}$. we project transformed points to the image plane, and the pixel values of the projected locations are preserved in a vector a^i_t

$$a^i_t = \{I^i_t(P_i T^i_t X) \mid X \in \Omega^i_{t_0}\} \tag{4}$$

where I^i_t is the image at t of view i, and P_i is the projection matrix of camera i. This procedure is carried out in every view. We calculate for each view the NCC score between a^i_t and the corresponding reference r_i. By summing all the NCC scores of all the views together we have

$$C^t_1 = \sum_{i=1}^{N_v} NCC(a^i_t, r_i) \tag{5}$$

where N_v is the number of cameras. And the probability $p(z_t|s_t)$ using the appearance cue alone can be written as

$$p_{app}(z_t|s_t) \propto \exp C^t_1. \tag{6}$$

Silhouette. When a 3D object projects onto the image plane, silhouette is the area of the projection in the image. Like the appearance, with a known

3D model, silhouette can be obtained by simply projecting the 3D model onto the image plane. If the foreground/background segmentation has been perfectly done we can then check the shape consistency of the predicted silhouette and the segmented silhouette. However accurate 3D model is difficult to obtain and the segmented area may contain the projections of several targets, so computing the similarity between shapes does not always make sense.

Even so, we have managed to make full use of the coarse silhouette, because they are obtained by subtracting static background and indicates there are moving things (probably being the targets we want to track) in that area. We seek to check if the predicted silhouette is in the area of segmented foreground, or in another word compute the proportion of the predicted silhouette that is in the segmented foreground (see Fig 1(b))

$$C_2^t = \sum_{i=1}^{N_v} \frac{\|\{F_t^i(P_i T_t^i X) \mid X \in \Omega_i, F_t^i(P_i T_t^i X) > thre\}\|}{\|\Omega_i\|}, \tag{7}$$

where $thre$ is a threshold used to threshold the foreground probabilistic map F_t^i, and $\|\cdot\|$ measures the cardinality of a set. Using the silhouette cue, the probability $p(z_t|s_t)$ can be written as

$$p_{sil}(z_t|s_t) \propto \exp C_2^t. \tag{8}$$

By combining the two different cues together, we can build an observation model as

$$p(z_t|s_t) = \alpha p_{app}(z_t|s_t) + \beta p_{sil}(z_t|s_t), \alpha + \beta = 1, \tag{9}$$

where α and β are the weights that are set experimentally. In our experiment, we set $\alpha = 0.7$ and $\beta = 0.3$, and the radius of window is set to 6.

3.4 Particle Filtering

Under the Markov assumption and by Bayes' rule, the posterior probability $p(s_t|z_{1:t})$ can be formulated recursively [18]

$$p(s_t|z_{1:t}) \propto p(z_t|s_t) \int p(s_t|s_{t-1}) p(s_{t-1}|z_{1:t-1}) dx_{t-1}. \tag{10}$$

Instead of making strong assumptions on the above distribution such as linear Gaussian in Kalman filter, particle filter approximates the posterior probability with a set of particles $\{(s_t^n, w_t^n)\}_{n=1...M}$, each particle is associated with a weight w_t^n. New samples are drawn from particles in the previous step using importance sampling and moved independently using the transition model, and then they are reweighted as

$$w_t^n \propto p(z_t^n|\tilde{s}_t^n), \sum_{n=1}^{M} w_t^n = 1. \tag{11}$$

After we have a particle set that approximates $p(s_t|z_{1:t})$, we simply compute the expectation as

$$E(s_t|z_{1:t}) = \sum_{n=1}^{M} w_t^n s_t^n. \tag{12}$$

3.5 Automatic Tracking System

We have introduced the probabilistic models that we use for tracking a single target. In this section we will present the techniques that make the system fully automatic.

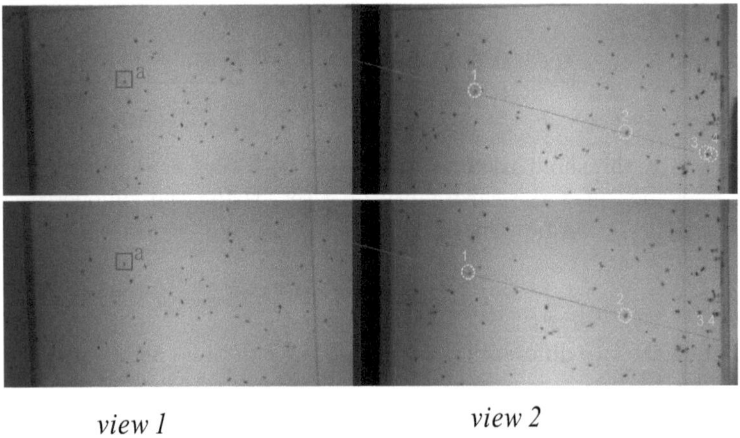

Fig. 2. Top: At time t, a detected target a in the left image finds 4 candidate correspondences in the right image using the epipolar constraint. Bottom: If correspondences can be found in the previous time step $t-1$ for a and the its 4 candidates, and the epipolar constraint is used again, ambiguities have been reduced with only two candidates remaining. Candidate 3 and 4 are removed. And then two trackers are started for the target.

Multiple Hypothesis Generation. First of all, we build a target queue Q which contains the targets that have been detected and are under tracking. We then carry out detection on images of all the views at time t, the result is a set of connected regions for each view. Some of the regions have been associated to targets in Q, and we are now interested in those haven't been assigned whose barycenters are calculated as $\{g_i^t\}$. We find their 2D locations $\{g_i^{t-1}\}$ in the previous time $t-1$ using a fast template matching algorithm [19]. This works because the target's appearance does not change much between two consecutive frames. The result is a set of point pairs $G_i = \{(g_i^t, g_i^{t-1})\}$ for view i.

For every point pair in G_1, we search in another set G_j, only those point pairs whose two points in both time steps are close enough to the corresponding epipolar lines are selected as candidates (see Fig 2). And the corresponding

3D point pairs can be obtained through triangulation. These 3D points in this set are projected onto other views to check if there is a target there (for the binocular case, this step is ignored). The final candidates are those 3D point pairs which both satisfy the two time step epipolar constraints between view 1 and view j and are visible by at least one other camera (for the binocular case, the last condition is ignored). Ambiguities cannot be avoided in this step, although we have done plenty of work to reduce them. We handle remaining ambiguities using a strategy similar to MHT, that is, we associate for this target multiple hypothetic trackers which are initialized using the candidates we have found, and push the target into the Q and each tracker work independently and is tested in later tracking. The angles in the state are simply set to zero. Wrongly associated trackers are expected to terminate in several time steps.

Hypothesis Verification. Thus each target in Q may maintain several hypothetic trackers after initialization. Each time after the particles of a tracker have been reweighted, a score is counted to decide whether this tracker is working properly for the target it belongs to. We count the percentage of particles whose computed appearance score C_1^t and silhouette score C_2^t are both below predetermined thresholds. If the percentage is higher than some threshold for 5 consecutive time steps, the tracker is terminated. Setting these parameters seems troublesome at first glance, but in our experiments we found that there is distinct difference between a properly working tracker and an incorrectly managing one.

Key Frame Selection. Sometimes the target's appearance change dramatically and abruptly, tracking with a fixed reference texture may cause problem. So we update reference at an interval of 8 frames but with much caution. We update reference only when the above mentioned termination score is sufficiently low. This ensures that the reference is selected when the tracker is in good condition.

3.6 System Workflow

The workflow of the proposed tracking system is summarized in Fig 3, where *bg subtraction* is short for background subtraction, and *bg maps* is the probabilistic maps output by the background subtraction method.

4 Experiments

We use fruit flies as targets in our experiment. About two hundred insects are put into a $35cm \times 35cm \times 25cm$ transparent acrylic box to freely fly within the cube. Three OPAL-1000 digital CCD cameras were used to synchronously capture videos at a frame rate of 120 fps and a resolution of 1024×1024. We implemented the proposed tracking method with Matlab and run it on a PC with an intel i7 3.4 GHZ CPU and 8 GB RAM.

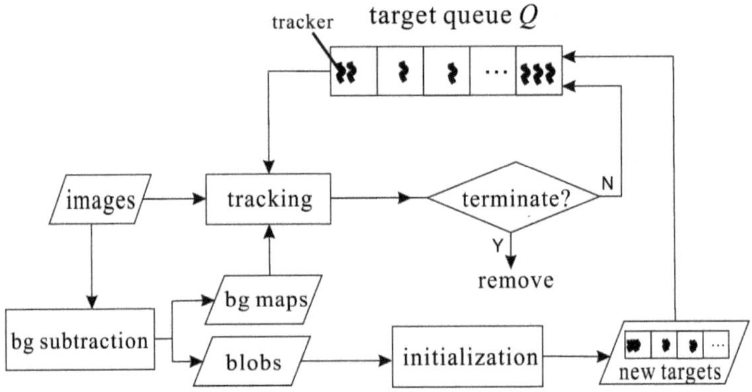

Fig. 3. One loop of the tracking system. The results of background subtraction are used by both tracking and detection procedures. Tracking results are taken into consideration in detection to avoid repetitive detection. Before tracking results are returned to the target queue, some trackers that satisfy the termination condition are terminated.

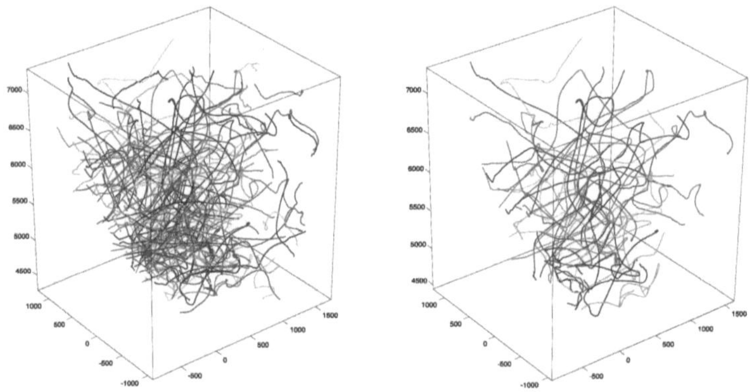

Fig. 4. Some of the trajectories obtained by the proposed method. Left: 142 trajectories that are longer than 40 frames. Right: 44 trajectories that are longer than 80 frames.

We captured videos of the flying fruit flies for about 2 seconds after they were stimulated. All the resulted videos had a length of 234 frames. We obtained 1371 targets in our target queue, some targets were assigned several trackers, and we only kept the longest of them. Most of trajectories that are too short were created mistakenly, so we abandoned those targets whose longest trajectory was short than 20 frames. And finally we got 239 trajectories, we display some of them in Fig 4.

Because of lack of ground truth, it is difficult to evaluate the accuracy of the computed 3D trajectories. But their projections on videos are observable. If a trajectory is observed to be correct in more than one view until the target is not visible to at least two view, we consider it a **completed** trajectory. Here we also define two types of tracking errors. Target **lost:** when the target is still moving and captured by at least one camera, but the tracker fails to track it. When this occurs, the tracker is expected to terminate in several time steps. Tracker **distracted:** when the target is still moving and visible by at least one camera, but the tracker is distracted and tracks another target. In this case, the tracker will not stop.

In order to evaluate the capability of the proposed method in handling occlusions and distractions, we compare the proposed method with two 2D tracking methods. The first one is a 2D particle filter method with template matching as observation model (2DPF+TM), that is, the particles are reweighted according to the NCC score of matching. And the state space is defined as $(x_t, y_t, x_{t-1}, y_{t-1})$. The other is template matching which is a pure deterministic method without Bayesian filtering, and we update the template in every 5 frames. This method is termed 2DTM. Both of the two methods adopted a 10×10 window. The 142 trajectories which are longer than 40 frames from our results were used for test. We initialized the 2D trackers with projection of the start points of trajectories. We checked whether the trajectories for test were correctly initialized by observing their projections on each view. If there is a corresponding target for that trajectory on each view for a sufficiently long time, then the chance of the trajectory being an outlier is negligible. We carried out this 3 times to reduce random disturbance.

Table 1. Comparison results. > 40 **percentage** means the percentage of trackers that track the right target for more than 40 frames.

Methods	Distracted	Lost	> 40 percentage	Completed	Total
2DPF+TM	44	20	69%	54.9%	142
2DTM	61	37	52%	30.9%	142
Proposed method	2	7	100%	93.6%	142

The results of this experiment is in Table 1. We can see in this table that while 2D tracking methods suffered from occlusion and distraction in 2D images, the proposed method was generally not affected by them. That's because our trackers work directly in 3D space and integrates information from multiple-views (see Fig 5). We only found two distractions in our result, both of them were caused by targets flying too close to each other in 3D space (Fig 6(a)).

It should be noted that the detection result was not perfect in our experiments, not all the targets were immediately detected once they entered the scene. But most of them were detected in the time steps afterwards. We can see in Fig 6(b), it is a diagram of the nunber of active trackers varying with time. At the beginning, the number is 89, after 5 time steps it climbs to 140, that's because during that period a large number of targets were detected in the later frames and no tracker was terminated. The variation of the number is the joint results of detection and termination.

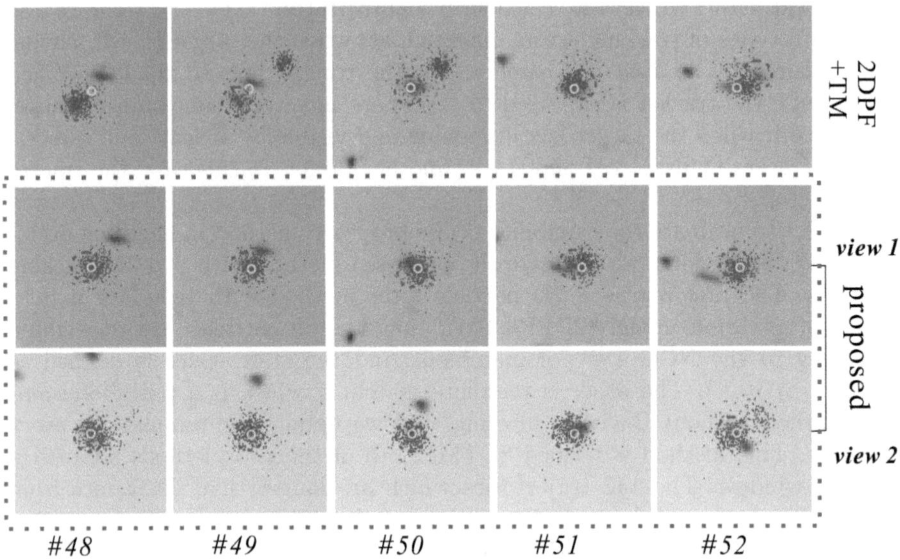

Fig. 5. Particle distributions (red dots) when tracking under distraction. The yellow circles are the estimated 2D locations, and the blue dashed circles are the target positions which have been marked manually. Top: in 2D tracking, distraction occurs when one target is occluded by another target. Middle and bottom: By integrating data from multiple views, the proposed method is generally immune from distraction in 2D image.

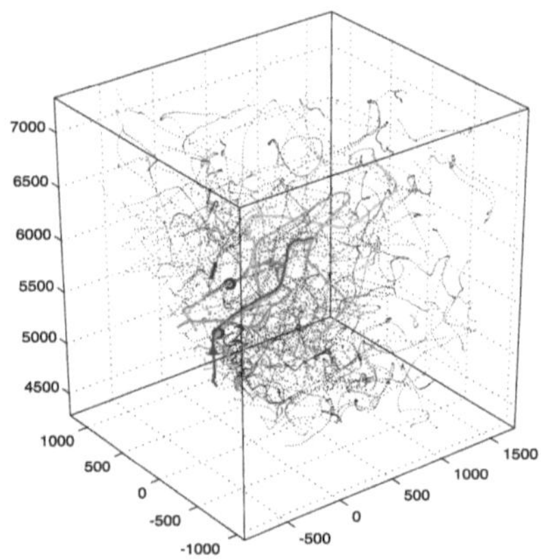

(a) 3D distractions

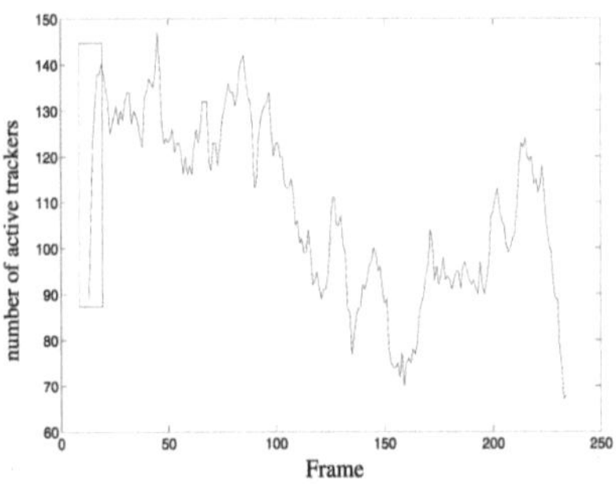

(b) Number of active trackers

Fig. 6. (a) Two 3D distractions are found which causes the failures (1 and 2) of the tracker. 1 happened because two targets moved close and flied in nearly one direction. 2 happened because two targets went close and one of them (orange) changed its direction instantly. (b) Plot of the number of active trackers. The boxed curve shows a dramatic increase in the number.

5 Conclusion and Future Work

We have proposed in this paper a tracking system to automatically track a large number of moving targets in 3D scene. Tracking is carried out directly in 3D space and information from multiple views is integrated reasonably. We have proposed several effective mechanisms which make the system fully automatic and stabe. With our Matlab implementation and PC, the system took around 15 second to process the data of one time step when the target queue maintaining about 140 active trackers. Our future work is to develop a GPU version of the system, which can be used in long-period tracking of targets in some natural particle-like systems.

Acknowledgement. The research work presented in this paper is supported by National Natural Science Foundation of China, Grant No. 61175036, and Education Commission of Shanghai Municipality, Grant No. 10ZZ03. The authors would like to thank Nan Jiang from Institute of Neuroscience, CAS for providing fruit flies in the experiments, and Qi Wang from Fudan University for helpful discussions.

References

1. Salzmann, M., Urtasun, R.: Physically-based motion models for 3d tracking: A convex formulation. In: IEEE 13th International Conference on Computer Vision. IEEE (2011)
2. Scharstein, D., Szeliski, R.: A taxonomy and evaluation of dense two-frame stereo correspondence algorithms. International Journal of Computer Vision 47(1), 7–42 (2002)
3. Du, H., Zou, D., Chen, Y.: Relative epipolar motion of tracked features for correspondence in binocular stereo. In: IEEE 11th International Conference on Computer Vision, pp. 1–8. IEEE (2007)
4. Isard, M., Blake, A.: Condensation conditional density propagation for visual tracking. International Journal of Computer Vision 29(1), 5–28 (1998)
5. Pérez, P., Hue, C., Vermaak, J., Gangnet, M.: Color-Based Probabilistic Tracking. In: Heyden, A., Sparr, G., Nielsen, M., Johansen, P. (eds.) ECCV 2002, Part I. LNCS, vol. 2350, pp. 661–675. Springer, Heidelberg (2002)
6. Okuma, K., Taleghani, A., de Freitas, N., Little, J.J., Lowe, D.G.: A Boosted Particle Filter: Multitarget Detection and Tracking. In: Pajdla, T., Matas, J. (eds.) ECCV 2004. LNCS, vol. 3021, pp. 28–39. Springer, Heidelberg (2004)
7. Hue, C., Le Cadre, J., Perez, P.: Sequential monte carlo methods for multiple target tracking and data fusion. IEEE Transactions on Signal Processing 50(2), 309–325 (2002)
8. Khan, Z., Balch, T., Dellaert, F.: Mcmc-based particle filtering for tracking a variable number of interacting targets. IEEE Transactions on Pattern Analysis and Machine Intelligence 27(11), 1805–1819 (2005)
9. Reid, D.: An algorithm for tracking multiple targets. IEEE Transactions on Automatic Control 24(6), 843–854 (1979)

10. Fortmann, T., Bar-Shalom, Y., Scheffe, M.: Sonar tracking of multiple targets using joint probabilistic data association. IEEE Journal of Oceanic Engineering 8(3), 173–184 (1983)
11. Veenman, C., Reinders, M., Backer, E.: Resolving motion correspondence for densely moving points. IEEE Transactions on Pattern Analysis and Machine Intelligence 23(1), 54–72 (2001)
12. Fleuret, F., Berclaz, J., Lengagne, R., Fua, P.: Multi-camera people tracking with a probabilistic occupancy map. IEEE Transactions on Pattern Analysis and Machine Intelligence 30(2), 267–282 (2008)
13. Mittal, A., Davis, L.: M 2 tracker: a multi-view approach to segmenting and tracking people in a cluttered scene. International Journal of Computer Vision 51(3), 189–203 (2003)
14. Khan, S.M., Shah, M.: A Multiview Approach to Tracking People in Crowded Scenes Using a Planar Homography Constraint. In: Leonardis, A., Bischof, H., Pinz, A. (eds.) ECCV 2006. LNCS, vol. 3954, pp. 133–146. Springer, Heidelberg (2006)
15. Zou, D., Zhao, Q., Wu, H., Chen, Y.: Reconstructing 3d motion trajectories of particle swarms by global correspondence selection. In: IEEE 12th International Conference on Computer Vision, pp. 1578–1585. IEEE (2009)
16. Wu, H., Zhao, Q., Zou, D., Chen, Y.: Automated 3d trajectory measuring of large numbers of moving particles. Optics Express 19(8), 7646–7663 (2011)
17. Wu, Z., Hristov, N., Hedrick, T., Kunz, T., Betke, M.: Tracking a large number of objects from multiple views. In: IEEE 12th International Conference on Computer Vision, pp. 1546–1553. IEEE (2009)
18. Ristic, B., Arulampalam, S., Gordon, N.: Beyond the Kalman filter: Particle filters for tracking applications. Artech House Publishers (2004)
19. Lewis, J.: Fast normalized cross-correlation. In: Vision Interface, vol. 10, pp. 120–123 (1995)

Towards Optimal Non-rigid Surface Tracking

Martin Klaudiny, Chris Budd, and Adrian Hilton

Centre for Vision, Speech and Signal Processing, University of Surrey, UK
{m.klaudiny,chris.budd,a.hilton}@surrey.ac.uk

Abstract. This paper addresses the problem of optimal alignment of non-rigid surfaces from multi-view video observations to obtain a temporally consistent representation. Conventional non-rigid surface tracking performs frame-to-frame alignment which is subject to the accumulation of errors resulting in drift over time. Recently, non-sequential tracking approaches have been introduced which re-order the input data based on a dissimilarity measure. One or more input sequences are represented in a tree with reducing alignment path length. This limits drift and increases robustness to large non-rigid deformations. However, jumps may occur in the aligned mesh sequence where tree branches meet due to independent error accumulation. Optimisation of the tree for non-sequential tracking is proposed to minimise the errors in temporal consistency due to both the drift and jumps. A novel cluster tree enforces sequential tracking in local segments of the sequence while allowing global non-sequential traversal among these segments. This provides a mechanism to create a tree structure which reduces the number of jumps between branches and limits the length of branches. Comprehensive evaluation is performed on a variety of challenging non-rigid surfaces including faces, cloth and people. This demonstrates that the proposed cluster tree achieves better temporal consistency than the previous sequential and non-sequential tracking approaches. Quantitative ground-truth comparison on a synthetic facial performance shows reduced error with the cluster tree.

Keywords: dense motion capture, non-rigid surface alignment, non-sequential tracking, minimum spanning tree, cluster tree, dissimilarity.

1 Introduction

Over the last decade, there has been an increasing research effort in spatio-temporal reconstruction of dynamic surfaces using multi-view video and/or depth acquisition. An important challenge is to transform the sequences of independent surface measurements at each frame into the aligned sequences with consistent temporal structure and correspondence. The problem of dense tracking for surfaces undergoing fast complex non-rigid motions over longer time periods has been tackled by a number of techniques. They can be divided into two broad groups according to the type of information they are primarily based on: image-based techniques work directly with multi-view video sequences; geometry-based techniques with a sequence of unregistered meshes reconstructed per frame.

A. Fitzgibbon et al. (Eds.): ECCV 2012, Part IV, LNCS 7575, pp. 743–756, 2012.

Image-based techniques commonly estimate a scene flow [1] between pairs of frames based on image constraints from multiple views. Multi-view 2D optical flows combined with per-frame geometry of the surface yield a 3D motion field which deforms a template mesh throughout the sequence [2]. Pons et al.[3] use a variational formulation of matching image information across views and over time to directly compute the surface shape and its motion field in alternation. The shape and motion computation can also be joined into a single complex optimisation [4]. Carceroni and Kutulakos [5] propose more efficient 3D tracking of independent surface patches with their own shape and appearance properties. Neumann and Aloimonos [6] iteratively refine shape and motion of the multi-resolution subdivision surface model by optimisation of individual surface patches. The patches can also be associated with triangle fans of a mesh deformed over time [7, 8]. Their shape changes with the tracked mesh which improves alignment of their textures with changing surface appearance in multi-view videos. Accumulation of tracking errors is reduced by fixed patch textures from the reference frame.

Geometry-based techniques directly create a temporally consistent representation of unregistered surface geometries [9–11] or fit a prior shape model to the unregistered sequence [12]. Cagniart et al.[10] perform hierarchical matching of overlapping rigid surface patches to sequentially track a sequence of multi-view reconstructions. Wand et al.[9] propose so-called urshape representing the surface and optimise its time-varying deformation field to fit a point cloud sequence. The animation cartography approach [11] employs geometric feature tracking to map surface regions to the 2D embedding space and build up a map of the complete surface from partial observations. Existing image-based or geometry-based approaches process input data sequentially which results in error accumulation causing a drift of the tracked mesh or a complete failure if the frame-to-frame alignment cannot handle rapid non-rigid deformation of the surface.

Non-sequential methods for surface tracking have been proposed which re-order the input sequence to overcome the problems of drift and failure. Beeler et al. [13] identify similar frames across a sequence of facial performance and use them to anchor a sequential alignment of intermediate frames using multi-view optic flow. In contrast, Budd et al. [14] optimise the traversal among all frames of whole-body performance by introducing the use of a minimum spanning tree in shape similarity space to re-order the frame-to-frame alignment process. Non-sequential alignment has been extended to register multiple non-rigid mesh sequences [14, 15].

Non-sequential approaches reduce the drift and improve robustness to tracking failures compared to sequential approaches. However, the independent accumulation of errors along different alignment paths can lead to jumps in the resulting mesh sequence where different paths meet. This paper addresses the problem of optimising the tree structure for non-sequential tracking to balance between drift and jump errors. The proposed concept is generalised for any frame-to-frame alignment method and variety of non-rigid surfaces. This is demonstrated by extensive evaluation on challenging datasets of faces, cloth and people.

2 Problem Statement

Input is a sequence of measurements $\{O_t\}_{t=1}^N$ of a deforming surface for frames $\{t_1, ..., t_N\}$. It can consist of multiple segments from independent motions of the surface. Each measurement O_t consists of a set of images from multiple viewpoints I_t^c and a mesh G_t representing the current shape of the surface. The mesh sequence $\{G_t\}_{t=1}^N$ is temporally unregistered, thus each mesh $G_t = (\hat{X}_t, \hat{C}_t)$ has time-varying vertex positions $\hat{X}_t$ and time-varying connectivity $\hat{C}_t$. The required output is a *temporally consistent mesh sequence* $\{M_t\}_{t=1}^N$ where the vertex positions X_t of mesh M_t correspond to the same set of surface points in every frame t and the connectivity of vertices C is fixed throughout the sequence.

Conventionally, the output mesh sequence $\{M_t\}_{t=1}^N$ is obtained by *sequential tracking* which concatenates *frame-to-frame non-rigid alignment* between successive frames t_i, t_{i+1}. The frame-to-frame alignment estimates the correspondence between observations $O_{t_i}, O_{t_{i+1}}$. *Non-sequential tracking* processes the input sequence $\{O_t\}_{t=1}^N$ in an order different from the temporal order. The reordering of $\{O_t\}_{t=1}^N$ is guided by a measure which estimates difficulty of non-rigid alignment of measurements O_t between any two frames. Intuitively, the difficulty of transition between frame t_i and t_j is represented by the *dissimilarity* between respective measurements $d(O_{t_i}, O_{t_j})$. Given $d(O_{t_i}, O_{t_j})$ between all pairs of frames, paths to every frame are jointly optimised to have minimal length. This reduces accumulation of alignment errors when the tracking is performed along the paths.

The paths are represented by a *traversal tree* $T = (\mathcal{N}, \mathcal{E})$ which is a spanning tree with the nodes $\mathcal{N} = \{n_1, ..., n_N\}$ corresponding to all frames $\{t_1, ..., t_N\}$ (Figure 1). The edges $\mathcal{E} = \{(n_i, n_j), ...\}$ are directed and weighted by the dissimilarity $d(O_{t_i}, O_{t_j})$. The non-sequential nature of tracking using the traversal tree leads to the presence of *cuts* in the sequence at places where two different alignment paths meet (marked red in Figure 1). Independent accumulation of tracking errors along these paths can potentially manifest as glitches or jumps in the resulting sequence $\{M_t\}_{t=1}^N$. There is a trade-off between the minimisation of tracking path length and a large number of cuts. Longer paths lead to larger gradual drift but large amount of cuts introduce sudden glitches and jitter. The proposed method reflects this trade-off and allows calculation of the traversal tree which balances between these two kinds of artefacts.

The non-sequential traversal of the input sequence using T can be combined with any frame-to-frame surface tracking technique working with $\{O_t\}_{t=1}^N$. The dissimilarity measure d has to be proportional to the alignment error of the selected technique so it is valid for calculating T. However, d is designed as an approximate measure which is significantly easier to compute than direct alignment of the mesh M. Given T, a user needs to specify a shape and topology of the mesh $M_{t_r} = (X_{t_r}, C)$ for the root node n_r. M_{t_r} is subsequently tracked between the pairs of frames along the branches of T from n_r towards the leaves. The result is a temporally consistent mesh sequence $\{M_t\}_{t=1}^N$ which can span across multiple separate captures of the same surface.

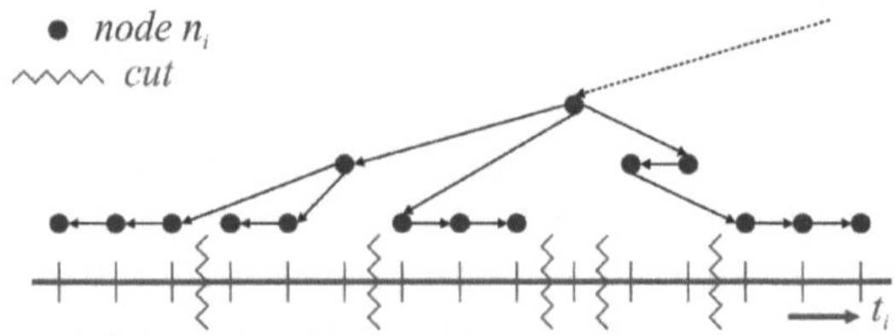

Fig. 1. Structure of a traversal tree T on the input frame sequence $\{t_1, ..., t_N\}$. The cuts separate adjacent frames which have different alignment paths along tree branches.

3 Minimum Spanning Tree

Non-sequential traversal of an input sequence based on the minimum spanning tree has been introduced by Budd et al.[14]. It is computed in a shape dissimilarity space and used for global alignment of multiple unregistered mesh sequences. This concept is generalised here for an arbitrary dissimilarity d between multi-modal measurements O_t in every frame. The space of all possible pair-wise transitions between frames of the sequence is represented by a dissimilarity matrix D of size $N \times N$ where both rows and columns correspond to individual frames (Figure 2(a)). The elements $D(i,j) = d(O_{t_i}, O_{t_j})$ define a cost of alignment between frames t_i and t_j. The matrix is symmetric ($d(O_{t_i}, O_{t_j}) = d(O_{t_j}, O_{t_i})$) and has zero diagonal ($d(O_{t_i}, O_{t_i}) = 0$). The optimal traversal in this space can be found through graph formulation of the problem as suggested in [14].

A fully-connected undirected graph $G = (\mathcal{N}, \mathcal{D})$ is built from the matrix D. The nodes $\mathcal{N} = \{n_1, ..., n_N\}$ are associated with frames and interconnecting edges $(n_i, n_j) \in \mathcal{D}$ have the weight $D(i,j)$. A traversal visiting all frames is described by an undirected spanning tree $T'_s = (\mathcal{N}, \mathcal{E}')$ where $\mathcal{E}' \subset \mathcal{D}$. The optimal tree T'_{MST} is defined as the *minimum spanning tree* (MST) which minimises the total cost of pair-wise alignment given by d as outlined in Equation 1. This objective describes total non-rigid deformation of the surface which has to be overcome following the traversal tree, and is optimised by Prim's algorithm.

$$T'_{MST} = \underset{\forall T'_s \subset G}{\operatorname{argmin}} \left(\sum_{\forall (n_i, n_j) \in T'_s} D(i,j) \right) \tag{1}$$

The benefit of MST is that low-cost transitions are close to the root and the edges with larger d are pushed towards the leaves. This reduces the accumulation of errors along the branches and also limits the extent of a failure due to large inter-frame dissimilarity to the ends of branches. The drawback of MST is that it does not take into account the introduction of cuts and tends to temporally over-fragment the sequence. T'_{MST} then contains short off-shoots or re-shuffling of consecutive frames on a single branch as illustrated in the lower right corner of Figure 2(b). This happens mostly in slow-motion periods where T_{MST} over-fits to small changes in low range of d.

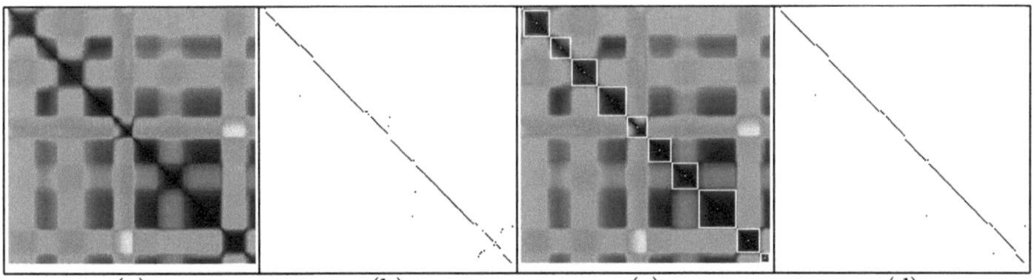

(a) (b) (c) (d)

Fig. 2. Dissimilarity matrix D for a part of the dataset SyntheticFace (blue - low values, red - high values) (a). Traversal tree T_{MST} depicted in D (each directed edge (t_i, t_j) is marked black at respective location $D(i, j)$). T_{MST} is the directed T'_{MST} with optimal root by Equation 7 (b). Clustering S_β illustrated in D as white squares for individual clusters (c). Traversal tree T_β based on the clustering S_β (notice less fragmentation and longer sequential segments than in (b)) (d).

4 Cluster Tree

To address shortcomings of MST the notion of temporal order of frames needs to be incorporated into the algorithm generating the traversal tree. MST is independent from the order of frames because the weight of edges in G does not change with re-ordering of the sequence $\{O_t\}_{t=1}^N$. A novel *cluster tree* is proposed which enforces sequential tracking locally to reduce the fragmentation of the sequence. The tree structure is still used to link the sequential segments together to obtain global non-sequential traversal of the sequence. The resulting tree shape is simpler with a smaller number of cuts which reduces the jumps/jitter in favour of relatively smooth sequential drift which is perceptually more acceptable.

4.1 Frame Clustering

Intuitively, the segments traversed sequentially should contain little or no deformation of the surface, thus there is a minimal accumulation of errors. Clusters of similar successive frames form blocks with low d around the diagonal in the matrix D (Figure 2(a)). Ideally, large clusters should be generated in slow-motion segments and small clusters (even down to individual frames) in the segments with significant surface motion. The summarisation method by Huang et al. [16] is modified for the purpose of frame clustering. The clusters do not have any representative key-frames but all frames are compared to each other to measure overall intra-cluster consistency. This provides a more general clustering approach which suits our purpose better than grouping frames around a few distinct exemplars.

A sequence of frames $\{t_1, ..., t_N\}$ can be represented by a clustering $S = \{F_1, ..., F_L\}$ where a frame cluster $F_i(t_{ci}, \Delta t_i)$ is a set of successive frames $\{t_{ci} - \Delta t_i, ..., t_{ci} + \Delta t_i\}$. All L clusters have to cover together the whole sequence $F_1 \cup ... \cup F_L = \{t_1, ..., t_N\}$ and be pair-wise disjoint $F_i \cap F_j = \emptyset$. The inconsistency of frames within cluster $A(F_i)$ is defined in Equation 2 as a sum of dissimilarities among them (the main difference to [16]).

$$A(F_i) = \frac{1}{2} \sum_{k=t_{ci}-\Delta t_i}^{t_{ci}+\Delta t_i} \left(\sum_{l=t_{ci}-\Delta t_i}^{t_{ci}+\Delta t_i} D(k,l) \right) \tag{2}$$

The clustering S is described by two costs: total intra-cluster inconsistency for all clusters and the number of clusters L. They are weighted against each other by the parameter $\beta \in <0,1>$ to provide a combined cost which is minimised in Equation 3.

$$S_\beta = \underset{S}{\operatorname{argmin}} \left(\beta L + (1-\beta) \sum_{\forall F_i \in S} A(F_i) \right) \tag{3}$$

The optimal set of clusters S_β for the dissimilarity matrix D (Figure 2(c)) depends on β which influences granularity of the clustering. A value closer to 1 returns smaller number of large clusters while a value closer to 0 returns larger number of small clusters. For a given β Equation 3 is minimised through a graph-based formulation as in [16].

4.2 Tree Calculation

A non-sequential traversal can be computed on the sequence of clusters instead of the original frame sequence using MST as described in Section 3. The dissimilarity matrix D is collapsed to a cluster dissimilarity matrix D_F of size $L \times L$ where rows and columns correspond to the individual clusters from S_β. Equation 4 defines the dissimilarity $D_F(i,j)$ between the clusters F_i and F_j as the minimal cost of transition between the respective clusters in the full matrix D. A cluster pair (F_i, F_j) is then linked by the pair of frames (t_k, t_l) with minimal dissimilarity.

$$D_F(i,j) = min(D(k,l)) \qquad \forall t_k \in F_i, \forall t_l \in F_j \tag{4}$$

The matrix D_F is symmetric with zero diagonal elements as for D. A fully-connected graph $G_F = (\mathcal{N}_F, \mathcal{D}_F)$ with nodes corresponding to the clusters $\{F_1, ..., F_L\}$ is built from D_F. The minimum spanning tree $T'_F = (\mathcal{N}_F, \mathcal{E}'_F)$ among the clusters is computed as in Equation 1.

Afterwards, the tree among clusters T'_F needs to be transformed to a full spanning tree T'_β interconnecting all frames. The set of nodes $\mathcal{N}$ for T'_β is expanded to the full sequence of frames $\{t_1, ..., t_N\}$. The set of edges $\mathcal{E}'$ for T'_β firstly contains a sparse set of links $\mathcal{E}'_1$ interconnecting the original clusters which is derived from $\mathcal{E}'_F$ (Equation 5). Secondly, $\mathcal{E}'$ contains a set of edges $\mathcal{E}'_2$ linking the rest of the frames within the clusters to T'_β. Because of low intra-cluster dissimilarity of frames sequential traversal is enforced among them. Thus, $\mathcal{E}'_2$ defines chains of frames in temporal order for all clusters (Equation 6).

$$\mathcal{E}'_1 = \{(n_k, n_l) : (n_i, n_j) \in \mathcal{E}'_F, (F_i, F_j) \sim (t_k, t_l)\} \tag{5}$$

$$\mathcal{E}'_2 = \bigcup_{\forall F_i \in S_\beta} \{(n_k, n_l) : t_k, t_l \in F_i, |t_k - t_l| = 1\} \tag{6}$$

The construction of T'_β does not strictly create cuts at all boundaries between the clusters. Typically, the minimal transition between temporally adjacent clusters is the one linking the last frame of the first cluster to the first frame of the second cluster. Therefore, the algorithm has an option to chain together several neighbouring clusters into a single sequential segment if it is deemed optimal.

The tree T'_β does not exactly define a traversal of the input sequence because it is undirected and has no root node. The root node n_r has to be selected to set directions along the paths in T'_β. The selection is made by minimisation of Equation 7 which is derived from the criterion for a shortest path tree. The length of weighted paths $n_l \to n_k$ from a candidate root node n_l to all other nodes n_k has to be minimal.

$$n_r = \underset{n_l \in \mathcal{N}}{\operatorname{argmin}} \left(\sum_{\forall n_k \in T'_\beta} \sum_{\forall (n_i, n_j) \in n_l \to n_k} D(i,j) \right) \tag{7}$$

The final traversal tree T_β (Figure 2(d)) is created from T'_β by setting the direction of the edges in $\mathcal{E}'$ according to the expansion of breadth-first search from n_r towards the leaves.

The shape of T_β is influenced by the clustering parameter β. The granularity of clustering S_β influences a number of branches for T_β. The cluster tree T_0 for $\beta = 0$ is equivalent to T_{MST} because all clusters contain one frame. With increasing β trees become generally thinner with longer sequential branches. T_1 for $\beta = 1$ is equivalent to purely sequential traversal because a single cluster for the whole sequence is generated. The spectrum of possible cluster trees allows a selection of T_β which balances the trade-off between drift and jumps/jitter for a given dataset. However, the optimal value of β has to be manually tuned according to visual evaluation of the tracked mesh sequence.

5 Experiments

The proposed approach has been extensively tested under several different scenarios of deformable surfaces undergoing complex non-rigid motions. Table 1 summarises the datasets used which contain facial performances (SyntheticFace, Face, DisneyFace [13]), whole-body performances (StreetDance [17]) and cloth deformation (Garment). All datasets provide multi-view image sequences with camera calibration and an unregistered mesh sequence. The absence of ground-truth for real data is a common issue in dense surface tracking. To allow quantitative evaluation of the methods the dataset SyntheticFace is artificially created.

Two different frame-to-frame tracking techniques are used according to the nature of individual datasets. Image-oriented surface tracking (IOST) is used for the face and cloth datasets [8]. The dissimilarity measure d_{IOST} for IOST is derived from the 3D trajectories of a sparse set of strong features robustly tracked in $\{I_t^c\}_{t=1}^N$. Geometry-oriented surface tracking (GOST) is used for the whole-body performance [14]. The dissimilarity measure d_{GOST} for GOST is

Table 1. Description of datasets and frame-to-frame alignment methods used for their evaluation. StreetDance [17] and DisneyFace [13] are publicly available. $|X|$ denotes the number of vertices of the tracked mesh M.

Dataset	No. of cameras	Resolution	Fps	No. of frames	Method	$\lvert X \rvert$
SyntheticFace	4	800×950	25	355	IOST	2689
Face	4	1920×1080	25	355	IOST	2689
DisneyFace	7	1176×864	46	346	IOST	2700
Garment	4	1920×1080	25	320	IOST	425
StreetDance	8	1920×1080	25	1050	GOST	3484

based on comparison of G_t between frames using a shape histogram. Details of IOST, GOST and d-measures are given in the supplementary material[1].

The following traversals of the input sequence are compared across all datasets: the standard sequential traversal (represented by $\beta = 1$), the non-sequential traversal based on MST (represented by $\beta = 0$) and the non-sequential traversal based on cluster tree. Multiple traversal trees T_β are generated for the proposed cluster-based approach to explore the spectrum of possible tree shapes between the sequential traversal and MST. Figure 3 shows the number of clusters for the tested values of β across individual datasets. The aligned sequence $\{M_t\}_{t=1}^N$ is obtained by applying the respective frame-to-frame alignment algorithm along the branches of T_β. The temporal consistency of mesh sequences resulting from the individual T_β has been visually assessed from the perspective of gradual drift versus severity of jitter and rapid glitches (the best traversal tree is noted in Figure 3). Due to the visual nature of results the reader is encouraged to watch supplementary videos[1].

5.1 Synthetic Facial Performance

The dataset SyntheticFace is derived from the real performance Face to achieve realistic face motion. The aligned mesh sequence obtained for the dataset Face is temporally smoothed across cuts to remove jumps. This represents the ground-truth $\{M_t^{GT}\}_{t=1}^N$ which is textured with a fixed face texture to avoid introduction of any inconsistencies between appearance changes and underlying motion. The textured $\{M_t^{GT}\}_{t=1}^N$ is rendered into 4 virtual views to create $\{I_t^c\}_{t=1}^N$ and the ground-truth meshes serve as $\{G_t\}_{t=1}^N$. The dissimilarity d_{IOST} is computed from 3D trajectories of the vertices selected from $\{M_t^{GT}\}_{t=1}^N$. The initial mesh M_{t_r} is taken directly from $\{M_t^{GT}\}_{t=1}^N$ in the root frame, so that the resulting $\{M_t\}_{t=1}^N$ can be compared directly the ground-truth.

To be valid for tree computation, d_{IOST} needs to be proportional to the difficulty of frame-to-frame alignment observed by IOST technique. This is analysed by comparing the values of d_{IOST} with the tracking errors E_{IOST} reported by the alignment algorithm. The graph in Figure 4(right) aggregates pairs of

[1] Supplementary material including videos is available under: `http://cvssp.org/projects/face3d/eccv2012/index.html`

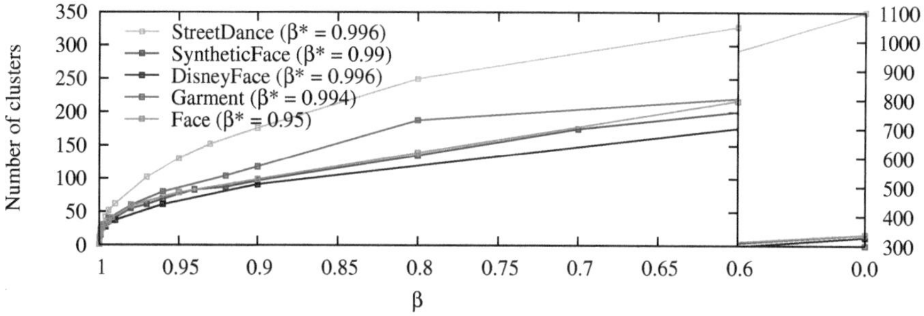

Fig. 3. Number of generated clusters for the tested values of β across the datasets. The amount of clusters increases from the sequential traversal ($\beta = 1$) towards MST ($\beta = 0$). β^* corresponds to the tree which gives the visually best tracking outcome.

(d_{IOST}, E_{IOST}) for every frame-to-frame transition across all traversals compared for SyntheticFace. The relationship has a scattered monotonically increasing trend. Low dissimilarities ($d_{IOST} < 0.4$) do not affect the quality of tracking and E_{IOST} linearly increases for higher values of d_{IOST}. The monotonic profile validates the use of d_{IOST} with IOST.

The ground-truth error of $\{M_t\}_{t=1}^{N}$ with respect to $\{M_t^{GT}\}_{t=1}^{N}$ is an average Euclidean distance of corresponding vertices across all frames $\{t_1, ..., t_N\}$. Figure 4(left) shows the graph of error for different β. The sequential tracking ($\beta = 1$) leads to the highest error due to accumulated drift. The profile for cluster trees demonstrates an improvement over MST ($\beta = 0$). In general, all non-sequential traversals achieve similar average imprecision $0.25 - 0.26mm$ per vertex which reflects the high quality of tracking. The ground-truth error reflects accumulation of the drift, however it does not quantify glitches due to the cuts. Despite this fact the graph of error correlates with visual assessment of the results and the cluster tree $T_{0.99}$ is selected as the best. The sequential result clearly suffers from significant mesh distortions built up during fast expression changes. The qualitative differences between $T_{0.99}$ and MST are fairly small because of the high-quality alignment achieved by IOST.

5.2 Facial Performance

The dataset Face containing fast changes of facial expressions poses a problem for sequential tracking which results in mesh distortions in the most deforming eye and mouth regions. The fragmentation in MST does not show as visible jumps in most cases because IOST produces accurate alignments in spite of weak skin texture. The best $T_{0.95}$ yields accurate mesh sequence which improves over MST by eliminating several small glitches around the eyes and on the lips. The monotonic relationship of d_{IOST} and E_{IOST} shown in Figure 5(left) validates d_{IOST} for IOST on real data as well. The tracking errors are generally higher than for SyntheticFace because of large changes in the face appearance during deformations.

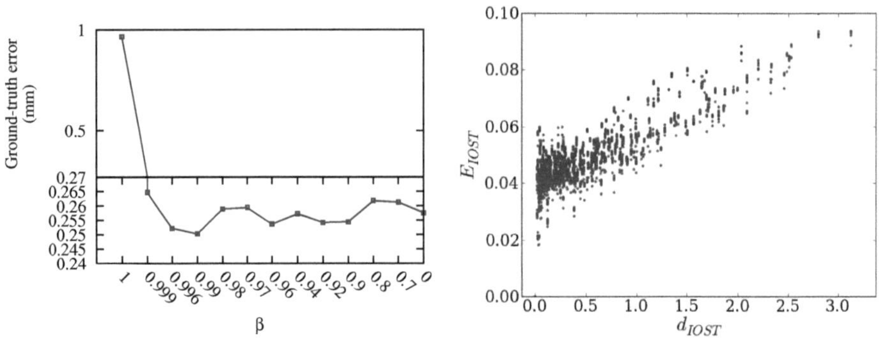

Fig. 4. Graph of the ground-truth error for SyntheticFace across different traversals given by β (left). The relationship of dissimilarity d_{IOST} and tracking error E_{IOST} for SyntheticFace (right). Colour scheme marks data samples from the sequential traversal (red) through $\beta = 1 \rightarrow 0$ to MST(blue).

The dataset DisneyFace contains moderately expressive speech which is tracked even by sequential traversal with small drift. Due to relatively low difficulty of the sequence the visual differences between MST and the best cluster tree $T_{0.996}$ amount to few noticeable glitches on the neck. Although the improvement by the cluster tree is relatively small (similarly for the dataset Face), it is significant because of the importance of accurate facial tracking for visual effects. Quantitative comparison has been performed on DisneyFace with the state-of-the-art non-sequential method for facial performance capture [13]. The difference to the temporally consistent mesh sequence released by Beeler et al.is calculated as for the dataset SyntheticFace with ground truth. The average vertex distance across all frames is $0.312mm$ with the standard deviation $0.357mm$ for the cluster tree $T_{0.996}$. Note that the difference may be due to the errors in either approach. Qualitatively, both techniques achieve comparable accuracy and temporal consistency.

5.3 Cloth

The dataset Garment contains fast free-form motions of a textured top on a subject's upper torso. Sequential alignment leads to fast degradation of the mesh at the beginning of sequence during rapid waving. Due to the partially repetitive motion pattern the number of branches of MST is excessive in some parts of the sequence. The increased presence of cuts causes many noticeable jumps. The cleaner structure of the cluster tree $T_{0.994}$ largely eliminates these artefacts apart from a few visible glitches at the peaks of complicated motions. The difference between MST and the cluster tree is more apparent than for the face because of the more challenging surface deformations complicated by motion blur.

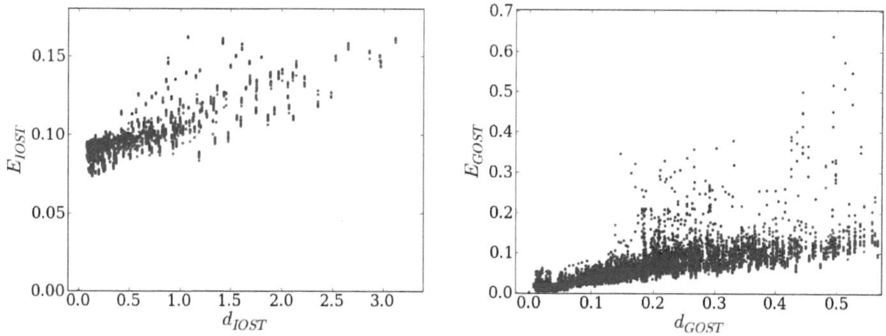

Fig. 5. The relationship of $d_{IOST} - E_{IOST}$ for Face (left) and $d_{GOST} - E_{GOST}$ for StreetDance (right)

5.4 Whole-Body Performance

The subject performing break-dance moves in loose uniform clothing is captured in the dataset StreetDance [17]. The sequence is composited from 3 different performances (Free, KickUp and FlashKick) to demonstrate the ability of non-sequential approaches to align the data across separate motions. The monotonic trend in Figure 5(right) validates the dissimilarity measure d_{GOST} for the GOST technique. However, the graph is more scattered in comparison to Figure 5(left) which caused by a more challenging dataset and use of geometry-based alignment.

The sequential tracking gradually distorts the structure of the mesh but the result by MST does not suffer from this severe slippage on the real surface. However, the mesh jitters during static segments of the performance because of significant re-ordering of frames. The best cluster tree $T_{0.996}$ enforces sequential processing of these segments which leads to a more coherent alignment. Figure 6 shows quantitatively this improvement by means of average acceleration across all vertices. The peaks represent high acceleration related to fast changes of mesh motion manifested as the jitter. $T_{0.996}$ significantly reduces acceleration spikes in a slow-motion segment of StreetDance in comparison to MST. In addition, gross errors in the mesh shape (e.g. artificial connections between limbs) occur frequently for MST during complex movements such as back-flip. They are largely eliminated by $T_{0.996}$ for the price of increased local drift at the peaks of motion. However, this is perceptually more plausible than fast alternation between quite differently distorted meshes. Overall, there is a clear superiority of results by the cluster tree in comparison to MST.

5.5 Discussion

The experimental results across different types of surfaces prove the existence of a trade-off between the accumulation of drift and the severity of glitches

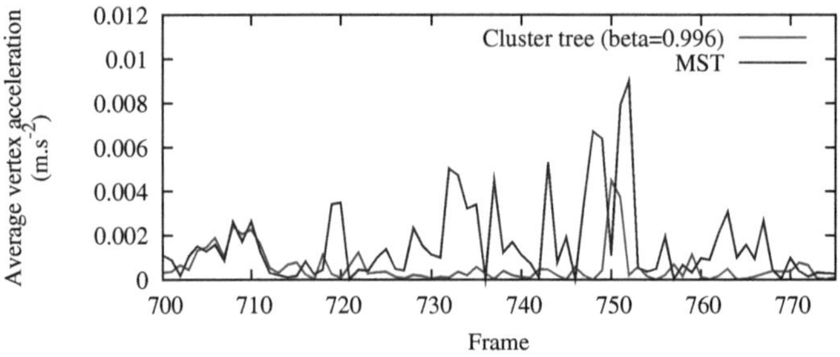

Fig. 6. Average vertex acceleration for MST and the best cluster tree $T_{0.996}$ for a segment in StreetDance where the subject stands still. The peaks representing fast change in motion correspond to high-frequency jitter in the aligned mesh sequence.

caused by cuts in temporal ordering. Perceptually, it is beneficial to increase the amount of local drift in the temporally consistent mesh sequence in exchange for the reduced amount of high-frequency jitter or glitches. Cluster trees provide a mechanism to balance this trade-off and therefore achieve results superior to fully sequential traversal or MST.

To analyse the trade-off between jumps and drift across the spectrum of trees, two quantitative measures representing each aspect are proposed. The measure SPL reflects the amount of potential drift in individual frames by a sum of path lengths between the root node and all other nodes (similar to Equation 7). The magnitude of potential glitch between adjacent frames separated by a cut is expressed as a sum of the non-overlapping parts of paths leading to them from the root node. The measure CUT is the total of these sums for all cuts created by the tree. Examples of SPL and CUT profiles across the tree spectrum are depicted in Figure 7 for the dataset SyntheticFace (graphs for the other datasets available online[1]). The trend of SPL across the datasets has a clear maximum for the completely accumulative sequential approach and generally decreases with some fluctuations towards MST. The measure CUT decreases from MST with a large amount of fragmentation towards the sequential traversal without any cuts. The middle range of both measures fluctuates because the different granularity of frame clustering given by β can lead to similar tree shapes. Some cluster trees have worse properties than MST in each measure but the majority of trees show an improvement in both. Intuitively, SPL and CUT should be combined into a single criterion which would express optimality of a tree with respect to the drift and jumps. This would enable automatic selection of the clustering parameter β defining a tree shape. However, any straightforward combination of the measures does not rank the trees consistently across different datasets, so that the order correlates with visual assessment of the tracking results. A combined criterion defining the optimal traversal tree for sequences with different types of surface deformation is an open problem.

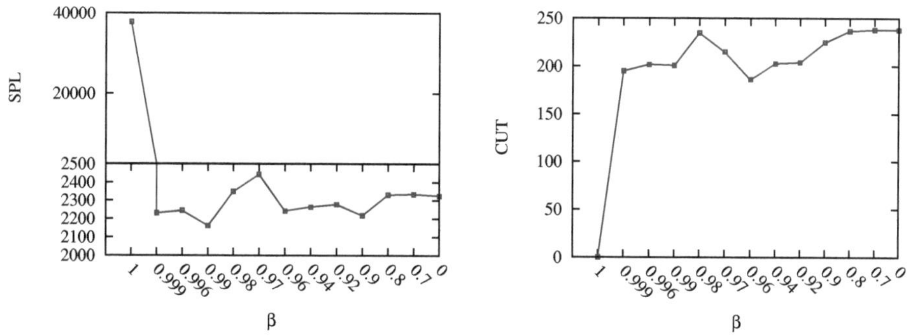

Fig. 7. SPL measure (left) and CUT measure (right) for SyntheticFace across different traversals given by β ($\beta = 1$ - sequential; $\beta = 0$ - MST)

Even with the single criterion reflecting sequential drift versus non-sequential jumps the selected tree is optimal only with respect to the dissimilarity d used. Because it is an approximate measure, the relationship to the actual difficulty of frame-to-frame tracking is not likely to be perfectly linear. This is indicated by the graphs between d and the tracking error E (Figures 4(right),5(left) for IOST and Figure 5(right) for GOST) where the correlation is monotonic but non-linear. This trend validates the use of the chosen measures for guiding the tracking. However, the non-linearity can bias the tree shape away from the ideal result (such as excessive branching due to over-fitting in low range of d which does not influence much the quality of tracking). The consequences of the non-ideal relationship can be alleviated by tuning of the tree shape through β. Even with a perfect dissimilarity the problem of distributing alignment errors across the sequence remains and needs to be optimised by the cluster tree.

6 Conclusion

This paper proposes a cluster tree to non-sequential tracking of non-rigid surface sequences which balances accumulation of errors in frame-to-frame alignment against jumps due to re-ordering of the data. The approach is generalised for any type of non-rigid surface tracked by an arbitrary frame-to-frame method. Evaluation is performed on a variety of datasets including facial, whole-body performances and deformation of cloth. Results demonstrate qualitatively and quantitatively improved temporal alignment against previous sequential and non-sequential minimum-spanning tree approaches.

Acknowledgement. This work was partly supported by EU ICT project SCENE and EPSRC Visual Media Platform Grant.

References

1. Vedula, S., Baker, S., Rander, P., Collins, R., Kanade, T.: Three-dimensional scene flow. TPAMI 27, 475–480 (2005)
2. Zhang, L., Snavely, N., Curless, B., Seitz, S.M.: Spacetime faces: high resolution capture for modeling and animation. ACM TOG 23, 548–558 (2004)
3. Pons, J.P., Keriven, R., Faugeras, O.: Multi-view stereo reconstruction and scene flow estimation with a global image-based matching score. IJCV 72, 179–193 (2007)
4. Courchay, J., Pons, J.-P., Monasse, P., Keriven, R.: Dense and Accurate Spatio-temporal Multi-view Stereovision. In: Zha, H., Taniguchi, R.-I., Maybank, S. (eds.) ACCV 2009, Part II. LNCS, vol. 5995, pp. 11–22. Springer, Heidelberg (2010)
5. Carceroni, R., Kutulakos, K.: Multi-view scene capture by surfel sampling: From video streams to non-rigid 3d motion, shape and reflectance. IJCV 49, 175–214 (2002)
6. Neumann, J., Aloimonos, Y.: Spatio-temporal stereo using multi-resolution subdivision surfaces. IJCV 47, 181–193 (2002)
7. Furukawa, Y., Ponce, J.: Dense 3D motion capture from synchronized video streams. In: CVPR, pp. 1–8. IEEE (2008)
8. Klaudiny, M., Hilton, A.: Cooperative patch-based 3D surface tracking. In: Conference for Visual Media Production, pp. 67–76. IEEE Computer Society (2011)
9. Wand, M., Adams, B., Ovsjanikov, M., Berner, A., Bokeloh, M., Jenke, P., Guibas, L., Seidel, H., Schilling, A.: Efficient reconstruction of nonrigid shape and motion from real-time 3D scanner data. ACM TOG 28, 15:1–15:15 (2009)
10. Cagniart, C., Boyer, E.: Free-form mesh tracking: A patch-based approach. In: CVPR, pp. 1339–1346. IEEE (2010)
11. Tevs, A.R.T., Berner, A., Wand, M., Ihrke, I.V.O., Bokeloh, M., Kerber, J., Seidel, H.P.: Animation Cartography - Intrinsic Reconstruction of Shape and Motion. ACM TOG 31, 12:1–12:15 (2011)
12. Vlasic, D., Baran, I., Matusik, W., Popović, J.: Articulated mesh animation from multi-view silhouettes. ACM TOG 27, 97:1–97:9 (2008)
13. Beeler, T., Hahn, F., Bradley, D., Bickel, B.: High-quality passive facial performance capture using anchor frames. ACM TOG 30, 75:1–75:10 (2011)
14. Budd, C., Huang, P., Klaudiny, M., Hilton, A.: Global Non-rigid Alignment of Surface Sequences. International Journal of Computer Vision, 1–15 (2012) ISSN 0920-5691, doi: 10.1007/s11263-012-0553-4, `http://dx.doi.org/10.1007/s11263-012-0553-4`
15. Huang, P., Budd, C., Hilton, A.: Global temporal registration of multiple non-rigid surface sequences. In: CVPR, pp. 3473–3480. IEEE (2011)
16. Huang, P., Hilton, A., Starck, J.: Automatic 3d video summarization: Key frame extraction from self-similarity. In: 3DPVT. IEEE Computer Society (2008)
17. Starck, J., Hilton, A.: Surface capture for performance-based animation. Computer Graphics and Applications 27, 21–31 (2007)

Full Body Performance Capture under Uncontrolled and Varying Illumination: A Shading-Based Approach

Chenglei Wu[1,2], Kiran Varanasi[1], and Christian Theobalt[1]

[1] Max Planck Institute for Informatik
[2] Intel Visual Computing Institute

Abstract. This paper presents a marker-less method for full body human performance capture by analyzing shading information from a sequence of multi-view images, which are recorded under uncontrolled and changing lighting conditions. Both the articulated motion of the limbs and then the fine-scale surface detail are estimated in a temporally coherent manner. In a temporal framework, differential 3D human pose-changes from the previous time-step are expressed in terms of constraints on the visible image displacements derived from shading cues, estimated albedo and estimated scene illumination. The incident illumination at each frame are estimated jointly with pose, by assuming the Lambertian model of reflectance. The proposed method is independent of image silhouettes and training data, and is thus applicable in cases where background segmentation cannot be performed or a set of training poses is unavailable. We show results on challenging cases for pose-tracking such as changing backgrounds, occlusions and changing lighting conditions.

1 Introduction

Marker-less capture of human skeletal motion from images is one of the well-studied problems of computer vision, with recent advances being able to reconstruct human motion at increasing speed and accuracy and under lesser controlled situations [1–7]. These methods have several applications in industry: ranging from game and movie productions to use in biomechanics, ergonomy and sports sciences. However, despite great algorithmic advances, even latest approaches can not yet be applied in arbitrary environments with possibly changing lighting conditions, occlusions and starkly varying scene backgrounds. This is why purposefully placing markers in the scene is still the method of choice under such more challenging conditions [8]. Special effects professionals and producers of 3D video content are sometimes interested beyond kinematic motion parameters - demanding faithful and detailed dynamic 3D shape models of captured scenes, such that believable virtual actors or convincing novel viewpoint renderings can be created. The research community has responded to this requirement by developing so-called *performance capture* approaches, *i.e,* methods that simultaneously capture shape, motion and possibly appearance

A. Fitzgibbon et al. (Eds.): ECCV 2012, Part IV, LNCS 7575, pp. 757–770, 2012.

of people in general apparel from a handful of video recordings [9–13]. Unfortunately, many state-of-the-art performance capture approaches are limited to studio settings with controlled lighting, controlled background, and to scenes without static or dynamic occluders. This has prevented the use of performance capture in practical applications such as outdoor movie sets or sports stadiums.

In this paper, we make a principal contribution towards the goal of model-based performance capture under less controlled conditions. We propose an algorithm that analyzes shading information to simultaneously estimate (a) human skeletal motion parameters, (b) arbitrary and time-varying incident scene illumination, (c) an approximation of surface reflectance, and (d) detailed dynamic shape geometry - such as folds and muscle bulges. We accept as input a multi-view video recorded from a synchronized and calibrated set of cameras, along with a rough initial shape-template of the person given as a 3D mesh fit to a kinematic skeleton. We do not require the subject to wear specific clothing or markers. Unlike previous performance capture methods [9–13], we do not require a fully controlled scene background, such as green screen, and thus do not expect exact foreground-background segmentations. We handle changing background and even some occlusions in the scene (Fig. 1). We do not rely on image features such as SIFT; our method is suitable even when the subject wears sparsely textured clothing.

The main idea in our paper is to mathematically formulate the image shading constraint in terms of its differential towards the motion parameters of the kinematic chain representing human body pose. Along with pose, we simultaneously estimate time-varying incident illumination, surface albedo and detailed surface geometry in a joint framework. Thus, we integrate the human motion estimation problem into the broader framework of multi view shape-from-shading.

Our major contributions in this paper are as follows.

1. We present a new theoretical formulation of performance capture that simultaneously recovers human articulated motion and time-varying incident illumination, by a minimization of shading-based error.
2. We provide a solution to reconstruct both skeletal motion estimates and finely detailed time-varying 3D surface geometry for human performances that are recorded under general and changing illumination and in front of less constrained background.

2 Related Work

For a thorough discussion and a historical perspective on human motion capture from images, one should consult any of the surveys [5, 7, 14]. Research efforts today can be broadly distinguished into studio-based methods which use multiple synchronized and calibrated cameras to achieve a high level of accuracy, and general purpose methods that work under fewer cameras in potentially cluttered surroundings - albeit producing pose estimates of lower accuracy. Many of the successful methods [15–17] validated on the HumanEva dataset [5] rely on a set

(a) (b) (c)

Fig. 1. Shading based pose tracking: (a,b) Overlay of estimated pose with recorded images - the actor is partially occluded by a person moving in the background (c) Reconstructed high-detail 3D geometry. The inset shows folds of the yellow T-shirt captured in 3D.

of training poses of tracking which limits their generalizability to new poses not observed in the training set. Methods for *performance capture* [9–13], *i.e,* detailed reconstruction of 3D surfaces along with skeletal motion, required studio conditions and green-screen to facilitate background segmentation. By contrast, in this paper we propose a shading-based approach that requires neither silhouettes nor training data. Silhouette estimation is sometimes integrated into the pose-estimation pipeline [18, 19] where 3D shape estimates are incorporated as a prior into image segmentation step. In particular, Hasler et al. [18] use this idea for an outdoor motion capture method. However, their approach does not capture detailed time-varying surface geometry. Also, background segmentation is an inherently error-prone step that fails in many cases; and hence should be avoided if possible for 3D shape reconstruction. Stoll et al [6] recently proposed a sums-of-Gaussian based holistic image and shape representation for pose tracking without silhouettes. But unlike them, we handle dynamic lighting changes, and recover not only body pose but also dense 3D surface detail, by analyzing image shading information.

Works in dynamic photometric stereo [20, 21] relied on specially engineered illumination to recover normal orientations that could be integrated to obtain the 3D surface. For example, a light-stage [21] captures images under temporally multiplexed illumination : with the shape being recorded under multiple known lighting conditions that provide a basis for describing light variations. These works analyze image shading information at a dense scale and thus recover true dynamic surface detail, instead of interpolating it from sparse image information such as silhouettes. However, finding a temporally coherent parameterization of the dynamic surface, despite some recent efforts [22, 23], remains a difficult task - especially when skeletal articulated motion need also be simultaneously captured. Wilson et al [24] use stereo and optical flow in a light-stage setup to obtain a temporally coherent parameterization for facial performance capture. They compute optical flow amidst a subset of *tracking frames* that are all captured under the same incident lighting. By contrast, in this work, we address arbitrary and unknown lighting conditions which can vary from frame-to-frame.

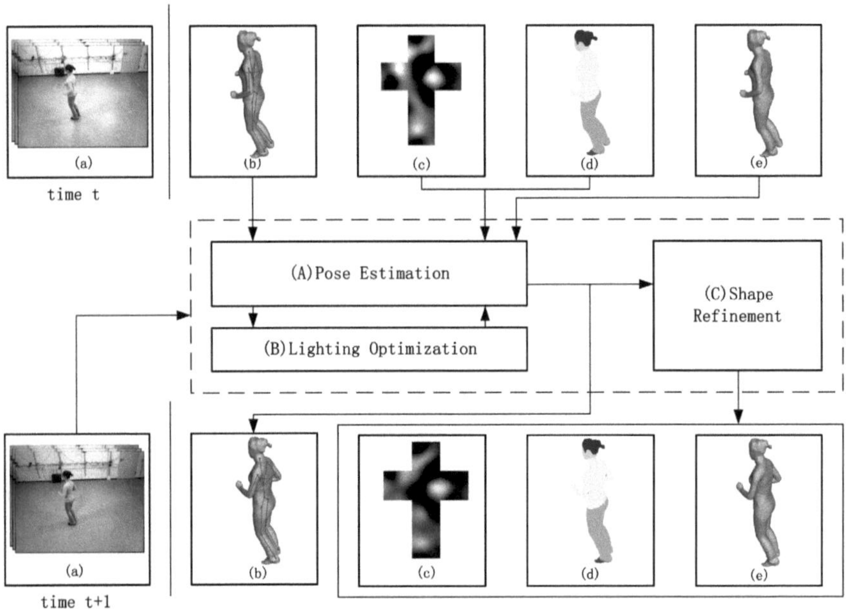

Fig. 2. Overview: (a) input multi-view images (b) skeletal pose (c) incident illumination (d) surface albedo (e) refined surface geometry. (b-e) are outputs of our method. Steps (A,B) for estimating pose and lighting are alternated in a joint optimization framework. In the step (C), final estimates of lighting, albedo and surface geometry are obtained. These estimates at t are provided as input for the optimization at $t+1$.

Wu et al.[25] have recently published a work that combines the strengths of model based performance capture with the inverse-rendering approaches of photometric stereo to reconstruct dynamic 3D surface detail that approaches the quality of light-stage reconstructions, albeit under arbitrary and unknown lighting conditions. The reconstructed surfaces are temporally coherent and aligned with simultaneous skeletal motion estimates. However, in that method, performance capture of the coarse geometry and dynamic shape refinement were treated as subsequent and independent problems, and the first part required the scene to be covered in green screen to enable coarse geometry estimation via silhouettes. By contrast, we use illumination estimation and shading constraints throughout the performance capture pipeline, *i.e,* for skeletal pose estimation and detailed shape reconstruction.

Our work is also relevant to the broader problem of dynamic shape from shading. Zhang et al.[26] provide an elegant formulation for shape and motion estimation under varying illumination, but the number of unknowns in the problem make it severely under-constrained, limiting their approach to only rigid motion estimates. However, as mentioned by them and others, shading variations provide cues for estimating flow even in texture-less regions. In this work, we build upon this insight to estimate complete articulated human motion under unknown and time-varying incident illumination, without relying on silhouettes or training data. To the best of our knowledge, this has not been attempted before, to achieve results of even lower quality.

3 Overview

The input to our method is a multi-view video sequence of a moving actor captured using a sparse set of synchronized and calibrated cameras. Lighting in the scene can be arbitrary and time-varying, and since no background subtraction is required, no green-screen is expected and other potentially occluding elements can be in the scene. A rigged 3D mesh model with an embedded skeleton is provided as a template for tracking. We only need a smooth template mesh at a low resolution; the fine-scale detail is added later by our method. Similar to [13], the smooth template is built from a static laser scan of a person, alternatively image-based reconstruction methods are also feasible. The embedded bone skeleton as well as the skinning weights for each vertex, which connect the mesh to the skeleton, are obtained using standard tools.

An outline of the processing pipeline is given in Fig. 2. Given a set of captured multi-view images (a) as input, at each time-step $t+1$ we estimate skeletal pose (b), incident illumination (c), surface albedo (d), and detailed surface geometry (e). For each of these variables, we solve an inverse-rendering problem that attempts to make the rendered images as-close-as-possible to the captured image data. In Step-A, starting with the skeleton and the refined mesh from time t, the skeletal pose is optimized by assuming incident lighting and surface albedo from t, thereby exploiting temporal coherence. In Step-B, the incident illumination at time $t+1$ is estimated based on the skinned coarse mesh in the new skeletal pose. The Step-A is then repeated by taking the newly estimated lighting which results in a better pose estimate. The steps A and B constitute the main part of our method and are described in Sec. 5. In Step-C, we re-estimate incident lighting, surface albedo and then refine the surface geometry. The refined surface now captures folds and bulges not describable by articulated motion. For the initialization of the very first frame, we refer readers to Gall et al. [13] for pose estimation based on the manually segmented silhouettes and Wu et al. [25] to calculate the albedo value for each albedo segment, which could be provided by the user or any albedo segmentation method.

4 Image Formation Model

Assuming the object being tracked is a non-emitter of light (*i.e*, no surface interreflections), the reflectance equation describing the light transport at a certain surface point on the object can be defined as [27]

$$I(q,\omega_o) = \int_{\Omega} L(\omega_i)V(q,\omega_i)\rho(q,\omega_i,\omega_o)\max(\omega_i \cdot n(q), 0)d\omega_i, \qquad (1)$$

where $I(q,\omega_o)$ is the reflected radiance, and the variables q, $\boldsymbol{n}$, ω_i and ω_o are the spatial location, the surface normal, and the incident and outgoing light directions, respectively. The symbol Ω represents the domain of all possible directions, $L(\omega_i)$ represents the incident lighting, $V(q, \omega_i)$ is a binary visibility function, and $\rho(q, \omega_i, \omega_o)$ is the bidirectional reflectance distribution function of the surface at q. To simplify the reflectance equation, we assume the reflectance to be Lambertian *i.e*, $\rho(q, \omega_i, \omega_o) = \rho(q)$, and represent the light transport with spherical harmonics (SH) so that the integral in the spatial domain will be converted to a dot product in the frequency domain.

We define the variable $G = LV$ and represent it with SH coefficients g_k. Then Eq. (1) will be simplified as follows:

$$I(q) = \rho(q) \sum_{k=1}^{d^2} g_k(q) S_k(n(q)), \tag{2}$$

where $S_k(n(q))$ is the scaled SH basis function depending on the surface normal directions $n(q)$, and $d - 1$ is the order of SH used. When visible lighting and albedo are known, the rendering value is determined by the surface normal only. This equation is employed to provide the shading constraints for pose estimation (Sec. 5) and later used for surface geometric refinement (Sec. 6).

5 Pose Estimation under Varying Illumination

At each time-step $t+1$, we perform a simultaneous estimation of body pose and incident lighting, both of which may change from time t. In order to keep the optimization tractable, we assume that changes in body pose are independent from changes in lighting, and alternate between the optimization of these variables.

We take as initialization the refined mesh and the embedded skeleton of time t, as well as the estimated incident lighting and surface albedo. In Sec. 5.1, we introduce how the mesh changes according to pose-changes. In Sec. 5.2, we define the shading constraint used to estimate the pose parameters, given the incident lighting. The optimization to minimize the shading error is described afterwards. The method to estimate incident lighting is described in Sec. 5.3.

5.1 Surface Parameterization with Respect to Pose

We use the popular linear blend skinning approach to deform the mesh to a skeletal pose. Similar to [1], we represent the articulated pose to be estimated by a set of twists $\theta_k \hat{\xi}_k$. The state of a kinematic chain is determined by a global twist $\hat{\xi}$ and the joint angles $\Theta = (\theta_1, \cdots, \theta_m)$. Assuming the state of the kinematic skeleton of the previous time-step to be known, the unknowns for pose estimation are the rigid motion of the root node and changes in joint angles which we denote as $\phi = (\Delta\hat{\xi}, \Delta\theta_1, \cdots, \Delta\theta_m)$. Let q_i^t be the position of vertex i at t. By using exponential maps to represent each joint's rigid motion and by linearizing the rigid body transforms, the pose of the vertex i at $t+1$ can be expressed with the skinning equation as

$$\begin{pmatrix} q_i^{t+1} \\ 1 \end{pmatrix} = \sum_{j=1}^{m} w_j e^{\Delta\hat{\xi}} \prod_{k \in T(j)} e^{\hat{\xi_k} \cdot \Delta\theta_k} \begin{pmatrix} q_i^t \\ 1 \end{pmatrix}$$
$$\approx \begin{pmatrix} q_i^t \\ 1 \end{pmatrix} + \left(\Delta\hat{\xi} + \sum_{j=1}^{m} w_j \sum_{k \in T(j)} \hat{\xi_k} \cdot \Delta\theta_k \right) \begin{pmatrix} q_i^t \\ 1 \end{pmatrix} = \begin{pmatrix} q_i^t \\ 1 \end{pmatrix} + M_q(i) \cdot \phi, \tag{3}$$

where $T(j)$ determines the indices of joints preceding the joint k in the kinematic chain, and $M_q(i)$ is the matrix determining how the pose change influences the change of vertex position. Each vertex i is assigned a set of skinning weights w_j that determine how much influence bone (or joint) j has on the deformation of vertex i. Skinning weights are once defined during template building using standard techniques [13]. A similar equation can be derived for the vertex normal n_i^{t+1} at time $t+1$

$$\begin{pmatrix} n_i^{t+1} \\ 0 \end{pmatrix} \approx \begin{pmatrix} n_i^t \\ 0 \end{pmatrix} + M_n(i) \cdot \phi, \tag{4}$$

where $M_n(i)$ is a matrix that determines how the pose change ϕ results in a change in normal orientation.

5.2 Shading Constraint for Pose Estimation

Our shading constraint requires the rendered images of the optimal pose according to our lighting model to be as-close-as-possible to the image data captured. Following Eq. (2), the shading constraint for a single camera c is defined as

$$E_c^s = \sum_i (\rho_i g(q_i^{t+1}) \cdot S(n_i^{t+1}) - I_c^{t+1}(x_i^{t+1}, y_i^{t+1}))^2, \tag{5}$$

where (x_i^{t+1}, y_i^{t+1}) is the projection of the surface vertex q_i^{t+1}, and $g(q_i^{t+1})$ and $S(n_i^{t+1})$ are the vectors of SH coefficients g_k and S_k of Eq. (2). We assume the albedo ρ_i at time $t+1$ is the same as that at time t, thereby exploiting temporal coherence in scene motion. However, both the lighting and geometry at time $t+1$ are unknown. We attempt to estimate both of them in a unified framework in order to properly account for shading changes due to changes in either lighting or pose. Since simultaneous estimation of both of them is computationally challenging, we alternate between error minimization with respect to either of these two variables. First we minimize the shading error to estimate the pose, by assuming the lighting of the previous time-step, and thereafter we solve for lighting. To do this, we linearize the SH term $S(n_i^{t+1})$ and the image intensity term I_c^{t+1}. The SH term is expressed in a first-order Taylor-series expansion, and using the terms of Eq. (4).

$$S(n_i^{t+1}) \approx S(n_i^t) + \frac{\partial S(n_i^t)}{\partial n_i^t} \Delta n_i^t = S(n_i^t) + \frac{\partial S(n_i^t)}{\partial n_i^t} M_n(i) \cdot \phi, \tag{6}$$

where $\frac{\partial S(n_i^t)}{\partial n_i^t}$ is derivative of scaled SH function with respect to normal changes Δn_i^t, which are expressed in terms of pose changes ϕ.

Inspired by the formulation of optical flow, we linearize $I^{t+1}(x_i^{t+1}, y_i^{t+1})$ as:

$$I^{t+1}(x_i^{t+1}, y_i^{t+1}) = I^{t+1}(x_i^t + u_i, y_i^t + v_i) \approx I^{t+1}(x_i^t, y_i^t) + I_x^{t+1} u_i + I_y^{t+1} v_i. \quad (7)$$

Next, we derive the linear approximation for the flow (u_i, v_i) in an image from the motion parameters ϕ. This is similar to the derivation in [1], but we use the full perspective camera model instead of scaled orthographic projection [1], as camera calibration is available for our system. Then, the image motion from time t to time $t+1$ can be linearized as:

$$\begin{pmatrix} u_i \\ v_i \end{pmatrix} \approx \begin{pmatrix} \frac{s_1}{Z_i^t} & 0 & 0 & s_3 \\ 0 & \frac{s_2}{Z_i^t} & 0 & s_4 \end{pmatrix} \cdot \boldsymbol{e}^{\hat{\xi_c}} \cdot \begin{pmatrix} \Delta q_i^t \\ 0 \end{pmatrix} + \begin{pmatrix} \frac{s_1}{Z_i^{t2}} & 0 & 0 & 0 \\ 0 & \frac{s_2}{Z_i^{t2}} & 0 & 0 \end{pmatrix} \cdot \boldsymbol{e}^{\hat{\xi_c}} \cdot \begin{pmatrix} q_i^t \\ 1 \end{pmatrix} \cdot \Delta Z_i^t, \quad (8)$$

where s_1, s_2, s_3, s_4 are the acquired camera intrinsic parameters, $\boldsymbol{e}^{\hat{\xi_c}}$ acts as the extrinsic matrix of the camera's pose, Z_i^t is the depth of q_i^t for the current camera. The linearization is based on the assumption that the rigid motion Δq_i^t as well as the relative depth change ΔZ_i^t are small enough. As both of them can be expressed through pose change ϕ (from Eq. (3)), the flow (u_i, v_i) can ultimately be expressed as a linear function of ϕ.

The shading constraint in Eq. (5) can be further improved by considering the color similarity between the rendered color and the image color. The color similarity is computed as the Euclidean distance in HSV space and appears as a weighting factor α_i in our shading constraint. This helps us avoid optimizing the model where the template material does not yet match to its projection in the image. Combining terms from multiple cameras, our non-linear multi-view shading energy function is given as

$$E = \frac{1}{N} \sum_c \sum_i \{\alpha_i^c (\rho_i g(q_i^{t+1}) \cdot S(n_i^{t+1}) - I_c^{t+1}(x_i^{t+1}, y_i^{t+1}))\}^2, \quad (9)$$

where N is the total number of constraints for error normalization (*i.e,* the number of pixels in all cameras getting the projection from the mesh), and α_i^c is the color similarity for pixel i in camera c. Using the previously described recipe of linearization, this can be expressed in terms of pose parameters ϕ as a linear system:

$$\boldsymbol{H} \cdot \phi = \boldsymbol{b} \quad (10)$$

Specifically, the kth rows of matrix $\boldsymbol{H}$ and vector $\boldsymbol{b}$ have the following form (detailed derivation is in the supplementary document, $r_3^\top$ refers to the last row of the rotation matrix of the camera pose) :

$$\begin{aligned} \boldsymbol{H}_k = \alpha_i^c \rho_i g(q_i^{t+1}) \cdot \frac{\partial S(n_i^t)}{\partial n_i^t} M_n(i) - \alpha_i^c \left[\tfrac{s_1}{Z_i^t} I_x^{t+1},\ \tfrac{s_2}{Z_i^t} I_y^{t+1},\ 0,\ s_3 I_x^{t+1} + s_4 I_y^{t+1}\right] \boldsymbol{e}^{\hat{\xi_c}} M_q(i) \\ + \alpha_i^c \left[\tfrac{s_1}{Z_i^{t2}} I_x^{t+1},\ \tfrac{s_1}{Z_i^{t2}} I_y^{t+1},\ 0,\ 0\right] \boldsymbol{e}^{\hat{\xi_c}} \begin{bmatrix} q_i^t \\ 1 \end{bmatrix} \cdot \left[r_3^T\ 0\right] \cdot M_q(i), \\ \boldsymbol{b}_k = \alpha_i^c I^{t+1}(x_i^t, y_i^t) - \alpha_i^c \rho_i g(q_i^{t+1}) \cdot S(n_i^t). \end{aligned} \quad (11)$$

Coarse-to-Fine Optimization. To minimize the non-linear error function of Eq. (9), we iteratively solve Eq. (10) and linearize around the new solution. Note that here after solving Eq. (10), we check if the original energy in Eq. (9) decreases to decide the appropriate step size for updating the solution, in a fashion similar to Newton-Raphson style minimization with adaptive step size. Besides, as given in Eq. (7), the linearization assumes that the local image intensity variations can be approximated by a first-order Taylor expansion. So we adopt a coarse-to-fine strategy for pose estimation - by building an image pyramid through successively downsampling each captured image, and running the pose estimation from coarsest images to the finest images. This helps us track big motions and reduces the chance of getting stuck in local minima.

5.3 Lighting Optimization

In the general case, lighting changes can be abrupt and impossible to model. However, for most cases, it can be assumed that the lighting at $t+1$ changes gradually from lighting at t. In our method, we optimize for pose and lighting in a two pass strategy. For the first pass, we use the lighting at t to optimize for pose at $t+1$, as described in the previous section. For the second pass, we estimate the lighting at $t+1$ based on the new pose, and then use it to refine the pose estimates. We have empirically observed that one additional iteration of alternating optimization is sufficient for getting good estimates.

We derive the constraint for lighting optimization from the image formation model defined in Eq. (1). But instead of Eq. (2), following Wu et al. [25], we use a different type of linearization. We define $T(q,\omega_i) = V(q,\omega_i)\max(\omega_i \cdot n(q), 0)$ and then represent it with SH coefficients t_k, while representing the incident lighting L with SH coefficients l_k. This gives the linearization:

$$I(q) = \rho(q) \sum_{k=1}^{d^2} l_k t_k. \tag{12}$$

We compare the rendered intensity values with the captured image I_c and solve for the lighting coefficients l_k. In order to deal with outliers, i.e. erroneous projection due to the inaccuracy of the pose, we solve a ℓ_1 norm minimization problem defined as:

$$\hat{l} = \operatorname*{argmin}_{l} \sum_{i} \sum_{c \in Q(i)} |\sum_{k=1}^{d^2} l_k t_k - I_c(P_c(x_i))|. \tag{13}$$

Here, i is the vertex index, c is the camera index, $Q(i)$ is the set of cameras that can see the i-th vertex $\boldsymbol{x}_i$, and P_c is the projection matrix for camera c.

6 Dynamic Surface Refinement

After the pose and lighting estimation step, we have a coarse template model that strikes the correct pose, as parameterized by the respective skeleton pose parameters. Different from linear skinning that we used in skeletal pose estimation for its simplicity, we here use quaternion blend skinning[28] to render the final shape of the surface mesh in the current pose, as it leads to higher quality surface deformation, in particular around joints. When we have the coarse mesh of time $t + 1$, we refine the vertex positions q_i from shading cues as given in Eq. (3). We refer to [25] for detailed explanation of this step. A minor difference is that temporal consistency is taken into account for assigning albedo labels, by formulating this as a Markov-Random-Field (MRF) problem with the data term consisting of two values (i) the similarity of vertex color to the average color in the material label and (ii) the label similarity with previous time-step.

7 Results

7.1 Quantitative Evaluation

In order to quantitatively evaluate our method, we generated a synthetic sequence of 100 frames with 10 camera views. The ground-truth skeleton and mesh geometry are taken from the results of a previous performance capture method of a human walking sequence. The ground-truth surface albedo map and dynamically changing illumination are manually assigned. With these generated synthetic images as input, and given the mesh, skeleton, albedo segmentations for the first frame, we run our algorithm on the remaining 99 frames. In Fig. 3, we report the accuracy of our approach, with the mean joint position error of only around 6 mm.

7.2 Real-Word Sequences

We use three real captured sequences for qualitatively evaluating our method. The sequences were captured with 11 cameras in a studio, but unlike in the input data of previous performance capture methods, the subject can wear sparsely textured apparel, there is no need for green-screen background, and there may be potentially occluding objects in the scene and dynamic background (Fig. 1). Cameras recorded at a resolution of 1296×972 pixels, and at a frame rate of $40fps$. Each sequence shows major illumination changes; they are induced by an operator randomly setting control knobs for various lights in the studio - these readings are not taken nor provided in any way to our method. Please also note that some of the captured images are saturated, which our method handles robustly. As can be seen in the overlayed images of our estimated skeleton and 3D shape in Fig. 4, good pose estimates are obtained despite the challenging scene conditions. Even when a few cameras are partially occluded, our method still works quite well thanks to the use of shading cues and multiple cameras setup. High quality surface detail such as deforming cloth folds are also captured (Fig. 6). We invite the readers to see the results in our accompanying video, which is better suited for observing temporal information. Minor errors in skeletal joint positions might cause the surface to jitter over time, which we remove in our video results by temporal smoothing of the vertices.

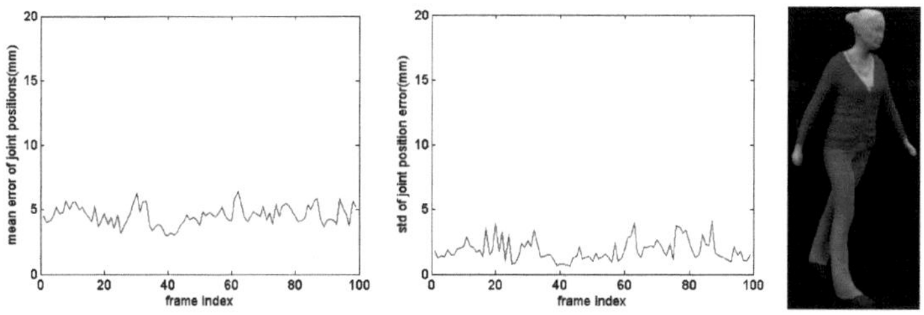

(a) (b) (c)

Fig. 3. Quantitative evaluation: (a) The mean error of joint positions. (b) The standard deviation of joint position errors. (c) A generated synthetic image.

We compare the results of our method with a texture-based tracker that does not estimate lighting explicitly at each frame. Instead, it assumes texture from the first frame and uses optical flow for tracking; it loses track after a few frames as the lighting changes significantly (see Fig. 5-b). We also implemented a silhouette-based tracker [13] that explicitly performs background segmentation using chroma-keying on the captured images. Due to changing lighting and moving background objects, the extracted silhouettes are sometimes misleading and result in inaccurate pose estimates (see Fig. 5-c).

7.3 Computation Time

The computation time of our method depends on image resolution, mesh resolution and the order of SH used for representation. In our experiments, we represented 3D shape using meshes of 80000 vertices, and used a 4th order SH for representing lighting. With these values, our method takes about 10 min per each frame on a standard CPU with a 2.6 GHz processor and 8 GB RAM. Specifically, the computation times are 3 min for one-pass of pose estimation, which we do twice for each frame. The lighting estimation step is quite fast, taking only 10 seconds. The other time-consuming part is the dynamic shape refinement, which takes 4 min, of which 1 min is spent on visibility calculation. Striking a trade-off between representation accuracy and computation time, we utilized a low-resolution mesh (around 5000 vertices) to render the visibility map for each vertex on the high-resolution mesh. As our code is unoptimized, we believe the computational time can be further reduced by parallelizing the algorithm.

7.4 Limitations and Future Work

Our algorithm becomes less effective when the underlying shape template is not accurate. For example, the rotation of the upper arm may not be modeled in the skeleton. We corrected for such errors by manually adjusting the pose where the algorithm failed (roughly one frame per 200 frames needed such correction in our experiments). Please note that a global optimization strategy such as that used in [13] can automatically handle such cases. Also since we estimate lighting

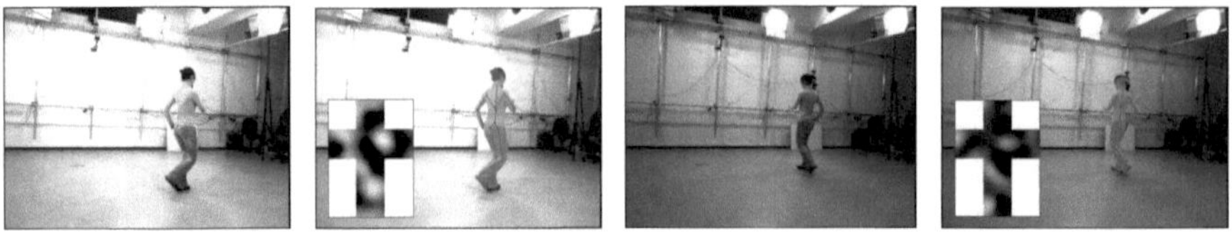

(a) (b) (c) (d)

Fig. 4. Illumination changes in a real captured sequence: (a,c) Frames showing widely different incident illumination (b,d) The output skeletal pose and mesh overlayed onto the images. The insets show estimated illumination at each frame.

(a) (b) (c)

Fig. 5. Comparison with alternative tracking methods: (a) Our method (b) Texture-based tracking (c) Silhouette-based tracking [13]

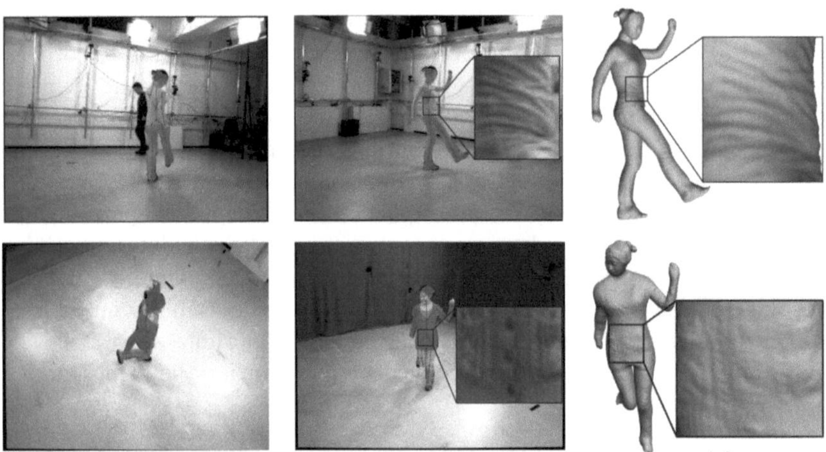

(a) (b) (c)

Fig. 6. Results of pose and 3D shape estimation: (a,b) Overlayed skeletal pose at different frames and camera views (c) Fine-scale 3D shape reconstruction. The inset shows dynamic cloth deformations captured from shading.

and pose sequentially at each time-step, error accumulation may cause drift of the tracker. In future work, we would like to address this issue by stronger priors from data-driven modeling. Our assumptions of Lambertian reflectance and local shading model may not be justified in some cases. Abrupt lighting changes, e.g, the illumination generated by a controlled light stage, are also hard to model. However, in such cases, the lighting pattern is known beforehand and can be directly provided as input to our method. A final limitation is the computation time for running our method which is too high for real-time deployment. We would like to address these and other limitations in future work.

8 Conclusion

In this paper, we provide a novel shading based frame-work for human performance capture under uncontrolled and dynamic lighting. Starting from synchronized multi-view images, we estimate both the articulated human pose and fine-scale time varying surface geometry. Key innovation is a novel iterative pose optimization framework that exploits estimated lighting and shading cues. Our approach does not expect carefully engineered backgrounds as it does not perform silhouette extraction or any other form of background segmentation. Ultimately, one of the goals of vision based motion capture is to obtain high quality motion reconstructions using a very limited set of cameras in outdoor situations. Even though we do not explicitly evaluate our method in outdoor scenes, we believe that our work provides a crucial step towards this goal.

References

1. Bregler, C., Malik, J., Pullen, K.: Twist based acquisition and tracking of animal and human kinematics. IJCV 56(3), 179–194 (2004)
2. Sidenbladh, H., Black, M.J., Fleet, D.J.: Stochastic Tracking of 3D Human Figures Using 2D Image Motion. In: Vernon, D. (ed.) ECCV 2000. LNCS, vol. 1843, pp. 702–718. Springer, Heidelberg (2000)
3. Deutscher, J., Blake, A., Reid, I.: Articulated body motion capture by annealed particle filtering. In: CVPR, pp. 1144–1149 (2000)
4. Balan, A., Sigal, L., Black, M., Davis, J., Haussecker, H.: Detailed human shape and pose from images. In: CVPR (2007)
5. Sigal, L., Balan, A., Black, M.: Humaneva: Synchronized video and motion capture dataset and baseline algorithm for evaluation of articulated human motion. IJCV 87, 4–27 (2010)
6. Stoll, C., Hasler, N., Gall, J., Seidel, H.P., Theobalt, C.: Fast articulated motion tracking using a sums of gaussians body model. In: ICCV (2011)
7. Poppe, R.: Vision-based human motion analysis: An overview. CVIU 108(1-2) (2007)
8. Raskar, R., Nii, H., de Decker, B., Hashimoto, Y., Summet, J., Moore, D., Zhao, Y., Westhues, J., Dietz, P., Barnwell, J., Nayar, S., Inami, M., Bekaert, P., Noland, M., Branzoi, V., Bruns, E.: Prakash: lighting aware motion capture using photosensing markers and multiplexed illuminators. ACM Trans. Graph. 26 (July 2007)

9. Vlasic, D., Baran, I., Matusik, W., Popovic, J.: Articulated mesh animation from multi-view silhouettes. ACM TOG (Proc. SIGGRAPH), 97:1–97:9 (2008)
10. de Aguiar, E., Stoll, C., Theobalt, C., Ahmed, N., Seidel, H.P., Thrun, S.: Performance capture from sparse multi-view video. In: Proc. SIGGRAPH (2008)
11. Cagniart, C., Boyer, E., Ilic, S.: Free-form mesh tracking: a patch-based approach. In: CVPR (2010)
12. Starck, J., Hilton, A.: Surface capture for performance based animation. IEEE Computer Graphics and Applications 27(3), 21–31 (2007)
13. Gall, J., Stoll, C., de Aguiar, E., Theobalt, C., Rosenhahn, B., Seidel, H.P.: Motion capture using joint skeleton and surface estimation. In: CVPR (2009)
14. Moeslund, T., Hilton, A., Krüger, V.: A survey of advances in vision-based human motion capture and analysis. CVIU 104(2), 90–126 (2006)
15. Li, R., Tian, T.P., Sclaroff, S., Yang, M.H.: 3D human motion tracking with a coordinated mixture of factor analyzers. IJCV 87, 170–190 (2010)
16. Lee, C.S., Elgammal, A.: Coupled visual and kinematic manifold models for tracking. IJCV 87, 118–139 (2010)
17. Bo, L., Sminchisescu, C.: Twin gaussian processes for structured prediction. IJCV 87, 28–52 (2010)
18. Hasler, N., Rosenhahn, B., Thormählen, T., Wand, M., Gall, J., Seidel, H.P.: Markerless motion capture with unsynchronized moving cameras. In: CVPR (2009)
19. Liu, Y., Stoll, C., Gall, J., Seidel, H.P., Theobalt, C.: Markerless motion capture of interacting characters using multi-view image segmentation. In: CVPR (2011)
20. Hernandez, C., Vogiatzis, G., Cipolla, R.: Multiview photometric stereo. IEEE TPAMI 30(3), 548–554 (2008)
21. Wenger, A., Gardner, A., Tchou, C., Unger, J., Hawkins, T., Debevec, P.: Performance relighting and reflectance transformation with time-multiplexed illumination. ACM TOG (Proc. SIGGRAPH) 24(3), 756–764 (2005)
22. Vlasic, D., Peers, P., Baran, I., Debevec, P., Popovic, J., Rusinkiewicz, S., Matusik, W.: Dynamic shape capture using multi-view photometric stereo. ACM TOG (Proc. SIGGRAPH) 28(5), 174 (2009)
23. Popa, T., South-Dickinson, I., Bradley, D., Sheffer, A., Heidrich, W.: Globally consistent space-time reconstruction. In: SGP (2010)
24. Wilson, C., Ghosh, A., Peers, P., Chiang, J.Y., Busch, J., Debevec, P.: Temporal upsampling of performance geometry using photometric alignment. ACM TOG (Proc. SIGGRAPH) 29(2) (March 2010)
25. Wu, C., Varanasi, K., Liu, Y., Seidel, H.P., Theobalt, C.: Shading-based dynamic shape refinement from multi-view video under general illumination. In: ICCV (2011)
26. Zhang, L., Curless, B., Hertzmann, A., Seitz, S.: Shape and motion under varying illumination: unifying structure from motion, photometric stereo, and multiview stereo. In: ICCV, vol. 1, pp. 618–625 (October 2003)
27. Kajiya, J.T.: The rendering equation. In: Proc. ACM SIGGRAPH 20(4) (1986)
28. Kavan, L., Collins, S., Žára, J., O'Sullivan, C.: Skinning with dual quaternions. In: Symposium on Interactive 3D Graphics and Games, pp. 39–46 (2007)

Automatic Exposure Correction of Consumer Photographs

Lu Yuan and Jian Sun

Microsoft Research Asia

Abstract. We study the problem of automatically correcting the exposure of an input image. Generic auto-exposure correction methods usually fail in individual over-/under-exposed regions. Interactive corrections may fix this issue, but adjusting every photograph requires skill and time. This paper will automate the interactive correction technique by estimating the image specific S-shaped non-linear tone curve that best fits the input image. Our first contribution is a new Zone-based region-level optimal exposure evaluation, which would consider both the visibility of individual regions and relative contrast between regions. Then a detail-preserving S-curve adjustment is applied based on the optimal exposure to obtain the final output. We show that our approach enables better corrections comparing with popular image editing tools and other automatic methods.

1 Introduction

Exposure is one of the most important factors of determining the quality of a photograph. In over-exposed or under-exposed regions, details are lost, and colors are washed out. Despite that sophisticated metering techniques have been equipped on the cameras, taking well-exposed photos remains a challenge for normal users. There are several reasons: 1) the camera's metering (*e.g.*, spot, center-weighted, average, or multi-zone metering) is not perfect. If the metering points/areas are not targeting the subject or there are multiple subjects, the metering may fail. Fig. 1(a) is a failure case caused by the backlit; 2) the assumption that the mid-tone of the subject is gray is sometimes invalid due to the complex reflectance of the world (*e.g.*, a snow-white rabbit is often captured as an undesired grayish rabbit without exposure compensation); 3) in-camera post-processing capability is limited, especially for the low-end cameras.

To address this issue, some automatic methods like auto-level stretch [1] and histogram equalization [1] have been proposed to correct the exposure. For example, auto-level stretch linearly maps the brightness to the maximum tonal range (*e.g.*, [0, 255]). This method, however, only uses the statistics of the whole image, without considering each image region individually. For the backlit case in Fig. 1, auto-level stretch does not take effect (see Fig. 1 (b)) since the image histogram has reached the maximum tonal range (top-left of Fig. 1(a)). Histogram equalization [1] (and its variations [2]) better distributes the intensity values over the histogram. Unfortunately, it would produce unrealistic effects in photographs (see Fig. 1(c)).

If user assistance is allowed, the interactive correction method is more effective. For instance, most photo editing software allow the user to manually adjust a non-linear tone

A. Fitzgibbon et al. (Eds.): ECCV 2012, Part IV, LNCS 7575, pp. 771–785, 2012.

Fig. 1. A typical under-exposed photo. On the top-left of (a), we show the luminance histogram of the input image which has the maximum tonal range and peaks in shadows and highlights.

curve [3] (*e.g.*, S-curve) to correct the dark/mid-tone/bright regions separately. Fig. 1(d) is the assisted result by expert. But the best shape of the curve varies a lot from image to image. Touching up every single image is impractical for typical consumers.

In this paper, we present an *automatic* exposure correction method that can estimate the best image specific non-linear tone curve (the S-curve in our case) for a given image. Unlike [4], we need no training data. Note that it is a non-trivial task since the variation of input consumer photographs is so large. The key to the success of an automatic correction is to know what the best exposure should be for every image region.

To address this fundamental issue, we borrow the concept of "Zone" from the well-developed Zone System [5] in photography. The Zone system quantizes the whole exposure range as eleven discrete zones. We formulate the exposure correction as a zone estimation problem - we optimize a global objective function to estimate the desired zone in each image region by simultaneously considering two goals: maximizing the local details in each region, and preserving the relative contrast between regions.

After getting the estimated zone of every region, we propose a new non-linear curve-based correction algorithm called *detail-preserving S-curve adjustment*, to push each region to its desired zone, as much as possible. Compared with generic S-curve adjustment [6][7][8], our detail-preserving S-curve adjustment can maintain local details and avoid halo effects. Fig. 1(e) shows our estimated curve and final corrected result.

Like most automatic approaches, our approach does not address the user preference issue [9]. The "correct" exposure may be defined as the one that achieves the effect the photographer intended. However, our user studies show that an automatic correction still benefits most typical consumers - especially for their daily photos processing. We also show our new exposure optimization provides significant visual quality improvement over pervious work. Since our correction is simple and robust, it can be chosen as a better alternate in photo editing tools and a built-in camera component.

2 Related Work

Automatic exposure control is one of the most essential research issues for camera manufacturers. The majority of developed techniques are hardware-based. Representative work include HP "Adaptive Lighting" technology [10] , Nikon "D-Lighting" technology [11]. These methods compress the luminance range of images by a known tone mapping curve (*e.g.*, Log curve) and further avoid local contrast distortion by "Retinex" processing [12]. Specific hardware has been designed to perform per-pixel exposure control [13] or scene-based (*e.g.*, backlit, frontlit [14] or face [15]) exposure control. Some automatic techniques (*e.g.* [16]) are proposed to estimate the optimal exposure parameters (shutter speed and aperture) during taking photos.

There are numerous techniques about software-based exposure adjustment, including most popular global correction (*e.g.*, auto-level stretch, histogram equalization [1]) and local exposure correction [17][18]. However, these methods only use some heuristic histogram analysis to map per-pixel exposure to the desired one, without considering the spatial information of pixels (or regions). An interesting work [19] tries to enhancement image via frequency domain (*i.e.*, block DCT). But some fixed tone curves are used for each image and blocking artifacts occasionally occur in their results.

Some algorithms [8][20] only consider the exposure of the regions of interest (ROI) and assume it is most important to the whole image correction. Different from ours, they use a known and predefined tone curve but we will estimate the specific curve for every image. Some tone mapping algorithms [21] can also be used to estimate the key of scene and infer a tone curve to map its original exposure to the desired key. However, the key estimation is based on the global histogram analysis and is sometimes inaccurate. Exposure fusion [22] combines well-exposed regions together from an image sequence with bracketed exposures. In contrast, we only use a single image as the input.

Since the exposure correction is kind of *subjective*, recent methods [23][4][9] enhance the input image using training samples from internet or personalized photos. However, our exposure correction is not relied on the selection of training images and only focuses on the input image itself. Another issue worth mentioning is that our approach does not aim to restore completely saturated pixels like [24].

3 Automatic Exposure Correction Pipeline

Our exposure correction pipeline is depicted in Fig. 2 and divided to two main steps: exposure evaluation and S-curve adjustment. Both components are performed in the luminance channel. To avoid bias due to different camera metering systems, or user's manual settings, we would linearly normalize the input tonal range to [0, 1] at first.

The heart of our system is an optimization-based, region-level exposure evaluation (see Section 4). In the exposure evaluation, we apply a Zone-based exposure analysis to estimate the desired zone (*i.e.*, exposure) for each image region. We first segment the input image into individual regions (*i.e.*, super-pixels). In each region, we measure visible details, region size, and relative contrast between regions. Then we formulate the optimal zone estimation as a global optimization which takes into account all these factors. We also use the high level information (*e.g.*, face) to set the priority of the regions.

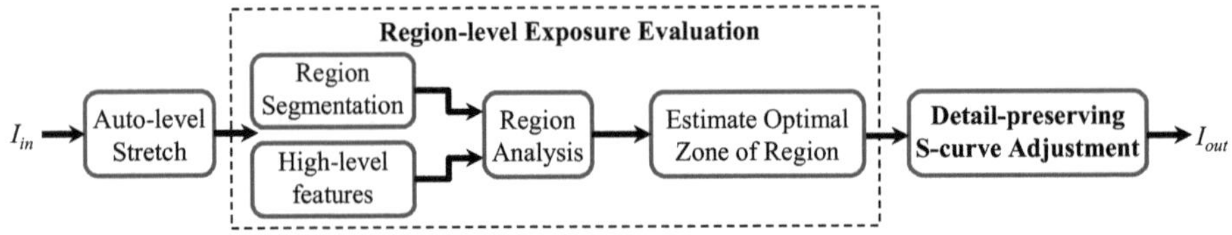

Fig. 2. Our automatic exposure correction pipeline

After the exposure evaluation, we estimate a best non-linear curve (S-curve) mapping for the entire image to push each region to its optimal zone. We further introduce a detail-preserving S-curve adjustment (see Section 5) instead of naïve S-curve mapping to preserve local details and suppress halo effects in the final result.

4 Region-Level Exposure Evaluation

The aim of our exposure evaluation is to infer the image specific tone curve for the consequent detail-preserving S-curve adjustment. To achieve this goal, we first need to know what is the "best" exposure of each region and how to estimate them all together.

4.1 Zone Region

To measure the exposure, we borrow the concept of "Zone" from Ansel Adams' Zone System [5], which is shown in Fig. 3(d). In Zone System, the entire luminance range [0, 1] is equally divided into 11 zones, ranging from 0 to X denoted by Roman numbers, with 0 representing black, V middle gray, and X pure white; these values are known as zones. In each zone, the mean intensity value is referred as its corresponding exposure. This concept was also used in recent HDR tone mapping applications [21][25] and realistic image composition [26].

We represent the image by a number of zone regions. We first decompose the image into a set of regions by graph-based segmentation [27]. Each region falls into one of the zones. Then, we merge the neighboring regions with the same zone value. To extract high-level information (*e.g.*, face/sky) for high priority of adjustment, we need to detect facial regions [28] and sky regions [29]. All connected regions belonging to face/sky regions are also merged. We call the final merged region as "zone region". Fig. 3(a-c) shows the procedure of the zone region extraction.

4.2 Optimal Zones Estimation

The optimal zone estimation can be formulated as a global optimization problem by considering two aspects: maximizing the visual details and preserving the original relative contrast between neighboring zone regions.

Measure of Visible Details. The amount of visible details in under-/over-exposed regions can be measured by the difference of the detected edges in these images which are generated by applying different gamma-curves on the input image I (the process is

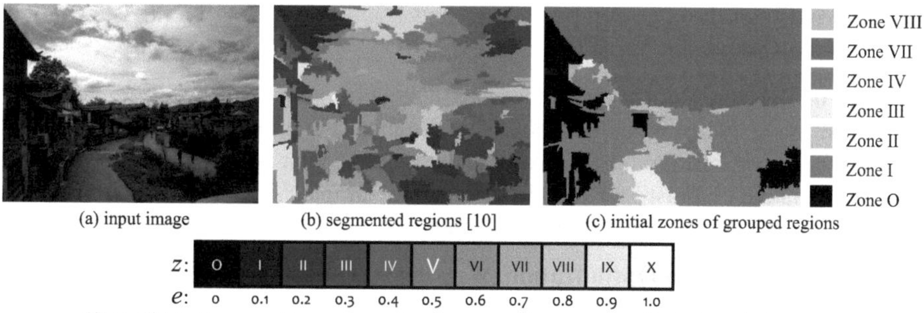

(a) input image (b) segmented regions [10] (c) initial zones of grouped regions

(d) Ansell Adam's zones z (Roman numeral) and corresponding exposures e (decimal number)

Fig. 3. Zone region extraction. In (c), different colors denote different zone regions, in which the Roman numbers denote corresponding zone values.

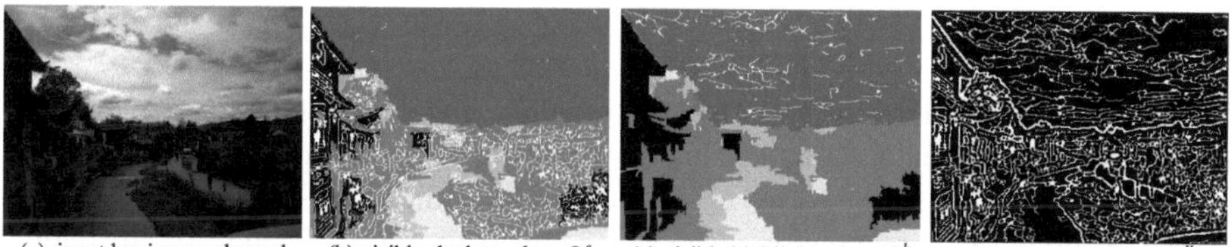

(a) input luminance channel (b) visible shadow edges Ω^s (c) visible highlight edges Ω^h (d) all visible edges Ω^{all}

Fig. 4. Measure of visible details. In (b-d), white lines are detected edges by Canny operator.

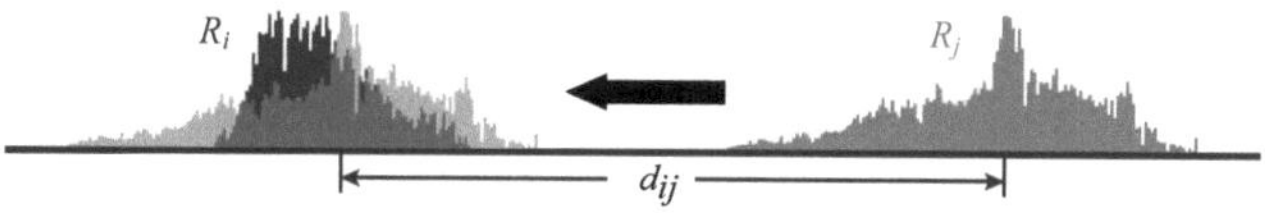

Fig. 5. Relative contrast d_{ij} is the histogram distance between two neighboring regions R_i, R_j

denoted as $I_{gamma} = I^{\gamma}$). It is based on an observation: in an under-exposed region, we can detect more/less visible edges after the gamma correction when the gamma γ is smaller/larger, and the edge number difference between two gamma-corrected images (one with small gamma, the other with large gamma) indicates the amount of recoverable details. The similar process can be applied to the over-exposed region as well.

In our implementation, we use two default gamma values $\gamma = 2.2$ and $\gamma^{-1} = 0.455$. We first detect edges on three images $I, I^{\gamma}, I^{\gamma^{-1}}$ by the same Canny operator [1] to obtain three edge sets: $\Omega_1, \Omega_{\gamma}, \Omega_{\gamma^{-1}}$. The visible details in the shadow region (zone value $<$ V) and the highlight region (zone value $>$ V) are measured by: $\Omega^s = \Omega_{\gamma^{-1}} - \Omega_{\gamma^{-1}} \bigcap \Omega_{\gamma}$ and $\Omega^h = \Omega_{\gamma} - \Omega_{\gamma^{-1}} \bigcap \Omega_{\gamma}$, shown in Fig. 4 (b)(c).

Note that the absolute differences Ω^s and Ω^h cannot be directly used since they vary from image to image. To obtain a comparable measure, we compute the relative visibility of details:

$$\nu^s = |\Omega^s| / |\Omega^{all}|, \qquad \nu^h = |\Omega^h| / |\Omega^{all}| \tag{1}$$

where $|\cdot|$ indicates the edge number in a set, and $\Omega^{all} = \Omega_1 \bigcup \Omega_\gamma \bigcup \Omega_{\gamma-1}$ is the union of all three sets, shown in Fig. 4 (d).

Measure of Relative Contrast. We measure the relative contrast between zone regions using their intensity histogram distance. This distance is defined as the minimum shifting distance of two histograms to maximize their intersection (shown in Fig. 5). We use the term "relative contrast" for this distance. For example, when their histograms are too close, we say their relative contrast is small.

Zones Estimation as an Optimization. With the two measures defined, we formulate the best zone estimation as a graph-based labeling problem. Each zone region is regarded as a node and any two neighboring zone regions are connected by a link. The optimal labels $Z = \{z_i^*\}$ of nodes are the final desired zones. We define the Markov Random Field (MRF) energy function $E(Z)$ of the graph as:

$$Z^* = \arg\min_Z E(Z) = \arg\min_Z (\sum_i E_i + \lambda \sum_{i,j} E_{ij}),$$

where E_i is the data term of an individual region i, and E_{ij} is the pairwise term between two adjacent regions i and j. In our work, the data term and pairwise term are respectively specified by the form: $E_i = -log(P(i))$ and $E_{ij} = -log(P(i,j))$.

The likelihood $P(i)$ of a region i is measured by its visibility of details ν_i, the region size C_i (normalized by the whole image size), and the important region size θ_i (normalized by the whole image size). The important region is directly computed from the probability map of facial/sky detector. We take into account all the three factors:

$$P(i) = \begin{cases} \nu_i^s \times C_i \times \theta_i \times \rho\left(\hat{z}_i - z_i\right), & (z_i < \mathrm{V}) \\ \nu_i^h \times C_i \times \theta_i \times \rho\left(z_i - \hat{z}_i\right), & (z_i > \mathrm{V}) \end{cases}, \tag{2}$$

where z_i is the original zone, $\hat{z}_i$ is the new zone and $\rho(t) = 1/\left(1 + \exp(-t)\right)$ is a sigmoid function. The likelihood would encourage shadow/highlight regions to move to higher/lower zones. For mid-zones (zone V), it takes no effect.

The coherence $P(i,j)$ is defined by the change of relative contrast between two neighboring regions, from the original relative contrast d_{ij} (before the optimization) to the new relative contrast $\hat{d}_{ij}$ (after the optimization), which is denoted by

$$P(i,j) = C_j \times \mathcal{G}(\hat{d}_{ij} - d_{ij}), \tag{3}$$

where $\mathcal{G}(\cdot)$ is a zero-mean gaussian function with variance 0.15 and the weight C_j is used so that relatively smaller regions contribute less. The coherence would penalize the dramatic change of relative contrast.

To obtain the global optimum, we use a brute-force searching method to travel all combinations of zone candidates for all regions because the total number of zone regions is not very high after region merging. To automatically estimate the weight λ, we first calculate the sum of data terms and the sum of pairwise terms across all combinations of zone candidates. Then we set λ to the ratio of two summations. We found it works very well in our experiments and does not require any tuning.

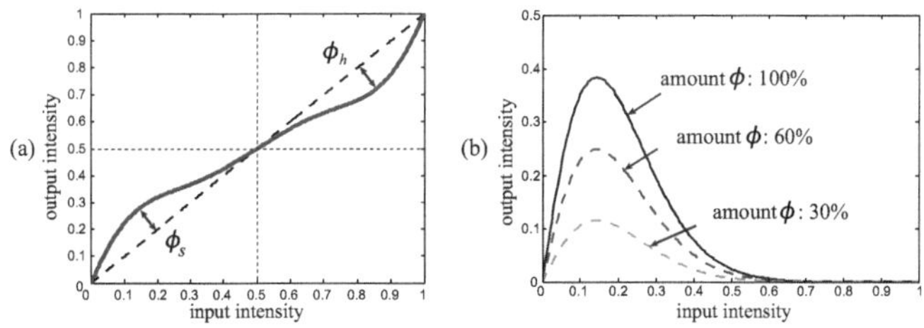

Fig. 6. (a) S-curve, ϕ_s, ϕ_h control the magnitude of S-curve adjustment in the shadow range and the highlight range respectively. (b) the curves of $f_\Delta(x)$ weighted by different amount ϕ.

5 Detail-Preserving S-Curve Adjustment

After getting the optimal zone for every region, we might have mapped the zone value (*i.e.*, exposure) of each region to its desired zone individually. However, this local mapping has the risk to produce exposure distortion in relatively small regions because these regions often contain insufficient information to estimate their optimal zones. To address this issue, we use a non-linear tone curve to globally map the brightness of every pixel to its desired exposure. We further preserve local contrast by fusion between the global curve mapping and an adaptive local detail enhancement.

S-Curve Adjustment. Most photographers often use an S-shaped non-linear curve (S-curve) to manually adjust the exposure in shadow/mid-tone/highlight areas. Fig. 6 (a) shows a typical (inverse) S-curve. This kind of S-curve can be simply parameterized by two parameters: shadow amount ϕ_s and highlight amount ϕ_h, which is denoted by:

$$f(x) = x + \phi_s \times f_\Delta(x) - \phi_h \times f_\Delta(1 - x), \tag{4}$$

where x and $f(x)$ are the input and output pixel intensities. $f_\Delta(x)$ is the incremental function and empirically defined as: $f_\Delta(x) = \kappa_1 x \exp\left(-\kappa_2 x^{\kappa_3}\right)$, where κ_2 and κ_3 control the modified tone range of the shadows or highlights. We use the default parameters ($\kappa_1 = 5, \kappa_2 = 14, \kappa_3 = 1.6$) of $f_\Delta(x)$ to make the modified tonal range fall in $[0, 0.5]$. The effect of shadow/highlight amounts (ϕ_s, ϕ_h) is shown in Fig. 6 (b).

Inference of Correction Amounts. We infer the amounts (ϕ_s, ϕ_h) from the estimated optimal zone in every region. For the shadow regions, we want to set the amount ϕ_s so that the original zone value of each shadow region can be moved to its optimal zone value, as much as possible. The amount ϕ_h can be estimated in a similar way.

Suppose the original exposure and new exposure of a shadow region i are respectively e_i and $\hat{e}_i$. (The relationship between the exposure and its corresponding zone value is shown on Fig. 3(d)). The original exposure is calculated by the intensity mean: $e_i = \sum I/c_i$, where I is original intensity and c_i is the region size. After the S-curve adjustment (by Eqn. 4), the new exposure $\hat{e}_i = \sum f(I)/c_i = \sum (I + \phi_s \times f_\Delta(I))/c_i$. Thus, the shadow amount ϕ_s of this region should be: $\phi_s = (\hat{e}_i - e_i) \times c_i \times \sum f_\Delta(I)$. To consider all regions, we take the weighted average of the estimated shadow amounts of all regions. We use the percentage of region size as the weight.

(a) input image I (b) naive S-curve mapping $f(I)$ (c) detail-preserving S-curve $\hat{I}$

Fig. 7. Comparison between direct S-curve mapping and detail-preserving S-curve adjustment

(a) input image (b) using Gaussian filter (c) using guided filter

Fig. 8. Comparisons of halo effects reduction between Gaussian filter and guided filter [30]

Detail-Preserving S-Curve Adjustment. If we directly apply the S-curve mapping (in Eqn. 4) to the input image, we may lose local details. Fig. 7(b) shows such a case, where the result looks too flat although dark areas are lightened. This undesired effect is due to: moving the intensities from shadows and highlights to the middle will compress the mid-tones. Since the S-curve is usually monotonic, the contrast between two neighboring pixels in the mid-tones could be reduced.

To address this issue, we propose a detail-preserving S-curve adjustment. Given an input image I, we adaptively fuse its S-curve result $f(I)$ with a local detail image ΔI. Note that ΔI is the difference between the input image I and its low-pass filtered version I_F: $\Delta I = I - I_F$. Here, we compute I_F by a fast edge-preserving low-pass filter, the so-called guided filter [30] to suppress halo effects. In Fig. 8, we show the result against a Gaussian filter. In our implementation, the radius is set to 4% of the short side of the image I. The final output image $\hat{I}$ is a weighted linear combination:

$$\hat{I} = f(I) + [2 \times f(I)(1 - f(I))] \times \Delta I, \quad (5)$$

where the second term on the right side adaptively compensates for the reduction of local details. The weight $f(I)(1 - f(I))$ reaches its maximum (when $f(I) = 0.5$) in the mid-tone range where there is notable loss in local details. In other words, we add more details back to the mid-tone than the shadow or highlight range. Specially in smooth regions, the output is mainly determined by the S-curve results. Such an adaptive adjustment mechanism can help us produce more natural-looking results (Fig. 7(c))

For a color image, we need to compensate the possible reduction of color saturation caused by the luminance adjustment, especially on shadows. To avoid this issue, we transform it to YIQ color space and then scale the corresponding I, Q chroma values by the adjustment of Y luminance values.

Efficient Implementation. For efficient computation, we enforce two extra constraints to largely reduce our search space of possible zone values: 1) Our adjustment uses the global S-curve which would map the same input pixel values to the same output. Thus we can consider the change of zone should be the same for the regions with the same original zone values; 2) Since our employed S-curve won't change values across the middle gray (0.5), we can consider that the change of every zone is not allowed across zone V. In addition, our exposure is evaluated on the down-scaled image with their long edge no more than 400 pixels. So our segmentation and face/sky detection can be very efficient. For an 16-megapixel RGB image, the whole evaluation and correction time is 0.3 second on Core2 Duo CPU 3.16GHz with single-thread, no SSE acceleration.

6 Experiments

6.1 Usability Study

Dataset: We perform our evaluation using a database of 4,000 images taken by our friends (including amateur and professional photographers) with direct camera output. These images varies on scenes, locations, lighting conditions and camera models (*e.g.*, DSLR, compact, mobile cameras). We ask five subjects to divide all images into three groups according to different extents of exposure problem. Three groups are "severely badly-exposed, definitely need correction" (Group A), "slightly badly-exposed photos, may require a little correction" (Group B), and "well-exposed, no more correction" (Group C). Finally, we obtain three different datasets respectively: "Group A" (975 images), "Group B" (1,356 images) and "Group C" (1,669 images) according to the majority agreement of five subjects. Fig. 9 (a) shows several examples.

Procedure: We will compare with automatic exposure corrections in several popular photo editing tools to manifest our method would become a better candidate. All of results are achieved by default parameters. We invite other 12 volunteers (7 males and 5 females) with balanced expertise in photography and camera use to perform pairwise comparison between our result and one of three other images: 1) input image, 2) result by Windows Live Photo Gallery's *Auto-adjust, exposure only* (http://download.live.com/photogallery), 3) result by Google Picasa's *Auto-contrast* (http://picasa.google.com/). For each pairwise comparison, the subject has three options: better, or worse, or no preference. Subjects are allowed to view each image pair back and forth for the comparison. To avoid the subjective bias, the group of images, the order of pairs, and the image order within each pair are randomized and unknown to each subject. This usability study is conducted in the same settings (room, light, and monitor).

Usability Study Results: The main user study results are summarized in Fig. 9 (b). Each color bar is the averaged percentage of the favored image over all 12 subjects (I-shape error bar denotes the standard deviation). From results on "All Groups" (without distinguishing the photos from different groups), we can see that the participants overwhelmingly select our result over the input (70.2% vs. 5.9%), Photo Gallery (60.5% vs. 29.6%), and Picasa (58.3% vs. 12.5%).

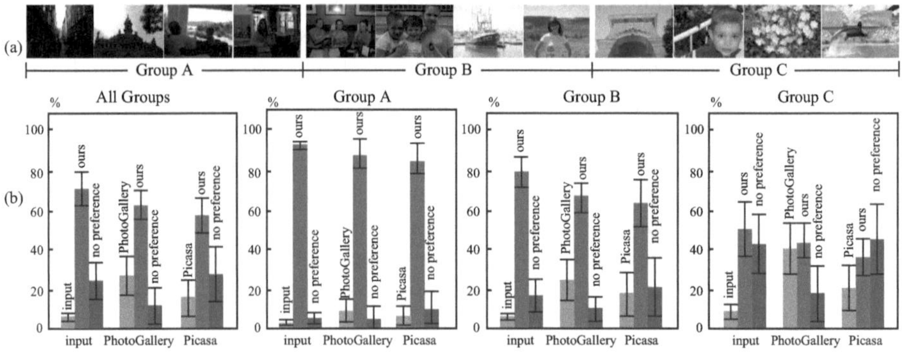

Fig. 9. Usability studies. (a) Examples from three groups: A (severely badly-exposed), B (slightly badly-exposed), C (well-exposed). (b) pairwise comparison of ours against the input, Photo Gallery, and Picasa, in all groups and three different groups respectively. Each color bar denotes the average percentage of favored image (with I-shape standard deviation bars).

Fig. 10. Examples randomly chosen from Group **A**. We can notice more details on foreground faces (a), foreground audiences (b) and street scene (c). **(Better View in Electronic Version)**.

Fig. 11. Two examples randomly chosen from Group **B** (a-b) and two from Group **C** (c-d)

"Group A" results show that our approach works significantly better for severely badly-exposed photos. The participants show a strong bias in preference towards our correction when compared to input images (92.3% vs. 2.7%) and other automatic tools (87% vs. 8.5% against Photo Gallery, 84% vs. 6.4% against Picasa). The results from "Group B" indicate that slightly badly-exposed photos can benefit more from our correction than other methods as well. In "Group C", our approach also performs very well - for near 92% photos, our method does not make the result worse. It is quite nontrivial and very important for practical use, especially for batch-processing photos.

Fig. 9 (b) also graphically show two phenomenons on "Group C" compared with "Group A": 1) the margin between our result favored and no preference is smaller, and 2) all standard derivations are larger. They both indicate that the exposure correction itself is somewhat *subjective* especially for "not bad" photos. Subjects show different tastes for good photos correction, which has been discussed in [9][4], but most of these subjects consistently agree with our correction for relatively bad photos.

After the user study, we also ask all participants to articulate the criteria for their feedbacks. We conclude the main criteria: 1) the over-/under-exposed regions of interest should be well corrected; 2) well-exposed regions should not be over-corrected; and 3) the colors in corrected images should look natural. Other feedbacks include "the color of a few individual regions sometimes looks slightly unrealistic", "in some cases, the corrected results bring in some noise", and "I want some parameters tuning so that I can control the results.". Overall, most participants like our correction and want to use it for their daily photos processing.

Visual Quality Comparisons: Fig. 10 shows three examples from "Groups A". These photos show several common badly-exposed scenarios, such as outdoor backlit, dim-light indoor environment, which are very challenging for existing tools. As we can see, their corrections take no effect, but our method brings more visible details into badly-exposed areas while preserving the original appearance in well-exposed areas. Fig. 11(a)(b) show two examples from "Groups B", whose exposures look somewhat problematic. Our results look much more appealing, especially on important areas, *e.g.*, over-exposed sky (Fig. 11(a)) and under-exposed face (Fig. 11(b)). Fig. 11(c)(d) show two well-exposed examples from "Groups C". Our corrections seem to be imperceptible because the dark silhouette regions (Fig. 11(c)) have few detectable visible details and the black clothes (Fig. 11(d)) have lower priority than well-exposed faces, which would contribute little to the change of zone in our optimization.

6.2 Comparisons with Other Academic Methods

In consequent comparisons, our results are generated by the same parameters used in useability study. In Fig. 12(b)(c), we compare with two traditional histogram equalization algorithm [1][2] (by Matlab function *histeq*, *adapthisteq*). We can notice local contrast reduction and undesired halo effects in their correction results shown in Fig. 12(b)(c). However, our result shown in Fig. 12(e) looks more natural. We also compare our method with a well-known tone-mapping operator [21] (shown in Fig. 12(d)). Since their automatically estimated scene key is not accurate and tends to be higher than the actual key in this case, their result looks a little over-exposed.

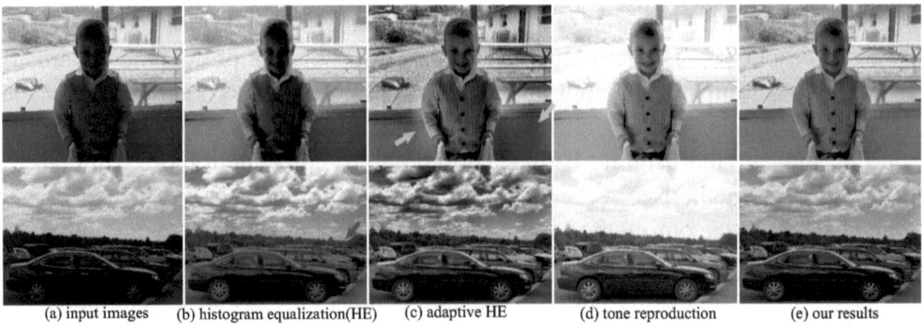

Fig. 12. Comparisons with histogram equalizations [1], adaptive histogram equalization [2] and tone reproduction [21]. The yellow/red arrows show unwanted halo effect/contrast reduction.

Fig. 13. Comparison with internet-based restoration [23]. Images (a-c) are taken from their paper. The reference result (b) is applied a fixed key. The yellow/red arrows show under-/over-exposed.

Fig. 14. Comparison with Exposure Fusion [22] on input image sequence (taken from their paper). Our algorithm only uses the single frame (b) as the input.

Fig. 15. Comparison with Exposure Fusion [22] on a single input image. We only use the input image (depicted in Green box) while Exposure Fusion uses the synthesized image sequence with different exposures from the input image. The red arrow shows unwanted artifacts.

(a) input image (b) V. Bychkovsky et. al. [5] (c) our result (d) Retoucher E

Fig. 16. Comparisons with learning-based tonal adjustment [4]. Images (a,b,d) are taken from [4].

input image our result input cropped patch our croppred patch close-up views

Fig. 17. Our failure case on noise amplification

In Fig. 13, we directly use the image and result from internet-based image restoration [23] for comparison. In this case, we can see our result has more visual details in local under-exposed areas than their provided result. Besides, their approach exaggerates over-exposed sky areas while our method can preserve their original appearance.

Exposure Fusion [22] is a fairly new concept that fuses all well-exposed regions together from a series of bracketed exposures. The good exposure is measured by some features: contrast, saturation and closeness to middle gray. Fig. 14 shows an example from their paper. We can see our result is visually approaching theirs, but our input is only a single frame from their input sequence. To perceive how well their algorithm works on a single input image, we make a modification of their method for comparison: (1) applying a series of global brightness adjustment (*e.g.*, multiplying luminance with 1/4, 1/2, 1, 2, 4) in Fig. 15(a); (2) applying a set of different gamma curves (*e.g.*, gamma values -3, -1.5, 1, 1.5, 3) in Fig. 15(b). Their results look either less vivid, or have lower global contrast than ours.

We show the comparison with learning-based adjustment [4] and assisted correction by expert in Fig. 16. As we can see, our result has more luminance details than their result on under-exposed areas and even much closer to the assisted result (from "Retoucher E" mentioned in [4]). Here, please ignore the difference in colors and focus on the luminance modification since the assisted adjustment includes both exposure correction and white balance. Without the need of training images, our approach obtain appealing results as well.

Fig. 17 (d) shows the limitation of our method. Since the correction does not consider the noise issue in our exposure evaluation, noise would become noticeable after we lighten dark areas. The issue may be addressed by suppressing the excessive noise amplification or applying denoising for these regions as preprocessing. We will further explore this issue in the future work.

7 Conclusions

We have presented an automatic method for the exposure correction of consumer photographs. The heart of this method is an optimization-based exposure evaluation and a detail-preserving curve adjustment algorithm. By simultaneously considering visible details in each region and relative contrast between regions, we are able to obtain appropriate exposure at the region level and produce natural-looking results.

References

1. Russ, J.C.: Image Processing HandBook, 3rd edn. CRC Press (1998)
2. Zuiderveld, K.: Contrast limited adaptive histograph equalization. In: Graphic Gems IV, pp. 474–485. Academic Press Professional, San Diego (1994)
3. CS5, A.P.: Adjust color and tonality with curves, Adobe Systems Inc. San Jose, CA (2010)
4. Bychkovsky, V., Paris, S., Chan, E., Durand, F.: Learning photographic global tonal adjustments with a database of input/output image pairs. In: CVPR (2011)
5. Ansel, A.: The Negative. The Ansel Adams Photography Series (1981)
6. Battiato, S., Bosco, A., Castorina, A., Messina, G.: Automatic image enhancement by content dependent exposure correction. Journal on Applied Signal Processing 12, 1849–1860 (2004)
7. Bhukhanwala, S.A., Ramabadran, T.V.: Automated global enhancement of digitized photographs. IEEE Trans. on. Consumer Electronics 40, 1–10 (1994)
8. dong Lee, K., Kim, S., Kim, S.D.: Dynamic range compression based on statistical analysis. In: ICIP (2009)
9. Kang, S.B., Kapoor, A., Lischinski, D.: Personalization of image enhancement. In: CVPR (2010)
10. Sobol, R.: Improving the retinex algorithm for rendering wide dynamic range photographs. Journal of Electronic Imaging 13(1) (2004)
11. Chesnokov, V.: Dynamic range compression preserving local image contrast. GB Patent 2417381 (2006)
12. Jobson, D.J., Rahman, Z., Woodell, G.A.: Properties and performance of a center/surround retinex. IEEE Trans. on Image Processing 6, 451–462 (1997)
13. Nayar, S.K., Branzoi, V.: Adaptive dynamic range imaging: Optical control of pixel exposures over space and time. In: ICCV (2003)
14. Shimizu, S., Kondo, T., Kohashi, T., Tsuruta, M., Komuro, T.: A new algorithm of exposure control based on fuzzy logic for video cameras. In: ICCE (1992)
15. Yang, M., Wu, Y., Crenshaw, J., Augustine, B., Mareachen, R.: Face detection for automatic exposure control in handheld camera. In: ICVS (2006)
16. Ilstrup, D., Manduchi, R.: One-Shot Optimal Exposure Control. In: Daniilidis, K., Maragos, P., Paragios, N. (eds.) ECCV 2010, Part I. LNCS, vol. 6311, pp. 200–213. Springer, Heidelberg (2010)
17. Brajovic, V.: Brightness perception, dynamic range and noise: a unifying model for adaptive image sensors. In: CVPR (2004)
18. Safonov, I.: Automatic correction of amateur photos damaged by backlighting. GraphiCon (2006)
19. Mukherjee, J., Mitra, S.K.: Enhancement of color images by scaling the dct coefficients. IEEE Trans. on Image Processing 17, 1783–1794 (2008)
20. Ovsiannikov, I.: Backlit subject detection in an image. US Patent 7813545 (2010)
21. Reinhard, E., Stark, M., Shirley, P., Ferwerda, J.: Photographic tone reproduction for digital images. SIGGRAPH (2002)

22. Mertens, T., Kautz, J., Reeth, F.V.: Exposure fusion. In: Pacific Conf. on Computer Graphics and Applications (2007)
23. Dale, K., Johnson, M.K., Sunkavalli, K., Matusik, W., Pfister, H.: Image restoration using online photo collections. In: ICCV (2009)
24. Guo, D., Cheng, Y., Zhuo, S., Sim, T.: Correcting over-exposure in photographs. In: Proc. IEEE CVPR, pp. 515–521 (2010)
25. Lischinski, D., Farbman, Z., Uyttendaele, M., Szeliski, R.: Interactive local adjustment of tonal values. ACM Trans. on Graph. 25(3), 646–653 (2006)
26. Xue, S., Agarwala, A., Dorsey, J., Rushmeier, H.: Understanding and improving the realism of image composites. ACM Trans. Graph. (2012)
27. Felzenszwalb, P.F., Huttenlocher, D.P.: Efficient graph-based image segmentation. IJCV 59 (2004)
28. Viola, P., Jones, M.: Rapid object detection using a boosted cascade of simple features. In: CVPR (2001)
29. Tao, L., Yuan, L., Sun, J.: Skyfinder: Attribute-based sky image search. ACM Trans. Graph. 28(3), 68:1–68:5 (2009)
30. He, K., Sun, J., Tang, X.: Guided Image Filtering. In: Daniilidis, K., Maragos, P., Paragios, N. (eds.) ECCV 2010, Part I. LNCS, vol. 6311, pp. 1–14. Springer, Heidelberg (2010)

Image Guided Tone Mapping with Locally Nonlinear Model

Huxiang Gu, Ying Wang, Shiming Xiang, Gaofeng Meng, and Chunhong Pan

Institute of Automation, Chinese Academy of Science
{hxgu,ywang,smxiang,gfmeng,chpan}@nlpr.ia.ac.cn

Abstract. In this paper, we propose an effective locally nonlinear tone mapping algorithm for compressing the High Dynamic Range (HDR) images. Instead of linearly scaling the luminance of pixels, our core idea is to introduce local gamma correction with adaptive parameters on small overlapping patches over the entire input image. A framework for HDR image compression is then introduced, in which the global optimization problem is deduced and two guided images are adopted to induct the optimum solution. The optimal compression can finally be achieved by solving the optimization problem which can be transformed to a sparse linear equation. Extensive experimental results on a variety of HDR images and a carefully designed perceptually evaluation have demonstrated that our approach can achieve better performances than the state-of-the-art approaches.

Keywords: high dynamic range, tone mapping, locally nonlinear model, guided image.

1 Introduction

HDR images can capture greater dynamic range of real world scenes than LDR images by using 16 bit or even higher bits with floating point type. This wide dynamic range allows HDR images to more accurately represent the intensity levels in real world. Unfortunately, most of the modern display devices have limited dynamic range. Hence, a number of tone mapping operators have been proposed to compress the high dynamic range of HDR images to the displayable range while preserve the visual contents[1–3]. These tone mapping operators are useful not only for HDR photography but also for lighting simulation in realistic rendering [4]. Therefore, the last three decades enjoy a boom of tone mapping algorithms in both the computational photography community and computer vision community [5, 4, 6–8].

In literature, the tone mapping operators can be roughly classified into two categories: global operators and local operators. Global operators [9–13] can be regarded as spatially uniform methods because the same mapping function is used for all the pixels of the input HDR image. They are simple and fast. However, they suffer from losing visual details in both bright areas and dark regions because they compress all the structures and details without considering

A. Fitzgibbon et al. (Eds.): ECCV 2012, Part IV, LNCS 7575, pp. 786–799, 2012.

the local luminance variation. Therefore a variety of local operators which model spatial adaptation by using locally changing functions have been proposed to compress the dynamic range while maintain or enhance the details [6, 14, 15, 2, 3]. Most local operators decompose the input HDR image into different layers [1] or areas [16]. Different mapping functions for each layer or area are adopted to compress the dynamic range and final results are achieved by a combination of these layers or scales after contrast reduction. Most of these local operators suffer from halo effects which are critical in HDR images. Then several operators have been proposed to improve this flaw [15, 2, 14, 3].

Although many excellent tone mapping operators have been proposed, tone mapping algorithm is still far beyond perfection. None of the present approaches have met the most challenging goal that an ideal tone mapping operator should achieve perceptually natural LDR images with precise details as well as free of any kinds of distortions or halo effect.

The main purpose of this paper is to introduce an effective tone mapping operator which can achieve perceptually pleasing results with fine details. The output LDR image has a high contrast and free of distortions or halo effects. Instead of linearly scaling the luminance of pixels, we propose a new tone mapping algorithm based on local gamma correction with adaptive parameters. Our method is based on the Weber-Fechner Law [17] that the human eye's subjective perception of brightness is related to the physical stimulation of light intensity in a manner which is similar with the power function used for gamma correction.

Our method benefits from the following two main contributions:

(1). An effective locally nonlinear model based on the Weber-Fechner Law [17] is proposed. Our model coincides with the nonlinear relationship between the physical magnitudes of stimuli and the perceived intensity of the stimuli. Compared with the locally linear model [8], our model has not only a more reasonable physical explanation, but also a wider applicability.

(2). When solving our locally nonlinear model, we add two constraint items into our energy function to avoid distortions and then achieve perceptually pleasing LDR images. Two guided images are creatively adopted in these two constraint items. These two guided images are critical for a natural LDR image which has fine details but no distortions.

2 Previous Work

Because of the great advantages over LDR images[4, 7], HDR images as well as tone mapping algorithms are therefore drawing a world of excellent researchers' attention [4, 15, 2, 3, 5, 1, 6].

Debevec and Malik [4] proposed that a HDR image can be created from three or more LDR images of the same scene under different exposures. With the development of photograph technology, we can get access to HDR cameras which can take HDR photos and videos directly now. Therefore, there is an increasing demand for tone mapping algorithms. These tone mapping algorithms can be roughly classified into two categories: global operators and local operators.

The global tone mapping methods are simply mapped the input HDR image $I^h(x,y)$ to an output LDR image $I^l(x,y) = f(I^h(x,y))$, where $f()$ is a global compression function which is spatially invariant, such as linear function, gamma function [18], histogram based function [10] and the function adapted to tone reproduction curves [12]. These methods are simple and fast, but always fail in balancing between unveiling visual contents and preserving details.

Hence, local tone mapping methods are the recent literature to compress the high dynamic range while maintain or enhance the details. Most of the local tone mapping methods decompose the input HDR image into several layers or areas, apply different compressing algorithm in different layers or areas and recombine all the layers or areas into a LDR image. Similar with Durand [6], Farbman [14] decomposed the HDR image into a base layer and a detail layer, while the base layer is obtained by an alternative edge-reserving smoothing operator and the detail layer is got by subtracting the base layer from the input HDR image. Recently, Lee [16] segmented the input HDR image into different parts using K-means algorithm and then applied automatic gamma correction in different parts. However, how to appropriately deal with the scale decomposition, layer separation or image segmentation is an another difficult problem. Besides, these methods have a reputation of causing halo artifacts.

Later, Li [2] improved the condition of halo artifacts by using a symmetrical analysis-synthesis filter bank and applying local gain control to the sub-bands. Results illustrated that the method of Li can achieve more satisfactorily than other multi-scale based methods. An alternative approach was also proposed by Fattal [15]. In their framework, the gradient field of the luminance image is manipulated by attenuating the magnitudes of large gradients as well as magnifying the small ones. Satisfactory results can be finally achieved by solving a Poisson equation. This gradient domain method is good at preserving fine details in dark regions and avoiding common artifacts.

More recently, Shan [8] provided us with a totally new tone mapping operator that performs locally linear adjustments on small overlapping windows over the entire input HDR image. They cast the compression task as a global optimization problem and achieve an optimal solution by solving a sparse equation. Locally linear method can effectively suppress local high contrast even in challenging HDR images. However, this method fails when luminance value of a local patch changes abruptly. An another impressive tone mapping method is the Local Laplacian filters [3]. Paris proposed a set of image filters using standard Laplacian pyramids to achieve edge-aware tone mapping. Local Laplacian filters can produce consistently high-quality results, especially in details manipulation. However, the complexity of this algorithm is a little high. Another imperfect point is that high-frequency textures are amplified by their detail-enhancing filter so that their result does not have a natural appearance.

As analyzed above, all these local operators firstly define a local measurement and then find a simple mapping function such as linear scaling. Although these tone mapping operators have achieved great success in many cases, the ideal target is still far away.

3 Motivation and Model

3.1 Motivation

We are motivated mainly by the following facts. On the one hand, the Weber-Fechner Law [17] states that subjective sensation is proportional to the logarithm of the stimulus intensity. Compared with LDR image, HDR image can more precisely model the illumination variation in the real world. Thus it implies that the relationship between the input HDR image and the desired output LDR image is nonlinear and can be represented in a manner that is similar to the power function used for gamma correction. On the other hand, locally linear hypothesis which achieves great success in LDR image can not guarantee that it is still reasonable in HDR image because luminance value of a HDR image may vary a lot even in a local patch. The existing locally linear operator [8] (see Figure 1(a)) abruptly adopts locally linear hypothesis and therefore causes some distortions when a patch is bright enough or contains both dark and bright pixels. For instance, when a patch contains both dark and bright pixels (see Figure 1(c)), the dynamic range of the dark pixels will be compressed at the same rate as the bright ones, which results in losing details in this patch, as shown in Figure 2(c) and Figure 3(d).

Hence, a new locally nonlinear operator is needed to compress the contrast of a local patch as well as enhance the visual contents, even when luminance in this patch changes abruptly. Local gamma correction with adaptive parameters is therefore proposed to meet this demand, as shown in Figure 1(b). Extensive experimental results on a variety of HDR images have demonstrated the correctness of our motivation.

3.2 Model

In this part, we introduce our local gamma correction model. Given an input HDR image with radiance map $\mathbf{I}$, we compute the radiance map $\mathbf{J}$ of the output LDR image through $\mathbf{J} = f(\mathbf{I})$, where $f(\cdot)$ is a local compression function which should satisfy the local monotonic constraint. Considering a local patch Ω_t centering at pixel t, the local gamma correction model is

$$\mathbf{j}(i) = \alpha_t \mathbf{i}(i)^{\beta_t} \qquad i \in \Omega_t, \tag{1}$$

where $\mathbf{j}$ is a vector of luminance values in the local patch Ω_t of the output LDR image $\mathbf{J}$ and $\mathbf{i}$ is a vector of luminance values in the same local patch of the input HDR image $\mathbf{I}$. $\mathbf{j}(i)$ denotes the i-th element of $\mathbf{j}$ and the same with $\mathbf{i}(i)$. Parameter α_t and β_t are constant values in each local patch, while α_t denotes the multiplier and β_t is the index value. From the image's perspective, α and β are named guided images in this paper, as shown in Figure 3(e) and Figure 3(f) respectively, which we will introduce in details in Section 4.3.

Note that the locally linear model is a particular case of our locally nonlinear model. Actually, when parameter β equals 1, our model turns into the locally linear model.

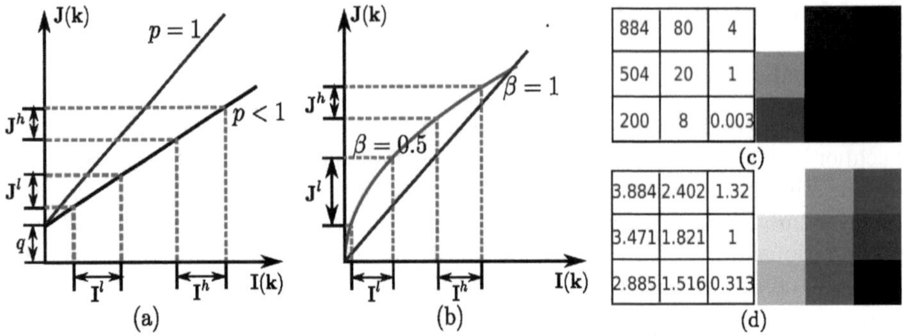

Fig. 1. Illustration of the locally linear model and our locally nonlinear model. (a) the locally linear model. (b) locally nonlinear model. (c) a local patch of the input HDR image, the left are relevant digital numbers and the right are luminance values. (d) the output local patch after tone mapping using our locally nonlinear method.

Fig. 2. Comparisons with the locally linear model [8]. (a) input HDR image. (b) result of Shan(β_1=0.7). (c) result of Shan(β_1=0.9). (d) our result.

Following we illustrate the advantage of our locally nonlinear model over the locally linear model in details. Instead of linearly compressing the contrast of a patch in an input HDR image, we adopt the local gamma correction strategy which can not only effectively compress the bright pixels but also enhance the dark ones in one hit even in challenging patches, as shown in Figure 1(d) and the sky-leaves part in Figure 3(h). The locally linear model usually fails when luminance value of a local patch changes abruptly, as shown in Figure 2(d) and Figure 5(c). In this situation, the dark pixels will turn bright because of q(intercept item of local linear model [8]) which determines the base radiance level (see Figure 1(a)). That is the reason why we adopt a new constraint item of q. Meanwhile, the dynamic range of the dark region will be compressed at the same rate as the bright pixels, which results in losing details in this patch. These flaws can be witnessed in the black area of the cow in Figure 2(c) and the sky-leaves in Figure 3(d). That is another reason why we introduce locally nonlinear model instead of locally linear model.

4 Algorithm and Implementation

4.1 Model Transformation

When dealing with nonlinear model, we generally transform them to another domain in which nonlinear model turns to be linear model. After applying logarithmic transformation on both sides of Eq. (1),we get:

$$\log \mathbf{j}(i) = \beta_t \log \mathbf{i}(i) + \log \alpha_t \qquad i \in \Omega_t. \tag{2}$$

Set $\mathbf{y}(i) = \log \mathbf{j}(i)$, $\mathbf{x}(i) = \log \mathbf{i}(i)$, $w_t = \beta_t$, $b_t = \log \alpha_t$, we get

$$\mathbf{y}(i) = w_t \mathbf{x}(i) + b_t \qquad i \in \Omega_t. \tag{3}$$

Comparing Eq. (3) with Eq. (1), we find that locally nonlinear model in image domain is equivalent to linear compression in logarithmic domain.

4.2 Model Solution

The most common way to solve the parameters of linear regression problem can be described as

$$\min_{w_t, b_t} \sum_{i \in \Omega_t} \left(\|\mathbf{y}(i) - w_t \mathbf{x}(i) - b_t\|^2 + \lambda \|w_t\|^2 \right). \tag{4}$$

However, the optimal solution of problem (4) are not so good, as shown in Figure 3(b). Therefore, inspired by [8], we adopt some prior information which are presented as the guided images to guide parameter w_t and b_t. In order to get no distortion results, we add a new constraint item in which b^* (namely the α image) is adopted to constrain the variation of parameter b_t. We also introduce a new approach to calculate w^* (namely the β image) to guide parameter w_t. These two guided images will be discussed in details in Section 4.3. As a result, the question now turns into minimize the local regression error e_t as follows

$$\min_{w_t, b_t} e_t, \tag{5}$$

where

$$e_t = \|\mathbf{y_t} - w_t \mathbf{x_t} - b_t\|^2 + \lambda_t \|w_t - w_t^*\|^2 + \tau_t \|b_t - b_t^*\|^2). \tag{6}$$

Here $\lambda_t = \mu {w_t^*}^{-2}$ and $\tau_t = \nu {b_t^*}^{-2}$ are regularization parameters in which $\mu = \nu = 0.1$. Denote $\mathbf{y_t} = [y(1), y(2), \ldots, y(K)]^T$ and $\mathbf{x_t} = [x(1), x(2), \ldots, x(K)]$ in which K is the pixel number in each window. Extend $\mathbf{x_t} = [\mathbf{x_t}; \mathbf{1}] \in \mathbf{R}^{2 \times K}$, $\mathbf{w_t} = [w_t, b_t]^T \in \mathbf{R}^{2\times 1}$, $\mathbf{w_t^*} = [w_t^*, b_t^*]^T \in \mathbf{R}^{2\times 1}$, $\mathbf{D_t} = \begin{bmatrix} \lambda_t, 0 \\ 0, \tau_t \end{bmatrix} \in \mathbf{R}^{2\times 2}$, we get

$$e_t = \|\mathbf{x_t}^T \mathbf{w_t} - \mathbf{y_t}\|^2 + \frac{1}{2}(\mathbf{w_t} - \mathbf{w_t^*})^T \mathbf{D_t} (\mathbf{w_t} - \mathbf{w_t^*}). \tag{7}$$

The second term in Equation (7) is a variation of typical manifold regularization [19]. Similar with classical optimization of manifold learning, we can solve

Equation (7) in derivation or iterative forms. Here we adopt the derivation form [20]. By taking the partial derivatives of e_t with respect to $\mathbf{w_t}$ and setting it to zero, we have

$$\mathbf{w_t} = (\mathbf{x_t}\mathbf{x_t}^T + \mathbf{D_t})^{-1}(\mathbf{x_t}\mathbf{y_t} + \mathbf{D_t}\mathbf{w_t^*}), \tag{8}$$

Substituting Eq. (8) into (7) and then taking the partial derivatives of e_t with respect to $\mathbf{y_t}$, we can get

$$\frac{de_t}{d\mathbf{y_t}} = (\mathbf{I_t} - \mathbf{x_t}^T(\mathbf{x_t}\mathbf{x_t}^T + \mathbf{D_t})^{-1}\mathbf{x_t})\mathbf{y_t} - \mathbf{x_t}^T(\mathbf{x_t}\mathbf{x_t}^T + \mathbf{D_t})^{-1}\mathbf{D_t}\mathbf{w_t^*}, \tag{9}$$

where $\mathbf{I_t} \in \mathbf{R}^{K\times K}$ is an identity matrix. Then the total regression error of the input HDR image can be evaluated as

$$E(\mathbf{Y}) = \sum_t \mathbf{e_t}. \tag{10}$$

Note that $\mathbf{y_t}$ is just a subvector of the target LDR luminance image $\mathbf{Y}$. Define a selection matrix $\mathbf{S_t} \in \mathbf{R}^{K\times N}$ (N is the total number of pixels in the input HDR image) as

$$\mathbf{S_t}(i,j) = \begin{cases} 1 & \text{if } \mathbf{y_t}(i) \text{ is the } j\text{-th element of } \mathbf{Y}, \\ 0 & \text{otherwise.} \end{cases}$$

So $\mathbf{y_t} = \mathbf{S_t}\mathbf{Y}$. By taking the derivatives of Eq. (10) with respect to t and setting it to zero we get

$$\mathbf{UY} = \mathbf{V}, \tag{11}$$

where

$$\mathbf{U} = \sum_t \mathbf{S_t}^T \left(\mathbf{I_t} - \mathbf{x_t}^T(\mathbf{x_t}\mathbf{x_t}^T + \mathbf{D_t})^{-1}\mathbf{x_t}\right) \mathbf{S_t}, \tag{12}$$

and

$$\mathbf{V} = \sum_t \mathbf{S_t}^T\mathbf{x_t}^T(\mathbf{x_t}\mathbf{x_t}^T + \mathbf{D_t})^{-1}\mathbf{D_t}\mathbf{w_t^*}. \tag{13}$$

Now we conclude that the optimal compression can be computed by solving a sparse linear Eq. (11). After we get the LDR luminance image $\mathbf{Y}$ in logarithmic domain, we can achieve the LDR luminance image $\mathbf{J}$ in image domain by setting $\mathbf{J} = \exp(\mathbf{Y})$.

As mentioned earlier, our method operates on the input HDR image's luminance channel $\mathbf{I}$. In order to reconstruct the RGB channels, we adopt an approach similar to method of Schlick[21]

$$\mathbf{J}_c = \left(\frac{\mathbf{I}_c}{\mathbf{I}}\right)^s \mathbf{J} \qquad c \in \{r, g, b\}, \tag{14}$$

where $\mathbf{I}_c$ and $\mathbf{J}_c$ denote one of the RGB color channels before and after tone mapping. The parameter s is the saturation factor. Our results show that $s \in [0.5, 0.8]$ works well for most HDR images.

The matrix $\mathbf{U} \in \mathbf{R}^{N\times N}$ in Eq. (12) is symmetric and sparse, and the number of nonzero elements of each row is $(2\sqrt{K} - 1)^2$. The computation complexity of constructing matrix $\mathbf{U}$ is about $O(NK^2)$.

Fig. 3. Guided images and its affection. (a) input HDR image. (b) Shan's result without guidance map. (c) Shan's guidance map[8]. (d)Shan's result. (e) our α image. (f) our β image. (g) result of local linear model with our two guided images. (h) our result.

4.3 Guided Image

In order to guide the modification of local contrast, Shan [8] proposed the concept of guidance map. With the help of guidance map, they can get more satisfactory result, as shown in Figure 3(b), (d). Bright regions in the guidance map indicate that the same areas of the input HDR image should be enhanced, otherwise should be compressed.

However, their approach usually fails when pixel values in a patch is bright enough, as shown in Figure 2(b),(c) and Figure 5(b),(c). Therefore we add a new contraint item b^* (namely guided image α) to constrain the variation of our intercept item b. From Figure 3(e), we can see that the guided image α has given a reasonable restriction to our intercept item b which denotes the luminance base. Figure 3(g) is achieved by the locally linear model with our two guided images. Compared with Figure 3(d), Figure 3(g) is free of the distortions caused by improper intercept item, as shown in sky parts in the rectangle.

A good estimation of guided images becomes very important since they are so critical for a satisfactory result. Fortunately, we find that there are several proper formulations. Following we discuss two essential components in constructing guided images. Since illumination is the main reason of causing the high dynamic range problem, local mean value is needed to estimate the illumination [5]. Local variance is critical to preserve the details because the target of tone mapping is compressing the high dynamic range while preserving the details. If we take these two components into consideration, the explicit formulation of guided image is less critical. Finally, we choose the formulation of our two guided images as follows:

$$w_t^* = \frac{1}{u_t^{\rho_1} + \lambda \sigma_t^{\rho_2}}. \quad (15)$$

$$b_t^* = u_t^{\rho_3} + \lambda \sigma_t^{\rho_4}, \quad (16)$$

where u_t and σ_t denotes the mean value and variation of the local patch centering in pixel t respectively. $\lambda = 0.1$ balances between the contribution of mean and value and $\rho_i (i \in \{1, 2, 3, 4\})$ are parameters which need to be toned.

Compared with the guidance map of Shan [8], our guided image has two advantages. Firstly, our approach is not sensitive to parameters. Default value $\rho_1 = 0.5, \rho_2 = 0.2, \rho_3 = 0.25, \rho_4 = 0.05$ works well for most HDR images. Secondly, our approach can achieve more natural results, as shown in Figure 3(g). From Figure 3(c),(f), we can find that our guided image is more sensitive to illumination changes, especially at the leaves parts and the path.

5 Experimental Results

In our experiments, it takes most of the time to construct the sparse matrix **U**, similarly with soft matting [20]. Therefore a multigrid method [22] is adopted to accelerate the computation. It takes about 5 seconds to process a 600×800 pixel image on a PC with a 2.83GHz Intel Core2 Processor using Matlab. We have tested several window size of 3*3, 5*5, 7*7, 9*9 and found that our algorithm was not sensitive to window size. In order to see structures of input HDR images more clearly, most of the input images are enhanced by global linear scaling. The codes of the compared methods are downloaded from their homepage with default parameters recommended by their original authors.

In Figure 4, we compare our approach with three typical global operators and locally linear method [8]. Compared with global linear scaling, global gamma correction can enhance more details. Global gamma correction in logarithmic domain can get a more natural result. However, all these global results are still unpleasing because of losing details or contrast. The locally linear model can get a high contrast result, but it sometimes causes distortions, as shown in red rectangle of Figure 4(e). On the contrary, our method can achieve a natural high contrast result without distortion or halo effects.

Next, we compare our method with locally linear approach in Figure 5. Locally linear method has some distortions in white regions, such as the white area in Figure 2(b), (c) and Figure 5(c). This kind of distortions, to some extent, can be improved by tuning the parameters. But it is really difficult to find proper parameters which can balance between unveiling the details in dark region and avoiding distortions in bright areas. Locally linear method also fails in patches which contain both dark pixels and bright pixels, for instance the sky-leaves in Figure 3(d). We have further found that local linear model is sensitive to patch size since the luminance value is more likely to vary abruptly in a larger window. Our method does not have these problems.

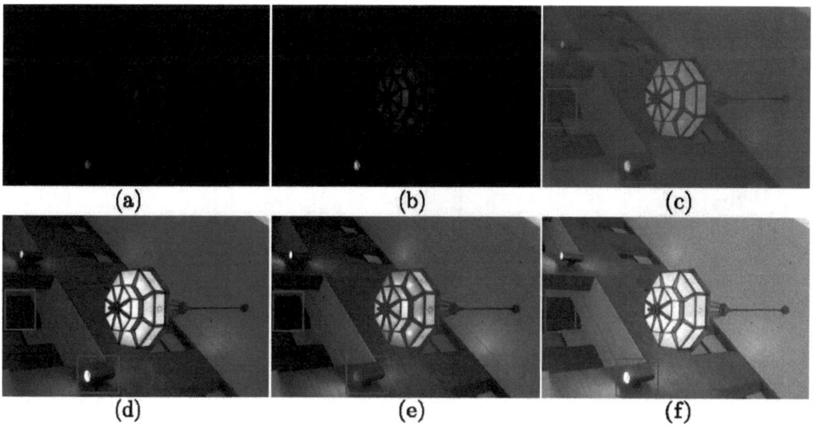

Fig. 4. Results compared with global operators and locally linear algorithm[8]. (a) input HDR image. (b) result of global linear scaling. (c) result of global gamma correction (β=0.2). (d) result of global gamma correction in logarithmic domain(β=0.6). (e) result of the locally linear method (β_1=0.9)[8] (f) our result. HDR image courtesy of Mark D. Fairchild[23].

In Figure 6 and Figure 7, we compare our method to six state-of-the-art tone mapping operators. Both Durand's Fast Bilateral Filtering method [6] and Farbman's edge-preserving multi-scale decompositions [14] have good performance in terms of preserving the details in bright regions. However, Farbman's method outperforms in details enhancing and details reproduction in dark regions. Compared with these two methods, our operator is better at preserving the details as well as getting a higher contrast, as shown in the statue part in the middle rectangle. Kuang [23] incorporates the spatial processing models in human visual system and propose a new image appearance model which is based on the iCAM framework. Their method does well in some other HDR images, but fails in Figure 6(d). Their result seems a little dim. Locally linear method [8] works quite well in the roof areas but has some distortions in the window parts. Their image has a high contrast but is not good at unveiling the dark regions with the recommended parameters of his paper. Li [2] compresses HDR images with subband architectures and successfully get a quite satisfactory result. Li's subband method can get a high contrast image with precise details in most HDR images. However, in many cases, her method does not enhance details in dark regions very well, as shown in the roof areas in the top rectangle. Figure 7(b) also shows that the red channel of her result is a little abnormal. Paris [3] has proposed an impressive method of tone mapping in terms of details enhancing. Their method also does well in unveiling the dark regions as well as preserving the details in bright areas. Unfortunately, their result does not have a high contrast or a perceptually pleasing appearance. Some distortions can also be found in Figure 7(e). Compared to those state-of-the-art approaches, our approach can effectively compress the dynamic range of the bright areas as well as enhance

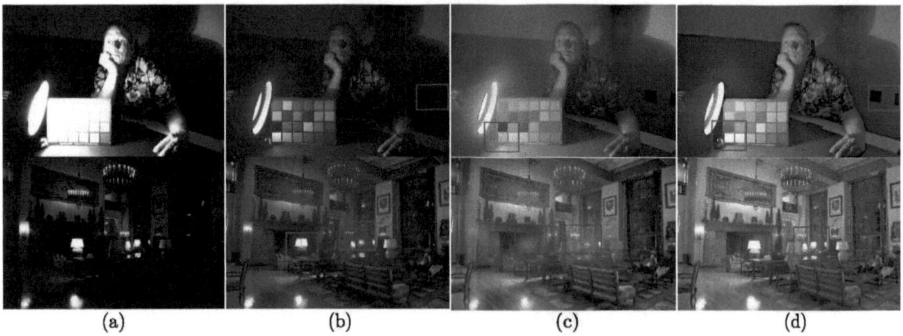

Fig. 5. Results compared with the locally linear model. (a) input HDR image. (b) the best results of the locally linear model balanced between compression and distortion: β_1=0.7. (c) results of the locally linear model using his recommendatory parameter: β_1=0.6,β_2=0.2,β_3=0.1. (d) our result. HDR image courtesy of Mark D. Fairchild[7].

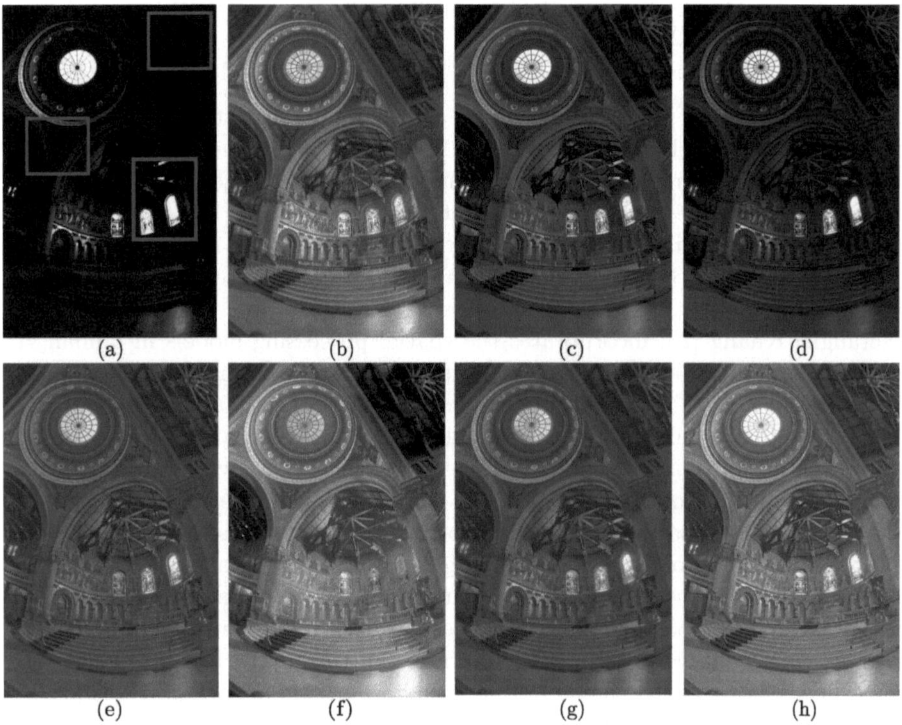

Fig. 6. Results compared with six state-of-the-art approaches. (a) input HDR image. (b) result of Durand [6]. (c) result of Li [2]. (d) result of Kuang [23]. (e) result of Farbman [14]. (f) result of Shan(β_1 = 0.6,β_2 = 0.2,β_3 = 0.1) [8]. (g) result of Paris[3]. (h) our result. HDR image courtesy of Paul Debevec[4].

Fig. 7. More comparisons with Li[2] and Paris[3]. (a),(d) input HDR image. (b) result of Li [2]. (e) result of Paris[3]. (c),(f) our result.

the details in dark regions without distortions or artifacts. From the perceptual perspective, our result has a high contrast and looks natural.

6 User Study

Finding whether a tone mapping operator suffers from distortions or halo effects is an easy work. However, it is quite difficult to evaluate whether this tone mapping operator is better than that operator because there is no convincing objective criteria. Fortunately, Yoshida[24] has done a perceptual evaluation of tone mapping operators. Therefore, we designed a similar perceptual evaluation of the above six state-of-the-art tone mapping operators.

The experiment was performed on the Internet with the participation of 23 human observers. The original input HDR image and output LDR images of seven operators were displayed on four web pages. Four perceptually criteria were tested in this experiment, namely naturalness, overall contrast, detail reproduction in dark and bright regions. The observer was asked to vote at most two images to the displayed seven LDR results according to one of the above four criteria. In each web page, eight images were displayed randomly in case of interact. All of the 23 participants were graduate students and researchers of our Lab. None of them were known for the goal of our experiment or tone mapping operators. Table 1 shows the vote results on Figure 6. Due to the limited space, more details about the experiments and more vote results on other tested images will be illustrated in the supplementary.

From Table 1, we can find that our method achieved better performances than the state-of-the-art approaches in terms of naturalness and detail reproduction in dark regions. Methods of Shan[8] and Paris[3] did well in detail reproduction in bright regions while Li's approach[2] outperformed in overall contrast.

Table 1. Perceptual evaluation of the seven tone mapping operators on Figure 6

Criteria \ Author	Durand	Li	Kuang	Farbman	Shan	Paris	**Our**
Naturalness	2	7	1	8	1	4	**15**
Overall Contrast	1	15	0	4	1	4	**9**
Details in Dark Regions	3	2	2	4	1	8	**12**
Details in Bright Regions	6	2	1	3	13	10	**1**
Total Votes	15	26	4	19	16	26	**37**

7 Conclusions

In this paper, we have introduced a new local operator for HDR image compression. The main contributions of our work are from two aspects. First, we propose an effective locally nonlinear model-local gamma correction with adaptive parameters. Our model has three properties: reasonable physical explanation, wide applicability and easy implementation. Second, we introduced two constraint items into our energy function and induced a close form solution by solving a sparse linear equation. With two guided images, our algorithm can not only effectively preserve the fine details but also achieve a natural high contrast result without any distortions or halo effects. Comparisons with six state-of-the-art methods have demonstrated that our approach can achieve better performances than the state-of-the-art approaches. Future work will concentrate on expanding our locally nonlinear model and applying it to different possible applications.

Acknowledgments. This work was supported in part by the National Basic Research Program of China under Grant 2012CB316304, and the NSFC under Grant 61175025,61075016.

References

1. Tumblin, J.E.J.: Three methods of detail-preserving contrast reduction for displayed images. Morgan Kaufmann Publishers Inc., San Francisco (1999)
2. Li, Y., Sharan, L., Adelson, E.H.: Compressing and companding high dynamic range images with subband architectures. ACM Trans. Graph. 24, 836–844 (2005)
3. Paris, S., Hasinoff, S.W., Kautz, J.: Local laplacian filters: edge-aware image processing with a laplacian pyramid. ACM Trans. Graph. (30), 68:1–68:12
4. Debevec, P.E., Malik, J.: Recovering high dynamic range radiance maps from photographs. In: SIGGRAPH 1997, NY, USA, pp. 369–378 (1997)
5. Stockham Jr., T.G.: Image processing in the context of a visual model. Proceedings of the IEEE 60, 828–842 (1972)
6. Durand, F., Dorsey, J.: Fast bilateral filtering for the display of high-dynamic-range images. ACM Trans. Graph. 21, 257–266 (2002)
7. Fairchild, M.D.: The HDR Photographic Survey. MDF Publications, Rochester Institute of Technology, NY, USA (2008)

8. Shan, Q., Jia, J., Brown, M.S.: Globally optimized linear windowed tone mapping. IEEE Trans. on Visualization and Computer Graphics 16, 663–675 (2010)
9. Drago, F., Myszkowski, K., Annen, T., Chiba, N.: Adaptive logarithmic mapping for displaying high contrast scenes. Computer Graphics Forum 22, 419–426 (2003)
10. Larson, G., Rushmeier, H., Piatko, C.: A visibility matching tone reproduction operator for high dynamic range scenes. IEEE Trans. on Visualization and Computer Graphics 3, 291–306 (1997)
11. Pattanaik, S.N., Tumblin, J., Yee, H., Greenberg, D.P.: Time-dependent visual adaptation for fast realistic image display. In: SIGGRAPH, NY, USA, pp. 47–54 (2000)
12. Qiu, G., Guan, J., Duan, J., Chen, M.: Tone mapping for hdr image using optimization a new closed form solution. In: Proceedings of the 18th International Conference on Pattern Recognition, Washington, DC, USA, pp. 996–999 (2006)
13. Tumblin, J., Rushmeier, H.: Tone reproduction for realistic images. IEEE Comput. Graph. Appl. 13, 42–48 (1993)
14. Farbman, Z., Fattal, R., Lischinski, D., Szeliski, R.: Edge-preserving decompositions for multi-scale tone and detail manipulation. ACM Trans. Graph. 27, 67:1–67:10 (2008)
15. Fattal, R., Lischinski, D., Werman, M.: Gradient domain high dynamic range compression. ACM Trans. Graph. 21, 249–256 (2002)
16. Lee, J.W., Park, R.H., Chang, S.: Local tone mapping using k-means algorithm and automatic gamma setting. In: IEEE International Conference on Consumer Electronics (ICCE), pp. 807–808 (2011)
17. Wagenaar, W.: Stevens vs fechner: A plea for dismissal of the case. Acta Psychologica 39, 225–235 (1975)
18. Reinhard, E., Ward, G., Pattanaik, S., Debevec, P.: High Dynamic Range Imaging: Acquisition, Display, and Image-Based Lighting. Morgan Kaufmann Publishers Inc., San Francisco (2005)
19. Xiang, S., Nie, F., Pan, C., Zhang, C.: Regression reformulations of lle and ltsa with locally linear transformation. IEEE Transactions on Systems, Man, and Cybernetics, Part B: Cybernetics 41, 1250–1262 (2011)
20. Levin, A., Lischinski, D., Weiss, Y.: A closed-form solution to natural image matting. IEEE Trans. on Pattern Analysis and Machine Intelligence 30, 228–242 (2008)
21. Schlick, C.: A customizable reflectance model for everyday rendering. In: Fourth Eurographics Workshop on Rendering, pp. 73–83 (1993)
22. Hager, W.W., Huang, S.J., Pardalos, P.M., Prokopyev, O.A.: Multiscale Optimization Methods and Applications. Springer (2005)
23. Kuang, J., Johnson, G.M., Fairchild, M.D.: icam06: A refined image appearance model for hdr image rendering. J. Vis. Comun. Image Represent. 18, 406–414 (2007)
24. Yoshida, A., Blanz, V., Myszkowski, K., Peter Seidel, H.: Perceptual evaluation of tone mapping operators with real-world scenes. In: Human Vision and Electronic Imaging X, pp. 192–203. SPIE (2005)

A Comparison of the Statistical Properties of IQA Databases Relative to a Set of Newly Captured High-Definition Images

Javier Silvestre-Blanes[1], Ian van der Linde[2], and Rubén Pérez-Lloréns[1]

[1] Instituto Tecnológico de Informática (ITI), Universitat Politècnica de València (UPV), Ferrandiz y Carbonell s/n, 03801 Alcoy, Spain
{jsilves,ruperez}@disca.upv.es

[2] Vision & Eye Research Unit (VERU), Postgraduate Medical Institute, Anglia Ruskin University, East Road, Cambridge CB1 1PT, United Kingdom
i.v.d.linde@anglia.ac.uk

Abstract. A broad range of image processing applications require image databases during development and testing. Whilst some image databases have been assembled with specific applications in mind, others are intended for more general use, with image content that is purposefully not application-specific. General-purpose image databases are in frequent use in the development of new compression algorithms, including in the evaluation of the efficacy of lossy compression techniques via statistical and human (perceptual) image quality assessment methods. The question of how the images featuring in standard image databases are selected is important, but is rarely quantitatively justified. In this article, we describe the compilation of a new image database of high-definition color images. We present statistical analyzes both of the images that feature in the most widely used extant databases, and the new database that we have compiled, in order to evaluate how broad a range of the statistics measured each database spans.

1 Introduction

The development of new image processing algorithms often requires image databases for testing and validation. Often, algorithms under development are quite specific, such as those for face recognition and stereo correlation, and correspondingly specific databases for these and other narrowly defined problems exist. However, a number of general-purpose image databases exist, wherein the content of the specific images selected for inclusion is not tailored to satisfy a particular final application, but aims to be useful in a broad range of applications, such as in the development of new compression algorithms, image quality assessment (**IQA**), and in the analysis of the statistical properties of natural images.

Several IQA image databases are in widespread use. These include LIVE [1][2][3], IRCCyN/IVC [4], CSIQ [5], TID [6], A57 [7], Toyama [8] and WIQ [9]. These databases comprise a number of lossless images (not always exclusive

A. Fitzgibbon et al. (Eds.): ECCV 2012, Part IV, LNCS 7575, pp. 800–813, 2012.

to each database, see below), along with a set of degraded versions of each image, typically distorted to different degrees with a range of different distortion methods. In studies examining the limits of the human visual system (HVS), one common database was assembled by van Hateren [10], comprising a set of calibrated grayscale images of natural scenes. Since this database contains some man-made structures, in some studies, a subset of the available images is used (e.g. DOVES [11]). A further calibrated natural image database for color images, without the objective of being for general use, or being a representative subset of the real world, is also available: the McGill Calibrated Colour Image Database [12] (Tabby). Calibration ensures that observed luminance and chrominance are veridically represented when images are digitized, but is unnecessary for most applications.

In Table 1, the size and constitution of a number of common image databases are provided. All incorporate images at a relatively low spatial resolution. Historically, one reason for this is that several core applications (such as IQA, and the study of HVS properties) require that image are presented to observers on a monitor without resampling (which introduces imperfections), i.e., are shown at their native resolution on a display device that has a corresponding spatial resolution, thereby imposing a limit on the maximum useful spatial resolution of images featuring in the database. When image resampling is not a concern, other resolutions may be used, as is the case with databases used for in development of new image compression algorithms, such as [13], in which images up to 7116×5412 at 16-bits per plane are provided. In almost all common databases, image from Kodak Lossless True Color Image Suite [14] are used, which possess relatively low spatial resolutions (768×512 or 512×768).

Clearly, both the number and content of the images provided in each database will influence the results of specific studies to some degree. In IQA studies, quality metrics will fluctuate significantly, contingent upon the database used for testing. In [15], the authors propose that statistical metrics (such as PSNR and SSIM) work better in databases incorporating images at a wide range of quality settings, since findings will be less informative where very high quality images are used, in which distortions may be barely perceptible, as a consequence of the limited acuity of the HVS. In addition to image resolution, and the severity of distortion introduced, it is also likey that the content of each of the images featuring in standard image databases will affect performance, potentially limiting the generalizability of results.

A common characteristic of all databases is the apparently arbitrary (or at least scantily documented) protocol for the selection of images. For CSIQ, described in [5], nothing is said about the selection of the 30 original images, except that they are divided into five categories: animals, landscape, people, plants and urban. The same can be said about the 10 images selected in IVC database [17], although many of these are standard images in widespread use by the image processing community. The images in LIVE [3] were selected to ensure diverse image content, and originate from the Kodak Lossless True Color

Image Suite, the Internet and CD-ROMs. Specifically, images include pictures of faces, people, animals, close-up shots, wide-angle shots, natural scenes, man-made objects, images with distinct foreground/background configurations, and also images without any specific object of interest. Almost all images featuring in the Toyama database originate from the Kodak Suite, and all-bar-three also feature in the LIVE database. Reference images used in TID20008 are obtained by cropping from the Kodak Suite. Once again, the selection procedure is largely undocumented. Furthermore, the image cropping performed to reduce image size will alter global image statistics, reducing scope for the comparison of results with those of LIVE and Toyama. The WIQ database is restricted to special distortion cases [18], such as those produced by packet loss in wireless communication, comprising a number of images well-known to the image processing community, rather like IVC, although in grayscale form. In Fig. 1 eight common images featuring in the LIVE, Toyama and TID2008 (which uses cropped versions) databases are shown, along with the names used in each database; the ubiquitous nature of these images means that they have borne a significant influence on the IQA field.

Our objective in this study is to compile a new database, denoted GID (General Image Database [16]), in which the selection of images is justified through the objective analysis of low-level scene statistics (rather than selecting images by hand that appear to possess a range of desirable properties), and in which images may be further categorized by their semantic content. By labeling test images according to a range of statistical metrics, the image processing community may test algorithms under development by selecting images with specific statistical properties, enabling them to triangulate the efficacy of algorithms across a range of input conditions, look for input statistic-performance correlations, and so on.

Fig. 1. Common images from LIVE, Toyama & TID2008 Databases

Table 1. Properties

Name	LIVE	Toyama	CSIQ	IVC	A57	TID	WIQ
resolution	<768x512	768x512	512x512	512x512	512x512	512x384	512x512
original images	29	14	30	10	3	25	7
Distorted imag.	779	168	866	235	54	1700	80
Distortions	5	2	5	3	6	17	1
Observers[1]	23	16	25	15	838		
Color	RGB	RGB	RGB	RGB	Gray	RGB	Gray
Name [2]	**van Hateren**	**DOVES**	**Tabby**				
resolution	1526x1024	1024x768	786x576				
original images	4168	101	850				
Color	Gray	Gray	Color				

[1] In average number of observers per image.
[2] Not IQA databases.

2 Image Statistics

In image processing, 2D images are represented in Cartesian space as matrix of $M \times N$ pixels, such that M is taken as the image width, and N the image height. Grayscale images are constructed from a single 2D plane, and color images from multiple planes. Examples include RGB, the standard colorspace for image acquisition and display systems, and HSV, the cylindrical coordinate system useful for color analysis, feature extraction, and other procedures that benefit from the independent representation of chrominance and luminance. Each image plane may be represented with 8 (the most usual), 10, 12 or even 16 bits per pixel (bpp). In HSV colorspace, the V plane represents image luminance, and is therefore functionally equivalent to a grayscale image; the H plane represents of the color of each pixel (pixel hue), and S represents the saturation (vibrancy) of that color [19][20]. In Fig. 2, the relationship between H, S and V coordinates are shown. H is often measured from 0 to 360. However, in many image processing operations, only the V plane is used.

In recent years, for a variety of applications, the statistical properties of natural images have become important, and the pictures that feature in common image databases have been subject to frequent analysis. Applications requiring that the statistical properties of images are examined include the development

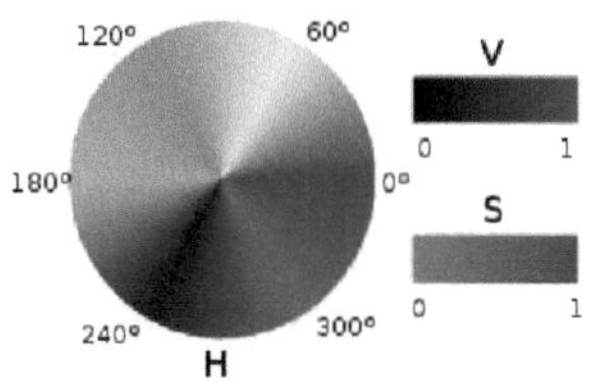

Fig. 2. Color planes in HSV model

Table 2. Pearson Product-Moment Correlation Coefficients (r) for V and H planes

V						**H**					
	SD	**SK**	**U**	**E**	C_{RMS}		**SD**	**SK**	**U**	**E**	C_{RMS}
M	0.51	-0.76	-0.63	0.70	0.51	**M**	-0.49	-0.69	-0.10	-0.15	-0.49
SD		-0.33	-0.42	0.58	0.99	**SD**		-0.38	-0.27	0.57	0.90
SK			0.60	-0.53	-0.32	**SK**			0.63	0.05	0.24
U				-0.82	-0.42	**U**				-0.83	-0.27
E					0.58	**E**					0.57

of perceptual image compression algorithms, gaze prediction [21], biometrics and automated indexing and categorization systems. Images may be subject to a wide range of first order, second order and higher order statistics; commonly reported statistics include mean luminance (M), standard deviation (SD), or variance, RMS contrast (C_{RMS}), histogram skewness (SK), uniformity (U), and entropy (E), along with power spectrum analysis (e.g., via the Discrete Fourier Transform). Formulas for calculating a number of basic statistics are provided below, where if $I(i,j)$ is the intensity value of the plane I being analyzed, at coordinate (i,j) in an image size of $M \times N$, then $\bar{I}$ is the average in the plane analyzed, and p_k the cumulative frequency of intensity k of the L possible values in the image:

$$M = \frac{1}{MN}\sum_{i=1}^{M}\sum_{j=1}^{N} I(i,j); \tag{1}$$

$$SD = \sqrt{\frac{1}{MN-1}\sum_{i=1}^{M}\sum_{j=1}^{N}(I(i,j)-\bar{I})^2}; \tag{2}$$

$$C_{RMS} = \sqrt{\frac{1}{MN}\sum_{i=0}^{N-1}\sum_{j=0}^{M-1} I(i,j)-\bar{I}} \tag{3}$$

$$SK = \sqrt{\sum_{k=1}^{L-1}(k-\bar{I})^3 p_k} \tag{4}$$

$$U = \sum_{k=1}^{L-1} p_k^2; \tag{5}$$

$$E = \sum_{k=1}^{L-1} p_k log_2 p_k; \tag{6}$$

Spatial frequency analyzes typically use the V plane (assuming we are working in HSV colorspace), since chrominance planes are known to exhibit similar spectral behavior [22]. A number of image statistics are correlated - for instance, an image with a very skewed (high or low) luminance distribution is unlikely to

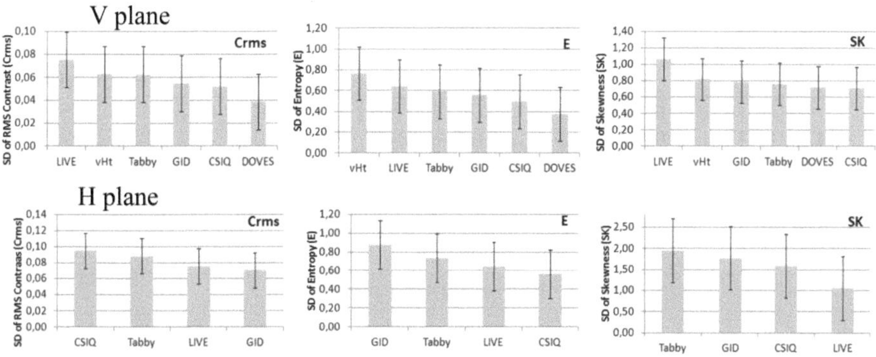

Fig. 3. Ranked image statistic dispersions (SD) for each image database. Error bars are +/- 1.96 SEM.

possess high RMS contrast. Table 2 shows the degree of correlation [23] between these statistics (in V and H planes) for all images in all image databases listed above. We see strong correlations (r >0.5) between many of the image statistics calculated, with many other medium sized correlations (r =0.3-0.5). In particular, SD and C_{RMS} appear to be colinear, so we take C_{RMS} as an indicator of contrast. Likewise, since E and U are very closely correlated, we take E as an indicator image complexity.

In Fig. 3, the dispersion of each image statistic defined is shown for each image plane. Normalized ranking each database (0 for lowest and 1 for the highest. See Table 3) reveals that the LIVE and van Hateren database (vHt) have the greatest variability across the statistics measures, and DOVES (a subset of the van Hateren database) the lowest variability. The same analysis in the H plane reveals that the CSIQ database has the greatest variability across the statistics measures, whereas LIVE have the lowest. At this point, the choice of IQA database for the highest variability is between GID and CSIQ, however, further image properties are to be examined.

Sometimes, log intensity is considered, so charts of the histograms of $ln(I(i,j)) - average(ln(I))$ [24][25] were calculated. In Fig. 4, histograms of some representative databases for the plane V are shown. In the database with the greatest number of images, van Hateren, positive skew is appreciable ($\varsigma = 2.7$). This is attributed by some authors [24] to the presence of (high intensity) daytime sky in many images. Similar skewness values are obtained for IQA databases. GID yields the lowest skewness value ($\varsigma = 2.29$), whereas LIVE, CSIQ and Tabby have $\varsigma = 2.46$, $\varsigma = 2.50$, and $\varsigma = 2.49$, respectively. In these cases, high intensity values that predominate over low intensity values are not only due to sky, but to many other parts of image content, such as clothes, stones, or sails. The intensity distribution shows a uniform distribution for all databases, except for CSIQ which has irregularities in the tails of histograms. This could be due to the inclusion of images with many pixels with intensities concentrated in the extremes, like in snow_leaves, roping (note that green pixels have high intensity in the V plane), sunsetcolor, or family. This kind of image should be included in a database for IQA, since despite being

Table 3. Image databases ranked for each image statistic in V and in H plane, and ranked overall

Name	C_{RMS}	E	M	SK	points	Name	C_{RMS}	E	M	SK	points
vHt[1]	0.65	0.76	0.35	0.31	2.07	**CSIQ**	1.00	0.00	0.58	1	2.58
LIVE	1	0.68	0	1	2.68	Tabby [1]	0.74	0.54	1	0	2.28
Tabby[1]	0.64	0.55	0.70	0.15	2.04	**GID**	0.00	1	0.80	0.16	1.96
GID	0.43	0.47	0.65	0.22	1.77	**LIVE**	0.20	0.25	0	0.03	0.48
CSIQ	0.36	0.31	1	0	1.67						
DOVES[1]	0	0	0.31	0.02	0.33						

[1] Not an IQA database.

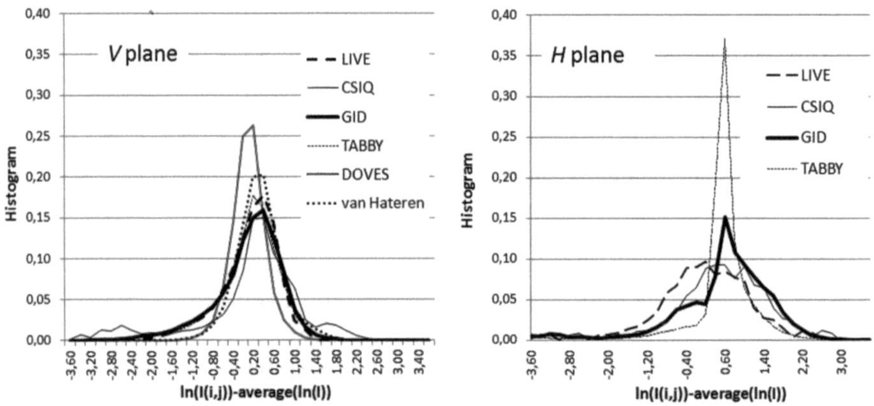

Fig. 4. Histograms of $ln(I(i,j)) - average(ln(I))$ for V and H planes

statistically unusual, it is entirely natural. However, where the number of images in a set it as a premium, such images should be relatively sparse. In GID, statistically unusual images exist, producing a higher dispersion in the distributions of core image statistic, but at the same time, due to the small proportion of such images overall, our histograms don't have marked irregularities.

Histograms of some representative databases for pixels in the H plane are shown in right Fig. 4. We observe higher skewness for Tabby in this plane ($\varsigma = 4.91$), which could be explained by the concentration of some colors in the images, since this database is not intended as a representation of the real world and is not specifically intended for use in the development of image processing algorithms. LIVE and CSIQ have $\varsigma = 1.62$ and $\varsigma = 1.66$ respectively. The shape of the histograms shows irregularities in both cases, which could be due to their low number of images, and a wide range in LIVE database. GID has a $\varsigma = 2.3$ and uniformly wide shape, so we can conclude that from the point of view of color information, GID has rich uniform distribution with respect to other IQA databases.

Concerning other statistics, gradients are the simplest way to analyze the relationship between pairs of pixels. The forward difference gradient at a pixel (i, j) in the plane I can be calculated as:

$$Dx(i,j) = ln(I(i+1,j)) - ln(I(i,j)); Dy(i,j) = ln(I(i,j+1)) - ln(I(i,j)) \quad (7)$$

$$D(i,j) = \sqrt{Dx(i,j)^2 + Dx(i,j)^2} \quad (8)$$

It is accepted that the gradient histogram has a very sharp peak at zero, and falls off quickly [26]. This distribution can be modeled as $e^{-x^{\alpha}}$ with $\alpha < 1$ [27]. The reason for this shape is connected to the general mixture of large smooth surfaces with few high contrast edges. Analyzing the α values in the databases available, it tends to be higher where a greater proportion of natural images are used, since then the edges are similarly distributed in all images and directions. Thus, we get $\alpha = 0.853$ for van Hateren, $\alpha = 0.82$ for CSIQ, $\alpha = 0.79$ for LIVE and Tabby, and $\alpha = 0.76$ for GID. In Fig. 5 the log(histogram) is shown in order to appreciate differences in the tails. Note the assymetry exhibited in the van Hateren database, which is due to many sky portions in images, although this could be due to other image properties. The CSIQ database has symmetrical tails, indicating that, on average, edges go all directions and are generally less noticeable. LIVE has concave tails on both sides, which could be due to the fact that edges are a strong component in images. GID and Tabby, like van Hateren, have a concave tail only on the left, indicating that the gradients of these databases may be a better representation of real world. The analysis of gradients in the H plane do not give different properties between the color images databases.

The analysis of Fourier power spectrum is also usually done to obtain image statistics. These analyses show how low frequencies contain the most power, which decrease as a function of frequency. Analyzing the amplitude as a function of frequency (P) in a log-log scale over a sufficient number of images, the result can be modeled as $P = 1/f^{\beta}$, where $P = 1/f^{\beta}$ is the spectral slope. Some works obtain β for different image ensembles (man-made, vegetation, etc.), and it can be assumed that the average spectral slope varies from 1.8 to 2.4, with most values clustering around 2.0 (a brief review of this and the related references can be found in [26]). Other studies analyze the shape of the power spectrum signature. Fig 6 shows the V plane power spectrum signatures of with 50% (red), 60% (blue), 75% (green) an 90% (yellow) of the energy over the power spectrum of the databases analyzed. It can be seen how signatures are coarse when the number of images are low, whereas it is well defined if the number of images is high. Also, the red signature is small when the number of images is high, indicating that the low frequencies are the main component of the images, so particular properties of some image of the dataset do not change this. In [28] it is shown how the kind of images produce special shapes for their signatures. Thus, it can be seen how van Hateren and DOVES have the shape of natural objects, though the lower number of images in DOVES makes these shapes wider. Tabby has a mixture of man-made objects and natural objects, which is an expected result, since it is a mixture of different types of images. GID shows similar behavior, although weighted slightly towards the natural shape.

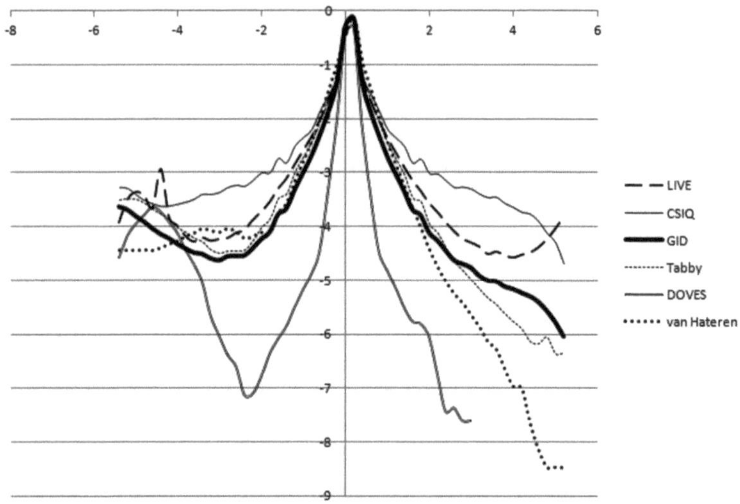

Fig. 5. Log-histograms of D for V plane

Higher order statistics are only valid if the image exhibits stationary statistics, like Wavelets or Gabor. These statistics cannot be used to select individual images of a big set, but the final results have to be coherent with the results shown, and there must not be significant differences in the new set defined with respect to the figures presented.

3 Image Selection

The image selection process aims to find a global representation of the real world, including natural scenes and other image types (see Fig. 7). Furthermore, multi-dimensional classification enable studies to focus upon different types of images. The number of images N is limited due to the main target of these images, that is, development and validation of IQA metrics. It is necessary to take into account that each original image has to be distorted using n distortion types. For each distortion, m different levels are applied, such that each one of the Nmn images is evaluated by one of O observers. Finally, $NmnO$ observations are compiled for analysis. For each distortion types, n, artifacts that reflect common coding and transmission systems are included, sometimes via simulation. The number of distortion levels, m, may be high, but it is typically considered unnecessary to include a large number of levels, since subjective evaluation is often limited to 5 rating categories (imperceptible, perceptible, slightly annoying, annoying, very annoying) [29]. The number of observers, O, should be large enough to be statistically representative. Thus, N should be chosen in order to achieve a sufficiently representative set of real world images, and span a range of image statistics, but at the same time ensure that subjetive experiments are feasible (both in terms of time and cost).

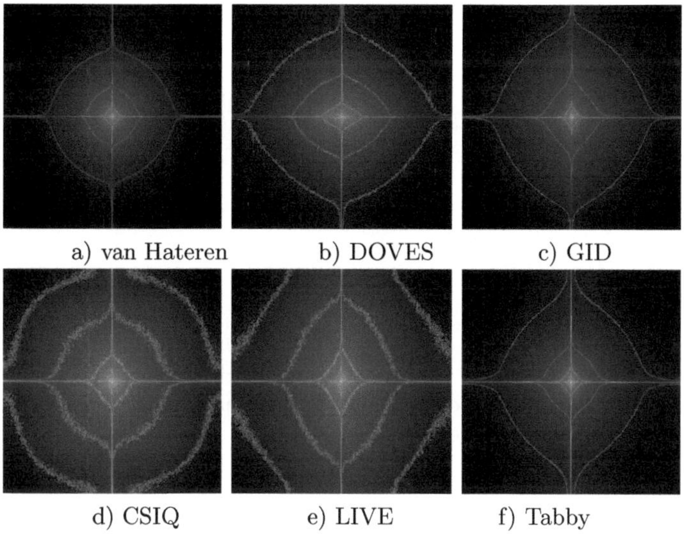

Fig. 6. Mean power spectrum signature for each image database

Fig. 7. Example GID images

The set of 500 images provided in GID may be reduced without loss of representivity. We use a random selection process to reduce the number of images from the original collection required without loss of global statistical characteristics. Of the common subsampling methods available: Simple Random Sampling, Stratified Random Sampling, and Cluster Sampling, since we only consider the image as a set (without exclusive subsets), simple random sampling was used with the reservoir sampling algorithm [30]. First, we get a subset of 200 images, denominated GID_{200}. From this subset, we repeat the random process to select 50 images, this is the GID_{50} subset. Iteratively, we try to reduce the value of N, in this case to 12, and from GID_{50} we repeat the random process four different times, to select GID_{12}^A, GID_{12}^B, GID_{12}^C and GID_{12}^D. In Fig. 8 the first order statistics of the V plane for GID and for all the mentioned subsets can be seen. We can see how the dispersion and complexity represented by the parameters mentioned in the previous section are mantained in GID_{200} and have a slight

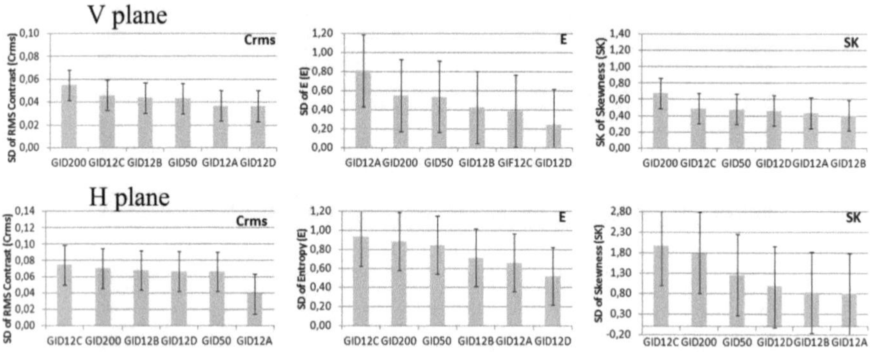

Fig. 8. Ranked image statistic dispersions *(SD)* for each image subset images. Error bars are 1.96 SEM. subset images.

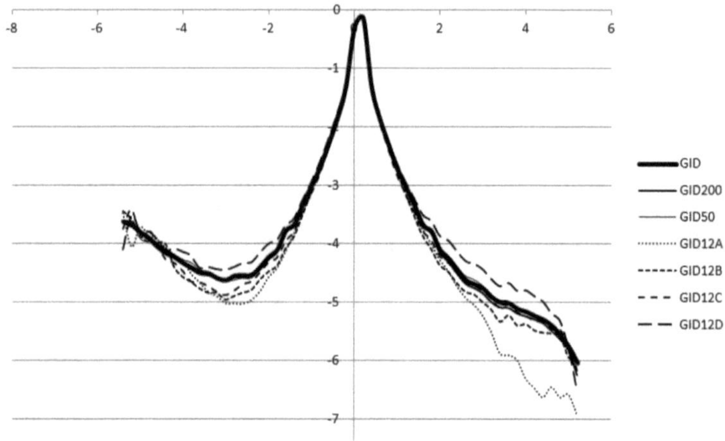

Fig. 9. Log-histograms of D for the V plane for subsets

reduction in GID_{50}, especially in C_{RMS}, and is significant in the other subsets, especially in entropy and skewness. Similar behavior is obtained in the H plane, as we can see in Fig. 8. The skewness of log intensity histograms on ln(I(i,j))-average(ln(I)) for GID_{200}, GID_{50}, GID_{12}^{A}, GID_{12}^{B}, GID_{12}^{C}, GID_{12}^{D} are $\varsigma = 2.29$, $\varsigma = 2.28$, $\varsigma = 2.11$, and $\varsigma = 2.44$, $\varsigma = 2.42$, $\varsigma = 2.39$, and $\varsigma = 2.33$. Significant differences with the reduction of number of images in the subsets were not found.

The gradients in the subsets, even in the smaller subsets, gave similar results to the full set GID, as we can see in Fig. 9. The power spectrum of signatures of the subsets are shown in Fig. 10. We can see how the main properties are maintained for GID_{200} and GID_{50}, while we get quite different shapes when we reduce the number of images to 12, changing then the average image type.

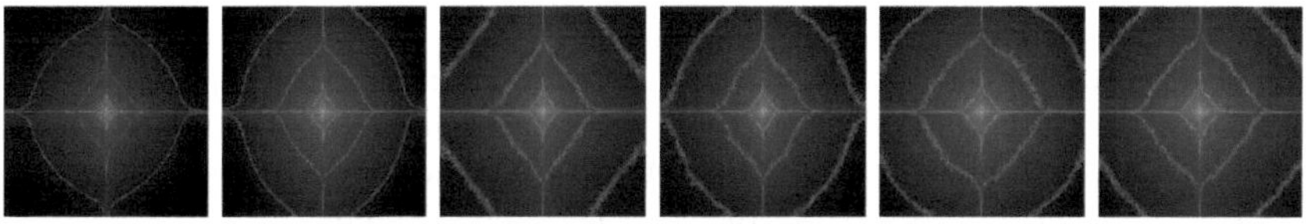

a) GID_{200} b) GID_{50} c) GID_{12}^{A} d) GID_{12}^{B} e) GID_{12}^{C} f) GID_{12}^{D}

Fig. 10. Spectral signatures of GID subsets

4 Conclusions and Future Work

We have analyzed several sets of images databases that are used for different purposes, and we have seen how they have very different properties. The images contained in these databases are used for the development of new image processing algorithms, including lossy compression, image quality assessment, etc. The properties of the set can have an influence on the algorithms developed. In this paper we have compiled a new set of images, with two important differences with respect to previous databases: the use of high definition resolution, and the use of a large number of images. We have analysed this set and compared their statistics with other databases.

After this, we obtained some subsets of the original one, and it was seen that their representativity is maintained when N is reduced from 500 to 200 and even to 50, rendering subjective image quality rating feasible. The reduction of N to 12 had an impact on some statistics.

Our next task is to complete subjective image quality evaluation for these images (spefically, GID_{50}). With this analysis, we will obtain the results for smaller subsets (GID_{12}^{A}, GID_{12}^{B}, GID_{12}^{C}, GID_{12}^{D}), so we can determine the influence of the number of images, and of the image statistics, on the evaluation of image quality.

Acknowledgement. This work is supported by the MCYT of Spain under the project TIN2010-21378-C02-02 and by Universidad Politècnica de Valècia under PAID-00-11.

References

1. Sheikh, H.R., Wang, Z., Cormack, L.K., Bovik, A.C.: LIVE image quality assessment database release 2, `http://live.ece.utexas.edu/research/quality`
2. Wang, Z., Bovik, A.C., Sheikh, H.R., Simoncelli, E.P.: Image quality assessment: from error visibility to structural similarity. IEEE Trans. Image Process. 13(4), 600–612 (2004)
3. Sheikh, H.R., Sabir, M.F., Bovik, A.C.: A statistical evaluation of recent full reference image quality assessment algorithms. IEEE Trans. Image Process. 11(15), 3440–3451 (2006)
4. Le Callet, P., Autrusseau, F.: Image quality evaluation database, `http://www.irccyn.ecnantes.fr/ivcdb`

5. Larson, E.C., Chandler, D.M.: Most apparent distortion: full-reference image quality assessment and the role of strategy. J. Electron. Imaging 19(19), 011006 (2010)
6. Ponomarenko, N., Lukin, V., Zelensky, A., Egiazarian, K., Carli, M., Battisti, F.: TID2008 - A Database for Evaluation of Full-Reference Visual Quality Assessment Metrics. Advances of Modern Radioelectronics, 30–45 (2009)
7. Chandler, D.M., Hemami, S.S.: VSNR: A Wavelet-Based Visual Signal-to-Noise Ratio for Natural Images. IEEE Trans. Image Process. 16(9), 2284–2298 (2007)
8. Horita, Y., Kawayoke, Y., Parvez Sazzad, Z.M.: Image quality evaluation database, `ftp://guest@mict.eng.utoyama.jp`
9. Engelke, U., Zepernick, H.-J., Kusuma, M.: Wireless Imaging Quality Database, `http://www.bth.se/tek/rcg.nsf/pages/wiq-db`
10. van Hateren, J., van der Schaaf, A.: Independent component filters of natural images compared with simple cells in primary visual cortex. Proc. R. Soc. B-Biol. Sci. 265(1394), 359–366 (1998)
11. van der Linde, I., Rajashekar, U., Bovik, A.C., Cormack, L.K.: DOVES: A database of visual eye movements. Spatial Vis. 22(2), 161–177 (2009)
12. Olmos, A., Kingdom, F.A.A.: A biologically inspired algorithm for the recovery of shading and reflectance images. Perception 33, 1463–1473 (2004)
13. Rawzor, `www.imagecompression.info`
14. Kodak, `http://r0k.us/graphics/kodak/`
15. Tourancheu, S., Autrusseau, F., Parvez Sazzad, Z.M., Horita, Y.: Impact of subjective dataset on the performance of image quality metrics. In: IEEE Int. Conf. in Image Processing (ICIP), San Diego, California, USA (2008)
16. Silvestre-Blanes, J.: `http://muro1.alc.upv.es/eccv12/gid.html`
17. Ninassi, A., Le Callet, P., Autrusseau, F.: Pseudo No Reference image quality metric using perceptual data hiding. In: SPIE Electronic Imaging, Human Vision and Electronic Imaging Conference XI, HVEI 2006, San Jose, USA (2006)
18. Engelke, U., Kusuma, M., Zepernick, H.J., Caldera, M.: Reduced-Reference Metric Design for Objective Perceptual Quality Assessment in Wireless Imaging. Signal Process.-Image Commun. 24(7), 525–547 (2009)
19. Cubero, S., Aleixos, N., Molt, E., Gómez-Sanchis, J., Blasco, J.: Advances in Machine Vision Applications for Automatic Inspection and Quality Evaluation of Fruits and Vegetables. Food Bioprocess Technol., 487–504 (2011)
20. Blasco, J., Aleixos, N., Molt, E., Gómez-Sanchis, J.: Citrus sorting by identification of the most common defects using multispectral computer vision. J. Food Eng., 384–393 (2007)
21. Rajashekar, U., van der Linde, I., Bovik, A.C., Cormack, L.K.: GAFFE: A gaze-attentive fixtion finding engine. IEEE Trans. Image Process. 17(4), 564–573 (2008)
22. Párraga, C.A., Brelstaff, G., Troscianko, T.: Color and luminance information in natural scenes. J. Opt. Soc. Am. A-Opt. Image Sci. Vis. 15, 563–569 (1998)
23. Cohen, J.: Statistical Power Analysis for the Behavioral Sciences. Lawrence Erlbaum Associates, Inc. (1988)
24. Huang, J., Mumford, D.: Statistics of Natural Images and Models. In: IEEE Computer Society Conference on Computer Vision and Pattern Recognition (CVPR 1999), Ft. Collins, CO, USA, vol. 1, pp. 541–547 (1999)
25. Brady, M., Field, J.D.: Local constrast in natural images: normalization and coding efficiency. Perception 29, 1041–1055 (2000)

26. Pouli, T., Cunningham, D.W., Reinhard, E.: Image Statistics and their Applications in Computer Graphics. In: Eurographics, Norrkping, Sweden, pp. 83–112 (2010)
27. Simoncelli, E.: Statistical modeling of photographic images. In: Bovik, A. (ed.) Handbook of Image and Video Processing, pp. 431–443. Elsevier Academic Press (2005)
28. Torralba, A., Oliva, A.: Statistics of natural image categories. Network: Comput. Neural Syst. 14, 391–412 (2003)
29. ITU-R BT.500-7 Methodology for the Subjective Assessment of the Quality of Television Pictures
30. Vitter, J.S.: Random sampling with a reservoir. ACM Trans. Math. Softw. 11(11), 37–57 (1985)

Supervised Assessment of Segmentation Hierarchies

Jordi Pont-Tuset and Ferran Marques*

Universitat Politècnica de Catalunya BarcelonaTech,
Jordi Girona, 1-3, 08034, Barcelona, Spain
`http://imatge.upc.edu`

Abstract. This paper addresses the problem of the supervised assessment of hierarchical region-based image representations. Given the large amount of partitions represented in such structures, the supervised assessment approaches in the literature are based on selecting a reduced set of representative partitions and evaluating their quality. Assessment results, therefore, depend on the partition selection strategy used. Instead, we propose to find the partition in the tree that best matches the ground-truth partition, that is, the upper-bound partition selection. We show that different partition selection algorithms can lead to different conclusions regarding the quality of the assessed trees and that the upper-bound partition selection provides the following advantages: 1) it does not limit the assessment to a reduced set of partitions, and 2) it better discriminates the random trees from actual ones, which reflects a better qualitative behavior. We model the problem as a Linear Fractional Combinatorial Optimization (LFCO) problem, which makes the upper-bound selection feasible and efficient.

1 Introduction

Region-based hierarchical image representations have proven their applicability in many fields such as segmentation, filtering, information retrieval [1]; object detection [2–4], contour detection [5, 6], etc.

Any hierarchy of nested regions based on a set of non-overlapping regions can be represented by a binary tree of regions (such as *Binary Partition Trees* (BPT) [1] or *Ultrametric Contour Map* (UCM) trees [5]), so although this work is focused on this type of trees, the results are generalizable to any hierarchy of regions such as quad trees [7].

A supervised assessment has been the most used to prove the validity of these representations, that is, comparing the results to a set of manually-generated partitions known as *ground truth*. However, comparing the large collection of partitions represented in a hierarchy to a non-hierarchical partition is not straightforward.

The approaches found in the literature consist in selecting a set of *representative* partitions from the tree and comparing them to the ground-truth partitions. This way, for each partition of the ground-truth database, there will be a set of values that indicate the quality of that particular tree.

* This work has been partially supported by the Spanish *Ministerio de Ciencia e Innovación*, under project TEC2010-18094 and FPU grant AP2008-01164.

A. Fitzgibbon et al. (Eds.): ECCV 2012, Part IV, LNCS 7575, pp. 814–827, 2012.

To average these results on a whole database, the representative partitions of the tree on each image of the database have to be put in correspondence (*align*) with the representative partitions of the trees of the rest of images, that is, there has to be a common parameter that *indexes* each set of representative partitions (e.g. their number of regions). Overall, aggregate results depend on a **partition selection algorithm** and an **alignment** procedure.

For instance, in [8, 9], the set of selected partitions are the ones formed in the merging sequence, aligned by their number of regions. The latter proposes a second alignment based on the accumulated merging cost threshold. In [5], the selected regions are also the ones in the merging sequence, but the alignment parameter is the confidence threshold on the ultrametric contour map.

Ideally, assessment results should depend mainly on the trees themselves, otherwise it is not clear whether the obtained results are due to the tree itself, or to the alignment and partition selection algorithms. To make results independent of the former, [5] proposes the *Optimal Image Scale* (OIS) analysis, which averages the best result in the representative set of each tree.

This paper proposes a technique to make the assessment results independent of the partition selection algorithm via the **upper-bound partition selection**, that is, computing the optimal results that can be achieved by any partition selection procedure.

In the case of the OIS, the maximum performance for each image is searched by brute force among all possible partitions in the merging sequence [5]. However, exhaustively searching the upper-bound performance among all possible partitions in a tree to make results independent of the partition selection algorithm is not computationally feasible. To overcome this limitation, we propose to model the problem of finding the best partition selection as a *Linear Fractional Combinatorial Optimization* (LFCO), which can be efficiently solved by the procedure presented in [10].

We show that the upper-bound partition selection has the following advantages in the assessment of region-based hierarchies. First, it expands the range of partitions assessed beyond the merging sequence. Note that this is a relevant feature, since there are image analysis works such as [2, 1] that extract partitions that are not in the merging sequence, and so such partitions would not be covered by the previous selection approaches. Second, we demonstrate that the partition selection technique may mislead the assessment of the tree quality, in the sense that the ranking between results is different from the upper-bound in a significant number of cases of the experiments. Finally, we show that the upper-bound partition selection has a better discriminative power between the baseline method of computing the hierarchy randomly and actual hierarchies.

The remainder of the paper is organized as follows: Section 2 presents the different trees that are used in this work and Section 3 expounds on the supervised techniques found in the literature to assess these hierarchies. Then, in Section 4 we present the step-by-step deduction and motivation of the LFCO model that we propose to find the upper-bound partition selection. Section 5 presents the experiments performed to evaluate and compare our algorithm and in Section 6 we draw the conclusions.

2 Hierarchy Creation Algorithm

In this paper we explore a region-based hierarchical image representation consisting of a binary tree, where each node represents a region in the image, and the parent node of a pair of regions represents their merging. This structure is referred to as *Binary Partition Tree* (BPT) in [1, 2, 8, 9]. The *Ultrametric Contour Map* (UCM) [5] hierarchy of regions is also a binary tree.

The algorithm to build both BPT and UCM is a greedy region merging algorithm that, starting from an initial partition P_0, iteratively merges the most similar pair of neighboring regions. The concept of region *similarity* is what makes the difference between both approaches.

In the case of the BPT, each region is represented by a model such as the color mean and contour complexity [8] or the color histogram [9], and the region similarity is obtained comparing their models. The UCM [5], in contrast, defines the dissimilarity between two neighboring regions as the strength of the *Oriented Watershed Transform* (OWT) of the *globalized Probability of boundary* (gPb) in the common boundary.

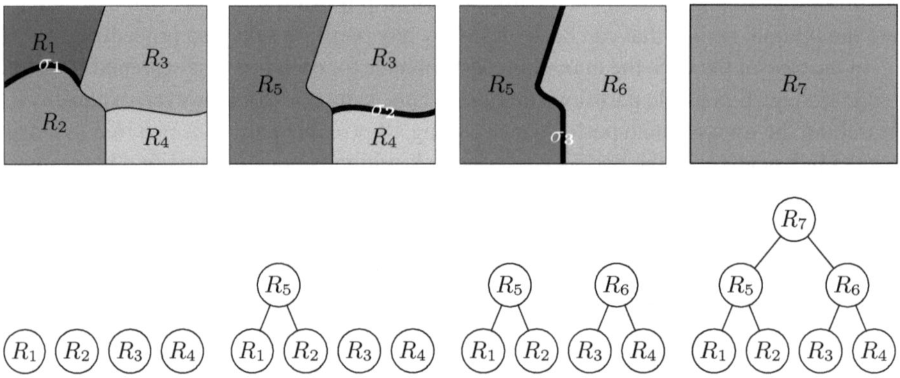

Fig. 1. BPT creation process: Above, the merging sequence partition set where, from left to right, two neighboring regions are merged at each step. The common boundary between them is highlighted. Below, the BPT representation depicted by a tree, where the region formed from the merging of two segments is represented as the parent of the two respective nodes.

The merging process ends when one single region remains, the whole image, which is represented by the root of the tree. The set of mergings that create the tree, from the starting partition to the whole image, is usually referred to as *merging sequence* and the set of partitions that are iteratively formed in the process is known as *merging-sequence partition set.*

To illustrate the process of creation of the hierarchies, Figure 1 shows the tree and the partition at each step of the merging sequence. In this example, the merging sequence is $\{R_1+R_2\rightarrow R_5\, , R_3+R_4\rightarrow R_6\, , R_5+R_6\rightarrow R_7\}$, and the merging-sequence partition set is formed by the four represented partitions.

3 Hierarchy Quality Assessment

The quality of a hierarchical region-based image representation is usually assessed in a supervised environment, that is, comparing how *accurate* the representation is with respect to a human-generated ground truth. Given that a hierarchical region-based image representation is a structured set of image partitions from the most detailed ones (more regions) to the coarsest ones (less regions), an intuitive approach to assess the representation could be to compare *a set* of representative partitions *selected* from the hierarchy and *aligned* by an index that represents the level of detail.

This is the approach followed in [8, 9], where the quality of the tree is represented by the assessment of the set of selected partitions in the so-called *merging-sequence partition set*, that is, the partitions formed at each step of the tree merging sequence. The number of regions is the index that represents the level of detail of the partitions. In other words, to assess the trees for various ground-truth images, the sets of partitions are put in correspondence by their number of regions to obtain an average result.

In [5], the same selection approach applies, but in this case the partitions to be assessed are selected via the thresholding of the Ultrametric Contour Map (UCM) at different levels of confidence. Therefore, the difference here is that the partitions are *aligned* with respect to this threshold value.

In other words, the same threshold for two UCM trees can correspond to different number of regions. This way, the aggregate results on a database will be different depending on the alignment used.

The strategy to average the results *aligning* them with respect to a certain parameter is referred to as Optimal Dataset Scale (ODS) in [5]. To avoid the dependence of the results of an alignment process, the same work proposes the Optimal Image Scale (OIS) which, in contrast, averages the quality of the best partition *in the selected set* for each image. That is, the rationale behind the OIS is to average the upper-bound performance of the UCM trees, avoiding the use of an *alignment*.

However, limiting the partitions assessed to those of a reduced set among all found in a hierarchy is also masking the real upper-bound performance of the technique, since this approach is not assessing all the partitions represented in the tree.

The proposal of this work is to find the upper-bound performance regardless also of the representative partition set selection, that is, independently of whether we assess those partitions from a thresholding of the UCM, those forming the set of merging-sequence partitions, etc. We will refer to the resulting selection strategies as upper-bound ODS and upper-bound OIS (ubODS and ubOIS, respectively).

The number of partitions represented in a binary tree, however, grows rapidly with respect to the number of initial regions, so it would not be feasible to assess all of them using brute force. To do so, the main objective of this paper is to model the problem as a *Linear Fractional Combinatorial Optimization* (LFCO) problem [10], which allows us to find the partitions that entail the upper-bound quality using a feasible algorithm.

The *F measure for boundary detection* (F_b) [5] measures the trade-off between the precision and recall of the matching between the boundary pixels of the ground truth and the assessed partition. Although this measure was initially designed to assess contour detectors, [5] states that: "While the relative ranking of segmentation algorithms remains fairly consistent across different benchmark criteria, the boundary benchmark appears most capable of discriminating performance."

As we will present on the following section, F_b can be written in the fractional form of an LFCO, and thus fulfills the objective of feasibility. Therefore, adding the good behavior of this measure perceived by [5], we will base our assessment on the F measure for boundary detection F_b.

4 Upper-Bound Partition Selection

The computation of F_b is based on a global optimal matching between the set of boundary pixels of the partition to be assessed and those of the ground truth. To avoid performing a matching for each of the partitions represented in a tree, which is computationally prohibitive, we propose an algorithm that performs a local matching between the ground truth and each of the *pieces* of region boundaries of the tree. This allows us to efficiently find the upper bound of the optimal global matching for any represented partition.

Formally, let P_0 be the partition on which a hierarchy H is built and $R_1 \ldots R_n$ its regions. Let $\{R_{i_1} + R_{i_2} \rightarrow R_{i_3}\}, i = 1 \ldots n-1$ be the merging sequence that forms H. We define σ_i as the common boundary between the regions that are merged at step i of the merging sequence. (Figure 1 depicts σ_1, σ_2, and σ_3 of the example tree.) Note that this set of common boundaries is not the full set of common boundaries between pairs of regions of P_0, but only those between regions merged in the hierarchy H.

Let $\mathcal{P}$ be the set of all partitions represented in the hierarchy H. Any partition $P \in H$ can be unequivocally described by the set of σ_i that forms its boundaries. Let $\mathbf{p} \in \{0,1\}^{n-1}$ be a binary vector such that $p_i = 1$ if the boundaries of P contain σ_i. In Figure 1, for example, the set of merging-sequence partitions can be identified by the vectors: $\mathbf{p} = (1, 1, 1)$, $(0, 1, 1)$, and $(0, 0, 1)$.

This way, one can define a bijection between the set of partitions $\mathcal{P}$ and a subset $\chi \subset \{0,1\}^{n-1}$. Our approach to find the partition that entails the best matching relies on modeling the problem as a binary search in χ and solving it using computationally feasible techniques.

Specifically, we will model the upper-bound partition selection as a Linear Fractional Combinatorial Optimization (LFCO) problem [10]:

$$\text{LFCO:} \quad \underset{\mathbf{x}}{\text{maximize}} \ \frac{\mathbf{t} \cdot \mathbf{x}^T}{\mathbf{f} \cdot \mathbf{x}^T} \qquad \text{s.t. } \mathbf{x} \in \chi \subset \{0,1\}^{n-1} \tag{1}$$

being $\mathbf{f},\mathbf{t} \in \mathbb{R}^{n-1}$ and all the constraints that define χ linear.

Section 4.1 explores the constraints that have to be put to the vector $\mathbf{p}$ in order for the corresponding partition to be valid within the hierarchy (that is, define χ) and how to make them linear. Next, Section 4.2 presents how the F_b of a partition with respect to a ground truth can be obtained from $\mathbf{p}$ in the form of an LFCO such as that of Equation 1. Finally, Section 4.3 adds the needed constraints to be able to find the ubODS.

4.1 Forcing the Partition to Be in the Hierarchy

Not all combinations of boundaries σ_i form a valid partition of the hierarchy and thus not all $\mathbf{p} \in \{0,1\}^{n-1}$ correspond to feasible solutions of our problem. Recalling the example of Figure 1, for instance, the partition corresponding to $[1\ 0\ 1]$ is a valid partition in the hierarchy, while the ones corresponding to $[1\ 0\ 0]$ or $[1\ 1\ 0]$ are not.

Let $\Sigma_i = \{i_j | j = 1 \ldots n_i\}$ be the indices of the set of boundaries σ_{i_j} between pairs of regions among the children of the two regions that define σ_i. In the example, for σ_3, $\Sigma_3 = \{1,2\}$.

Then, if the two regions that form σ_i are merged ($p_i = 0$), all the pairs of regions that form the boundaries indexed by Σ_i are forced to be also merged ($p_{i_j} = 0$). Formally $p_i = 0 \Rightarrow p_{i_j} = 0 \quad \forall\, i_j \in \Sigma_i$, or equivalently the following constraints:

$$p_i = 1 \quad \text{or} \quad \sum_{i_j \in \Sigma_i} p_{i_j} = 0 \tag{2}$$

In other words, if the boundary between two regions is not in the partition, the boundaries between any pair of their children cannot be in the partition either.

The binary search problem we are modeling will be much more efficient to solve if it is linear. The following linear constraint is equivalent to Equation 2:

$$\sum_{i_j \in \Sigma_i} p_{i_j} \le K\, p_i \tag{3}$$

where K is a *sufficiently large* constant, which in our problem can be set to n, the number of regions.

To conclude, the set of partitions represented in the hierarchy H can be identified with the set:

$$\chi = \left\{ \mathbf{p} \in \{0,1\}^{n-1} \,\middle|\, \sum_{i_j \in \Sigma_i} p_{i_j} \le n\, p_i \right\}.$$

In the sequel, any partition P in the hierarchy H will be identified by its corresponding binary vector $\mathbf{p} \in \chi$.

4.2 Upper-Bound Partition Selection as an LFCO

For a given partition $P \in H$ ($\mathbf{p} \in \chi$), let TP be the set of matched boundary pixels with the boundary pixels of a ground truth partition, i.e. true positives, and FP the false positives set. We can write that $|TP| = \sum_{i=1}^{n-1} p_i\, |\sigma_i^m|$, $|FP| = \sum_{i=1}^{n-1} p_i\, |\sigma_i^u|$, where $\sigma_i = \sigma_i^m \cup \sigma_i^u$ is a division of the boundary pixels between *matched* and *unmatched*, respectively.

The first approach we propose is to perform a single matching between the boundary pixels of the original partition P_0 and those of the ground-truth partition, and define σ_i^m and σ_i^u as those sets of pixels of σ_i matched or unmatched, respectively.

If we define $\boldsymbol{\sigma}^m = \left(|\sigma_1^m|, \ldots, |\sigma_{n-1}^m|\right) \in \mathbb{N}^{n-1}$, $\boldsymbol{\sigma} = \left(|\sigma_1|, \ldots, |\sigma_{n-1}|\right) \in \mathbb{N}^{n-1}$, the problem of finding the partition in the hierarchy with the best F_b with respect to the ground truth can be written as:

$$\mathcal{F}: \underset{\mathbf{p}}{\text{maximize}}\ F_b = 2\frac{(\boldsymbol{\sigma}^m,0) \cdot (\mathbf{p},1)^T}{(\boldsymbol{\sigma},|P_{gt}|) \cdot (\mathbf{p},1)^T}, \quad \text{s.t.} \quad (3)$$

This type of problem is referred to as a *Linear Fractional Combinatorial Optimization* (LFCO) problem in [10], which also presents an efficient way to solve it. The remainder of this section is devoted to present the limitation of this approach: the ground-truth multi-matching and the solution we propose.

Ground-Truth Multi-Matching

The previous matching strategy presents the following problem: the matching is carried out at the level of the original partition P_0, assuming it is optimal for all possible combinations of pieces of boundaries in the hierarchy. More precisely, this approach assumes that the sets σ_i^m and σ_i^u do not depend on the partition $\mathbf{p}$ being analyzed; or in other words, that the optimal matching for any partition $\mathbf{p}$ can be obtained from the initial matching on P_0.

In order to illustrate this problem, Figure 2 depicts an example partition (a) and the correspondent ground truth (b). If pixels are matched globally, as presented in the previous section, let us assume that all pixels in σ_1 are matched to all M ground-truth pixels. Then, we would have that $\sigma_1^m = M$ and $\sigma_2^m = 0$, that is, no pixel in σ_2 would be matched at the level of P_0. When computing the number of matched ground-truth pixels for the partition identified by $\mathbf{p} = (0,1)$, we would find that the number of matched pixels is $\boldsymbol{\sigma}^m \cdot \mathbf{p} = 0$, but the right portion of the ground-truth boundary should be matched to σ_2, that is, the correct result should be $\boldsymbol{\sigma}^m \cdot \mathbf{p} = M/2$.

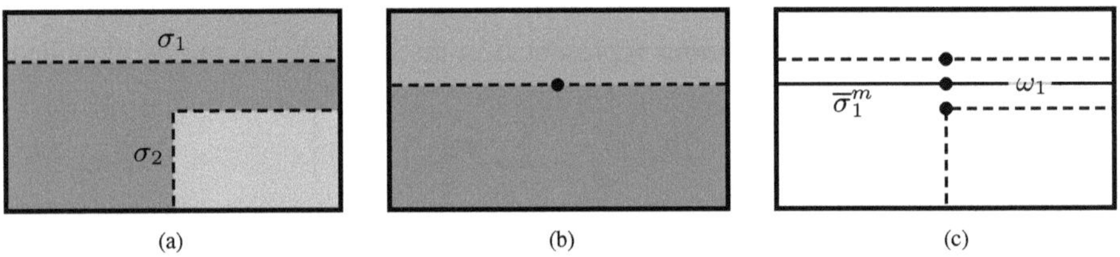

Fig. 2. Ground-truth multi-matching representation: (a) Partition being assessed, (b) ground truth, (c) both partitions overlaid. The points are plotted to highlight the division of the boundary pixels into sets.

The approach we propose to solve this issue is to perform $n-1$ matchings between the pixels of the ground-truth partition and those of each σ_i, and define σ_i^m and σ_i^u as those sets of pixels locally matched or unmatched, respectively. In other words, some pixels of the ground truth can be matched with more than one boundary segment, and thus we call it multi-matching.

Formally, once performed the $n-1$ matchings between the ground-truth boundary pixels and each σ_i, each boundary pixel of the ground truth may be matched to a boundary pixels of some σ_i (from 1 to $n-1$) of the partition. Understanding the set of indices of each σ_i involved in the multi matching as a *signature* of each of the ground-truth boundary pixels, we divide these ground-truth boundary pixels into groups of equal signature.

This way, for instance, we will have a set of unmatched pixels, $n-1$ sets of single-matched pixels which we will denote as $\overline{\sigma}_i^m$ (see Figure 2), and the rest will have more than one index in the signature. Intuitively, we will count a ground-truth boundary pixel as matched only if any of the σ_i in its signature is in the partition but not counting it more than once.

To do so, and in order to have a compact modeling, let us group the set of ground-truth boundary pixels with equal signature and define the set as ω_j. Moreover, let us assume we have m different multiple-index sets of pixels ω_j with signatures $\Omega_j = \{s_1^j, \ldots, s_k^j\}$. For instance, the pixels in the set ω_1 of the example of Figure 2 (see (c)) are each of them multi-matched to pixels in σ_1 and σ_2, then their signature is $\Omega_j = \{1, 2\}$. Let $\mathbf{q} \in \{0,1\}^m$ be a vector such that $q_j = 1$ if the set of pixels in ω_j should be considered as matched. The value of q_j is function of the values in the signature, that is, $q_j = 1$ if any $p_{s_i^j} = 1$ and 0 otherwise. Mathematically:

$$q_j = p_{s_1^j} \text{ or } p_{s_2^j} \text{ or } \cdots \text{ or } p_{s_{k_j}^j}$$

The equivalent linear constraints that define this equation are:

$$q_j \leq \sum_{s \in \Omega_j} p_s \tag{4}$$

$$q_j \geq p_s \qquad \forall\, s \in \Omega_j \tag{5}$$

Let us define $\overline{\boldsymbol{\sigma}} = \left(|\overline{\sigma}_1^m|, \ldots, |\overline{\sigma}_{n-1}^m|\right) \in \mathbb{N}^{n-1}$ be the vector of single-matched number of ground-truth boundary pixels for each σ_i, and $\boldsymbol{\omega} = (|\omega_1|, \ldots, |\omega_m|) \in \mathbb{N}^m$ the vector of the number of ground-truth boundary pixels with equal signature. Then, the problem $\mathcal{F}$ can be rewritten as:

$$\begin{aligned} \mathcal{F}: \underset{\mathbf{p},\mathbf{q}}{\text{maximize}} \;\; & F_b = 2\frac{(\overline{\boldsymbol{\sigma}}, \boldsymbol{\omega}, 0) \cdot (\mathbf{p}, \mathbf{q}, 1)^T}{(\boldsymbol{\sigma}, \mathbf{0}, |P_{gt}|) \cdot (\mathbf{p}, \mathbf{q}, 1)^T} \\ \text{subject to} \;\; & (3), (4), (5) \end{aligned} \tag{6}$$

which, as wanted, fulfills the form of an LFCO as in Equation 1, identifying $\mathbf{x} = (\mathbf{p}, \mathbf{q}, 1)$ as the binary-valued variable of the problem.

4.3 ubODS: Sweeping the Number of Regions

The problem 6 finds the optimal single partition in terms of F_b so, in other words, it finds the upper-bound Optimal Image Scale (ubOIS) partition. Given that a hierarchy represents a collection of partitions of varying number of regions, it would also be desirable to explore the upper-bound Optimal Dataset Scale (ubODS) from sweeping a varied range of number of regions.

To do so, we add the following constraint, that forces the result to have a specific number of regions N: $\sum_i p_i = N - 1$, and sweep all the values of N between 1 and n.

5 Experiments

We compare the upper-bound partition selection technique against the merging-sequence partition analysis on four different hierarchies. The first one is the Ultrametric Contour Map (UCM) tree [5]. Then, two different BPT: the Normalized Weighted Euclidean distance between Models with Contour complexity (NWMC) tree [8], and the Independent Identically Distributed - Kullback Leibler (IID-KL) tree [9]. As a baseline we use a randomly-generated tree (Random), that is, a tree that is formed by iteratively merging random pairs of neighboring regions.

The trees are built on the 200 test images of the BSDS500 [5]. Each tree is compared with each of the multiple ground-truth partitions available and the result averaged, as proposed by [11] to handle multiple-partition ground truths. In order for the comparison to be fair, the base partition P_0 on which the tree is built is the same for the four techniques: the one obtained with the UCM with 100 regions.

The upper-bound partition selection algorithm is implemented in MATLAB, publicly available at `https://imatge.upc.edu/web/?q=node/1352`. The optimization itself of the LFCO is done by the IBM ILOG CPLEX Optimizer (free of charge for academic use), which is called directly by the MATLAB code. The scripts to fully reproduce the experiments and figures of this paper are also released.

In turn, the boundary matching code used in all the experiments has been obtained from [12]. Note that, this original code represents the boundaries of a partition in the *pixel grid*, that is, as a mask in which the pixels swept by the boundaries moved half pixel up and left are activated, which leads to an ambiguous representation. This ambiguity can be solved using the *contour grid* [13], which we use in our code. The numerical impact of this change of representation is not significant but the code obtained is much simpler and more readable.

5.1 ODS and OIS

Table 1 shows the mean Optimal Dataset Scale (ODS) and Optimal Image Scale (OIS) F_b values for the 200 image ground-truth pairs, and for the four compared hierarchies. The two first columns refer to the merging-sequence partition selection technique and the two last columns show the values for the upper-bound partition selection technique.

Comparing the quality of the hierarchies, the UCM tree presents better results than the rest of hierarchies. However, the main objective of this paper is not to compare the hierarchies themselves, but the partition selection techniques on which the assessment is based.

Regarding the comparison between ODS and OIS, the latter is coherently higher than the former. An improvement is also observed between the merging-sequence and the upper-bound techniques, which is, again, coherent with the theory.

Moreover, what really makes the difference between comparison techniques is their relative values, that is, how well the assessment discriminates the quality between the

Table 1. ODS and OIS F_b values for the merging-sequence and upper-bound partition selection techniques

	Merging sequence		Upper bound	
	ODS	OIS	ubODS	ubOIS
UCM	0.587	0.622	0.669	0.695
NWMC	0.542	0.581	0.658	0.684
IID-KL	0.538	0.571	0.634	0.654
Random	0.523	0.537	0.589	0.603

Table 2. Relative ODS and OIS F_b values for the merging-sequence and upper-bound partition selection techniques

	Merging sequence		Upper bound	
	ODS	OIS	ubODS	ubOIS
UCM	1	1	1	1
NWMC	0.30	0.51	0.86	0.89
IID-KL	0.23	0.40	0.56	0.56
Random	0	0	0	0

different hierarchies. In particular, good assessment techniques should be able to correctly discriminate between a random tree and the other techniques. To evaluate this aspect, Table 2 shows the relative values of ODS and OIS, that is, assigning 0 to the random tree, 1 to UCM, and scaling the rest of the values accordingly.

If the measurement techniques were equivalent, the relative values should not change, but there are significant differences in these relative values, meaning that the conclusions extracted from the assessment can vary depending on the criterion used.

As introduced previously, a desirable property of the assessment techniques is a high discrimination of the random tree. In other words, it is obvious that the random trees must be far away from any *real* hierarchy. Under this point of view, the upper-bound assessment provides much better behavior.

As an example, the IID-KL tree is much closer to the random tree than to the UCM tree for ODS, while for the upper-bound ODS (ubODS), the IID-KL tree is halfway between the two, which is qualitatively more accurate.

The improvement obtained in the OIS with respect to the ODS highlights the relevance of the alignment algorithm on the results obtained. The same way, the improvement of the upper-bound analysis ubODS and ubOIS with respect to ODS and OIS is an indicator of the impact of the partition selection algorithm on the assessment.

Focusing on the sorting of the algorithm quality for the two top-rated hierarchies (UCM and NWMC), in 529 of the 1800 cases studied (9 parameterizations on 200 images), the ranking provided by the merging sequence analysis is not coherent with the one provided by the upper-bound. In other words, different partition selection strategies can lead to different decisions with respect to which is the best hierarchy based on a supervised assessment.

5.2 Upper-Bound Precision-Recall Curves

A region-based hierarchy is a structured set of image partitions at different scales, and thus comparing them to non-hierarchical partitions via the OIS and ODS F_b may obviate the assessment of some parts of the tree. The precision recall curves on boundary detection, instead, can give us a global picture of the quality of the hierarchy, sweeping the partitions at different scales.

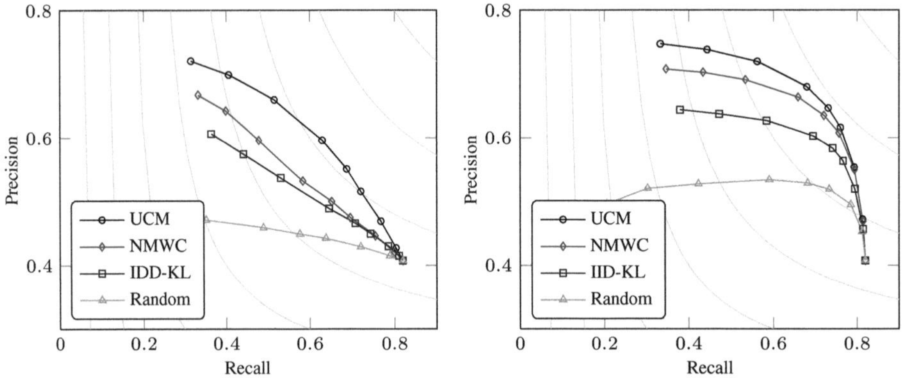

Fig. 3. Merging-sequence (left) and upper-bound (right) precision-recall curves

Figure 3 shows the precision-recall curves for the four hierarchies studied. In the figure of the left, the points have been obtained using the merging-sequence partition selection whereas, in the figure of the right, the proposed upper-bound partition selection has been used.

In the range of interest of the hierarchies, that is, the range of better F_b, similarly to the results of the previous section, the upper-bound precision-recall curves better discriminate between the random hierarchy and the rest of trees. In the range of higher number of regions, close to the leaves of the tree, the different curves are much closer than in the merging sequence, which reflects that, in this range, the original partition is more influent than the hierarchy itself. Note that, coherently, all curves meet in the point corresponding to 100 regions, because each tree contains only one partition with the maximum level of detail: P_0.

To better visualize the differences between the precision-recall curves and their upper-bound equivalents, Figure 4 shows them both in the same axis, leaving the IDD-KL tree out for the sake of clarity of the plot.

Note that, for each type of hierarchy, both curves start from the same point at high number of regions and tend to converge for few regions. In the middle range, corresponding also to the better F_b values, the gain obtained with the upper-bound assessment is much more relevant for the NWMC tree than for the rest of trees, which reinforces the possibility that different partition selection techniques can lead to discrepant results.

5.3 Computational Cost

Although a supervised assessment is usually performed offline, a reduced computational cost is of paramount importance. The faster the method is, the larger the datasets in which researchers will tune and test their algorithms, which results in a more solid research. This section compares the computational cost of the proposed evaluation techniques (ubODS and ubOIS) in front of ODS and OIS.

ODS requires computing the boundary matching for k different number of regions, thus the whole time is k times the cost of a boundary matching, which we will refer to as $t(BM)$. OIS requires the ODS computation and find the F_b maximum for

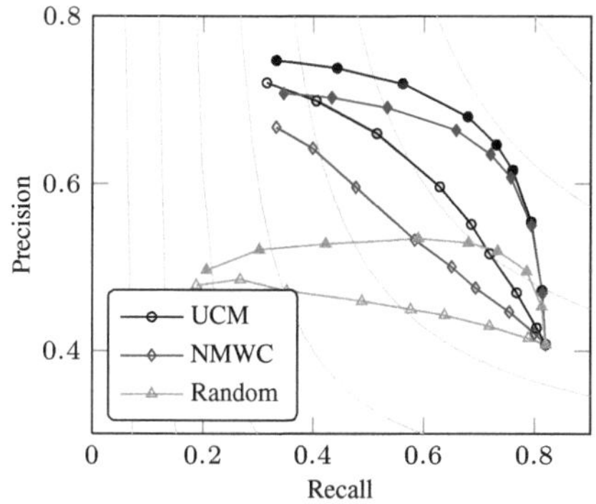

Fig. 4. Merging sequence (unfilled markers) versus upper-bound (filled markers)

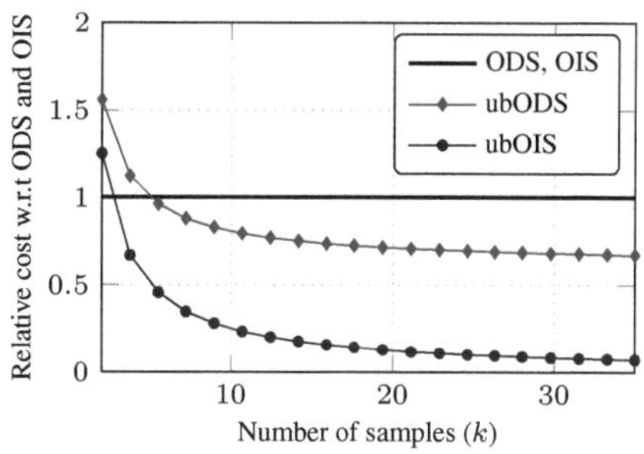

Fig. 5. Computational cost analysis for varying number of samples (k)

each image, so the cost is also $k \cdot t(BM)$. The cost of ubODS is one boundary multi-matching $t(BMM)$ and k LFCO optimizations $t(LFCO)$. Finally, the cost of ubOIS is $t(BMM) + t(LFCO)$, since one single optimization finds the optimal number of regions, thus not needing the computation of ubODS.

The mean values obtained in the experiments for each of these processes are: $t(BM) = 0.34\,s$, $t(BMM) = 0.64\,s$, and $t(LFCO) = 0.21s$. Thus, the mean time spent for each technique is $t(ODS)=t(OIS)=k \cdot 0.34\,s$, $t(ubODS)=0.64+k\cdot 0.21\,s$, and $t(ubOIS)=0.85\,s$. Figure 5 shows the relative cost of the upper-bound techniques with respect to the cost of the merging-sequence ones. The higher the number of samples k, the lower the relative cost of the upper-bound techniques. The computation of ubODS is approximately 25% faster than ODS and OIS, while ubOIS, thanks to the fact that a single optimization is enough, is considerably faster.

5.4 Worst-Discrepancy Graphical Results

To get a qualitative idea of the type of discrepancies between the region selection techniques, Figure 6 shows the most discrepant example of partition selection on the UCM tree for 6, 10, and 20 regions selected, that is, the three results whose partition selected in the merging sequence is more dissimilar with the upper-bound one.

The differences observed between the two strategies are visually relevant. In the first and second columns (6 and 10 regions), the merging sequence analysis obviates the main object of interest or part of it, while in the upper-bound partition selection the object is present in the selected partition. In the last column (20 regions) the upper-bound selection is capable of highlighting the higher importance of the background object with respect to the background as in the ground truth.

To sum up, the upper-bound partitions (Figure 6.d) represent the quality of the tree much better than those of the merging sequence (Figure 6.c), or in other words, the region selection masks the actual quality of the tree.

(a)
(b)
(c)
(d)

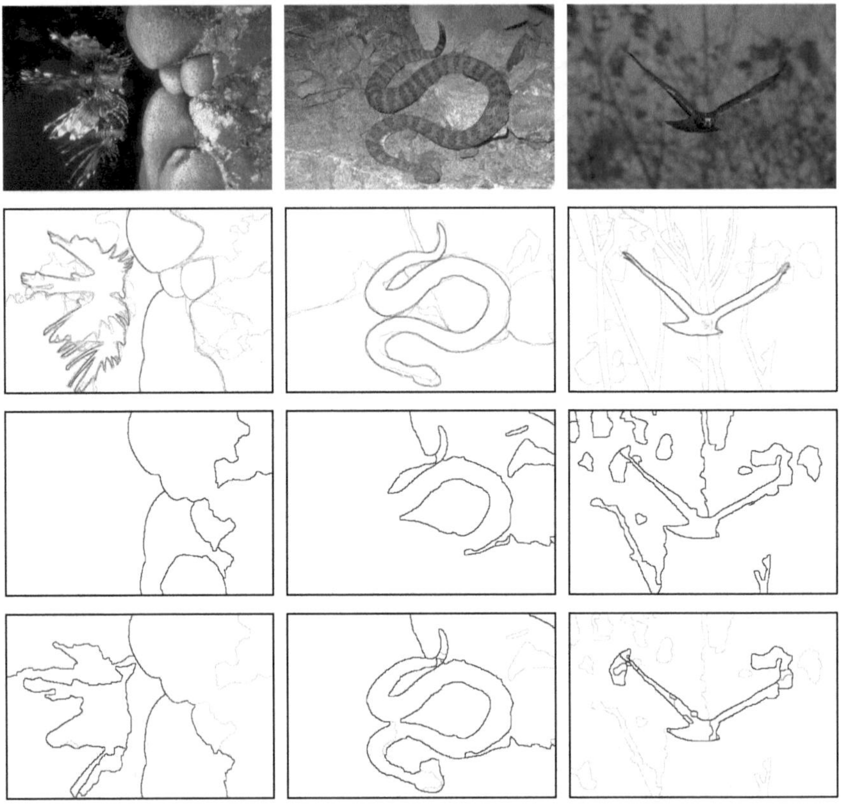

Fig. 6. Worst-case results on UCM trees: (a) images of the BSDS500 test set, (b) their multiple ground-truth partitions, (c) partitions selected from the merging sequence with 6, 10, and 20 regions, respectively, and (d) the upper-bound partitions with the same number of regions

6 Conclusions

This paper presents the upper-bound partition selection algorithm as a supervised assessment of hierarchical region-based image representations. It consists in finding, among all possible partitions represented in the hierarchy, the partition that best match the ground truth, instead of assessing just a reduced set of representative partitions.

The quality assessment measure used is the so-called F measure for boundary detection (F_b), which is known to present a good behavior among the existing measures. To be able to efficiently analyze all possible partitions in a hierarchy, we model the problem as a Linear Fractional Combinatorial Optimization (LFCO) problem.

The experiments show that the ubODS and ubOIS assessment techniques better represent the quality of the tree: 1) they cover partitions that are omitted in the merging sequence (and are used in image analysis works) and reach much better F_b values, 2) their performance discrimination between the random and the actual techniques is much better. Some visual examples corroborate that the merging-sequence selected partitions are not good representatives of the quality of the tress. Overall, an assessment based on the previous techniques in the literature can mislead the conclusions that can be extracted.

We make the MATLAB code to compute the ubODS and ubOIS publicly available, as well as all the scripts to fully reproduce the experiments and figures of this paper.

References

1. Salembier, P., Garrido, L.: Binary partition tree as an efficient representation for image processing, segmentation, and information retrieval. IEEE Transactions on Image Processing 9(4), 561–576 (2000)
2. Huihai, L., Woods, J.C., Ghanbari, M.: Binary partition tree analysis based on region evolution and its application to tree simplification. IEEE Transactions on Image Processing 16(4), 1131–1138 (2007)
3. Cardelino, J., Caselles, V., Bertalmio, M., Randall, G.: A contrario hierarchical image segmentation. In: IEEE International Conference on Image Processing, pp. 4041–4044 (2009)
4. McGuinness, K., O'connor: A comparative evaluation of interactive segmentation algorithms. Pattern Recognition 43, 434–444 (2010)
5. Arbeláez, P., Maire, M., Fowlkes, C.C., Malik, J.: Contour detection and hierarchical image segmentation. IEEE Transactions on Pattern Analysis and Machine Intelligence 33(5), 898–916 (2011)
6. Pont-Tuset, J., Marques, F.: Contour detection using binary partition trees. In: IEEE International Conference on Image Processing, pp. 1609–1612 (2010)
7. Hunter, G.M., Steiglitz, K.: Operations on images using quad trees. IEEE Transactions on Pattern Analysis and Machine Intelligence 1(2), 145–153 (1979)
8. Vilaplana, V., Marques, F., Salembier, P.: Binary partition trees for object detection. IEEE Transactions on Image Processing 17(11), 2201–2216 (2008)
9. Calderero, F., Marques, F.: Region merging techniques using information theory statistical measures. IEEE Transactions on Image Processing 19(6), 1567–1586 (2010)
10. Radzik, T.: Newton's method for fractional combinatorial optimization. In: Symposium on Foundations of Computer Science, pp. 659–669 (1992)
11. Unnikrishnan, R., Pantofaru, C., Hebert, M.: Toward objective evaluation of image segmentation algorithms. IEEE Transactions on Pattern Analysis and Machine Intelligence 29(6), 929–944 (2007)
12. Martin, D., Fowlkes, C., Malik, J.: Learning to detect natural image boundaries using local brightness, color, and texture cues. IEEE Transactions on Pattern Analysis and Machine Intelligence 26(5), 530–549 (2004)
13. Nunes, P., Marques, F., Pereira, F., Gasull, A.: A contour-based approach to binary shape coding using a multiple grid chain code. Signal Processing: Image Communication 15(7-8), 585–599 (2000)

Image Labeling on a Network: Using Social-Network Metadata for Image Classification

Julian McAuley and Jure Leskovec

Stanford University
{jmcauley,jure}@cs.stanford.edu

Abstract. Large-scale image retrieval benchmarks invariably consist of images from the Web. Many of these benchmarks are derived from online photo sharing networks, like Flickr, which in addition to hosting images also provide a highly interactive social community. Such communities generate rich metadata that can naturally be harnessed for image classification and retrieval. Here we study four popular benchmark datasets, extending them with social-network metadata, such as the groups to which each image belongs, the comment thread associated with the image, who uploaded it, their location, and their network of friends. Since these types of data are inherently relational, we propose a model that explicitly accounts for the interdependencies between images sharing common properties. We model the task as a binary labeling problem on a network, and use structured learning techniques to learn model parameters. We find that social-network metadata are useful in a variety of classification tasks, in many cases outperforming methods based on image content.

Keywords: Image Classification, Social Networks, Structured Learning.

1 Introduction

Recently, research on image retrieval and classification has focused on large image databases collected from the Web. Many of these datasets are built from online photo sharing communities such as Flickr [1,2,3,4] and even collections built from image search engines [5] consist largely of Flickr images.

Such communities generate vast amounts of metadata as users interact with their images, and with each other, though only a fraction of such data are used by the research community. The most commonly used form of metadata considered in multimodal classification settings is the set of *tags* associated with each image. In [6] the authors study the relationship between tags and manual annotations, with the goal of recovering annotations using a combination of tags and image content. The problem of recommending tags was studied in [7], where possible tags were obtained from similar images and similar users. The same problem was studied in [8], who exploit the relationships between tags to suggest future

A. Fitzgibbon et al. (Eds.): ECCV 2012, Part IV, LNCS 7575, pp. 828–841, 2012.

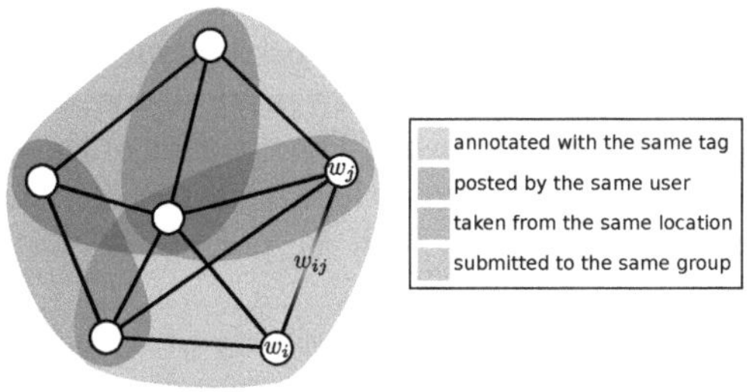

Fig. 1. The proposed relational model for image classification. Each node represents an image, with cliques formed from images sharing common properties. 'Common properties' can include (for example) *communities*, e.g. images submitted to a group; *collections*, e.g. sets created by a user; *annotations*, e.g. tag data; and *user data*, e.g. the photo's uploader and their network of friends.

tags based on existing ones. Friendship information between users was studied for tag recommendation in [9], and in [10] for the case of Facebook.

Another commonly used source of metadata comes directly from the camera, in the form of *exif* and *GPS* data [11,12,13,14]. Such metadata can be used to determine whether two photos were taken by the same person, or from the same location, which provides an informative signal for certain image categories.

Our goal in this paper is to assess what *other* types of metadata may be beneficial, including the groups, galleries, and collections in which each image was stored, the text descriptions and comment threads associated with each image, and user profile information including their location and their network of friends. In particular, we focus on the following three questions: (1) How can we effectively model relational data generated by the social-network? (2) How can such metadata be harnessed for image classification and labeling? (3) What types of metadata are useful for different image labeling tasks?

Focusing on the first question we build on the intuition that images sharing similar tags and appearance are likely to have similar labels [2]. In the case of image tags, simple nearest-neighbor type methods have been proposed to 'propagate' annotations between similar images [15]. However, unlike image labels and tags – which are categorical – much of the metadata derived from social networks is inherently *relational*, such as collections of images posted by a user or submitted to a certain group, or the networks of contacts among users. We argue that to appropriately leverage these types of data requires us to *explicitly* model the relationships between images, an argument also made in [16].

To address the relational nature of social-network data, we propose a graphical model that treats image classification as a problem of simultaneously predicting binary labels for a network of photos. Figure 1 illustrates our model: nodes represent images, and edges represent *relationships* between images. Our intuition that images sharing common properties are likely to share labels allows us to exploit techniques from supermodular optimization, allowing us to efficiently make binary predictions on all images simultaneously [17].

In the following sections, we study the extent to which categorical predictions about images can be made using social-network metadata. We first describe how we augment four popular datasets with a variety of metadata from Flickr. We then consider three image labeling tasks. The creators of these datasets obtained labels through crowdsourcing and from the Flickr user community. Labels range from objective, everyday categories such as 'person' or 'bicycle', to subjective concepts such as 'happy' and 'boring'.

We show that social-network metadata reliably provide *context* not contained in the image itself. Metadata based on common galleries, image locations, and the author of the image tend to be the most informative in a range classification scenarios. Moreover, we show that the proposed relational model outperforms a 'flat' SVM-like model, which means that it is essential to model the relationships between images in order to exploit these social-network features.

2 Dataset Construction and Description

We study four popular datasets that have groundtruth provided by human annotators. Because each of these datasets consists entirely of images from Flickr, we can enrich them with social network metadata, using Flickr's publicly available API. The four image collections we consider are described below:

- The *PASCAL Visual Object Challenge* ('PASCAL') consists of over 12,000 images collected since 2007, with additional images added each year [1]. Flickr sources are available only for training images, and for the test images from 2007. Flickr sources were available for 11,197 images in total.
- The *MIR Flickr Retrieval Evaluation* ('MIR') consists of one million images, 25,000 of which have been annotated [2]. Flickr sources were available for 15,203 of the annotated images.
- The *ImageCLEF Annotation Task* ('CLEF') uses a subset of 18,000 images from the MIR dataset, though the correspondence is provided only for 8,000 training images [3]. Flickr sources were available for 4,807 images.
- The *NUS Web Image Database* ('NUS') consists of approximately 270,000 images [4]. Flickr sources are available for all images.

Flickr sources for the above photos were provided by the dataset creators. Using Flickr's API we obtained the following metadata for each photo in the above datasets:

- The photo itself
- Photo data, including the photo's title, description, location, timestamp, viewcount, upload date, etc.
- User information, including the uploader's name, username, location, their network of contacts, etc.
- Photo tags, and the user who provided each tag
- Groups to which the image was submitted (only the uploader can submit a photo to a group)

Table 1. Dataset statistics. The statistics reveal large differences between the datasets, for instance images in MIR have more tags and comments than images in PASCAL, presumably due to MIR's bias towards 'interesting' images [2]; few images in PASCAL belong to galleries, owing to the fact that most of the dataset was collected before this feature was introduced in 2009. Note that the number of tags per image is typically slightly higher than what is reported in [2,3,4], as there may be additional tags that appeared in Flickr since the datasets were originally created.

	CLEF	PASCAL	MIR	NUS	ALL
Number of photos	**4546**	**10189**	**14460**	**244762**	**268587**
Number of users	2663	8698	5661	48870	58522
Photos per user	1.71	1.17	2.55	5.01	4.59
Number of tags	21192	27250	51040	422364	450003
Tags per photo	10.07	7.17	10.24	19.31	18.36
Number of groups	10575	6951	21894	95358	98659
Groups per photo	5.09	1.80	5.28	12.56	11.77
Number of comments	77837	16669	248803	9837732	10071439
Comments per photo	17.12	1.64	17.21	40.19	37.50
Number of sets	6066	8070	15854	165039	182734
Sets per photo	1.71	0.87	1.72	1.95	1.90
Number of galleries	1026	155	3728	100189	102116
Galleries per photo	0.23	0.02	0.27	0.67	0.62
Number of locations	1007	1222	2755	22106	23745
Number of labels	**99**	**20**	**14**	**81**	**214**
Labels per photo	11.81	1.95	0.93	1.89	2.04

- Collections (or sets) in which the photo was included (users create collections from their own photos)
- Galleries in which the photo was included (a single user creates a gallery only from *other* users' photos)
- Comment threads for each photo

We only consider images from the above datasets where *all* of the above data was available, which represents about 90% of the images for which the original Flickr source was available (to be clear, we include images where this data is *absent*, such as images with no tags, but not where it is *missing*, i.e., where an API call fails, presumably due to the photo having been deleted from Flickr). Properties of the data we obtained are shown in Table 1. Note in particular that the *ratios* in Table 1 are not uniform across datasets, for example the NUS dataset favors 'popular' photos that are highly tagged, submitted to many groups, and highly commented on; in fact all types of metadata are more common in images from NUS than for other datasets. The opposite is true for PASCAL, which has the least metadata per photo, which could be explained by the fact that certain features (such as galleries) did not exist on Flickr when most of the dataset was created. Details about these datasets can be found in [1,2,3,4].

In Figure 2 we study the relationship between various types of Flickr metadata and image labels. Images sharing common tags are likely to share common labels [15], though Figure 2 reveals similar behavior for nearly all types of metadata.

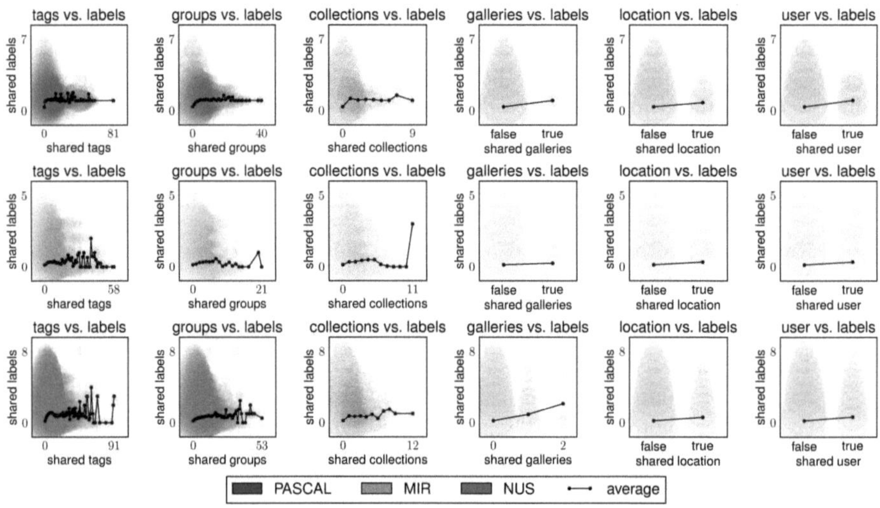

Fig. 2. Relationships between Flickr metadata and image labels provided by external evaluators. All figures are best viewed in color. Scatterplots show the number of images that share a pair of properties in common, with radii scaled according to the logarithm of the number of images at each coordinate. All pairs of properties have positive correlation coefficients. ImageCLEF data is suppressed, as it is a subset of MIR and has similar behavior.

Groups are similar to tags in quantity and behavior: images that share even a single group or tag are much more likely to have common labels, and for images sharing *many* groups or tags, it is very unlikely that they will not share at least one label. The same observation holds for collections and galleries, though it is rarer that photos have these properties in common. Photos taken at the same location, or by the same user also have a significantly increased likelihood of sharing labels [11]. Overall, this indicates that the image metadata provided by the interactions of the Flickr photo-sharing community correlates with image labels that are provided by the external human evaluators.

All code and data is available from the authors' webpages.[1]

3 Model

The three tasks we shall study are label prediction (i.e., predicting groundtruth labels using image metadata), tag prediction, and group recommendation. As we shall see, each of these tasks can be thought of as a problem of predicting *binary* labels for each of the images in our datasets.

Briefly, our goal in this section is to describe a binary graphical model for each image category (which might be a label, tag, or group), as depicted in Figure 1.

[1] `http://snap.stanford.edu/`, `http://i.stanford.edu/~julian/`

Table 2. Notation

Notation	Description
$\mathcal{X} = \{x_n \dots x_N\}$	An image dataset consisting of N images
$\mathcal{L} = \{-1, 1\}^L$	A label space consisting of L categories.
$y^n \in \mathcal{L}$	The groundtruth labeling for the image x_n.
$y_c^n \in \{-1, 1\}$	The groundtruth for a particular category c.
$Y_c \in \{-1, 1\}^N$	The groundtruth for the entire dataset for category c.
$\bar{y}_c(x_n; \Theta_c) \in \{-1, 1\}$	The prediction made image x_n and category c.
$\bar{Y}_c(\mathcal{X}; \Theta_c) \in \{-1, 1\}^N$	Predictions across the entire dataset for category c.
$\theta_c^{\text{node}} \in \mathbb{R}^{F_1}$	Parameters of first-order features for category c.
$\theta_c^{\text{edge}} \in \mathbb{R}^{F_2}$	Parameters of second-order features for category c.
$\Theta_c = (\theta_c^{\text{node}}; \theta_c^{\text{edge}})$	Full parameter vector for category c.
$\phi_c(x_i) \in \mathbb{R}^{F_1}$	Features of the image x_i for category c.
$\phi_c(x_i, x_j) \in \mathbb{R}^{F_2}$	Features of the pair of images (x_i, x_j) for category c.
$\Phi_c(\mathcal{X}, Y) \in \mathbb{R}^{F_1+F_2}$	Aggregate features for labeling the entire dataset $\mathcal{X}$ as $Y \in \{-1, 1\}^N$ for category c.
$\Delta(Y, Y_c) \in \mathbb{R}_+$	The error induced by making the prediction Y when the correct labeling is Y_c.

Each node represents an image; the weight w_i encodes the potential for a node to belong to the category in question, given its features; the weights w_{ij} encode the potential for two images to have the *same* prediction for that category. We first describe the 'standard' SVM model, and then describe how we extend it to include relational features.

The notation we use throughout the paper is summarized in Table 2. Suppose we have a set of images $\mathcal{X} = \{x_n \dots x_N\}$, each of which has an associated groundtruth labeling $y^n \in \{-1, 1\}^L$, where each y_c^n indicates positive or negative membership to a particular category $c \in \{1 \dots L\}$. Our goal is to learn a classifier that predicts y_c^n from (some features of) the image x_n.

The 'Standard' Setting. Max-margin SVM training assumes a classifier of the form

$$\bar{y}_c(x_n, \Theta_c) = \underset{y \in \{-1,1\}}{\operatorname{argmax}}\, y \cdot \langle \phi_c(x_n), \Theta_c \rangle, \tag{1}$$

so that x_n has a positive label whenever $\langle \phi_c(x_n), \Theta_c \rangle$ is positive. $\phi_c(x_n)$ is a *feature vector* associated with the image x_n for category c, and Θ_c is a *parameter vector*, which is selected so that the predictions made by the classifier of (eq. 1) match the groundtruth labeling. Note that a *different* parameter vector Θ_c is learned for each category c, i.e., the model makes the assumption that the labels for each category are independent.

Models similar to that of (eq. 1) (which we refer to as 'flat' models since they consider each image independently and thus ignore relationships between images) are routinely applied to classification based on image features [18], and have also been used for classification based on image tags, where as features one can simply create indicator vectors encoding the presence or absence of each tag [2]. In practice this means that for each tag one learns its influence on the presence of each label. For image tags, this approach seems well motivated, since tags are *categorical* attributes. What this also means is that the tag vocabulary – though large – ought to grow sublinearly with the number of photos (see Table 1), meaning that a more accurate model of each tag can be learned as the dataset grows. Based on the same reasoning, we encode group and text information (from image titles, descriptions, and comments) in a similar way.

Modeling Relational Metadata. Other types of metadata are more naturally treated as *relational*, such as the network of contacts between Flickr users. Moreover, as we observed in Table 1, even for the largest datasets we only observe a very small number of photos per user, gallery, or collection. This means it would not be practical to learn a separate 'flat' model for each category. However, as we saw in Figure 2, it may still be worthwhile to model the fact that photos from the same gallery are likely to have similar labels (similarly for users, locations, collections, and contacts between users).

We aim to learn *shared* parameters for these features. Rather than learning the extent to which membership to a particular collection (resp. gallery, user) influences the presence of a particular label, we learn the extent to which a pair of images that belong to the *same* gallery are likely to have *the same* label. In terms of graphical models, this means that we form a *clique* from photos sharing common metadata (as depicted in Figure 1).

These relationships between images mean that classification can no longer be performed independently for each image as in (eq. 1). Instead, our predictor $\bar{Y}_c(\mathcal{X}, \Theta_c)$ labels the entire dataset at once, and takes the form

$$\bar{Y}_c(\mathcal{X}, \Theta_c) = \operatorname*{argmax}_{Y \in \{-1,1\}^N} \sum_{i=1}^{N} y_i \cdot \underbrace{\langle \phi_c(x_i), \theta_c^{\text{node}} \rangle}_{w_i} + \sum_{i=1}^{N} \sum_{j=1}^{N} \delta(y_i = y_j) \underbrace{\langle \phi_c(x_i, x_j), \theta_c^{\text{edge}} \rangle}_{w_{ij}}, \tag{2}$$

where $\phi_c(x_i, x_j)$ is a feature vector encoding the relationship between images x_i and x_j, and $\delta(y_i = y_j)$ is an indicator that takes the value 1 when we make the same binary prediction for both images x_i and x_j. The first term of (eq. 2) is essentially the same as (eq. 1), while the second term encodes relationships between images. Note that (eq. 2) is linear in $\Theta_c = (\theta_c^{\text{node}}; \theta_c^{\text{edge}})$, i.e., it can be rewritten as

$$\bar{Y}_c(\mathcal{X}, \Theta_c) = \operatorname*{argmax}_{Y \in \{-1,1\}^N} \langle \Phi_c(\mathcal{X}, Y), \Theta_c \rangle. \tag{3}$$

Since (eq. 2) is a binary optimization problem consisting of pairwise terms, we can cast it as *maximum a posteriori* (MAP) inference in a graphical model, where each node corresponds to an image, and edges are formed between images that have some property in common.

Despite the large maximal clique size of the graph in question, we note that MAP inference in a pairwise, binary graphical model is tractable so long as the pairwise term is *supermodular*, in which case the problem can be solved using graph-cuts [17,19]. A pairwise potential $f(y_i, y_j)$ is said to be supermodular if

$$f(-1,-1) + f(1,1) \geq f(-1,1) + f(1,-1), \tag{4}$$

which in terms of (eq. 2) is satisfied so long as

$$\langle \phi_c(x_i, x_j), \theta_c^{\text{edge}} \rangle \geq 0. \tag{5}$$

Assuming positive features $\phi_c(x_i, x_j)$, a sufficient (but not necessary) condition to satisfy (eq. 5) is $\theta_c^{\text{edge}} \geq \mathbf{0}$, which in practice is what we shall enforce when we learn the optimal parameters $\Theta_c = (\theta_c^{\text{node}}; \theta_c^{\text{edge}})$. Note that this is a particularly weak assumption: all we are saying is that photos sharing common properties are *more likely* to have similar labels than different ones. The plots in Figure 2 appear to support this assumption.

We solve (eq. 2) using the graph-cuts software of [20]. For the largest dataset we consider (NUS), inference using the proposed model takes around 10 seconds on a standard desktop machine, i.e., less than 10^{-4} seconds per image. During the parameter learning phase, which we discuss next, memory is a more significant concern, since for practical purposes we store all feature vectors in memory simultaneously. Where this presented an issue, we retained only those edge features with the most non-zero entries up to the memory limit of our machine. Addressing this shortcoming using recent work on distributed graph-cuts remains an avenue for future study [21].

4 Parameter Learning

In this section we describe how popular *structured learning* techniques can be used to find model parameter values Θ_c so that the predictions made by (eq. 2) are consistent with those of the groundtruth Y_c. We assume an estimator based on the principle of regularized risk minimization [22], i.e., the optimal parameter vector Θ_c^* satisfies

$$\Theta_c^* = \underset{\Theta}{\operatorname{argmin}} \Bigg[\underbrace{\Delta(\bar{Y}(\mathcal{X};\Theta), Y_c)}_{\text{empirical risk}} + \underbrace{\frac{\lambda}{2} \|\Theta\|^2}_{\text{regularizer}} \Bigg], \tag{6}$$

where $\Delta(\bar{Y}(\mathcal{X};\Theta), Y_c)$ is some *loss function* encoding the error induced by predicting the labels $\bar{Y}(\mathcal{X};\Theta)$ when the correct labels are Y_c, and λ is a hyperparameter controlling the importance of the regularizer.

We use an analogous approach to that of SVMs [22], by optimizing a convex upper bound on the structured loss of (eq. 6). The resulting optimization problem is

$$[\Theta^*, \xi^*] = \underset{\Theta,\xi}{\operatorname{argmin}} \left[\xi + \lambda \|\Theta\|^2 \right] \tag{7a}$$

$$\text{s.t. } \langle \Phi(\mathcal{X}, Y_c), \Theta \rangle - \langle \Phi(\mathcal{X}, Y), \Theta \rangle \geq \Delta(Y, Y_c) - \xi, \tag{7b}$$

$$\theta_c^{\text{edge}} \geq \mathbf{0} \quad \forall Y \in \{-1,1\}^N.$$

Note the presence of the additional constraint $\theta_c^{\text{edge}} \geq \mathbf{0}$, which enforces that (eq. 2) is supermodular (which is required for efficient inference).

The principal difficulty in optimizing (eq. 7a) lies in the fact that (eq. 7b) includes exponentially many constraints – one for every *possible* output $Y \in \{-1, 1\}^N$ (i.e., two possibilities for every image in the dataset). To circumvent this, [22] proposes a constraint generation strategy, including at each iteration the constraint that induces the largest value of the slack ξ. Finding this constraint requires us to solve

$$\hat{Y}_c(\mathcal{X}; \Theta_c) = \underset{Y \in \{-1,1\}^N}{\operatorname{argmax}} \langle \Phi_c(\mathcal{X}, Y), \Theta_c \rangle + \Delta(Y, Y_c), \tag{8}$$

which we note is tractable so long as $\Delta(Y, Y_c)$ is also a supermodular function of Y, in which case we can solve (eq. 8) using the same approach we used to solve (eq. 2). Note that since we are interested in making simultaneous binary predictions for the entire dataset (rather than *ranking*), a loss such as the average precision is not appropriate for this task. Instead we optimize the *Balanced Error Rate*, which we find to be a good proxy for the average precision:

$$\Delta(Y, Y_c) = \frac{1}{2}\Bigg[\underbrace{\frac{|Y^{\text{pos}} \setminus Y_c^{\text{pos}}|}{|Y_c^{\text{pos}}|}}_{\text{false positive rate}} + \underbrace{\frac{|Y^{\text{neg}} \setminus Y_c^{\text{neg}}|}{|Y_c^{\text{neg}}|}}_{\text{false negative rate}}\Bigg], \tag{9}$$

where Y^{pos} is shorthand for the set of images with positive labels (Y^{neg} for negatively labeled images, similarly for Y_c). The Balanced Error Rate is designed to assign equal importance to false positives and false negatives, such that 'trivial' predictions (all labels positive or all labels negative), or random predictions have loss $\Delta(Y, Y_c) = 0.5$ on average, while systematically incorrect predictions yield $\Delta(Y, Y_c) = 1$.

Other loss functions, such as the 0/1 loss, could be optimized in our framework, though we find the loss of (eq. 9) to be a better proxy for the average precision.

We optimize (eq. 7a) using the solver of [23], which merely requires that we specify a loss function $\Delta(Y, Y_c)$, and procedures to solve (eq. 2) and (eq. 8). The solver must be modified to ensure that θ_c^{edge} remains positive. A similar modification was suggested in [24], where it was also used to ensure supermodularity of an optimization problem similar to that of (eq. 2).

5 Experiments

We study the use of social metadata for three binary classification problems: predicting image labels, tags, and groups. Note some differences between these three types of data: labels are provided by human annotators outside of Flickr, who provide annotations based purely on image content. Tags are less structured, can be provided by any number of annotators, and can include information that is difficult to detect from content alone, such as the camera brand and the photo's location. Groups are similar to tags, with the difference that the groups to which a photo is submitted are chosen entirely by the image's author.

Data Setup. As described in Section 3, for our first-order/node features $\phi_c(x_i)$ we construct indicator vectors encoding those words, groups, and tags that appear in the image x_i. We consider the 1000 most popular words, groups, and tags across the entire dataset, as well as any words, groups, and tags that occur at least twice as frequently in positively labeled images compared to the overall rate (we make this determination using only *training* images). As word features we use text from the image's title, description, and its comment thread, after eliminating stopwords.

For our relational/edge features $\phi_c(x_i, x_j)$ we consider seven properties:

- The number of common tags, groups, collections, and galleries
- An indicator for whether both photos were taken in the same location (GPS coordinates are organized into distinct 'localities' by Flickr)
- An indicator for whether both photos were taken by the same user
- An indicator for whether both photos were taken by contacts/friends

Where possible, we use the training/test splits from the original datasets, though in cases where test data is not available, we form new splits using subsets of the available data. Even when the original splits are available, around 10% of the images are discarded due to their metadata no longer being available via the Flickr API. This should be noted when we report results from other's work.

Evaluation. Where possible we report results directly from published materials on each benchmark, and from the associated competition webpages. We also report the performance obtained using image tags alone (the most common form of metadata used by multimodal approaches), and a 'flat' model that uses an indicator vector to encode collections, galleries, locations, and users, and is trained using an SVM; the goal of the latter model is to assess the improvement that can be obtained by using metadata, but not explicitly modeling *relationships* between images. To report the performance of 'standard' low-level image models we computed 1024-dimensional features using the publicly-available code of [25]; although these features fall short of the best performance reported in competitions, they are to our knowledge state-of-the-art in terms of publicly available implementations.

We report the Mean Average Precision (MAP) for the sake of comparison with published materials and competition results. For this we adopt an approach commonly used for SVMs, whereby we rank positively labeled images followed by negatively labeled images according to their first-order score $\langle \phi_c(x_i), \theta_c^{\text{node}} \rangle$. We also report performance in terms of the Balanced Error Rate Δ (or rather, $1 - \Delta$ so that higher scores correspond to better performance).

5.1 Image Labeling

Figure 3 (left) shows the average performance on the problem of predicting image labels on our four benchmarks. We plot the performance of the tag-only flat model, all-features flat model and our all-features graphical model.

For ImageCLEF, the graphical model gives an 11% improvement in Mean Average Precision (MAP) over the tag-only flat model, and a 31% improvement over the all-features flat model. Comparing our method to the best text-only method reported in the ImageCLEF 2011 competition [3], we observe a 7% improvement in MAP. Our method (which uses no image features) achieves similar performance to the best visual-only method. Even though the images were labeled by external evaluators solely based on their *content*, it appears that the social-network data contains information comparable to that of the images themselves. We also note that our graphical model outperforms the best visual-only method for 33 out of 99 categories, and the flat model on all but 9 categories.

On the PASCAL dataset we find that the graphical model outperforms the tag-only flat model by 71% and the all-features flat model by 19%. The performance of our model on the PASCAL dataset falls short of the best visual-only methods from the PASCAL competition; this is not surprising, since photos in the dataset have by far the least metadata, as discussed in Section 2 (Table 1).

On the MIR dataset the graphical model outperforms the tag-only and all-features flat models by 38% and 19%, respectively. Our approach also compares favorably to the baselines reported in [26]. We observe a 42% improvement in MAP and achieve better performance on all 14 categories except 'night'.

On the NUS dataset our approach gives an approximately threefold improvement over our baseline image features. While the graphical model only slightly outperforms the tag-only flat model (by 5%), we attribute this to the fact that some edges in NUS were suppressed from the graph to ensure that the model could be contained in memory. We also trained SVM models for six baseline features included as part of the NUS dataset [4], though we report results using the features of [25], which we found to give the best overall performance.

Overall, we note that in terms of the Balanced Error Rate Δ the all-features flat model reduces the error over the tag-only model by 18% on average (the all-features flat model does not fit in memory for the NUS data), and the graphical model performs better still, yielding a 32% average improvement over the tag-only model. In some cases the flat model exhibits relatively good performance, though upon inspection we discover that its high accuracy is primarily due to the use of words, groups, and tags, with the remaining features having little influence. Our graphical model is able to extract additional benefit for an overall reduction in loss of 17% over the all-features flat model. Also note that our performance measure is a good proxy for the average precision, with decreases in loss corresponding to increases in average precision in all but a few cases.

Although we experimented with simple methods for combining visual features and metadata, in our experience this did not further improve the results of our best metadata-only approaches.

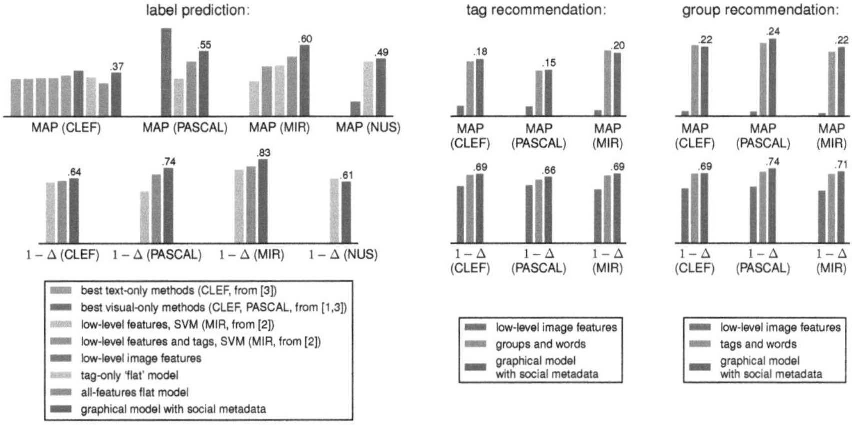

Fig. 3. Results in terms of the Mean Average Precision (top), and the Balanced Error Rate (bottom). 'Flat' models use indicator vectors for all relational features and are trained using an SVM. Recall that using our performance measure, a score of 0.5 is no better than random guessing. Comparisons for the ImageCLEF and PASCAL datasets are taken directly from their respective competition webpages; SVM comparisons for the MIR dataset are taken directly from [26].

5.2 Tag and Group Recommendation

We can also adapt our model to the problem of suggesting tags and groups for an image, simply by treating them in the same way we treated labels in Section 5.1. One difference is that for tags and groups we only have 'positive' groundtruth, i.e., we only observe whether an image *wasn't* assigned a particular tag or submitted to a certain group, not whether it *couldn't* have been. Nevertheless, our goal is still to retrieve as many positive examples as possible, while minimizing the number of negative examples that are retrieved, as in (eq. 9). We use the same features as in the previous section, though naturally when predicting tags we eliminate tag information from the model (sim. for groups).

Figure 3 (center and right) shows the average performance of our model on the 100 most popular tags and groups that appear in the ImageCLEF, PASCAL, and MIR datasets. Using tags, groups, and words in a flat model already significantly outperforms models that use only image features; in terms of the Balanced Error Rate Δ, a small additional benefit is obtained by using relational features.

While image labels are biased towards categories that can be predicted from image contents (due to the process via which groundtruth is obtained), a variety of popular groups and tags can be predicted much more accurately by using various types of metadata. For example, it is unlikely that one could determine whether an image is a picture of the uploader based purely on image contents, as evidenced by the poor performance of image features the 'selfportrait' tag; using metadata we are able to make this determination with high accuracy. Many of the poorly predicted tags and groups correspond to properties of the camera

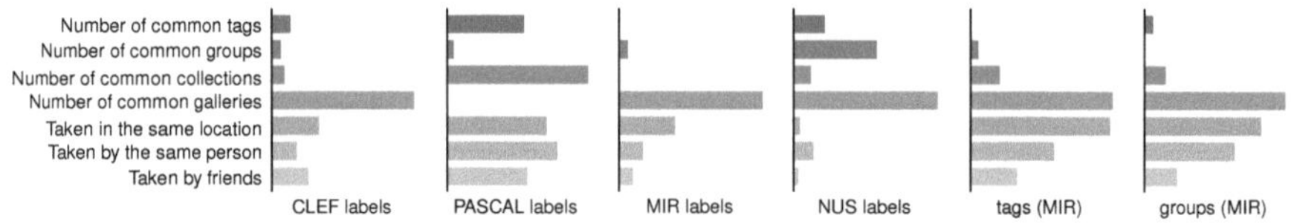

Fig. 4. Relative importance of social features when predicting labels for all four datasets, and groups, and tags on the MIR dataset (weight vectors for tags and groups on the remaining datasets are similar). Vectors were first normalized to have unit sum before averaging, as the models are scale-invariant.

used ('50mm', 'canon', 'nikon', etc.). Such labels could presumably be predicted from exif data, which while available from Flickr is not included in our model.

5.3 Social-Network Feature Importance

Finally we examine which types of metadata are important for the classification tasks we considered. Average weight vectors for the relational features are shown in Figure 4. Note that different types of relational features are important for different datasets, due to the varied nature of the groundtruth labels across datasets. We find that shared membership to a gallery is one of the strongest predictors for shared labels/tags/groups, except on the PASCAL dataset, which as we noted in Section 2 was mostly collected before galleries were introduced in Flickr. For tag and group prediction, relational features based on location and user information are also important. Location is important as many tags and groups are organized around geographic locations. For users, this phenomenon can be explained by the fact that unlike labels, tags and groups are *subjective*, in the sense that individual users may tag images in different ways, and choose to submit their images to different groups.

Acknowledgements. We thank the creators of each of the datasets used in our study for providing Flickr image sources. We also thank Jaewon Yang and Thomas Mensink for proofreading and discussions. This research has been supported in part by NSF CNS-1010921, IIS-1016909, IIS-1159679, CAREER IIS-1149837, AFRL FA8650-10-C-7058, Albert Yu & Mary Bechmann Foundation, Boeing, Allyes, Samsung, Yahoo, Alfred P. Sloan Fellowship and the Microsoft Faculty Fellowship.

References

1. Everingham, M., Van Gool, L.J., Williams, C., Winn, J., Zisserman, A.: The PASCAL visual object classes (VOC) challenge. IJCV (2010)
2. Huiskes, M., Lew, M.: The MIR Flickr retrieval evaluation. In: CIVR (2008)
3. Nowak, S., Huiskes, M.: New strategies for image annotation: Overview of the photo annotation task at ImageCLEF 2010. In: CLEF (Notebook Papers/LABs/Workshops) (2010)

4. Chua, T.S., Tang, J., Hong, R., Li, H., Luo, Z., Zheng, Y.T.: NUS-WIDE: A real-world web image database from the National University of Singapore. In: CIVR (2009)
5. Deng, J., Dong, W., Socher, R., Li, L.J., Li, K., Fei-Fei, L.: ImageNet: A large-scale hierarchical image database. In: CVPR (2009)
6. Guillaumin, M., Verbeek, J., Schmid, C.: Multimodal semi-supervised learning for image classification. In: CVPR (2010)
7. Lindstaedt, S., Pammer, V., Mörzinger, R., Kern, R., Mülner, H., Wagner, C.: Recommending tags for pictures based on text, visual content and user context. In: Internet and Web Applications and Services (2008)
8. Sigurbjörnsson, B., van Zwol, R.: Flickr tag recommendation based on collective knowledge. In: WWW (2008)
9. Sawant, N., Datta, R., Li, J., Wang, J.: Quest for relevant tags using local interaction networks and visual content. In: MIR (2010)
10. Stone, Z., Zickler, T., Darrell, T.: Autotagging Facebook: Social network context improves photo annotation. In: CVPR Workshop on Internet Vision (2008)
11. Luo, J., Boutell, M., Brown, C.: Pictures are not taken in a vacuum – an overview of exploiting context for semantic scene content understanding. IEEE Signal Processing Magazine (2006)
12. Li, Y., Crandall, D., Huttenlocher, D.: Landmark classification in large-scale image collections. In: ICCV (2009)
13. Kalogerakis, E., Vesselova, O., Hays, J., Efros, A., Hertzmann, A.: Image sequence geolocation with human travel priors. In: ICCV (2009)
14. Joshi, D., Luo, J., Yu, J., Lei, P., Gallagher, A.: Using geotags to derive rich tag-clouds for image annotation. In: Social Media Modeling and Computing (2011)
15. Mensink, T., Verbeek, J., Csurka, G.: Trans media relevance feedback for image autoannotation. In: BMVC (2010)
16. Denoyer, L., Gallinari, P.: A ranking based model for automatic image annotation in a social network. In: ICWSM (2010)
17. Kolmogorov, V., Zabih, R.: What Energy Functions Can Be Minimized via Graph Cuts? In: Heyden, A., Sparr, G., Nielsen, M., Johansen, P. (eds.) ECCV 2002, Part III. LNCS, vol. 2352, pp. 65–81. Springer, Heidelberg (2002)
18. Chapelle, O., Haffner, P., Vapnik, V.: Support vector machines for histogram-based image classification. IEEE Trans. on Neural Networks (1999)
19. Boros, E., Hammer, P.L.: Pseudo-boolean optimization. Discrete Applied Mathematics (2002)
20. Boykov, Y., Kolmogorov, V.: An experimental comparison of min-cut/max-flow algorithms for energy minimization in vision. IEEE Trans. on PAMI (2001)
21. Strandmark, P., Kahl, F.: Parallel and distributed graph cuts by dual decomposition. In: CVPR (2010)
22. Tsochantaridis, I., Joachims, T., Hofmann, T., Altun, Y.: Large margin methods for structured and interdependent output variables. JMLR (2005)
23. Teo, C.H., Smola, A., Vishwanathan, S., Le, Q.: A scalable modular convex solver for regularized risk minimization. In: KDD (2007)
24. Petterson, J., Caetano, T.: Submodular multi-label learning. In: NIPS (2011)
25. van de Sande, K., Gevers, T., Snoek, C.: Evaluating color descriptors for object and scene recognition. IEEE Trans. on PAMI (2010)
26. Huiskes, M., Thomee, B., Lew, M.: New trends and ideas in visual concept detection: the MIR Flickr retrieval evaluation initiative. In: CIVR (2010)

Segmentation Based Particle Filtering for Real-Time 2D Object Tracking

Vasileios Belagiannis[1], Falk Schubert[2], Nassir Navab[1], and Slobodan Ilic[1]

[1] Computer Aided Medical Procedures, Technische Universität München, Germany
{belagian,navab,slobodan.ilic}@in.tum.de
[2] EADS Innovation Works, Germany
falk.schubert@eads.net

Abstract. We address the problem of visual tracking of arbitrary objects that undergo significant scale and appearance changes. The classical tracking methods rely on the bounding box surrounding the target object. Regardless of the tracking approach, the use of bounding box quite often introduces background information. This information propagates in time and its accumulation quite often results in drift and tracking failure. This is particularly the case with the particle filtering approach that is often used for visual tracking. However, it always uses a bounding box around the object to compute features of the particle samples. Since this causes the drift, we propose to use segmentation for sampling. Relying on segmentation and computing the colour and gradient orientation histograms from these segmented particle samples allows the tracker to easily adapt to the object's deformations, occlusions, orientation, scale and appearance changes. We propose two particle sampling strategies based on segmentation. In the first, segmentation is done for every propagated particle sample, while in the second only the strongest particle sample is segmented. Depending on this decision there is obviously a trade-off between speed and performance.

We perform an exhaustive quantitative evaluation on a number of challenging sequences and compare our method with the number of state-of-the-art methods previously evaluated on those sequences. The results we obtain outperform majority of the related work, both in terms of the performance and speed.

1 Introduction

Visual object tracking is one of the major research problems in Computer Vision. It is essential for numerous applications, such as surveillance [1], action recognition [2] or augmented reality [3]. One of the classical approaches for object tracking is particle filtering. It generalizes well to any kind of objects, models well non-Gaussian noise and is able to run in real-time. The observation models that have been used with particle filtering are either colour histograms [4] or histograms of oriented gradients [5]. These observation modes are computed from the bounding boxes surrounding the target object. While using bounding boxes is fast and convenient, they often capture undesirable background information

A. Fitzgibbon et al. (Eds.): ECCV 2012, Part IV, LNCS 7575, pp. 842–855, 2012.

Fig. 1. Tracking results for some of our evaluation sequences. From top to the bottom row respectively sequences are named: *Mountain-bike*, *Entrance*, *UAV*, *Cliff-dive 1*. The *Entrance* sequence has been captured with a stationary camera while in the other three sequences both the object and camera are moving.

as most objects do not fit into a rectangle very well. This information is further propagated to all sample particles and often causes drift. This is particularly true for deformable objects, like humans, where the bounding box sometimes includes very large portions of the background.

The recent trend in visual tracking is related to learning the object's appearance. The tracking then becomes a classification problem where the goal is to discriminate the object of interest from the background [6]. The appearance of the object can be learned offline or online. These approaches are traditionally called *tracking-by-detection* or online learning approaches and have performed very well on demanding tracking scenarios, e.g. sport activities, pedestrian tracking or vehicle tracking. Although they are often robust against occlusions, deformations, orientation, scale and appearance changes, their computational cost makes most of them inefficient for real-time applications. In addition, the presence of false positive detections causes drifting. The drifting is closely related to the area from which the object's features are extracted. It is usually determined from a rectangular bounding box. However, the object does not usually fit perfectly inside the box, so the additional background information is included in the extracted features. For instance, this results in learning background in the trackers based on the online learning of the object appearance. Again, the presence of the background information becomes more critical for deformable objects where the bounding box always includes that type of noise. To overcome this problem

Godec et al. [7] recently proposed an approach that removes a bounding box constraint and combines segmentation and online learning. However, due to the very expensive learning procedure based on Hough forests the efficiency of this tracker is far from real time.

Our objective is to overcome majority of these limitations and provide a general purpose tracker that can track arbitrary objects whose initial shape is not a priori known in challenging sequences in real-time. These sequences contain clutter, partial occlusions, rapid motion, significant viewpoint and appearance changes (Fig. 1). We propose to use the standard particle filter approach based on colour and gradient histograms and incorporate the object shape into the state vector. Since the classical particle filter based on bounding box surrounding particle samples drifts due to sometime abrupt amount of captured background, we propose to use segmentation at the particle sample locations propagated by a basic dynamic motion model. This allows having particle samples of arbitrary shapes and collecting more relevant regions features than when the bounding box is used. Consequently the object state vector strongly depends on the object's shape. Relying on segmentation allows the tracker to easily adapt to the object's deformations, occlusions, orientation, scale and appearance changes. We propose two particle sampling strategies based on segmentations. In one case the segmentation is done for every propagated particle sample and therefore is more robust to large displacements, scales and deformations, but it is more time consuming. The other strategy is to do the segmentation on the particle sample with the highest importance weight and propagate its shape to all other samples. This is definitely less robust and more critical in difficult sequences where object shape and position change dramatically from frame to frame, but in all other sequences, where this is not the case, is sufficient and comes with the great computational complexity reduction leading to very fast runtime of up to 50 fps. Depending on this decision, there is obviously a trade-off between speed and performance.

We tested our method on a number of available sequences used by the recent state-of-the-art methods. We demonstrated the advantage of our method over normal particle filtering based on bounding box and made a comparison with many state-of-the-art trackers. This analysis showed that in many cases our method outperforms related approaches both in terms of speed and performance.

1.1 Related Work

There is notable literature on visual object tracking. Given the limited space, we focus on work mostly related to particle filtering and learning-based approaches as well as methods that do not rely on rectangular bounding boxes. Starting from the probabilistic methods, Isard and Blake [8] introduced the particle filter, namely condensation algorithm, for tracking curves. Later on, the method was also applied to colour based tracking [9]. Similarly, Pérez et al. [4] proposed a colour histogram based particle filtering approach. However, the colour distribution fails to describe an object in situations where the object is of a similar colour as the background. For that reason, Lu et al. [5] incorporated a gradient orientation histogram in the particle filter. The most common particle filtering algorithm, the bootstrap filter [10], has been combined with a classifier [11] in order to be created an advanced motion model. All these methods rely on bounding boxes for sampling and therefore are sensible to the particle samples erroneously taken from the background. A more recent approach combines an off-line and an online classifier in the bootstrap filter's importance weight estimation [1]. In all cases, incorporating a classifier into the particle filter has an important impact on the runtime.

In the domain of a unified tracking and segmentation, the object is presented from a segmented area instead of a bounding box. Particularly impressive is the probabilistic approach of Bibby and Reid [12]. They have combined the bag-of-pixels image representation with a level-set framework, where the likelihood term has been replaced from the posterior term. Even though this approach adapts the model online and is not based on the bounding box, it is susceptible to the background clutter and occlusions. Chockalingam et al. [13] divided the object into fragments based on level-sets as well. Recently, Tsai et al. [14] have proposed a multi-label Markov Random Field framework for segmenting the image data by minimizing an energy function, but the method works only offline. The complexity of all these methods increases their computational cost significantly. In addition to the object segmentation, Nejhum et al. [15] have used a block configuration for describing the object. Each block corresponds to an intensity histogram and all together share a common configuration. This representation forms the searching window which is iteratively updated. Nevertheless, the bounding box representation is still present but in a small scale.

The first work on learning-based approaches was published by Avidan [6] and Javed et al. [16], where tracking is defined as a binary classification problem. A set of weak classifiers is trained online and afterwards boosted to discriminate the foreground object from the background. The idea of online training has been continued by Grabner et al. [17] for achieving a real-time performance in a semi-supervised learning framework. In this approach, the samples from the initialization frame are considered as positive for online training and during the runtime the classifier is updated with unlabelled data. Babenko et. al [18] have proposed a multiple instance learning (MIL) approach for dealing with the incorrectly labelled data during the training process. The MIL classifier is trained with bags of positive and negative data, where a positive bag contains at least one positive instance. More recently, Kalal et al. [19] have combined the KLT tracker [20] with an online updated randomized forest classifier for learning the appearance of the foreground object. The tracker updates the classifier and the classifier reinitializes it in case of a drift. Similarly in [21], the appearance model of the tracker evolves during time. All the above approaches present mechanisms for preventing the drifting effect in some form. However, they are all trained with data extracted from a bounding box. As a result, background information is highly probable to penetrate into the training process which will eventually lead to drift assuming arbitrarily shaped objects.

Godec et al. [7] have gone a step further into online learning by removing the rectangular bounding box representation. They have employed the Hough Forests [22] classification framework for online learning. In this approach, the classification output initializes a segmentation algorithm for getting a more accurate shape of the object. The approach is relatively slow, but it delivers promising results on demanding tracking sequences. In the proposed work, we similarly make use of the segmentation concept as well but we incorporate this into a much faster particle filter tracker instead of using a non-bounding box classification approach.

2 Particle Filter Based Visual Object Tracking

The particle filter has shown to be a robust tracking algorithm for deformable objects with non-linear motion [8]. The tracking problem is defined as a Bayesian filter that recursively calculates the probability of the state $\mathbf{x}_t$ at time t, given the observations $\mathbf{z}_{1:t}$ up to time t. This requires the computation of the (probability density function) pdf $p(\mathbf{x}_t \mid \mathbf{z}_{1:t})$. It is assumed that the initial pdf $p(\mathbf{x}_0 \mid \mathbf{z}_0) = p(\mathbf{x}_0)$ of the state vector, also known as the prior, is available. $\mathbf{z}_0$ is an empty set indicating that there is no observation. In our problem the state consists of the object's shape S and 2D position of the shape's centre of mass x_c, y_c and is defined as $\mathbf{x}_t = [x_c, y_c, S]^T$. The prior distribution is estimated from the initial object shape. The initial shape can be either manually drawn or estimated from segmenting a bounding box which surrounds the object. Finally, the pdf $p(\mathbf{x}_t \mid \mathbf{z}_{1:t})$ can be computed from the Bayesian recursion, consisting of two phases called prediction and update. Assuming that the pdf $p(\mathbf{x}_{t-1} \mid \mathbf{z}_{1:t-1})$ is available and the object state evolves from a transition model $\mathbf{x}_t = f(\mathbf{x}_{t-1}, \mathbf{v})$, where $\mathbf{v}$ is a noise model, then in the prediction phase the prior pdf $p(\mathbf{x}_t \mid \mathbf{z}_{1:t-1})$ at time t can be computed using the Chapman-Kolmogorov equation:

$$p(\mathbf{x}_t \mid \mathbf{z}_{1:t-1}) = \int p(\mathbf{x}_t \mid \mathbf{x}_{t-1}) p(\mathbf{x}_{t-1} \mid \mathbf{z}_{1:t-1}) d\mathbf{x}_{t-1} \tag{1}$$

The probabilistic model of the state evolution $p(\mathbf{x}_t \mid \mathbf{x}_{t-1})$ is defined by the transition model. When at time t an observation $\mathbf{z}_t$ becomes available, the prior can be updated via Bayes' rule:

$$p(\mathbf{x}_t \mid \mathbf{z}_{1:t}) = \frac{p(\mathbf{z}_t \mid \mathbf{x}_t) p(\mathbf{x}_t \mid \mathbf{z}_{1:t-1})}{p(\mathbf{z}_t \mid \mathbf{z}_{1:t-1})} = \tag{2}$$
$$= \frac{p(\mathbf{z}_t \mid \mathbf{x}_t) \int p(\mathbf{x}_t \mid \mathbf{x}_{t-1}) p(\mathbf{x}_{t-1} \mid \mathbf{z}_{t-1}) \mathrm{d}\mathbf{x}_{t-1}}{\int p(\mathbf{z}_t \mid \mathbf{x}_t) p(\mathbf{x}_t \mid \mathbf{z}_{1:t-1}) \mathrm{d}\mathbf{x}_t}$$

where the likelihood $p(\mathbf{z}_t \mid \mathbf{x}_t)$ is defined by the observation model $\mathbf{z}_t = \mathbf{h}(\mathbf{x}_t, \mathbf{n}_t)$ with known statistics $\mathbf{n}_t$. In the update phase, the observation $\mathbf{z}_t$ is used to update the prior density in order to obtain the desirable posterior of the current state. The observation in our method comes from colour $p(\mathbf{z}_t^{col} \mid \mathbf{x}_t)$ and gradient orientation $p(\mathbf{z}_t^{or} \mid \mathbf{x}_t)$ histograms.

Since posterior density cannot be computed analytically, it is represented by a set of random particle samples $\{\mathbf{x}_i^t\}_{i=1\cdots N_s}$ with associated weights $\{\mathbf{w}_i^t\}_{i=1\cdots N_s}$. The most standard particle filter algorithm is Sequential Importance Sampling (SIS). Theoretically, when the number of samples becomes very large, this so called Monte Carlo sampling becomes an equivalent representation to the usual analytical description of the posterior pdf. Each particle sample represents a hypothetical object state and it is associated with an importance weight. The calculation of the weight is based on the observation likelihood and weight from the previous time step.

However, a common problem with the SIS particle filter algorithm is the degeneracy phenomenon. This means that after a few iterations the majority of particles will have negligible weight. To overcome this problem the bootstrap filter, which is based on the Sampling-Importance-Resampling (SIR) technique, aims to remove low importance samples from the posterior distribution. When the number of particle samples with high importance weight drops under a constant threshold, the resampling step is executed. There, every sample contributes to the posterior with proportion to its importance weight. The weight estimation is given by:

$$\mathbf{w}_t^{(i)} = \mathbf{w}_{t-1}^{(i)} \cdot p(\mathbf{z}_t \mid \mathbf{x}_t^{(i)}) = \mathbf{w}_{t-1}^{(i)} \cdot p(\mathbf{z}_t^{col} \mid \mathbf{x}_t^{(i)}) p(\mathbf{z}_t^{or} \mid \mathbf{x}_t^{(i)}), \sum_{i=1}^{N_s} \mathbf{w}_t^{(i)} = 1 \quad (3)$$

After the resampling step, the samples are equally weighted with $\mathbf{w}_{t-1}^{(i)}$ being constant (i.e. $1/N_s$). The importance weight calculation cost is increased linearly with the number of the the particle samples. Detailed description and discussion of particle filtering can be found in [10]. Next, we detail elements of our particle filtering approach including observation and transition model as well as the segmentation of the particle samples.

2.1 Observation Model

Our observation model relies on two components, the colour and gradient orientation histograms. Concerning the colour information, we use the HSV space similar to [4] since it is less sensitive to illumination changes. The colour distribution is invariant to rotation, scale changes and partial occlusion. For the gradient orientation histogram, we compute the histogram of oriented gradients (HOG) descriptor [23]. The strong normalization of the descriptor makes it invariant to illumination changes.

The likelihood of the observation model $p(\mathbf{z}_t \mid \mathbf{x}_t^{(i)})$ for each particle sample $i = 1 \ldots N_s$ is calculated from the similarity between the current $\mathbf{q}(\mathbf{x}_{t-1}) = \{q_n(\mathbf{x}_{t-1})\}_{n=1,\ldots,N_c}$ and the predicted state $\mathbf{q}(\mathbf{x}_t) = \{q_n(\mathbf{x}_t)\}_{n=1,\ldots,N_c}$ distributions represented by colour histograms, where N_c is the number of colour bins. The state distribution of the gradient orientation histogram is formulated in the same way. We use the Bhattacharyya coefficient $\rho[\mathbf{q}(\mathbf{x}_{t-1}), \mathbf{q}(\mathbf{x}_t)] = \sum_{i=1}^{N_c} \sqrt{q_i(\mathbf{x}_{t-1}) q_i(\mathbf{x}_t)}$ for measuring the similarity of two distributions. As a result, the distance measure is equal to $d = \sqrt{1 - \rho[\mathbf{q}(\mathbf{x}_{t-1}), \mathbf{q}(\mathbf{x}_t)]}$. In the proposed method, likelihoods of both colour and gradient orientation histograms are estimated using the Bhattacharyya coefficient and an exponential distribution, resulting in $p(\mathbf{z}_t^{col} \mid \mathbf{x}_t^{(i)}) = e^{-\lambda d_{col}}$ being the colour likelihood and $p(\mathbf{z}_t^{or} \mid \mathbf{x}_t^{(i)}) = e^{-\lambda d_{or}}$ being the gradient orientation likelihood. The final importance weight is consequently given by:

$$\mathbf{w}_t^{(i)} = p(\mathbf{z}_t^{col} \mid \mathbf{x}_t^{(i)}) p(\mathbf{z}_t^{or} \mid \mathbf{x}_t^{(i)}) = e^{-\lambda d_{col}} e^{-\lambda d_{or}} \tag{4}$$

where λ is a scaling factor. While d_{col} and d_{or} are the distances of the colour and orientation histogram respectively.

2.2 Transition Model

The transition model of the particle filter has the same importance as the observation model for achieving an accurate forward inference. The variance and/or non-linearity of the motion of different objects do not allow to use a simplified motion model, like the constant velocity in [1]. In our work, the transition model of the particle filter is based on a learnt second order autoregressive model. The Burg method [24] is used for deriving two second order autoregressive functions, independently for the x and y direction. The last term of the object's state, the shape, is represented by a constant term in state space, which is estimated from the segmentation.

2.3 Segmentation of the Particle Samples

The particle filter algorithm treats the uncertainty of the object's state by estimating the state's distribution. In the state model we introduce the shape term S for discriminating the foreground object from the background information during sampling. The shape term is assumed to be known while a segmentation algorithm is employed for estimating it. Finally, the sample's observation is free of background during the likelihood $p(\mathbf{z}_t \mid \mathbf{x}_t^{(i)})$ estimation.

In the current work, the choice of the segmentation algorithm is important. We require that the segmentation algorithm is fast, generic and provides two-class segmentation output. Therefore, we chose the *GrabCut* algorithm, a graph-cut segmentation approach [25]. The algorithm is incorporated with the particle filter for refining the shape of the particle samples.

The area to be segmented is always slightly larger than the area of the sample's shape. Based on the current shape, an initial bounding box is specified where everything outside of it is considered as background and the interior area is considered uncertain. With such input, *GrabCut* segments the foreground object inside the rectangular area occupied by the particle.

The computational cost of the *GrabCut* algorithm scales with the size of the area which has to be segmented. Even though the speed of the GrabCut is appropriate for small regions of interests like our particle samples, the overall computational complexity grows with the number of particle samples. For that reason we have implemented two different sampling strategies.

2.4 Sampling Strategies

To investigate the approximation of the state distribution, we propose two sampling strategies based on the segmentation output. In the first strategy each particle sample is segmented in every iteration in order to refine its shape. We name this sampling strategy a multiple particle filter samples segmentation (*Multi-PaFiSS*) strategy and use this name in our experimental evaluation. The second sampling strategy that we call the single particle filter samples segmentation (*Single-PaFiSS*) strategy is based on segmentation of the sample with the highest importance weight and then propagating its shape to the rest particle samples.

The first sampling strategy is more robust and better adapts to the object's large deformations and scale from frame to frame. However, it comes at the price of increased computational complexity. On the contrary, the second strategy is not that robust to large appearance and scale changes, but it is extremely fast and in many situations also performs well as our experimental validation indicates.

2.5 Segmentation Artifacts and Failure

The proposed algorithm is dependent on the segmentation output for refining the shape of the particle samples. Subsequently, a segmentation failure could obstruct the algorithm's pipeline. We identify two possible failure modes. In one case, the segmentation delivers more than one segmented areas of the same class (Fig. 2b). In the second case, the segmentation explodes by including almost the whole area to a single class or segments everything as background. These two common problems can occur when the *GrabCut* algorithm is used.

The first failure mode provides a successful segmentation output. However, there are some small isolated areas, which we call artifacts, that are often present in the output (Fig. 2b). In our experiments, it never happened to have artifacts with an area larger than 5% of the segmented area. By applying a two-pass connected component labelling, we locate the shape with the largest area and exclude the smaller artifacts.

The second failure mode is more critical because we cannot recover a meaningful segmentation (Fig. 2d). The reason for the failure of the *GrabCut* algorithm is poor quality of the image, failure of the edge extraction and when the colour of the object is not discriminative enough from the background color. Hopefully, this type of failure is easily identified in our algorithm by comparing the current output with the segmentation of the particle sample in the previous time instant based on a threshold. The overlap of the two areas is being compared. In the case of a segmentation failure, the shape of the particle samples becomes rectangular until a new shape is estimated. Thereby, the algorithm continues the tracking task without segmentation refining.

Fig. 2. Segmentation artifacts and failure: The figures (a) and (c) show input images. (b) The red car is correctly segmented, but there are two connected components. One is a car and the other is a line marking that is an artifact. We eliminate it by keeping the largest connected component. (d) The segmentation algorithm failed to segment (c) and labeled background as foreground object. In this case the shape of the particle samples becomes rectangular until a new shape is estimated

3 Experiments

In order to demonstrate the advantages of the proposed algorithm, we evaluate it on standard tracking sequences used in other related work and we also offer five new challenging sequences[1]. For evaluating our algorithm, we have implemented two versions of our method according to the sampling strategy. The evaluation dataset includes videos with objects of different classes that undergo deformations, occlusions, scale and appearance changes. The test video sequences come from the following datasets: *ETH Walking Pedestrians (EWAP)* [26], *Pedestrian dataset* [27], *Comets project* [28] and the *Aerial Action Dataset* [29]. In total, we used 13 sequences for evaluation. The comparison is done with the standard particle filter and three recent approaches. We compare the two versions of our method with the *TLD* [19], *MIL* [18] and *HoughTrack* [7] algorithms.

The evaluation dataset includes the ground-truth annotations in which the target object is outlined by a bounding box in every frame. We use this type of annotation for all test sequences. This type of annotation is not the appropriate way to describe complex objects (e.g. articulated), but it is the standard annotation method. Therefore, our ground-truth are bounding box representations centered on the centre of mass of the segmented area. *HoughTrack* [7] segmentation based tracking algorithm produces bounding boxes for evaluation in the same way. *TLD* [19] and *MIL* [18] have already a bounding box output and they do not require any modification. Then the overlap between the tracker's bounding box and the annotated one is calculated, based on the *PASCAL VOC* challenge [30] overlap criterion. In all experiments, we set the overlap threshold to 50%. Additionally, we evaluate the computational cost of each method by estimating the average number of tracked frames per second (fps) for every sequence.

3.1 System Setup

Both versions of our method have fixed parameters for all sequences. There are two parameters which affect the performance of the system: the number of

[1] The evaluation dataset can be found at `http://campar.in.tum.de/Chair/PaFiSS`

particle samples and the threshold indicating the segmentation failure. Since we do not depend on the bounding box, we found out experimentally that the performance of our method does not increase with the number of the samples. Hence, the number of samples is set to 50 and the segmentation failure threshold to the 40% overlap between two successful consecutive segmentation. All methods have been downloaded from the web and executed with their default settings. All experiments are carried out on a standard Intel i7 3.20 GHz desktop machine.

3.2 Comparison to the Standard Particle Filter

The proposed method is compared to the standard particle filter (*SPF*) to prove the superiority of the non-rectangular sampling. For comparison, we implemented the standard bootstrap particle filter [10]. We tested it on all of our sequences but choose the *Entrance* sequence for comparison, since it nicely demonstrates that the amount of background, captured with the bounding box, causes drift. Based on the 50% overlap criterion of the *PASCAL VOC* challenge [30], the standard way of sampling totally fails (Fig 3). Since we also noticed that the increase of the number of samples does not increase the performance of *SPF*, we also set it to 50. In contrast, the proposed method excludes the background information from the likelihood estimation and keeps tracking the object until the end of the sequence.

(a) (b) (c) (d)

Fig. 3. Failure of the Standard Particle Filter (*SPF*). (a): The overlap over time plot, based on the *PASCAL VOC* challenge [30] criterion, shows the performance of the *SPF* and the two versions of our method. Other images: *SPF* tracker gradually drifts due to collecting background information

3.3 Comparison to the state-of-the-Art

The comparison to the latest online learning methods aims to show the outstanding performance of the computationally inexpensive single sampling *Single-PaFiSS* strategy and the more accurate multiple segmentation *Multi-PaFiSS* strategy of our method. Table 1 shows that both strategies of our method outperform the other approaches. While Table 2 shows that Single-PaFiSS is considerably faster than the other approaches.

We introduce the sequences *Entrance*, *Exit 1*, *Exit 2* and *Bridge* for evaluation of occlusions, scale and appearance changes. All of them come from outdoor and

Table 1. Results for 13 sequences: Percentage of correct tracked frames based on the overlap criterion (> 50%) of the *PASCAL VOC* challenge [30]. The average perentage follows in the end.

Sequence	Frames	Single-PaFiSS	Multi-PaFiSS	TLD [19]	MIL [18]	HT [7]
Actions 2 [29]	2113	82.30	**89.87**	8.18	8.42	8.61
Entrance	196	96.42	**98.46**	35.20	35.20	64.79
Exit 1	186	**100**	**100**	74.19	17.74	**100**
Exit 2	172	96.51	98.83	59.88	95.93	**100**
Skiing [7]	81	13.50	**48.14**	6.17	8.64	46.91
UAV [28]	716	64.26	**88.68**	47.90	58.10	73.46
Bridge	55	10.90	10.90	10.9	**12.72**	12.65
Pedestrian 1 [27]	379	1.84	11.60	**66.22**	56.20	12.40
Pedestrian 2 [26]	352	83.23	94.73	**98.57**	89.20	96.30
Cliff-dive 1 [7]	76	**100**	94.73	55.26	63.15	56.57
Mountain-bike [7]	228	18.85	40.35	36.84	**82.89**	39.03
Motocross 2 [7]	23	**95.65**	69.56	73.91	60.86	91.65
Head	231	82.68	**84.41**	77.05	33.34	61.47
Average		65.53	**70.92**	49.88	47.87	58.73

Table 2. Speed results for 13 sequences: Average frames per second (fps) for every sequence. The total average fps follows in the end.

Sequence	Frames	Single-PaFiSS	Multi-PaFiSS	TLD [19]	MIL [18]	HT [7]
Actions 2 [29]	2113	6.07	0.50	3.76	**19.09**	1.35
Entrance	196	**51.17**	5.79	5.44	20.60	1.75
Exit 1	186	**39.73**	4.17	5.29	21.10	1.83
Exit 2	172	**21.07**	1.92	4.57	17.79	1.57
Skiing [7]	81	**83.67**	4.71	4.25	24.65	2.93
UAV [28]	716	**36.50**	4.30	6.50	27.3	4.58
Bridge	55	**22.17**	1.46	4.38	19.4	1.67
Pedestrian 1 [27]	379	18.82	2.51	5.87	**24.43**	1.56
Pedestrian 2 [26]	352	**29.46**	3.14	2.73	18.72	1.73
Cliff-dive 1 [7]	76	6.46	0.55	8.97	**30.24**	2.48
Mountain-bike [7]	228	**37.79**	3.22	4.53	26.53	2.81
Motocross 2 [7]	23	10.05	1.45	3.95	**23.28**	1.78
Head	231	7.50	0.76	9.74	**34.40**	7.51
Average		**28.23**	2.65	5.38	23.64	2.20

dynamic environments where the illumination varies. Furthermore, the main characteristic of the sequences is the simultaneous motion and deformations of the target objects.

There is a number of sequences where we have achieved better results than the other methods. For instance, in *Actions 2* sequence both of our sampling versions outperform the other methods because of the adaption to the scale changes.

Fig. 4. Additional tracking results (first row: *Motocross 2*, second row: *Exit 2*, third row: *Skiing*, fourth row: *Head*). The *Exit 2* and *Head* sequences have been captured with a stationary camera while in the other two sequences both the object and camera are moving.

In *Exit 1* and *Exit 2* sequences, both versions of our method and *HoughTrack* give similar results, while *TLD* partially drifts. *MIL* succeeds in *Exit 2* but it does not scale in *Exit 1* sequence. Next, in the *Skiing* sequence the abrupt motion leads *TLD* and *MIL* to complete failure while only *HoughTrack* tracks partially the object until the end. In our algorithm, the segmentation fails to refine the object's shape after some time and the algorithm completely drifts.

In general, we face the segmentation failure problem when the quality of the image data is low, like in the *Pedestrian 1* sequence. As long as the tracker is dependent on the segmentation output for getting the object's shape, a possible failure can cause drift. However, our algorithm continues tracking the object by fitting a bounding box to the most recent object shape and sampling using the bounding box, up to small scale changes. This behavior can be observed in the *Single-PaFiSS* sampling strategy while in *Multi-PaFiSS*, it rarely occurs.

Another segmentation failure can be observed in *Cliff-dive 1* sequence where there is an articulated object in low qualitative image data. Consequently there is high probability that the segmentation can provide incorrect information about the shape of the object. For that reason *Single-PaFiSS* performs better than *Multi-PaFiSS* where there are multiple segmentations per frame. In *Bridge* sequence, our algorithm failed to track the object because there is full occlusion. It is a situation which we do not treat with the current framework. The same failure result occurred with the other approaches.

Taking into consideration the evaluation results, one can conclude that the idea of using a probabilist searching method with the combination of shape based sampling produces a robust tracker. The two evaluated implementations of our method give similar results but *Single-PaFiSS* is considerably faster than all the other methods. Fig. 1 and 4 show some of our results for selected frames.

4 Conclusion

We have presented a simple yet effective method for tracking deformable generic objects that undergo a wide range of transformations. The proposed method relies on tracking using a non-rectangular object description. This is achieved by integrating a segmentation step into a bootstrap particle filter for sampling based on shapes. We investigated two sampling strategies which allow a great trade-off between performance and speed. In the first version, we have reached a better performance by segmenting every particle sample while in the second, we have a less accurate but significantly faster algorithm. During the evaluation on a wide variety of different sequences, our method outperforms recent state-of-the-art object tracking approaches on most sequences or performs at least on par. In future work, we will increase the robustness of the segmentation (e.g. by using spatio-temporal information) and speed by parallelizing our method.

References

1. Breitenstein, M., Reichlin, F., Leibe, B., Koller-Meier, E., Van Gool, L.: Online multiperson tracking-by-detection from a single, uncalibrated camera. IEEE Trans. on PAMI (2011)
2. Ikizler, N., Forsyth, D.: Searching video for complex activities with finite state models. In: CVPR (2007)
3. Wagner, D., Langlotz, T., Schmalstieg, D.: Robust and unobtrusive marker tracking on mobile phones. In: ISMAR (2008)
4. Pérez, P., Hue, C., Vermaak, J., Gangnet, M.: Color-Based Probabilistic Tracking. In: Heyden, A., Sparr, G., Nielsen, M., Johansen, P. (eds.) ECCV 2002, Part I. LNCS, vol. 2350, pp. 661–675. Springer, Heidelberg (2002)
5. Lu, W., Okuma, K., Little, J.: Tracking and recognizing actions of multiple hockey players using the boosted particle filter. Image and Vision Computing (2009)
6. Avidan, S.: Ensemble tracking. In: CVPR (2005)
7. Godec, M., Roth, P., Bischof, H.: Hough-based tracking of non-rigid objects. In: ICCV (2011)
8. Isard, M., Blake, A.: Condensation-conditional density propagation for visual tracking. IJCV (1998)
9. Nummiaro, K., Koller-Meier, E., Van Gool, L.: An adaptive color-based particle filter. Image and Vision Computing (2003)
10. Doucet, A., De Freitas, N., Gordon, N.: Sequential Monte Carlo methods in practice. Springer (2001)
11. Okuma, K., Taleghani, A., de Freitas, N., Little, J.J., Lowe, D.G.: A Boosted Particle Filter: Multitarget Detection and Tracking. In: Pajdla, T., Matas, J. (eds.) ECCV 2004. LNCS, vol. 3021, pp. 28–39. Springer, Heidelberg (2004)

12. Bibby, C., Reid, I.: Robust Real-Time Visual Tracking Using Pixel-Wise Posteriors. In: Forsyth, D., Torr, P., Zisserman, A. (eds.) ECCV 2008, Part II. LNCS, vol. 5303, pp. 831–844. Springer, Heidelberg (2008)
13. Chockalingam, P., Pradeep, N., Birchfield, S.: Adaptive fragments-based tracking of non-rigid objects using level sets. In: ICCV (2009)
14. Tsai, D., Flagg, M., Rehg, J.: Motion coherent tracking with multi-label mrf optimization. Algorithms (2010)
15. Shahed Nejhum, S., Ho, J., Yang, M.: Visual tracking with histograms and articulating blocks. In: CVPR (2008)
16. Javed, O., Ali, S., Shah, M.: Online detection and classification of moving objects using progressively improving detectors. In: CVPR (2005)
17. Grabner, H., Leistner, C., Bischof, H.: Semi-supervised On-Line Boosting for Robust Tracking. In: Forsyth, D., Torr, P., Zisserman, A. (eds.) ECCV 2008, Part I. LNCS, vol. 5302, pp. 234–247. Springer, Heidelberg (2008)
18. Babenko, B., Yang, M., Belongie, S.: Visual tracking with online multiple instance learning. In: CVPR (2009)
19. Kalal, Z., Matas, J., Mikolajczyk, K.: Pn learning: Bootstrapping binary classifiers by structural constraints. In: CVPR (2010)
20. Lucas, B., Kanade, T.: With an application to stereo vision. In: Proceedings DARPA Image Understanding Workrhop (1998)
21. Kwon, J., Lee, K.: Tracking of a non-rigid object via patch-based dynamic appearance modeling and adaptive basin hopping monte carlo sampling. In: CVPR (2009)
22. Gall, J., Lempitsky, V.: Class-specific hough forests for object detection. In: CVPR (2009)
23. Dalal, N., Triggs, B.: Histograms of oriented gradients for human detection. In: CVPR (2005)
24. Stoica, P., Moses, R.: Introduction to spectral analysis, vol. 51. Prentice Hall, Upper Saddle River (1997)
25. Rother, C., Kolmogorov, V., Blake, A.: Grabcut: Interactive foreground extraction using iterated graph cuts. ACM Transactions on Graphics, TOG (2004)
26. Pellegrini, S., Ess, A., Schindler, K., Van Gool, L.: You'll never walk alone: Modeling social behavior for multi-target tracking. In: ICCV (2009)
27. Leibe, B., Schindler, K., Van Gool, L.: Coupled detection and trajectory estimation for multi-object tracking. In: ICCV (2007)
28. Ollero, A., Lacroix, S., Merino, L., Gancet, J., Wiklund, J., Remuss, V., Perez, I., Gutierrez, L., Viegas, D., Benitez, M., et al.: Multiple eyes in the skies: architecture and perception issues in the comets unmanned air vehicles project. IEEE Robotics & Automation Magazine (2005)
29. Lockheed-Martin: Ucf lockheed-martin uav dataset (2009), `http://vision.eecs.ucf.edu/aerial/index.html`
30. Everingham, M., Van Gool, L., Williams, C.K.I., Winn, J., Zisserman, A.: The pascal visual object classes (voc) challenge. IJCV (2010)

Online Video Segmentation by Bayesian Split-Merge Clustering

Juho Lee[1], Suha Kwak[1], Bohyung Han[1,3], and Seungjin Choi[1,2,3]

[1] Department of Computer Science and Engineering
[2] Division of IT Convergence Engineering
[3] Department of Creative IT Excellence Engineering,
Pohang University of Science and Technology,
77 Cheongam-ro, Nam-gu, Pohang 790-784, Korea
{stonecold,mercury3,bhhan,seungjin}@postech.ac.kr

Abstract. We present an online video segmentation algorithm based on a novel nonparametric Bayesian clustering method called Bayesian Split-Merge Clustering (BSMC). BSMC can efficiently cluster dynamically changing data through split and merge processes at each time step, where the decision for splitting and merging is made by approximate posterior distributions over partitions with Dirichlet Process (DP) priors. Moreover, BSMC sidesteps the difficult problem of finding the proper number of clusters by virtue of the flexibility of nonparametric Bayesian models. We naturally apply BSMC to online video segmentation, which is composed of three steps—pixel clustering, histogram-based merging and temporal matching. We demonstrate the performance of our algorithm on complex real video sequences compared to other existing methods.

1 Introduction

Clustering is a primitive problem widely used in many computer vision applications. While clustering algorithms have typically been invented for static data, some applications involve dynamic data evolving over time, which often makes the problem much more difficult; clustering results should be consistent in the temporal domain and adaptive to the changes of existing data and the arrivals of new data. Clustering with such constraints is called *evolutionary clustering* [1] and most of existing algorithms are limited to simple extensions of standard clustering techniques by enforcing temporal smoothness [1, 2].

In computer vision, video segmentation is an important example of evolutionary clustering. As a generalization of image segmentation, it aims to cluster the pixels into related groups throughout an input video. However, video segmentation is not straightforward to be handled by ordinary evolutionary clustering techniques because natural videos often involve drastic changes and complex cluster structures. Due to this challenge, many video segmentation algorithms are designed in batch method, which process the entire spatio-temporal video volume offline [3–5]. However, batch processing on the spatio-temporal volume is generally expensive in time and space, and often intractable; the development

A. Fitzgibbon et al. (Eds.): ECCV 2012, Part IV, LNCS 7575, pp. 856–869, 2012.

of fast and robust online video segmentation algorithm would be essential for the situations with limited resources and real-time requirements.

On the other hand, many video segmentation algorithms suffer from the choice of the proper number of segments as it dynamically changes over time. One possible solution is using nonparametric Bayesian methods such as Dirichlet Process Mixture (DPM) [6] based on the Dirichlet process [7]. There is a prior work to apply the DPM to adapting the number of clusters over time in evolving datasets [8]. For video segmentation, a DPM based algorithm was proposed by extending the static DPM using MCMC for inference [9]. However, both generalizations assume slow evolutions of data. Especially in [9], videos are assumed to be moderately changing and relatively simple because of the limitation of the expensive MCMC steps for inference.

In this paper, we propose an online video segmentation technique based on a novel clustering algorithm called Bayesian Split-Merge Clustering (BSMC). BSMC efficiently organizes clusters through split and merge processes and determines the number of clusters in evolving data, based on the Dirichlet process. It is inspired from Bayesian Hierarchical Clustering (BHC) [10]—a probabilistic version of agglomerative hierarchical clustering. BSMC is a probabilistic version of top-down and bottom-up split-merge clustering, where the initial clustering of the current data is given by the model at the previous time step. The proposed algorithm efficiently handles the temporal variations of data by incremental update of clustering through split and merge operations from the initial clusters at each time step; it maintains structural consistencies in time and adapts to substantial changes from old clusters. Note that BHC is a bottom-up clustering algorithm, which is not easily extended for evolving data. BSMC is nicely applied to the online video segmentation problem and efficiently handles the drastic variations in real-world video sequences with greater accuracy compared to other online segmentation method [9]. The advantages of our video segmentation algorithm are as follows:

- Contrary to many existing algorithms, the proposed algorithm is an online algorithm.
- It performs cluster-wise split-merge inference for clustering in contrast to point-wise inference in DP mixture models; at each time step, it can rapidly adapt to dynamic changes in video, while MCMC methods require many iterations to converge to the solution.
- It sidesteps the difficult problem of finding the proper number of segments by employing flexible nonparametric Bayesian models.

This paper is organized as follows. We first describe general nonparametric Bayesian clustering in Section 2 and discuss BSMC algorithm in Section 3. Section 4 describes the application of our algorithm to video segmentation. Our technique is tested on synthetic data and real video sequences, and its performance is illustrated in Section 5.

2 Nonparametric Bayesian Clustering

2.1 Mixture over Partitions

Clustering on the input dataset $\boldsymbol{X} = \{\boldsymbol{x}_1, \dots, \boldsymbol{x}_N\}$ is a task to find a mutually-exclusive partition $\{\boldsymbol{X}_1, \dots, \boldsymbol{X}_K\}$ of $\boldsymbol{X}$, where K can vary from 1 to N. The number of possible partitions is $\mathcal{O}(N^N)$. In nonparametric Bayesian clustering models, each partition of $\boldsymbol{X}$ is given a probability that measures how well the partition reflects the structure of a dataset. Hence, one can write the marginal probability of $\boldsymbol{X}$ as a mixture over partitions as

$$p(\boldsymbol{X}) = \sum_{\phi \in \Phi(\boldsymbol{X})} p(\boldsymbol{X}, \phi) = \sum_{\phi \in \Phi(\boldsymbol{X})} p(\boldsymbol{X}|\phi) p(\phi), \tag{1}$$

where $\Phi(\boldsymbol{X})$ is a set of all partitions of $\boldsymbol{X}$, and $p(\phi)$ is a prior distribution over partition ϕ. $p(\boldsymbol{X}|\phi)$ is a likelihood for $\boldsymbol{X}$ given a partition ϕ, which is given by

$$p(\boldsymbol{X}|\phi) = \prod_{k=1}^{K_\phi} p(\boldsymbol{X}_k^\phi), \tag{2}$$

where $\{\boldsymbol{X}_k^\phi\}_{k=1}^{K_\phi}$ is a set of K_ϕ clusters corresponding to ϕ. Each cluster is characterized by its parameter θ_k, which defines a probabilistic model generating the data that belong to the kth cluster.[1] In non-Bayesian models, we find the optimal parameters for all clusters by point estimation. In Bayesian models, we place a prior distribution over parameters and integrate them out. Therefore, the probability of cluster $p(\boldsymbol{X}_k^\phi)$—in other words, the probability that the data in $\boldsymbol{X}_k^\phi$ are independently drawn from the same model—is computed as

$$p(\boldsymbol{X}_k^\phi) = \int \Bigg\{ \prod_{\boldsymbol{x}_n \in \boldsymbol{X}_k^\phi} p(\boldsymbol{x}_n|\theta_k) \Bigg\} p(\theta_k) d\theta_k, \tag{3}$$

which is computed easily provided that $p(\theta_k)$ is a conjugate prior for $p(\boldsymbol{x}_n|\theta_k)$. Using these probabilities, we compute a score for a partition ϕ by the joint probability $p(\boldsymbol{X}, \phi)$. As a result, finding the optimal partition of $\boldsymbol{X}$ reduces to finding the partition with maximum joint probability as

$$\phi^* = \arg\max_{\phi \in \Phi(\boldsymbol{X})} p(\boldsymbol{X}, \phi). \tag{4}$$

Note that we do not place any hypothesis on the number of clusters, which means that solving Eq. (4) bypasses the model selection problem. However, finding ϕ^* is often impractical because of the huge search space and the intractable computation of posterior $p(\boldsymbol{X}|\phi)$. The most popular approach to solve the problem is MCMC sampling, which draws indefinite number of samples from $p(\phi|\boldsymbol{X})$ and finds reasonable partitions based on the samples.

[1] For example, if the underlying probabilistic model is Gaussian, the parameter would be the mean and covariance of a cluster.

2.2 Prior for Partitions

To define the joint probability $p(\boldsymbol{X}, \phi)$, we need a prior $p(\phi)$ that is a probability distribution over partitions ϕ. One of choices for the prior is Dirichlet process (DP) [7], which is a random measure on discrete distributions with infinite supports; Dirichlet Process Mixture (DPM) refers to the nonparametric Bayesian models with the DP prior. Under the DP, a random partition of dataset is easily drawn by Chinese restaurant process [6], which is a predictive distribution of DP. Suppose that $\boldsymbol{x}_{<n} = \{\boldsymbol{x}_1, \ldots, \boldsymbol{x}_{n-1}\}$ are partitioned into K clusters $\{\boldsymbol{X}_k\}_{k=1}^{K}$. Then, for the nth point $\boldsymbol{x}_n$,

$$p(\boldsymbol{x}_n \in \boldsymbol{X}_k, 1 \leq k \leq K | \boldsymbol{x}_{<n}) = \frac{N_k}{n + \alpha - 1} \quad (5)$$

$$p(\boldsymbol{x}_n \in \boldsymbol{X}_{K+1} | \boldsymbol{x}_{<n}) = \frac{\alpha}{n + \alpha - 1}, \quad (6)$$

where $N_k = |\boldsymbol{X}_k|$. This implies that $\boldsymbol{x}_n$ may belong to the existing clusters or create a new cluster. Here, α is a *concentration parameter* that controls the tendency to create a new cluster. Using these conditional distributions, the joint distribution of ϕ is given as

$$p(\phi) = \frac{\alpha^{K^\phi} \Gamma(\alpha)}{\Gamma(N + \alpha)} \prod_{k=1}^{K^\phi} \Gamma(N_k^\phi), \quad (7)$$

where Γ denotes the gamma function. Note that this probability is not affected by the ordering of the data, which is referred to as *exchangeability.*

2.3 Bayesian Hierarchical Clustering (BHC)

Instead of drawing indefinite number of samples from $p(\phi|\boldsymbol{X})$, one can reduce the search space and find the optimal solution by selecting the best among the possible partitions. BHC [10], a probabilistic version of agglomerative hierarchical clustering, reduces the search space using a tree representing the hierarchical structure of the dataset. It computes the *probability* of merging based on the posterior distribution of DPM and merges the pairs whose merging probability is the largest. Unlike traditional hierarchical clustering methods, it automatically determines whether the tree requires additional merging or not by means of the posterior probability. Therefore, it is free from the model selection problem.

More specifically, let $\boldsymbol{X}$ be a dataset to be clustered. BHC computes $p(\boldsymbol{X}|T)$, where T is the tree composed of the elements in $\boldsymbol{X}$. Instead of summing all possible partitions, BHC sums over the tree-consistent partitions, which are the partitions existing under the tree, representing the hierarchical cluster structure of the dataset. $p(\boldsymbol{X}|T)$ is computed recursively from the bottom, where each data point corresponds to one node. Let $\boldsymbol{X}_i$ be a set of data in the subtree rooted by T_i, $\boldsymbol{X}_j$ be another node in the same level and $\boldsymbol{X}_k = \boldsymbol{X}_i \cup \boldsymbol{X}_j$.

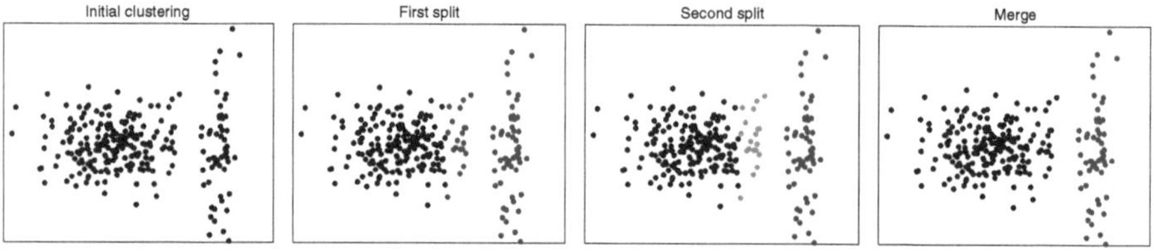

Fig. 1. Example of clustering by BSMC. A single cluster is split and merged through the split and merge stage to perform clustering.

There are two possible options: $\boldsymbol{X}_i$ and $\boldsymbol{X}_j$ belong to the one cluster $\boldsymbol{X}_k$ or they are separate clusters. Therefore, $p(\boldsymbol{X}_k|T_k)$ is recursively computed as

$$p(\boldsymbol{X}_k|T_k) = \pi_k p(\boldsymbol{X}_k|H_k) + (1-\pi_k)p(\boldsymbol{X}_i|T_i)p(\boldsymbol{X}_j|T_j), \tag{8}$$

where H_k is a hypothesis that $\boldsymbol{X}_k$ is a single cluster and π_k is a prior probability for H_k that is recursively computed from the DP prior. (Note that $p(\boldsymbol{X}_k|H_k)$ is equivalent to (3).) By the Bayes rule, the posterior probability for H_k is

$$P(H_k|\boldsymbol{X}_k) = \frac{\pi_k p(\boldsymbol{X}_k|H_k)}{\pi_k p(\boldsymbol{X}_k) + (1-\pi_k)p(\boldsymbol{X}_i|T_i)p(\boldsymbol{X}_j|T_j)}, \tag{9}$$

and $p(H_k|\boldsymbol{X}_k) > 0.5$ means that $\boldsymbol{X}_i$ and $\boldsymbol{X}_j$ should be merged. Therefore, the algorithm can determine the stopping level naturally while greedily merging the pair with the largest posterior probability in Eq. (9) at each iteration.

3 Bayesian Split-Merge Clustering (BSMC)

BHC is a batch clustering algorithm that always starts its merge process from the bottom level; it is not desirable for evolving data since previous clustering results are ignored completely. Therefore, we propose an alternative hierarchical clustering algorithm called *Bayesian Split-Merge Clustering (BSMC)*. BSMC is a probabilistic version of traditional split-merge clustering algorithm such as ISO-DATA [11]. As its name implies, BSMC obtains the optimal partition through split and merge procedures. The decision of splitting or merging depends on the approximate posterior of partitions based on Bayesian clustering model. Therefore, it can bypass the model selection problem. Moreover, BSMC is appropriate for evolving data since it can start clustering from any intermediate level of the propagated tree.

Given an initial partition, we recursively split clusters in so-called the *split stage* as long as the probability of splitting is larger than 0.5. After that, pairs of clusters are merged in a recursive manner as long as the probability of merging is larger than 0.5, which is done in the *merge stage*. The procedure for BSMC is illustrated in Fig. 1.

3.1 Initial Partitions

At each time step, the initial partition ϕ_0 is obtained from the previous clustering result. If a new data point enters, a new cluster is created for the new data point. If no initial partition is given—for example, at the first time step, ϕ_0 is set to a single cluster containing all data.

3.2 Split Stage

Let $\boldsymbol{X} = \{\boldsymbol{x}_1, \ldots, \boldsymbol{x}_N\}$ be a dataset, ϕ_0 be an initial partition and ϕ be the incumbent solution at a new time step. (The time index is omitted for simplicity.) Initially, we set $\phi = \phi_0$, which corresponds to $\{\boldsymbol{X}_k^{\phi}\}_{k=1}^{K_\phi}$. In the split stage, we test whether any of these clusters should be split into two or more clusters. By the Bayesian clustering model, the posterior probability of ϕ is given by

$$p(\phi|\boldsymbol{X}) = \frac{p(\boldsymbol{X}|\phi)p(\phi)}{\sum_{\phi' \in \Phi(\boldsymbol{X})} p(\boldsymbol{X}|\phi')p(\phi')}. \tag{10}$$

To estimate this posterior without considering all partitions, we test the partitions made by splitting current clusters. Let ϕ^{s} be a partition that the current cluster $\boldsymbol{X}_k^{\phi}$ is split into two clusters $\boldsymbol{X}_i^{\phi^{\mathrm{s}}}$ and $\boldsymbol{X}_j^{\phi^{\mathrm{s}}}$ and other clusters remain unchanged. One can propose ϕ^{s} by any appropriate bisecting algorithm such as k-means clustering, spectral clustering or graph cut. Then, we obtain

$$p(\phi|\boldsymbol{X}) < \frac{p(\boldsymbol{X}|\phi)p(\phi)}{p(\boldsymbol{X}|\phi)p(\phi) + p(\boldsymbol{X}|\phi^{\mathrm{s}})p(\phi^{\mathrm{s}})} = \left\{1 + \frac{p(\boldsymbol{X}|\phi^{\mathrm{s}})p(\phi^{\mathrm{s}})}{p(\boldsymbol{X}|\phi)p(\phi)}\right\}^{-1}, \tag{11}$$

which computes a loose upper bound of $p(\phi|\boldsymbol{X})$ using ϕ^{s} only. The upper bound gets tighter as $p(\boldsymbol{X}, \phi^{\mathrm{s}})$ increases. Although the bound is not tight for the accurate computation of $p(\phi|\boldsymbol{X})$, it is sufficient to check the optimality of ϕ.

Suppose that we define the split probability p_{split} as

$$p_{\text{split}} = 1 - \left\{1 + \frac{p(\boldsymbol{X}|\phi^{\mathrm{s}})p(\phi^{\mathrm{s}})}{p(\boldsymbol{X}|\phi)p(\phi)}\right\}^{-1}. \tag{12}$$

If $p_{\text{split}} > 0.5$, $p(\phi|\boldsymbol{X}) < 0.5$ by Eq. (11). Therefore, we conclude that ϕ is not optimal. The ratio in p_{split} can easily be computed since the terms for clusters other than $\boldsymbol{X}_k^{\phi}$ are canceled out. Using DP prior in Eq. (7), p_{split} is given by

$$p_{\text{split}} = 1 - \left\{1 + \frac{\alpha\Gamma(N_i^{\phi^{\mathrm{s}}})\Gamma(N_j^{\phi^{\mathrm{s}}})p(\boldsymbol{X}_i^{\phi^{\mathrm{s}}})p(\boldsymbol{X}_j^{\phi^{\mathrm{s}}})}{\Gamma(N_k^{\phi})p(\boldsymbol{X}_k^{\phi})}\right\}^{-1}. \tag{13}$$

If $p_{\text{split}} > 0.5$, we set $\phi = \phi^{\mathrm{s}}$. Then, for the two split clusters $\boldsymbol{X}_i^{\phi^{\mathrm{s}}}$ and $\boldsymbol{X}_j^{\phi^{\mathrm{s}}}$, we repeat the same procedure recursively as long as $p_{\text{split}} > 0.5$. The recursion for all initial clusters achieves the partition that is not desirable to split any further.

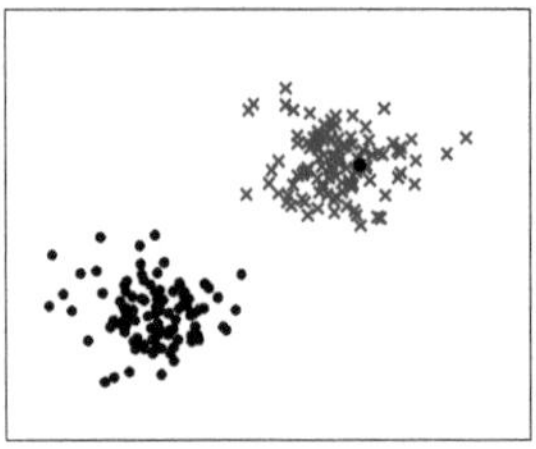

Fig. 2. A partition that requires postprocessing. The isolated black circle in the red cross cluster can simply be allocated to the red cross cluster in the postprocessing stage.

3.3 Merge Stage

In the merge stage, we determine whether any pairs of split clusters should be merged—for example, the [blue] and the [green] clusters in Figure 1 are more natural to be merged after split stage. Let $\boldsymbol{X}_i^\phi$ and $\boldsymbol{X}_j^\phi$ be a pair of clusters under the current optimal partition. By the similar arguments in Section 3.2, we check whether $p(\phi|\boldsymbol{X})$ is large enough by proposing a merged partition. Let ϕ^{m} be a partition that merges $\boldsymbol{X}_i^\phi$ and $\boldsymbol{X}_j^\phi$ into $\boldsymbol{X}_k^{\phi^{\mathrm{m}}}$ and leaves other clusters unchanged. Similar to the split stage, p_{merge} is given by

$$p_{\mathrm{merge}} = 1 - \left\{ 1 + \frac{\Gamma(N_k^{\phi^{\mathrm{m}}}) p(\boldsymbol{X}_k^{\phi^{\mathrm{m}}})}{\alpha \Gamma(N_i^\phi)\Gamma(N_j^\phi) p(\boldsymbol{X}_i^\phi) p(\boldsymbol{X}_j^\phi)} \right\}^{-1} . \tag{14}$$

If $p_{\mathrm{merge}} > 0.5$, we conclude that ϕ needs to be improved. As in BHC, we compute p_{merge} for all pairs of clusters and merge the pairs with the largest p_{merge}. We repeat the same procedure as long as the largest $p_{\mathrm{merge}} > 0.5$.

3.4 Quality of the Solution

We can prove that $p(\phi|\boldsymbol{X})$ always increases by the splitting and merging:

$$1 - \left\{ 1 + \frac{p(\boldsymbol{X}|\phi')p(\phi')}{p(\boldsymbol{X}|\phi)p(\phi)} \right\}^{-1} > \frac{1}{2} \iff p(\boldsymbol{X}|\phi')p(\phi') > p(\boldsymbol{X}|\phi)p(\phi), \tag{15}$$

where $\phi' \in \{\phi^{\mathrm{s}}, \phi^{\mathrm{m}}\}$. Although this does not guarantee the optimality, it justifies the use of BSMC for the situations where good initial solutions are given, like video segmentation. According to our observation, BSMC provides quality solutions for complex and fast changing videos.

3.5 Postprocessing

Contrary to other point-wise inference algorithms, BSMC is a cluster-wise algorithm. Although this cluster-wise operations make BSMC efficient, some point-wise errors might occur as presented in Fig. 2. Since the overall cluster structure is found after the split and merge stage, these errors are easily fixed by allocating each point to the clusters having the closest center. The entire procedure of BSMC is summarized in Algorithm 1.

Algorithm 1. Bayesian Split-Merge Clustering

Input: Initial partition ϕ_0 and dataset $\boldsymbol{X} = \{\boldsymbol{x}_1, \ldots, \boldsymbol{x}_N\}$.
Output: Optimal partition ϕ^*.
  Initialize $\phi = \phi_0$.
  • **Split stage**
  for $k = 1, \ldots, K_\phi$ **do**
    Propose ϕ^s by bisecting $\boldsymbol{X}_k^\phi$ into $\boldsymbol{X}_i^{\phi^\text{s}}$ and $\boldsymbol{X}_j^{\phi^\text{s}}$.
    if $p_\text{split} > 0.5$ **then**
      Split $\boldsymbol{X}_k^\phi$ into $\boldsymbol{X}_i^{\phi^\text{s}}$ and $\boldsymbol{X}_j^{\phi^\text{s}}$ (Set $\phi \leftarrow \phi^\text{s}$.)
      Recursively split $\boldsymbol{X}_i^{\phi^\text{s}}$ and $\boldsymbol{X}_j^{\phi^\text{s}}$.
    end if
  end for
  • **Merge stage**
  Compute p_merge for all pairs of split clusters.
  while The maximum $p_\text{merge} > 0.5$ and $K_\phi > 1$ **do**
    Merge the maximum p_merge pair ($\phi \leftarrow \phi^\text{m}$) and update p_merge.
  end while
  • **Postprocessing**
  for $n = 1, \ldots, N$ **do**
    Allocate $\boldsymbol{x}_n$ to the cluster with the closest mean.
  end for
  $\phi^* \leftarrow \phi$.

4 Video Segmentation

BSMC can be naturally applied to video segmentation in the spatio-temporal domain. In this section, we describe three steps to accomplish video segmentation results perceptually consistent and temporally coherent.

4.1 Pixel Clustering

We first extract RGB color values (or xy-RGB vectors to incorporate spatial constraints) from all pixels in the input image and cluster them. Since our method does not suffer from the problem of choosing the proper number of segments, it can deal with changing number of segments throughout the video. Furthermore, we can provide the clustering result in the previous frame as an initial partition when a new frame arrives. Then, the initial clusters are typically split near the boundaries of moving objects and the split clusters merge to build new clusters. This approach gives segmentation results that are consistent in the major boundaries. We call this procedure *pixel clustering.*

4.2 Second Merge Stage by Histogram Feature

Since pixel clustering employs local features only, clustering results may not be consistent temporally due to the jitters in the regions involving complex textures and coherent with human perception that often treats semantically related but textured areas as a single segment.

To overcome such limitations, we adopt the idea of region-based segmentation proposed in [4]. We run the second merge stage, based on *histogram features* obtained from regions resulting from the pixel clustering. Using these histogram features, the similarities between regions are measured by color distributions of the regions. Therefore, two textured regions with similar color distributions may have high probability of merging. To define the similarity between histograms, we introduce a probabilistic model for histograms. Let $\boldsymbol{h} = [h_1 \dots h_K]^\top$ be a K-bin color histogram. Following [12], we use the multinomial distribution for the likelihood of histograms, which is given by

$$p(\boldsymbol{h}|\boldsymbol{\beta}) = \frac{M!}{\prod_{k=1}^{K} h_k!} \prod_{k=1}^{K} \beta_k^{h_k}, \tag{16}$$

where $M = \sum_k h_k$ is a normalization constant[2], $\boldsymbol{\beta} = [\beta_1 \dots \beta_K]^\top$ is a parameter that defines the probability of each bin. We use the Dirichlet distribution for $\boldsymbol{\beta}$ that is a conjugate prior of multinomial distribution as

$$p(\boldsymbol{\beta}|\boldsymbol{\pi}) = \frac{\Gamma\left(\sum_{k=1}^{K} \pi_k\right)}{\prod_{k=1}^{K} \Gamma(\pi_k)} \prod_{k=1}^{K} \beta_k^{\pi_k - 1}, \tag{17}$$

where $\boldsymbol{\pi}$ is a hyperparameter for Dirichlet distribution. Now, we can define p_{merge} under these probabilistic models. Denoting two sets of histograms by $\boldsymbol{H}_i = \{\boldsymbol{h}_{i,1}, \dots, \boldsymbol{h}_{i,N_i}\}$ and $\boldsymbol{H}_j = \{\boldsymbol{h}_{j,1}, \dots, \boldsymbol{h}_{j,N_j}\}$, which represent two clusters of regions, the probability of merging these two clusters is given by

$$p_{\text{merge}} = 1 - \left\{1 + \frac{\Gamma(N_i + N_j) p(\boldsymbol{H}_i \cup \boldsymbol{H}_j)}{\alpha \Gamma(N_i) \Gamma(N_j) p(\boldsymbol{H}_i) p(\boldsymbol{H}_j)}\right\}^{-1}. \tag{18}$$

We iteratively merge regions as long as the maximum p_{merge} is greater than 0.5. Note that we can restrict candidates pairs to be adjacent to each other to incorporate spatial constraints.

4.3 Matching Clusters between Frames

Since our algorithm is based on the splitting and merging process, maintaining segment identities across frames is not straightforward . We present a simple solution to match clusters between adjacent frames to maintain cluster identity. Suppose that $\boldsymbol{H}_t$ and $\boldsymbol{H}_{t+1}$ are the sets of histograms extracted from the regions made by clustering at the frame t and $t+1$, respectively. We perform another merge stage on $\boldsymbol{H}_t \cup \boldsymbol{H}_{t+1}$; if $\boldsymbol{h}_{t,i}$ and $\boldsymbol{h}_{t+1,j}$ belong to the same cluster, they are matched and identified as a same segment. An additional benefit of this strategy is improved temporal coherency; erroneously separated segments in $\boldsymbol{H}_t$ can be merged using additional information given by $\boldsymbol{H}_{t+1}$. The entire process of segmentation is summarized in Fig. 3.

[2] We normalize $\boldsymbol{h}$ and multiply M to compare regions with different sizes.

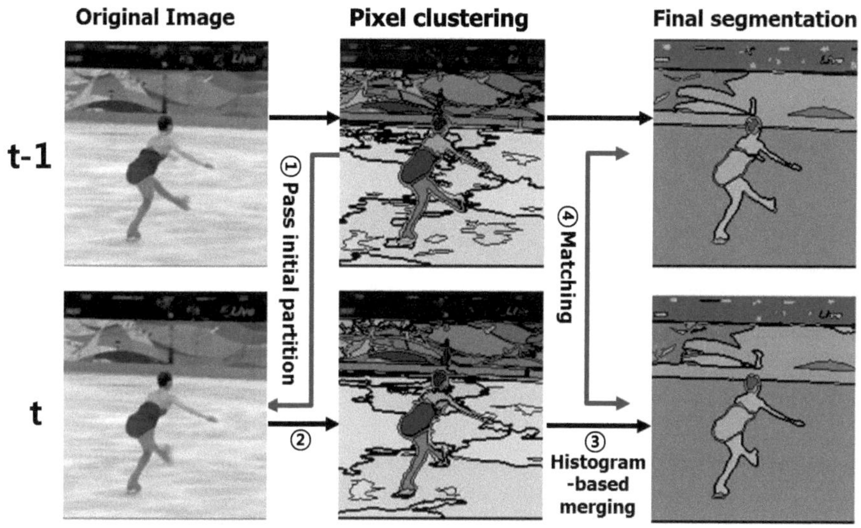

Fig. 3. Video segmentation process. 1. Passing initial partition 2. Pixel segmentation using BSMC 3. Histogram-based merging. 4. Matching two frames.

5 Experiments

5.1 Clustering Simulation

To evaluate the solutions by BSMC, we compared BSMC with collapsed Gibbs sampler for DPM [13], BHC [10] and DPChain [8] on a synthetic dataset. The dataset is composed of 16 frames evolving over time where points in each frame are generated from a Gaussian mixture model (Fig.4(a)). Throughout the sequence, the characteristics of data including the number of clusters change drastically over time, which violates the assumption of temporal smoothness in evolutionary clustering.

For all algorithms, we used the Gaussian likelihood and Gaussian-Wishart prior as parameters:

$$p(\boldsymbol{x}|\boldsymbol{\mu}, \boldsymbol{\Lambda}) = \mathcal{N}(\boldsymbol{x}|\boldsymbol{\mu}, \boldsymbol{\Lambda}^{-1}) \tag{19}$$

$$p(\boldsymbol{\mu}, \boldsymbol{\Lambda}) = \mathcal{N}(\boldsymbol{\mu}|\boldsymbol{m}, (\tau\boldsymbol{\Lambda})^{-1})\mathcal{W}(\boldsymbol{\Lambda}|\boldsymbol{W}, \nu) \tag{20}$$

where $\boldsymbol{\mu}$ is the mean of a cluster, $\boldsymbol{\Lambda}$ is a precision and $\{\boldsymbol{m}, \tau, \nu, \boldsymbol{W}\}$ are hyperparameters. In all experiments, we set $\boldsymbol{m}$ and $\boldsymbol{W}$ to the sample mean and precision of the dataset and fixed $\tau = 0.01$ and $\nu = 15$. BSMC employed k-means clustering for bisection. We iterated 100 times for the collapsed Gibbs sampler and DPChain. For DPChain, initial labels are given by the result of the previous time step. We controlled the smoothness parameter λ to 0.5 (DPChain1) and 1 (DPChain2). Smaller λ means more temporal smoothness. For all algorithms except BHC, we conducted clustering 10 times and averaged the results to handle randomness.

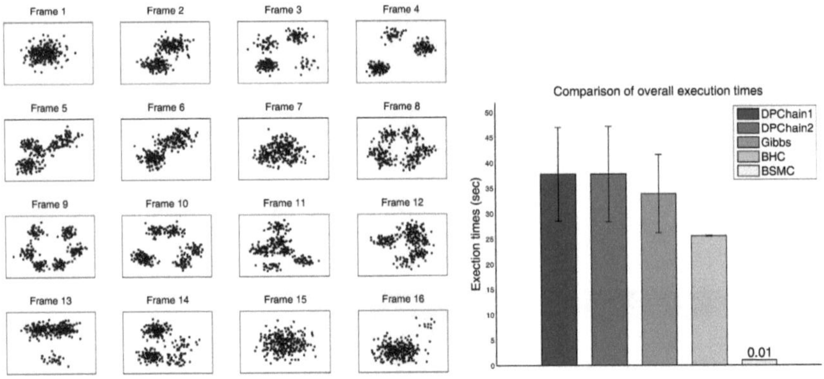

(a) (b)

Fig. 4. (a) Synthetic dataset generated using Gaussian mixture models with moving centers. (b) Average computing time in seconds.

According to our experiments, the accuracies of all algorithms are almost identical. However, in terms of running time, BSMC is faster at least by three orders of magnitude than all other algorithms (Fig. 4(b)). The computing time of BSMC is dominated by the bisecting algorithm due to its cluster-wise inference. Therefore, provided that the bisecting algorithm is efficient, BSMC would be significantly faster while maintaining comparable clustering performance.

5.2 Video Segmentations

We tested our algorithm on real world video sequences, which include dynamic movements and complex patterns. We compared our method with a offline algorithm, hierarchical graph-based video segmentation (EHGBVS) [4], and an online algorithm, Bayesian order-adaptive clustering (BOAC) [9].

For pixel clustering, we used k-means clustering in the split stage, and the Gaussian likelihood and Gaussian-Wishart prior for underlying probabilistic models. For color histograms in histogram merging, we employed 3D color histograms. For the BOAC, we used 4-bin RGB histograms for each channel and set the window radius to 2. We iterated 100 times for the first frame and $2 \sim 5$ times for the rest of frames. For EHGBVS, we used the default settings provided in the project website.[3]

Qualitative Comparison. We tested five sequences: *skating* (180×320, 185 frames), *jump* (224×352, 157 frames), *sprint* (320×480, 442 frames), *matrix* (272×480, 171 frames) and *earth* (170×400, 98 frames).[4] Note that, contrary to the online algorithms such as BSMC and BOAC, EHGBVS is a batch algorithm

[3] `http://neumann.cc.gt.atl.ga.us/segmentation/`

[4] All videos are downloaded from YouTube except the *earth* sequence, which is obtained from `http://cpl.cc.gatech.edu/projects/videosegmentation/` [4].

Fig. 5. Comparison of three video segmentation algorithms. From top to bottom, *skating, jump, sprint, matrix* and *earth* sequence are presented. From left to right, original sequence and the results by BSMC, BSMC with spatial constraints, BOAC and EHG-BVS are illustrated. Frame numbers are shown at upper-left corners.

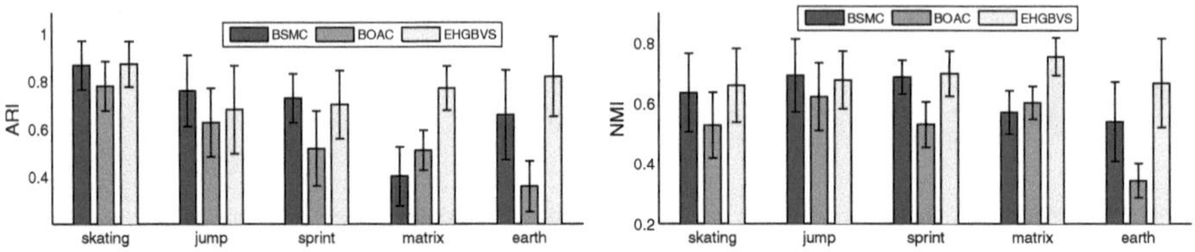

Fig. 6. Average ARI and NMI values of three algorithms for five sequences

that performs a global optimization for segmentation. Also, it can maintain segment identities in 3D spatio-temporal volume and has advantage to visualize results with less flickering. However, our algorithm still demonstrates visually good performance compared to EHGBVS with consistency in region boundaries while BOAC produces many noisy segments (Fig. 5). As the tested videos involve nontrivial patterns and drastic motions, BOAC requires many iterations for convergence. BSMC was approximately 4 $\sim$ 8 times faster than BOAC in our MATLAB implementation; for the *skating* sequence, ours took 207 secs while BOAC took 1647 secs. EHGBVS is implemented and run on a completely different systems with parallel architecture; direct comparison of running time is unavailable.

Quantitative Evaluation. We compared three algorithms quantitatively based on ground-truths manually constructed by five people. We evaluated the segmentation result by Adjusted Rand Index (ARI) [14] and Normalized Mutual Information (NMI) [15] for randomly selected frames from each sequence. We emphasize again that EHGBVS is an offline method which is expected to outperform online methods since it clusters past, present and future frames simultaneously. BSMC outperforms the BOAC except for the *matrix* sequence for both ARI and NMI, while being comparable to EHGBVS as illustrated in Fig. 6.

6 Conclusion

We proposed a novel on-line clustering algorithm called Bayesian split-merge clustering. BSMC can cluster evolving data efficiently and flexibly, while preserving temporal consistency and adapting to drastic changes. We applied our algorithm to online video segmentation through three steps—pixel clustering, merge by histogram, and temporal matching—and obtained good segmentation results with significantly improved efficiency.

Acknowledgments. This work was supported by MEST Basic Science Research Program through the NRF of Korea (2012-0003697), NIPA ITRC Support Program (NIPA-2012-H0301-12-3002), NIPA Program of Software Engineering Technologies Development and Experts Education, MEST Converging Research Center Program (2012K001343), MKE and NIPA "IT Consilience Creative Program" (C1515-1121-0003), and NRF WCU Program (R31-10100).

References

1. Chakrabarti, D., Kumar, R., Tomkins, A.: Evolutionary clustering. In: Proceedings of the ACM SIGKDD Conference on Knowledge Discovery and Data Mining (KDD), Philadelphia, PA (2006)
2. Chi, Y., Song, X., Zhou, D., Hino, K.: Evolutionary spectral clustering by incorporating temporal smoothness. In: Proceedings of the ACM SIGKDD Conference on Knowledge Discovery and Data Mining (KDD), San Jose, CA (2007)
3. DeMenthon, D., Megret, R.: Sptio-temporal segmentation of video by hierarchical mean shift analysis. Technical Report LAMP-TR-090,CAR-TR-978,CS-TR-4388,UMIACS-TR-2002-68, University of Maryland, College Park (2002)
4. Grundmann, M., Kwatra, V., Han, M., Essa, I.: Efficient hierarchical graph-based video segmentation. In: Proceedings of the IEEE International Conference on Computer Vision and Pattern Recognition (CVPR), San Francisco, CA (2010)
5. Wang, J., Thiesson, B., Xu, Y., Cohen, M.: Image and Video Segmentation by Anisotropic Kernel Mean Shift. In: Pajdla, T., Matas, J. (eds.) ECCV 2004. LNCS, vol. 3022, pp. 238–249. Springer, Heidelberg (2004)
6. Antoniak, C.E.: Mixtures of Dirichlet processes with applications to Bayesian nonparametric problems. The Annals of Statistics 2, 1152–1174 (1974)
7. Ferguson, T.S.: A Bayesian analysis of some nonparametric problems. The Annals of Statistics 1, 209–230 (1973)
8. Xu, T., Zhang, Z., Yu, P.S., Long, B.: Dirichlet process based evolutionary clustering. In: Proceedings of the IEEE International Conference on Data Mining (ICDM), Pisa, Italy (2008)
9. Orbanz, P., Braendle, S., Buhmann, J.M.: Bayesian Order-Adaptive Clustering for Video Segmentation. In: Yuille, A.L., Zhu, S.-C., Cremers, D., Wang, Y. (eds.) EMMCVPR 2007. LNCS, vol. 4679, pp. 334–349. Springer, Heidelberg (2007)
10. Heller, K.A., Ghahrahmani, Z.: Bayesian hierarchical clustering. In: Proceedings of the International Conference on Machine Learning (ICML), Bonn, Germany (2005)
11. Jain, A.K., Murty, M.N., Flynn, P.J.: Data clustering: A review. ACM Computing Surveys 31, 264–323 (1999)
12. Orbanz, P., Buhmann, J.M.: Smooth Image Segmentation by Nonparametric Bayesian Inference. In: Leonardis, A., Bischof, H., Pinz, A. (eds.) ECCV 2006. LNCS, vol. 3951, pp. 444–457. Springer, Heidelberg (2006)
13. Escobar, M.D., West, M.: Bayesian density estimation and inference using mixtures. Journal of the American Statistical Association 90, 577–588 (1995)
14. Hubert, L., Arabie, P.: Comparing partitions. Journal of Classification 2, 193–218 (1985)
15. Xu, W., Liu, X., Gong, Y.: Document clustering based on non-negative matrix factorization. In: Proceedings of the ACM SIGIR Conference on Research and Development in Information Retrieval (SIGIR), Toronto, Canada (2003)

Joint Classification-Regression Forests for Spatially Structured Multi-object Segmentation

Ben Glocker[1], Olivier Pauly[2,3], Ender Konukoglu[1], and Antonio Criminisi[1]

[1] Microsoft Research, Cambridge, UK
[2] Institute of Biomathematics and Biometry, Helmholtz Zentrum München, Germany
[3] Computer Aided Medical Procedures, Technische Universität München, Germany

Abstract. In many segmentation scenarios, labeled images contain rich structural information about spatial arrangement and shapes of the objects. Integrating this rich information into supervised learning techniques is promising as it generates models which go beyond learning class association, only. This paper proposes a new supervised forest model for joint classification-regression which exploits both class and structural information. Training our model is achieved by optimizing a joint objective function of pixel classification and shape regression. Shapes are represented implicitly via signed distance maps obtained directly from ground truth label maps. Thus, we can associate each image point not only with its class label, but also with its distances to object boundaries, and this at no additional cost regarding annotations. The regression component acts as spatial regularization learned from data and yields a predictor with both class and spatial consistency. In the challenging context of simultaneous multi-organ segmentation, we demonstrate the potential of our approach through experimental validation on a large dataset of 80 three-dimensional CT scans.

1 Introduction

Semantic image segmentation consists of assigning a categorical label to each pixel in an image. A common approach is to cast segmentation as a multi-label classification problem and employ a classification algorithm. In this context, supervised learning techniques have gained increased interest. Relying on the availability of annotated data, they permit to learn the relationship between visual features of pixels and their class labels during their training phase. Given an unseen image, the learned classifier is then able to predict the correct label assignment for each pixel.

Decision forests have emerged as a promising, flexible model for image understanding [1–4]. In particular, classification and regression forests have shown great performance in the tasks of supervised classification and regression such as human pose estimation [5], recognition [6], localization [7], or classification [8, 9]. Classification forests are popular because they are probabilistic and efficient, and naturally handle multi-class problems. Moreover, they often compare favorably with respect to other techniques [10, 11].

A. Fitzgibbon et al. (Eds.): ECCV 2012, Part IV, LNCS 7575, pp. 870–881, 2012.

In their original implementation classification forests provide as output a class posterior distribution for each pixel independently. Recent work has started to investigate new and more complex models of structured-output forests to enable spatially consistent predictions [12–15]. However, accessible structural information about the shapes and spatial arrangement of objects present in ground truth annotations, *i.e.* label maps, is not fully exploited in previous approaches.

The main contribution of this paper is a novel joint classification-regression formulation based on decision forests which incorporates this extra information. In each tree, we learn a discrete-continuous predictor based on class *and* spatial consistency by extracting structural information from label maps. The key innovation within our approach is a simple yet elegant modification of the training objective function which enables joint learning of classification and regression. We employ signed distance maps (SDMs) in a regression objective as efficient representations of information about shapes and spatial arrangement.

Similar to pictorial structures [16] our model is particularly suited for images with multiple objects whose organization shows some consistency (*e.g.* facial features, limbs in a human body, internal organs in medical scans, etc.).

Classification and regression have been combined before in the context of decision forests for body joint prediction [17] and object detection [18]. Both approaches are quite different to ours. In [17], the prediction model is a single continuous regressor, for which training is performed *either* based on a classification or regression objective function. In [18], the training objective alternates between classification and regression, but is not based on a joint objective function.

There are many other methods which aim at solving the problem of structured multi-object segmentation. Active shape and appearance models [19], or random fields [20] are among the most successful ones. A comparison with these methods is beyond the scope of this paper. Here, we focus on one particular approach based on classification forests, and demonstrate how performance can be substantially improved through simple modifications. We believe that an isolated view on this particular modification yields more insights than a broader comparison with substantially different methods. Further, we believe that our proposed modifications can be easily integrated in existing, more complex approaches.

Experimental validation of our model is carried out on multi-organ segmentation on a challenging labeled dataset of 3D medical CT scans of 80 patients.

2 Classification-Regression Forests

In the following, we will derive a general formulation for joint classification-regression in the context of decision forests. At the same time, we will provide the necessary details for our application of multi-object segmentation. We refer the interested reader to [2] for more details on forests.

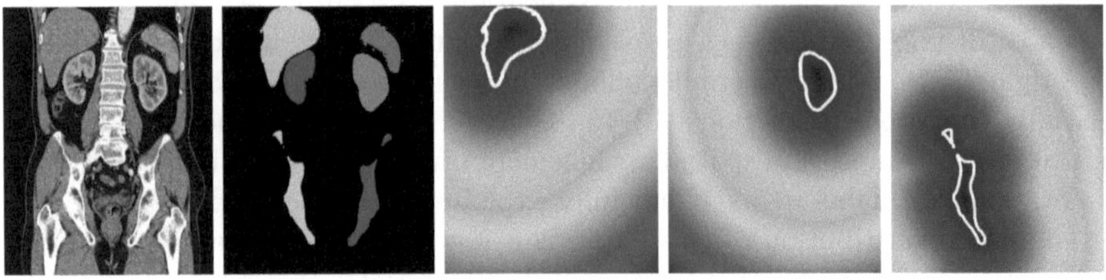

(a) CT scan (b) Label map (c) SDM liver (d) SDM kidney (e) SDM pelvis

Fig. 1. An example slice of a 3D input image in (a) with ground truth label map in (b). Besides class membership, the label map contains additional information such as a distance for each pixel to all objects of interest obtained from signed distance maps as shown in (c)-(e). The zero-level is overlaid on the distance maps for clarity. Pixels inside an object have negative distances.

2.1 Decision Forests for Supervised Learning

In its most general form, the goal of supervised, discriminative learning is to obtain the posterior distribution $p(\mathbf{y}|\mathbf{x})$, where $\mathbf{x} \in \mathbb{R}^m$ is some observation represented by a *feature vector*, and $\mathbf{y} \in \mathbb{R}^n$ is the output or *prediction* variable. Learning this distribution allows us to make predictions for new (unseen) data, *e.g.* by inferring the maximum-a-posteriori (MAP) estimate $\hat{\mathbf{y}} = \arg\max_{\mathbf{y}} p(\mathbf{y}|\mathbf{x})$.

We assume that a set of K training examples $\mathcal{S} = \{(\mathbf{x}_k, \mathbf{y}_k)\}_{k=1}^K$ is available, from which we can learn the distribution $p(\mathbf{y}|\mathbf{x})$. In image segmentation, the entity $\mathbf{x}_k$ corresponds to a collection of image features – *e.g.* intensity or textural information – extracted for an individual pixel k. The output variable is the (one-dimensional) discrete class label $\mathbf{y}_k \in \mathcal{C}$, where $\mathcal{C}$ is a finite set of labels (or objects). The aim is then to learn a predictor that determines the probability for assigning a particular class label to a pixel of a previously unseen test image.

We employ the decision forest framework which tackles the learning problem in a divide-and-conquer fashion. A decision forest is an ensemble of (probabilistic) decision trees, where each tree t yields its own distribution $p_t(\mathbf{y}|\mathbf{x})$. By iteratively subdividing the training set within the associated features space $\mathbb{R}^m$, posterior distributions can be learned "locally" on smaller training subsets. Injecting randomness into the training phase decreases the correlation between individual trees, and increases generalization (see [1] for details).

Tree testing: A (binary) decision tree is a set of two types of nodes, the *split nodes* and the *leaf nodes.* While split nodes store decision functions, leaf nodes store empirical distributions. In order to make a prediction for previously unseen data $\mathbf{x}$, we push $\mathbf{x}$ through the tree, starting at the root node. At each split node, a (binary) decision function is applied to $\mathbf{x}$, which determines whether it is sent to the left or right child node. Once the data point reaches a leaf node, we can simply read out the stored distribution $p_t(\mathbf{y}|\mathbf{x})$. The overall prediction of the forest with T trees can be obtained by averaging the individual tree predictions:

$$p(\mathbf{y}|\mathbf{x}) = \frac{1}{T}\sum_{t=1}^{T} p_t(\mathbf{y}|\mathbf{x}) \ . \tag{1}$$

Tree training: The role of training is to optimize the parameters of the decision functions and to determine the leaf node distributions. To this end, a (possibly random sub-) set of training examples $\mathcal{S}$ is simultaneously pushed through the tree. Let us denote by $\mathcal{S}_i$ the training set reaching node i, where $\mathcal{S}_0 = \mathcal{S}$ at the root node with index 0. At each split node the incoming set $\mathcal{S}_i$ is divided into two disjunct, outgoing sets $\mathcal{S}_i^L$ and $\mathcal{S}_i^R$ which are sent to the left and right child nodes. The split is based on a decision function operating on the feature vectors of incoming training examples. Most commonly used split functions are so called axis-aligned functions $f_{\mathbf{v},\tau}$, defined as:

$$f_{\mathbf{v},\tau} \hat{=} (\mathbf{v} \cdot \mathbf{x} \geq \tau) \ , \tag{2}$$

where $\mathbf{v}$ is a m-dimensional binary (random) vector and $\tau \in \mathbb{R}$ is a threshold. Note that $\mathbf{v}$ has only one non-zero entry and permits thereby to select one dimension from the m-dimensional feature space. τ is then either (randomly) drawn from the range of the feature values, or optimized via exhaustive search. Based on the decision function the training examples are separated into two subsets.

Following a greedy optimization strategy, different (randomly generated) split function candidates are evaluated and the most discriminative one is found based on maximizing an objective function such as the information gain:

$$I(\mathcal{S}_i, \mathcal{S}_i^L, \mathcal{S}_i^R) = H(\mathcal{S}_i) - \sum_{j \in \{L,R\}} \frac{|\mathcal{S}_i^j|}{|\mathcal{S}_i|} H(\mathcal{S}_i^j) \ , \tag{3}$$

where $H(\cdot)$ is the entropy. In case of classification with a finite set of discrete labels $\mathcal{C}$, H is defined as the Shannon entropy

$$H(\mathcal{S}) = -\sum_{\mathbf{y} \in \mathcal{C}} p(\mathbf{y}|\mathbf{x}) \log p(\mathbf{y}|\mathbf{x}) \ , \tag{4}$$

where $p(\cdot)$ is the empirical class distribution estimated from the training set $\mathcal{S}$. Good split functions should maximize the information gain which minimizes the uncertainty of the empirical distributions. When the tree growing process reaches a predefined depth, iterative splitting of the training data stops. The current node becomes a leaf where the empirical distribution over the incoming training examples is stored. The tree depth has an impact on the generalization of the tree as it directly influences the resolution of the partition of the feature space.

As a consequence of the objective function in Eq. (3), the training procedure yields leaf nodes with peaked class distributions. At test time, an unseen data point should take the same path along the tree nodes as training examples with similar features. The empirical distribution over those training examples would then provide a good prediction for the test point.

After setting out the basics of decision forests in a classification scenario, next we discuss our main contribution: a joint classification-regression model employed within the same forest.

2.2 Joint Classification-Regression

Classification forests have been widely used in practice. In this paper we argue that in some applications their discriminative power can be improved by a simple yet elegant modification within the learning procedure. So far, the training of classification forests is only based on the ground truth class labels. The key idea of our approach is to explore also the spatial structure of objects. In fact, the same ground truth, *i.e.* label maps, contain information about the shapes of objects, and in multi-class problems, about relative positions and spatial arrangement (see Fig. 1 for an example). The integration of this rich information into the supervised learning can yield better predictions. To this end, we formulate a joint classification-regression approach where the training objective is to increase both class and spatial consistency. We introduce two prediction variables where $\mathbf{c} \in \mathcal{C}$ corresponds to a one-dimensional discrete classification output, and $\mathbf{r} \in \mathbb{R}^n$ is a n-dimensional continuous regression variable. The role of this variable is described in detail in Sec. 2.3. For now, let us assume it captures some continuous shape parameters. Given the same input variable $\mathbf{x}$ as before, our goal is now to learn the joint probability $p(\mathbf{c},\mathbf{r}|\mathbf{x})$. Using the chain rule, we can rewrite this joint distribution as $p(\mathbf{c},\mathbf{r}|\mathbf{x}) = p(\mathbf{r}|\mathbf{c},\mathbf{x})\, p(\mathbf{c}|\mathbf{x})$. In order to learn this distribution within the framework of decision forests, we define the joint entropy as

$$\begin{aligned} H(\mathcal{S}) &= -\sum_{\mathbf{c}\in\mathcal{C}} \int_{\mathbf{r}\in\mathbb{R}^n} p(\mathbf{c},\mathbf{r}|\mathbf{x}) \log p(\mathbf{c},\mathbf{r}|\mathbf{x})\, d\mathbf{r} \\ &= \underbrace{-\sum_{\mathbf{c}\in\mathcal{C}} p(\mathbf{c}|\mathbf{x}) \log p(\mathbf{c}|\mathbf{x})}_{\text{Shannon Entropy: } H_{\mathbf{c}}} + \underbrace{\sum_{\mathbf{c}\in\mathcal{C}} p(\mathbf{c}|\mathbf{x}) \left(- \int_{\mathbf{r}\in\mathbb{R}^n} p(\mathbf{r}|\mathbf{c},\mathbf{x}) \log p(\mathbf{r}|\mathbf{c},\mathbf{x})\, d\mathbf{r} \right)}_{\text{Weighted Differential Entropy: } H_{\mathbf{r}|\mathbf{c}}} . \end{aligned} \tag{5}$$

During training, we maximize the same objective function as defined in Eq. (3), where now the entropy becomes $H(\mathcal{S}) = H_{\mathbf{c}}(\mathcal{S}) + H_{\mathbf{r}|\mathbf{c}}(\mathcal{S})$.

The two entropies $H_{\mathbf{c}}$ and $H_{\mathbf{r}|\mathbf{c}}$ may live within quite different ranges depending on the problem and its dimensionality, and one of them could easily overrule the other one during optimization. Hence, we propose the following normalization step

$$H(\mathcal{S}) = \frac{1}{2} \left(\frac{H_{\mathbf{c}}(\mathcal{S})}{H_{\mathbf{c}}(\mathcal{S}_0)} + \frac{H_{\mathbf{r}|\mathbf{c}}(\mathcal{S})}{H_{\mathbf{r}|\mathbf{c}}(\mathcal{S}_0)} \right) , \tag{6}$$

where each entropy is normalized w.r.t. the root node entropy. This normalization maps both initial entropies at the root node to one, and the information gain measures the relative improvement w.r.t. the inherent entropy of the training set.

2.3 Spatial Consistency via Distance Regression

In order to capture the spatial information contained in the label maps, we employ Euclidean signed distance maps (SDMs) as an implicit representation of shape. Assuming there are n different objects to be segmented, we can determine n distance maps per training image. Note that we treat the background as an extra class, so we have $|\mathcal{C}| = n+1$ number of classes, and no distance map is computed for the background class. Also note, that it is not necessary that all objects are present in all images. In practice, we can make use of indicator variables encoding the presence of an object which allows us to ignore missing data in the computation of statistics. For sake of simplicity, in the following we assume that all objects are present in all images.

The distance maps allow us to assign n-dimensional vectors $\mathbf{r} = (d_1, ..., d_n)^\top$ to each pixel in the training set, where $d_\mathbf{c}$ is the distance of a pixel to the closest boundary point of the object with class index $\mathbf{c}$. Negative distances are assigned to pixels inside an object. This is an efficient way of enriching the training set to $\mathcal{S} = \{(\mathbf{x}_k, \mathbf{c}_k, \mathbf{r}_k)\}$, where now each data point carries both information about its class membership and its relative positions w.r.t. the shapes of all objects. The regression component $\mathbf{r}$ captures both shape and spatial layout of the objects, which in a common classification approach would remain hidden in the label maps. This supplementary information comes at no additional cost regarding annotations. This is a major advantage since acquiring ground truth data can be tedious and time-consuming, in particular, in the medical domain.

For efficient training of our joint model, we need a compact representation for the conditional distribution $p(\mathbf{r}|\mathbf{c}, \mathbf{x})$ which can be efficiently stored in the leaf nodes. We employ n-dimensional multivariate Normal distributions $p(\mathbf{r}|\mathbf{c}, \mathbf{x}) \mathrel{\hat=} \mathcal{N}(\mu_{\mathbf{r}|\mathbf{c}}, \Sigma_{\mathbf{r}|\mathbf{c}}|\mathbf{r}, \mathbf{c}, \mathbf{x})$, one distribution per class label $\mathbf{c}$. Those can be efficiently stored by keeping only the means and covariance matrices. Additionally, Gaussian distributions have a closed-form definition for the differential entropy such that

$$H_{\mathbf{r}|\mathbf{c}} = \sum_{\mathbf{c}\in\mathcal{C}} p(\mathbf{c}|\mathbf{x}) \left(\frac{1}{2} \log \left[(2\pi e)^n |\Sigma_{\mathbf{r}|\mathbf{c}}| \right] \right) , \tag{7}$$

where $|\cdot|$ denotes the determinant of a matrix.

Optimizing the information gain w.r.t. this entropy encourages splits which reduce the covariance over spatial location. This is the case when elements within subsets belonging to the same class are also spatially consistent. In fact, the regression component acts as a *learned* spatial regularization. In order to demonstrate this effect, we perform a small experiment. We take one 2D image (a coronal slice from a 3D CT scans) for training a single tree using the standard

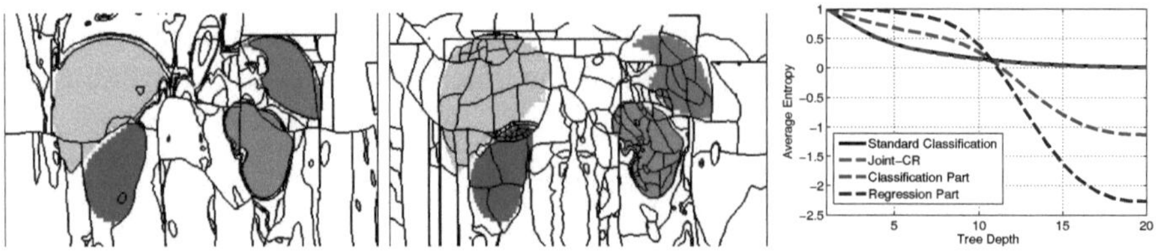

(a) Classification (b) Joint CR (c) Entropy Progression

Fig. 2. (a,b) Leaf node region maps overlaid on ground truth segmentation. The maps illustrate the spatial regularization effect of the regression component. **(c)** Progression of different parts of the joint entropy (Eq. (6)) compared to standard classification.

classification objective function, and another tree using our joint objective function. To visualize the resulting "clustering" of training points, we use the same image at test time and store for each pixel the index of the reached leaf node. From these index maps we extract the cluster regions as shown in Fig. 2(a,b). Each closed region corresponds to a particular leaf node in the corresponding tree. At the same tree depth, training jointly on the combined classification-regression objective yields leaf nodes with clusters of training examples which are both consistent in terms of class membership *and* spatial location.

Robust Parameter Estimation. The regression part of our joint predictor model requires estimation of means and covariances of the corresponding Gaussians $\mathcal{N}(\mu_{\mathbf{r}|\mathbf{c}}, \Sigma_{\mathbf{r}|\mathbf{c}}|\mathbf{r}, \mathbf{c}, \mathbf{x})$. This is commonly done via maximum likelihood (ML) estimation. Since we estimate the empirical distributions conditioned on the class label, the sample size for a particular distribution can become quite small. In order to overcome statistical problems when only few samples are available, we employ a more robust Bayesian estimation where the parent distribution of a child node plays the role of the prior. The mean is then estimated as

$$\mu^{\text{child}}_{\mathbf{r}|\mathbf{c}} = \frac{|\mathcal{S}^{\text{child}}_{\mathbf{r}|\mathbf{c}}|}{\kappa + |\mathcal{S}^{\text{child}}_{\mathbf{r}|\mathbf{c}}|}\,\bar{\mu}^{\text{child}}_{\mathbf{r}|\mathbf{c}} + \frac{\kappa}{\kappa + |\mathcal{S}^{\text{child}}_{\mathbf{r}|\mathbf{c}}|}\,\mu^{\text{parent}}_{\mathbf{r}|\mathbf{c}} \quad . \tag{8}$$

The covariance matrix is then computed as

$$\Sigma^{\text{child}}_{\mathbf{r}|\mathbf{c}} = \frac{|\mathcal{S}^{\text{child}}_{\mathbf{r}|\mathbf{c}}|}{Z}\,\bar{\Sigma}^{\text{child}}_{\mathbf{r}|\mathbf{c}} + \frac{\nu + n - 1}{Z}\,\Sigma^{\text{parent}}_{\mathbf{r}|\mathbf{c}} + \frac{\kappa\,|\mathcal{S}^{\text{child}}_{\mathbf{r}|\mathbf{c}}|}{Z\,(\kappa + |\mathcal{S}^{\text{child}}_{\mathbf{r}|\mathbf{c}}|)}\,\Psi_{\mathbf{r}|\mathbf{c}} \quad , \tag{9}$$

where $Z = \nu + n - 1 + |\mathcal{S}^{\text{child}}_{\mathbf{r}|\mathbf{c}}|$ and $\Psi_{\mathbf{r}|\mathbf{c}} = (\mu^{\text{parent}}_{\mathbf{r}|\mathbf{c}} - \bar{\mu}^{\text{child}}_{\mathbf{r}|\mathbf{c}})(\mu^{\text{parent}}_{\mathbf{r}|\mathbf{c}} - \bar{\mu}^{\text{child}}_{\mathbf{r}|\mathbf{c}})^{\top}$. Variables $\bar{\mu}^{\text{child}}_{\mathbf{r}|\mathbf{c}}$ and $\bar{\Sigma}^{\text{child}}_{\mathbf{r}|\mathbf{c}}$ are ML estimates of mean and covariance computed over the subset $\mathcal{S}^{\text{child}}_{\mathbf{r}|\mathbf{c}}$. Variables $\mu^{\text{parent}}_{\mathbf{r}|\mathbf{c}}$ and $\Sigma^{\text{parent}}_{\mathbf{r}|\mathbf{c}}$ correspond to the mean and covariance of the parent node. κ and ν are two parameters which permit to control the trade-off between the prior and the empirical information w.r.t. sample size. In fact, when the number of training examples $|\mathcal{S}^{\text{child}}_{\mathbf{r}|\mathbf{c}}|$ is sufficiently large ($|\mathcal{S}^{\text{child}}_{\mathbf{r}|\mathbf{c}}| >>

$\kappa, \nu)$, the ML estimates dominate. When the number of training samples gets closer to the values of κ and ν the estimate of $\Sigma_{\mathbf{r}|\mathbf{c}}^{\text{child}}$ relies more on the parent.

2.4 Forest Predictions

Our joint classification-regression model allows to make two kinds of predictions at test time. The obvious one is regarding the most probable class label given a new data point, *i.e.* a pixel of a test image. This MAP estimate can be obtained by simply computing

$$\hat{\mathbf{c}} = \arg\max_{\mathbf{c}\in\mathcal{C}} p(\mathbf{c}|\mathbf{x}) \ . \tag{10}$$

Note, that test efficiency from a computational perspective is exactly the same as with standard classification forests. By obtaining the labels for all pixels, we determine the multi-object segmentation of the image.

We can also make predictions regarding the regression component. The most probable estimate of object distances for a pixel can be obtained by

$$\begin{aligned}\hat{\mathbf{r}} &= \arg\max_{\mathbf{r}} p(\mathbf{r}|\mathbf{x}) \\ &= \arg\max_{\mathbf{r}} \sum_{\mathbf{c}\in\mathcal{C}} p(\mathbf{r}|\mathbf{c},\mathbf{x})p(\mathbf{c}|\mathbf{x}) \ ,\end{aligned} \tag{11}$$

which requires some sort of mode finding algorithm. Based on our Gaussian model, an alternative, robust estimate can be obtained via the mixture mean

$$\tilde{\mathbf{r}} = \sum_{\mathbf{c}\in\mathcal{C}} p(\mathbf{c}|\mathbf{x})\mu_{\mathbf{r}|\mathbf{c}} \ . \tag{12}$$

The regression allows us to estimate SDMs which could be of great use for instance in object alignment applications. One could think of defining a (weighted) matching criterion on both image intensities and regressed SDMs. The SDM part could potentially make the alignment less sensitive to initialization and more robust w.r.t. large transformations. The focus in this paper is on the segmentation part, and we are mainly interested in the label maps obtained via Eq. (10). However, we will also show results of SDM regression in the following section.

3 Experimental Validation

We evaluate our approach on the task of multi-organ segmentation in 3D medical CT scans. To this end, we collected a large dataset of 80 highly variable patient scans, in which 6 major organs have been manually delineated by an expert. The set of organs include liver, spleen, left and right kidney, left and right pelvic bone. To demonstrate the potential of our joint classification-regression strategy, we aim at isolating the effect of the proposed objective function, and therefore compare it directly with standard classifcation forests. The challenges in multi-organ segmentation arise from overlapping intensity profiles of different organs, variability in patient anatomy, presence of pathologies, and image noise. However, the human anatomy exhibits a highly structured spatial arrangement of inner parts. Hence, our approach is paricularly suitable for this task.

3.1 Experimental Setup and Training Parameters

For both methods, standard classification forest and our joint approach, we use the same fixed set of parameters. We train decision forests with 50 trees and a maximum tree depth of 20. We use bagging during training, which means each tree is trained on a random subset containing 10% of the total number of training image points. At each split node, we evaluate 100 different features from a pool of 1000 randomly generated features. For each feature, and the corresponding set of feature responses from the training points, we try 10 different thresholds uniformly distributed along the range of responses.

We employ five different types of features, where four of them are variants of 3D box features efficiently computed on integral images [21]: (i) a simple look-up of intensity in a smoothed version of the input image (Gaussian smoothing with $\sigma = 2$mm), (ii) average intensity in a randomly sized box centered at the image point, (iii) average intensity in a randomly sized box displaced by a random offset from the image point, (iv) intensity difference between the local intensity and a displaced box as in feature (iii), (v) intensity difference between two displaced boxes as defined in (iii). These features can capture both local and long-range contextual visual information. The range of the box sizes varies between 10 and 100mm. The displacements of boxes are drawn from an [0,100]mm interval. Concerning the Gaussian update for the mean and covariance estimation within the nodes, we choose $\kappa = 10$ and $\nu = 10$.

Fig. 2(c) shows the progress along tree depth of different parts of the entropy averaged over all trees. We make the following observations: i) the classification part $H_{\mathbf{c}}$ progresses almost identical compared to standard classification; ii) the regression part $H_{\mathbf{r}|\mathbf{c}}$ decreases mainly after a tree depth of 10.

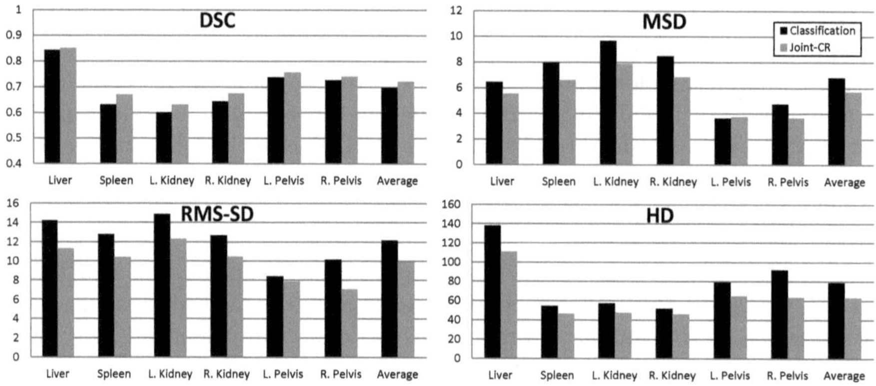

Fig. 3. Segmentation errors over four different scores. DSC measures the agreement between prediction and ground truth where 1 indicates perfect results. MSD, RMS-SD, and HD determine the surface distance in millimeters between prediction and ground truth where 0 indicates perfect results. Scores for classification forests are the black bars on the left, scores for our joint classification-regression are the gray bars on the right. All four scores indicate improved segmentation results for our approach.

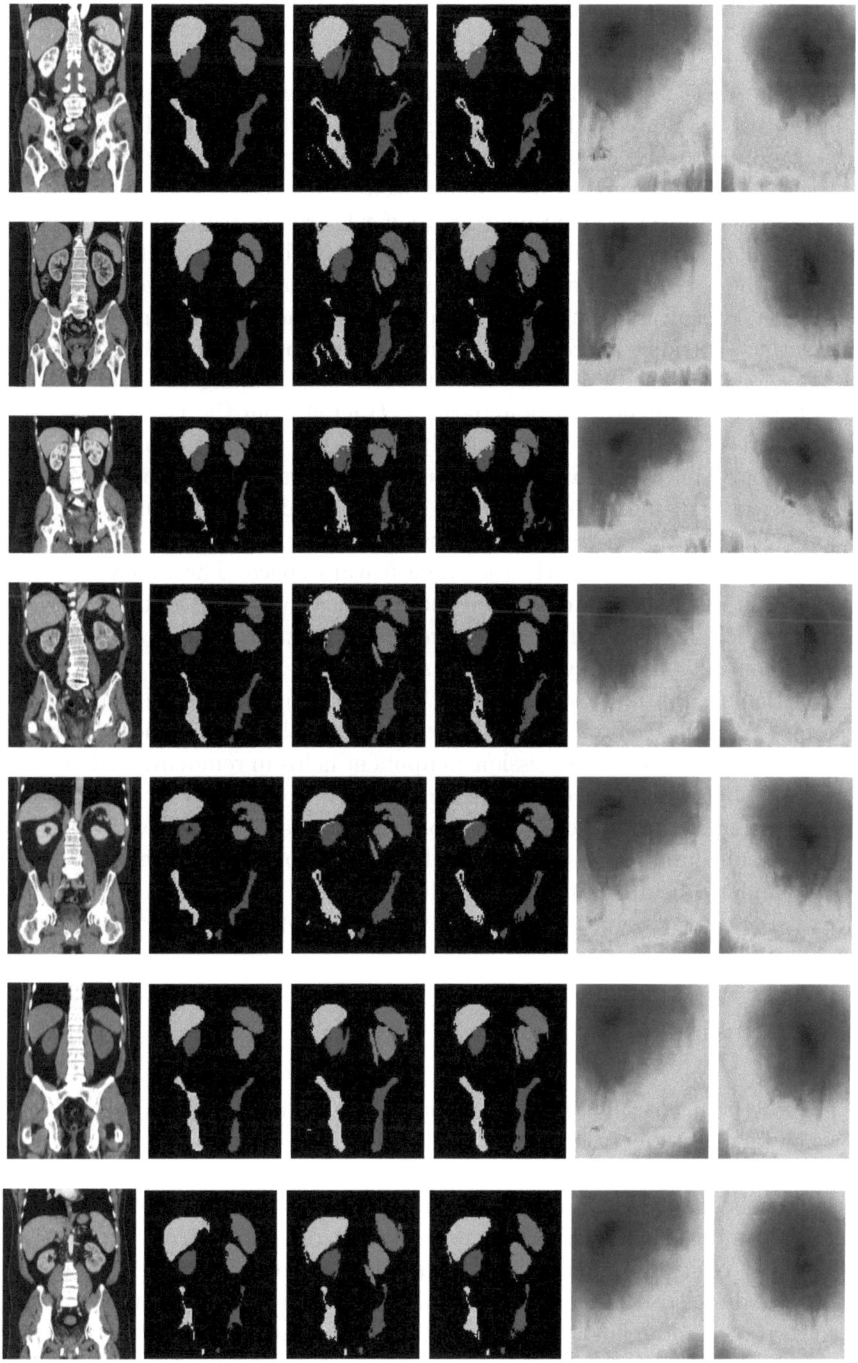

Fig. 4. From left to right: Slice from 3D input image, ground truth segmentation, MAP estimate of standard classification forest, MAP estimate of our joint approach, regressed distance maps for liver and left kidney obtained via Eq. (12).

3.2 Results

We split the 80 CT scans in two non-overlapping sets with each 40 scans and then perform a two-fold cross-validation. Hence, we can report overall segmentation errors computed on all 80 scans. The quantitative results for individual organs and the average performance are summarized in Fig. 3. Further qualitative results are shown in Fig. 4. We report errors w.r.t. ground truth annotations over four different segmentation scores, namely Dice's similarity coefficient (DSC) measuring the agreement between label maps (also known as F-score combining precision and recall into one value), and three surface distance measures. The mean surface distance (MSD), root-mean-square surface distance (RMS-SD), and Hausdorff distance (HD) are computed by determining the euclidean distances between segmentation boundaries extracted from the label maps. Note, that medical scans are always metrically calibrated (while the actual physical resolution between images varies). The unit of the last three errors is therefore in millimeters. All four scores indicate an improved performance when using our joint classification-regression approach. It is important to note, that both methods have access to exactly the same feature space. The difference in the segmentation results stems only from the modification of the training objective function, which favors features in the greedy optimization which are yield both class and spatial consistency in the splits.

In particular, the improvement w.r.t. RMS-SD and HD is important. Both measures are sensitive to segmentation errors with larger distances. Here, the regularization effect of the regression component helps in removing outliers. This is confirmed by visual inspection of the qualitative results in Fig. 4. We observe that the segmentations for our joint approach are spatially more consistent and spurious results present in the standard classification are suppressed. We also show exemplary distance maps for the liver and left kidney. The regressed distance at each image point is the mixture mean as defined in Eq. (12).

4 Conclusion

We propose joint classification-regression forests as a novel supervised learning approach for the segmentation of spatially structured objects. Our experiments demonstrate that joint optimization yields superior results with both class and spatial consistency. This is achieved via a simple modification of the training objective combined with efficient representation of shape regression at no additional cost regarding annotations. A promising direction, where our method could be of direct use, is learning application-specific energy functions – *e.g.* in the context of random fields [12, 15]. Here, our joint model could be used to learn strong unaries which exhibit spatial smoothness learned from the training data. Other tasks, such as human pose estimation [5, 17] could also benefit from joint learning. In conclusion, we believe our model adds an important component to the framework of decision forests beyond the task of pixel-wise classification.

References

1. Breiman, L.: Random Forests. Machine Learning 45(1), 5–32 (2001)
2. Criminisi, A., Shotton, J., Konukoglu, E.: Decision Forests: A Unified Framework. Foundations and Trends in Computer Graphics and Vision 7(2-3) (2011)
3. Ho, T.K.: Random Decision Forests. In: ICDAR, vol. 1, pp. 278–282 (1995)
4. Ho, T.K.: The Random Subspace Method for Constructing Decision Forests. PAMI 20(8), 832–844 (1998)
5. Shotton, J., Fitzgibbon, A., Cook, M., Sharp, T., Finocchio, M., Moore, R., Kipman, A., Blake, A.: Real-Time Human Pose Recognition in Parts from a Single Depth Image. In: CVPR, pp. 1297–1304 (2011)
6. Amit, Y., Geman, D.: Shape Quantization and Recognition with Randomized Trees. Neural Computation 9, 1545–1588 (1997)
7. Criminisi, A., Shotton, J., Robertson, D., Konukoglu, E.: Regression Forests for Efficient Anatomy Detection and Localization in CT Studies. In: Menze, B., Langs, G., Tu, Z., Criminisi, A. (eds.) MICCAI 2010. LNCS, vol. 6533, pp. 106–117. Springer, Heidelberg (2011)
8. Bosch, A., Zisserman, A., Munoz, X.: Image Classification Using Random Forests and Ferns. In: ICCV (2007)
9. Maree, R., Geurts, P., Piater, J., Wehenkel, L.: Random Subwindows for Robust Image Classification. In: CVPR (2005)
10. Caruana, R., Karampatziakis, N., Yessenalina, A.: An Empirical Evaluation of Supervised Learning in High Dimensions. In: ICML, pp. 96–103 (2008)
11. Yin, P., Criminisi, A., Essa, I., Winn, J.: Tree-based Classifiers for Bilayer Video Segmentation. In: CVPR, pp. 1–8 (2007)
12. Payet, N., Todorovic, S.: $(RF)^2$ Random Forest Random Field. In: NIPS (2010)
13. Kontschieder, P., Rota Buló, S., Bischof, H., Pelillo, M.: Structured class-labels in random forests for semantic image labelling. In: ICCV (2011)
14. Montillo, A., Shotton, J., Winn, J., Iglesias, J.E., Metaxas, D., Criminisi, A.: Entangled Decision Forests and Their Application for Semantic Segmentation of CT Images. In: Székely, G., Hahn, H.K. (eds.) IPMI 2011. LNCS, vol. 6801, pp. 184–196. Springer, Heidelberg (2011)
15. Nowozin, S., Rother, C., Bagon, S., Sharp, T., Yao, B., Kohli, P.: Decision Tree Fields. In: ICCV (2011)
16. Felzenszwalb, P.F., Huttenlocher, D.P.: Pictorial Structures for Object Recognition. IJCV 61(1), 55–79 (2005)
17. Girshick, R., Shotton, J., Kohli, P., Criminisi, A., Fitzgibbon, A.: Efficient Regression of General-Activity Human Poses from Depth Images. In: ICCV, pp. 415–422 (2011)
18. Gall, J., Yao, A., Razavi, N., Van Gool, L., Lempitsky, V.: Hough Forests for Object Detection, Tracking, and Action Recognition. PAMI 33(11), 2188–2202 (2011)
19. Cootes, T., Edwards, G., Taylor, C.: Active Appearance Models. PAMI 23(6), 681–685 (2001)
20. Boykov, Y., Funka-Lea, G.: Graph Cuts and Efficient N-D Image Segmentation. IJCV 70(2), 109–131 (2006)
21. Viola, P., Jones, M.J.: Robust Real-Time Face Detection. IJCV 57(2), 137–154 (2004)

Author Index

MIX
Papier aus verantwortungsvollen Quellen
Paper from responsible sources
FSC® C105338

If you have any concerns about our products,
you can contact us on
ProductSafety@springernature.com

In case Publisher is established outside the EU,
the EU authorized representative is:
Springer Nature Customer Service Center GmbH
Europaplatz 3, 69115 Heidelberg, Germany

Printed by Libri Plureos GmbH
in Hamburg, Germany